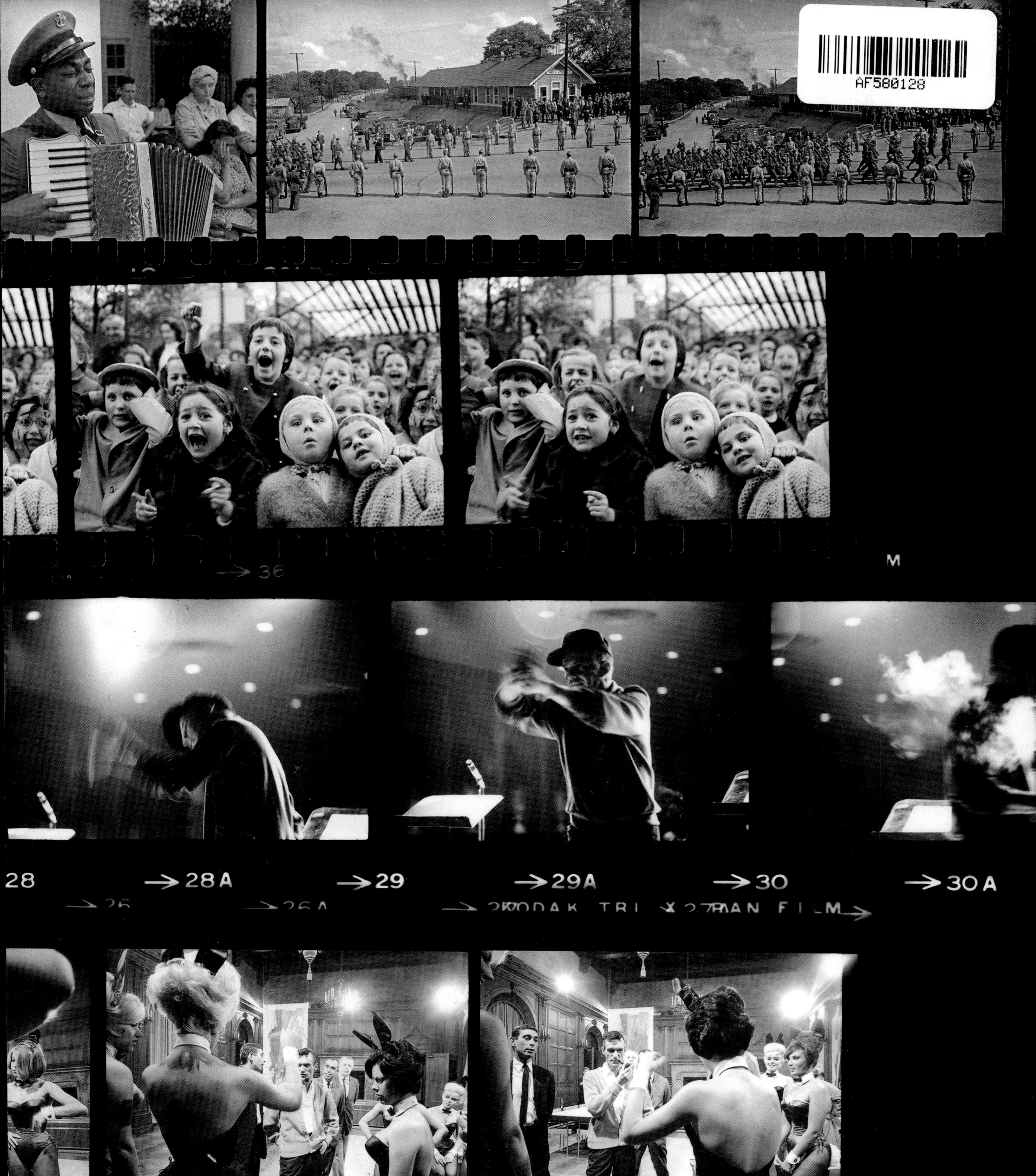

→36
M
28
→28A
→29
→29A
→30
→30A

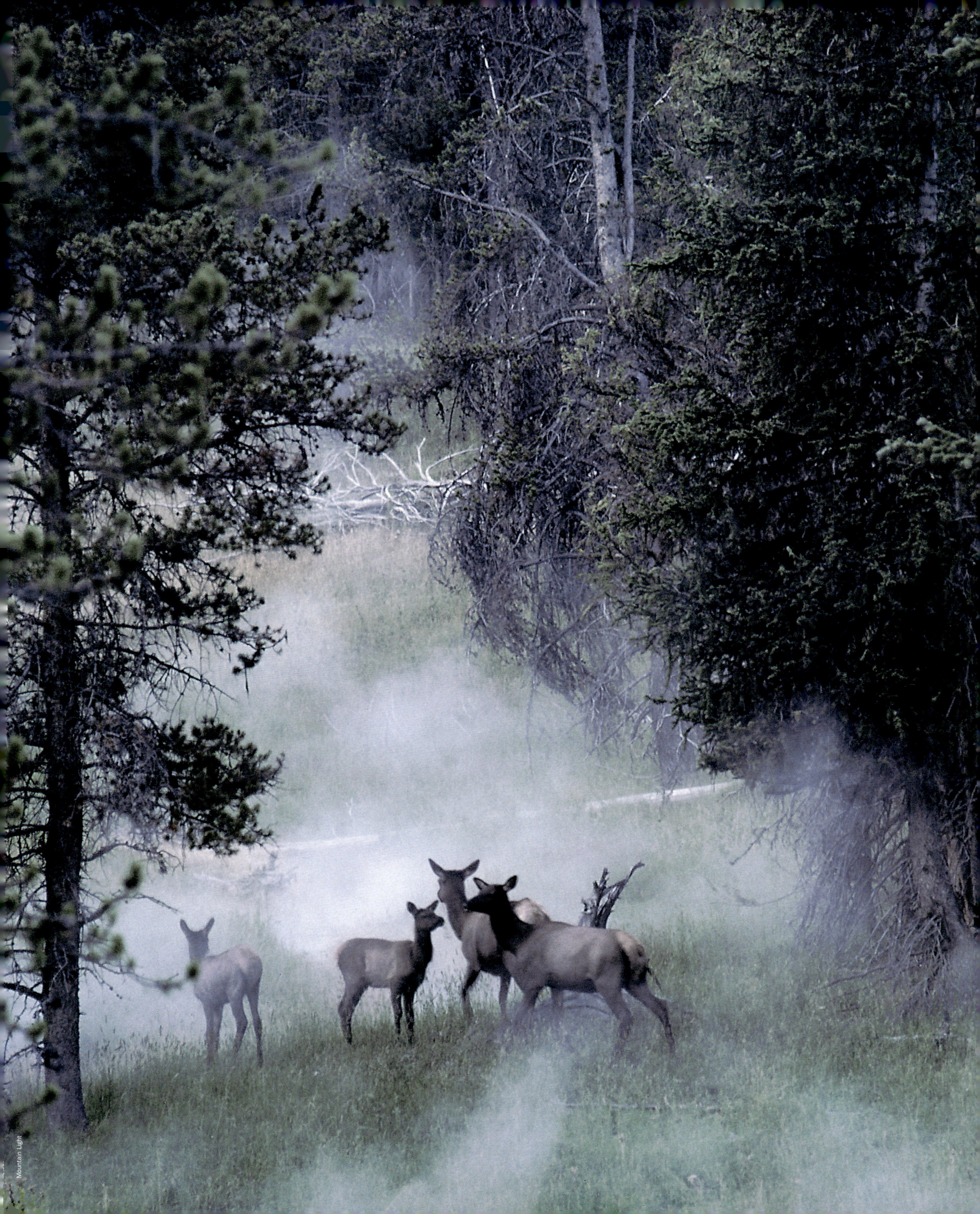

Mountain Light

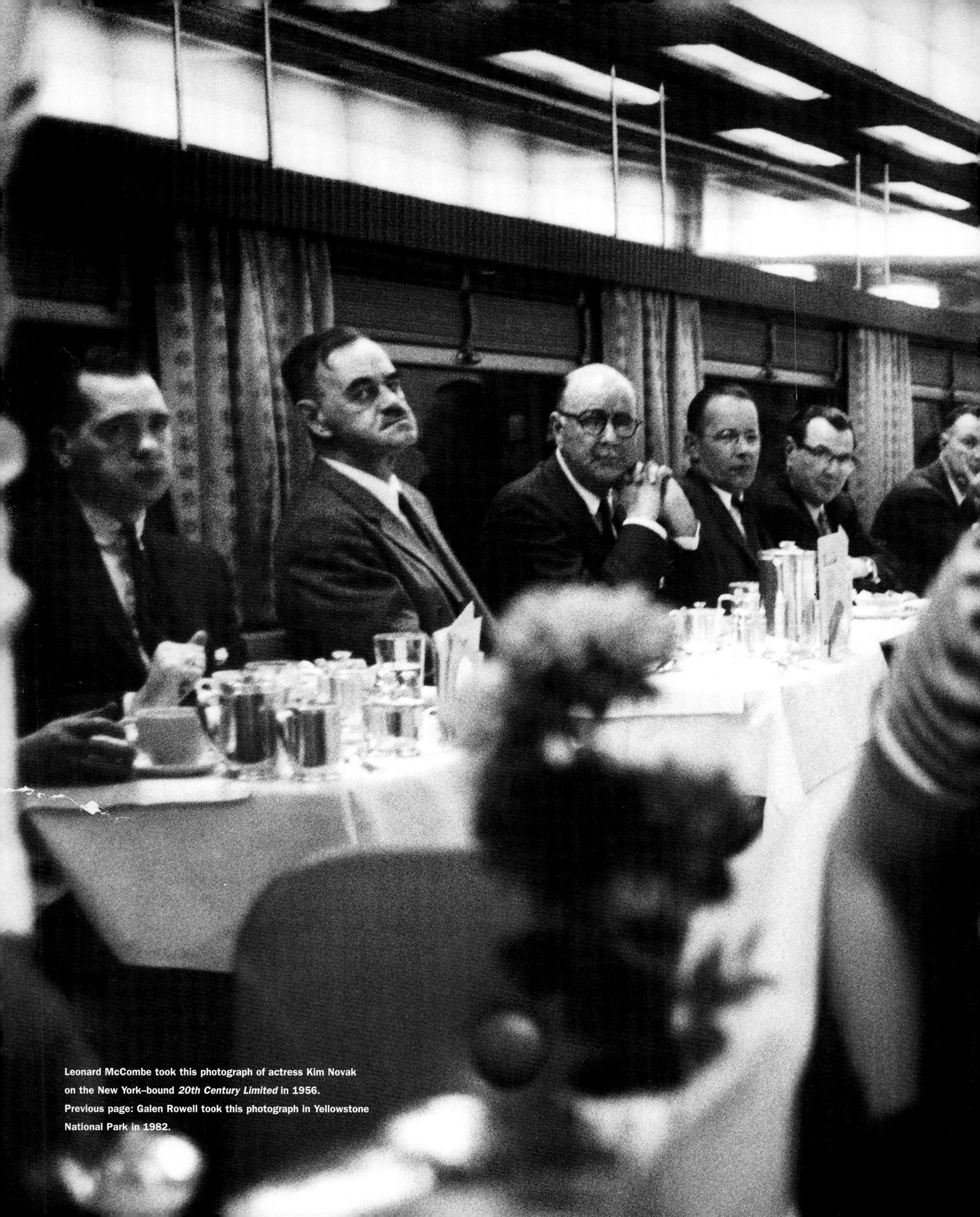

Leonard McCombe took this photograph of actress Kim Novak on the New York–bound *20th Century Limited* in 1956.
Previous page: Galen Rowell took this photograph in Yellowstone National Park in 1982.

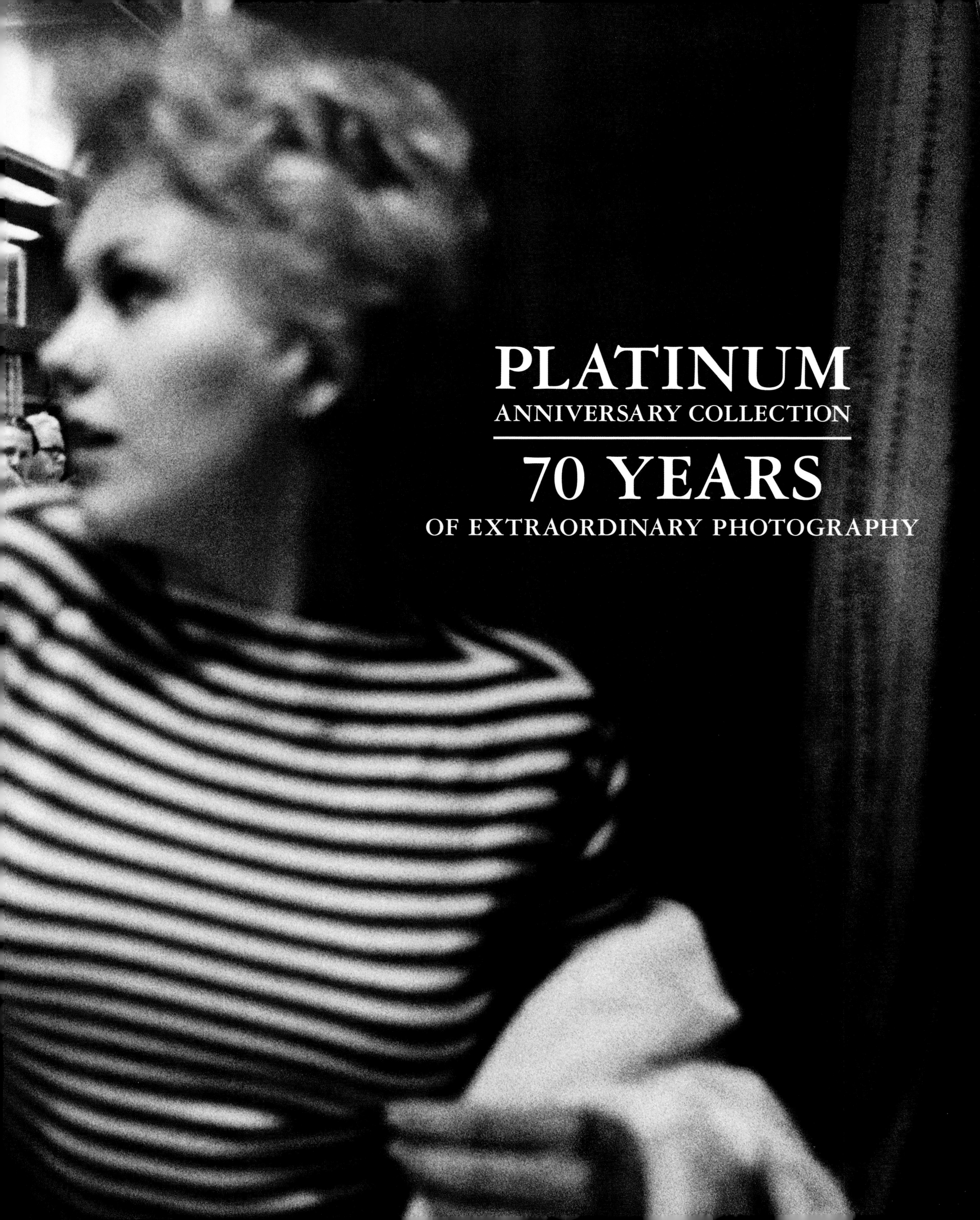

PLATINUM
ANNIVERSARY COLLECTION

70 YEARS
OF EXTRAORDINARY PHOTOGRAPHY

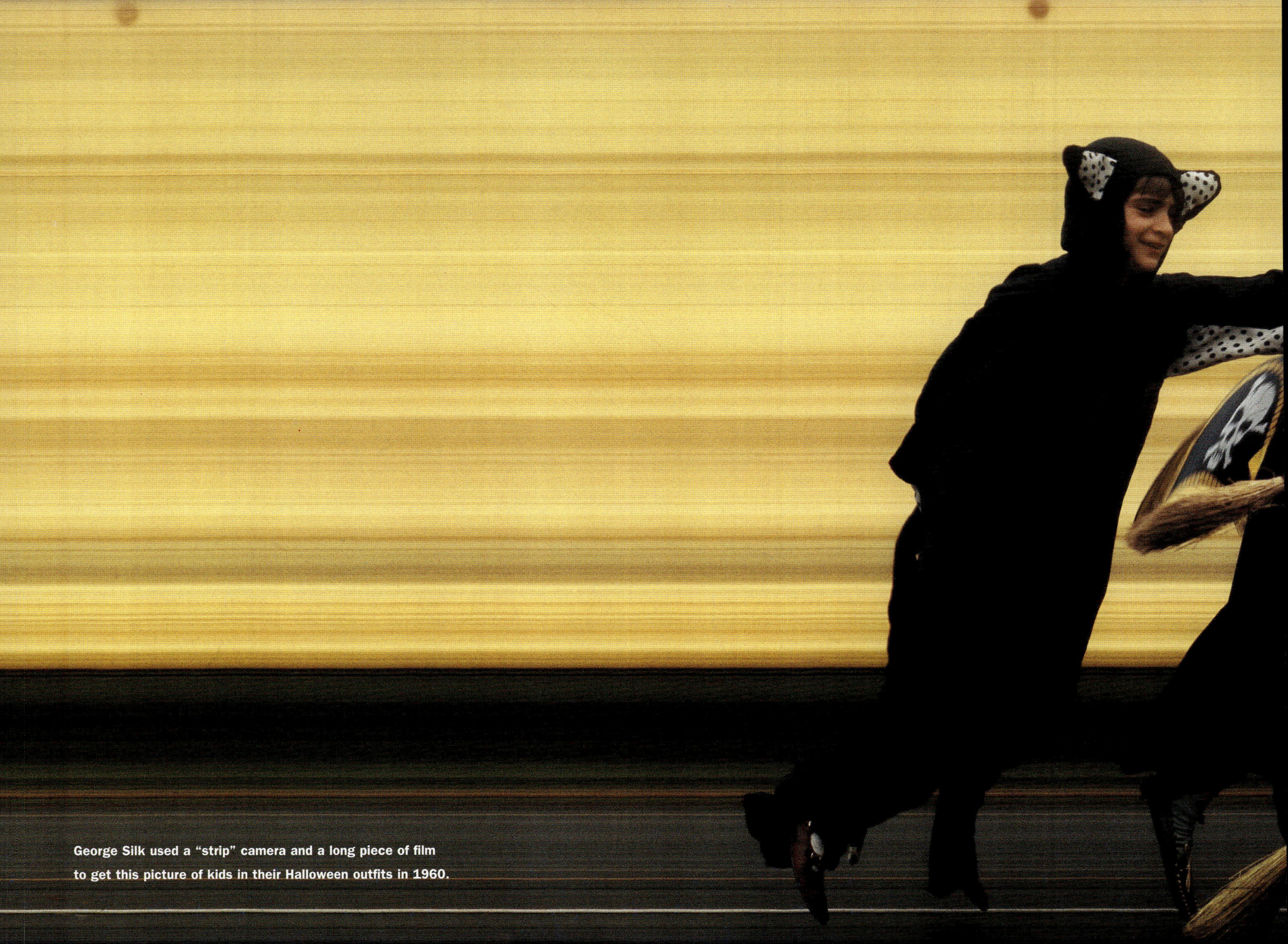

George Silk used a "strip" camera and a long piece of film to get this picture of kids in their Halloween outfits in 1960.

CONTENTS

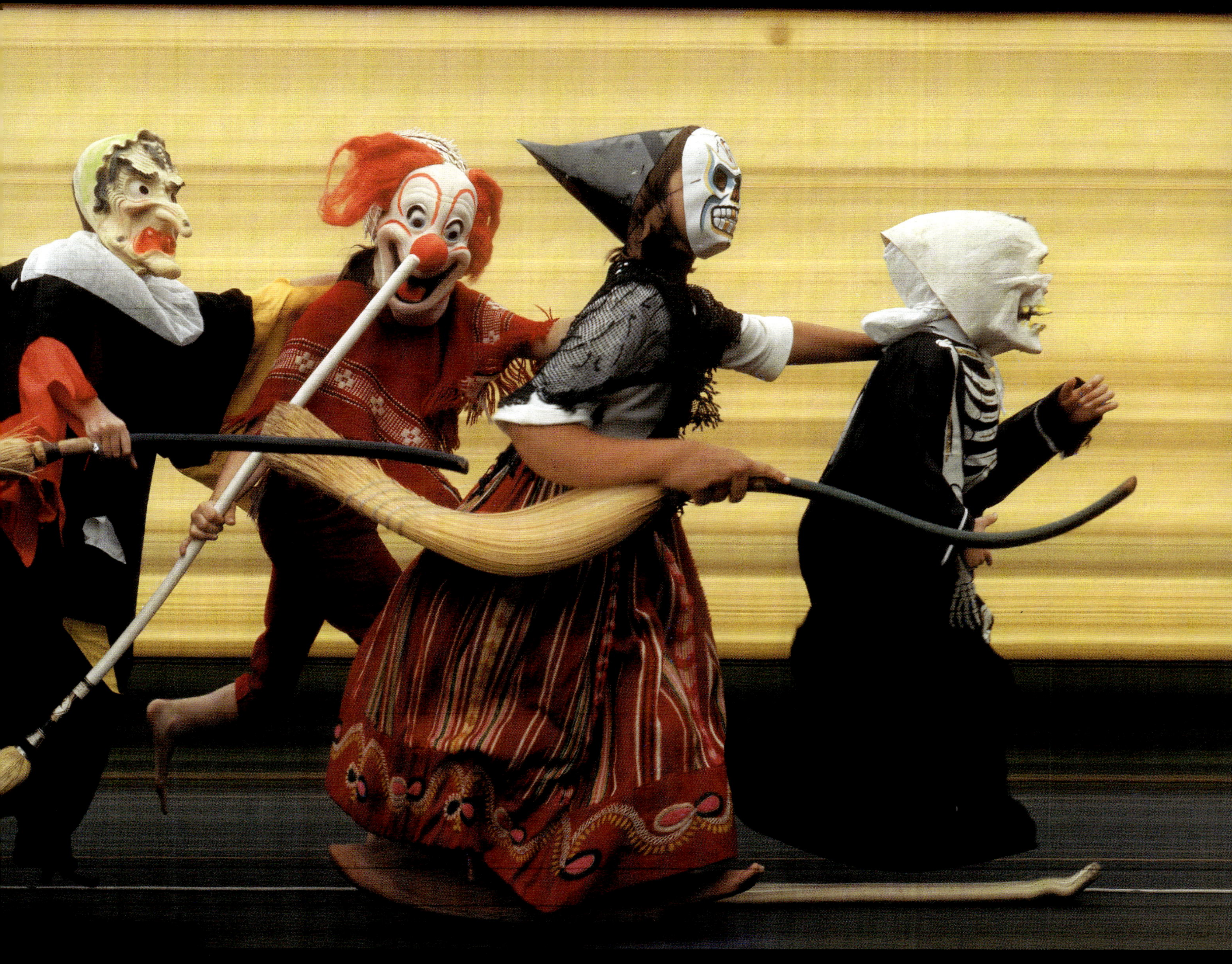

LIFE Books

Editor Robert Andreas
Director of Photography Barbara Baker Burrows
Creative Director Mimi Park
Deputy Picture Editor Christina Lieberman
Writer-Reporter Hildegard Anderson
Copy Lesley Gaspar (Chief), Christine Q. Brennan
Production Manager Michael Roseman
Assistant Production Managers Leenda Bonilla, Rachel Hendrick
Photo Research Joan Shweky
Photo Assistant Joshua Colow
Consulting Picture Editors Mimi Murphy (Rome), Tala Skari (Paris)

Editorial Director Robert Sullivan

Special thanks to John Loengard, Charles A. Whittingham

President Andrew Blau
Business Manager Roger Adler
Business Development Manager Jeff Burak

Editorial Operations Richard K. Prue (Director), Richard Shaffer (Manager), Brian Fellows, Raphael Joa, Stanley E. Moyse (Supervisors), Keith Aurelio, Charlotte Coco, Erin Collity, Scott Dvorin, Kevin Hart, Rosalie Khan, Marco Lau, Po Fung Ng, Barry Pribula, Albert Rufino, David Spatz, Vaune Trachtman, David Weiner

Time Inc. Home Entertainment

Publisher Richard Fraiman
Executive Director, Marketing Services Carol Pittard
Director, Retail & Special Sales Tom Mifsud
Marketing Director, Branded Businesses Swati Rao
Director, New Product Development Peter Harper
Financial Director Steven Sandonato
Assistant General Counsel Dasha Smith Dwin
Prepress Manager Emily Rabin
Book Production Manager Jonathan Polsky
Marketing Manager Laura Adam
Associate Prepress Manager Anne-Michelle Gallero
Associate Marketing Manager Danielle Radano

Special thanks to Bozena Bannett, Alexandra Bliss, Glenn Buonocore, Suzanne Janso, Robert Marasco, Brooke McGuire, Chavaughn Raines, Ilene Schreider, Adriana Tierno, Britney Williams

Published by LIFE Books

Time Inc., 1271 Avenue of the Americas, New York, NY 10020

ISBN: 1-933405-17-1
Library of Congress Control Number: 2006900123
"LIFE" is a trademark of Time Inc.

We welcome your comments and suggestions about LIFE Books. Please write to us at:
LIFE Books,
Attention: Book Editors,
PO Box 11016, Des Moines, IA 50336-1016

If you would like to order any of our hardcover Collector's Edition books, please call us at 1-800-327-6388 (Monday through Friday, 7:00 a.m.–8:00 p.m., or Saturday, 7:00 a.m.–6:00 p.m., Central Time).

Please visit us, and sample past editions of LIFE, at www.LIFE.com. Classic images from the pages and covers of LIFE are now available. Posters can be ordered at www.LIFEposters.com.

Fine art prints from the LIFE Picture Collection and the LIFE Gallery of Photography can be viewed at www.LIFEphotographs.com.

INTRODUCTION

To See the World

A BRIEF HISTORY OF LIFE

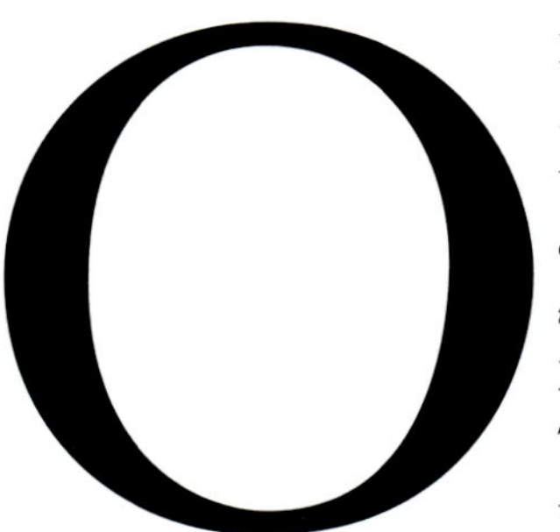

N THIS PAGE are copies of an historic document, Henry Luce's manifesto for THE SHOW-BOOK OF THE WORLD—a prospective magazine that, on Thursday, November 19, 1936, would hit the streets with a more elegant, far less grandiloquent but somehow more grandiose name: LIFE. What a debut! The pictorial weekly was a sellout (225,000 to charter subscribers, 200,000 more gone from newsstands overnight) and instantly part of the country's conversation. LIFE was nothing short of a phenomenon, and its launch was arguably the most sensational in magazine-publishing history.

This might have been predicted by any who had read Luce's remarkable, red-blooded, basso-throated prospectus. "To see life;" Luce wrote, boldly stating the magazine's mission and its mandate, "to see the world; to eyewitness great events; to watch the faces of the poor and the gestures of the proud; to see strange things—machines, armies, multitudes, shadows in the jungle and on the moon; to see man's work—his paintings, towers and discoveries; to see things thousands of miles away, things hidden behind walls and within rooms, things dangerous to come to; the women that men love and many children; to see and take pleasure in seeing; to see and be amazed; to see and be instructed . . ."

And Luce went on from there, continuing to evince not only a deep-dyed affinity for the semicolon but also an unswerving faith in photography and its power to educate, enlighten and entertain. Luce's *Time* magazine was about the week's news, and his *Fortune* was about business and industry. His "SHOW-BOOK"—his LIFE—would be about pictures, pictures of everything that might lend itself to a picture, which is to say: everything but the wind (though images of tornadoes and hurricanes, quickly plentiful in LIFE's pages, would take care of that). His new magazine "proposes to be the biggest picture show on earth—and the most vividly coherent. It proposes to scour the world for the best pictures of every kind; to edit them with a feeling for visual form, for history and for drama . . . By giving to pictures their own magazine, SHOW-BOOK intends that the camera shall at last take its place as the most convincing reporter of contemporary life."

A lofty goal and, despite LIFE's immediate success with the nation's masses, not one that was quickly attained. There were certainly some riveting features and individual pictures in the earliest editions of LIFE (Margaret Bourke-White's photo essay from inside a WPA shantytown in the very first issue was a stunner), but there were also dozens of examples of a young magazine finding its way and, regularly, stubbing its toe. Just as legendary in the Time & Life Building as the Bourke-White masterwork is a 1937 photo essay explicating the proper way a wife should undress for her husband, a blatant attempt by the editors to costume naughty pictures as a "service article"—and evidence all these years later that LIFE was ready and willing to pander for popularity.

It is perceived wisdom that LIFE found its true calling during World War II; Luce himself once commented, "Though we did not plan LIFE as a war magazine, it turned out that way." But if that is so, the magazine already was growing up in 1938 when it got a first taste of the momentous impact it could have with important material. New York State had banned a film about the birth of a baby, even though doctors had said the imagery was anything but obscene—was, in fact, praiseworthy. LIFE warned subscribers a week beforehand that it intended to run frames from the movie in its April 11 issue, which it did, 35 pictures in all, over four pages. The uproar was great, and action was taken to ban the issue in Boston (of course), Chicago, New Orleans, Tucson, more than 50 locales in all. LIFE fought the sanctions even as the public—and several public figures—weighed in. "[S]ome . . . feel that such information should be printed only in medical journals," said First Lady Eleanor Roosevelt. "But [it] must be given in mediums the public sees or listens to or reads . . . It is information to safeguard your people, to try to bring down the death rate of mothers and babies." A Gallup poll taken at the time showed

A PROSPECTUS

For A

NEW MAGAZINE

THE PURPOSE:

To see life; to see the world, the cockeyed world; to eyewitness great events; to watch the faces of the poor and the gestures of the proud; to see strange things -- machines, armies, multitudes, shadows in the jungle and on the moon; to see man's work -- ~~paintings, towers, harbors, courts of law,~~ his discoveries; to see things past, things thousands of miles away, things hidden behind walls and within rooms, things dangerous to come to; to see the women that men love; to see and to take pleasure in seeing; to see and be amazed; to see and be instructed; ~~to see, to laugh,~~ and ~~to wonder and reflect.~~ . . .

~~Thus~~ To see, and to be shown, is now the will and new expectancy of half mankind.

To see and to show is the mission now, for the first time, undertaken by a new kind of publication, SCOPE, The Show-Book Of The World, hereinafter described.

THE NEED & OPPORTUNITY:

I

In the course of a week the U.S. citizen sees many pictures. He sees a few in the newspapers and more on Sundays. He may see travel pictures in travel magazines, art pictures in art digests, cinema pictures in cinemagazines, scientific pictures in scientific journals. But nowhere can he see the cream of

- 2 -

all the world's pictures brought together for him to enjoy and study in one comfortable sitting. No publication devotes itself directly, without compromise and without conflicting purposes, to the business of supplying the biggest and best package of pictures which it is possible to produce at a popular price. Nowhere, therefore, does the insistent demand for pictures meet a direct and fully satisfying supply.

II

Pictures have become a dynamic ~~pawn~~ power in the Fourth Estate of the 20th Century. But, although people demand and get pictures in nearly every periodical; although the gravure section of The New York Times is the section most "read" by the distinguished clientele of that journal; although pictures stir the blood of the readers of FORTUNE: and although the superlatively successful Daily News is commonly regarded as a picture paper --

Nevertheless, people are missing relatively more of what the camera can tell than of what the reporter writes. With more or less success they "follow" the news -- i.e. the written news. They scarcely realize how fascinating it can be to "follow" pictures -- to be for the first time pictorially well-informed.

For this there are many reasons. Pictures are taken haphazardly. Pictures are published haphazardly. Naturally, therefore, they are looked at haphazardly. Cameramen who use their heads as well as their legs are rare. Rarer still are camera-editors. Thus, many a newsworthy picture which can be taken is not taken. Thus, too, only a fraction of the best pictures of widest interest are brought to the attention of any one alert U.S. citizen. And almost nowhere is there an attempt to edit pictures into a coherent story -- to make an effective mosaic out of the fragmentary documents which pictures, past and present, are.

The mind-guided camera can do a far better job of reporting current events than has been done. And, more than that, it can reveal to us far more explicitly the nature of the dynamic social world in which we live.

III

SCOPE, The Show-Book Of The World, undertakes to meet this challenge, this opportunity.

It proposes to be the biggest picture show on earth -- and the most vividly coherent. It proposes to scour the world for the best pictures of every kind; to edit them with a feeling for visual form, for history and for drama; and to publish them on fine paper, every week, for a dime.

It takes for its field not all the news but all the news which now and hereafter can be seen; and of these seen events it proposes to be the complete and reliable record.

It takes for its field all of the world which may be known by seeing -- and it promises to reveal, every week, aspects of human life and work which have never before been seen by the camera's miraculous second sight. By giving to pictures their own magazine, SCOPE intends that the camera shall at last take its place as the most convincing reporter of contemporary life.

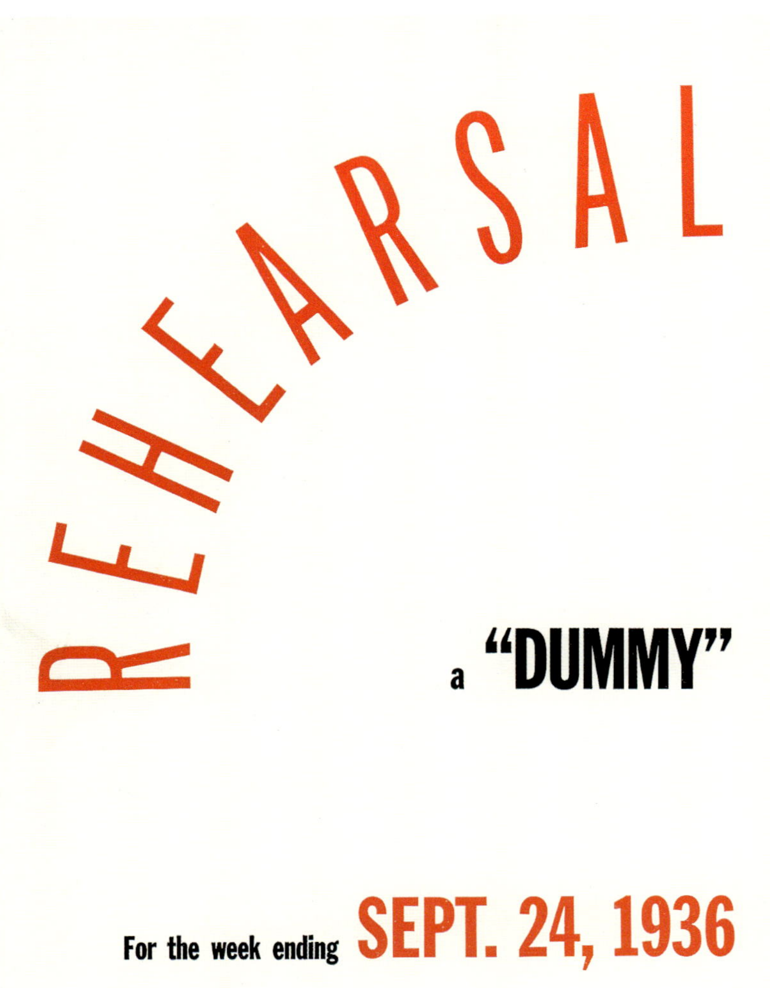

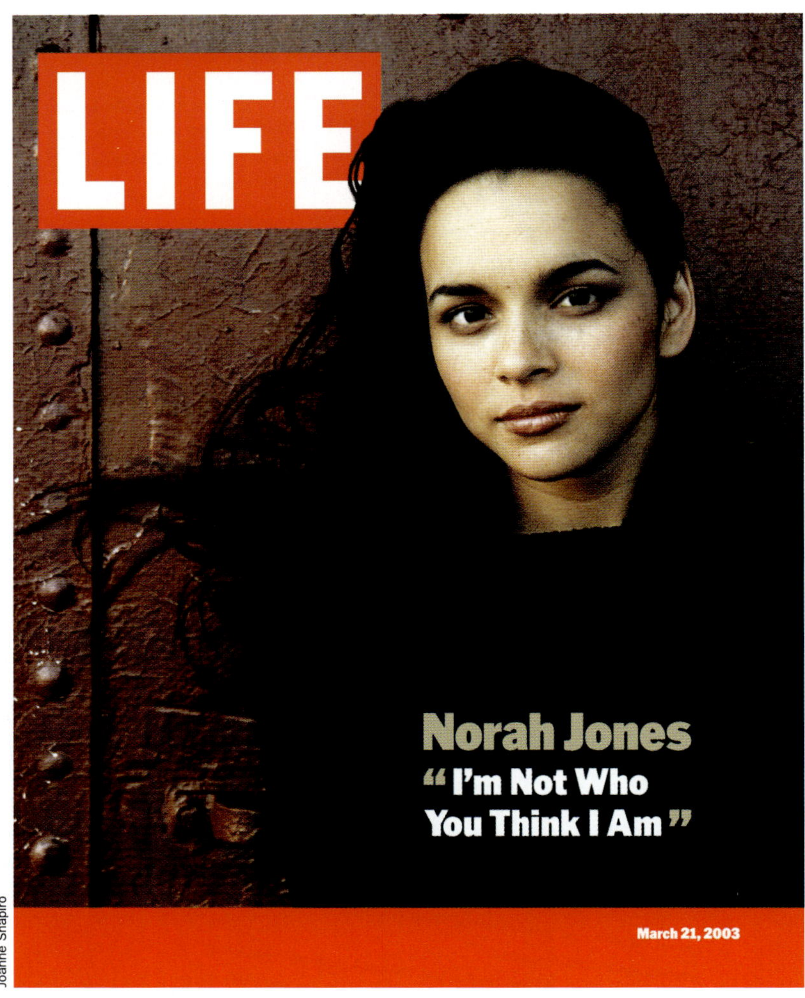

Joanne Shapiro

Two examples of starting up: the original working-version cover, and the cover that was used as a test sample for the weekly reincarnation in 2004

that 76 percent of Americans approved of the way LIFE had handled the story, and all legal charges of indecency against the magazine were eventually dropped. "The Birth of a Baby" can be seen now as a precursor to all the significant and controversial imagery that LIFE has put before the country over the decades—George Strock's and Ralph Morse's tough pictures from the Pacific theater, Bourke-White's from the death camps, David Douglas Duncan's intimate and harrowing photoreportage from the Korean War, Abraham Zapruder's film from the murder of President John F. Kennedy, Gordon Parks's inside look at Harlem street gangs and at the poorest within Brazil's slums, Lennart Nilsson's images from within the womb, Larry Burrows' color photography from deep inside the Vietnam War, Bill Eppridge's behind-closed-doors visits with heroin addicts, Mary Ellen Mark's unsparing look at the plight of America's homeless. After "The Birth of a Baby," LIFE knew what was coming when it decided to publish this harder stuff: criticism, certainly, but also acclaim and, not least, public notice (which can be translated: publicity). The magazine made its readers smarter with these stories, and made itself better and stronger.

From the 1940s through the early '60s LIFE was at peak power. More than a third of all U.S. families read the magazine, and it was in LIFE's pages that the country saw the defining moments of assassinations, wars, the civil rights movement, the quest for the moon. Plus, of course: the stars of Hollywood, who willingly answered the doorbell for LIFE; the everyman next door (the ranch hand in Texas, the career girl in Gotham, the general practitioner in rural Colorado); the sports heroes in their grand arenas; the giants of science and medicine in their laboratories; the awesome wonders of the natural world; the sweet or funny moments that make life worth living. It was well known to LIFE's editors that much of their readership traveled the magazine back-to-front each week, so as to get to the humorous pictures and the "LIFE Goes to a Party" feature first. The soldiers, the astronauts, the President himself: They could wait.

We have talked so far about pictures, and this 70th anniversary commemorative is dedicated nearly in its entirety to photographs. But LIFE also established, particularly in this middle period, a strong reputation for its words. Theodore H. White's important reporting from China distinguished LIFE in the 1940s, as did the appearance in 1952 of the entirety of Ernest Hemingway's *The Old Man and the Sea,* the powerful novella that secured for Papa his Nobel Prize. (Fun footnotes: Hemingway was happy to write captions for another LIFE feature, and the poet and playwright Archibald MacLeish also contributed caps to a Bourke-White photo essay.) In the 1960s staff writers Loudon Wainwright and Shana Alexander became regular columnists and developed avid national followings, and Hugh Sidey began his influential weekly reports from the White House. The literary legacy extended: In 1971, Norman Mailer covered the Ali-Frazier heavyweight championship fight for LIFE—to the tune of 13,000 words, which were accompanied by pictures taken for the magazine by none other than Frank Sinatra, an enthusiastic amateur shutterbug who just happened to have a ringside seat. Today, with the weekly LIFE reborn, Frank McCourt is a contributing writer, tackling subjects as large as the newest American immigrants and as small (and frisky) as his beagle Rory. John Updike, Melissa Fay Greene and other wordsmiths have also contributed anew to LIFE. To excerpt the work of all these writers in the pages that follow would do them scant justice. But we do, readily and proudly, salute them here.

What *can* retain all of their power and glory in an anniversary book of this size are the photographs.

The pictures.

The images that were and are LIFE's reason for being.

Their magical qualities made LIFE an indispensable part of the national fabric but were not enough to sustain the magazine when financial difficulties beset the weekly in the late 1960s and early '70s. LIFE's enormous circulation actually became a liability when advertising revenues began to decline. Eventually each issue cost more to produce and distribute than it brought in through subscription

William Sumits

fees and ads. And so, the painful decision was made at the end of 1972 to close down the shop.

Not for the last time, LIFE found another path, continuing to produce well-received books and specials. The sentiment gradually built within the halls of the Time & Life Building that readers out there—and certainly editors in here—missed visiting with LIFE on a regular basis. In 1978 (again not for the last time) the magazine was relaunched, sailing forth as a monthly. In this incarnation the magazine would last until the spring of 2000, and would, as had its weekly predecessor, produce much distinguished photojournalism, hit the occasional false note, and sometimes move the nation. Old friends like Eppridge, Nilsson and Parks brought their newest pictures to LIFE, and such as Harry Benson, Lynn Johnson, Brian Lanker, Joe McNally and Co Rentmeester were regularly represented in our pages and proved worthy successors to the original staff photographers (who were, for the sake of history: Alfred Eisenstaedt, Thomas McAvoy and Peter Stackpole, as well as Bourke-White). LIFE proceeded in this period with all of its old ambition. It found stories and told them the proper way; America came to know and care about the conjoined Hensel twins, Brittany and Abigail, through an exclusive 1996 cover story in LIFE. Five years earlier, the editors reacted to the first Iraq war by taking LIFE weekly once more. In four issues produced that winter, LIFE took the pulse of action in the desert and the homeland in a manner deeply reminiscent of the way that Robert Capa, Carl Mydans—and Strock, Morse, Bourke-White, Duncan, Burrows—had humanized previous conflicts for LIFE's readers.

As the so-called war weekly indicated, the notion that the weekly LIFE might one day reappear was never completely dead. Not long after LIFE had again embarked on a schedule of books and specials in 2000, the events of September 11, 2001, galvanized the editors to tackle what was, after all, the most photographed event in the history of war. When LIFE's book on that subject appeared, an old debate that had dogged the magazine since the 1960s was visited anew: With television showing live-action footage of events in the real world on a constant basis, what's the value, if any, of the still image? Certainly in an era of cable news and hundreds of stations, the photograph seemed an anachronism.

Nevertheless, September 11 proved to us that the power that Henry Luce saw in the still image in 1936 retained its potency in the postmodern age. People could contemplate an unmoving picture in a way that was impossible with a video feed. There was, as ever, something remarkable about freezing a moment in time.

With that as a solidly held principle, it was decided that a regularly appearing LIFE was coming back once more—this time, to be distributed in newspapers each weekend. And so we see on the adjacent page more artifacts linked in a continuum with the pages of Luce's manifesto: the prototype issues of the first LIFE, and the new LIFE, which debuted on October 1, 2004.

Its mission?

"To see life; to see the world . . ."

As ever.

—Robert Sullivan

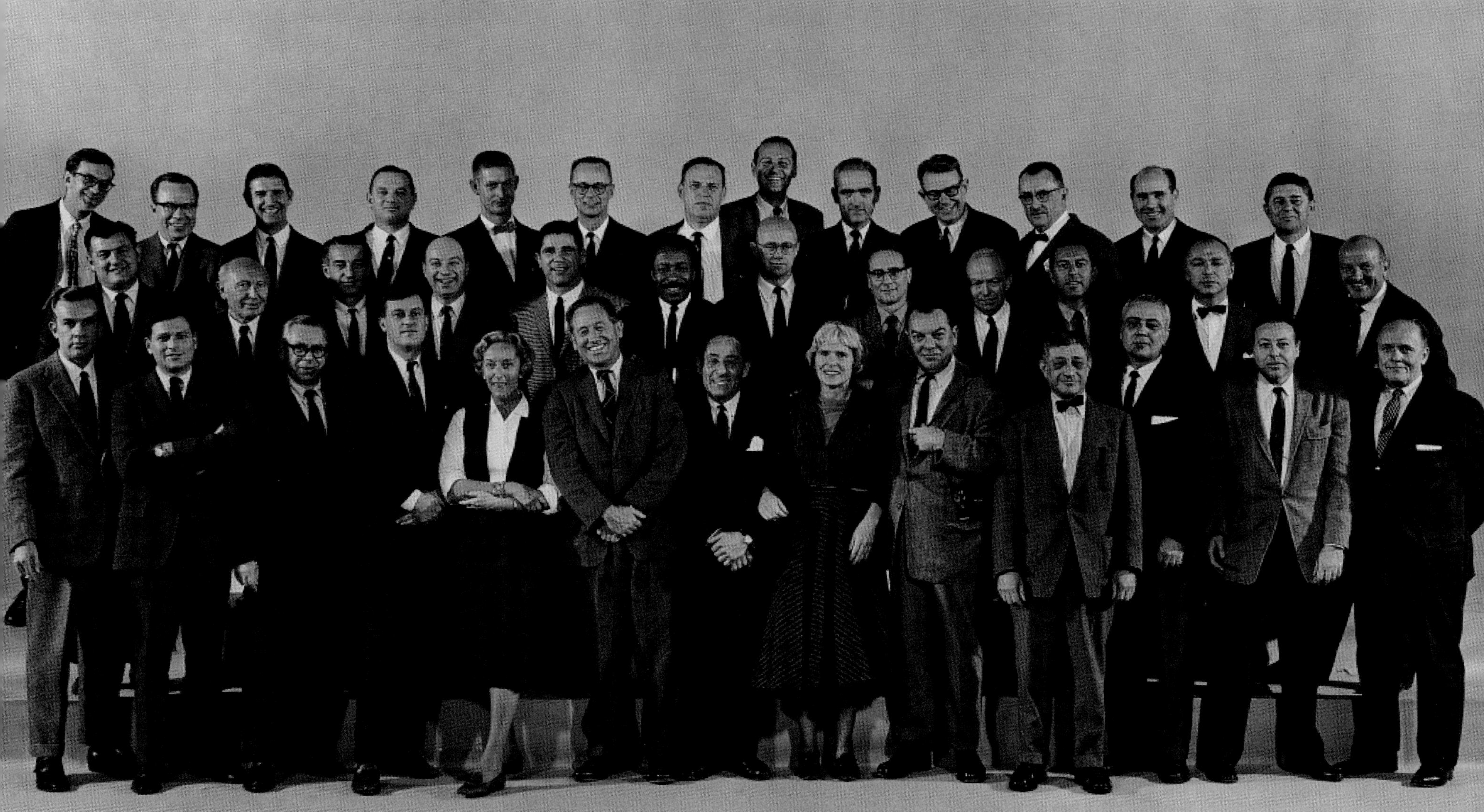

The LIFE staff photographers in 1960, front row, left to right: James Whitmore, Paul Schutzer, Walter Sanders, Michael Rougier, Nina Leen, Peter Stackpole, Alfred Eisenstaedt, Margaret Bourke-White, Thomas McAvoy, Carl Mydans, Al Fenn, Ralph Morse, Francis Miller; middle row: Hank Walker, Dmitri Kessel, N.R. Farbman, Yale Joel, John Dominis, Gordon Parks, James Burke, Andreas Feininger, Fritz Goro, Allan Grant, Eliot Elisofon, Frank Scherschel; back row: Grey Villet, Ed Clark, Loomis Dean, Joe Scherschel, Stan Wayman, Robert W. Kelley, J.R. Eyerman, Ralph Crane, Leonard McCombe, Howard Sochurek, Wallace Kirkland, Mark Kauffman, George Silk

The Power of LIFE

BY RICHARD B. STOLLEY

During the height of the school desegregation battle in the South, I was in the small eastern Tennessee town of Clinton, where violence had broken out over a handful of black high school students. The National Guard had been called in, several local rednecks had been jailed, and tension was as thick as the morning mountain fog. I was walking toward the police station when a rough-looking citizen in coveralls stepped in front of me and blocked my path. I moved to one side, then the other; he moved with me. Finally, I held up my LIFE magazine ID card and said, "Press. LIFE magazine."

His features twisted with rage as he snarled, "Press *this,* Mr. LIFE Magazine!" Then, miraculously, he got out of my way. He clearly did not want to tangle with America's famous picture magazine, which had already proved itself to be an important force in revealing the depths of racism in the South. LIFE got the story that day in Clinton, and would continue to chronicle the South's eventual and thrilling acceptance of the rule of law.

Everyone who has worked at the magazine has his or her own stories about just when the realization came: This magazine means something to people, this is really something special. Any LIFE staffer, past or present, has remarkable tales to tell. These are just a few of my own, and between the lines there may be something about that unique power of LIFE.

The kind of access the magazine enjoyed during my years there was astonishing, extending from Tennessee to Washington, D.C., to the rest of the world. LIFE was first—TV included—to be allowed to cover *Air Force One.* I was with photographer Bill Eppridge when he climbed aboard the Boeing 707 in Washington for a quick trip to New England. A big, big man suddenly emerged from a cabin, walked down the aisle, stuck out his enormous paw toward Bill, and graciously (if unnecessarily) said, "Lyndon Johnson." A dumbstruck Eppridge managed to stammer out his own name, and he solemnly shook the President's hand.

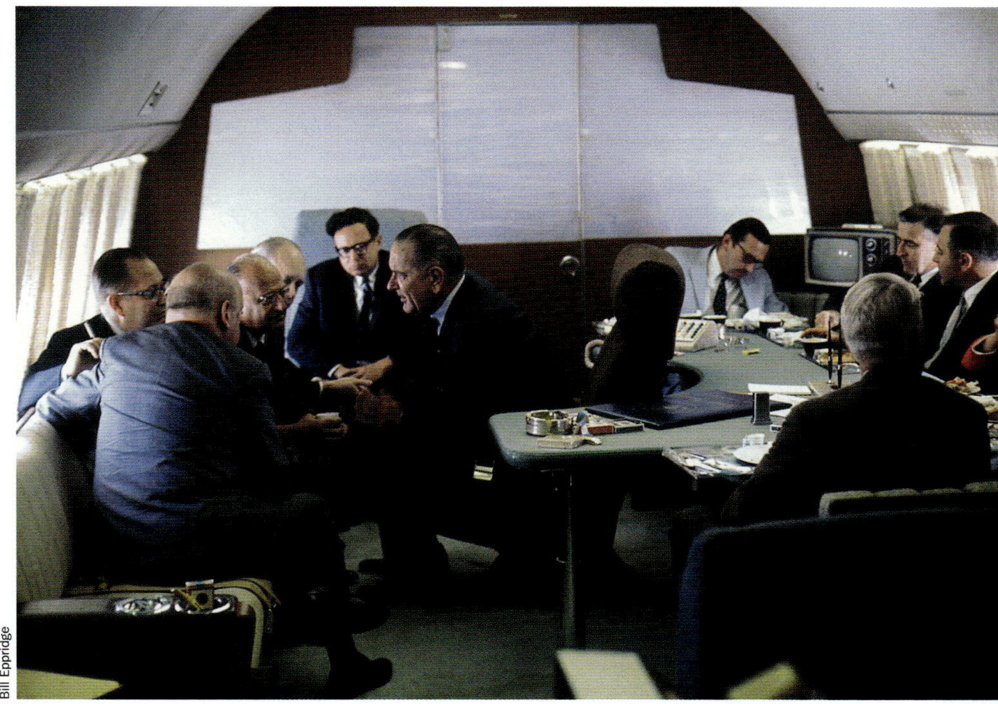

Bill Eppridge

President Johnson (center) talks with New York congressmen aboard *Air Force One.*

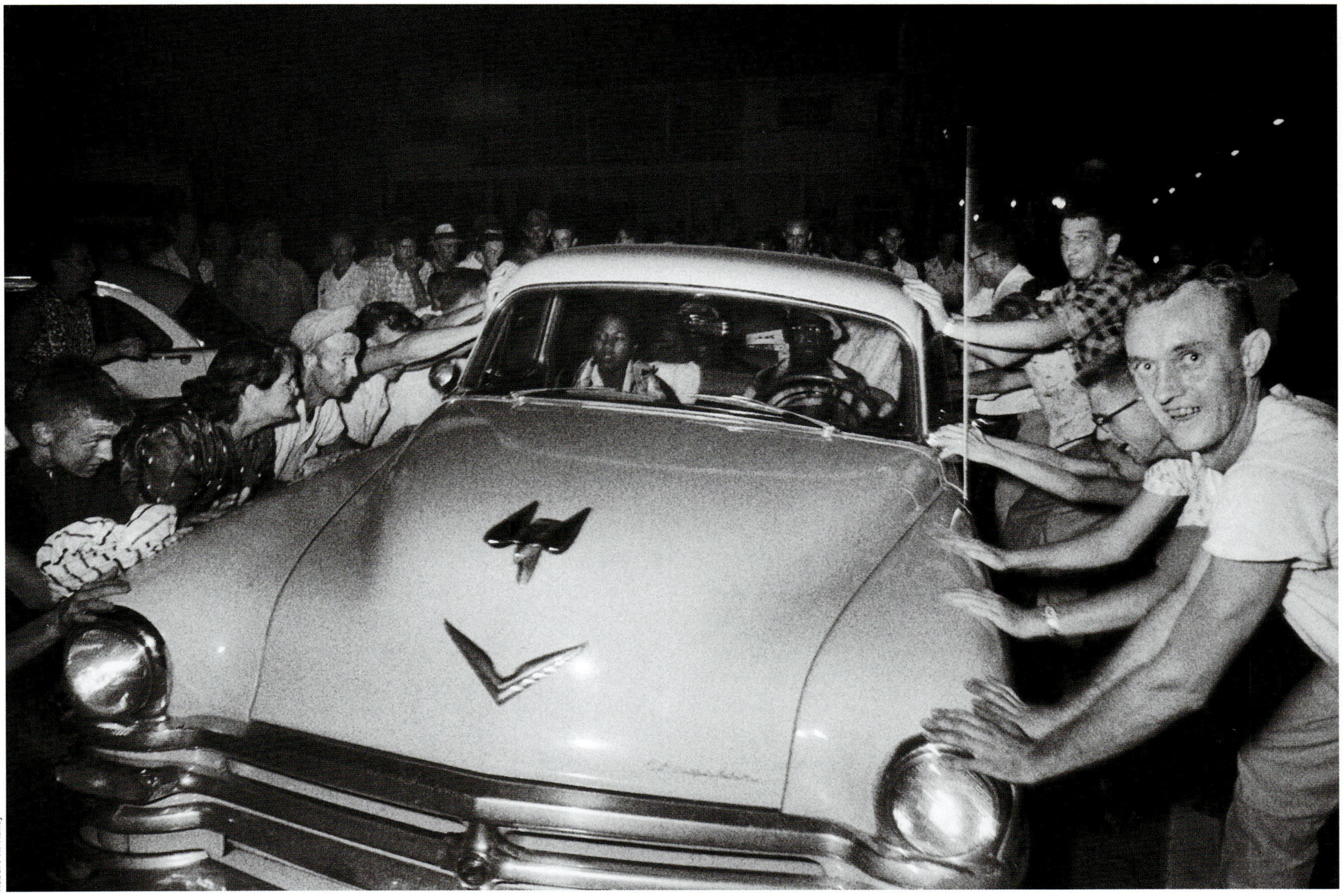

Robert W. Kelley

A mob rocks an out-of-state automobile during race riots in Clinton, Tenn.

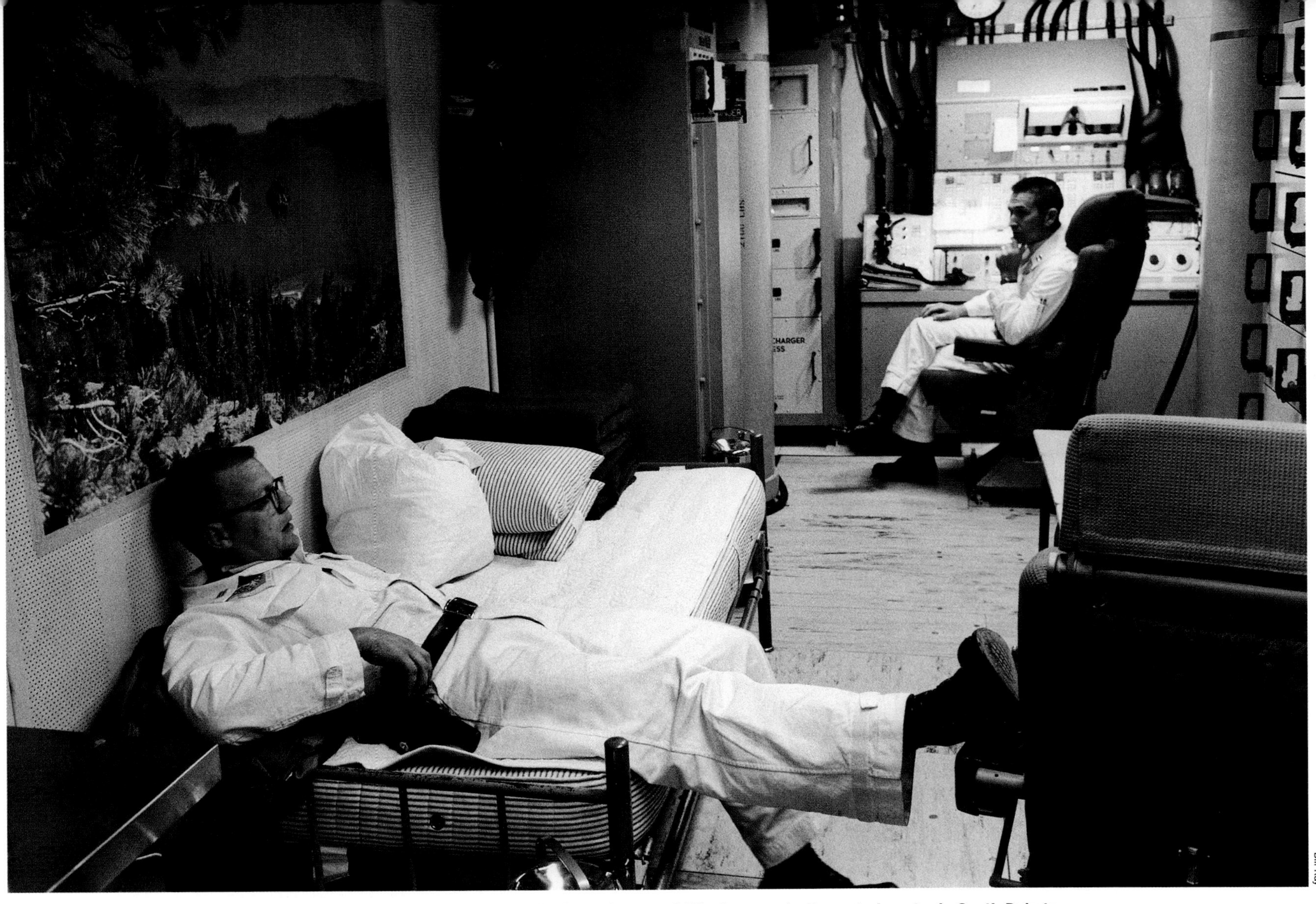

Bill Ray

Capt. William Christians, at left, rests in the underground Minuteman missile control center in South Dakota.

We saw fascinating things, went to strange places. At the height of the cold war, when America's first line of offense was a network of intercontinental ballistic missiles, the magazine asked the Pentagon for permission to document life in a Minuteman command capsule 60 feet below South Dakota farmland. Photographer Bill Ray and I spent 24 hours down there with two Air Force officers whose job was to press two buttons, if so ordered, to launch a nuclear warhead at the Soviet Union. I remember thinking, once we had finally returned to civilization, *whatever happened to the wild blue yonder?*

Sometimes, the LIFE name got us even farther than we expected. When London photographer Terry Spencer and I were covering Soviet Premier Nikita Khrushchev's visit to Stockholm in 1964, we decided on a mutual dare to crash the private reception afterward. We used our LIFE credentials in a fairly outrageous way to get past Swedish and Soviet security, arrived at Khrushchev's side, greeted him on behalf of the magazine—whose name he immediately recognized with a huge smile—and only then were we hustled away.

Much more recently, LIFE secured permission to cover the 1994 planned U.S. invasion of Haiti from a unique vantage. Photographer Harry Benson and I shadowed the commanding general (and later Army chief of staff), Hugh Shelton. We flew from Fort Bragg, N.C., to Guantánamo Bay with the 82nd Airborne, then went aboard the command ship, USS *Mount Whitney,* with General Shelton. Only a few hours before American soldiers and Marines were scheduled to hit the Haitian beaches, an American diplomatic mission in Port-au-Prince persuaded the Haitian dictator Raoul Cédras to step down. Benson and I—of course sworn to secrecy, and definitely not allowed to leave the room for any reason—were with Shelton and his top officers when the dramatic word came through. The invasion had been canceled, and next morning we helicoptered into Haiti with Shelton as peacekeepers.

These are not so much stories of derring-do—hardly a patch on some of the stories you will read in these pages—but of trust. I think it is safe to say that LIFE has long been not only the best-known magazine in the world, but the most trusted. That was never more clear to me than after the assassination of President John F. Kennedy. With the help of a LIFE stringer named Patsy Swank, I was the first reporter to contact Abraham Zapruder, the Dallas garment manufacturer who recorded the murder from beginning to end on his 8mm home movie camera. I reached him that November evening in 1963, about 10 hours after the President had died. I asked if I could go to his house to view the film. Exhausted and grieving, he said no. I did not persist.

By the next morning, other journalists, both print and broadcast, had discovered Zapruder. We all had gathered outside his office. He announced that because I had talked to him first, he would talk to me first. Our negotiations were gracious, low-key and sad. In the end, LIFE got the film, for a $50,000 fee (our competitors would have paid more, I am sure) plus our pledge that we would not exploit its shocking, grisly contents.

Our handling of his movie was crucial to Mr. Zapruder. He told me he had had a nightmare, only a few hours after the assassination. In it, he was walking through Times Square, and a huckster in a flashy suit stood outside a movie theater and squawked, "Come on in, folks, and see the President killed on the big screen . . ." I assured him that LIFE would treat his film with honor and respect, and the magazine did, selling the still images only to well-established foreign publications—and refusing to allow the film to be shown on television or in movie theaters at all—while it was in our possession. In short, LIFE scored one of the great exclusives of the 20th century because of Abraham Zapruder's trust in the magazine.

The public's confidence in the magazine was achieved partly because of the way we told stories—through photographs. People trusted pictures. Tampering with photographs, so easy now by electronic means, was virtually unheard of for much of LIFE's 70 years, and furthermore: It was (and remains) gospel that if a picture appeared in our publication, it was a genuine rendering of a scene or a

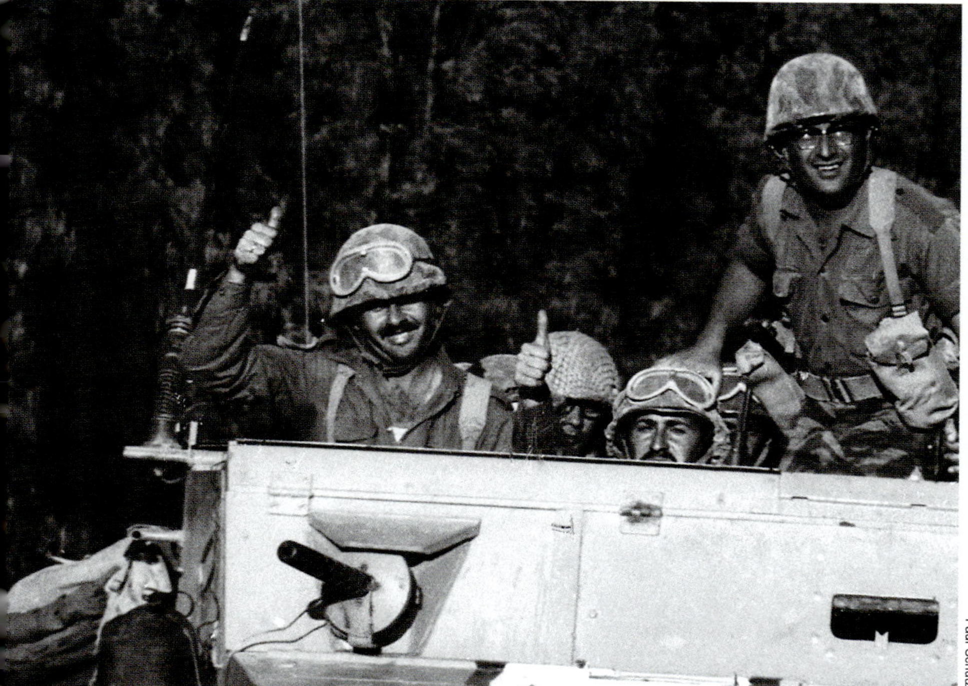

Paul Schutzer

This shot of Israeli soldiers during the Six-Day War was one of the last taken by Schutzer before he was killed.

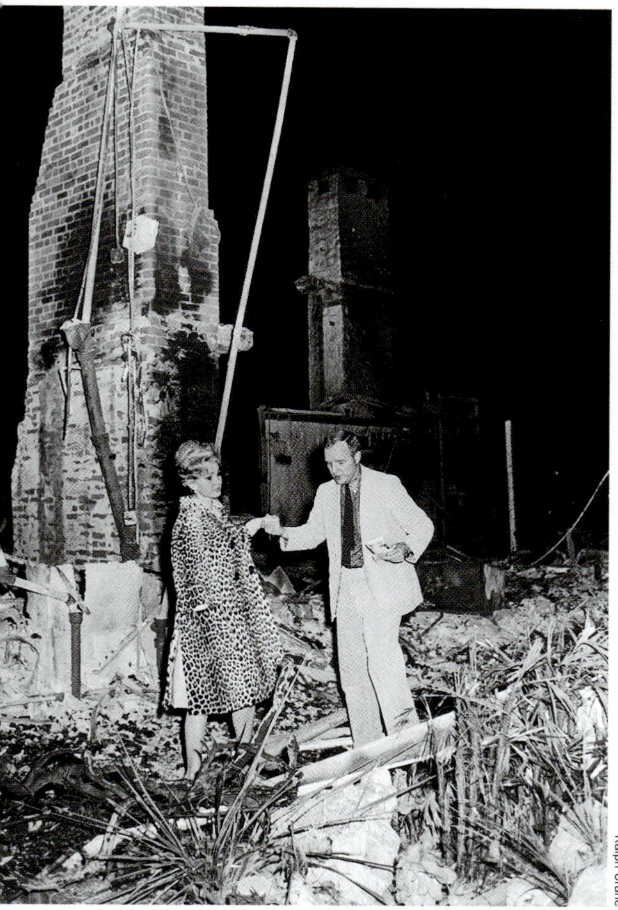

Ralph Crane

Stolley helps Zsa Zsa Gabor after her home was destroyed by brushfire in 1961.

human being. A hallmark of the photographers I generally worked with was eyeblink-by-eyeblink, unposed, spontaneous coverage.

Such coverage sometimes took courage. In Clinton, Tenn., photographer Bob Kelley was covering the segregationist rally from a truck when he was attacked. He broke his leg leaping from the vehicle. Kelley was one of the luckier ones. Three LIFE friends of mine were killed while working. One was Denver correspondent Terry Turner, who died in a small plane crash while on assignment. The other two lost their lives in wars—photographers Larry Burrows in Laos and Paul Schutzer in Israel during the Six-Day War. Paul's death was particularly ironic. A few years earlier, he had been badly injured during our coverage of Hurricane Audrey in Louisiana. Kelley and I were flying in a rescue helicopter when we spotted an emergency signal on the soggy ground below. We landed, and Schutzer was immediately flown to a Lake Charles hospital, where his hemorrhaging spleen was removed just in time. He was spared then, only to die in a Middle Eastern desert.

Partly because of the emotional and physical demands of their job, LIFE photographers lived life . . . shall we say, energetically? They ate well; they drank. They attracted women. I was sitting in a Charlotte, N.C., bar with an especially flirtatious photographer who was targeting two attractive women nearby. "Are these guys married?" one of the women asked the other.

"No," her friend replied, "but their wives are."

One photographer I worked with never went to bed without a six-pack of beer beside his pillow. He once got drunk in New Orleans and instead of flying home, as expected, decided to catch a plane to Cuba, where Fidel Castro had just taken over. I was desperately checking the morgue in New Orleans—not the photo morgue, the real morgue—when I received a call from Havana that my colleague was covering the story that had gripped the world.

On a different occasion, that hard-drinking photographer taught me an invaluable lesson: Great shooters see things that the rest of the world doesn't. Even veteran LIFE reporters standing right beside them taking notes don't have the same powers of observation. The two of us were at the time covering a nighttime political rally in the mountains of Jamaica. I was there all evening, eyes wide open, and yet when I looked at my friend's contact sheets later, I saw stunning pictures that I'd missed entirely at the time. That experience has always defined LIFE photography for me.

And that photography lives on—in the magazine and now in this commemorative 70th anniversary book. As was detailed in the Introduction, LIFE has been rendered in various versions and permutations—weekly, monthly, specials, now weekly again—this time delivered in newspapers every Friday. Whatever the future holds, that name and logo are a permanent part of American culture.

I was reminded of this a few years ago while playing Trivial Pursuit.

Some background: I edited the final issue of the weekly LIFE in December 1972. Its cover consisted of the names of people and places that had made news that year. In the bottom right-hand corner of that cover, I asked our art director Gene Light to insert the word "Goodbye" in small type. It seemed only fitting. He did so, and we never told anyone. That final issue came out, and slowly columnists began to notice the "Goodbye" and write about it. Now it was years later, and I picked up this Trivial Pursuit question and could not believe my eyes. It asked what the word was in the bottom right-hand corner of the last issue of the weekly LIFE. My entire career at the magazine—much of which is reflected in this amazing book—clearly prepared me for that precise moment.

Isn't that what we all call fate?

Perhaps so. But, of course, it wasn't Goodbye—not for LIFE. It came back as a monthly. When September 11 happened, America was again able to turn to LIFE, and its book *One Nation,* for the definitive photographic document of the day. And now it's back in weekly form yet again. Maybe that's fate too.

Or maybe the country needs and trusts this magazine in ways none of us fully understand.

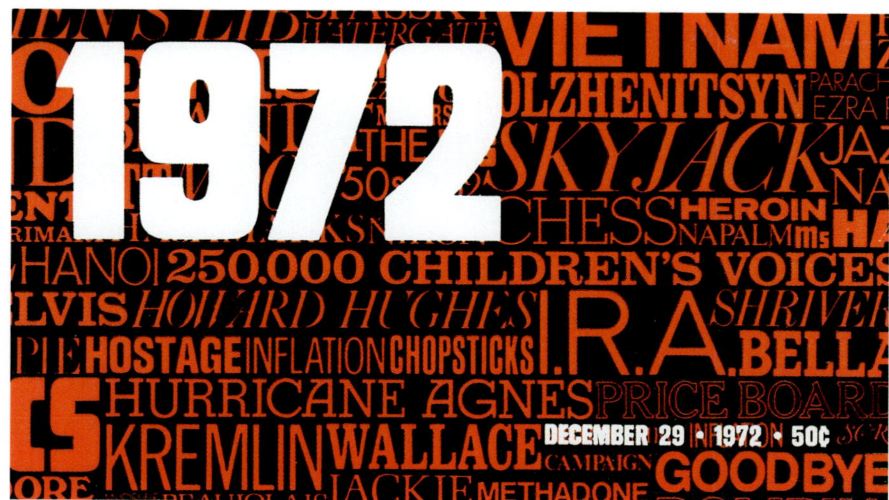

Richard B. Stolley *joined* LIFE *in 1953 as a reporter, and over the next 30 years served both the weekly and monthly versions of the magazine as a writer and editor. He was, as well, the founding managing editor of* People *magazine. He was inducted into the American Society of Magazine Editors' Hall of Fame in 1996.*

THE PRESIDENCY

LIFE and America's Chief Executives have enjoyed a long, durable relationship, one which began literally with the very first issue. Included in those pages was a section called "The President's Album," a kind of picture diary of Franklin D. Roosevelt. Apparently the editors were well pleased with the piece, judging from their gushing remarks in an introductory statement: "Luckily for LIFE, it can start its diary with a President who is a marvelous camera actor and is not above demonstrating his art." This presidential link has extended right through to the current man in office, George W. Bush, who provided an introduction for our 2002 book on the challenges of September 11, *The American Spirit*, and whose wife, Laura, took LIFE on a tour of her favorite White House room for a feature that ran last year.

If we may expand on the sentiments expressed by the earliest LIFE editors: Given that LIFE is, principally, a photographic endeavor, it's clearly not a bad thing for a LIFE subject—any LIFE subject—to be photogenic (which is another way of saying "a marvelous camera actor"). Looking back, our various treatments of, say, Richard Nixon, don't seem quite as fawning—nor were there as many of them—as those of, say, John Kennedy. Life, and LIFE, is not always fair.

The Kennedys and LIFE seemed made for each other. JFK's athletic handsomeness and easy grin were photographic dynamite, and the magazine happily went along on the fairytale stroll through our American Camelot. Even with his shocking death, President Kennedy and LIFE proved a potent tandem with the publication of the Zapruder images.

The surviving Kennedy clan continued to make regular appearances in LIFE. Jackie was, of course, the most glamorous example of all the First Ladies—dating back to Eleanor Roosevelt—to grace our pages, and America's interest in her continued long after her husband's death. The campaign trail has been a staple for the magazine, and staff photographer Bill Eppridge's shot of Bobby Kennedy dashing along the beach during the '68 race was the very stuff of LIFE. So, too, was Eppridge's famous, horrific image of RFK felled by an assassin's bullet later that same spring.

LIFE has enjoyed special entrée to the Oval Office, sometimes owing to the power of the publication, sometimes to the avidity and skills of its photographers. Indeed, several Presidents have forged warm personal relationships with particular LIFE photographers, and these have led to special, intimate pictures. There is, however, a presidential moment that we would prefer to forget. We see herein the famous picture of Harry Truman gleefully displaying the *Chicago Daily Tribune* with its embarrassing headline, DEWEY DEFEATS TRUMAN. Well, LIFE was so confident that the heavily favored Dewey would win that we went to press a few days before the election with a picture caption that referred to Dewey as "the next President."

Fortunately, Truman forgave us our sin and, as is the case with all Presidents, he appeared many times in our pages.

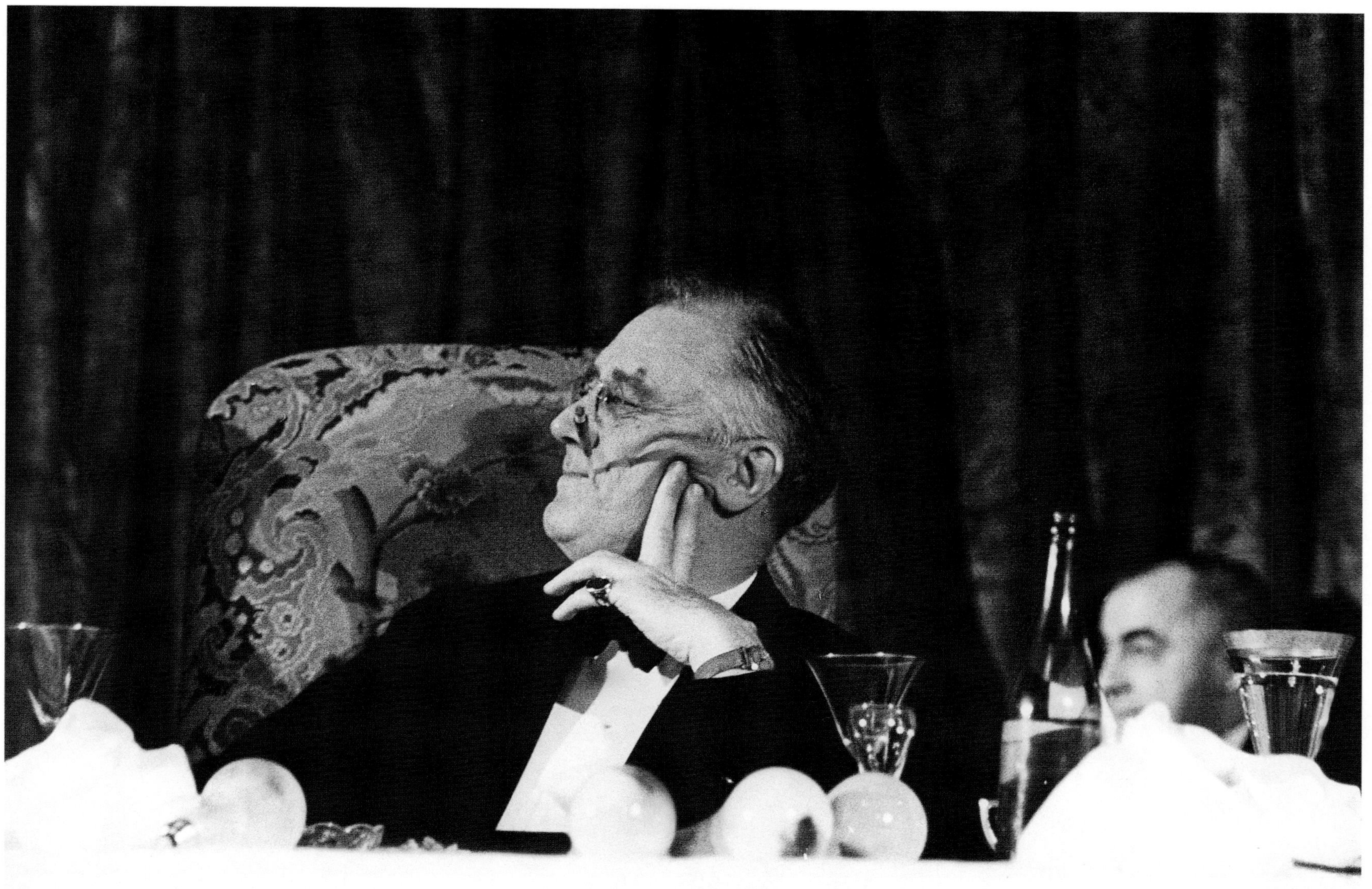

A CONFIDENT LEADER

President Roosevelt had already given his speech when this picture was taken on January 8, 1938, at a dinner in Washington, D.C., honoring Andrew Jackson. FDR's talk had reaffirmed his Jacksonian devotion to the good of the masses, and now he was savoring the positive response of the assembled Democrats. Note the photographers' spent flashbulbs littering the table.

THOMAS D. MCAVOY

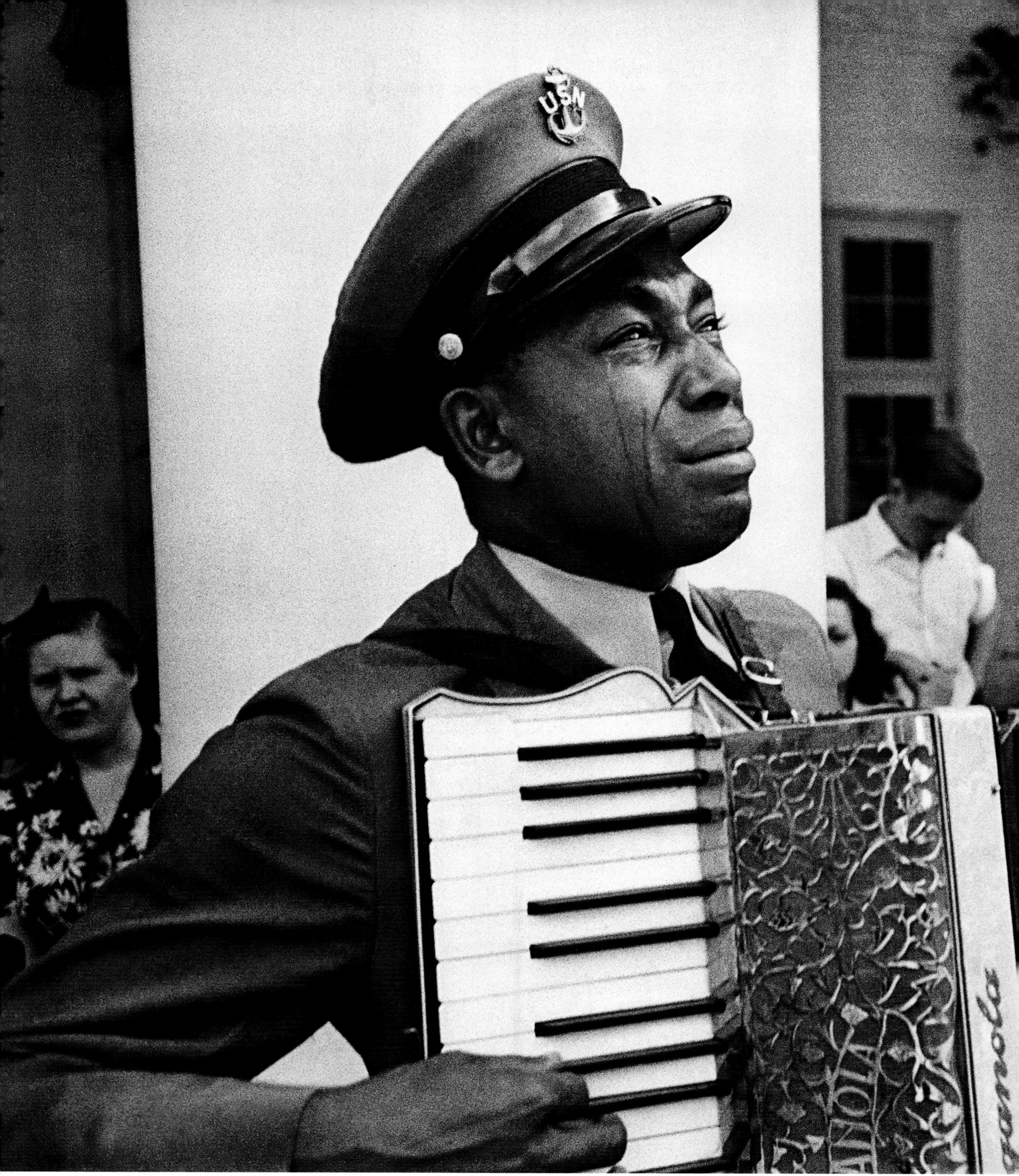
USN

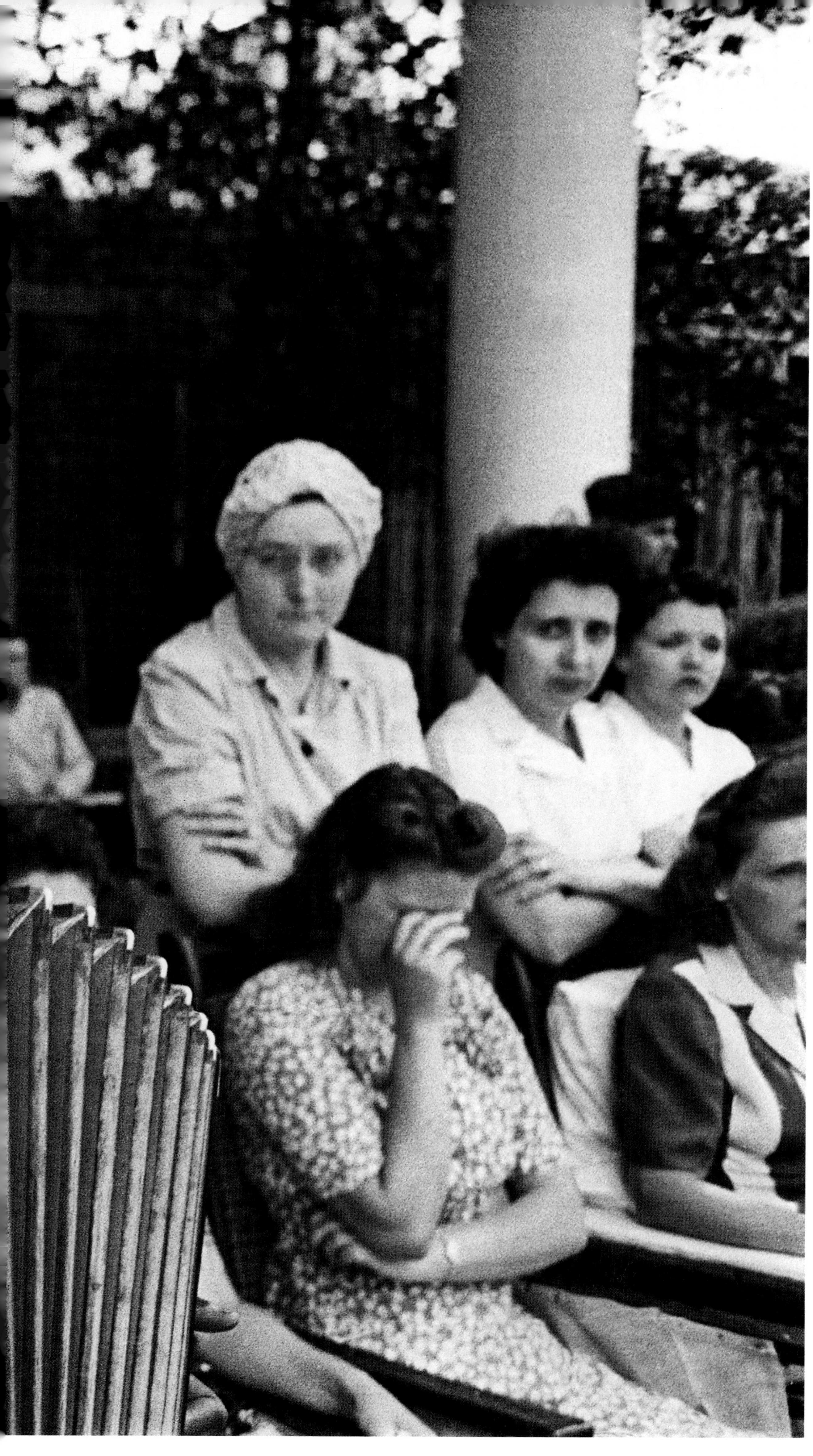

GRIEF

FDR's death in April 1945 was a terrible blow to America, the loss of a man who had led the nation out of the Depression and guided her through the Second World War. Here, in Warm Springs, Ga., where the President had been slated to attend a barbecue on the day he died, CPO Graham Jackson plays "Going Home" as FDR's body is borne past. "I heard this accordion start to play behind me," said photographer Clark. "I thought to myself, 'My God, what a picture.' "

EDWARD CLARK

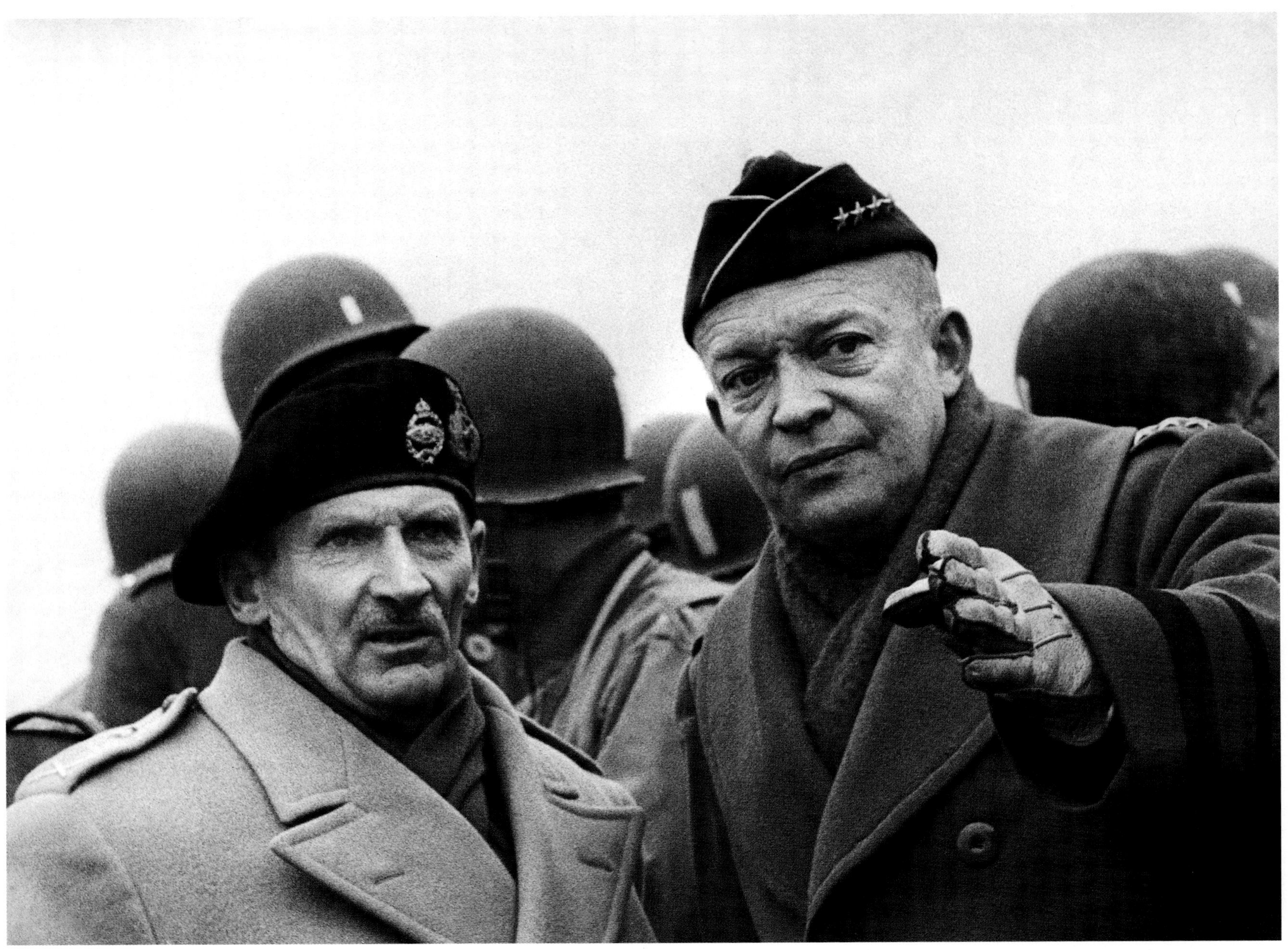

IN DEFENSE OF DEMOCRACY

Future President Dwight Eisenhower was in charge of Allied operations in Europe during WWII, and here in England in 1944, not long before D-Day, he discusses a point of strategy with British Field Marshal Bernard Montgomery. Frank Scherschel was one of LIFE's six accredited photographers at the invasion of Normandy.

FRANK SCHERSCHEL

A HEADLINE FOR THE AGES

Almost without exception, political experts across the land were in agreement that New York Governor Thomas Dewey would roll over the incumbent, Harry Truman, in the presidential election of 1948. Gallup, Roper and the other polls had, from the conventions to the morning of the vote, been unanimous in predicting a victory for the GOP. Of course, as we now know, you can't always believe what you read.

W. EUGENE SMITH

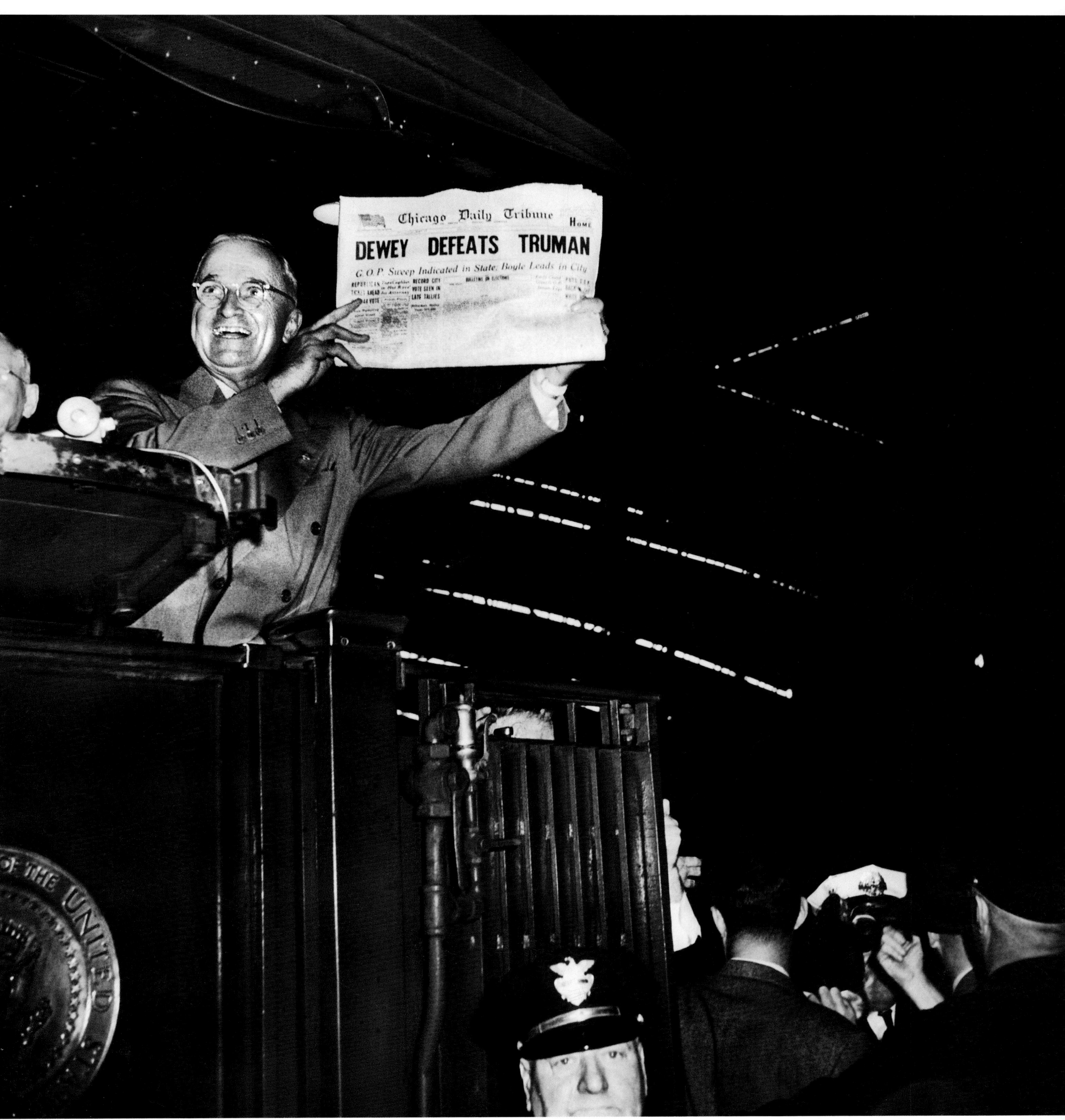
Chicago Daily Tribune
HOME
DEWEY DEFEATS TRUMAN
G.O.P. Sweep Indicated in State; Boyle Leads in City

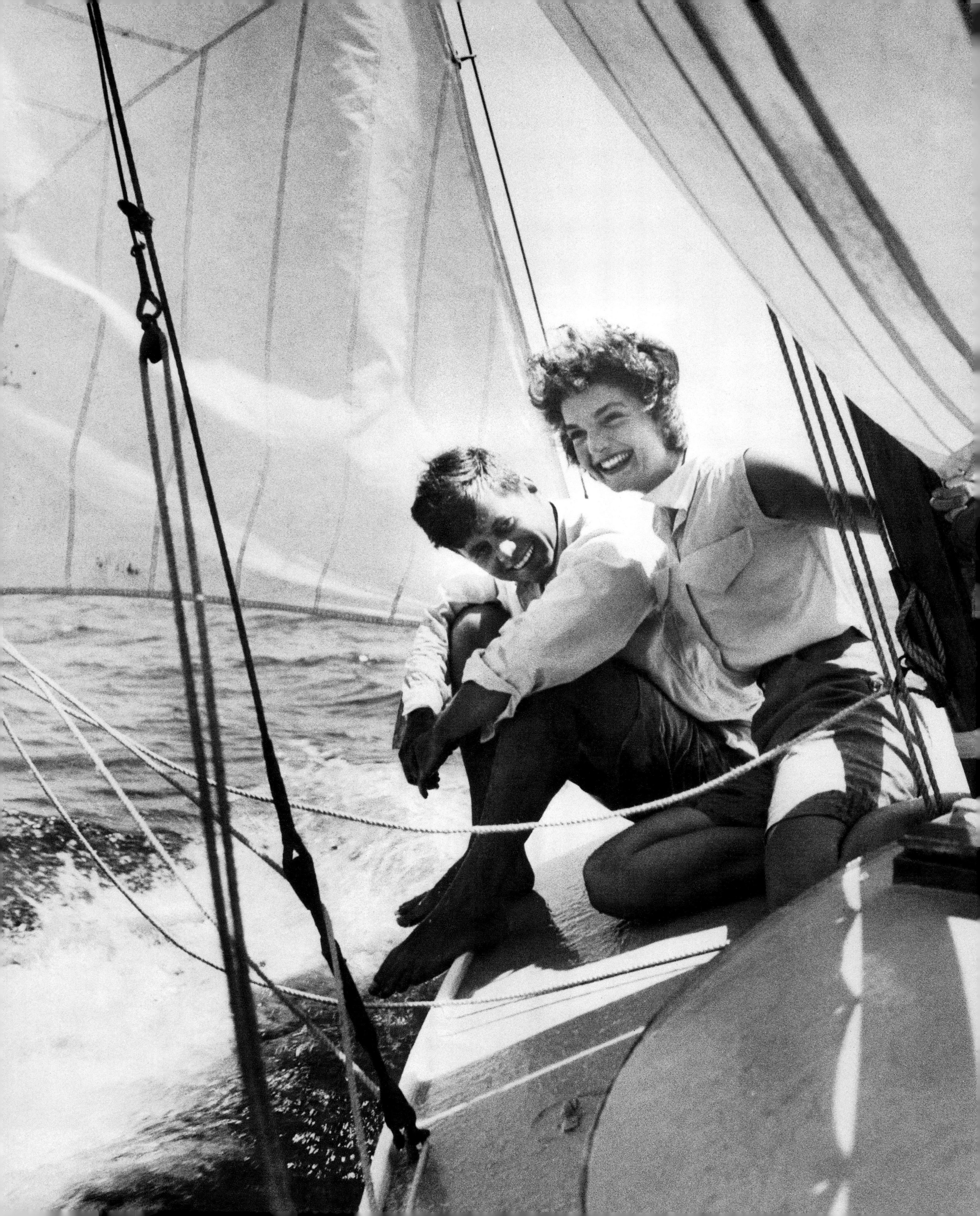

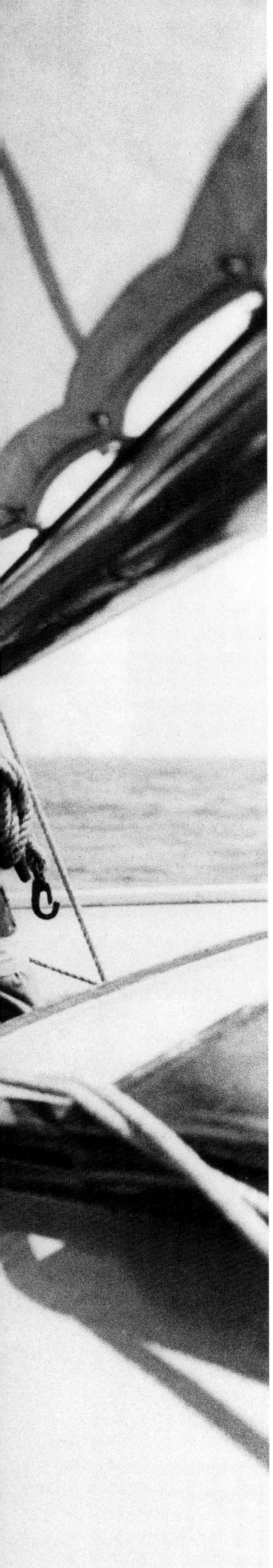

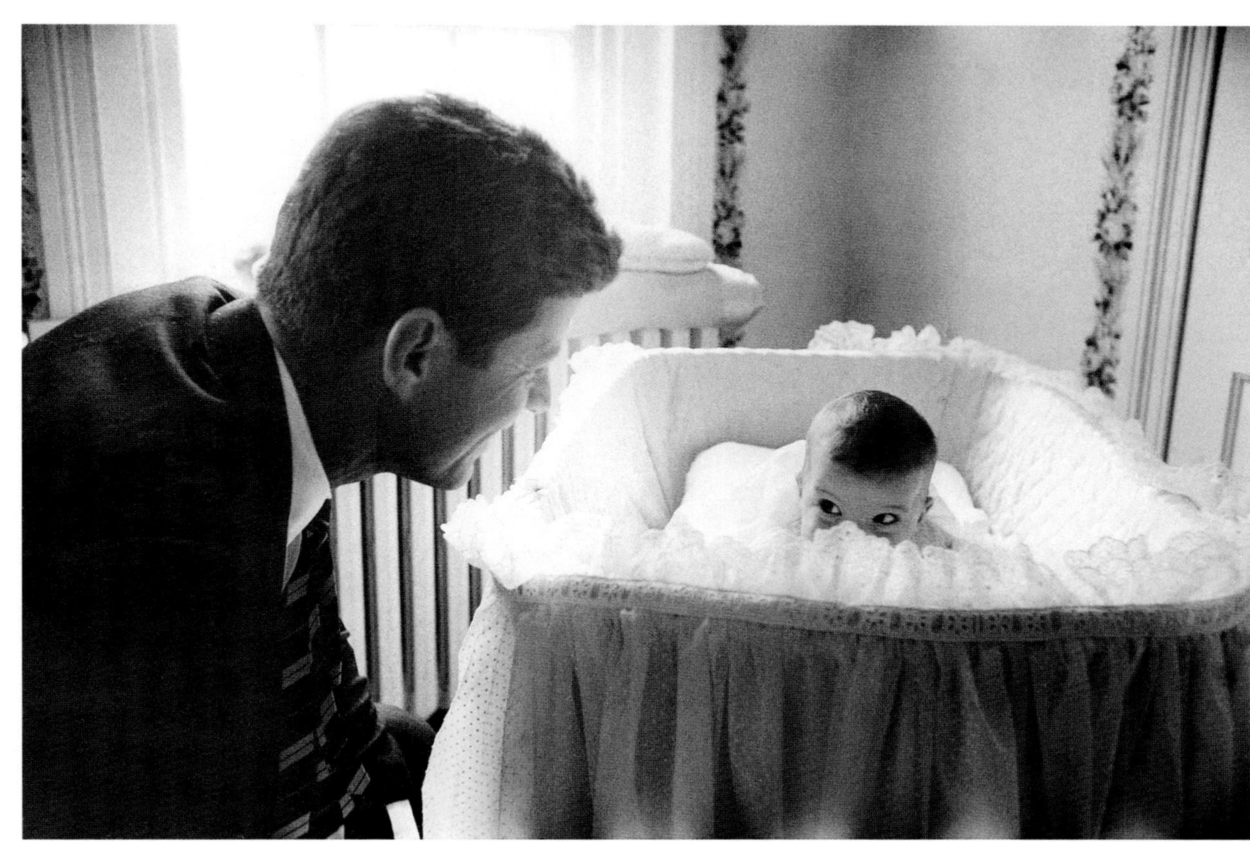

YOUTHFUL BEAUTIES

In July 1953, Senator Jack Kennedy and his betrothed, Jacqueline Bouvier, enjoy a sail off Cape Cod. Kennedy had brought his fiancée—they would wed in two months—to the family compound at Hyannis Port for a weekend of fun. This photo from the July 20 issue of LIFE marked the first time Jackie appeared on the cover of a national magazine. It would be difficult to calculate how many would follow; for LIFE alone there were more than two dozen. Above, in 1958, four-month-old Caroline peeks at Daddy. Said Kennedy, "I'm not home much, but when I am, she seems to like me."

LEFT **HY PESKIN** *ABOVE* **EDWARD CLARK**

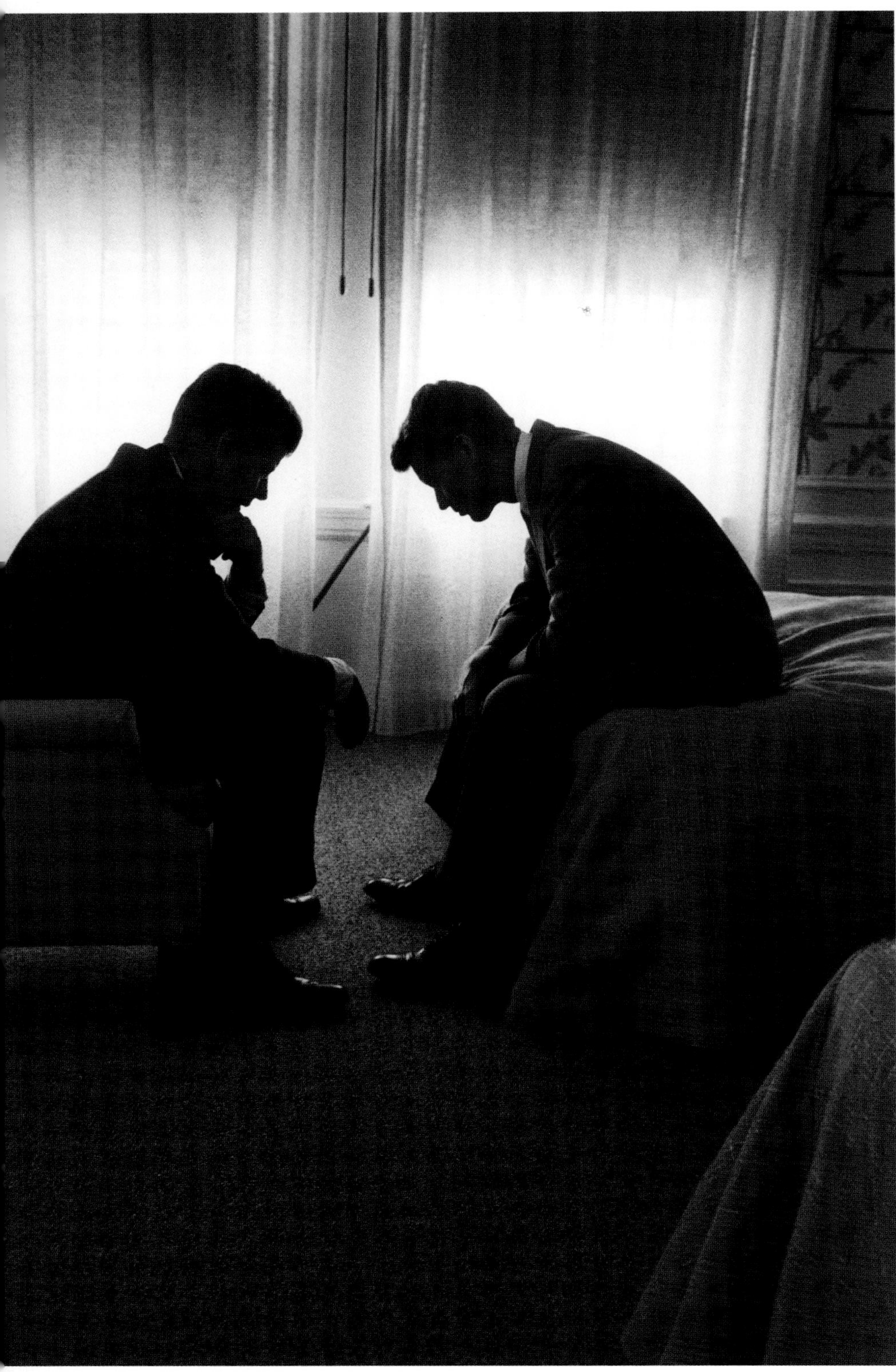

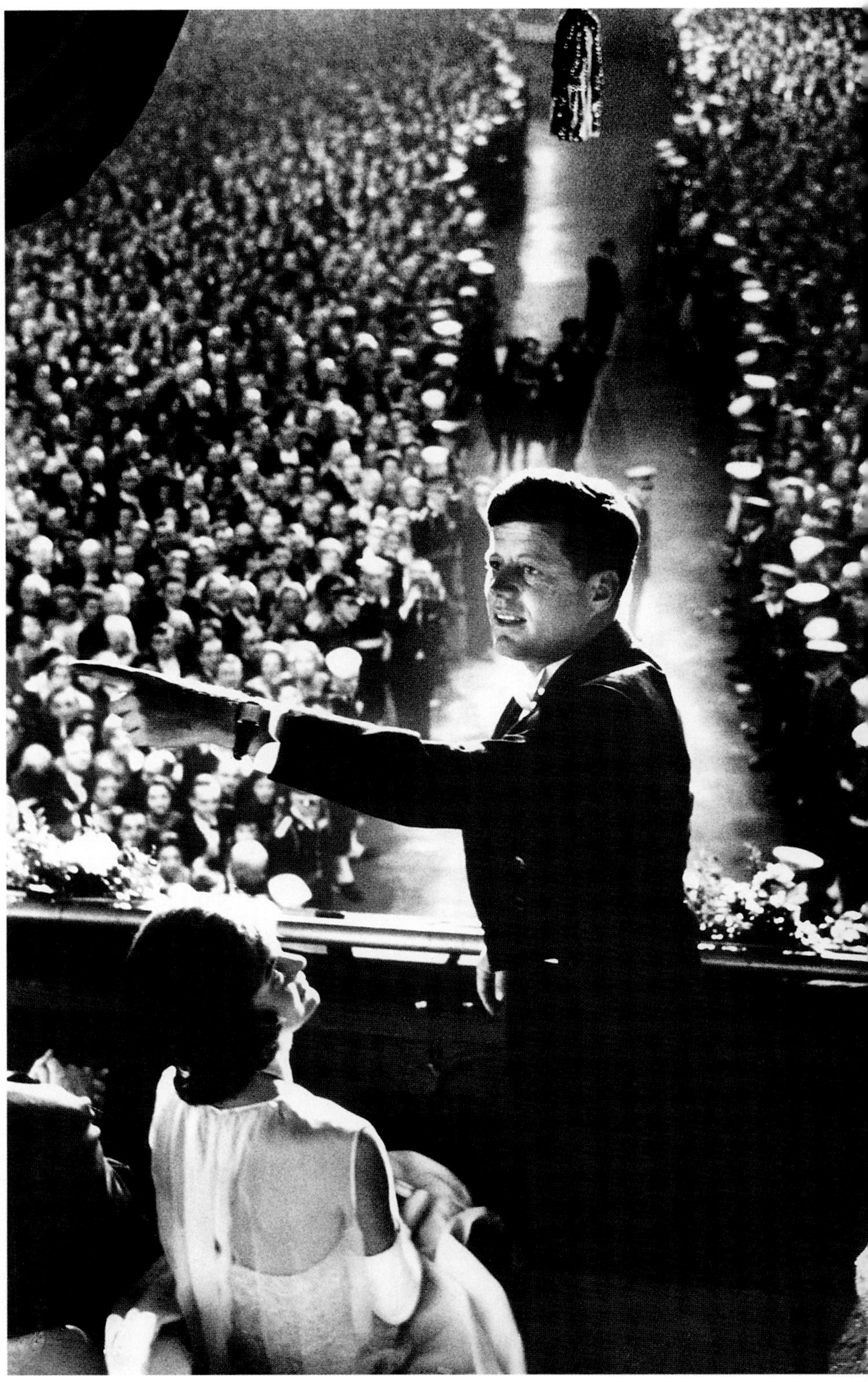

A MAN AND HIS FAMILY

The campaign for the presidency was a tough one. Richard Nixon was a formidable foe. It was good for Jack Kennedy that he had selected a tough campaign organizer: his brother Bobby. At left they confer in a Los Angeles hotel suite in 1960. At center, the new President and First Lady attend an inaugural ball. At the time, LIFE wrote under this photo, A NEW HAND, A NEW VOICE, A NEW VERVE. At right, the President savors the sight of Caroline and John Jr. gamboling in the Oval Office. Jackie was concerned that the children lead as normal lives as possible, but when her back was turned JFK would sneak photographers into the West Wing. He knew that America loved the kids and that these pictures were good for presidential popularity.

LEFT **HANK WALKER** *CENTER* **PAUL SCHUTZER** *OPPOSITE* **CECIL STOUGHTON**

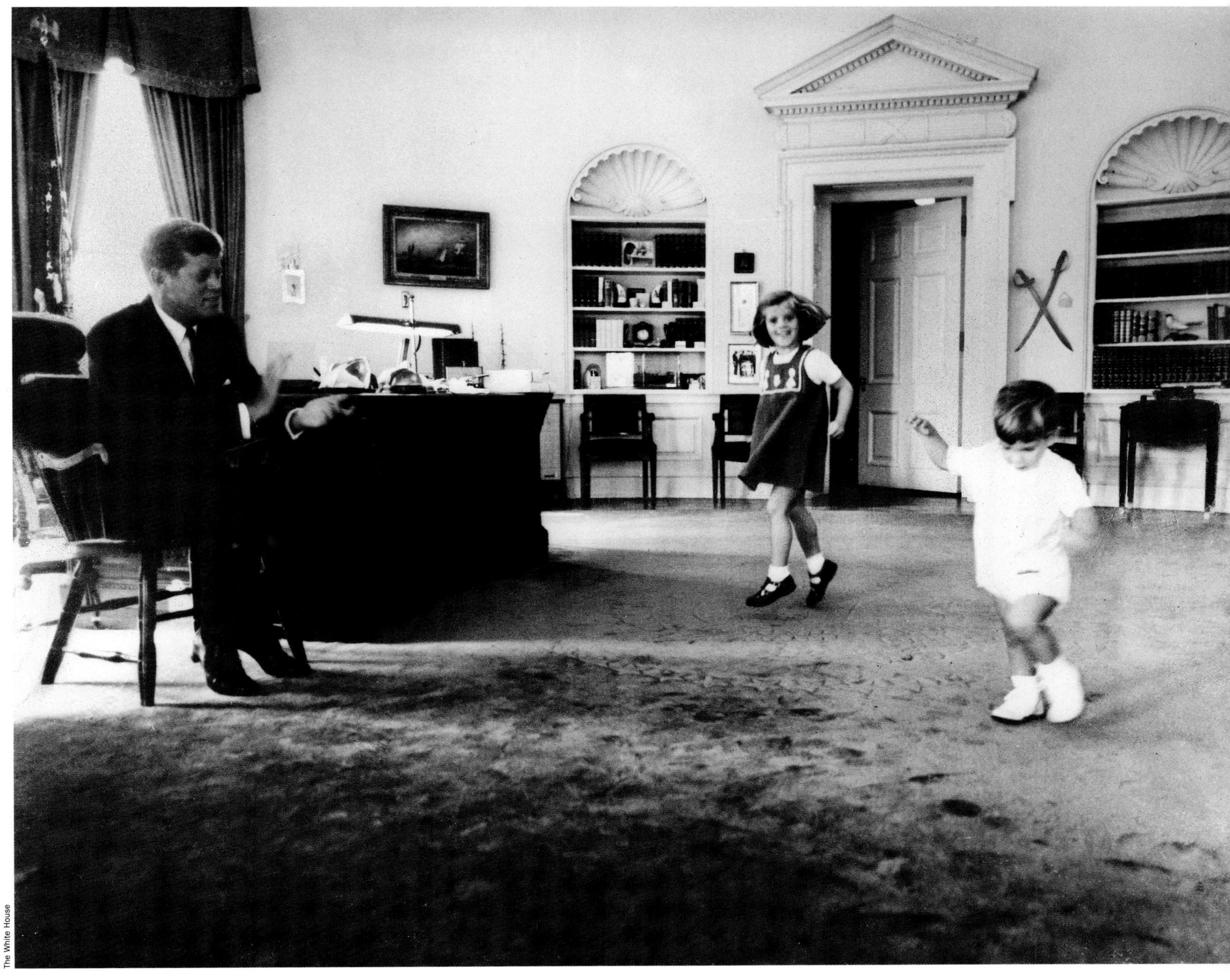
The White House

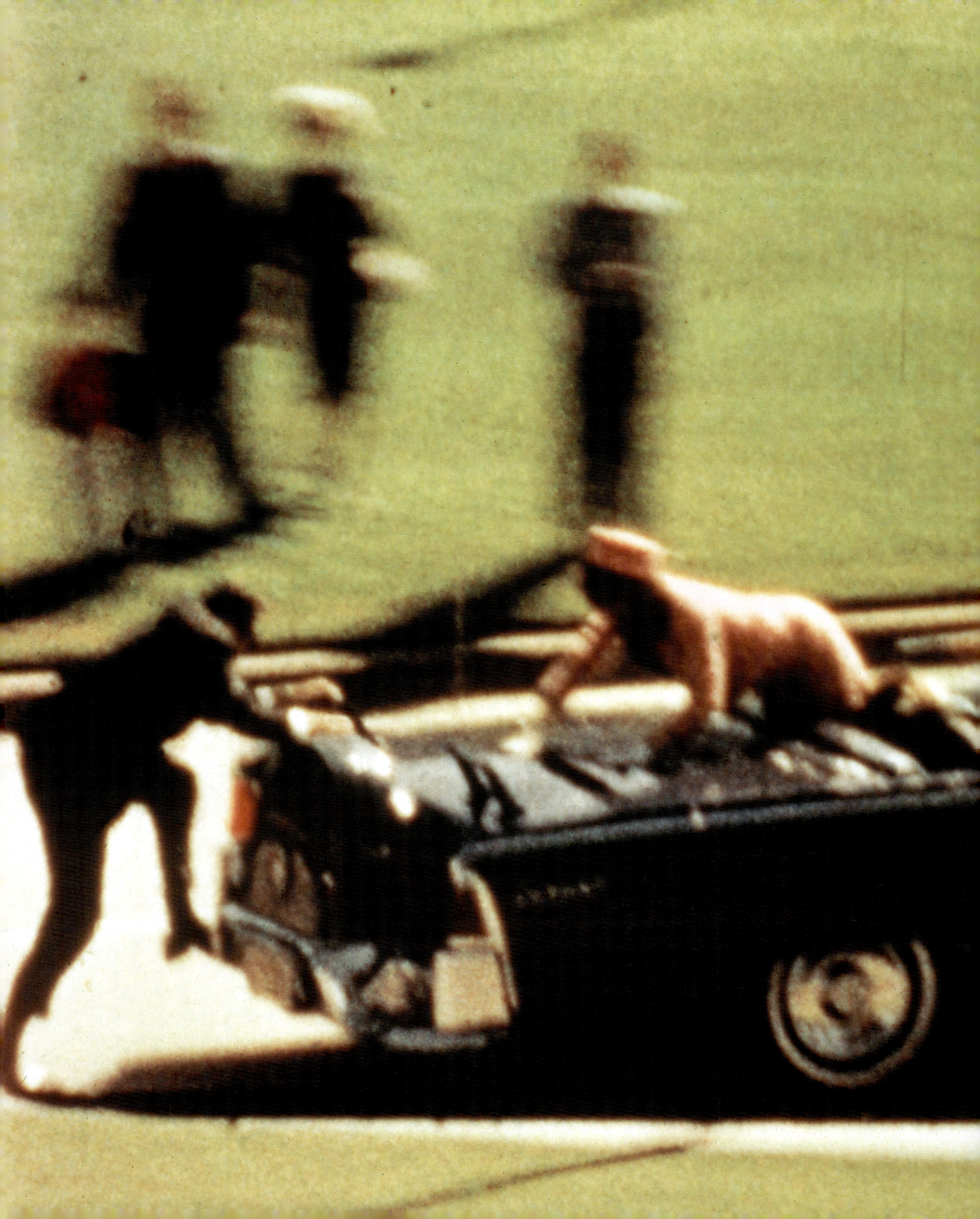

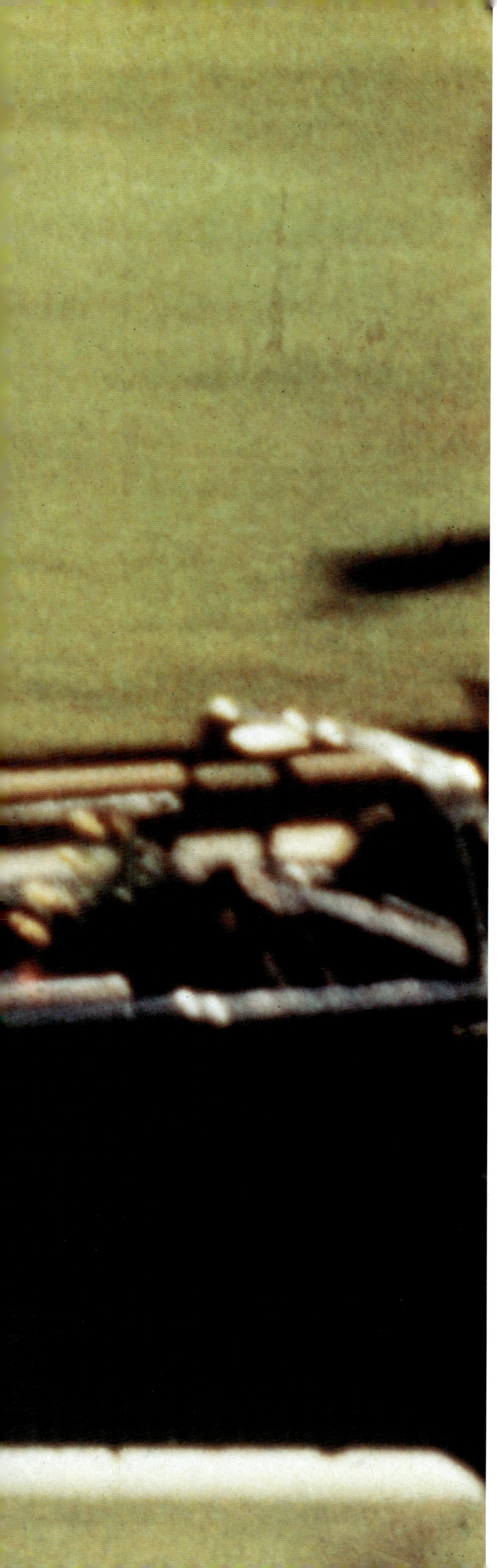

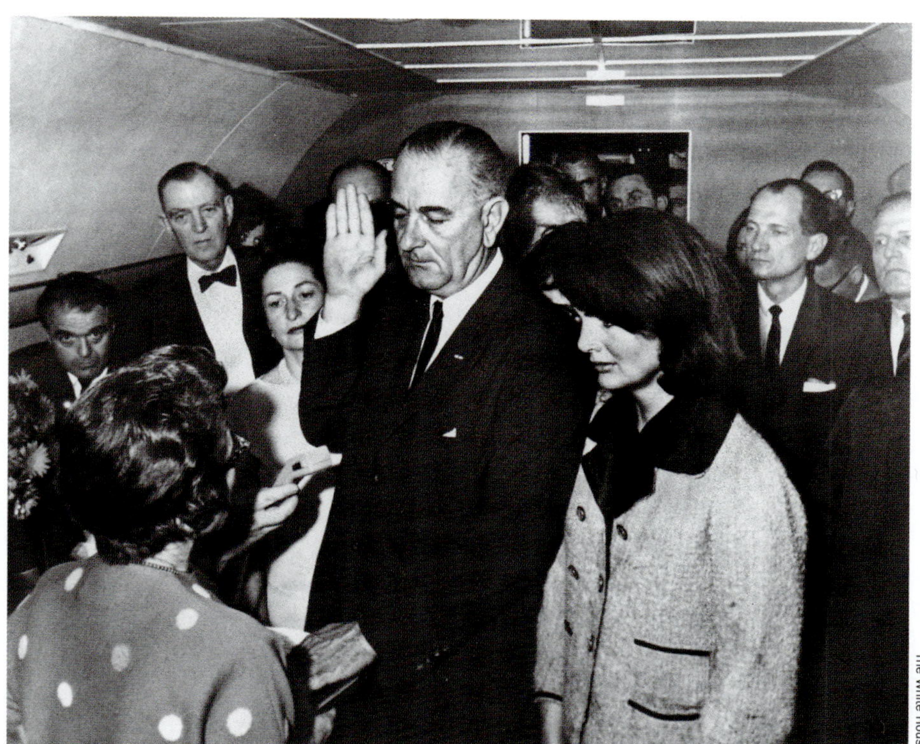

The White House

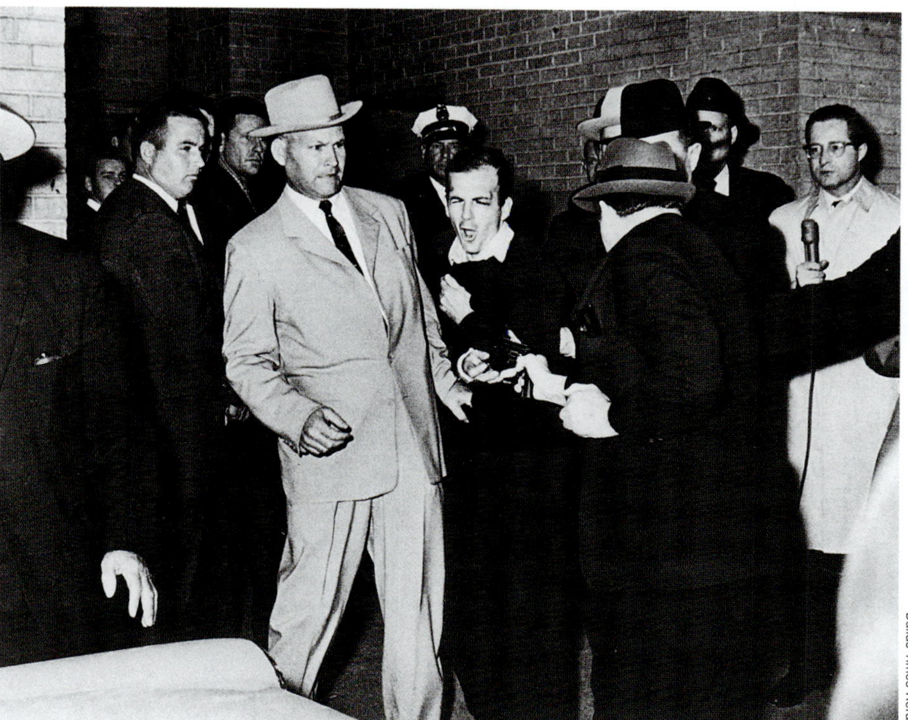

Dallas Times Herald

NIGHTMARE IN DALLAS

When the terrible word came that President Kennedy had been shot, LIFE dispatched a young editor named Dick Stolley to Dallas. He learned that an amateur photographer had made an 8mm film of the assassination. Stolley found Abraham Zapruder's number in the phone book and reached him at about midnight. The next morning, after looking at the film with Zapruder, Stolley delicately but swiftly secured the print rights, and LIFE ran 31 frames of the horrifying sequence. The film became a central point of focus in one of the century's darkest stories. Here, a Secret Service agent lunges for the car as the shocked First Lady crawls desperately onto the trunk. Just two hours later, at top, Lyndon Johnson is sworn in as President aboard *Air Force One.* He is flanked by his wife, Lady Bird, and Mrs. Kennedy. Two days later, the alleged assassin, Lee Harvey Oswald, is shot dead by Jack Ruby in the basement of the Dallas city jail.

LEFT **ABRAHAM ZAPRUDER** *TOP* **CECIL STOUGHTON** *ABOVE* **BOB JACKSON**

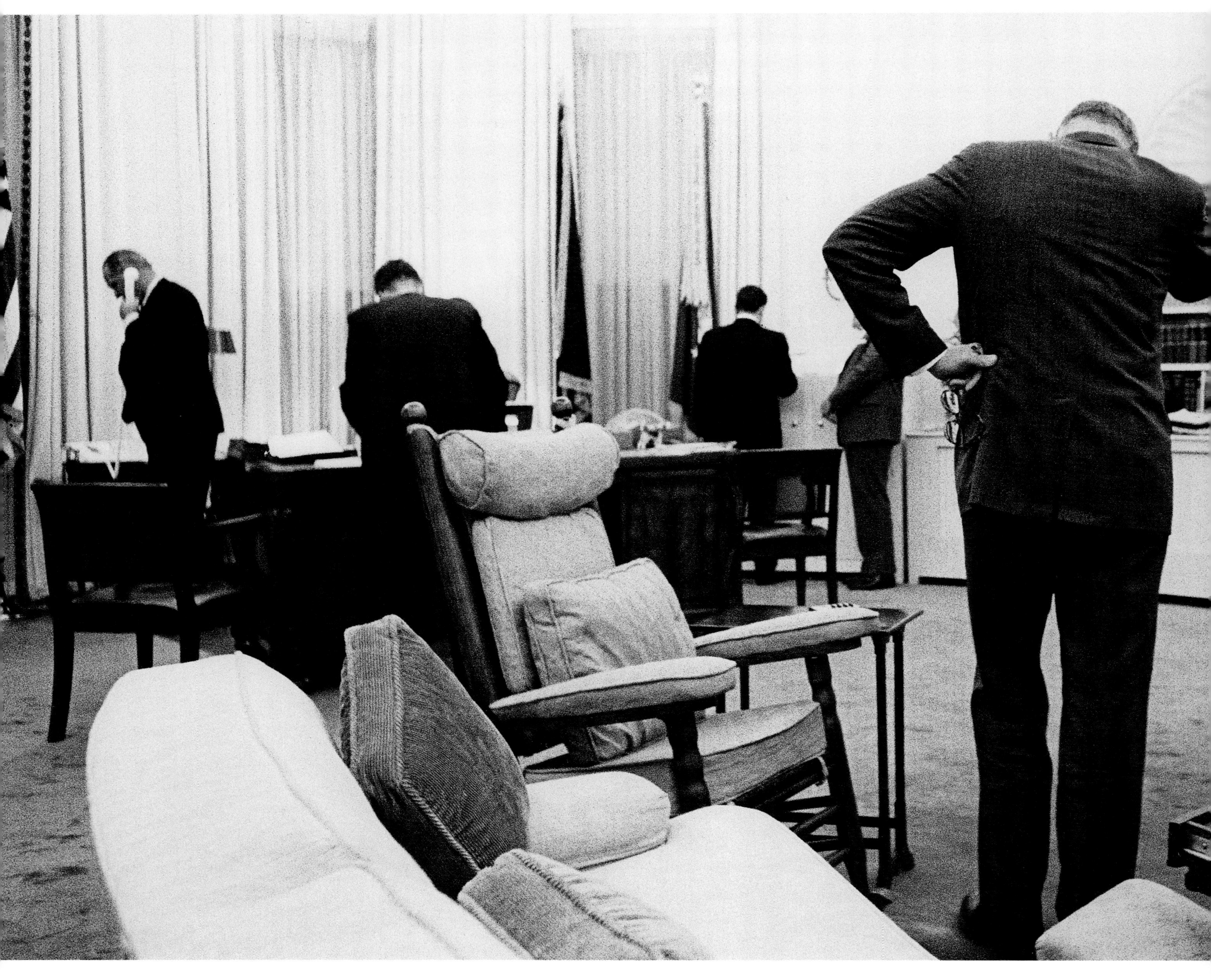

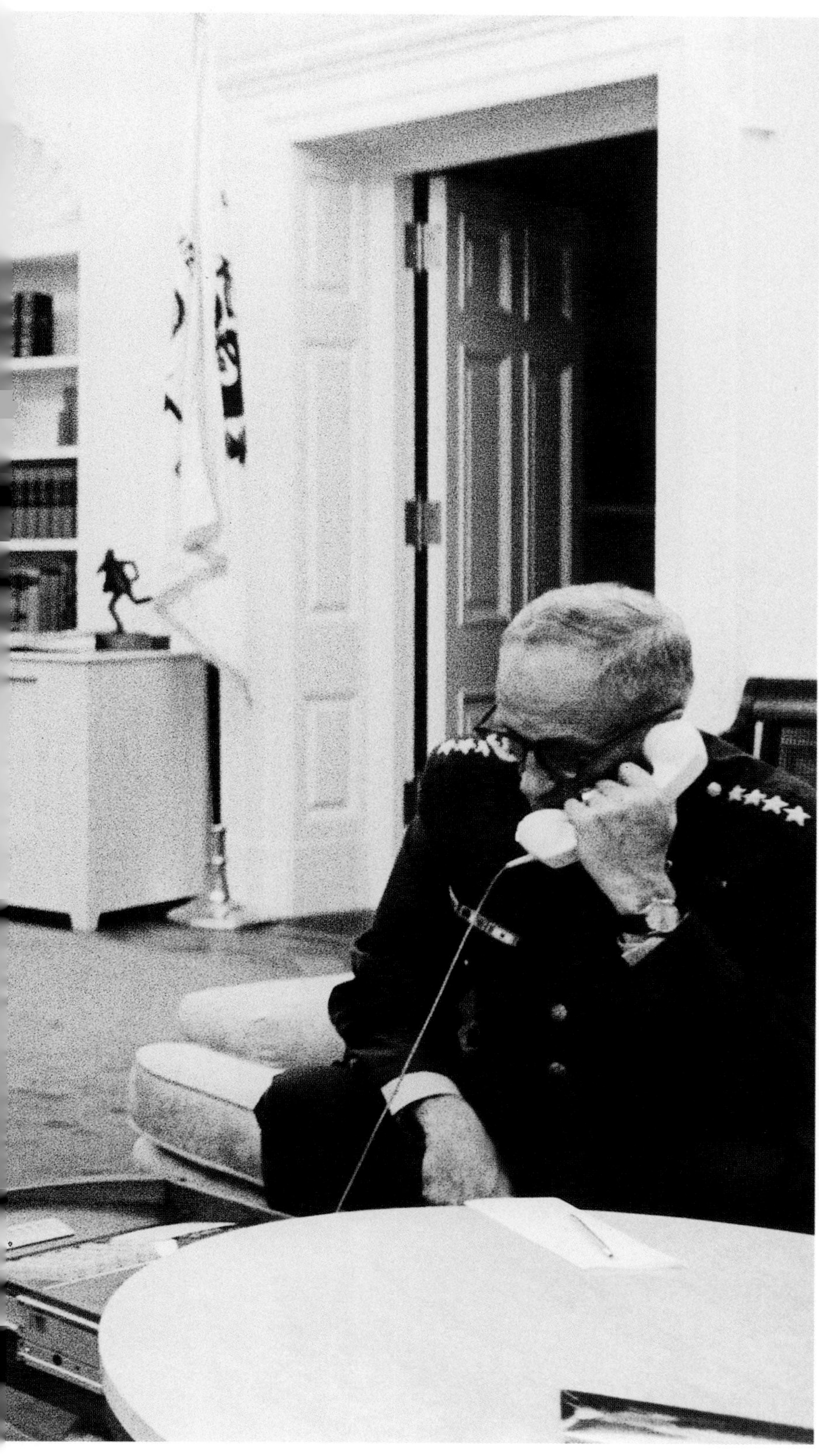

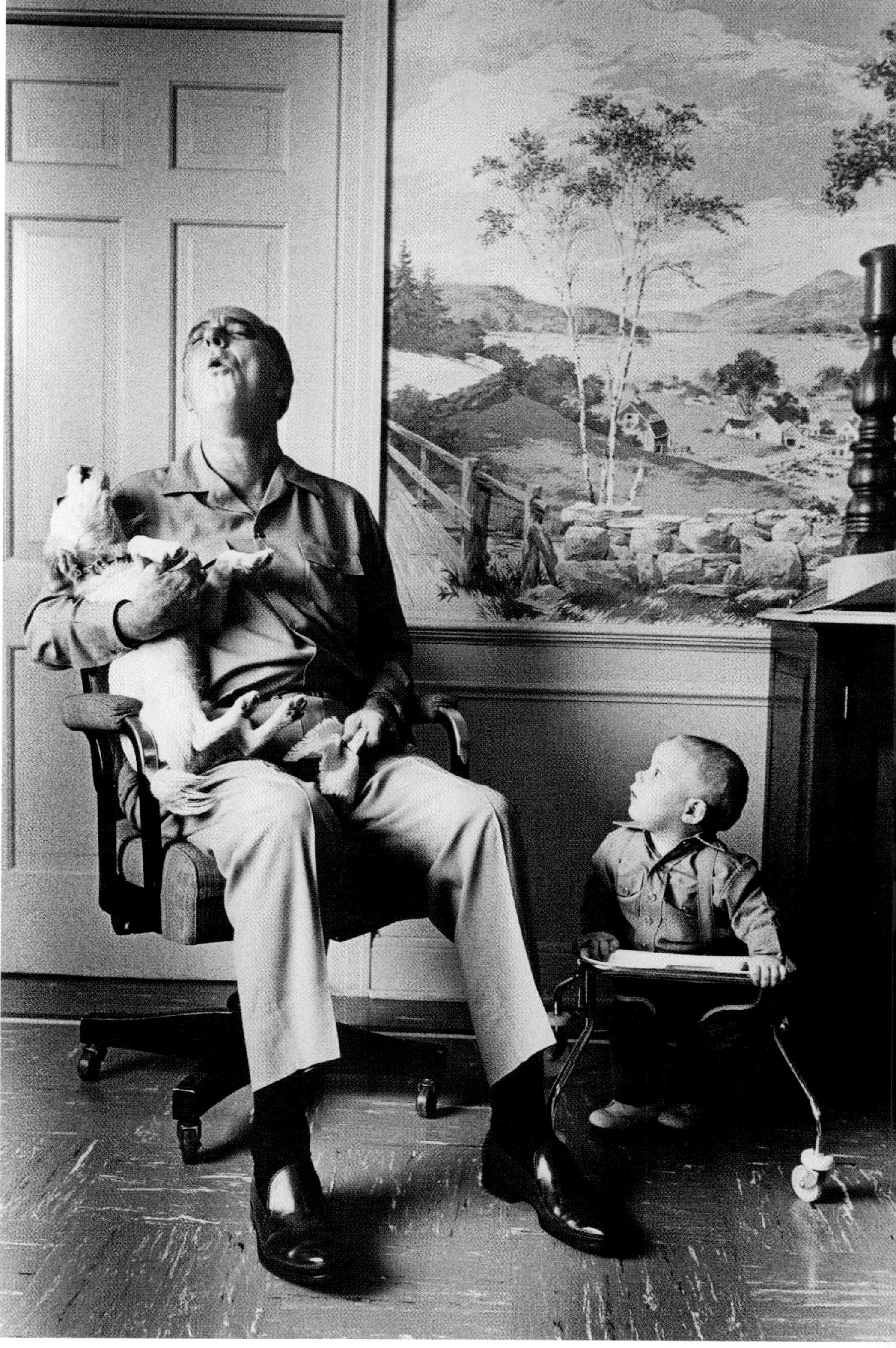

The White House (2)

THE GREAT SOCIETY

Johnson served as President during the turbulent 1960s, and although he was one tough hombre, he elected not to run for a final term. Vietnam was his overriding problem, but racial rioting was yet another complex matter. Here, in the Oval Office, Johnson (at far left) and staffers monitor riots in Detroit in 1967. Above, back home on his ranch in the months before his death, in January 1973, LBJ finally gets to relax. The former President enjoys a good howl with his dog, to the amazement of grandson Patrick Lyndon Nugent.

YOICHI OKAMOTO

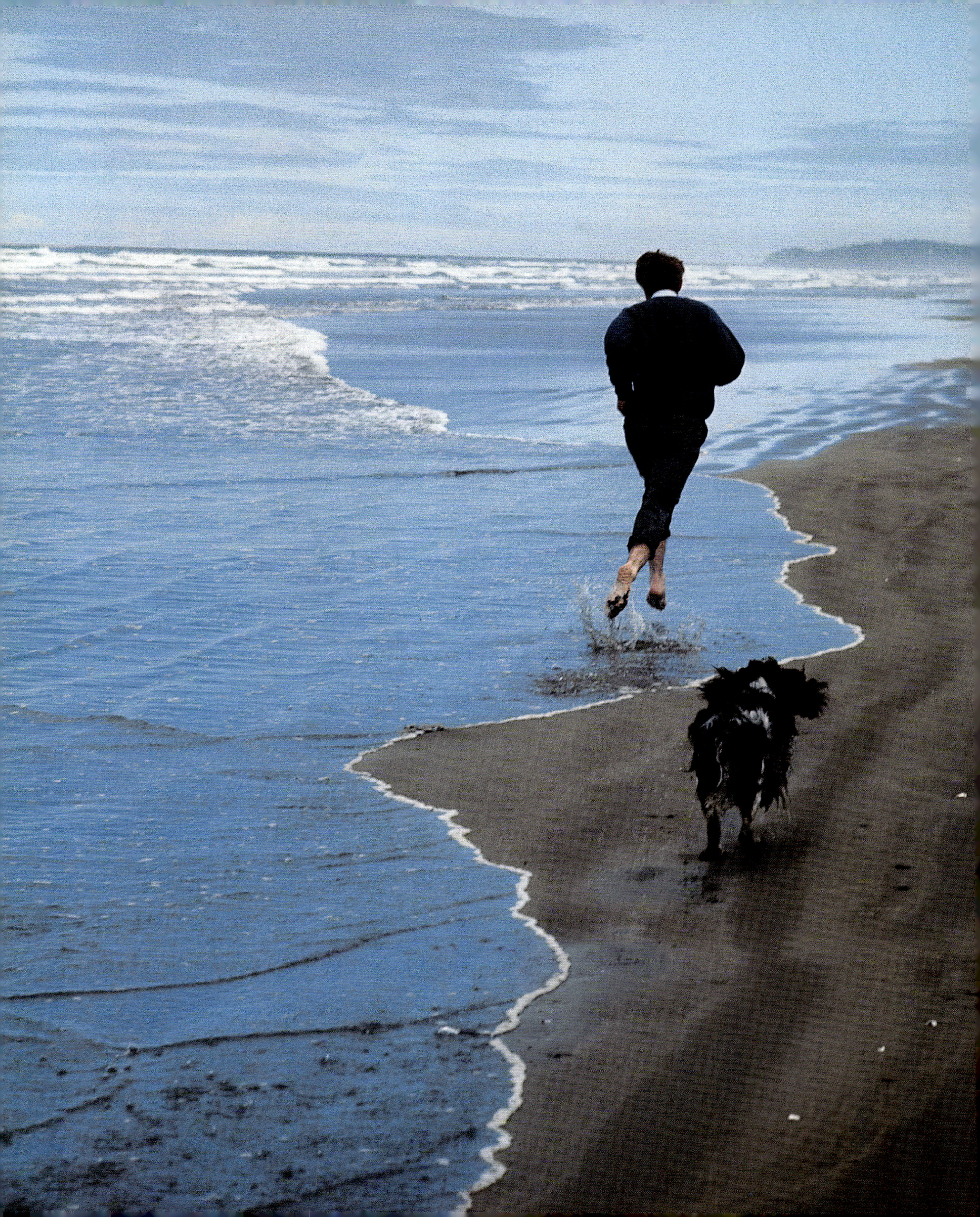

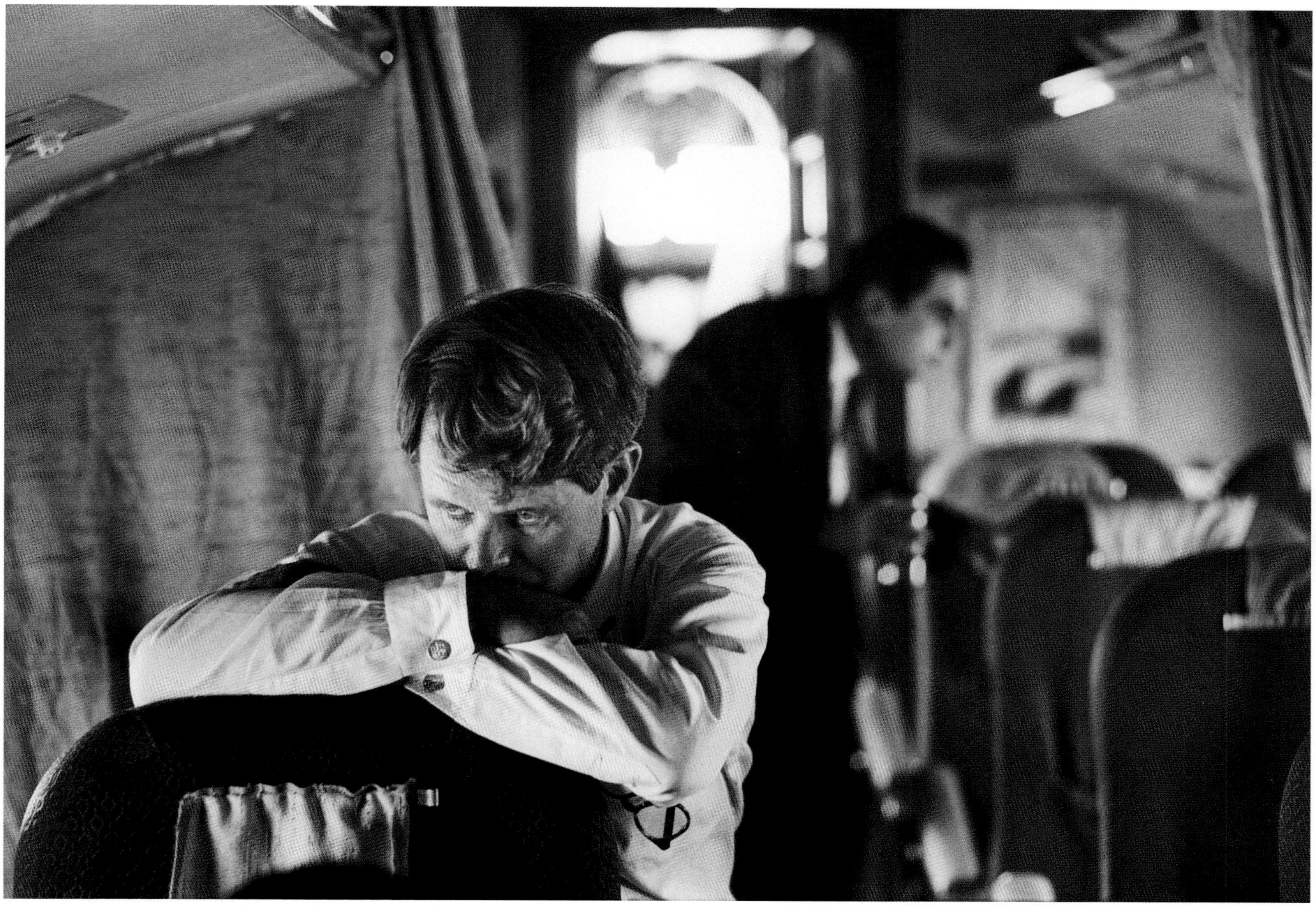

ROBERT F. KENNEDY

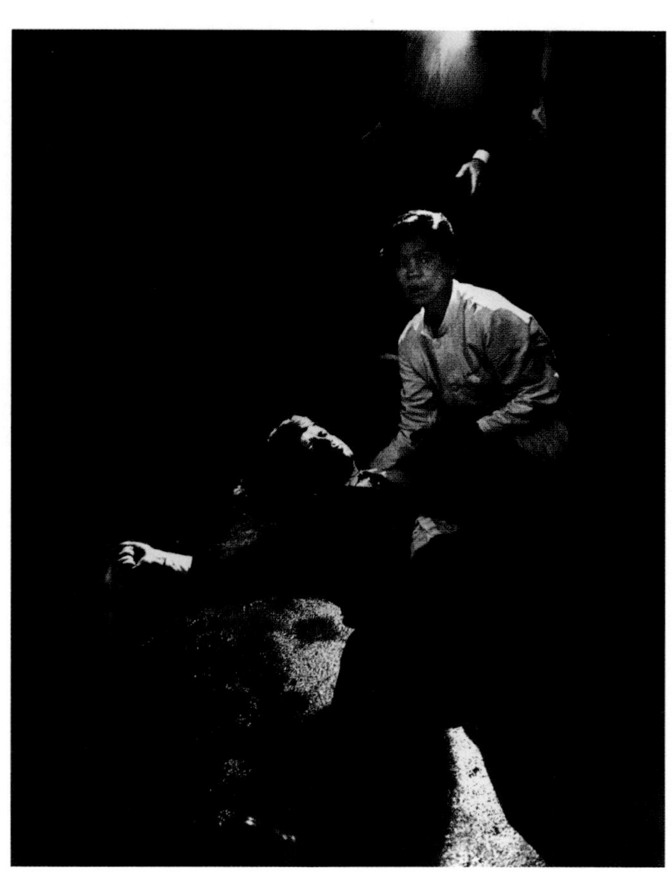

ANOTHER DREAM GONE WRONG

LIFE photographer Bill Eppridge was on hand to capture all three of these very different images of Bobby Kennedy. Above, in 1966, the intensely driven politician is seen on a campaign trip for local candidates. At left, in 1968, he is on his own campaign trail, for the Presidency, and his energy is funneled into a brisk run along the Oregon shore with his dog Freckles. In June of that same year, having delivered a speech in the Ambassador Hotel celebrating his victory in the crucial California primary, he is shot to death by Sirhan Sirhan. Kennedy had just shaken the hand of this busboy, Juan Romero. Photographer Eppridge recalled, "There was nobody else around . . . the busboy looked up, and he had this look in his eye. I made that picture, and then suddenly the whole situation closed in again. And it became bedlam."

BILL EPPRIDGE (3)

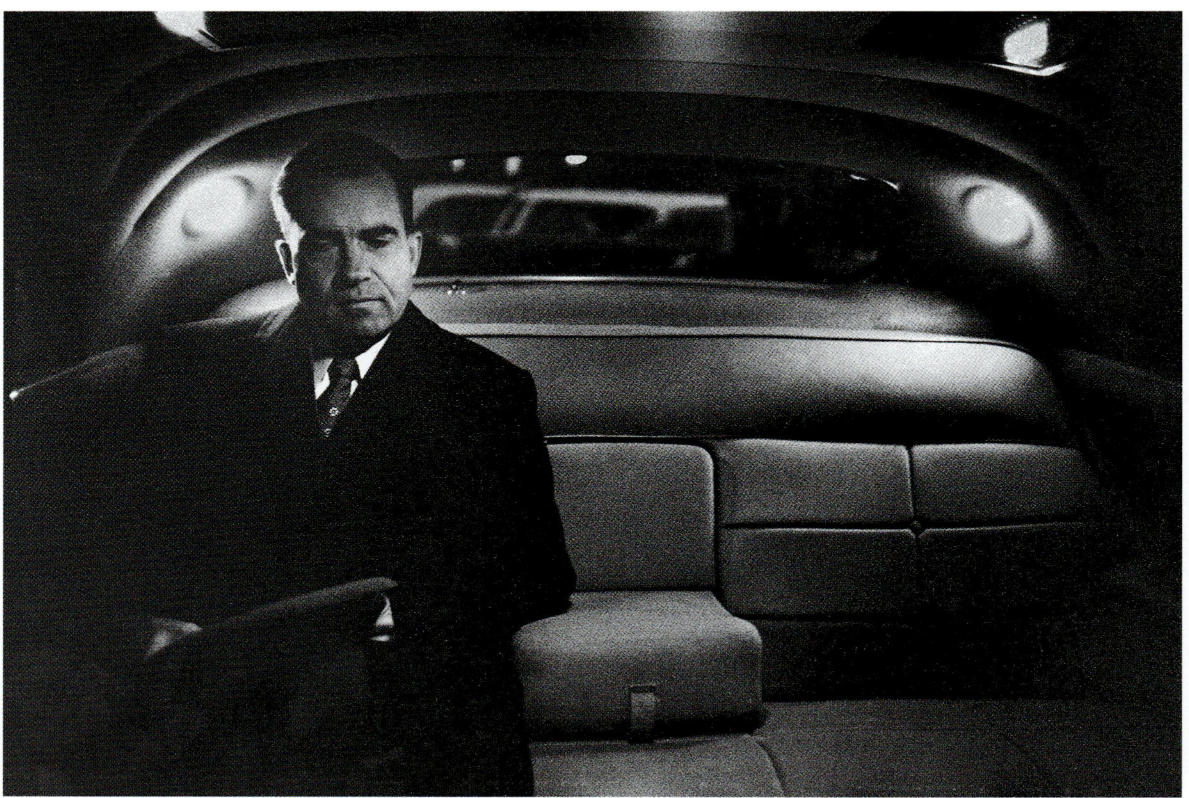

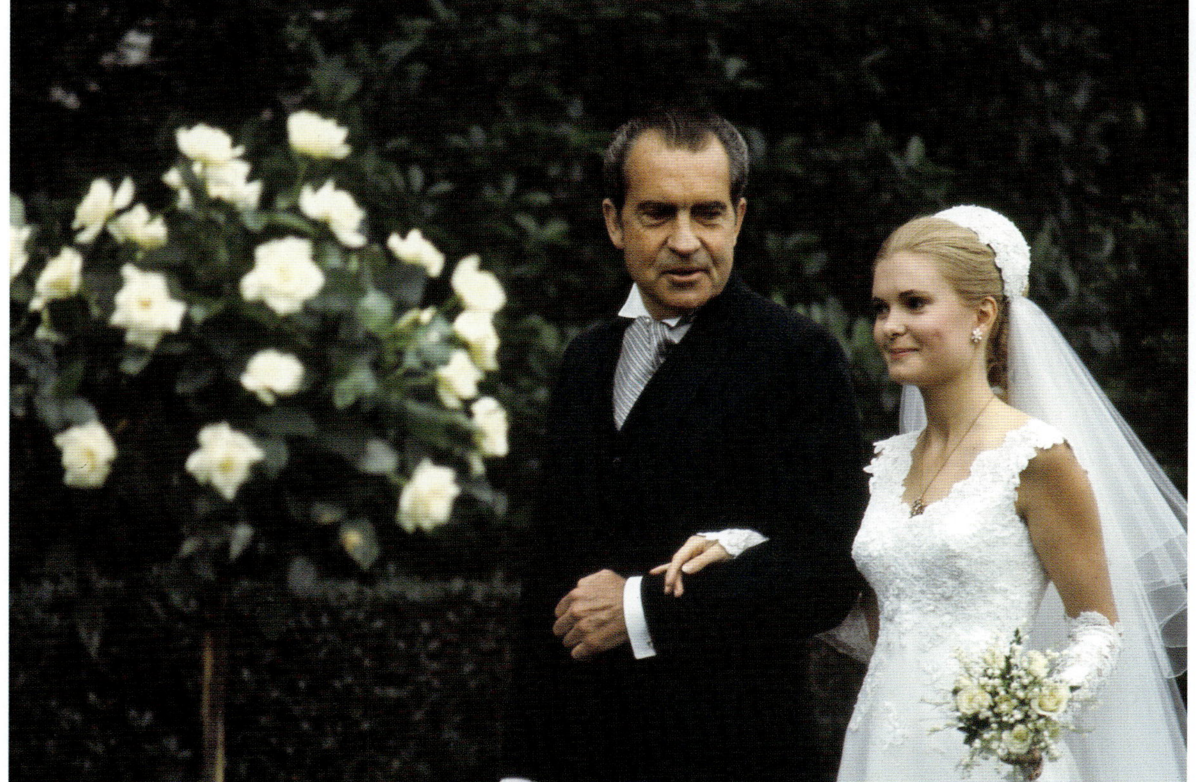

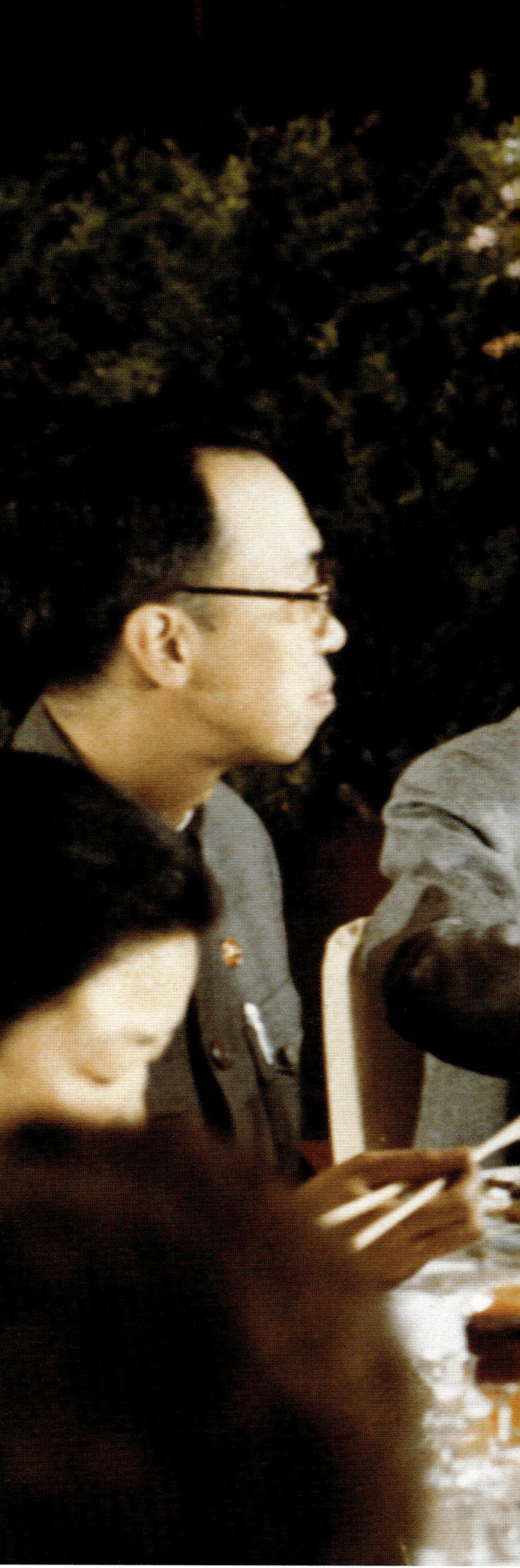

The White House

THREE CRISES

At top, in 1957, Vice President Nixon heads for home after a long day at the White House. He is filling in for President Eisenhower, who has (temporarily) been felled by a minor stroke. Is that a lean and hungry look on the Veep? Above, in June 1971, it seemed that the elements were against him, but then a rainy day relents just long enough for the President to escort his daughter Tricia across the White House lawn to the Rose Garden altar, where in 20 minutes she will become Mrs. Edward Cox. At right, in early '72, during the course of an historic visit to China, the consummate politician weighs the diplomatic pros and cons of that . . . thing . . . in his chopsticks.

TOP **HANK WALKER** *ABOVE* **CO RENTMEESTER** *RIGHT* **OLLIE ATKINS**

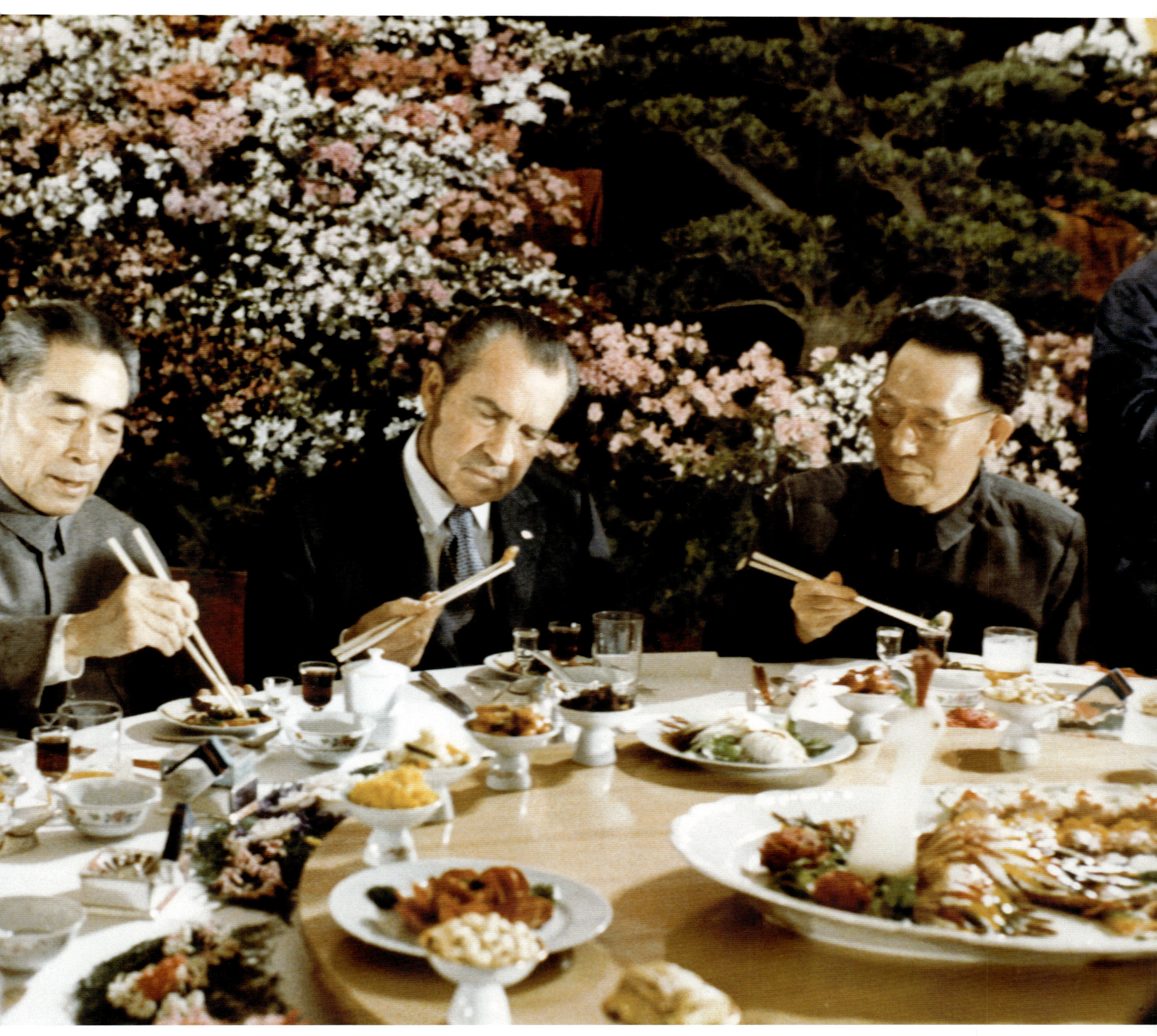

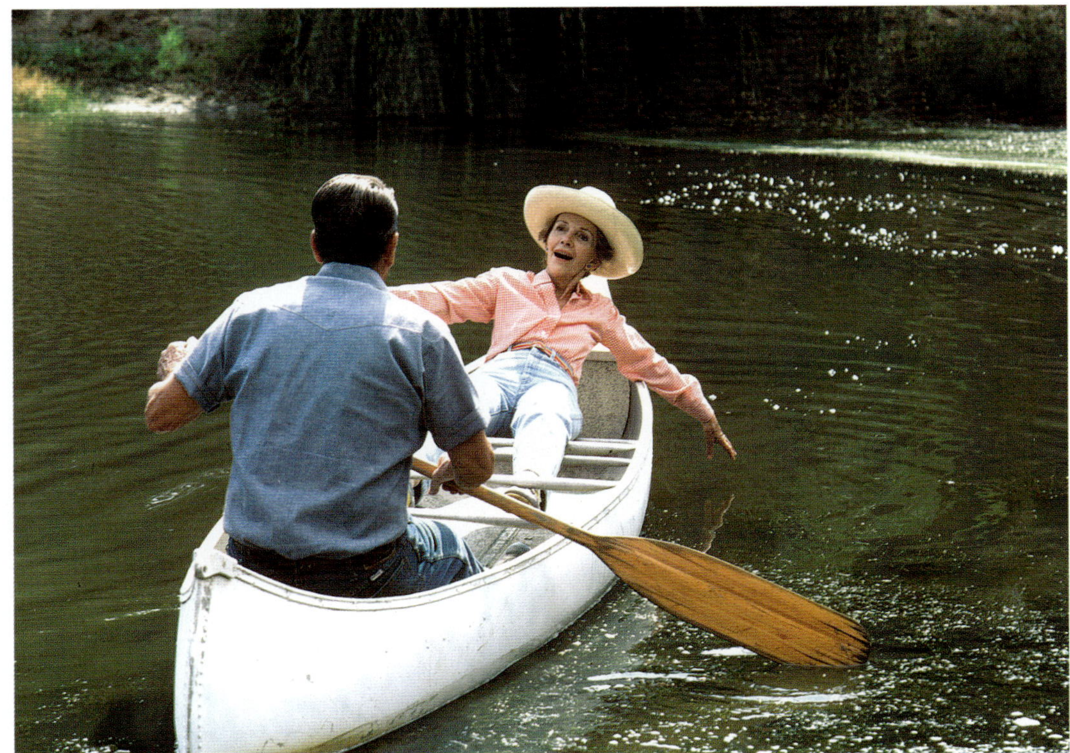

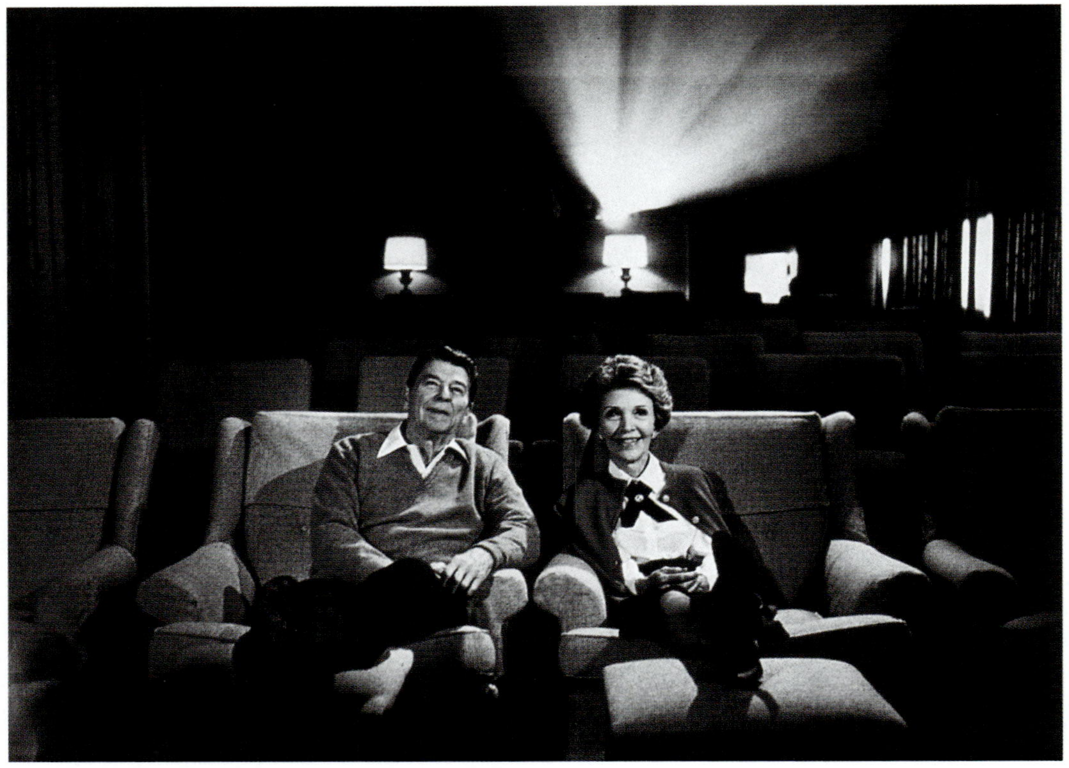

The White House

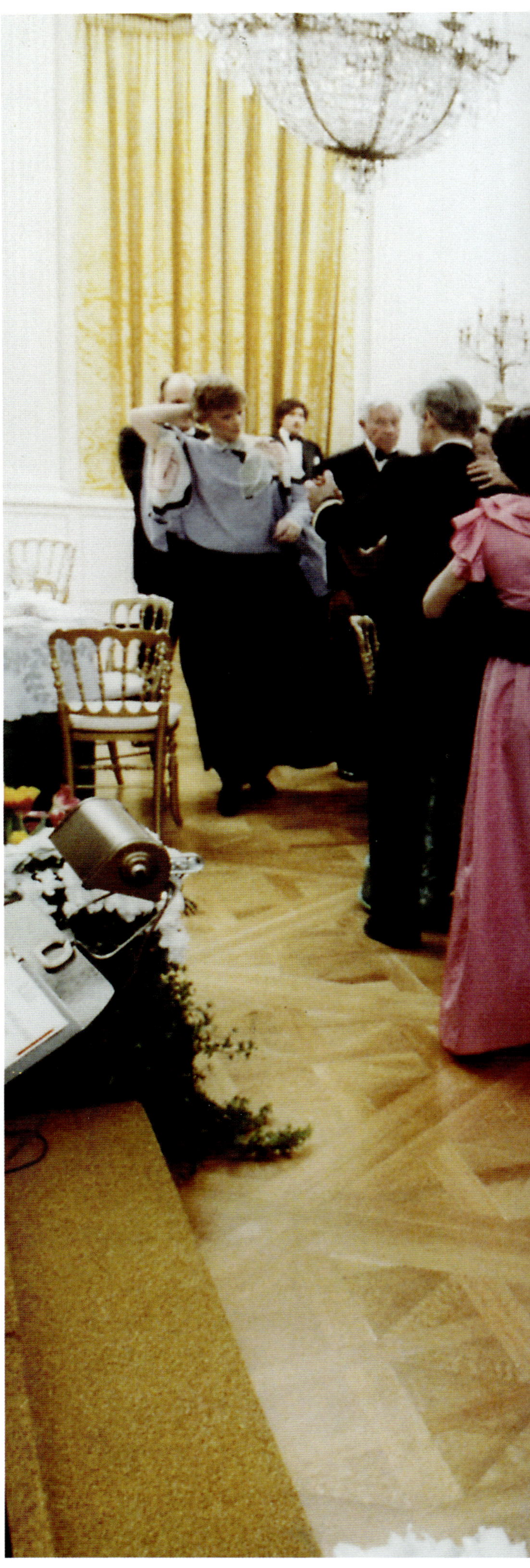

The White House

RONNIE AND NANCY

It is entirely fitting that the First Lady appears with the President in all three of these pictures. They may have been the closest such couple ever. Above, they take in a movie in the White House screening room. At top, in 1983, the President paddles his beloved about on Lake Lucky, an artificial pond at Rancho del Cielo, their spread in the Santa Ynez Mountains of California. When aide Michael Deaver suggested the President spend less time there, Reagan looked him in the eye and said he could question anything but visits to the ranch. Deaver was also less than pleased with the photo at right, taken in the East Room in 1981: He felt Frank Sinatra's alleged links to the mob made him an undesirable companion. The occasion was a surprise party to celebrate Reagan's 70th birthday.

TOP **HARRY BENSON** *ABOVE* **PETE SOUZA** *RIGHT* **MICHAEL EVANS**

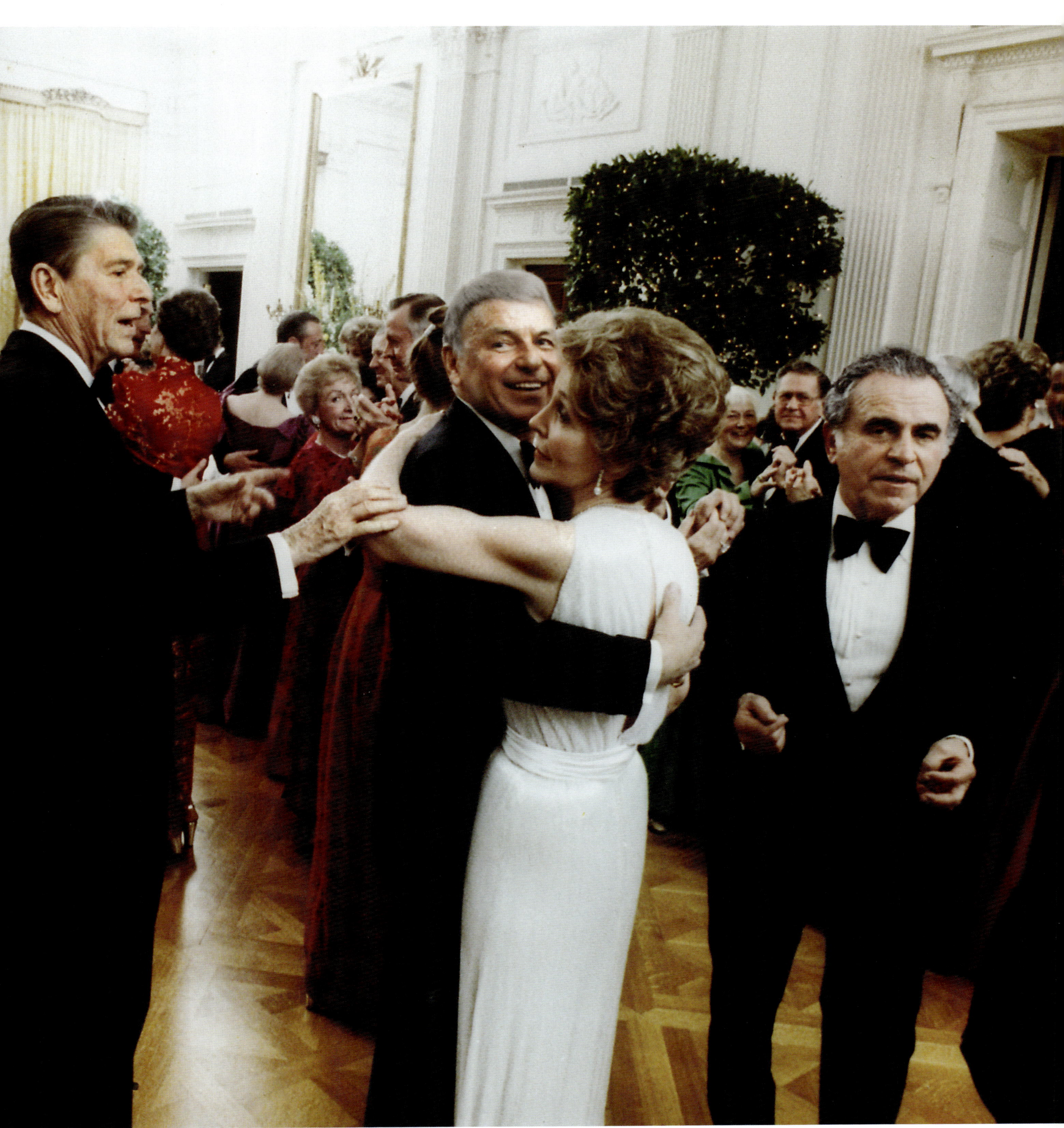

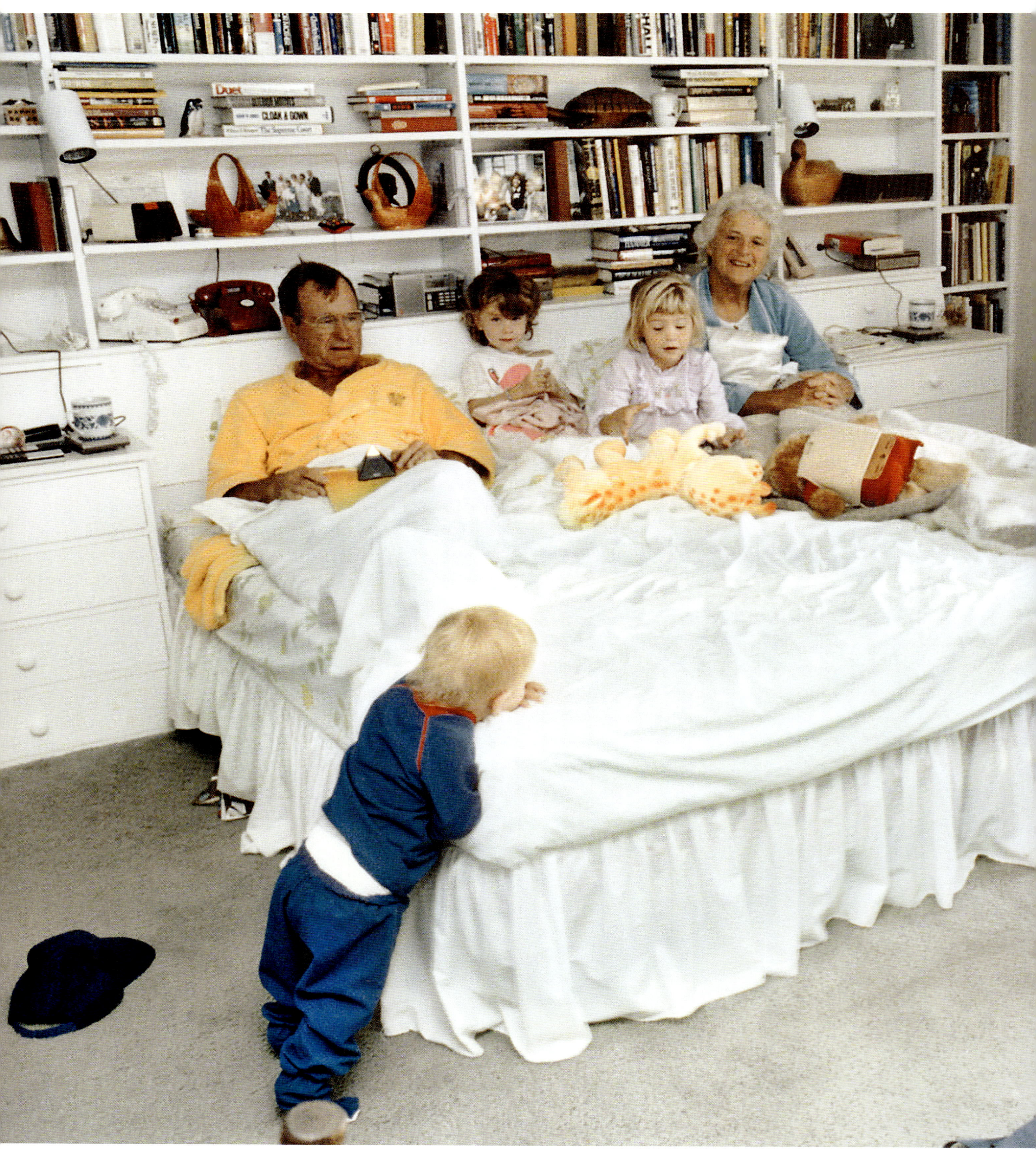
Duet
CLOAK & GOWN
The Supreme Court

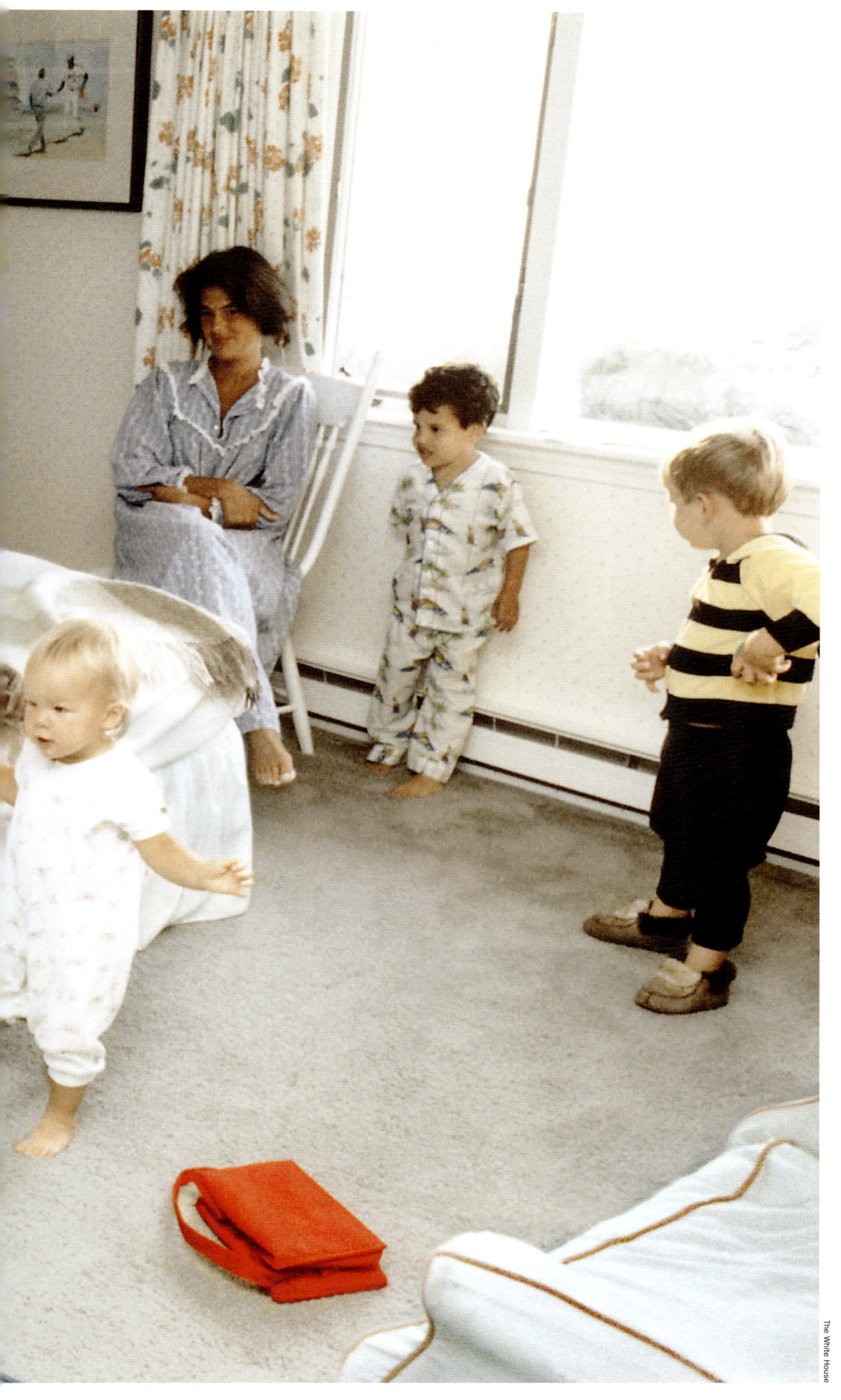

The White House

GEORGE H.W. BUSH

BUSH (GRAND) PÈRE

In August 1987, the Bush clan has gathered at the family's vacation home in Kennebunkport, Maine. At about six o'clock each morning, a gaggle of grandkids march into the master bedroom and awaken (then) Vice President Bush and wife Barbara for an hour of play. Accompanying the grandparents here are, from left, Pierce, twins Barbara and Jenna, Marshall, Jebby and Sam. Seated is Barbara and George's daughter, Dorothy.

DAVID VALDEZ

A SELECT FRATERNITY

November 4, 1991, marked the first time that five Presidents—Bush, Reagan, Carter, Ford, Nixon—were together in a single photograph. They had convened for the dedication ceremony of the Ronald Reagan Presidential Library in Simi Valley, Calif. The best quote of the day belonged to Carter: "At least all of you have met a Democratic President. I've never had that honor."

FOLLOWING PAGES **DAVID HUME KENNERLY**

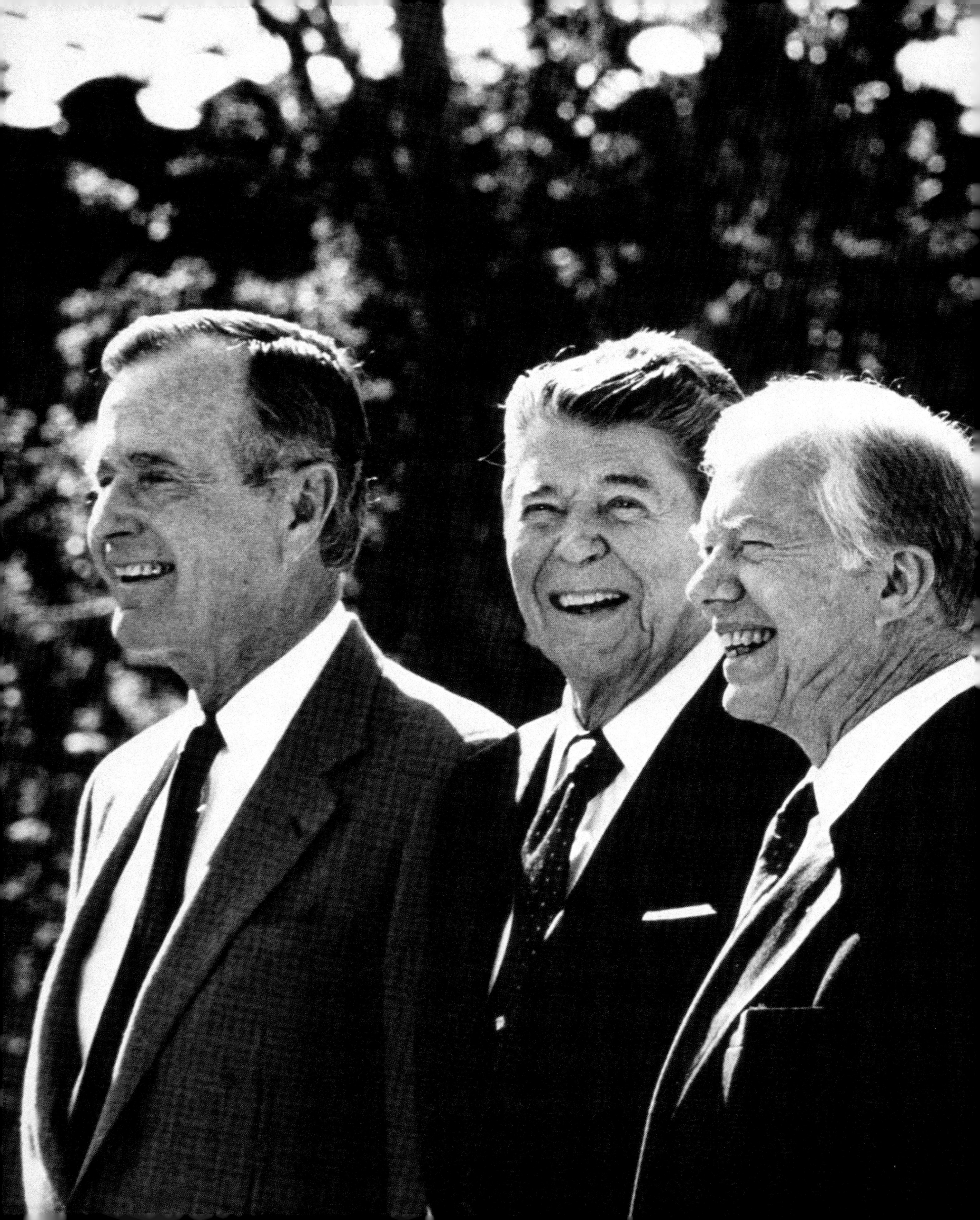

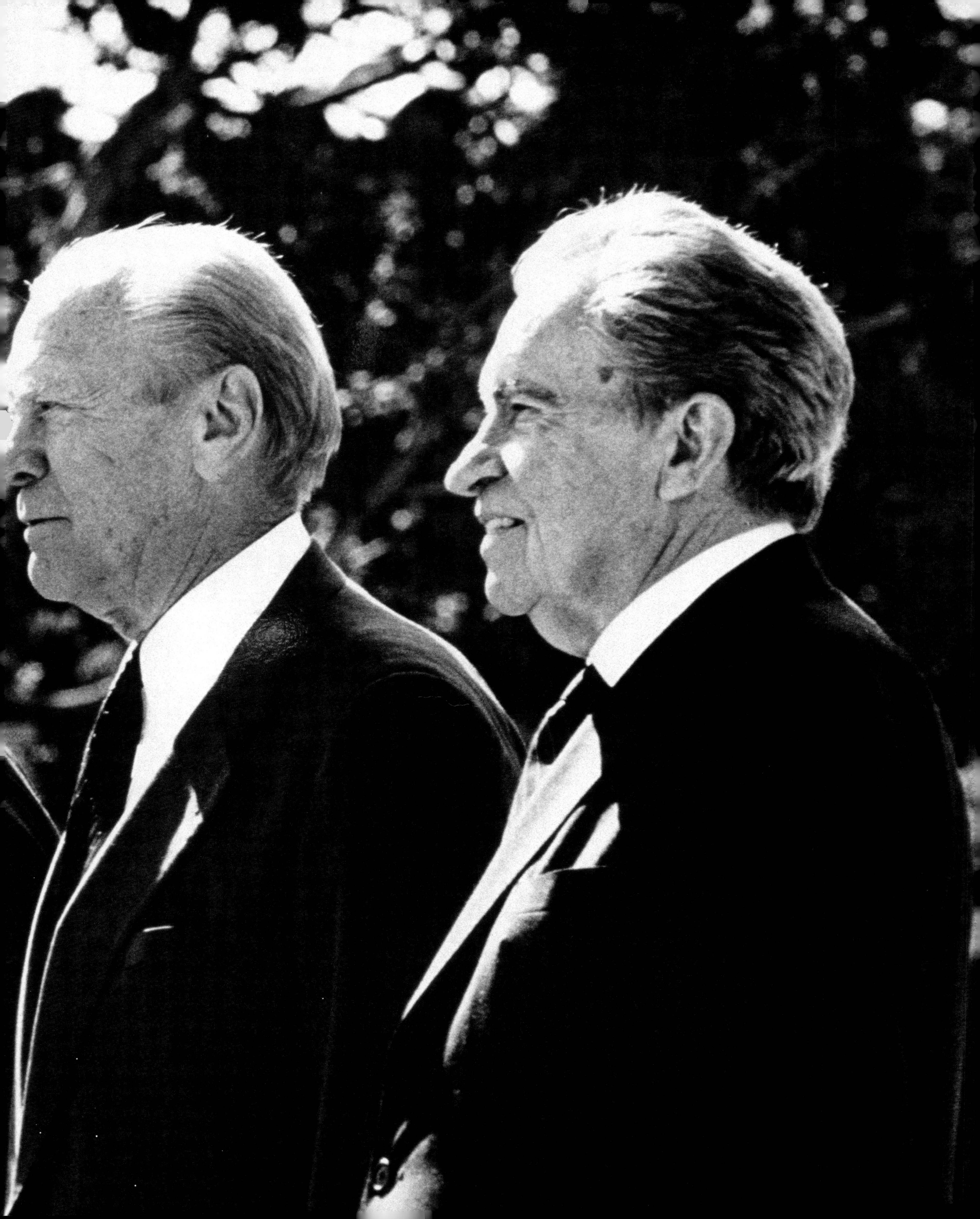

BILL CLINTON

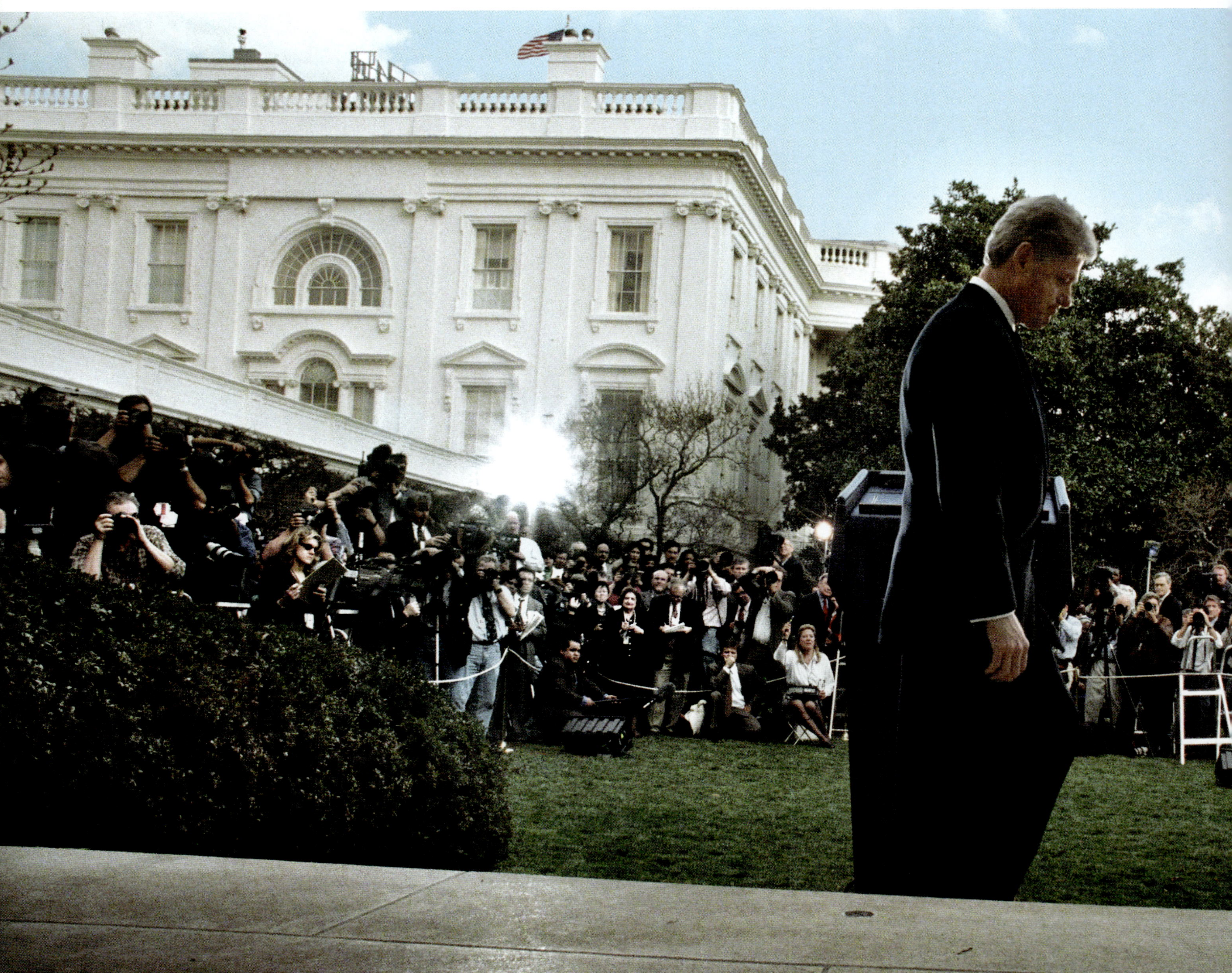

MEET THE PRESS

The occasion is Lincoln's birthday, the year 1999, the place the White House Rose Garden. President Clinton has just been acquitted by the Senate of perjury and obstruction of justice, and an effort to censure him has failed. Oddly, despite his being impeached, Clinton's approval rating stands at 66 percent, perhaps an indication that the nation has accepted his apologies for the Monica Lewinsky affair, perhaps an indication that the nation is desperate to move on.

CHRIS USHER

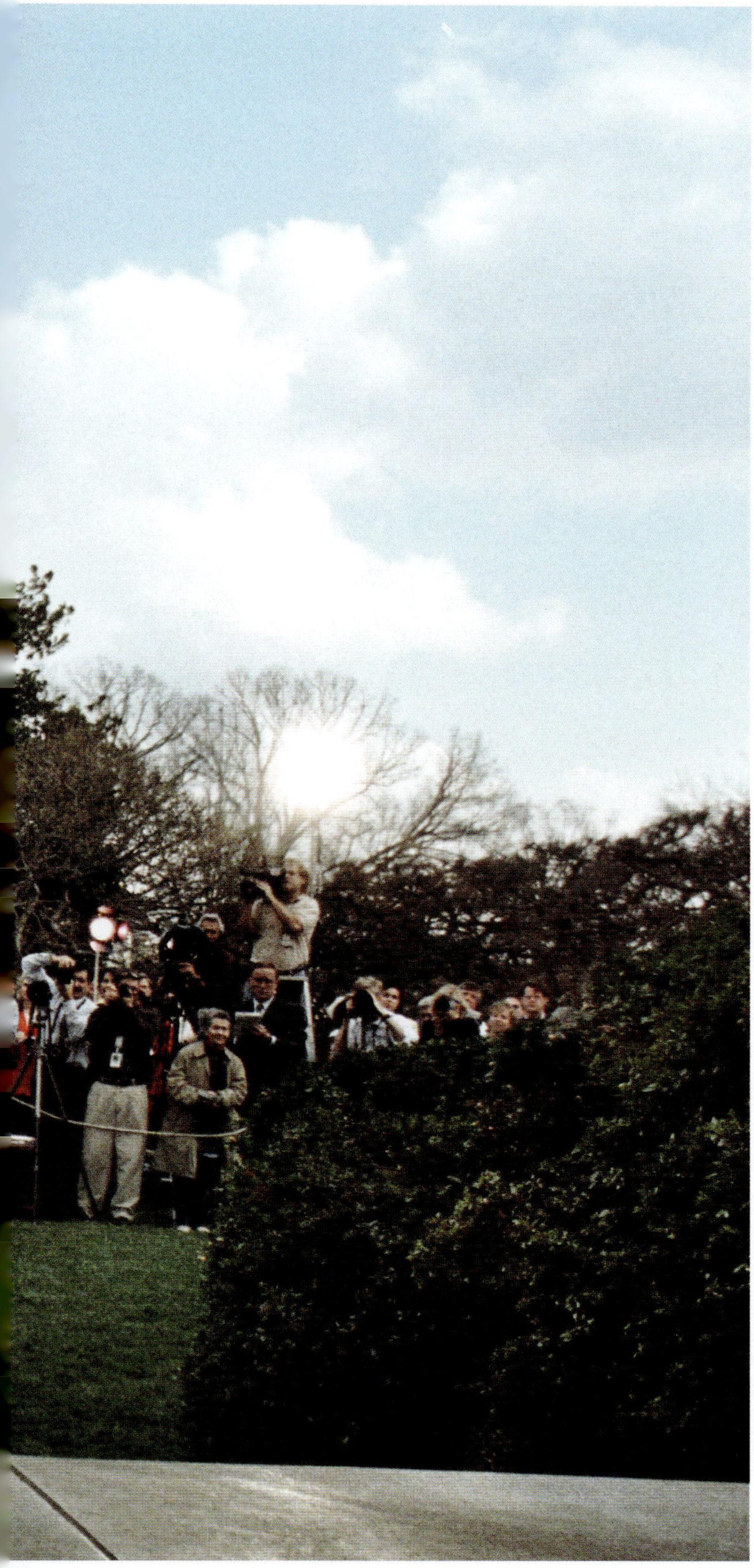

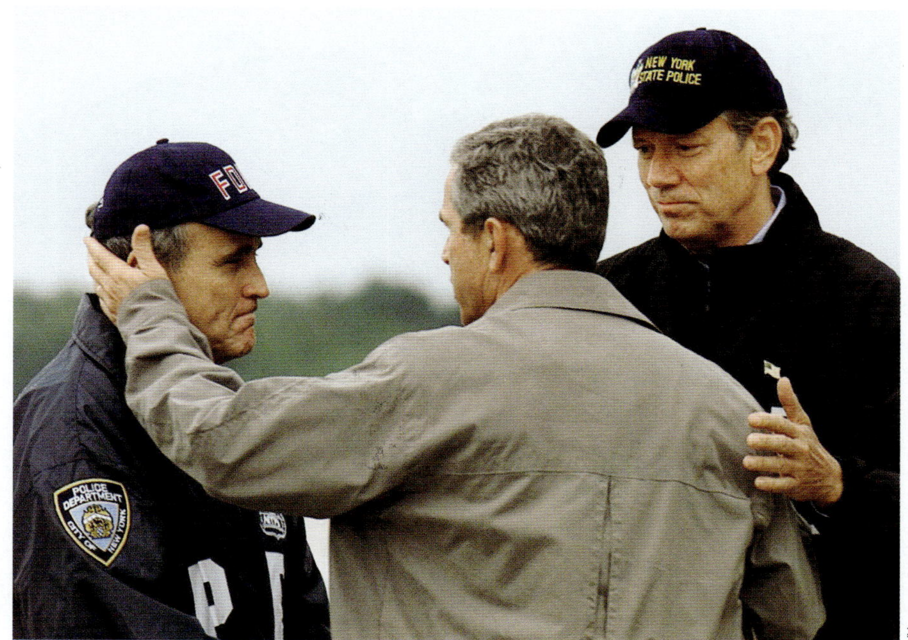

AP

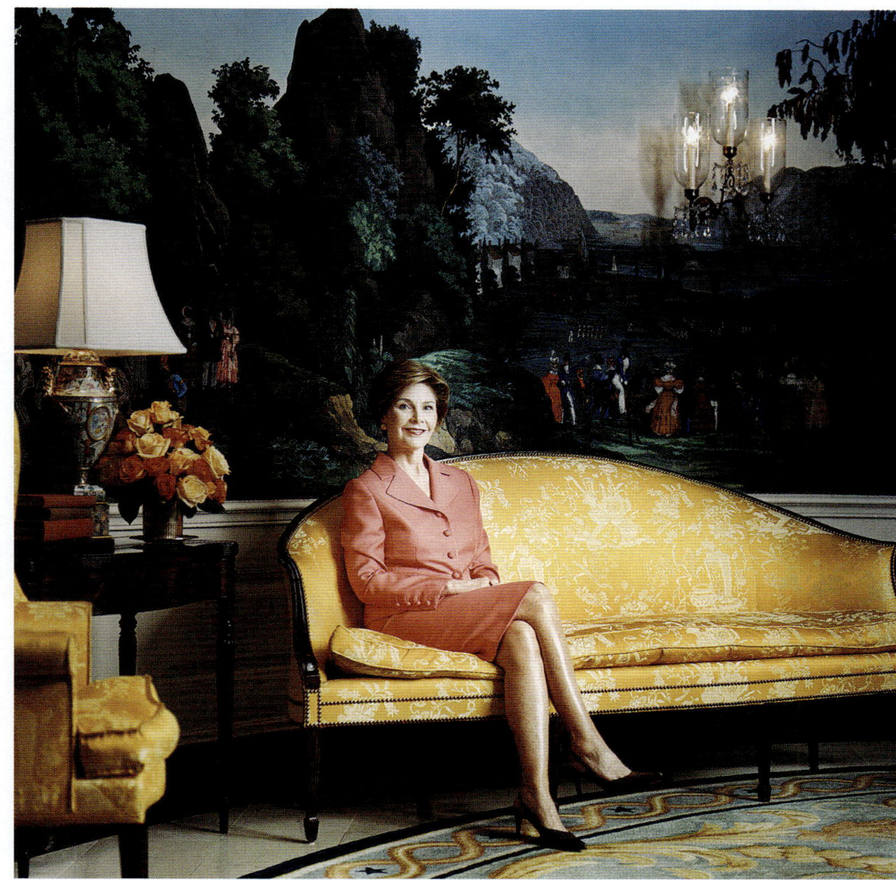

A TALE OF TWO CITIES

On September 14, 2001, three days after the terrorist attack on the World Trade Center, President Bush offers consolation to New York City Mayor Rudolph Giuliani and New York Governor George Pataki.
In the eyes of many, this was Giuliani's finest hour. Bush's initial response to the attack raised questions, but he showed a firm hand in the succeeding days.
Above, in early 2005, Laura Bush takes LIFE into her favorite place in the White House, the Diplomatic Reception Room, an oval-shaped chamber through which she and the President often pass: "There's just something comforting about this coming-in-and-going-out space."

TOP **DOUG MILLS** *ABOVE* **BRIGITTE LACOMBE**

THE
HOTO ESSAYS

In March 1937, with a dozen issues of LIFE put to bed, Time Inc. Editor-in-Chief Henry Luce took stock of his publication in a confidential memoir. Not surprisingly, there were things that pleased him, and things that didn't. One section in particular, though, had Luce confident that LIFE was heading in the right direction: the photo essay. "Here is where you get that 'pure pictorial journalism' that the picture-fanatics love . . . What I mean is this: You can pick practically any damn human or sub-human institution or phenomenon under the sun, turn a crack photographer on it (after a little lecture by a journalist) and publish with pleasure in eight pages the resultant *photographic essay.* Fifty or twenty years ago, people used to write 'essays' for magazines. Essays for example on the bee. The essay is no longer a vital means of communication. But what is vital is *the photographic essay.*"

The photo essay was indeed an essential development in the world of communications. The camera was wresting new ground in reportage. No longer were stories highlighted by an occasional picture, but rather the picture essentially told the story.

muckraking wake. The photo essay as we know it—on just about any topic, not necessarily for the purpose of exposé—was born in the late 1920s when two German magazines began to run picture stories that capitalized on the mobility of new miniature cameras, such as the Leica. An entire issue of the short-lived Parisian magazine *Vu* was devoted to the Spanish Civil War (replete with photographs from future LIFE star Robert Capa).

Having said that, it is reasonable to claim that LIFE, with its gifted and ambitious corps of photographers, elevated the photo essay to its apex. (Indeed, many others have claimed that for us.) And it didn't take long to get things going. Volume 1, No. 1 featured an assemblage of photos by Margaret Bourke-White that in nine pages let readers immediately grasp the day-to-day and night-to-night in the rough-hewn wild-west shantytowns that had sprung up around a work-relief project in Montana. The photographer had provided a coherent view of the subject; the images were laid out with assurance but without a lot of seeming effort—and therein lay the story's victory. The pictures dictated the narrative flow of the pages with a logic that derived from what Luce once called the "mind-guided camera."

The annals of LIFE are bursting with towering photo essays. Choosing from them has been difficult. With apologies to all that simply could not be included, here is our selection.

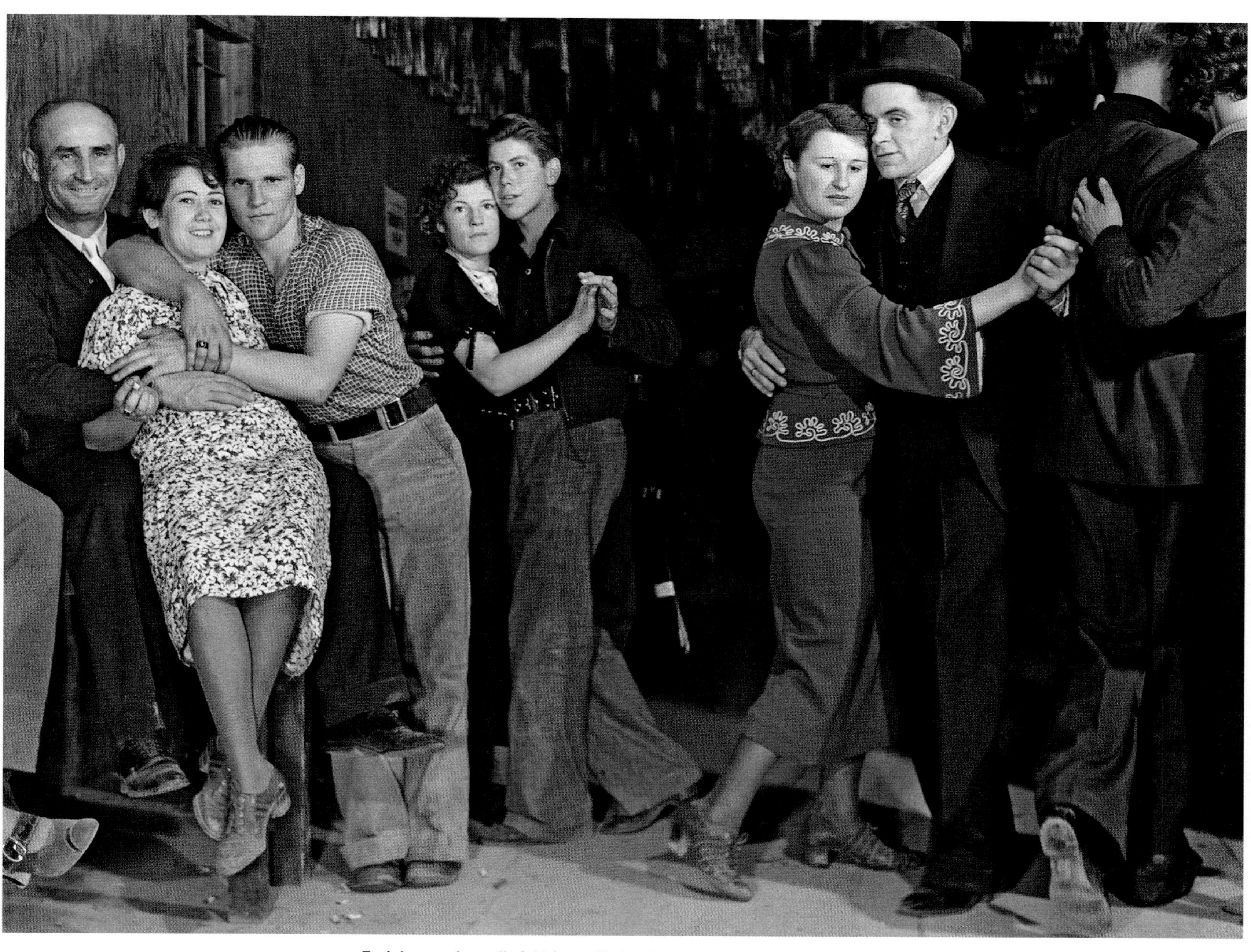

Taxi dancers lope all night in scuffed and dusty shoes for a nickel a song.

FRANKLIN ROOSEVELT'S WILD WEST

MARGARET BOURKE-WHITE
NOVEMBER 23, 1936

The first feature in the inaugural issue of LIFE brought into focus a work-relief project in northeastern Montana that was designed by FDR's planners to bring jobs to the unemployed of the state. The Fort Peck Dam project—the dam itself was featured on the cover, which in turn became a U.S. first-class stamp in 1998—provided for a decent town for the workers, with dorms, hospital and so on, but failed to consider their families. So, to make ends meet, a lot of workers and their friends moved a few miles away and created a half dozen shantytowns, with names such as New Deal, Delano Heights and Wheeler. Like the wild and woolly locales of Teddy Roosevelt's time, these Fort Peck towns had wide-open saloons and bad men with guns, a red-light area and quack doctors with patent medicines. Margaret Bourke-White's photographs gave the rest of the country a gimlet portrait of this 1936 throwback to frontier times.

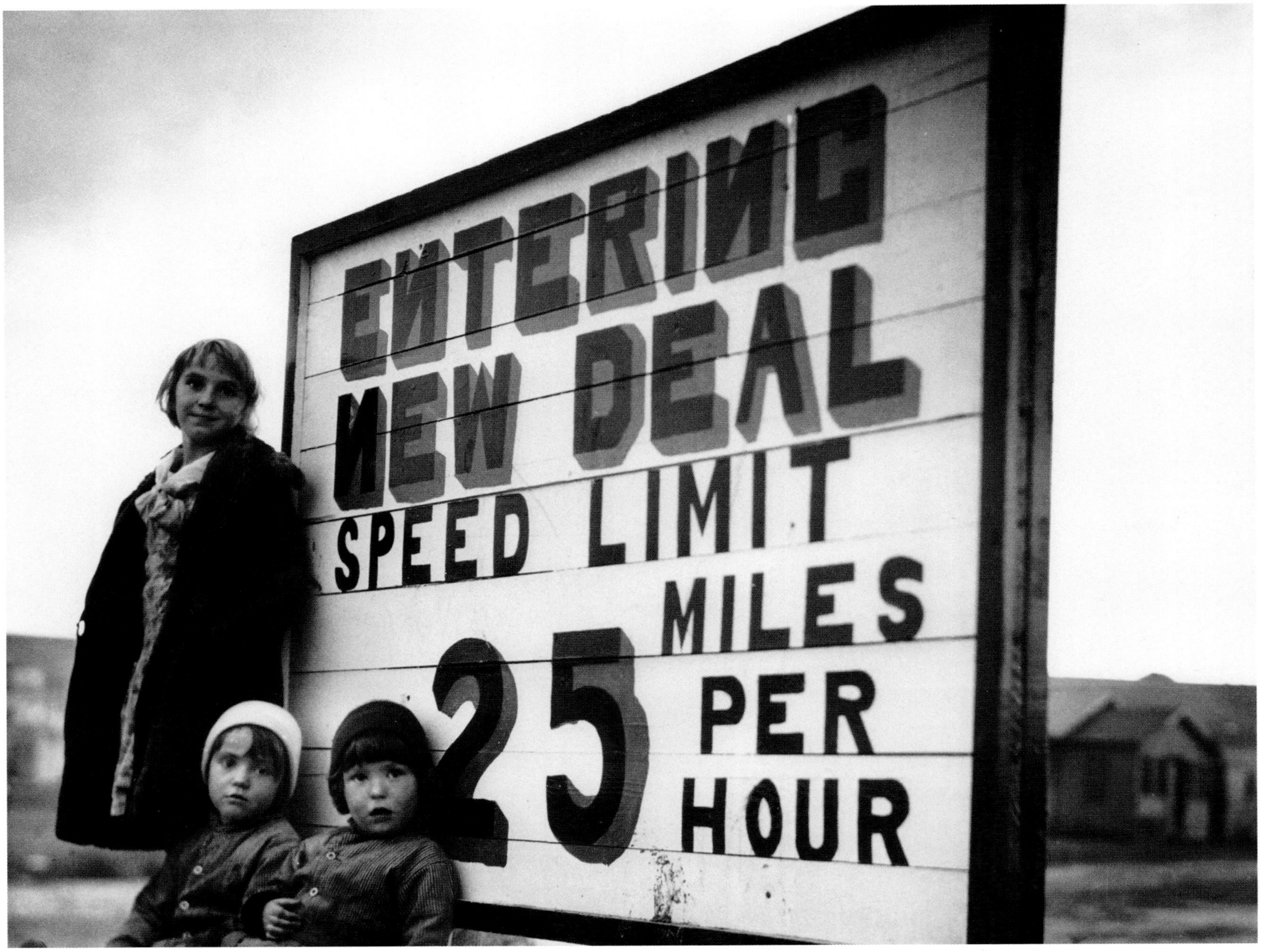

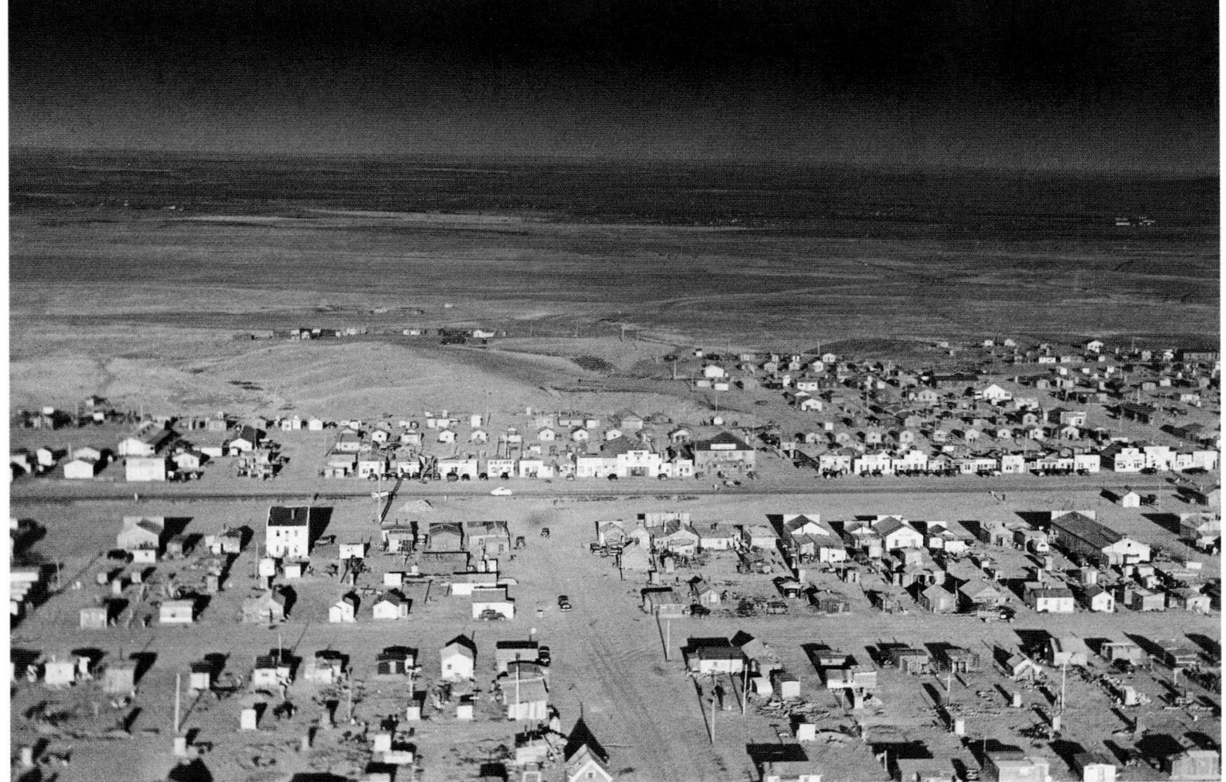

ABOVE

Welcome to a real Montana hot spot. Drive slow, and watch out for the kids.

LEFT

An aerial view of a new town, called Wheeler. Burton Kendall Wheeler was a U.S. senator from Montana.

OPPOSITE

Saturday night in the Fort Peck region. The woman at the bar is a waitress, or "hasher." She took her child to work because she couldn't leave her at home.

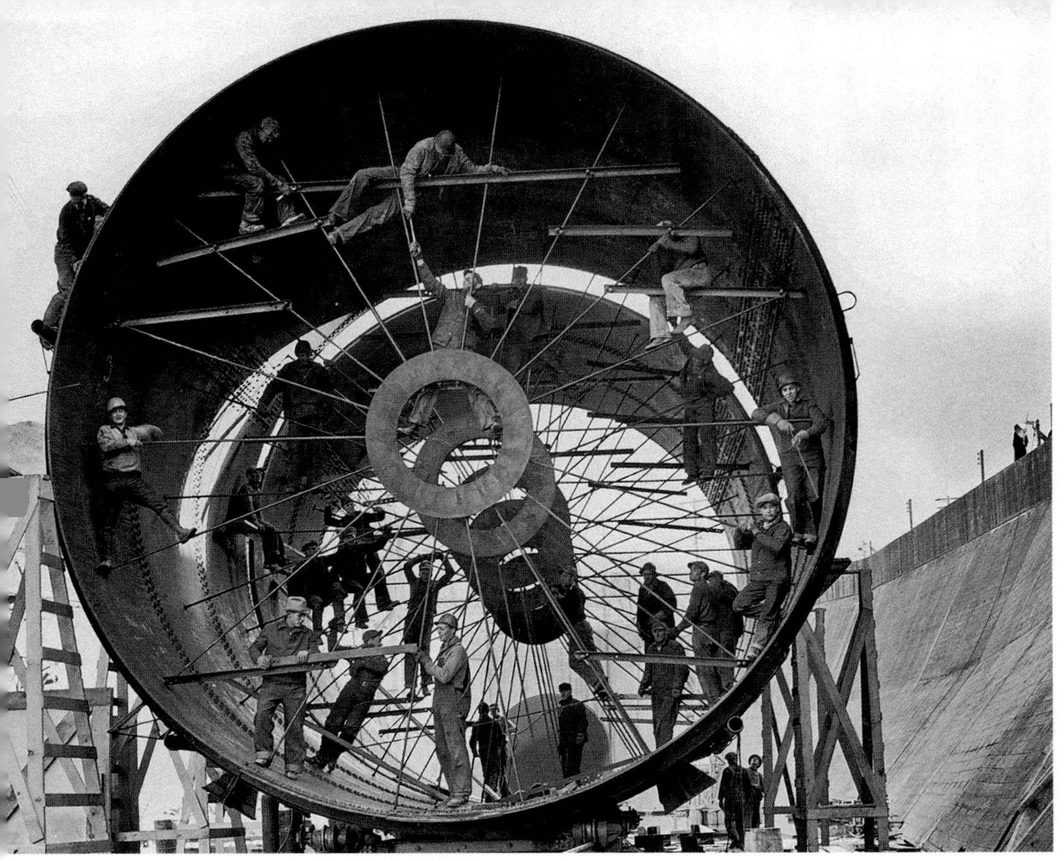

An apparatus for one of the four diversion tunnels needed to construct the Fort Peck Dam

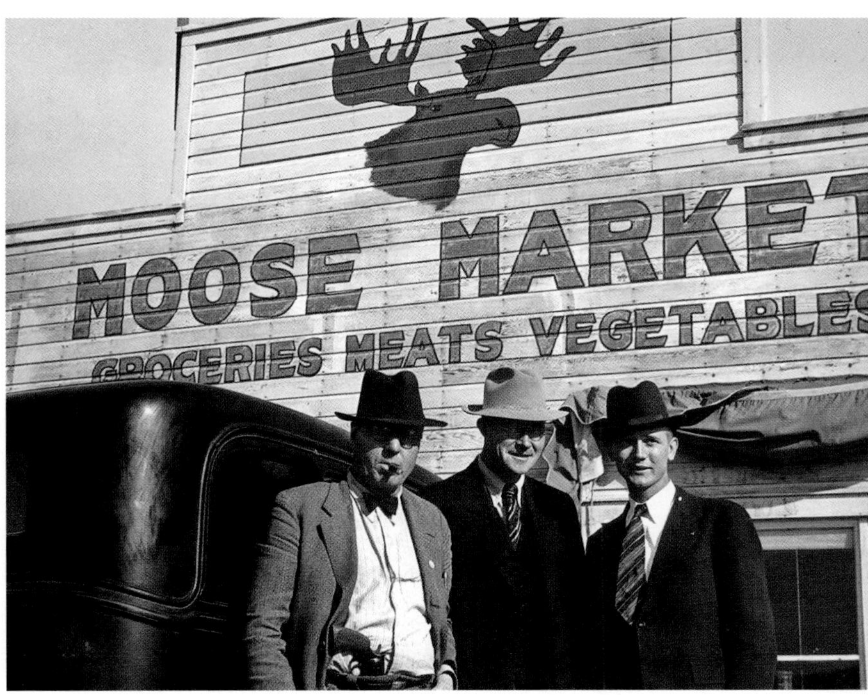

The law in Wheeler displays his gun. He used to be a traveling salesman.

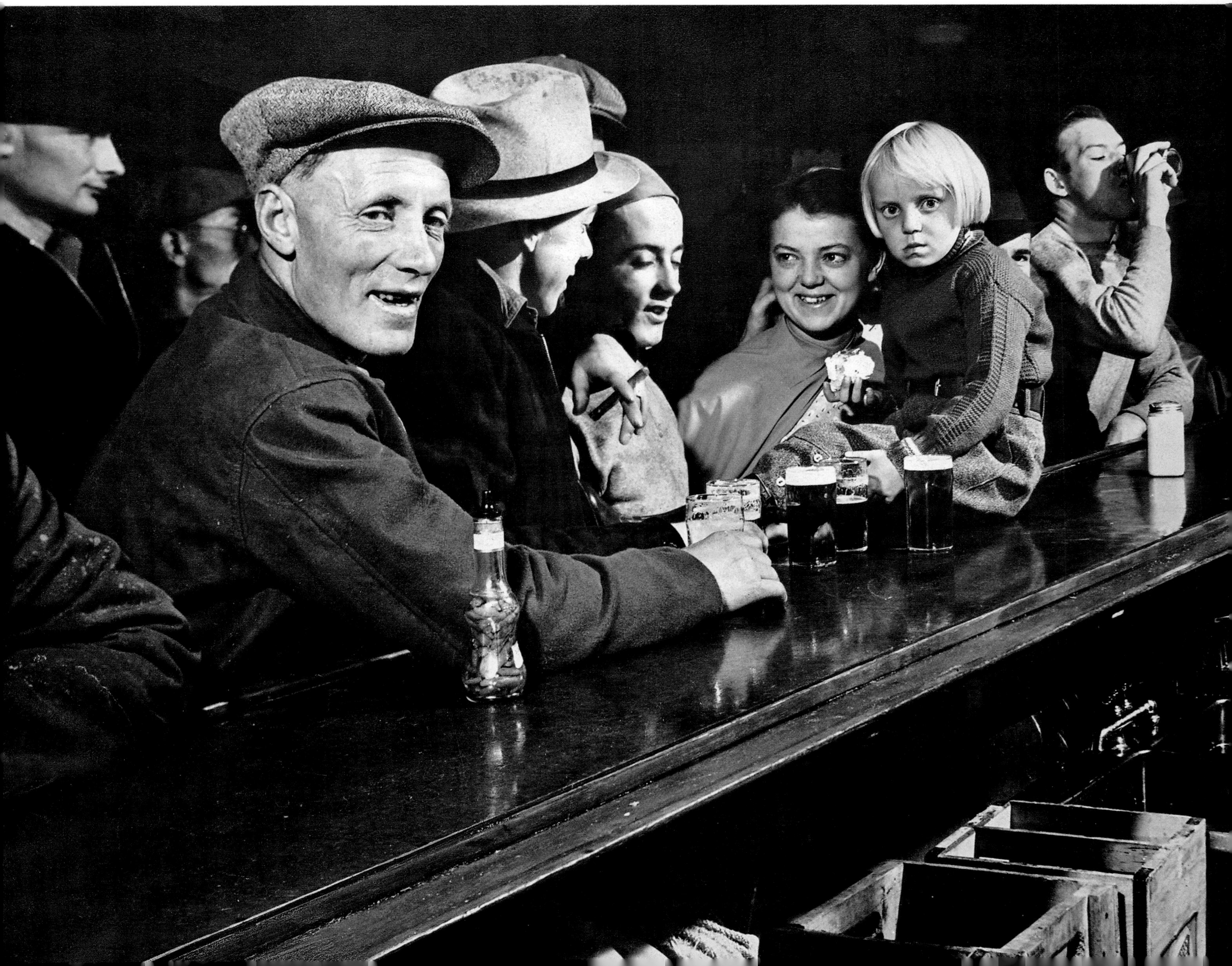

CAREER GIRL

LEONARD McCOMBE

MAY 3, 1948

Fresh from completing a course in advertising at the University of Missouri, Gwyned Filling departed the Show-Me State to show 'em her stuff in big, bad New York City. She was joined by her college roommate, Marilyn Johnson, and together they shared an 11-by-15-foot furnished room in Manhattan. It was a tough scrape for the young ladies to meet the $75 monthly rent and the other stiff prices that New York affords. After weeks of pounding the pavement, Gwyned finally found a job with an ad agency, but the pressures of a career, and being away from home, would take their toll. Nevertheless, the 23-year-old was doing what she always wanted to do. Never before had there been a story like this, ordinary people living their lives . . . in photographs.

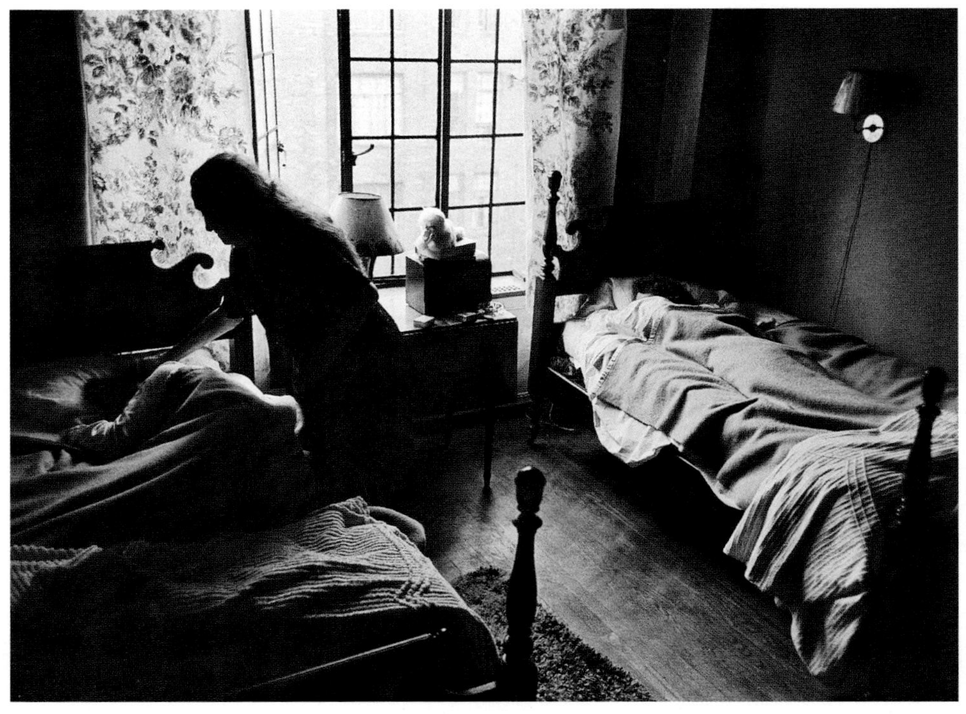

Gwyned has two alarm clocks but both are broken, and here, at 7:30, her landlady rouses her.

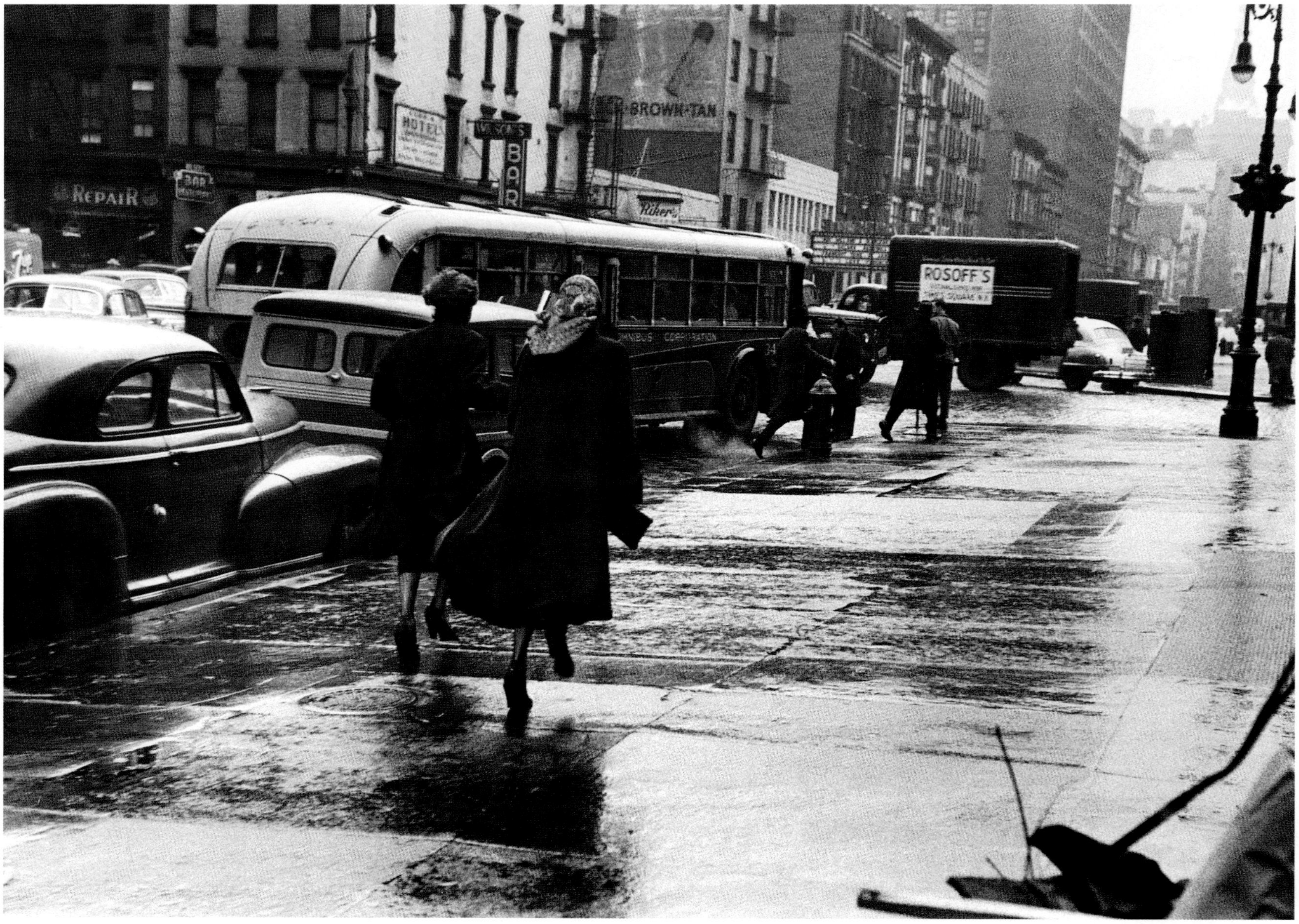

Heading for work, Gwyned and Marilyn run for the bus on a blustery, rainy morning. Sometimes, to save money, Gwyned walks the mile or so to her office.

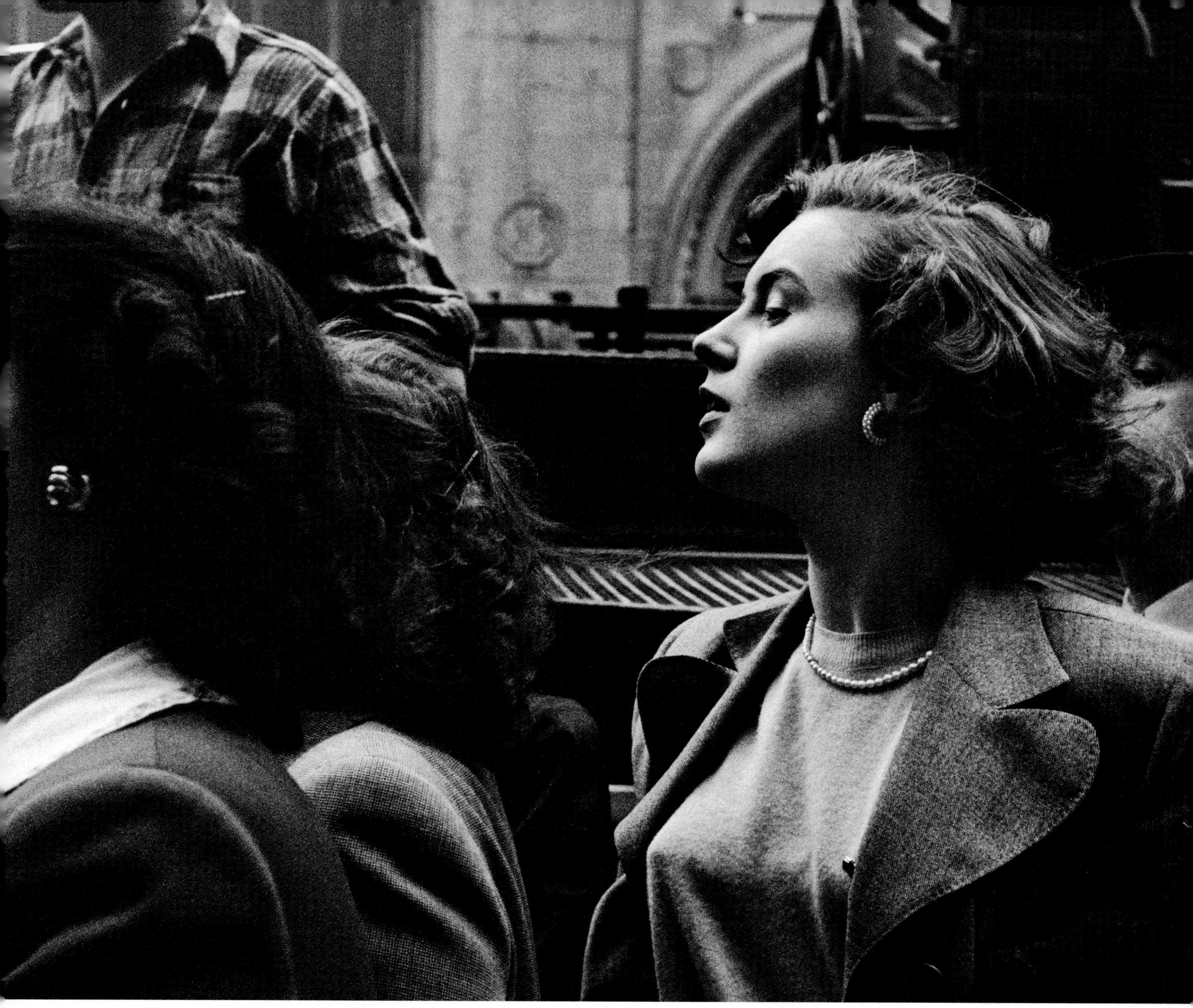

Amidst a sidewalk crowd that has gathered to look at a fire, Gwyned stands on tiptoe to get a better view.

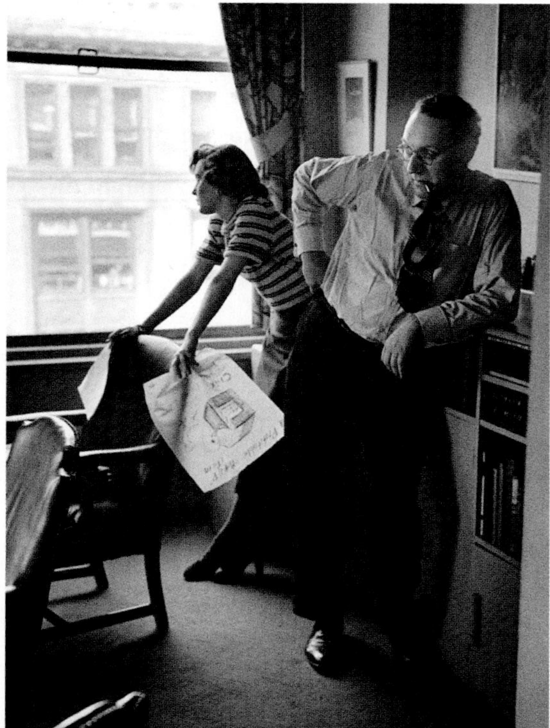

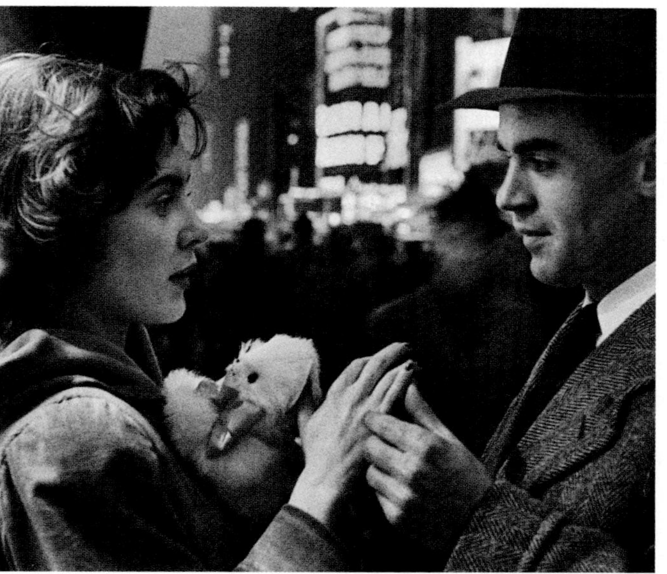

FAR LEFT

After racing to work, she must now put on the brakes and wait until her boss is ready to see her. With Gwyned is George Flanagan, a copy supervisor who often provides reassurance.

LEFT

Gwyned has been in love only once, and that was briefly in high school. In New York there are a number of young men attracted to her. Here, one of them has bought her a stuffed cat they had seen in a store window.

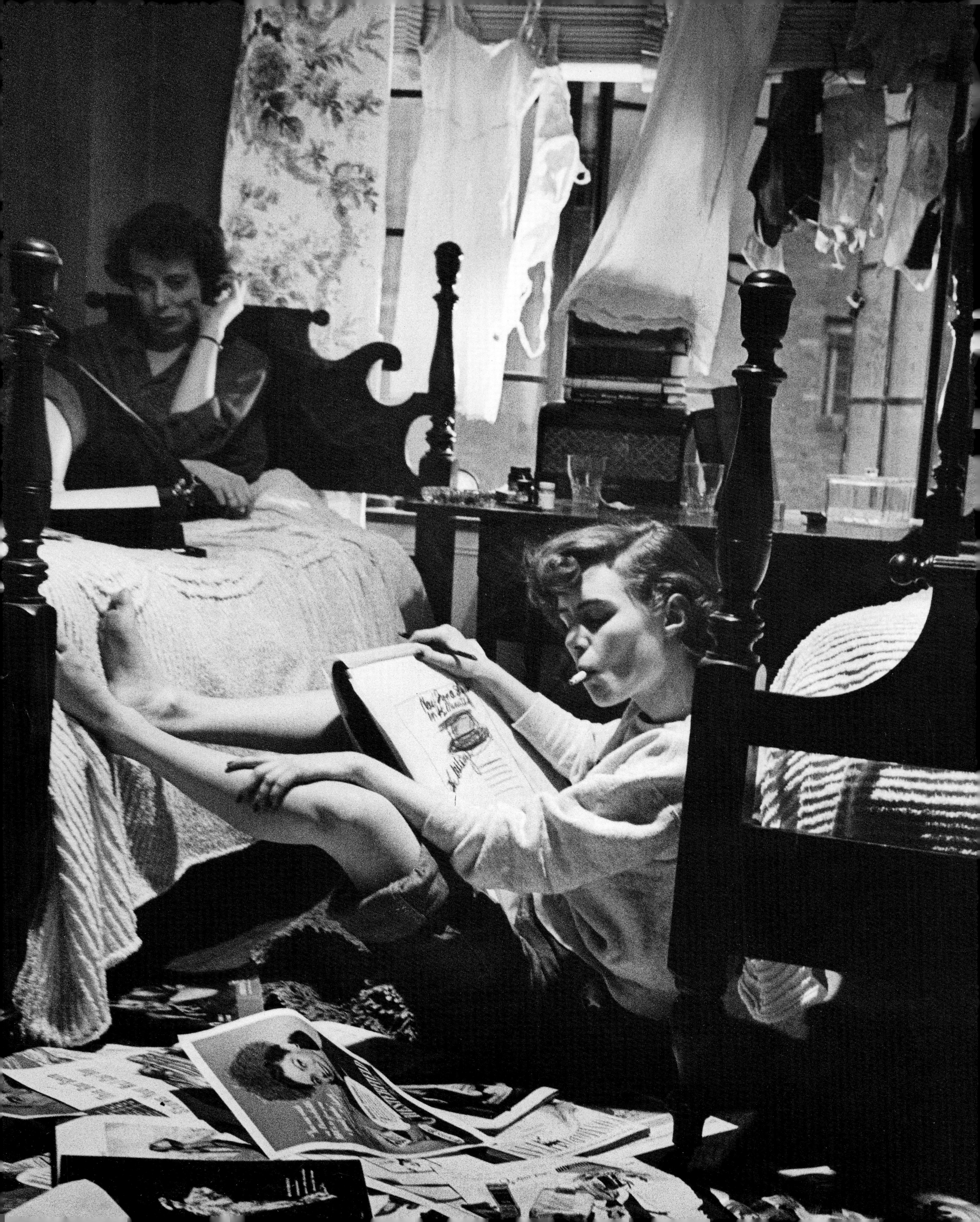

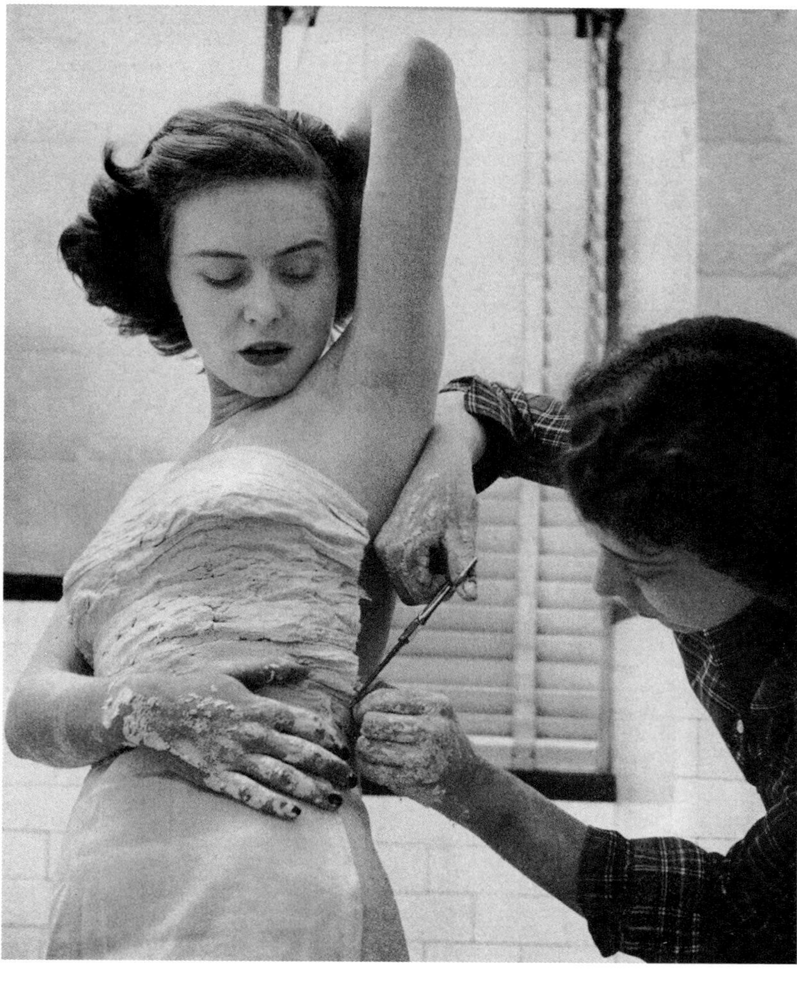

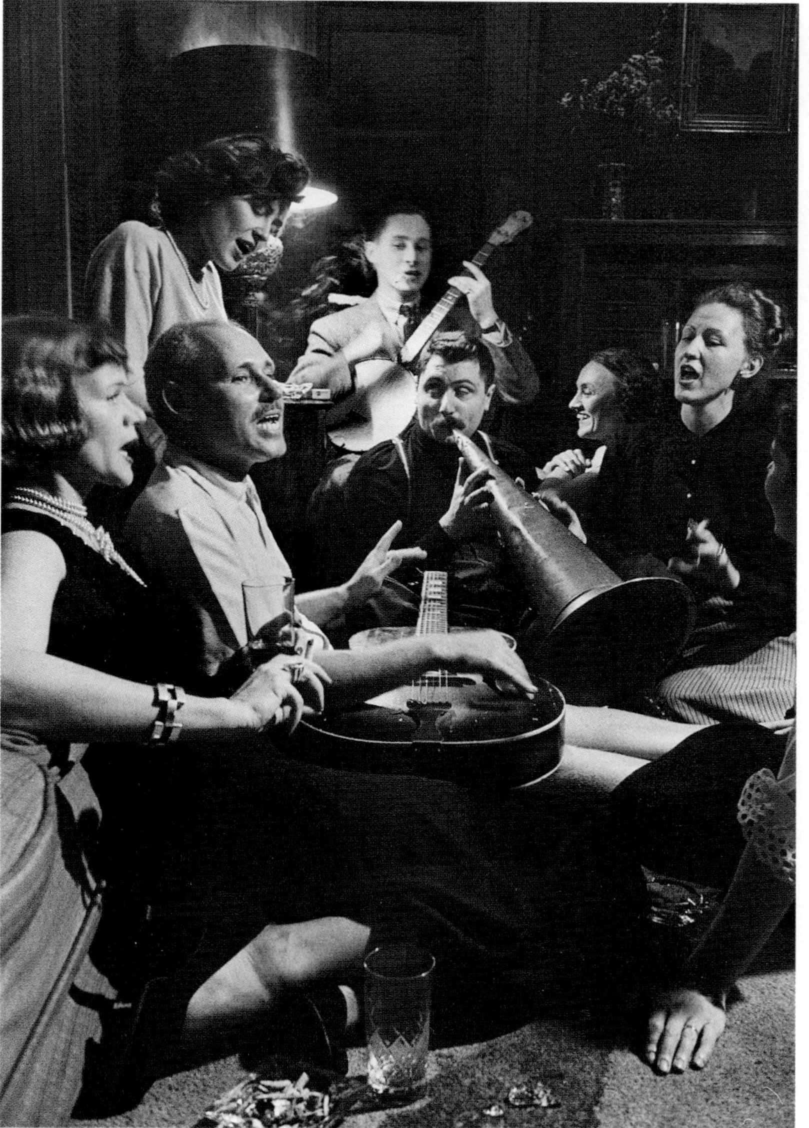

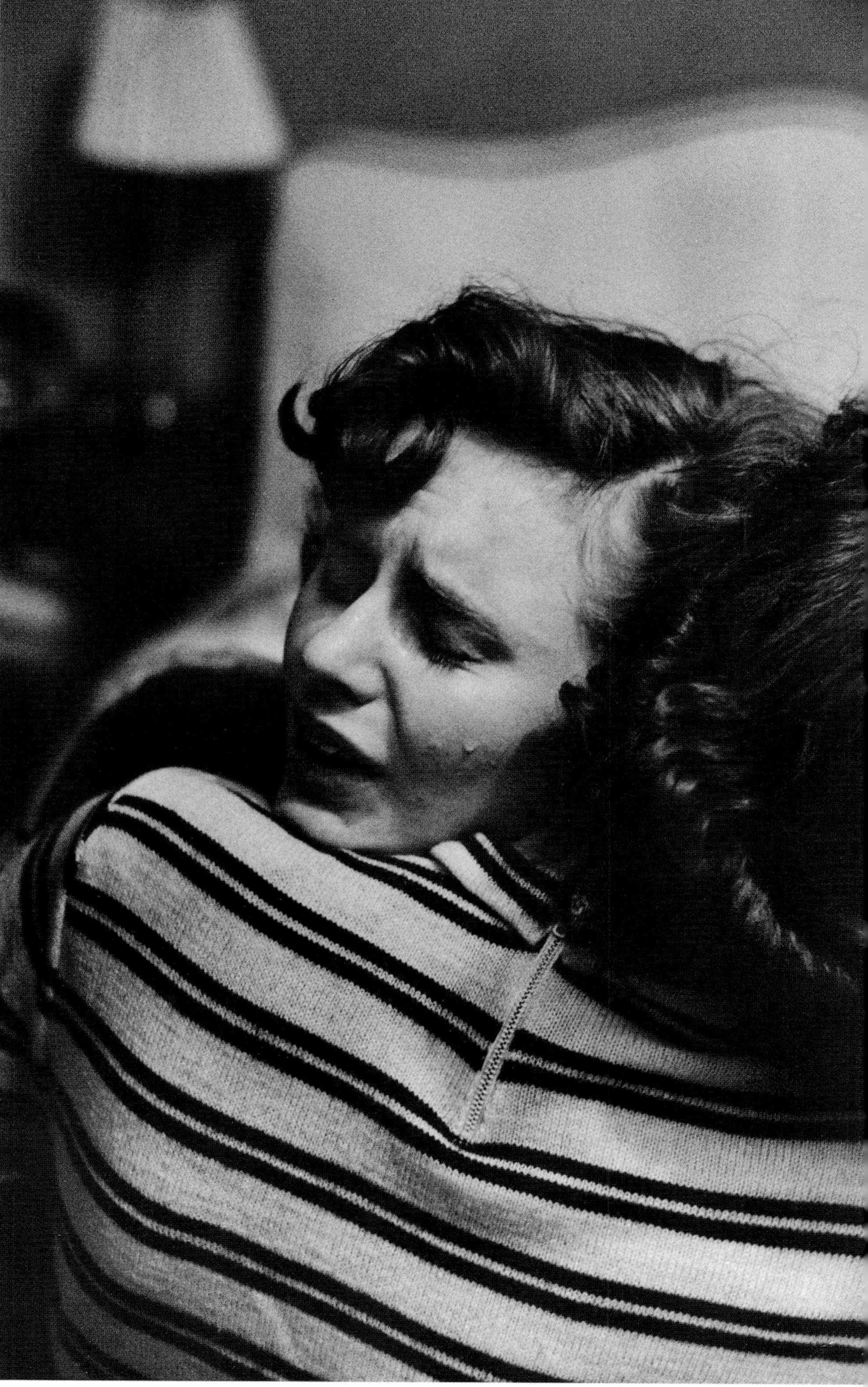

TOP LEFT

One blessing is that the roommates are the same size. Because they have very little money for clothes, they make much of their wardrobe on a gauze-and-plaster dressmaker's dummy, shown here in construction.

LEFT

Gwyned is able to unwind at parties thrown by friends she has made. Attendees include artists and illustrators, musicians and writers.

OPPOSITE

The earnest Gwyned often works for hours at night in her apartment, smoking up a storm among her papers, sketches and books. Marilyn supplies bright if occasionally acid comments. Gwyned is dead serious about her endeavors and doesn't always enjoy the banter.

ABOVE

Once in a while the strain is too much for Gwyned, and even a tiny thing gets to her. Here, she cries on Marilyn's shoulder after a seemingly innocuous conversation with one of her beaus. Despite everything, she insists she wants to work five more years.

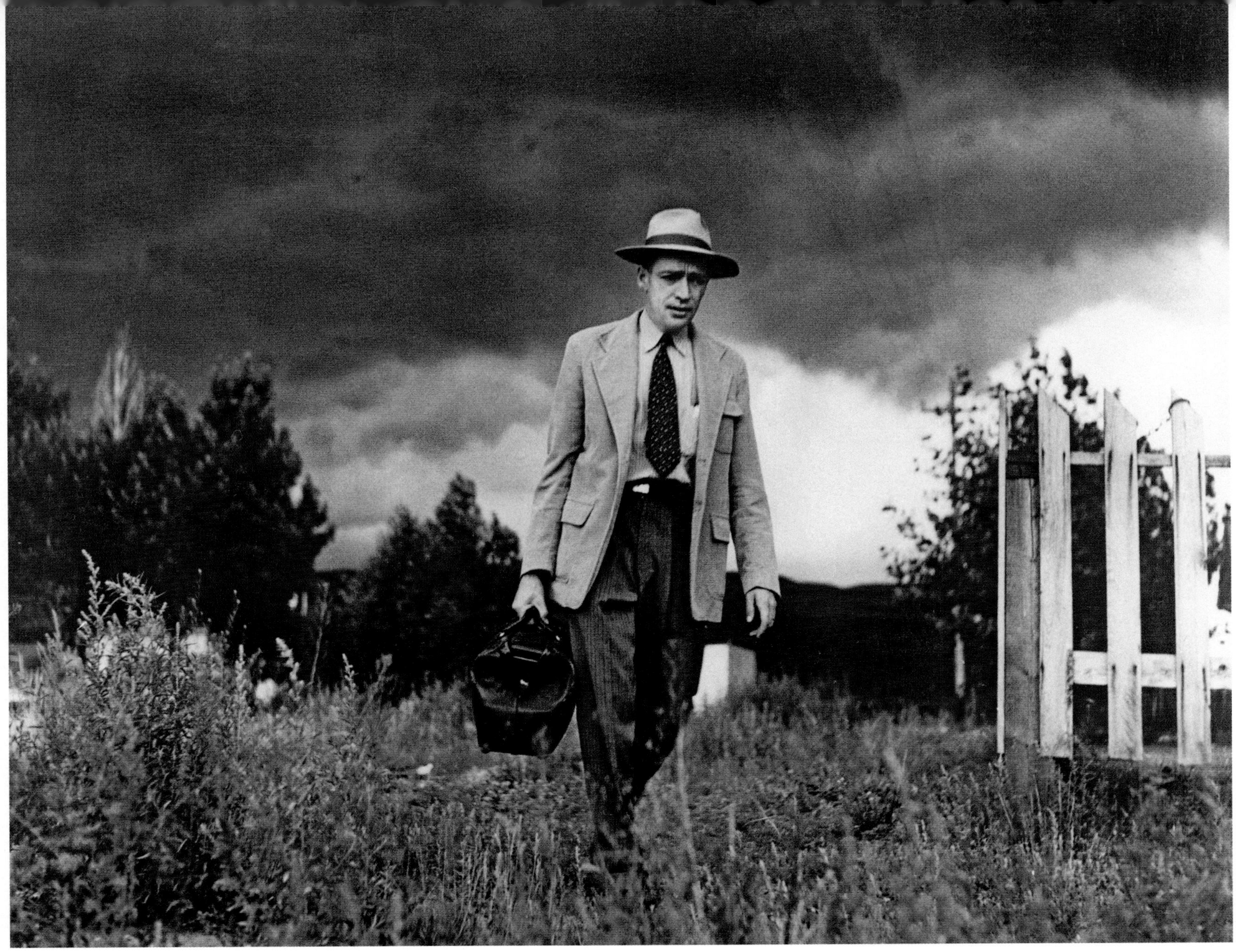

COUNTRY DOCTOR

W. EUGENE SMITH

SEPTEMBER 20, 1948

Kremmling, Colo., lies 115 miles west of Denver. In 1948, Gene Smith took his camera there and endowed LIFE's readers with an indelible portrait of Dr. Ernest Ceriani, a 32-year-old general practitioner who served as physician, surgeon, obstetrician, pediatrician, psychiatrist, dentist, oculist and lab technician for the 2,000 people who lived in that 400-square-mile area.

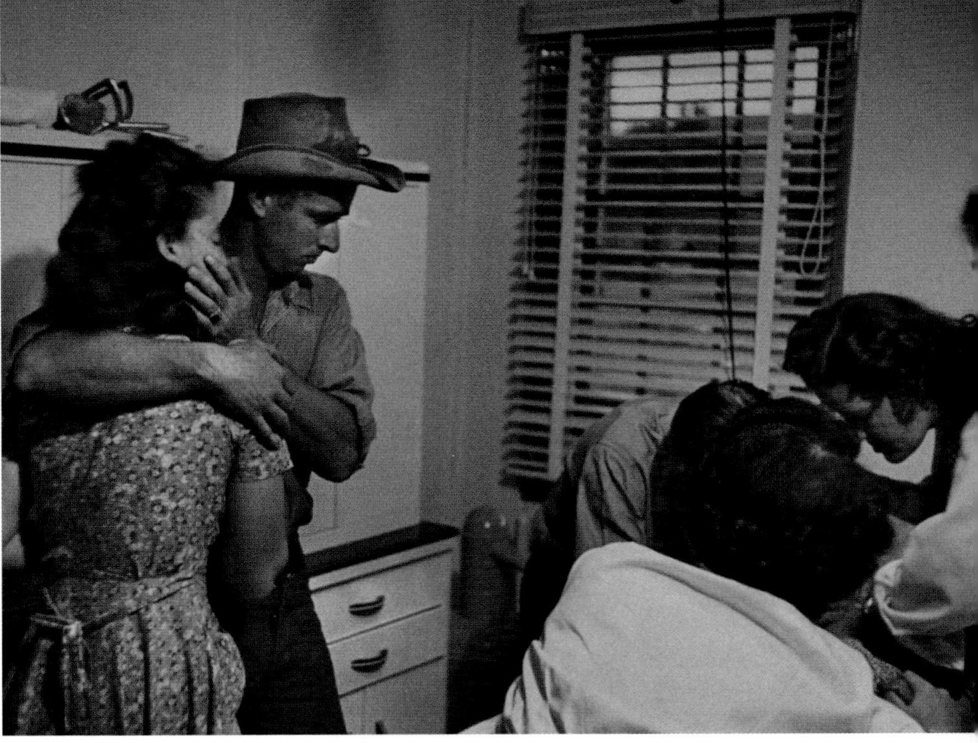

TOP

Though a young man, Ceriani already is slightly stooped as he makes his way through weeds growing rank in an unkempt yard.

ABOVE & OPPOSITE

Anxious parents watch as Ceriani treats their two-and-a-half-year-old girl, who has been kicked by a horse. He knows her eye cannot be saved.

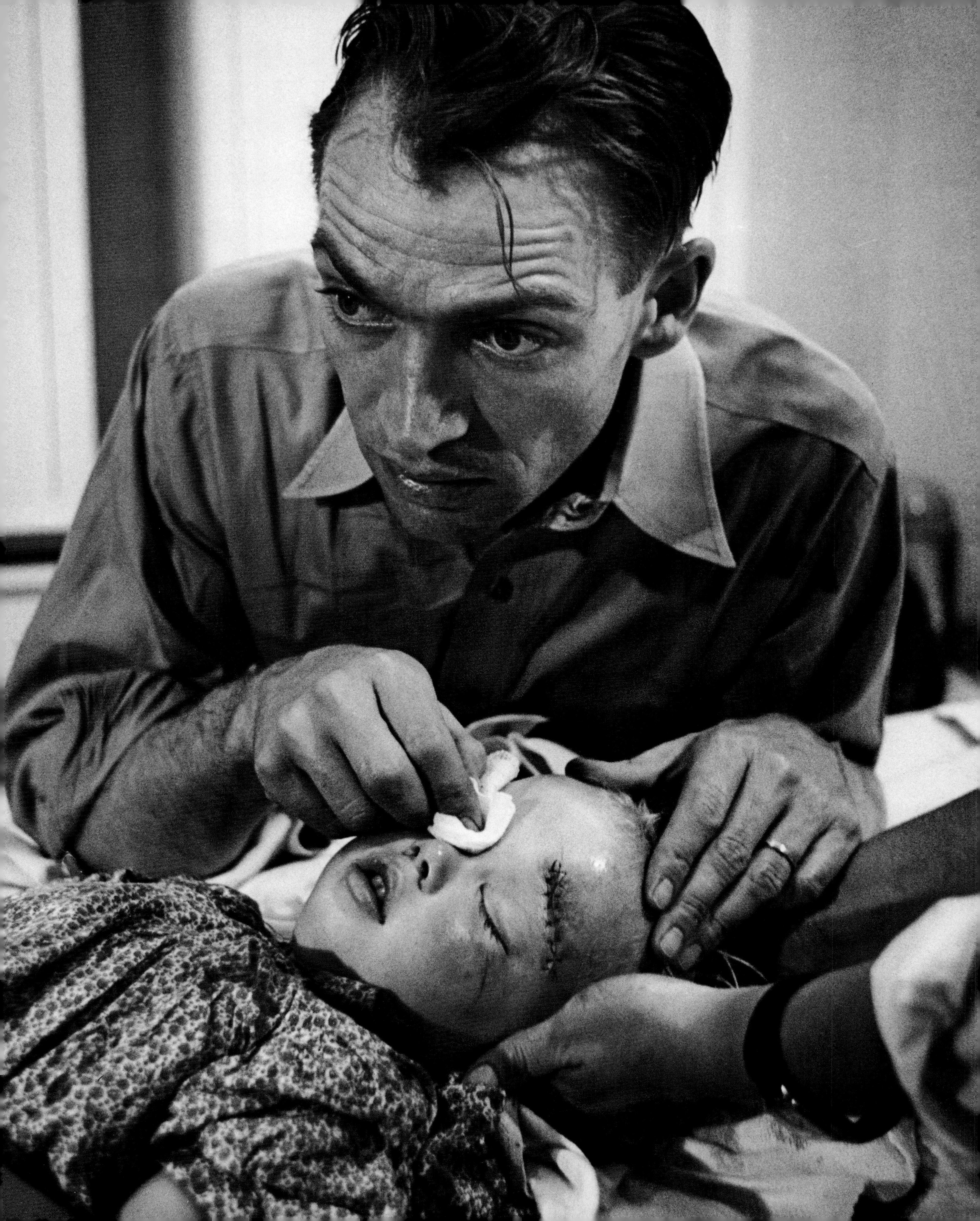

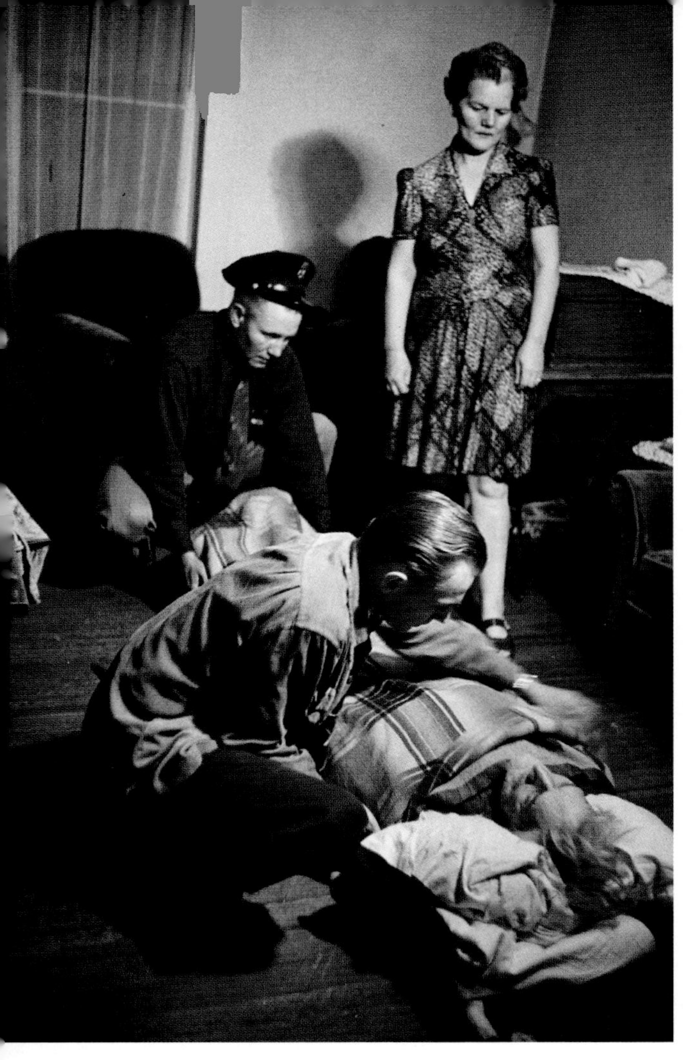

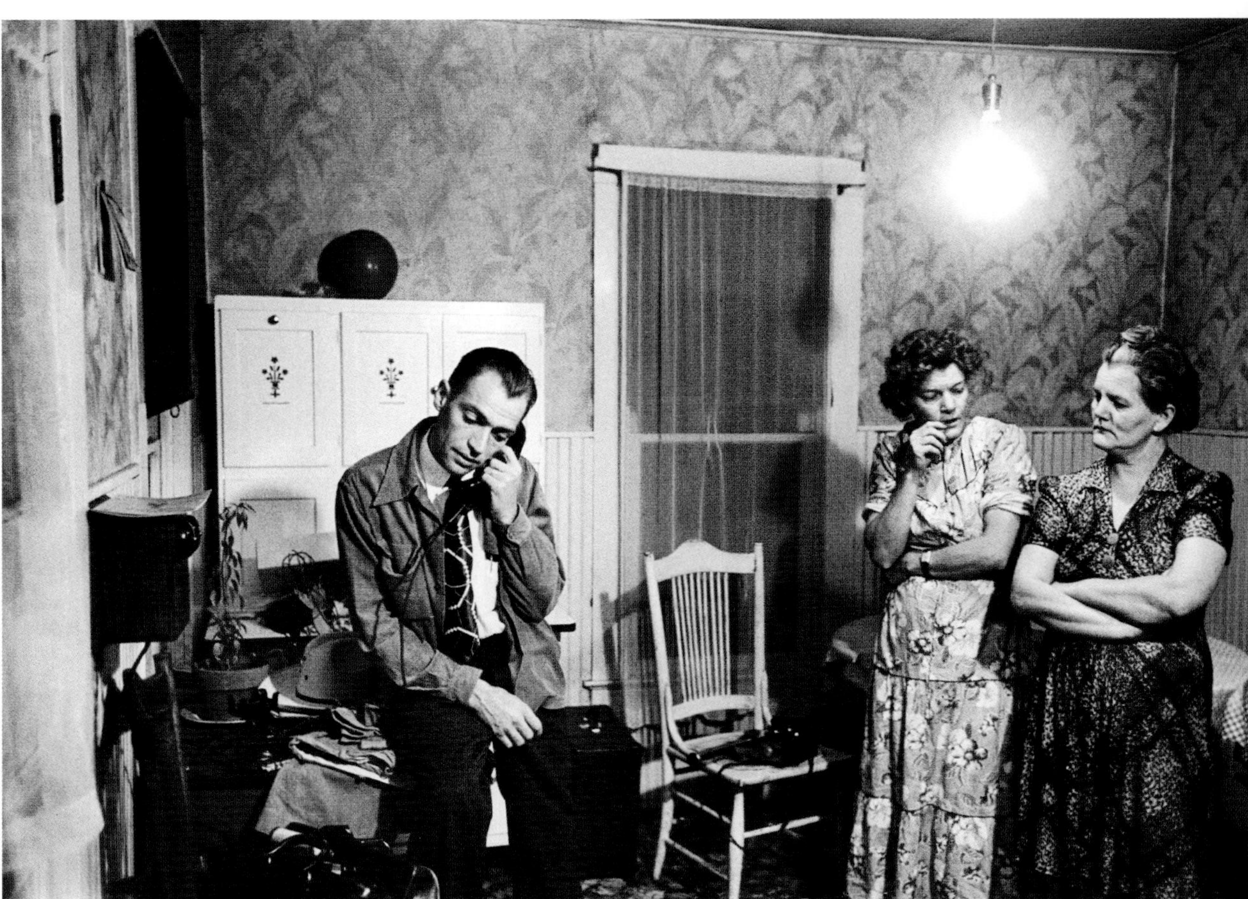

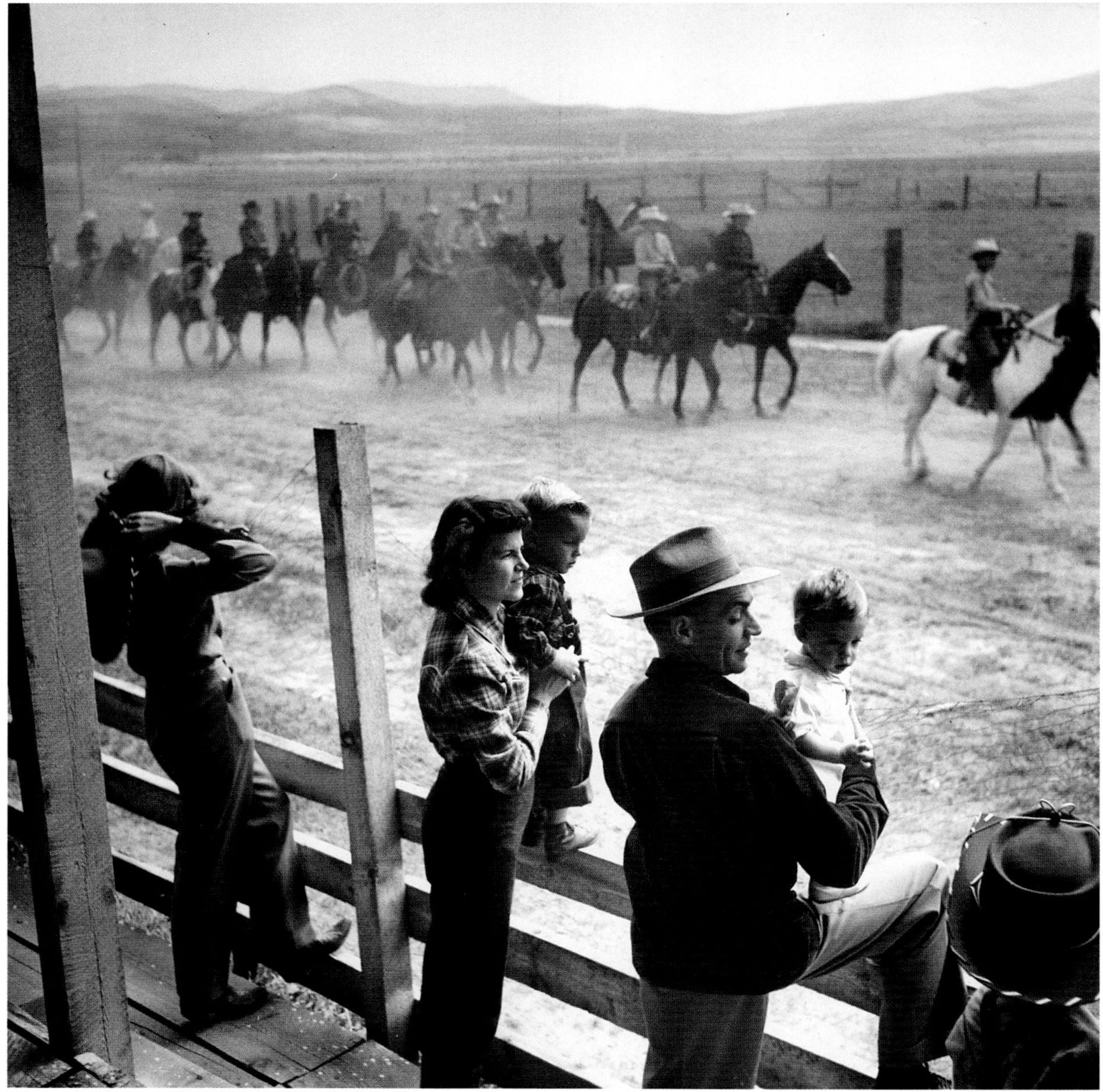

TOP LEFT & ABOVE

Minutes before midnight, Ceriani got a call that an 82-year-old man was very ill. The doctor donned a cloth jacket and at the house found the man had suffered a heart attack. After tucking a blanket around the doomed patient, Ceriani phones a priest, asking him to meet them at the hospital. The man died at 2:30 a.m.

LEFT

Ceriani, his wife, Bernetha, and their two boys watch a parade in Kremmling. After four years of marriage, Bernetha has learned to accept nearly all the problems presented by her husband's career, but is still dismayed that she sees him only on special occasions, such as this one.

OPPOSITE

After an operation that lasted until two a.m., Ceriani has a cup of coffee and a smoke. His nurses admonish him to relax, to rest, but they know better and always keep a potful of fresh coffee brewing.

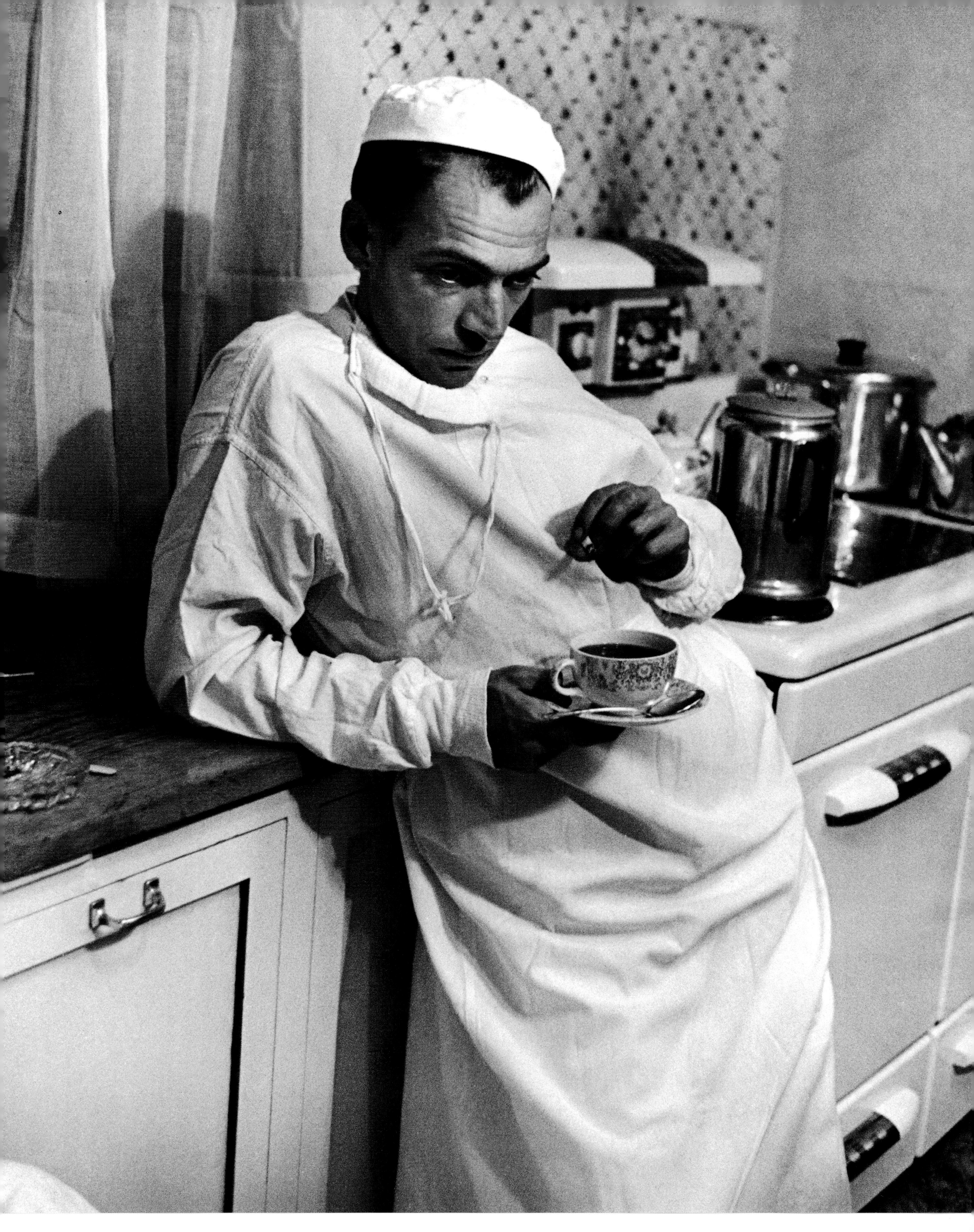

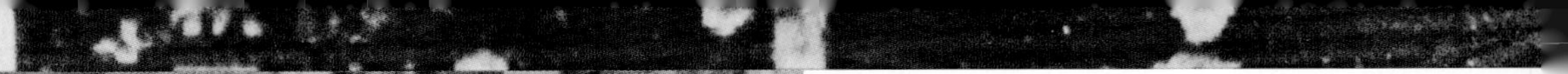

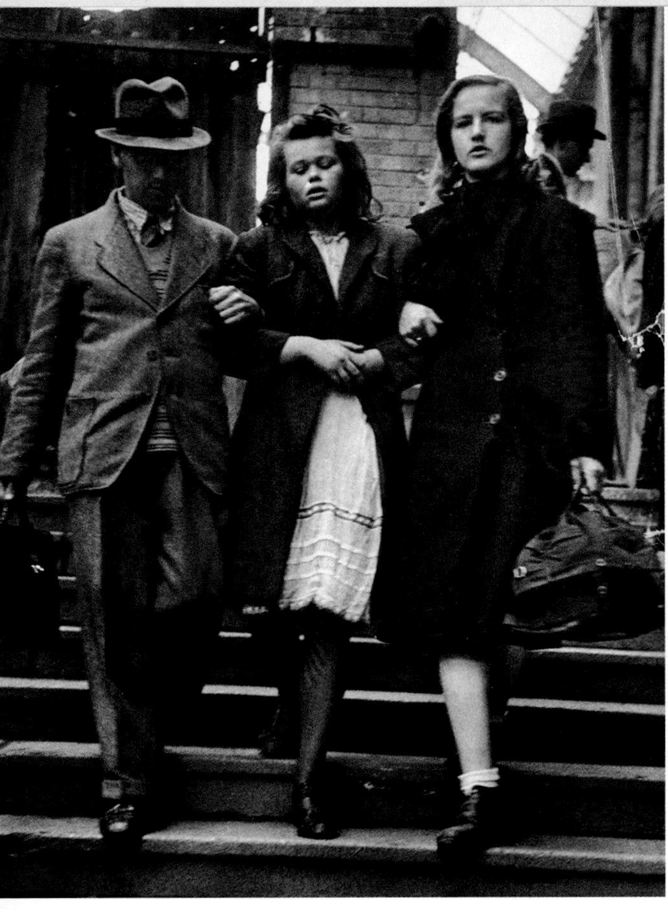

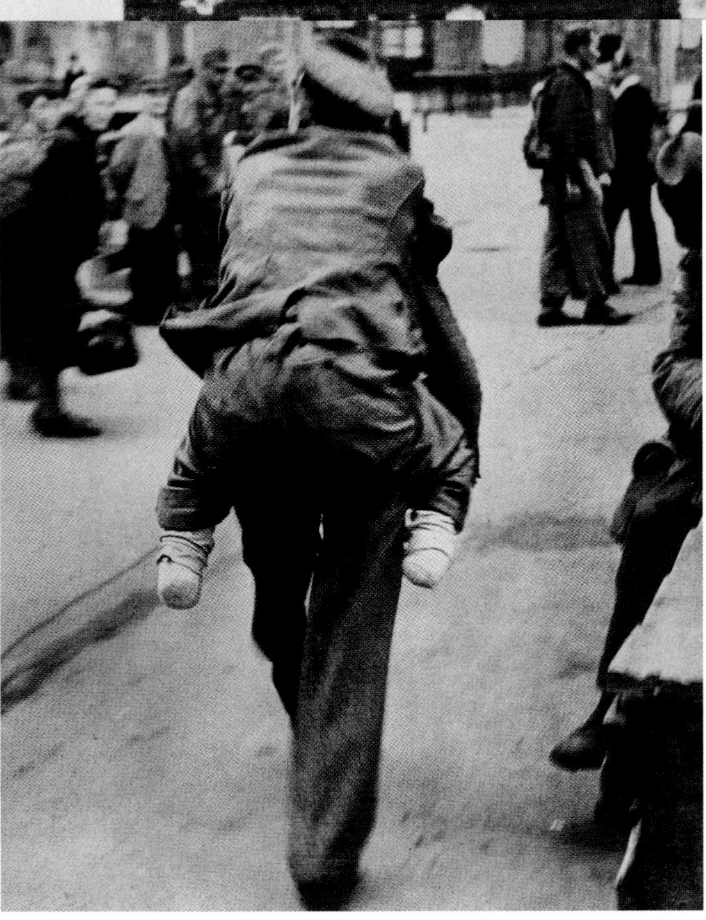

FAR LEFT

This teenage girl was raped by Polish hoodlums on a train that was taking her out of that country. Poles commonly boarded the trains to loot the German refugees.

LEFT

This footless German soldier, released by the Russians but without crutches, is taken from a train. Several other amputation cases had died on that train trip.

OPPOSITE

This orphaned German from the Sudetenland was about three when Hitler made the Czech region a rallying cry for war in 1938.

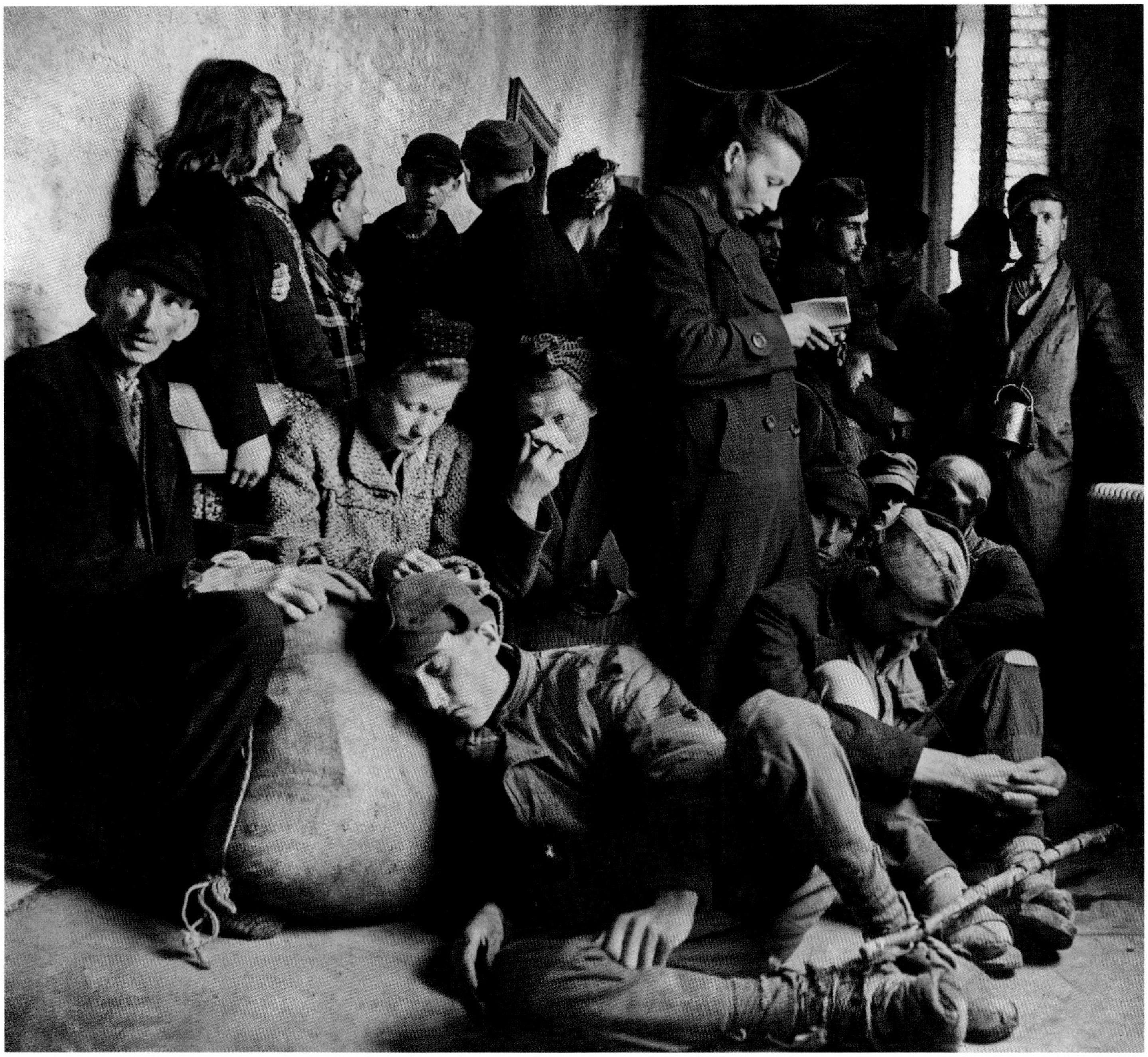

An exhausted group, including an old man with his sack, huddles in a Berlin municipal building.

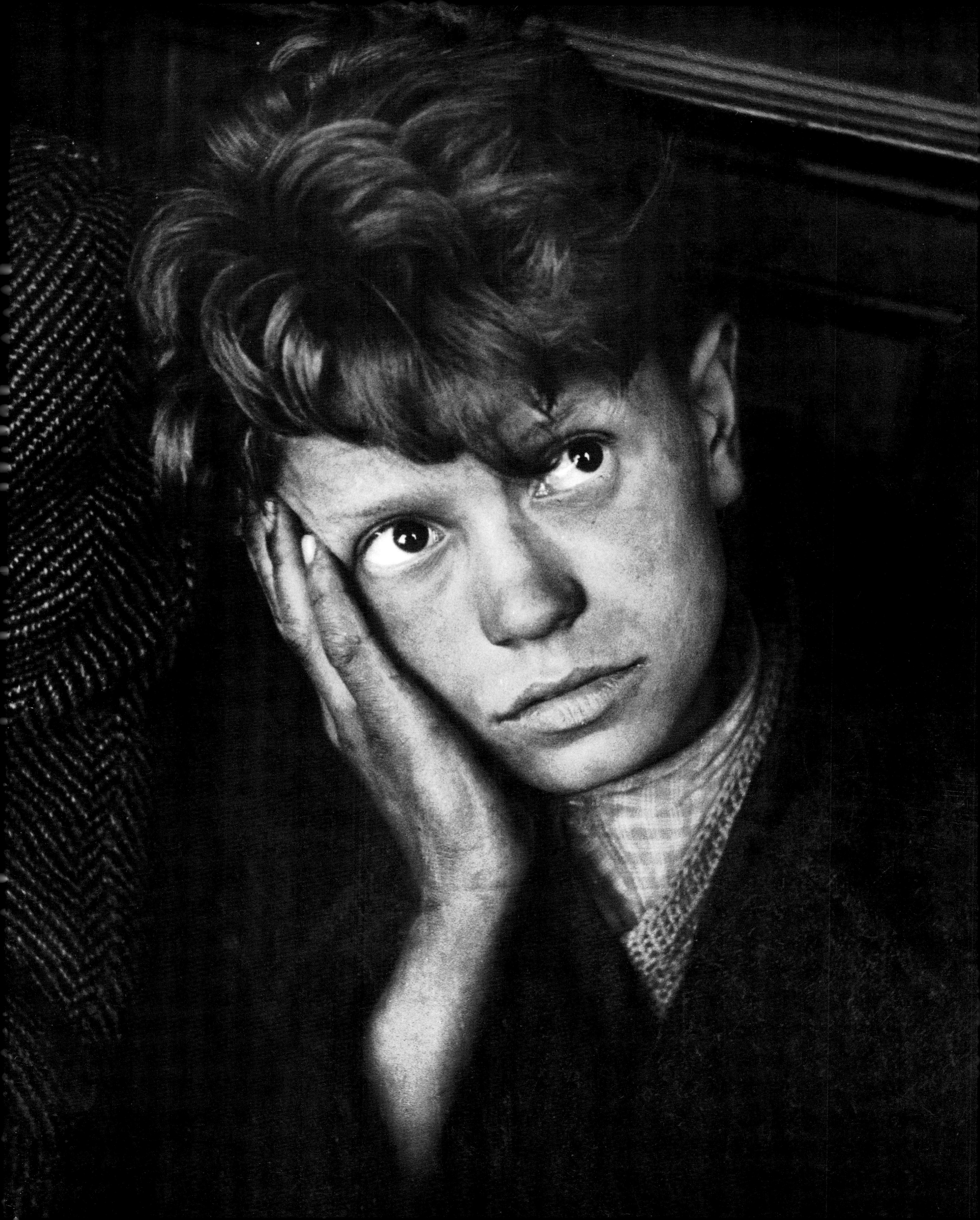

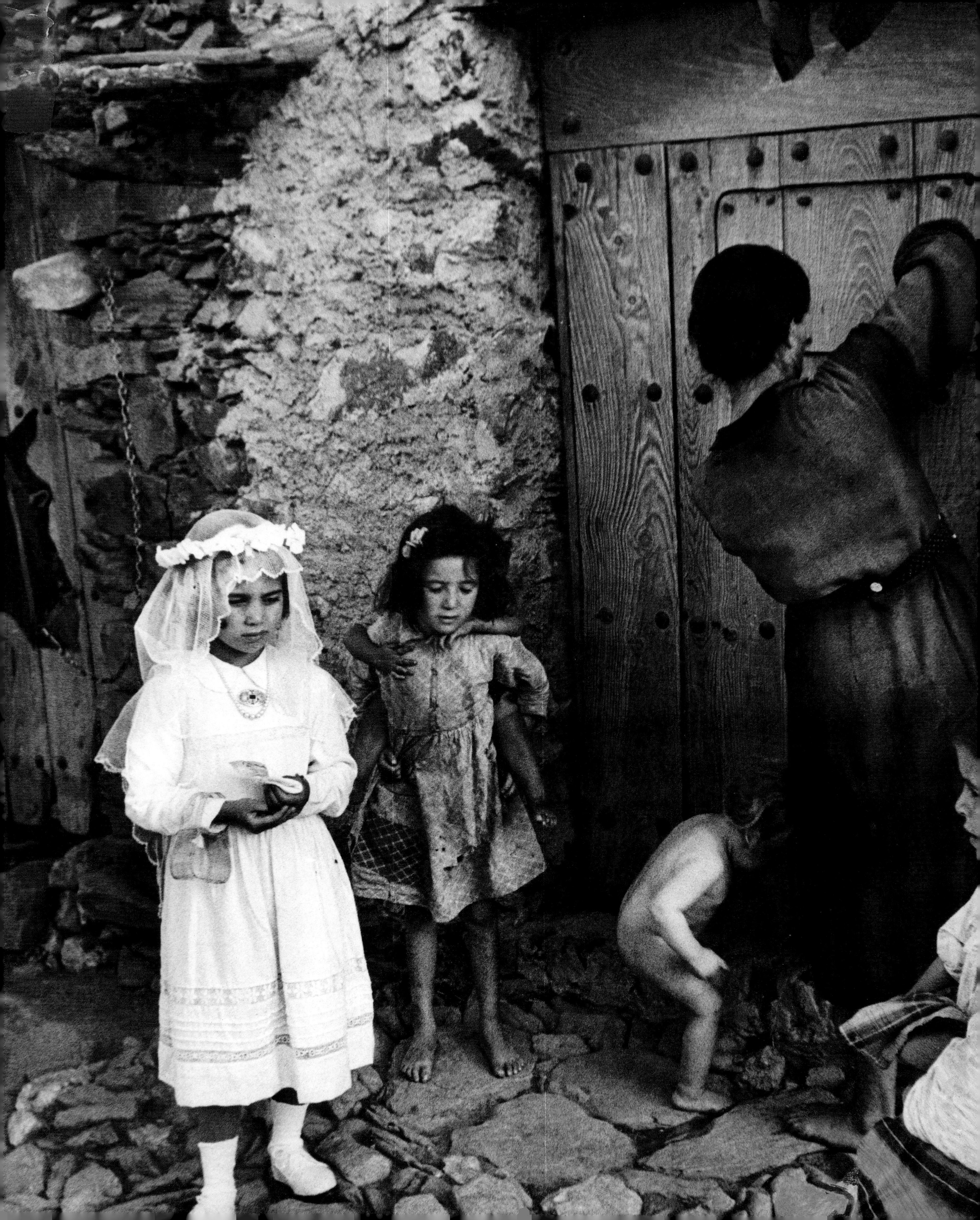

OPPOSITE

As her mother locks the door, seven-year-old Lorenza Curiel waits to go to church for her First Communion.

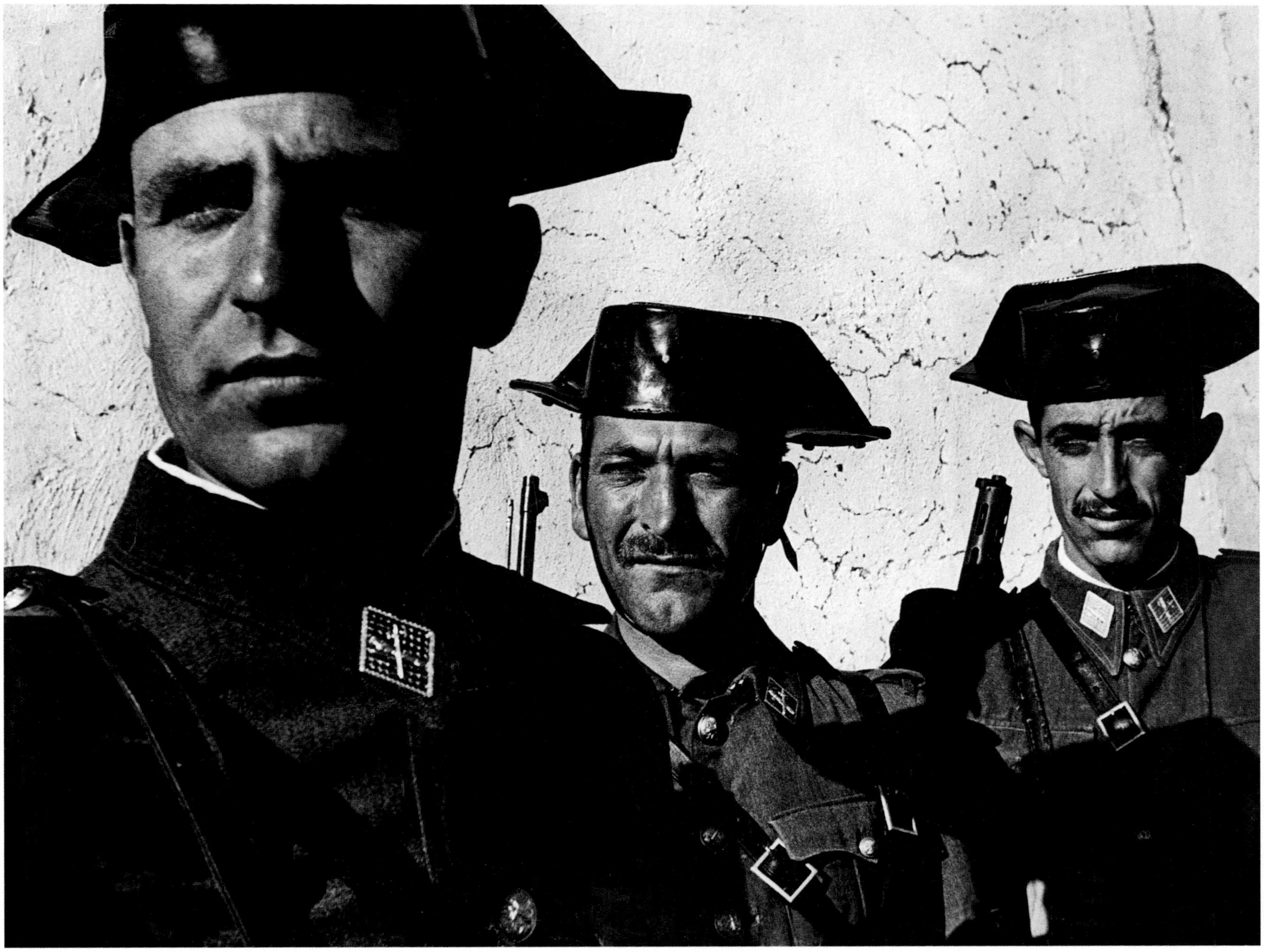

Francisco Franco's stern Guardia Civil is responsible for enforcing national law in the countryside. Villagers fear them.

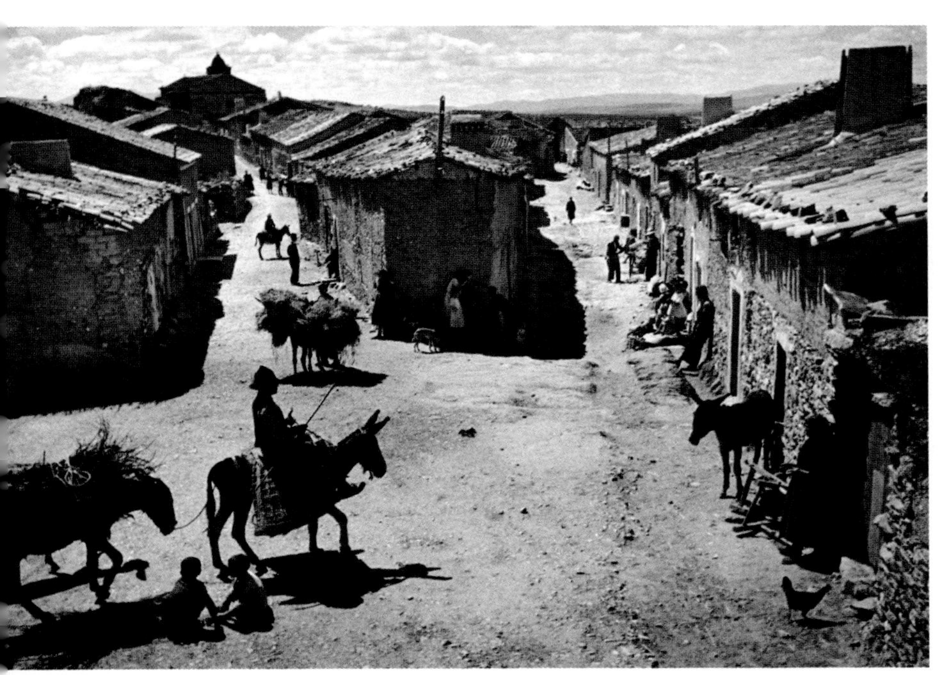

The midmorning sun beats down on a cluster of stone houses.

SPANISH VILLAGE

W. EUGENE SMITH

APRIL 9, 1951

According to fellow LIFE staffer Gordon Parks, Gene Smith possessed "a wonderful sense of humanity." In 1951, about halfway between Madrid and the Portuguese border, Gene wandered off the main road into a very old village called Deleitosa. The name means "Delightful," but for this community of 2,300 peasants, stranded on a high, dry tableland, that meaning no longer applied. There had been few advances since medieval times, and the daily grind of subsistence, along with a sustaining faith in their Catholic beliefs, dominated the lives of all the people. Here is a classic example of the human need, and will, to survive.

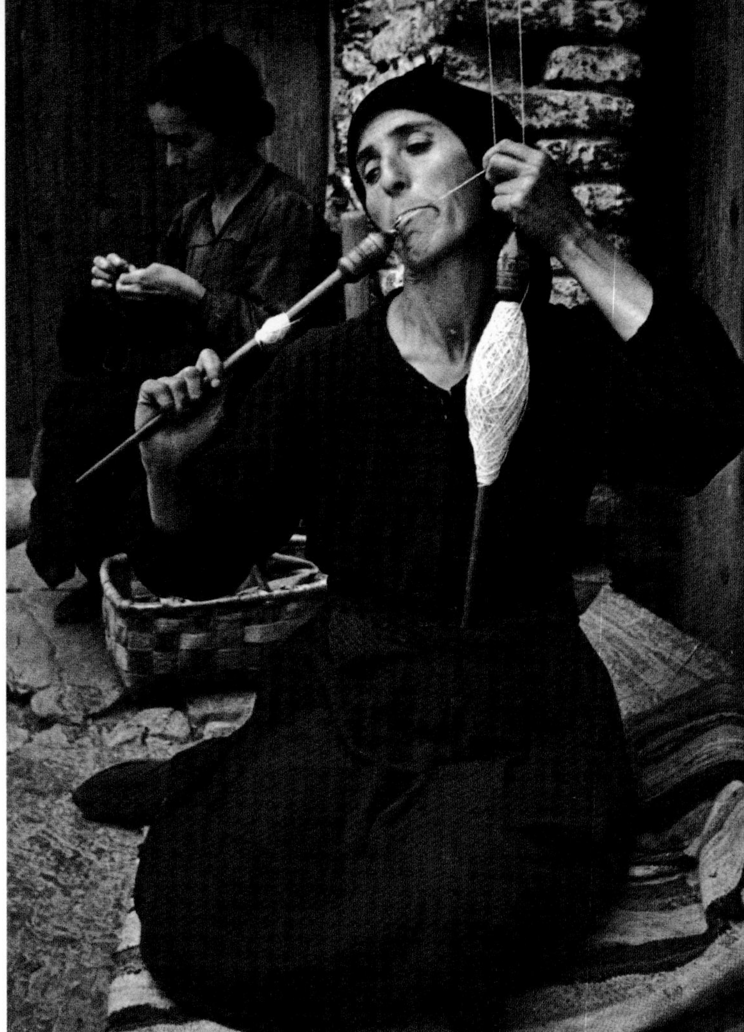

A woman moistens flax fibers in the process of making thread.

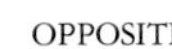

OPPOSITE

A teenage girl opens the door to the community oven. At least once a week, she bakes 24 loaves for her family of eight. The flour is made from family-grown grain.

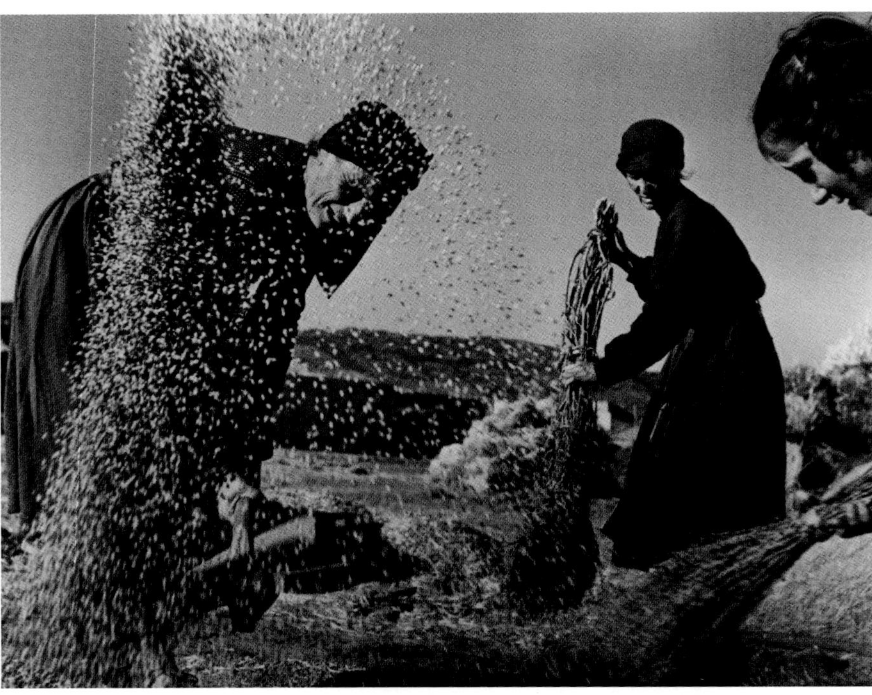

A thresher tosses wheat kernels into the air so that the breeze can carry off the chaff.

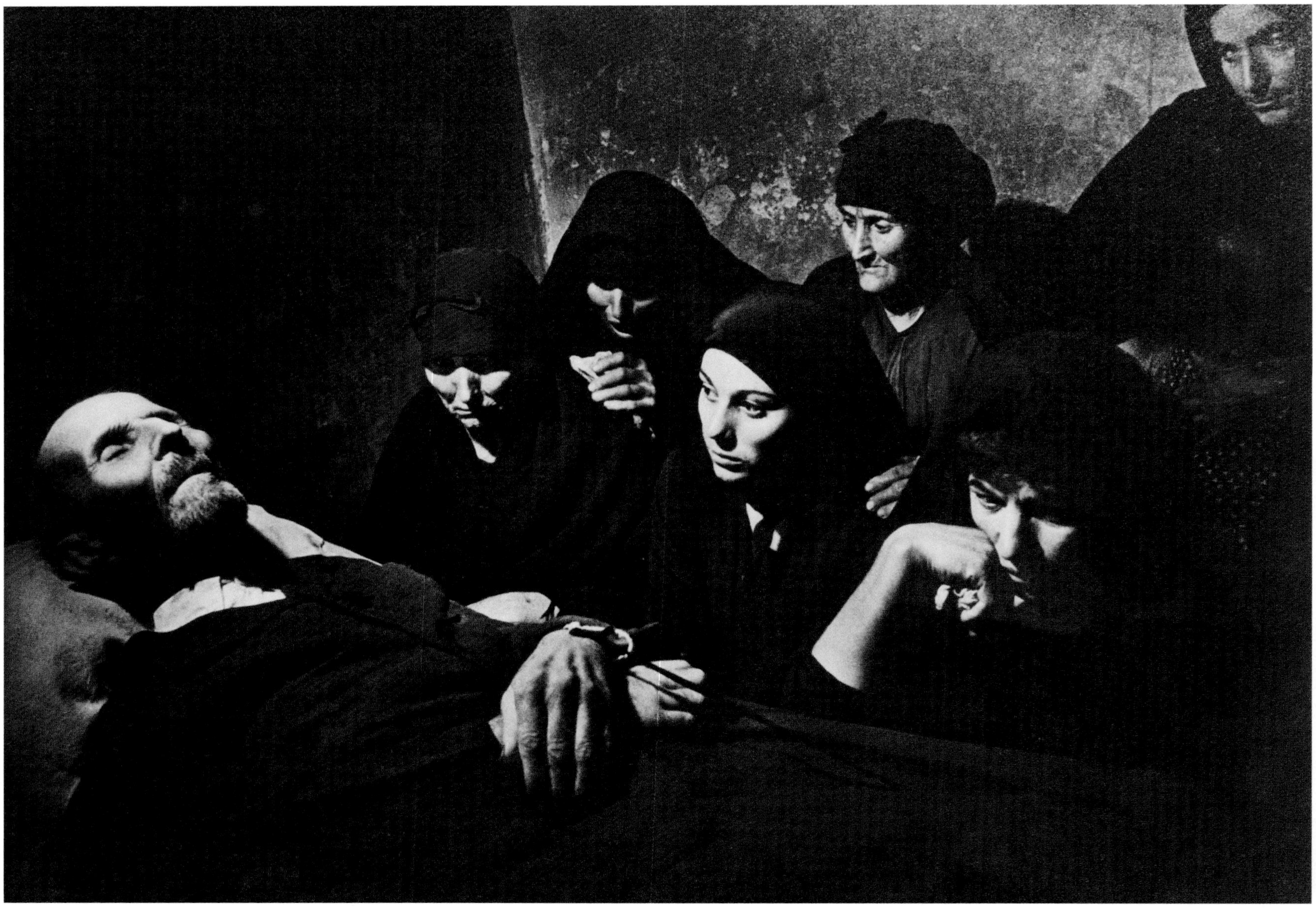

His wife, daughter, granddaughter and friends have a last earthly visit with a villager.

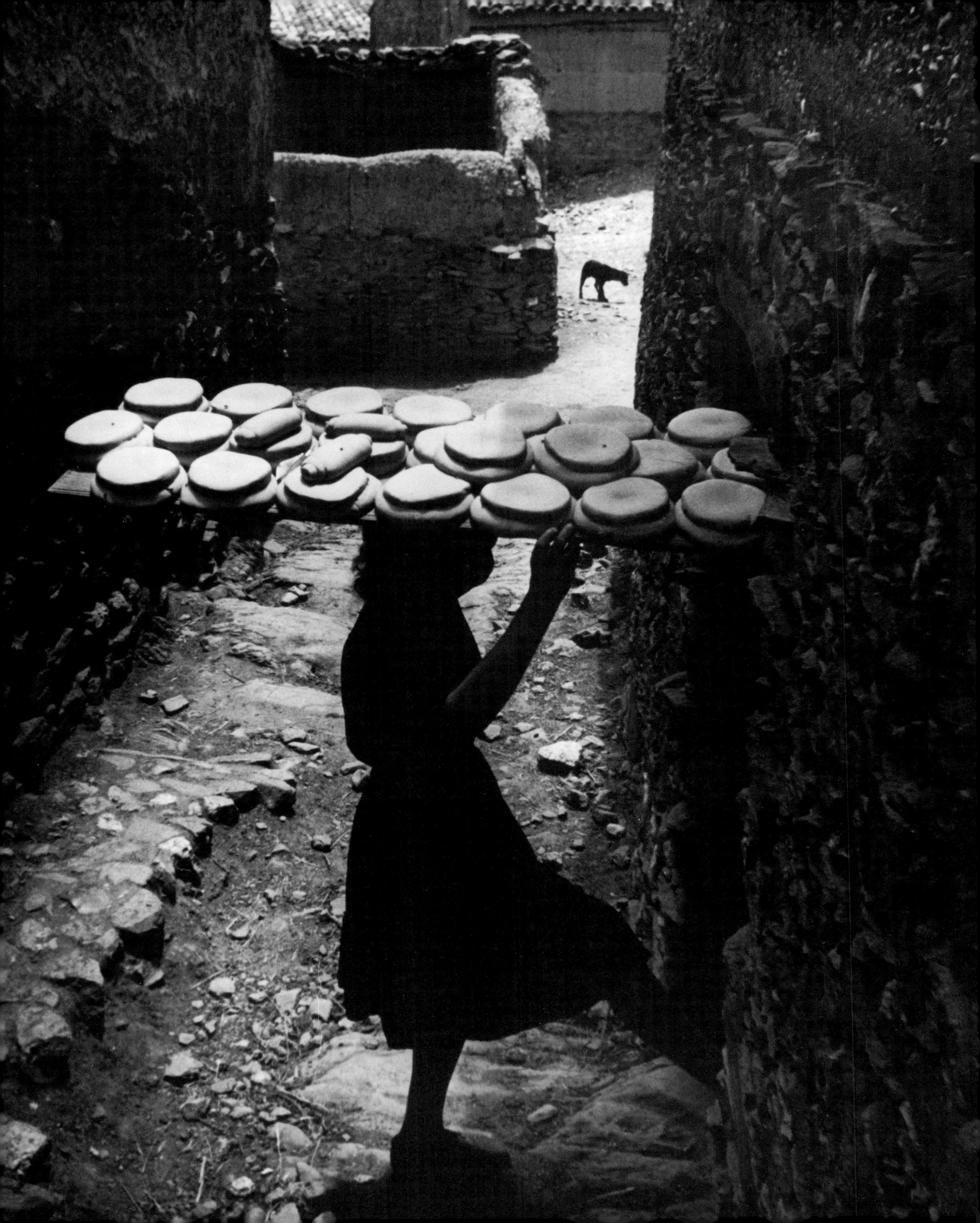

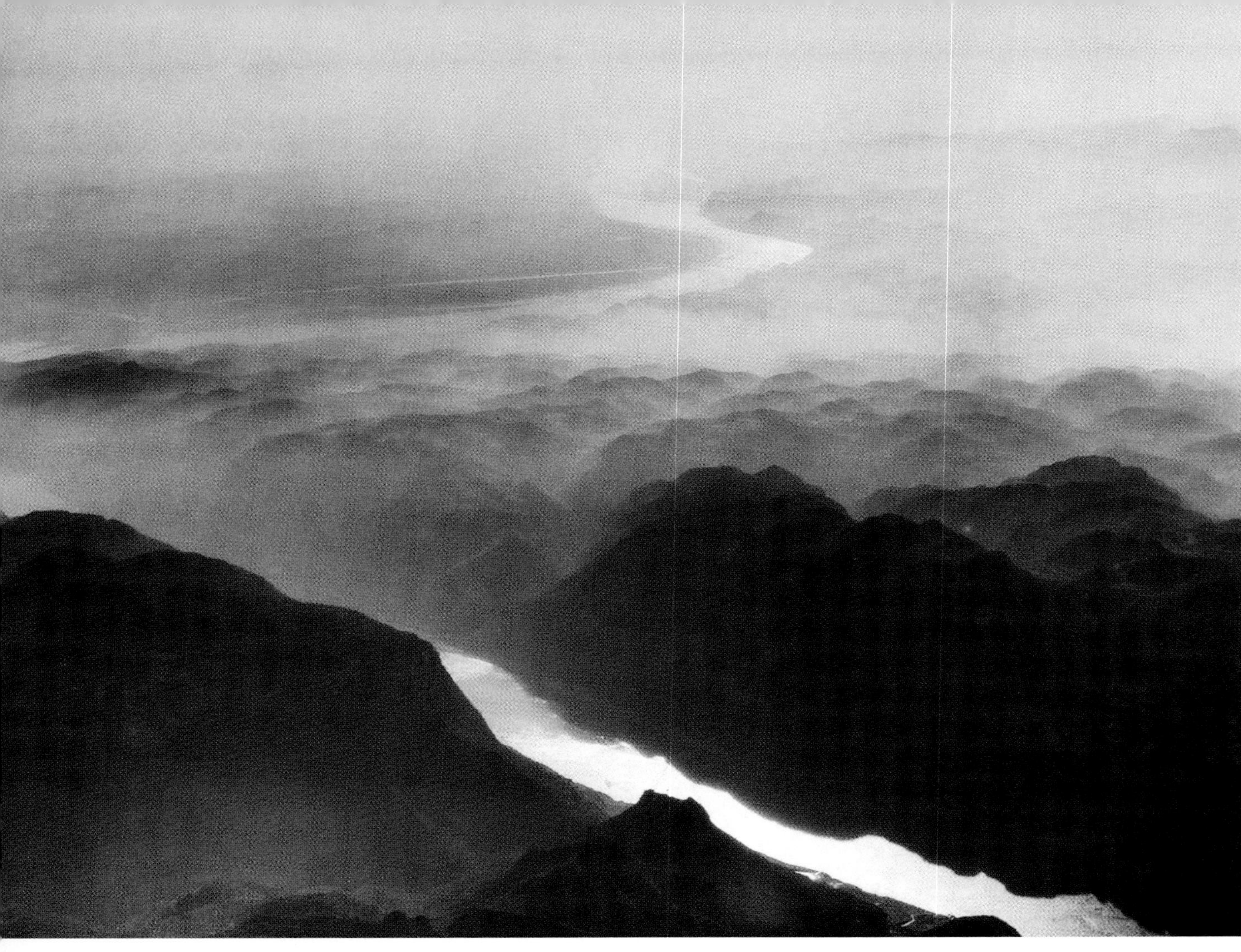

LEFT
With mists enshrouding the ancient mountains, the river makes its way through the land in graceful arcs.

OPPOSITE
Harnessed and bowed, trackers pad along the rough bank towing a junk up the waterway. Wrote Hersey, "The head tracker's formal title was Noise Suppressor. With a thread of sweet song he was supposed to suppress the groan-shout that marked each painful step."

BOTTOM LEFT
Women washing clothes along Duck Creek mingle in the confined and noisy bustle ashore.

BELOW
Shooting the low-water rapids, a junk and its hardy crew careen through a moraine of rocks that pierces the river's flow.

A STORY OF THE MIGHTY YANGTZE

DMITRI KESSEL
JUNE 11, 1956

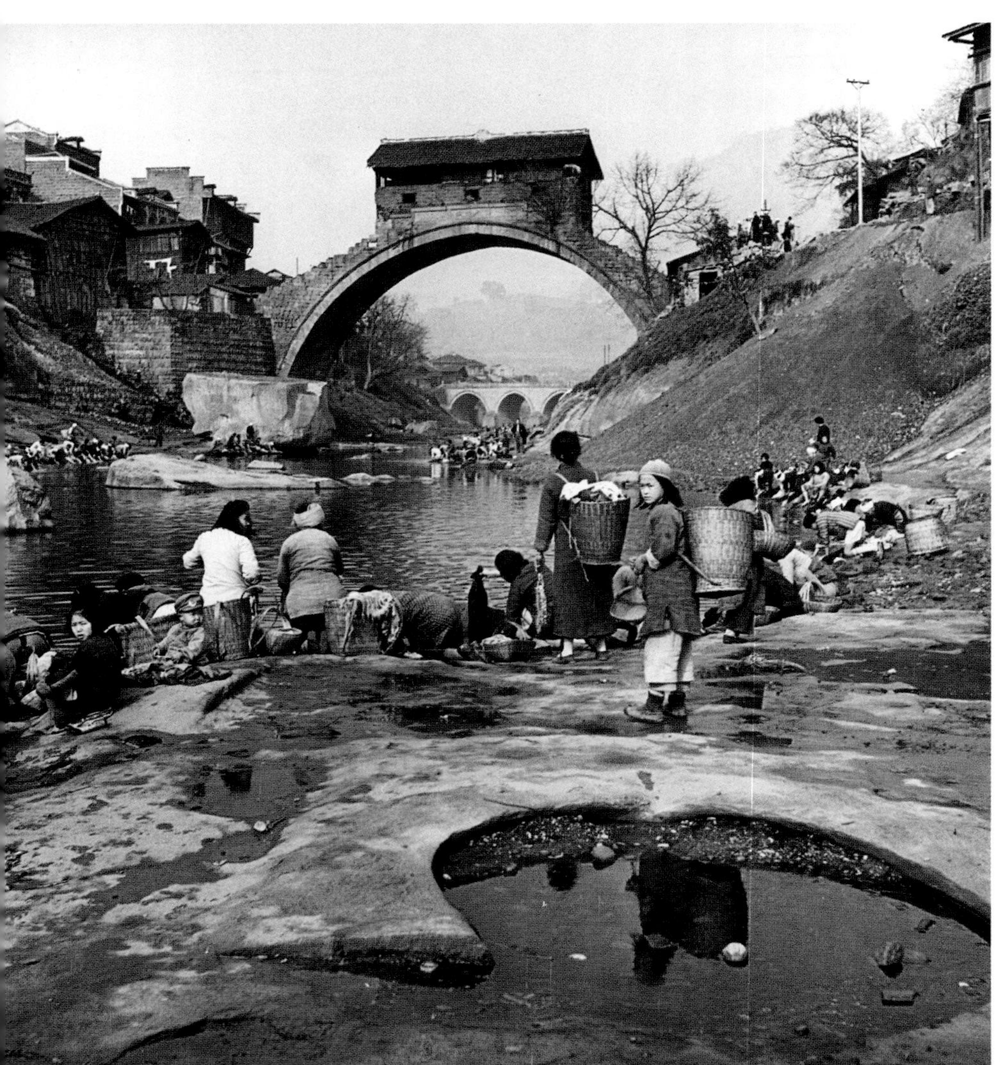

In 1946, LIFE photographer Kessel and editor John Hersey spent three weeks in the heart of China on the powerful, majestic Yangtze River. Ten years later, that trip culminated in a book by Hersey called *A Single Pebble,* and in this photo essay that spanned 10 pages in LIFE. The wonder is that these timeless photographs had remained unpublished for so long.

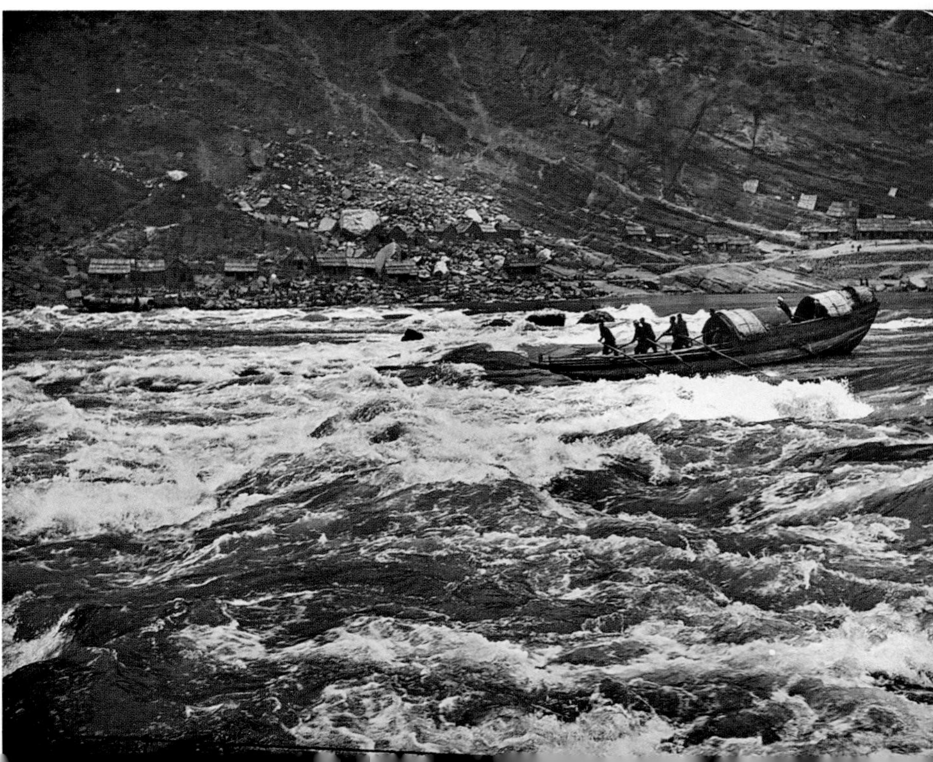

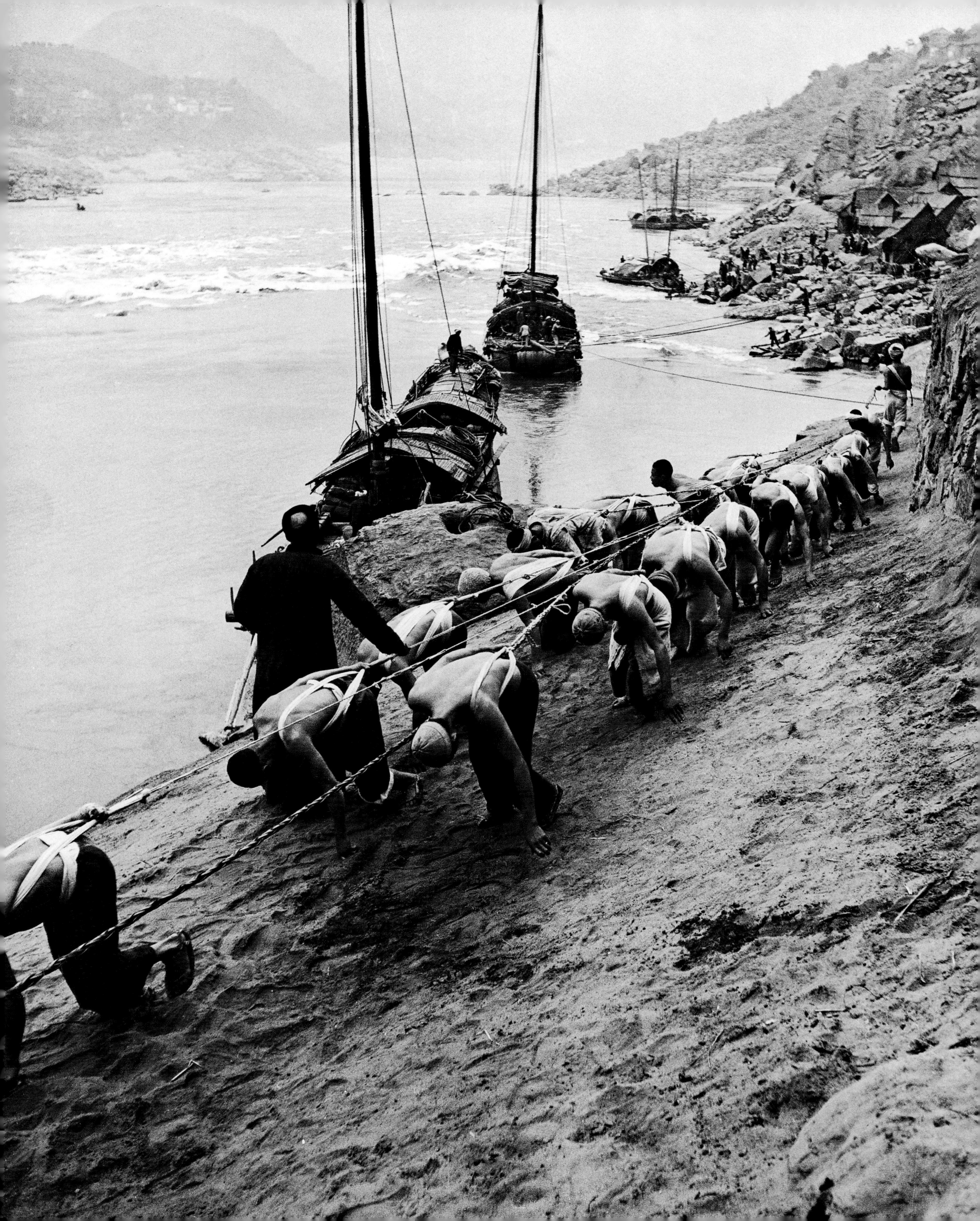

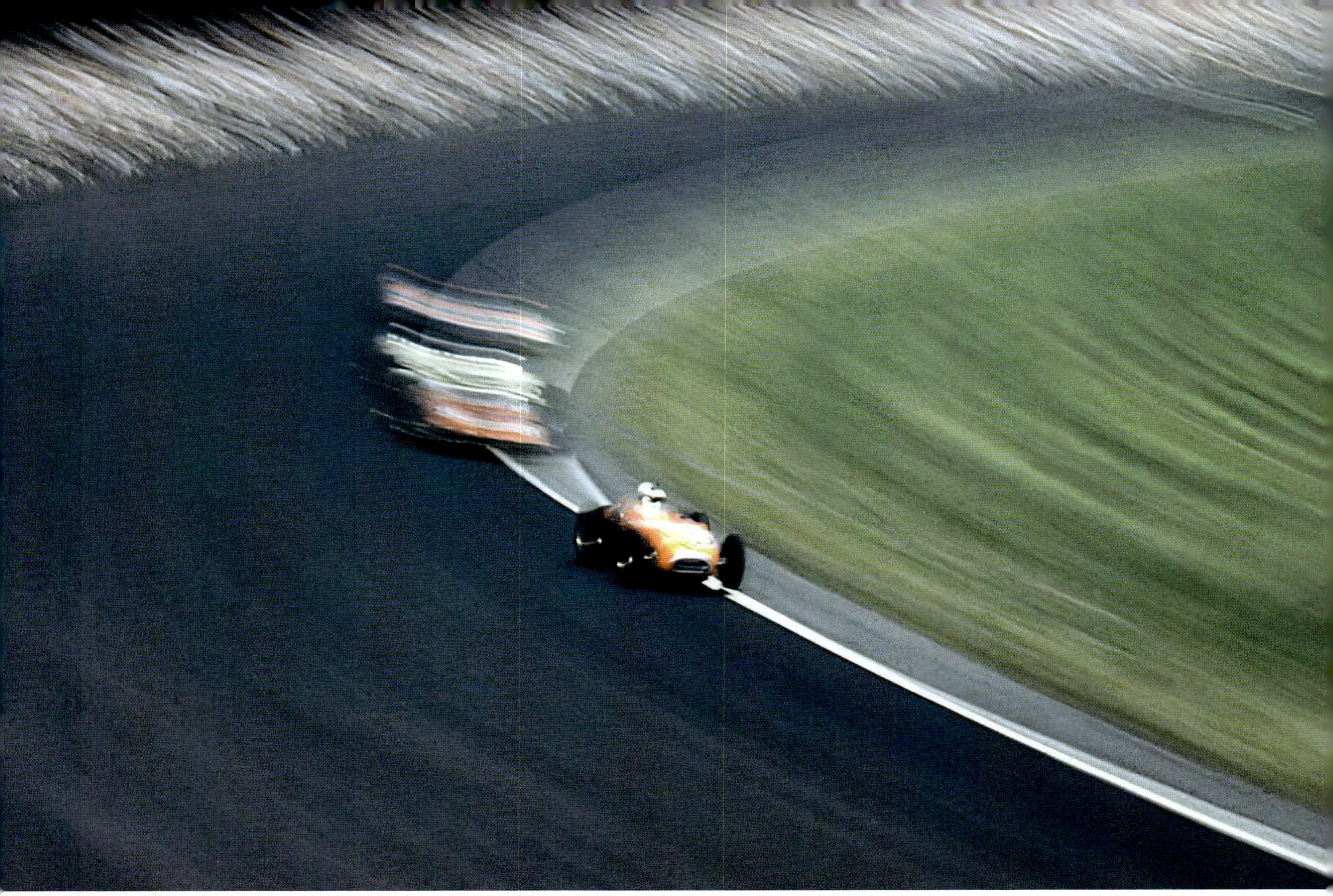

At Indianapolis Speedway, the lead car is clear but its pursuers and the grandstand are another matter.

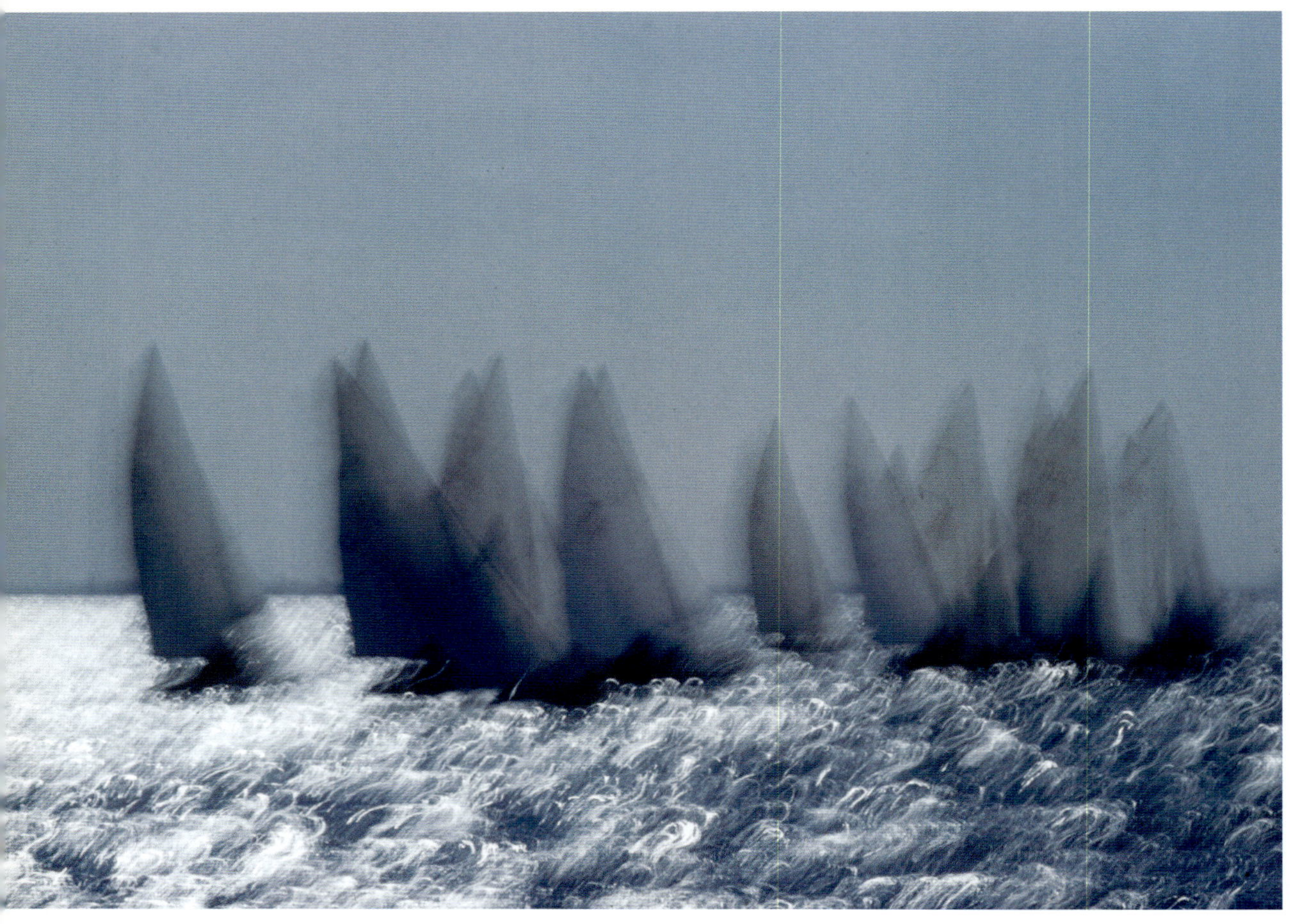

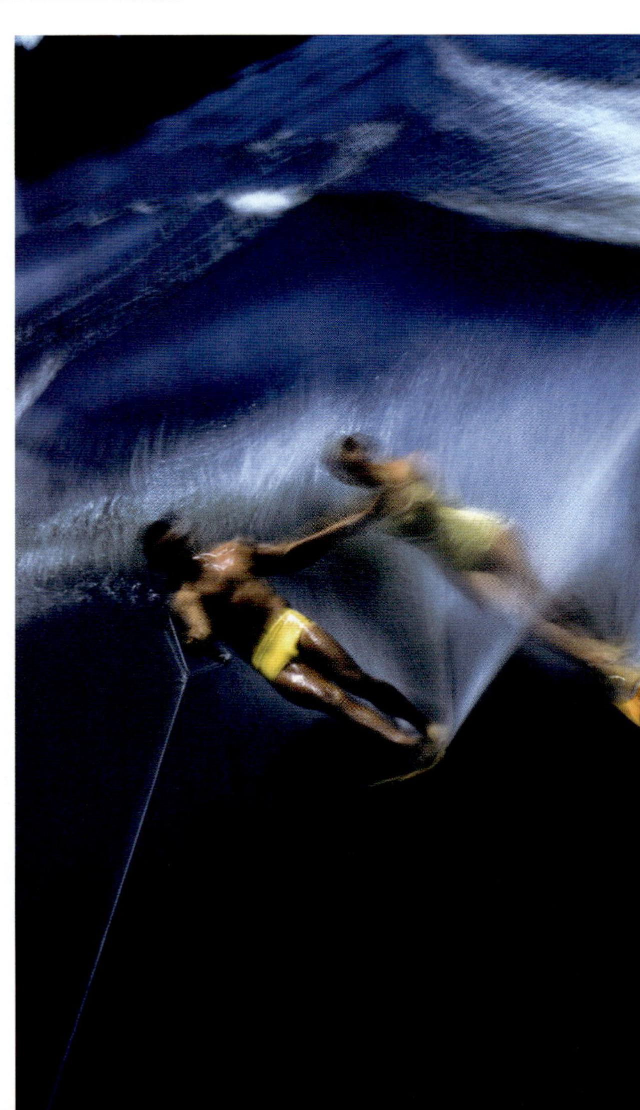

THE MAGIC OF COLOR IN MOTION

ERNST HAAS

AUGUST 11 & 18, 1958

Early attempts at incorporating color into photography were, in the main, static ventures because active subjects presented a spate of technical problems. But for Ernst Haas these hurdles were merely a welcome invitation to race with the wind. In these photos he sought to make the camera see color in motion as the eye sees it: not in fixed images but in a blended flow. Typically, Haas raised the bar by choosing types of movement whose courses were unpredictable, and along the way he freed the images from distractions of detail, thereby attaining a purification of color.

RIGHT

This tough cowboy's determination to stay in the saddle lends him a balletic quality.

OPPOSITE, FAR LEFT

Haas was on a boat himself when he took this photo of racing yachts on a swaying sea.

OPPOSITE, RIGHT

The photographer was inspired by the harmony and grace of a young couple as they skied along behind a speedboat.

Getty (4)

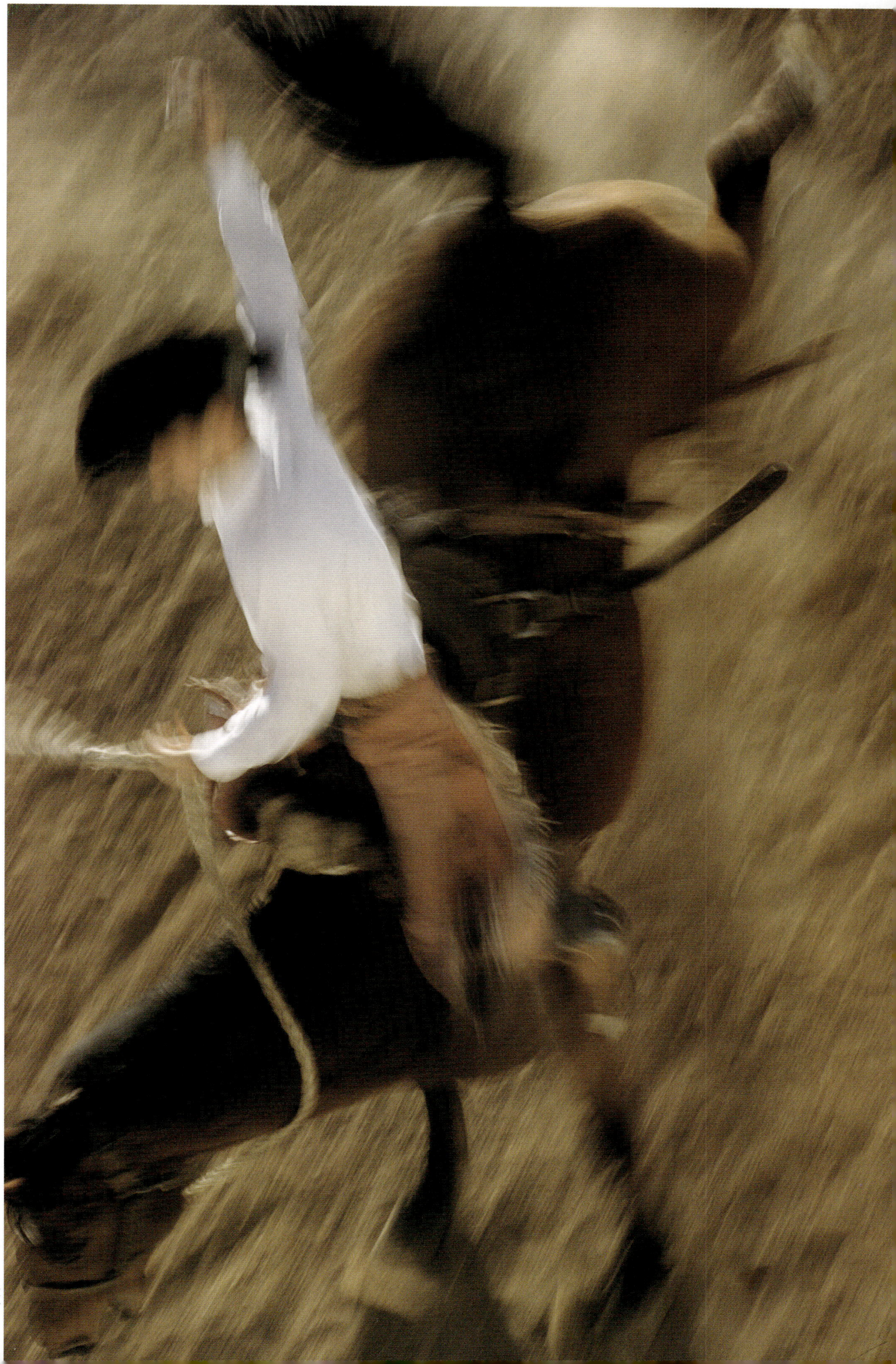

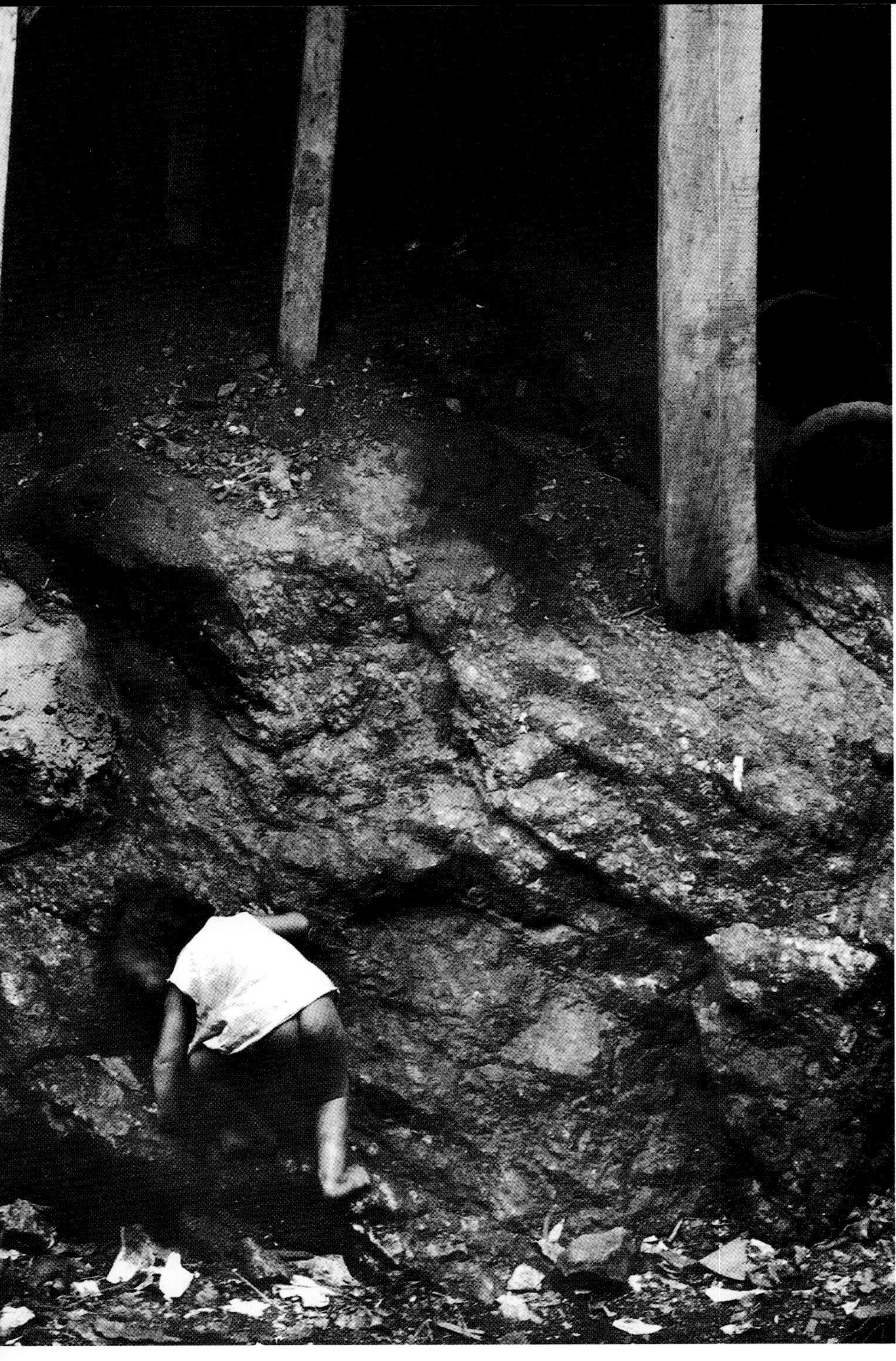

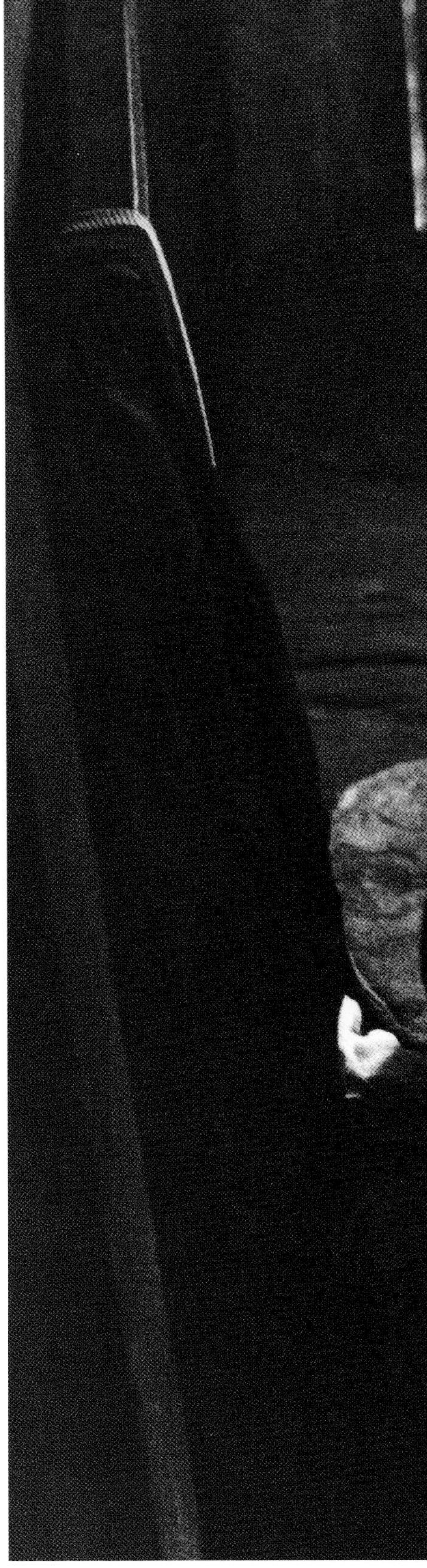

LEFT

Seventeen-month-old Zacarias, the youngest of the family, explores a path among the pilings that support the shack.

RIGHT

In the spreading shadows of yet another squalid evening, three-year-old Isabel cries to herself after vainly seeking comfort from her exhausted father, José.

OPPOSITE, BOTTOM

Pouring water into the family pot, Flavio starts to cook for his brothers and sisters. Virtually every meal is black beans and rice. The exception is breakfast—often just coffee.

BELOW

Flavio steadies Zacarias with one hand and feeds him with the other. The rest of the children must wait until Zacarias is fed to ensure that he gets enough.

BOTTOM LEFT

Completely spent after caring for the family all week, Flavio rests on a Sunday, when his mother is free to look after his brothers and sisters. Losing a battle against bronchial asthma and malnutrition, the 12-year-old says, "I am not afraid of death. But what will they do after?"

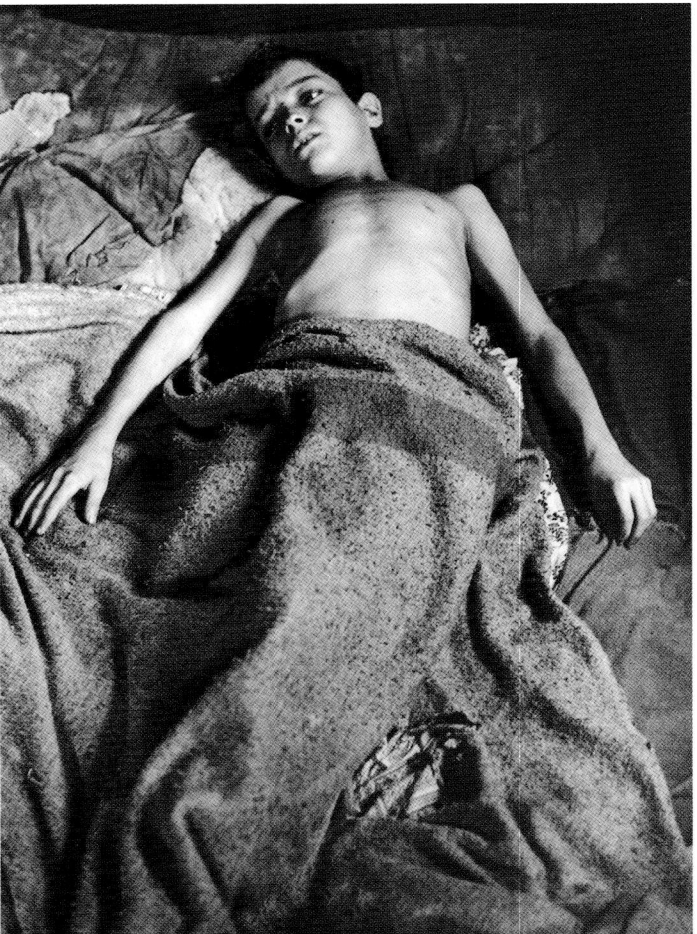

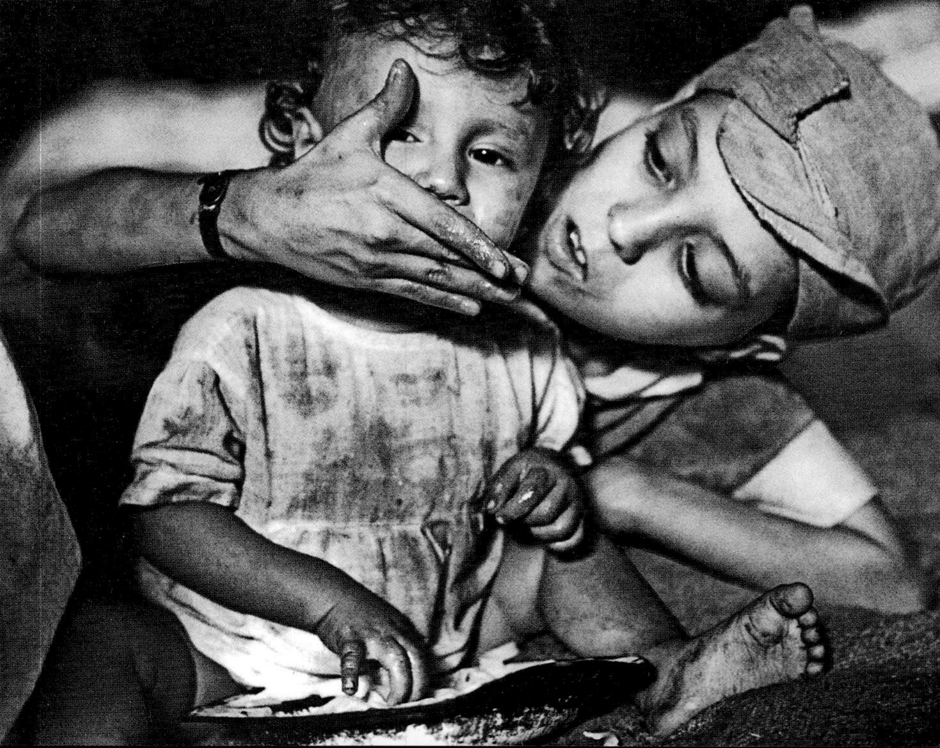

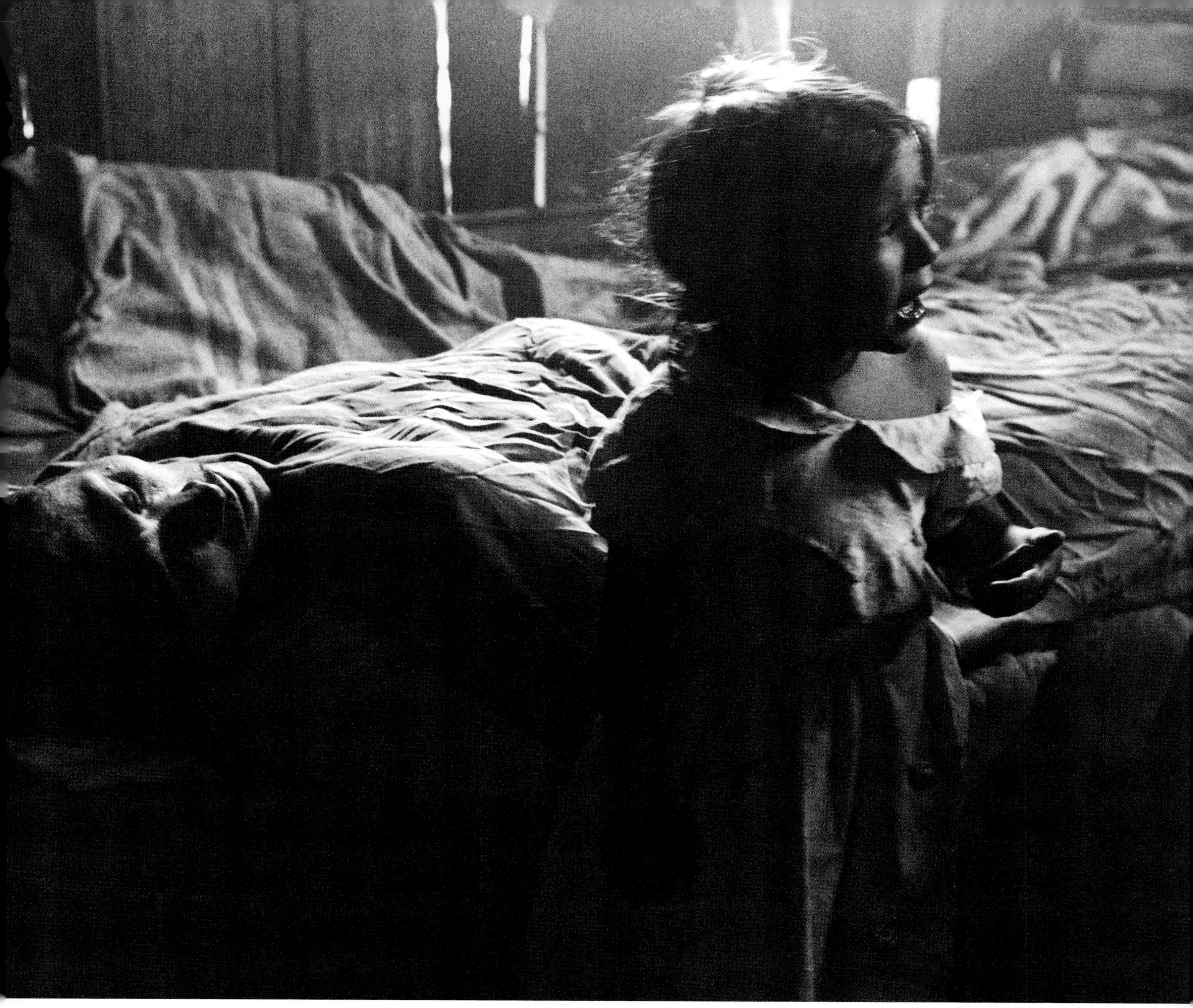

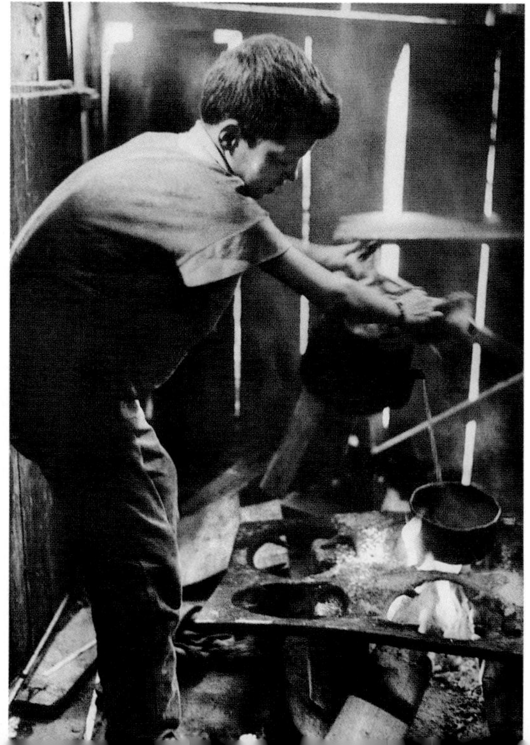

FREEDOM'S FEARFUL FOE: POVERTY

GORDON PARKS

JUNE 16, 1961

As part of a series on Latin America, LIFE sent photographer Gordon Parks to document the poor side of Rio de Janeiro, not because the penury there was worse than that of Bolivia, Chile or other such nations, but because the destitution in Rio was in such stark contrast to the florid elegance that thrived nearby. Parks spent 19 days with the Da Silva family of 10, soon to be 11, who lived in a cramped shack fashioned from odds and ends. Mother Nair did laundry at a hillside spigot. Father José had been a construction worker, then an accident forced him to sell kerosene and bleach from a tiny stall. They were gone all day, so it fell to the eldest child, 12-year-old Flavio, to tend to himself and his siblings.

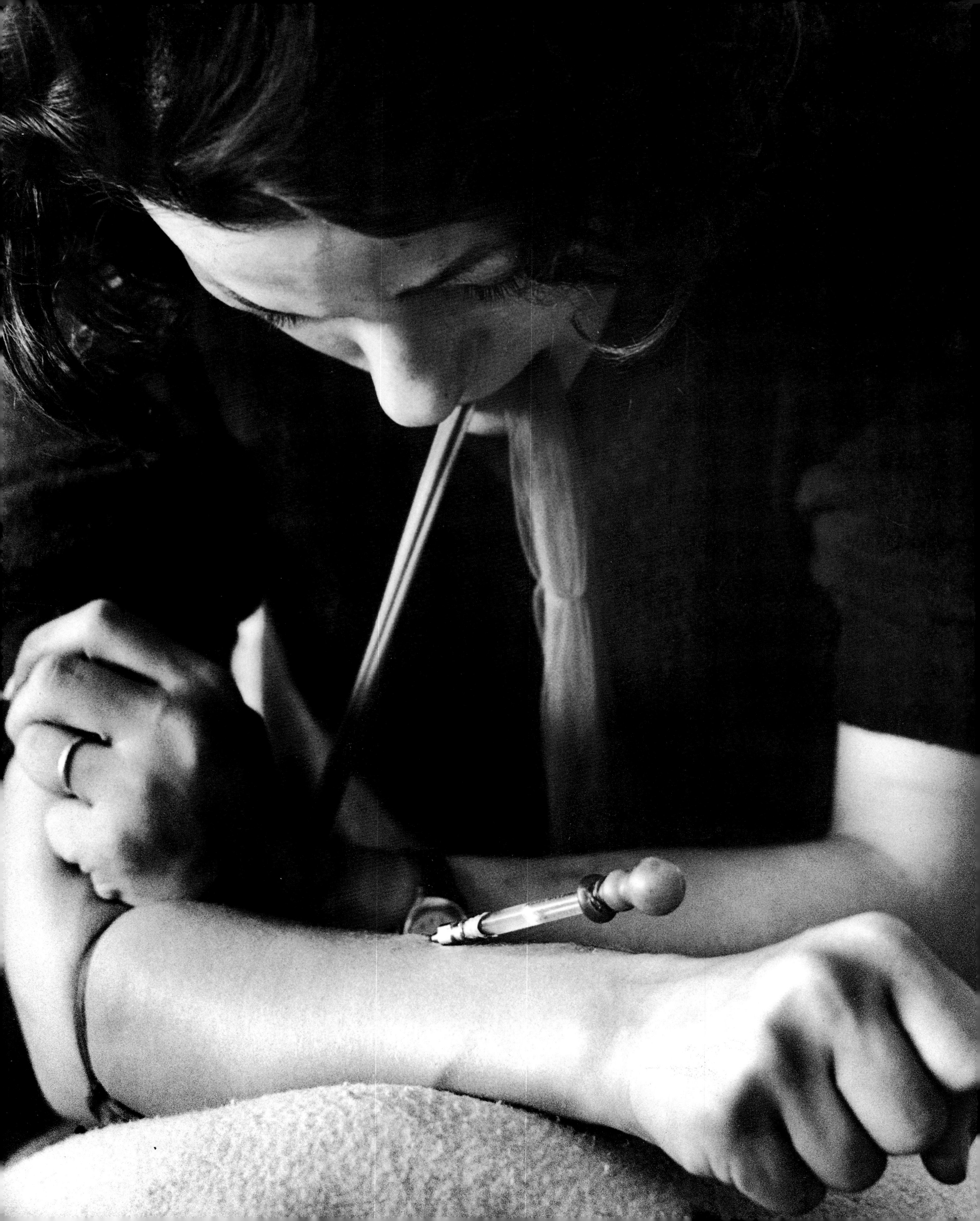

JOHN AND KAREN, TWO LIVES LOST TO HEROIN

BILL EPPRIDGE

FEBRUARY 26, 1965

In order to realize this story, photographer Eppridge spent two months living with John, 24, and Karen, 26, a pair of New York junkies. To gain uninhibited access to their desperate, seedy world, Eppridge had to convince them that this would be their chance to make some sort of contribution to society. The couple considered the proposal, and finally consented. Of the addicts who populate her driven existence, Karen said, "We are animals. We are all animals in a world no one knows." After this piece, and a film that was based on it called *The Panic in Needle Park,* the rest of society had an all-too-clear look into that world.

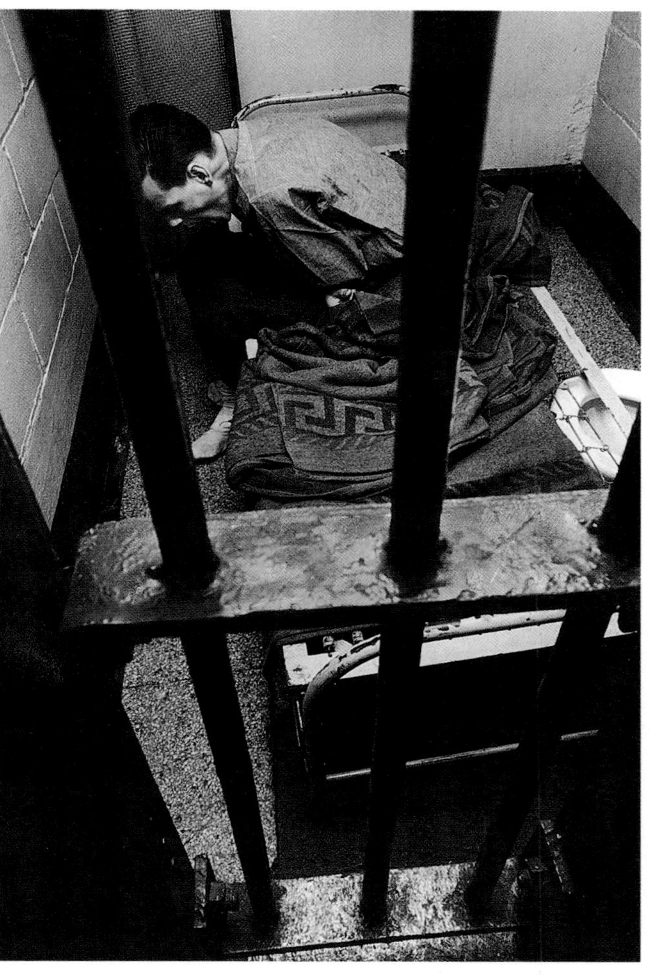

John goes through withdrawal in jail, a common occurrence.

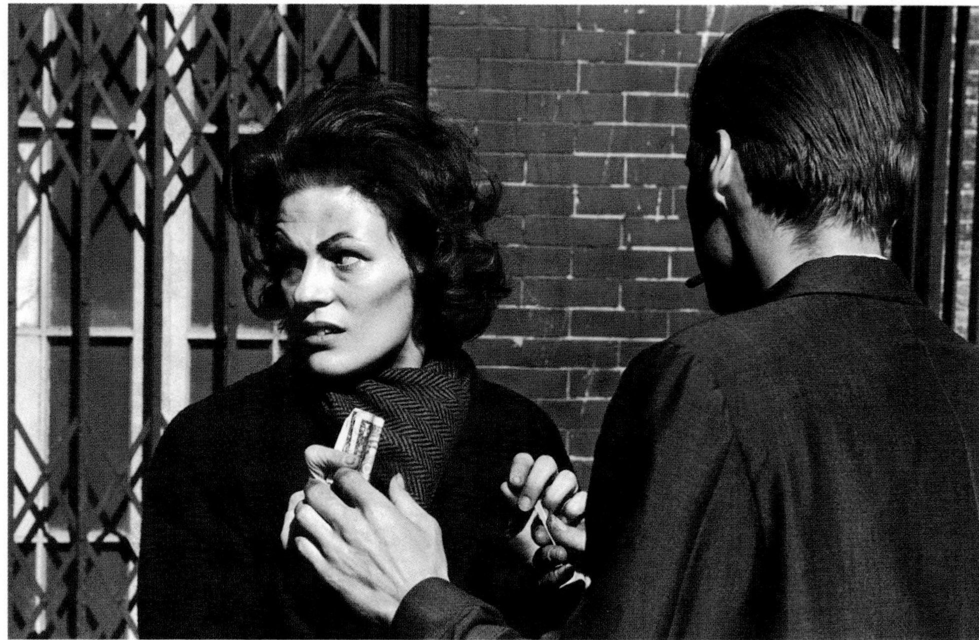

With an eye out for the police, Karen passes money to a pusher for a fix.

OPPOSITE

Four times a day, Karen injects heroin. If she doesn't, the potent withdrawal symptoms set in quickly. When she does, things seem all right—for a few hours.

RIGHT

Karen holds John and his brother, also a junkie, in a cheap hotel room. On the table are water to dissolve heroin and a bottle cap used to cook it.

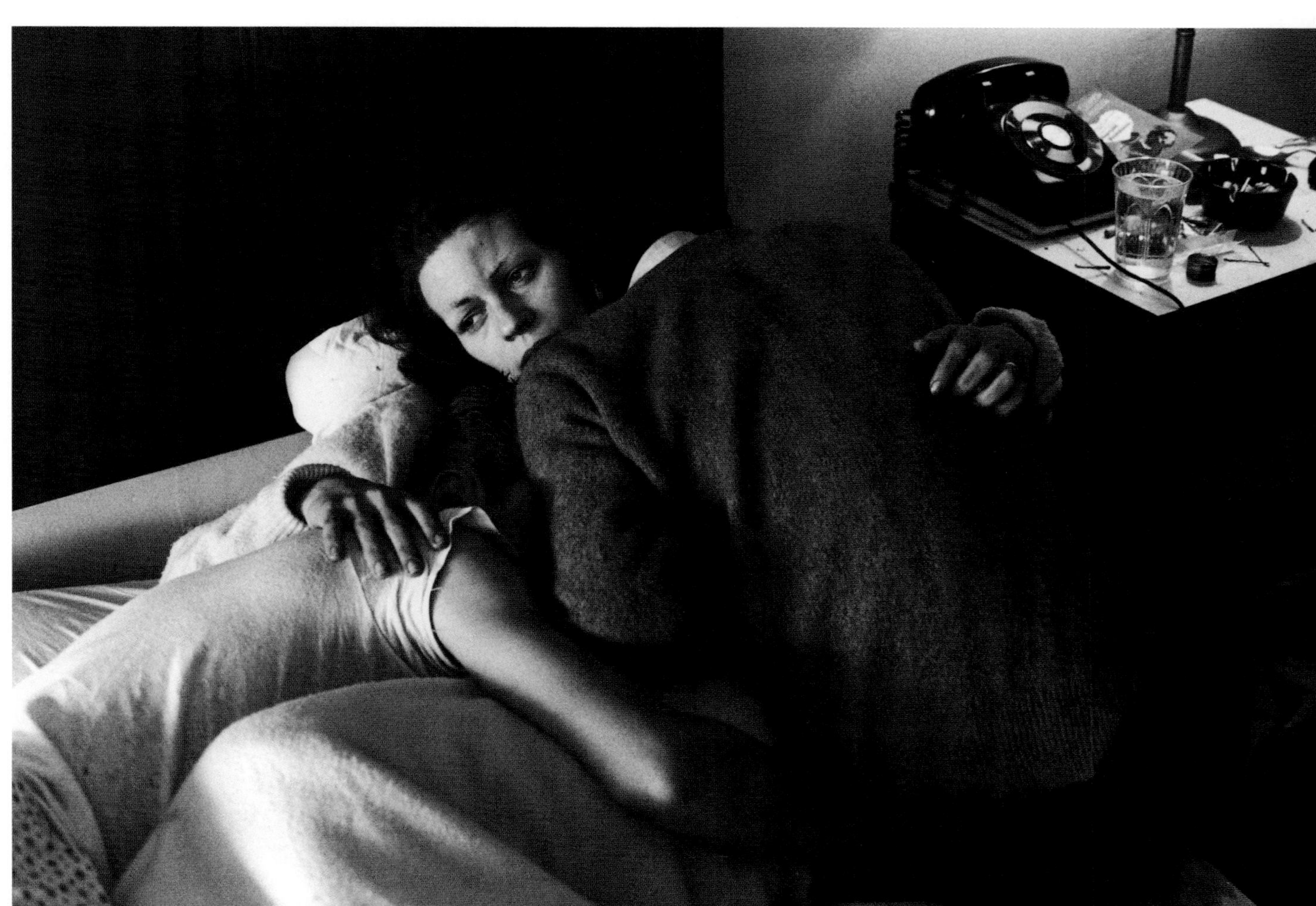

ONE RIDE WITH YANKEE PAPA 13

LARRY BURROWS

APRIL 16, 1965

Honored as perhaps "the greatest photo essay ever made," this was the masterpiece in the career of Larry Burrows, who was called by LIFE managing editor Ralph Graves "the single bravest and most dedicated war photographer I know of." *Yankee Papa 13* was the name of a Marine helicopter whose crew, a squadron of U.S. Marines, was given the job of ferrying a battalion of Vietnamese infantry to an isolated area 20 miles away. That area was a rendezvous point for enemy Vietcong forces. The day, like any other day, began typically, but by the end disaster had laid its cruel hand on several very young men. In turn, this photo essay sounded a clarion call to a naive America that serious trouble was brewing in a faraway land.

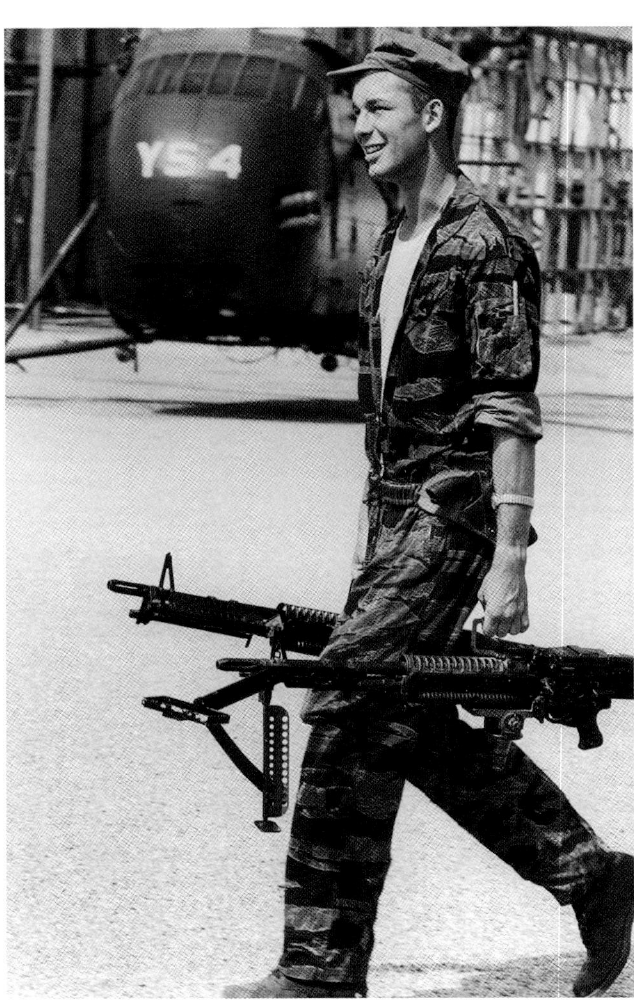

A seemingly carefree young warrior, crew chief Lance Cpl. James C. Farley totes two M-60 machine guns to the helicopter.

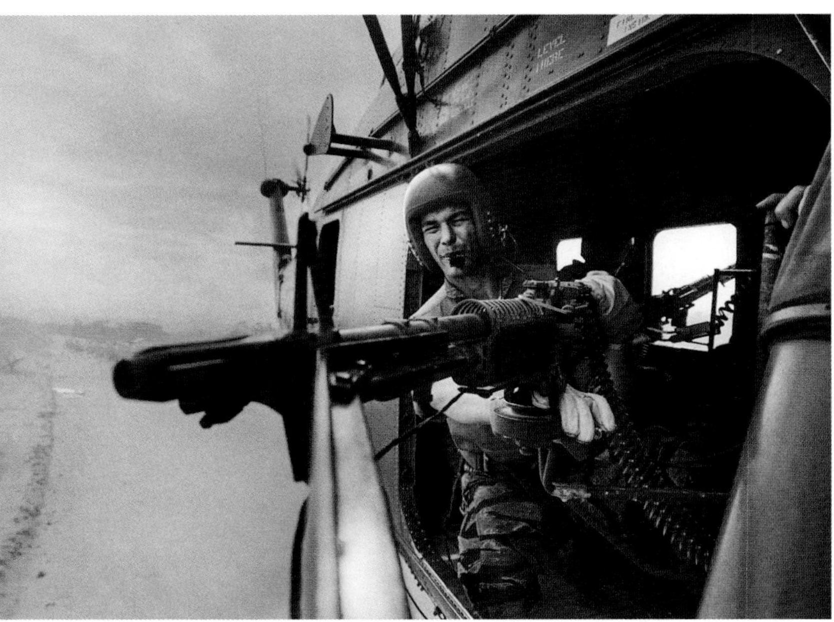

A camera Burrows mounted outside the copter shows Farley firing his M-60 on the approach to the landing zone.

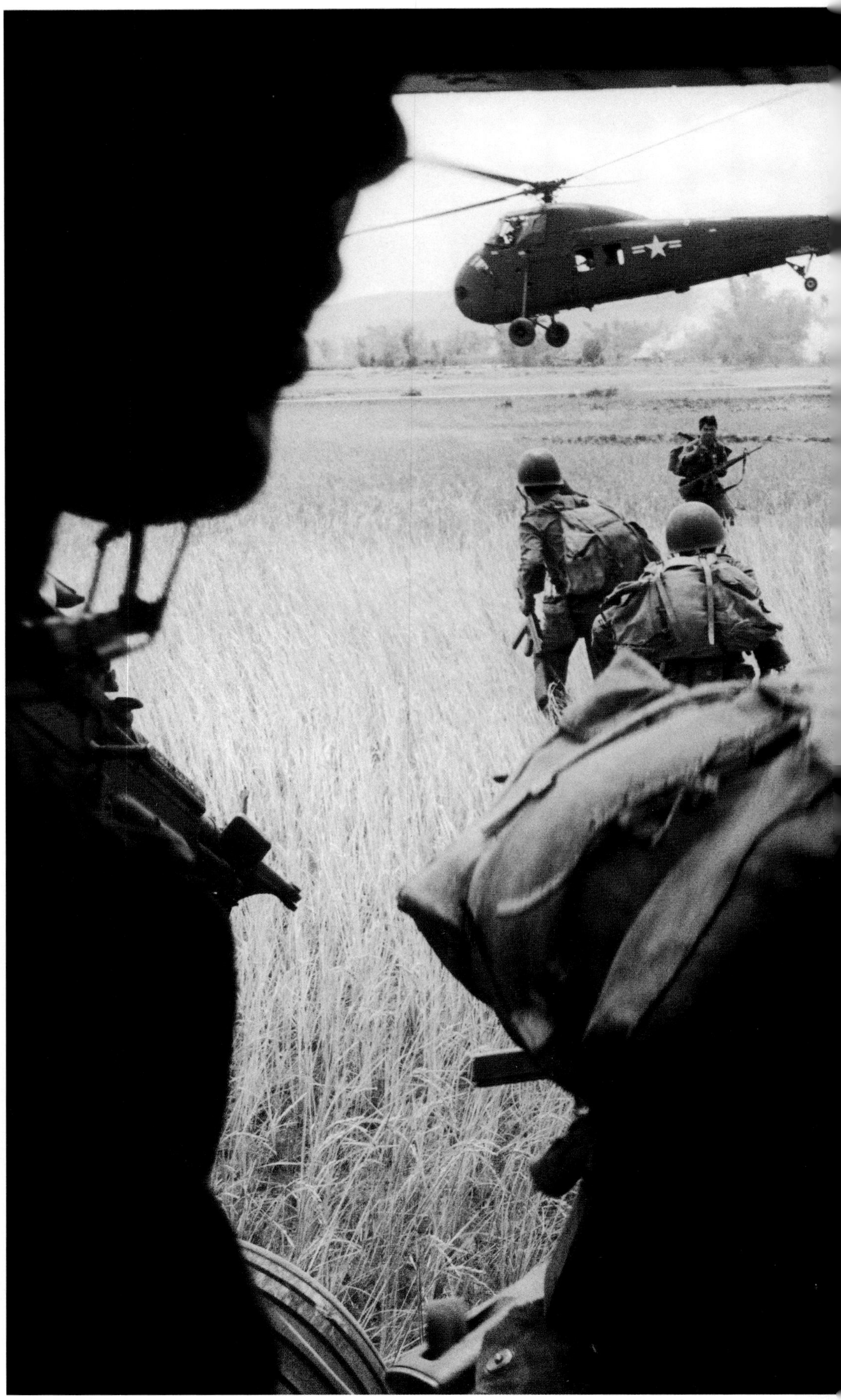

BELOW

South Vietnamese soldiers scramble out of the chopper to join in the assault against Vietcong forces hidden along the tree line in the background.

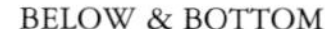

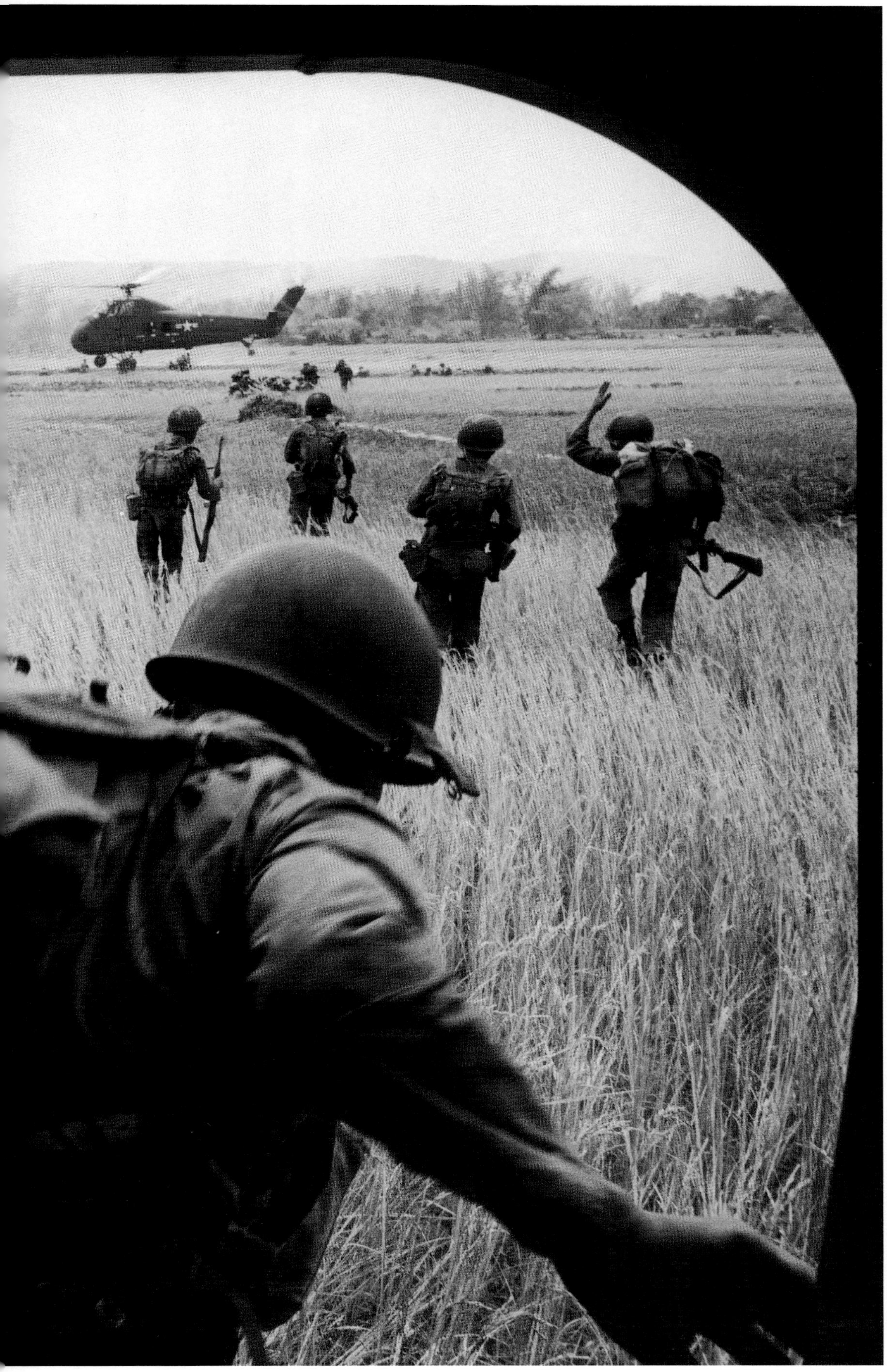

BELOW & BOTTOM

Farley climbs onto another craft, the downed *Yankee Papa 3*, in an attempt to rescue the pilot, who has been shot in the neck. Farley assumes he is dead and runs back to his copter. Note that Burrows must be unsheltered and in the path of gunfire.

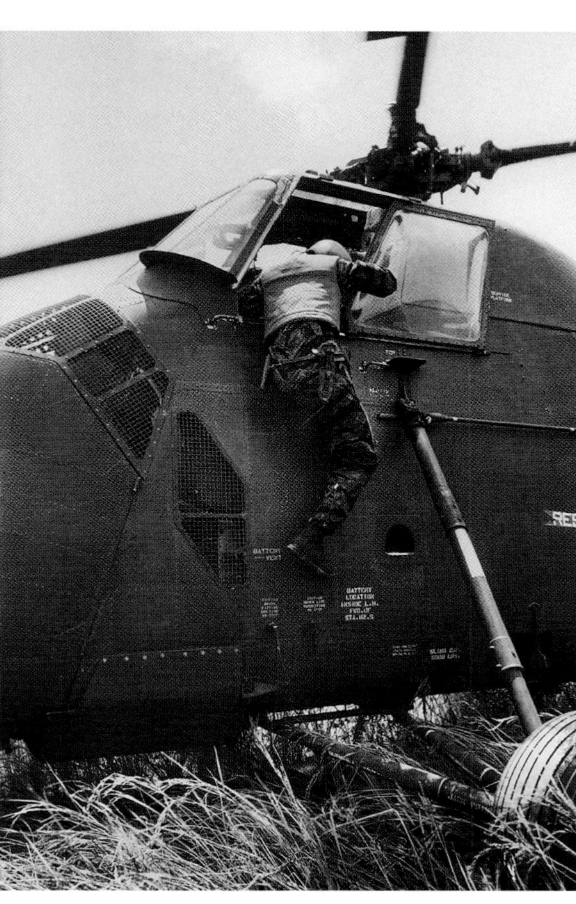

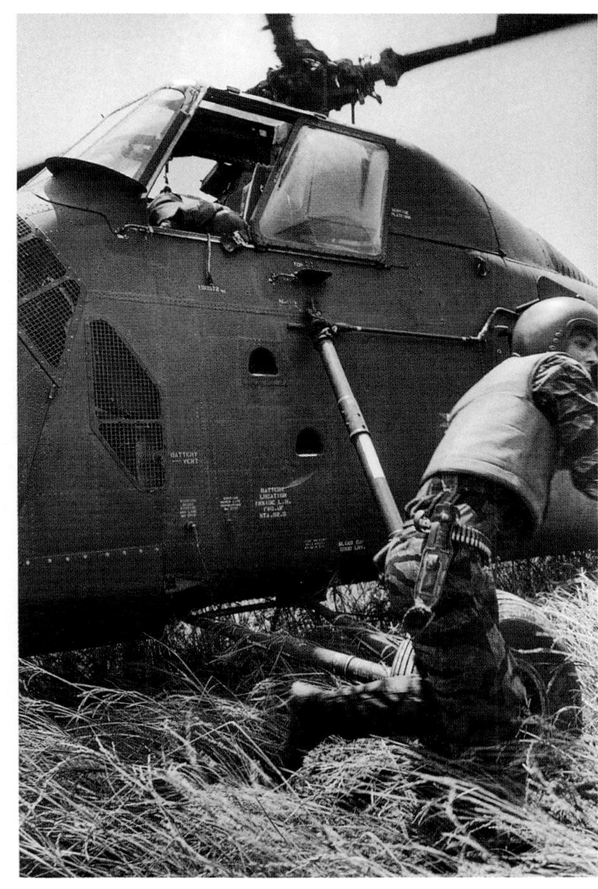

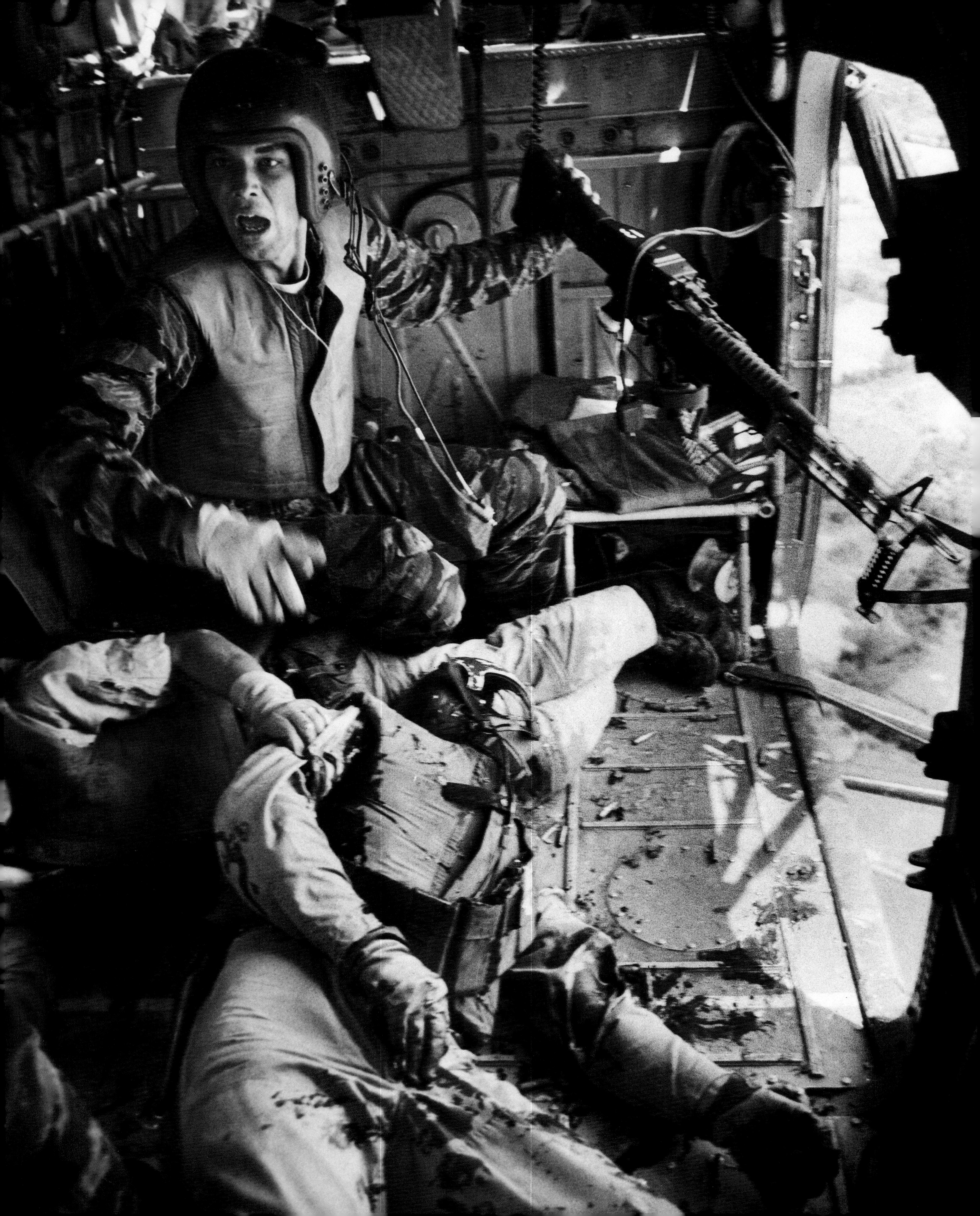

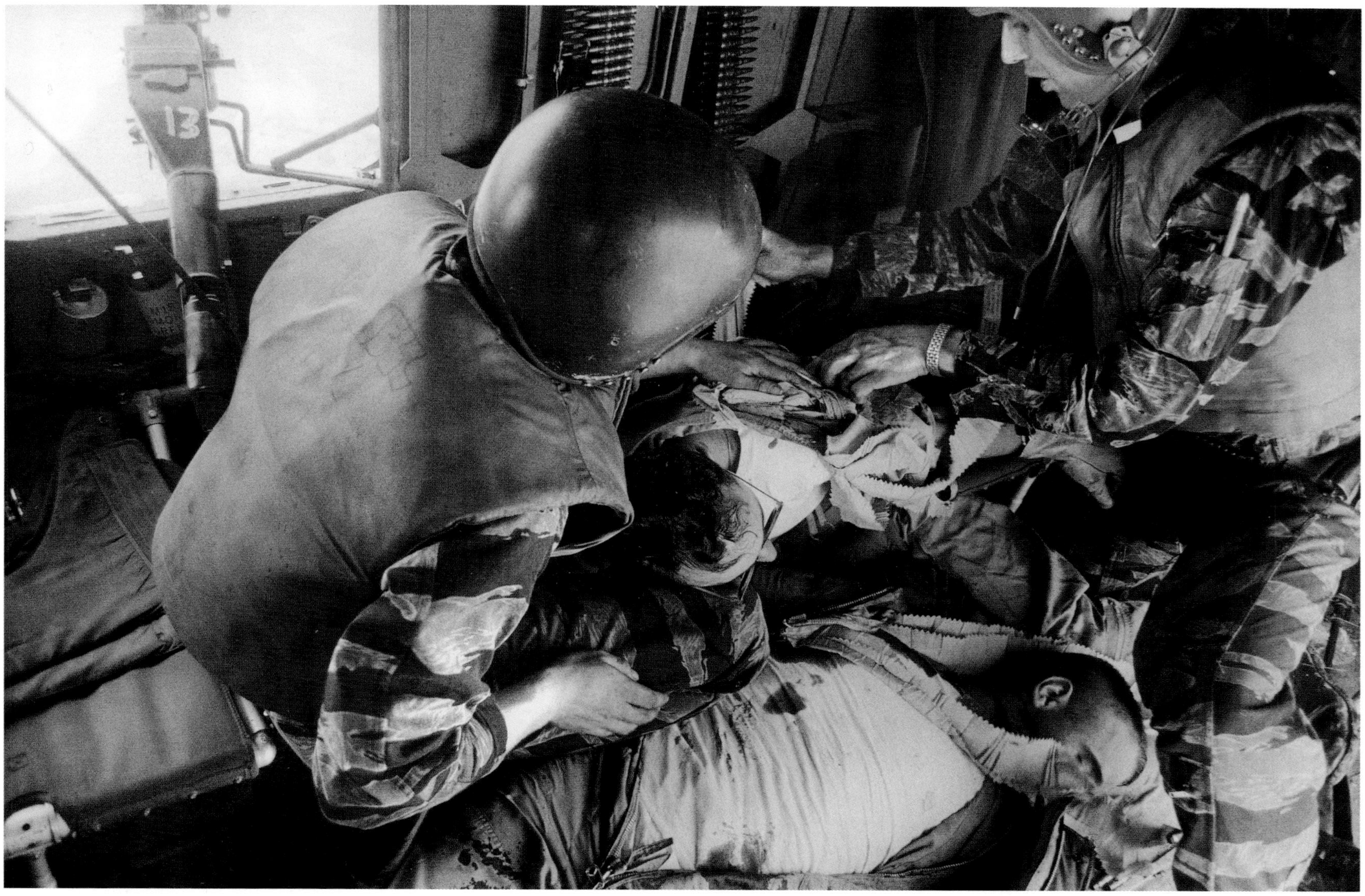

With a dead comrade in the foreground, Farley and Pfc. Wayne Hoilien attend to Sgt. Billie Owens, who has been badly wounded in the shoulder.

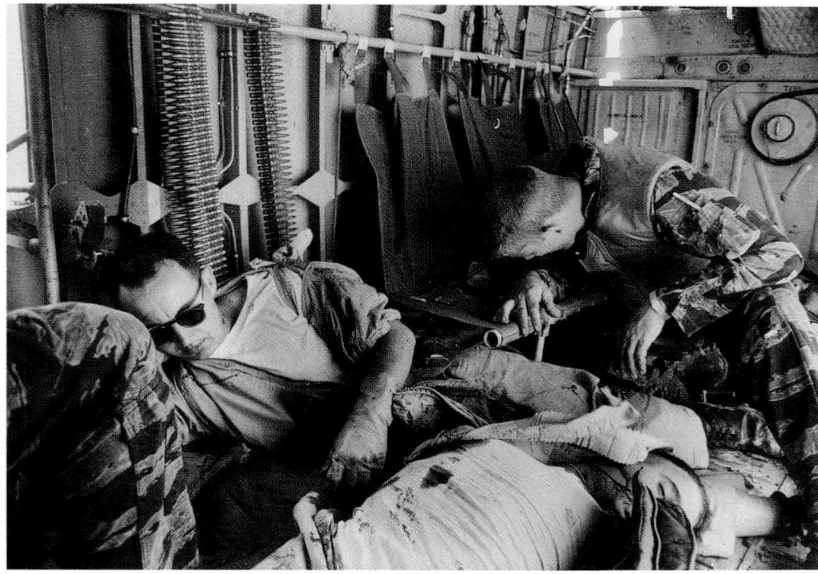

OPPOSITE

His rescue mission botched, Farley, heading back to base with two wounded comrades, discovers that his machine gun is now jammed.

ABOVE

Owens, his shoulder patched, leans against Hoilien. *Yankee Papa 13,* with 11 bullet holes in its skin and its radio knocked out, is making for home.

RIGHT

Back at the base, Farley has talked to his weary men and reported in. Finally, slumped over in a supply shack, Lance Corporal Farley yields to the day.

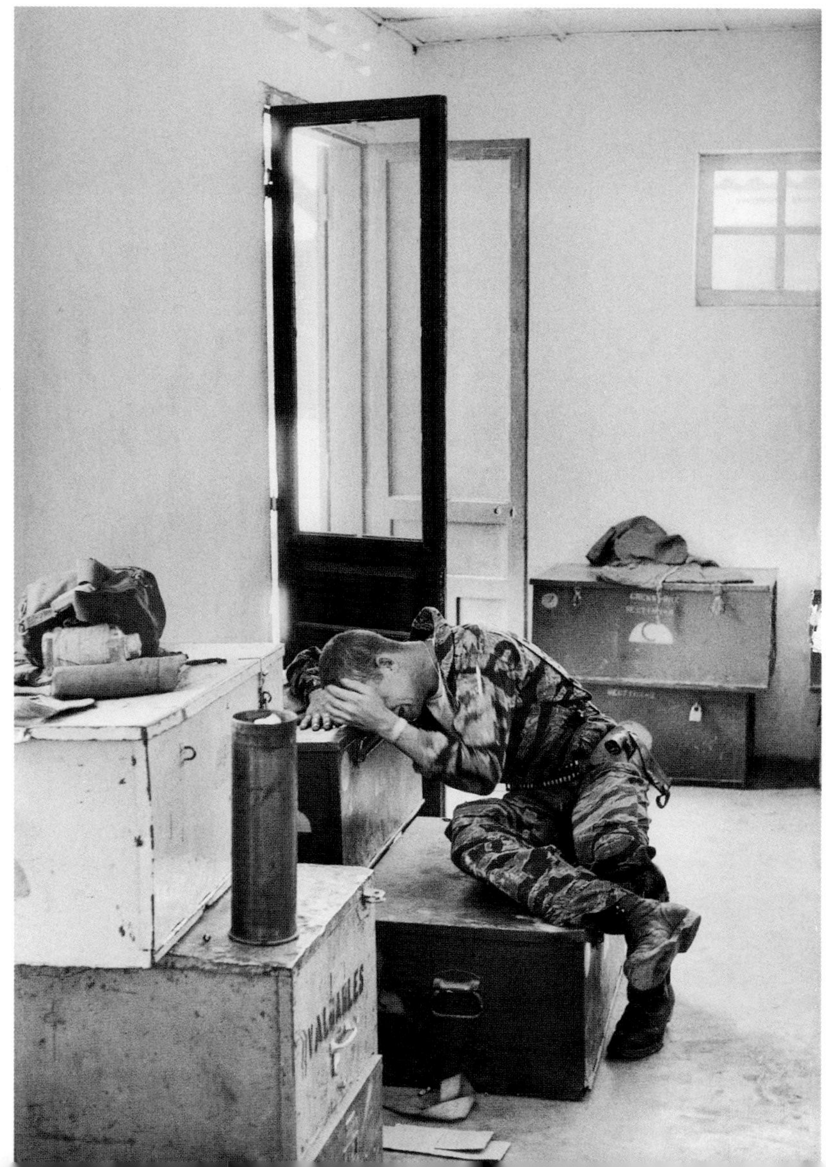

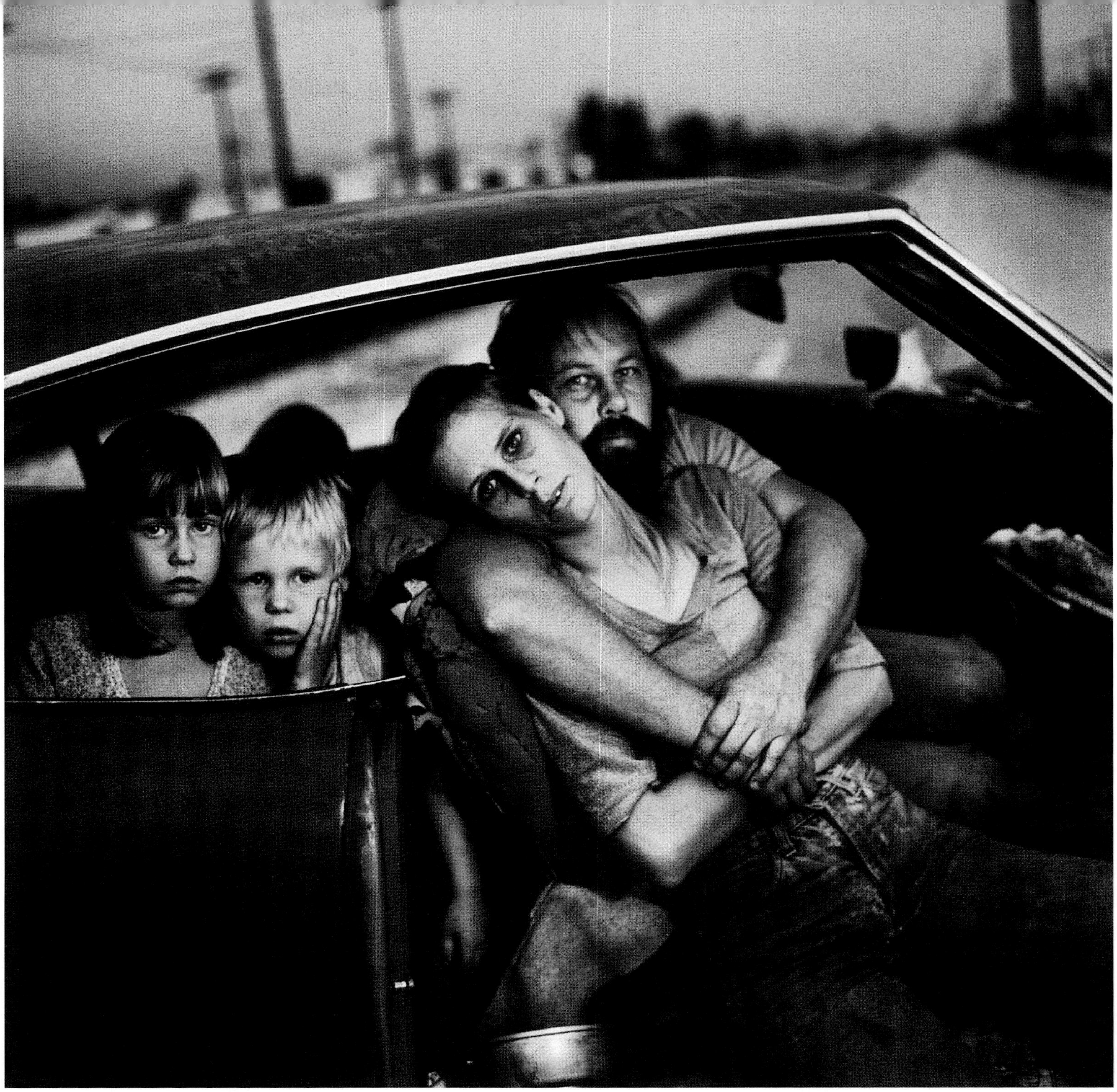

The Damm family: Crissy, six; Jesse, four; mother Linda, 27, a former nursing-home aide; and stepfather Dean, 33, an ex-trucker

A WEEK IN THE LIFE OF A HOMELESS FAMILY

MARY ELLEN MARK

DECEMBER 1987 & MAY 1995

America is a caring nation, but homeless families all too easily slip through the cracks, hidden away from the public eye in their lives eked out on the margin, one night after another in shelters, welfare hotels and cars. In 1987, LIFE spent a week with the Damm family, who a month earlier had moved from Colorado to California because that state's welfare allotments were the highest in the nation. The utter degradation of a human being is difficult to embrace, and here were the Damms, two adults and two children at the bottom, ceaselessly slipping yet lower. The question ultimately posed by the piece is, What future do these children have? Eight years later, LIFE revisited the Damms (right), and the answer had become chillingly apparent: The family, now even larger, still faced daily troubles and strife.

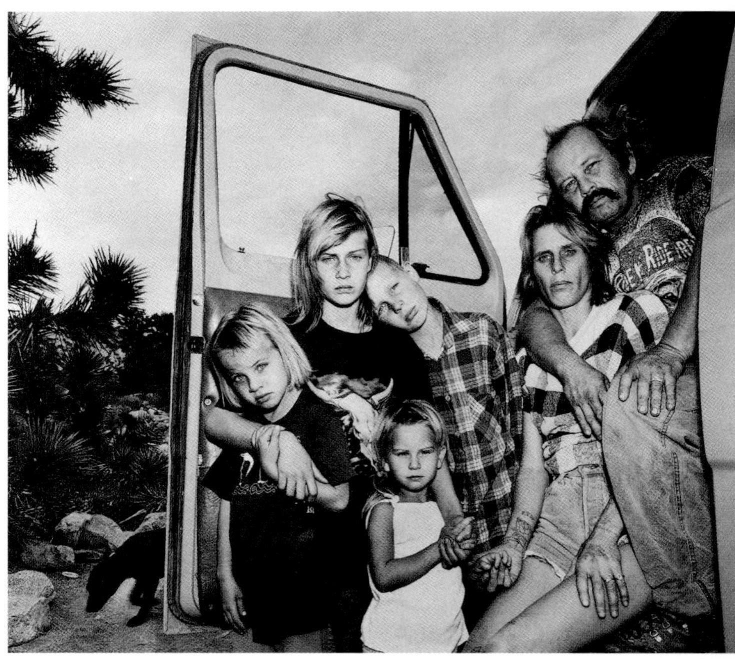

In 1995, there were two new Damms, Ashley, left, and Summer.

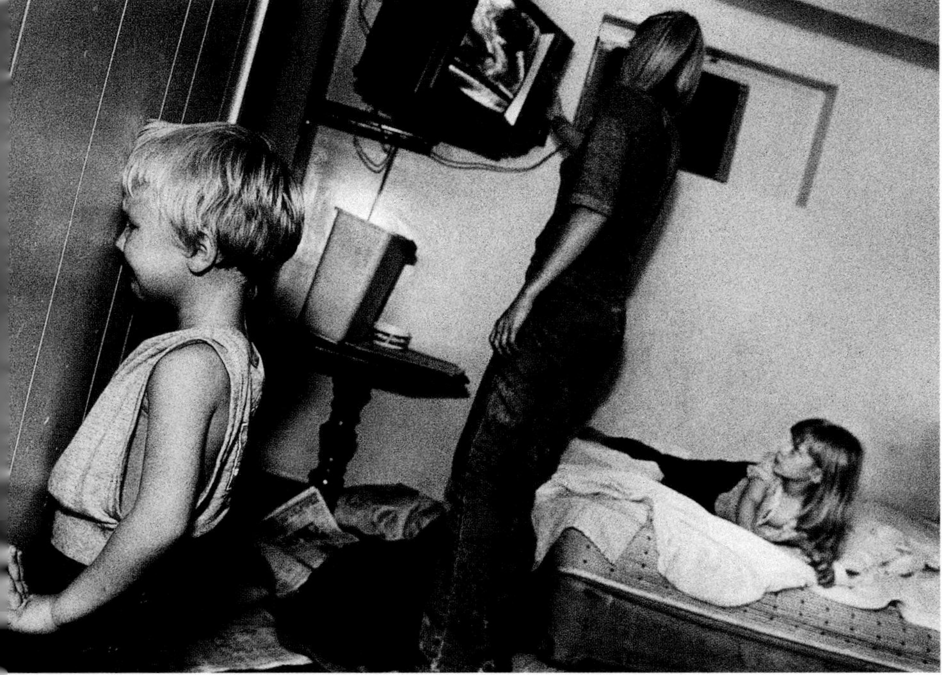

Jesse cries amid the unexpected comforts of a motel, provided by a charitable agency.

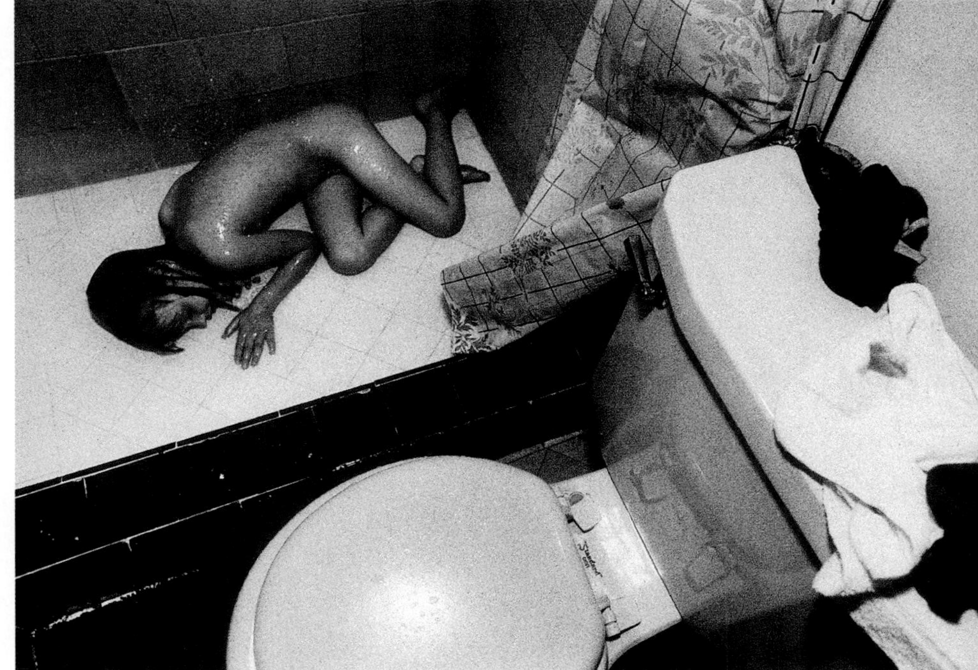

Soothed by the warm shower, Crissy stays there, curled up, for an hour.

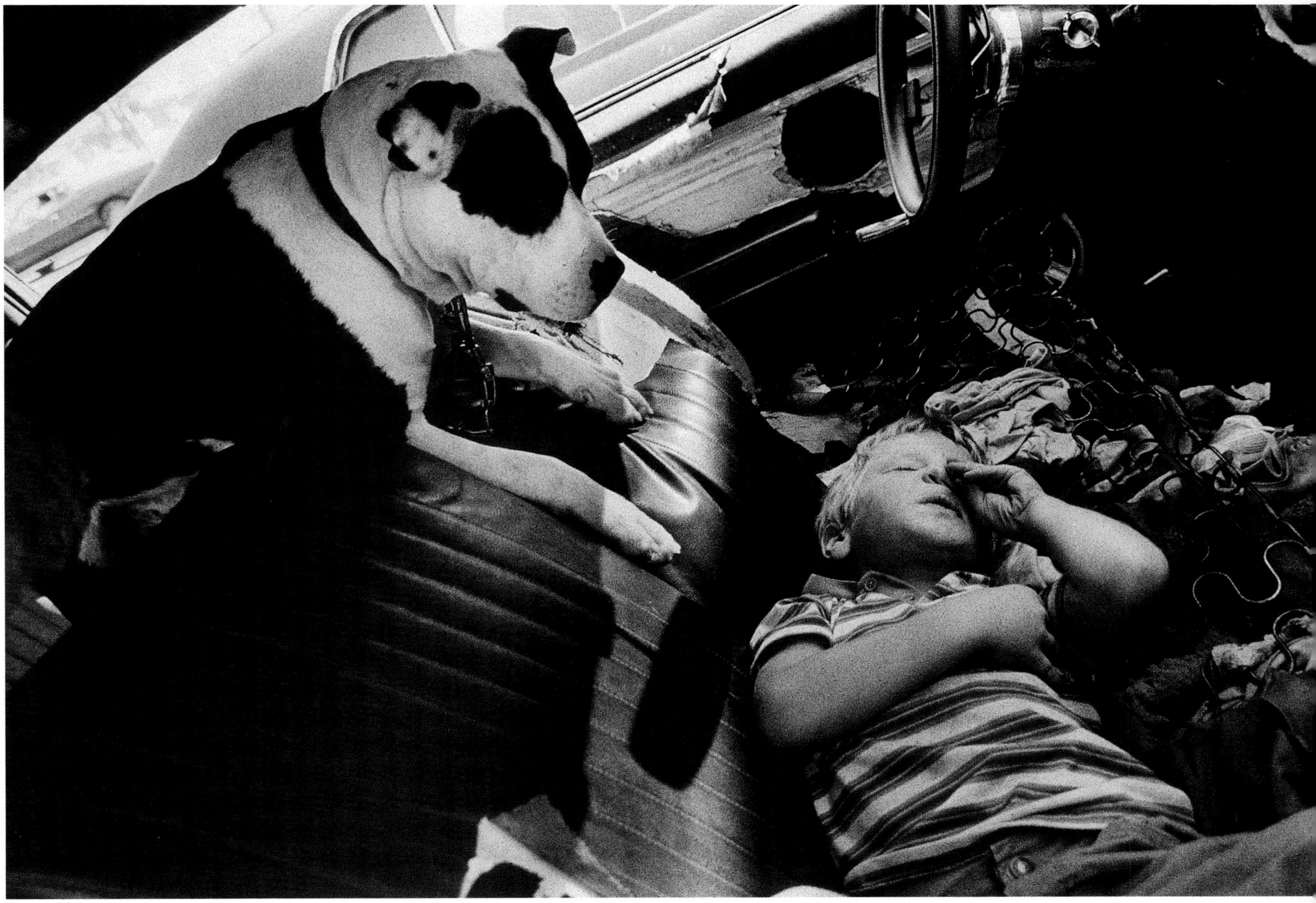

Jesse naps in the car under the guardianship of Runtley, a pit bull who spends most of his time chained to the front seat.

IN HOLLYWOOD

In America's ardent love affair with the movies, magazines featuring the bigger-than-life heroes and heroines have for decades provided us mere mortals with the chance to touch the stars, and to see the scrumptious sets behind the scenes. If some of these backstage glimpses have been carefully orchestrated, who cares? We're talking about Tinseltown here.

LIFE has long been a partner in this dance. Those beautiful faces from Hollywood have been very, very good to the magazine over the years, and we like to think the relationship has been mutually beneficial. There was a time when the biggest of the big—the Bogarts and Bergmans and Brandos and Hepburns and Gables and Lorens—were not only complicitous in creating the perfect shot but also trusted LIFE to play fair with the intimate moments, and therefore let our cameras in. That's happening again with today's stars, as we shall see.

The wonder from this vantage point, 70 years on, is that it took LIFE so long to realize the importance of the celluloid glamourpuss to its readers. Fully 23 issues were published before, on May 3, 1937, a movie star appeared on our cover. Let it be quickly noted, however, that when that first one arrived, she arrived with a bang: It was the original Platinum Blonde, Jean Harlow. But then, after that, the same doubting editors waited yet 18 more issues before putting another blond on the cover . . . and then it was Harpo Marx!

Perhaps we might best put this down to growing pains.

In any case, that initial coolness would soon enough melt away as LIFE forever more opened its pages to the particular light and heat that emanate from the motion-picture star. Film has been the dominant art form of the past several decades, and while movies have proceeded in many different directions, LIFE has always been on the chase—always there to chronicle the separate universe that is Hollywood. And that universe is about one thing above all others—its stars, stars aglow with celestial bodies, heavenly faces and a divine radiance their fans want to bask in.

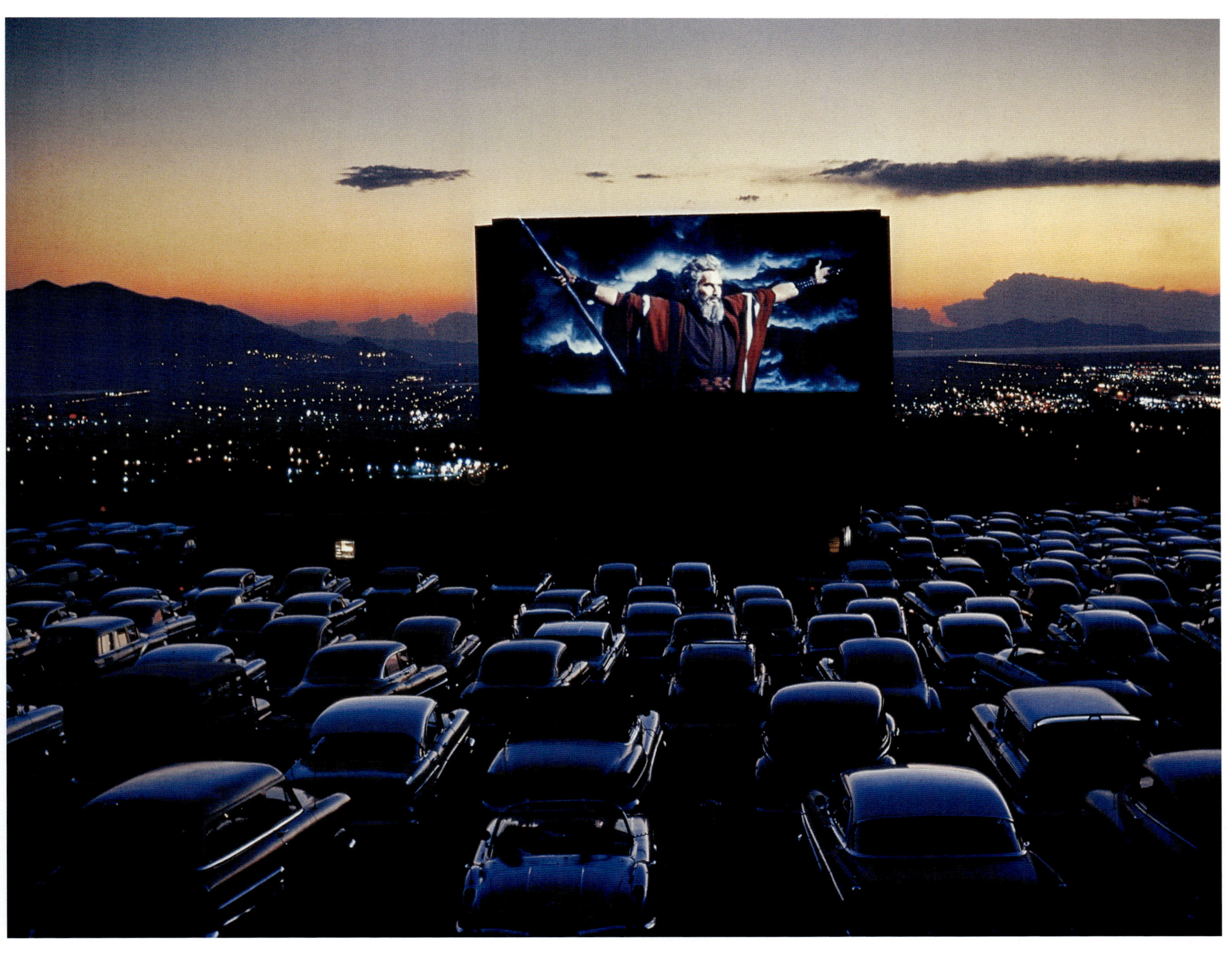

THE TEN COMMANDMENTS

Charlton Heston *is* Moses at this drive-in theater in Salt Lake City in 1958. Drive-ins may have gone the way of silent movies, but classic films like this Cecil B. DeMille epic continue to attract audiences on the little screen.

J.R. EYERMAN

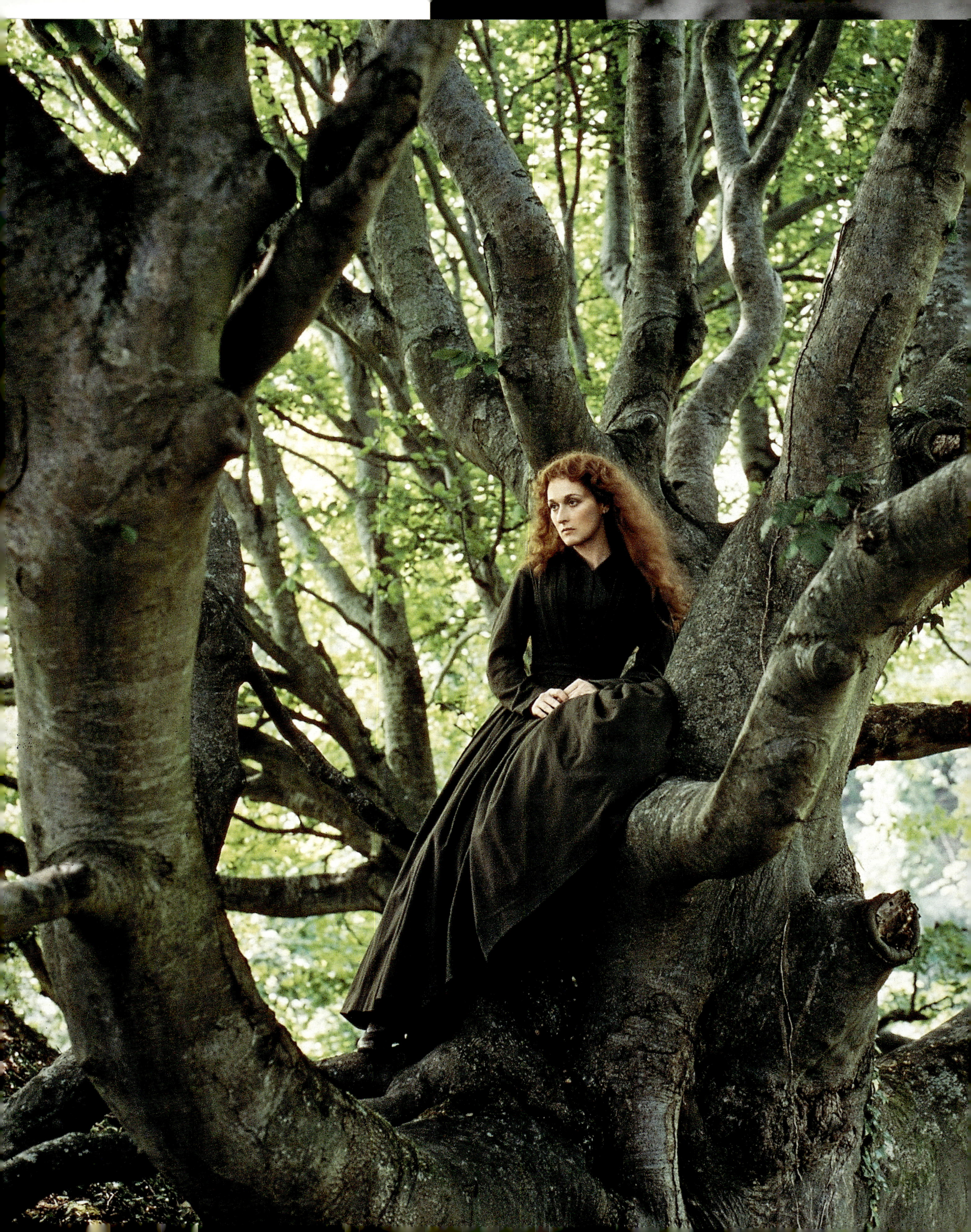

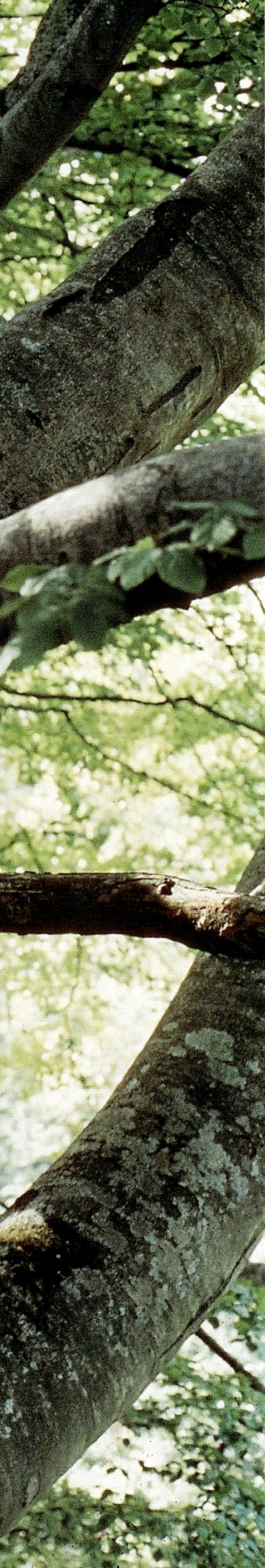

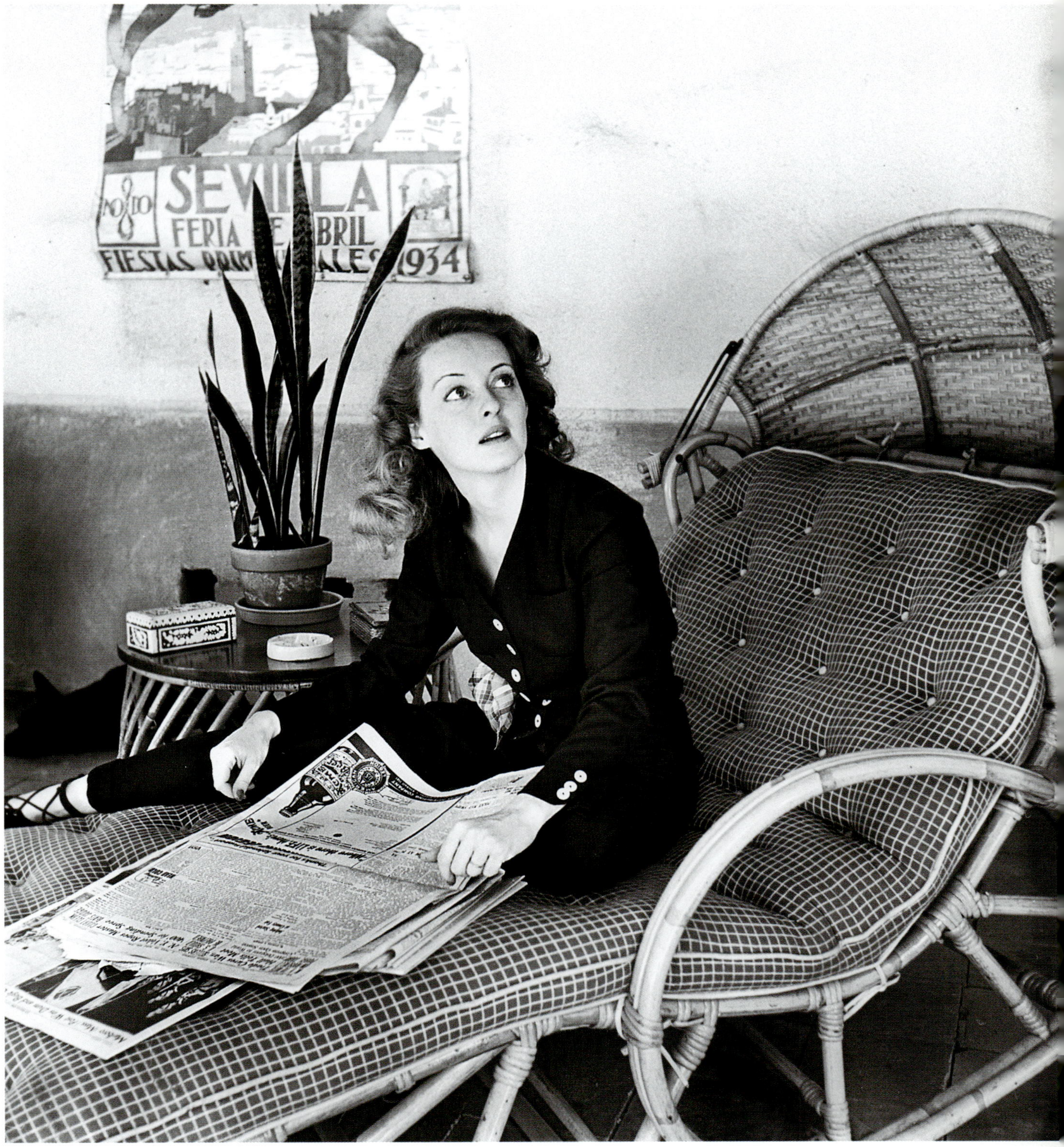

MERYL STREEP

Arguably the premier motion picture actress of the latter half of the 20th century, Meryl Streep reposes in Dorset, England, in 1980 during a break in the shooting of *The French Lieutenant's Woman.*

SNOWDON

BETTE DAVIS

Arguably the premier motion picture actress of the first half of the 20th century, Bette Davis reposes with the morning papers in the playroom of her Beverly Hills home in January 1939.

ALFRED EISENSTAEDT

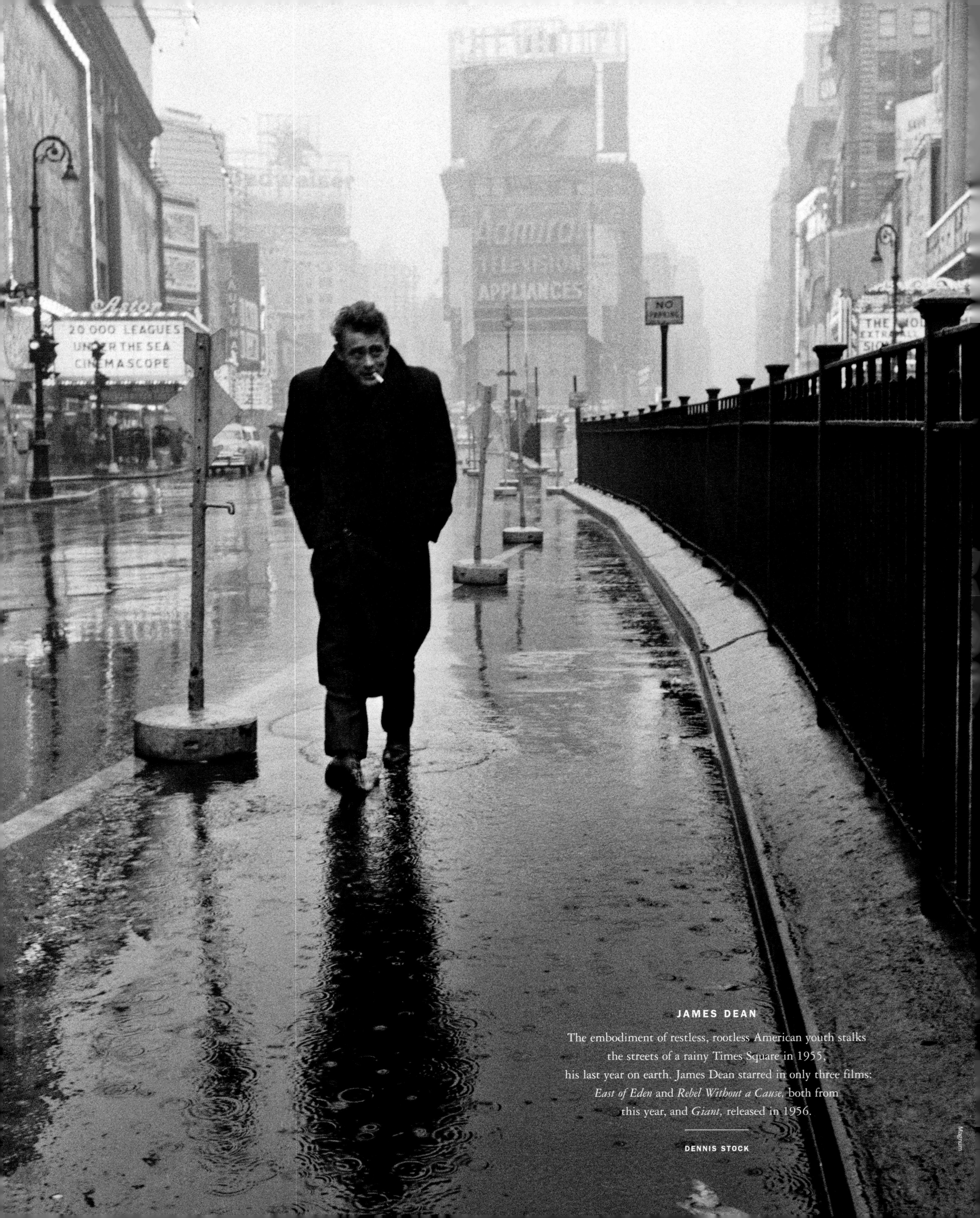

JAMES DEAN

The embodiment of restless, rootless American youth stalks the streets of a rainy Times Square in 1955, his last year on earth. James Dean starred in only three films: *East of Eden* and *Rebel Without a Cause,* both from this year, and *Giant,* released in 1956.

DENNIS STOCK

Magnum

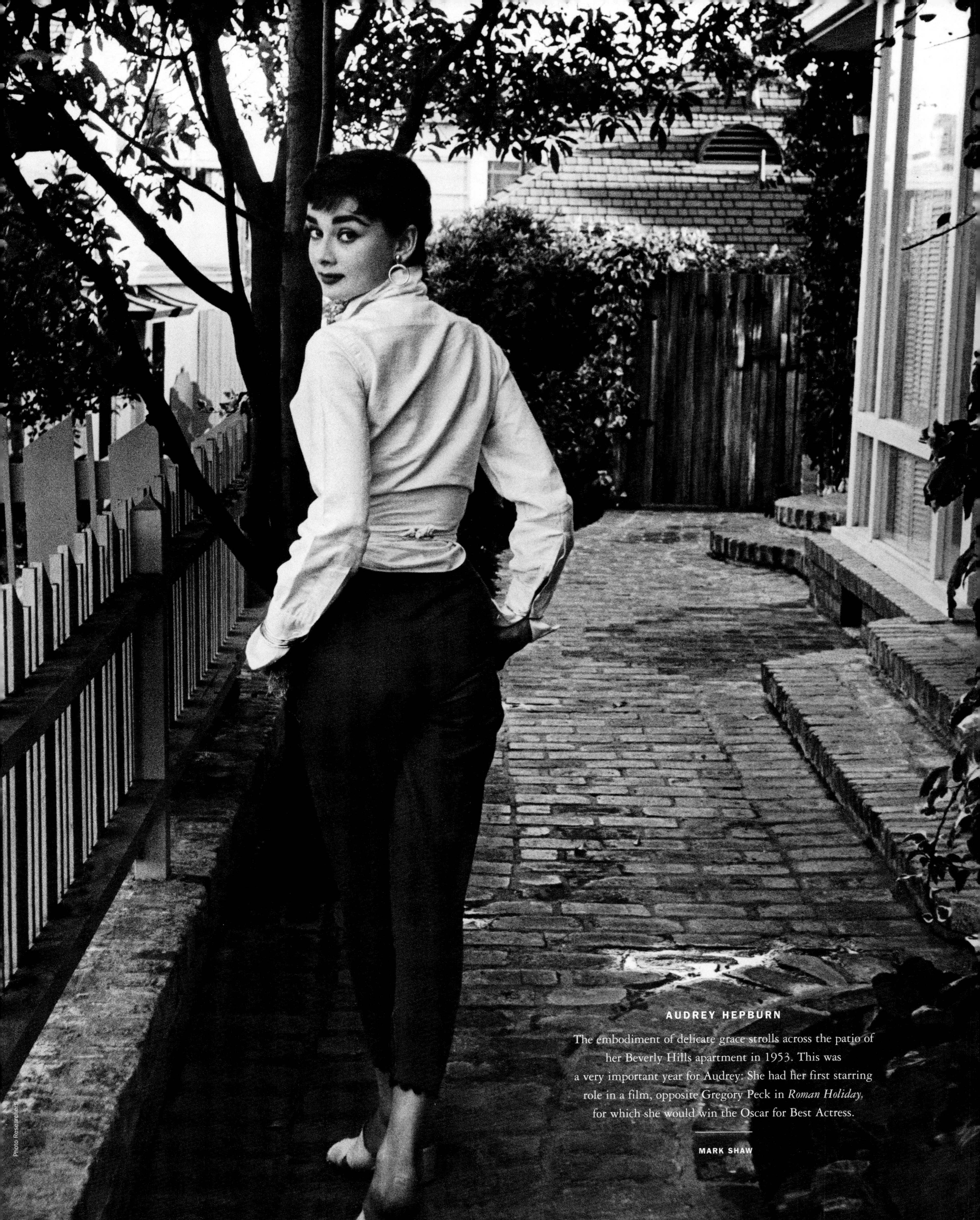

AUDREY HEPBURN

The embodiment of delicate grace strolls across the patio of her Beverly Hills apartment in 1953. This was a very important year for Audrey: She had her first starring role in a film, opposite Gregory Peck in *Roman Holiday,* for which she would win the Oscar for Best Actress.

MARK SHAW

Photo Researchers

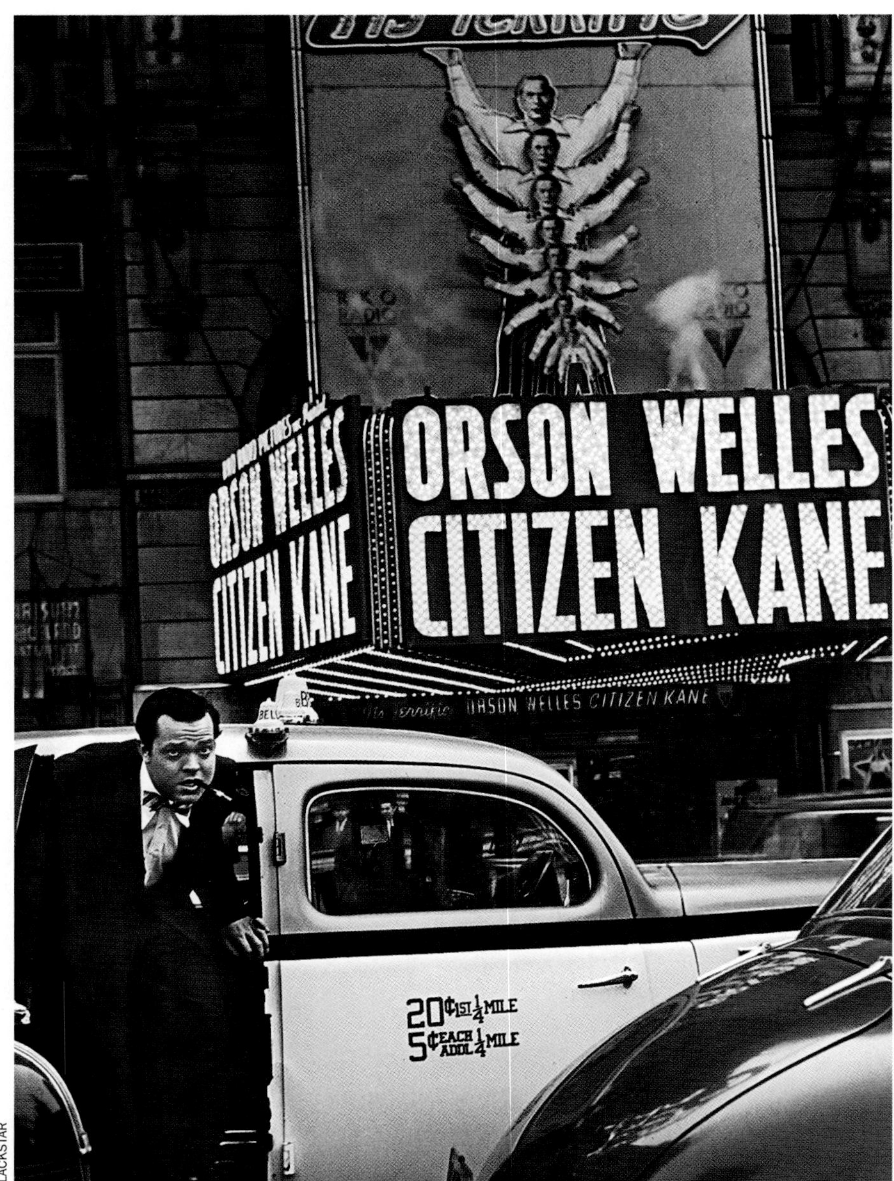

BLACKSTAR

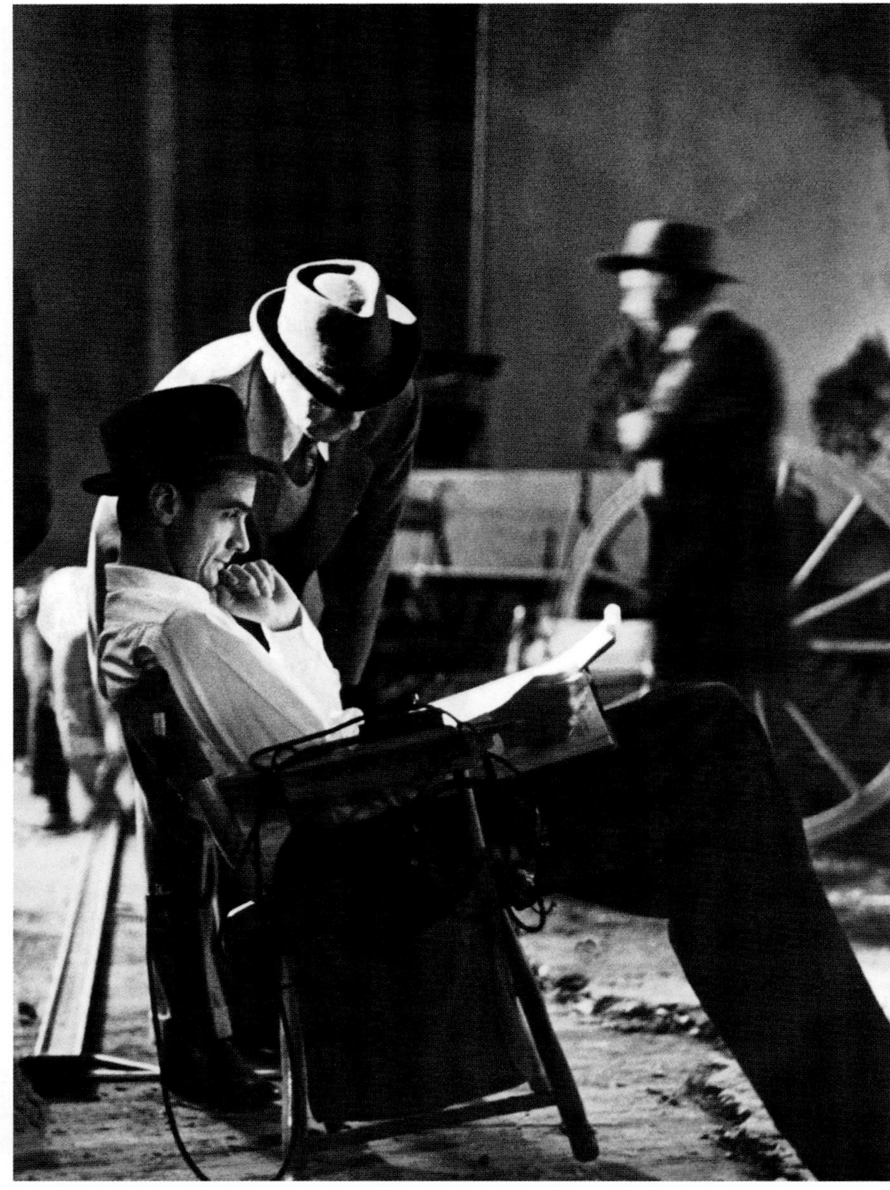

ORSON WELLES

A brilliant triple threat as actor-writer-director, Welles also checked out ticket sales at box offices, as here, in New York City, for his 1941 masterpiece. *Kane* lost money, then his next, *The Magnificent Ambersons,* was severely cut by the studio and tanked, setting the tone for years of wrangling with producers.

W. EUGENE SMITH

HOWARD HUGHES

On the set of *The Outlaw,* the eccentric Hughes mulls over script changes. The film was the first "sex western," and director Hughes made ample use of Jane Russell's cleavage, for which his aircraft engineers designed a cantilevered bra. *The Outlaw* was released in 1943, then shelved for censorial reasons till 1946.

BOB LANDRY

ALFRED HITCHCOCK

The Master of Suspense (and cinema in general) poses for a publicity still for his 1963 classic, *The Birds,* which he adapted from a Daphne du Maurier story. In this movie, Hitch relies, as so often, on turning seemingly ordinary, trustworthy things—our avian friends—into frightening agents of confusion.

PHILIPPE HALSMAN

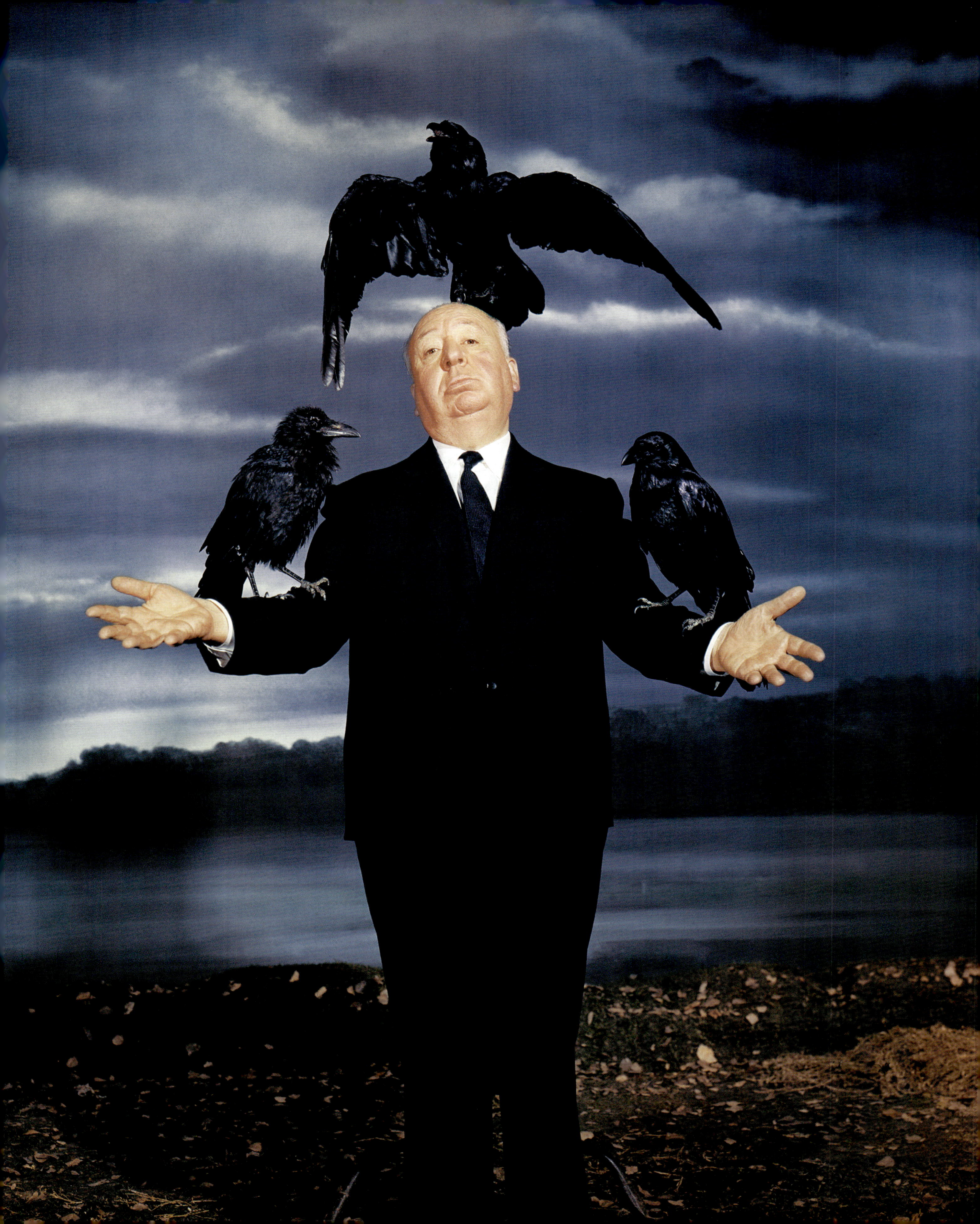

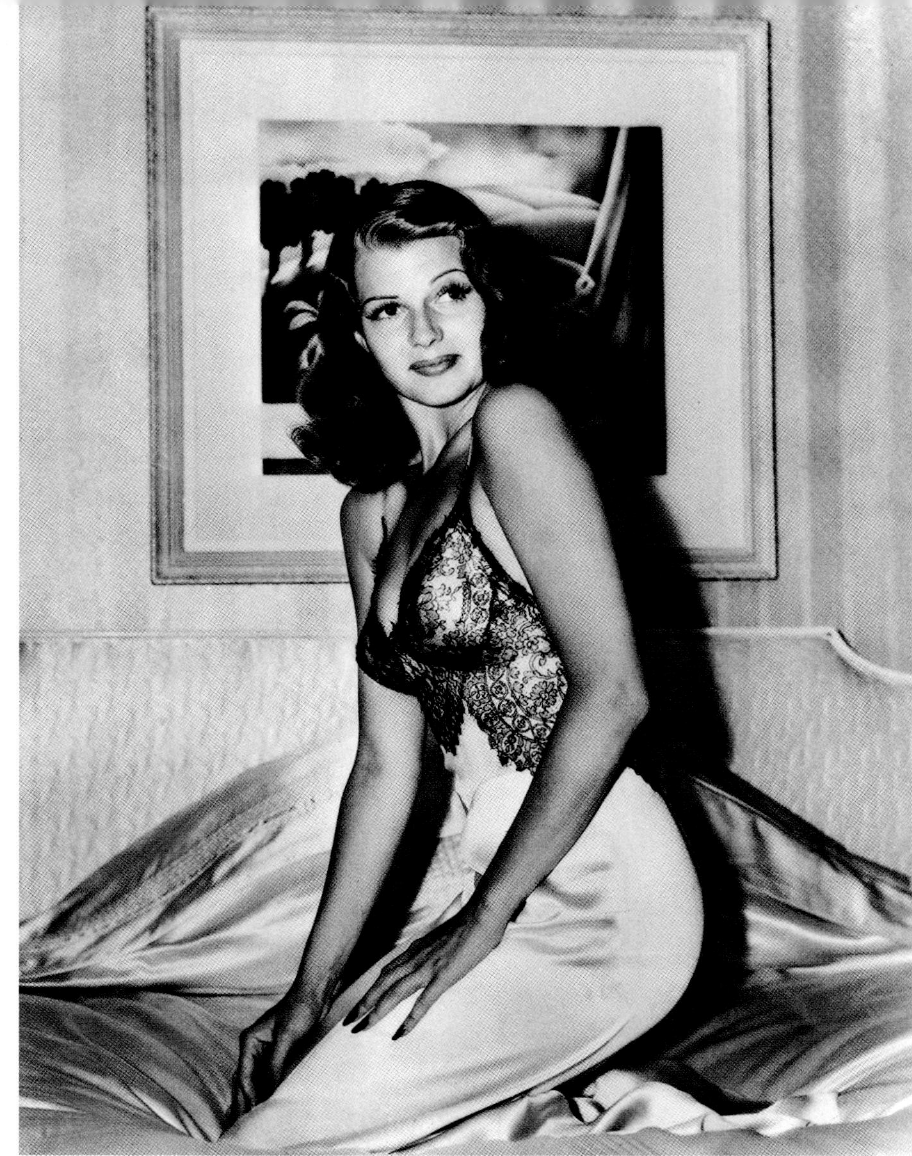

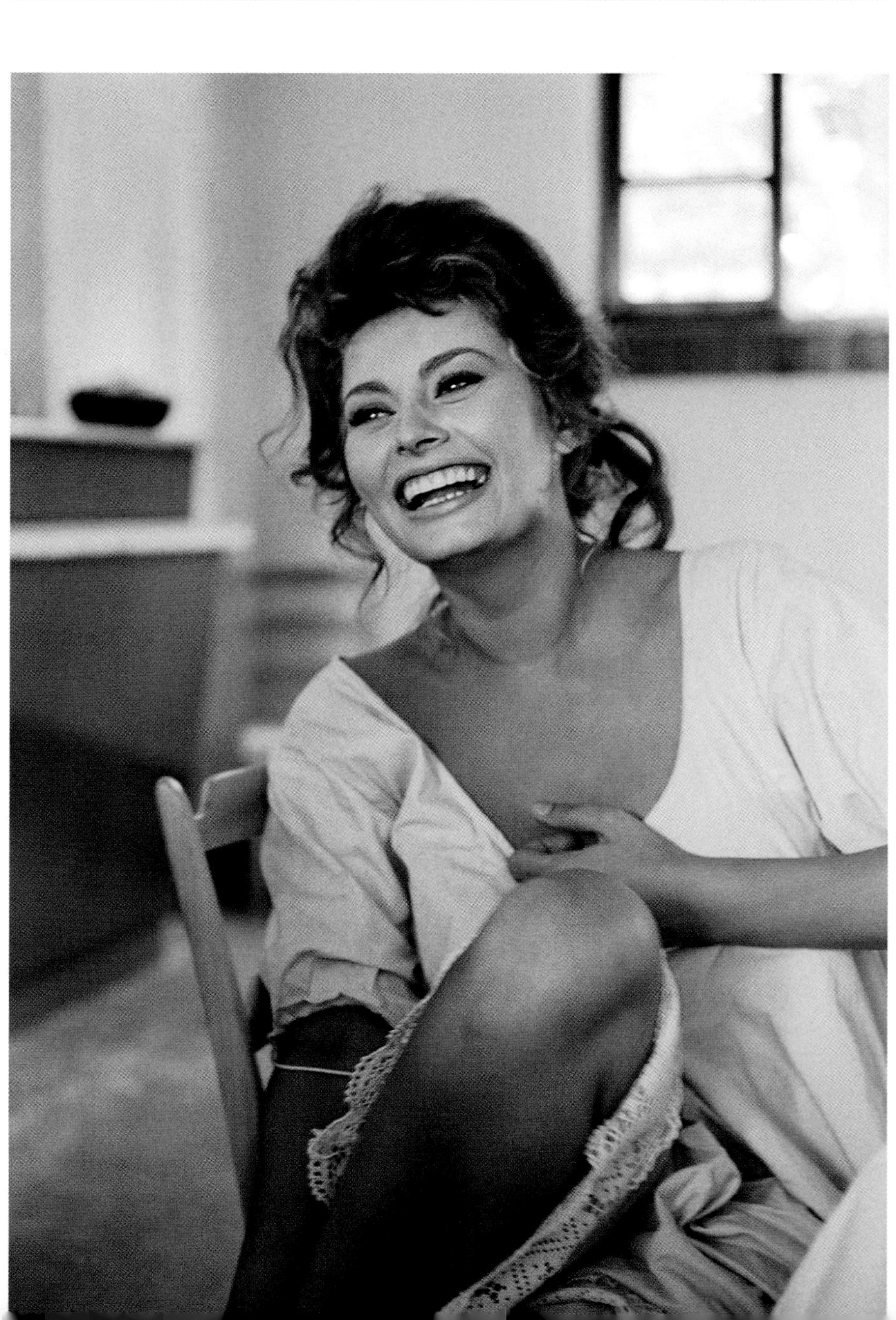

RITA HAYWORTH

In an obituary of Hayworth, this 1941 photograph was called "the *Mona Lisa* of pinups." On one hand, that is entirely apt: This is, after all, the most famous of all pinups, the one that we would send to an alien culture to represent the medium. On the other hand, however, where the intent of Leonardo's lady has inspired endless debate through the years, Landry's woman has left absolutely nothing to question.

BOB LANDRY

SOPHIA LOREN

Over the years, Loren and photographer Eisenstaedt had quite a special relationship, imbued with a warm affection. She visited Eisie in New York on more than one occasion, and was delighted to attend when LIFE celebrated our 50th anniversary at Radio City Music Hall. We think it is only because of their bond that this remarkable photograph was possible.

ALFRED EISENSTAEDT

ELIZABETH TAYLOR

She was only 15 years old when this was taken, at Malibu Beach in California, but she was clearly on her way to becoming, in the eyes of many, the most beautiful woman in the world. Elizabeth was about to costar in the delightful film *Life with Father;* in just two years, she would be dating Howard Hughes.

BOB LANDRY

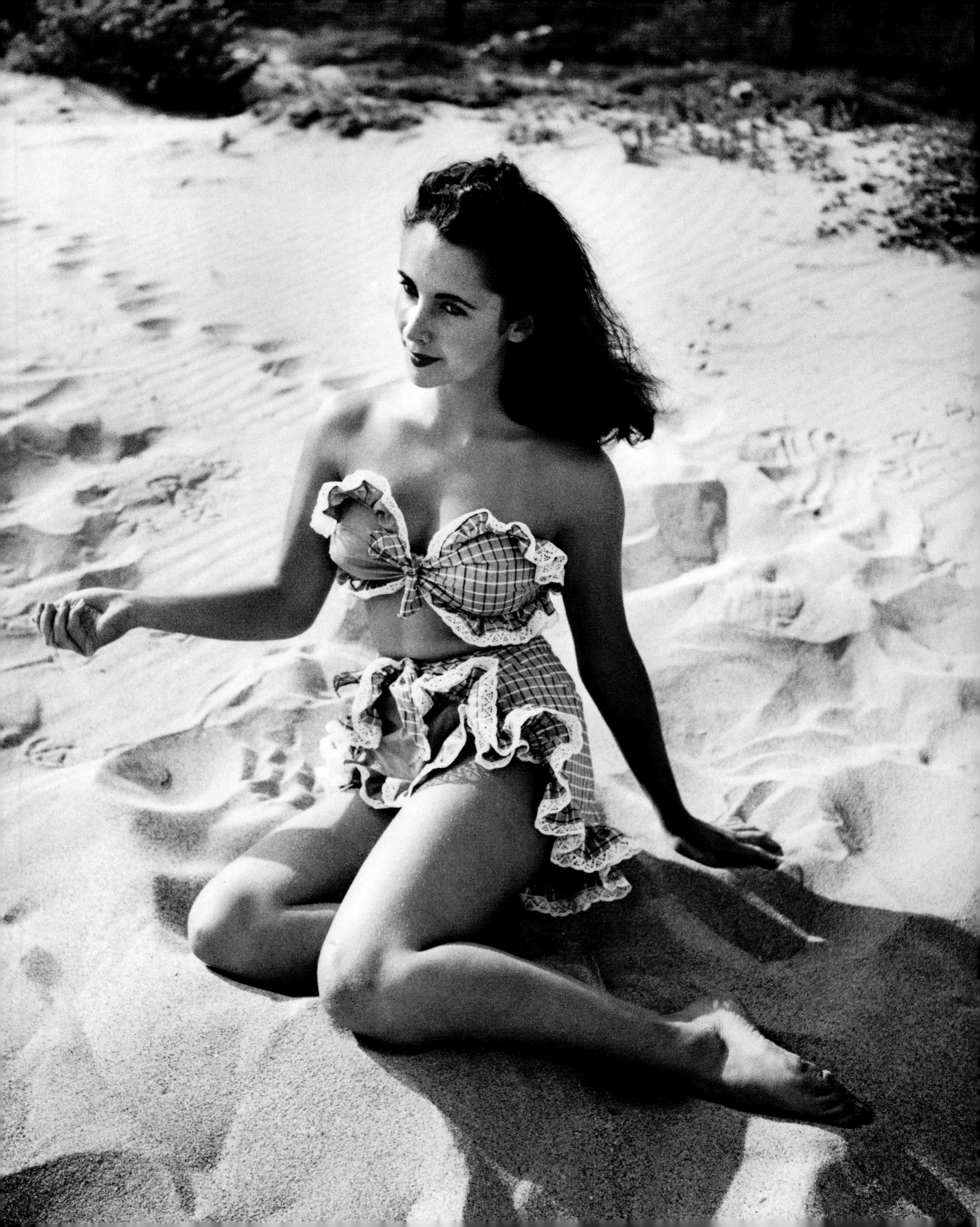

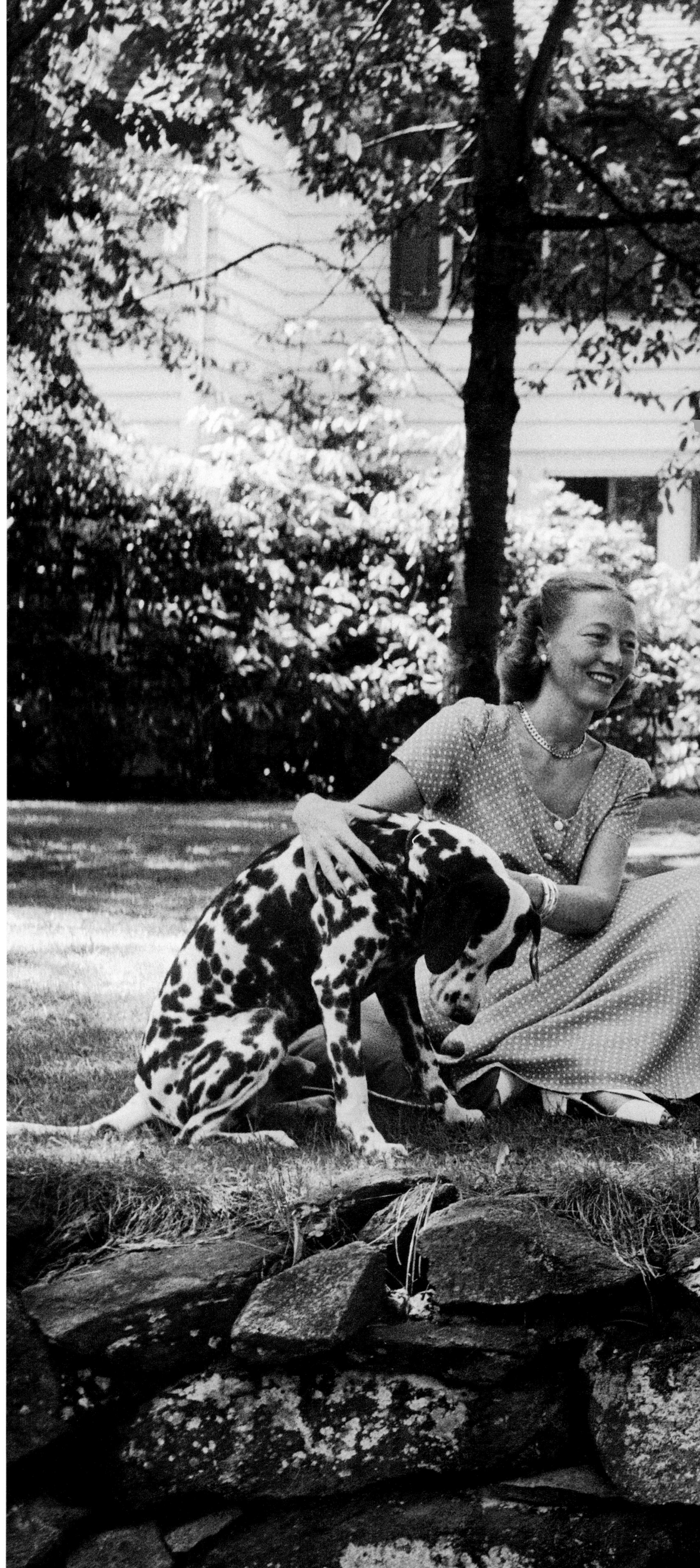

THE FONDAS

Ah, the serenity of suburban Connecticut in 1948. Here, enjoying a quiet, dappled morning is your typical American clan. That's dad Henry showing son Peter the aerodynamic ins and outs of a model plane, while daughter Jane plays with the family cat. Petting the dog is the matriarch, Frances, who sits next to Frances Brokaw, her daughter from a previous marriage. Henry's commitment to his work would grow into an obsession, while his kids were a couple of decades away from a long, strange trip.

PETER STACKPOLE

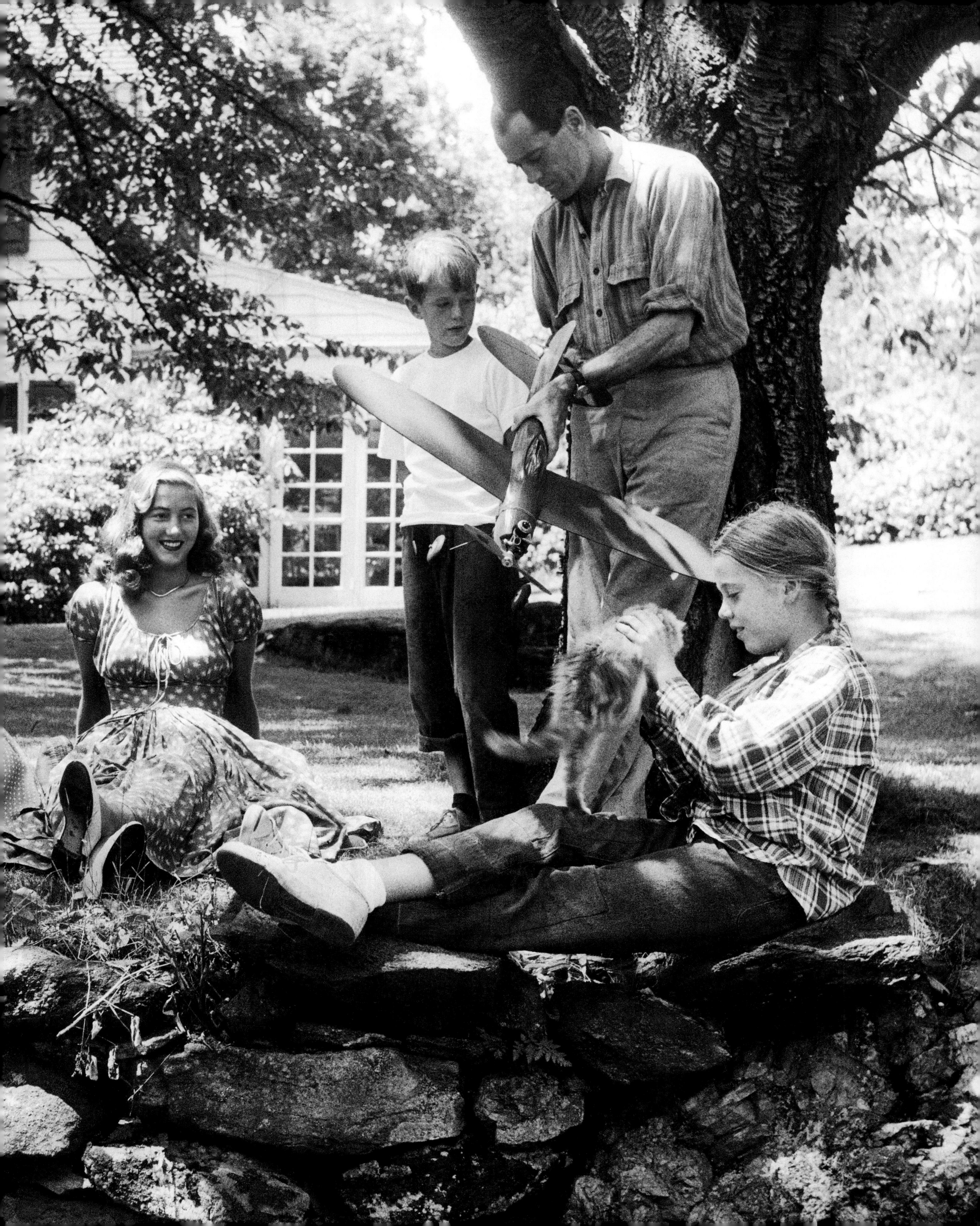

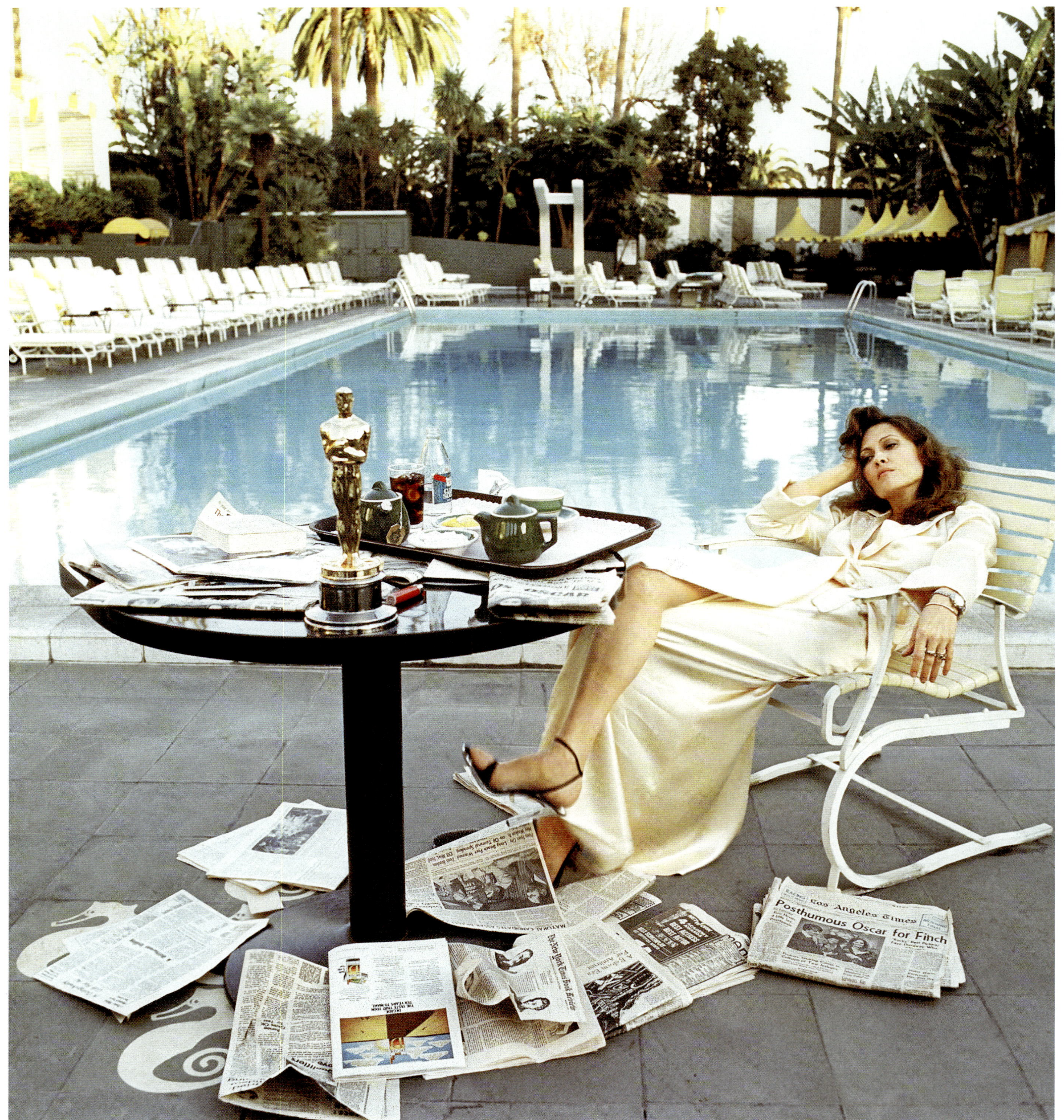

FAYE DUNAWAY

Amid a welter of stories on the Oscars, Faye Dunaway, after a night of revelry, takes stock of her 1976 Best Actress award for *Network.* This photo was taken by her future husband.

TERRY O'NEILL

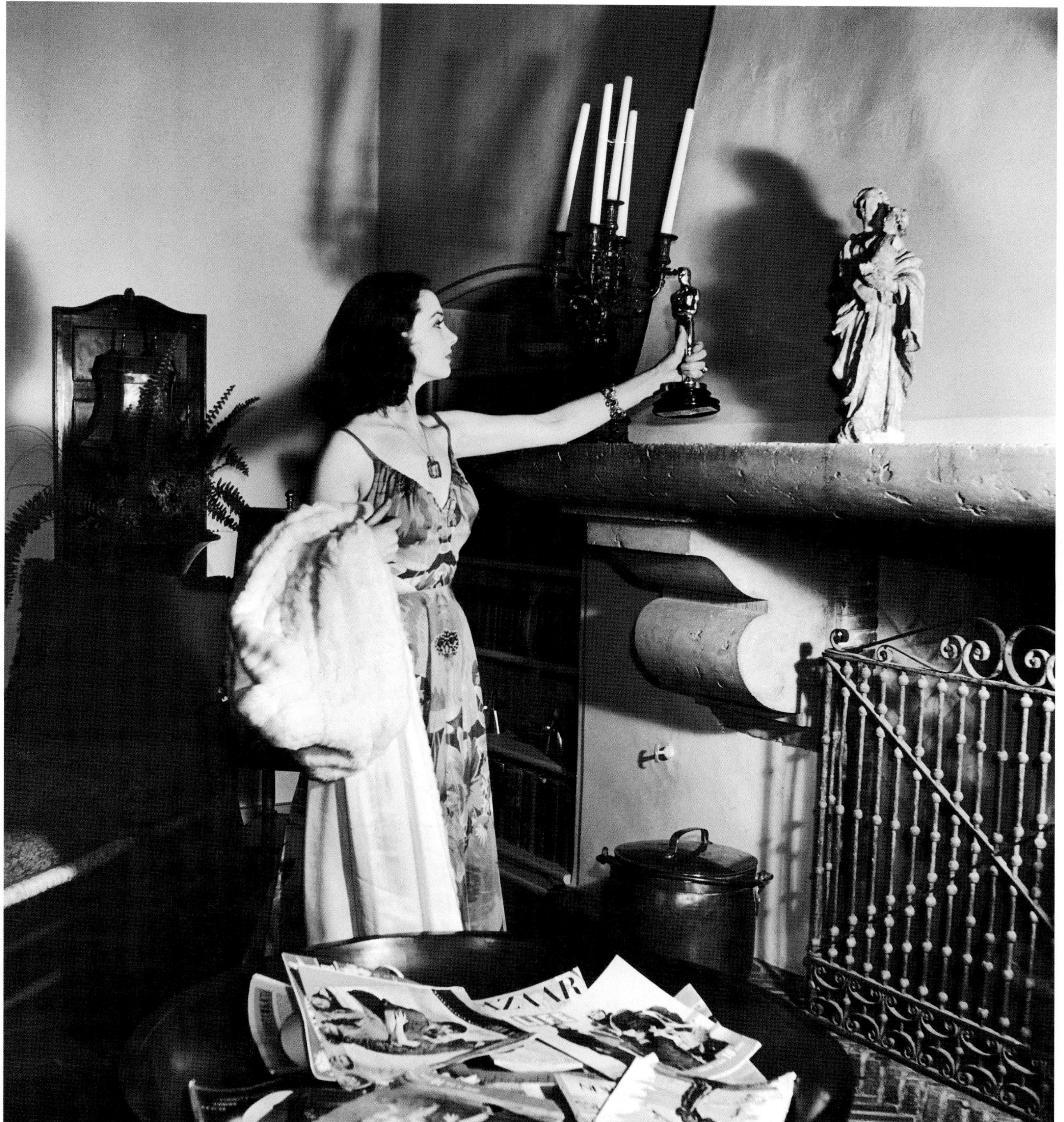

VIVIEN LEIGH

The radiant British star places her Best Actress Oscar on her mantel in 1940. She had won the award, along with international fame, for her portrayal of Scarlett O'Hara in *Gone with the Wind.*

PETER STACKPOLE

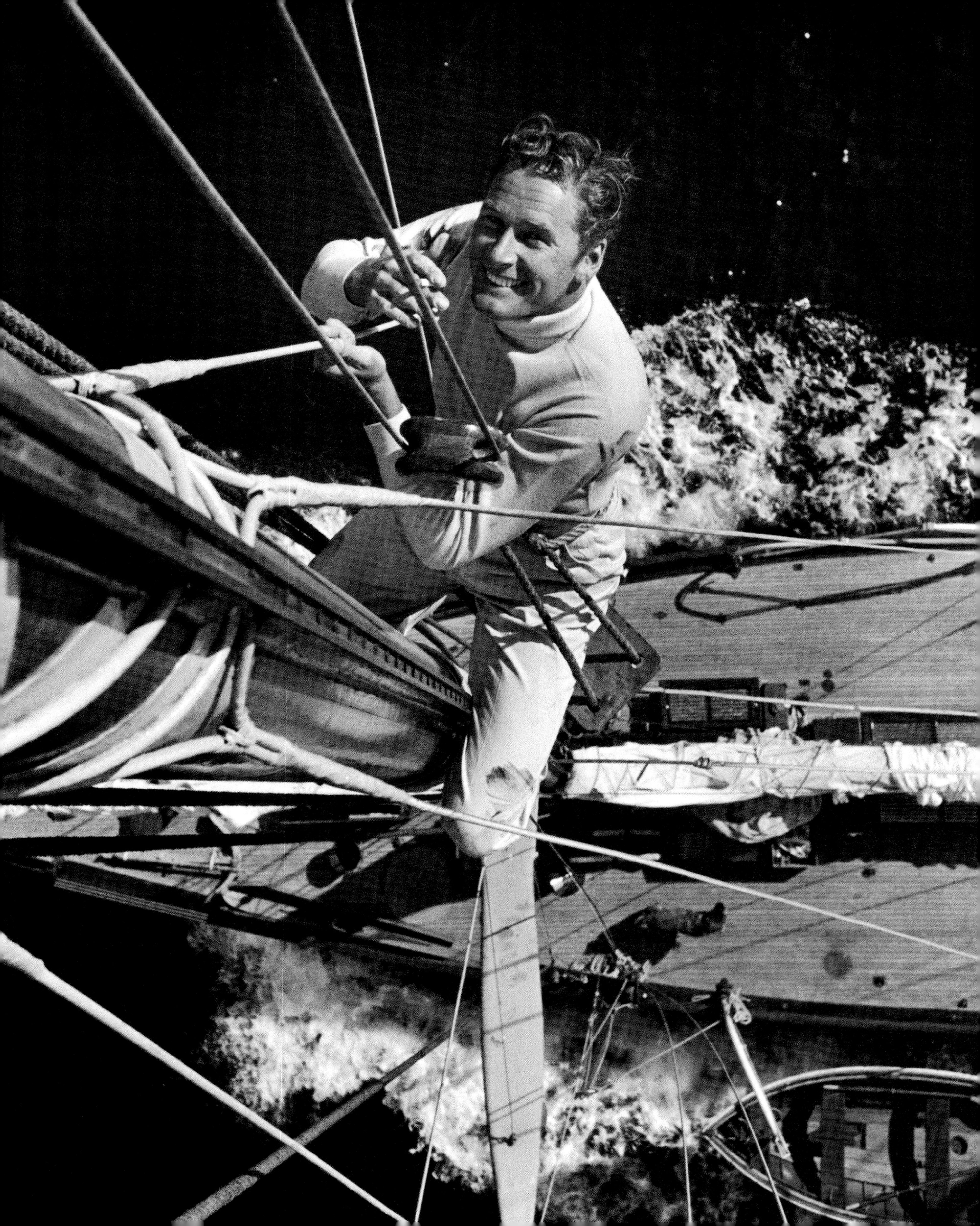

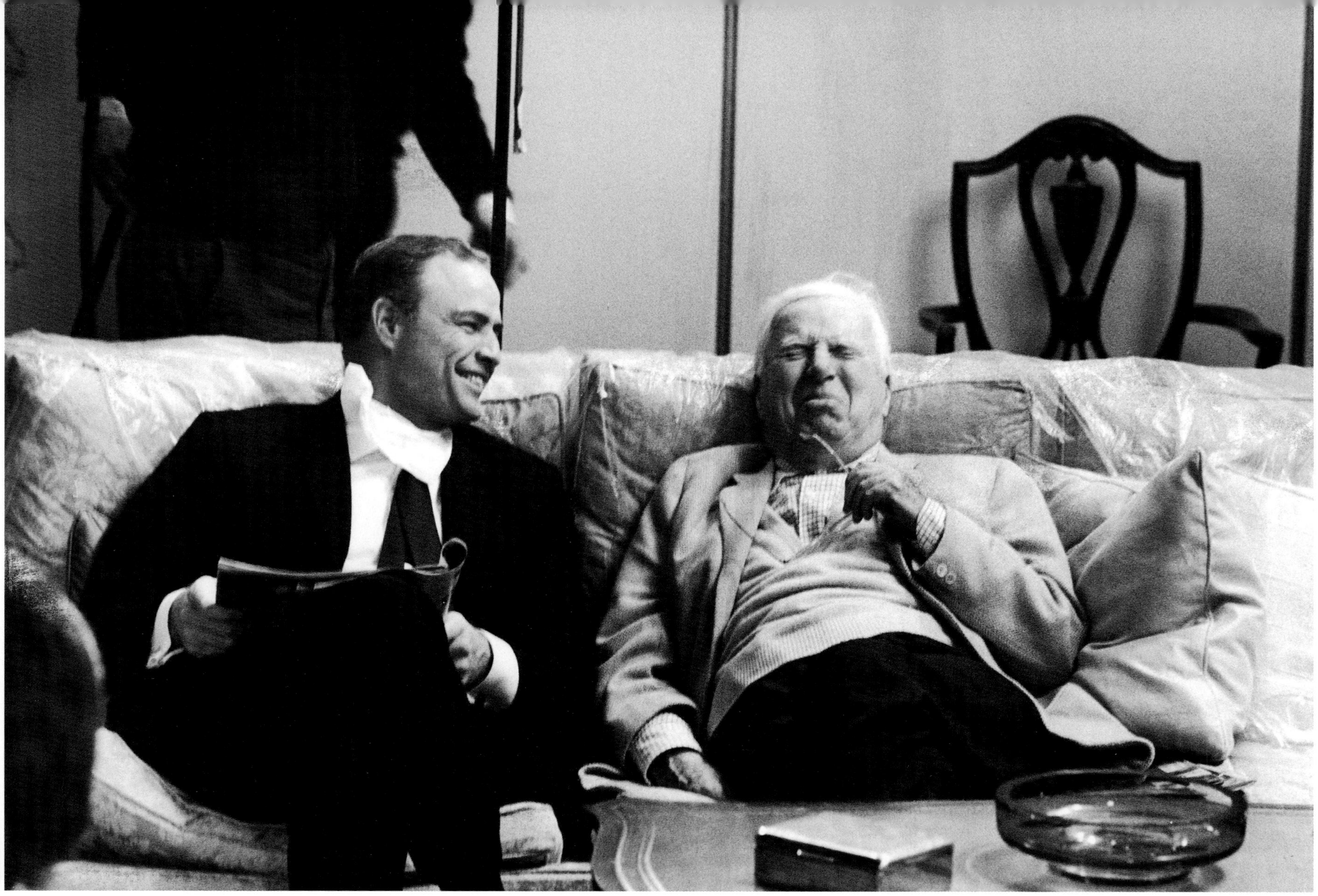

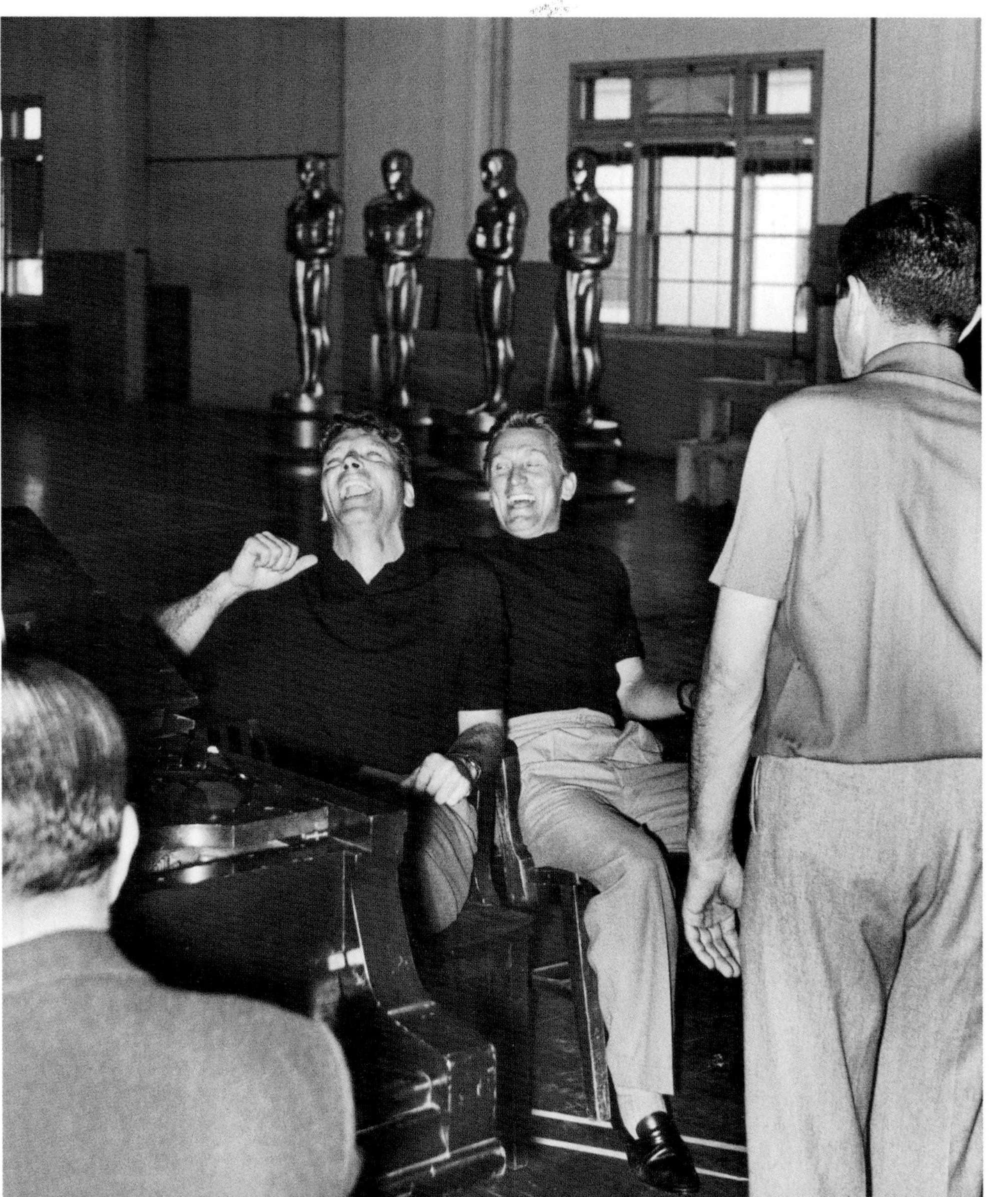

MARLON BRANDO & CHARLIE CHAPLIN

Two of the screen's true iconoclasts savor a moment on the set of *A Countess from Hong Kong* in 1966.

ALFRED EISENSTAEDT

BURT LANCASTER & KIRK DOUGLAS

Backstage at Oscar's 30th birthday, in 1958, these frequent action costars yuk it up during rehearsals for their musical number, "It's Great Not to Be Nominated."

LEONARD MCCOMBE

ERROL FLYNN

If there were a Hall of Fame for Hollywood Bad Boys, Flynn would be a charter member. Here, in 1941, the swashbuckler is aboard his yacht, *Sirocco,* off the coast of California.

PETER STACKPOLE

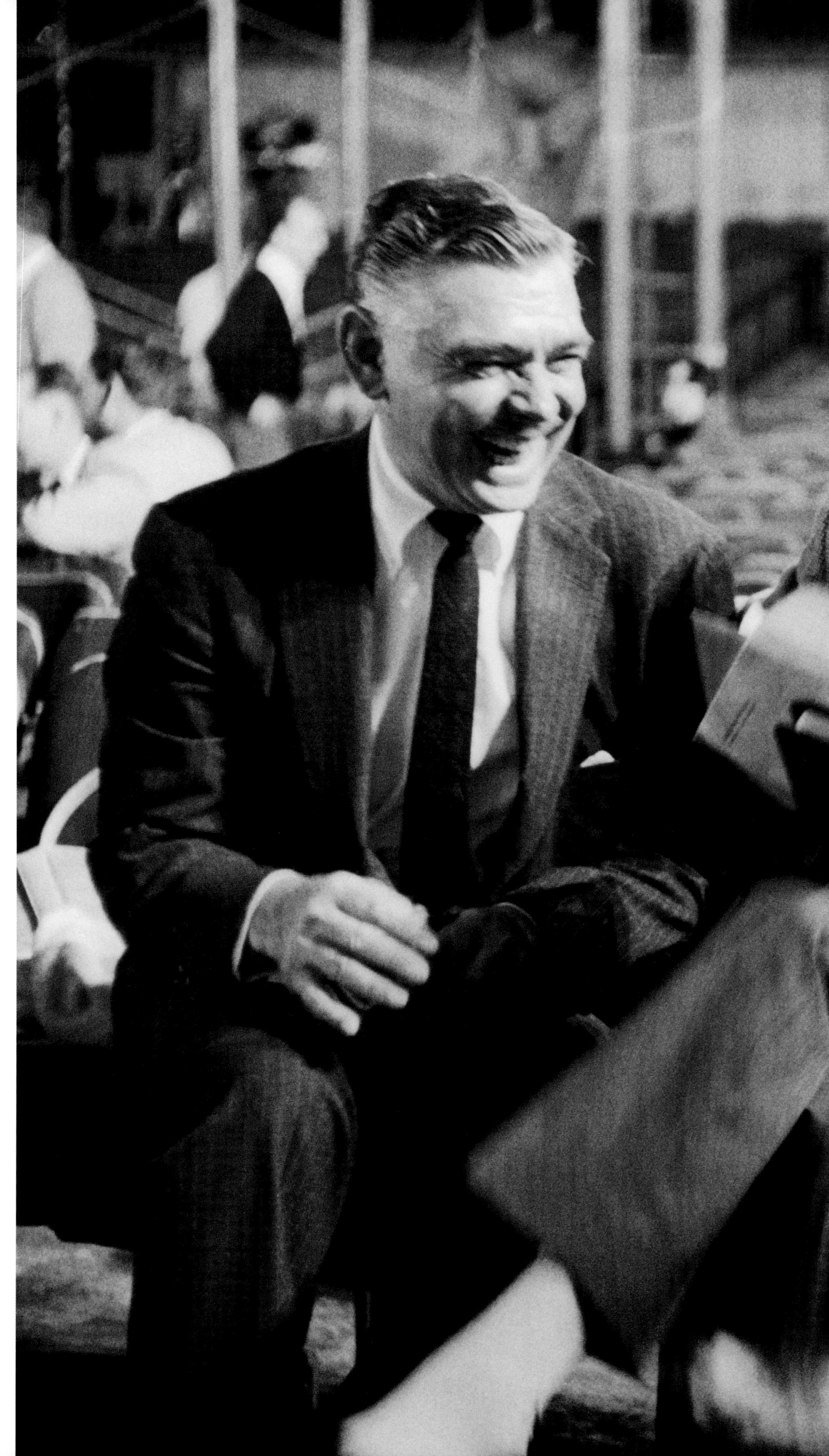

FOUR FOR THE AGES

The 1958 30th birthday bash for Oscar was quite an event. Here, a quartet of Hollywood's most durable, and popular, leading men share a ripe moment. From left, Clark Gable, Cary Grant, Bob Hope and David Niven.

LEONARD MCCOMBE

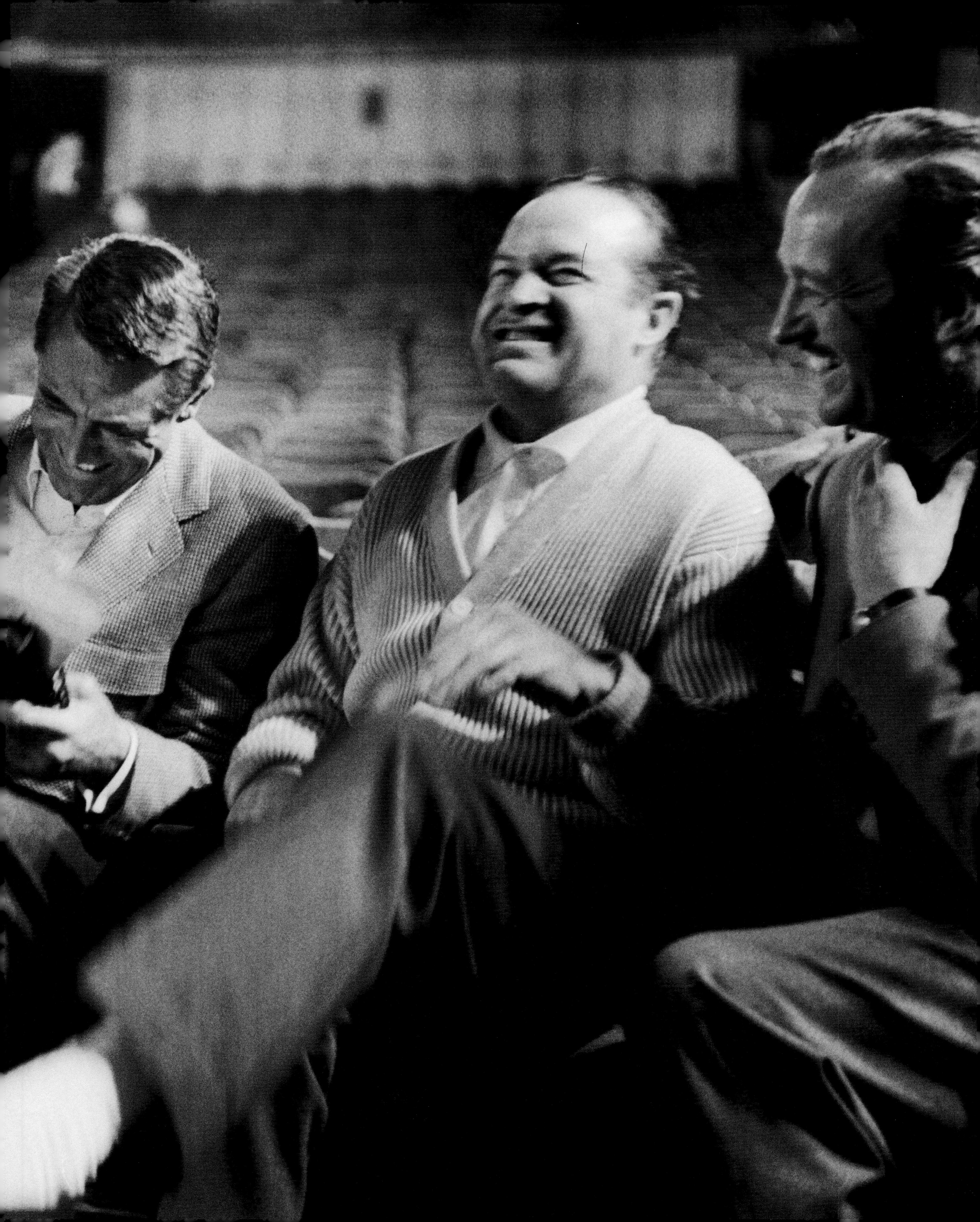

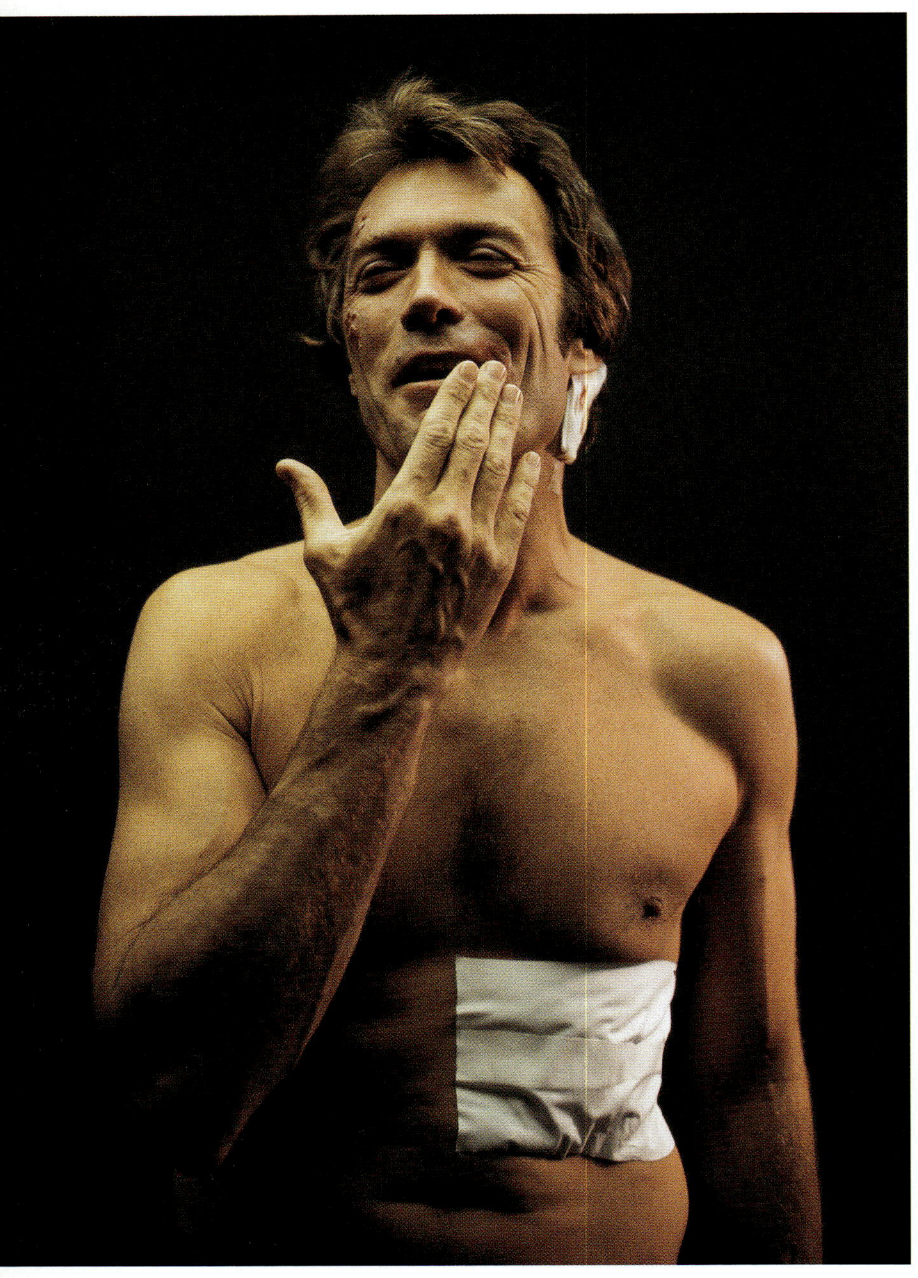

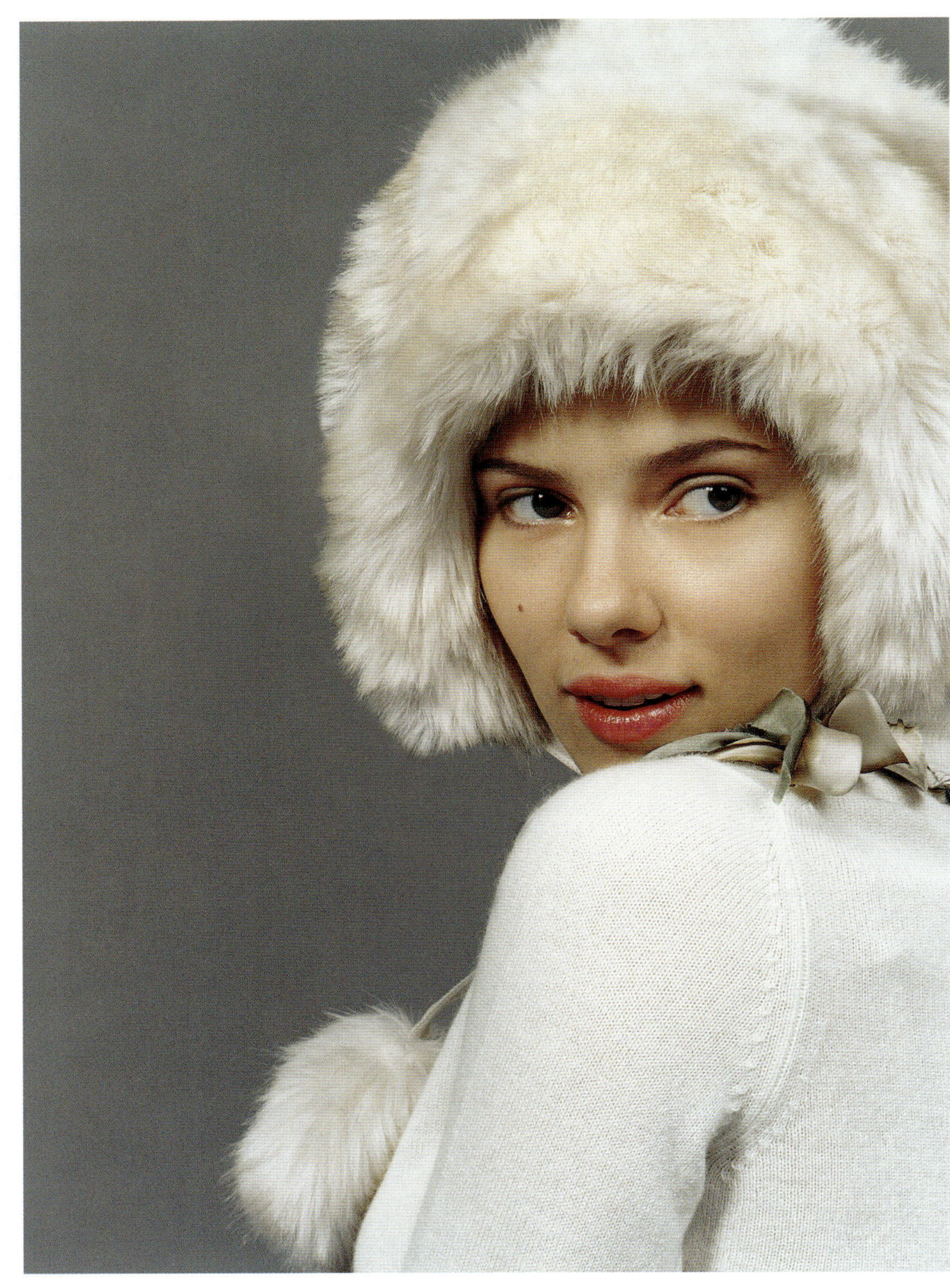

CLINT EASTWOOD

This picture was taken in 1971 after Clint finished a scene from *Dirty Harry,* the film that made him a superstar. Few people at the time had the slightest notion that he would develop into an accomplished actor and a sensitive, award-winning director.

BILL EPPRIDGE

SCARLETT JOHANSSON

This portrait is from a cover story that appeared in LIFE in December 2005. She was all of 21 years old at the time, but already her seductive sensuality had conspired with a winsome shyness to make her a full-blooded star.

KOTO BOLOFO

BILL MURRAY

This photo appeared on the December 24, 2004, cover of LIFE. In films like *Groundhog Day* and *Lost in Translation* (which costarred Johansson), Murray shows his keen genius for patiently extracting belly laughs from real pathos.

KARINA TAIRA

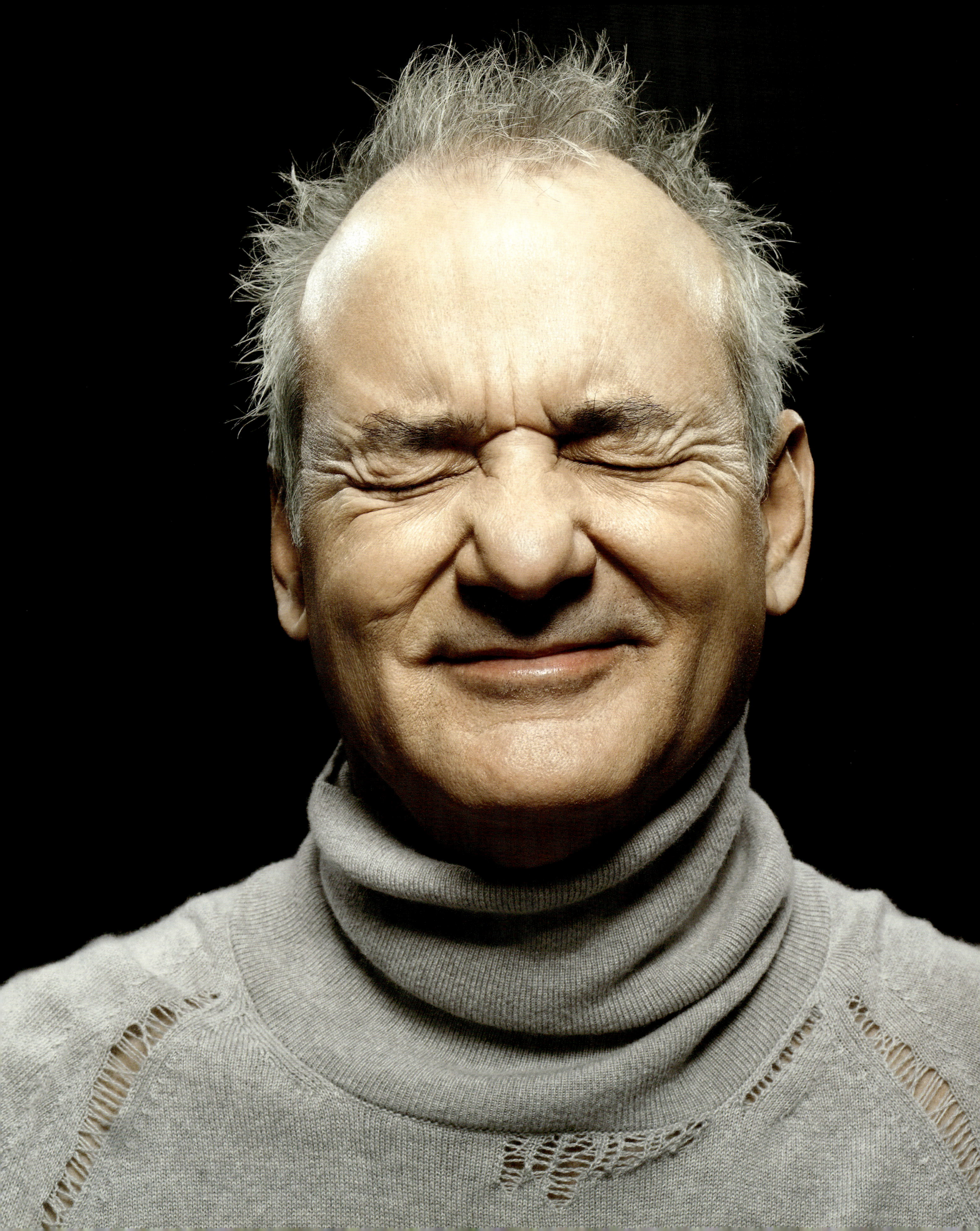

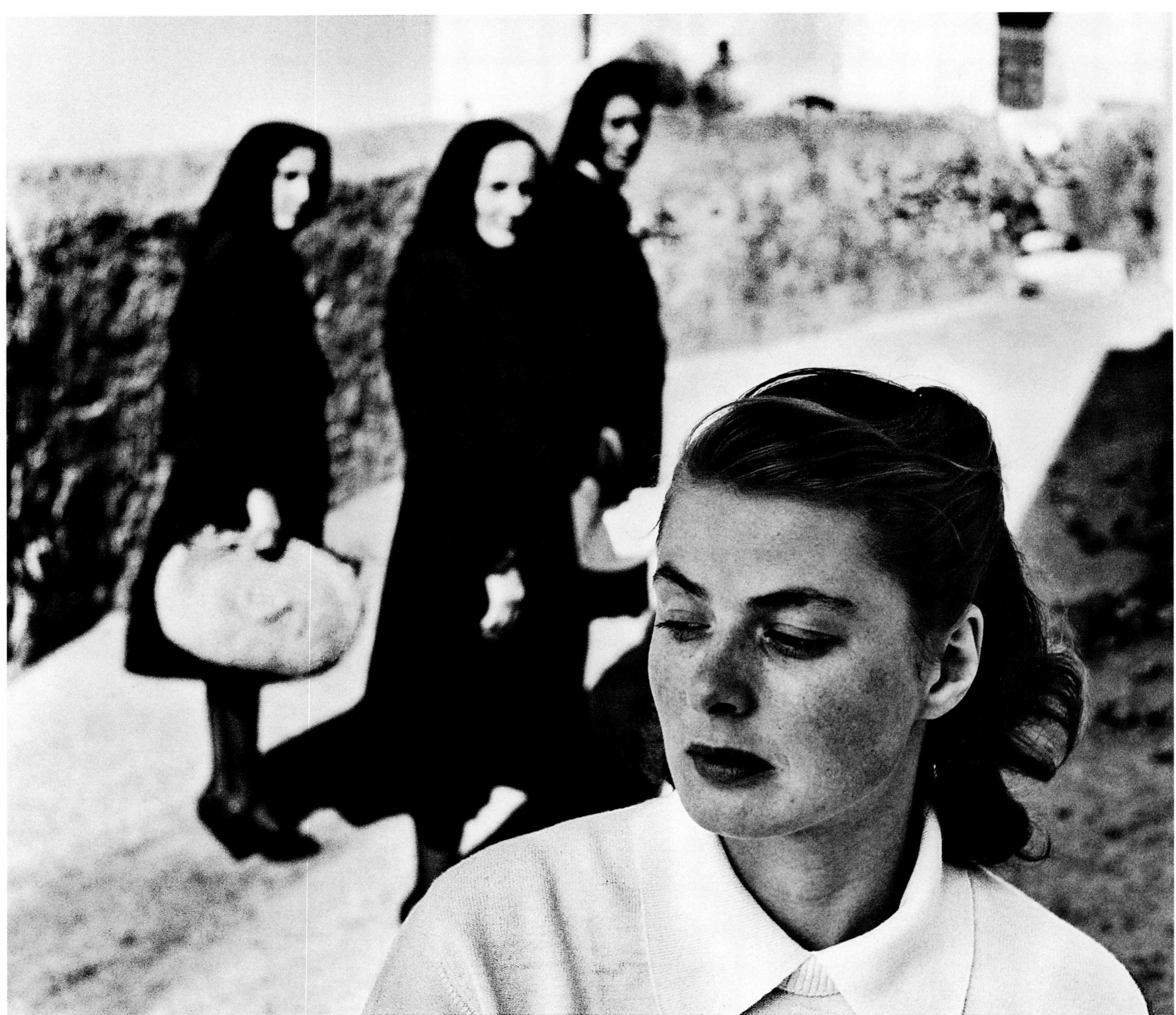

INGRID BERGMAN

She was one of the top stars of the 1940s (*Casablanca, Gaslight, Notorious*), but her career derailed in 1949 when she left her husband and daughter for director Roberto Rossellini. Bergman would not work in an American film for seven years, then she took home an Oscar for 1956's *Anastasia.* She had suffered, but that was no surprise. As director Jean Renoir said, "She will always prefer a scandal to a lie." Photographer Parks was a close friend, and took this photo in 1949 on location for the film *Stromboli,* in which Rossellini directed Bergman.

GORDON PARKS

AUDREY HEPBURN & GRACE KELLY

March 21, 1956. This is backstage at the RKO Pantages Theatre in Hollywood, and the event is the Academy Awards. You can feel the tension in the room, and these two stars aren't even up for Oscars. They are there to present: Kelly will handle Best Actor (Ernest Borgnine wins for *Marty*), while Hepburn will bestow Best Film (*Marty*).

ALLAN GRANT

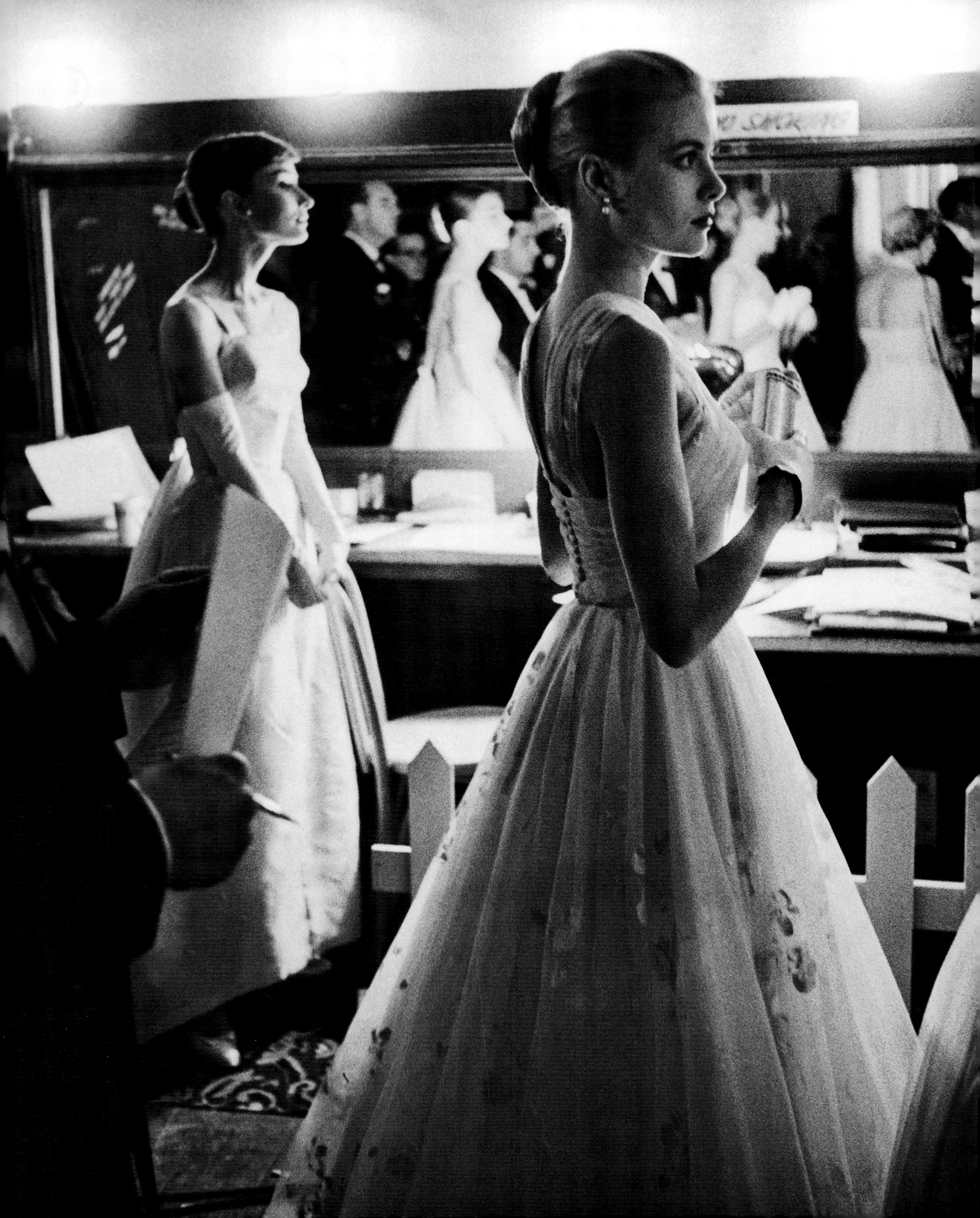

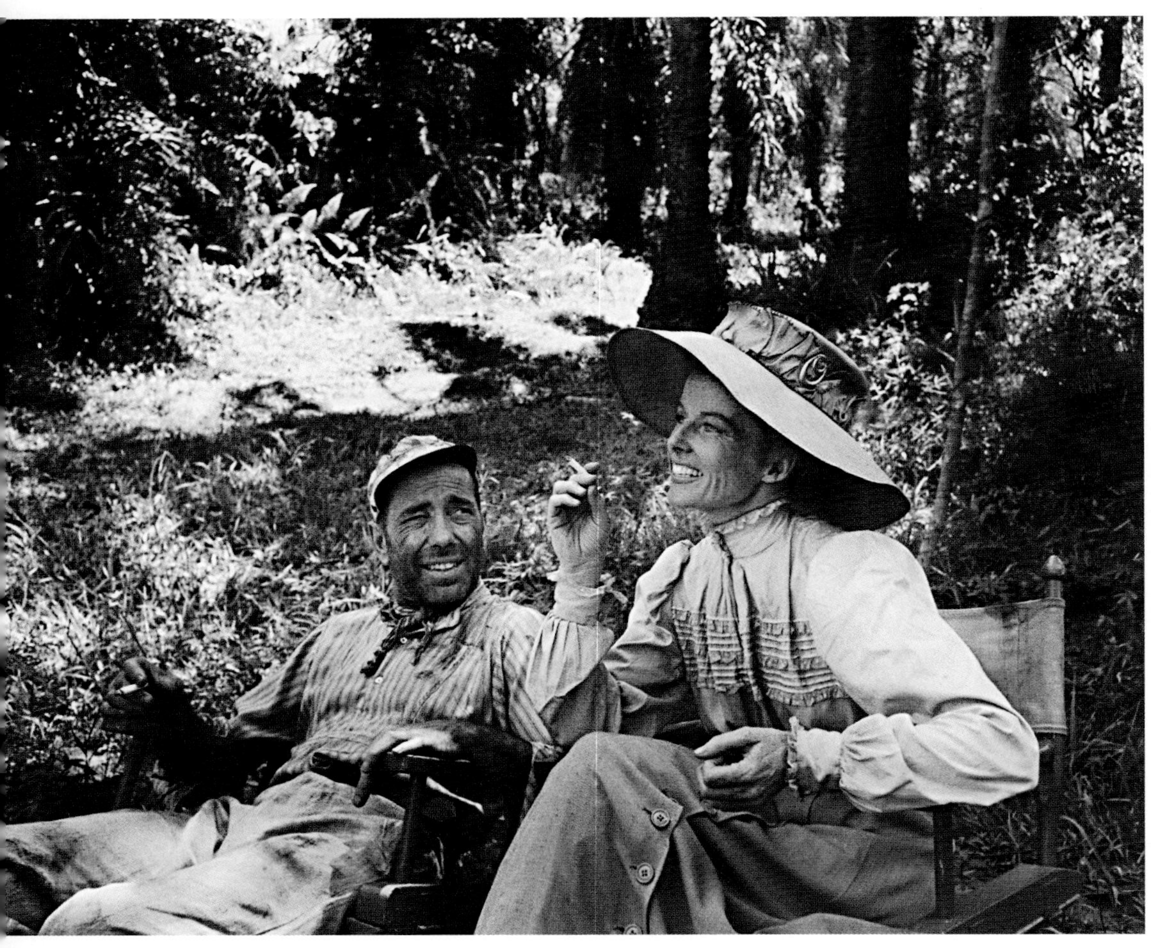

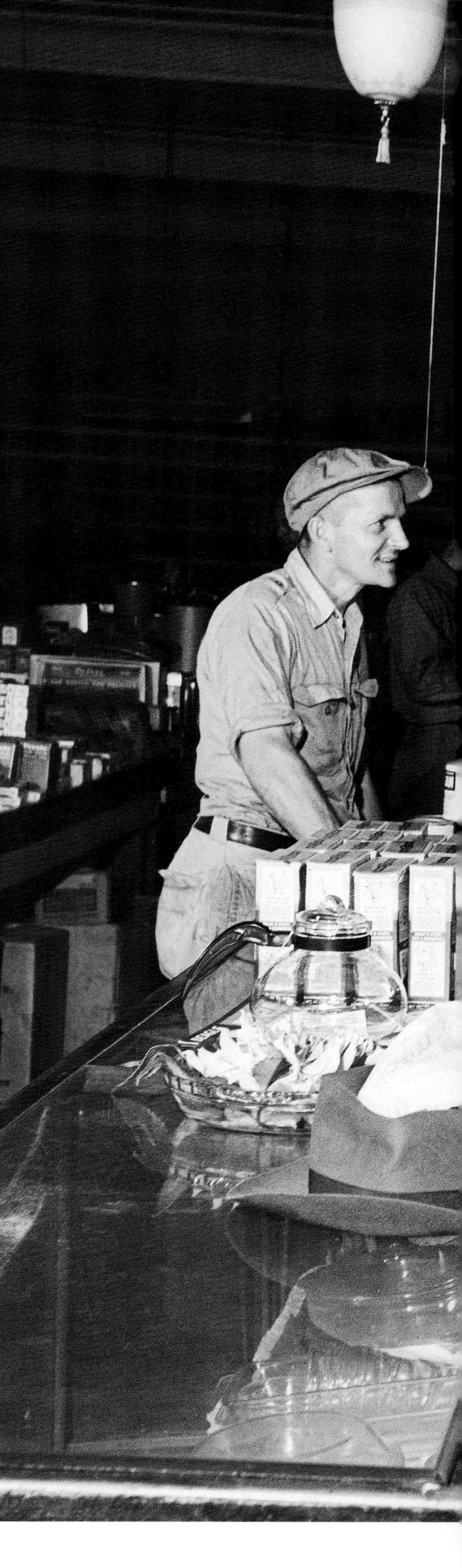

HUMPHREY BOGART & KATHARINE HEPBURN

The two stars take a break during the shooting of 1951's *The African Queen.* Director John Huston had insisted on using real locations in Africa, to which Bogey and Kate reacted quite differently. He decried the heat, mildew, bugs and bad water, while she, according to Bogart, found everything "divine."

ELIOT ELISOFON

JAMES STEWART

This picture from a September 1945 cover story shows Colonel Stewart paying a visit to his hometown of Indiana, Pa., not long before getting his Army discharge. Here, perched on a counter in his father's store, he calls an old friend to make a date to go fishing that afternoon. A real-life action hero, Jimmy Stewart had flown 20 combat missions during the war.

PETER STACKPOLE

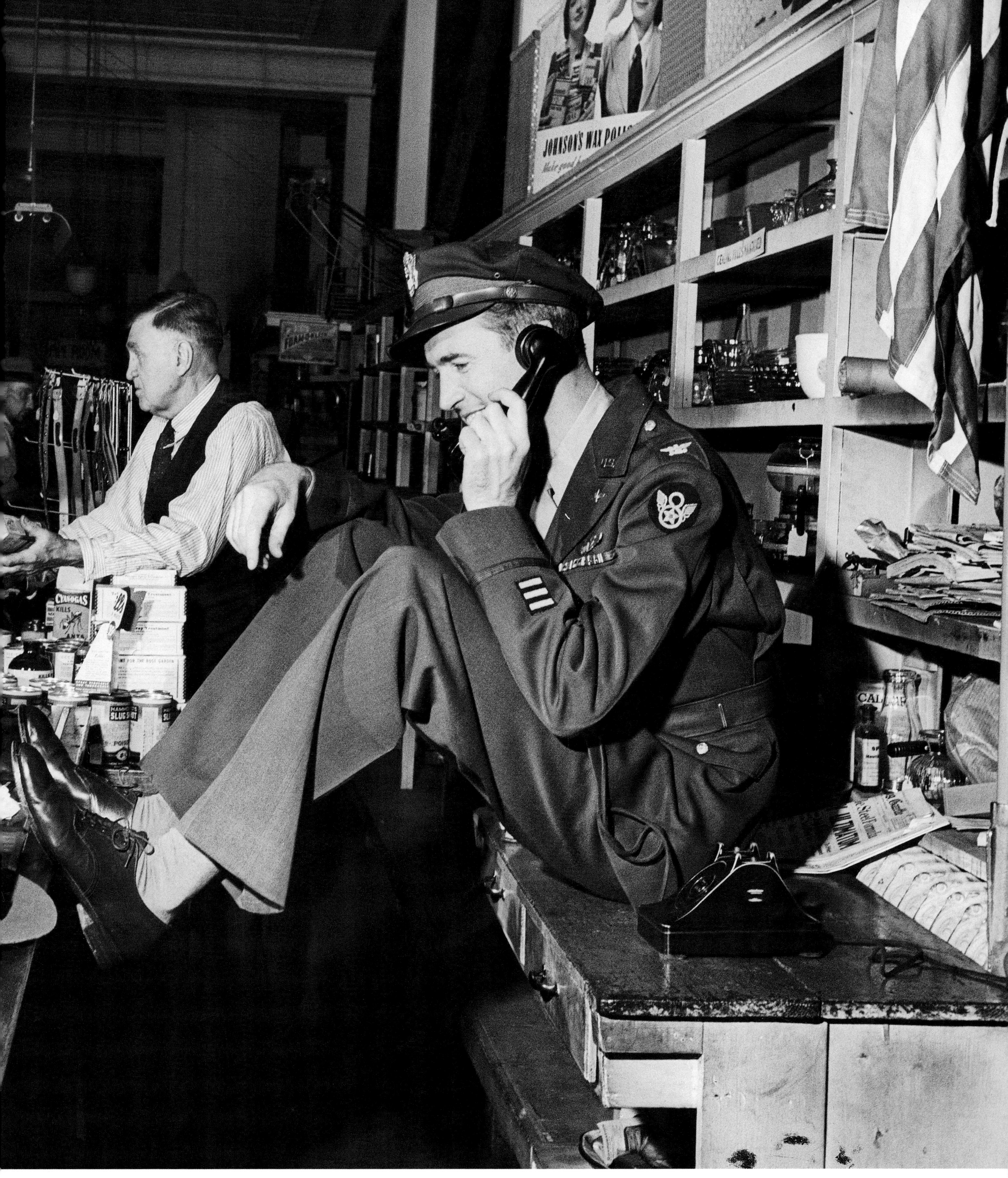
JOHNSON'S WAX
CYANOGAS
KILLS
SLUG SHOT
FOR THE ROSE GARDEN

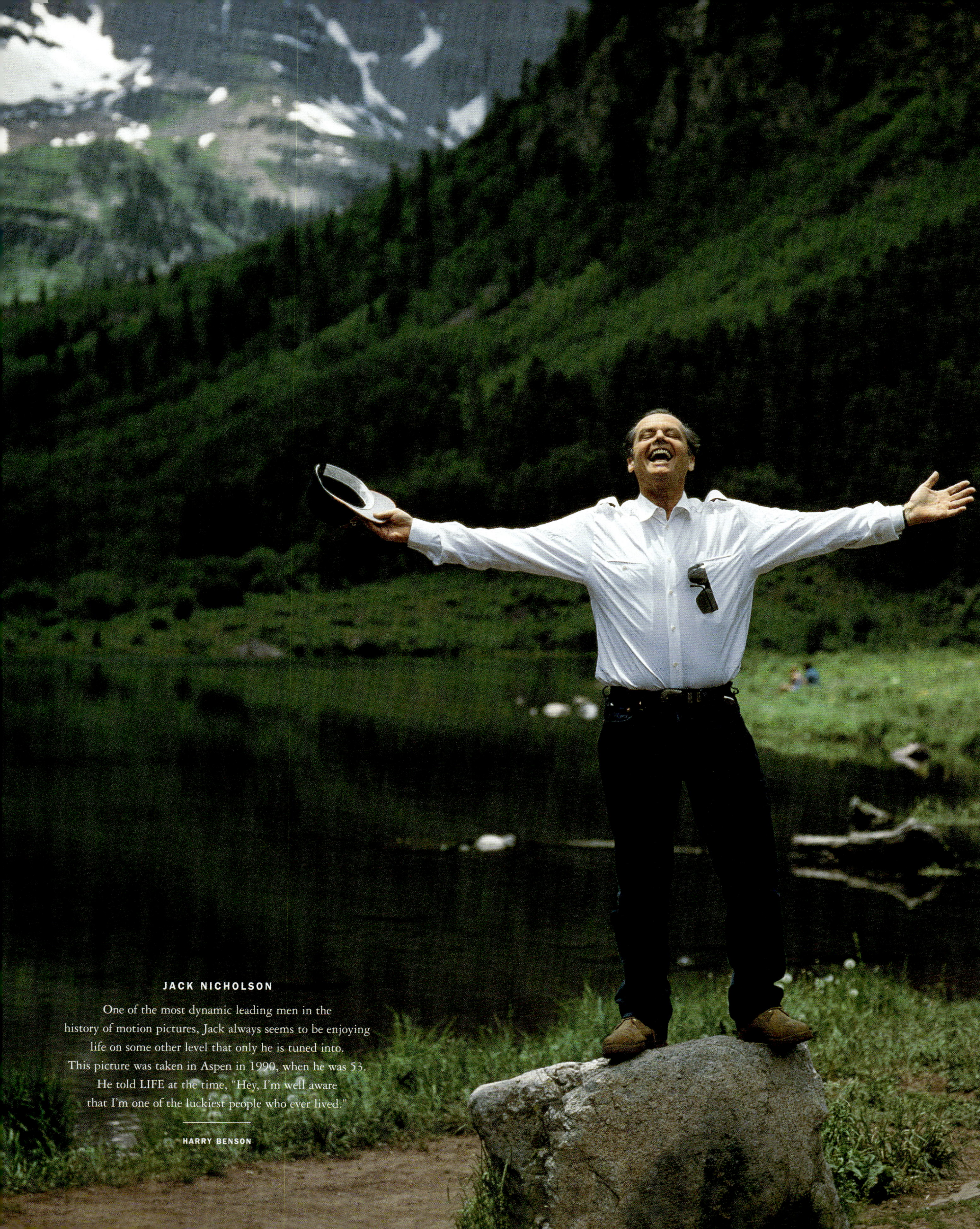

JACK NICHOLSON

One of the most dynamic leading men in the history of motion pictures, Jack always seems to be enjoying life on some other level that only he is tuned into. This picture was taken in Aspen in 1990, when he was 53. He told LIFE at the time, "Hey, I'm well aware that I'm one of the luckiest people who ever lived."

HARRY BENSON

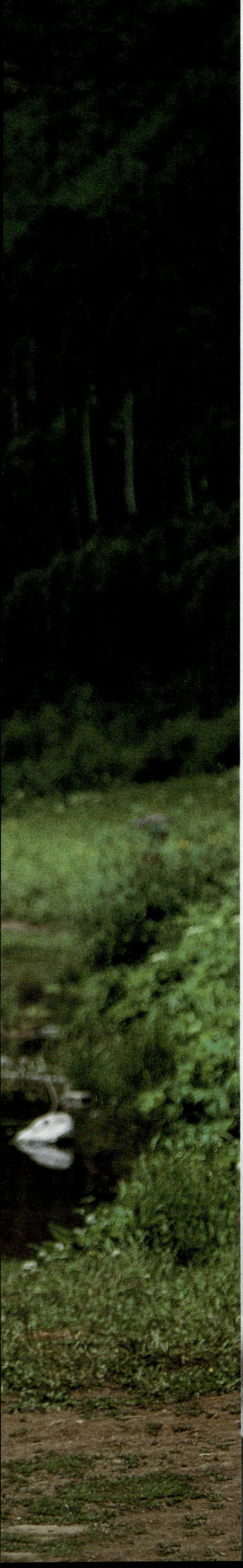

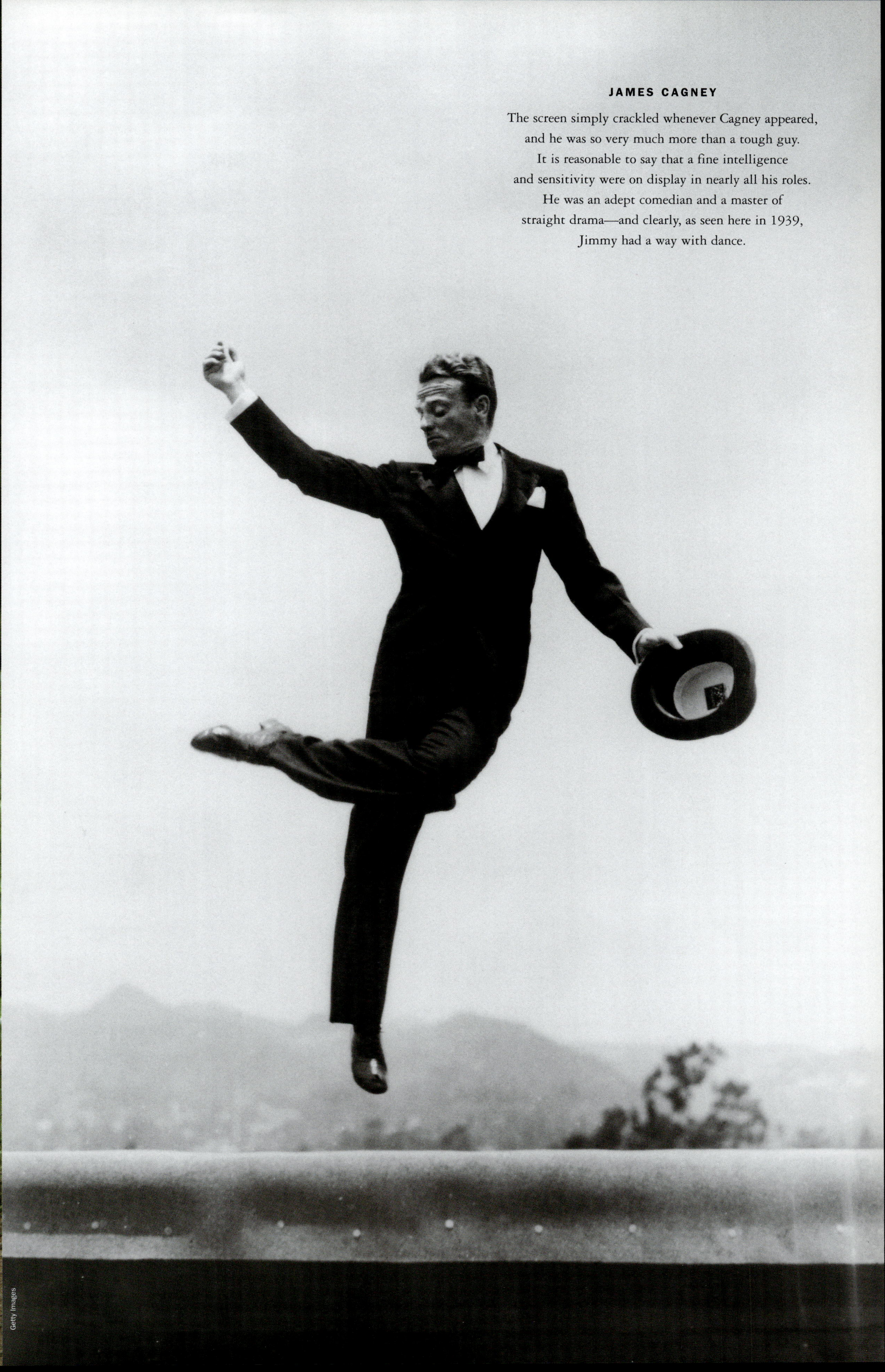

JAMES CAGNEY

The screen simply crackled whenever Cagney appeared, and he was so very much more than a tough guy. It is reasonable to say that a fine intelligence and sensitivity were on display in nearly all his roles. He was an adept comedian and a master of straight drama—and clearly, as seen here in 1939, Jimmy had a way with dance.

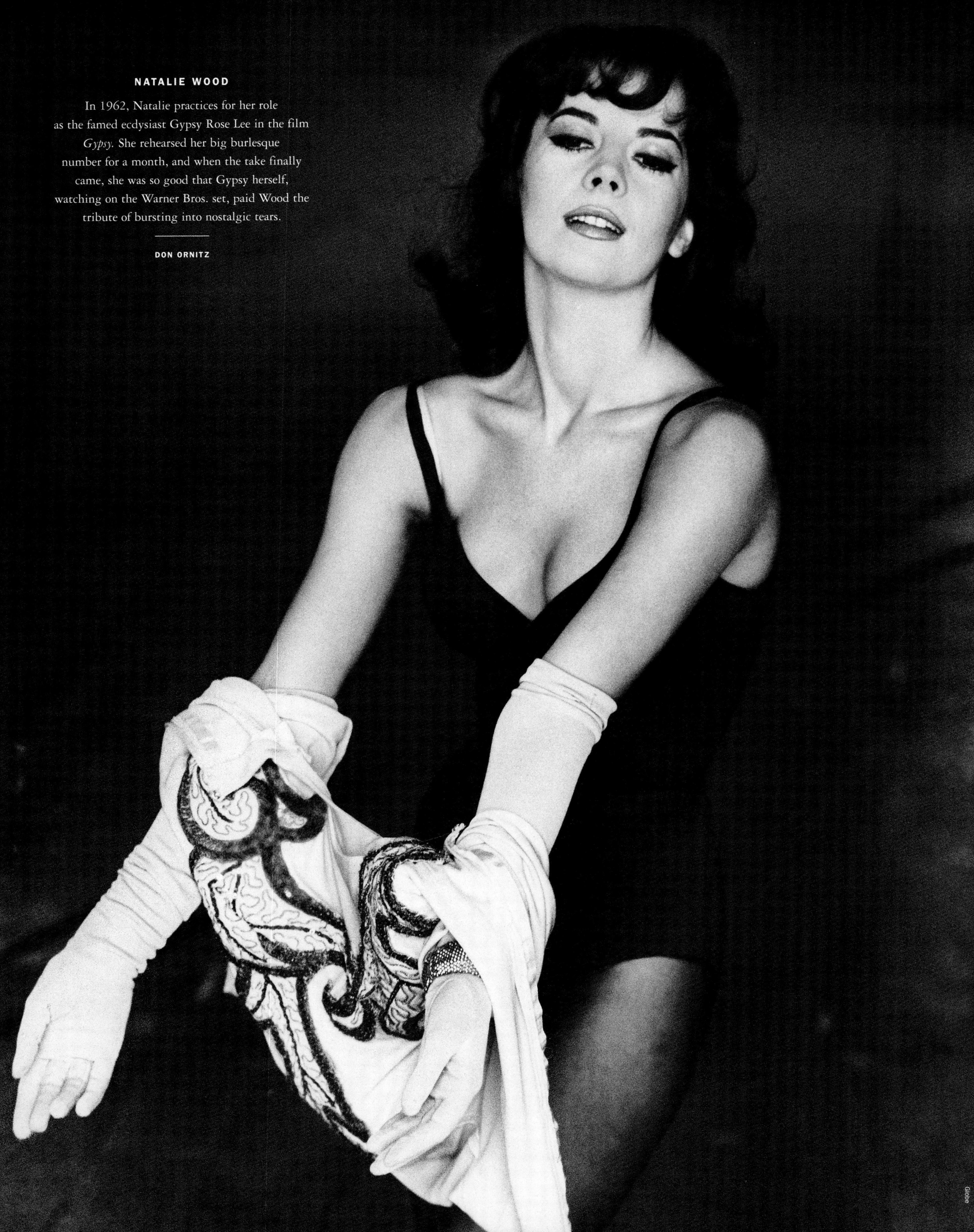

NATALIE WOOD

In 1962, Natalie practices for her role as the famed ecdysiast Gypsy Rose Lee in the film *Gypsy.* She rehearsed her big burlesque number for a month, and when the take finally came, she was so good that Gypsy herself, watching on the Warner Bros. set, paid Wood the tribute of bursting into nostalgic tears.

DON ORNITZ

Globe

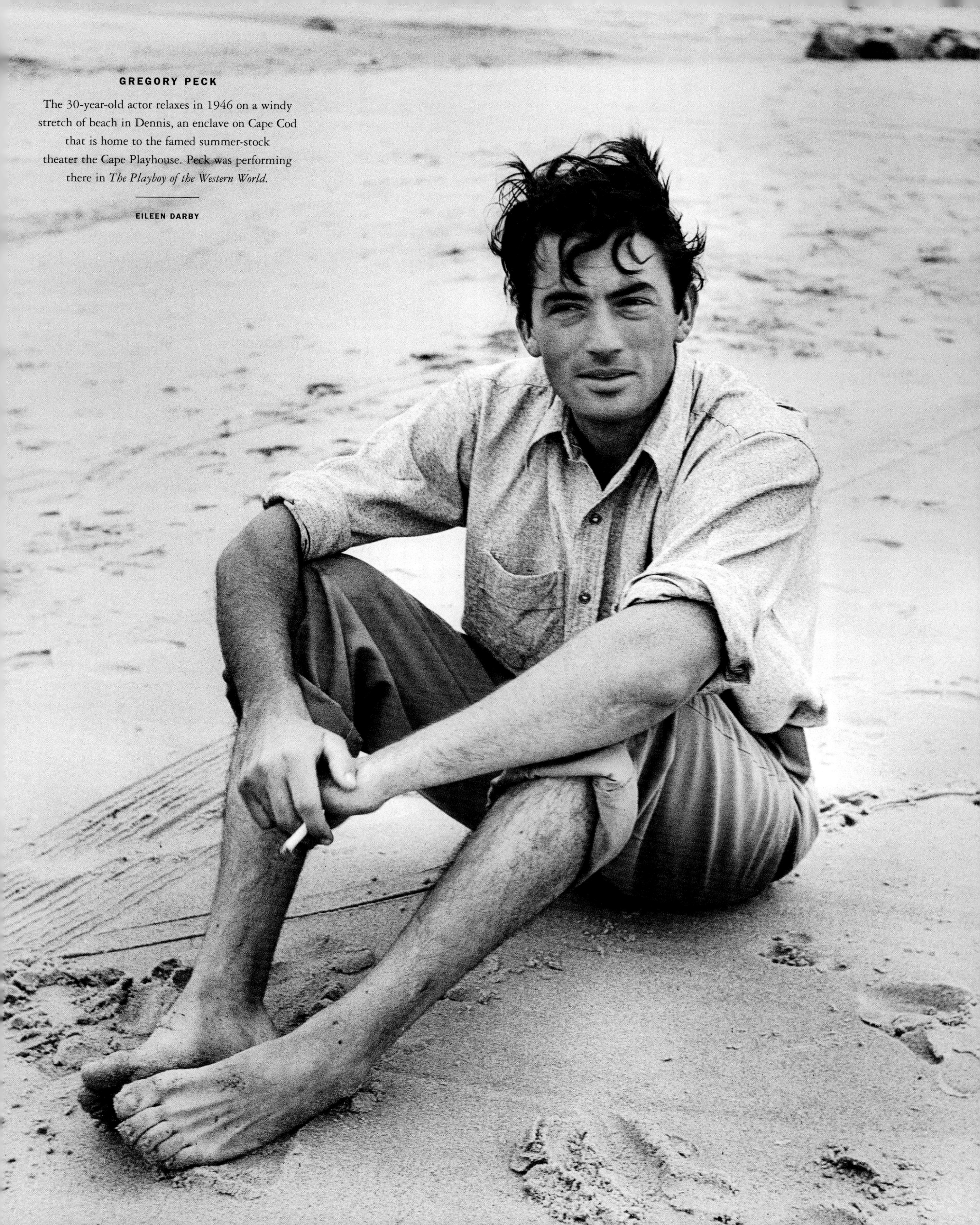

GREGORY PECK

The 30-year-old actor relaxes in 1946 on a windy stretch of beach in Dennis, an enclave on Cape Cod that is home to the famed summer-stock theater the Cape Playhouse. Peck was performing there in *The Playboy of the Western World.*

EILEEN DARBY

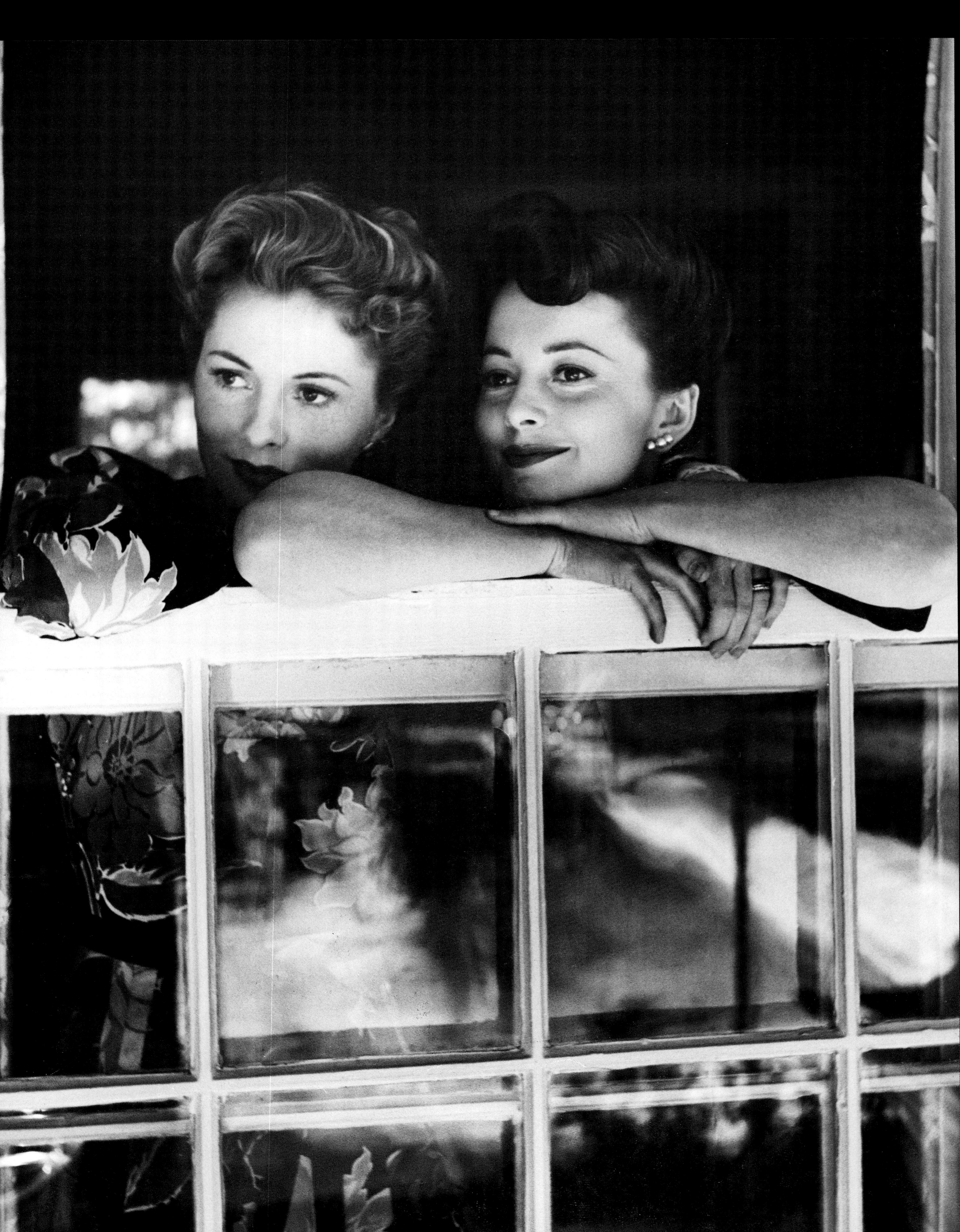

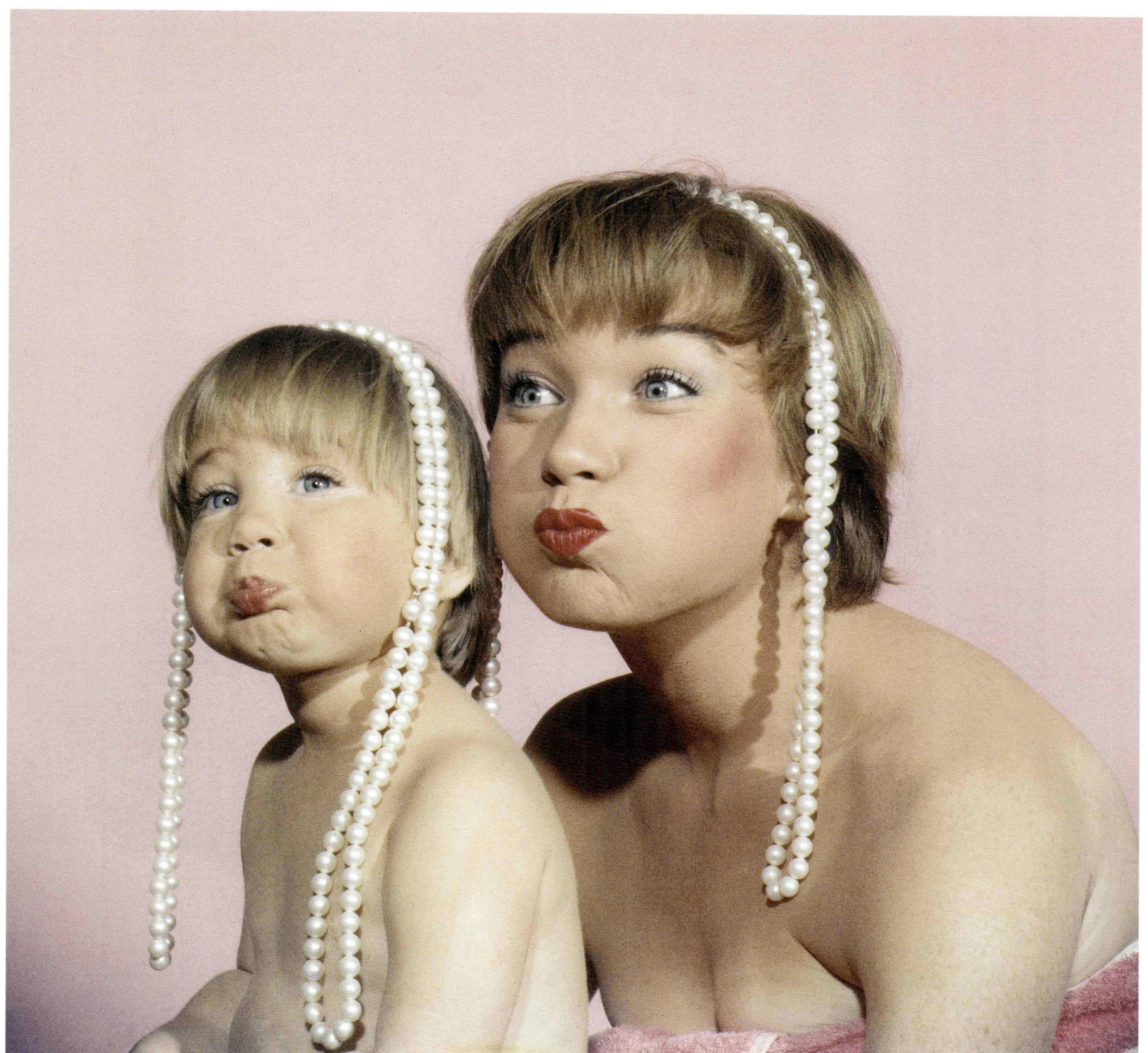

JOAN FONTAINE & OLIVIA DE HAVILLAND

In 1942, the two sisters look out from a window in Joan's home. In February, Joan had won the Best Actress Oscar for *Suspicion,* while Olivia was an also-ran for *Hold Back the Dawn.* The siblings famously never got along.

BOB LANDRY

SHIRLEY MACLAINE

In 1959, mother MacLaine poses with her daughter, Sachi Parker, who was born in Los Angeles in 1956. The adorable little girl grew into an attractive woman who herself appeared in a dozen movies in the 1980s and '90s.

ALLAN GRANT

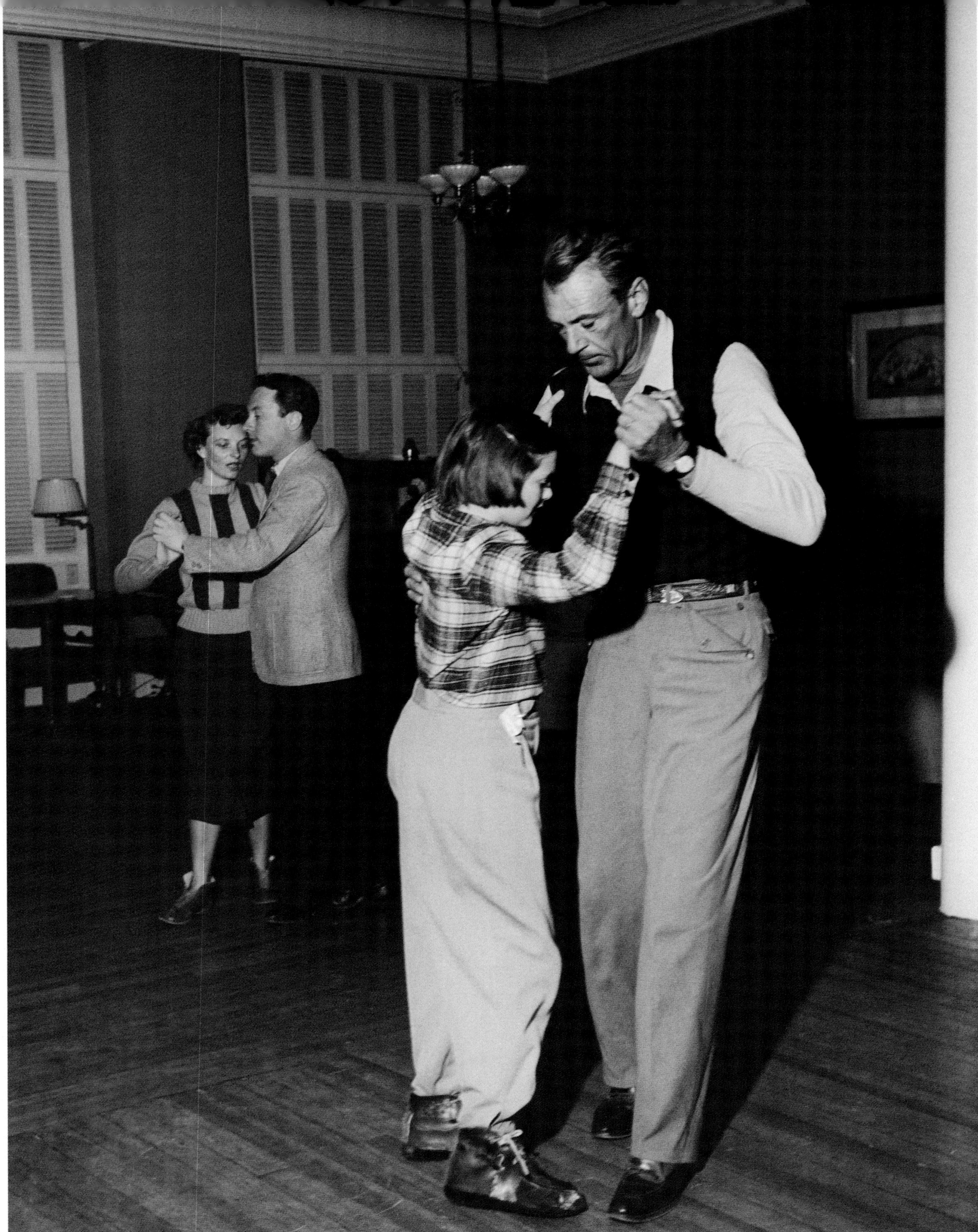

GARY COOPER

In March 1949 we ran a story called "LIFE Visits Gary Cooper," which was fashioned around a family holiday that Coop, his wife, Rocky, and their 11-year-old daughter, Maria, spent in Aspen. The caption for this photo read, "TEA DANCE finds Gary showing Maria a few steps. She was shy on the dance floor, but out on the snow could ski circles around her father."

PETER STACKPOLE

ANJELICA & JOHN HUSTON

One of Hollywood's most talented families, the Hustons started things off with Walter, an insightful, compelling actor; then came his son, John, a stellar director and fine actor himself; and finally granddaughter Anjelica, a mesmerizing performer. Other than talent, the three shared a fierce tenacity. Here, John and Anjelica take to the floor in Ireland in 1966.

LOOMIS DEAN

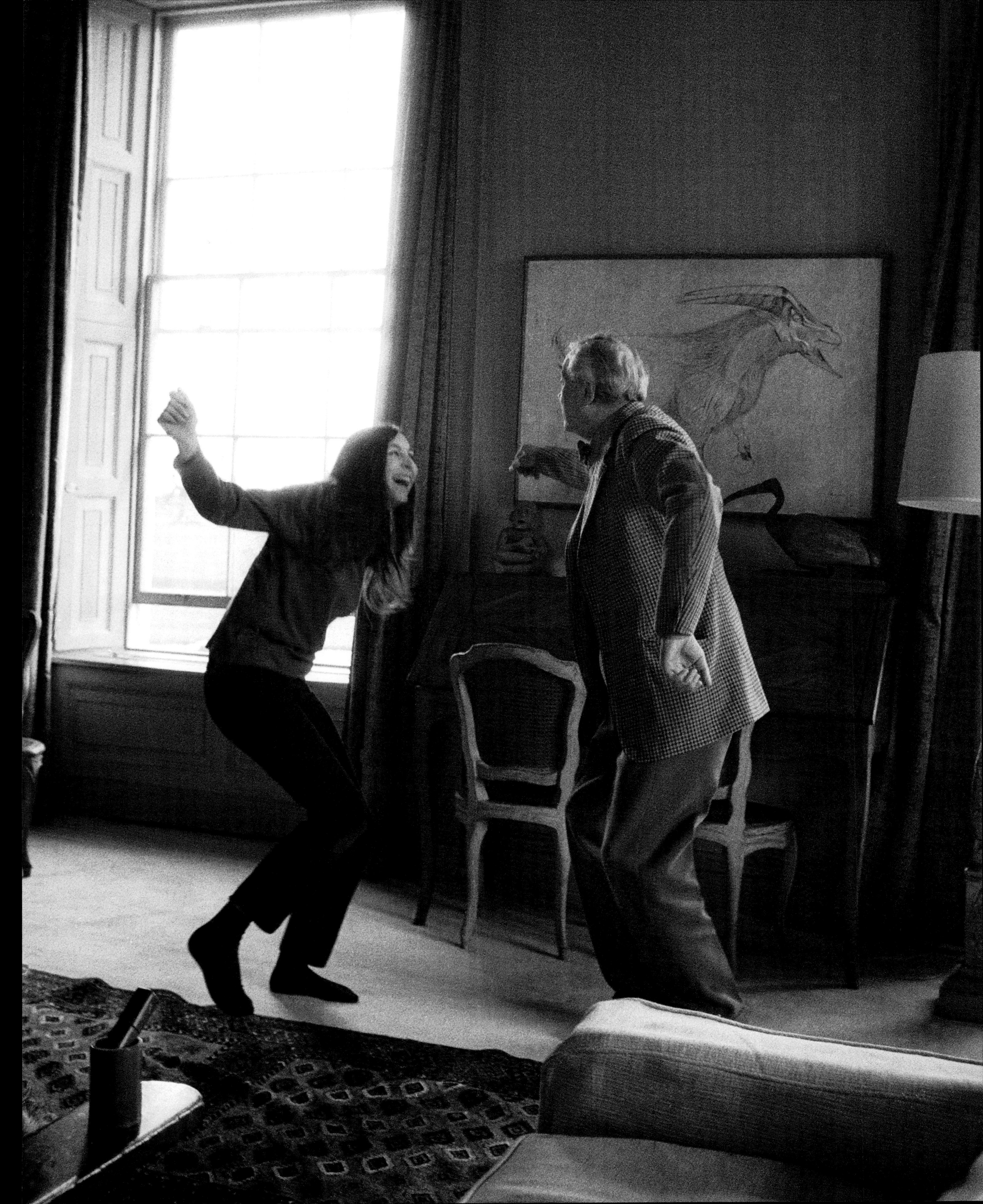

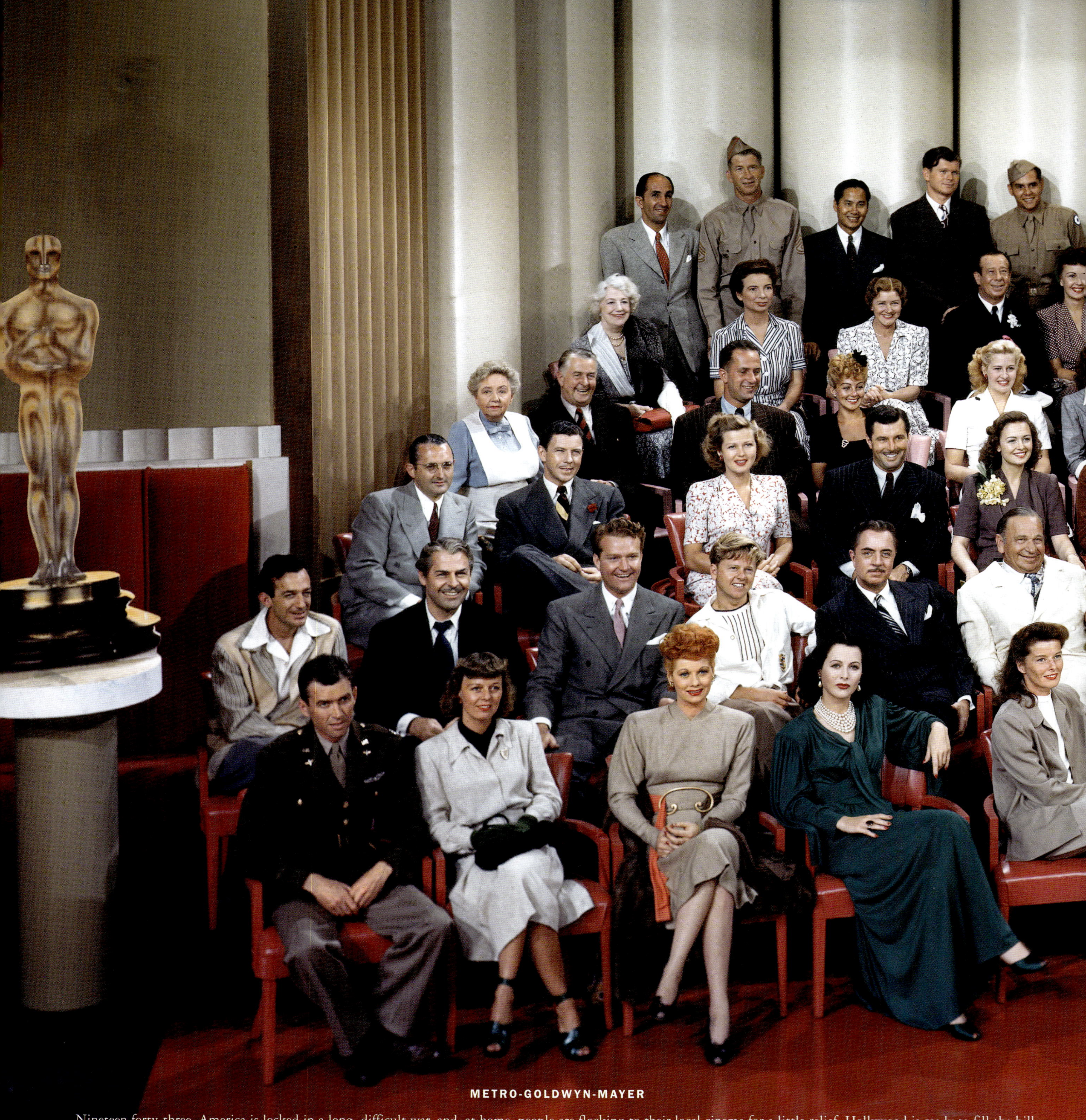

METRO-GOLDWYN-MAYER

Nineteen forty-three. America is locked in a long, difficult war, and, at home, people are flocking to their local cinema for a little relief. Hollywood is ready to fill the bill. Among the many studios providing the escapism, none is the equal of MGM, a sleek glamour machine powered by "More stars than there are in heaven." Here, MGM head Louis B. Mayer poses with his entourage. *Front row:* James Stewart, Margaret Sullavan, Lucille Ball, Hedy Lamarr, Katharine Hepburn, Mayer, Greer Garson, Irene Dunne, Susan Peters, Ginny Simms, Butch Jenkins, Lionel Barrymore; *second row:* Harry James, Brian Donlevy, Red Skelton, Mickey Rooney, William Powell, Wallace Beery, Spencer Tracy, Walter Pidgeon, Robert Taylor, Jean-Pierre Aumont, Lewis Stone, Gene Kelly; *third row:* Tommy Dorsey, George Murphy, Jean Rogers, James Craig, Donna Reed, Van Johnson, Fay Bainter, Marsha Hunt, Ruth Hussey, Marjorie Main, Robert Benchley; *fourth row:* Dame May Whitty, Reginald Owen, Keenan Wynn, Diana Lewis, Marilyn Maxwell, Esther Williams, Ann Richards, Martha Linden, Lee Bowman, Richard Carlson, Mary Astor; *fifth row:* Blanche Ring, Sara Haden, Fay Holden, Bert Lahr, Frances Gifford, June Allyson, Richard Whorf, Frances Rafferty, Spring Byington, Connie Gilchrist, Gladys Cooper; *sixth row:* Ben Blue, Chill Wills, Keye Luke, Barry Nelson, Desi Arnaz, Henry O'Neill, Bob Crosby, Rags Ragland.

WALTER SANDERS

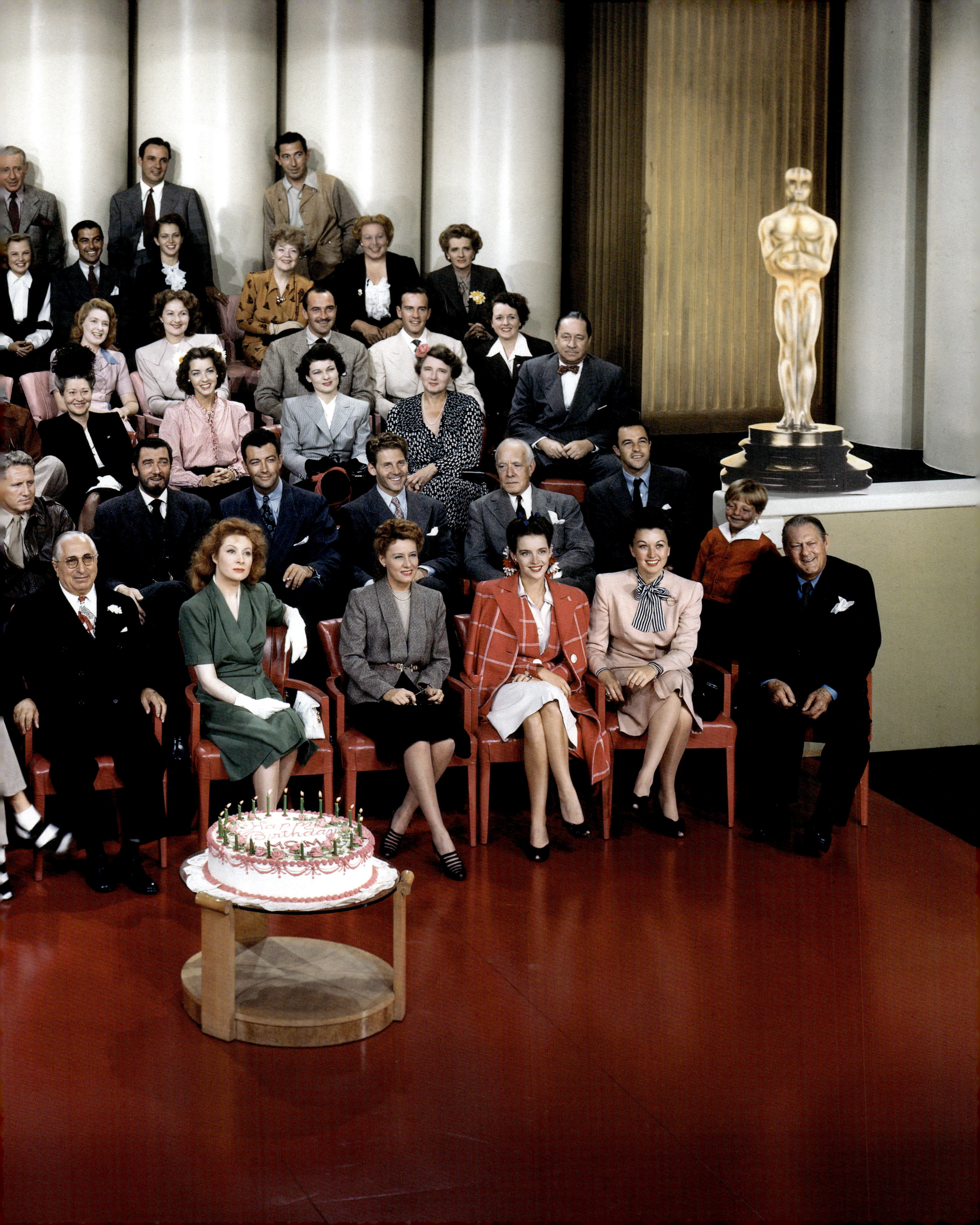
Birthday
MGM

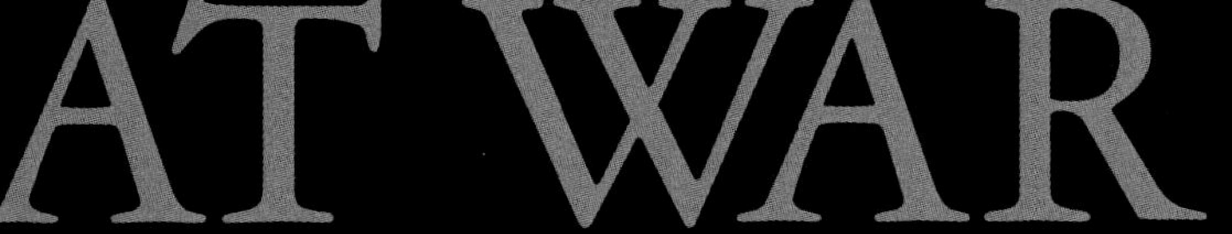

It seems that there is always a war somewhere. And while no one would argue with the notion that all war is hell, there are certain conflicts that are carried on less for reasons of pride, power or stupidity than in the pursuit of righteousness.

It may be deemed appropriate that the Spanish Civil War was the prevailing belligerency in the year that LIFE was born, 1936. This war was an example of the type that—at least from the point of view of those who favored democracy—had a "good" aspect, one that was even regarded somewhat romantically. Artists and intellectuals from America and Europe rallied to the cause of the Republic, while fascist Italy and Nazi Germany supported the Nationalists. A nice example may be drawn from the film *Casablanca,* in which we learn that Humphrey Bogart's character had fought with the Loyalists on the side of the Republic. The Spanish Civil War was that kind of a war, one with a heart, and that spirit has always been the overarching *raison d'être* at LIFE—that this is a publication with a heart. Henry Luce said it well long ago: "It is the nature of LIFE to be *for* things."

Unfortunately, the pursuit and protection of democracy is an endeavor without end; thus has there been one war after another for LIFE to attend to. The good news—again, if it may be so regarded—is that LIFE's photographers have always taken their heartbreaking "duty" to heart, with the result that the magazine from the beginning to this day has featured some of the world's most profound examples of images drawn from warfare. Please permit us to salute the work of a few of those brave men and women who have gone repeatedly into harm's way to show us what was really happening—the nightmares and hopes, the evil and the heroic.

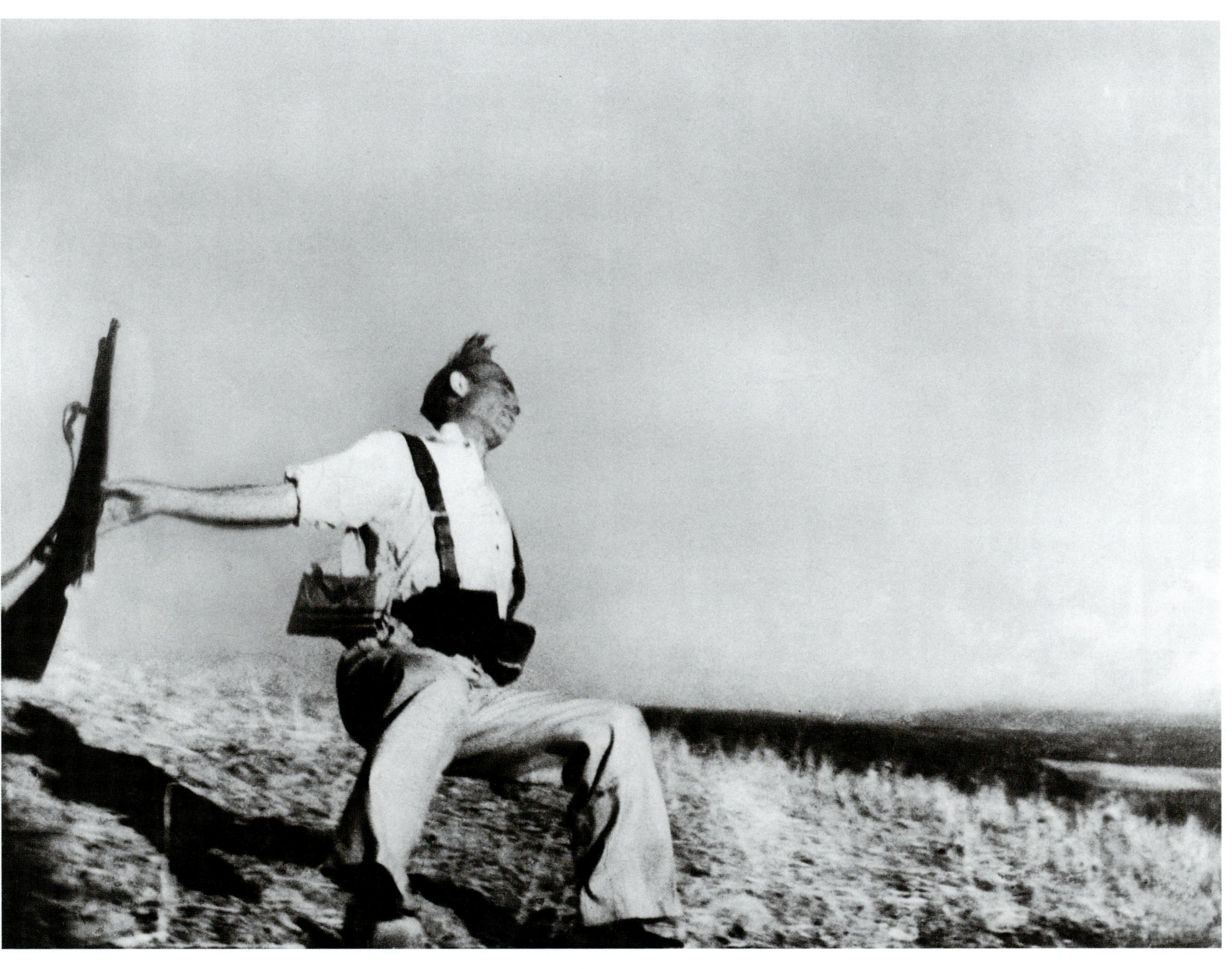

FALLING SOLDIER

The official title of this, the most famous war photograph of all time, is *Loyalist Militiaman at the Moment of Death, Cerro Muriano, September 5, 1936.* The photographer, mysterious, dashing Robert Capa, once said, "If your pictures aren't good enough, you're not close enough." Capa was most definitely near enough to this moment of sudden mortality, as this martyr for the Spanish Republic greets death with open arms. The instant is so ideally captured that there have been questions as to its authenticity, but the preponderance of opinion holds that it is legitimate, in every way.

ROBERT CAPA

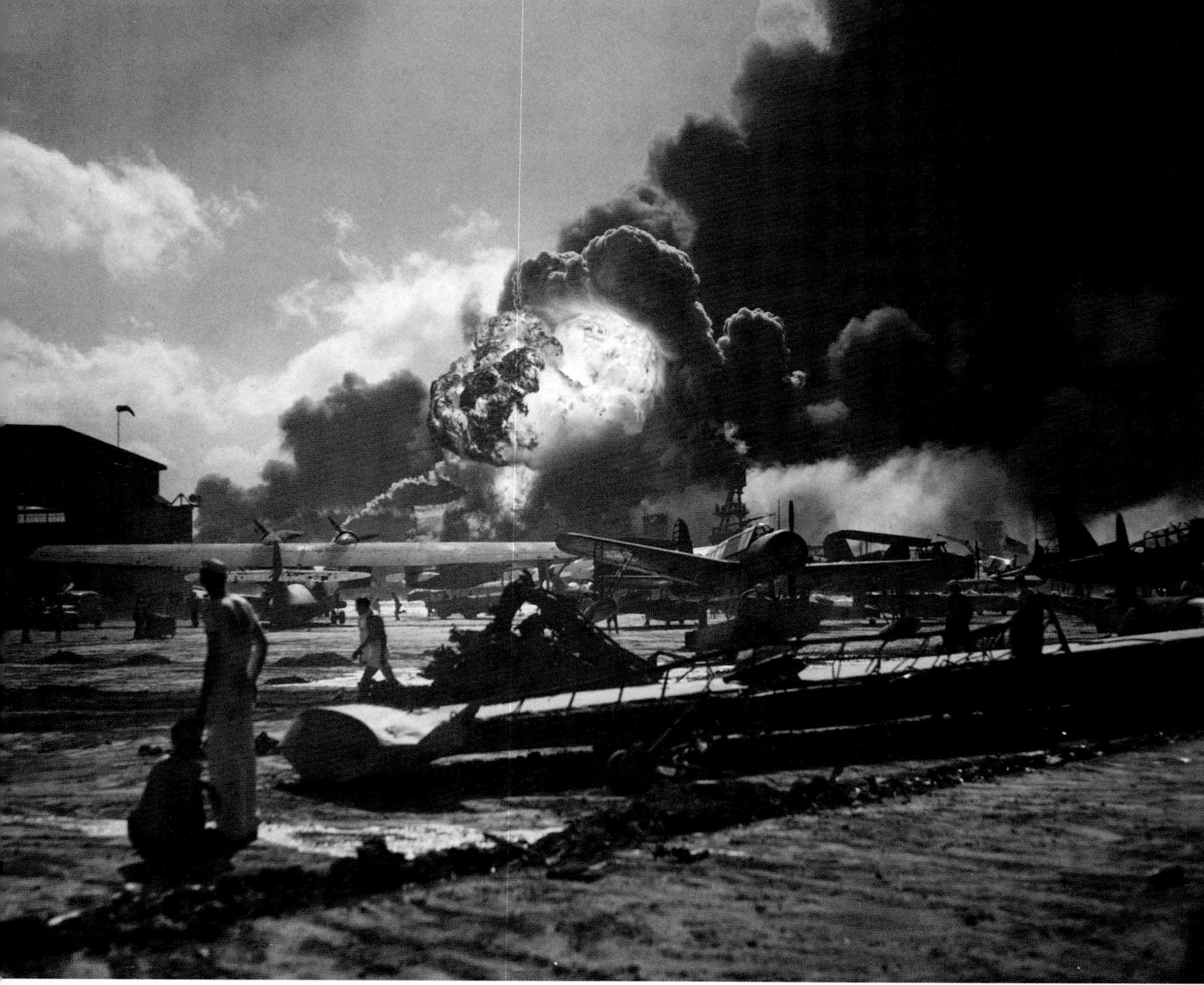

U.S. Navy

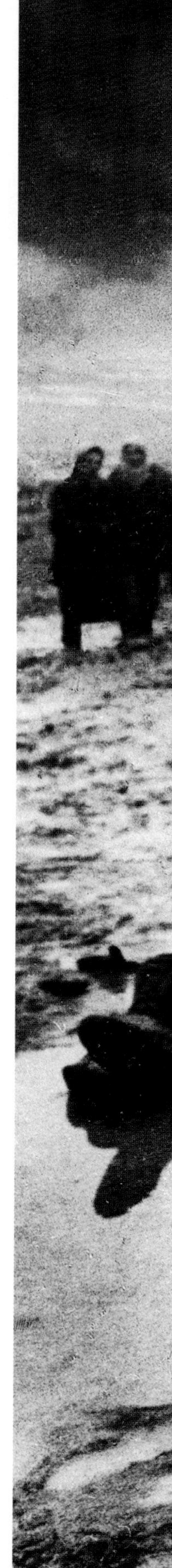

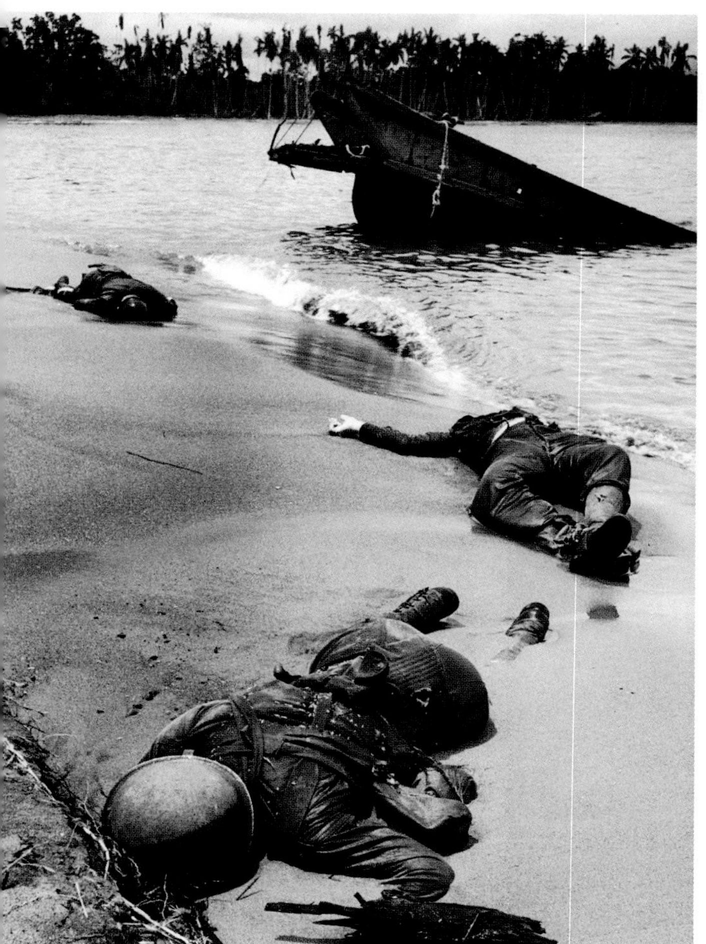

GRIEF, DESTRUCTION, DEATH

Right: More than 20 million Soviets would perish during the war. On or about December 1, 1941, Nazis overran the Crimea, and on the heels of the German army came the Einsatzgruppen, mobile units that murdered more than a million Jews, including 7,000 here on the Kerch Peninsula. (Photographer Baltermants' haunting image was suppressed until the 1960s. The photographer had by then added the ominous sky.) Above, a few days later, on a date which will live in infamy, December 7, 1941, sailors surrounded by damaged aircraft watch as a fireball from the bombed destroyer USS *Shaw* billows into the sky above Pearl Harbor. At left, three Americans lie dead on a beach in Papua New Guinea in 1943. LIFE published the photo with the blessing of President Franklin D. Roosevelt. The President had decided the public was growing too complacent about the war, so he lifted the ban on images depicting U.S. casualties.

LEFT **GEORGE STROCK** *RIGHT* **DMITRI BALTERMANTS**

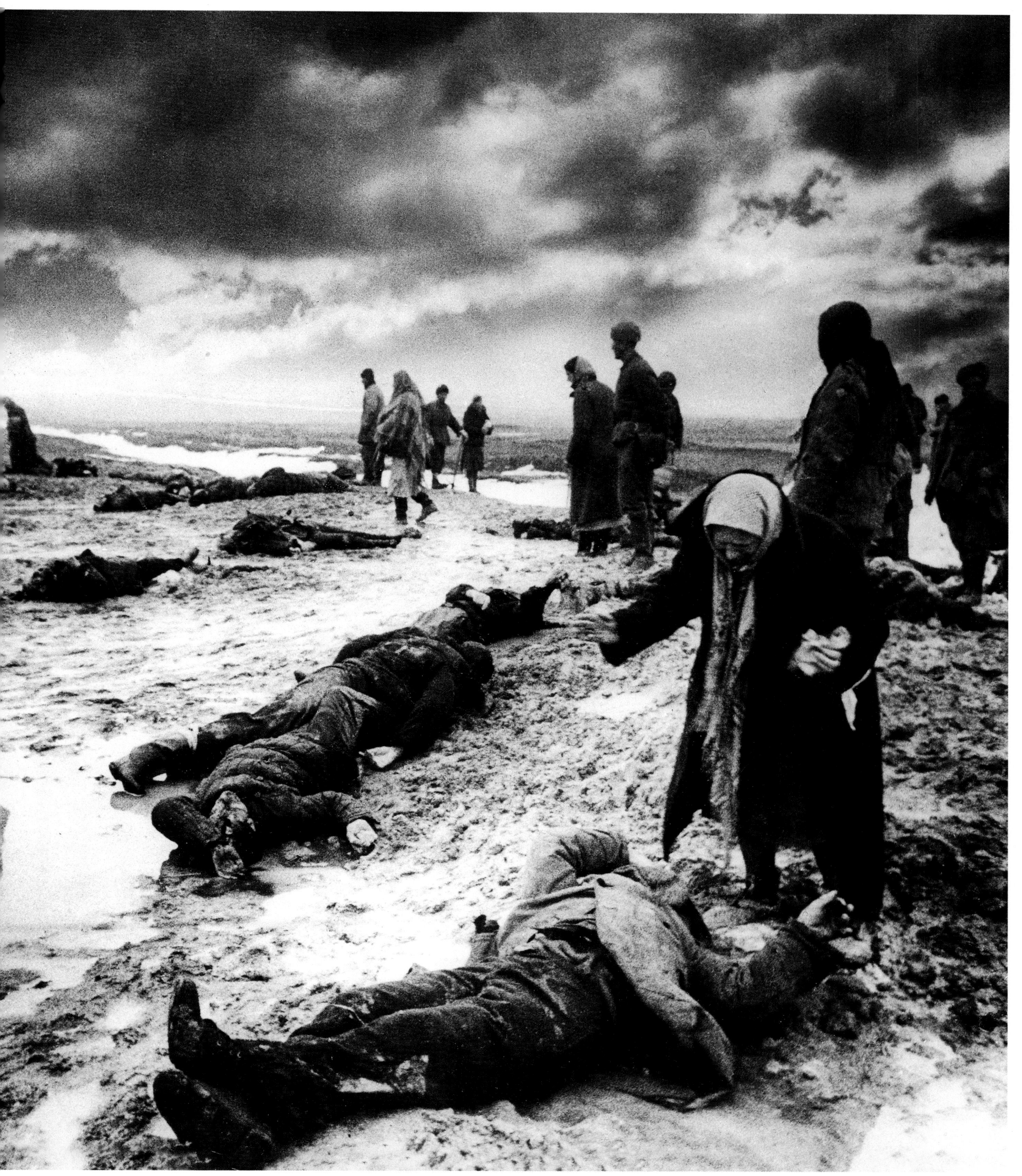

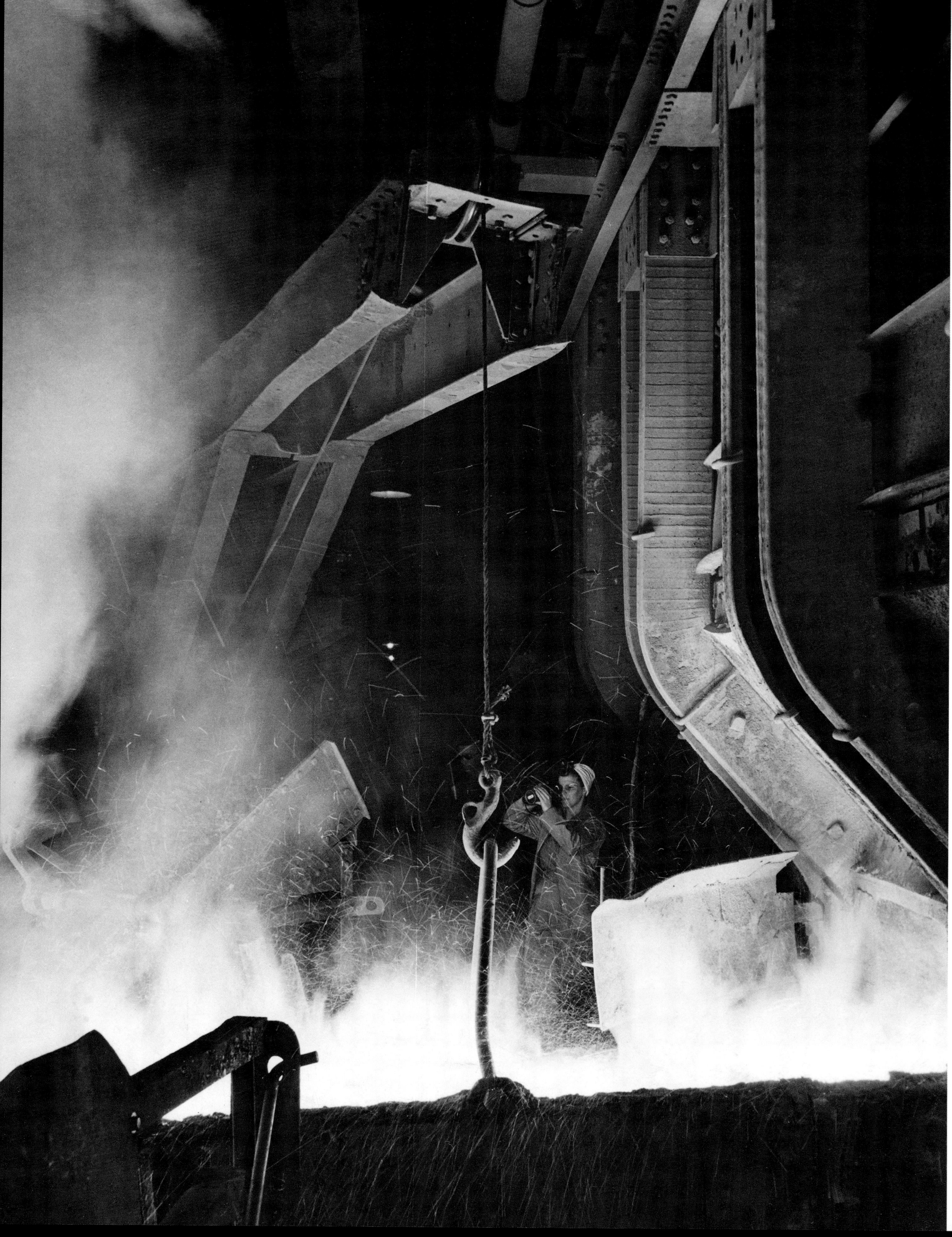

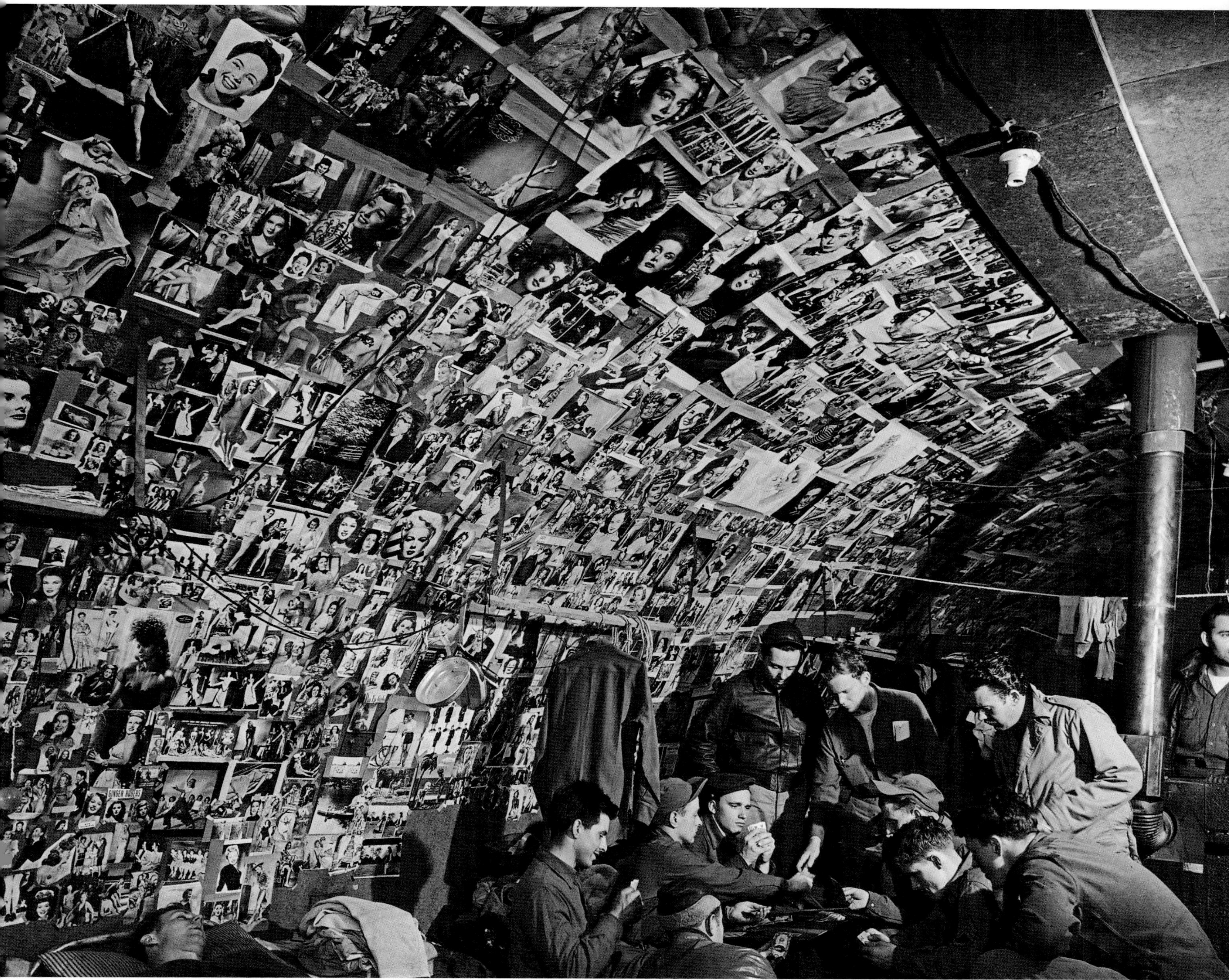

WOMEN AND THE WAR

As men entered the armed forces en masse in the months following Pearl Harbor, hundreds of thousands of women reported for duty at armament plants across America, and before long the nation was quite familiar with "Rosie the Riveter." By the end of the war more than six million women had joined the labor force. Here, in 1943, a female metallurgist peers through an optical pyrometer to determine the temperature of steel in an open-hearth furnace in Gary, Ind. Members of the American bomber crew above, serving in the frigid Aleutian Islands, relax with a game of cards. While they are glad that "Rosie" is taking care of business at home, they reap yet greater solace from the hundreds of pinups that adorn their Quonset hut.

OPPOSITE **MARGARET BOURKE-WHITE** *ABOVE* **DMITRI KESSEL**

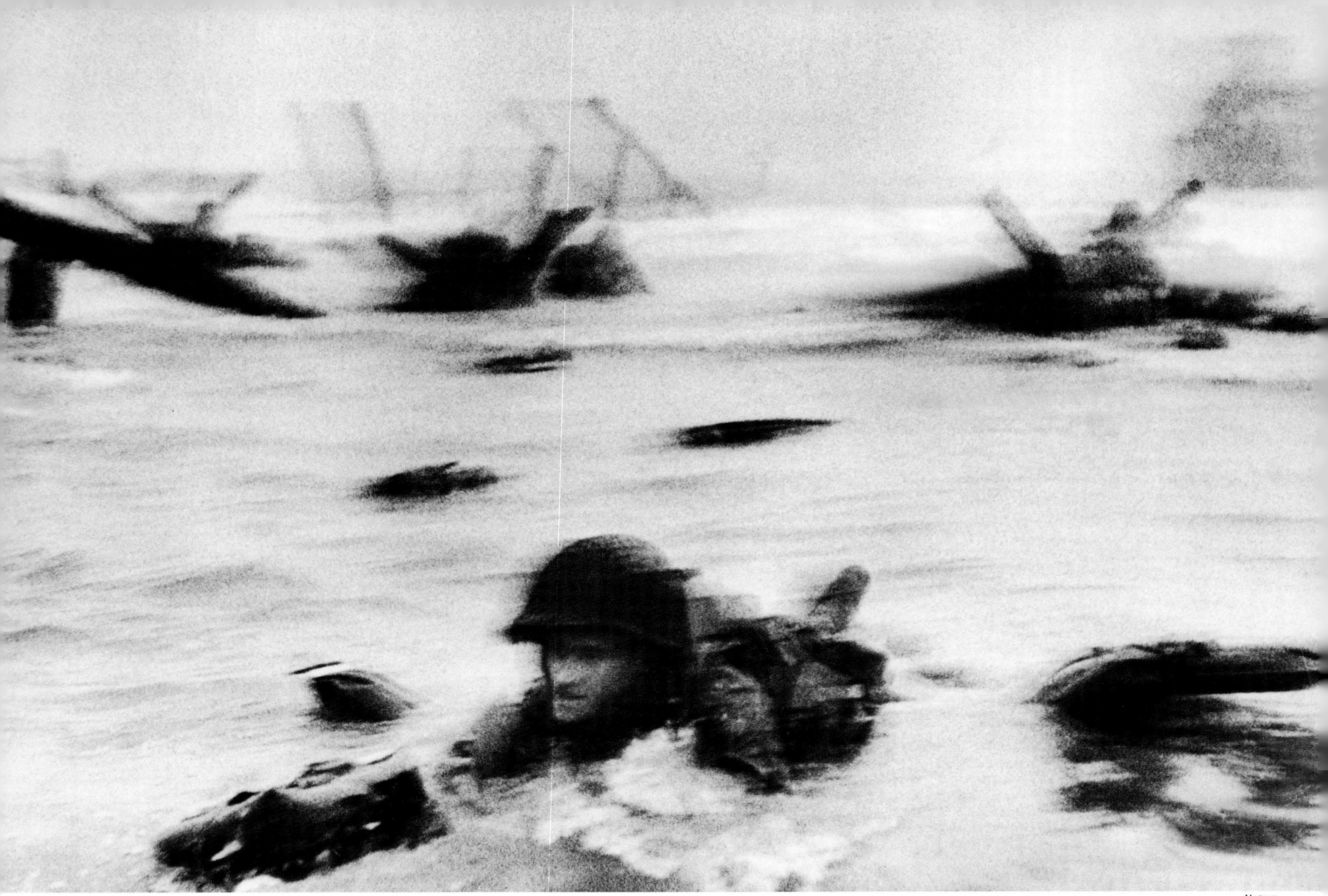

Magnum

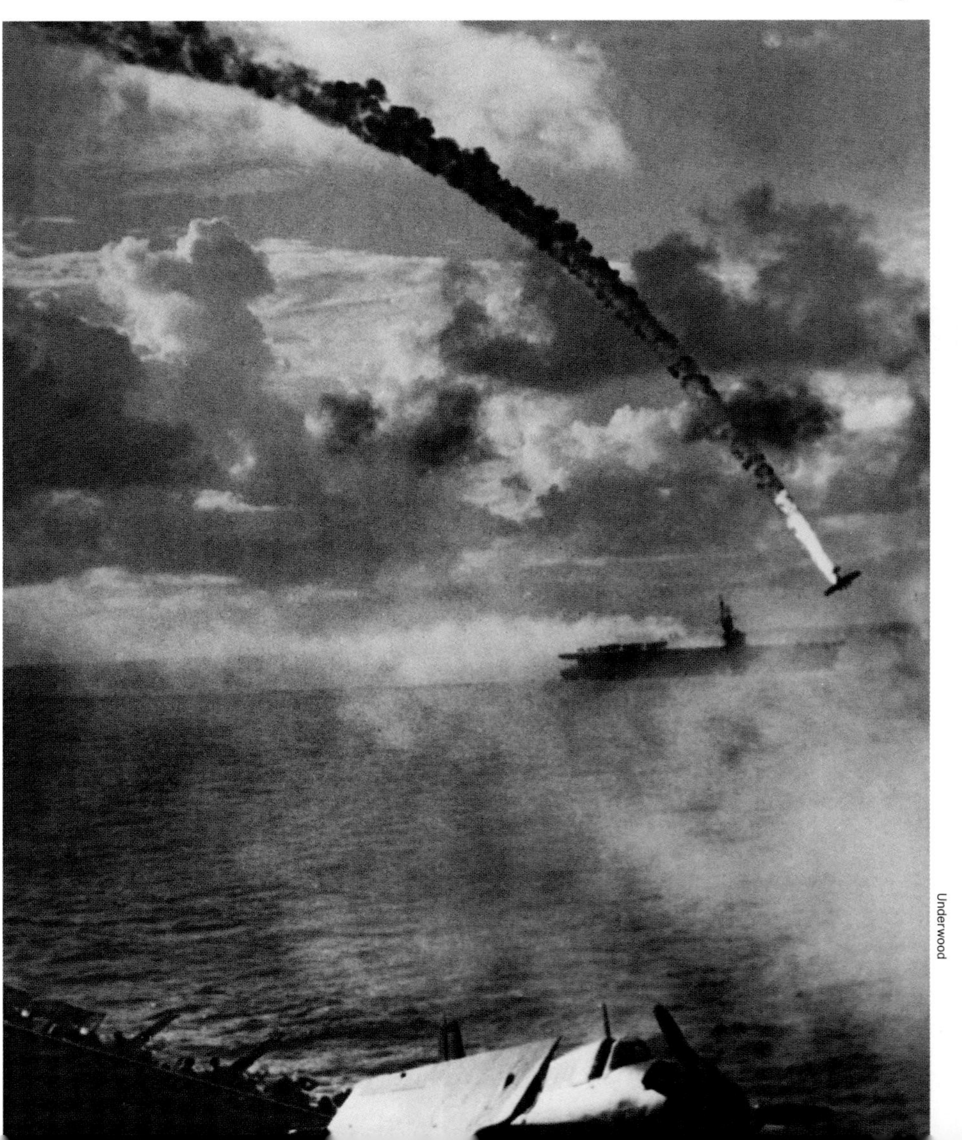

Underwood

THE ALLIES STRIKE BACK

LIFE photographer Capa was with the first wave of troops when they landed in the face of furious resistance at Omaha Beach on D-Day, June 6, 1944. He shot four rolls of film, but a photo assistant in London wrecked all but a dozen images. However, when this soon-to-be-famous picture ran in LIFE a week later, folks at home had a real sense of the perils of that Longest Day. At right, also in 1944, a Japanese torpedo plane goes down in action near Saipan.

ABOVE **ROBERT CAPA**

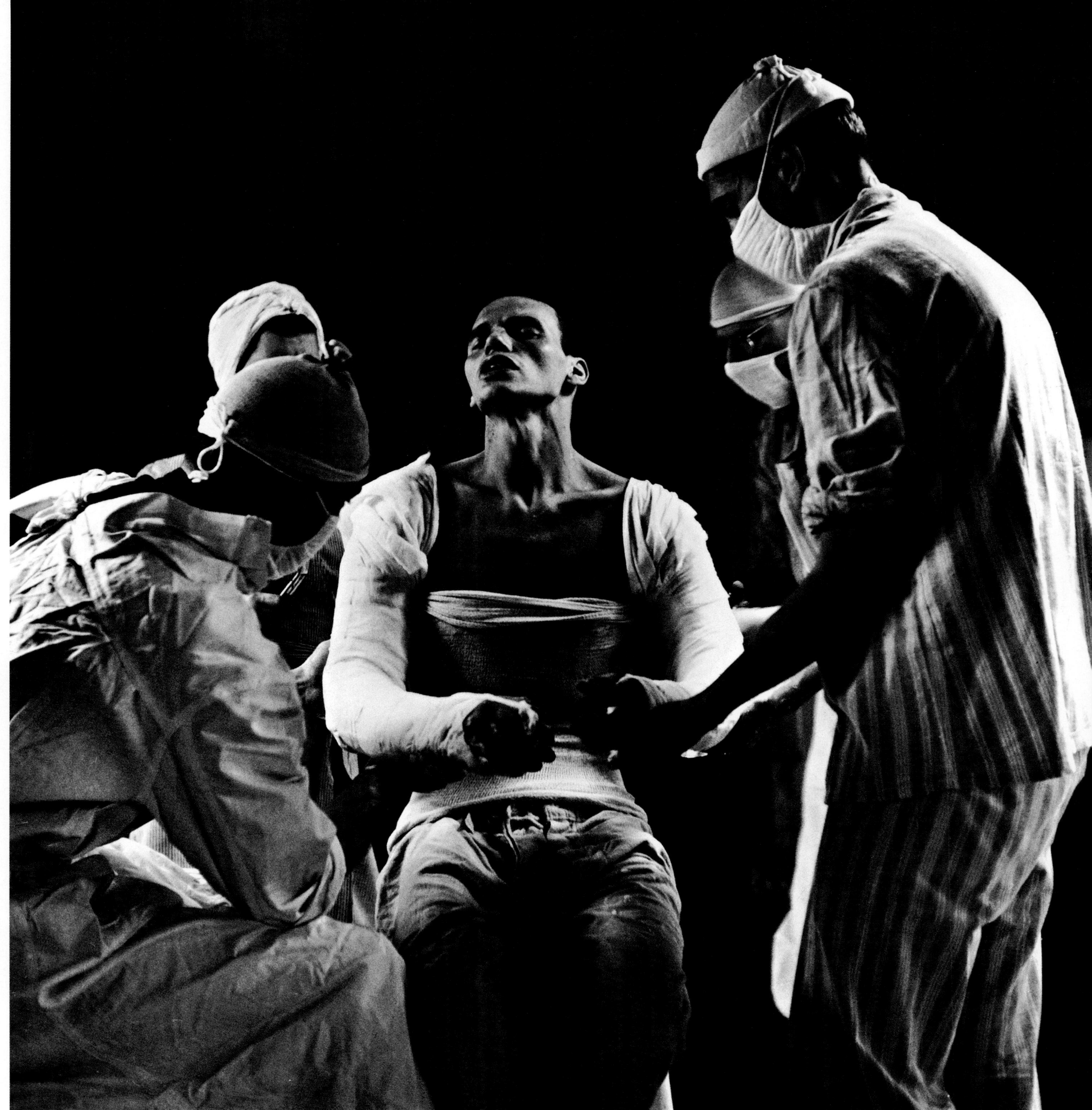

THE WAGES OF WAR

Twenty-two-year-old medic George Lott heard the cries of a wounded man on the battlefield in France on November 22, 1944. Lott hurried to the man, exposing himself to enemy fire, when fragments from a mortar ripped into him. Here, three weeks later, he has been moved to a U.S. Army hospital in England, and surgeons are completing a plaster cast.

RALPH MORSE

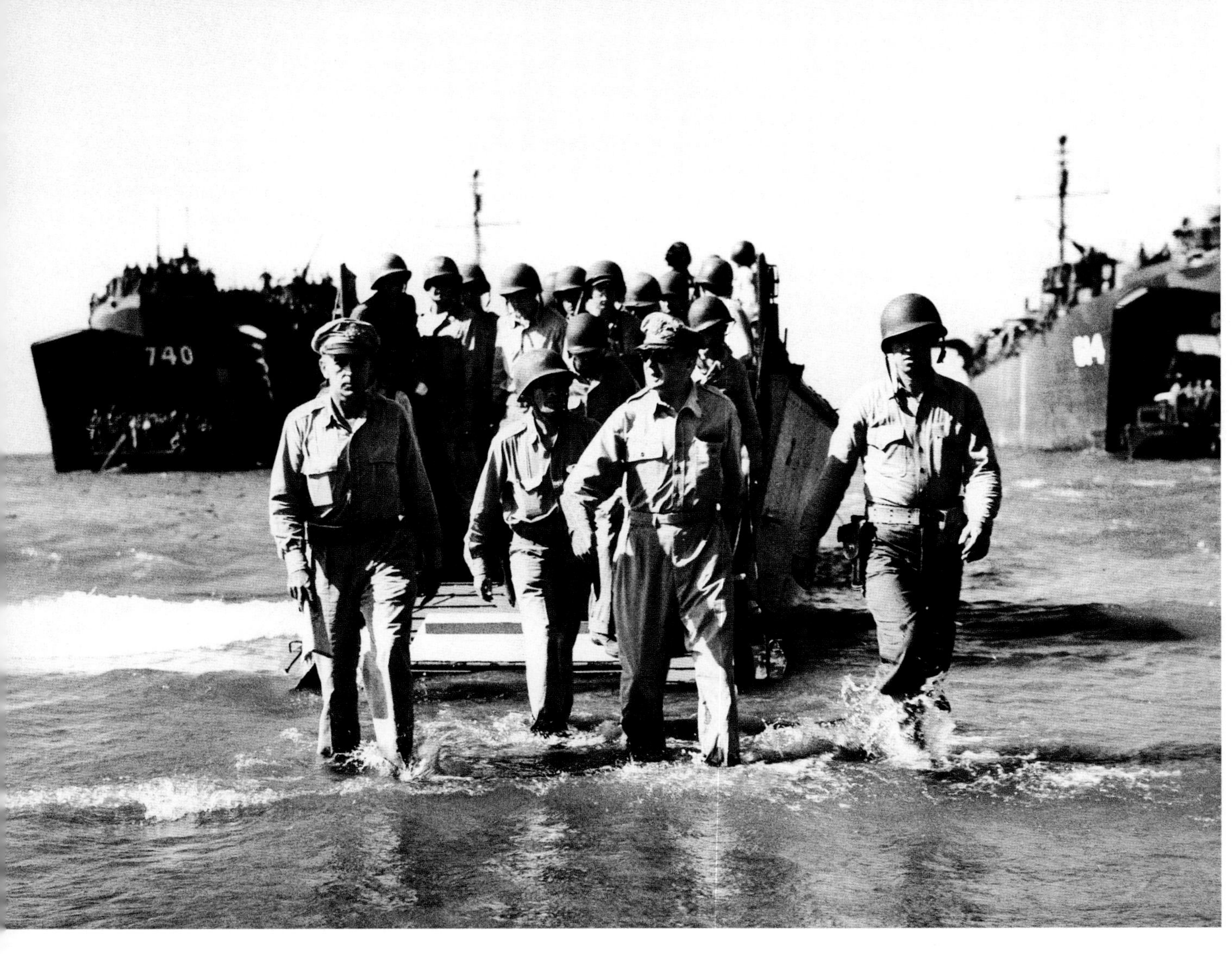

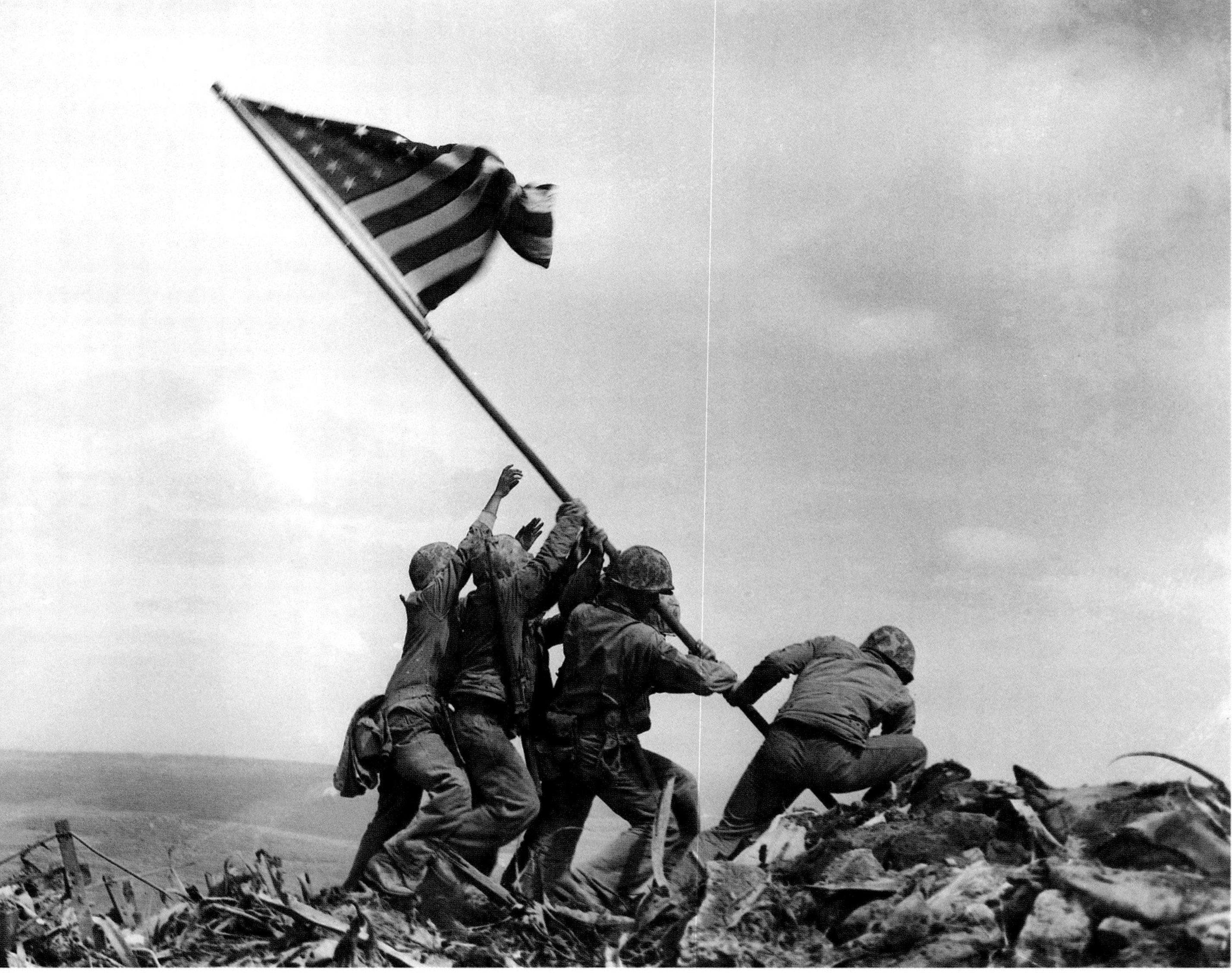

AP

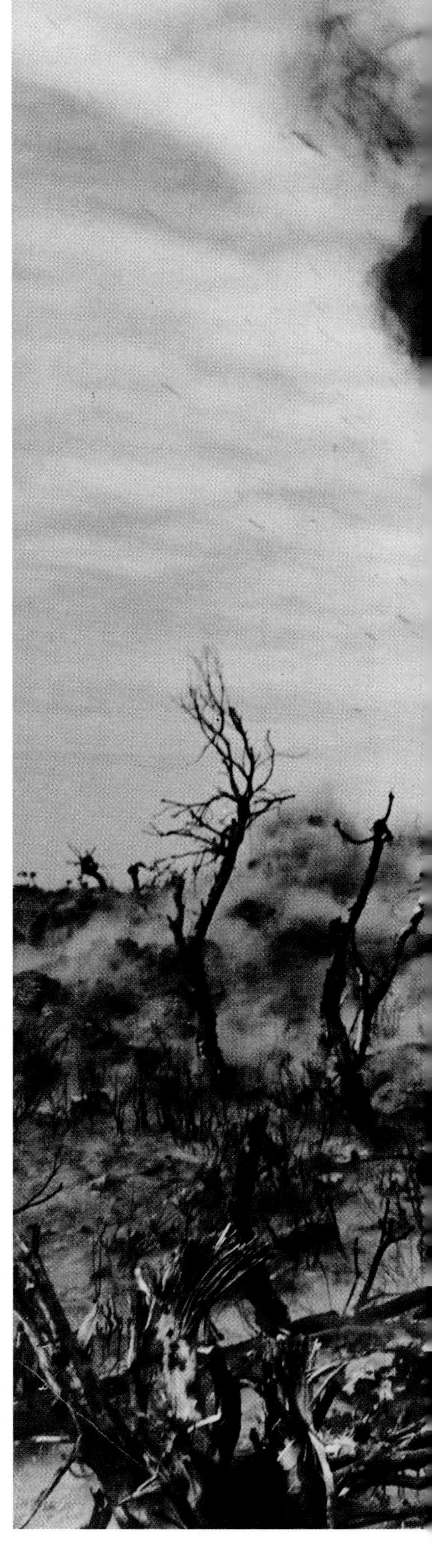

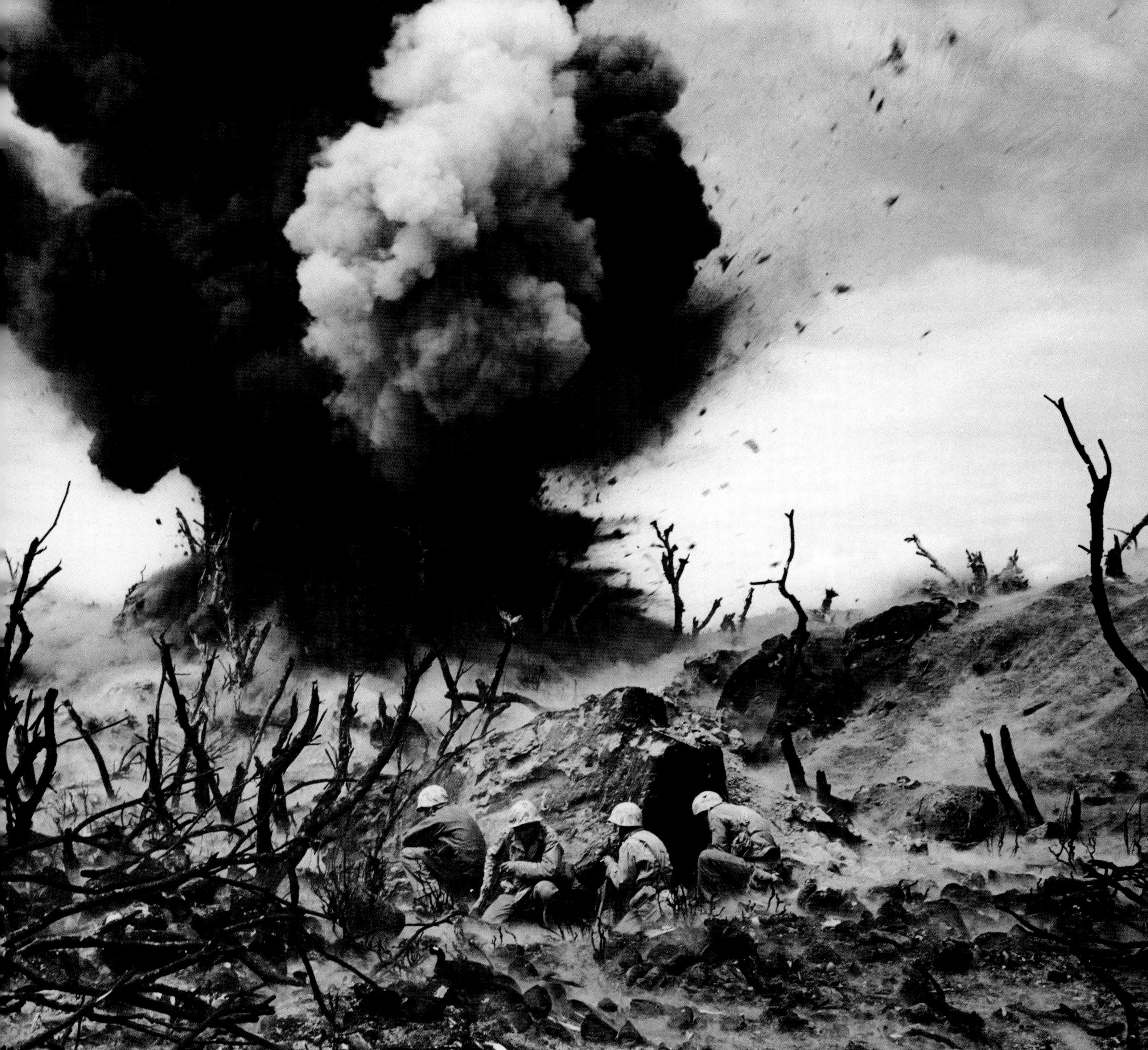

VALOR IN THE PACIFIC

At left are two of the century's most recognizable images. At top, Gen. Douglas MacArthur, who had been driven from the Philippines in March 1942 but declared, "I shall return," did indeed return in October of '44. This photo is invariably used to commemorate that event. However, it was actually taken three months later, at a different beach. The general apparently preferred his commanding mien in this version. In the bottom photo, U.S. Marines raise the flag atop Mount Suribachi on Iwo Jima on February 23, 1945. It has been suggested that this perfect composition was staged, but there is corroborating evidence from a (less sensational) photo taken at the same time by a Marine photographer. Above, Iwo Jima was one of the toughest battles of WWII. Here, Marines blow up a cave connected to a Japanese blockhouse.

OPPOSITE, TOP **CARL MYDANS** *OPPOSITE, LEFT* **JOE ROSENTHAL** *ABOVE* **W. EUGENE SMITH**

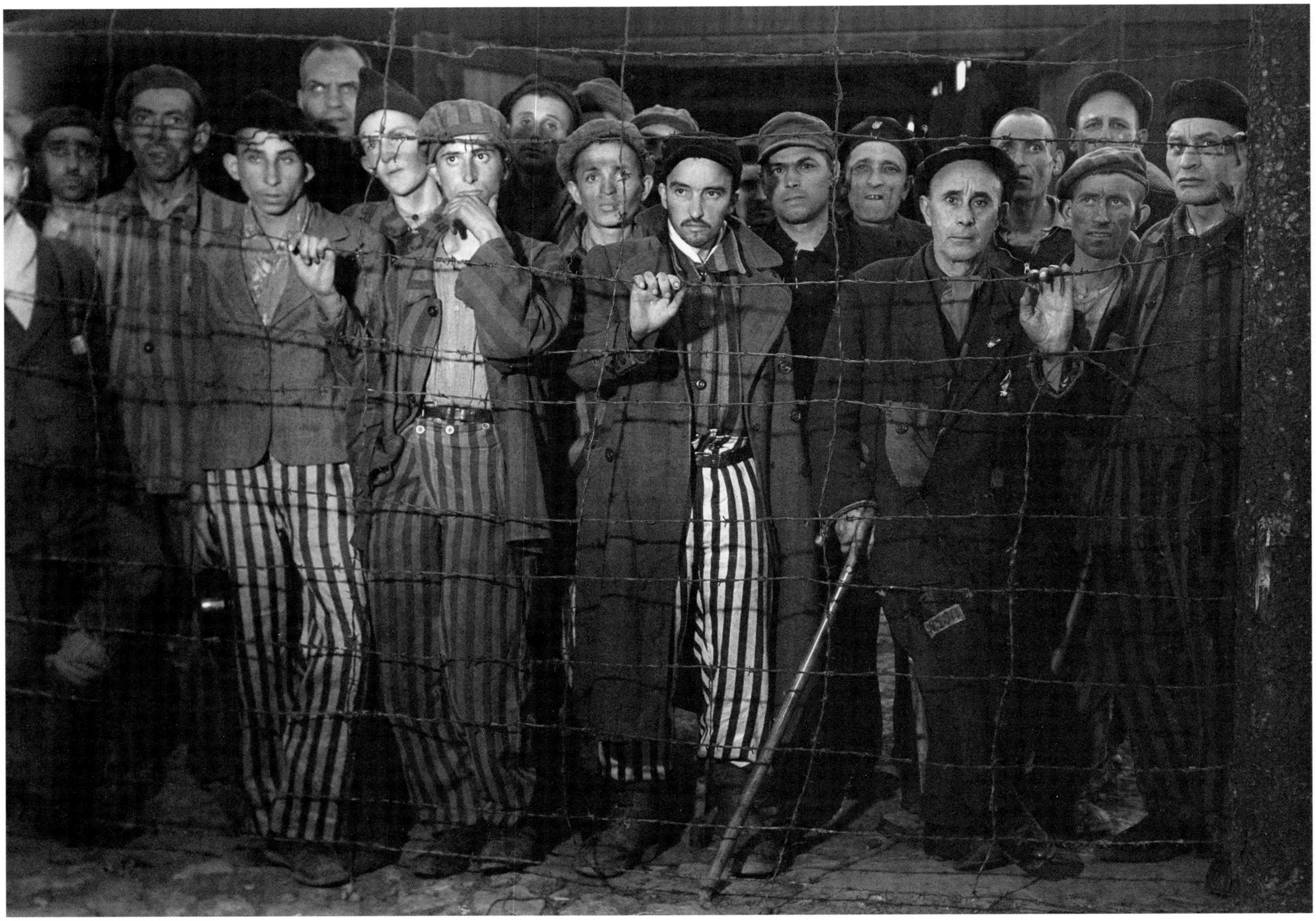

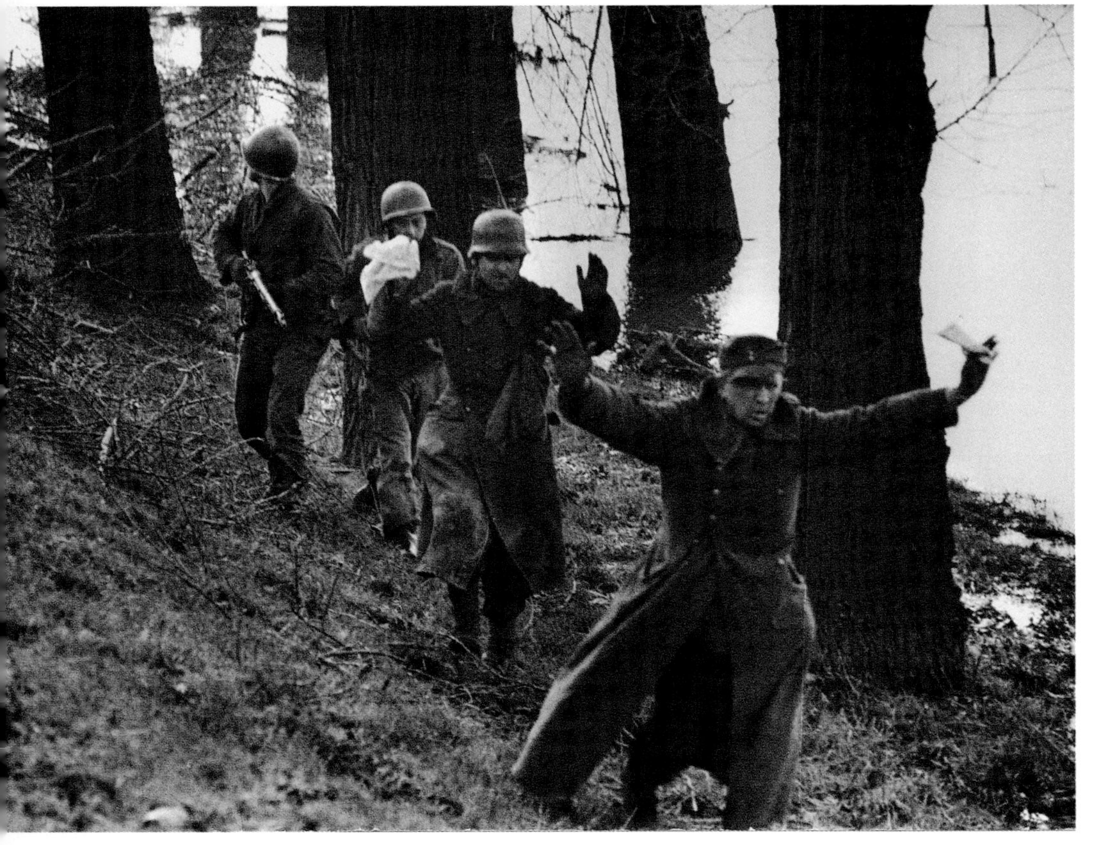

THE FINAL DAYS

As 1945 progressed, it was apparent that the Allies would win the war, but there was still plenty of time for misery. At left, an American soldier escorts German prisoners along the banks of the Roer River in March. The German forces were in tatters, but danger lurked everywhere. The terrible image above was taken at Buchenwald in April. Photographer Bourke-White was with Gen. George Patton's troops when they liberated the concentration camp. Her pictures were proof that the rumored Nazi atrocities against the Jews were true. At right, on August 10, one day after an atomic bomb blasted Nagasaki, a mother and son, rice balls in hand, wander through the devastation.

ABOVE **MARGARET BOURKE-WHITE** *LEFT* **GEORGE SILK** *OPPOSITE* **YOSUKE YAMAHATA**

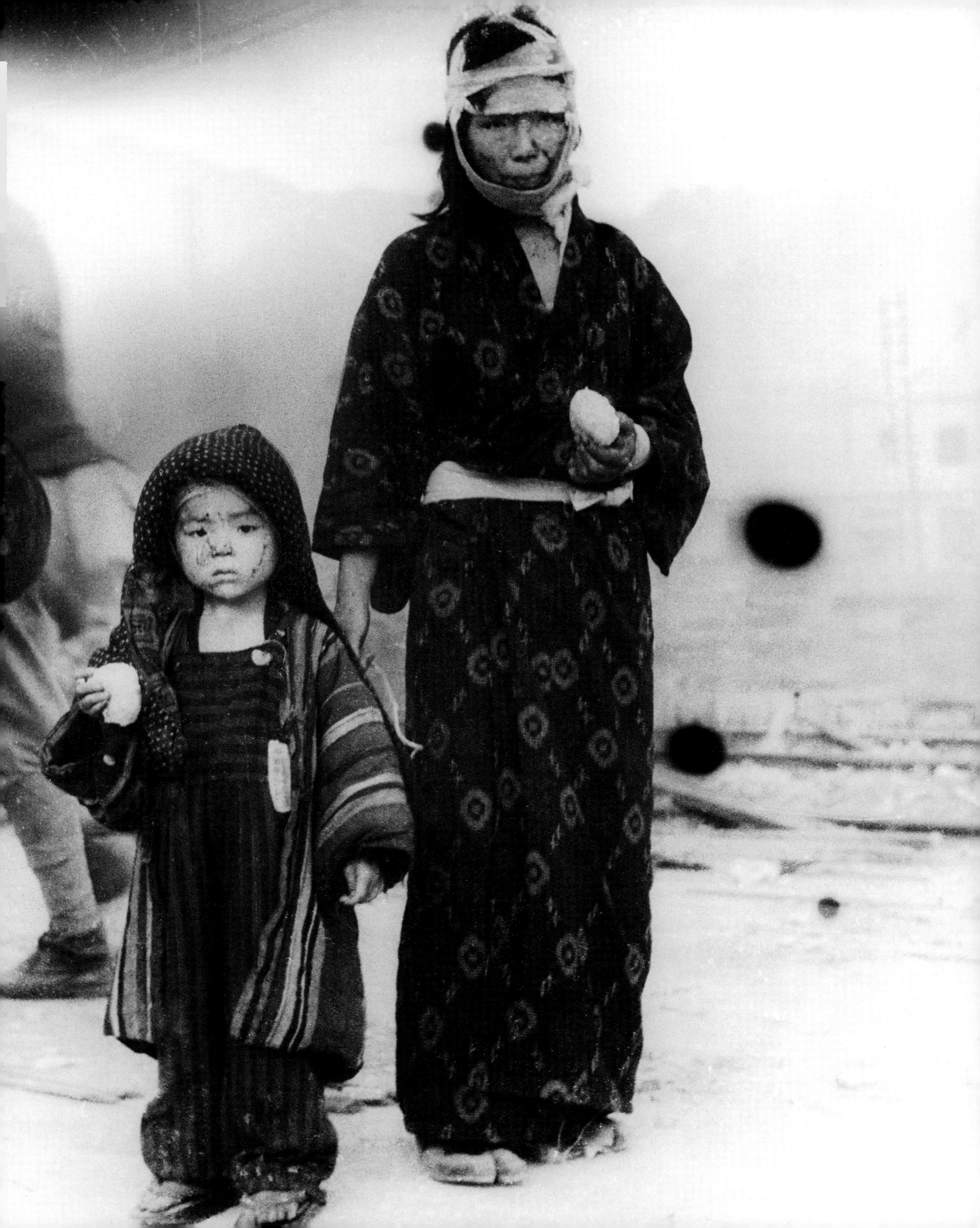

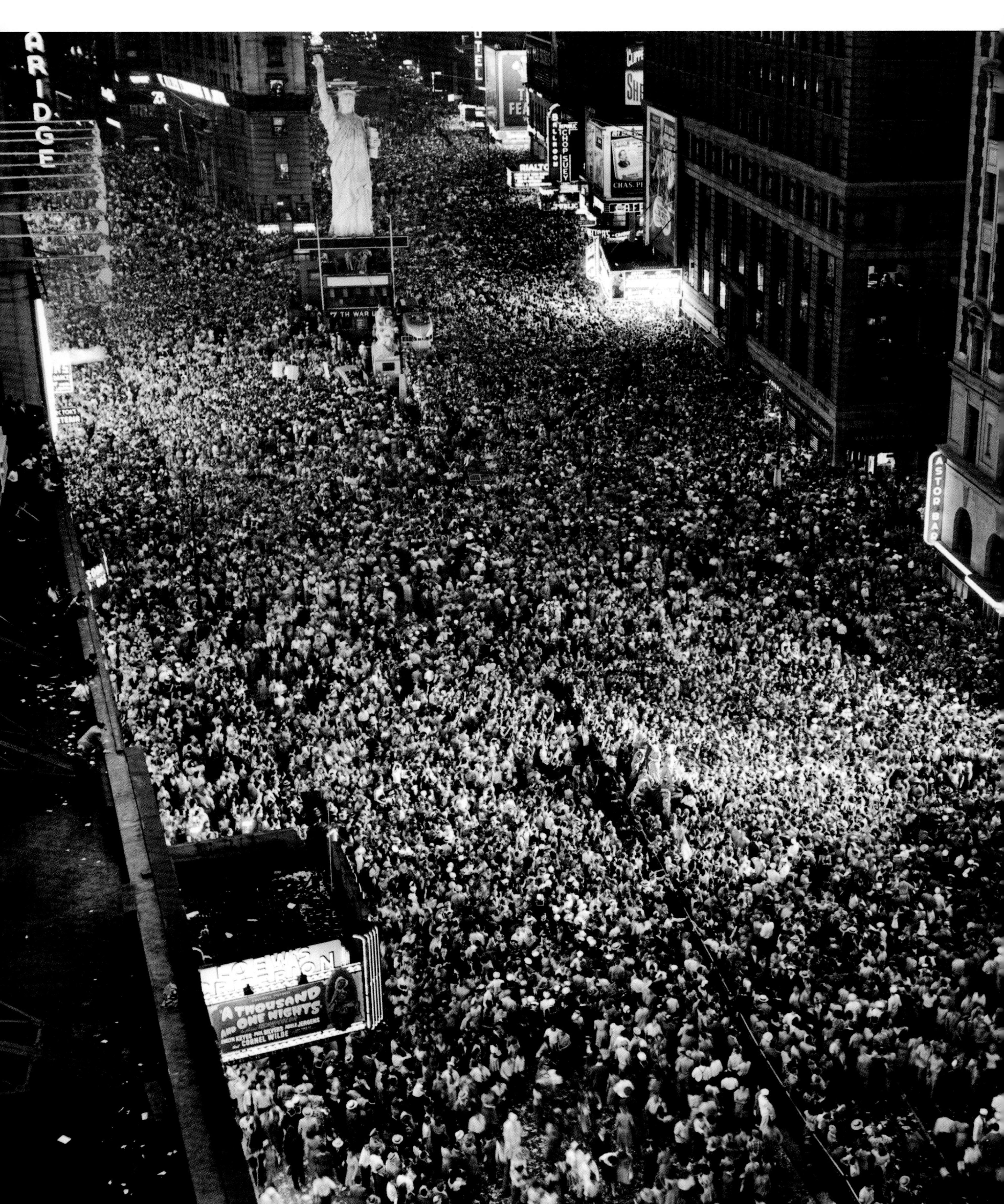
RIDGE
BALLROOM
CHOP SUEY
RIALTO
CHAS. P
CAFE
7TH WAR
ASTOR BAR
A THOUSAND AND ONE NIGHTS
CORNEL WILDE

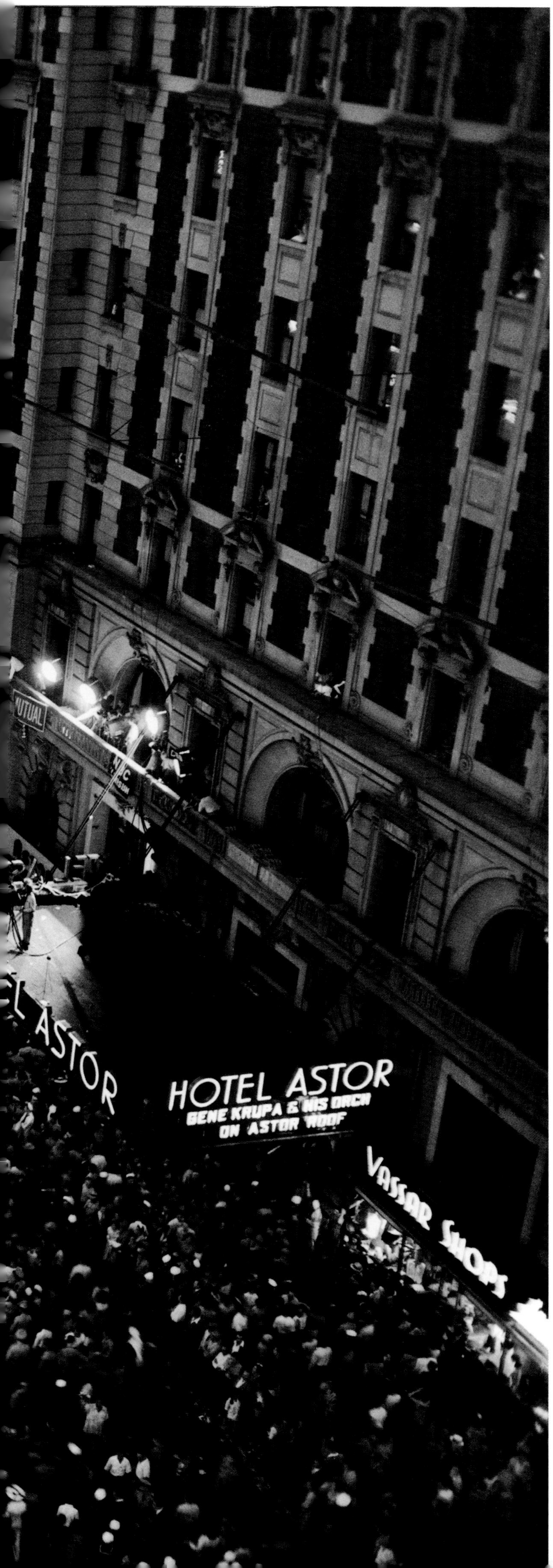

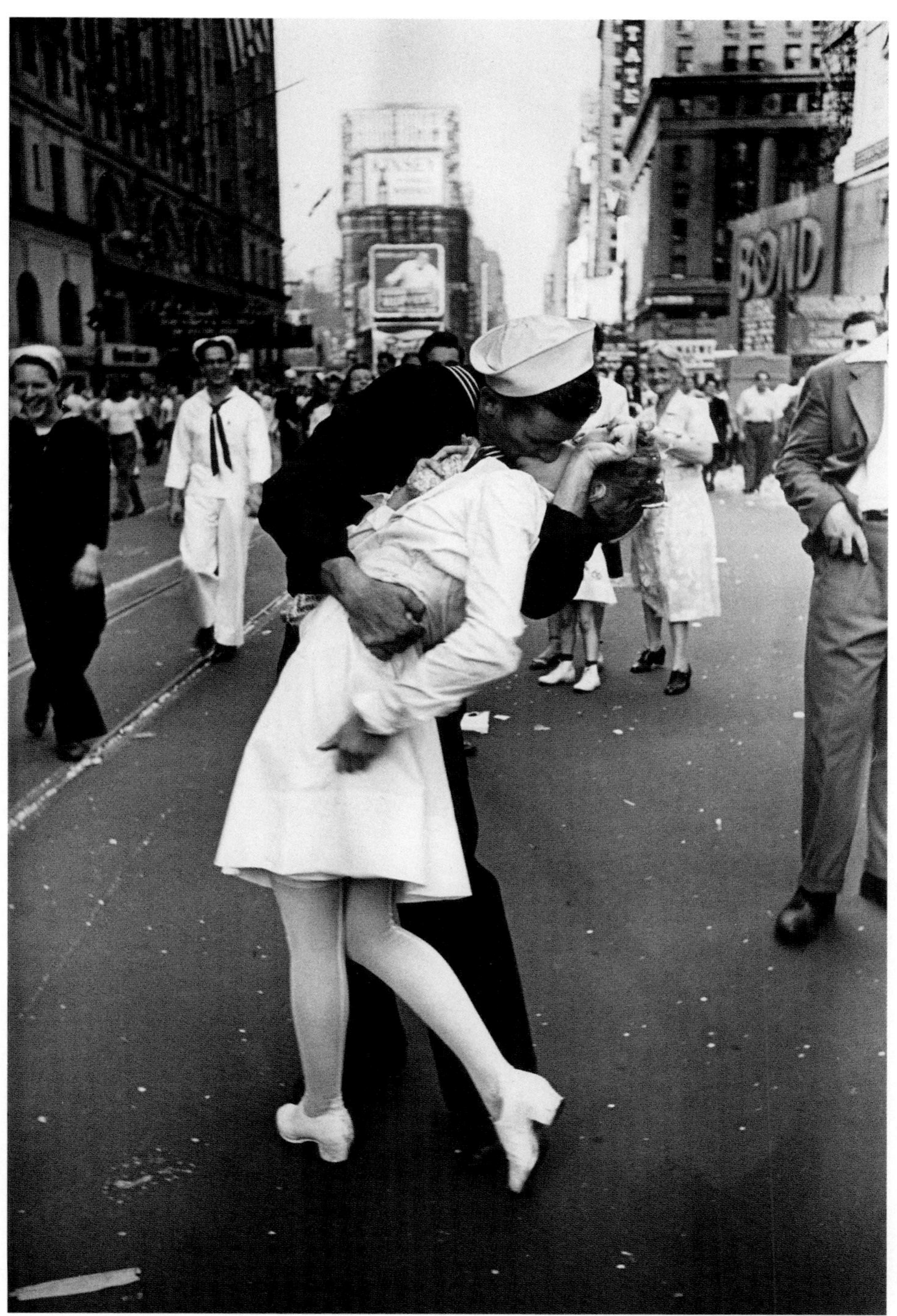

V-J DAY

It had been a long, dreadful struggle, but on August 14, 1945, victory in Japan could at last be celebrated. Above, Times Square in New York City is the setting for what we call The Picture. Said photographer Eisenstaedt, "There were thousands of people milling around, in side streets and everywhere. Everybody was kissing each other . . . I didn't even know what was going on until [the sailor] grabbed something in white. And I stood there, and they kissed. And I snapped five times." At left, two million people fill Times Square that night, a gathering truly to be remembered.

LEFT **HERBERT GEHR** *ABOVE* **ALFRED EISENSTAEDT**

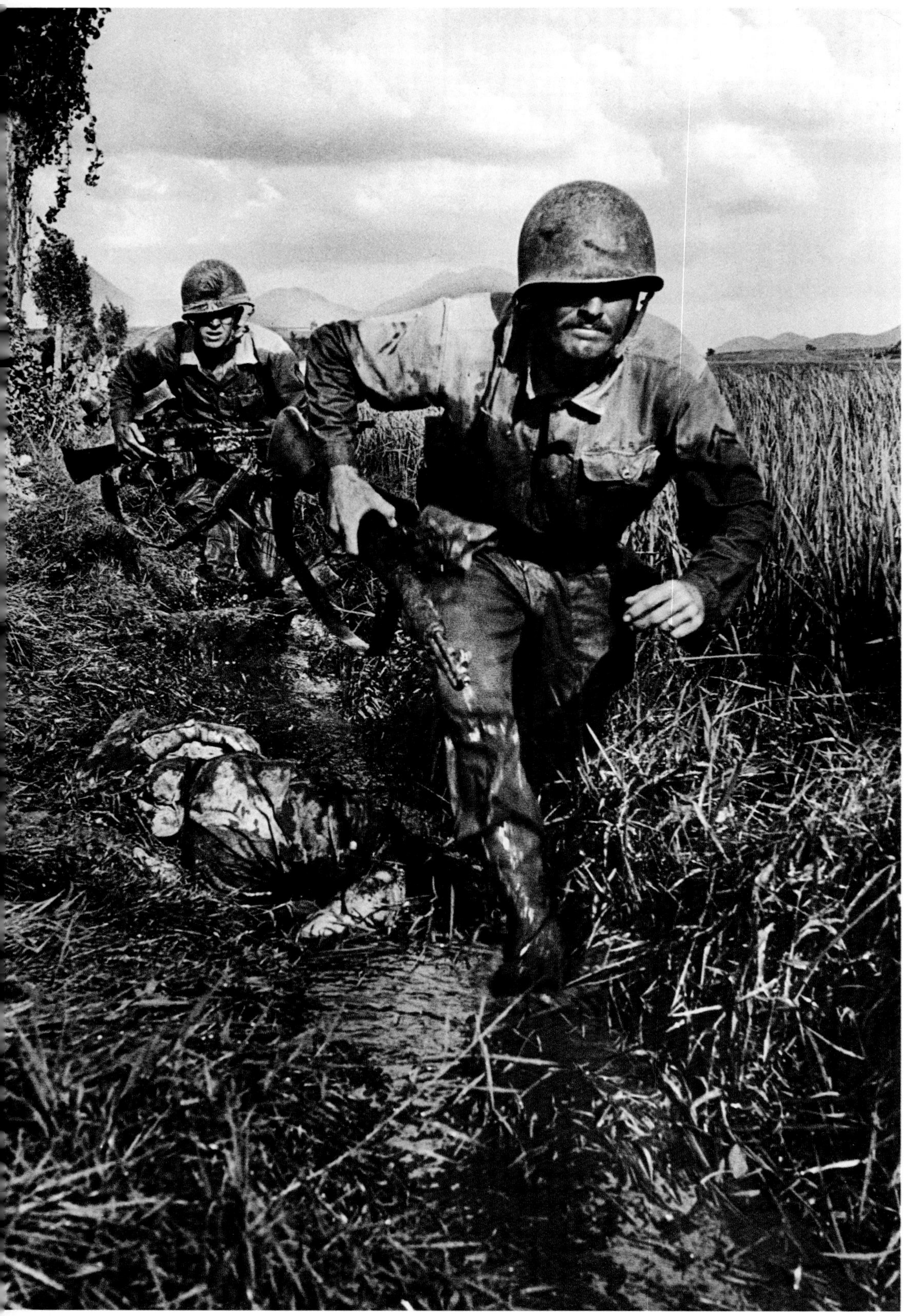

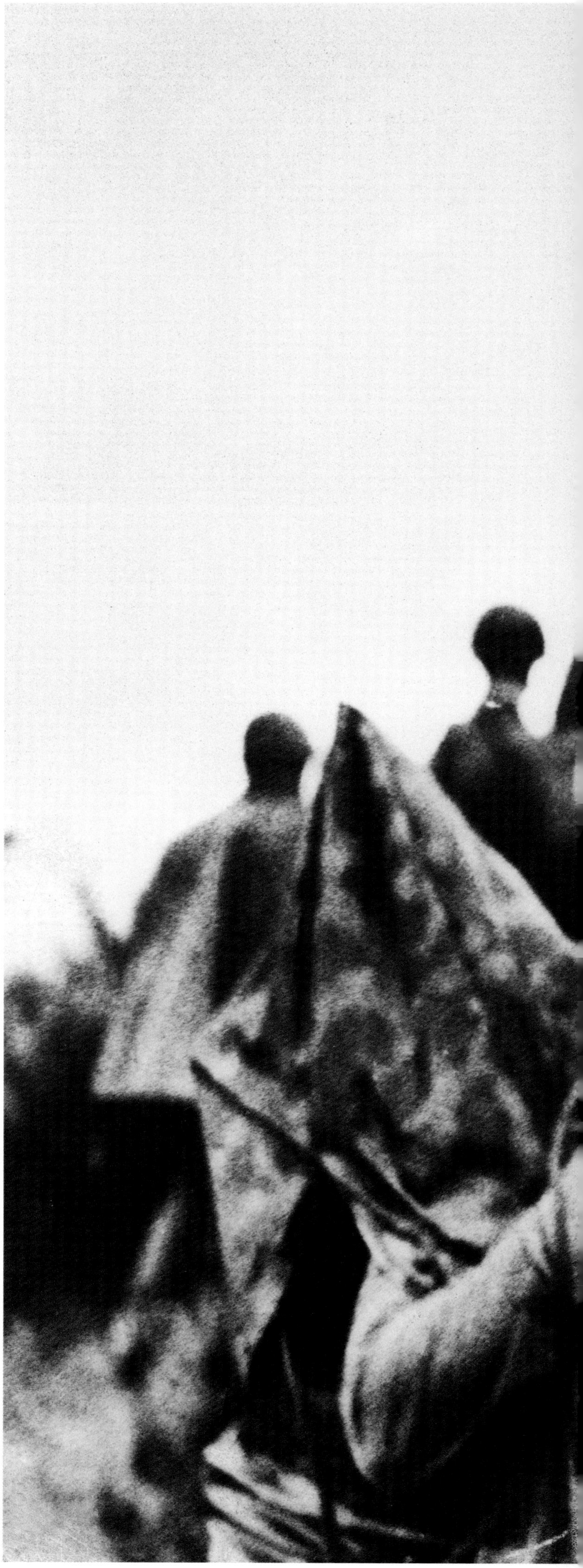

KOREA

It was only five years earlier that Americans were fighting a brutal war in Asia, then in 1950 it was time to go back, this time to Korea, to take on the North Koreans and the Chinese. There wasn't as much glory attached to this war, but there was a lot of suffering. At right, in the midst of an enemy counterattack, Marine Capt. Francis "Ike" Fenton has just learned that his company has lost radio contact and is out of ammunition. Supplies later arrived, and the men held their position. Above, Marines advance past an enemy corpse.

DAVID DOUGLAS DUNCAN (2)

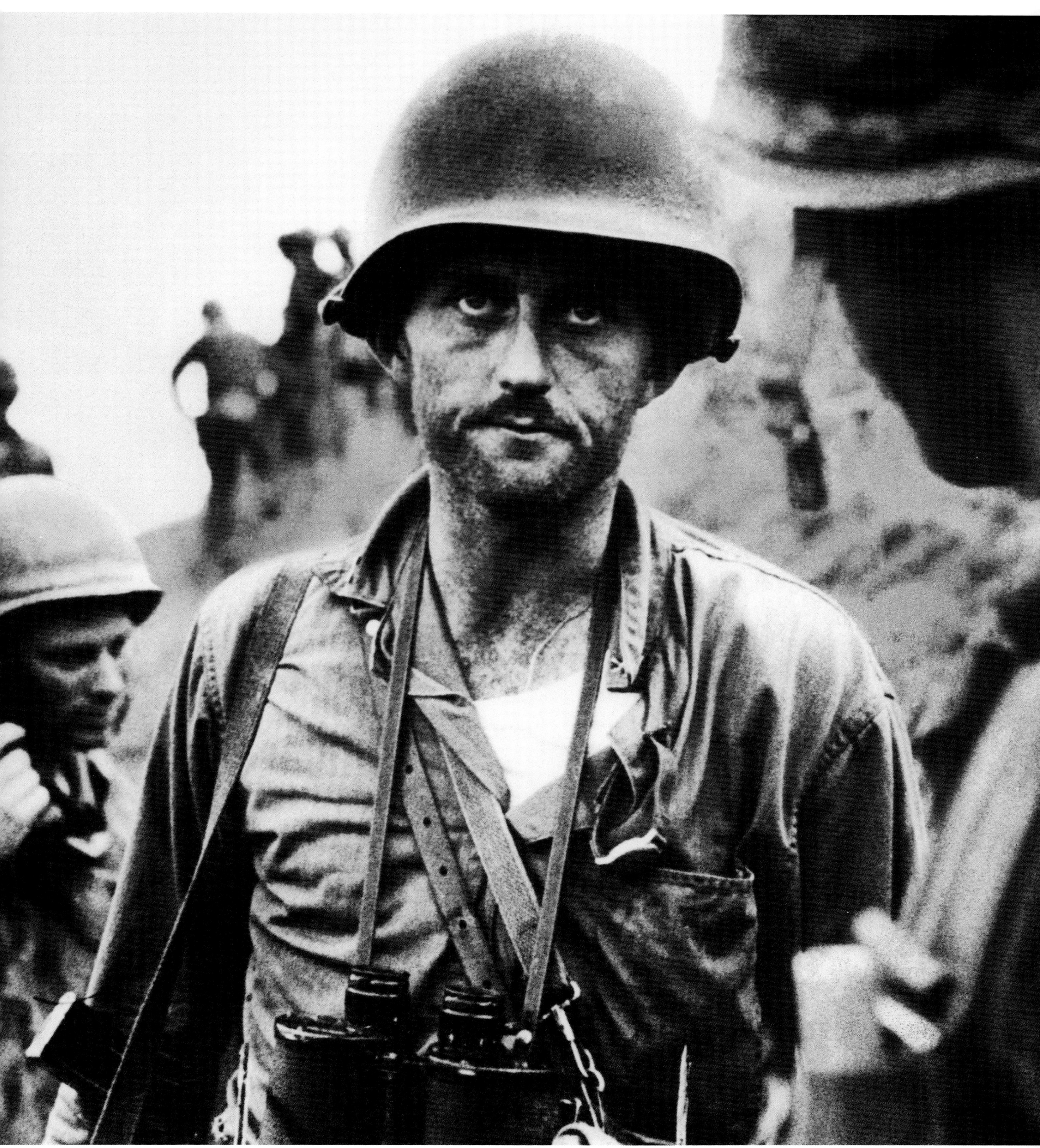

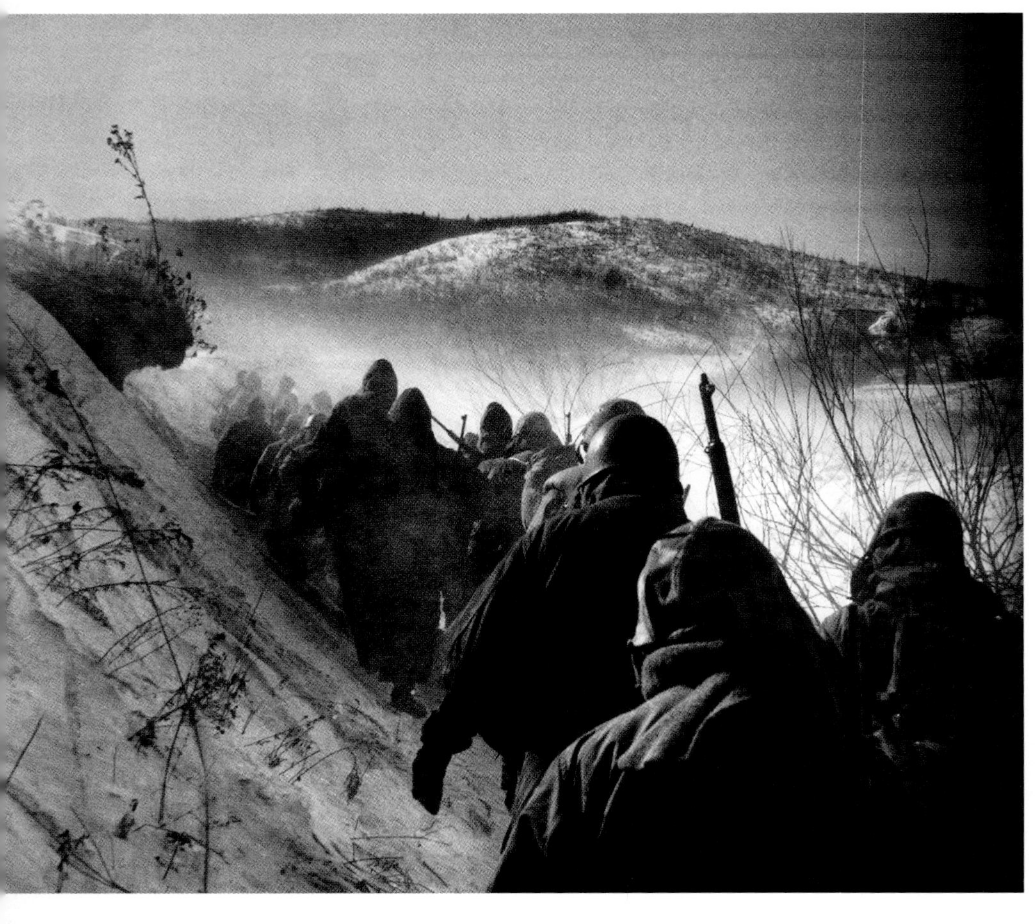

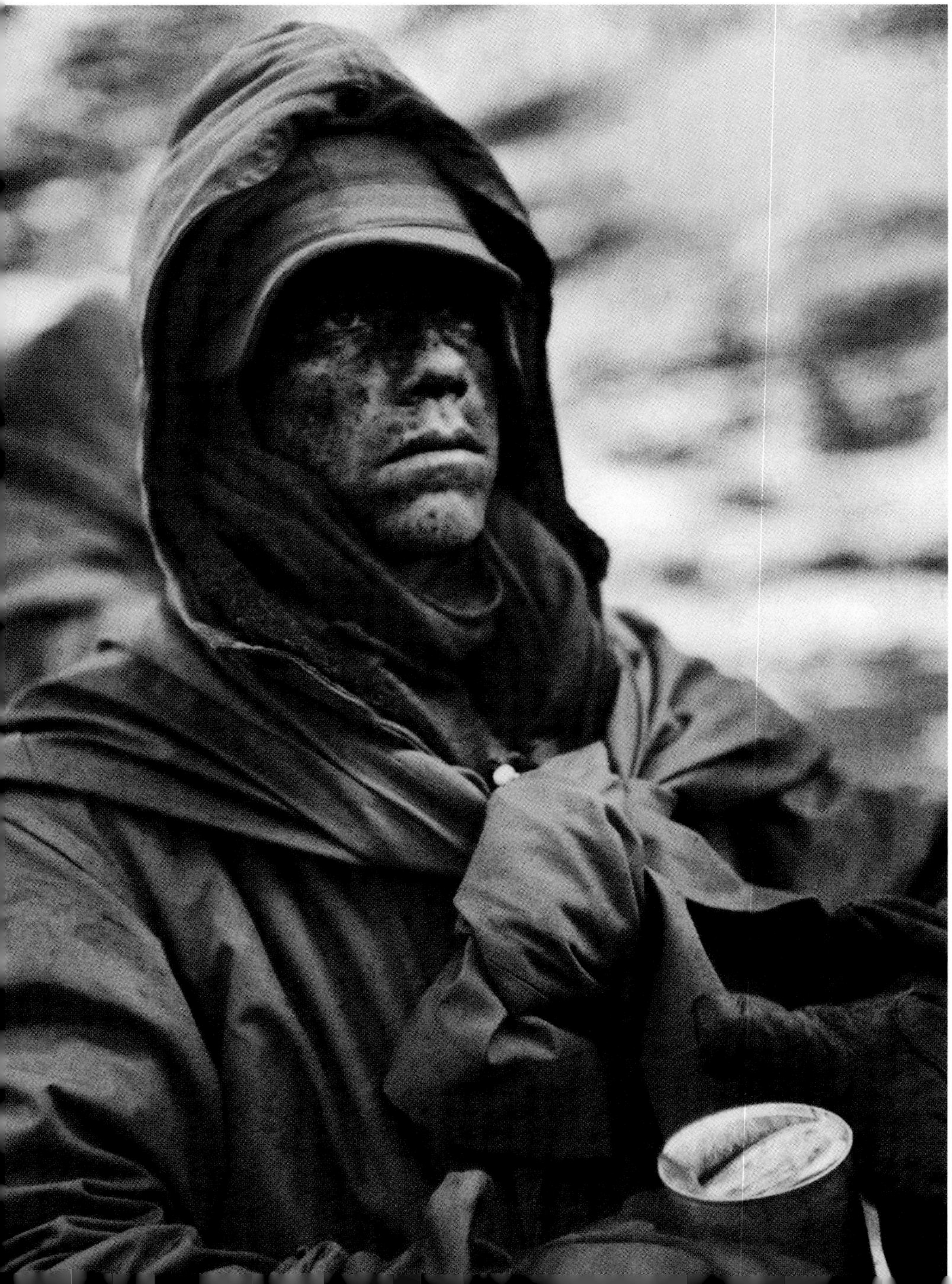

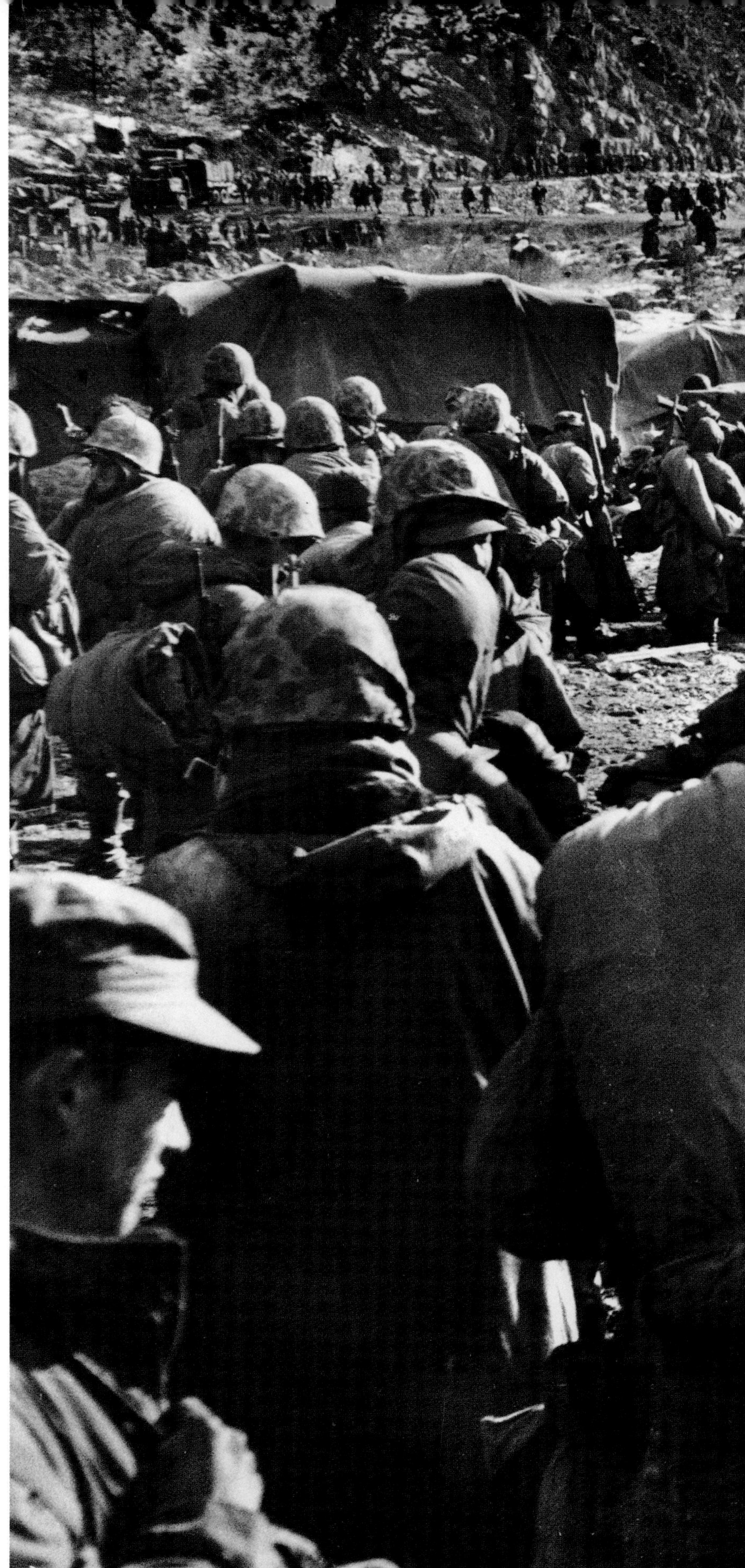

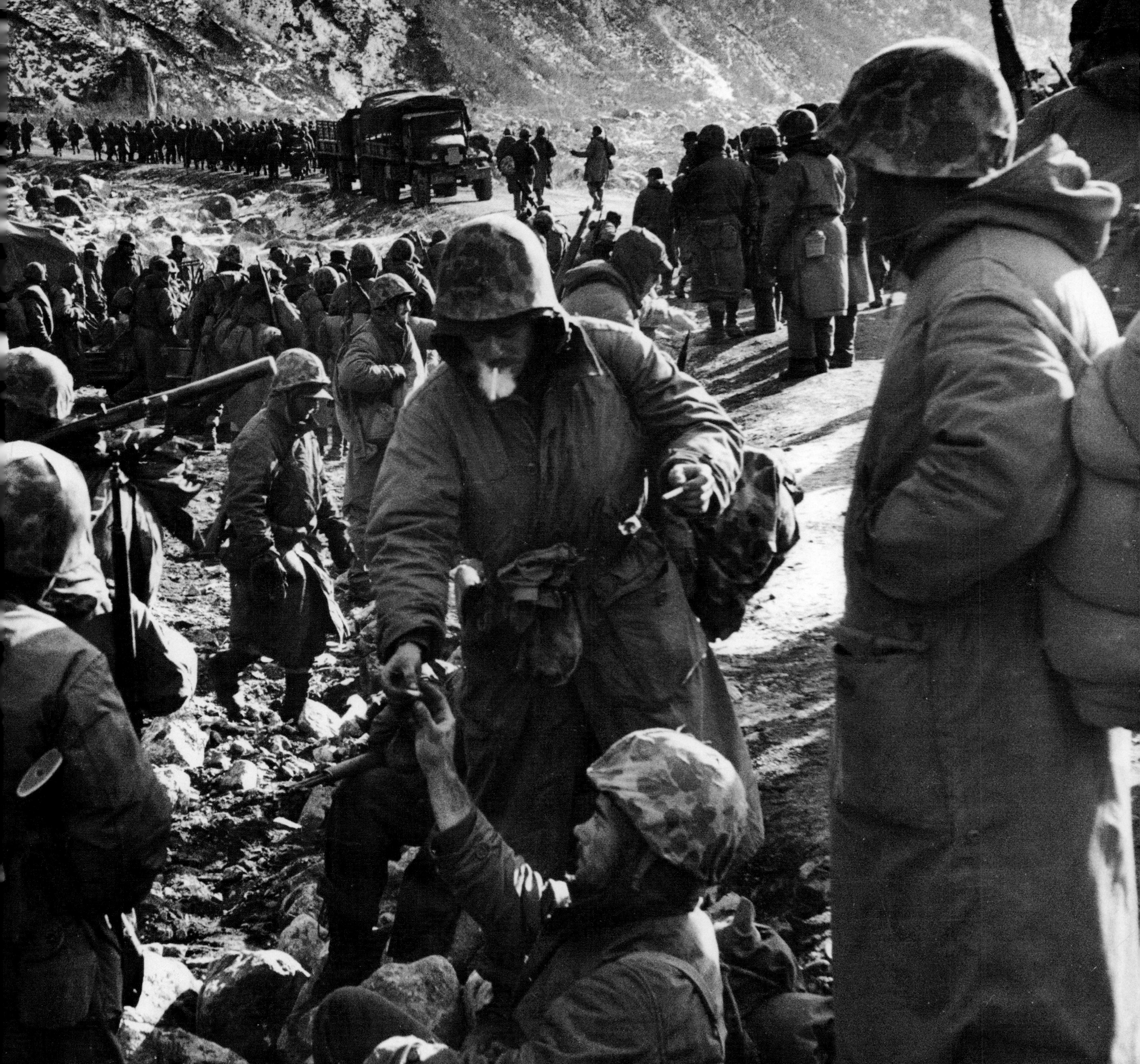

A WEARYING COLD

Photographer Duncan had joined the Marines during World War II and was the preeminent photographer of the Korean War. These pictures were taken in December 1950, as Marines made a long retreat from the Changjin Reservoir, where they had been cut off by the Chinese. Clockwise from left: This man shows the strain of fighting against heavy odds with minimal rations; heads bent against the bitter weather, Marines make their way along "Nightmare Alley"; after surviving Nightmare Alley, there is time for a smoke.

DAVID DOUGLAS DUNCAN (3)

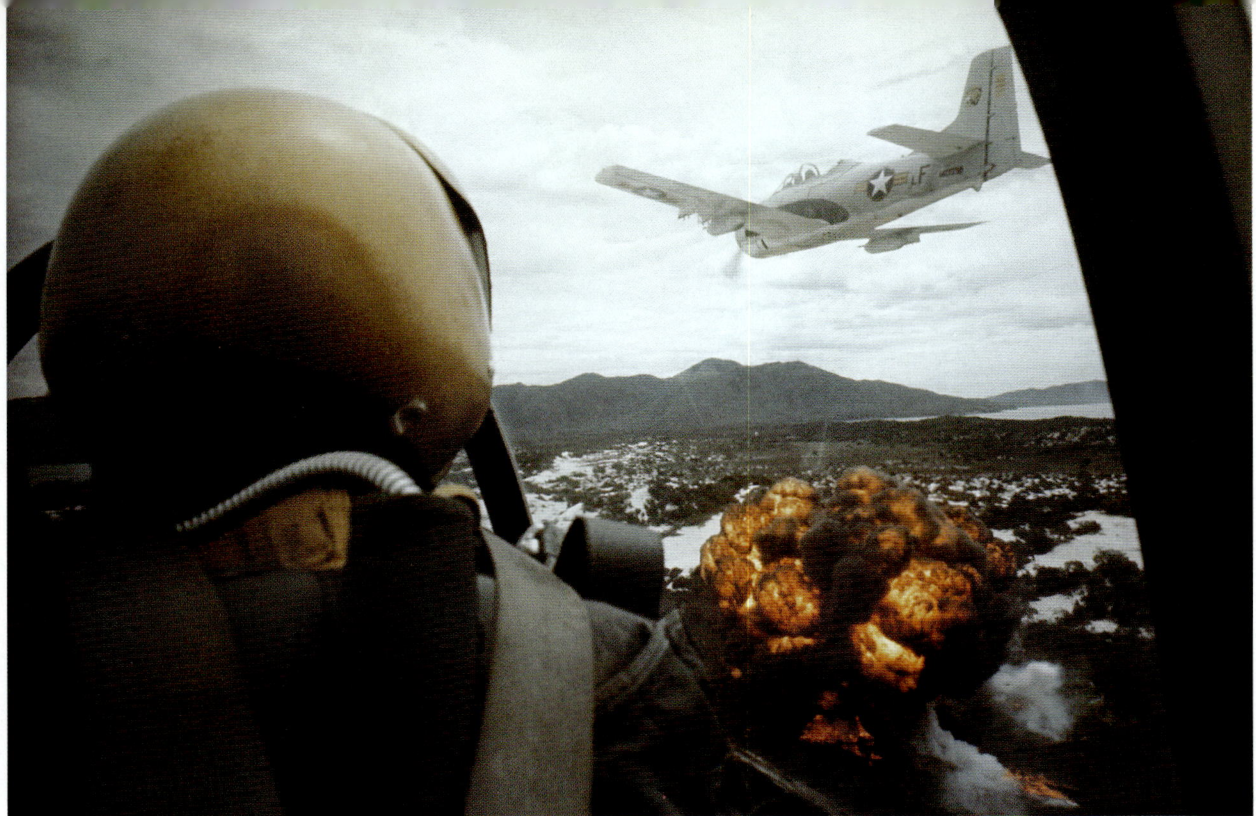

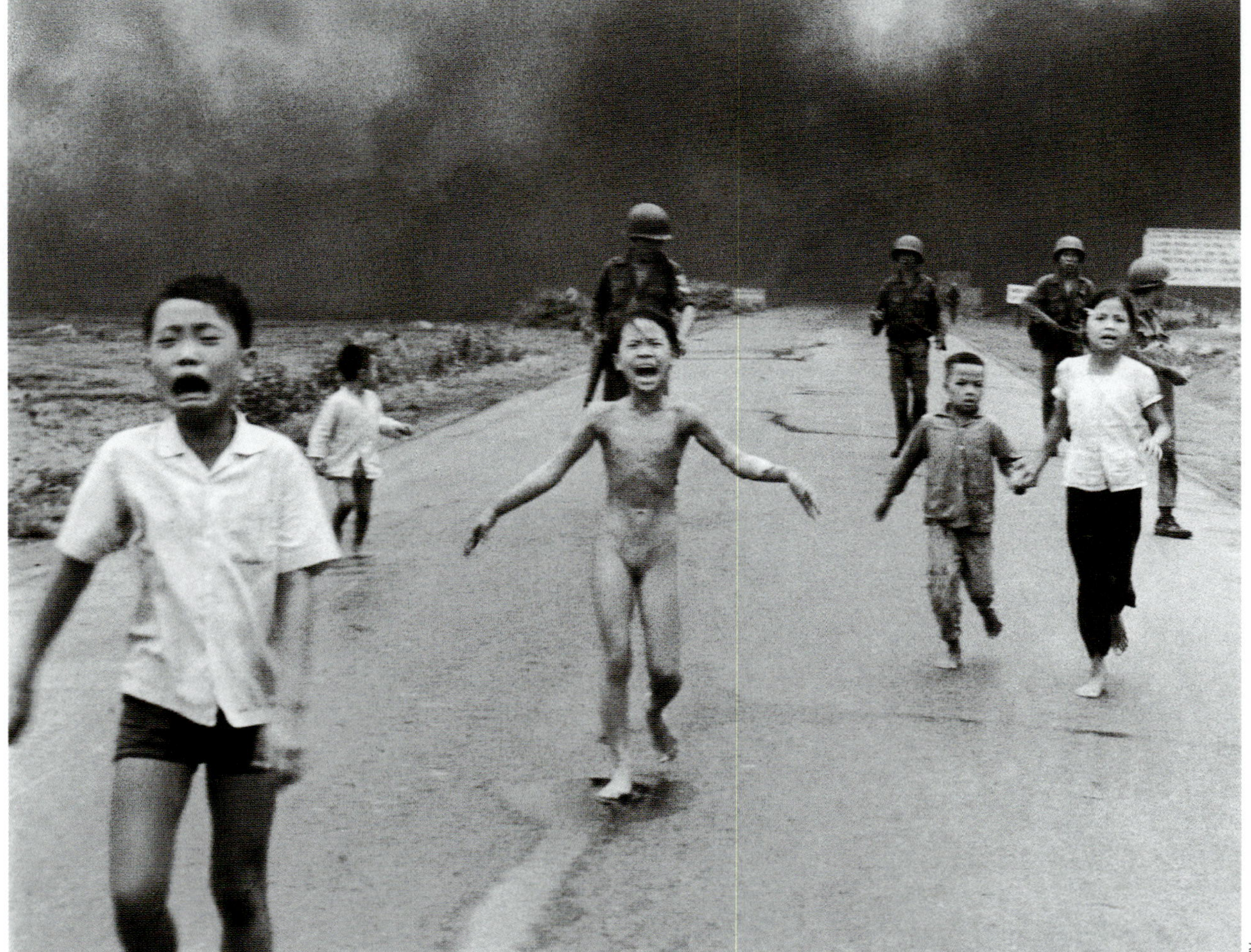

AP

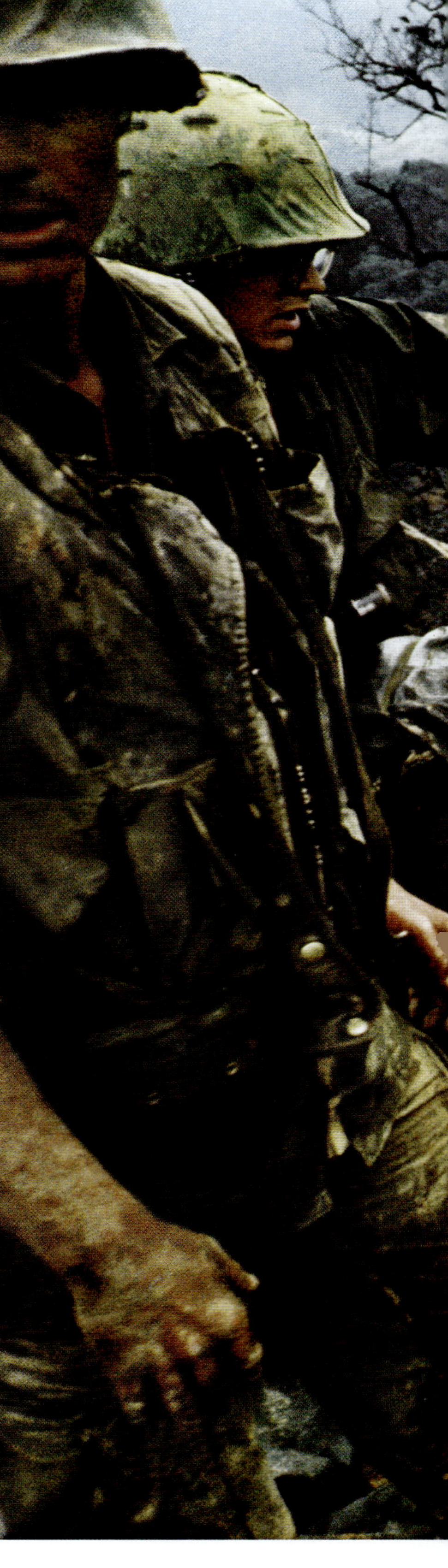

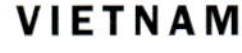

VIETNAM

In the photo at top, an American jet is releasing napalm over a Vietcong position early in the Vietnam War. This picture was taken by Larry Burrows, the LIFE photographer who exhibited unflagging courage and tenacity during the course of the war until his death in a helicopter crash in Laos in 1971. The picture above was taken by AP photographer Ut, who was in a village called Trang Bang when a South Vietnamese Skyraider let loose with four napalm bombs. Suddenly Ut heard a child screaming, *"Nong qua! Nong qua!"* which means "Too hot! Too hot!" Ut turned to see nine-year-old Kim Phuc, who had torn off her napalm-soaked clothes. When the girl reached him, and he saw that her skin was coming off, Ut put down his camera: "I didn't want to take any more pictures." He then rushed her and other injured children to a hospital.

TOP **LARRY BURROWS** *ABOVE* **NICK UT**

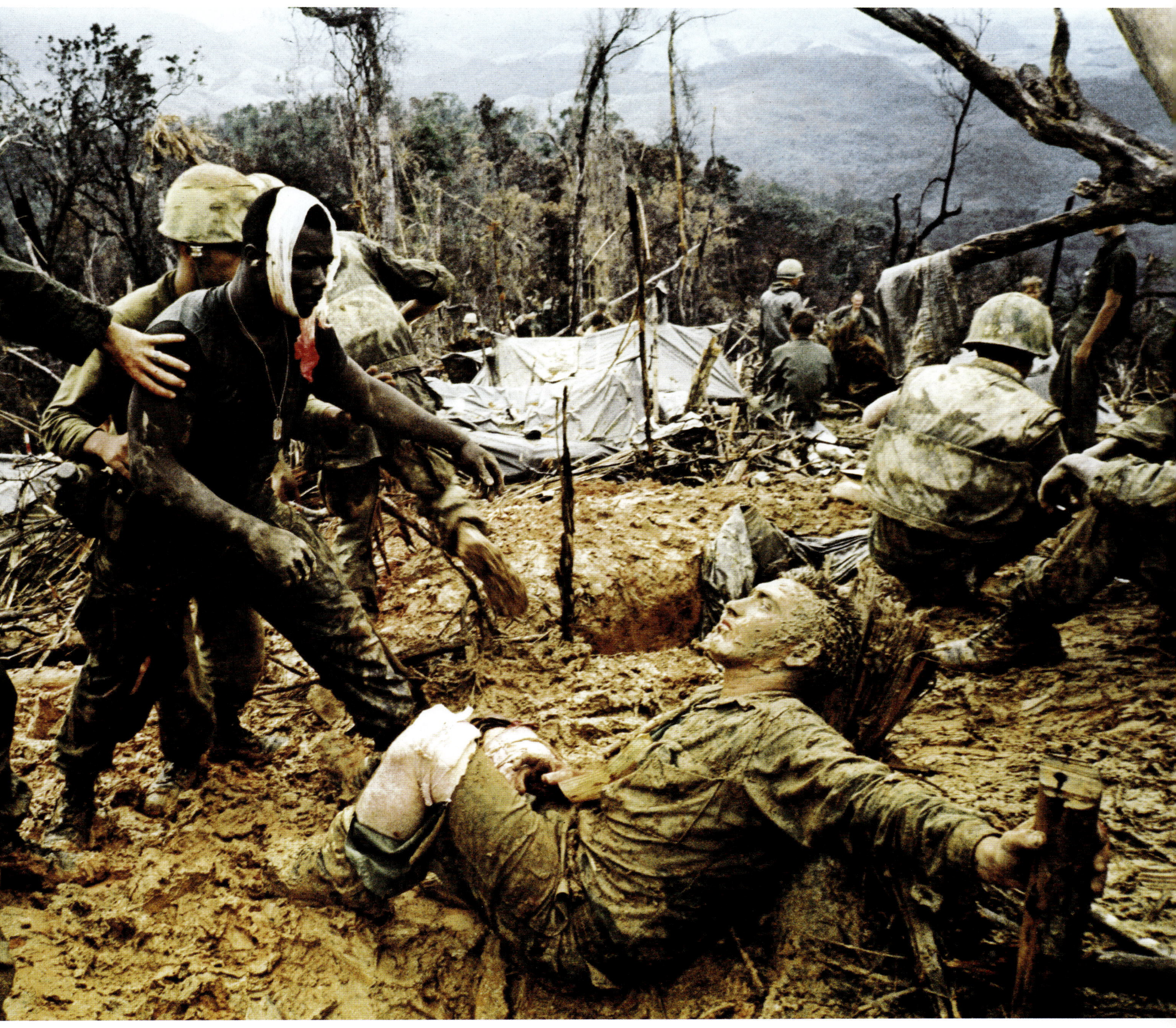

SEMPER FI

On October 5, 1966, a company of U.S. Marines was caught in an ambush on Mutter's Ridge. Casualties were heavy. In this photograph, now familiarly known as *Reaching Out,* Gy. Sgt. Jeremiah Purdie has just arrived at a first-aid station. Purdie's wounds are bad, but he seems more concerned with a fellow comrade who has also been hurt. This photo sat in a slide tray in LIFE's offices until Burrows died five years later. The picture then ran in an article devoted to his memory.

LARRY BURROWS

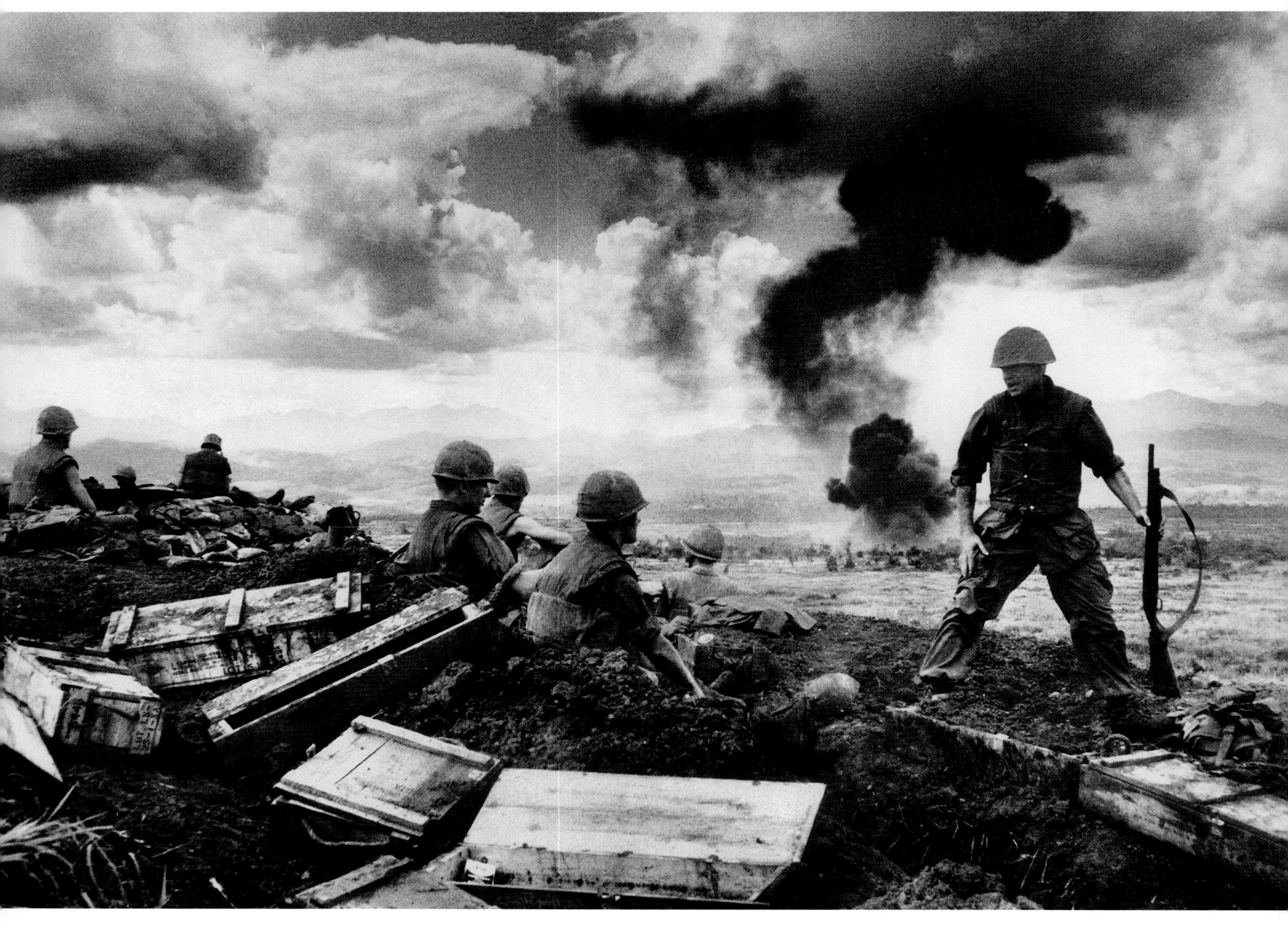

DISTANT FIRE

In 1967, a U.S. Marine unit waits quietly on a hillside as American planes bomb and strafe an enemy position in the valley below. LIFE photographer Duncan served with the Corps in World War II, and was present at Korea as well.

DAVID DOUGLAS DUNCAN

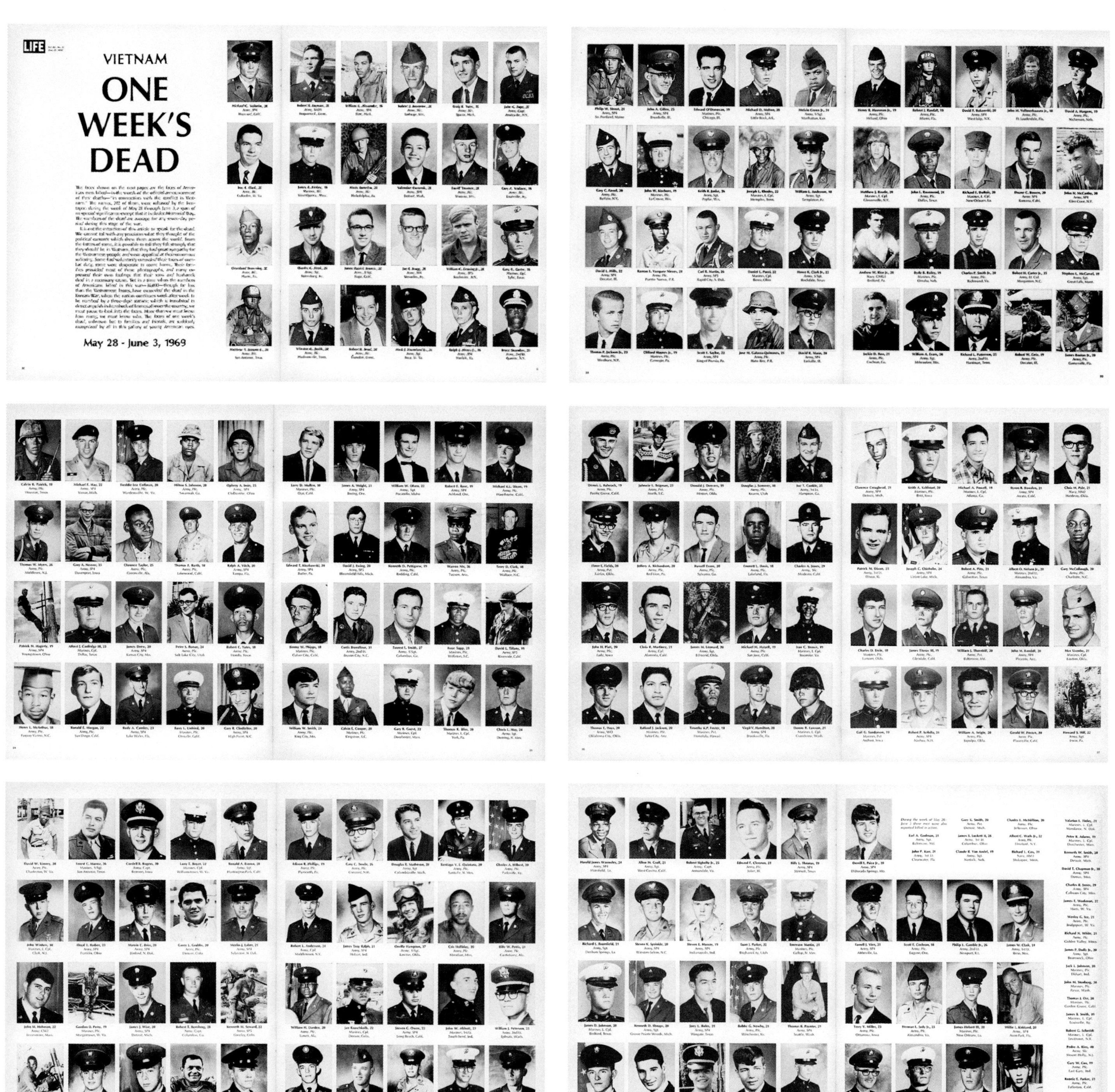
LIFE

VIETNAM

ONE WEEK'S DEAD

May 28 - June 3, 1969

ONE WEEK'S DEAD

This story was born in a conversation between editors Loudon Wainwright and Phil Kunhardt. LIFE had been running articles that were supportive of the war effort in Vietnam, including a pair by Time Inc. Editor-in-Chief Hedley Donovan with the titles "Vietnam: The War Is Worth Winning" and "Vietnam: Slow, Tough But Coming Along." By 1969, however, the death tolls had become unbearable. The question at LIFE became, how to handle it? The answer was simple, and devastating. The magazine secured from the Pentagon the names and hometowns of the 242 servicemen who had died during the week of May 28 to June 3, 1969. Where families chose not to be involved, LIFE ran only the names, rather than acquiring pictures from other sources. Most families, though, did want to be involved. The piece ran across 12 pages, and made the distant, anonymous casualties a ghastly, intimate matter.

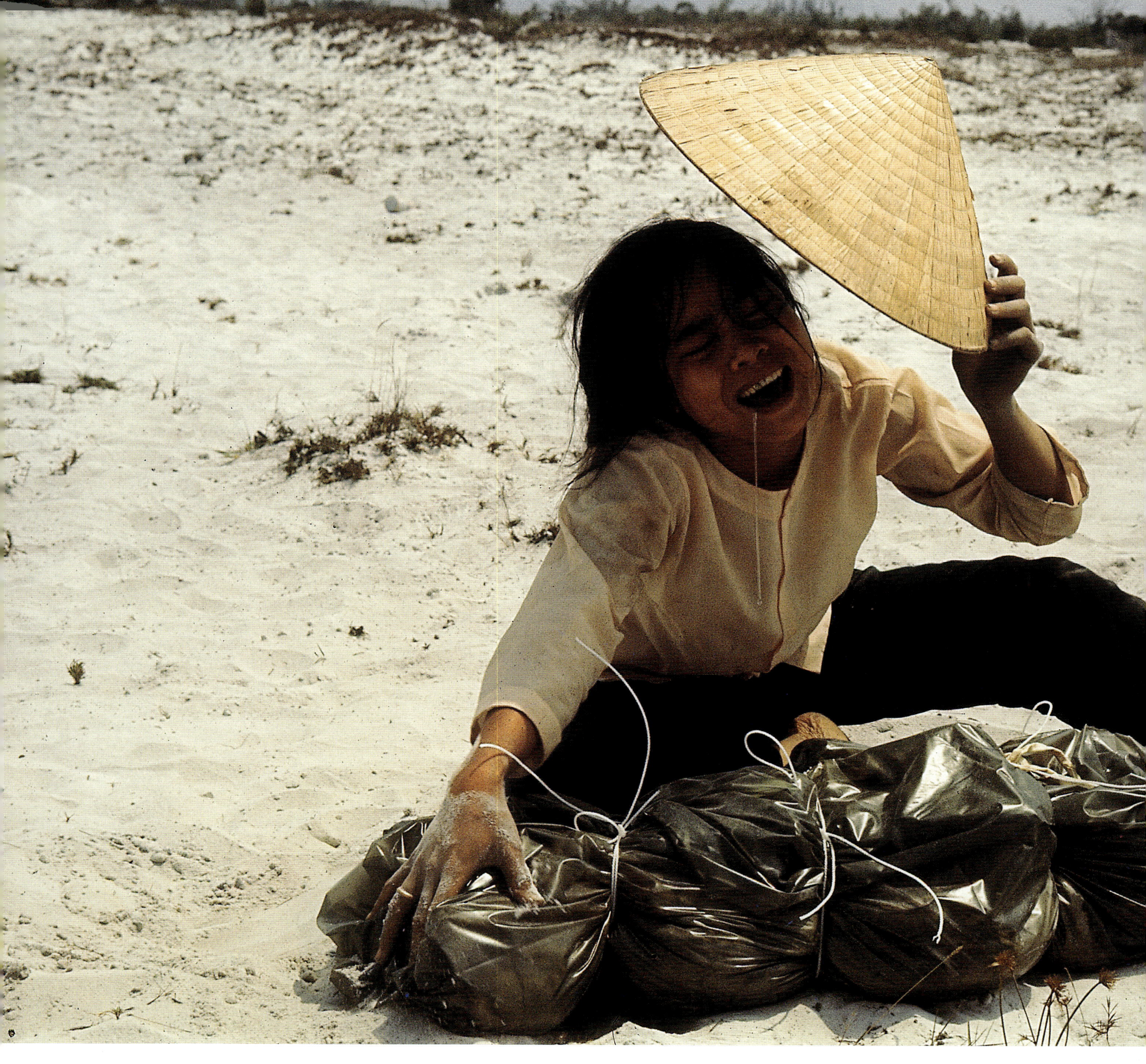

HORROR, RESOLVE, CHAOS

The South Vietnamese woman above laments over a recently discovered plastic bag containing the remains of her husband, who had been killed and tossed into a mass grave by the Vietcong during the Tet offensive of 1968. This image has been used by some as a counterpoint to the My Lai massacre. Opposite, top: In 1968 this Army helicopter is part of a (successful) mission to rescue Marines trapped in nearby Khe Sanh. At bottom, pilot Robert D. Hedrix punches a man desperately trying to board an already overcrowded plane out of Nha Trang. The date is April 2, 1975. South Vietnamese forces are in total disarray following the withdrawal of American troops. Hedrix, working for the State Department, is evacuating Americans, mostly journalists, and some Vietnamese kids and elderly. Shortly after this plane departed, North Vietnamese troops overran the city.

ABOVE & OPPOSITE, TOP **LARRY BURROWS**

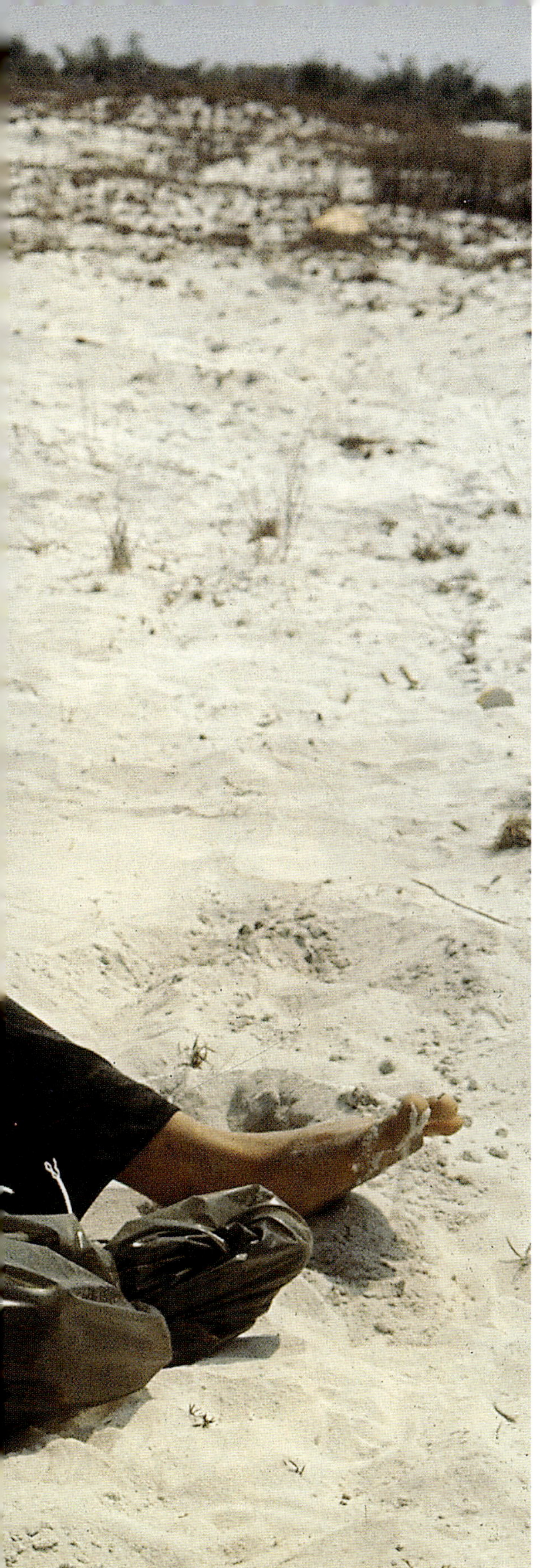

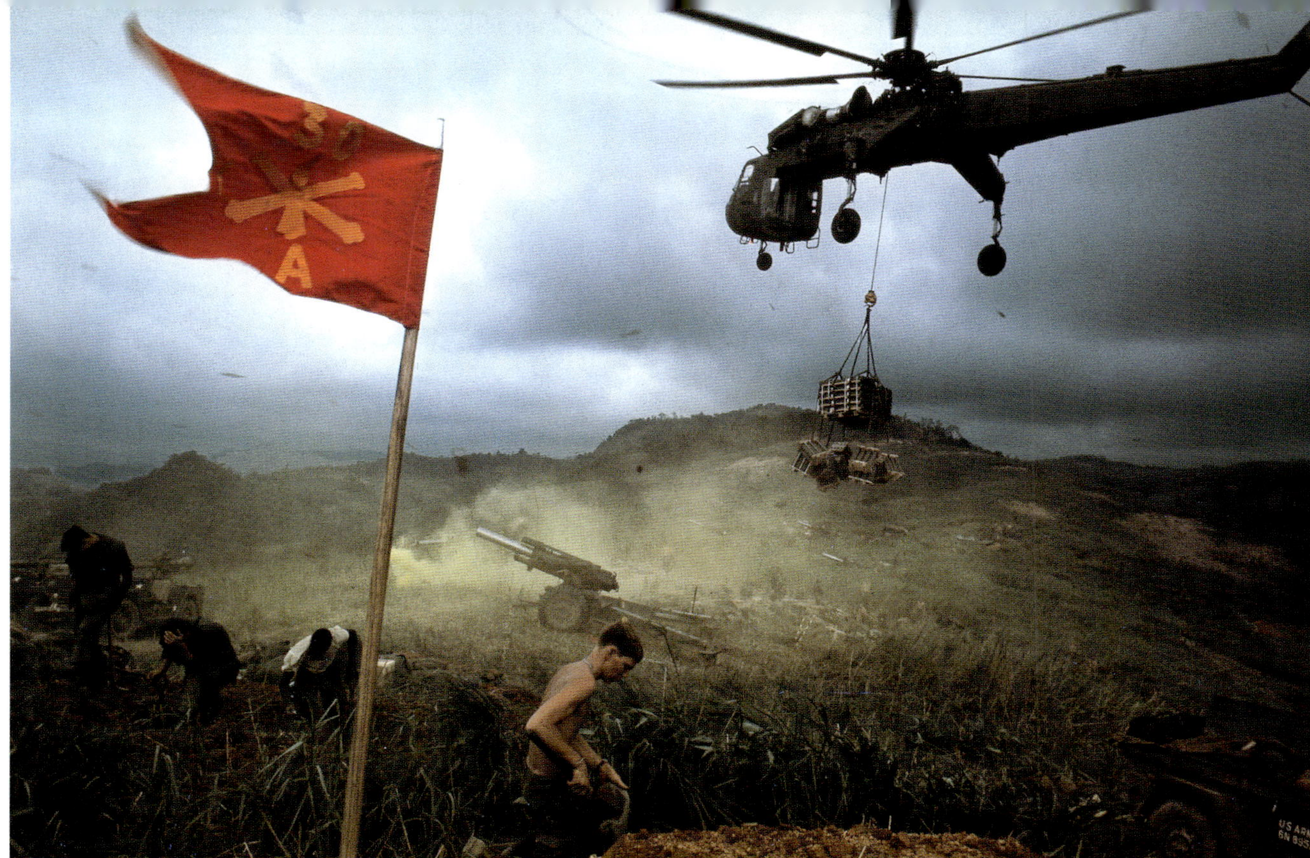

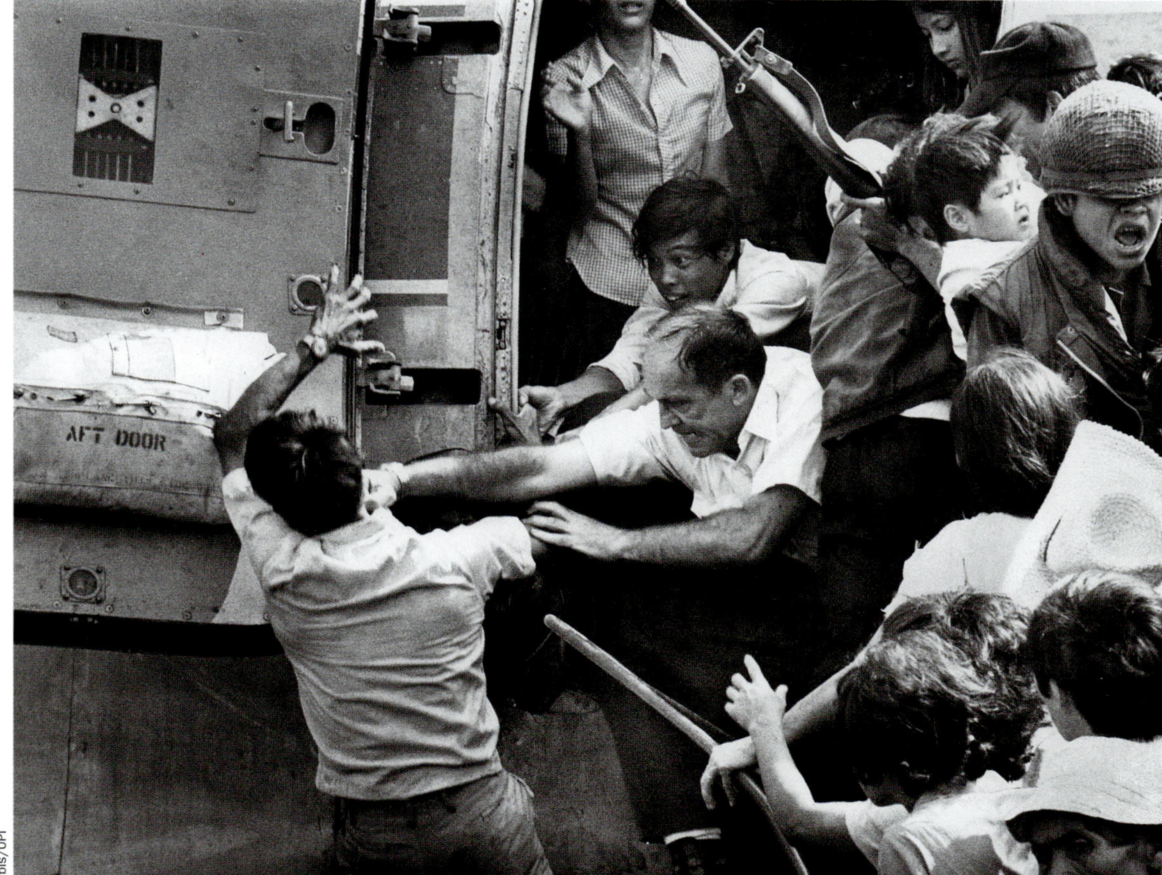

Corbis/UPI

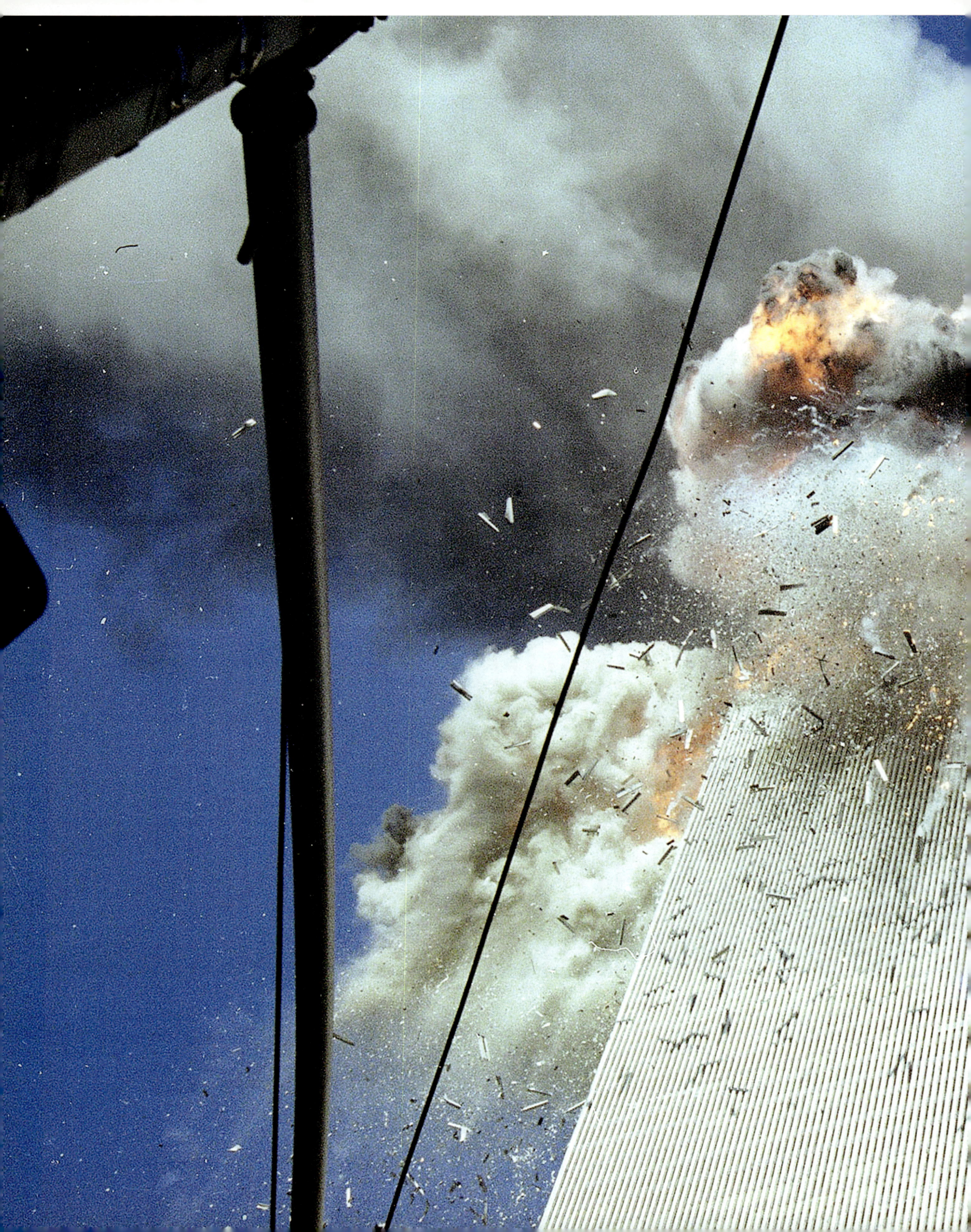

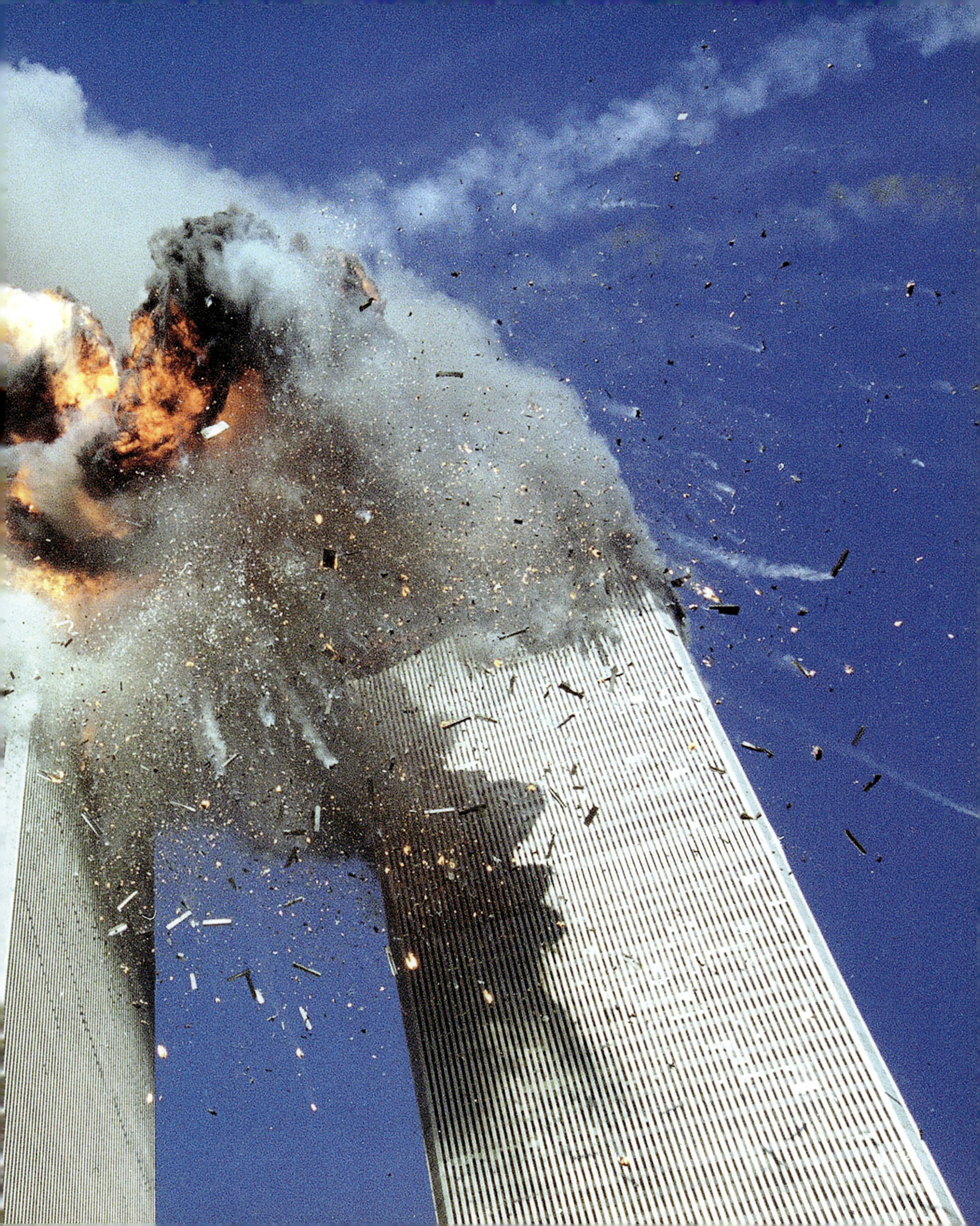

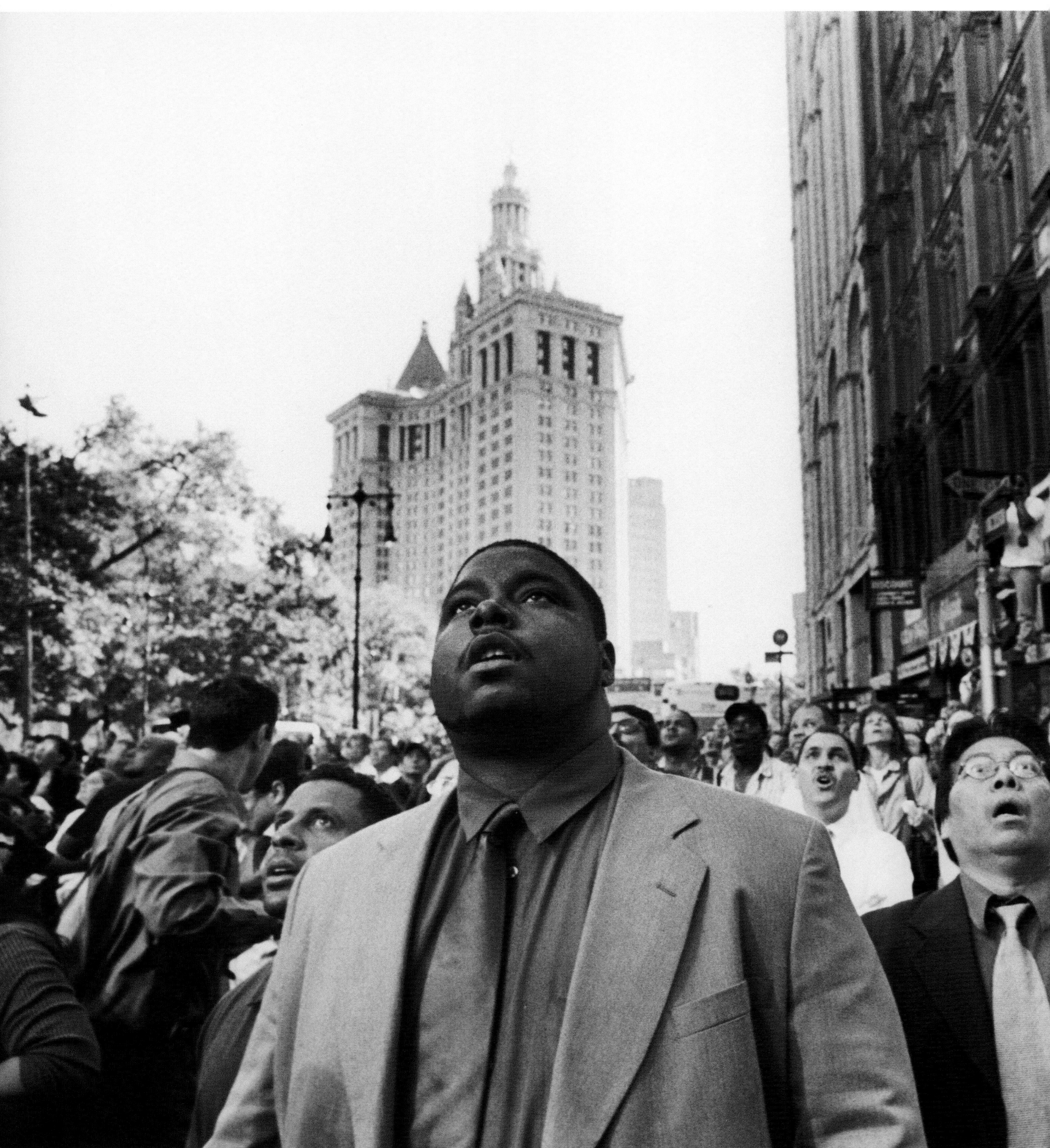

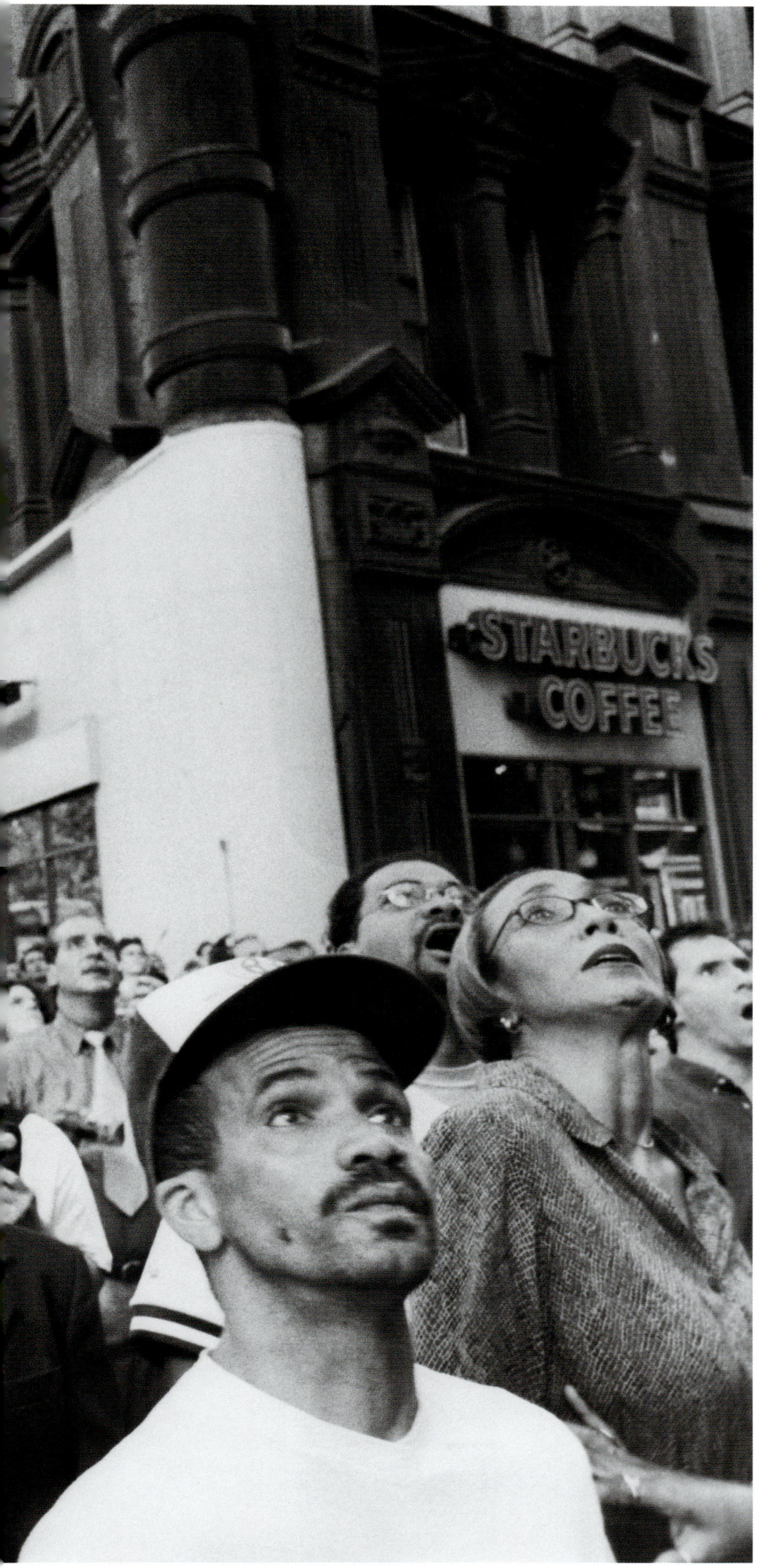

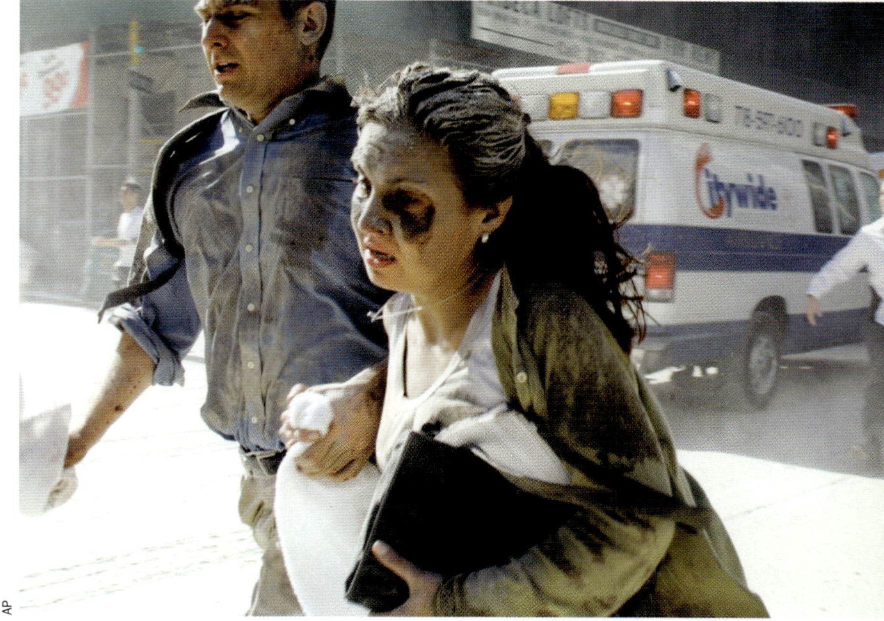

AP

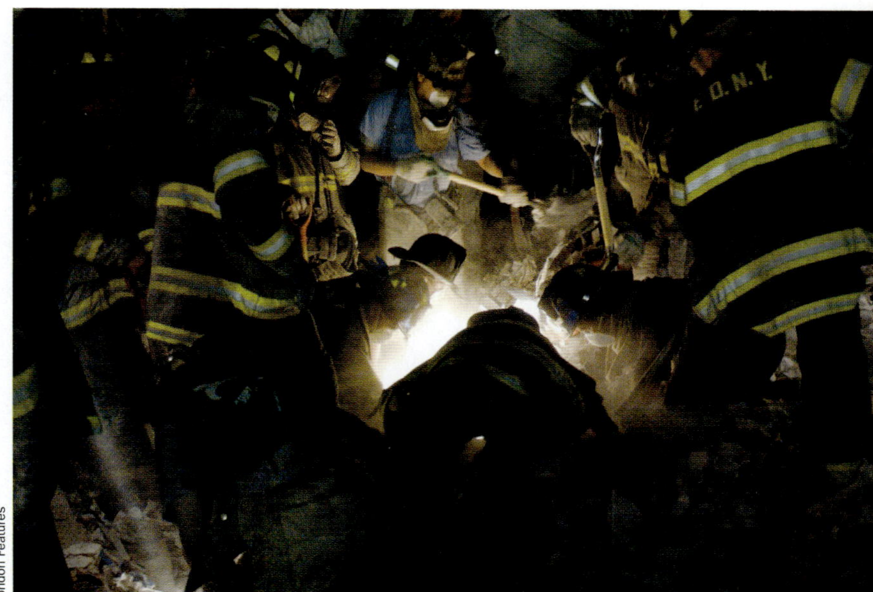

London Features

SEPTEMBER 11

It was a very pretty Tuesday morning in 2001 in Manhattan, and folks there, as elsewhere in America, were heading for work when out of the blue at 8:47 a jet crashed into the north tower of the World Trade Center. People watched from the streets as a massive plume of smoke extended from the skyscraper, and soon TV cameras were trained on the accident. Minutes later, as seen on the previous pages and at left, everything changes and a horrible truth hits home: There has been no accident. A different jet has rammed into the other tower, and people watch mesmerized as the towers present a nightmarish tableau and then collapse to the ground. In the photograph at top, coworkers scramble toward safety, while above, firefighters peer into the abyss as they endeavor to save two of their brethren. Soon the morning brings news of yet other plane crashes, at the Pentagon and in a Pennsylvania field, and the American people realize they have been struck by another Pearl Harbor. Once again, war . . . but this time different, endlessly complex, surely long-lasting.

LEFT **PATRICK WITTY** *TOP* **DIANE BONDAREFF** *ABOVE* **DENNIS VAN TINE**
PREVIOUS PAGES **NAOMI STOCK**

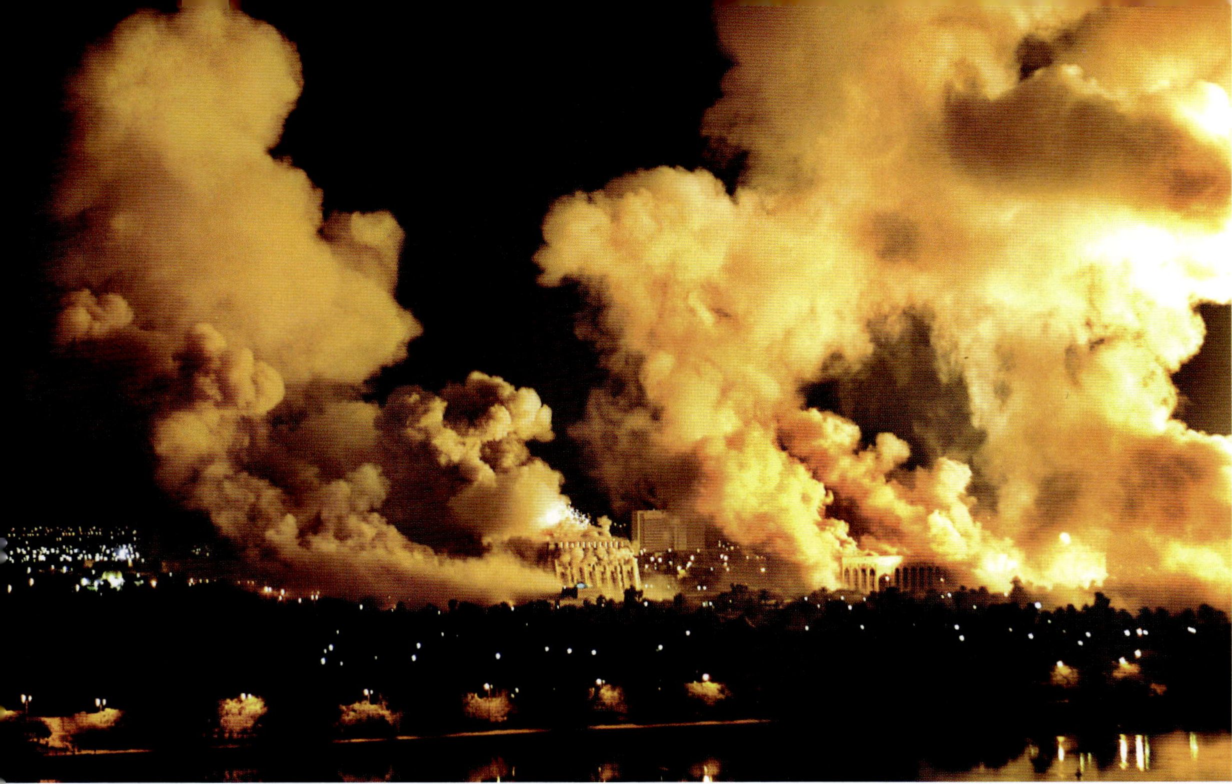

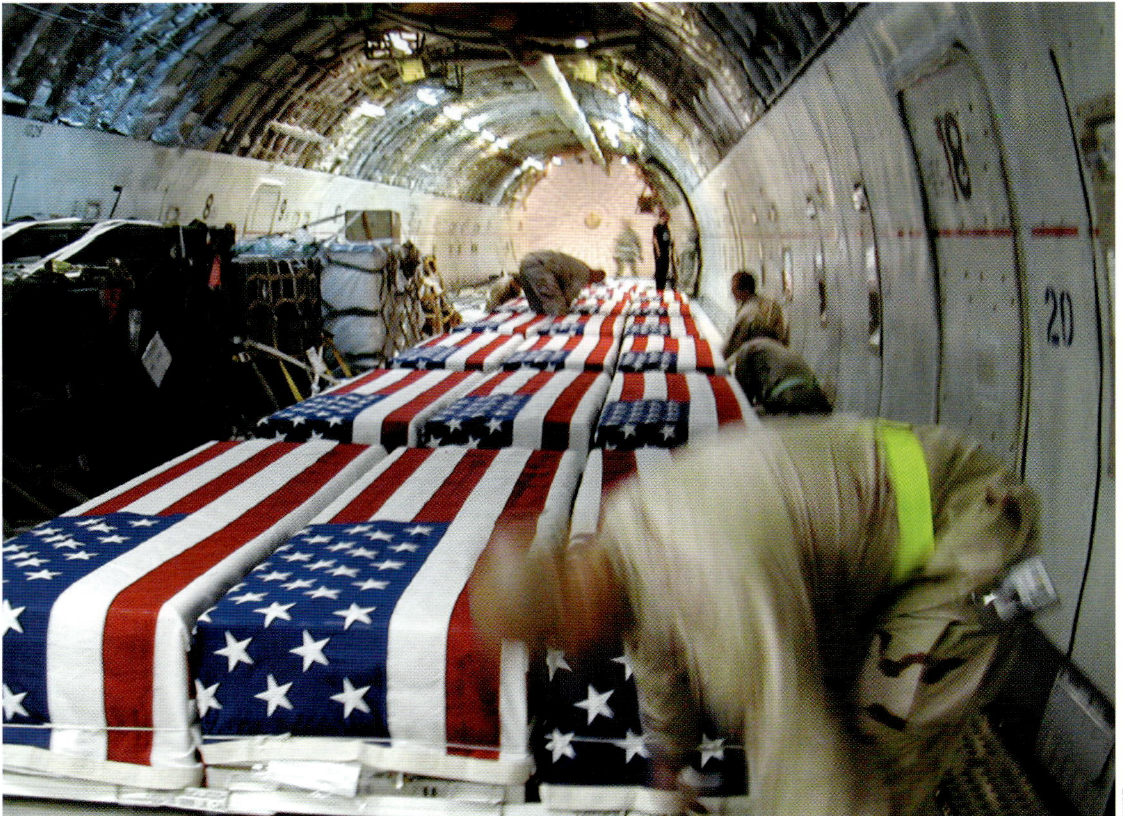

Zuma

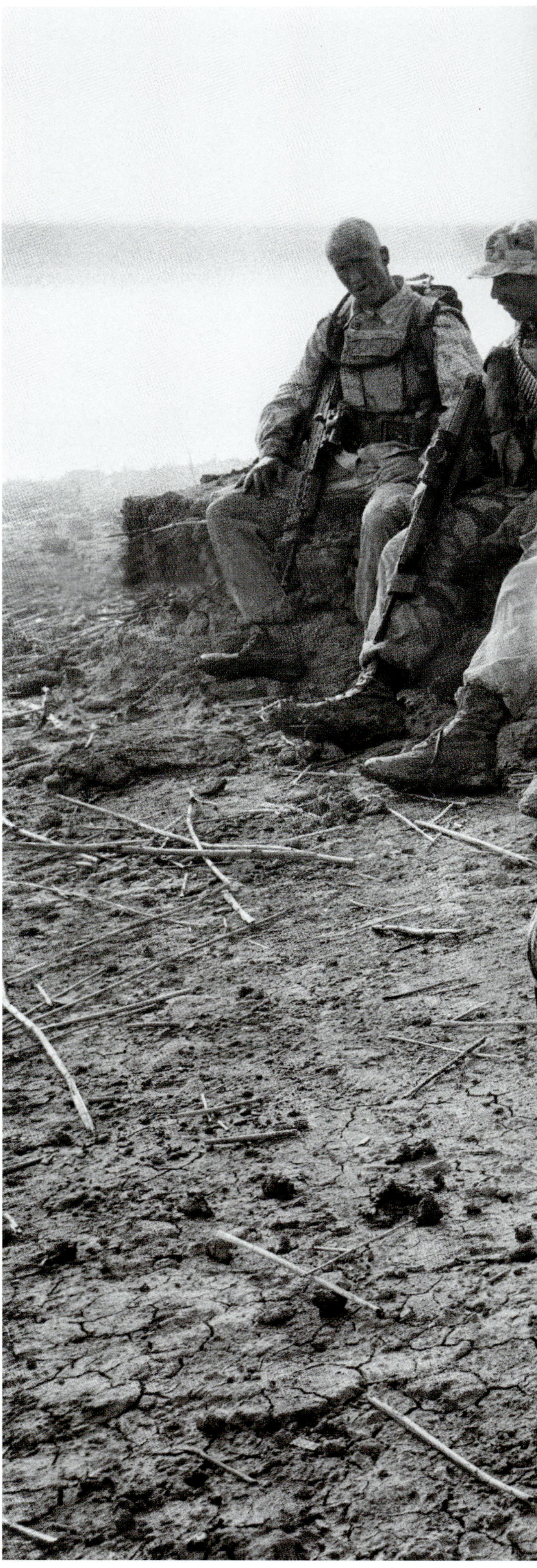

IPG

IRAQ

At top, on March 21, 2003, one day after Coalition forces entered Iraq, the first installment of "Shock and Awe" pummels the western bank of the Tigris River in Baghdad. By April 9, the capital city is secured. Fighting along the way is tough, as we see in the photo at right by Tom Stoddart, who was embedded with the 539 Assault Squadron of the British Royal Marines. The men have been fighting all night and have just been told that one of their comrades has been killed. The photo above was taken on April 7, 2004, by Tami Silicio, who worked the night shift at Kuwait International Airport for a defense contractor. She had seen a lot of coffins pass through, en route for burial in the States. She wanted to show that these young people were being treated with respect, and sent the picture to a friend. After it later appeared in print, she was fired because the Pentagon had banned photos or news coverage of dead servicemen.

ABOVE **TAMI SILICIO** *RIGHT* **TOM STODDART**

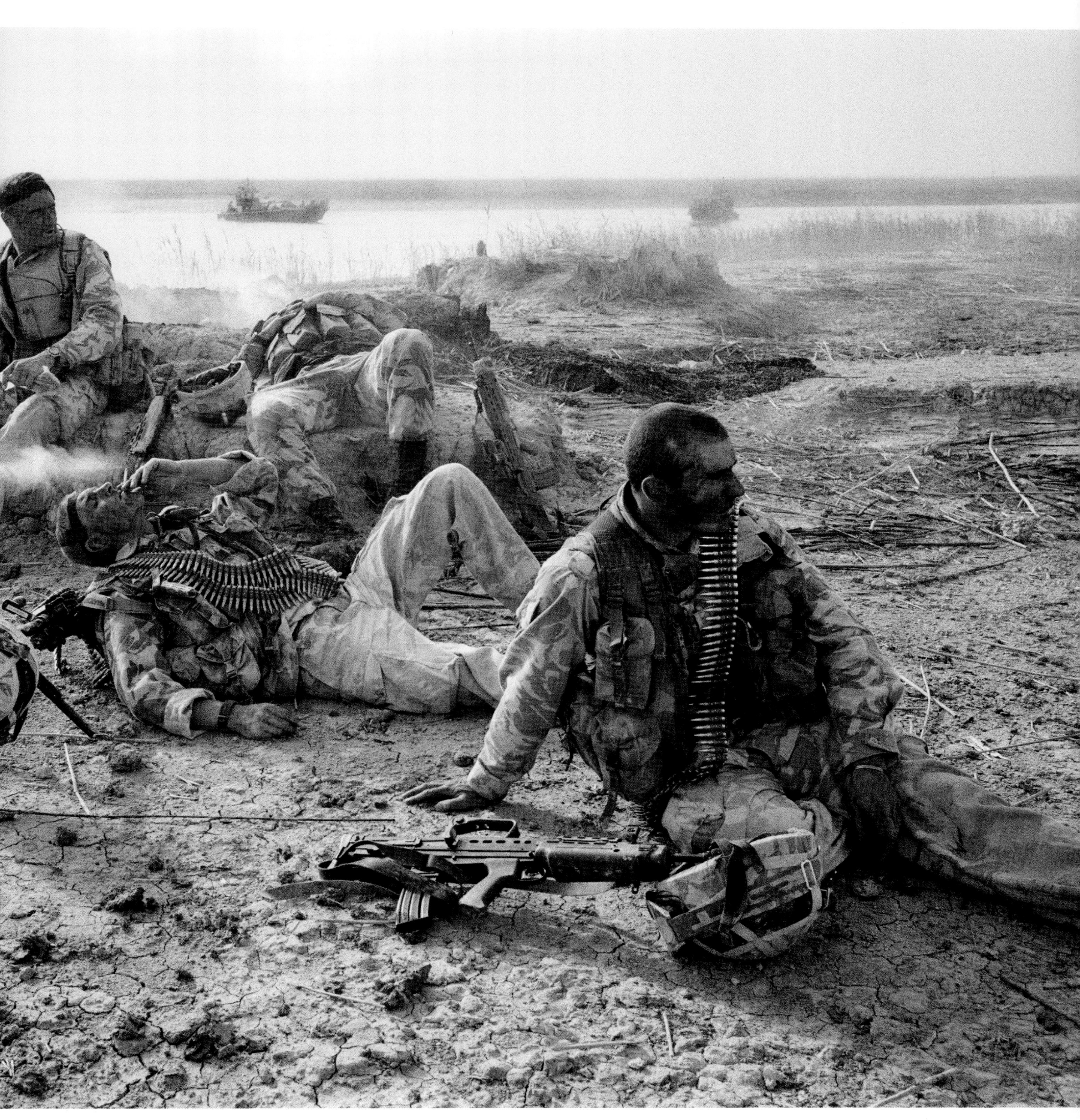

SCIENCE & NATURE

In that first written appraisal of his new baby, LIFE, composed a few months after its birth, Henry Luce considered the various segments of the magazine. When he reached the topic of science, he had this to say: "It is really amazing how little has come to us of a scientific nature which is really informative. But I have very little doubt that if we bend persistent and serious journalistic efforts to this task, we will develop a significant flow of scientific information—through pictures.

"We shall not insist that Science shall always be pictorially arresting . . . We will be happy to have pictures which, if given a little time and study by the reader, will yield information which sticks . . . The fact is that today most people—most educated people—walk through a world which has been amazingly analyzed by Science without having the least idea of what the world looks like to the eye of the Geologist, the Engineer, the Astronomer, the Biologist, the Chemist or the Bacteriologist. By learning only a little about how to see, LIFE can open many eyes.

"Here, as elsewhere, it is necessary in LIFE to achieve a reputation. Or perhaps what I mean is not so much that we must achieve a reputation as that we have first of all to put up our sign: HONEST SCIENCE SOLD HERE."

Luce was, of course, absolutely right. But even he had no idea what an important and multifaceted role science would play in the pages of LIFE. The advances in science—and photography—that have been realized in the past 70 years are dizzying, and the magazine has been punctilious in keeping abreast.

LIFE has always been entirely at home in the laboratory and in the wild. With flora and fauna, from the microscopic to the grand, as constant subjects, the pages of LIFE have always been truly alive.

SOLAR FRENZY

A sunspot is a vortex of gas on that star's surface involving immense magnetic activity capable of wreaking havoc on satellites and power grids. This photo, from July 2004, shows activity above the massive sunspot 652, which at this point was about 20 times the size of Earth.

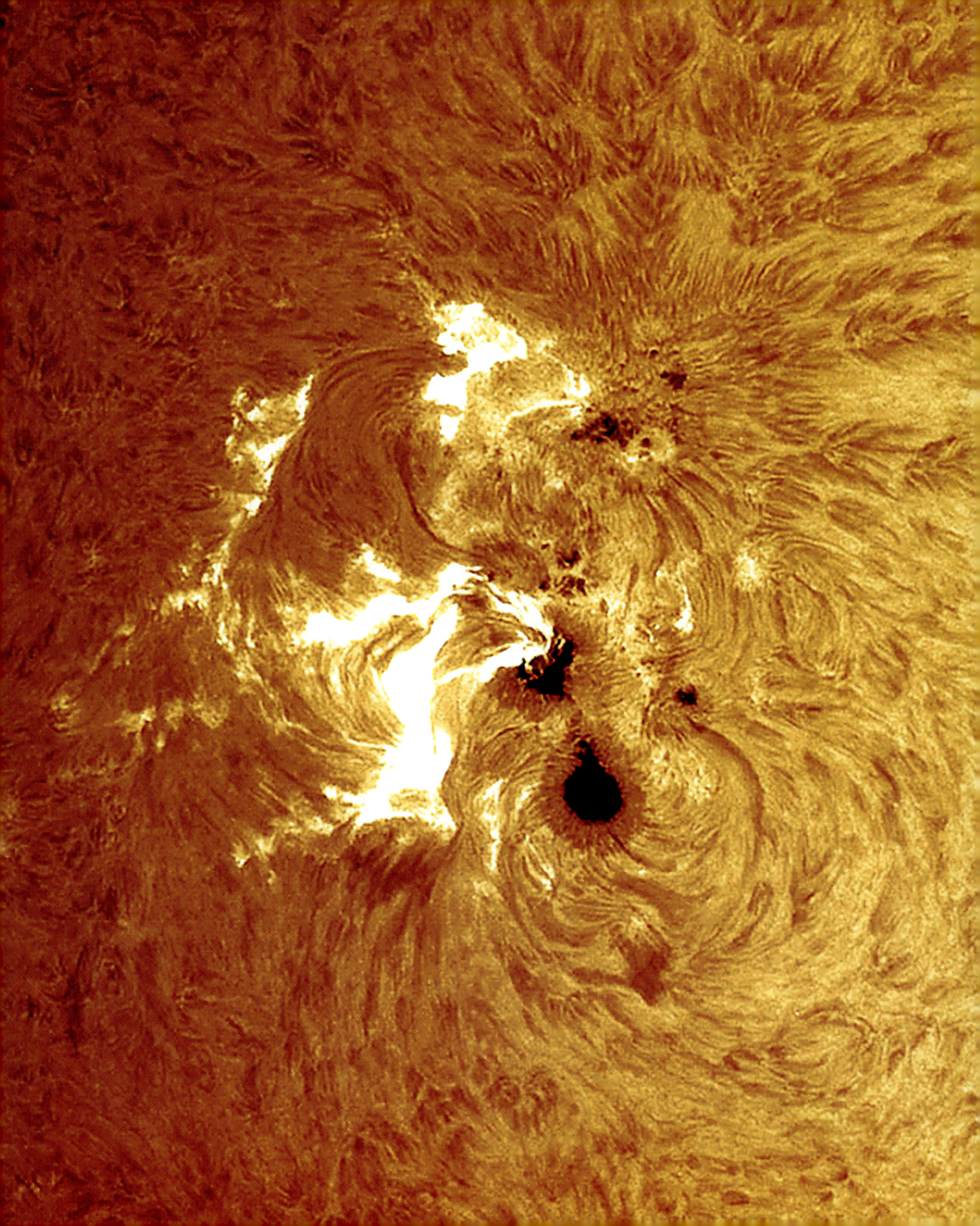

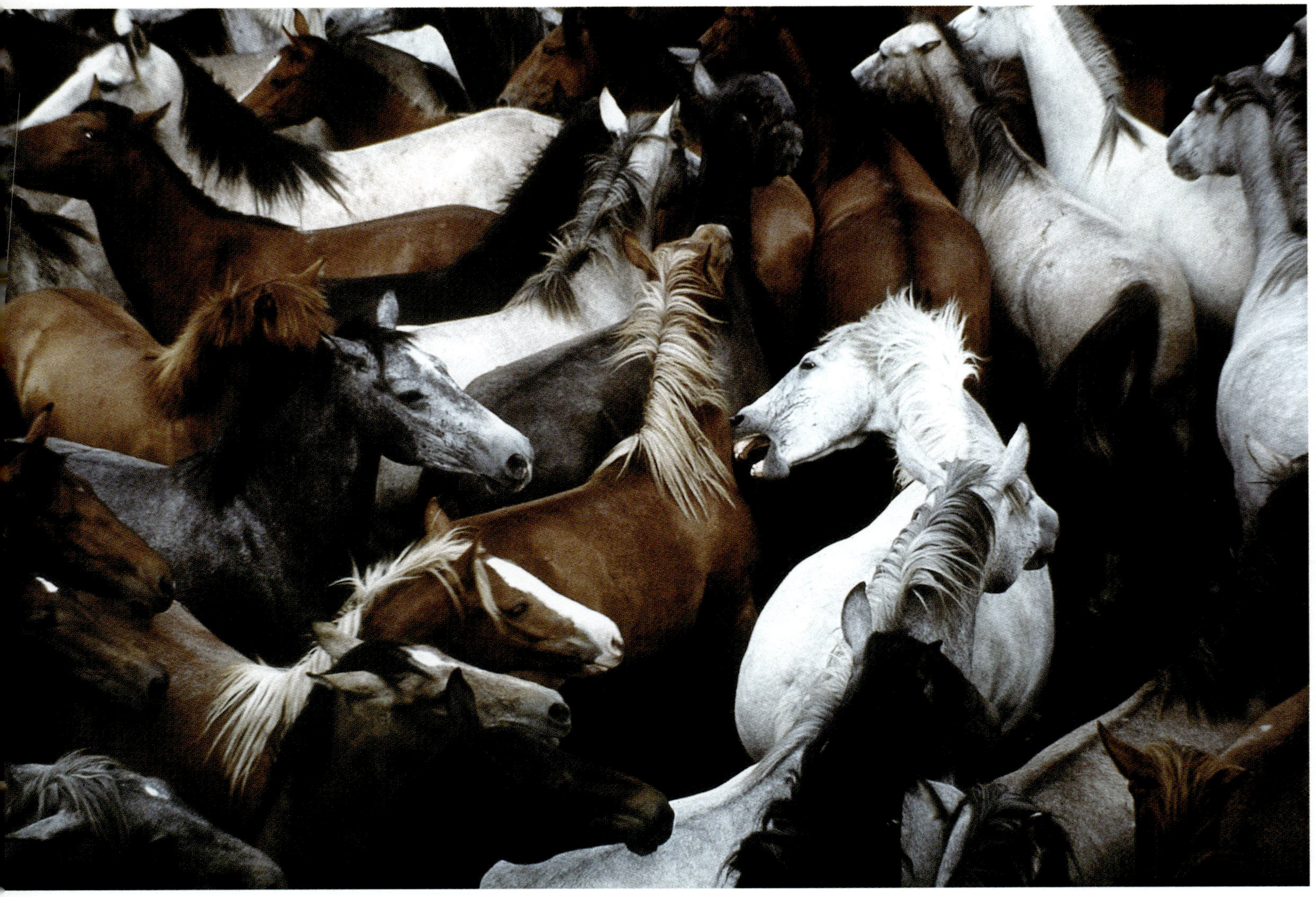

WILD HORSES

From the vantage point of a giant eucalyptus, photographer Vavra took this photograph of a herd of Arab and Andalusian mares as they make their busy way through a narrow ravine outside the city of Seville, in southern Spain.

ROBERT VAVRA

SWANSCAPE

For decades, photographer Saga devoted five months a year to whooper swans, which migrate annually to the northern Japanese island of Hokkaido. Here, in 1987, they are just awakening after the long flight.

TEIJI SAGA

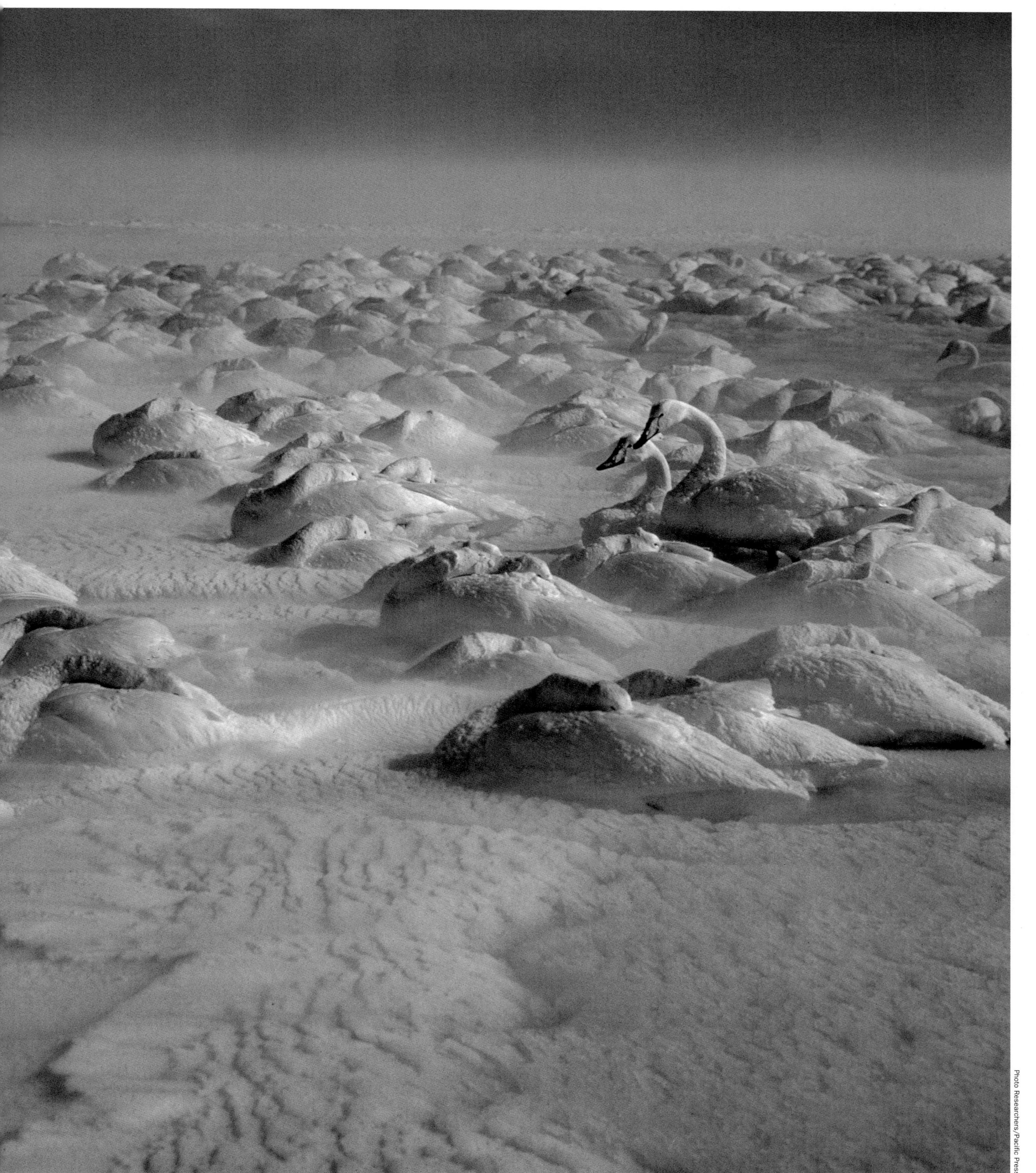

Photo Researchers/Pacific Press

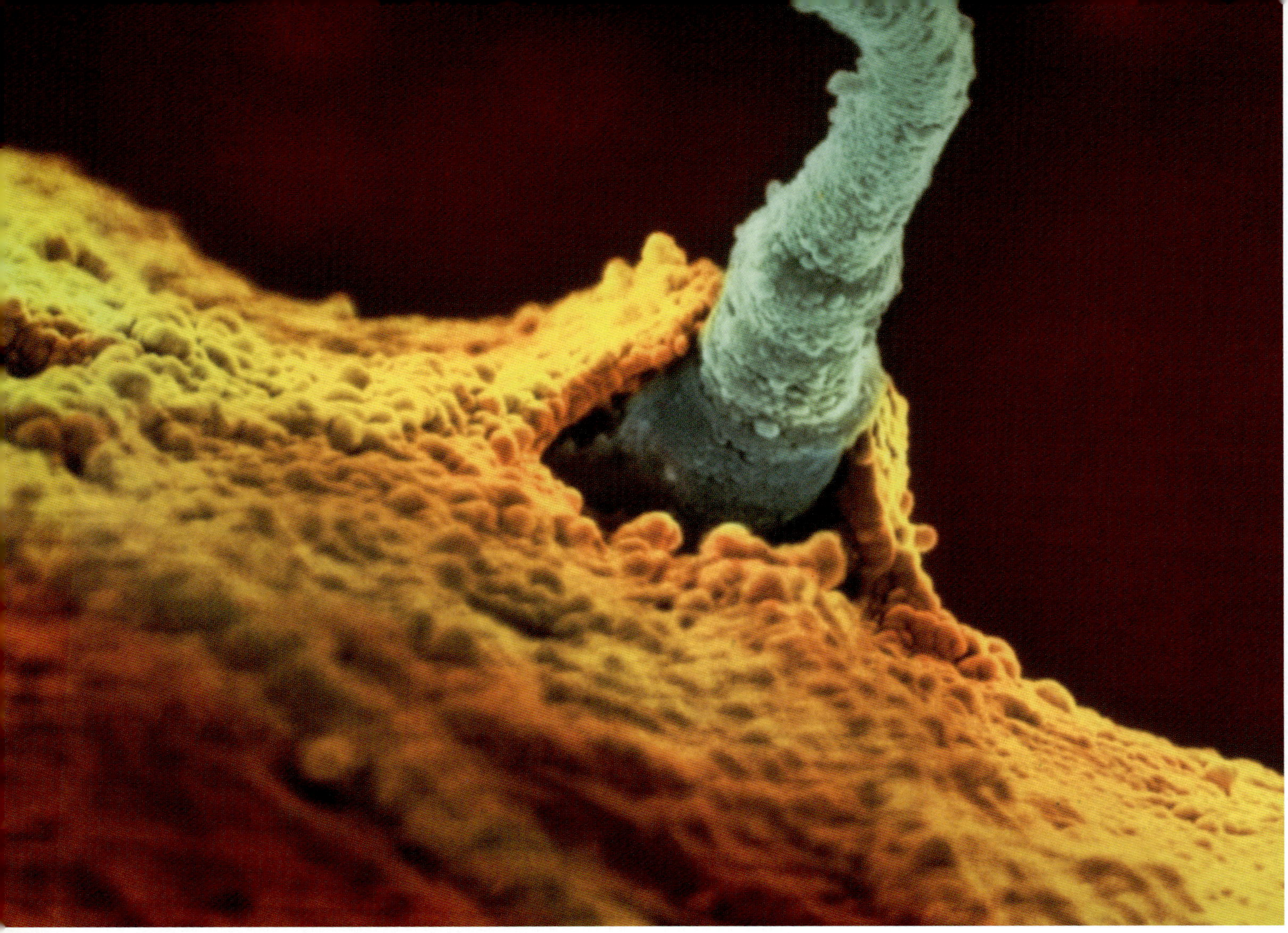

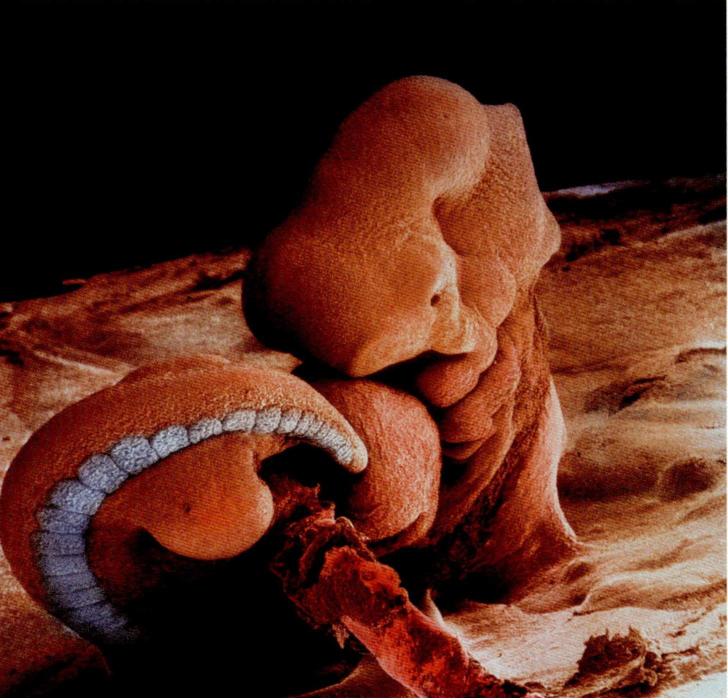

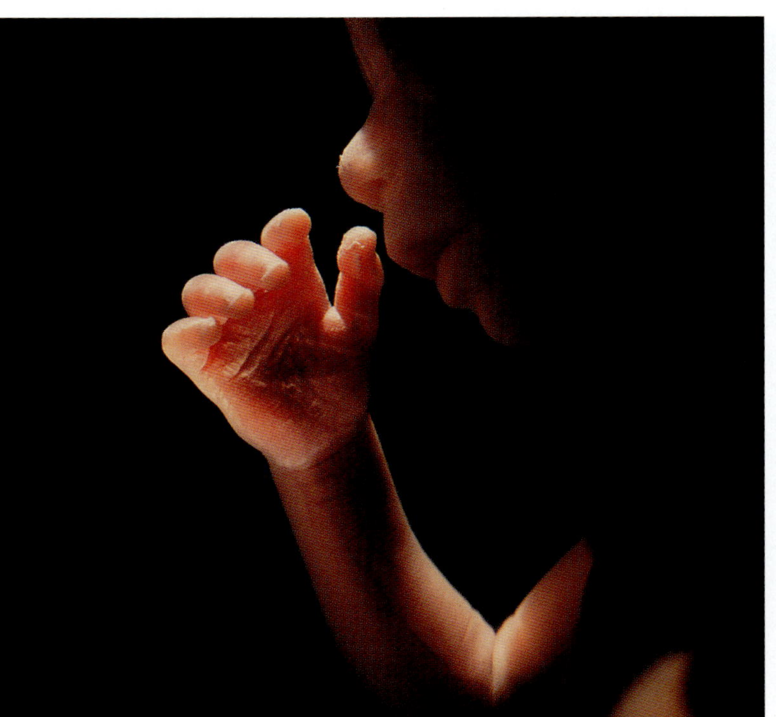

THE INCEPTION

Lennart Nilsson began his long fascination with the secrets of life as a boy. When he was in his early thirties, he saw a two-month-old fetus in a laboratory bottle: "In that same second I knew I would concentrate on the early development of the human." In 1965, LIFE published a piece that was 14 years in the making, "Drama of Life Before Birth." It became one of the magazine's most famous stories. Fortunately for all of us, Nilsson to this day continues his important work. Counterclockwise from top: A sperm forces its way into an egg; the embryo at four and a half weeks has a tail that will soon disappear; at 17 weeks, fingernails are visible; a living human fetus at 28 weeks.

LENNART NILSSON (4)

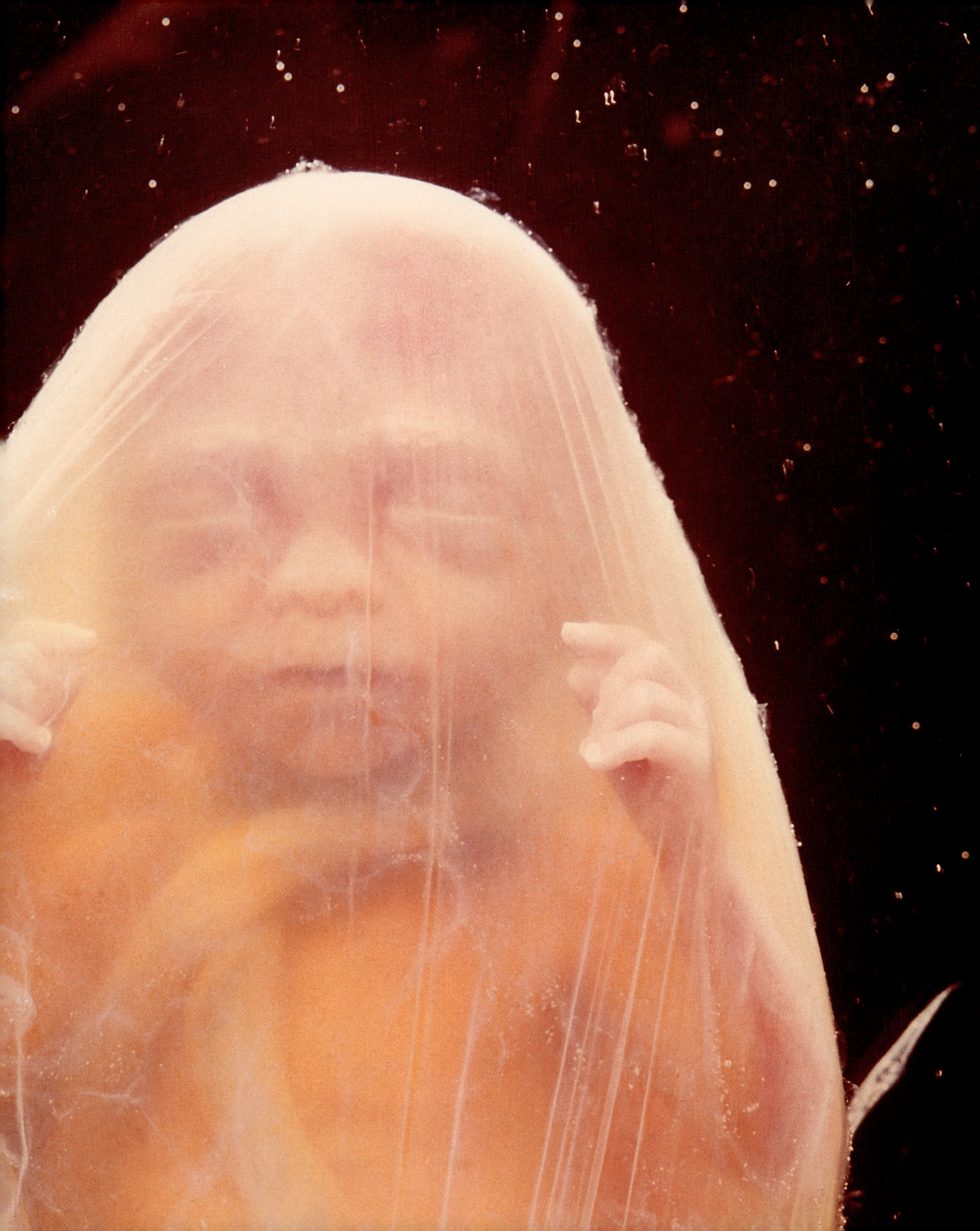

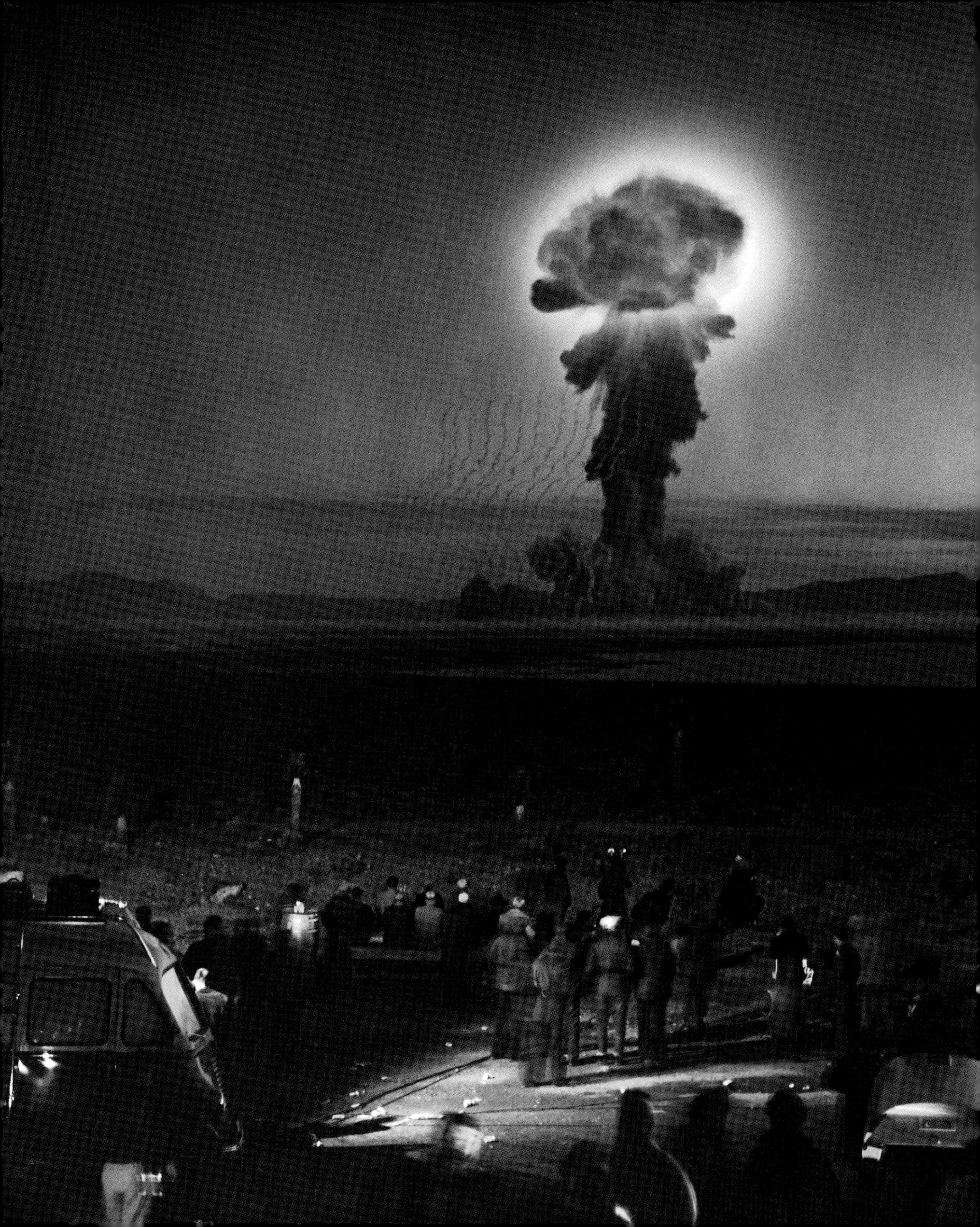

A TEST

The photo at left was taken in 1953, and is very much of its time. It easily could be a still from a '50s sci-fi flick in which some mutant monster will emerge from man's misguided nuclear trespasses. Or it could even be a shot of folks at a drive-in watching that same flick. Actually, it is civil defense officials in Yucca Flat, Nev., watching an atomic-bomb test seven miles away.

J.R. EYERMAN

MOUNT ST. HELENS

For two months scientists had monitored this Washington volcano as rising magma forced its north flank to swell a stunning five feet each day. The bulge exceeded 450 feet on May 18 when a 5.1 earthquake triggered the biggest recorded landslide in the history of the world, followed by a 20-mile lateral blast of superheated stone, ash and poisonous gas.

ROGER WERTH

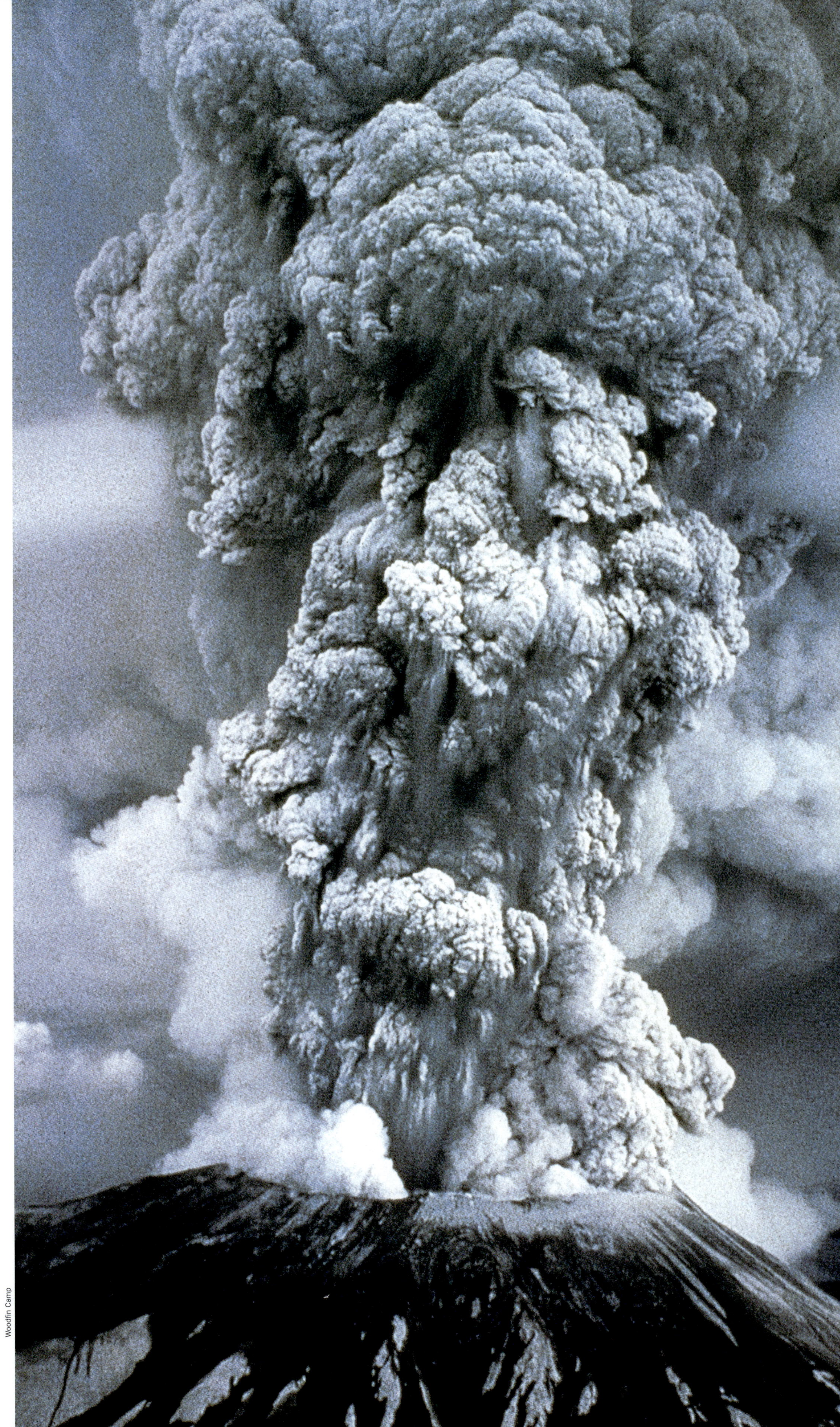

Woodfin Camp

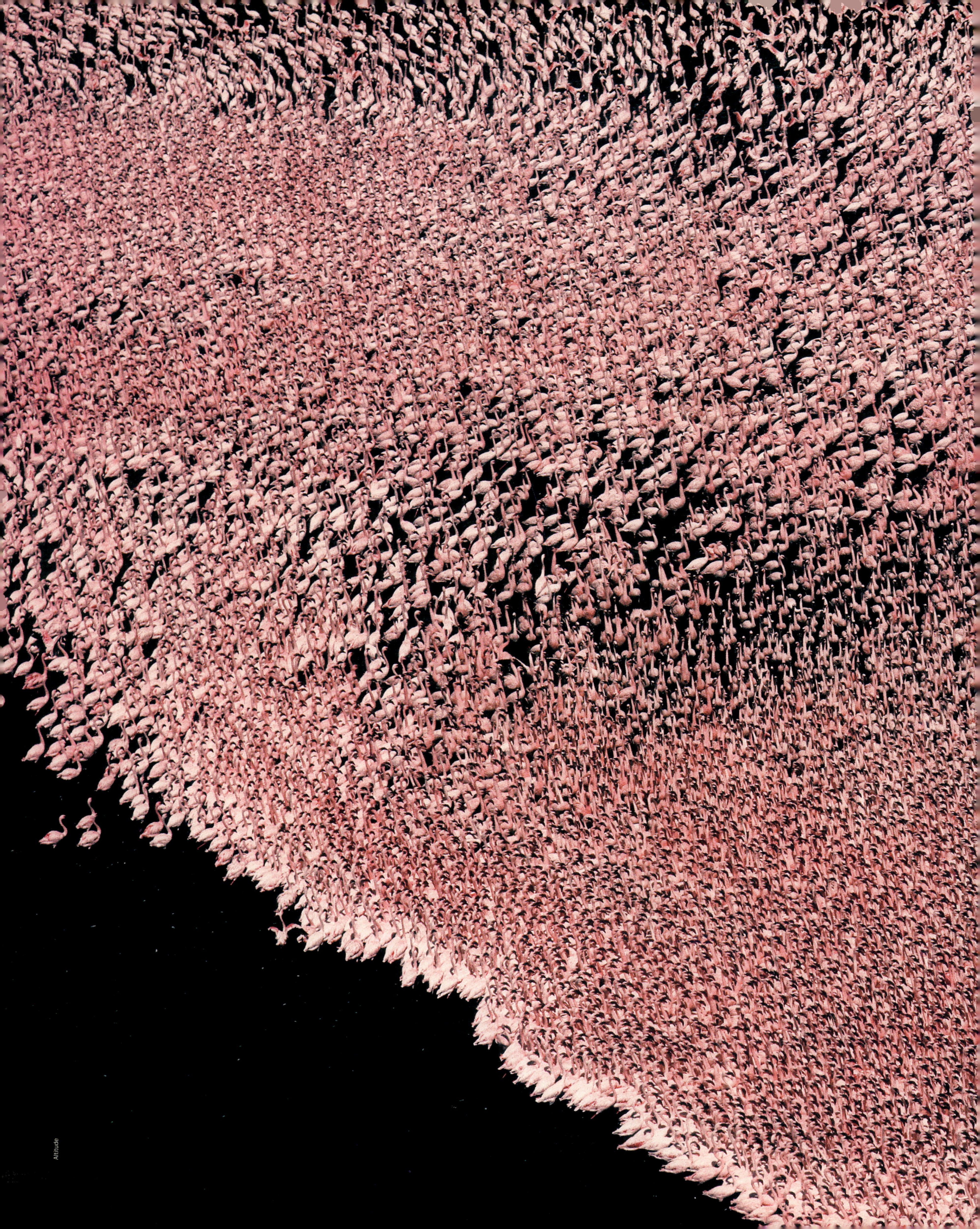

Altitude

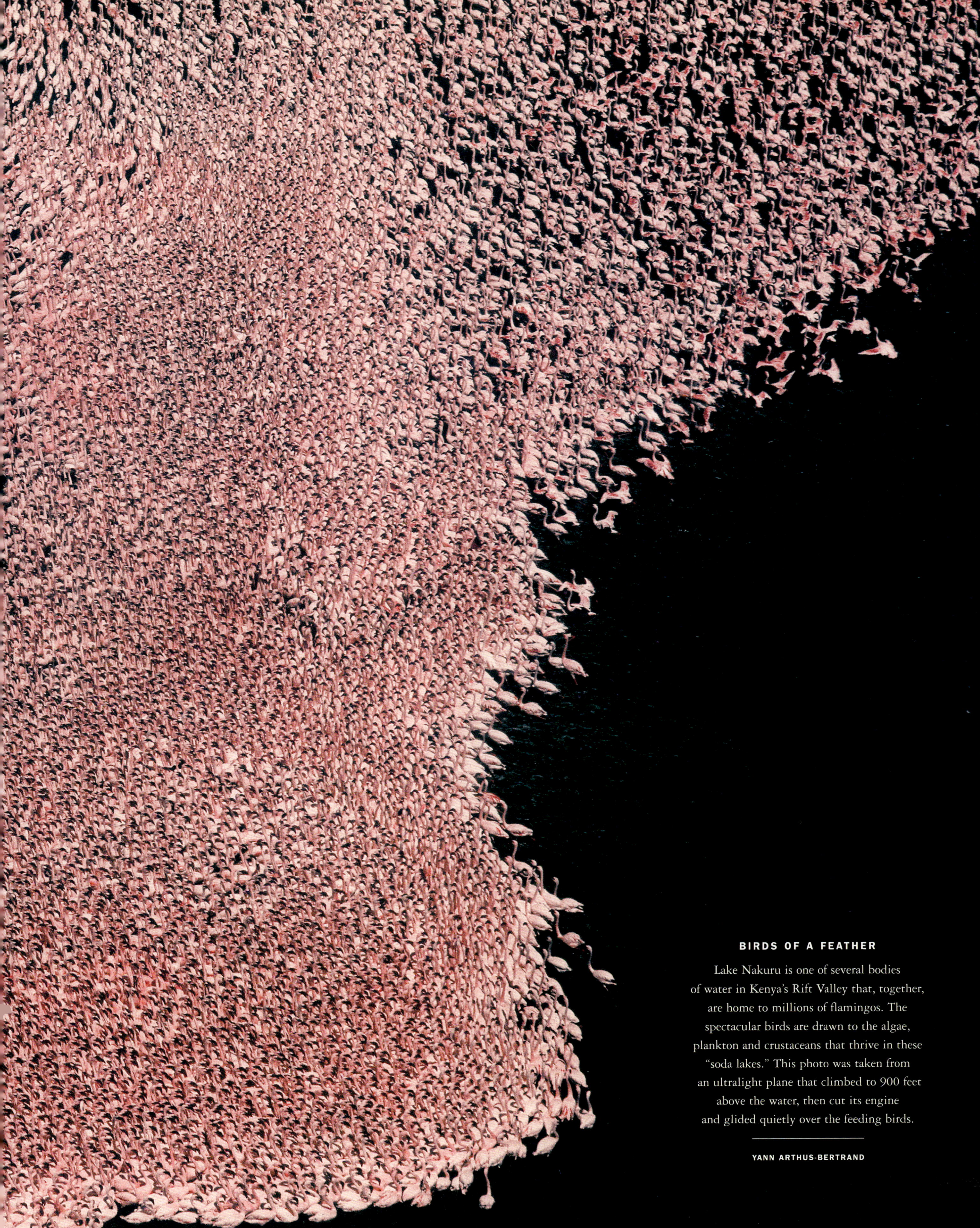

BIRDS OF A FEATHER

Lake Nakuru is one of several bodies of water in Kenya's Rift Valley that, together, are home to millions of flamingos. The spectacular birds are drawn to the algae, plankton and crustaceans that thrive in these "soda lakes." This photo was taken from an ultralight plane that climbed to 900 feet above the water, then cut its engine and glided quietly over the feeding birds.

YANN ARTHUS-BERTRAND

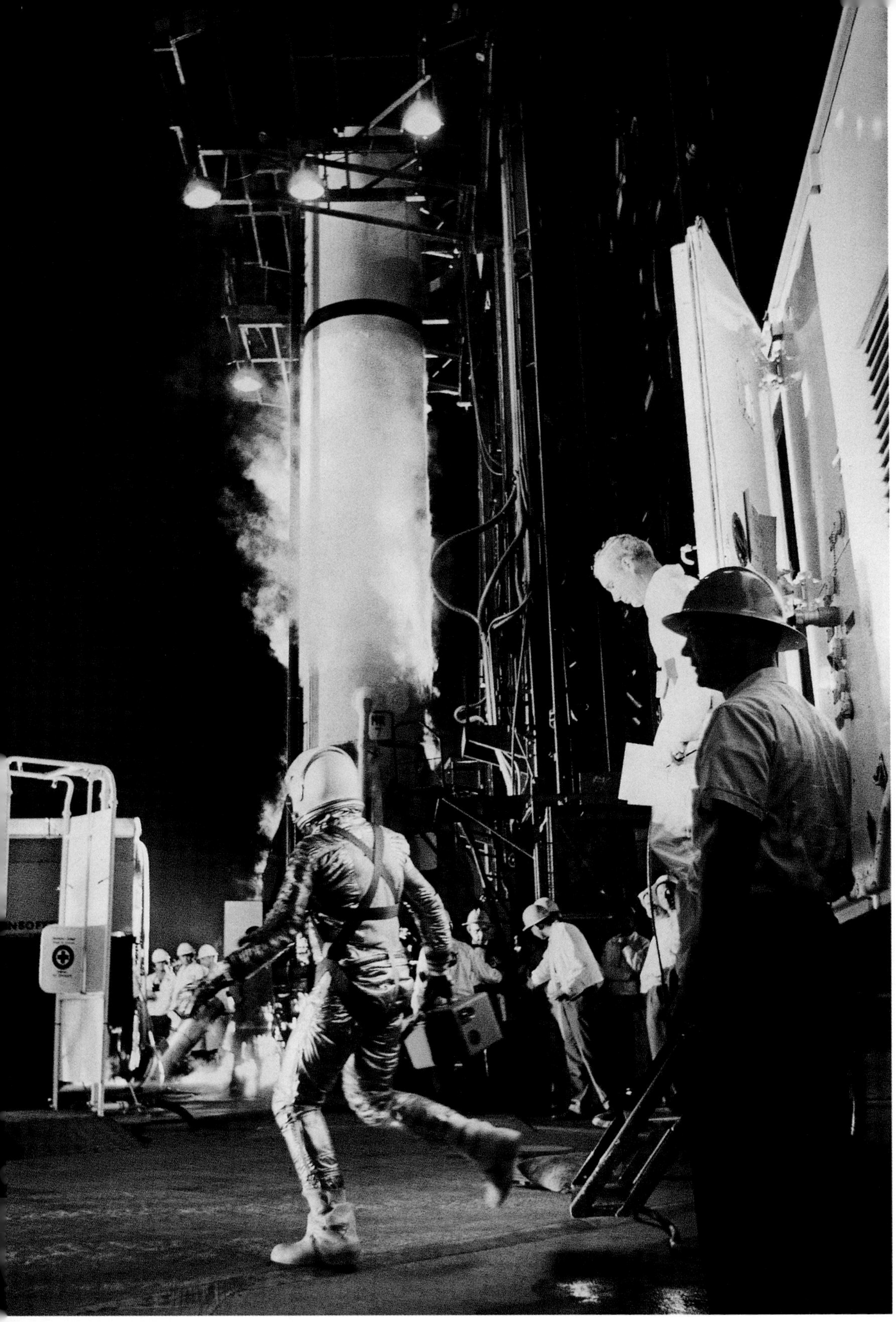

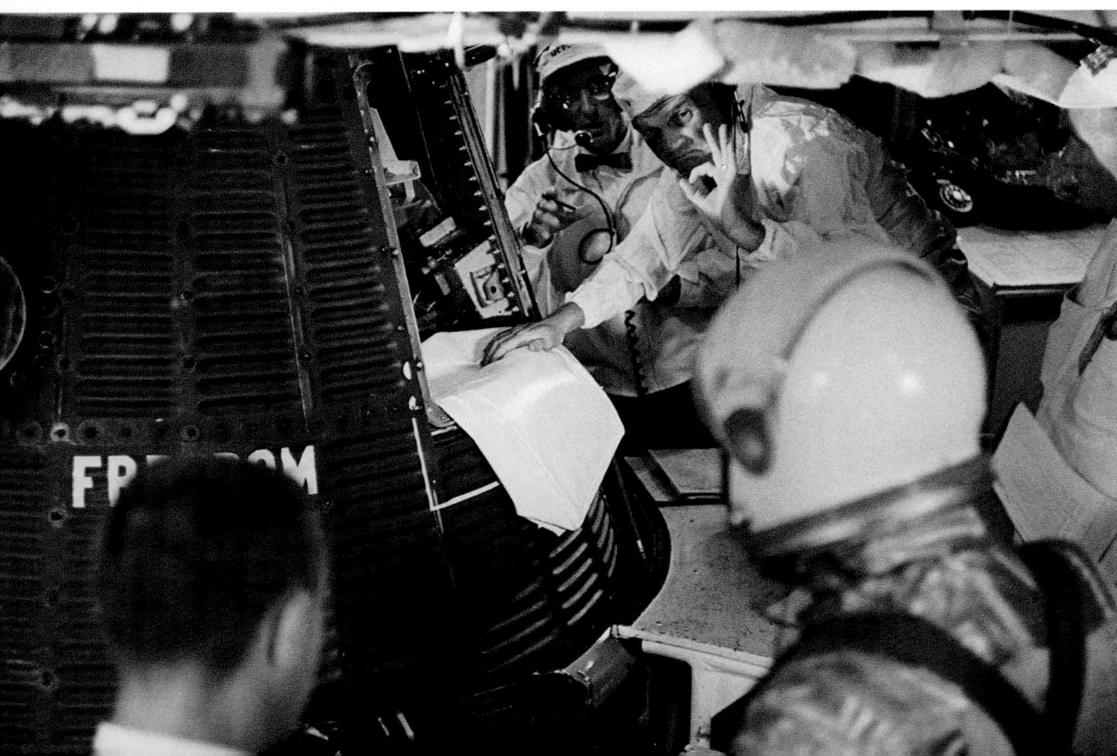

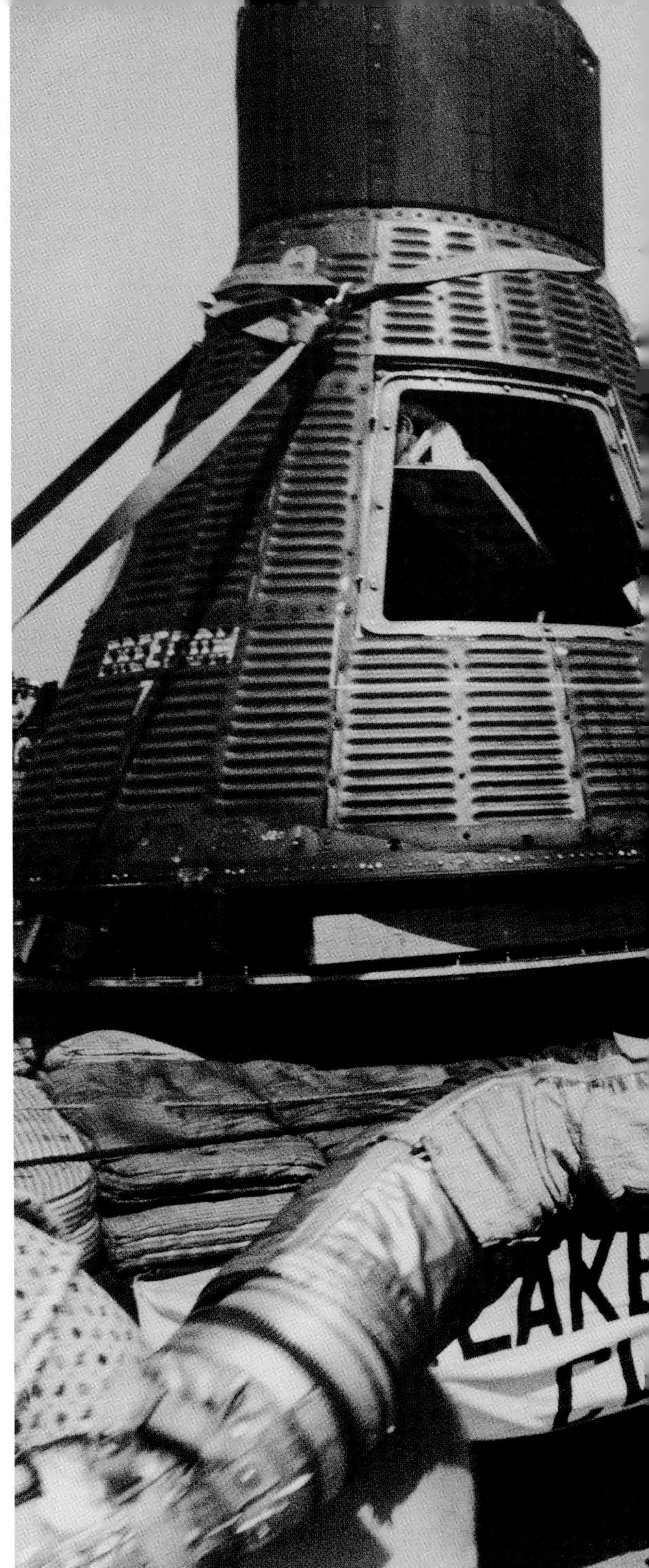
FREEDOM

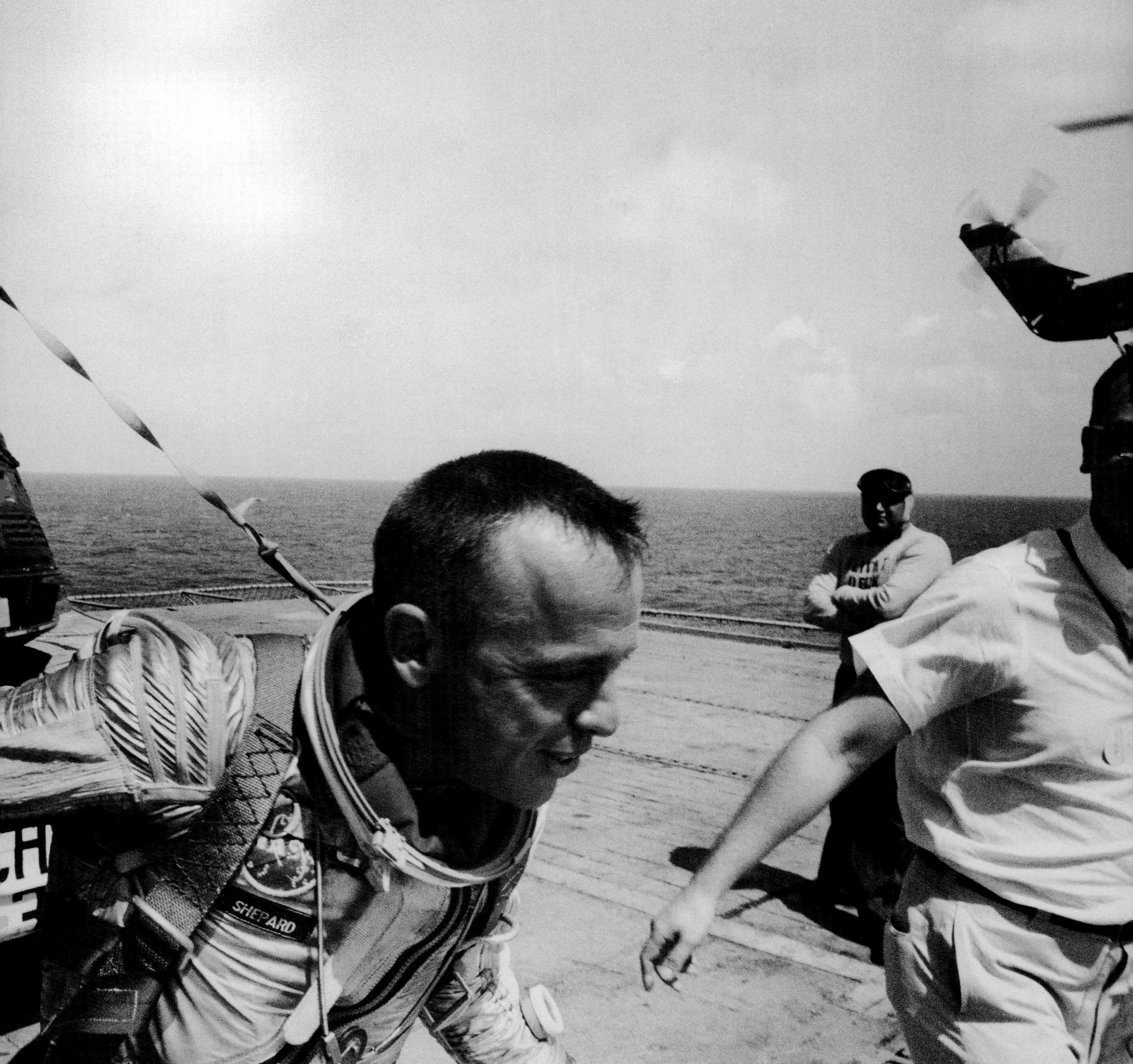

CAN-DO

On April 12, 1961, the space race was at full tilt when America was shaken to learn that the Soviets had put a man into orbit and brought him back safely. The U.S. Mercury program shifted into higher gear, and on May 5 was ready to respond. Opposite, top: In the predawn hours, Navy Cmdr. Alan Shepard hurries toward a Redstone booster rocket. Bottom: John Glenn, having checked out the *Freedom 7* capsule, gives Shepard the A-O.K. Above: Shepard is back from a trip that lasted only about 15 minutes, but which made him the first American in space.

OPPOSITE, TOP & BOTTOM **RALPH MORSE** *ABOVE* **DEAN CONGER**

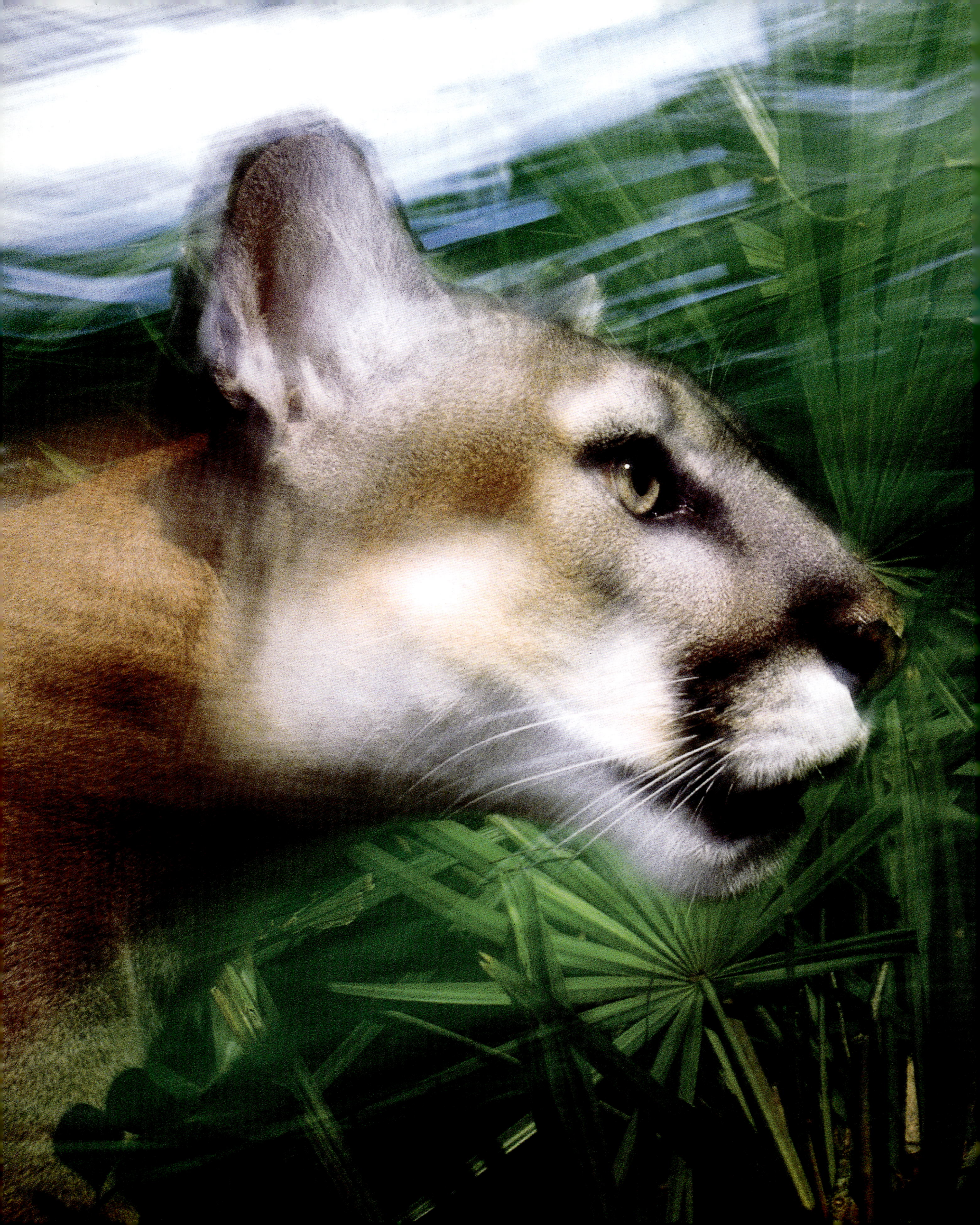

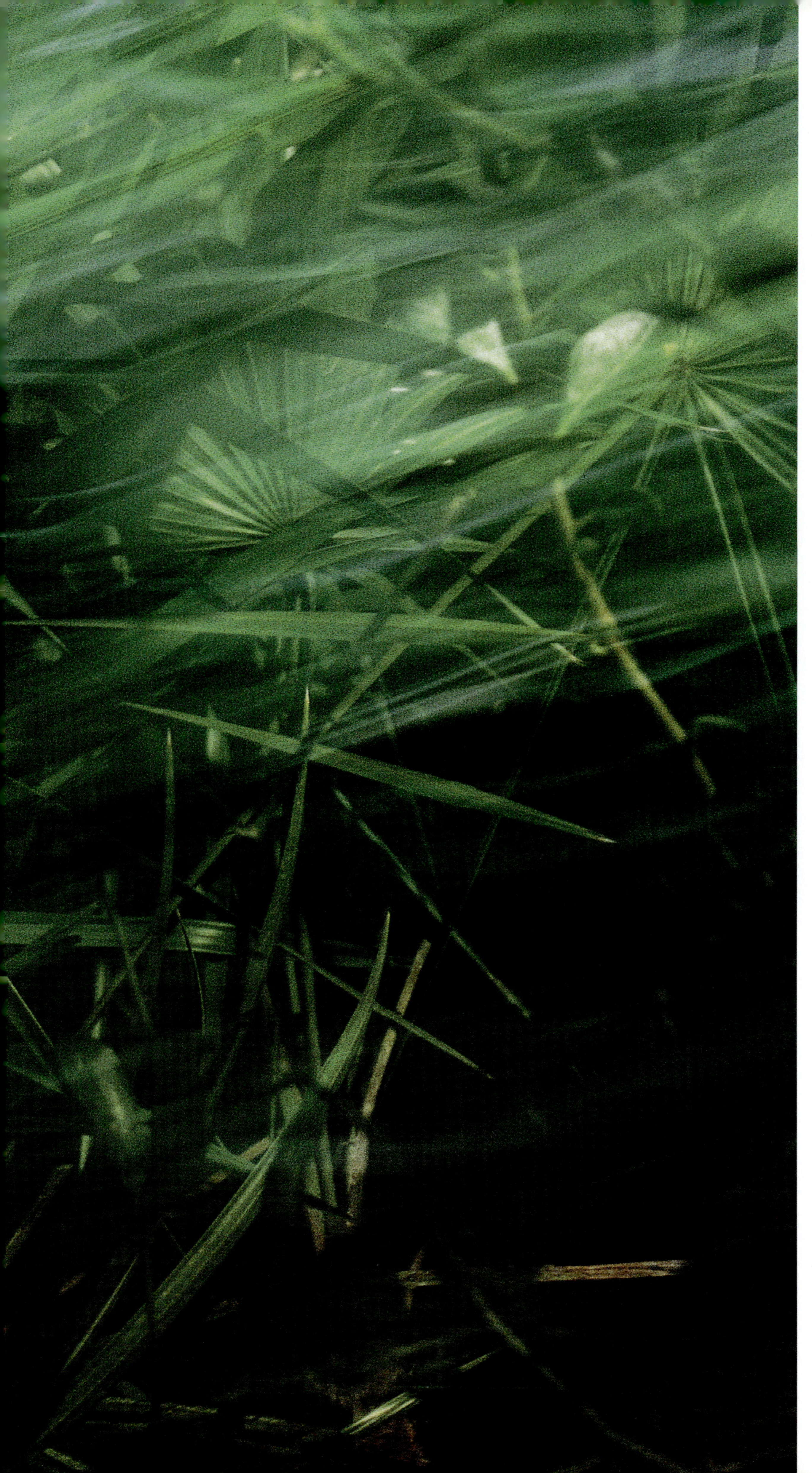

TROUBLED BEAUTY

There are perhaps 100 Florida panthers remaining in the world, and they are all living in the southwest part of that state. Given Florida's roundheeled approach to development, the future of this species looks none too bright, though because of Balog's fine 1995 photograph, this particular creature will forever entrance.

JAMES BALOG

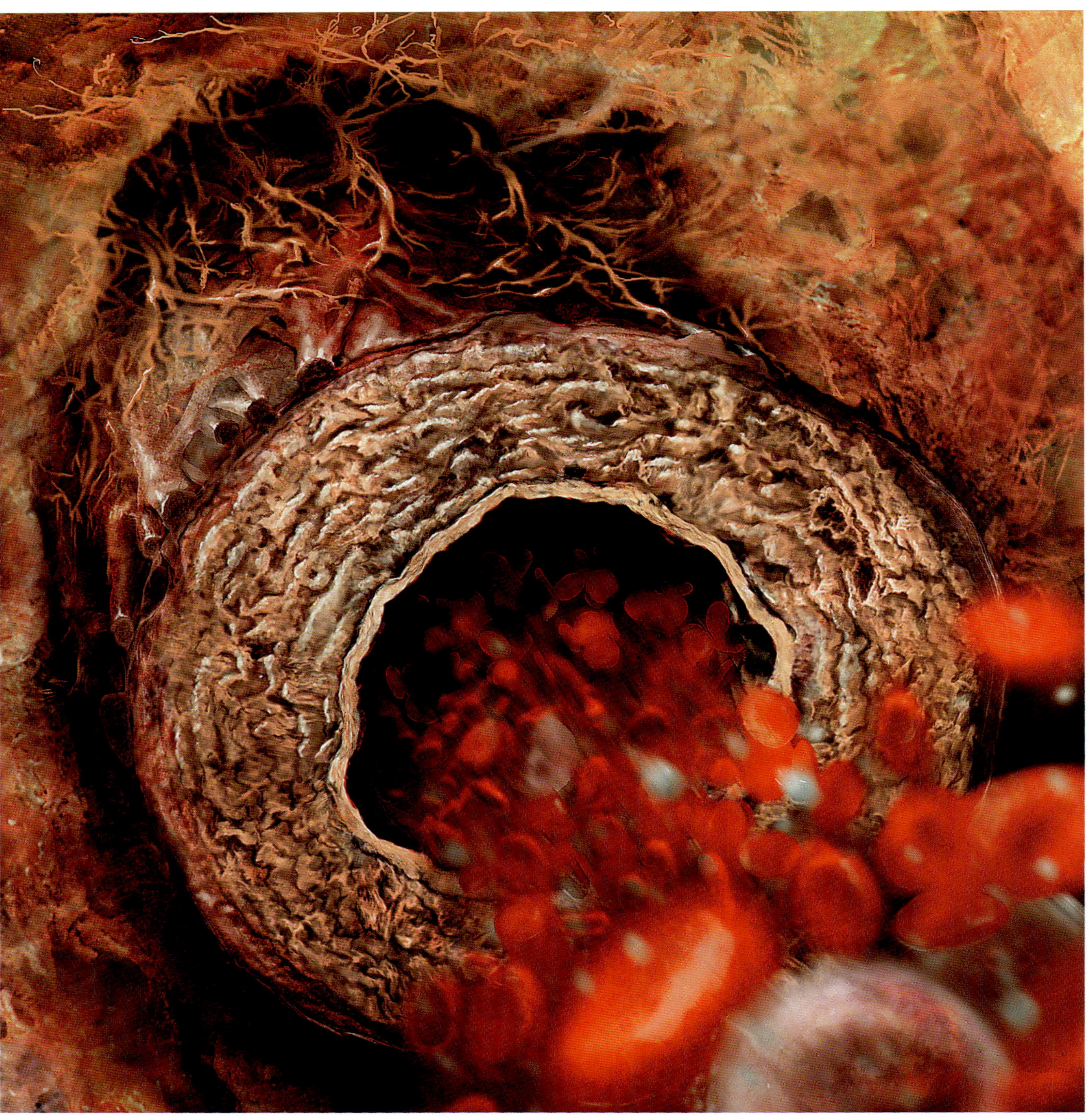

ARTERY

As a child, photographer Tsiaras was captivated by the Visible Man model. Today he co-opts medical-imaging techniques, enhances them with digital color and shadow, and creates photolike renderings of anatomical precision and visual wonder. The image above, which ran in LIFE in 2005, shows a healthy artery with its flow of trillions of blood cells.

ALEXANDER TSIARAS

LOUSE

There are thousands of different types of lice, and whether they're preying on African warthogs or some other godforsaken creature, the little parasites spend their entire life on the body of their host. The only exception is the human body louse, seen at right in a photo from 1994. This pinhead-size insect resides in clothing and moves to a person only when hungry.

DAVID SCHARF

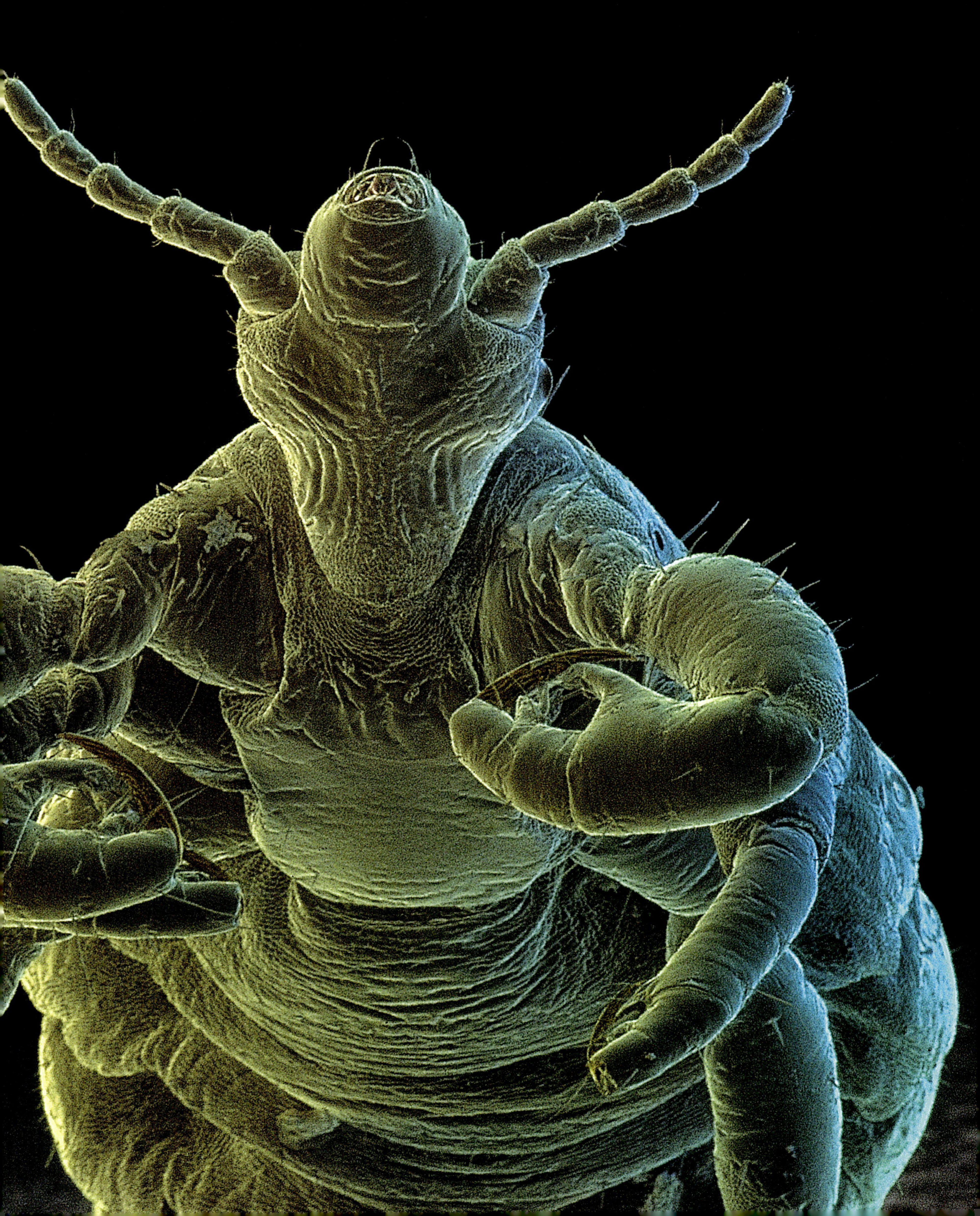

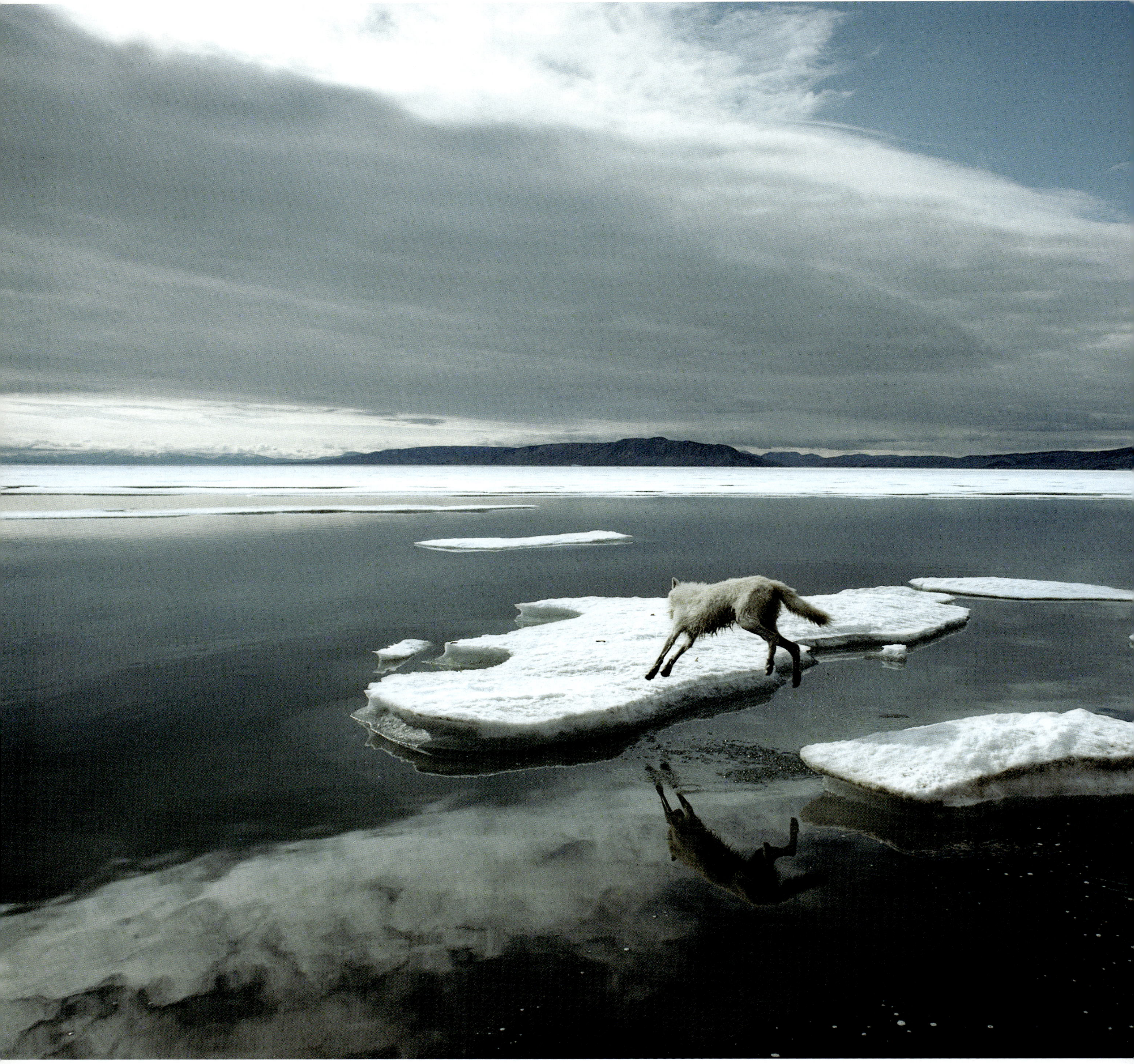

WHERE WOLVES MAY WANDER

"Patience and passion" are the prerequisites of getting a good nature shot, according to photographer Brandenburg, who has spent long periods in frigid climes taking pictures of the beautiful, haunting arctic wolf. This was taken on remote Ellesmere Island in Canada's Northwest Territories.

JIM BRANDENBURG

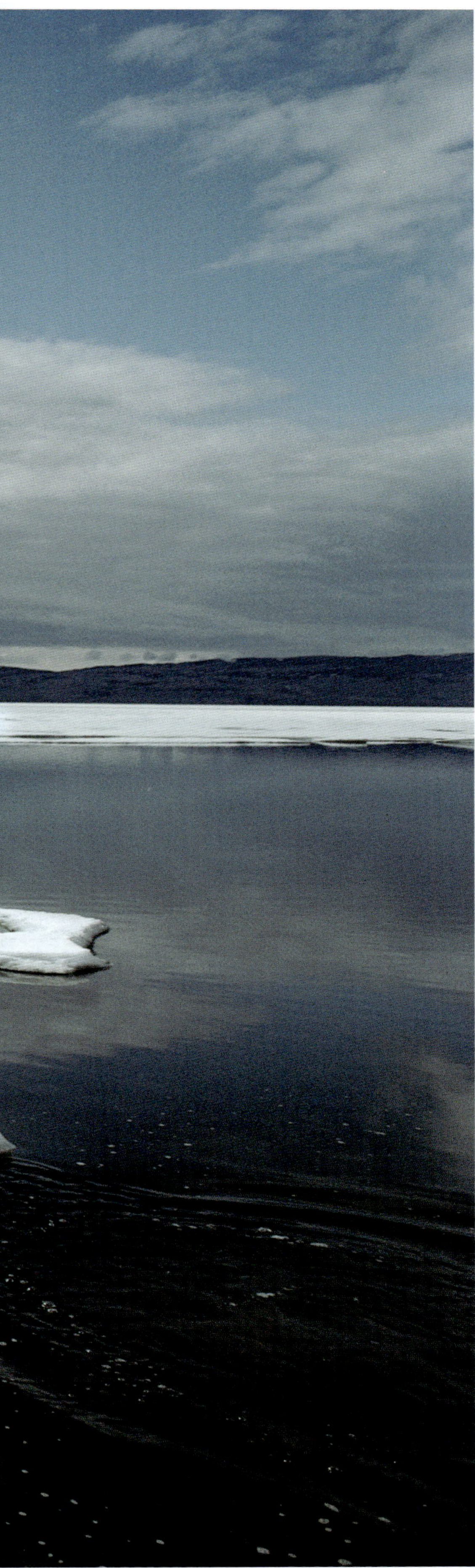

Minden Pictures

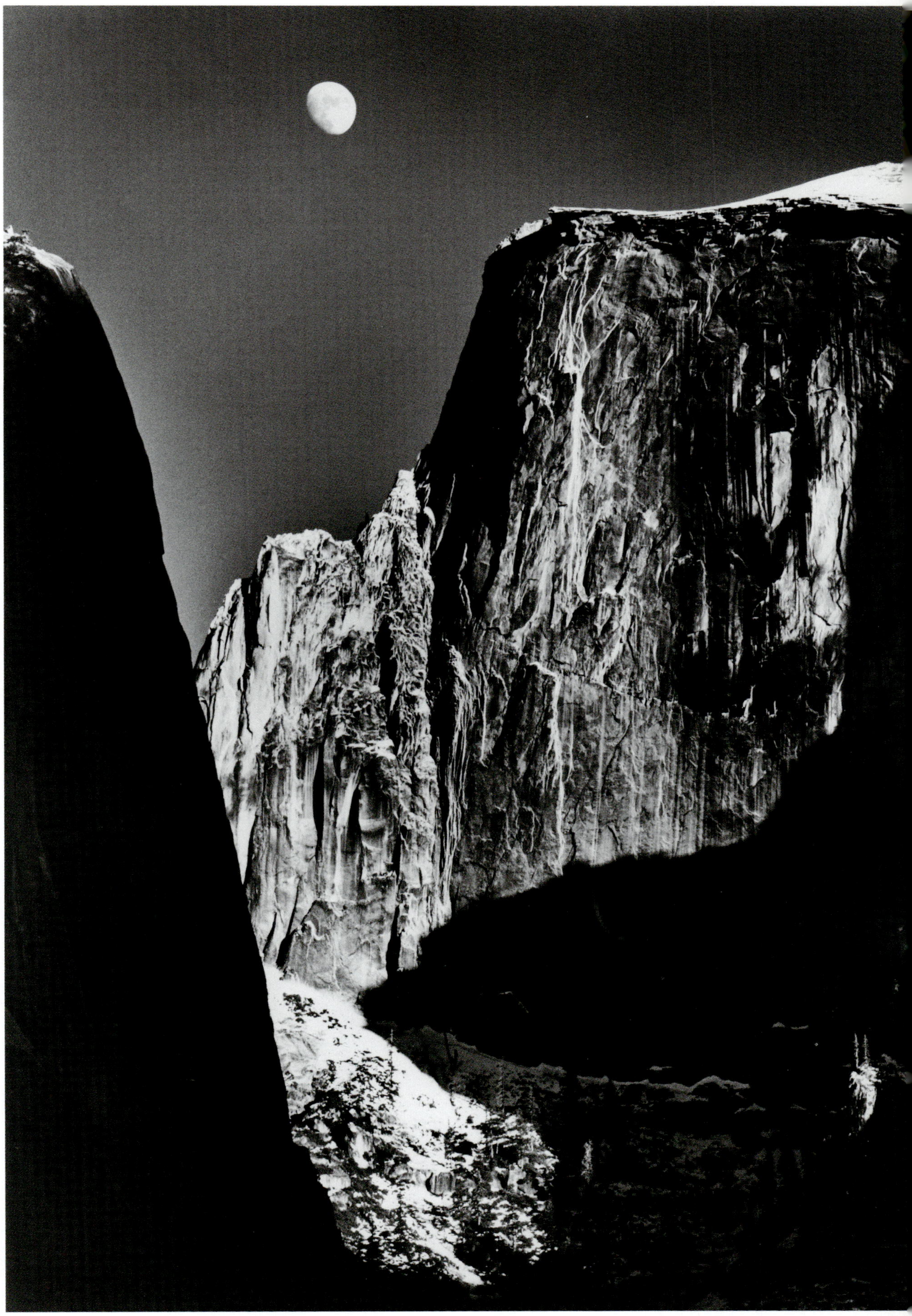

SPIRIT OF NOCTURNE

The iconic photographer of America's most iconic landscapes, Ansel Adams was a crusader with a camera, deeply devoted to the preservation of the environment. Here, in a photograph taken in 1970, the moon is at play over California's Yosemite.

ANSEL ADAMS

APOLLO 17

This last of the Apollo missions to the moon was made in December 1972. In this panoramic composite of photographs taken by astronaut Gene Cernan, his colleague Jack Schmitt is foraging for samples near Split Rock, with the lunar module beyond. The mountain at right rear is known as South Massif, while East Massif is to the left.

EUGENE CERNAN/NASA

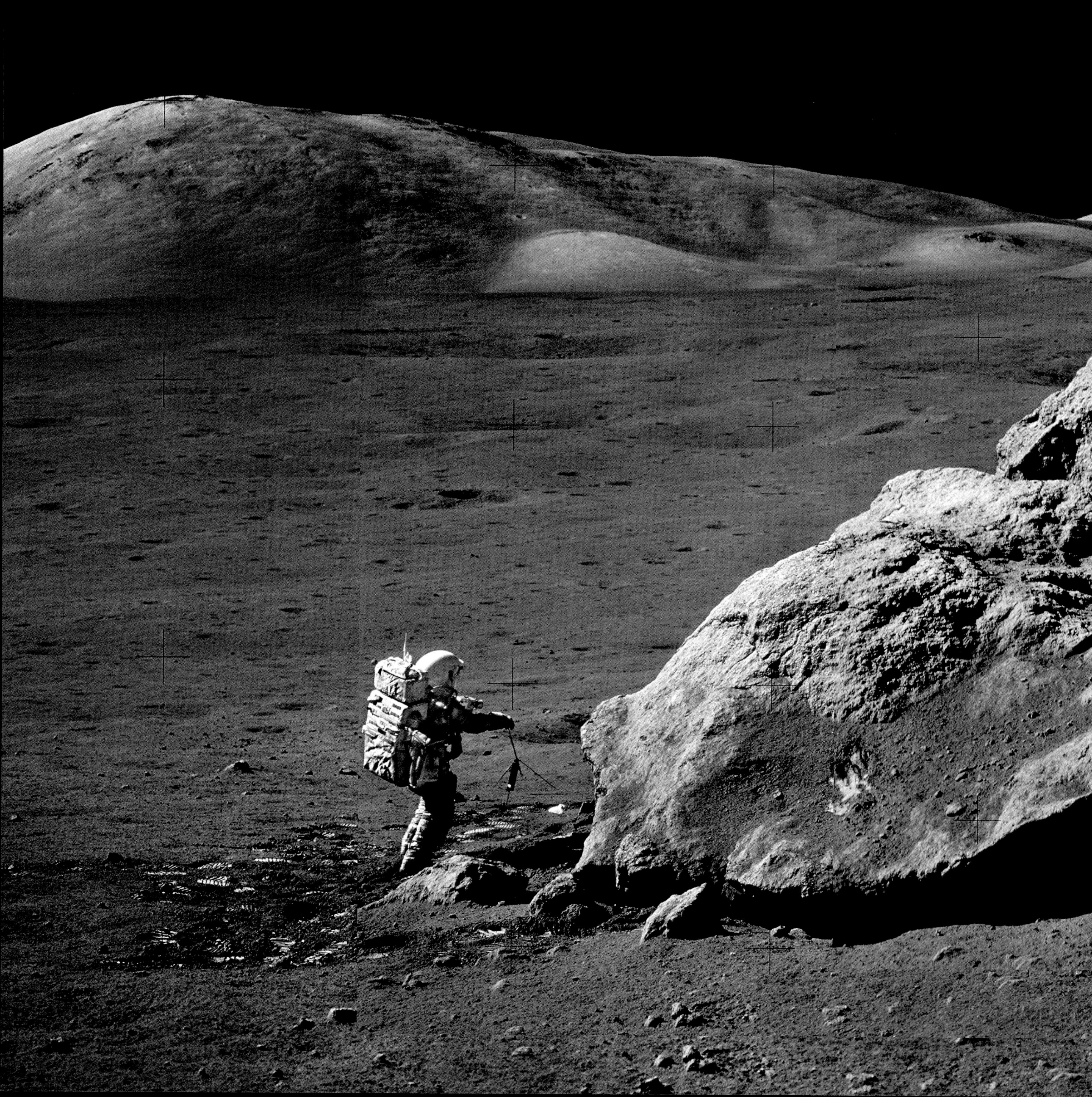

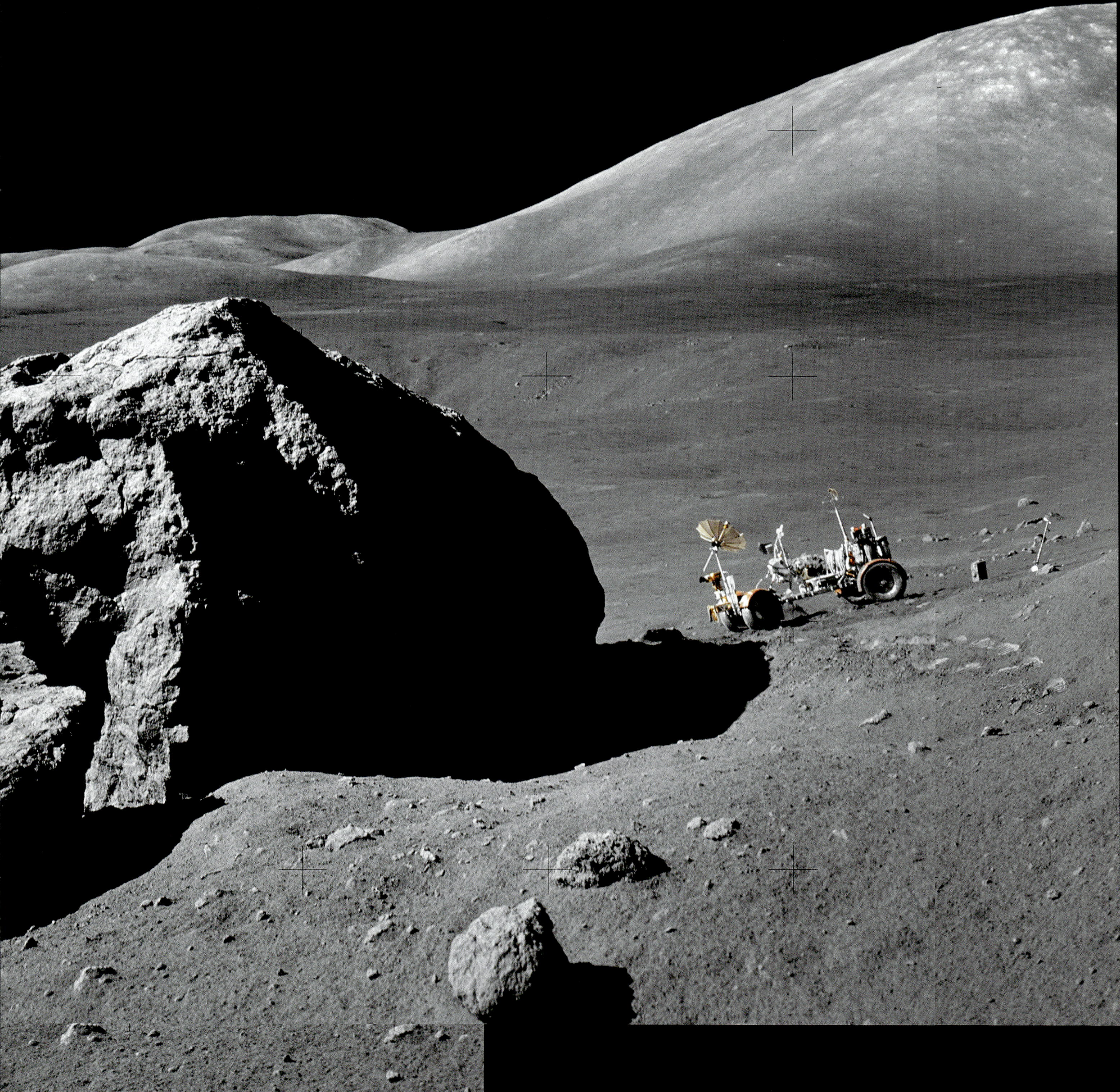

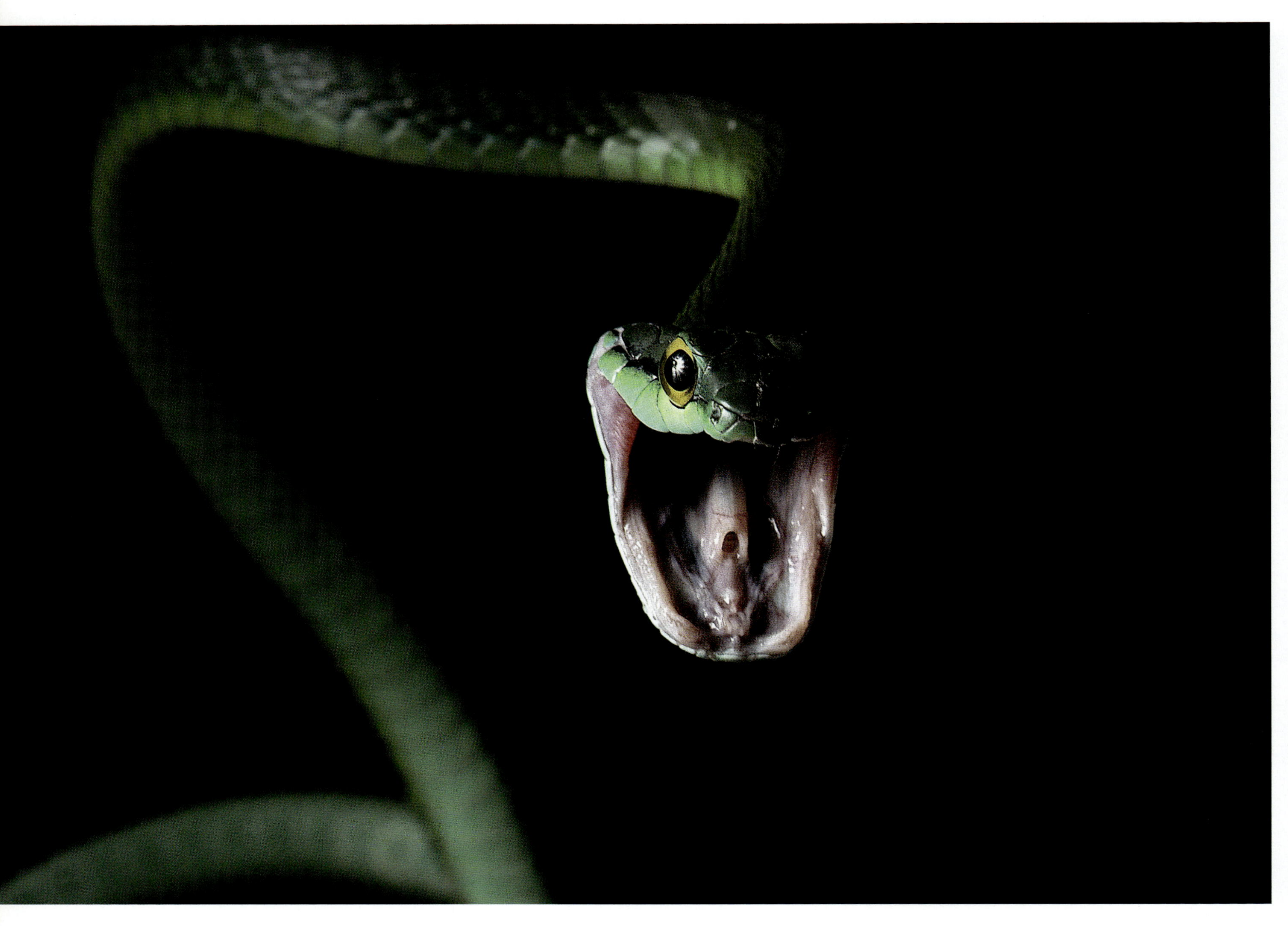

THE SERPENT

In 1982 photographer Melford was on a photo shoot of creatures inhabiting the floor of a rainforest in Costa Rica. Although fond of snakes, he quickly had a series of very unpleasant encounters with some serious customers, including the deadly fer-de-lance. Melford decided to retreat to a local research center, where he took this portrait of an arresting, but gentle, green vine snake.

MICHAEL MELFORD

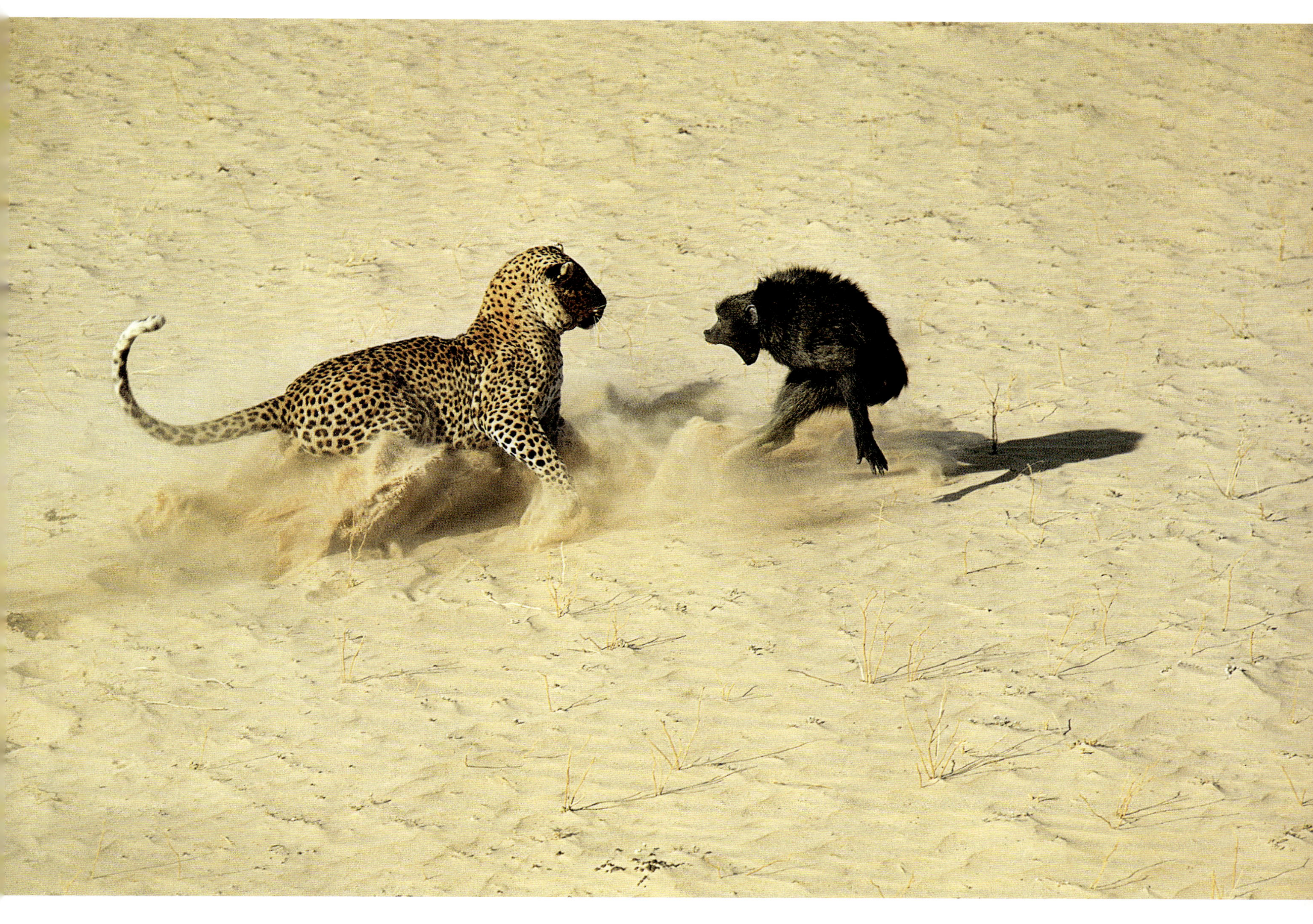

"NATURAL" ENCOUNTER

It is not beyond the pale in wildlife photography for events to be staged. For example, a ferocious tiger snarling at arm's length is indeed at arm's length, except that it may be in a game park or some such place, and not all that ferocious. Above is a rather different example of helping the photo along. This picture of a confrontation between a leopard and a baboon was taken in Botswana in 1966. These two creatures are ancient enemies, but in this case the cat was a rental dropped in among the simians. In any case, the photograph remains famous, and exceptional.

JOHN DOMINIS

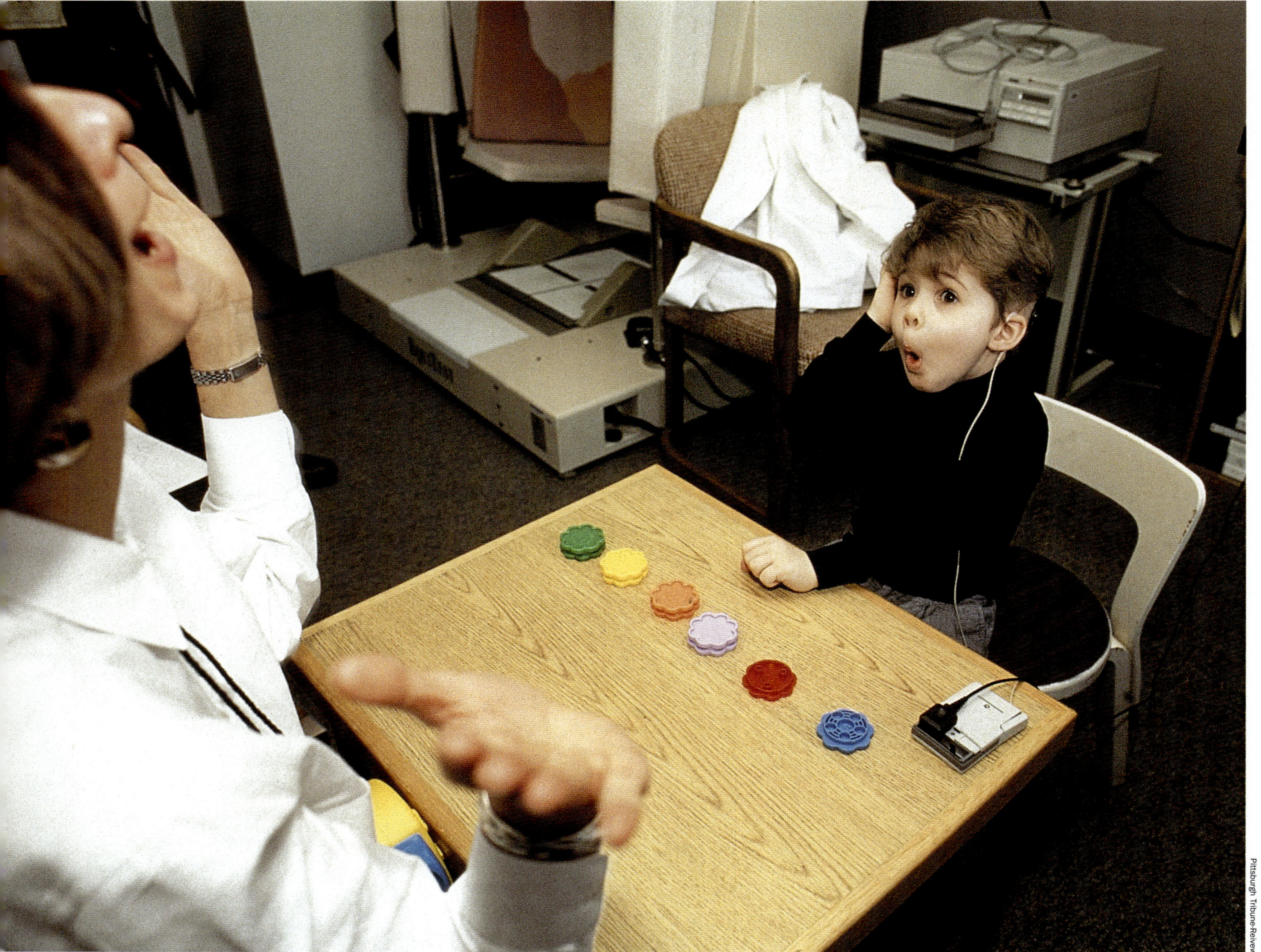

Pittsburgh Tribune-Reivew

WOW!

In 1993 four-year-old Brian Siclare, who has been deaf since birth, hears sound for the first time thanks to a surgical implant that stimulates his inner ear.

JAMES M. KUBUS

WOW!!

In 1954 pregnant Mrs. Jane Dill has just been told that, judging from the response of a chemical wafer on her tongue, she is going to have a baby girl.

WALLACE KIRKLAND

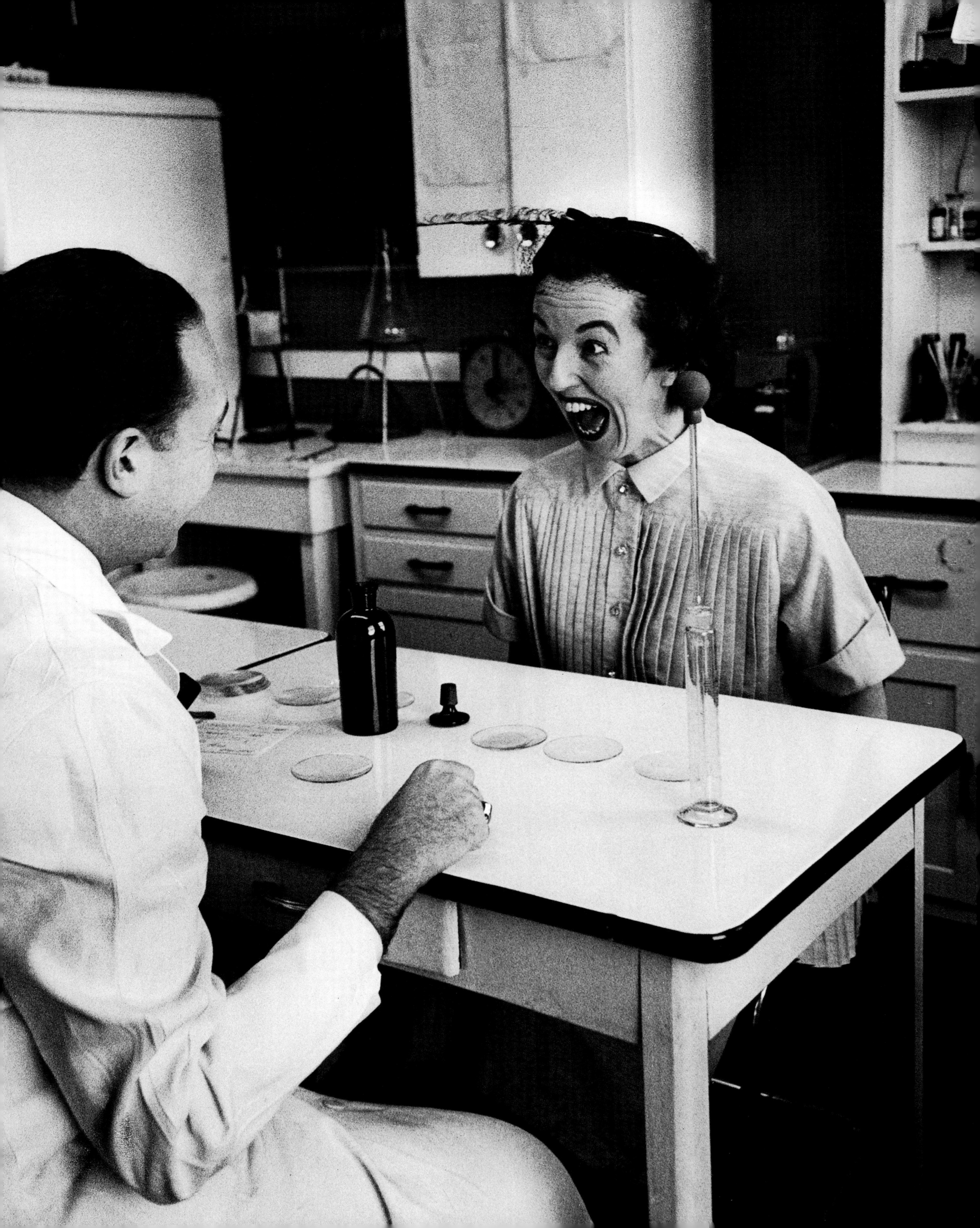

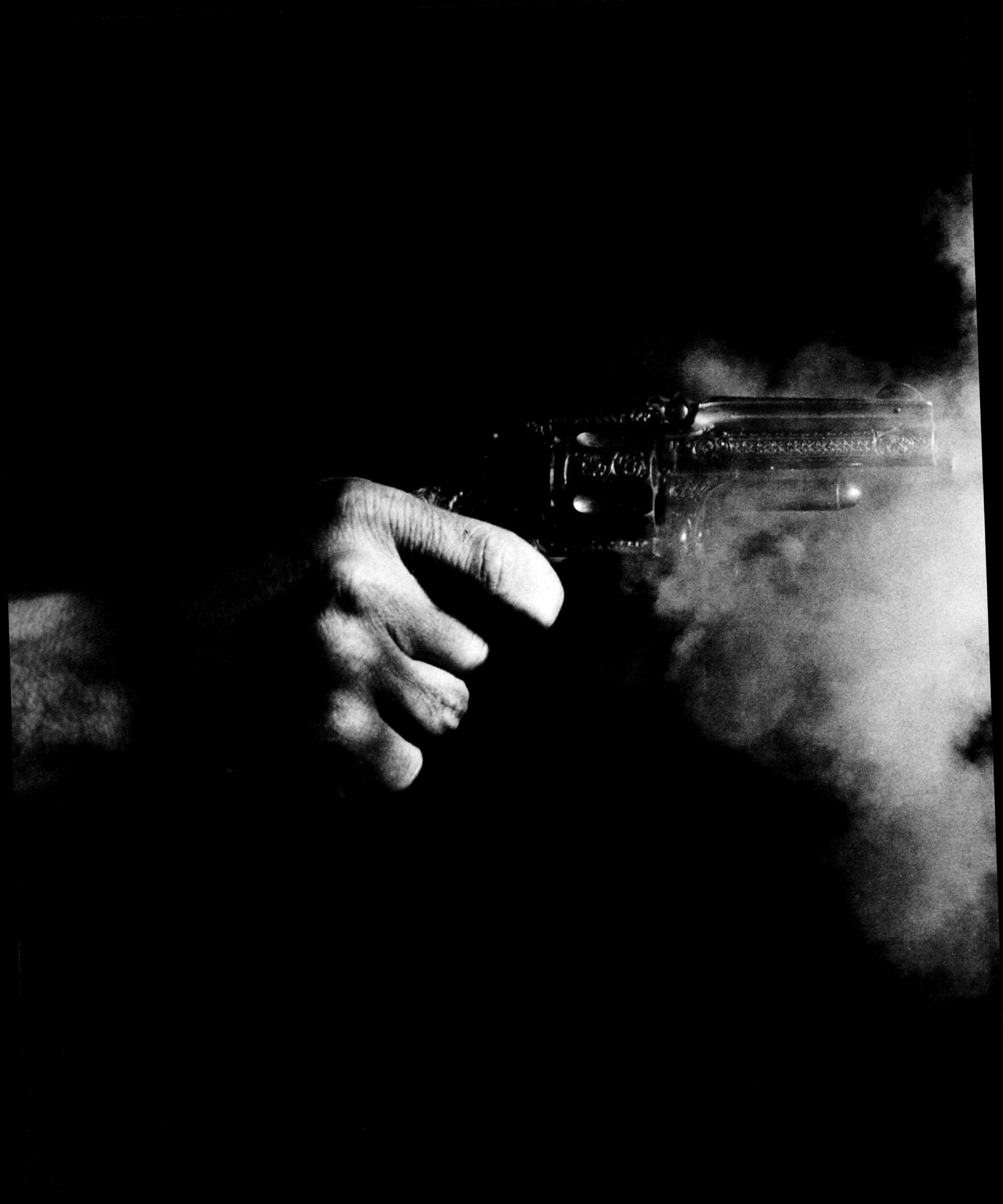

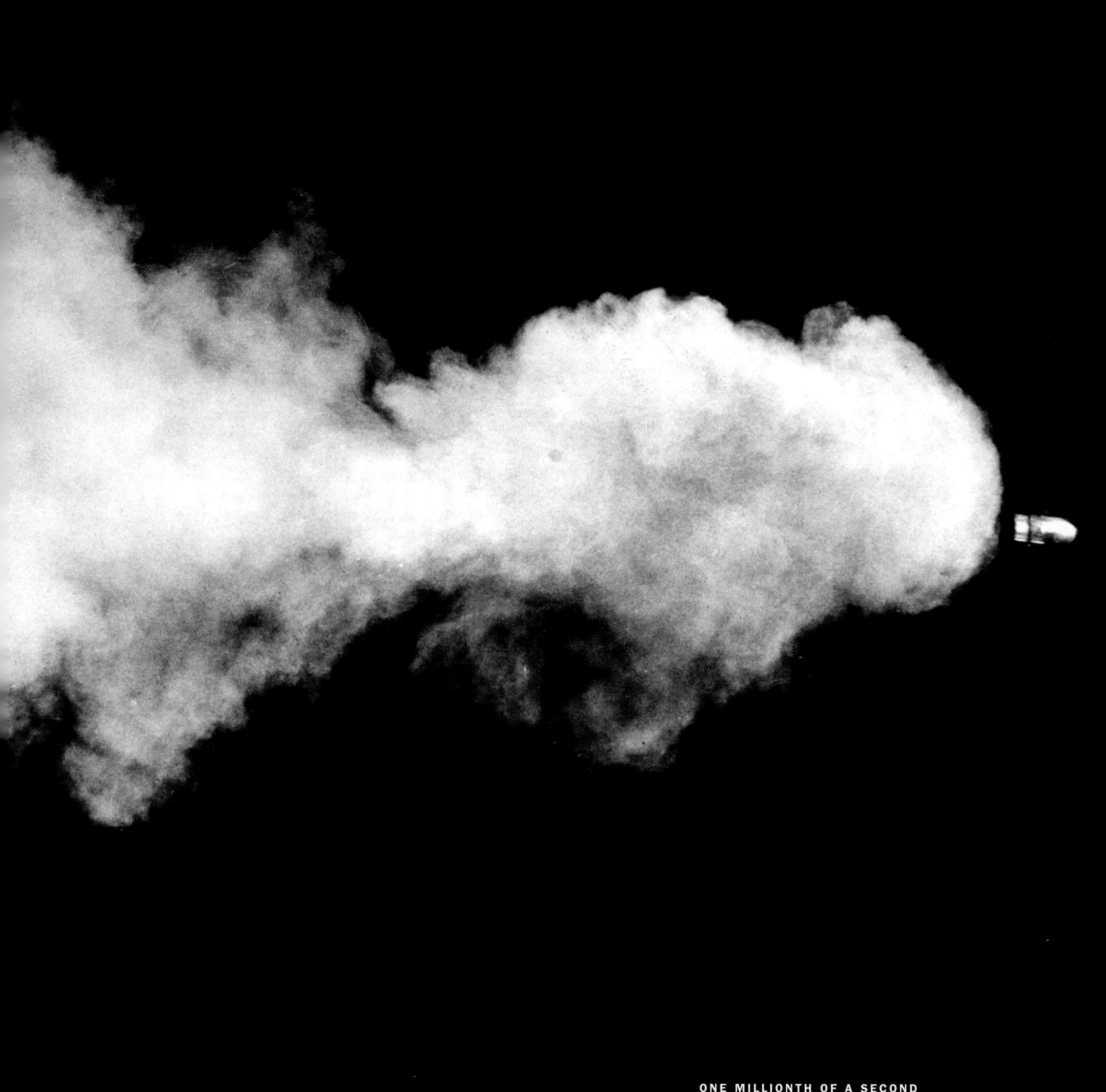

ONE MILLIONTH OF A SECOND

Prior to 1931, the fastest stop-action picture was only about one thousandth of a second. Then Harold Edgerton, who was a grad student in electrical engineering at MIT, invented the high-speed electronic flash, or stroboscope. Edgerton's skill was not confined to scientific wizardry, however. He also had an artist's touch with a photograph, as in this 1939 portrait of a speeding bullet.

HAROLD EDGERTON

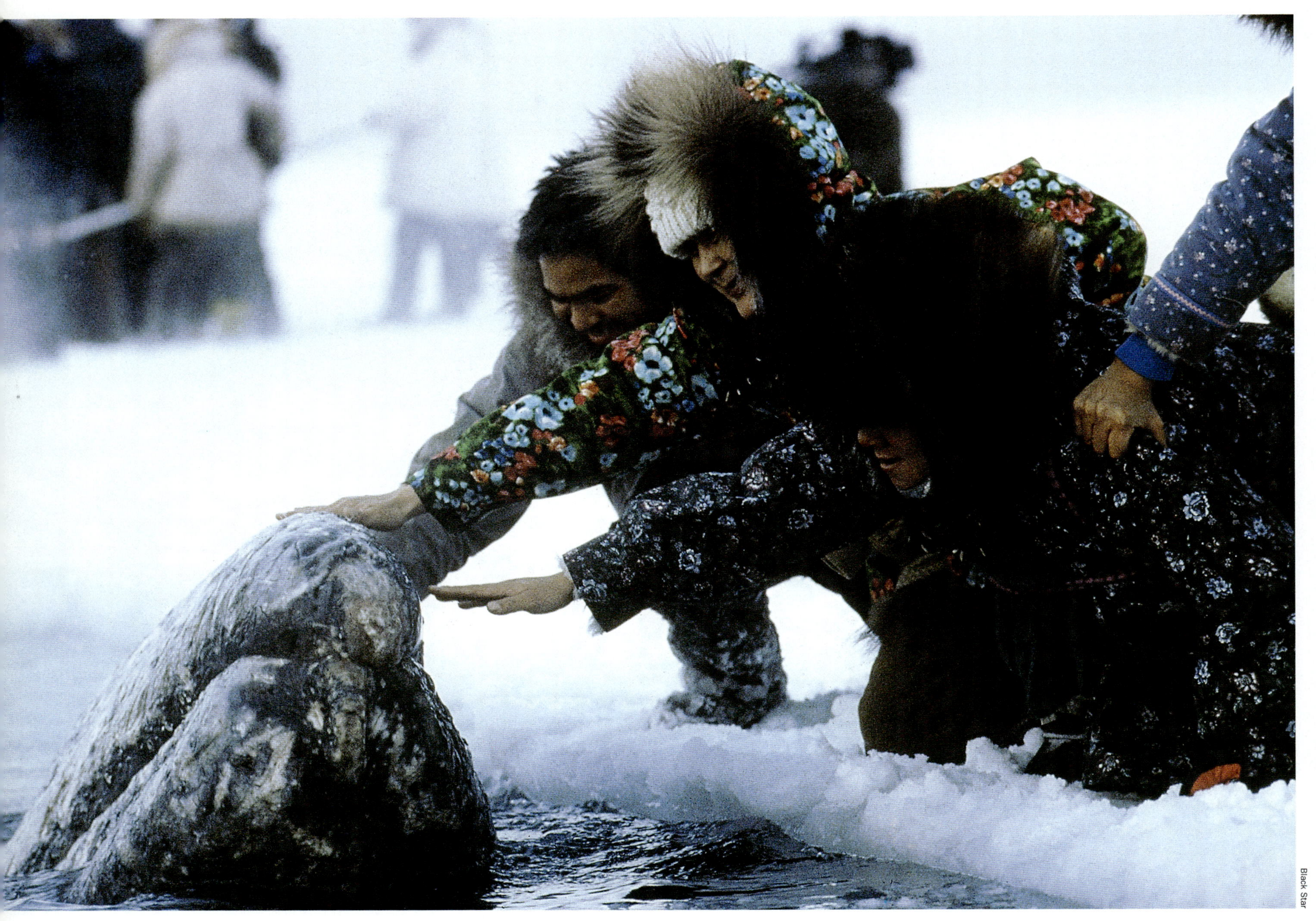
Black Star

A WHALE'S FRIENDS

Point Barrow, Alaska, always gets cold in the winter—some years earlier than usual. Such was the case in 1988, which sent thousands of gray whales scurrying southward to their wintering grounds off Baja California. However, three young ones failed to get the message and were rapidly encircled by ice. The plight of the whales became a cause, and a three-week, $1 million rescue effort ensued. The town's residents, mostly Eskimos, cut ice and poked holes, while a helicopter and two icebreakers did what they could. Two weeks in, the smallest whale vanished beneath the ice. Six days later, a channel was at last cleared to open water. Above, hopeful goodbyes are made. The fate of the weakened animals remains unknown.

CHARLES MASON

DOG'S BEST FRIEND

One day in 1947 the Olson family in Yakima, Wash., brought home a duckling, and "Donald" instantly became fast friends with the family dog—to the extent that Donald emulated everything the dog did, including chasing children and other dogs from the yard. Donald actually became rather a nuisance in the town, so the Olsons gave him to a rancher a dozen miles away. There, he became pals with a Chesapeake Bay retriever named Trigger (opposite). However, whenever the ranchers tossed Donald into the pond so that he could be with the other ducks, Trigger would immediately dash in and retrieve him. Trigger was as gentle as possible, but ultimately it was decided that Donald would be best back with the Olsons.

LOOMIS DEAN

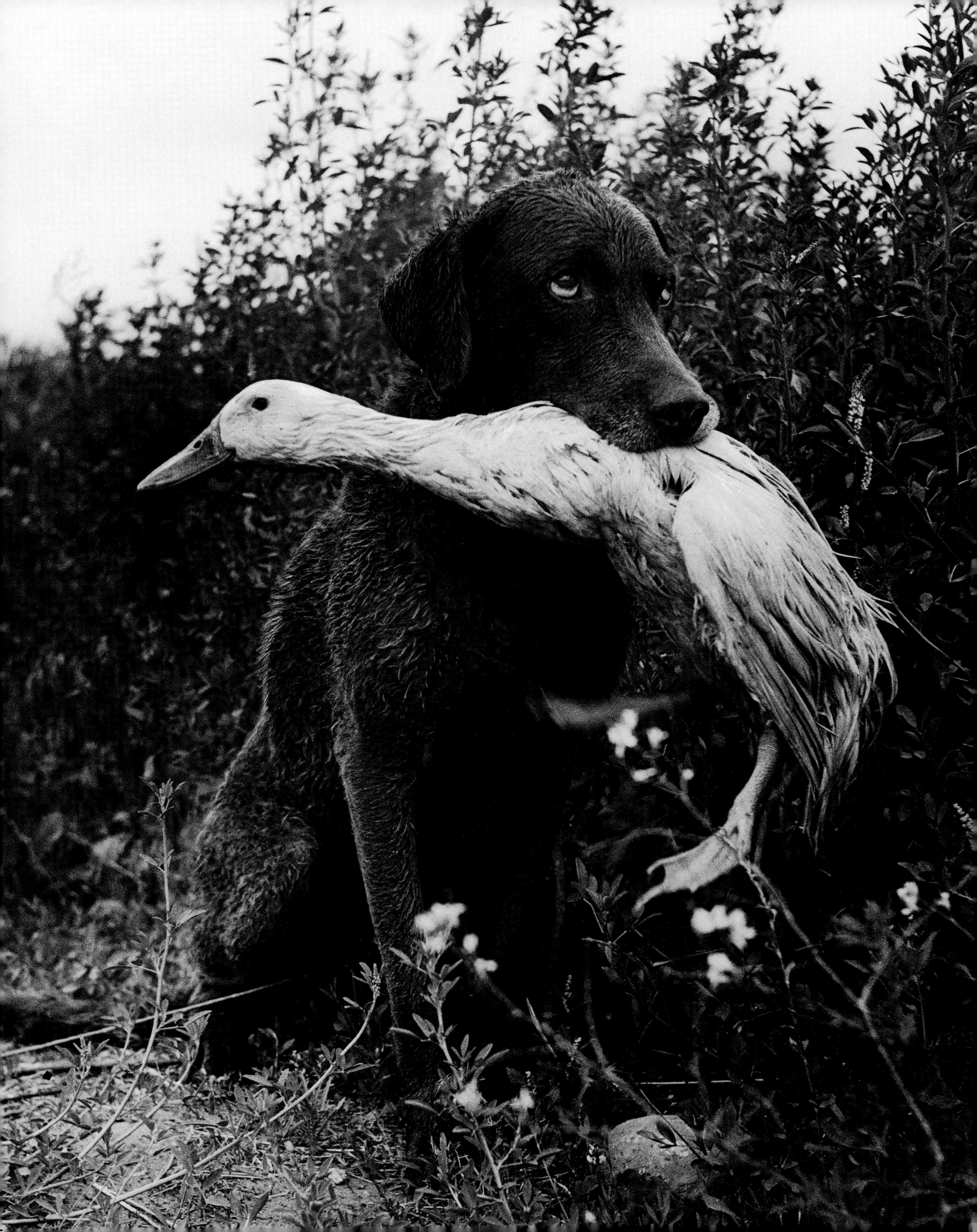

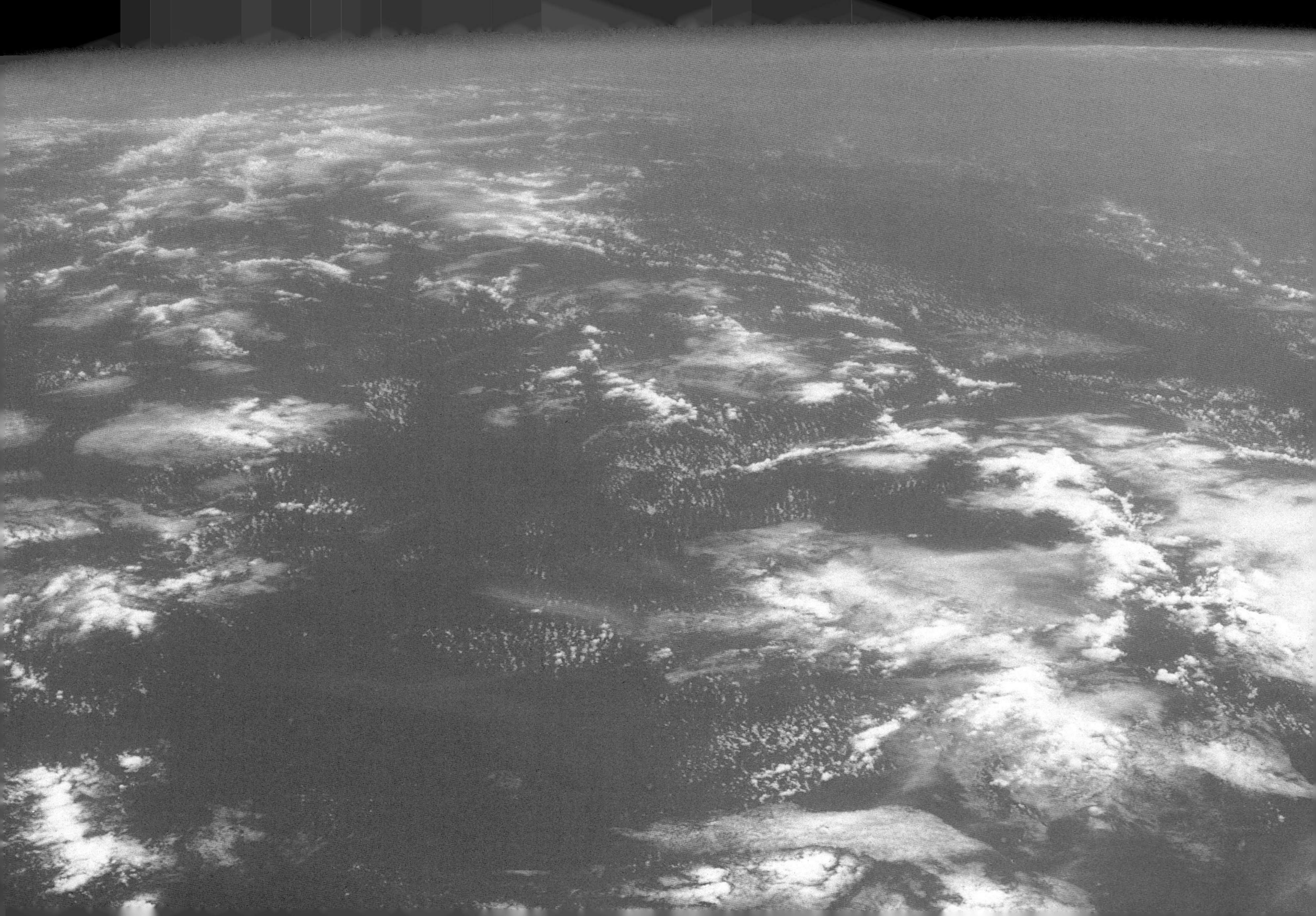

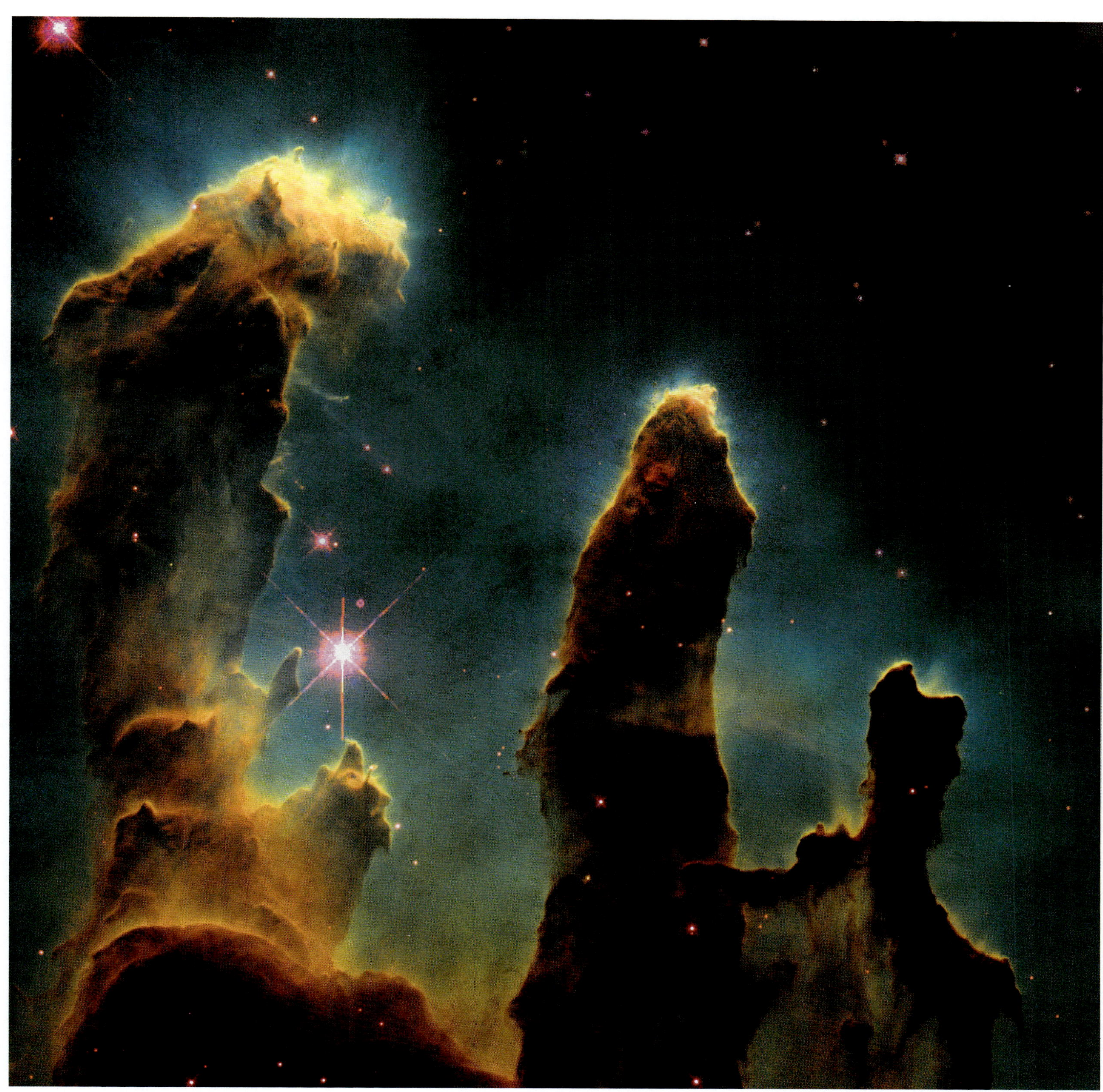

WITHOUT A NET

At 8:25 a.m. on February 7, 1984, Navy Capt. Bruce McCandless stepped from the shuttle *Challenger* and became the first free-flying human in space. McCandless had no tether and used a nitrogen-propelled backpack to venture 300 feet from *Challenger* as he and the spaceship orbited Earth at about 17,000 mph.

ROBERT L. GIBSON/NASA

THE HUBBLE

In 1990 another space shuttle, *Discovery,* carried into Earth's orbit an extraordinary optical device known as the Hubble Space Telescope, which has sent back images and data providing important clues to the origin and development of our universe. The image above, from 1995, shows part of the Eagle Nebula, a star-forming region that is 7,000 light-years away.

JEFF HESTER & PAUL SCOWAN/NASA

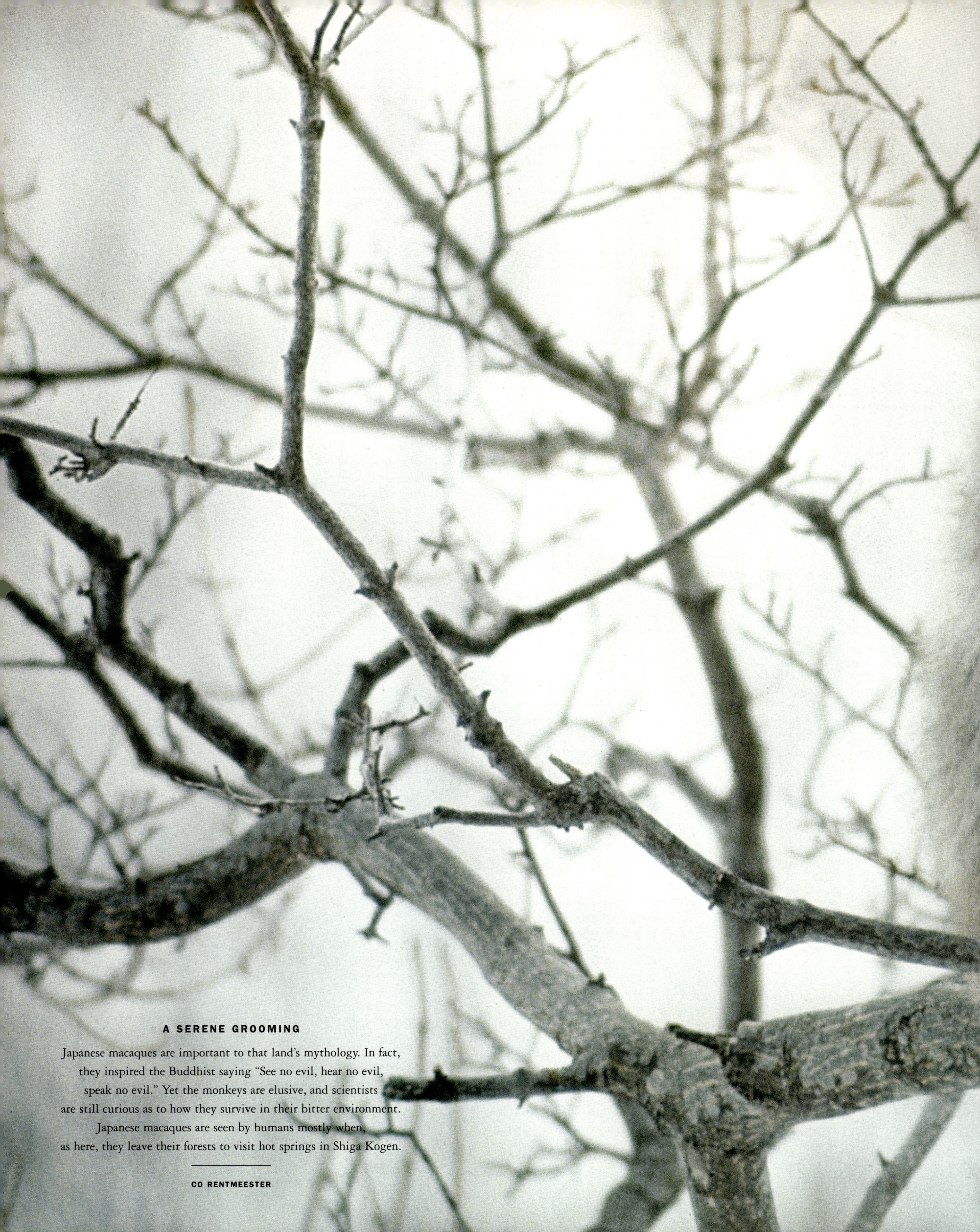

A SERENE GROOMING

Japanese macaques are important to that land's mythology. In fact, they inspired the Buddhist saying "See no evil, hear no evil, speak no evil." Yet the monkeys are elusive, and scientists are still curious as to how they survive in their bitter environment. Japanese macaques are seen by humans mostly when, as here, they leave their forests to visit hot springs in Shiga Kogen.

CO RENTMEESTER

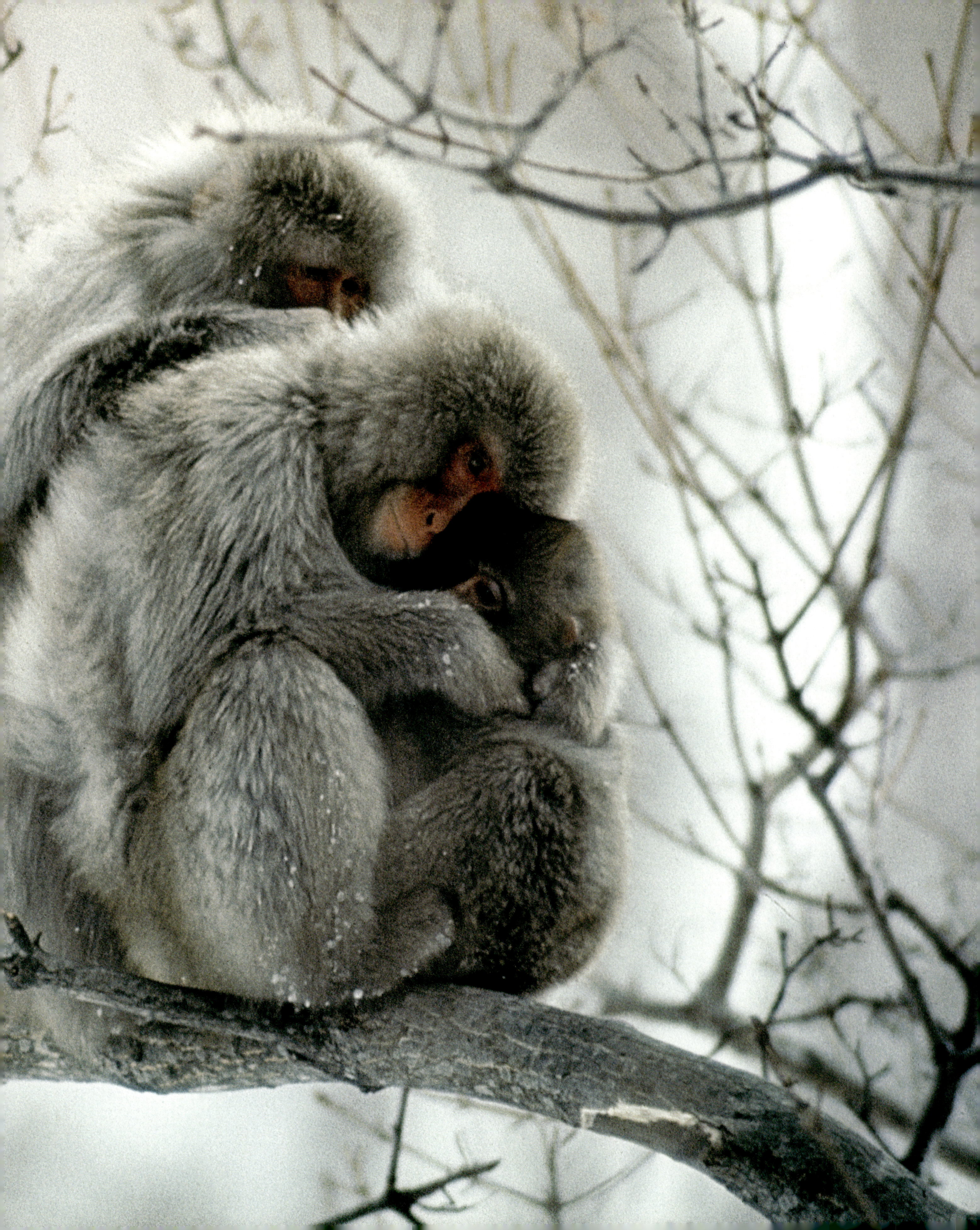

SPORT

When LIFE opened for business in 1936, there was considerable attention paid to the news of the day and, of course, to photo essays, and to science and art and fashion and other facets of society. This is not to say that the arena of sport was entirely ignored. After all . . . a sound mind in a sound body, and all that. But there was essentially no recognition of the realm of organized sport.

There were nods to certain sporting endeavors. LIFE's third cover featured skiing—now, there's a good, outdoorsy pursuit. Then, two dozen covers later it was time to showcase marbles—an excellent way to foster good hand–eye coordination. By the 36th week it was deemed time for another sports cover; this time the subject was polo—not a game for everyone, granted, but without question a test of spiritual and financial resolve. Finally, with nearly a year gone, there appeared on the cover a young man clad in gridiron gear with the words NO. 1 TROJAN. The lad's name wasn't actually mentioned, so the words came off more like a Southern Cal fight song, but at least a major sport had made an appearance on LIFE's cover.

It must be said that this sort of "gentlemen's" approach to athletics held sway for some years. Indeed, in the 1940s, one sports editor at LIFE averred with a twinkle that he had never even attended a major league baseball game until he landed the job. Having this fellow oversee your sports coverage is tantamount to hiring a food editor who has never set foot inside a restaurant.

Eventually, of course, the magazine's approach to sport did begin to change, however coincidentally, about the time that the nation changed its sports focus. Professional basketball and football were also-rans until the 1950s, as the collegiate versions had long dominated those games. In that decade though, the tactics, size and speed of the professionals began to attract the bulk of national attention, until today when even mediocre players are household names.

So, as time passed, LIFE increasingly embraced the athlete, and not simply the badminton or yachting whiz. Sport carved out its own niche at the magazine—not the same sort of coverage provided at sports weeklies, certainly, or even at the newsweeklies, but rather our own particular way of presenting this very human drama, this very special spectacle. And throughout our coverage, we like to think that we have never overlooked that place where sports has its genesis: in the hearts and minds of children.

FAMILY FARE

The fifth annual Pebble Beach, Calif., sports-car races are a perfect occasion in 1954 for these folks to savor picnic food and libations along with the elemental allure of speed.

ROBERT LACKENBACH

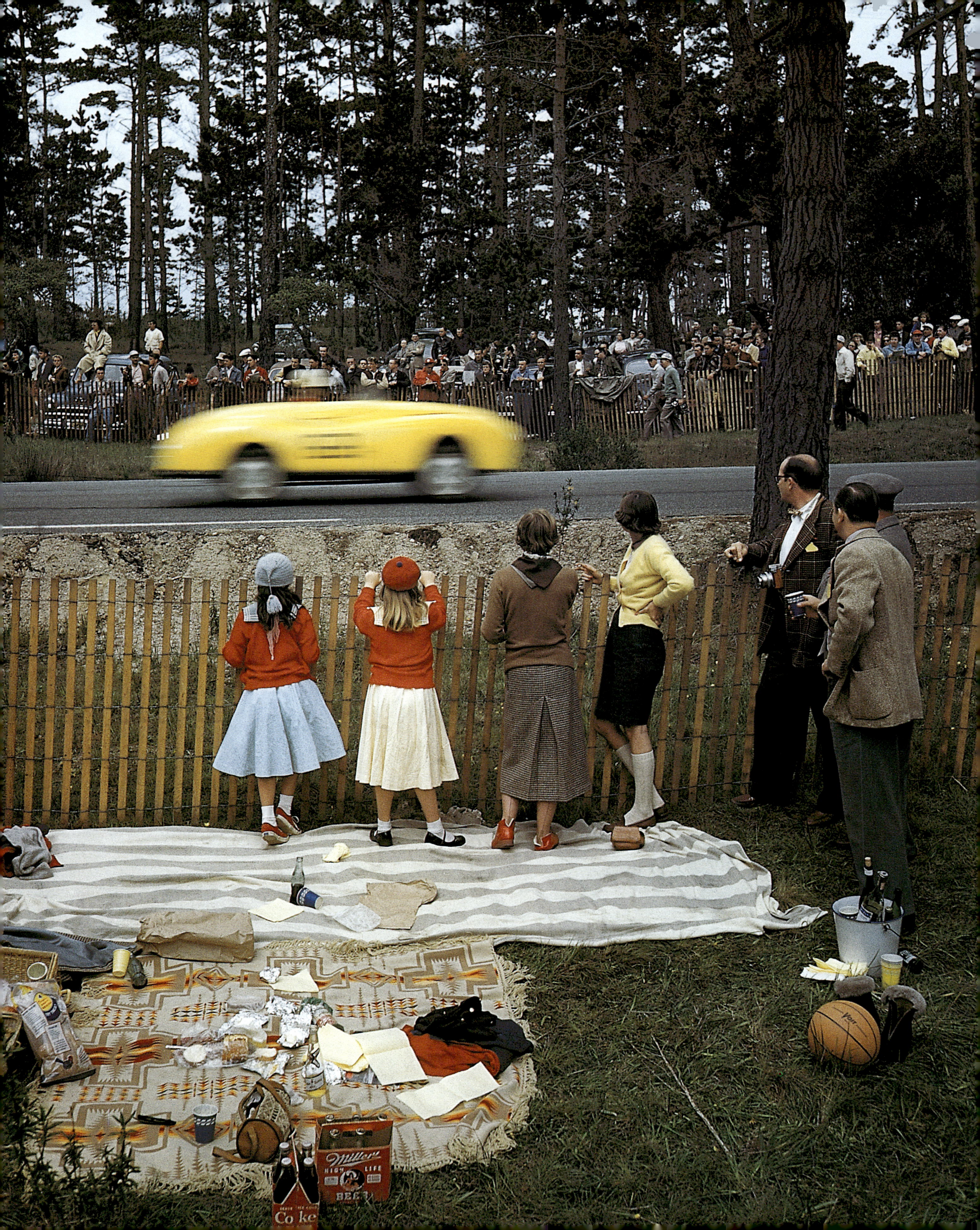
Miller
HIGH LIFE
BEER
Coke

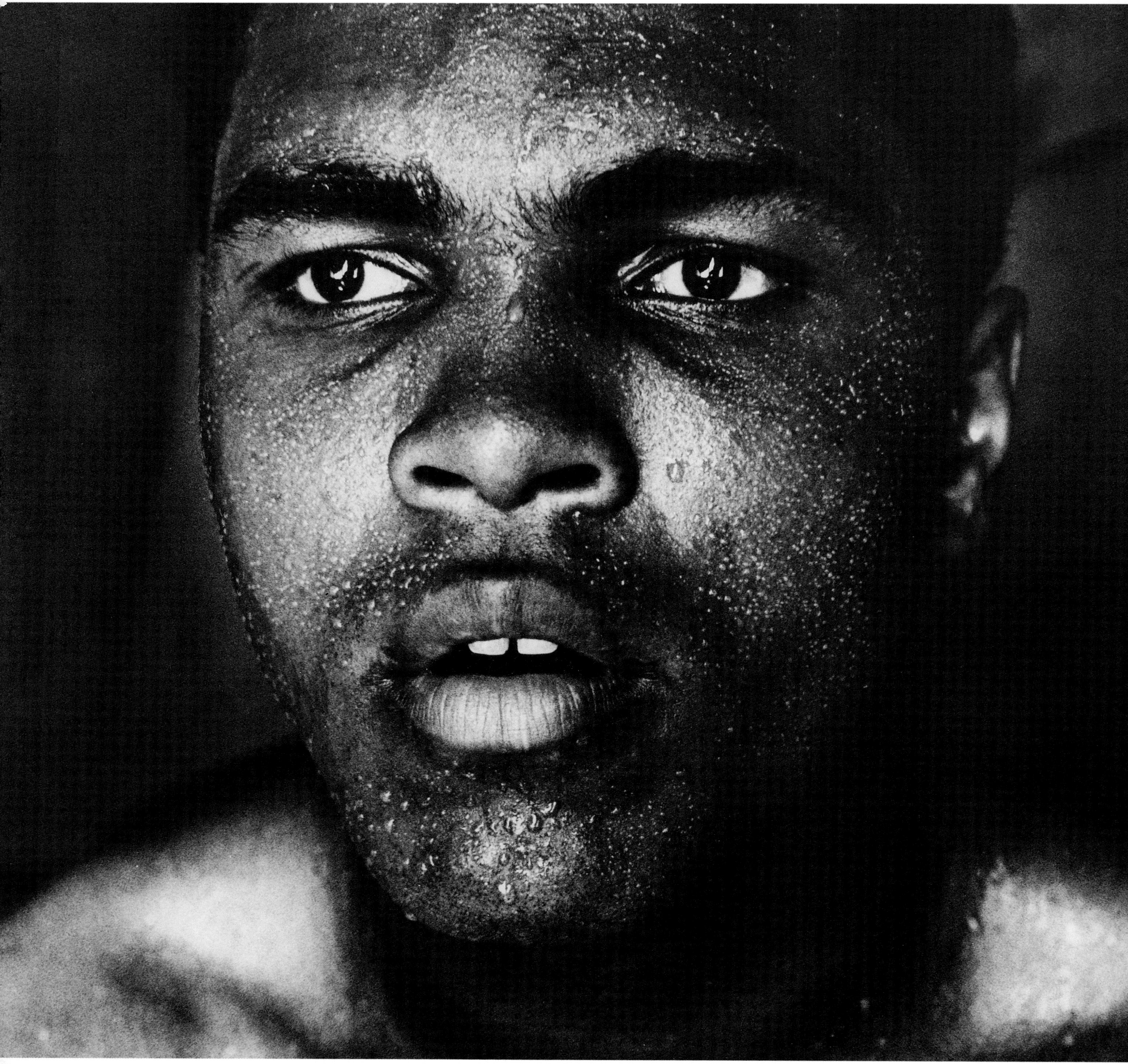

THE GREATEST

The intensity of Muhammad Ali is in full display in this photo taken in September 1966, as the champ prepares for a bout with Germany's Karl Mildenberger. Ali would win on a TKO in the 12th round, but would have his title stripped a half year later when he refused to enter the draft.

GORDON PARKS

DOWN, BUT NOT OUT

Jersey Joe Walcott stands over Joe Louis after knocking him to the mat in a December 1947 title match at Madison Square Garden. The Brown Bomber retained his crown with a controversial split decision, but in 1948 knocked Walcott out in a return match.

GJON MILI

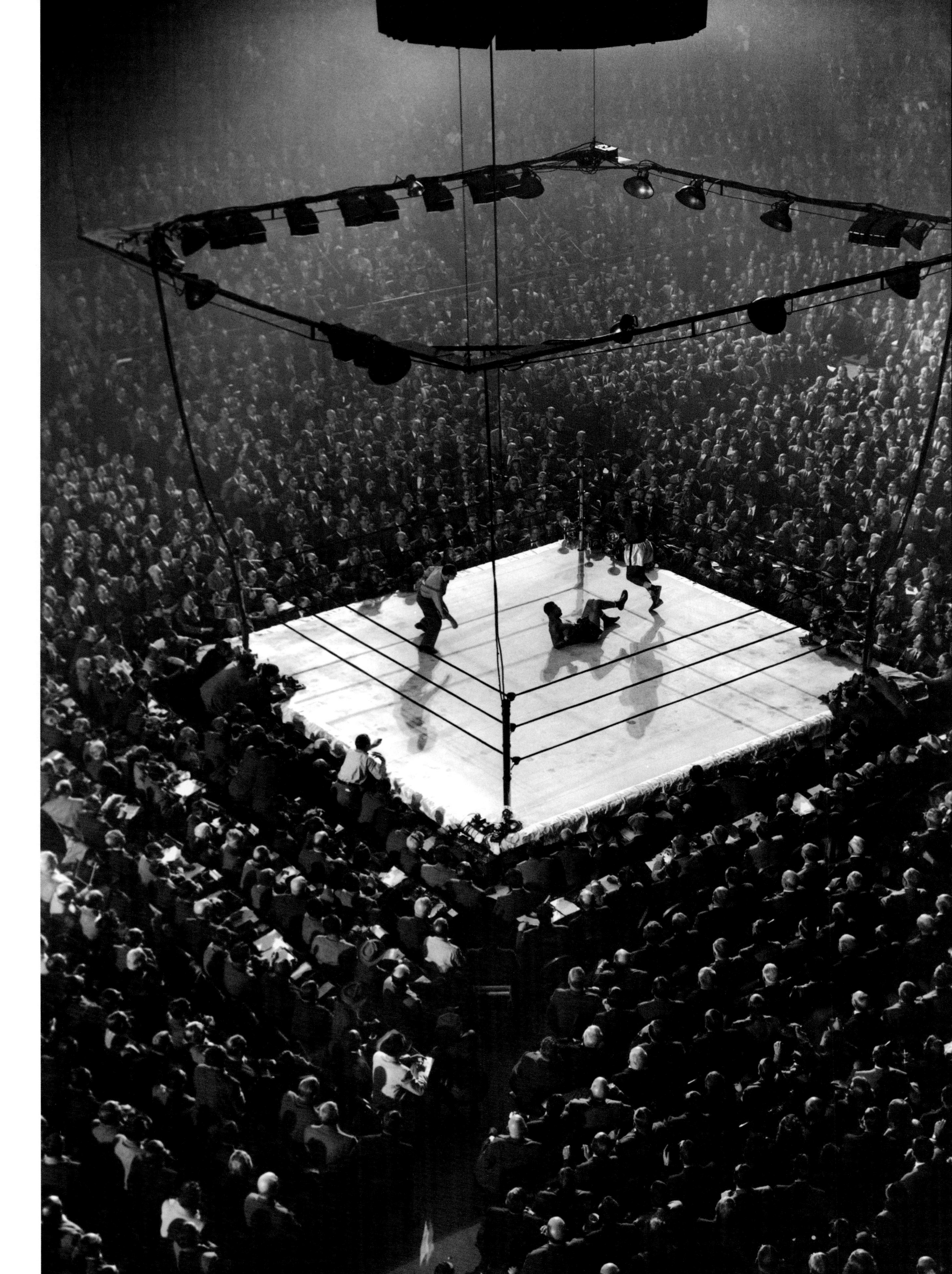

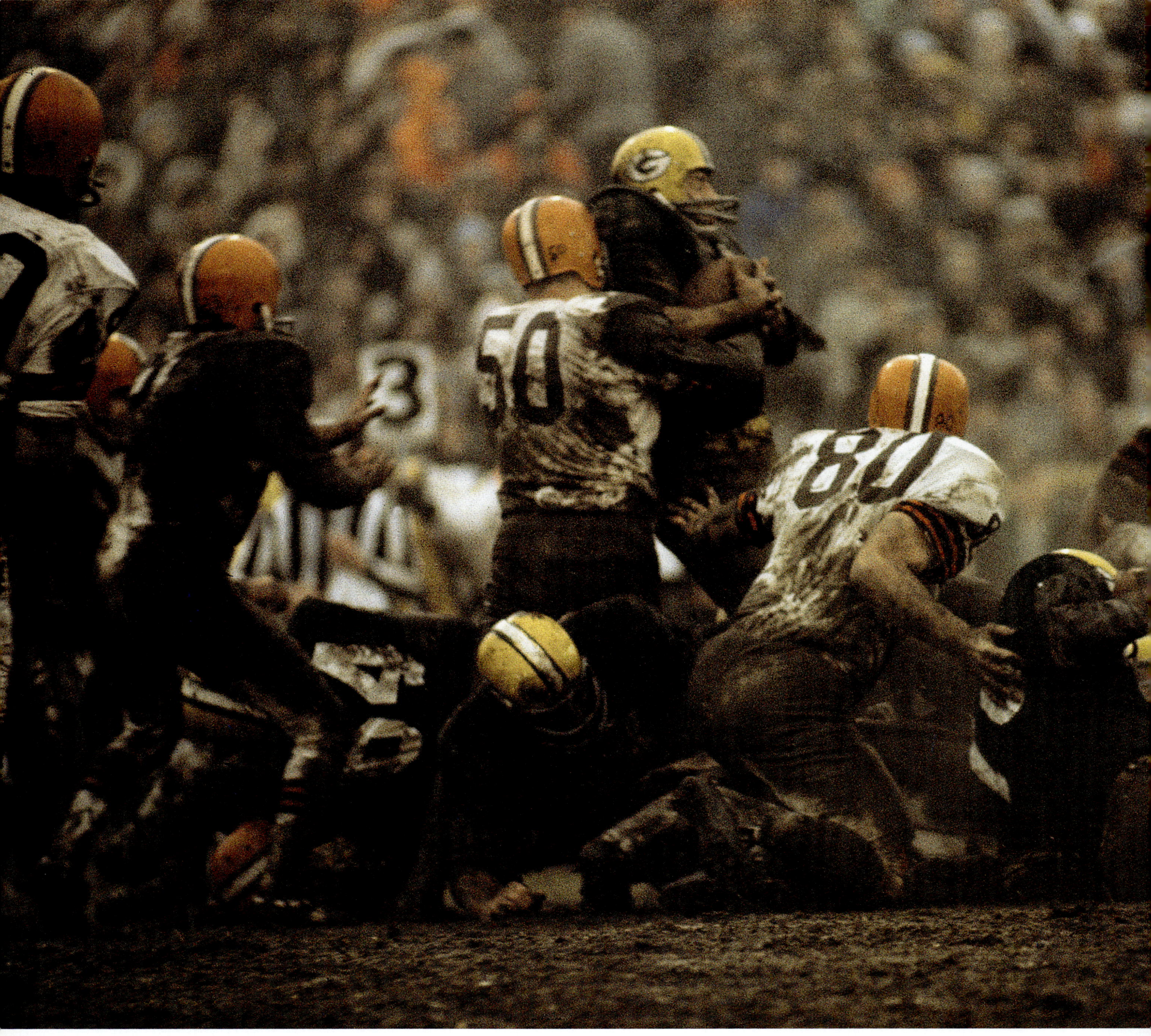

THE GLADIATORS

In the 1965 NFL title game, Vince Costello of the Cleveland Browns has Jim Taylor of the Green Bay Packers in a bear hug, but the Pack, under coach Vince Lombardi, would emerge victorious. Rickerby's photography helped bring the pro game, with all of its attendant strategy, speed and violence, into national prominence.

ARTHUR RICKERBY

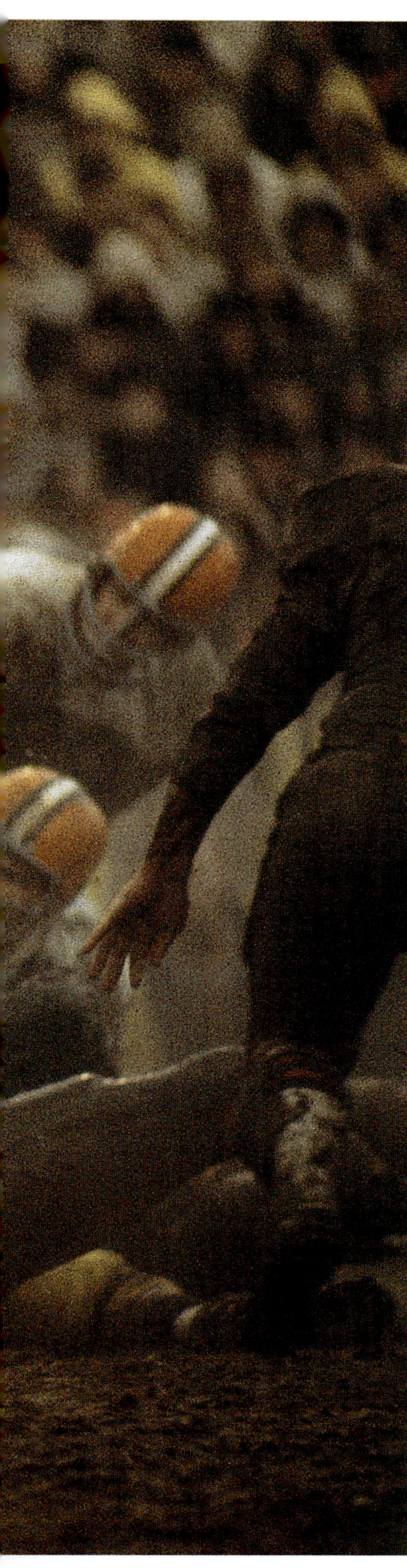

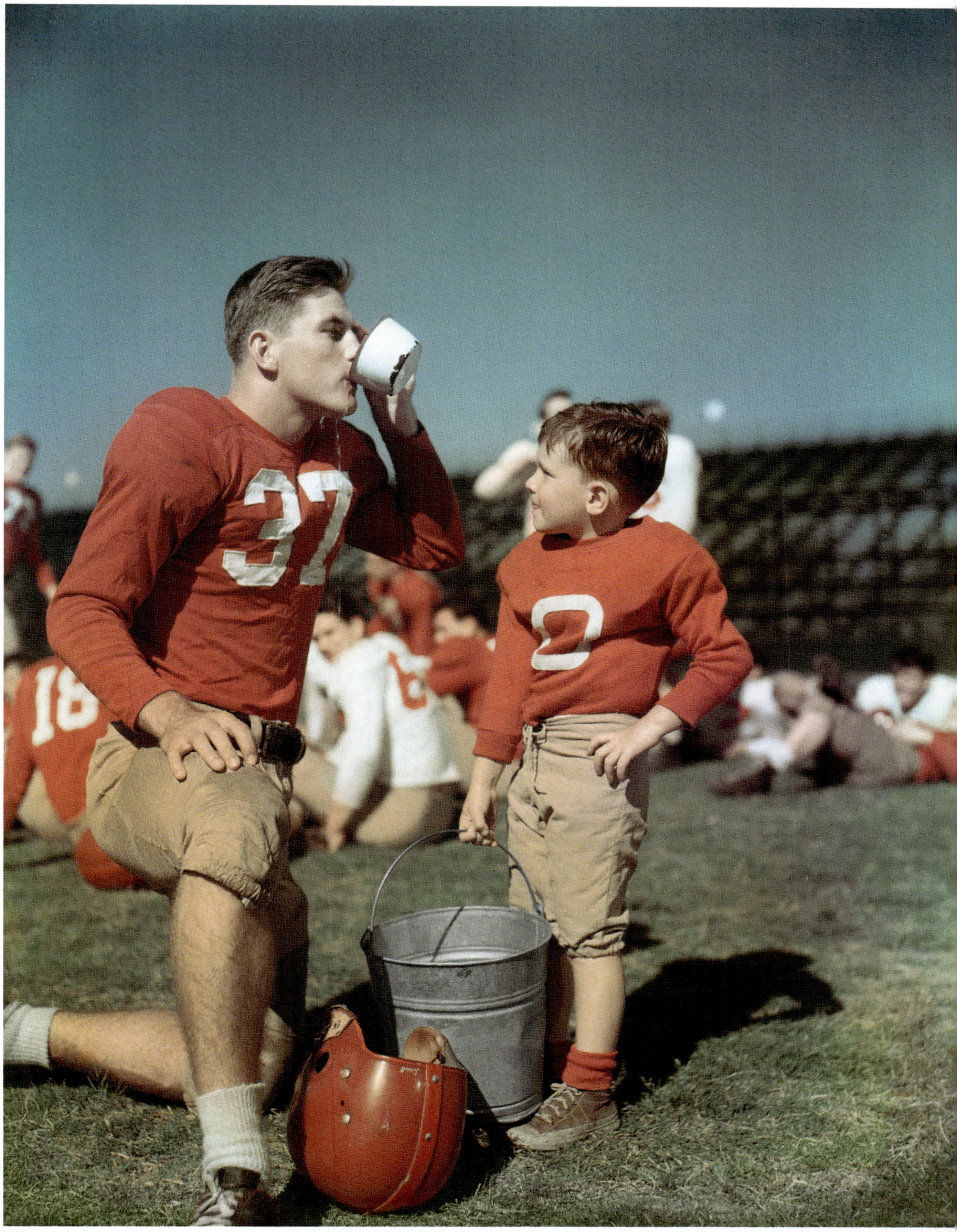

"MR. FOOTBALL"

Southern Methodist football great Doak Walker takes a break during practice in 1948 with the team's mascot, Thomas Timothy Tribble Jr., the son of an ex-GI who was attending SMU. Walker was a triple-threat runner, passer and kicker, and the embodiment of the all-American boy at a time when the college game was king. He was awarded the Heisman Trophy after the '48 season.

MICHAEL LAVELLE

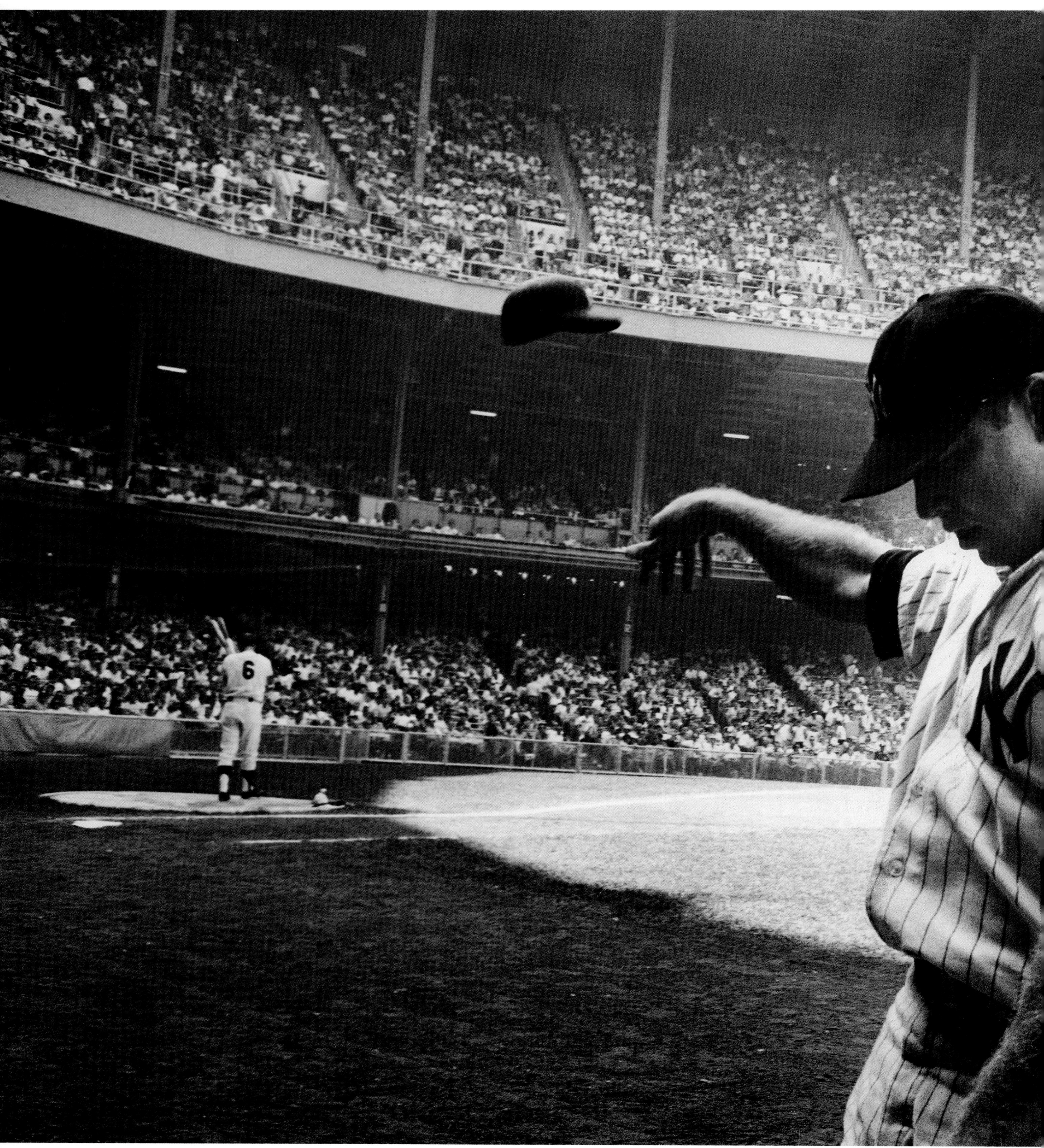

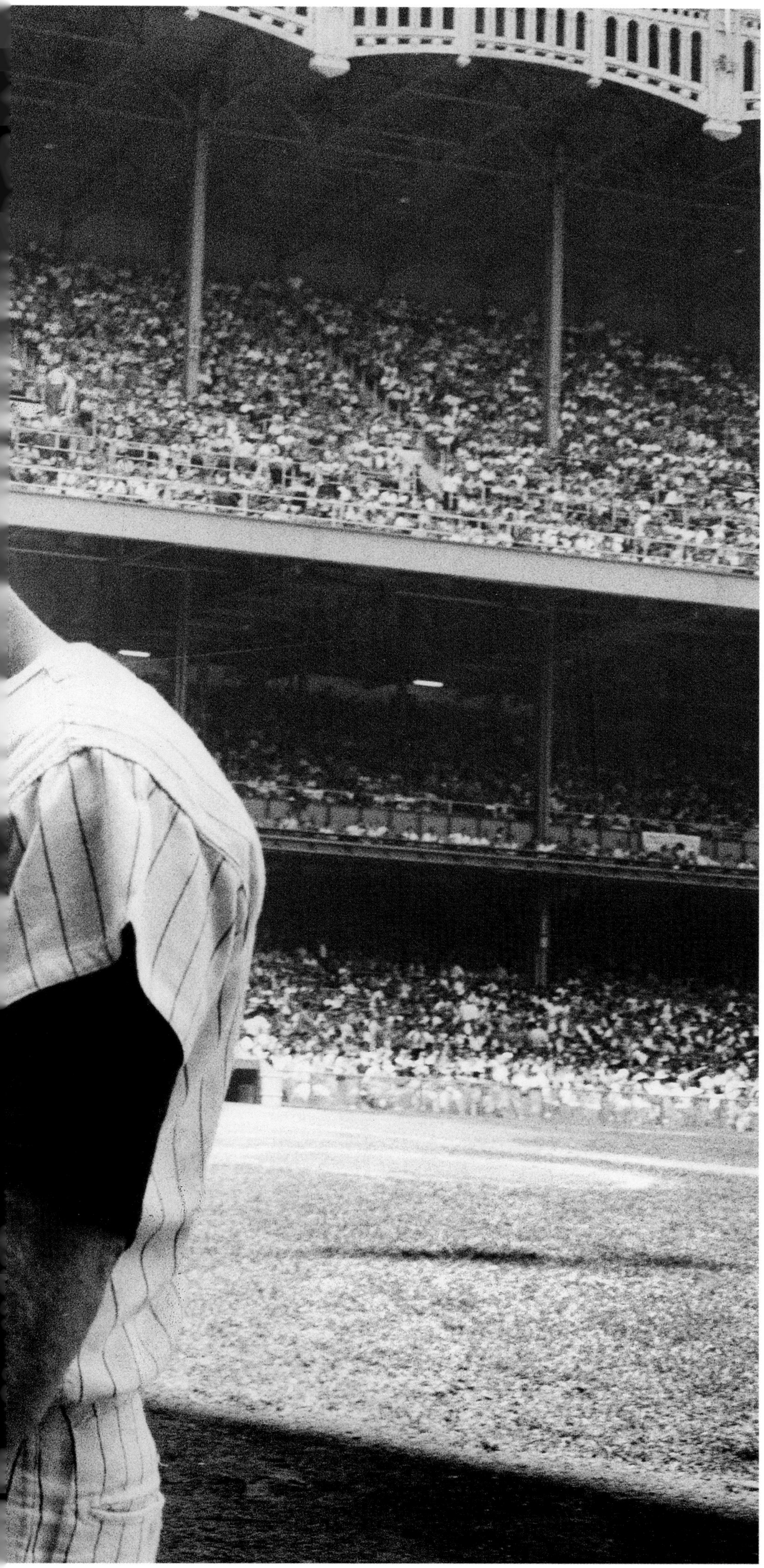

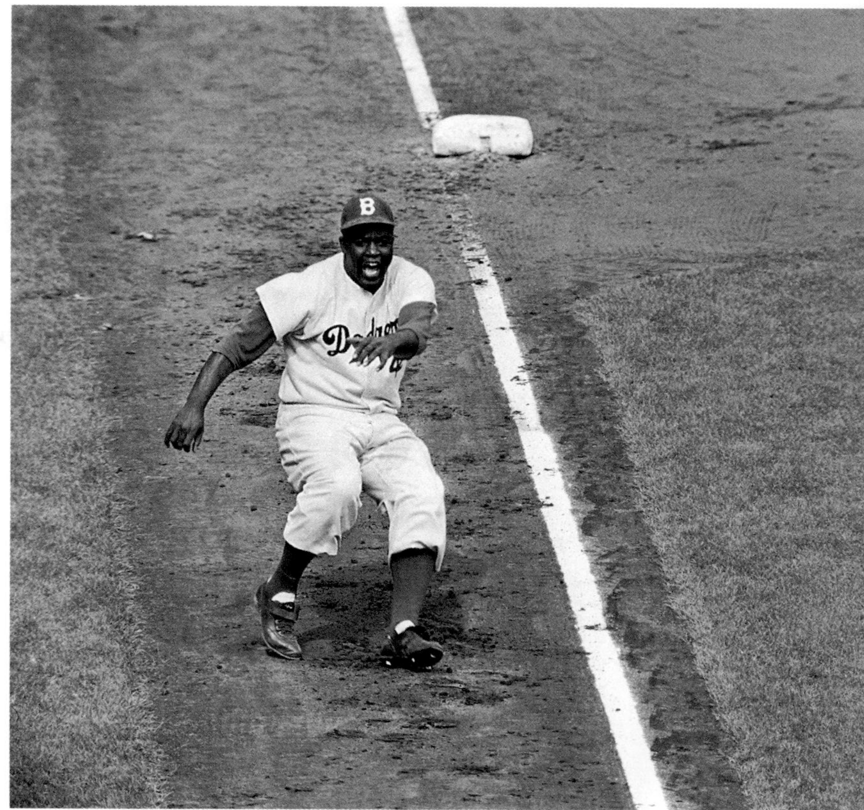

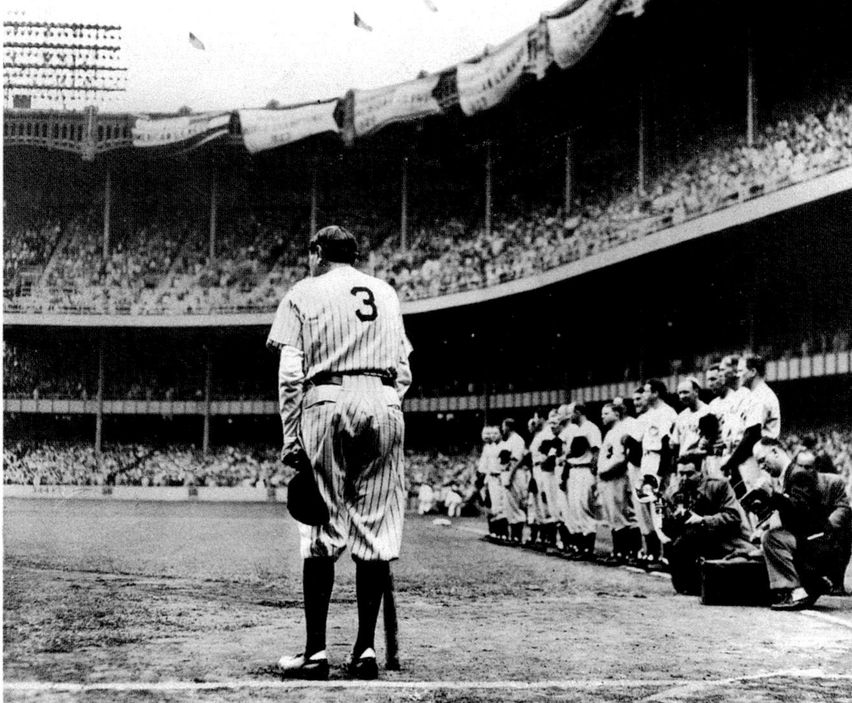

IMMORTALS OF THE DIAMOND

Here, at different points in their lives, are three of the most famous of all baseballers. At top, Jackie Robinson of the Dodgers strikes terror in the hearts of the Yankees en route to victory in the 1955 World Series. Above, on June 13, 1948, Babe Ruth bids a final farewell during the 25th anniversary of the opening of The House That Ruth Built. In a couple of months, the Sultan of Swat would be dead. At left, Mickey Mantle tosses his batting helmet after striking out during a midseason game in 1965. At this stage, The Mick was beginning his descent into the twilight of what had been a stellar career.

LEFT **JOHN DOMINIS** *TOP* **RALPH MORSE** *ABOVE* **NAT FEIN**

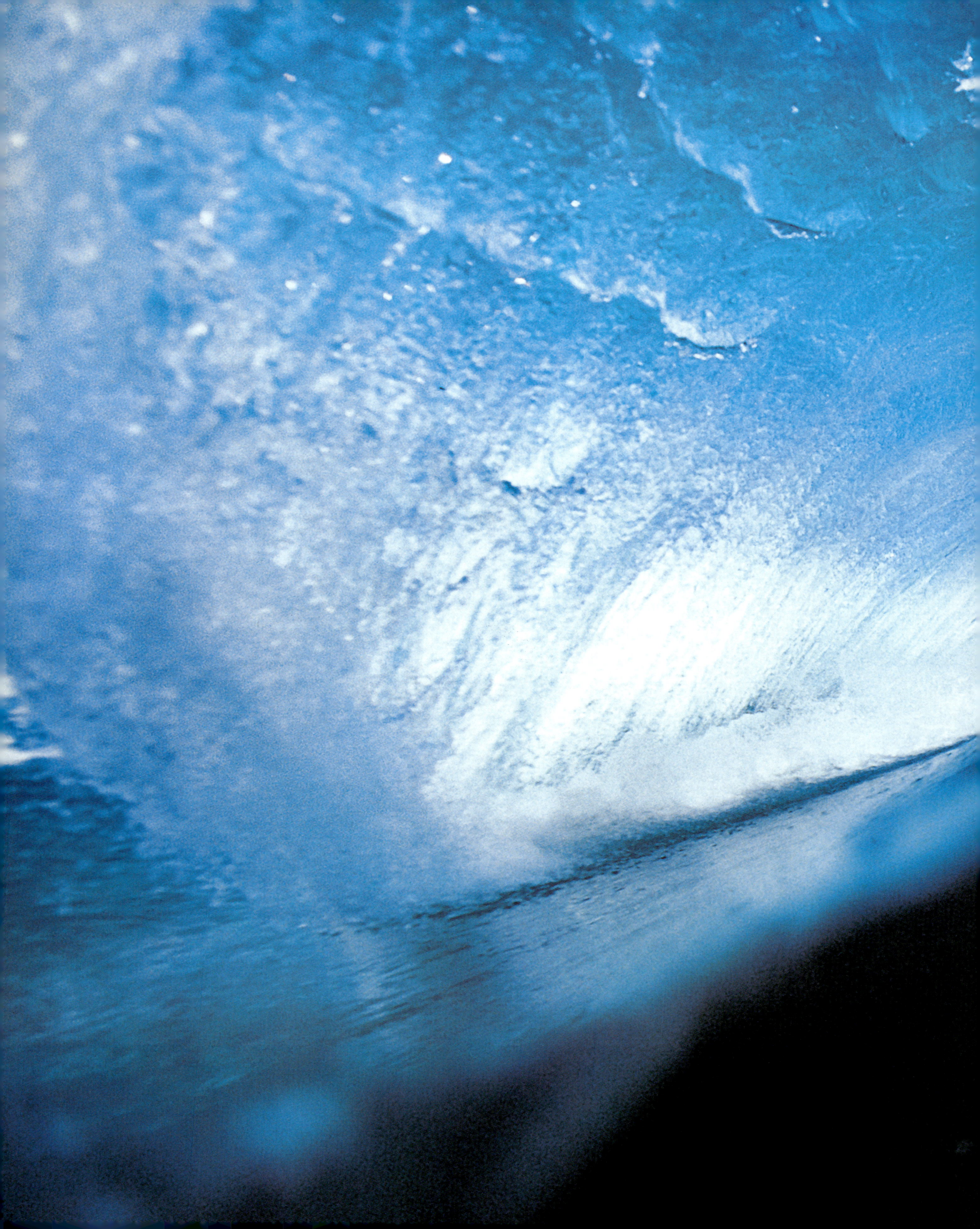

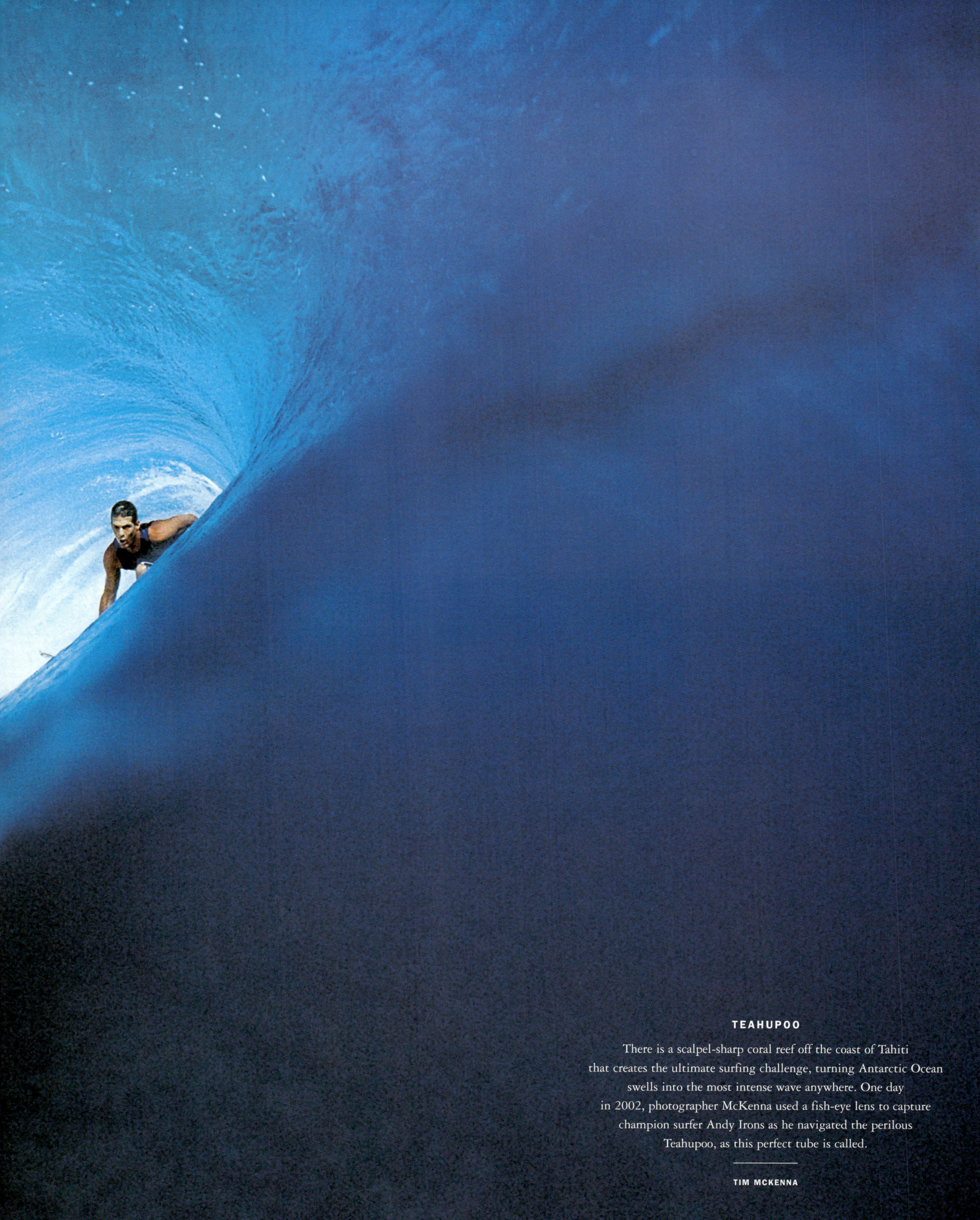

TEAHUPOO

There is a scalpel-sharp coral reef off the coast of Tahiti that creates the ultimate surfing challenge, turning Antarctic Ocean swells into the most intense wave anywhere. One day in 2002, photographer McKenna used a fish-eye lens to capture champion surfer Andy Irons as he navigated the perilous Teahupoo, as this perfect tube is called.

TIM MCKENNA

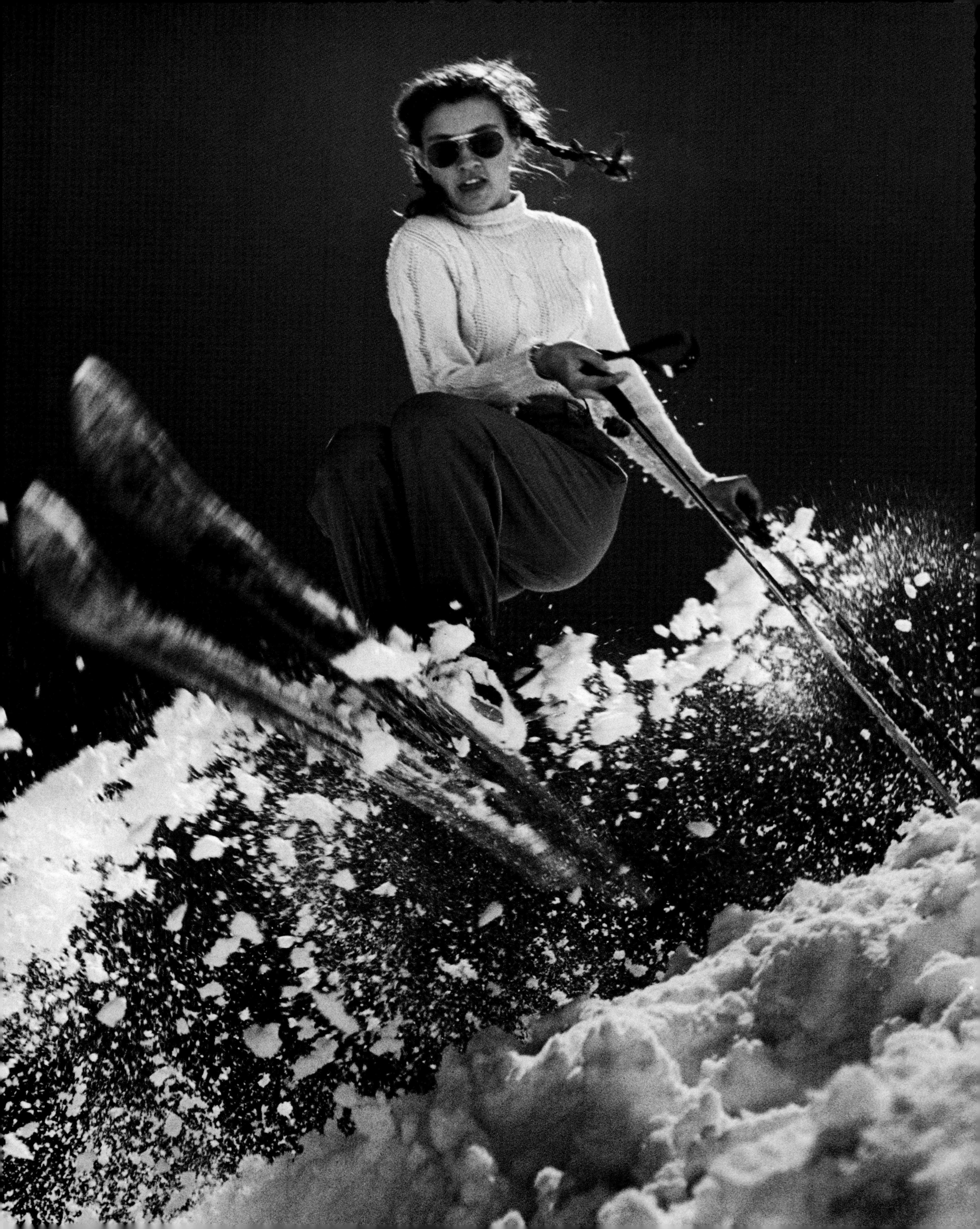

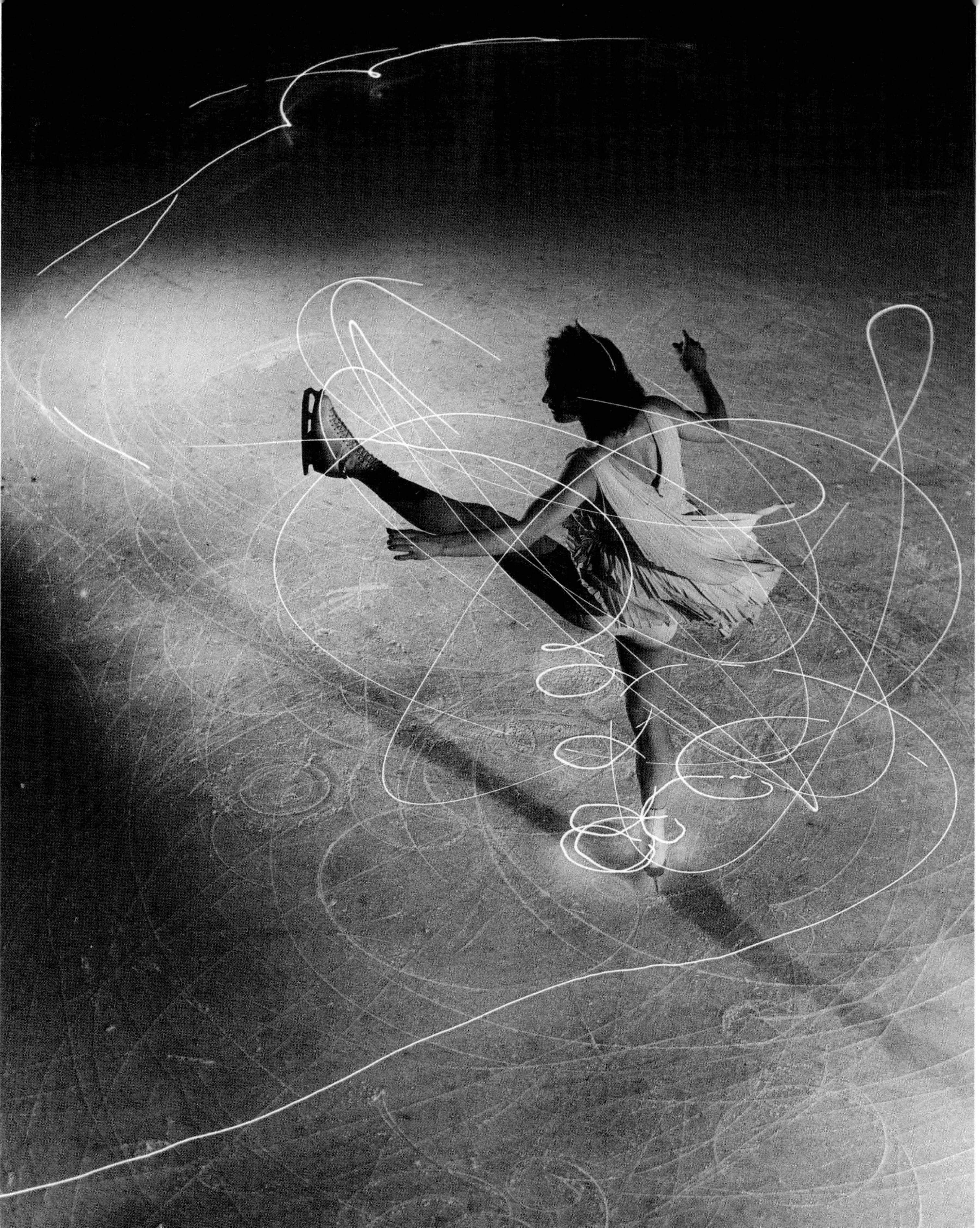

SLALOM SENSATION

Fifteen-year-old Andrea Mead Lawrence of Rutland, Vt., flashes past the camera in 1947 as she practices for the Winter Olympics. Although she didn't take home any medals at St. Moritz, four years later, at Oslo, she became the first American skier ever to win two gold medals, in the slalom and giant slalom.

GEORGE SILK

TRIPPING THE LIGHT FANTASTIC

In 1945, photographer Mili outfitted Carol Lynne with a three-quarter-pound flashlight in each of her boots, then the 19-year-old professional figure skater embarked on a routine from the long-running New York City show *Hats Off to Ice.* As she swept across the ice on a darkened stage, Mili used a stroboscopic light to record her patterns.

GJON MILI

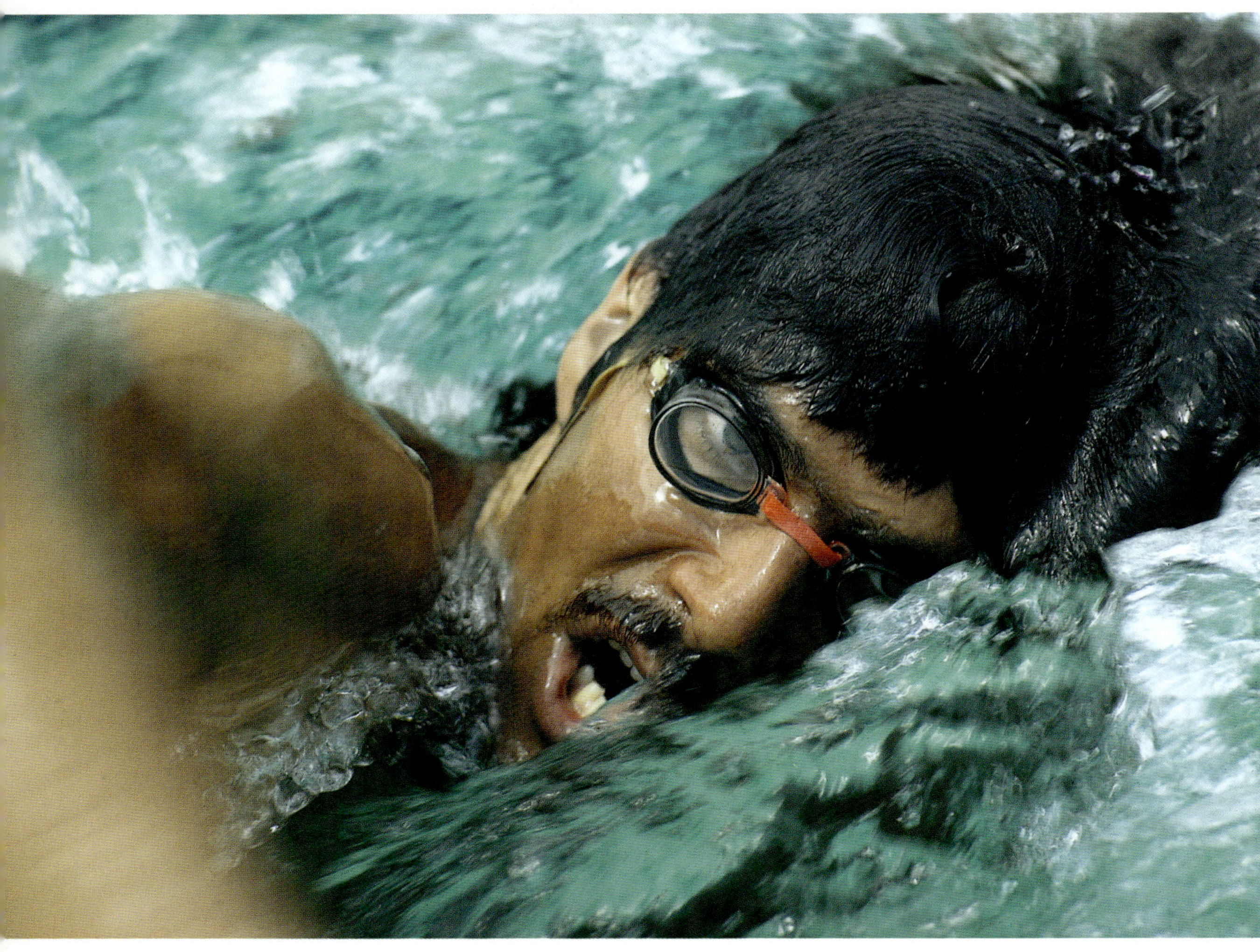

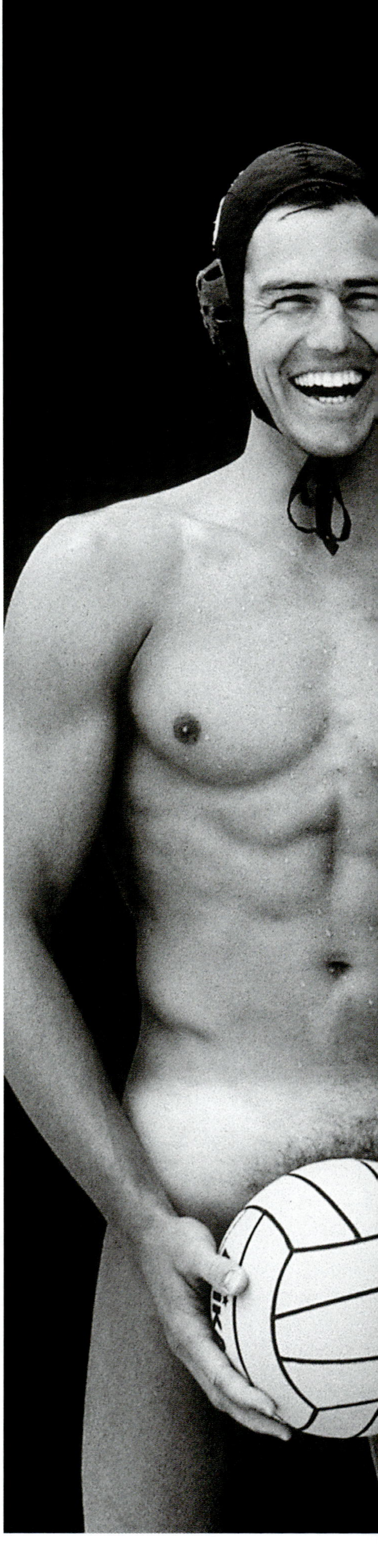

WATER WIZARD

This photograph was taken in Santa Clara, Calif., as Mark Spitz trained for the 1972 Munich Olympics. Not only did Spitz win seven gold medals—more than anyone else, ever—he also, incredibly, set a world record in each event.

CO RENTMEESTER

THE BOD SQUAD

Strength, size and stamina are the prerequisites of water polo. In 1996, photographer McNally captured the proud U.S. team au naturel: from left, Rick McNair, Alex Rousseau, Chris Humbert and Chris Duplanty.

JOE MCNALLY

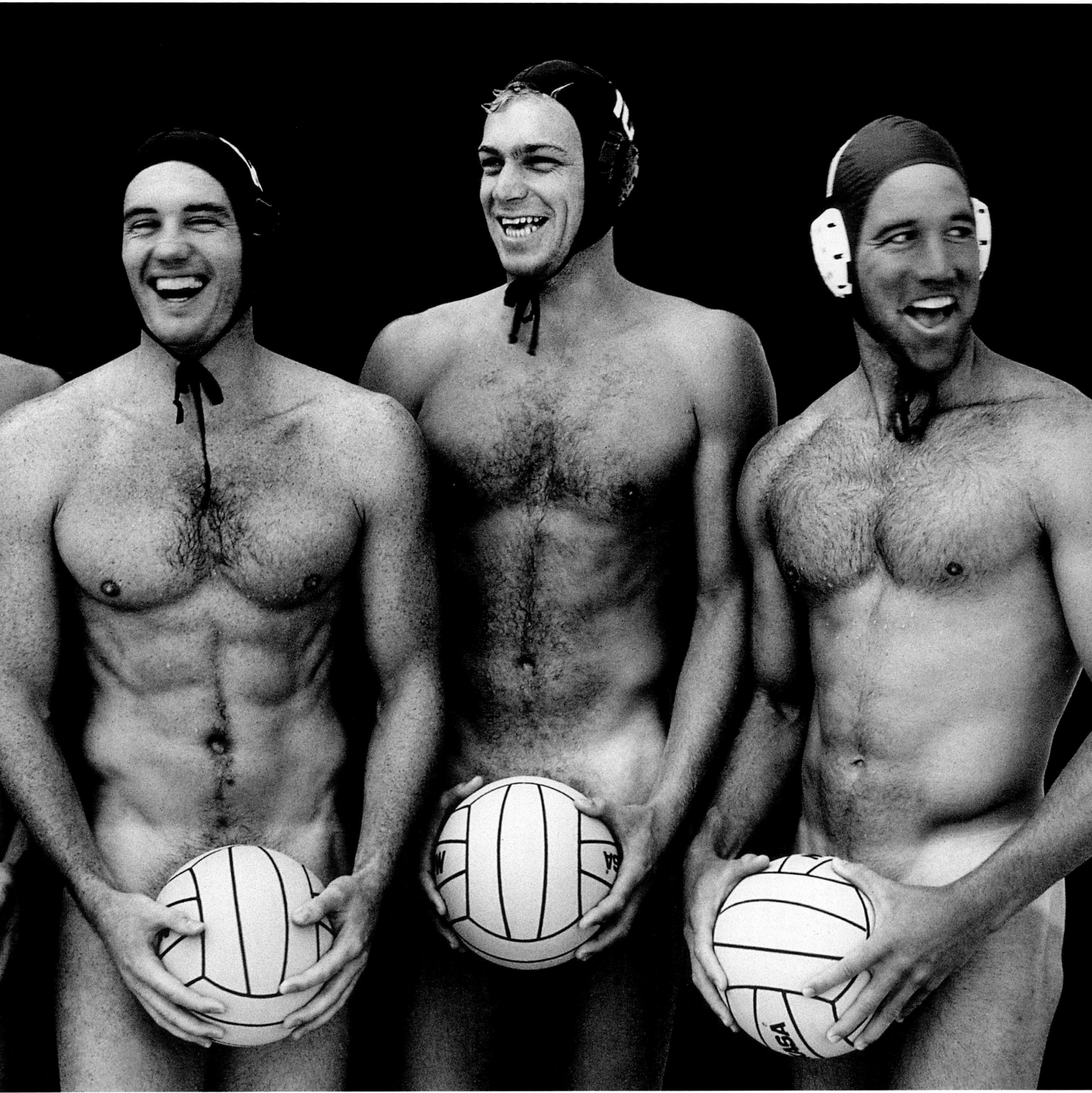

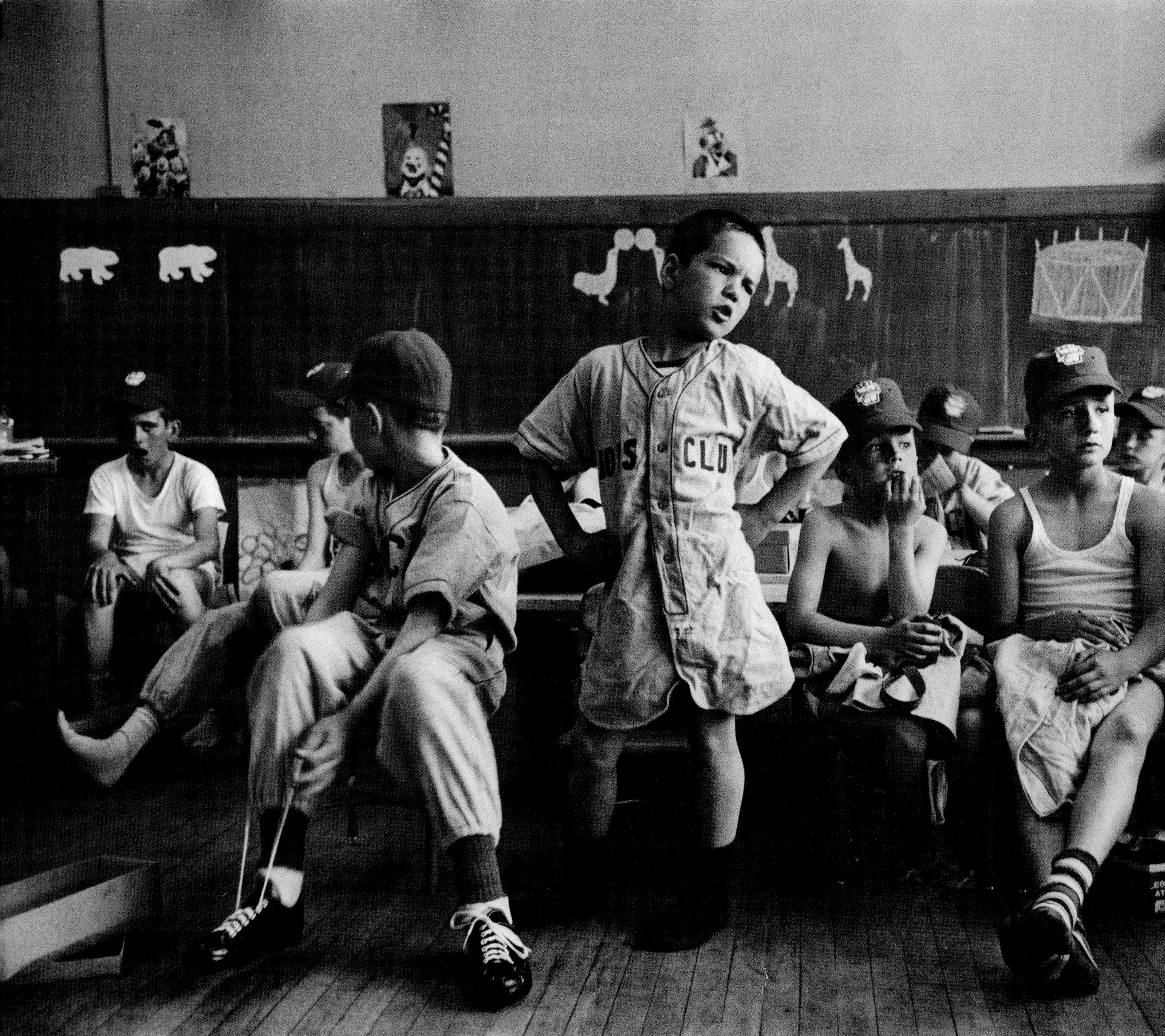

O.K., NOW WHAT?

These Little Leaguers in Manchester, N.H., were dressing in a schoolroom before a game in 1954 when they discovered, to their chagrin, that some of their new uniforms were not entirely complete.

YALE JOEL

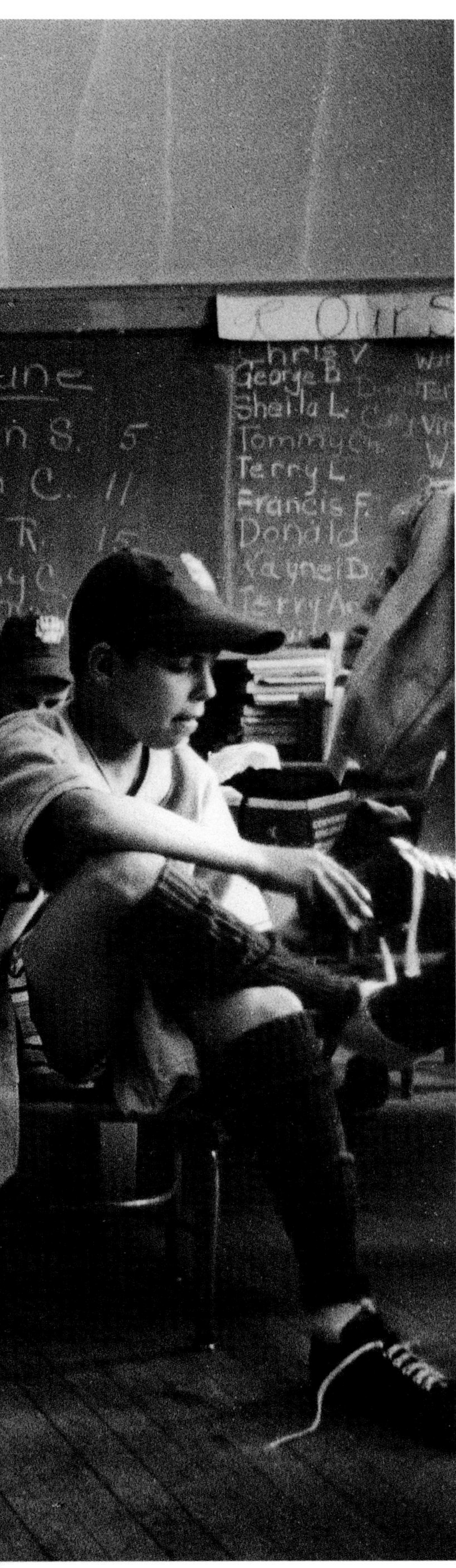

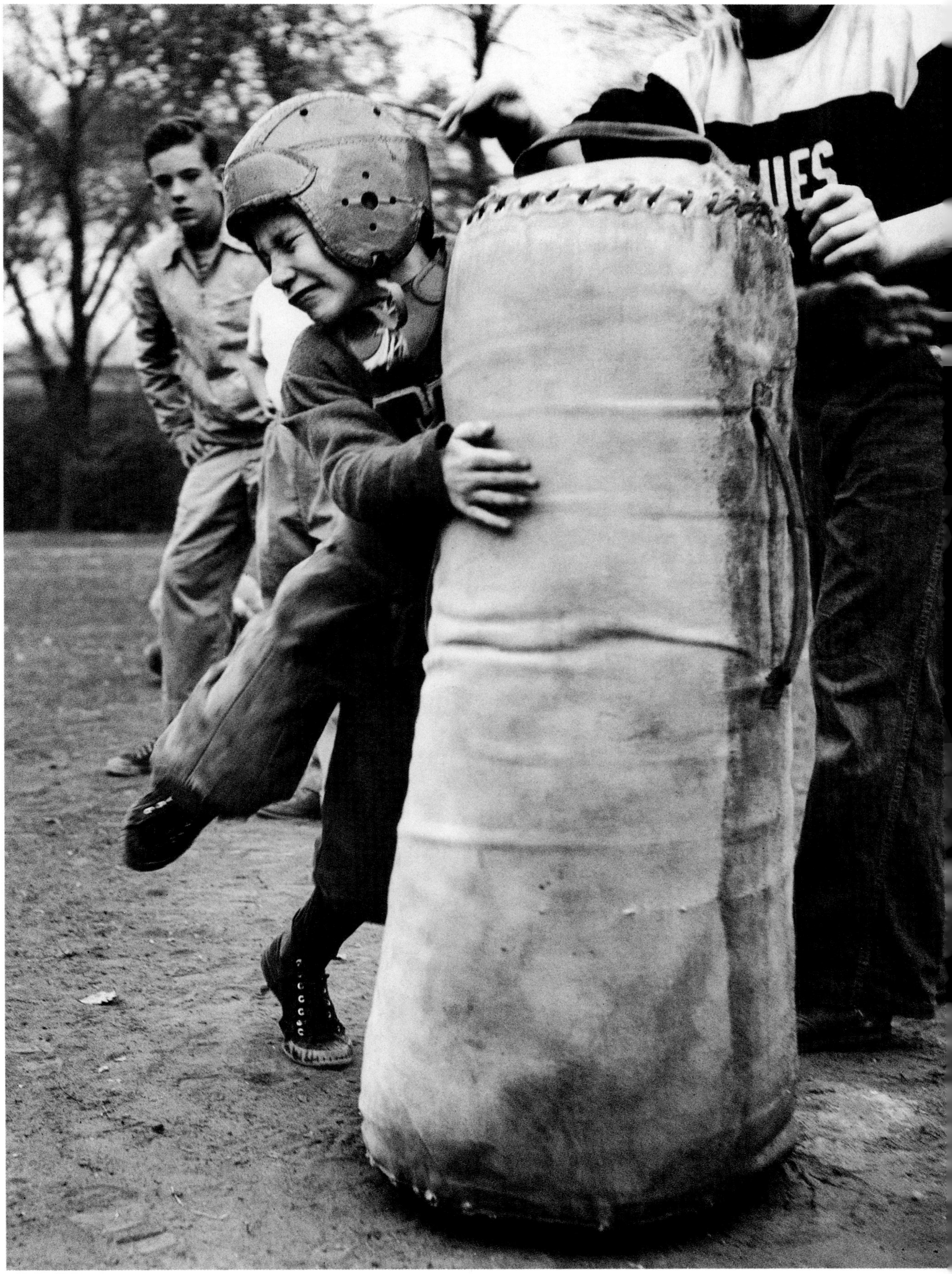

LITTLE GRIDDER

Seven-year-old Ray Denson readies for contact as he is about to take on a tackling dummy in 1947. At the time, all 167 boys in the eight grades at the Joseph Sears school in Kenilworth, Ill., participated in football.

WALLACE KIRKLAND

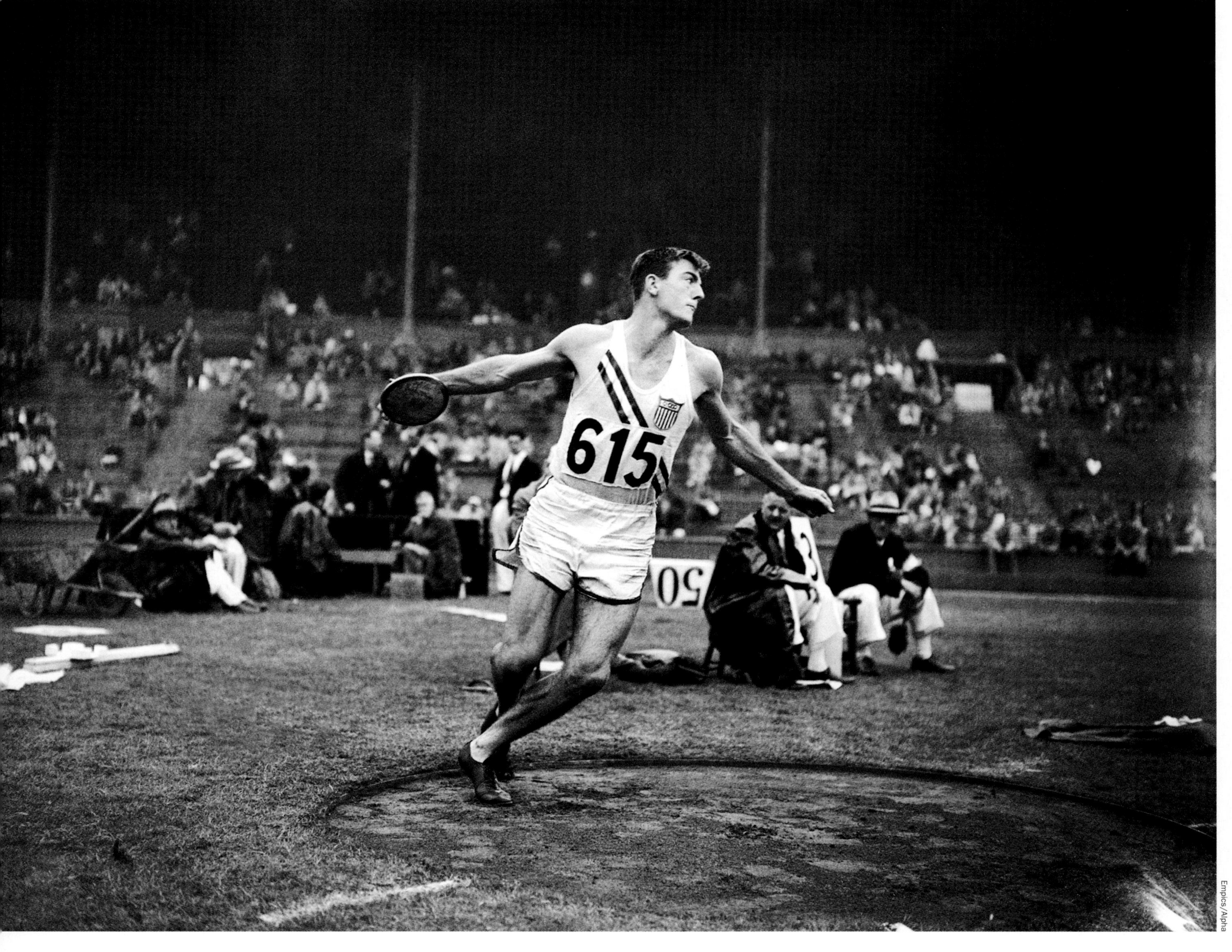

BOY WONDER

As a child, Bob Mathias suffered from anemia and was fed pills and special diets to boost his strength. Something worked, because in 1948, just months after first competing in the event, he won the Olympic decathlon at age 17. (He had to use a manual to learn the pole vault and javelin.) Mathias became a football star at Stanford, then won the decathlon again at the '52 Games.

EARLY AIR JORDAN

Back in 1984, when amateurs still made up the United States Olympic basketball team, the star of the squad was gravity-defying 21-year-old Michael Jordan, seen here in a classic photo from Co Rentmeester. The American team, which also included Chris Mullin and Patrick Ewing, easily won the gold medal at the Los Angeles Games.

CO RENTMEESTER

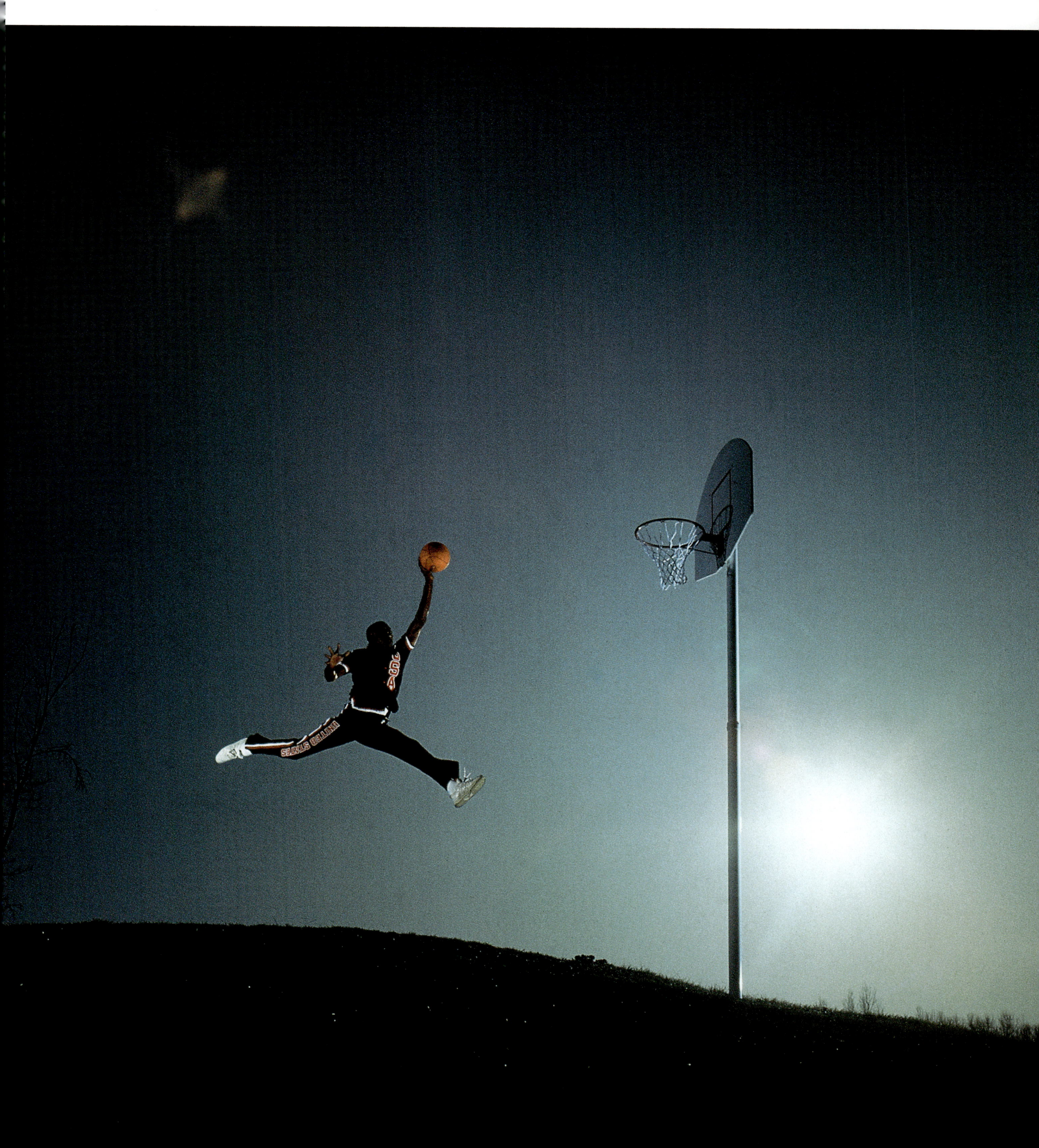

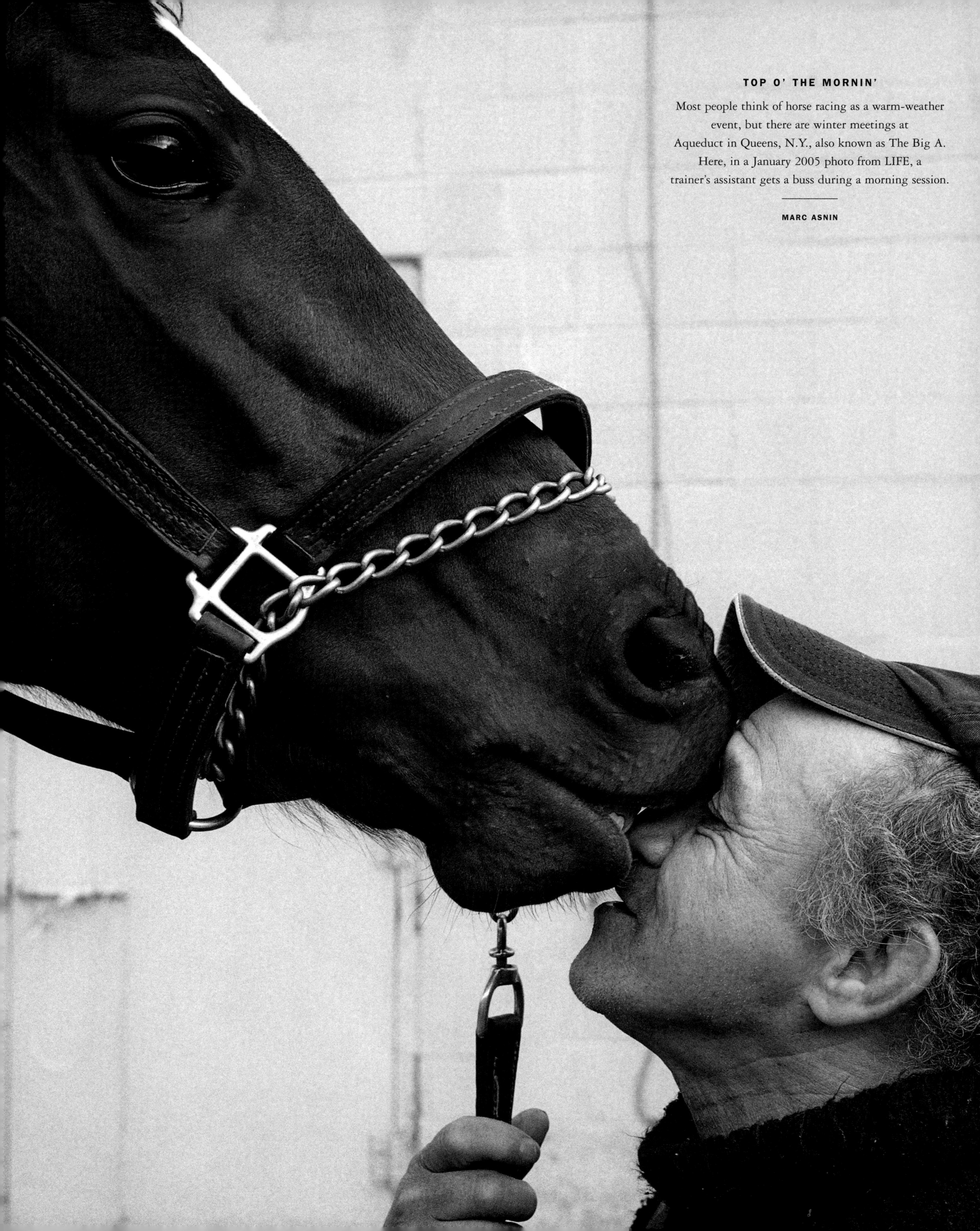

TOP O' THE MORNIN'

Most people think of horse racing as a warm-weather event, but there are winter meetings at Aqueduct in Queens, N.Y., also known as The Big A. Here, in a January 2005 photo from LIFE, a trainer's assistant gets a buss during a morning session.

MARC ASNIN

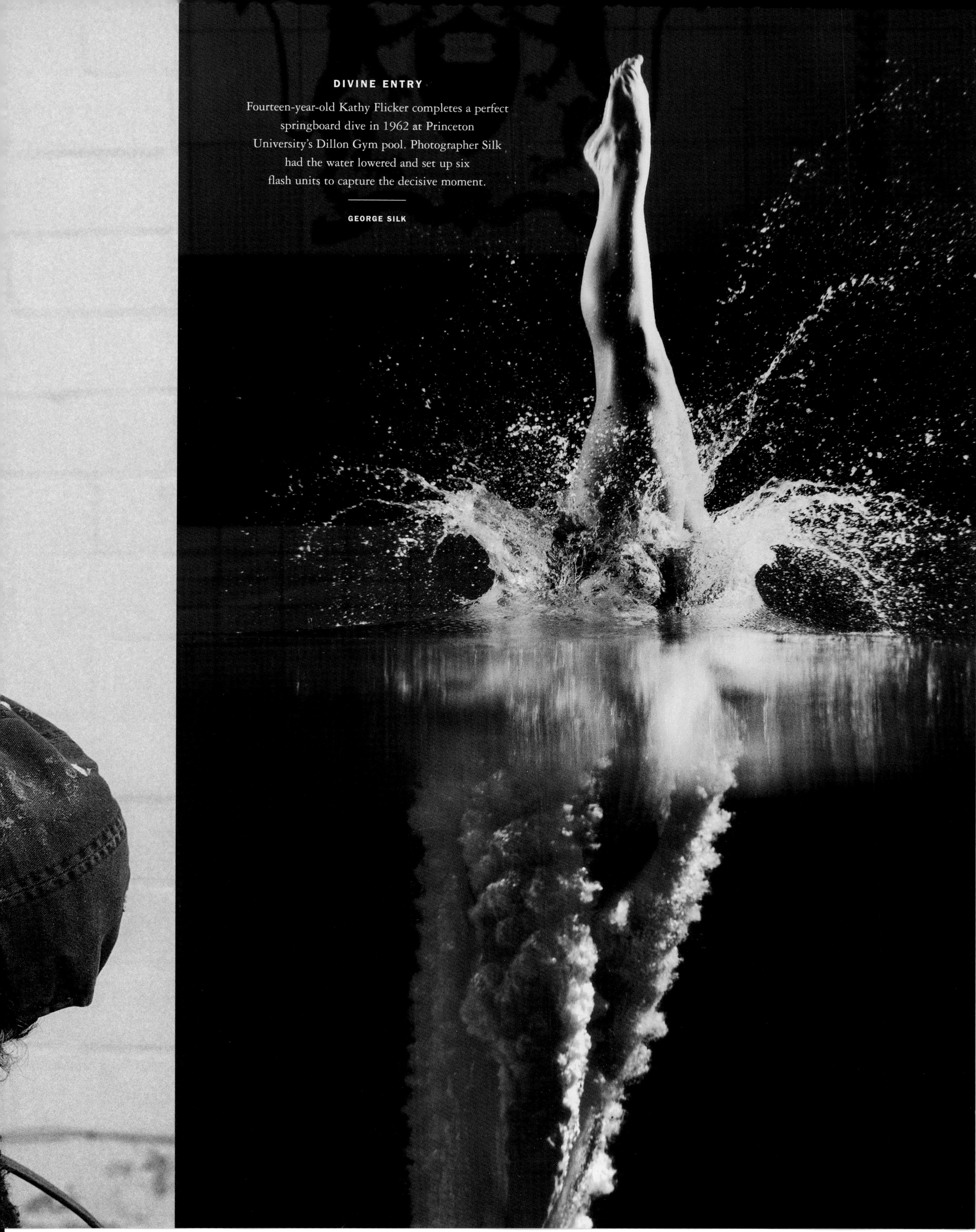

DIVINE ENTRY

Fourteen-year-old Kathy Flicker completes a perfect springboard dive in 1962 at Princeton University's Dillon Gym pool. Photographer Silk had the water lowered and set up six flash units to capture the decisive moment.

GEORGE SILK

GEORGE SILK

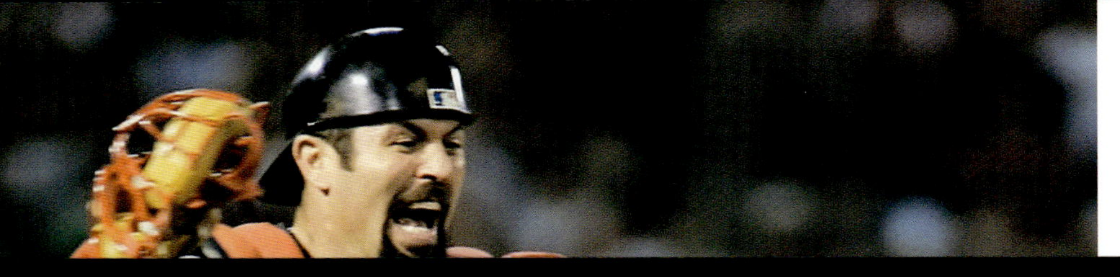

OUR CULTURE, OUR WORLD

In March 1937—with LIFE a few months old—Henry Luce wanted very much to ensure that his editors shared his views on where the magazine was headed and how its increasingly apparent power ought best be harnessed. In his first, private assessment of the publication, in a section he called Emotion, Luce wrote, "LIFE has a bias. LIFE is in favor of the human race, and is hopeful. LIFE likes life. LIFE is quicker to point with pride than to view with alarm. At some later time I will try to explain to myself why this is necessarily so. For the present, let it be acknowledged that this is inevitably LIFE's bias so that it may not be thwarted or inhibited."

A dozen years later, Luce made Edward M. Thompson LIFE's managing editor, and it would prove to be a wise decision. After a short time at the helm, Ed wrote a letter to Luce describing his thoughts about the magazine: "LIFE, to me, is a friendly neighbor, almost one of the family. He is kind of gabby, asks a lot of questions, always wants to get into a discussion, so there are bound to be some anti-social folks who don't like him too much. But where he is welcome he sidles up to the picket fence and says—

'Let me tell you about that big fire I saw on my way through the county seat tonight . . .

'I've been studying up about this fellow Tito, and I have a Jugo-Slav brother-in-law who tells me . . .

'Say, have you heard of a wonderful man named Schweitzer over in Africa? Well, he's doing fine things . . . but he's an expert on Goethe, too, and here's what he thinks . . .' "

Thompson then added, "In short, it seems to me that LIFE must be curious, alert, erudite and moral, but it must achieve this without being holier-than-thou, a cynic, a know-it-all or a Peeping Tom. LIFE must always feel *privileged* to be the bearer of information or thoughts."

It continues to be a very real privilege to be this messenger. Sometimes the news we bring is thrilling and sometimes it's a joy, but isn't always pretty, and it isn't always nice. Nevertheless, that is the way of the world we inhabit. Herein are some of the ways that LIFE has tried to represent these myriad cultural realities.

COWBOY

This is C.H. Long, the 39-year-old foreman of the JA ranch on the Texas panhandle. In 1949, in the story accompanying this cover photograph, LIFE described a cowboy as "one of the most purely functional human beings the world has ever developed." The writer ended up being correct on two counts. When an ad exec saw this picture, he came up with the idea of the Marlboro Man, and transformed what had been a women's cigarette into a top-ranking brand.

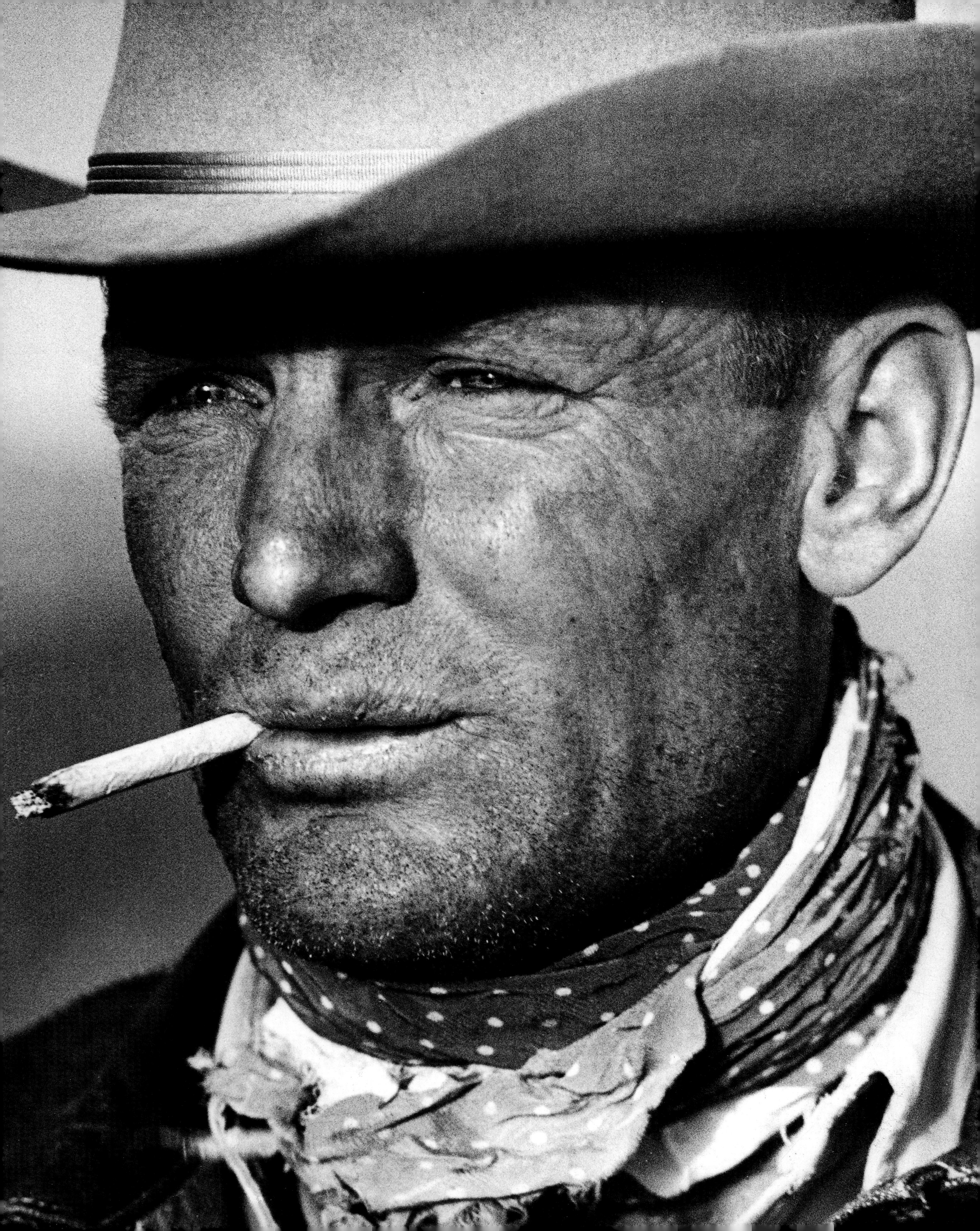

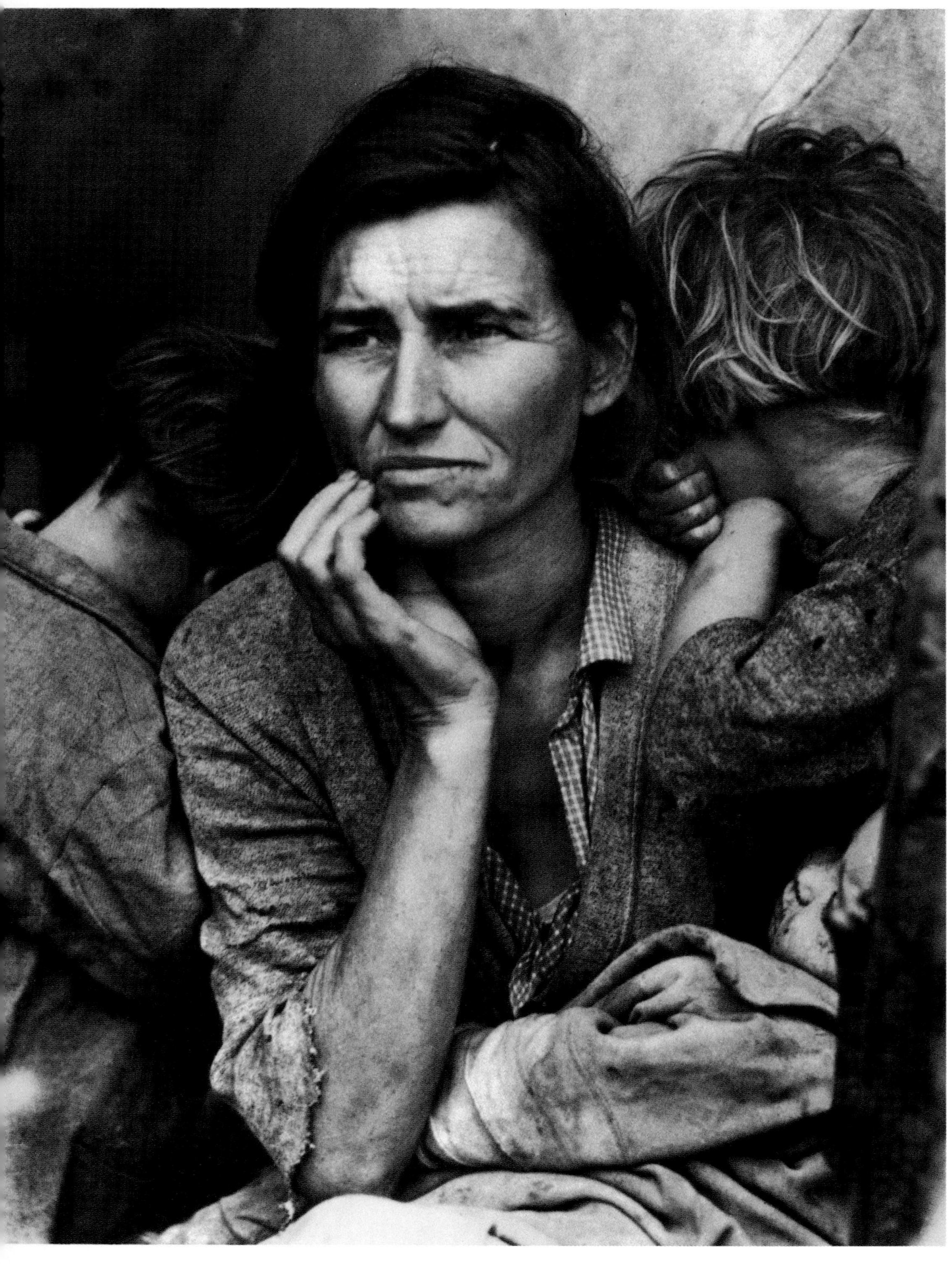

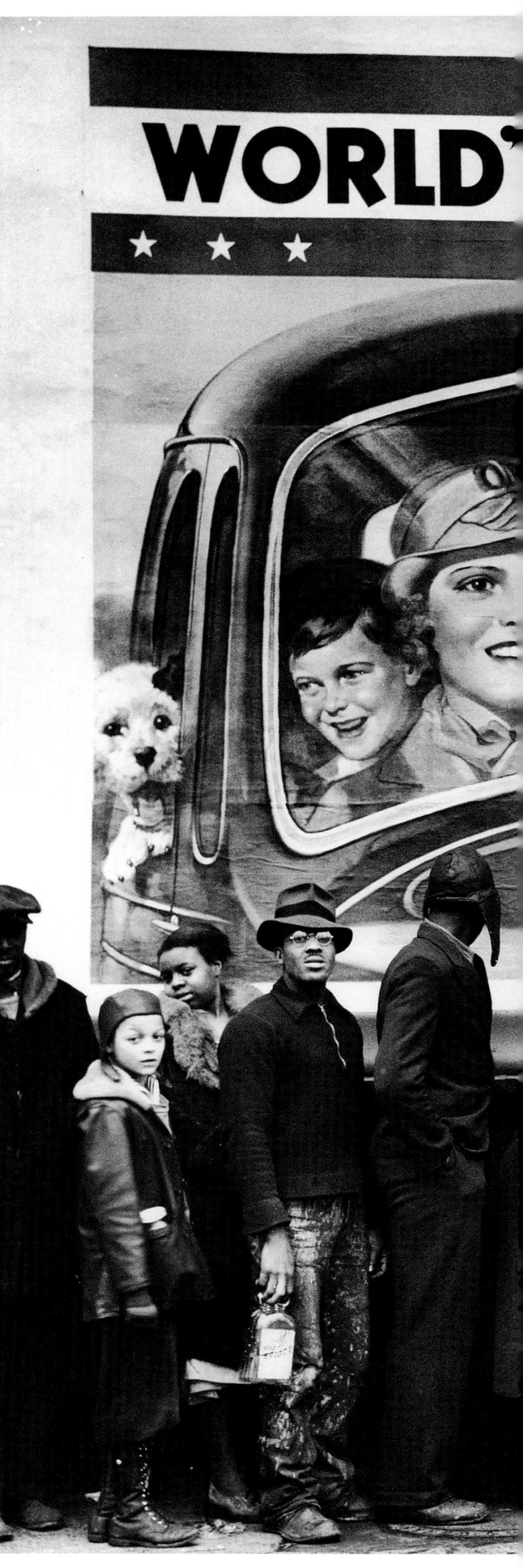

HARD TIMES

Here are two images from astute photographers that resonate with the bone-wearying despair of the Great Depression. Above, in 1936, this 32-year-old California farmworker has just sold her tent and the tires off her car to purchase food for her seven children. They have been subsisting on chance vegetables and wild birds. At right, victims of the Louisville Flood line up in 1937 to obtain food and clothing from a Red Cross relief station. The juxtaposition with the billboard is nothing short of surreal. Bourke-White later said that when Henry Luce saw the difference between her flood photos and those from the news services, he realized that his photographers deserved credit lines.

ABOVE **DOROTHEA LANGE** *RIGHT* **MARGARET BOURKE-WHITE**

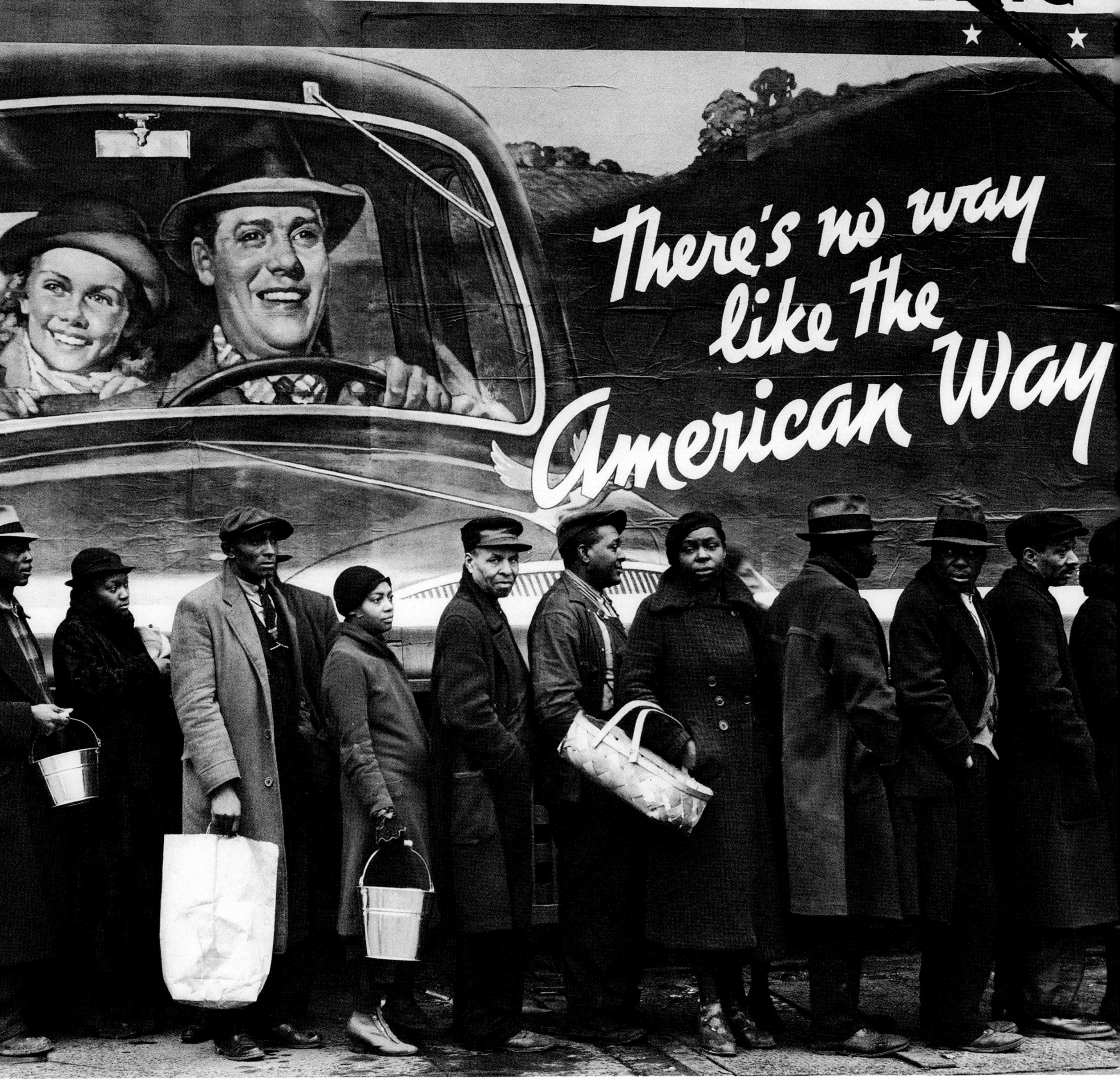
HIGHEST STANDARD OF LIVING
There's no way
like the
American Way

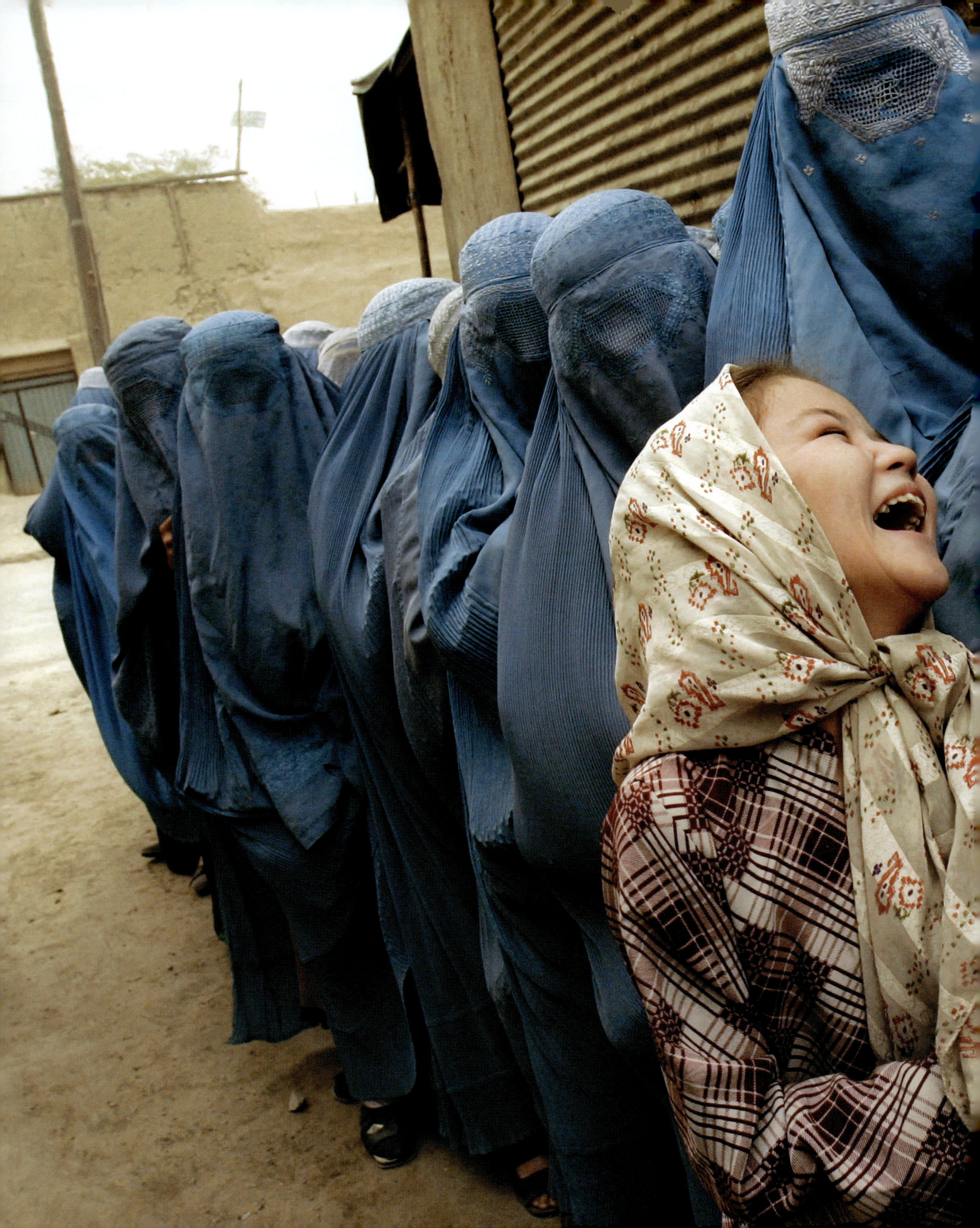

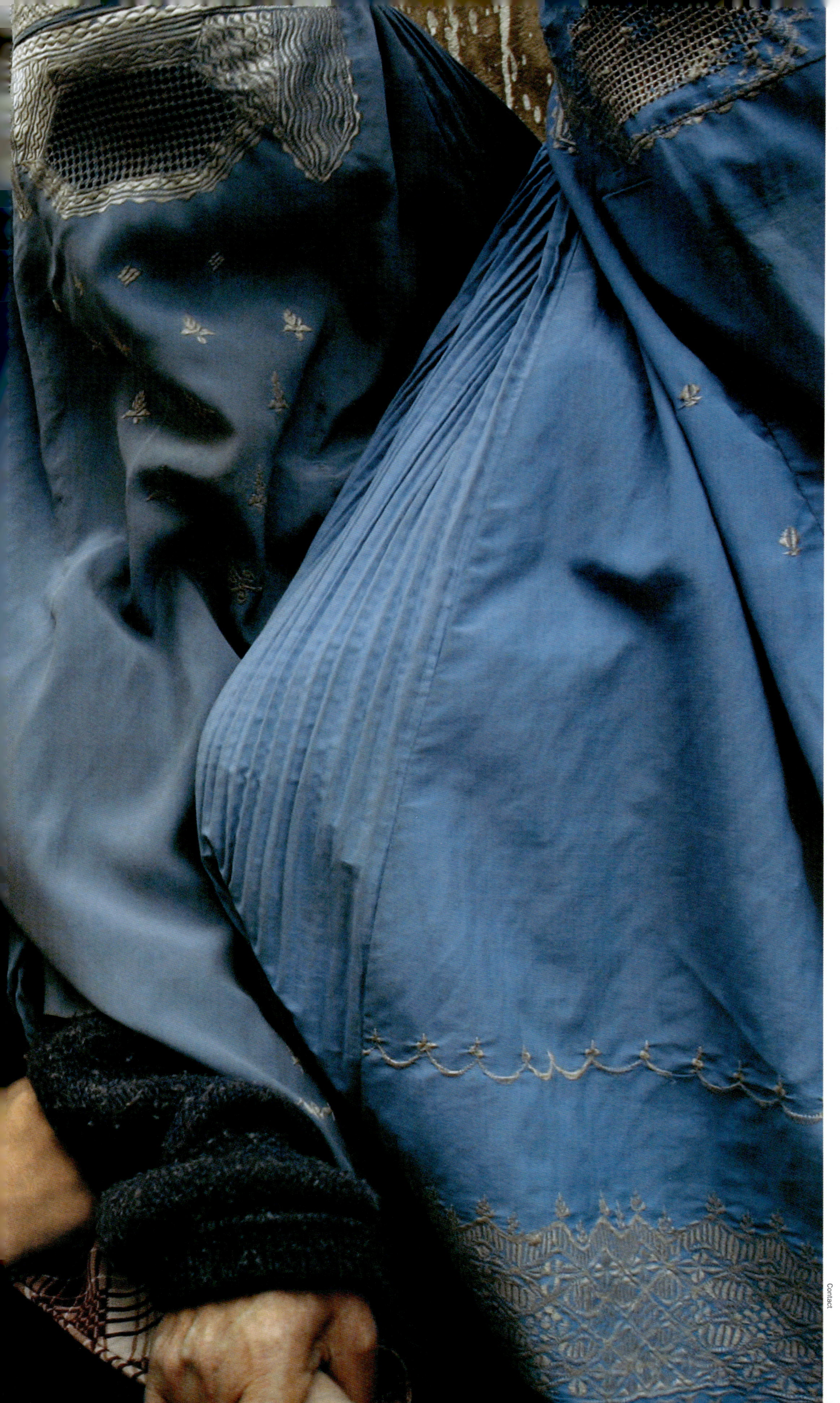

Contact

THE RIGHT TO CHOOSE

On October 9, 2004, an election was held in Afghanistan. The event was marked by controversy, extending even to the ephemeral quality of the ink used to indicate who had cast a vote. Nevertheless, it was an extraordinary day, as it was the country's first democratic presidential election. And yet, some things are very slow to change. Here, a young girl stands with her mother in a line of women waiting to vote, but still required to wear the head-to-toe burka.

YUNGHI KIM

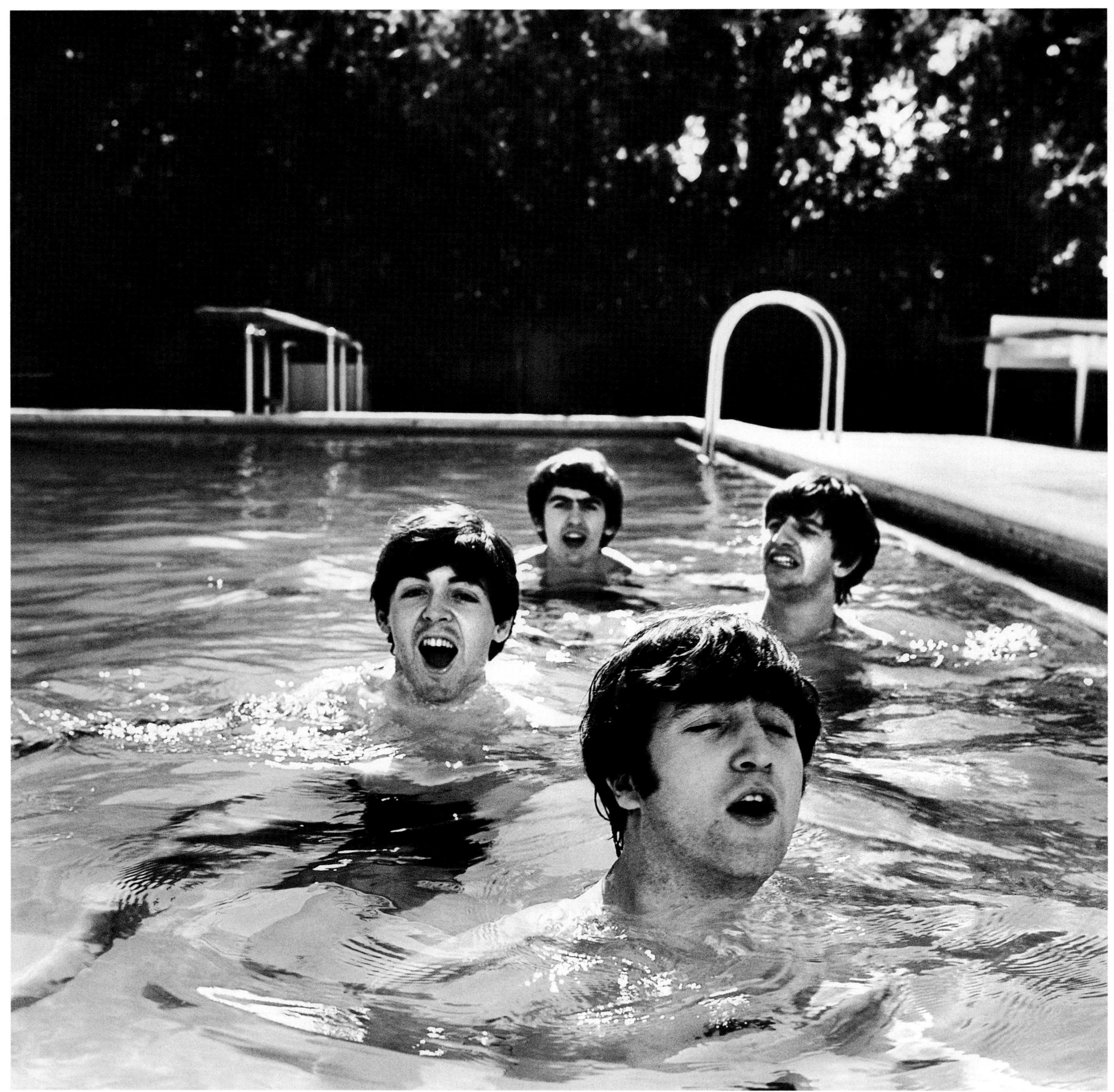

THE FAB FOUR

In 1964, LIFE arranged for Paul McCartney, George Harrison, John Lennon and Ringo Starr, a.k.a. the Beatles, to unwind in a Miami Beach swimming pool.

JOHN LOENGARD

3-D

In the 1950s, Hollywood tried to fight off the encroachments of television with a variety of innovations. Here, in 1952, viewers take in the first commercial 3-D feature, *Bwana Devil.*

J.R. EYERMAN

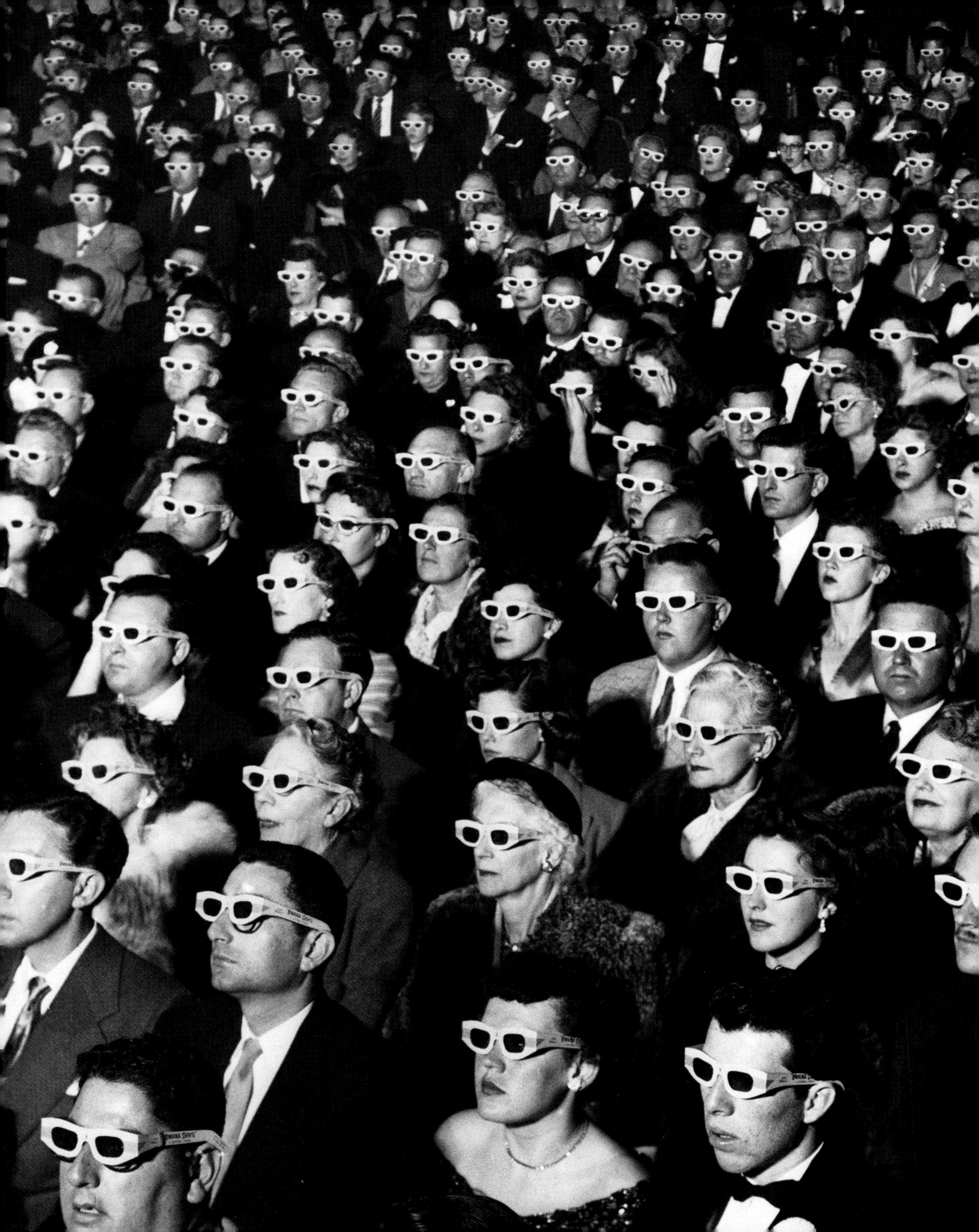

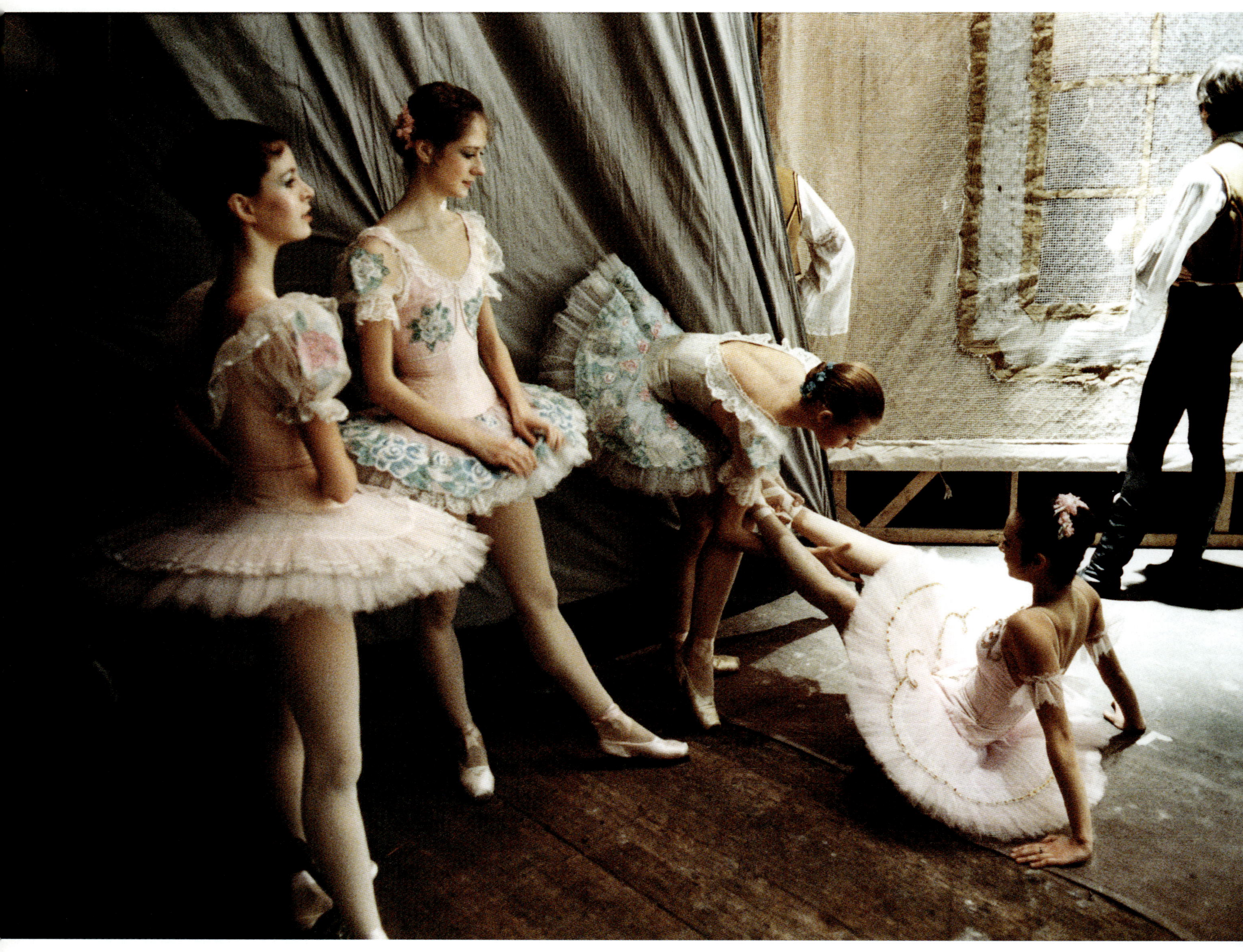

AN EYE FOR THE ARTS

Here are two quite different photos, each depicting a moment in a famed European theater that precedes the onset of the production itself. Above, members of the Bolshoi Ballet prepare backstage at Moscow's Bolshoi Theatre in 1989. Opposite, in one of Eisenstaedt's masterworks, patrons of Milan's La Scala opera house await a premiere in 1934. Eisie said he was looking about when "suddenly I saw a lovely young society girl sitting next to an empty box. From that box I took another picture, with the girl in the foreground. For years and years this has been one of my prize photographs. Without the girl I would not have had a memorable picture."

ABOVE **DAVID TURNLEY** *OPPOSITE* **ALFRED EISENSTAEDT**

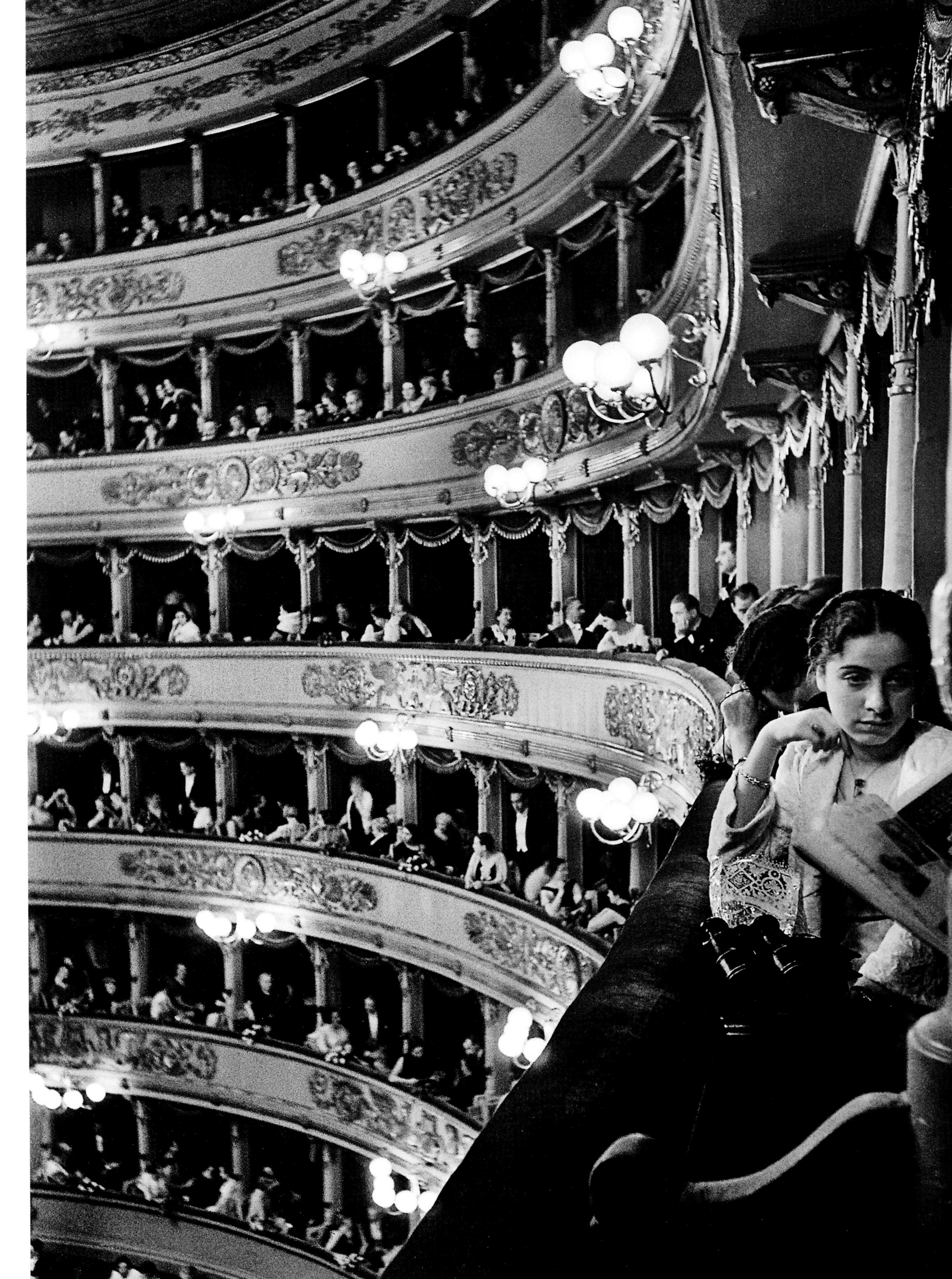

Corbis

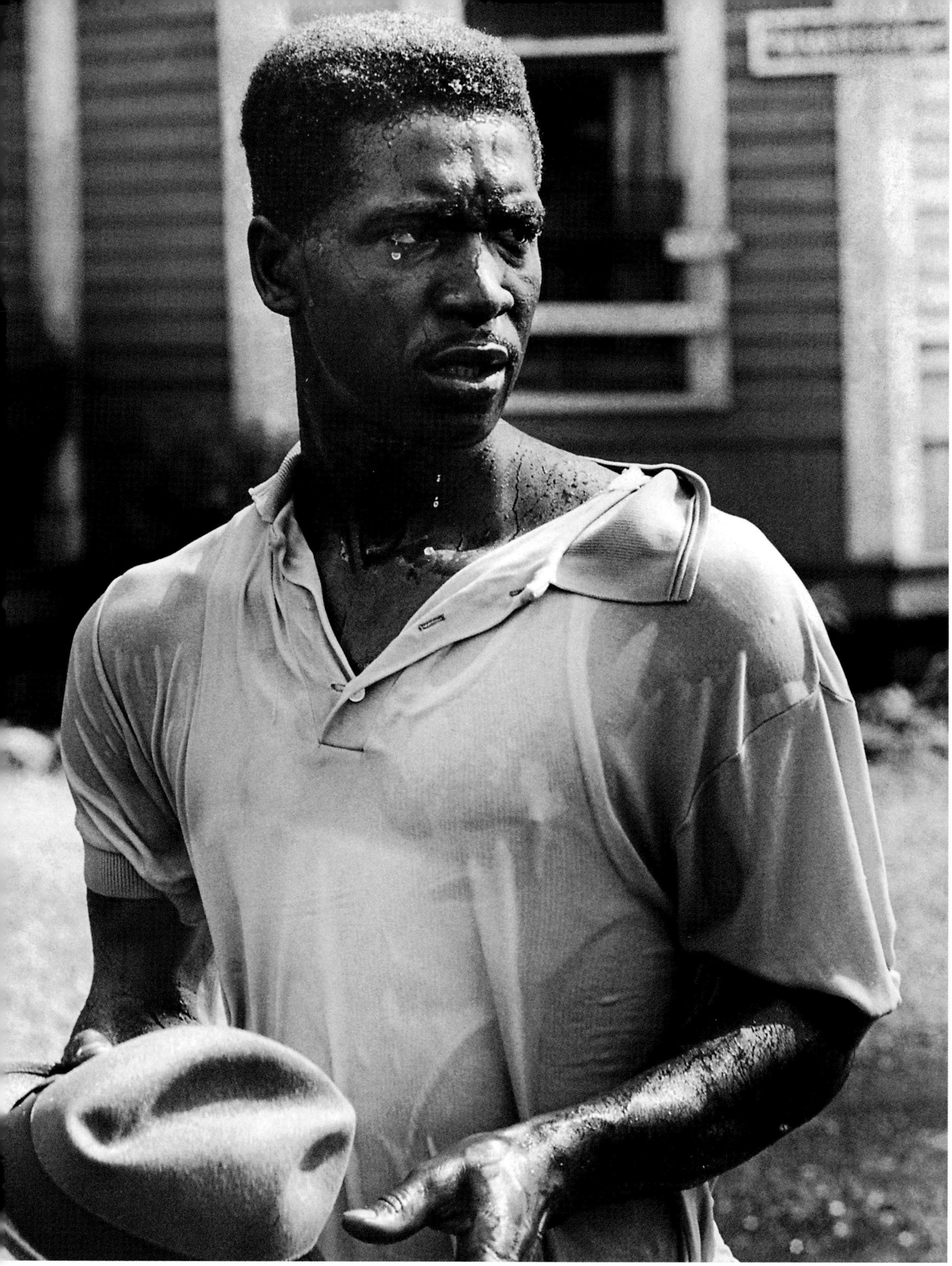

Black Star (2)

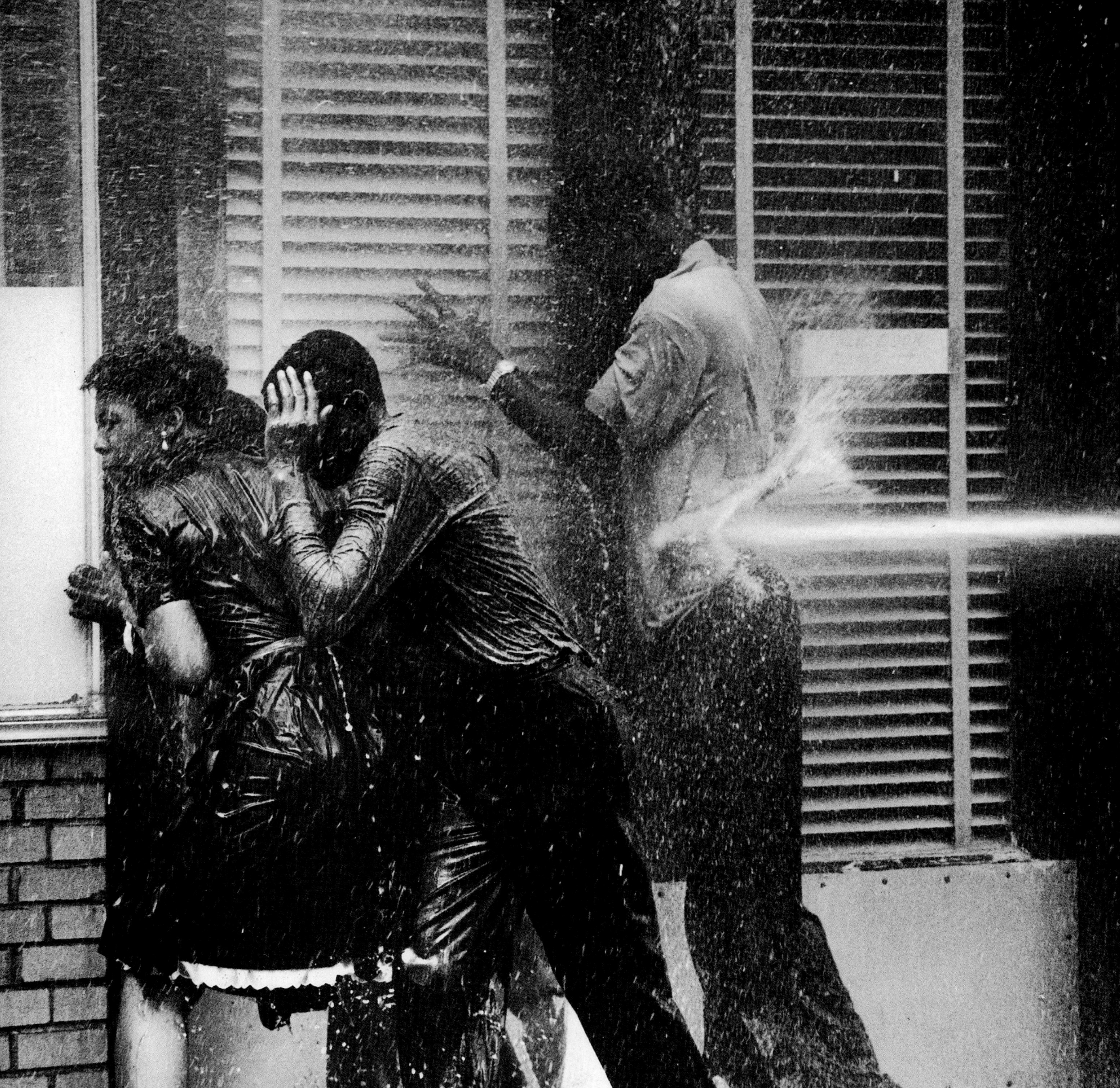

BIRMINGHAM, ALABAMA

For a long time, this city was considered one of the toughest in the South, as a sizable black population and a dominant white class frequently joined in overt hostility. By 1963, Birmingham had become a touchstone of the black civil rights movement, and nonviolent demonstrators led by Rev. Martin Luther King Jr. were met with police dogs and high-velocity hoses. The disturbing photo above helped bring support for the civil rights cause. Opposite: A world of emotions cross this man's face as he stands battered but unbowed after a police hosing.

CHARLES MOORE (2)

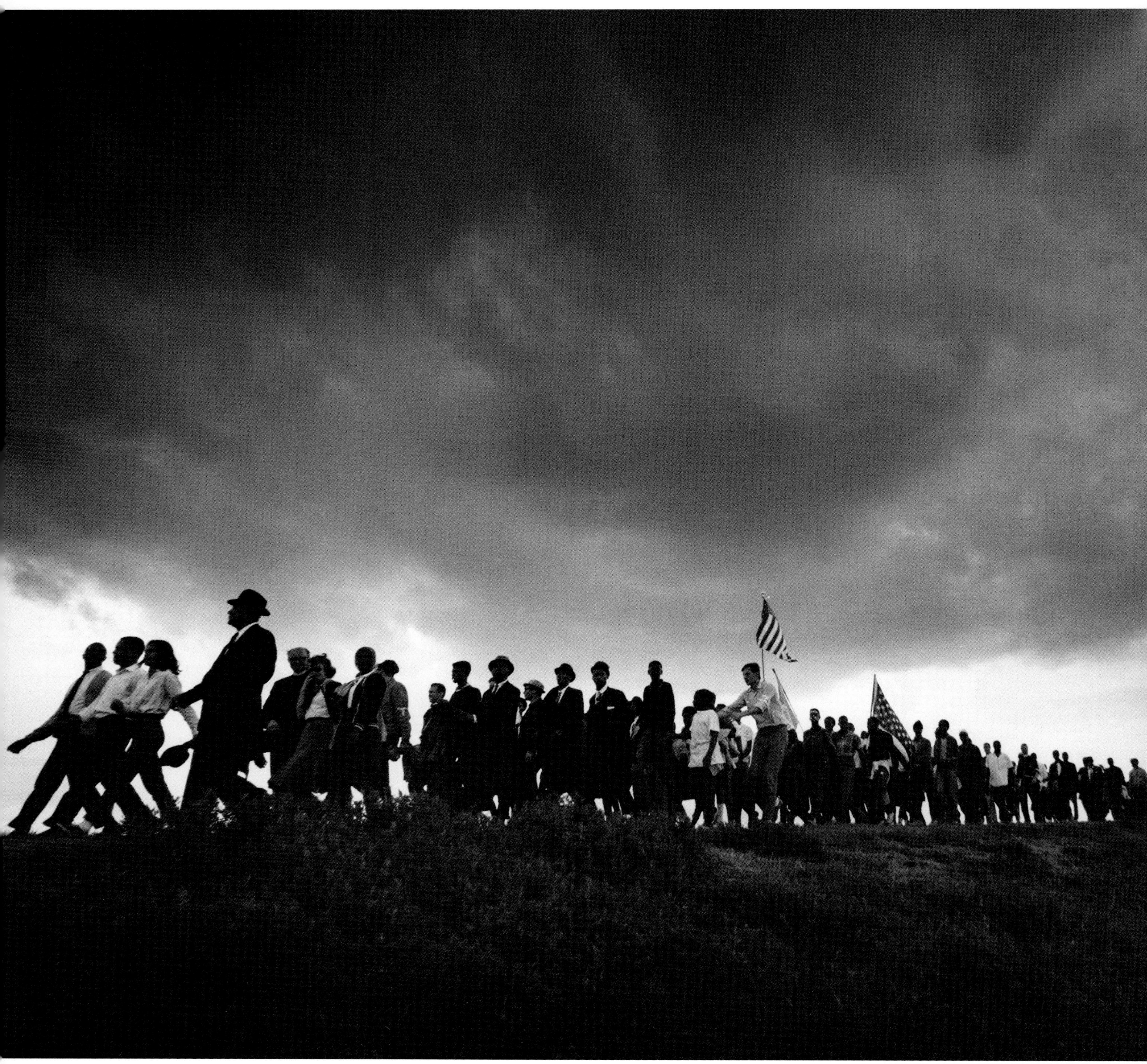

THE SELMA MARCH

From the mid-1950s, racial discord in America grew increasingly intense and widespread, as blacks sought their rightful place in society. Voting rights were a key issue, and in 1965, Reverend King organized a nonviolent march from the Alabama city of Selma to the state capital in Montgomery. Many of the demonstrators were beaten severely, but the march led to the Voting Rights Act of 1965.

JAMES H. KARALES

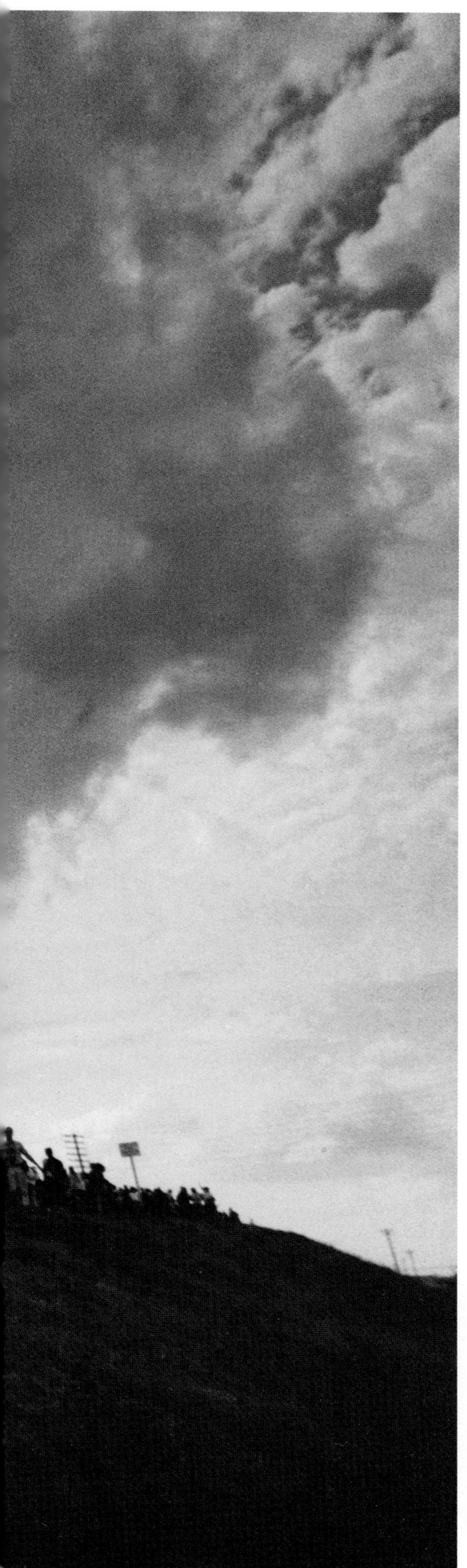

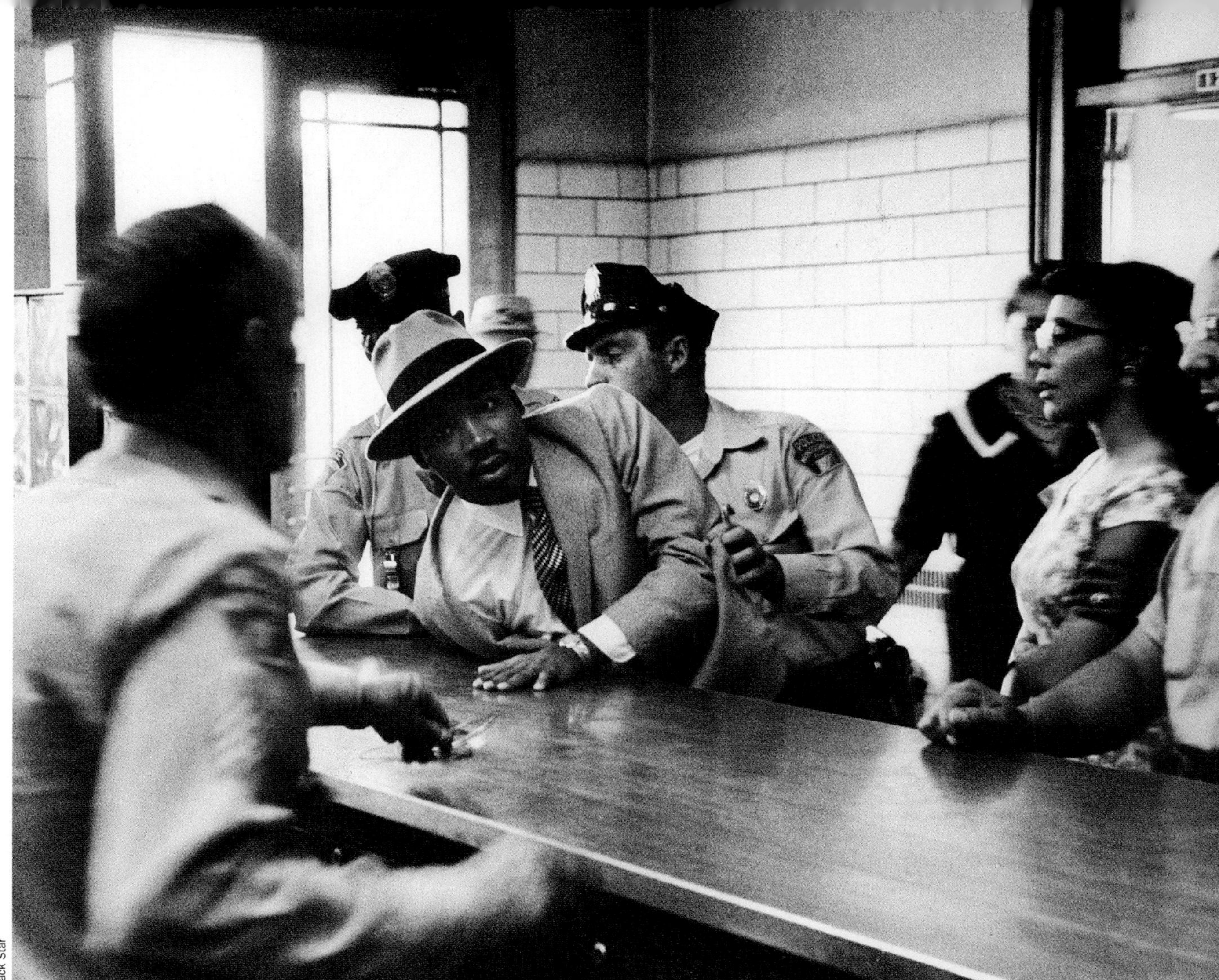

Black Star

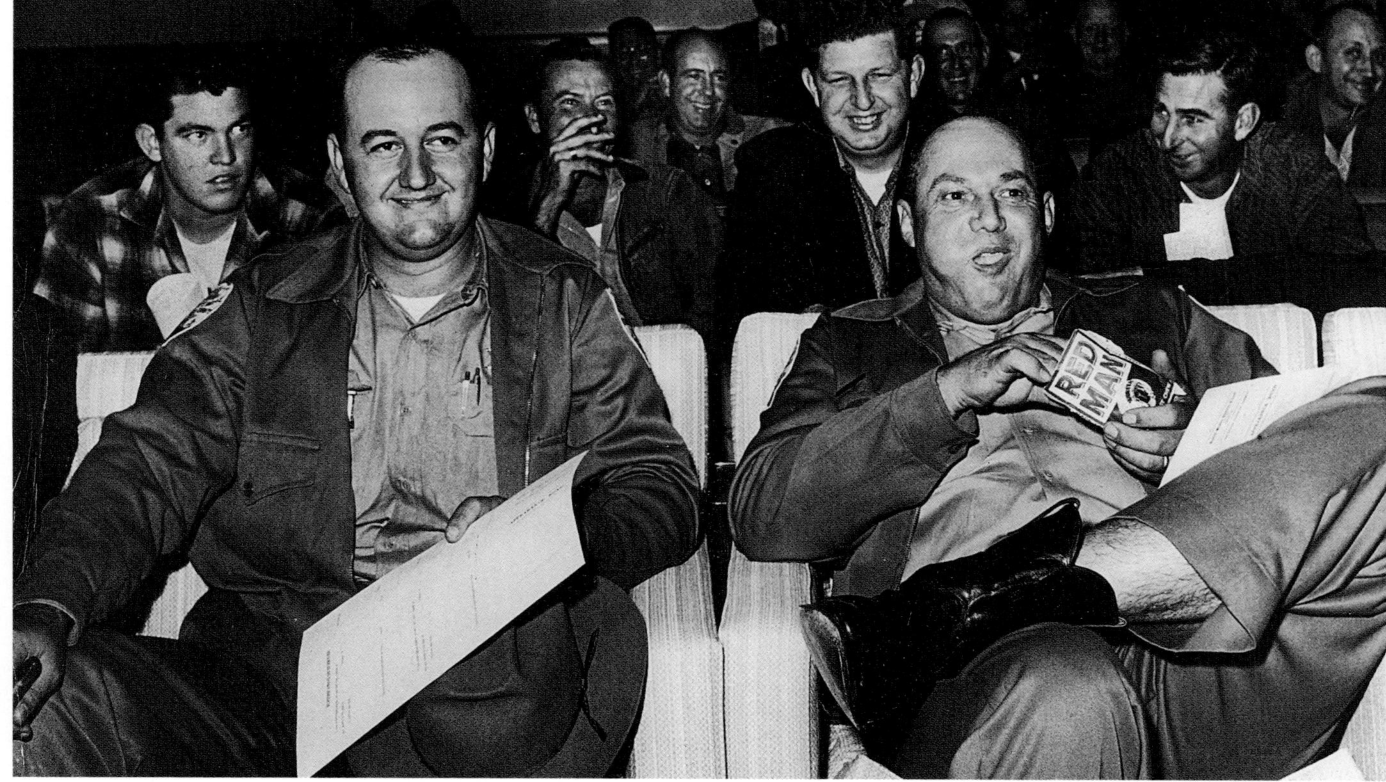

JUSTICE

At top, Reverend King is shoved against a police desk after being arrested for loitering in Montgomery in 1958. He was released when police learned his identity. Above, in 1964, Neshoba County, Miss., Sheriff Lawrence Rainey (right) is arraigned with 20 others on charges relating to the murder of civil rights workers. Rainey was acquitted, but seven others were convicted of conspiracy to violate civil rights.

TOP **CHARLES MOORE** *ABOVE* **BILL REED**

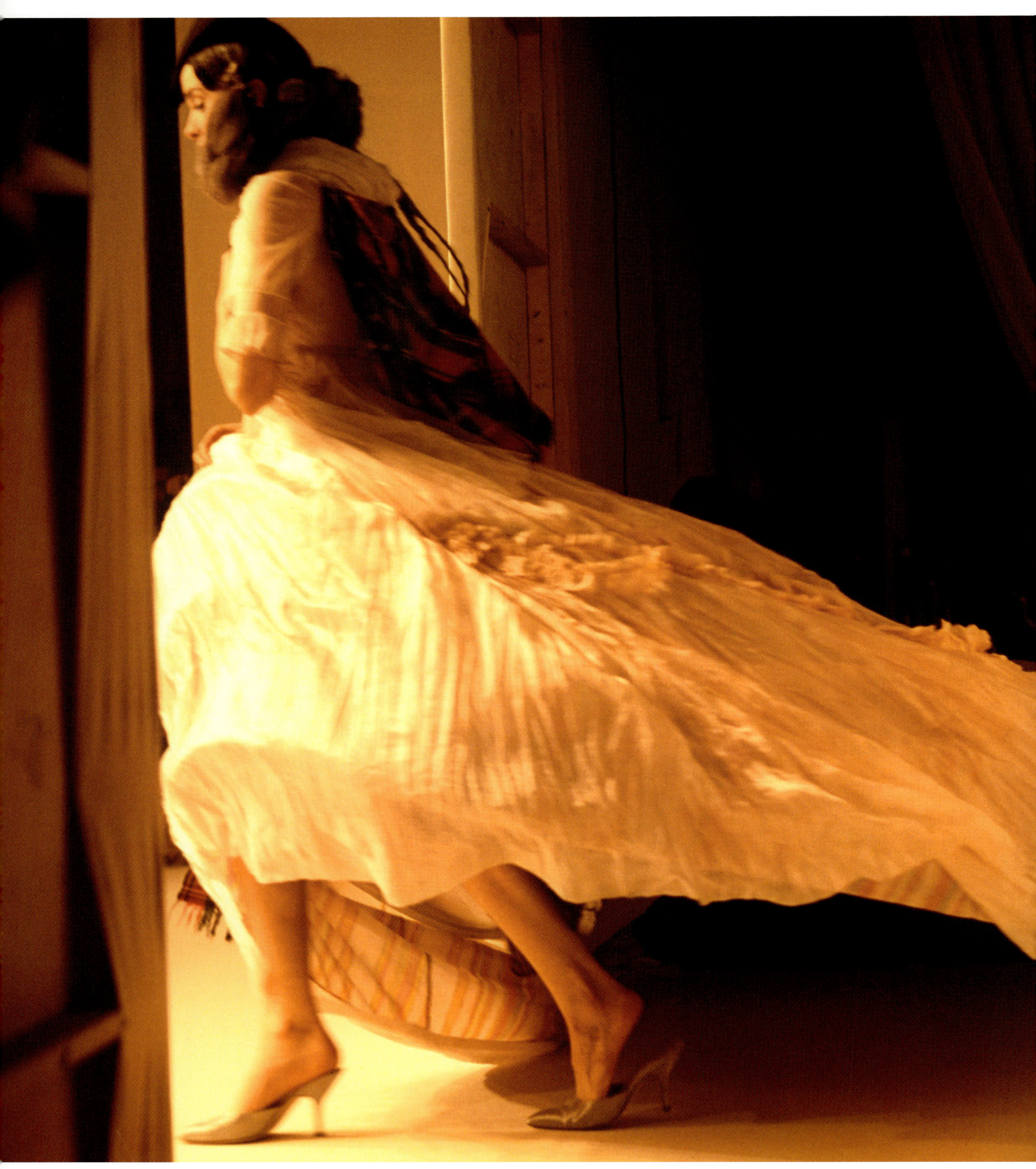

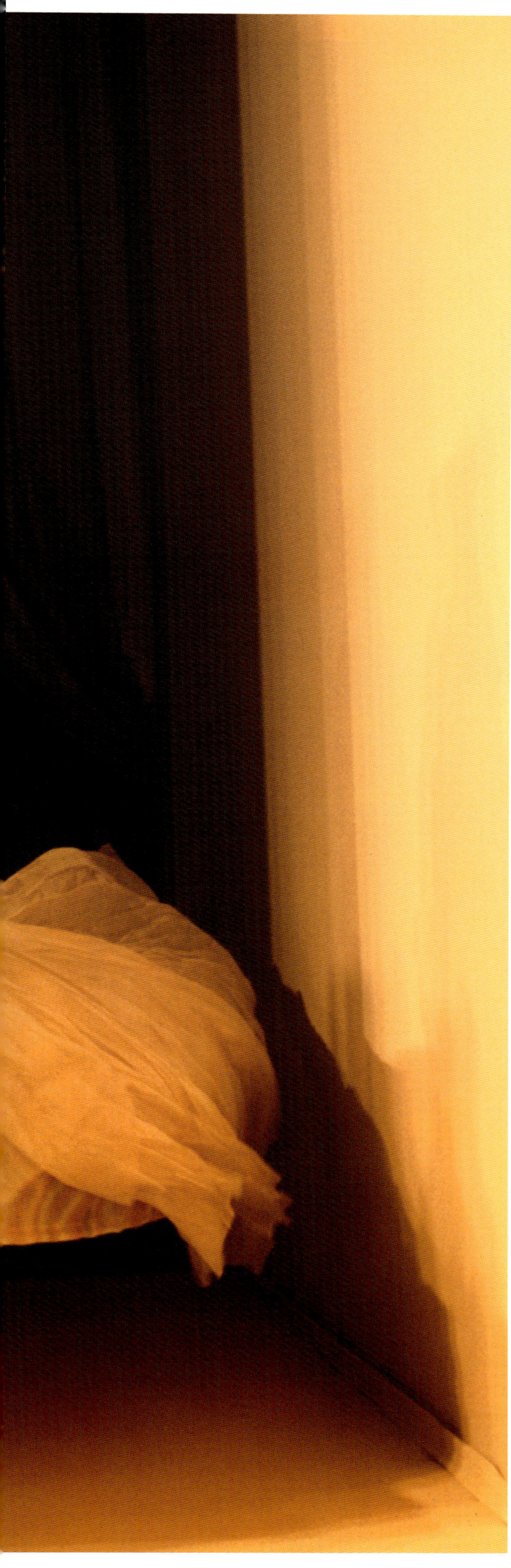

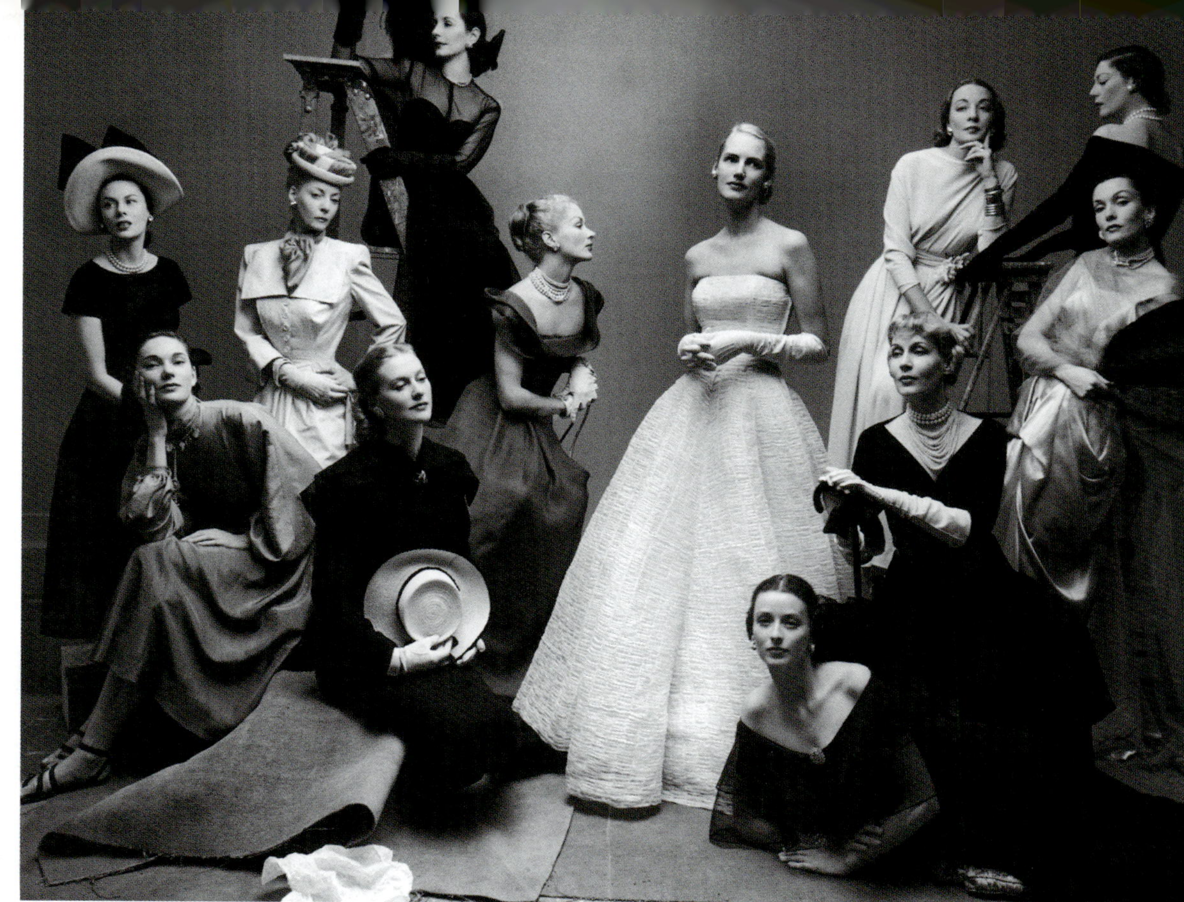

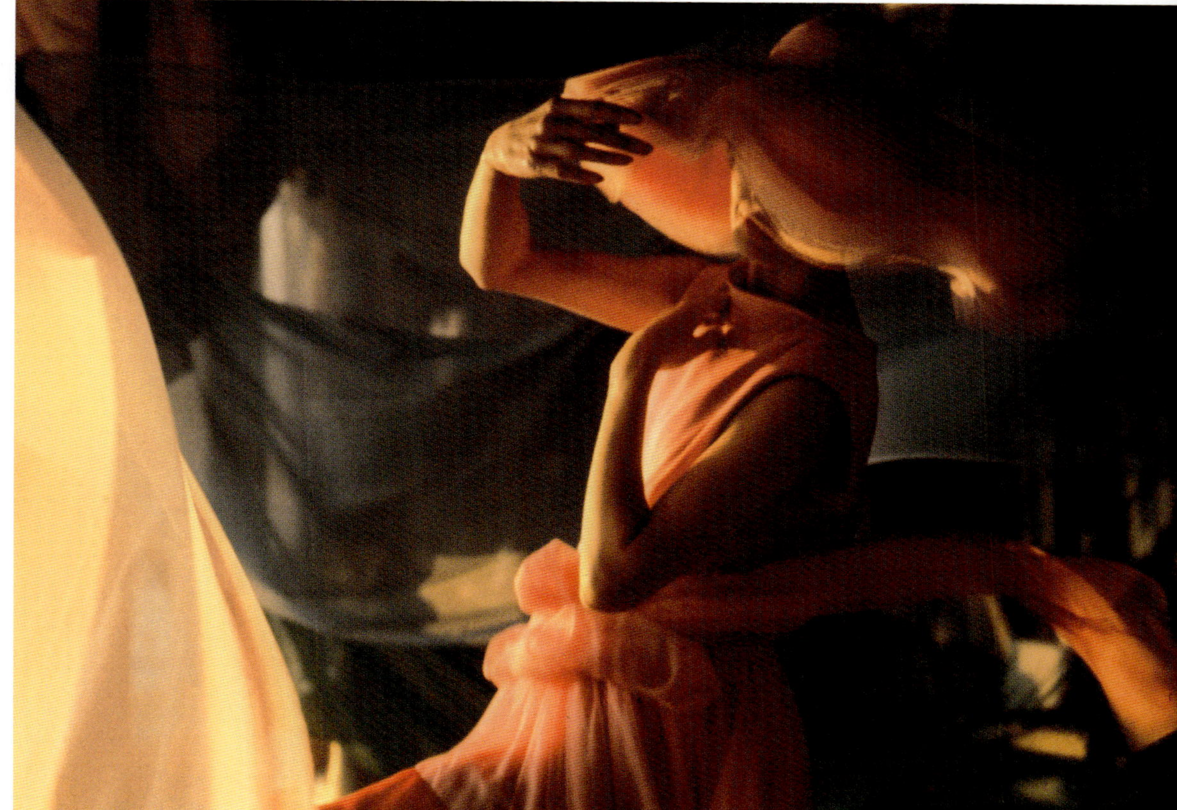

A REALM OF ALLURE

Fashion has made countless appearances in the pages of LIFE over the years. Clockwise from top: Irving Penn assembled this gorgeous group of *Vogue* models in New York City in 1947; Gordon Parks snapped this model in a James Galanos afternoon dress and 15-layer chiffon hat in 1961; Harry Benson caught this model, resplendent in a Galiano gown, in Paris in 1994.

LEFT **HARRY BENSON** *TOP* **IRVING PENN** *ABOVE* **GORDON PARKS**

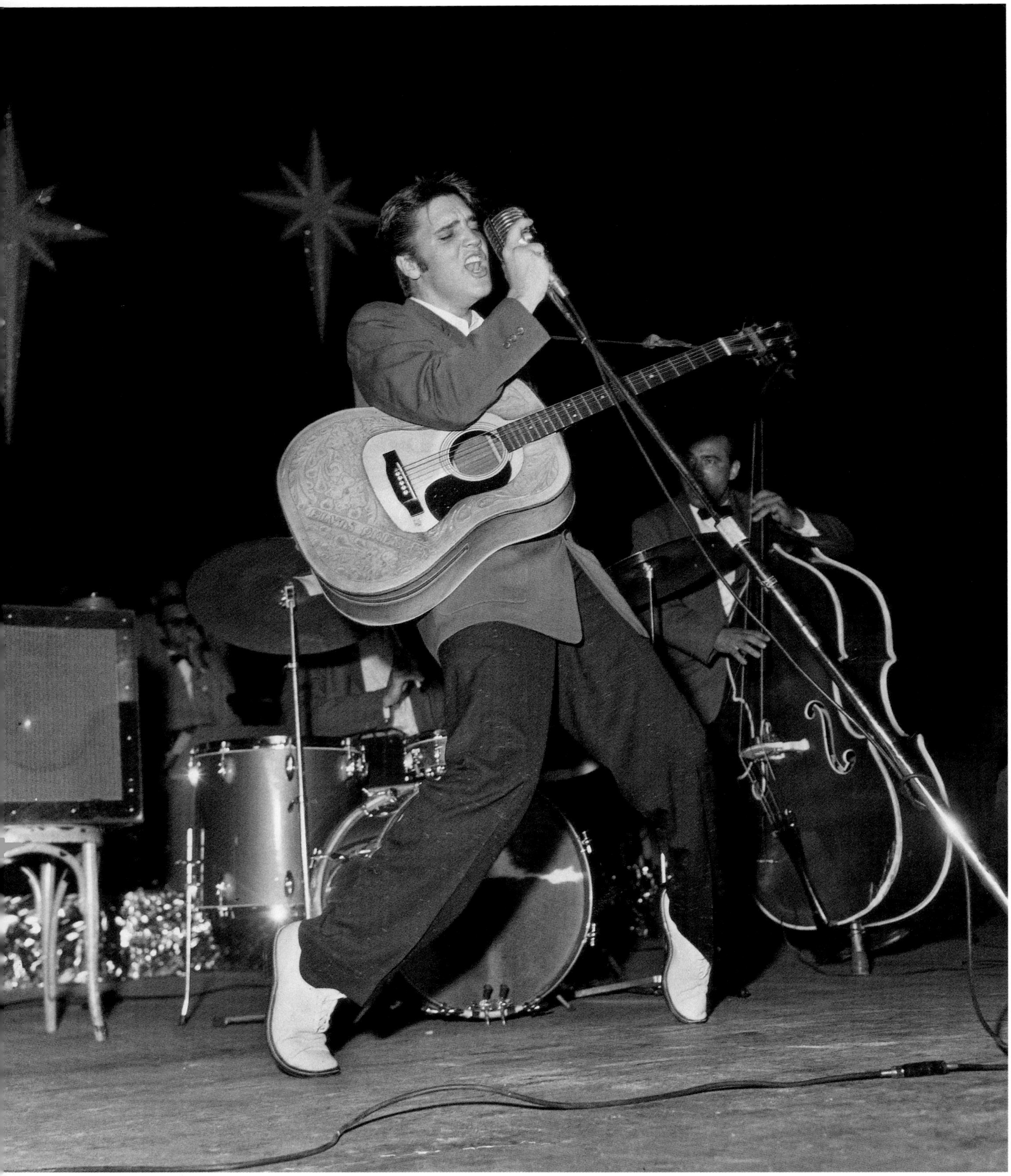

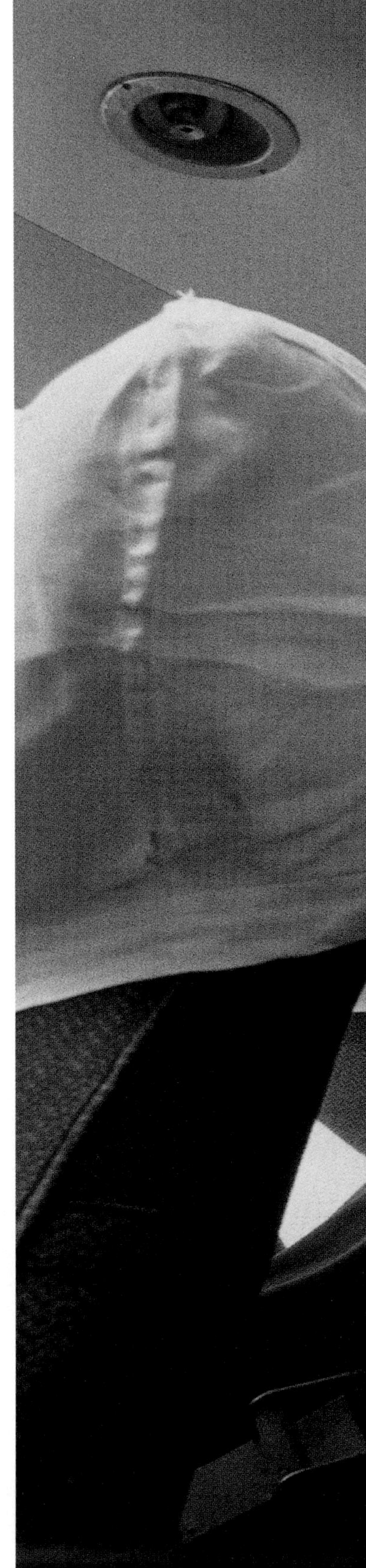

THE KING

There are some celebrities who seem never to take a bad photograph, and the young Elvis Presley was certainly at the forefront of these photogenic marvels. Here, the "white man with the black man's feel," as Sam Phillips put it, tears it up in Florida in 1956. LIFE was the first national magazine to showcase Elvis.

CHARLES TRAINOR

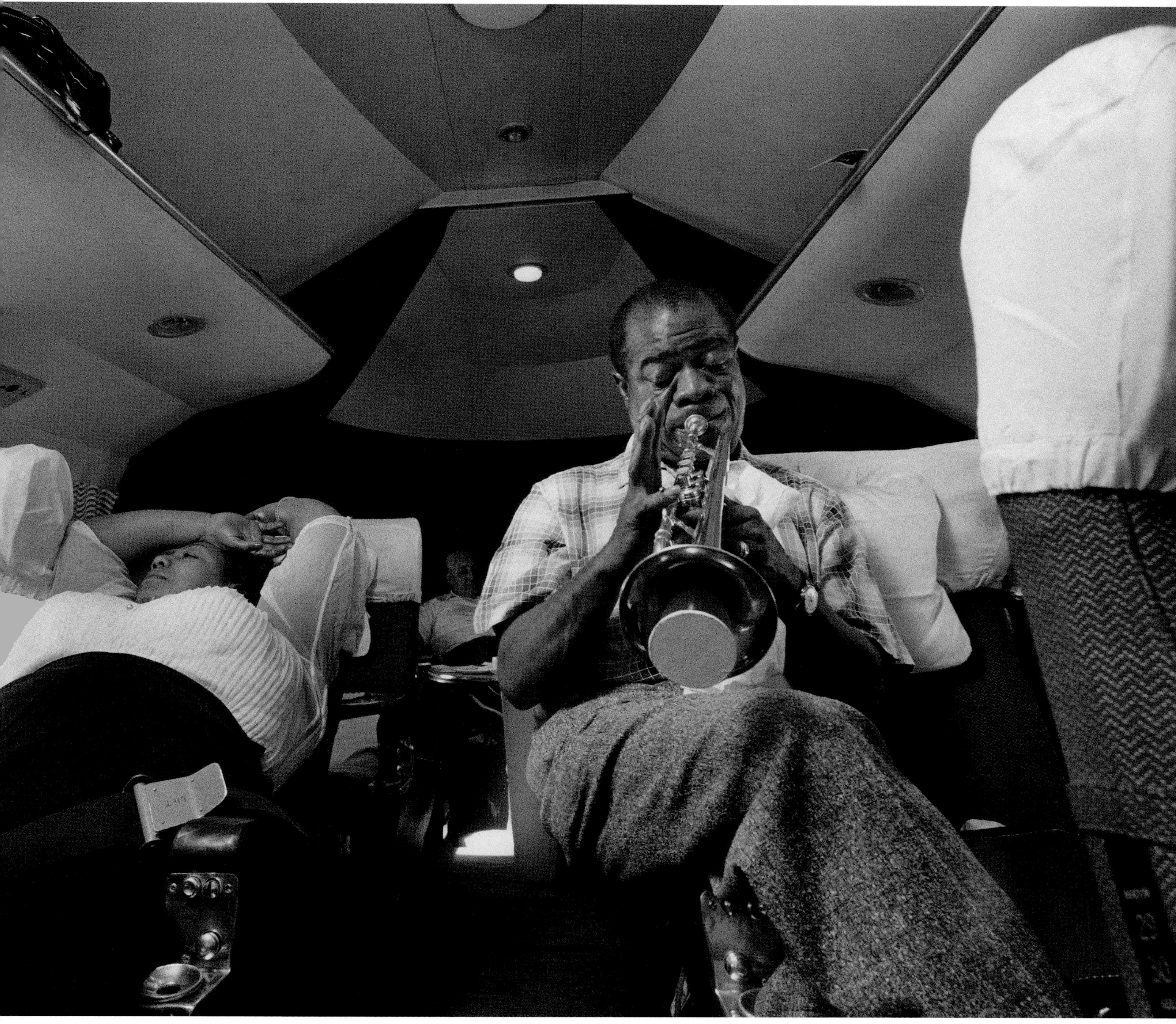

SATCHMO

Here, also in 1956, one of the century's musical titans is on a tour of Africa, but he's not too tired to squeeze a little more magic out of the day. On a plane from Nigeria to Gold Coast, Louis Armstrong, with singer Velma Middleton reclining to left, takes flight.

LARRY BURROWS

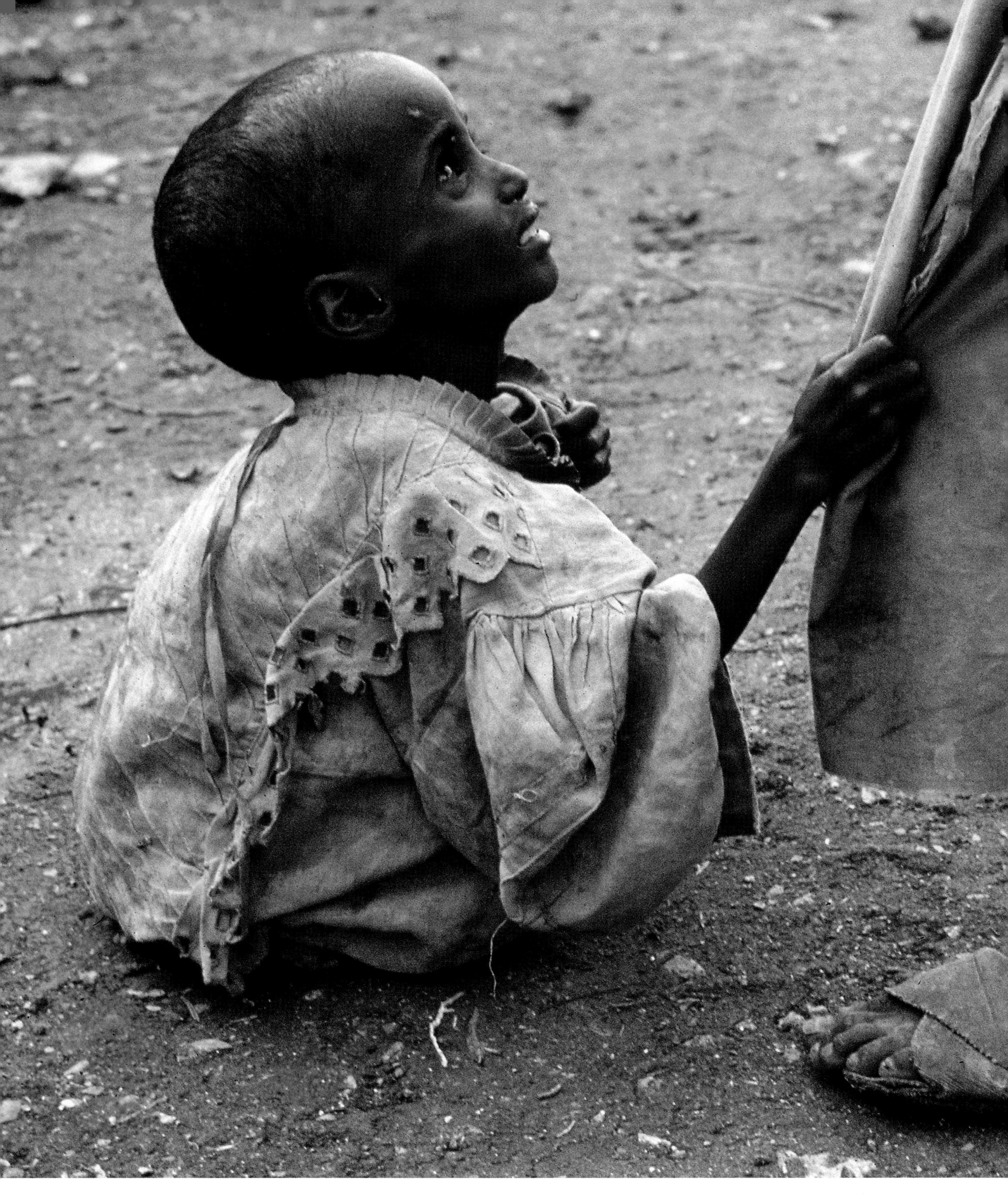

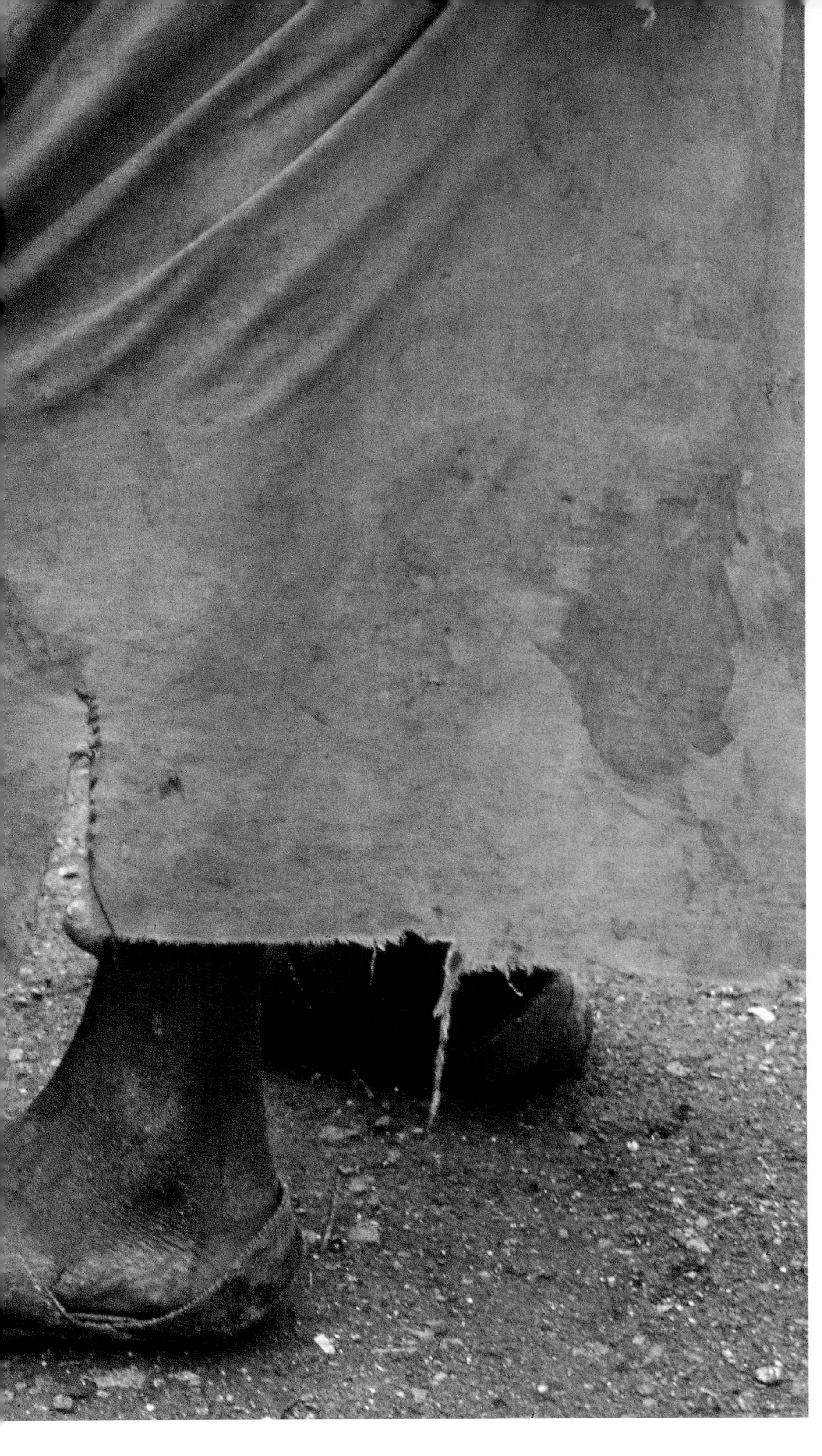

FAMINE

In the early 1990s the eastern African nation of Somalia, a land in which two thirds of the people are nomads, was wracked by drought and civil war. Here, at a feeding center in 1992, a starving girl tugs at the hem of her brother's garment.

ANDREW HOLBROOKE

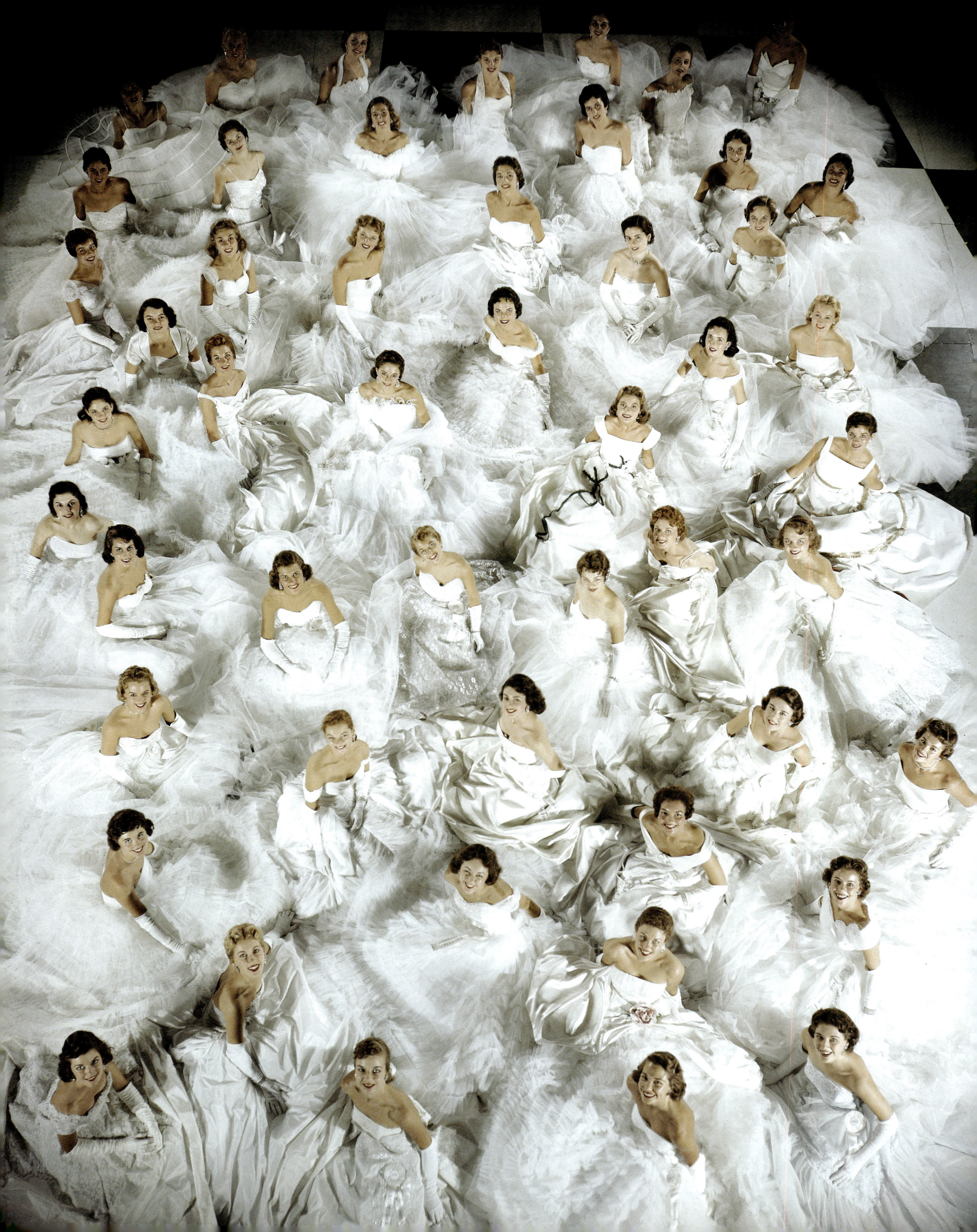

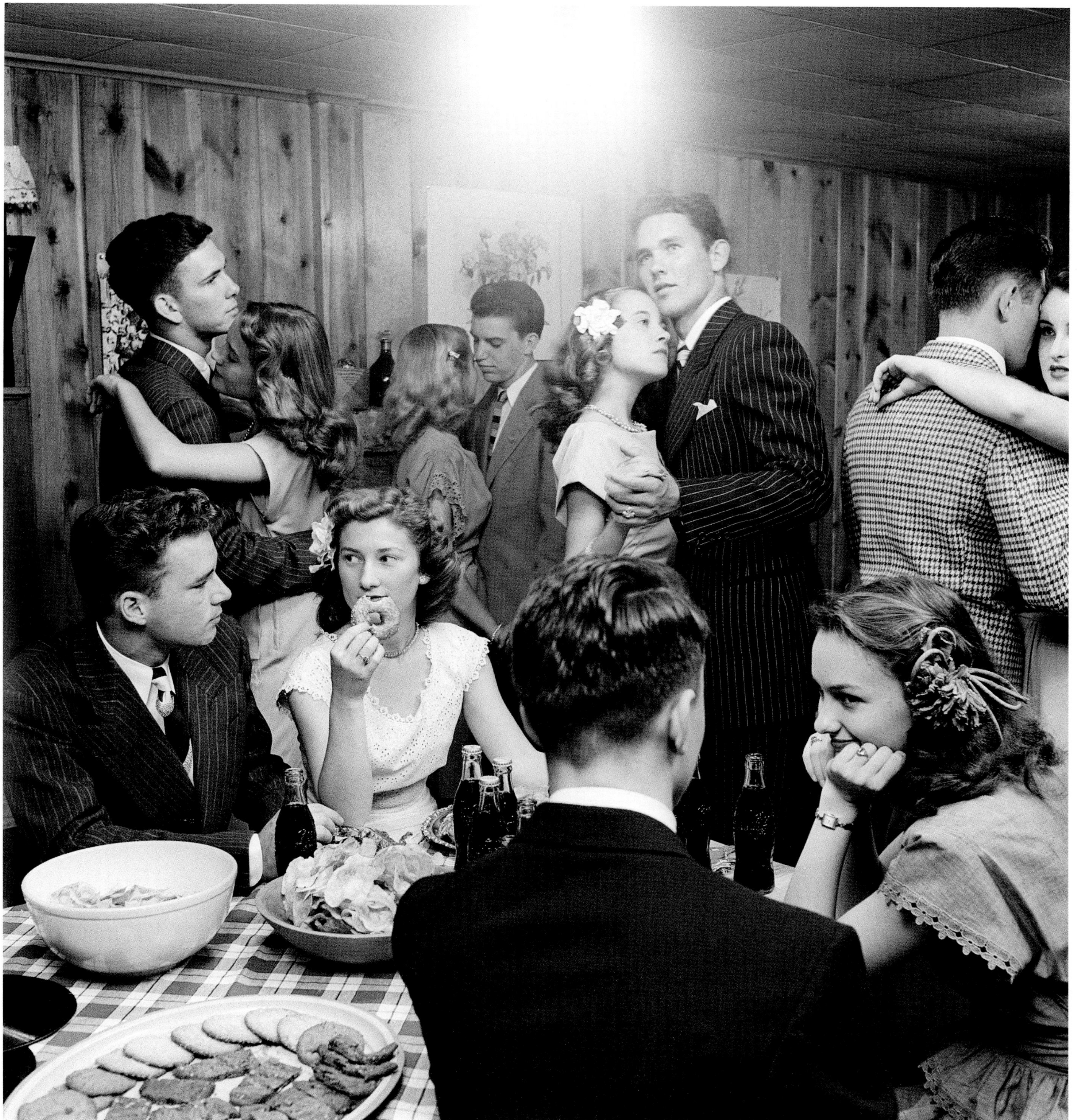

AN ATLANTIC CITY BOUQUET

The contestants in the 1956 Miss America pageant gather in a shimmering display of white evening gowns and high hopes. The winner was Marian McKnight of South Carolina, third row from the top, second from left, with wide shoulder straps.

YALE JOEL

SENTIMENTAL JOURNEY

These well-scrubbed teenagers are enjoying a lovely evening in Tulsa in 1947, fueled by a steady supply of Cokes 'n' snacks. As LIFE noted at the time, when they weren't eating and chatting, they were dancing to "dreamy tunes like 'Night and Day.' "

NINA LEEN

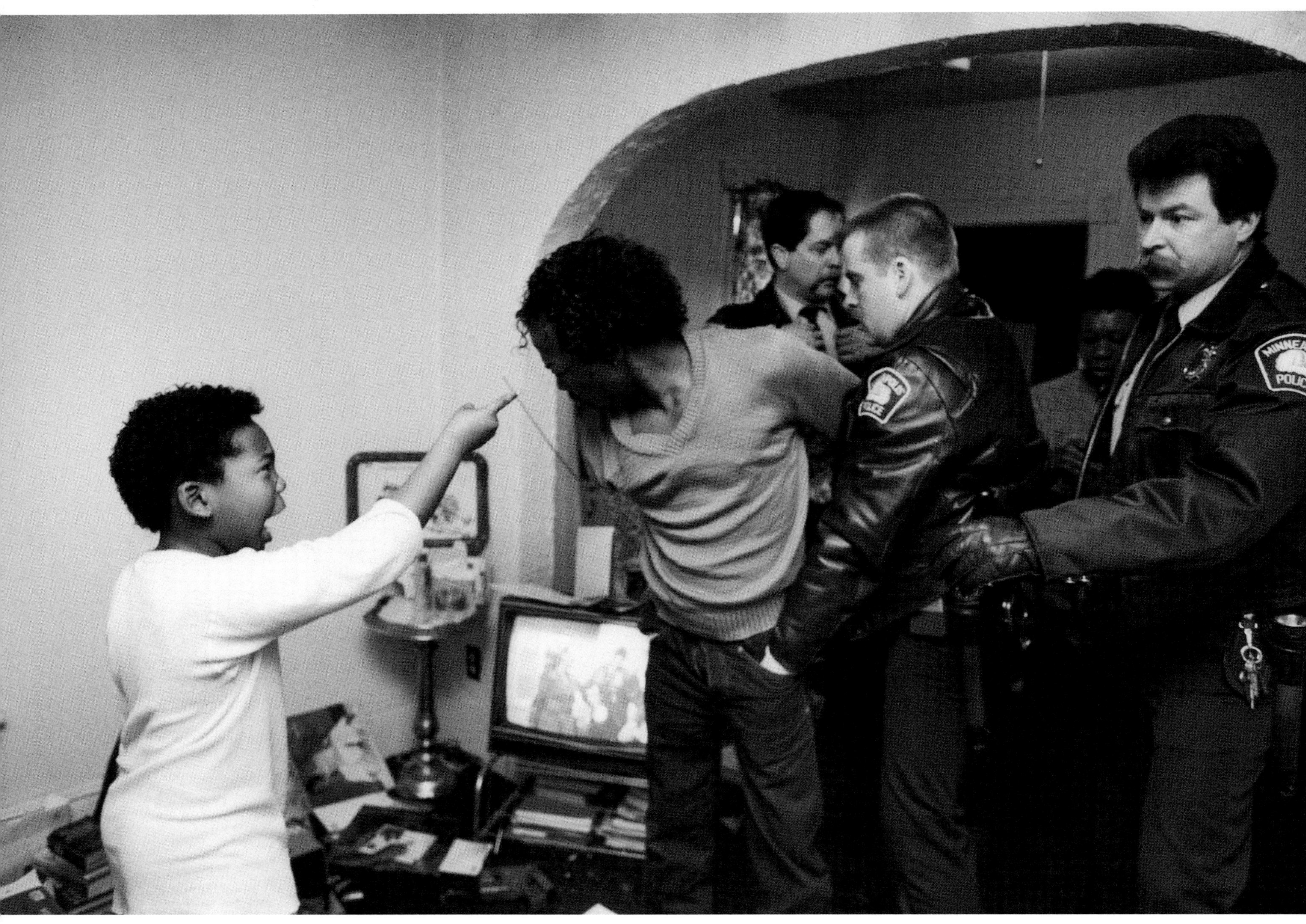

A VALIANT LAD

Photographer Ferrato was riding with Minneapolis police in 1988 when a call came in from an eight-year-old boy: His father was attacking his mother, and had a knife. As officers subdued the man, his son screamed, "I hate you! Don't you ever come back to my house!" Ferrato, a crusader for battered women, said of the child, "That's who we all need to be like."

DONNA FERRATO

FRIEND OR FOE?

In the summer of 1967 these women in eastern India were preparing their wheat fields for planting when the first drops of a monsoon began to drench them. "In India, there's more to monsoons than rains and floods," according to photographer Singh. "It's a whole way of life. A good monsoon means a good harvest. No monsoon means famine."

RAGHUBIR SINGH

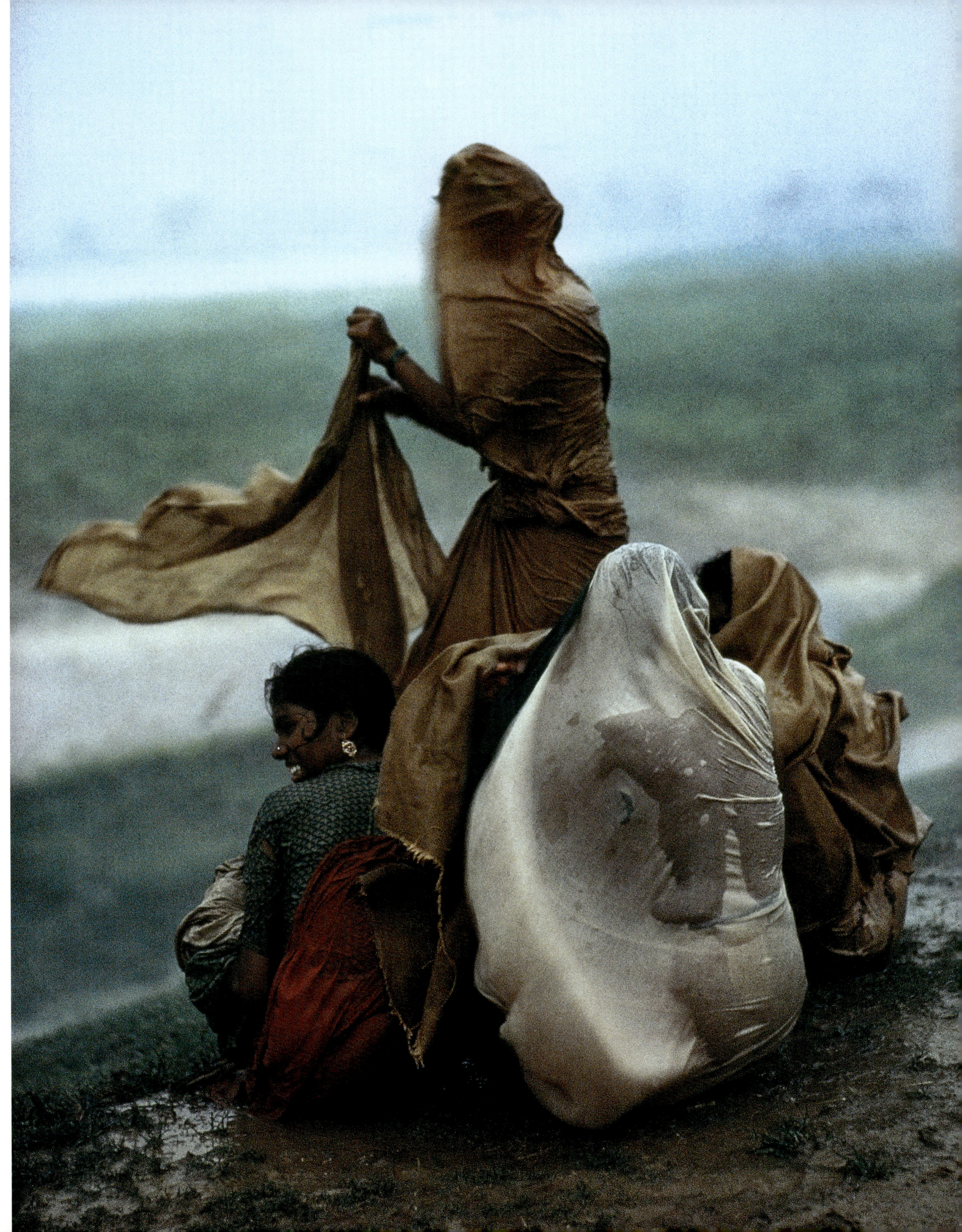

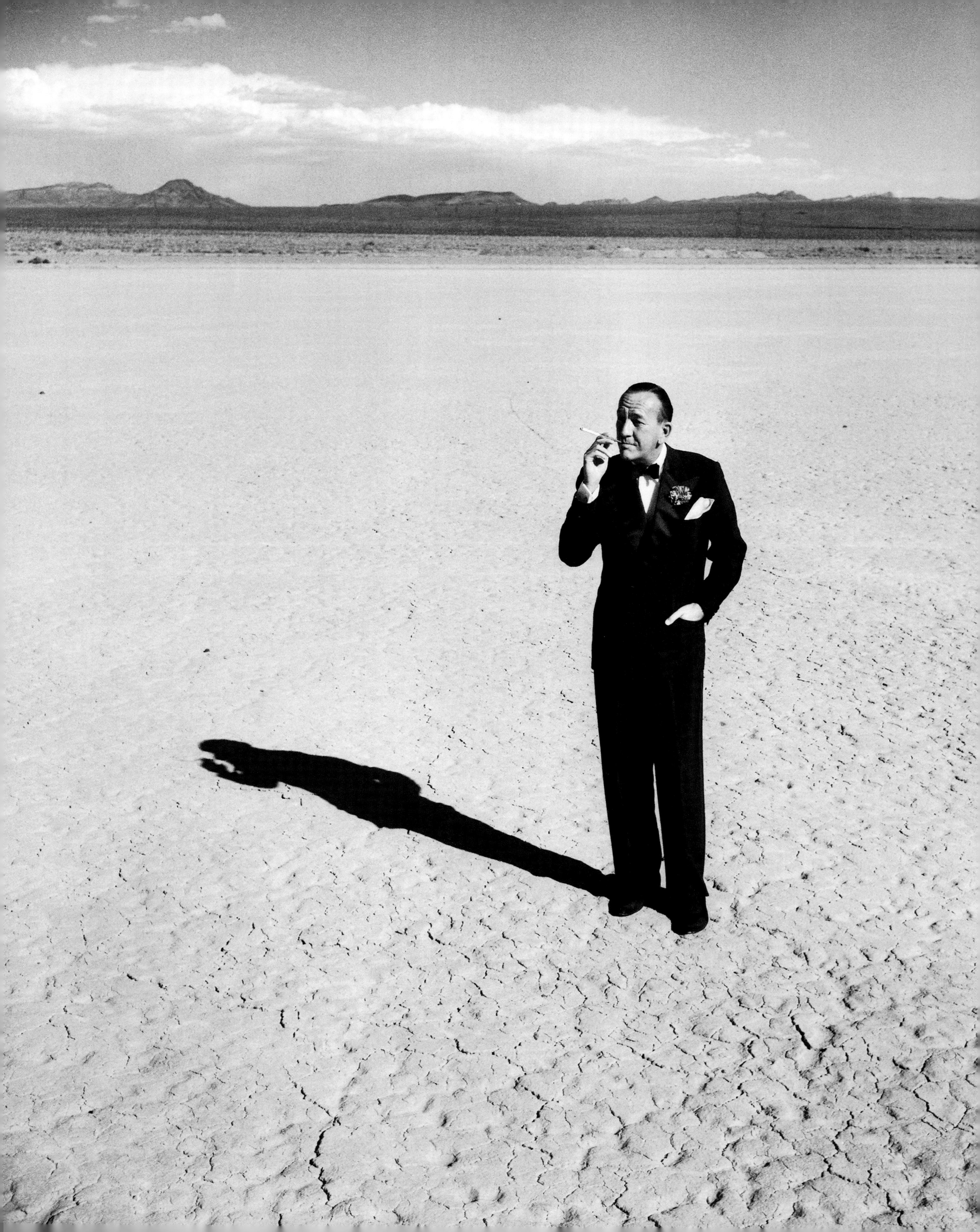

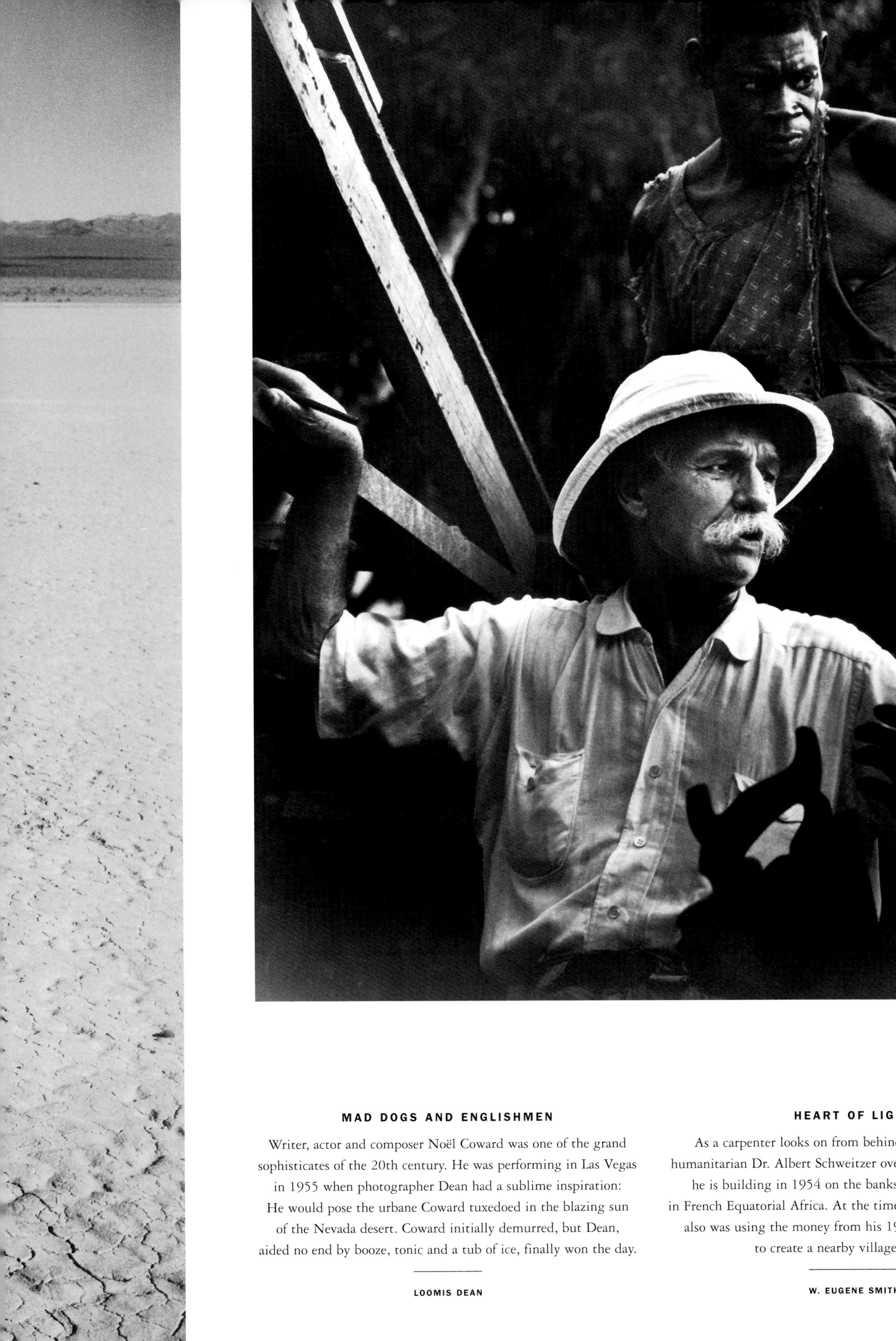

MAD DOGS AND ENGLISHMEN

Writer, actor and composer Noël Coward was one of the grand sophisticates of the 20th century. He was performing in Las Vegas in 1955 when photographer Dean had a sublime inspiration: He would pose the urbane Coward tuxedoed in the blazing sun of the Nevada desert. Coward initially demurred, but Dean, aided no end by booze, tonic and a tub of ice, finally won the day.

LOOMIS DEAN

HEART OF LIGHT

As a carpenter looks on from behind, the great Alsatian humanitarian Dr. Albert Schweitzer oversees work on a hospital he is building in 1954 on the banks of the Ogowe River in French Equatorial Africa. At the time, the medical missionary also was using the money from his 1952 Nobel Peace Prize to create a nearby village for lepers.

W. EUGENE SMITH

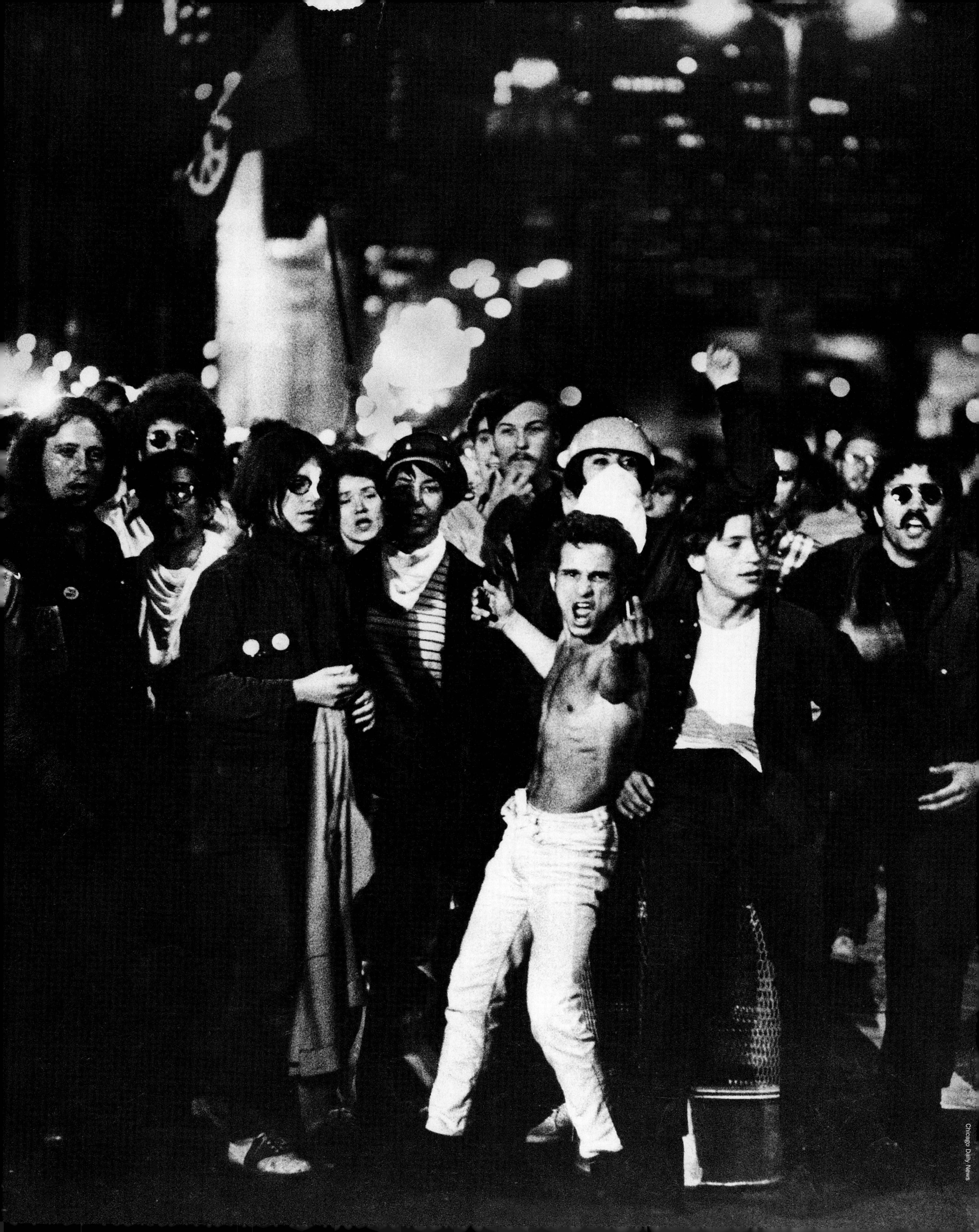

Chicago Daily News

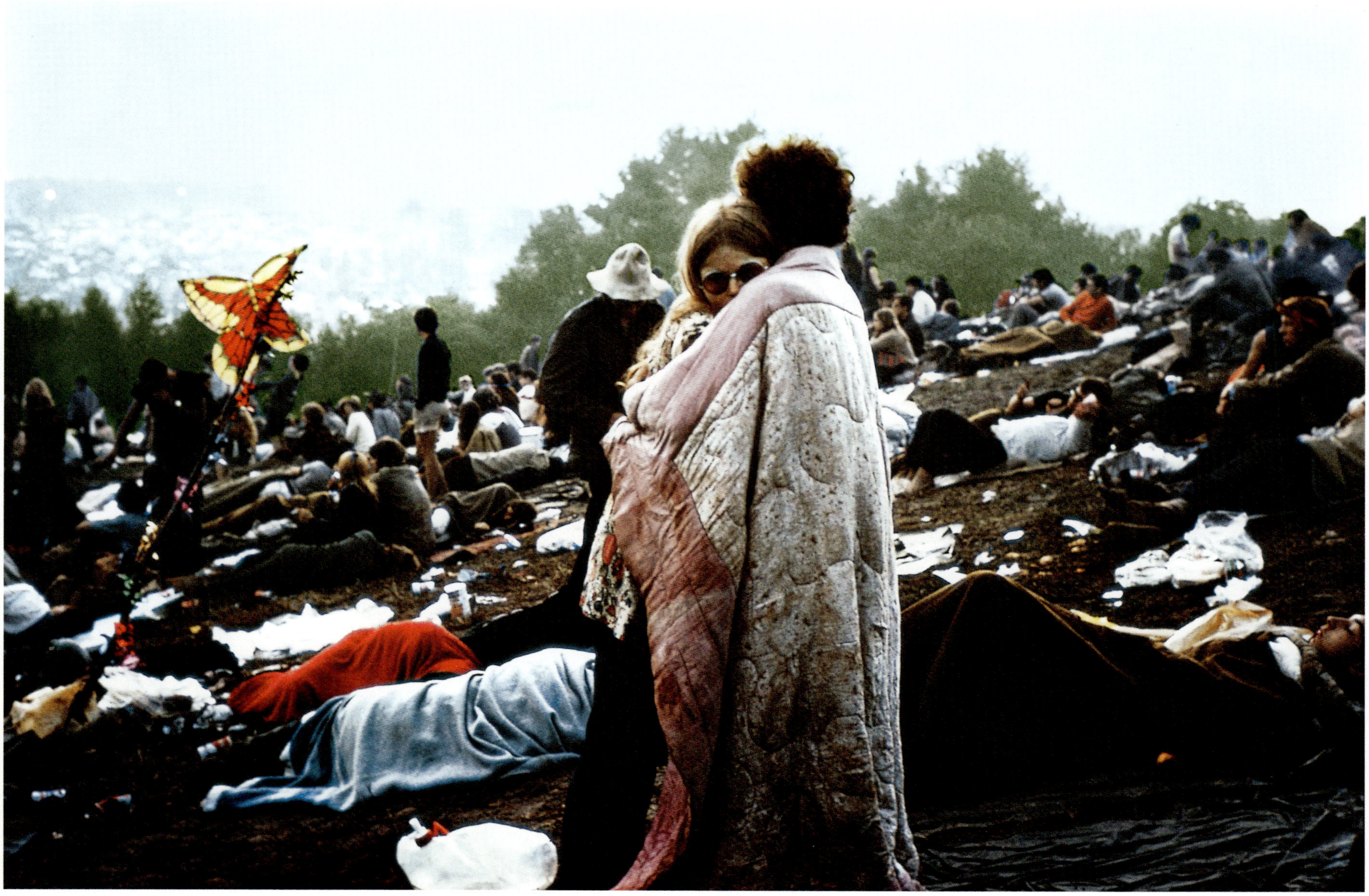

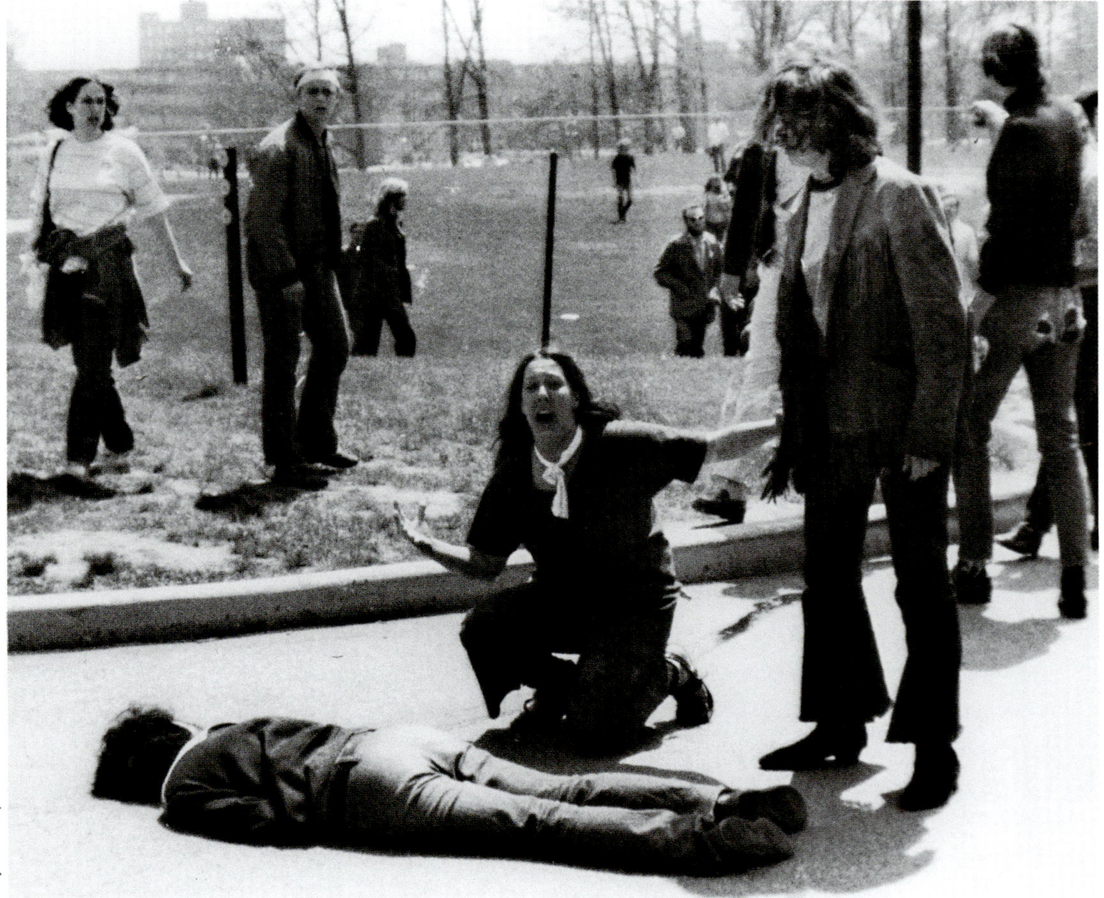

Valley News Dispatch

THE TIMES, THEY WERE A-CHANGIN'

In the 1960s, the Vietnam War collided with an increasingly defiant younger generation, and the results were complex and divisive. Opposite, at the 1968 Democratic national convention in Chicago, the chant "The whole world is watching!" fills the streets as antiwar demonstrators clash with the Chicago police force. Above, in 1969, hundreds of thousands of kids gather for a few days of peace, love, music and mud at the Woodstock festival in New York State. At left, the following year, Mary Ann Vecchio grieves over the body of a student shot by National Guardsmen at Kent State University in Ohio.

OPPOSITE **PERRY C. RIDDLE** *LEFT* **JOHN PAUL FILO** *ABOVE* **BURK UZZLE**

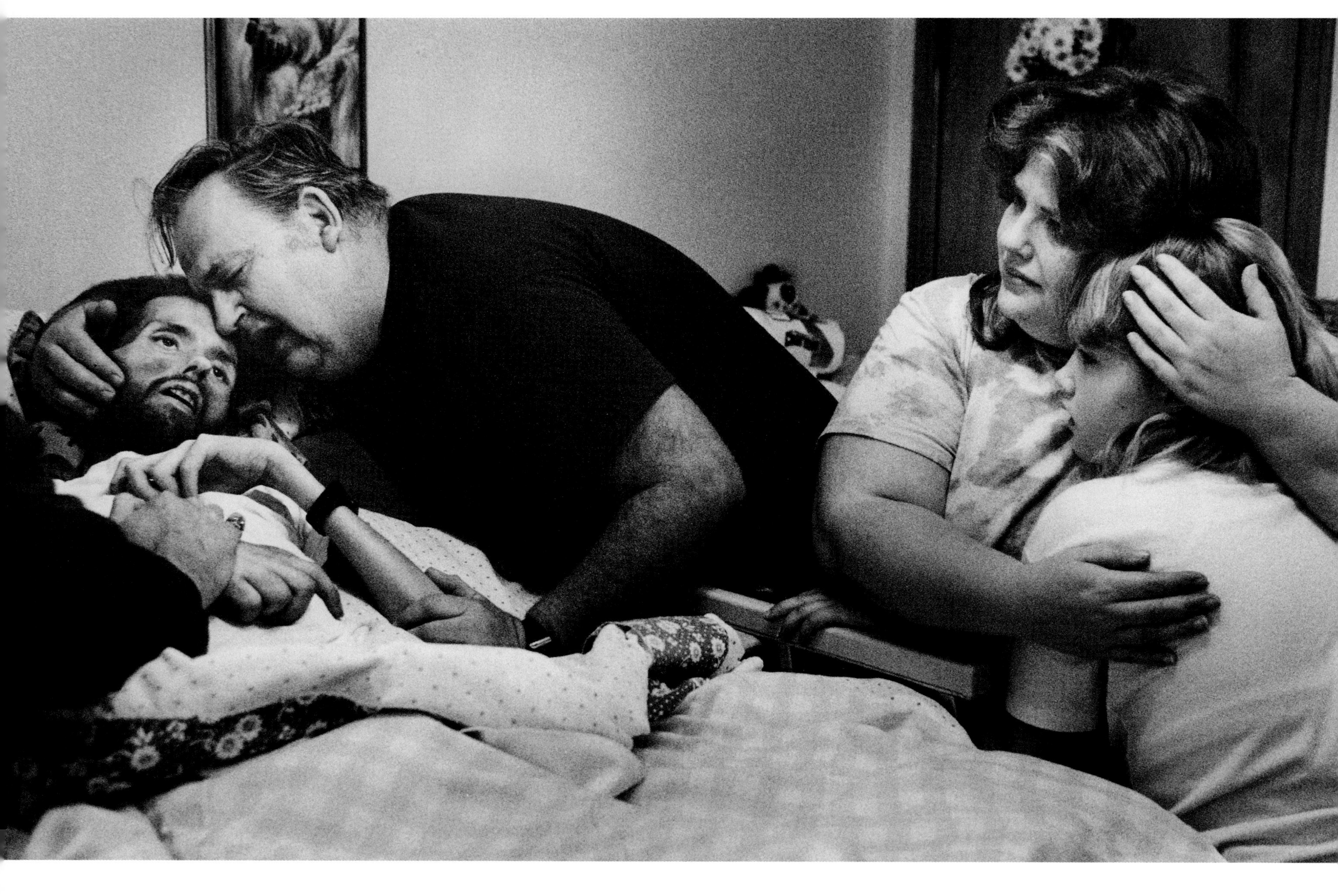

AIDS

In 1990, 32-year-old AIDS activist David Kirby is attended at his deathbed by family members. When this photograph ran in LIFE, the magazine was lauded for showing the dire effects of a plague in our midst. Then, with the family's permission, the Italian clothing company Benetton and designer Tibor Kalman colorized the image and used it in an ad. This commercialization of misery appalled many, though Benetton said it was trying to bring public awareness to the disease.

THERESE FRARE

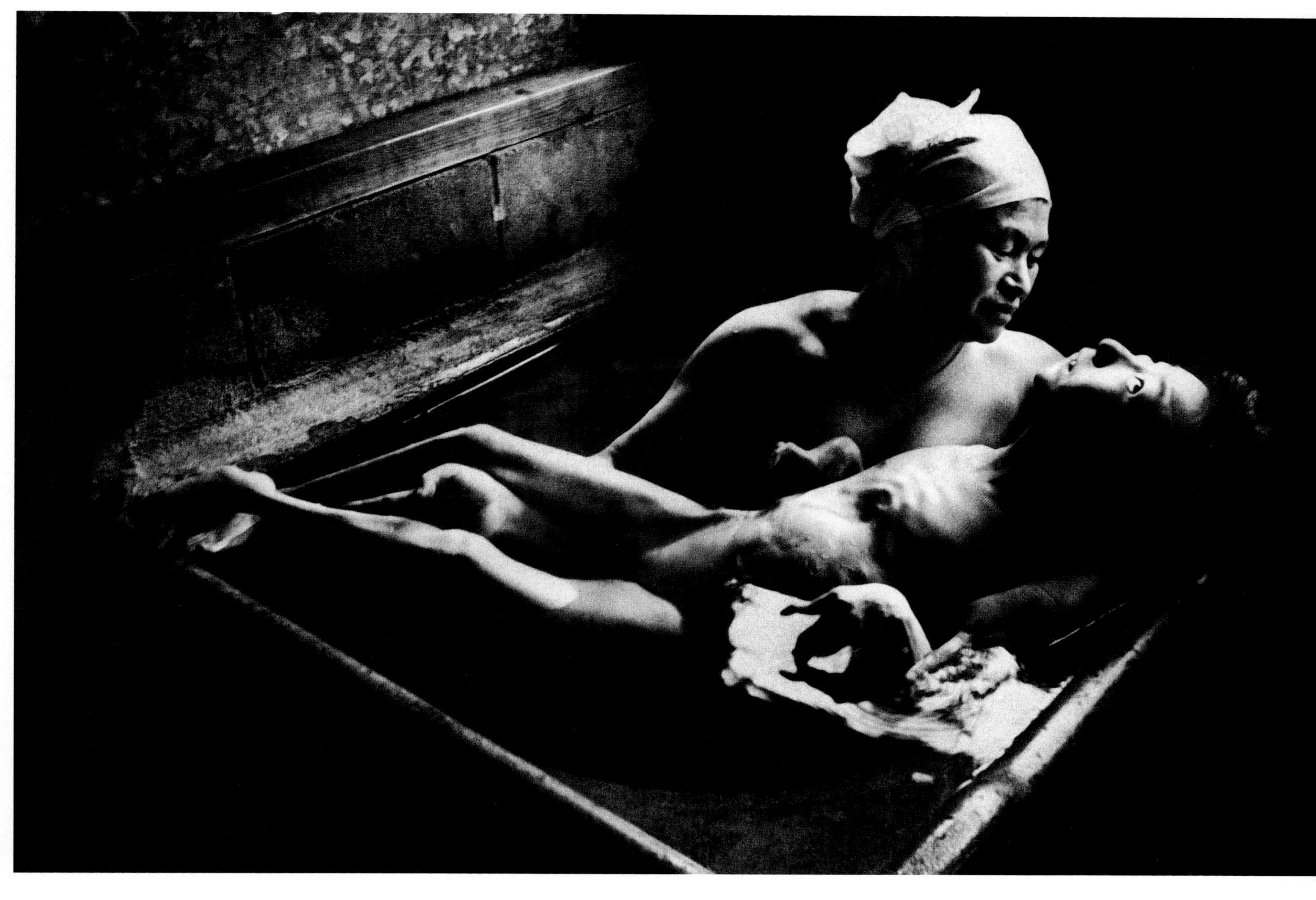

INDUSTRIAL WASTE

Some Japanese who resided in a fishing village called Minamata during the 1950s and '60s suddenly began to suffer from tremors and impaired sight and hearing. Soon many of them were dying from a mysterious ailment that translates as "ouch-ouch disease." It turned out that a chemical company called Chisso was dumping mercury into the coastal waters. Here, in 1971, Tomoko Uemura, who was poisoned in the womb and born blind, mute and mangled, is bathed with timeless tenderness by her mother.

W. EUGENE SMITH

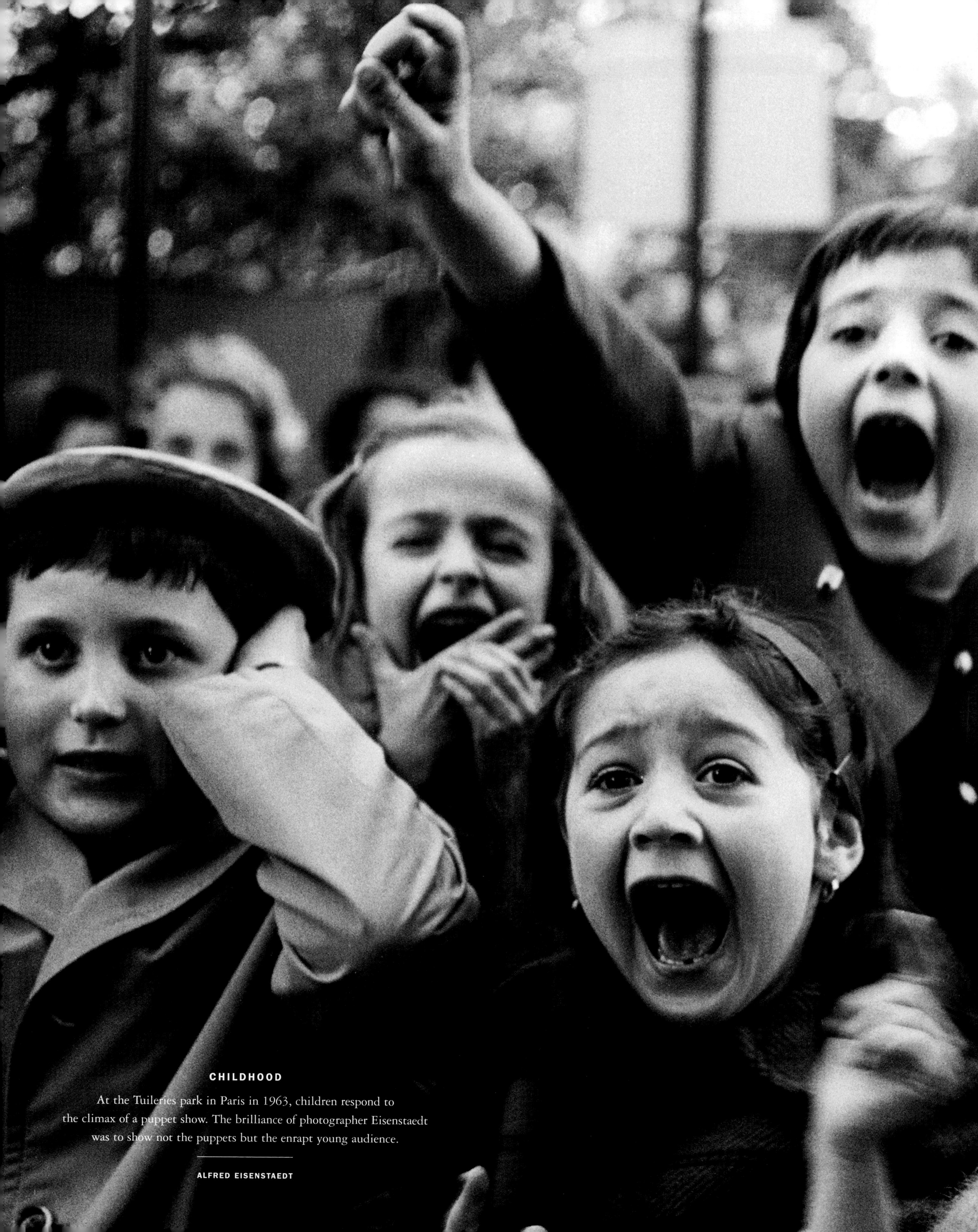

CHILDHOOD

At the Tuileries park in Paris in 1963, children respond to the climax of a puppet show. The brilliance of photographer Eisenstaedt was to show not the puppets but the enrapt young audience.

ALFRED EISENSTAEDT

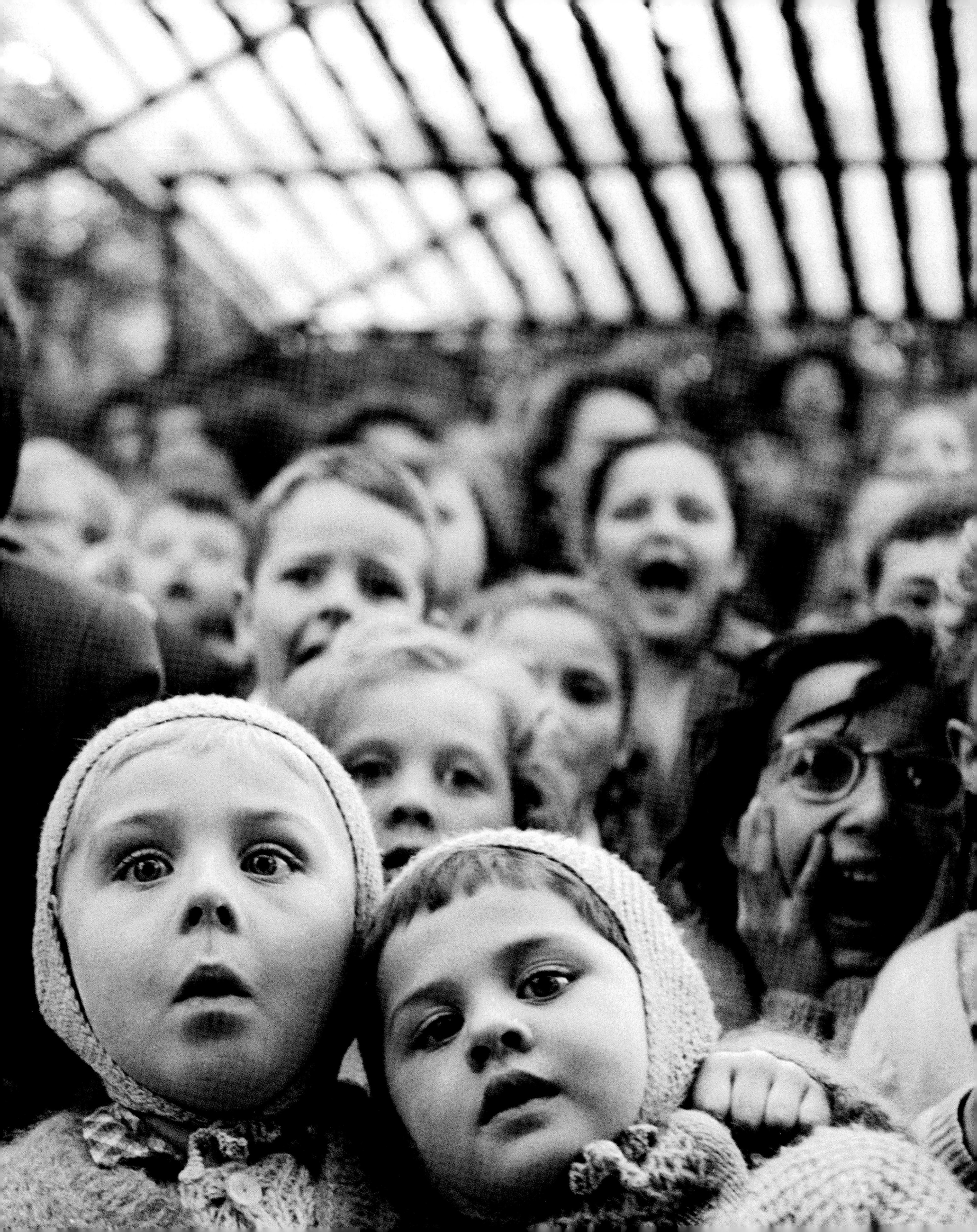

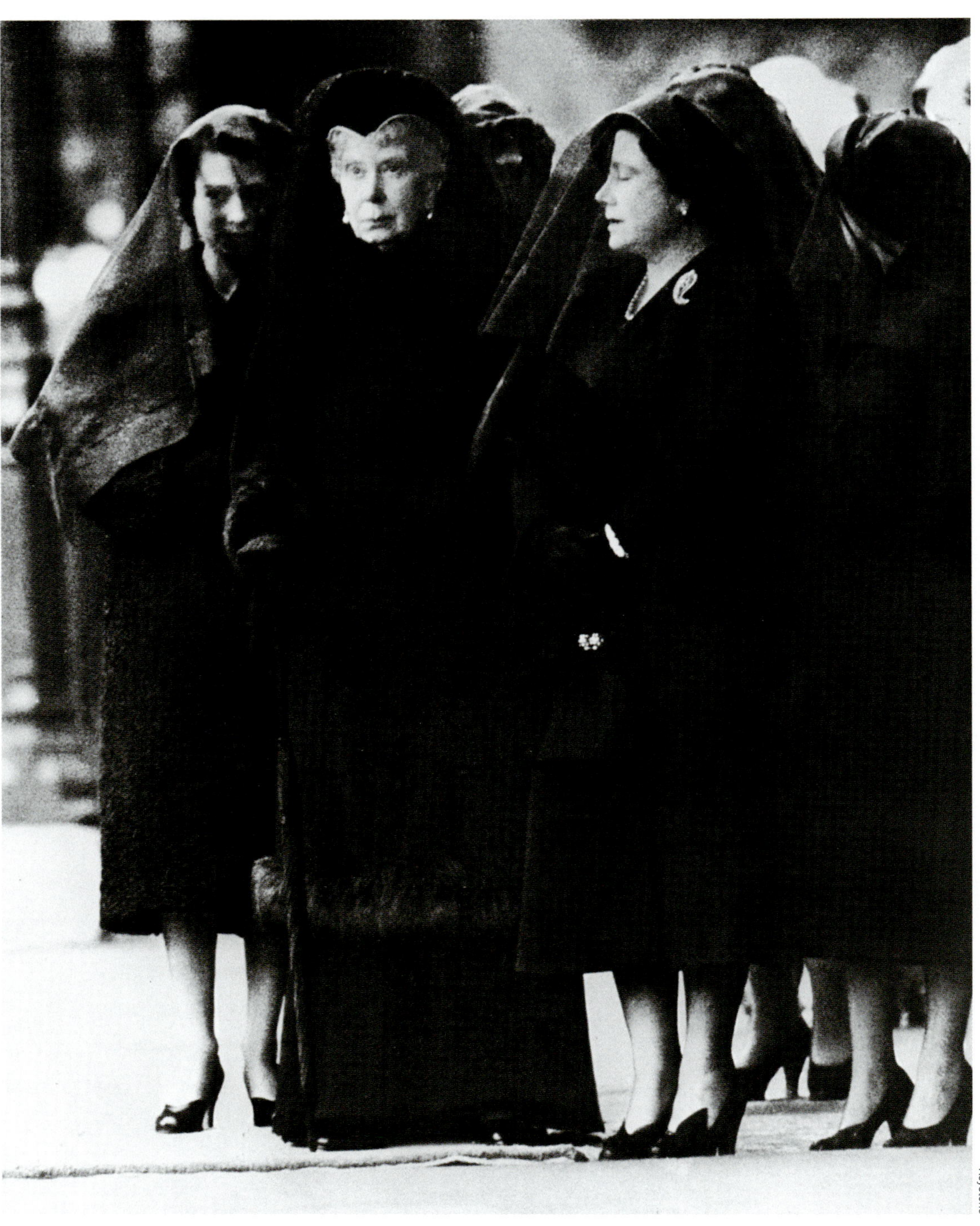

Keystone

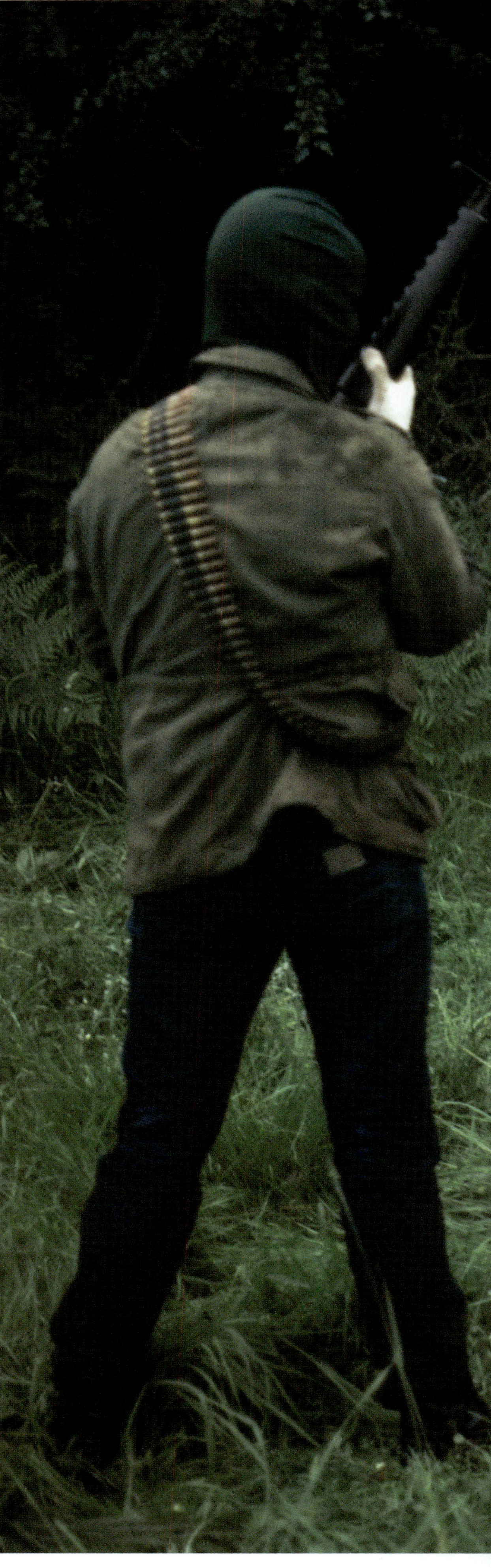

ROYALS IN DISTRESS

Above, with heavy veils barely concealing their grief, three English queens, (from left) Elizabeth II, Queen Mary and the Queen Mother, attend as the coffin of King George VI is borne into Westminster Hall in February 1952. Right: Photographer Benson and LIFE were allowed a look inside the Irish Republican Army in 1985. The visit began with these telephoned orders: "Don't worry about anything, just rent a fast car with four doors and we will take care of the rest." The 10-day underground tour ended with this bizarre scene in a field in Armagh, as an IRA commander donned a Prince Charles mask and joked about the royal heir's capture, while the group staged a rehearsal for an execution.

RIGHT **HARRY BENSON**

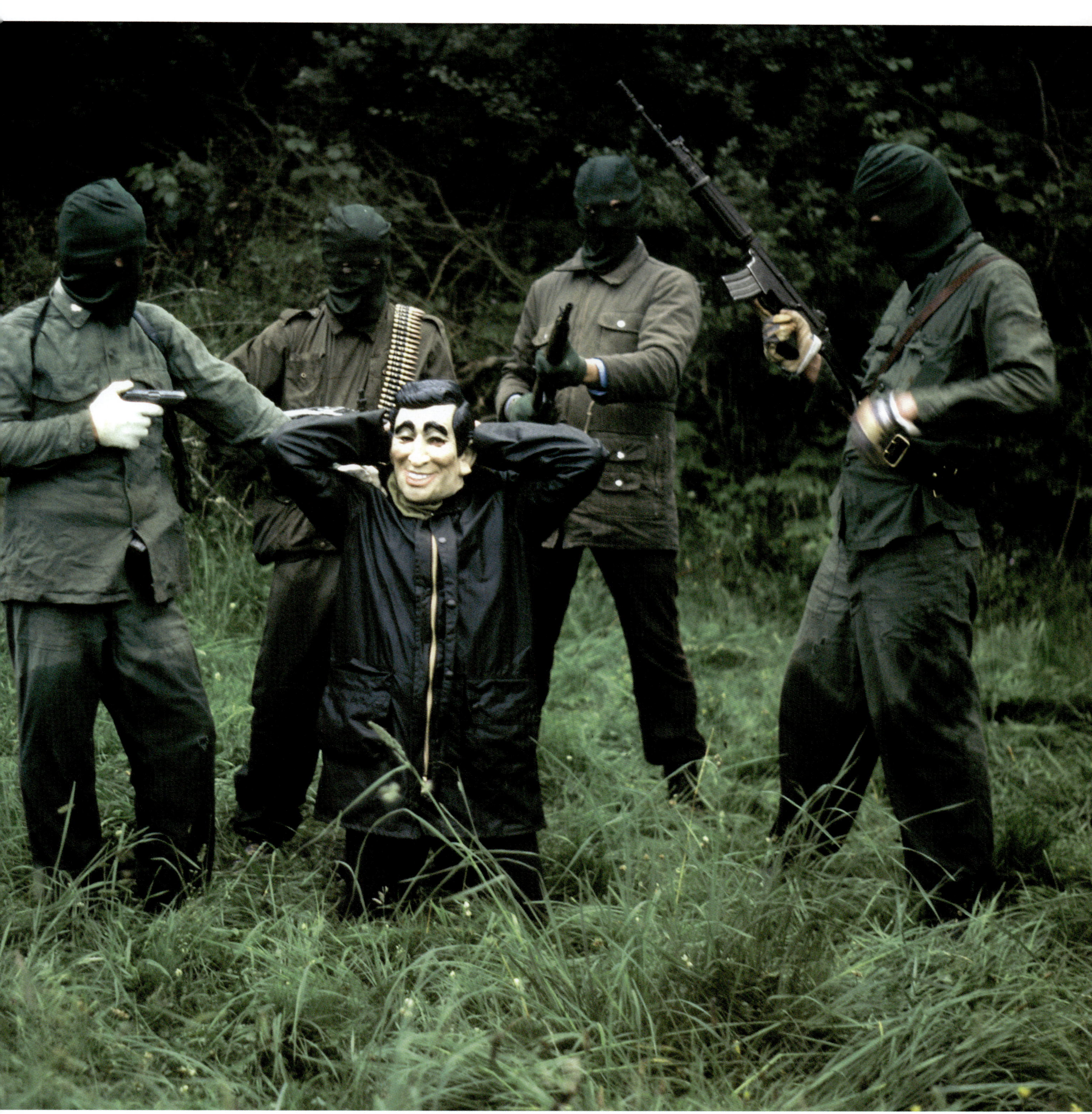

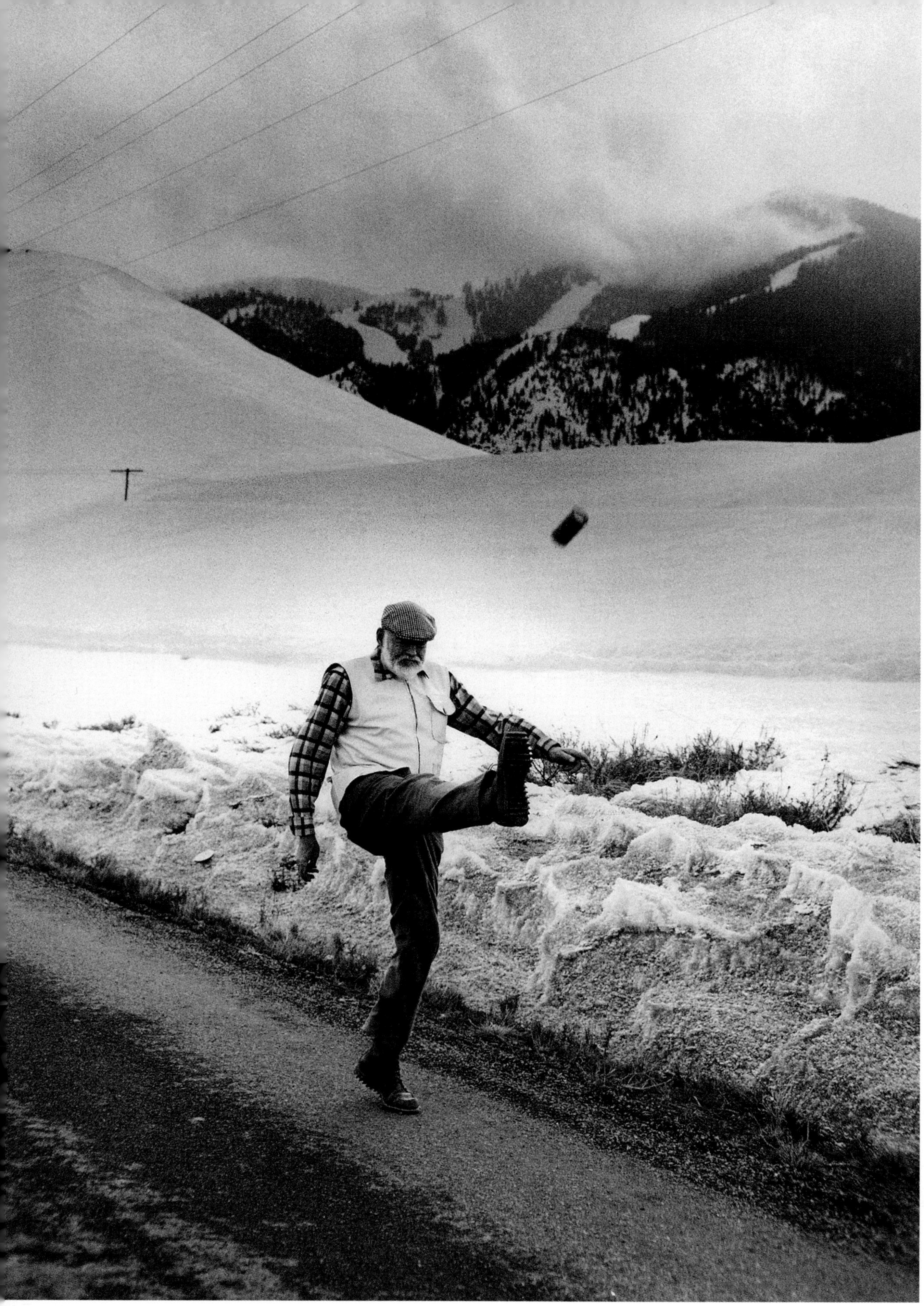

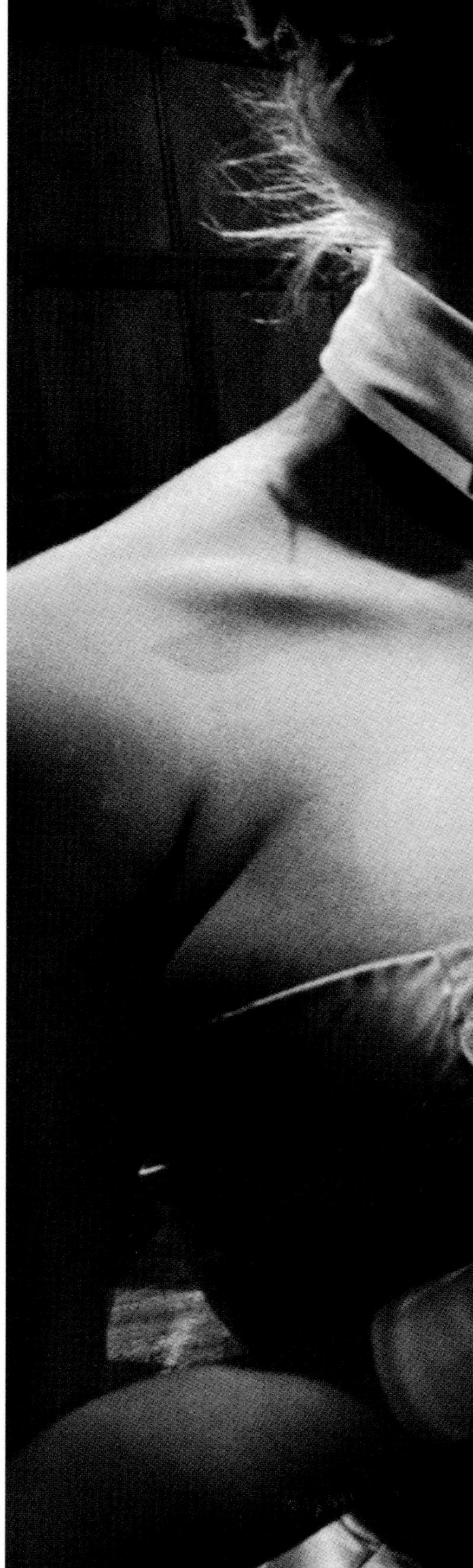

PAPA

Ernest Hemingway was 60 years old when this photo was shot in Ketchum, Idaho, and he later told us, "This was the best picture I ever had taken." LIFE had a long, cherished relationship with Hem, dating back to 1937 when he wrote captions for a story on the Spanish Civil War. In September 1952, a single issue introduced in its entirety his novella *The Old Man and the Sea.* "I'm very excited that it is coming out in LIFE," he wrote an editor, "so that many people will read it who could not afford to buy it. That makes me much happier than to have a Nobel Prize." That statement must have had some good karma, as *The Old Man and the Sea* helped win Hemingway his Nobel.

JOHN BRYSON

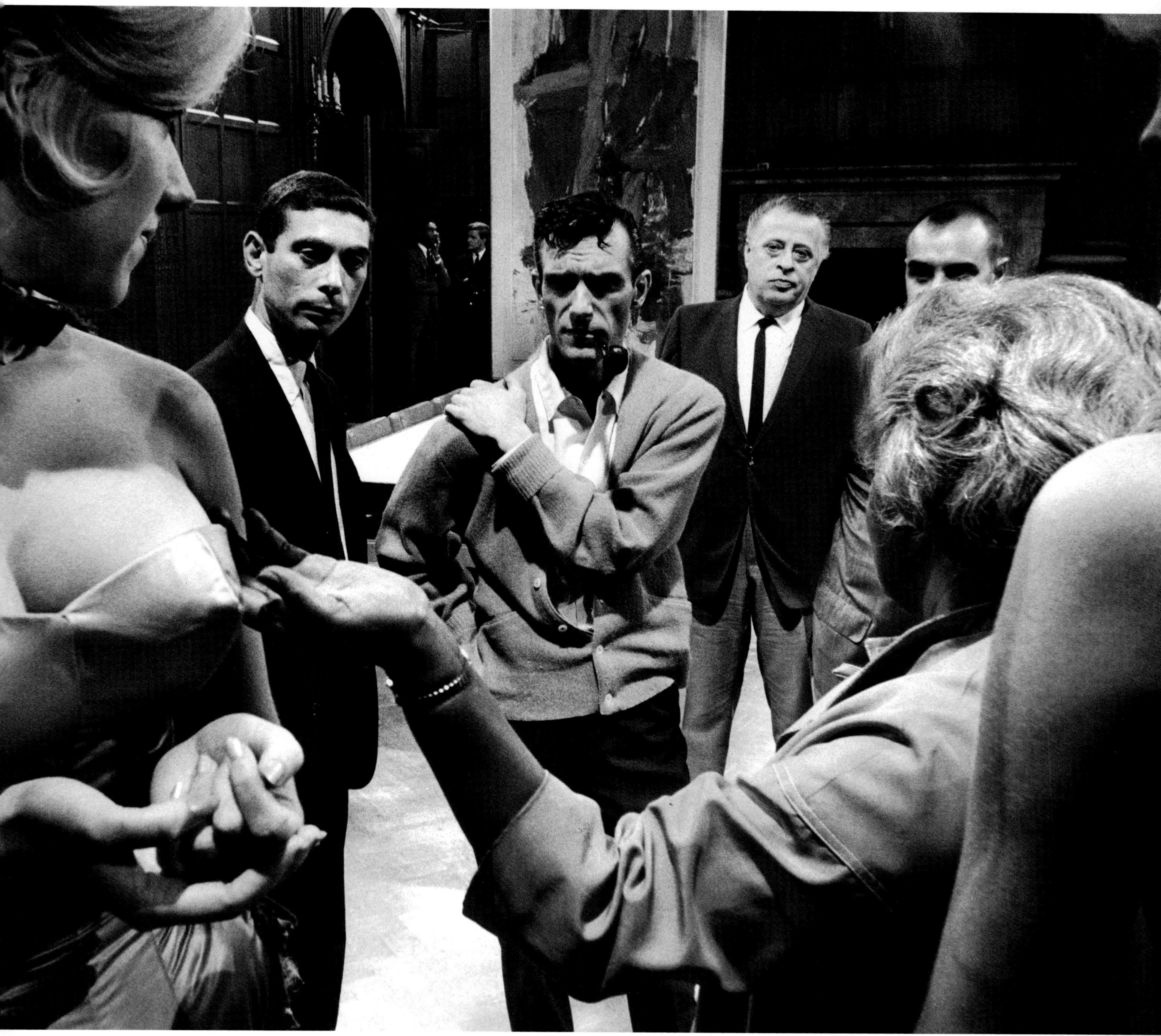

INSIDE THE HUTCH

Within the cozy confines of his 48-room mansion in Chicago, Hugh Hefner and staffers consider strategic alterations to the Playboy bunny outfit in 1965. Hef was 39 at the time, and his own attire here comes as something of a surprise, since he was known to prefer pajamas with his pipe. He was not merely the founder, editor and publisher of *Playboy* magazine but also the grand potentate of a Playboy empire that, at the time, was worth $70 million.

BURK UZZLE

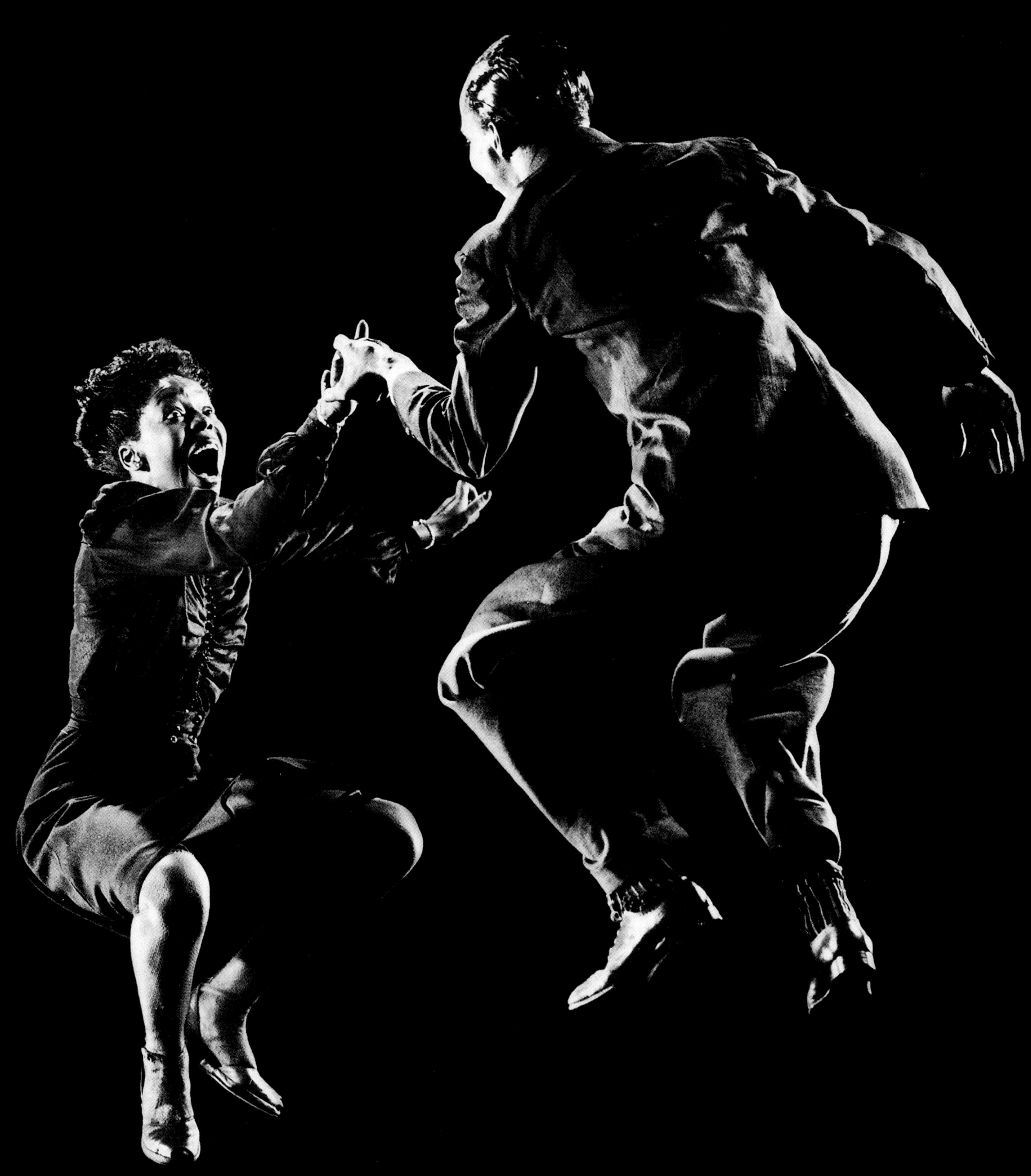

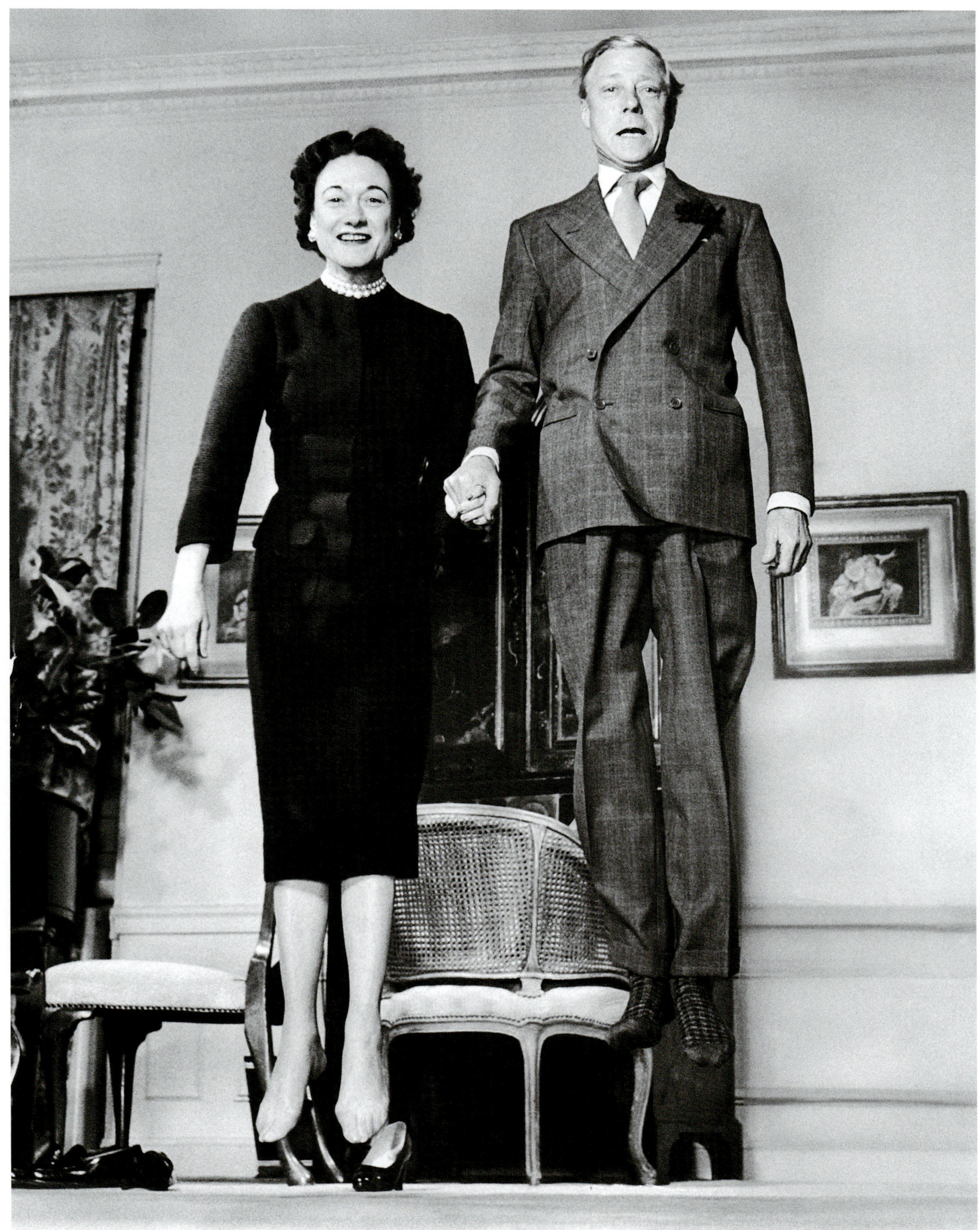

THE LINDY HOP

Not long after Charles Lindbergh's historic solo flight across the Atlantic in 1927, the pyrotechnics of dancers in Harlem's Savoy Ballroom moved one wag to observe that "it looks like they're doing the lindy hop." The lindy was a kind of jitterbug, and it is performed here, in 1943, by Willa Mae Ricker and Leon James.

GJON MILI

JUMPOLOGY

In 1950 photographer Halsman discovered during a long, difficult photo session that when he persuaded a subject to jump, "his attention is mostly directed toward the act of jumping and the mask falls so that the real person appears." Here, in 1959, he has a pair of unlikely jumpers in the duke and duchess of Windsor.

PHILIPPE HALSMAN

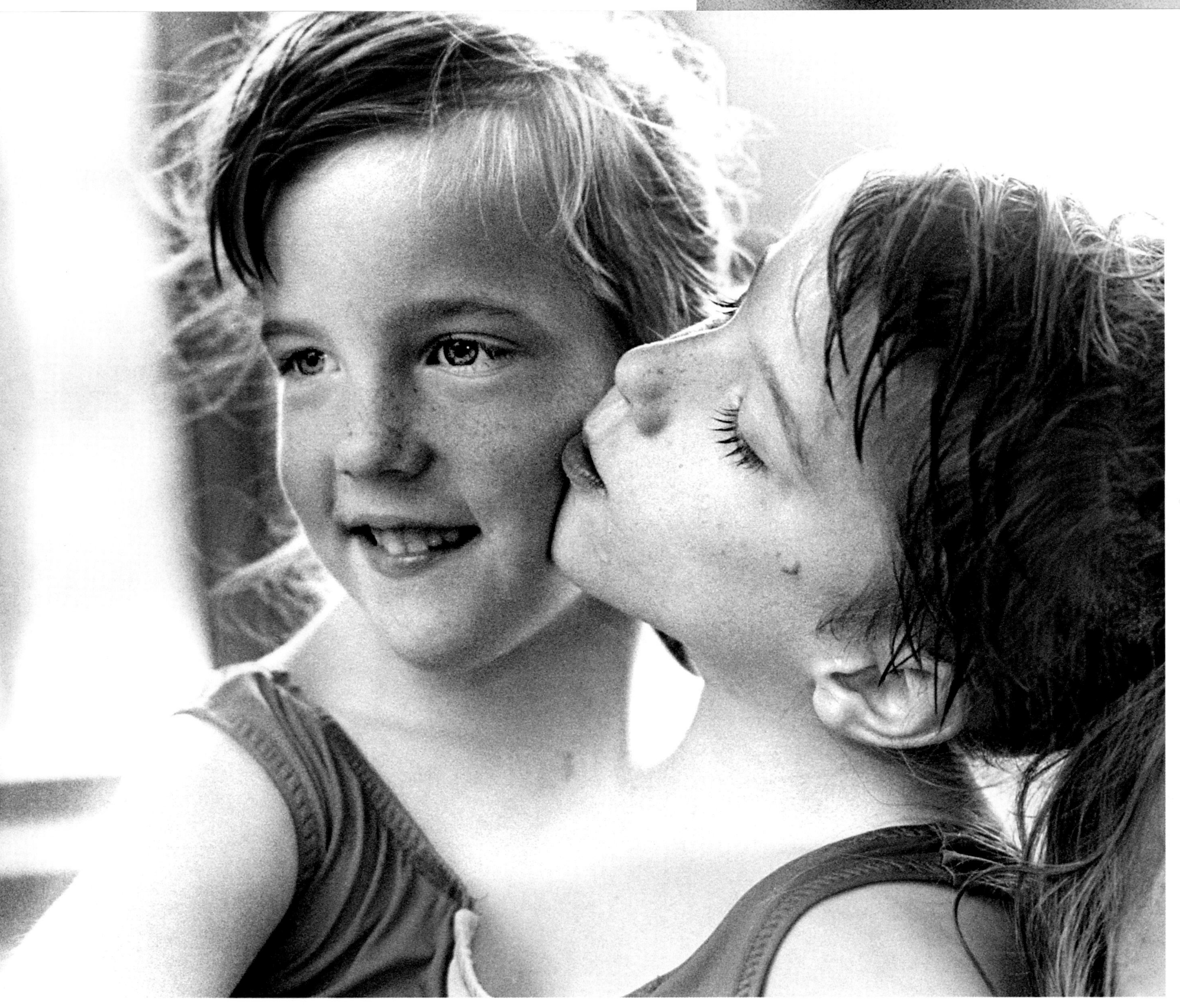

THE HENSELS

One of the most heartwarming, and provocative, pieces ever to appear in LIFE came in 1996 with the story of Abigail (left) and Brittany Hensel, six-year-old sisters from Minnesota who were born as conjoined twins. That is, they have an undivided torso and two legs, and while each has her own heart and stomach, they together rely on three lungs. Conjoined twins prompt far-reaching questions about human nature, about individuality, privacy and many other issues. But to anyone who saw Abby and Britty visit LIFE's offices back then, playing swimmingly with kids of staffers, these questions dissolved for a couple of hours, replaced by an easy smile.

STEVE WEWERKA

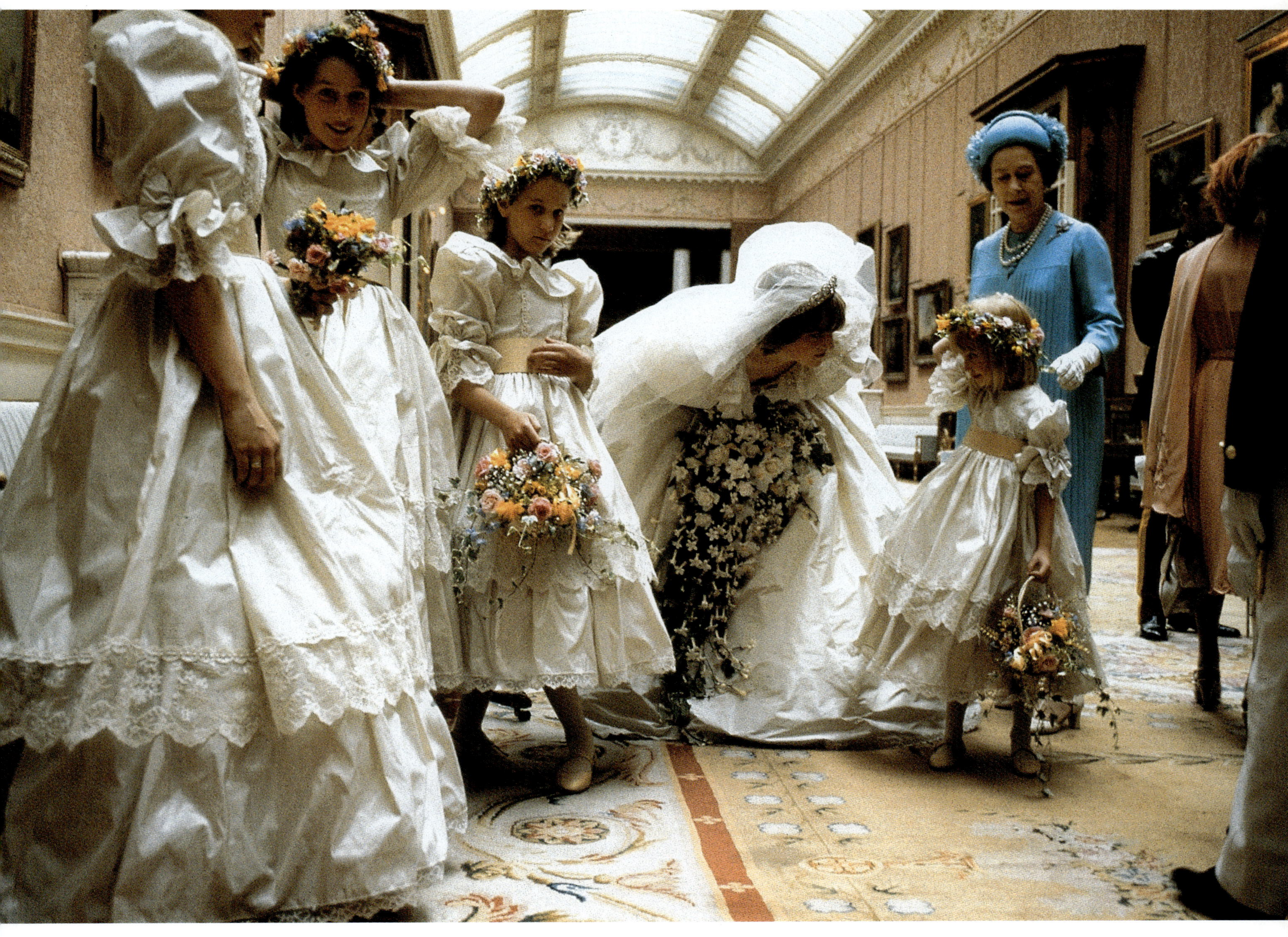

A PRINCESS . . . INDEED

It was, perhaps, the wedding of the century when Lady Diana Spencer married Prince Charles in 1981. Thomas Patrick John Anson, the fifth Earl of Lichfield, would have been on the guest list anyway, but Patrick Lichfield, as the fashion-celebrity photographer is more commonly known, also served as official photographer. There were countless posed tableaux, but the best picture came after five-year-old Clementine Hambro—the great-granddaughter of Winston Churchill—bumped her head and the solicitous Diana, newly a princess, leaned over to console her. Lichfield grabbed a simple little camera from his pocket, and voilà!

PATRICK LICHFIELD

UST
UN

In 1960, LIFE's founder Henry Luce said, "I always thought it was the business of *Time* to make enemies, and of LIFE to make friends." He meant, of course, that while *Time* was in the business of asking the hard questions and presenting the cold facts, the role of LIFE was to engage the reader in a manner that might ultimately make him feel a wee bit better.

One of the ways that LIFE has made so many friends through the years is with humor, sometimes sophisticated, sometimes outlandish, but more often slice-of-life images that prompt readers to hand the magazine across the table with a gentle chuckle and the words, "Did you see this?"

Not long after the magazine made its first appearance, Luce told his editors that there were two qualities they should ever be on the watch for: charm and relaxation. "We find that we must definitely plot and plan for Charm," he wrote. "Charm does not come naturally out of the news . . . Yet we intend that every issue of LIFE shall have the quality of Charm." As for the second quality, Luce said, "LIFE today does not come to its readers with any such burden of responsibility as does either *Time* or *Fortune* . . . And so the reader can relax—and does."

Well, at least we hope so. Sometimes the business of making friends just can't be orchestrated perfectly, and Charm and Relaxation aren't always as easily achieved as one might wish. In choosing the pictures for this section we did not go for the cat-up-a-tree or spaghetti-on-the-baby's-head photos—though scads of these have appeared in LIFE—but for images that would elicit a smile from any reader, perhaps even Luce himself, along with the thought, Yes. That's it.

Detrick was a summer photography intern with *The Baltimore Sun* in 2004, covering the annual crowning of the Howard Country Farm Bureau Queen. Fortunately for Chris, and for us, he had loved roller coasters as a kid, so he thought he would give The Fire Ball a whirl.

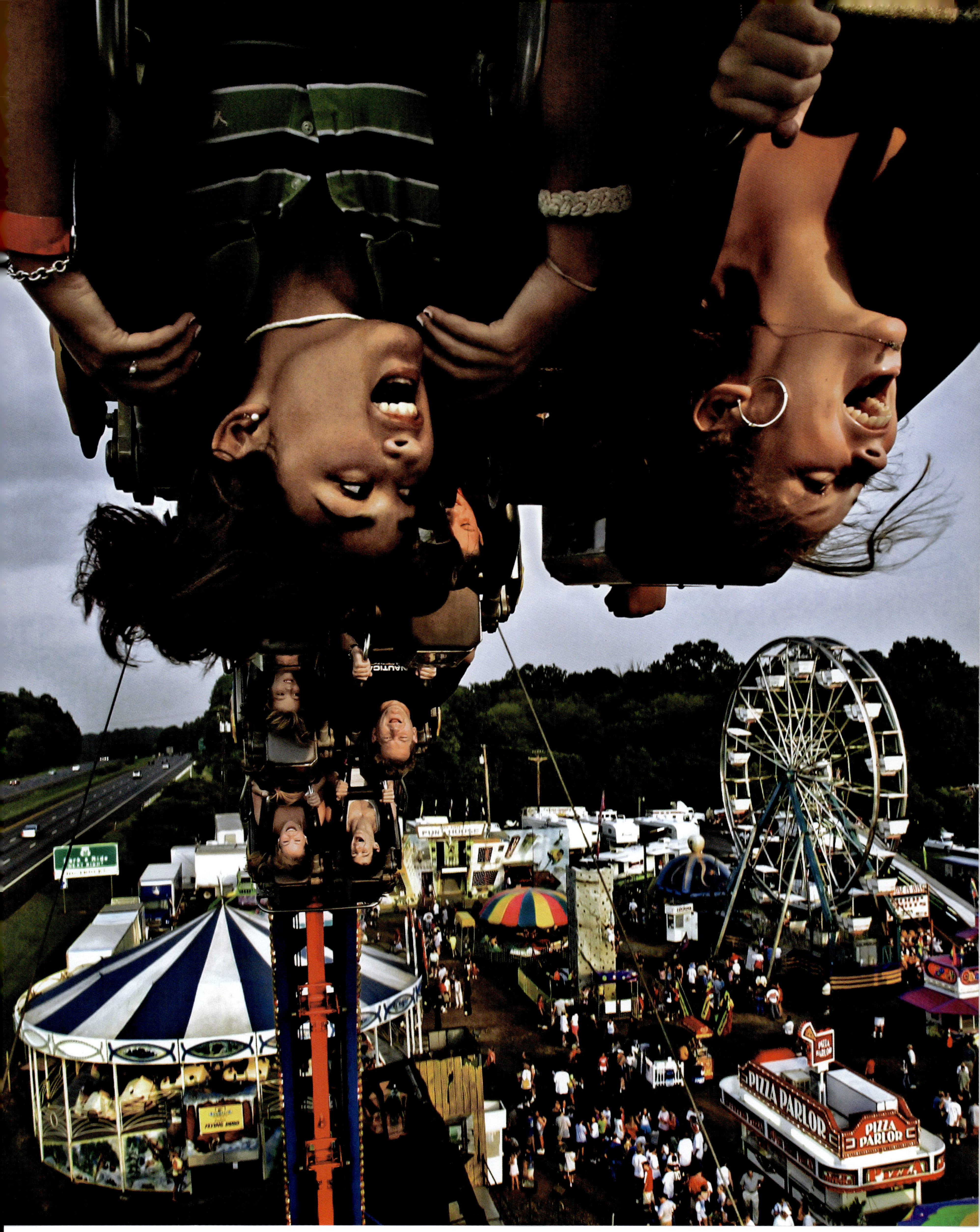
PIZZA PARLOR
PIZZA PARLOR

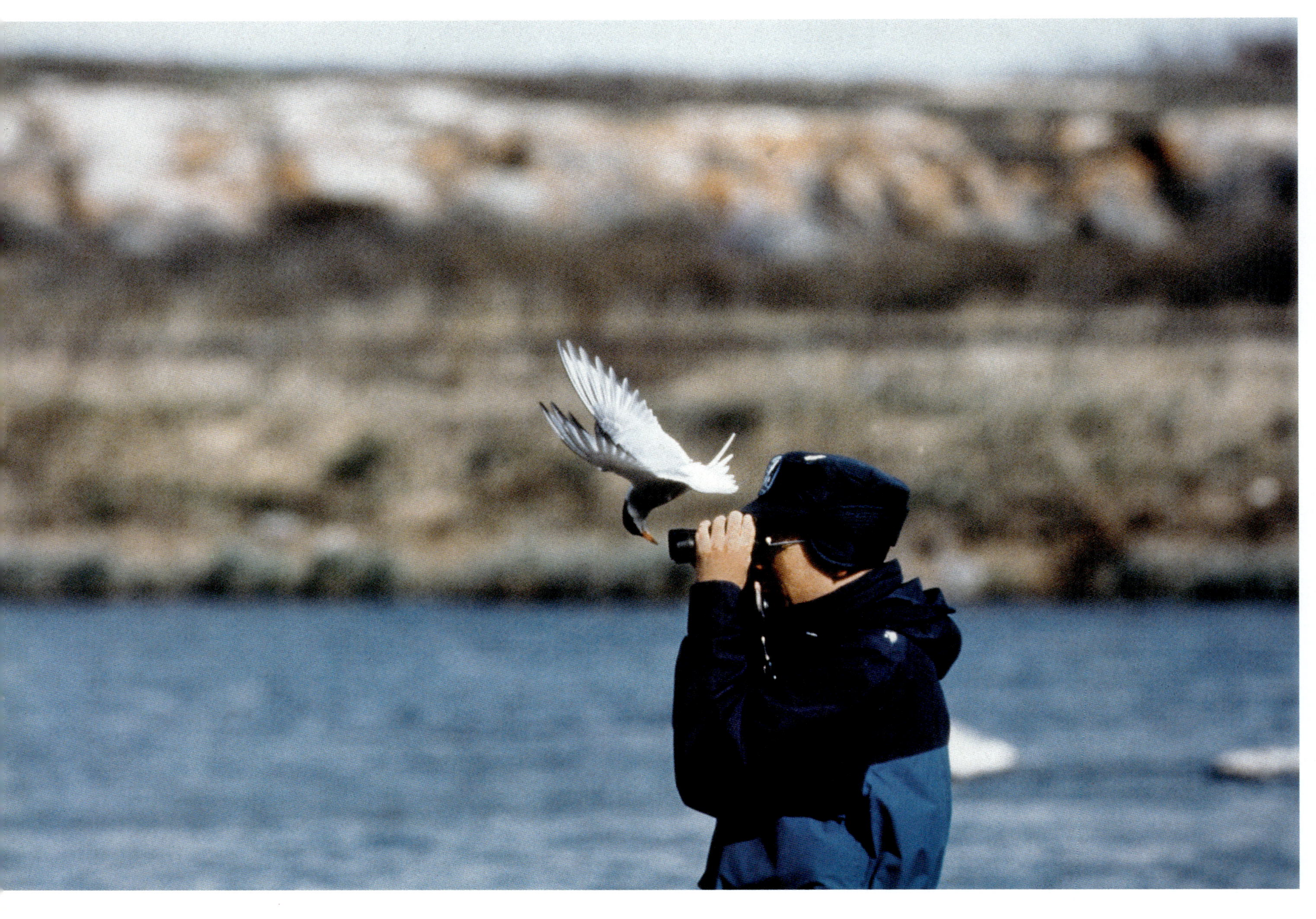

Birdwatching is a popular recreation, but it can be turned on its head, as Peter Deknijff discovered in Churchill, Manitoba, in 1990. Forty years earlier, in Valley Forge, Pa., Billy Petersen looks completely satisfied. And who wouldn't be, after trading two pieces of deer antler for this very fine horned toad?

ABOVE **NORBERT ROSING** *OPPOSITE* **ROBERT W. KELLEY**

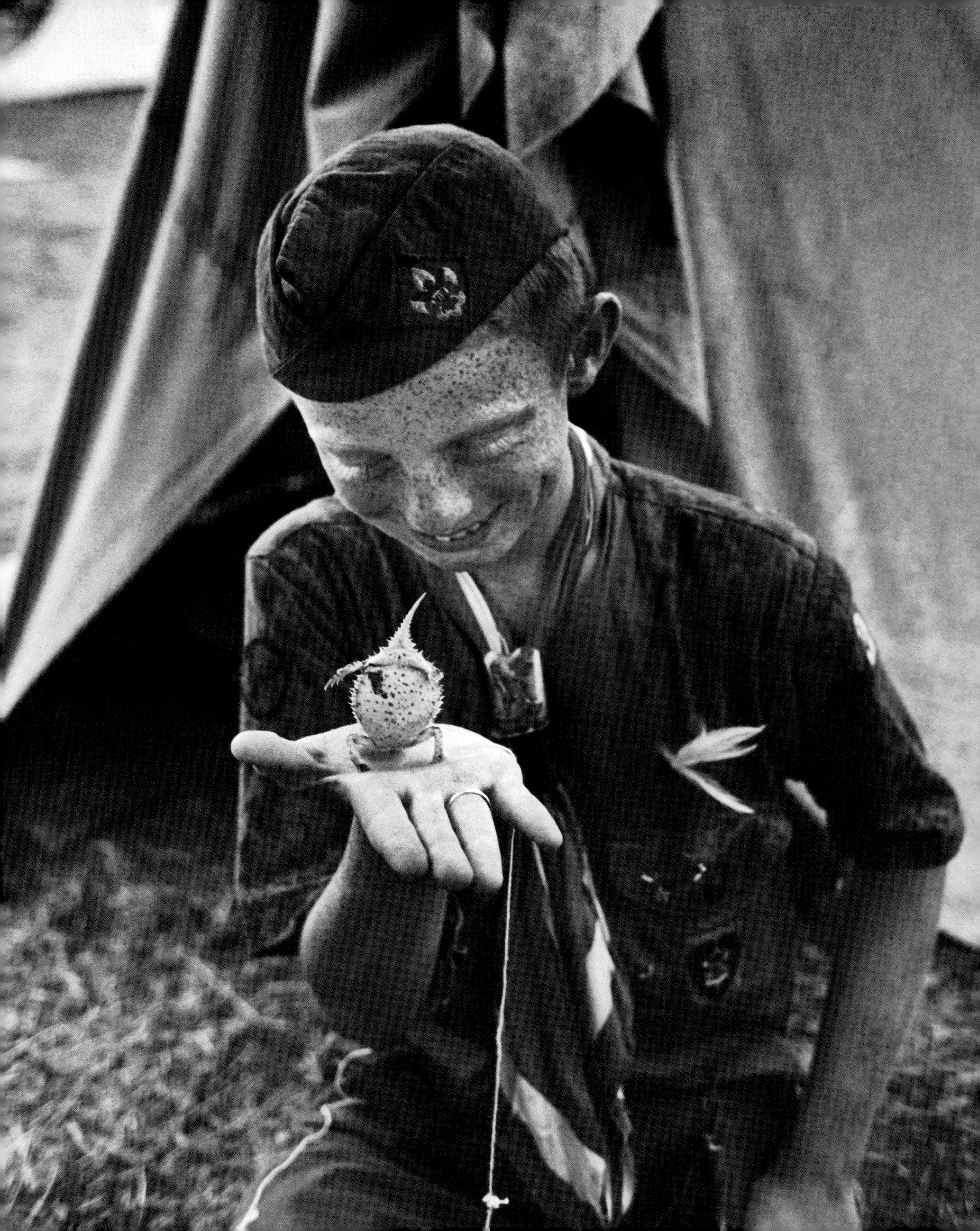

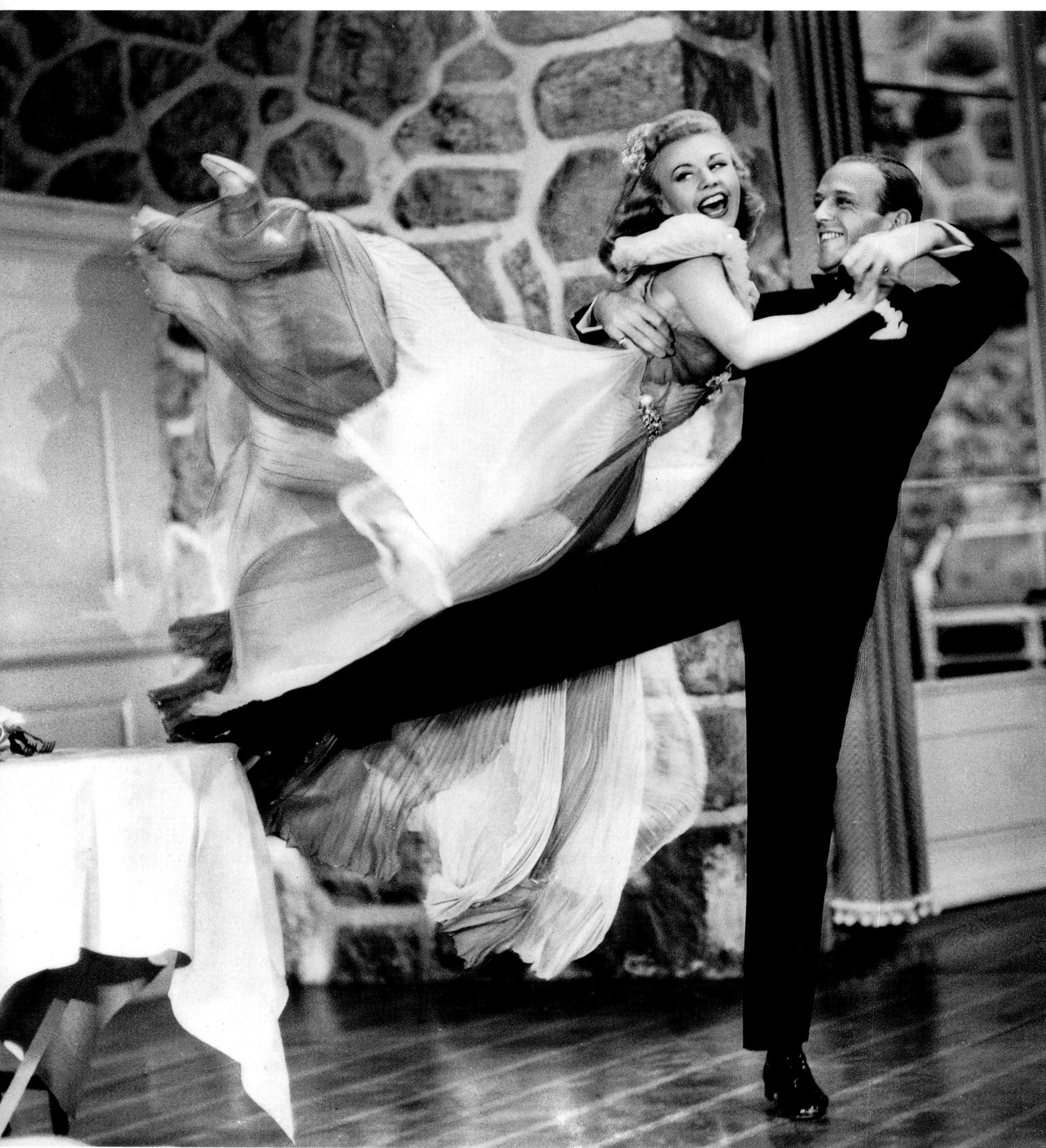

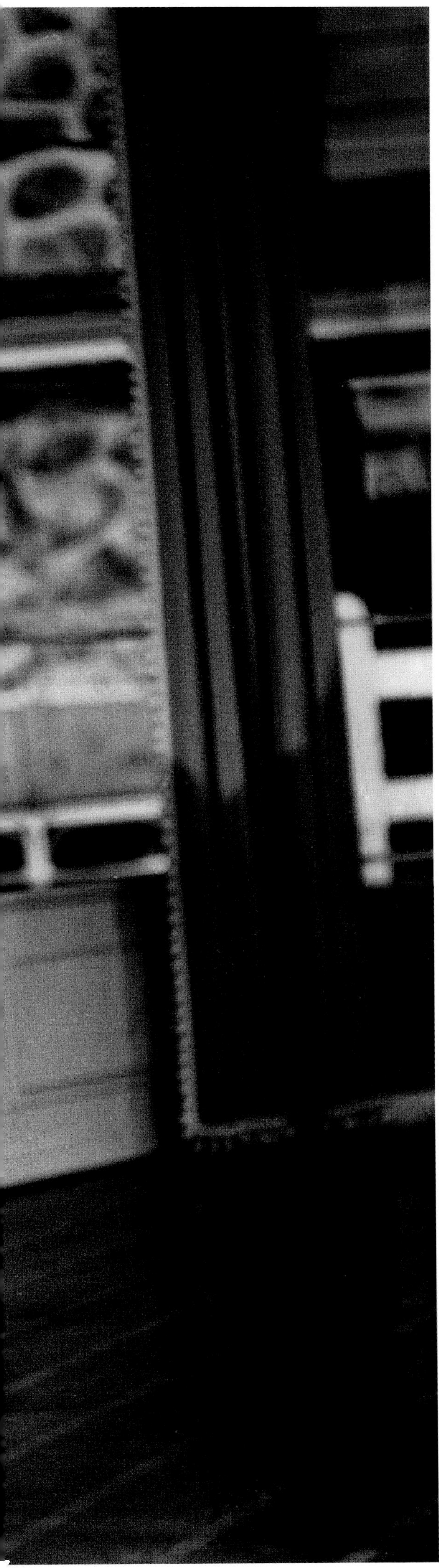

Everett Collection

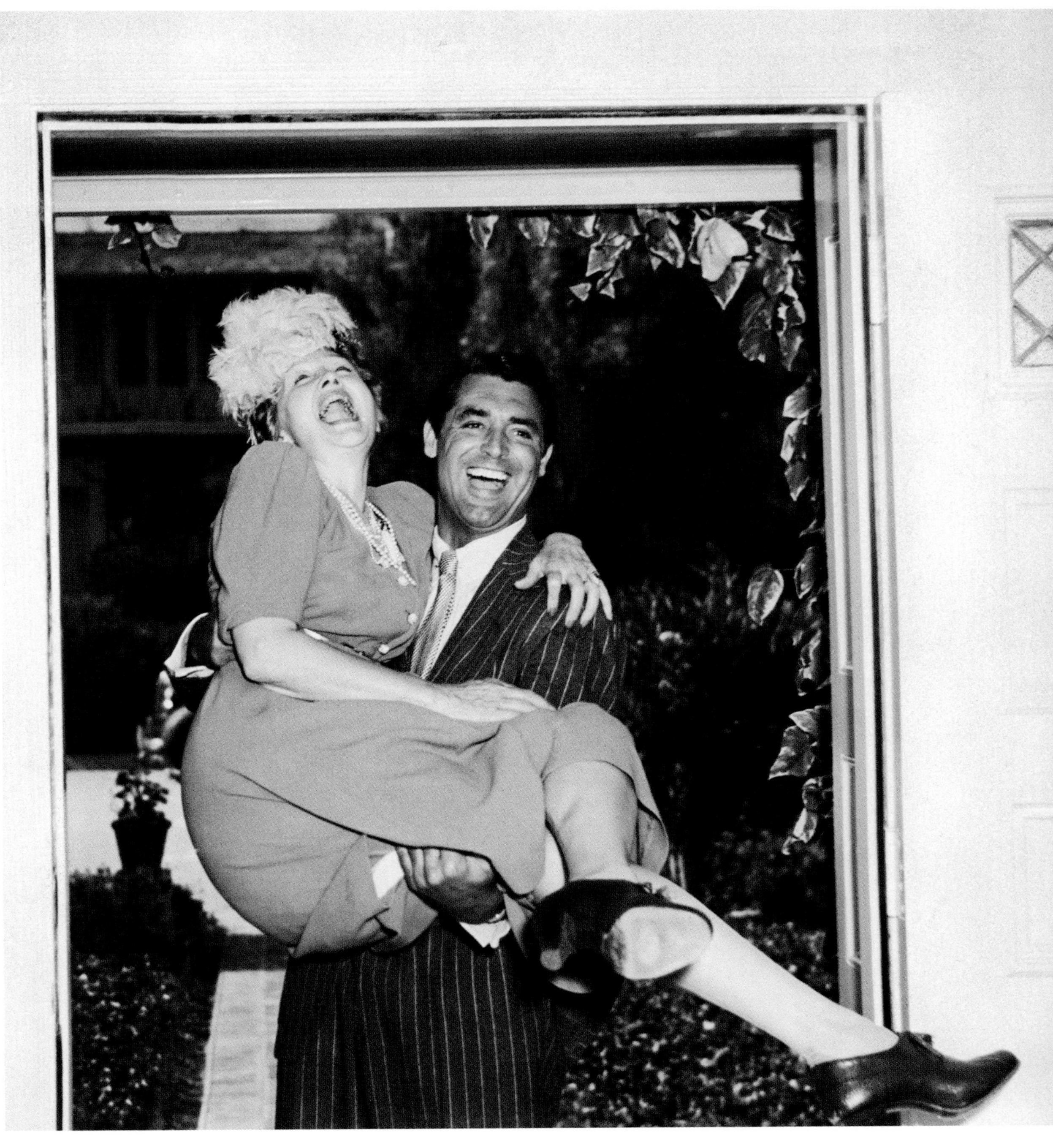

Fred Astaire and Ginger Rogers were simply *too diveen* in the 10 films they made together. Here, they perform an airy number called "The Yam" in 1938's *Carefree.* "Hedda Hopper is a gay, boisterous, impulsive woman in her fifties who knows more Hollywood gossip than any person alive," LIFE said in 1941. As a result, Cary Grant was more than happy to carry the influential columnist "over the threshold" when she moved into her new digs in Beverly Hills.

ABOVE **JEROME ZERBE**

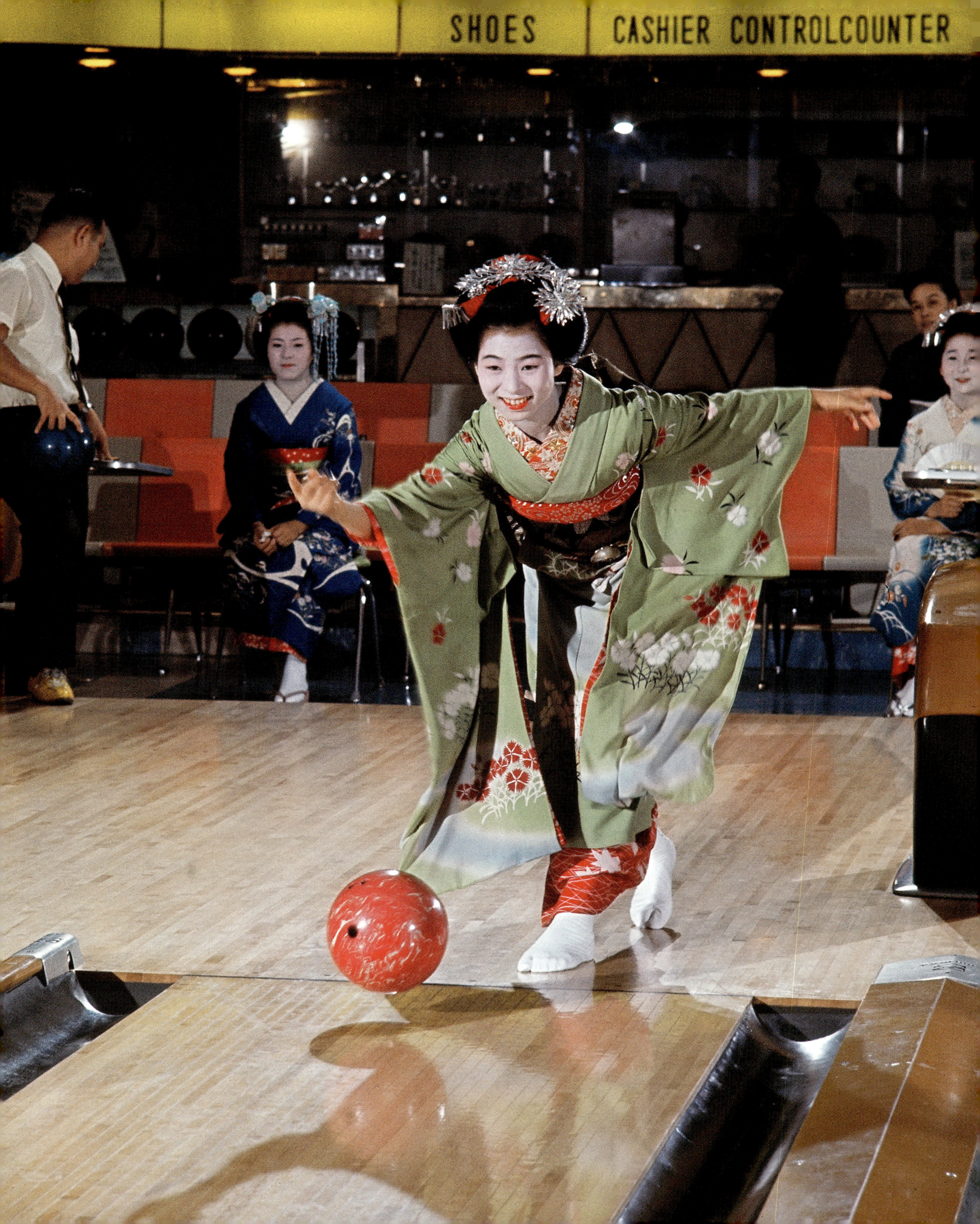
SHOES
CASHIER CONTROLCOUNTER

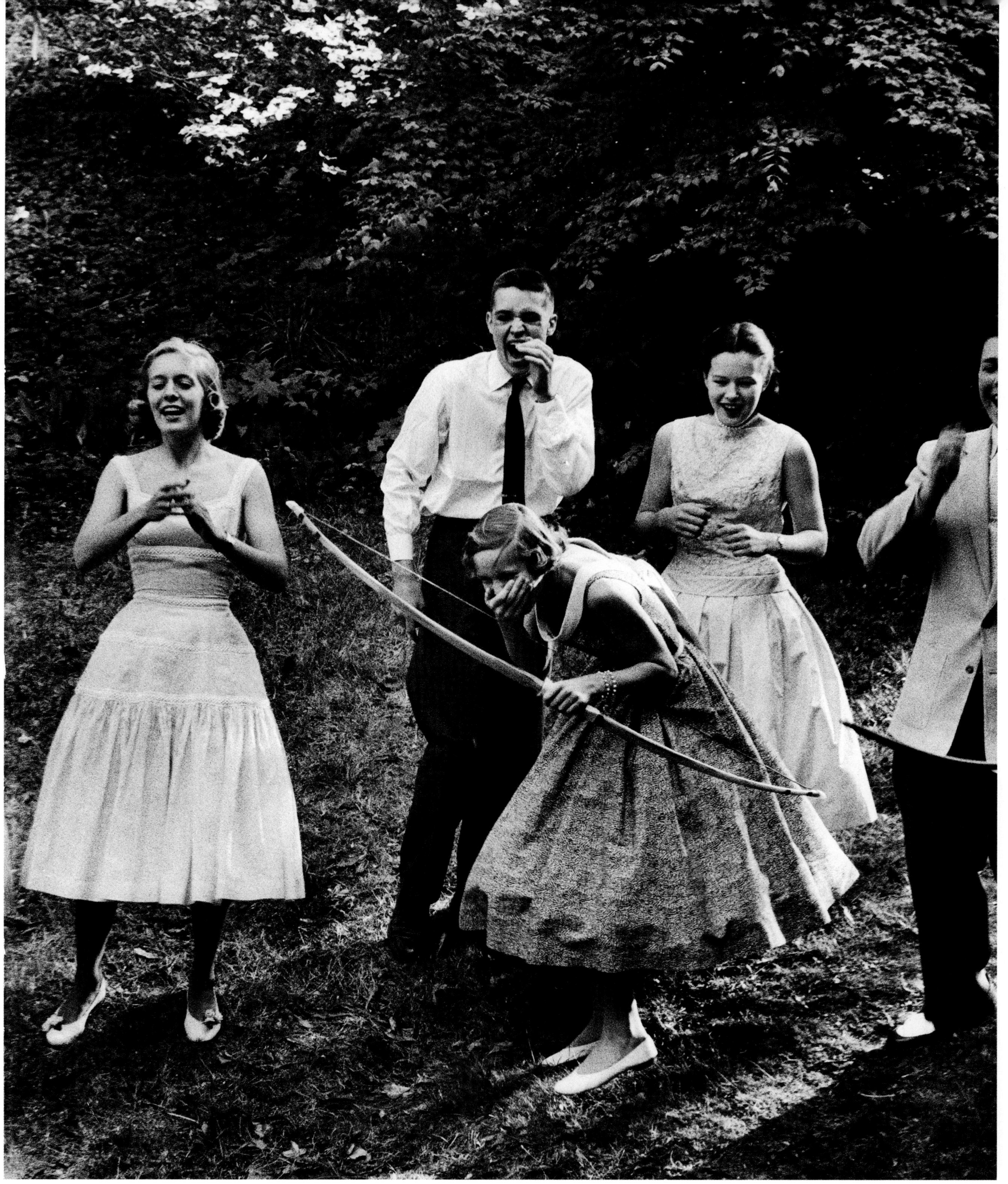

An apprentice geisha tackles a rather different discipline in Kyoto in 1964.
Meanwhile, in Briarcliff, N.Y., in 1956, it looks like somebody missed the mark.

OPPOSITE **LARRY BURROWS** *ABOVE* **YALE JOEL**

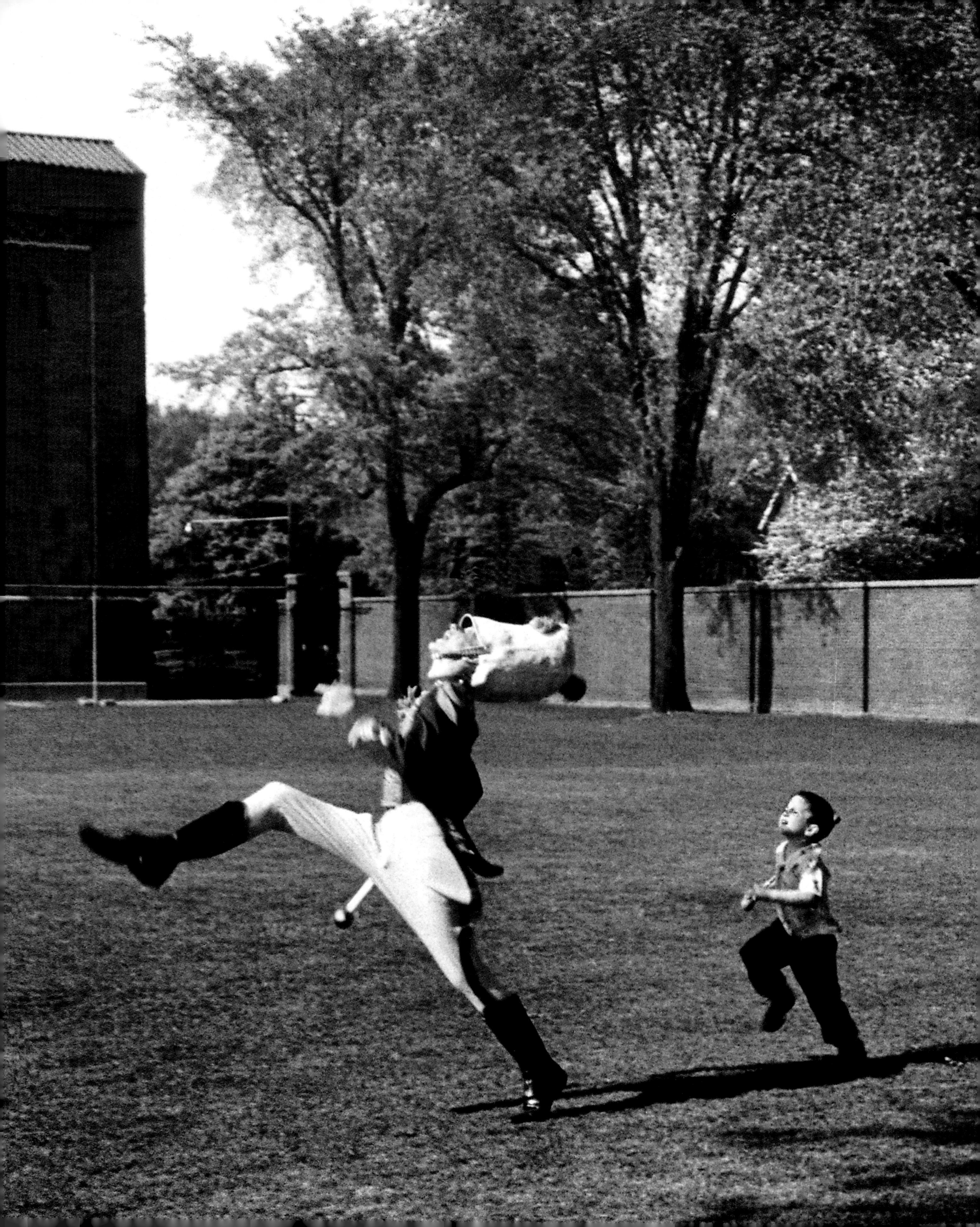

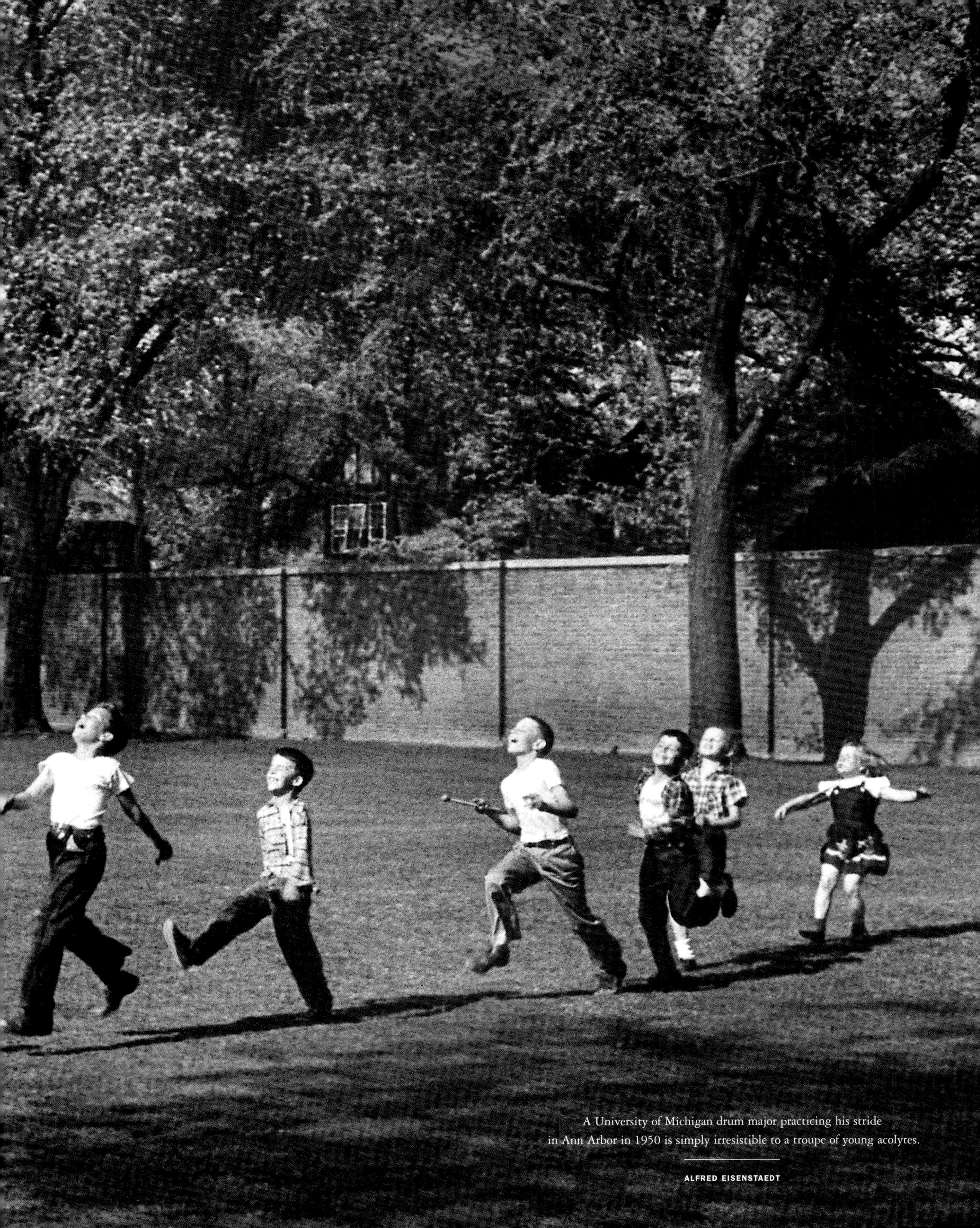

A University of Michigan drum major practicing his stride
in Ann Arbor in 1950 is simply irresistible to a troupe of young acolytes.

ALFRED EISENSTAEDT

THE COVERS

Here they are, thousands of them, from weeklies, monthlies, specials and books, and along the way is revealed a passion for subjects that are incisive, or frolicsome, or edifying, or sobering, or . . . well . . . having something to do with starlets. Here, the many faces of LIFE!

1936

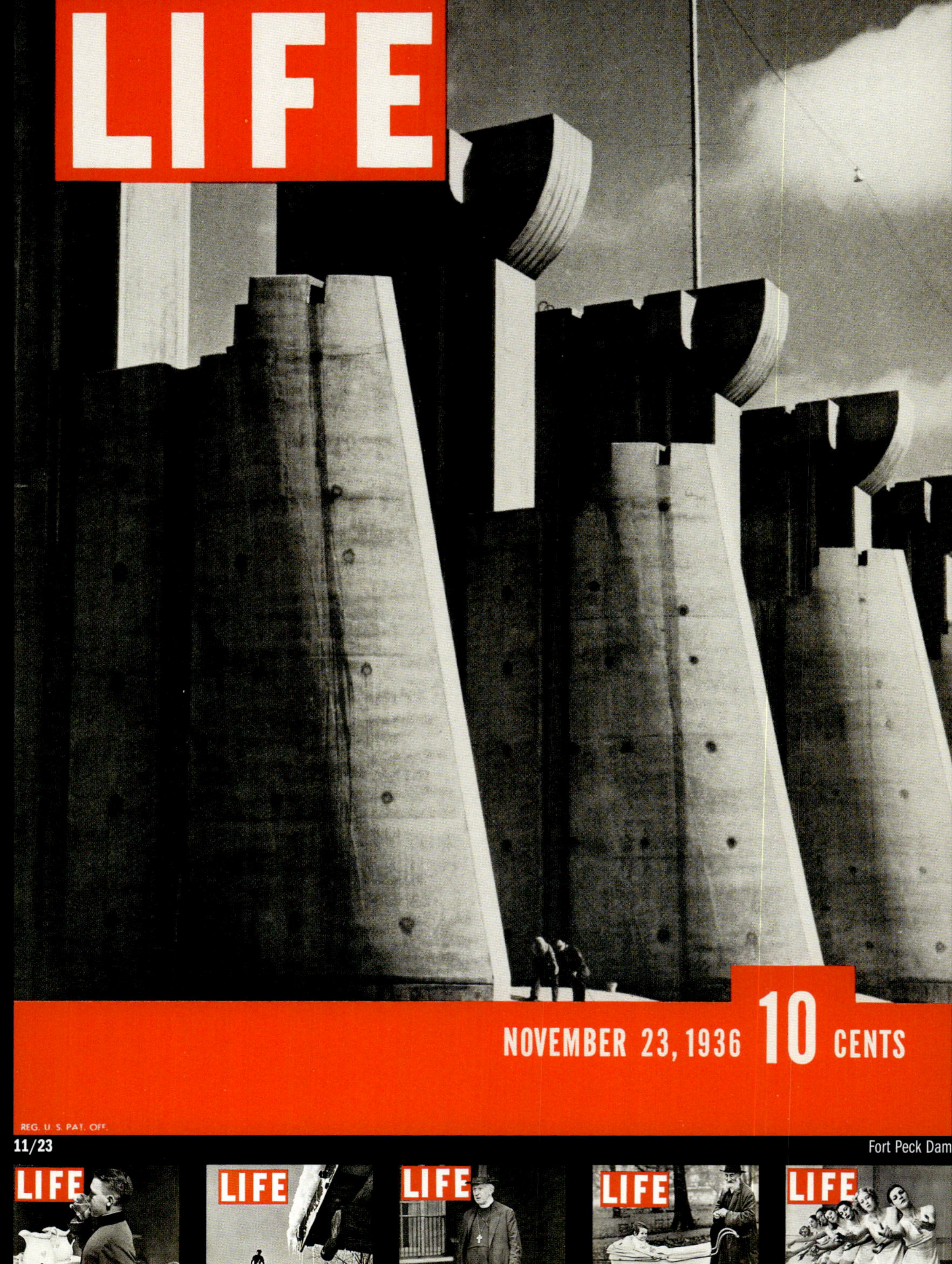

11/23 Fort Peck Dam

11/30 West Point Cadet
12/7 Skiing
12/14 Canterbury
12/21 Beaverbrook Baby
12/28 Ballet

The Spanish Civil War erupts • Jesse Owens wins four gold medals at the Berlin Olympic Games
Bruno Hauptmann is executed for kidnapping the Lindbergh baby • Dale Carnegie publishes his self-help book *How to Win Friends and Influence People*
The Dust Bowl exodus reaches its peak

1937

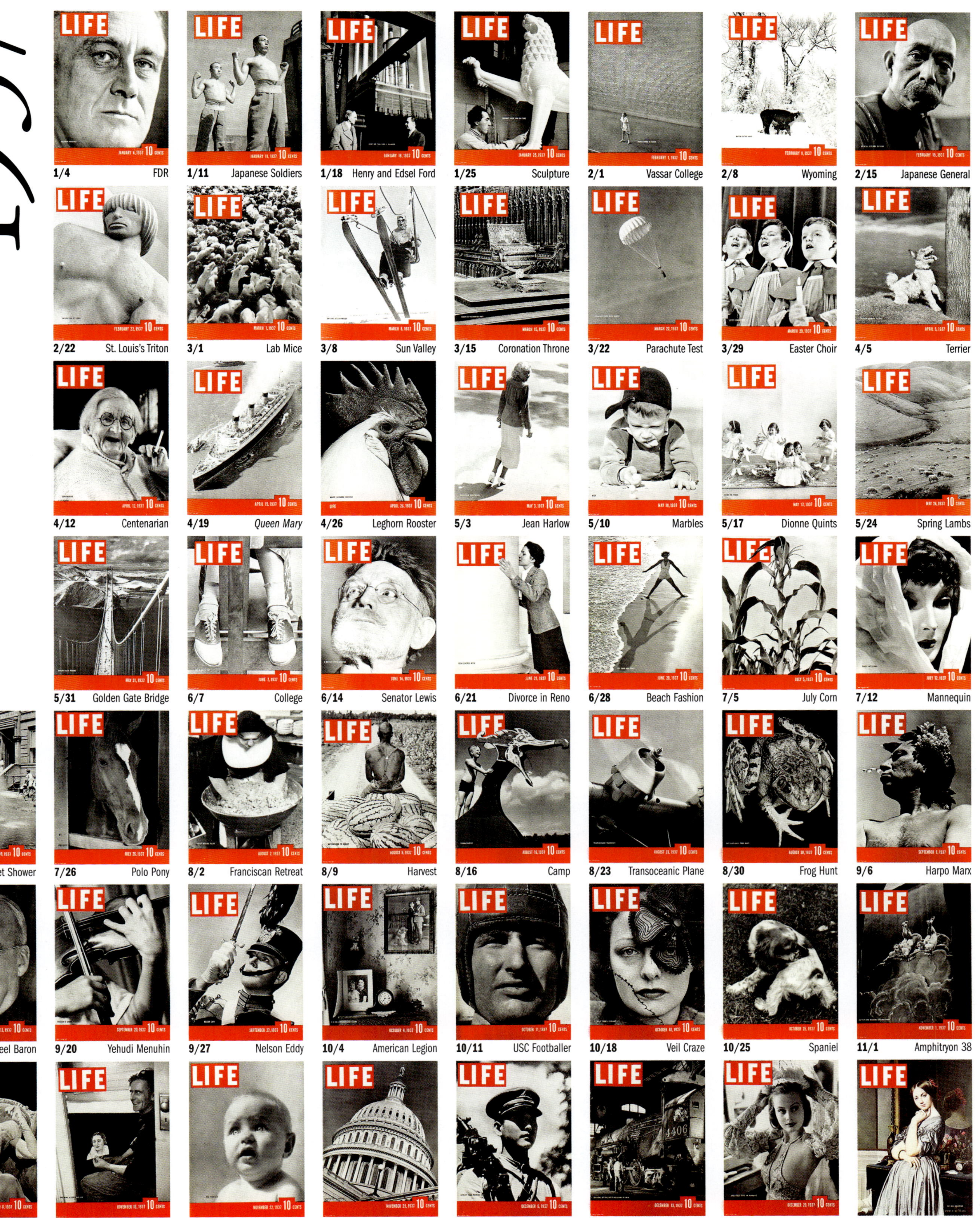

1/4 FDR
1/11 Japanese Soldiers
1/18 Henry and Edsel Ford
1/25 Sculpture
2/1 Vassar College
2/8 Wyoming
2/15 Japanese General
2/22 St. Louis's Triton
3/1 Lab Mice
3/8 Sun Valley
3/15 Coronation Throne
3/22 Parachute Test
3/29 Easter Choir
4/5 Terrier
4/12 Centenarian
4/19 *Queen Mary*
4/26 Leghorn Rooster
5/3 Jean Harlow
5/10 Marbles
5/17 Dionne Quints
5/24 Spring Lambs
5/31 Golden Gate Bridge
6/7 College
6/14 Senator Lewis
6/21 Divorce in Reno
6/28 Beach Fashion
7/5 July Corn
7/12 Mannequin
7/19 Street Shower
7/26 Polo Pony
8/2 Franciscan Retreat
8/9 Harvest
8/16 Camp
8/23 Transoceanic Plane
8/30 Frog Hunt
9/6 Harpo Marx
9/13 Steel Baron
9/20 Yehudi Menuhin
9/27 Nelson Eddy
10/4 American Legion
10/11 USC Footballer
10/18 Veil Craze
10/25 Spaniel
11/1 Amphitryon 38
11/8 Greta Garbo
11/15 Awaiting Wallis
11/22 LIFE Turns One
11/29 Capitol
12/6 Japanese Soldier
12/13 Railroads
12/20 Hope Chandler
12/27 Ingres Portrait

American aviatrix Amelia Earhart disappears over the Pacific • A store owner in Oklahoma introduces the grocery cart
DuPont Company patents nylon • *Snow White and the Seven Dwarfs* is the first full-length animated film
Picasso enters *Guernica* in a Paris exhibition

1938

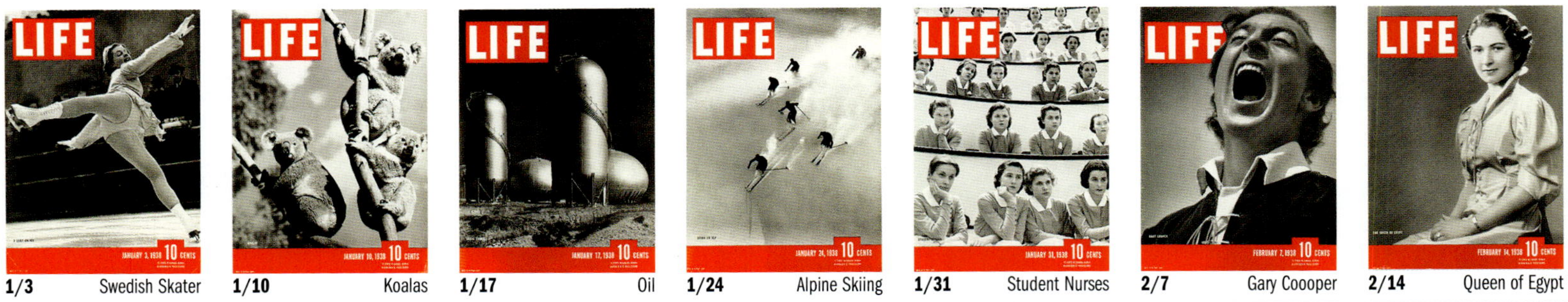

1/3 Swedish Skater
1/10 Koalas
1/17 Oil
1/24 Alpine Skiing
1/31 Student Nurses
2/7 Gary Coooper
2/14 Queen of Egypt
2/21 Carl Sandburg 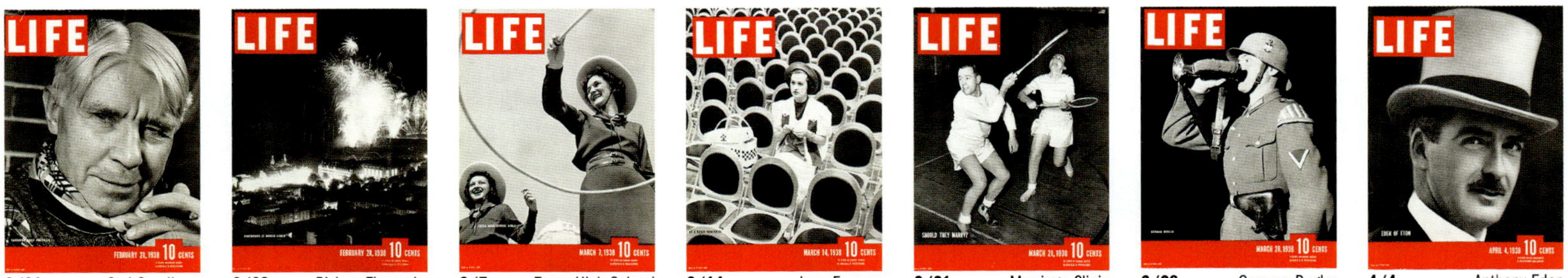
2/28 Riviera Fireworks
3/7 Texas High School
3/14 Jane Froman
3/21 Marriage Clinic
3/28 German Bugler
4/4 Anthony Eden
4/11 Monogram Craze 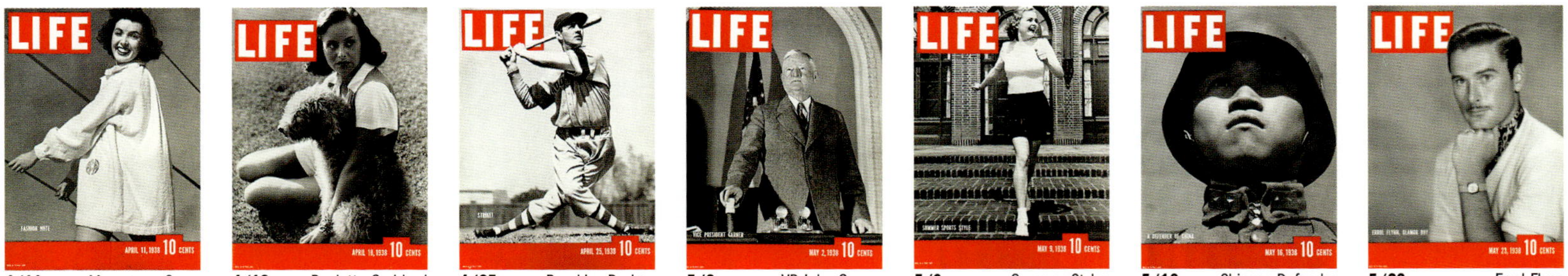
4/18 Paulette Goddard
4/25 Brooklyn Dodger
5/2 VP John Garner
5/9 Summer Styles
5/16 Chinese Defender
5/23 Errol Flynn
5/30 Czech General 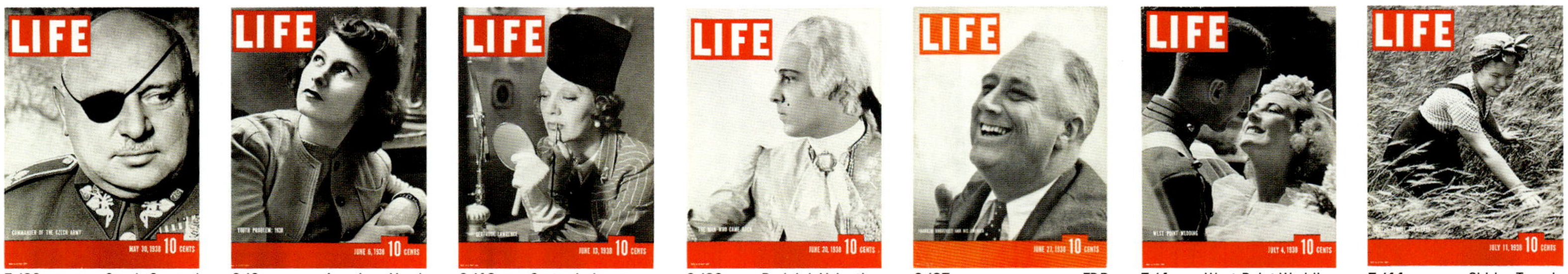
6/6 American Youth
6/13 Gertrude Lawrence
6/20 Rudolph Valentino
6/27 FDR
7/4 West Point Wedding
7/11 Shirley Temple
7/18 Camisoles 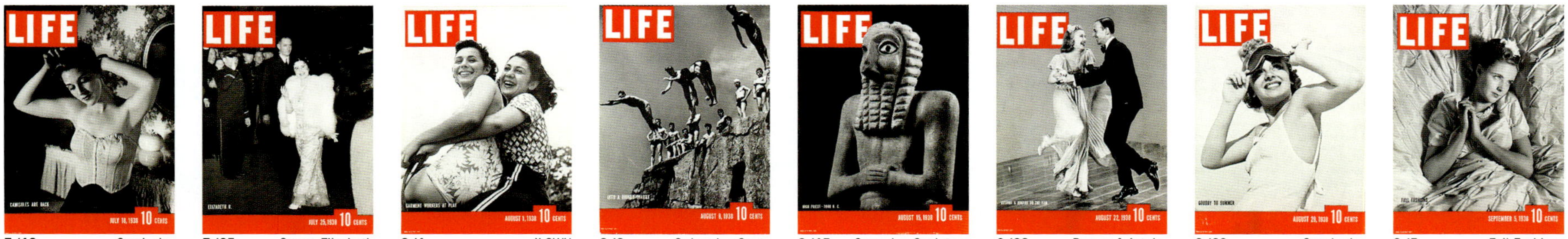
7/25 Queen Elizabeth
8/1 ILGWU
8/8 Swimming Spots
8/15 Sumerian Sculpture
8/22 Rogers & Astaire
8/29 Sunshades
9/5 Fall Fashions
9/12 Hungarian Guard 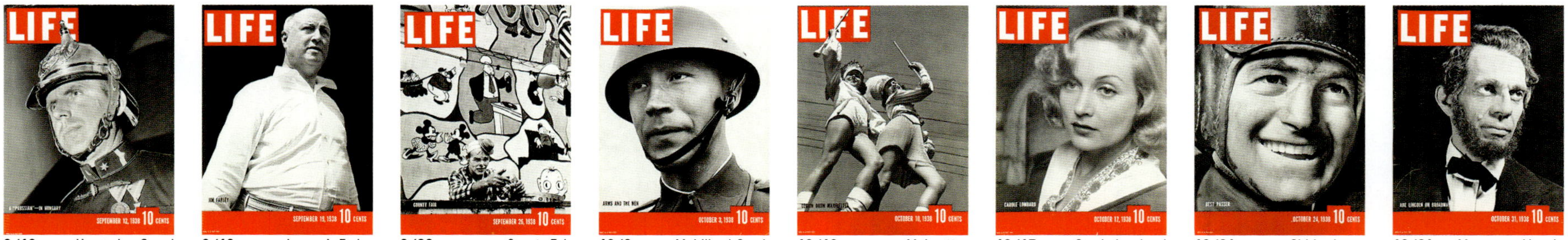
9/19 James A. Farley
9/26 County Fair
10/3 Mobilized Czech
10/10 Majorettes
10/17 Carole Lombard
10/24 Sid Luckman
10/31 Massey as Lincoln
11/7 Elections 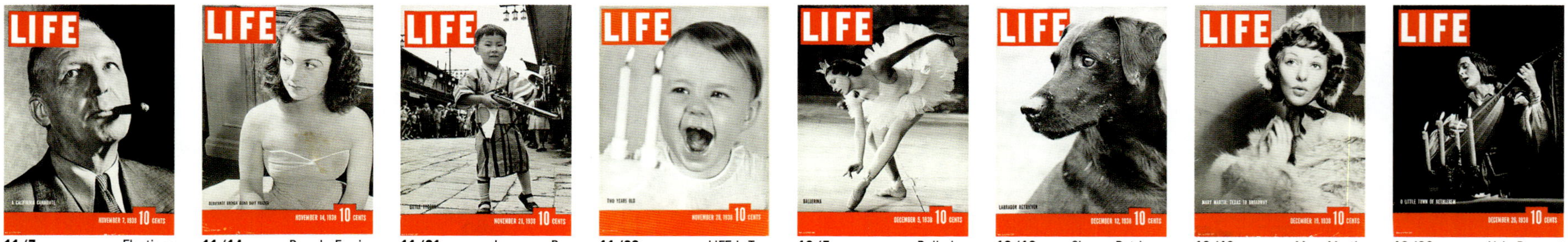
11/14 Brenda Frazier
11/21 Japanese Boy
11/28 LIFE Is Two
12/5 Ballerina
12/12 Champ Retriever
12/19 Mary Martin
12/26 Yule Pageant

The ballpoint pen is designed by Lazlo Biro of Hungary • Orson Welles' adaptation of *The War of the Worlds* panics listeners
A 40-hour workweek is established by The Fair Labor Standards Act
Roy J. Plunkett invents Teflon • Eddie Arcaro rides Lawrin, his first Kentucky Derby winner

1939

1/2 Wimples Return
1/9 Romanian Boy
1/16 Lucius Beebe
1/23 Bette Davis
1/30 Air Cadet
2/6 Peruke Hairstyle
2/13 Norma Shearer
2/20 Top French General
2/27 Twelve-Day Cruise
3/6 Tallulah Bankhead
3/13 World's Fair
3/20 Rep. Joe Martin
3/27 Pliofilm
4/3 Look-alike Dolls
4/10 Texas
4/17 Hildegarde
4/24 Neville Chamberlain
5/1 Joe DiMaggio
5/8 Cotton
5/15 Anne M. Lindbergh
5/22 World's Fair Guide
5/29 Eleanor Roosevelt
6/5 America's Future
6/12 Annapolis Grads
6/19 USC Sprinter
6/26 College Fads
7/3 Swimsuits
7/10 Japan Home Guard
7/17 Lord Halifax
7/24 Ann Sheridan
7/31 Diana Barrymore
8/7 FSA's Paul McNutt
8/14 Baby Actress
8/21 Day-coach Travel
8/28 Alice Marble
9/4 Rosalind Russell
9/11 Benito Mussolini
9/18 British Gunner
9/25 Britain's Ironside
10/2 Cordell Hull
10/9 Kids' Football
10/16 War on U-boats
10/23 Military Look
10/30 Veloz & Yolanda
11/6 English Air Defense
11/13 Claudette Colbert
11/20 German Raider
11/27 Grandpa Toscanini
12/4 UCLA Homecoming
12/11 Betty Grable
12/18 Canadian General
12/25 Skating Fashions

Folk artist Grandma Moses gains fame • John Steinbeck publishes *The Grapes of Wrath*
"God Bless America" is one of America's most popular songs
Greta Garbo stars in *Ninotchka* • World War II begins as Germany invades Poland

1940

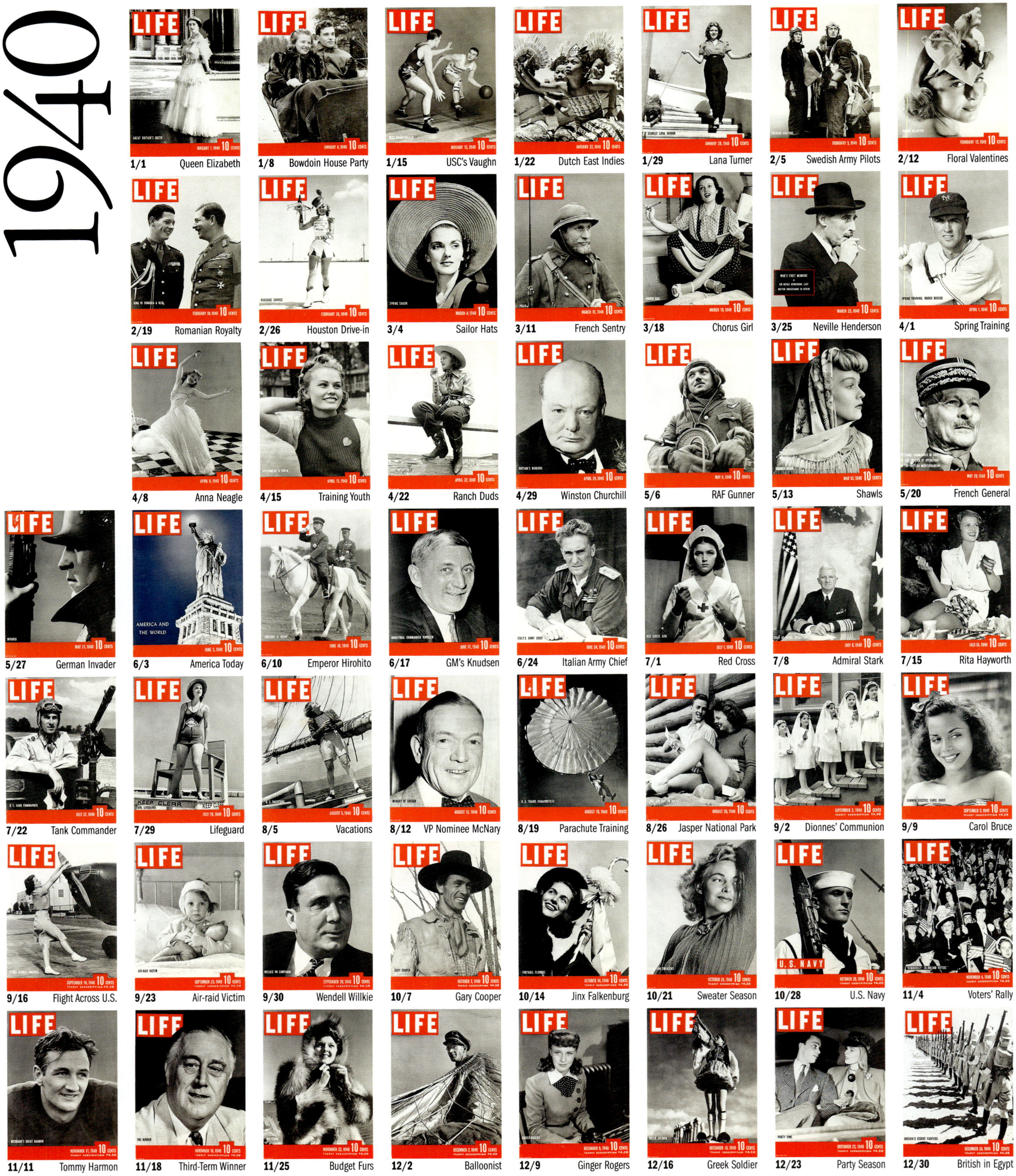

1/1 Queen Elizabeth
1/8 Bowdoin House Party
1/15 USC's Vaughn
1/22 Dutch East Indies
1/29 Lana Turner
2/5 Swedish Army Pilots
2/12 Floral Valentines

2/19 Romanian Royalty
2/26 Houston Drive-in
3/4 Sailor Hats
3/11 French Sentry
3/18 Chorus Girl
3/25 Neville Henderson
4/1 Spring Training

4/8 Anna Neagle
4/15 Training Youth
4/22 Ranch Duds
4/29 Winston Churchill
5/6 RAF Gunner
5/13 Shawls
5/20 French General

5/27 German Invader
6/3 America Today
6/10 Emperor Hirohito
6/17 GM's Knudsen
6/24 Italian Army Chief
7/1 Red Cross
7/8 Admiral Stark
7/15 Rita Hayworth

7/22 Tank Commander
7/29 Lifeguard
8/5 Vacations
8/12 VP Nominee McNary
8/19 Parachute Training
8/26 Jasper National Park
9/2 Dionnes' Communion
9/9 Carol Bruce

9/16 Flight Across U.S.
9/23 Air-raid Victim
9/30 Wendell Willkie
10/7 Gary Cooper
10/14 Jinx Falkenburg
10/21 Sweater Season
10/28 U.S. Navy
11/4 Voters' Rally

11/11 Tommy Harmon
11/18 Third-Term Winner
11/25 Budget Furs
12/2 Balloonist
12/9 Ginger Rogers
12/16 Greek Soldier
12/23 Party Season
12/30 British in Egypt

The U.S. population is 132,164,569 • Winston Churchill becomes Britain's prime minister • Ernest Hemingway publishes *For Whom the Bell Tolls*
Nylon stockings go on sale • The average life expectancy in the U.S. is 64, up from 49 in 1900

1941

1/6 Katharine Hepburn
1/13 Resort Styles
1/20 Army Ski Patrol
1/27 Churchills
2/3 Goebbels & Goering
2/10 Lord Halifax
2/17 Hollywood Party

2/24 Anzac Soldiers
3/3 Model & Mannequin
3/10 D.C. Workers
3/17 Panama Canal
3/24 Spring Hats
3/31 Carrier Bomber
4/7 Rainwear

4/14 New York City
4/21 Cavalry
4/28 Best-selling Red
5/5 Harvard
5/12 Army Paratrooper
5/19 Floppy Hats
5/26 Army Nurse

6/2 Sunday School
6/9 The Windsors
6/16 British Navy in U.S.
6/23 Lazy Fishing
6/30 Madam Chiang
7/7 Defense Issue
7/14 Sand Sailing

7/21 Singapore's Defender
7/28 The Circus
8/4 British Women
8/11 Rita Hayworth
8/18 Marine in Bermuda
8/25 Astaire & Son
9/1 Ted Williams
9/8 Campus Pigtails

9/15 Lord Mountbatten
9/22 Brazil's Top Dancer
9/29 Radio Quiz Kid
10/6 South Dakota
10/13 Turner & Gable
10/20 Pan Am Clipper
10/27 Air-raid Test
11/3 West Point

11/10 Gene Tierney
11/17 Texas Football
11/24 How to Knit
12/1 Air Power
12/8 General MacArthur
12/15 *Junior Miss*
12/22 U.S. Goes to War
12/29 Aerial Gunner

The Lend Lease Act allocates $7 billion in aid to Great Britain • Churchill and FDR meet and sign the Atlantic Charter
U.S. savings bonds and stamps go on sale • Joe DiMaggio hits safely in 56 consecutive games • Gary Cooper wins Best Actor Oscar for *Sergeant York*

1942

1/5 Nursing Shortage
1/12 Pacific Coast
1/19 North Atlantic
1/26 *This Above All*
2/2 U.S. *Thunderbolt*
2/9 Nightclub Chorus
2/16 USO
2/23 Brooklyn Navy Yard
3/2 Ginger Rogers
3/9 Barrage Balloons
3/16 Private Teed
3/23 Airplane Models
3/30 Shirley Temple
4/6 Bomber
4/13 Supply Chief
4/20 Slacks in Style
4/27 Nelson Rockefeller
5/4 Chinese Air Cadet
5/11 Joan Caulfield
5/18 Bombardier
5/25 Spring Planting
6/1 Hedy Lamarr
6/8 Nurse's Aide
6/15 General Stilwell
6/22 War-stamp Bride
6/29 USO Volunteer
7/6 United We Stand
7/13 Gunnery School
7/20 Short Coats
7/27 Atlantic Convoy
8/3 MacArthur's Son
8/10 General Chennault
8/17 Guerrilla Training
8/24 Fatigue Hats
8/31 Survivor's Tale
9/7 War Glider
9/14 OPA Chief
9/21 Iran's Queen
9/28 Admiral Leahy
10/5 Hats
10/12 War Worker
10/19 Sphinx
10/26 Joan Leslie
11/2 Navy Chaplain
11/9 Mountain Trooper
11/16 Winter Warmth
11/23 Puritan Spirit
11/30 Future Draftee
12/7 Marine Ace
12/14 Coast Guard Skipper
12/21 Wartime Wife
12/28 Raphael's *Madonna*

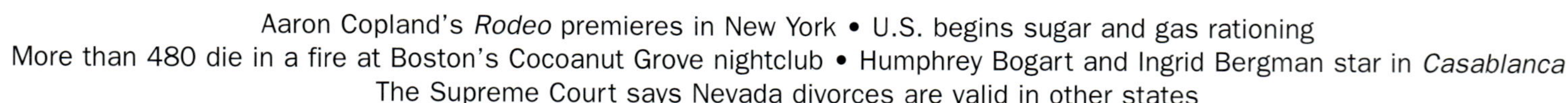

Aaron Copland's *Rodeo* premieres in New York • U.S. begins sugar and gas rationing
More than 480 die in a fire at Boston's Cocoanut Grove nightclub • Humphrey Bogart and Ingrid Bergman star in *Casablanca*
The Supreme Court says Nevada divorces are valid in other states

1943

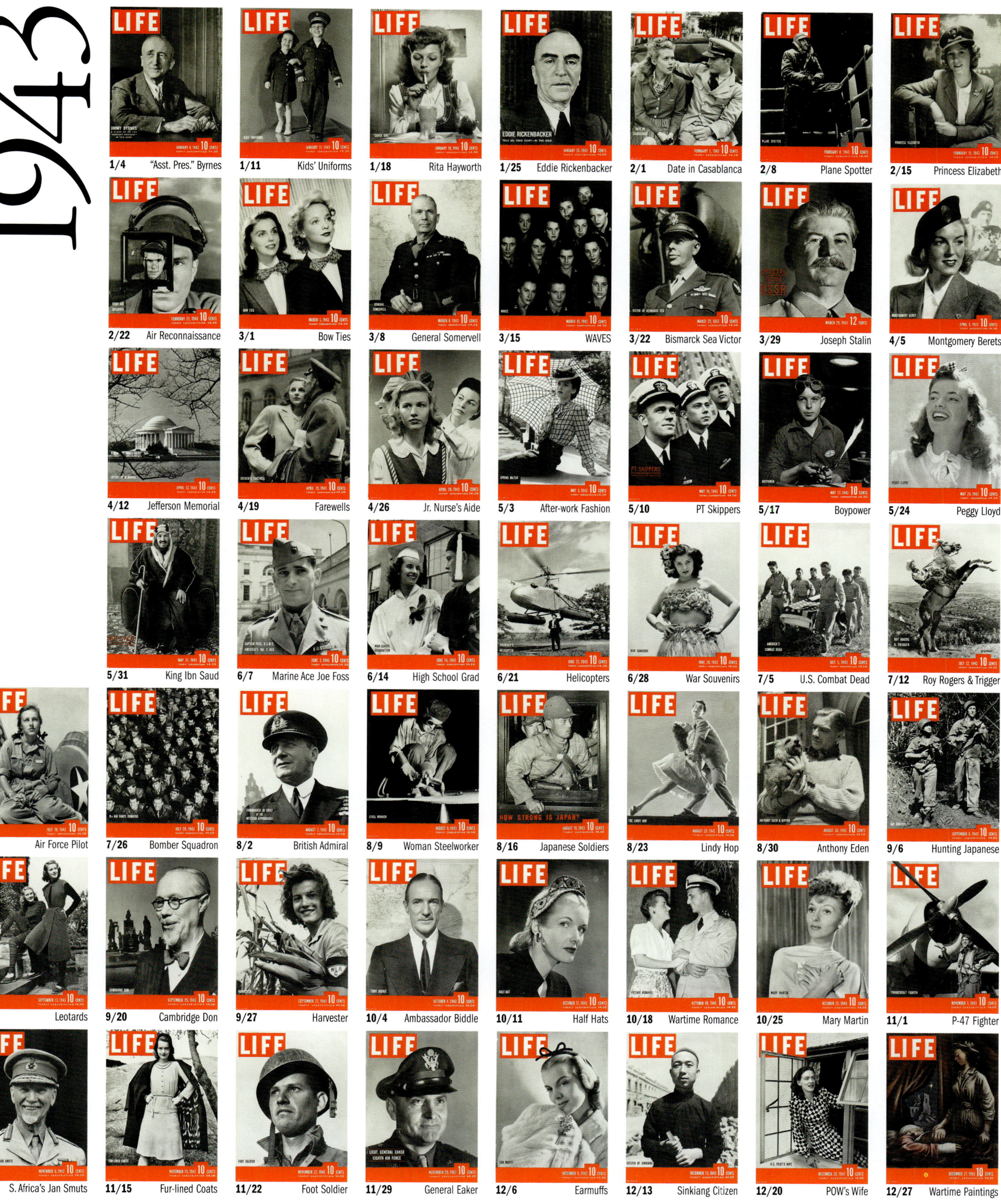

1/4 "Asst. Pres." Byrnes
1/11 Kids' Uniforms
1/18 Rita Hayworth
1/25 Eddie Rickenbacker
2/1 Date in Casablanca
2/8 Plane Spotter
2/15 Princess Elizabeth
2/22 Air Reconnaissance
3/1 Bow Ties
3/8 General Somervell
3/15 WAVES
3/22 Bismarck Sea Victor
3/29 Joseph Stalin
4/5 Montgomery Berets
4/12 Jefferson Memorial
4/19 Farewells
4/26 Jr. Nurse's Aide
5/3 After-work Fashion
5/10 PT Skippers
5/17 Boypower
5/24 Peggy Lloyd
5/31 King Ibn Saud
6/7 Marine Ace Joe Foss
6/14 High School Grad
6/21 Helicopters
6/28 War Souvenirs
7/5 U.S. Combat Dead
7/12 Roy Rogers & Trigger
7/19 Air Force Pilot
7/26 Bomber Squadron
8/2 British Admiral
8/9 Woman Steelworker
8/16 Japanese Soldiers
8/23 Lindy Hop
8/30 Anthony Eden
9/6 Hunting Japanese
9/13 Leotards
9/20 Cambridge Don
9/27 Harvester
10/4 Ambassador Biddle
10/11 Half Hats
10/18 Wartime Romance
10/25 Mary Martin
11/1 P-47 Fighter
11/8 S. Africa's Jan Smuts
11/15 Fur-lined Coats
11/22 Foot Soldier
11/29 General Eaker
12/6 Earmuffs
12/13 Sinkiang Citizen
12/20 POW's Wife
12/27 Wartime Paintings

Americans are limited to three pairs of leather shoes a year • *Oklahoma* opens on Broadway
Zoot suits are a new antiestablishment fashion • Nearly half of all vegetables in the U.S. come from victory gardens
Ernie Pyle publishes *Here Is Your War,* a collection of front-line dispatches

1944

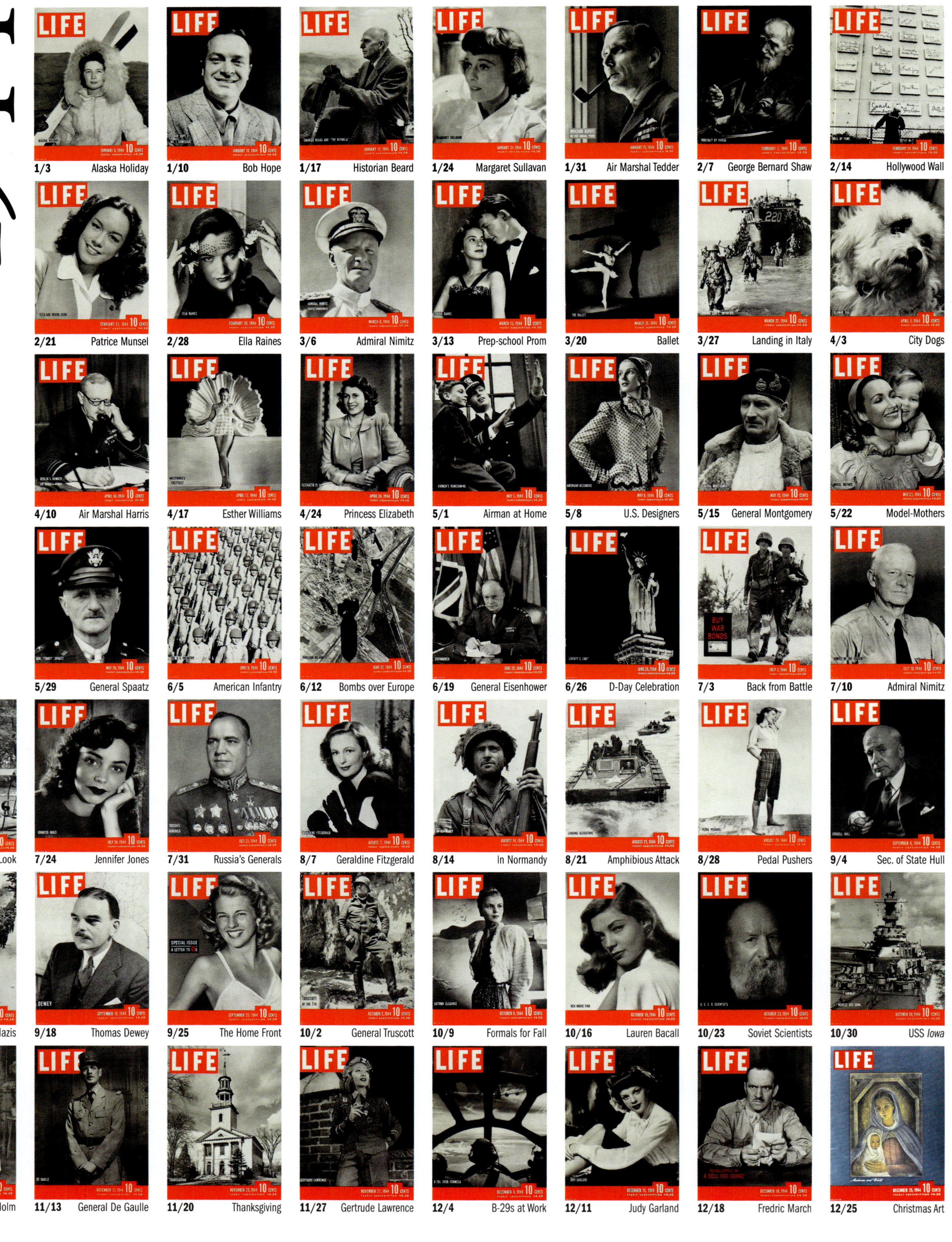

1/3 Alaska Holiday
1/10 Bob Hope
1/17 Historian Beard
1/24 Margaret Sullavan
1/31 Air Marshal Tedder
2/7 George Bernard Shaw
2/14 Hollywood Wall
2/21 Patrice Munsel
2/28 Ella Raines
3/6 Admiral Nimitz
3/13 Prep-school Prom
3/20 Ballet
3/27 Landing in Italy
4/3 City Dogs
4/10 Air Marshal Harris
4/17 Esther Williams
4/24 Princess Elizabeth
5/1 Airman at Home
5/8 U.S. Designers
5/15 General Montgomery
5/22 Model-Mothers
5/29 General Spaatz
6/5 American Infantry
6/12 Bombs over Europe
6/19 General Eisenhower
6/26 D-Day Celebration
7/3 Back from Battle
7/10 Admiral Nimitz
7/17 Peasant Look
7/24 Jennifer Jones
7/31 Russia's Generals
8/7 Geraldine Fitzgerald
8/14 In Normandy
8/21 Amphibious Attack
8/28 Pedal Pushers
9/4 Sec. of State Hull
9/11 Captured Nazis
9/18 Thomas Dewey
9/25 The Home Front
10/2 General Truscott
10/9 Formals for Fall
10/16 Lauren Bacall
10/23 Soviet Scientists
10/30 USS *Iowa*
11/6 Celeste Holm
11/13 General De Gaulle
11/20 Thanksgiving
11/27 Gertrude Lawrence
12/4 B-29s at Work
12/11 Judy Garland
12/18 Fredric March
12/25 Christmas Art

The cost of living rises nearly 30 percent in the U.S. • The GI Bill of Rights provides benefits for veterans
Bomb plot against Hitler fails
John Hersey publishes *A Bell for Adano* • Silly Putty is created by GE chemists

1945

1/1 Shortages at Front
1/8 Fancy Crochets
1/15 General Patton
1/22 St. John's Hoopsters
1/29 Casualty's Journey
2/5 Florida Poses
2/12 Soviet Soldier
2/19 Ski Styles
2/26 Winter Soldier
3/5 Over the Pacific
3/12 General Simpson
3/19 Dutch Floods
3/26 Carol Lynne
4/2 Subdeb Clubs
4/9 Iwo Jima
4/16 General Eisenhower
4/23 President Truman
4/30 War Artists
5/7 The German People
5/14 Victory in Europe
5/21 Winston Churchill
5/28 Barbara Bates
6/4 War-loan Drive
6/11 Teenage Boys
6/18 Congress
6/25 Kindergarten Ends
7/2 Sea Power
7/9 Swimsuit Review
7/16 Hero Audie Murphy
7/23 Peggy Ann Garner
7/30 Shadow Play
8/6 Yacht Club Youths
8/13 Fastest Fighter
8/20 General Spaatz
8/27 Aquatic Ballet
9/3 House Party
9/10 UAW
9/17 MacArthur in Japan
9/24 Col. Jimmy Stewart
10/1 June Allyson
10/8 General Eichelberger
10/15 Fall Jewelry
10/22 Ohio State Star
10/29 Autumn
11/5 The Fleet's In
11/12 Ingrid Bergman
11/19 Big belts
11/26 Champion Afghan
12/3 Spencer Tracy
12/10 Festive Finery
12/17 Paulette Goddard
12/24 Medici Treasures
12/31 Mountain Ascent

An atomic bomb is detonated in a secret test at Alamogordo, N.M. • Percy L. Spencer invents the microwave oven
13 people die when a B-25 bomber strikes the Empire State Building
The *Enola Gay* drops the first atom bomb on Hiroshima • The United Nations charter is signed in San Francisco

1946

1/7 Churchill's Paintings
1/14 Resort Fashions
1/21 Cardinal Spellman
1/28 Jan Clayton
2/4 Hope & Crosby
2/11 Lincoln Memorial
2/18 Dorothy McGuire
2/25 Bird Dogs
3/4 Figure Skater
3/11 Senator Vandenberg
3/18 Paris
3/25 Lucillle Bremer
4/1 Cardinal Hurler
4/8 Circus Preview
4/15 Easter Parading
4/22 Denver High School
4/29 Peiping
5/6 Margaret Leighton
5/13 Outdoor Fashions
5/20 Ice Show
5/27 Ozark Farmer
6/3 Child-size Chapels
6/10 Donna Reed
6/17 Play Dresses
6/24 Chief Justice Vinson
7/1 Sailing Season
7/8 "Little Girl" Clothes
7/15 Welded Plastics
7/22 Long Island Society
7/29 Vivien Leigh
8/5 Radio's *Juvenile Jury*
8/12 Loretta Young
8/19 Yellowstone Park
8/26 Campus Fashions
9/2 Cape Cod
9/9 Jane Powell
9/16 Davis & Blanchard
9/23 Cat's Playmate
9/30 Jeanne Crain
10/7 Crosby & Caulfield
10/14 Fall Styles
10/21 Gloria Grahame
10/28 One-room School
11/4 Palestine
11/11 High-school Model
11/18 Party Raincoats
11/25 LIFE Is 10
12/2 Ingrid Bergman
12/9 Jet Pilot
12/16 Teresa Wright
12/23 Fra Angelico
12/30 Dorothy Kirsten

Eniac, the first electronic computer, is unveiled • Winston Churchill delivers his Iron Curtain speech in Fulton, Mo. Top Nazi officials go on trial at Nuremberg • The bikini debuts in Paris • Eugene O'Neill's *The Iceman Cometh* opens on Broadway

1947

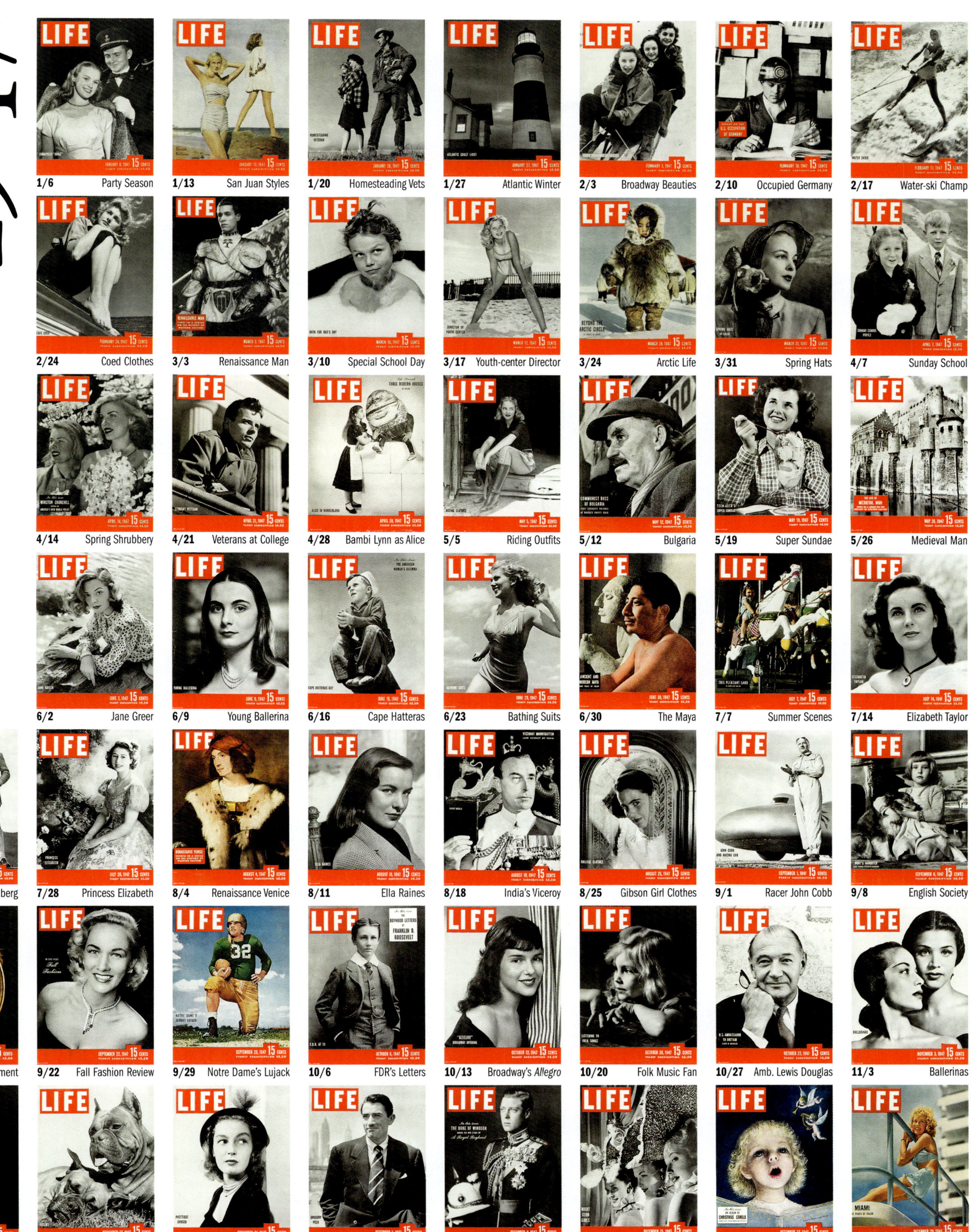

1/6 Party Season
1/13 San Juan Styles
1/20 Homesteading Vets
1/27 Atlantic Winter
2/3 Broadway Beauties
2/10 Occupied Germany
2/17 Water-ski Champ
2/24 Coed Clothes
3/3 Renaissance Man
3/10 Special School Day
3/17 Youth-center Director
3/24 Arctic Life
3/31 Spring Hats
4/7 Sunday School
4/14 Spring Shrubbery
4/21 Veterans at College
4/28 Bambi Lynn as Alice
5/5 Riding Outfits
5/12 Bulgaria
5/19 Super Sundae
5/26 Medieval Man
6/2 Jane Greer
6/9 Young Ballerina
6/16 Cape Hatteras
6/23 Bathing Suits
6/30 The Maya
7/7 Summer Scenes
7/14 Elizabeth Taylor
7/21 Yanks at Heidelberg
7/28 Princess Elizabeth
8/4 Renaissance Venice
8/11 Ella Raines
8/18 India's Viceroy
8/25 Gibson Girl Clothes
9/1 Racer John Cobb
9/8 English Society
9/15 Age of Enlightenment
9/22 Fall Fashion Review
9/29 Notre Dame's Lujack
10/6 FDR's Letters
10/13 Broadway's *Allegro*
10/20 Folk Music Fan
10/27 Amb. Lewis Douglas
11/3 Ballerinas
11/10 Rita Hayworth
11/17 Boxers
11/24 New York Subdeb
12/1 Gregory Peck
12/8 Windsor's Memoirs
12/15 Nightclubs
12/22 Christmas Carols
12/29 Miami

Jackie Robinson breaks baseball's color barrier • Thor Heyerdahl and a crew of five sail the *Kon-Tiki* from Peru to Polynesia
Meet the Press debuts on NBC • Chuck Yeager breaks the sound barrier in a rocket plane • Edwin Land demonstrates the Polaroid instant camera

1948

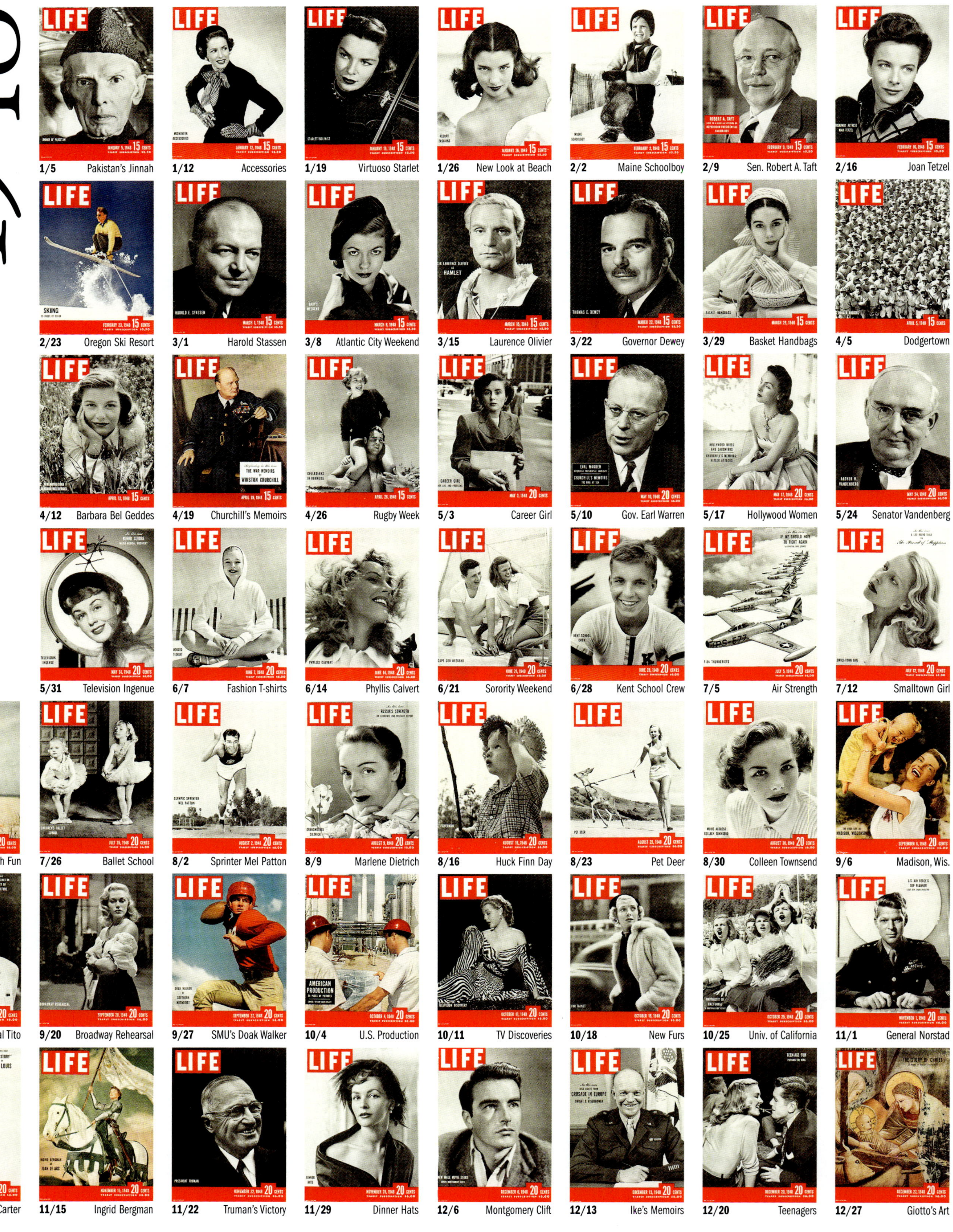

1/5 Pakistan's Jinnah
1/12 Accessories
1/19 Virtuoso Starlet
1/26 New Look at Beach
2/2 Maine Schoolboy
2/9 Sen. Robert A. Taft
2/16 Joan Tetzel
2/23 Oregon Ski Resort
3/1 Harold Stassen
3/8 Atlantic City Weekend
3/15 Laurence Olivier
3/22 Governor Dewey
3/29 Basket Handbags
4/5 Dodgertown
4/12 Barbara Bel Geddes
4/19 Churchill's Memoirs
4/26 Rugby Week
5/3 Career Girl
5/10 Gov. Earl Warren
5/17 Hollywood Women
5/24 Senator Vandenberg
5/31 Television Ingenue
6/7 Fashion T-shirts
6/14 Phyllis Calvert
6/21 Sorority Weekend
6/28 Kent School Crew
7/5 Air Strength
7/12 Smalltown Girl
7/19 Beach Fun
7/26 Ballet School
8/2 Sprinter Mel Patton
8/9 Marlene Dietrich
8/16 Huck Finn Day
8/23 Pet Deer
8/30 Colleen Townsend
9/6 Madison, Wis.
9/13 Marshal Tito
9/20 Broadway Rehearsal
9/27 SMU's Doak Walker
10/4 U.S. Production
10/11 TV Discoveries
10/18 New Furs
10/25 Univ. of California
11/1 General Norstad
11/8 Helena Carter
11/15 Ingrid Bergman
11/22 Truman's Victory
11/29 Dinner Hats
12/6 Montgomery Clift
12/13 Ike's Memoirs
12/20 Teenagers
12/27 Giotto's Art

Berlin airlift begins • Jackson Pollock's *Composition No. 1* is unveiled • Harry Truman upsets Thomas Dewey in the presidential election
135 million paperback books are sold in the U.S. • A Hindu fanatic assassinates Mahatma Gandhi

1949

1/3 Famous babies
1/10 Debutante Season
1/17 Resort Wear
1/24 French Skier
1/31 No. 1 Cocker
2/7 Churchill's Memoirs
2/14 Viveca Lindfors

2/21 Dean Acheson
2/28 Costume Clothes
3/7 The Champions
3/14 Three Hours Old
3/21 Teen Wardrobe
3/28 Films for TV
4/4 ECA's Paul Hoffman

4/11 Mississippi Spring
4/18 *South Pacific*
4/25 Parisian Styles
5/2 West Point Athlete
5/9 Missouri vs. Smith
5/16 Young Pugilists
5/23 Sarah Churchill

5/30 FDR Album
6/6 Shorts & Tops
6/13 Marta Toren
6/20 Hillsdale High
6/27 Inland Sailing
7/4 Seaside Date
7/11 Olympian Mathias

7/18 Hollywood's Kids
7/25 Beach Boats
8/1 Joe DiMaggio
8/8 Fairfield County
8/15 Aspiring Starlet
8/22 Cowboy
8/29 Campus Fashions
9/5 Ben Turpin

9/12 Marshal Tito
9/19 Arlene Dahl
9/26 Separates
10/3 Gridiron Roundup
10/10 J.R. Oppenheimer
10/17 Jeanne Crain
10/24 Swedish Ideal
10/31 Princess Margaret

11/7 Fontanne & Lunt
11/14 Pearls
11/21 Ricardo Montalban
11/28 Movie Dancer
12/5 Men's Sportswear
12/12 Fifth Ave. Belles
12/19 Girls' Clothing
12/26 Sistine Chapel

The first Emmy Awards are presented • NATO is established • Arthur Miller's *Death of a Salesman* wins the Pulitzer Prize for Drama
Mao Zedong proclaims the People's Republic of China • Perry Como and Arthur Godfrey have popular TV shows

1950

1/2 Midcentury Issue
1/9 Mexico
1/16 Ice Prodigy
1/23 Man-tailored Shirts
1/30 Natural Childbirth
2/6 Eva Gabor
2/13 Indonesia
2/20 Gregory Peck
2/27 Atomic War
3/6 Marsha Hunt
3/13 Spring Fashions
3/20 Young U.S. Artists
3/27 Mystery Flight
4/3 *The Innocents*
4/10 Young Horsewoman
4/17 Ike at Columbia
4/24 Inexpensive Blouses
5/1 Ruth Roman
5/8 Jackie Robinson
5/15 One-piece Suits
5/22 Windsor's Memoirs
5/29 Sloan S. O'Dwyer
6/5 Show-biz Mermaid
6/12 Hopalong Cassidy
6/19 Kids' Sand Styles
6/26 Cecile Aubry
7/3 The Revolution
7/10 Mexican Actress
7/17 U.S. Jets to Korea
7/24 Jamboree
7/31 On the Front
8/7 Peggy Dow
8/14 Admiral Hoskins
8/21 Bubble-bath Girls
8/28 U.N. Commander
9/4 Reconnaissance
9/11 American Elegance
9/18 Ezio Pinza
9/25 Swedish Red Cross
10/2 Stuart Symington
10/9 Jean Simmons
10/16 New Trier High
10/23 Ed Wynn
10/30 Faye Emerson
11/6 Horse Show
11/13 SMU's Kyle Rote
11/20 Nile River
11/27 UCLA Homecoming
12/4 West Berliners
12/11 Palmer & Harrison
12/18 George C. Marshall
12/25 Child's Christmas

The U.S. population is 151,325,798 • Masked robbers in Boston steal $2.8 million from a Brink's office
Senator Joseph McCarthy says the State Department is riddled with Communists • Antihistamines become popular as cold-relief medication
Peanuts makes its debut in seven U.S. newspapers

1951

1/1 GE's Charles Wilson
1/8 Janice Rule
1/15 Rose Parade Marshal
1/22 Air Defense
1/29 Betsy von Furstenberg
2/5 Police Commissioner
2/12 Hatless Hats
2/19 Adoption
2/26 Debbie Reynolds
3/5 Paris Fashions
3/12 Paul Douglas
3/19 Navy Couple
3/26 Cherub Choir
4/2 New World Riviera
4/9 Bradley's Memoirs
4/16 Esther Williams
4/23 Dalai Lama
4/30 General Ridgway
5/7 Phyllis Kirk
5/14 Sen. Blair Moody
5/21 Summer Styles
5/28 Paratrooper
6/4 Ursula Thiess
6/11 Vivian Blaine
6/18 Iran
6/25 Janet Leigh
7/2 Medal of Honor
7/9 Charlotte, N.C., Debs
7/16 Dagmar
7/23 Olympics Prospect
7/30 Gary Crosby
8/6 Summer Fun
8/13 Martin & Lewis
8/20 Swimming Champ
8/27 13-year-old Model
9/3 Gina Lollobrigida
9/10 Japan's PM Yoshida
9/17 TV's Roxanne
9/24 Gene Tierney
10/1 Princess Elizabeth
10/8 Slow Loris
10/15 Zsa Zsa Gabor
10/22 Bronc Rider
10/29 TV Gal Friday
11/5 Ginger Rogers
11/12 Anthony Eden
11/19 Great Stage Ladies
11/26 Photo Contest
12/3 Christmas Lingerie
12/10 Truman's Garb
12/17 Leigh & Olivier
12/24 Tintoretto's Art
12/31 Asia

The first disposable diapers go on the market • Gen. Douglas MacArthur is relieved of the Far East command
Edward R. Murrow's *See It Now* is the first TV news magazine
Cleveland disc jockey Alan Freed coins the term "rock 'n' roll" • Direct long-distance dialing goes into effect

1952

1/7 Hair Styles
1/14 Augustus John
1/21 Candidate Ike
1/28 Triple Talent
2/4 Barbara Ann Scott
2/11 Olympic Skiing
2/18 Queen Elizabeth II

2/25 Gloves
3/3 Patrice Munsel
3/10 Brandon de Wilde
3/17 Prettiest Showgirl
3/24 Democrats
3/31 Surprise Wedding
4/7 Marilyn Monroe

4/14 Italian Fashions
4/21 Tito's Story
4/28 Young Eisenhower
5/5 Diana Lynn
5/12 SHAPE's Ridgway
5/19 Starlet Kerima
5/26 Stewart Granger

6/2 Party Clothes
6/9 Weddings
6/16 A Soldier Retires
6/23 Mail-order Fashions
6/30 Nancy Kefauver
7/7 Arlene Dahl
7/14 The Night Before

7/21 Nominee Ike
7/28 British Starlets
8/4 Adlai Stevenson
8/11 Joan Rice
8/18 Daughter & Dietrich
8/25 Campus Fashions
9/1 Ernest Hemingway
9/8 Siren Look

9/15 Rita Gam
9/22 Arctic Base
9/29 *Jackie Gleason Show*
10/6 SF Opera Opening
10/13 Mamie Eisenhower
10/20 Italian Cinema
10/27 Jon Lindbergh
11/3 Completion of U.N.

11/10 Duck Hunter
11/17 Election Winners
11/24 Too Much Jewelry?
12/1 French Actresses
12/8 Earth's Birth
12/15 DP to College Queen
12/22 Wee Horse
12/29 Marionettes

The U.S. explodes the first hydrogen bomb on an atoll in the Pacific • Republican VP candidate Richard Nixon makes his Checkers speech
George Jorgenson becomes Christine Jorgenson in a sex-change operation
Grace Kelly and Gary Cooper star in the western *High Noon* • Christian Dior dominates Paris fashions

1953

1/5 $15,000 House
1/12 Majorca Clothing
1/19 Cabinet Designates
1/26 Ohrbach's Stylist
2/2 Inauguration
2/9 Miracle of the Sea
2/16 Queen's Soldiers
2/23 Prettiest Teacher
3/2 Chinese on Formosa
3/9 Vanessa Brown
3/16 Malenkov & Stalin
3/23 Elaine Stewart
3/30 Coronation Attire
4/6 The Arnaz Family
4/13 Face of the Land
4/20 Marlon Brando
4/27 Coronation Portrait
5/4 Africa
5/11 Dressy Denim
5/18 Arts in Midwest
5/25 Monroe & Russell
6/1 Hollywood Daughters
6/8 Roy Campanella
6/15 Coronation
6/22 Graduations
6/29 Cyd Charisse
7/6 Terry Moore
7/13 Everest
7/20 Kennedy & Bouvier
7/27 Cancan Lingerie
8/3 Nicole Maurey
8/10 Irish Fashions
8/17 Hollywood Sisters
8/24 Ballet Troupe
8/31 Donna Reed
9/7 Evolution
9/14 Casey Stengel
9/21 Photog's Child
9/28 Biarritz Ball
10/5 Italians in U.S.
10/12 Bare Backs
10/19 Age of Mammals
10/26 Working Mothers
11/2 Nobel Winner
11/9 Jill Corey
11/16 Greece's Queen
11/23 Art Student
11/30 Sea Creatures
12/7 Audrey Hepburn
12/14 Richard Nixon
12/21 Canasta Pajamas
12/28 Four Churches

Edmund Hillary and Tenzing Norgay conquer Mount Everest • Atomic spies Julius and Ethel Rosenberg are executed
James Watson and Francis Crick reveal the double-helix structure of DNA
Hugh Hefner runs a nude photo of Marilyn Monroe in his new magazine, *Playboy* • Tests on mice show that tars from cigarettes cause cancer

1954

1/4 The Economy
1/11 Deb Twins
1/18 Strategy Session
1/25 TV Dancer
2/1 Tropical Togs
2/8 Coral Reef
2/15 Hairstyles

2/22 Disney Movie
3/1 Rita Moreno
3/8 Arabella Churchill
3/15 Bobo Rockefeller
3/22 Emperors
3/29 Pat Crowley
4/5 The Desert

4/12 Subteen Styles
4/19 H-bomb Test
4/26 Grace Kelly
5/3 Rare Stamps
5/10 Germany
5/17 Dawn Addams
5/24 Kaye Ballard

5/31 William Holden
6/7 Arctic Barrens
6/14 California Look
6/21 Vegas Chorine
6/28 Beach Wear
7/5 Cartoon U.S.A.
7/12 Pier Angeli

7/19 Eva Marie Saint
7/26 Joseph Welch
8/2 Summer Show
8/9 Cowhand & Dad
8/16 Basutoland
8/23 Duke of Edinburgh
8/30 Anna Maria Alberghetti
9/6 Paris Collections

9/13 Judy Garland
9/20 Tropical Forests
9/27 Hydrofoils
10/4 Thai Visitor
10/11 Conquest of K2
10/18 Campaign Trail
10/25 Big 10 Look
11/1 Dorothy Dandridge

11/8 Woodland Life
11/15 Gina Lollobrigida
11/22 Judy Holliday
11/29 Twins in *Fanny*
12/6 Jet-age Man
12/13 Pope Pius XII
12/20 Starry Universe
12/27 Bruegel's Art

Brown v. *Board of Education* outlaws segregation in public schools • Jonas Salk begins human trials of his polio vaccine
Nautilus, the first atomic submarine, is launched • Roger Bannister breaks the four-minute mile • Frozen TV dinners hit the market

1955

1/3 Food
1/10 Greta Garbo
1/17 Russian Folk
1/24 Tahiti
1/31 Spencer Tracy
2/7 Hinduism
2/14 *Family of Man*

2/21 Princess Margaret
2/28 Shelley Winters
3/7 Buddhism
3/14 *The Good Shepherd*
3/21 Sheree North
3/28 Volcano
4/4 Confucianism

4/11 Grace Kelly
4/18 Cultural Heritage
4/25 PM & Lady Eden
5/2 *Oklahoma!*
5/9 Islam
5/16 Styles of Orient
5/23 *Daddy Long Legs*

5/30 Historic Cards
6/6 Henry Fonda
6/13 Judaism
6/20 Las Vegas
6/27 Peak Tourism
7/4 Fireworks
7/11 Susan Strasberg

7/18 Audrey Hepburn
7/25 Cathy Crosby
8/1 Big Four in Geneva
8/8 Ben Hogan
8/15 MacArthur's Memoirs
8/22 Sophia Loren
8/29 Grandson's Fun
9/5 Parisian Glamour

9/12 Joan Collins
9/19 *Guys and Dolls*
9/26 Truman's Memoirs
10/3 Rock Hudson
10/10 Princess Margaret
10/17 Venetian Wedding
10/24 *Ten Commandments*
10/31 Elegant Evenings

11/7 Man's Beginnings
11/14 Convalescent Ike
11/21 Broadway Talent
11/28 Carol Channing
12/5 Man-made Mink
12/12 Dawn of Religion
12/19 Holiday Buying
12/26 Christianity

Captain Kangaroo premieres on CBS • Despite 110° temperature, crowds rush to the opening of Disneyland • Velcro is patented
Rosa Parks refuses to relinquish her seat on a Montgomery, Ala., bus • The Brooklyn Dodgers beat the New York Yankees in the World Series

1956

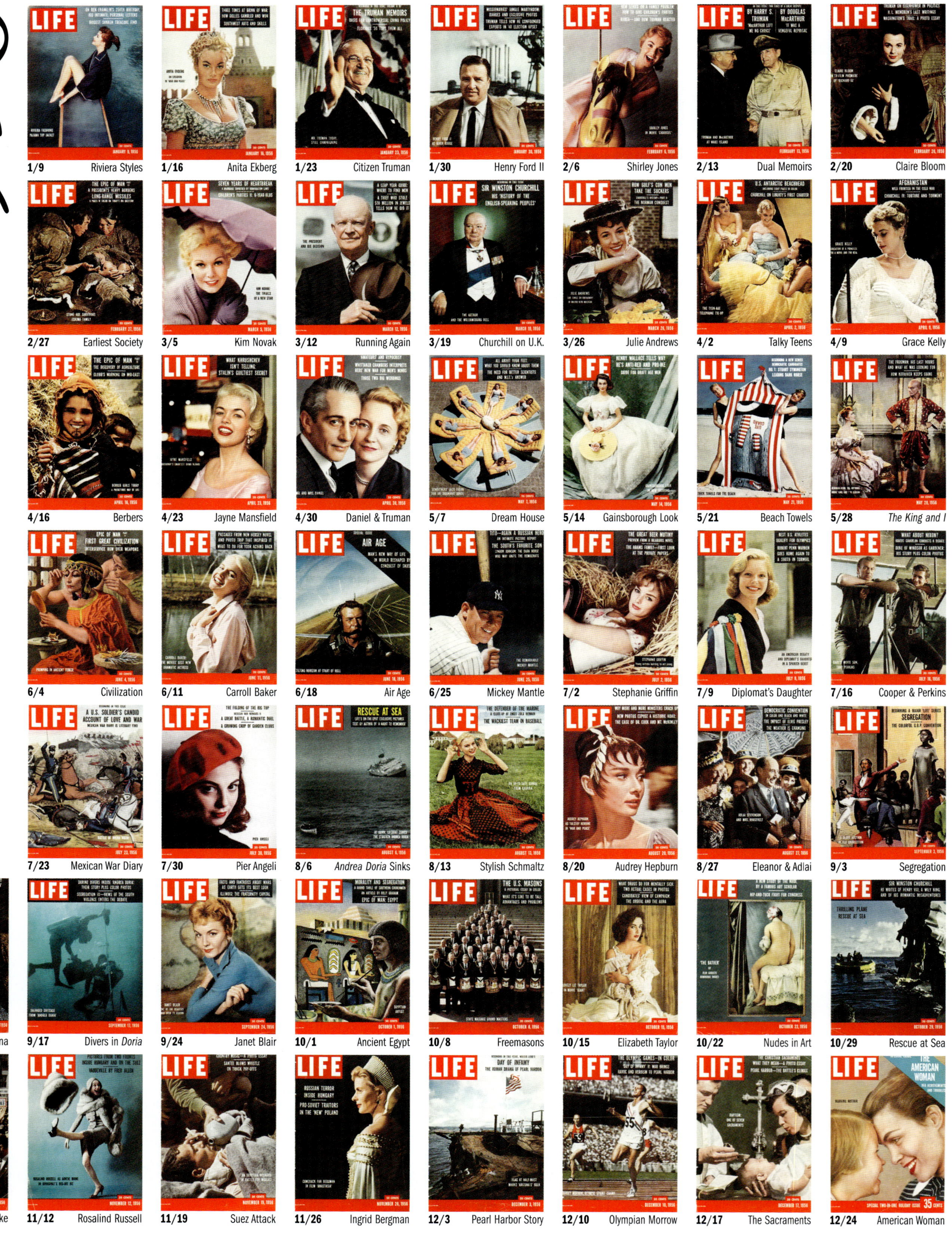

1/9 Riviera Styles
1/16 Anita Ekberg
1/23 Citizen Truman
1/30 Henry Ford II
2/6 Shirley Jones
2/13 Dual Memoirs
2/20 Claire Bloom
2/27 Earliest Society
3/5 Kim Novak
3/12 Running Again
3/19 Churchill on U.K.
3/26 Julie Andrews
4/2 Talky Teens
4/9 Grace Kelly
4/16 Berbers
4/23 Jayne Mansfield
4/30 Daniel & Truman
5/7 Dream House
5/14 Gainsborough Look
5/21 Beach Towels
5/28 *The King and I*
6/4 Civilization
6/11 Carroll Baker
6/18 Air Age
6/25 Mickey Mantle
7/2 Stephanie Griffin
7/9 Diplomat's Daughter
7/16 Cooper & Perkins
7/23 Mexican War Diary
7/30 Pier Angeli
8/6 *Andrea Doria* Sinks
8/13 Stylish Schmaltz
8/20 Audrey Hepburn
8/27 Eleanor & Adlai
9/3 Segregation
9/10 Siobhan McKenna
9/17 Divers in *Doria*
9/24 Janet Blair
10/1 Ancient Egypt
10/8 Freemasons
10/15 Elizabeth Taylor
10/22 Nudes in Art
10/29 Rescue at Sea
11/5 Campaigner Ike
11/12 Rosalind Russell
11/19 Suez Attack
11/26 Ingrid Bergman
12/3 Pearl Harbor Story
12/10 Olympian Morrow
12/17 The Sacraments
12/24 American Woman

Elvis Presley appears on *The Ed Sullivan Show* • Grace Kelly weds Prince Rainier • *My Fair Lady* opens on Broadway
In God We Trust is adopted as a national motto • Scientists isolate the human growth hormone

1957

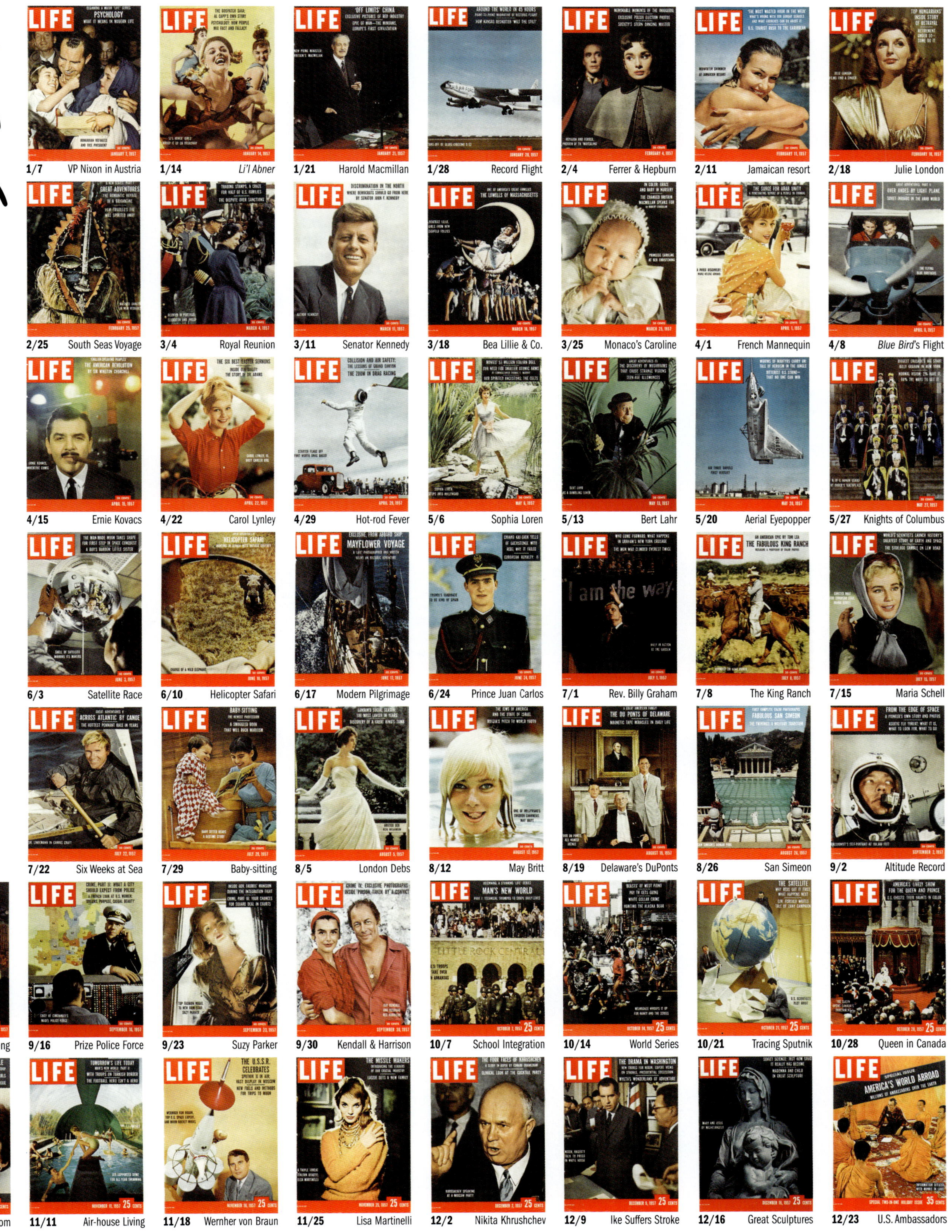

1/7 VP Nixon in Austria
1/14 *Li'l Abner*
1/21 Harold Macmillan
1/28 Record Flight
2/4 Ferrer & Hepburn
2/11 Jamaican resort
2/18 Julie London
2/25 South Seas Voyage
3/4 Royal Reunion
3/11 Senator Kennedy
3/18 Bea Lillie & Co.
3/25 Monaco's Caroline
4/1 French Mannequin
4/8 *Blue Bird*'s Flight
4/15 Ernie Kovacs
4/22 Carol Lynley
4/29 Hot-rod Fever
5/6 Sophia Loren
5/13 Bert Lahr
5/20 Aerial Eyepopper
5/27 Knights of Columbus
6/3 Satellite Race
6/10 Helicopter Safari
6/17 Modern Pilgrimage
6/24 Prince Juan Carlos
7/1 Rev. Billy Graham
7/8 The King Ranch
7/15 Maria Schell
7/22 Six Weeks at Sea
7/29 Baby-sitting
8/5 London Debs
8/12 May Britt
8/19 Delaware's DuPonts
8/26 San Simeon
9/2 Altitude Record
9/9 Street Gang
9/16 Prize Police Force
9/23 Suzy Parker
9/30 Kendall & Harrison
10/7 School Integration
10/14 World Series
10/21 Tracing Sputnik
10/28 Queen in Canada
11/4 Liza Todd & Mom
11/11 Air-house Living
11/18 Wernher von Braun
11/25 Lisa Martinelli
12/2 Nikita Khrushchev
12/9 Ike Suffers Stroke
12/16 Great Sculptures
12/23 U.S. Ambassadors

Leonard Bernstein's *West Side Story* makes its debut • Congress passes first Civil Rights Act • Jack Kerouac's *On the Road* is published
U.S., U.S.S.R. begin space race • President Eisenhower sends federal troops to Little Rock to enforce desegregation

1958

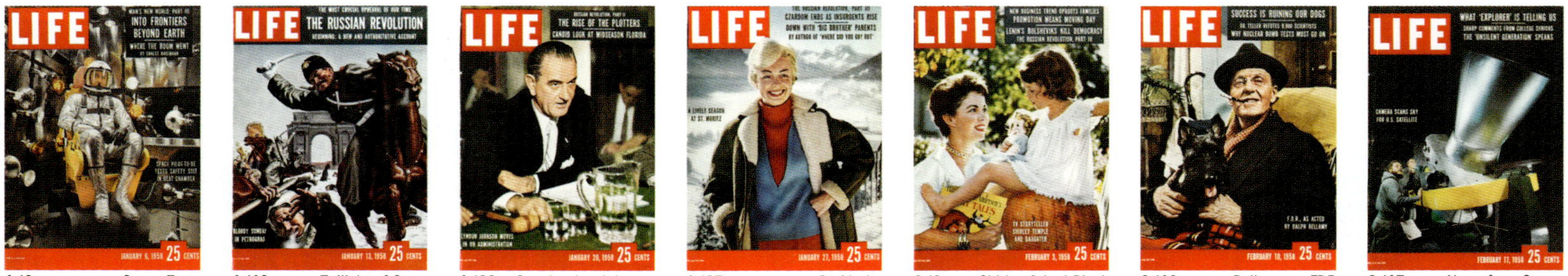

1/6 Space Tests
1/13 Twilight of Czars
1/20 Sen. Lyndon Johnson
1/27 St. Moritz
2/3 Shirley & Lori Black
2/10 Bellamy as FDR
2/17 News from Space

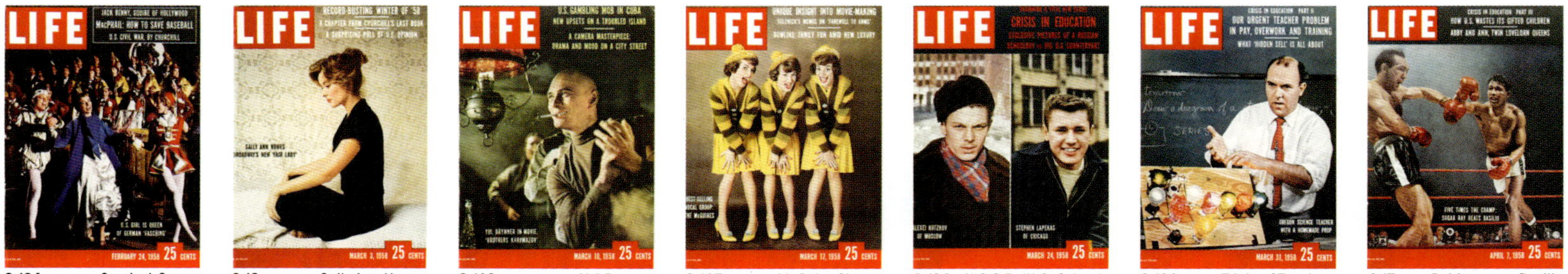

2/24 Carnival Queen
3/3 Sally Ann Howes
3/10 Yul Brynner
3/17 McGuire Sisters
3/24 U.S.S.R./U.S. Schools
3/31 Trials of Teachers
4/7 Robinson vs. Basilio

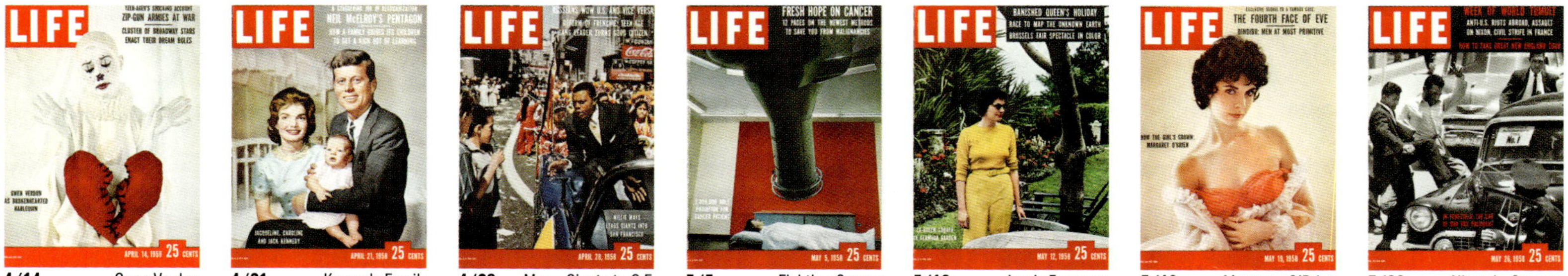

4/14 Gwen Verdon
4/21 Kennedy Family
4/28 Mays, Giants to S.F.
5/5 Fighting Cancer
5/12 Iran's Ex-queen
5/19 Margaret O'Brien
5/26 Nixon in Caracas

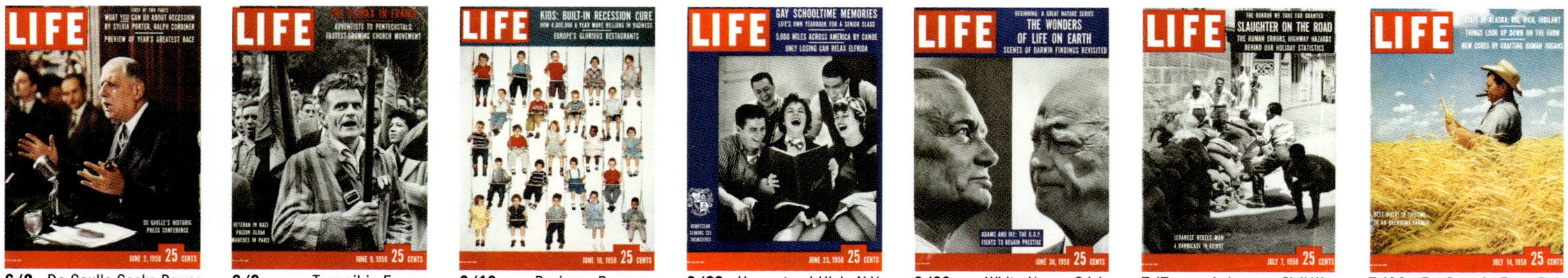

6/2 De Gaulle Seeks Power
6/9 Turmoil in France
6/16 Business Bonanza
6/23 Hempstead High, N.Y.
6/30 White House Crisis
7/7 Lebanese Civil War
7/14 Fat Days in Farm Belt

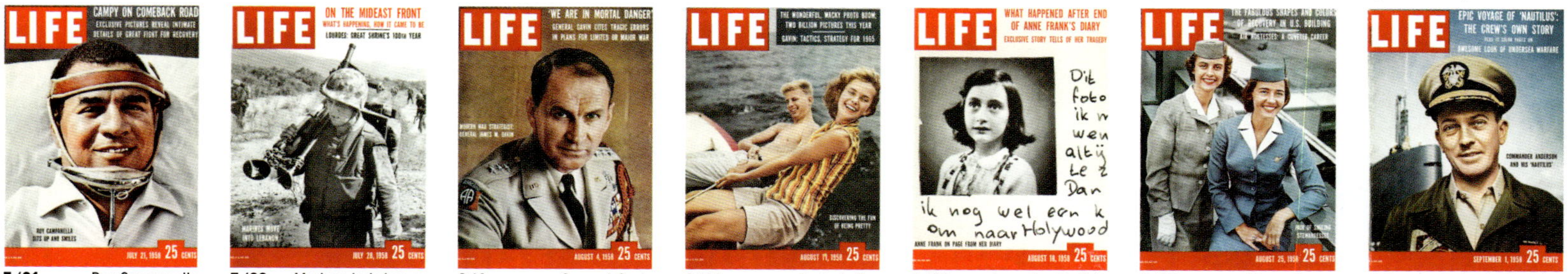

7/21 Roy Campanella
7/28 Marines in Lebanon
8/4 General Gavin
8/11 Pretty Is Fun
8/18 Anne Frank's Fate
8/25 Stewardesses
9/1 Subpolar Crossing

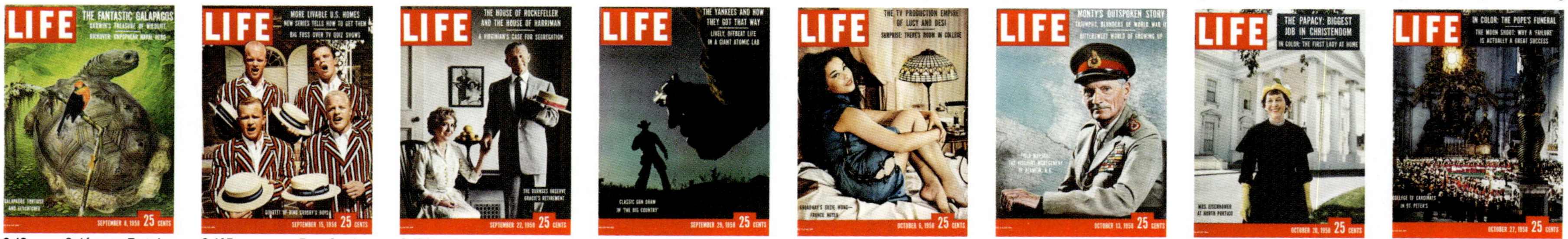

9/8 Galápagos Tortoise
9/15 Four Crosbys
9/22 Allen & Burns
9/29 *The Big Country*
10/6 France Nuyen
10/13 Monty's Memoirs
10/20 Mamie Eisenhower
10/27 Pius XII Funeral

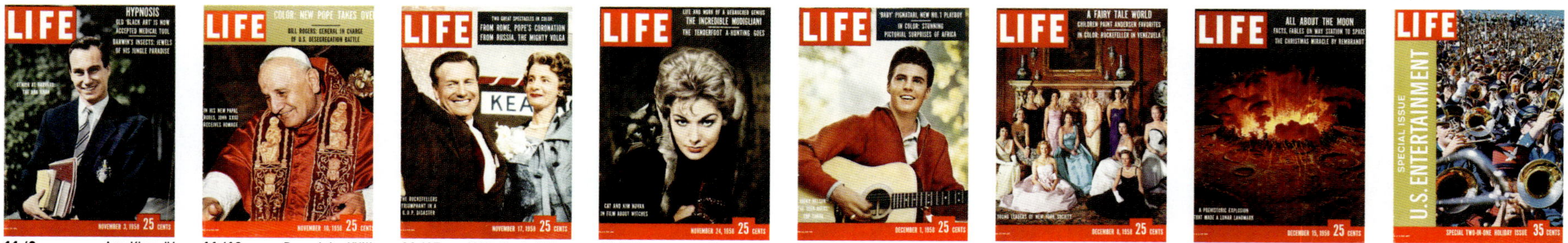

11/3 Aga Khan IV
11/10 Pope John XXIII
11/17 N.Y.'s Rockefellers
11/24 Kim Novak
12/1 Ricky Nelson
12/8 Charity Balls
12/15 Lunar Fact & Fancy
12/22 Show-biz

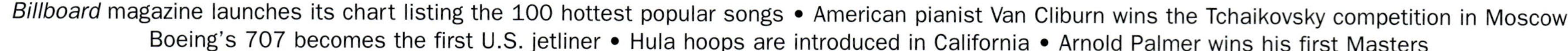

Billboard magazine launches its chart listing the 100 hottest popular songs • American pianist Van Cliburn wins the Tchaikovsky competition in Moscow
Boeing's 707 becomes the first U.S. jetliner • Hula hoops are introduced in California • Arnold Palmer wins his first Masters

1959

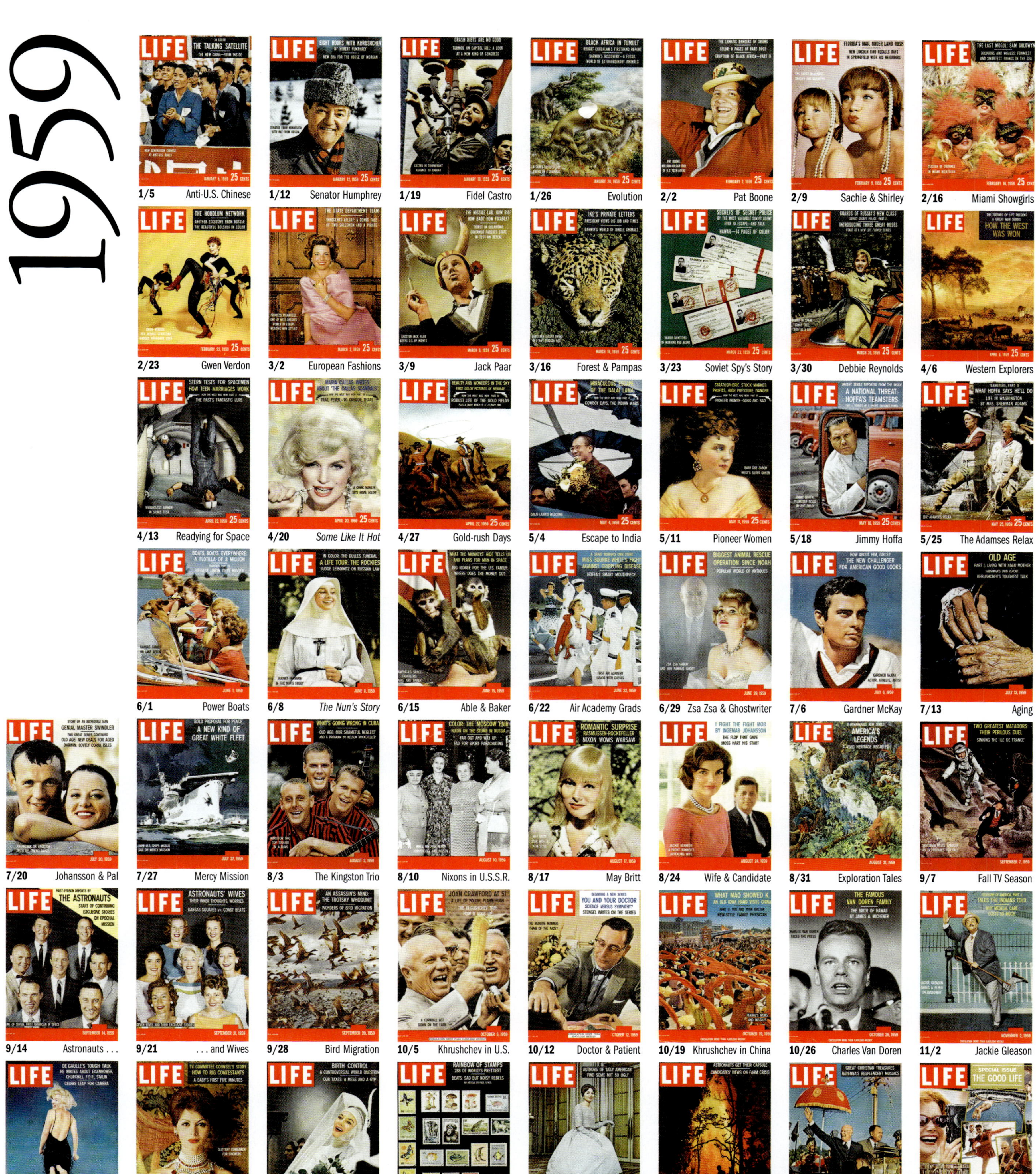

1/5 Anti-U.S. Chinese · 1/12 Senator Humphrey · 1/19 Fidel Castro · 1/26 Evolution · 2/2 Pat Boone · 2/9 Sachie & Shirley · 2/16 Miami Showgirls

2/23 Gwen Verdon · 3/2 European Fashions · 3/9 Jack Paar · 3/16 Forest & Pampas · 3/23 Soviet Spy's Story · 3/30 Debbie Reynolds · 4/6 Western Explorers

4/13 Readying for Space · 4/20 *Some Like It Hot* · 4/27 Gold-rush Days · 5/4 Escape to India · 5/11 Pioneer Women · 5/18 Jimmy Hoffa · 5/25 The Adamses Relax

6/1 Power Boats · 6/8 *The Nun's Story* · 6/15 Able & Baker · 6/22 Air Academy Grads · 6/29 Zsa Zsa & Ghostwriter · 7/6 Gardner McKay · 7/13 Aging

7/20 Johansson & Pal · 7/27 Mercy Mission · 8/3 The Kingston Trio · 8/10 Nixons in U.S.S.R. · 8/17 May Britt · 8/24 Wife & Candidate · 8/31 Exploration Tales · 9/7 Fall TV Season

9/14 Astronauts . . . · 9/21 . . . and Wives · 9/28 Bird Migration · 10/5 Khrushchev in U.S. · 10/12 Doctor & Patient · 10/19 Khrushchev in China · 10/26 Charles Van Doren · 11/2 Jackie Gleason

11/9 Jumpers Galore · 11/16 Chokers · 11/23 *The Sound of Music* · 11/30 Prettiest Postage · 12/7 Shah's Fiancée · 12/14 Kilauea Iki · 12/21 Ike in Pakistan · 12/28 Leisure

Pictures of the far side of the moon are published • Hawaii becomes the 50th state to enter the Union
Barbie debuts in a zebra-striped swimsuit and stiletto heels • Fidel Castro takes control of Cuba • The St. Lawrence Seaway opens

1960

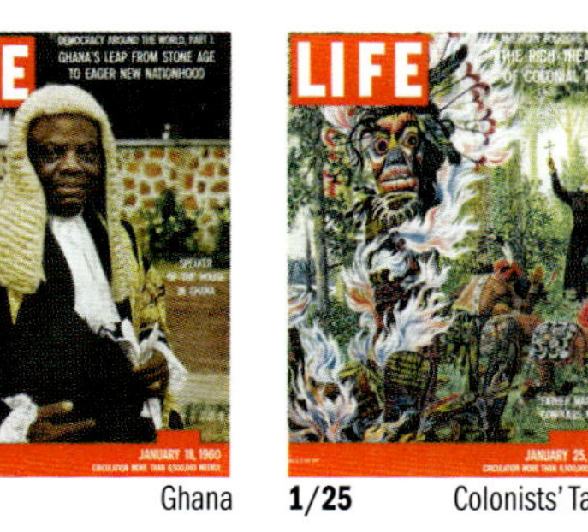
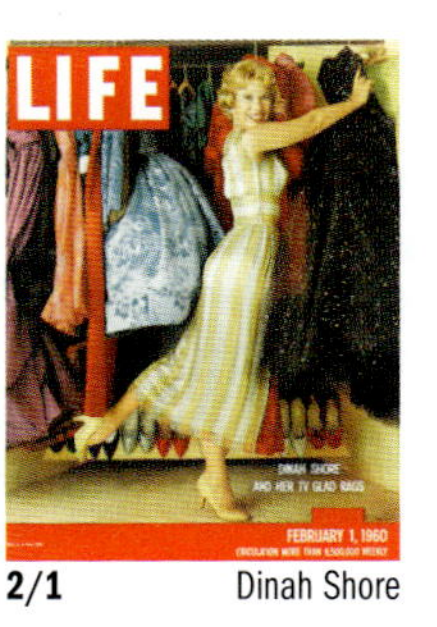
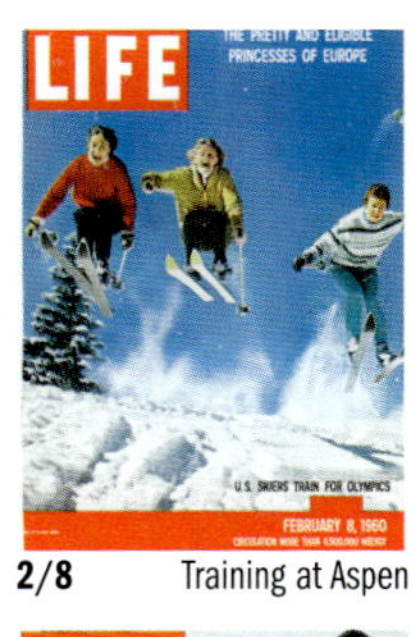
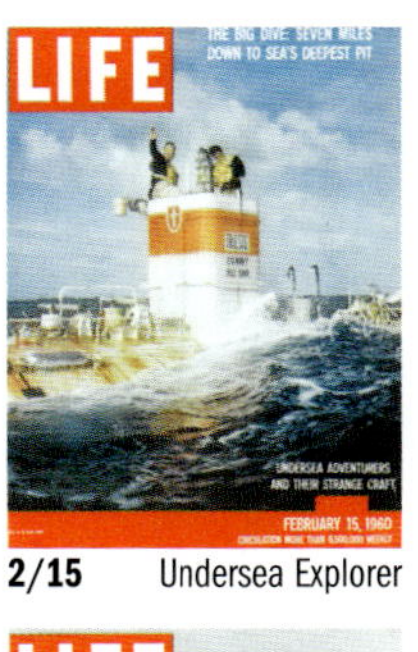

1/11 Dina Merrill · 1/18 Ghana · 1/25 Colonists' Tales · 2/1 Dinah Shore · 2/8 Training at Aspen · 2/15 Undersea Explorer · 2/22 Jane & Henry Fonda

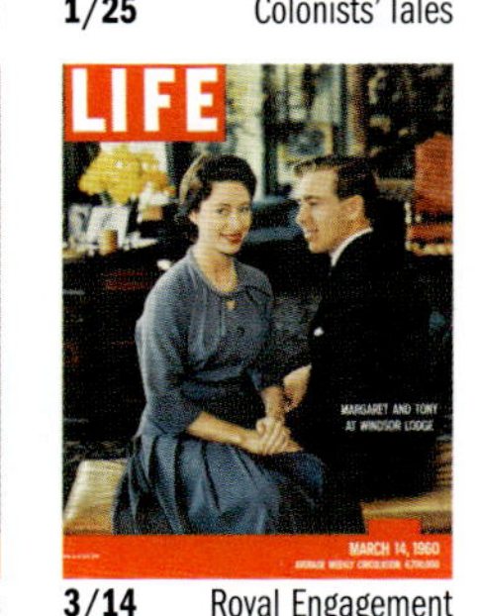
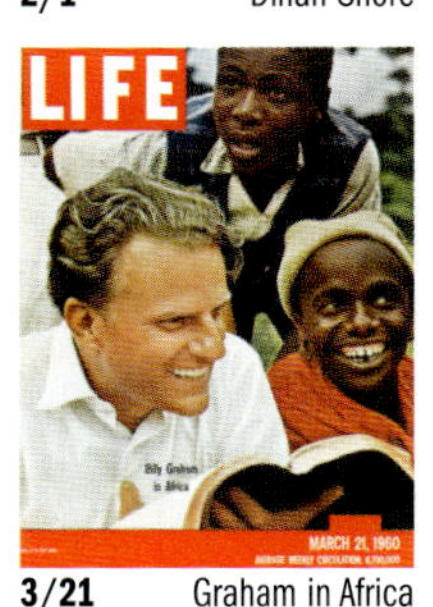
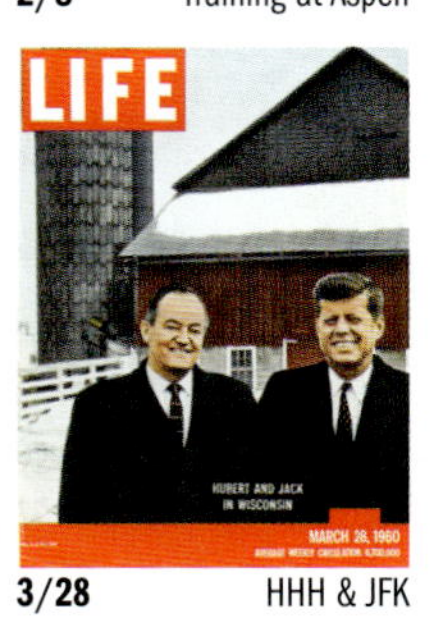
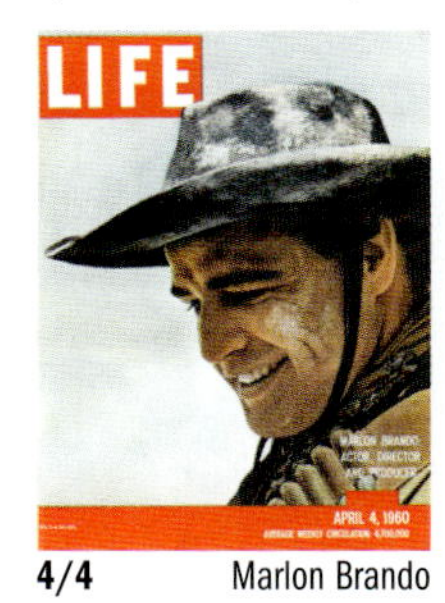
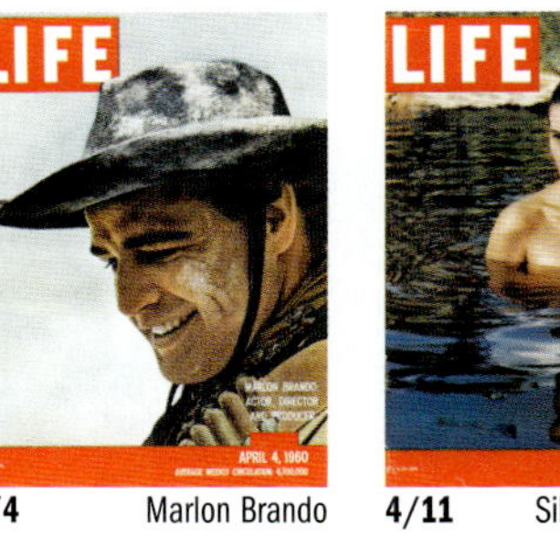

2/29 Winter Olympics · 3/7 Hypnosis · 3/14 Royal Engagement · 3/21 Graham in Africa · 3/28 HHH & JFK · 4/4 Marlon Brando · 4/11 Silvana Mangano

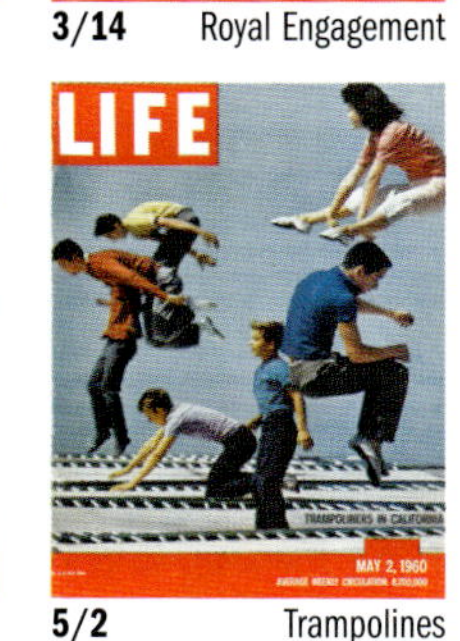
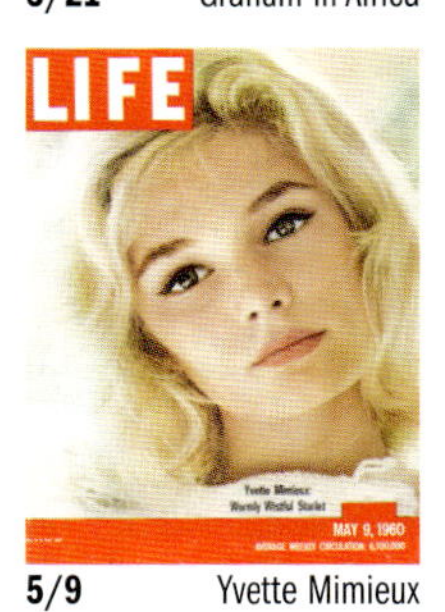
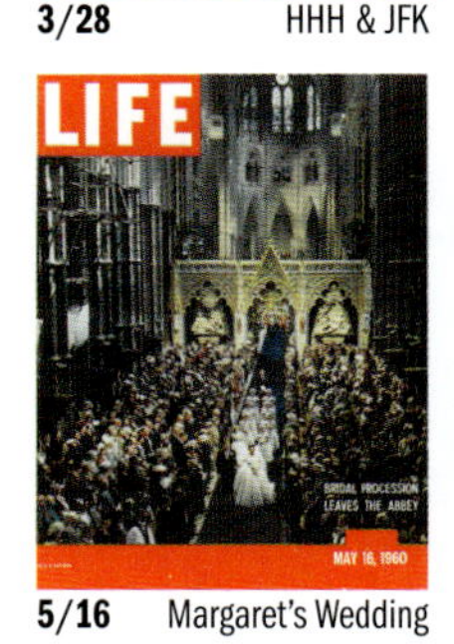
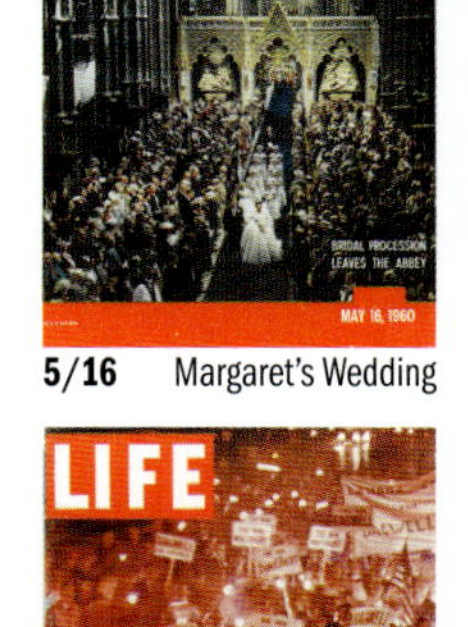
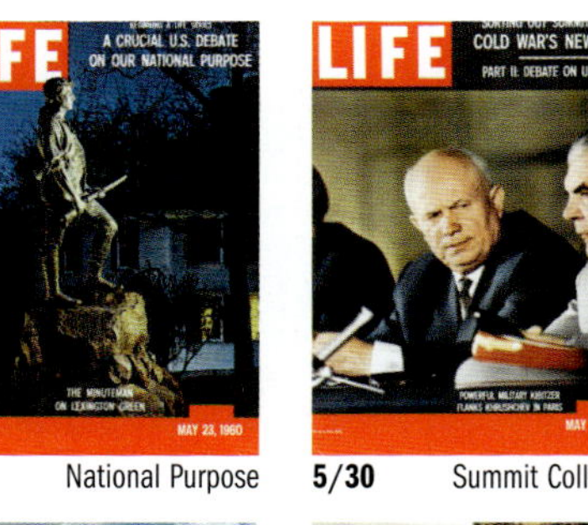

4/18 Elopement · 4/25 Southeast in Spring · 5/2 Trampolines · 5/9 Yvette Mimieux · 5/16 Margaret's Wedding · 5/23 National Purpose · 5/30 Summit Collapse

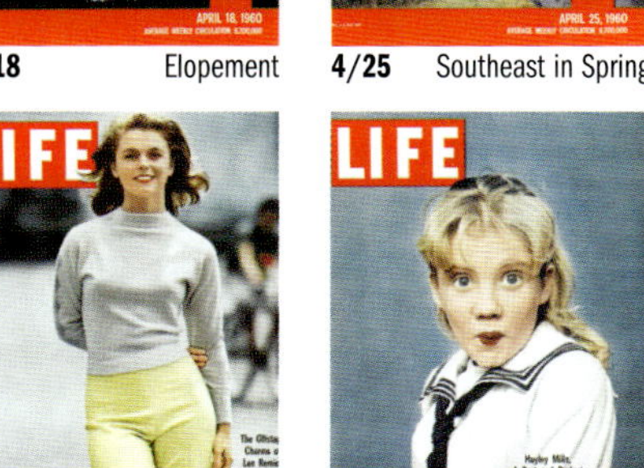
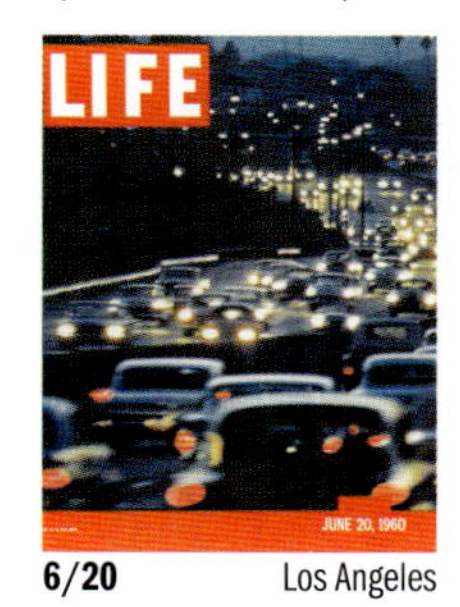
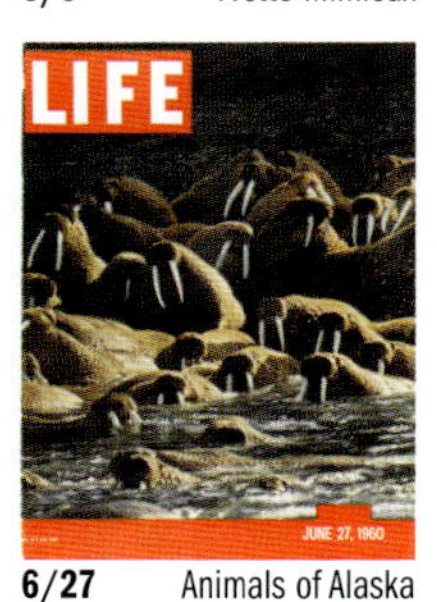
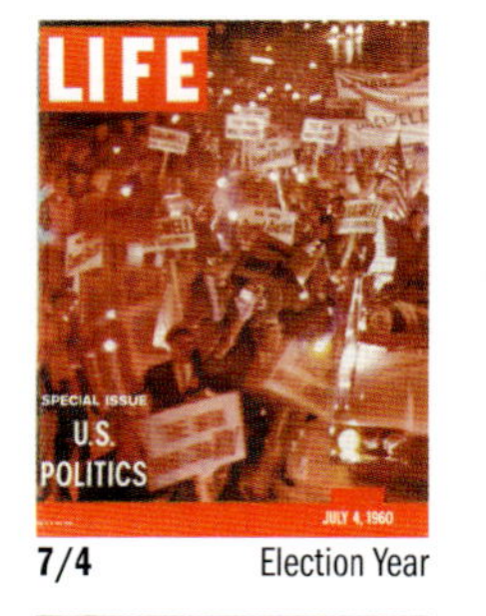
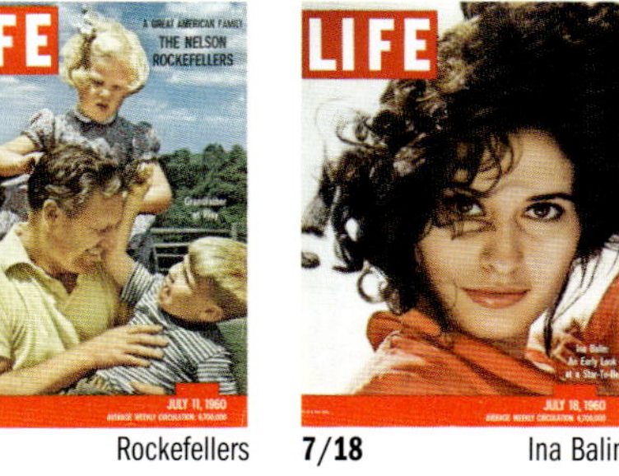

6/6 Lee Remick · 6/13 Hayley Mills · 6/20 Los Angeles · 6/27 Animals of Alaska · 7/4 Election Year · 7/11 Rockefellers · 7/18 Ina Balin

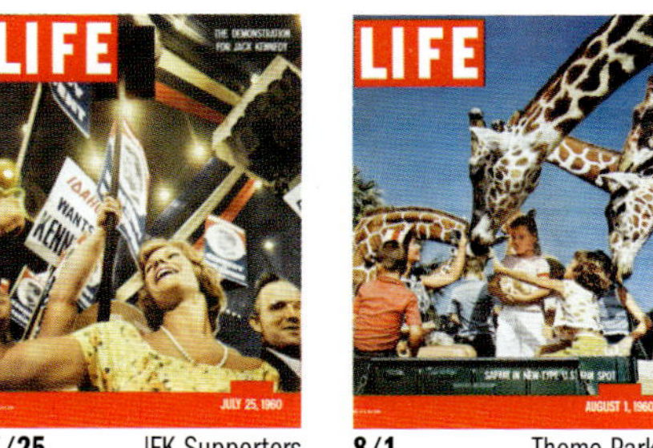
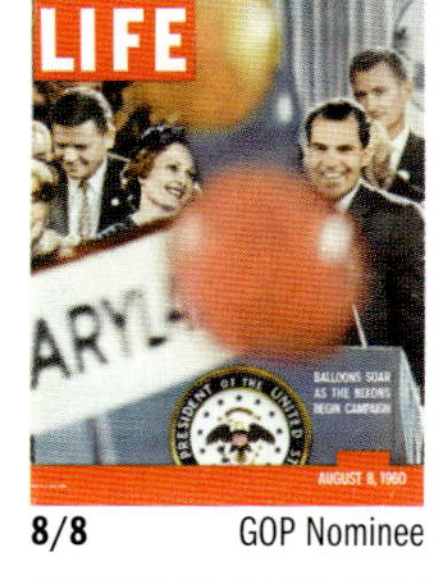
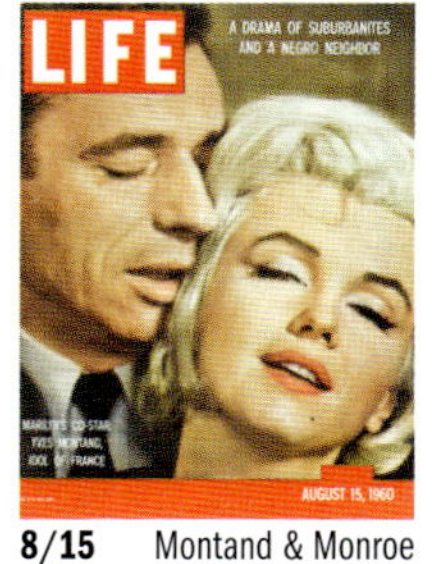
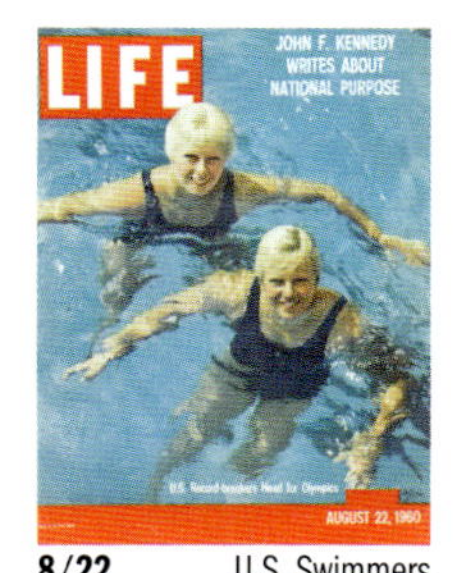
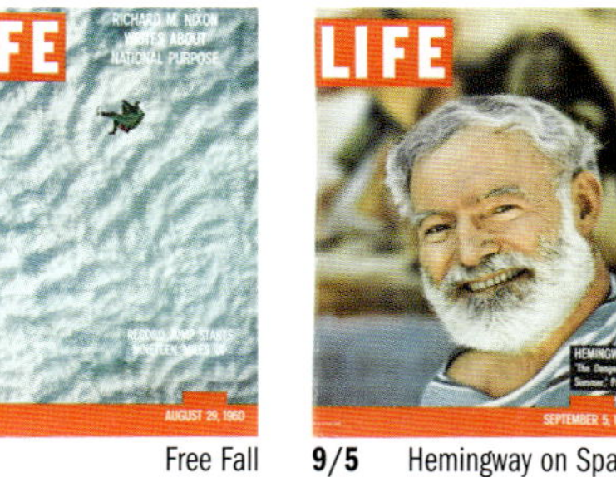

7/25 JFK Supporters · 8/1 Theme Parks · 8/8 GOP Nominee · 8/15 Montand & Monroe · 8/22 U.S. Swimmers · 8/29 Free Fall · 9/5 Hemingway on Spain

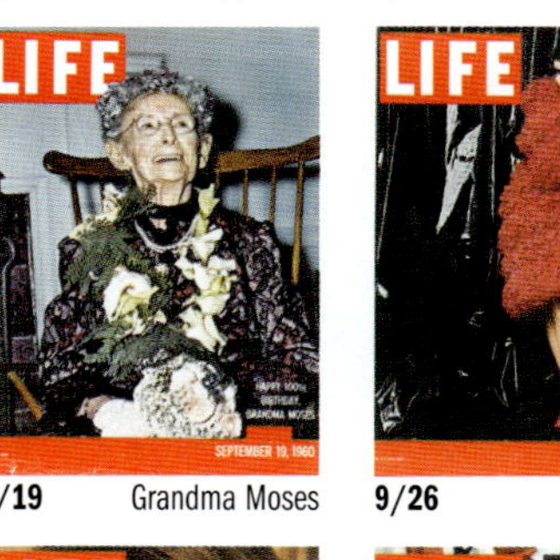
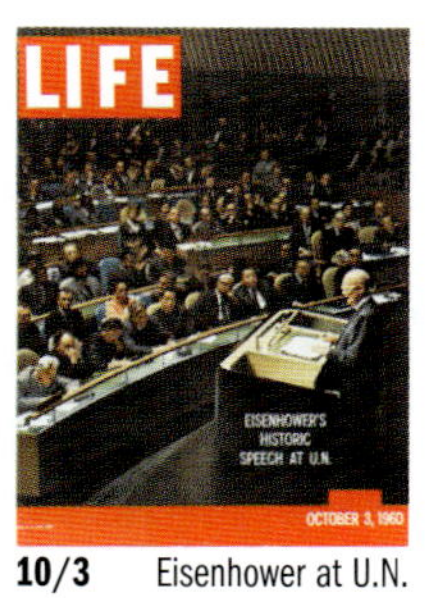
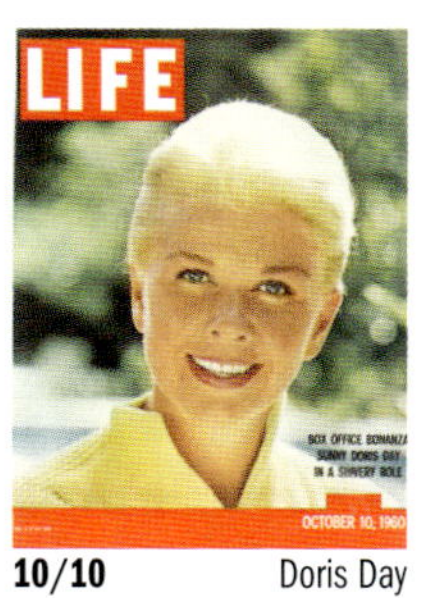
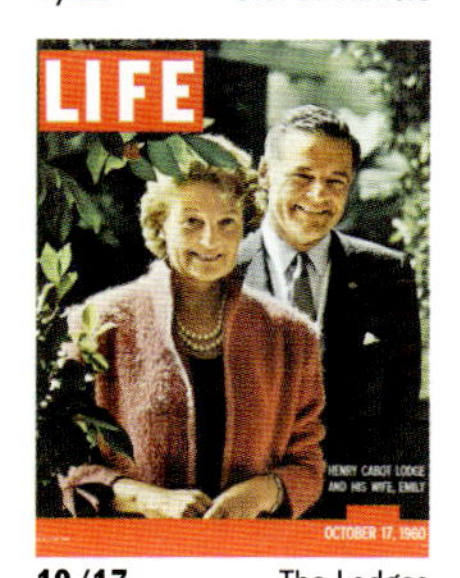
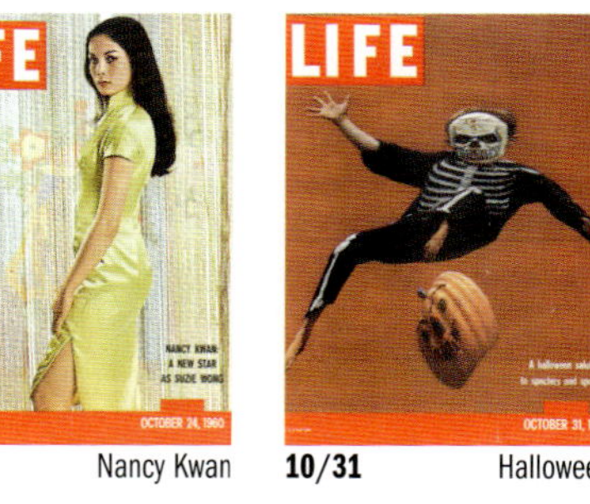

9/12 Gymnasts in Rome · 9/19 Grandma Moses · 9/26 Norell Styles · 10/3 Eisenhower at U.N. · 10/10 Doris Day · 10/17 The Lodges · 10/24 Nancy Kwan · 10/31 Halloween

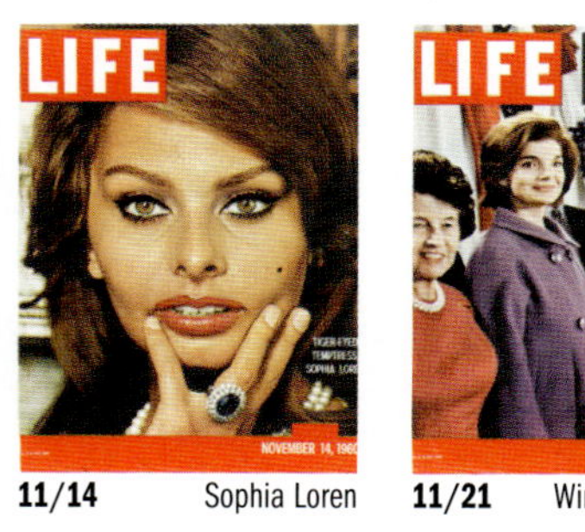
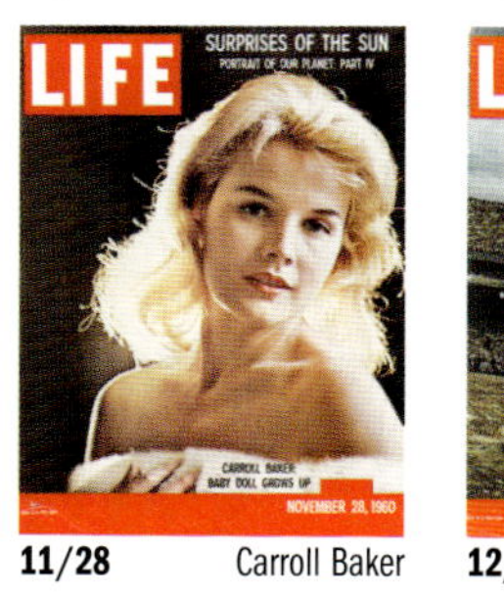
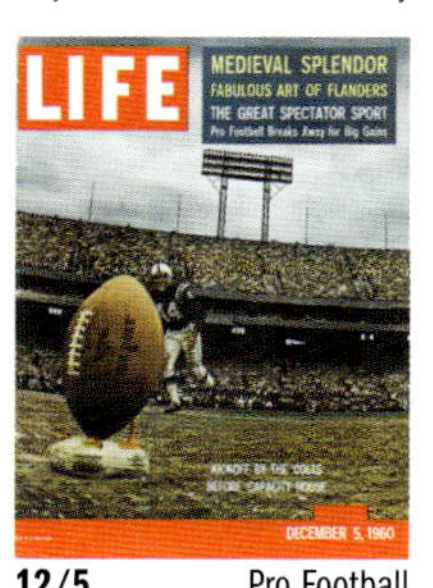
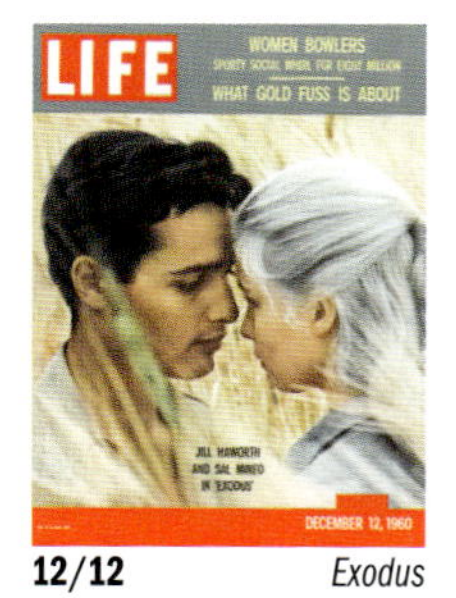
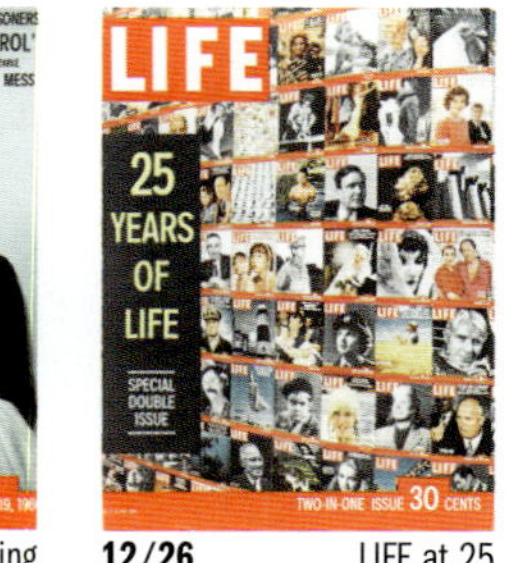

11/7 Planet Earth · 11/14 Sophia Loren · 11/21 Winner Kennedys · 11/28 Carroll Baker · 12/5 Pro Football · 12/12 *Exodus* · 12/19 Christening · 12/26 LIFE at 25

The U.S. population is 179,323,175 • 90 percent of American homes have a TV set • 70 million people watch the Kennedy-Nixon debates
Theodore Maiman creates the laser • Construction begins on the Aswan Dam

1961

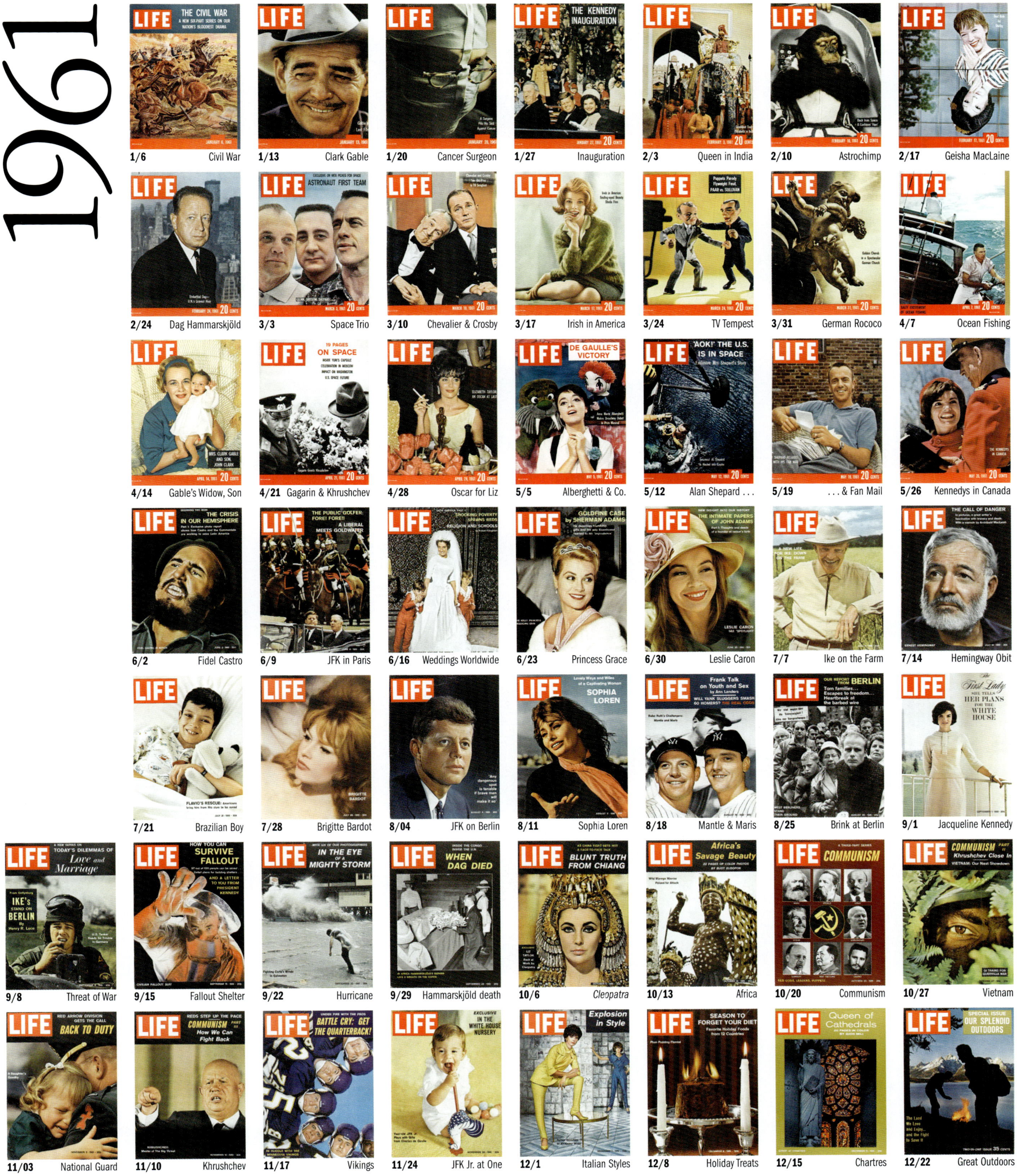

1/6 Civil War
1/13 Clark Gable
1/20 Cancer Surgeon
1/27 Inauguration
2/3 Queen in India
2/10 Astrochimp
2/17 Geisha MacLaine

2/24 Dag Hammarskjöld
3/3 Space Trio
3/10 Chevalier & Crosby
3/17 Irish in America
3/24 TV Tempest
3/31 German Rococo
4/7 Ocean Fishing

4/14 Gable's Widow, Son
4/21 Gagarin & Khrushchev
4/28 Oscar for Liz
5/5 Alberghetti & Co.
5/12 Alan Shepard . . .
5/19 . . . & Fan Mail
5/26 Kennedys in Canada

6/2 Fidel Castro
6/9 JFK in Paris
6/16 Weddings Worldwide
6/23 Princess Grace
6/30 Leslie Caron
7/7 Ike on the Farm
7/14 Hemingway Obit

7/21 Brazilian Boy
7/28 Brigitte Bardot
8/04 JFK on Berlin
8/11 Sophia Loren
8/18 Mantle & Maris
8/25 Brink at Berlin
9/1 Jacqueline Kennedy

9/8 Threat of War
9/15 Fallout Shelter
9/22 Hurricane
9/29 Hammarskjöld death
10/6 *Cleopatra*
10/13 Africa
10/20 Communism
10/27 Vietnam

11/03 National Guard
11/10 Khrushchev
11/17 Vikings
11/24 JFK Jr. at One
12/1 Italian Styles
12/8 Holiday Treats
12/15 Chartres
12/22 Great Outdoors

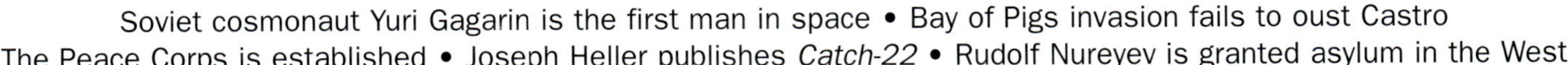

Soviet cosmonaut Yuri Gagarin is the first man in space • Bay of Pigs invasion fails to oust Castro
The Peace Corps is established • Joseph Heller publishes *Catch-22* • Rudolf Nureyev is granted asylum in the West

1962

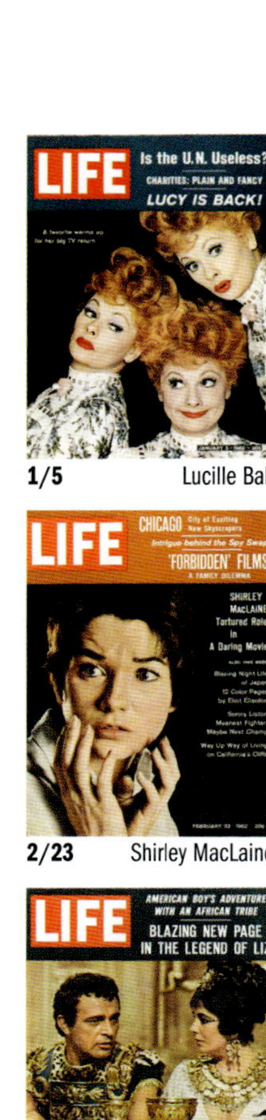
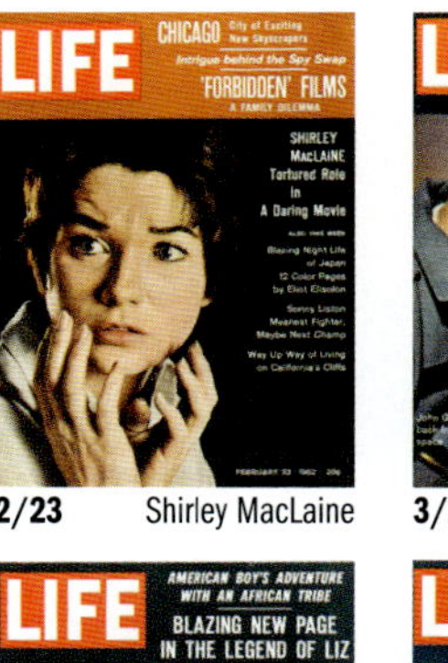
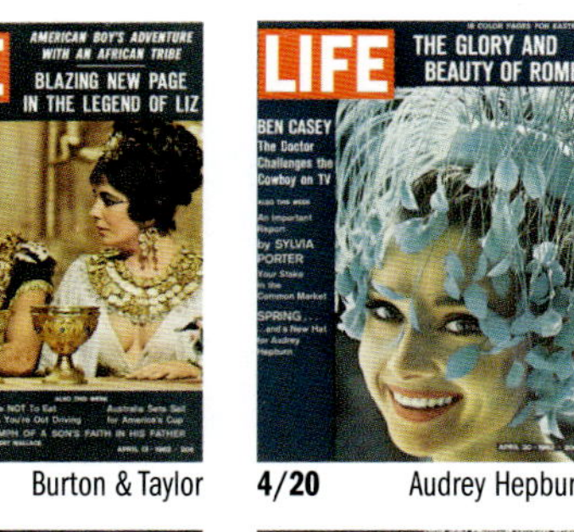
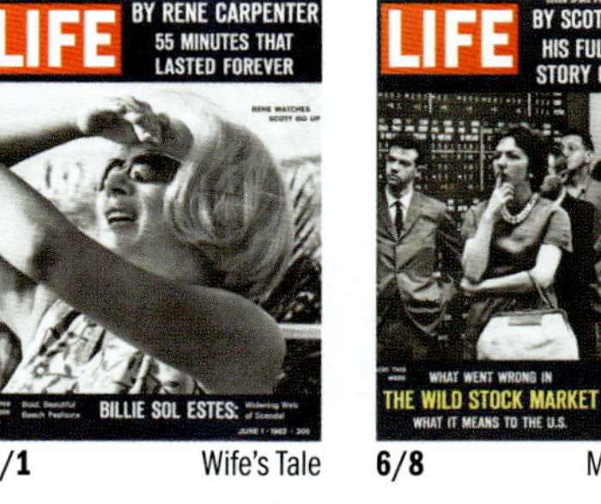
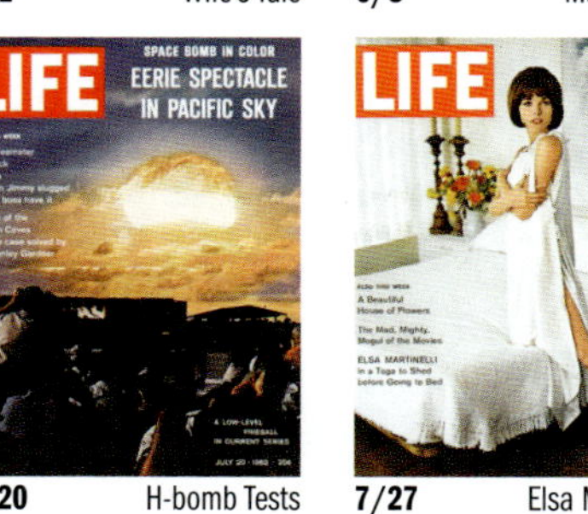
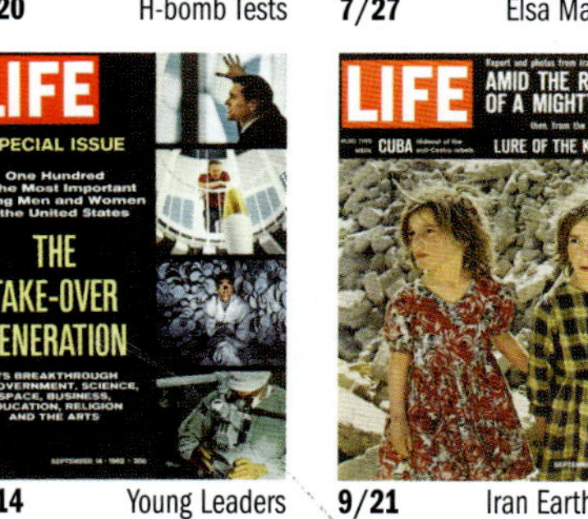
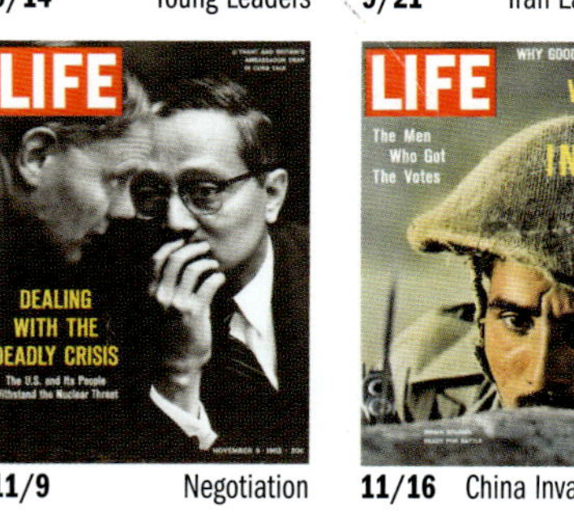
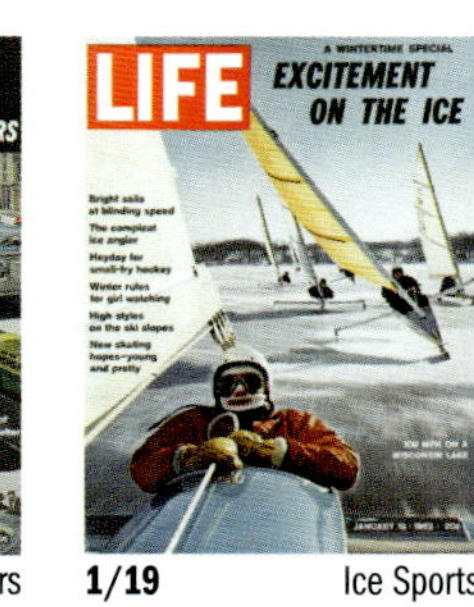
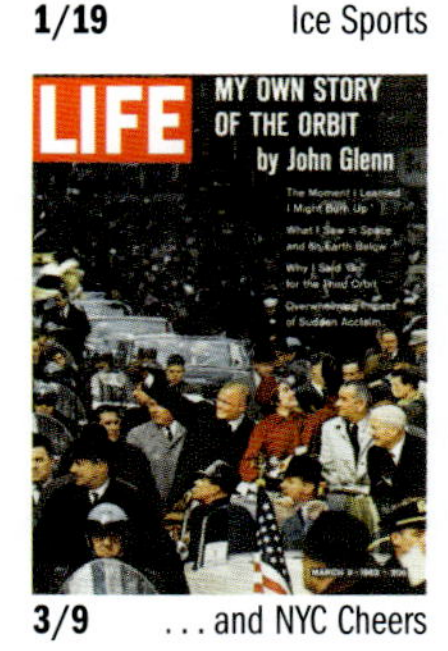
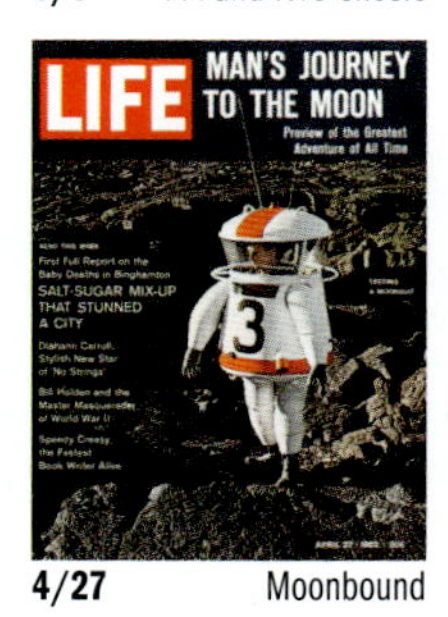
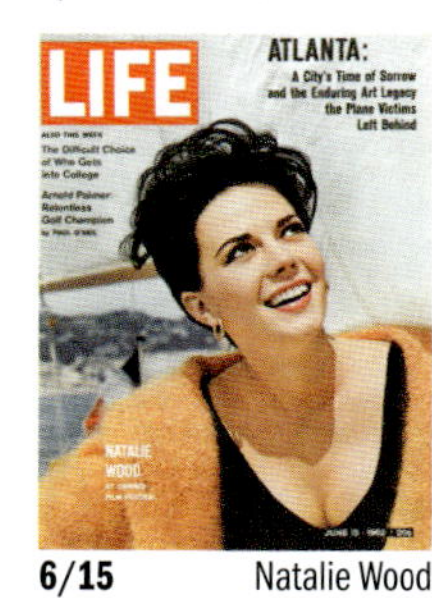
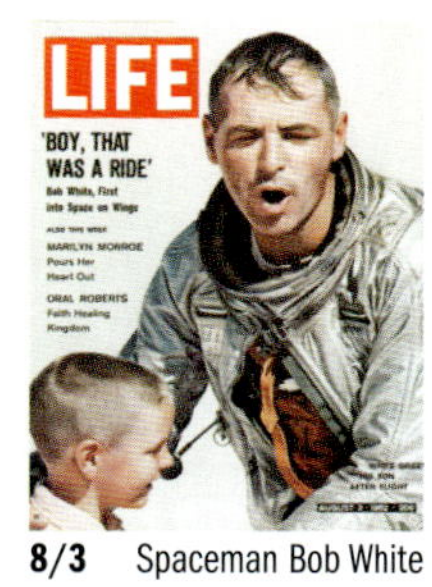
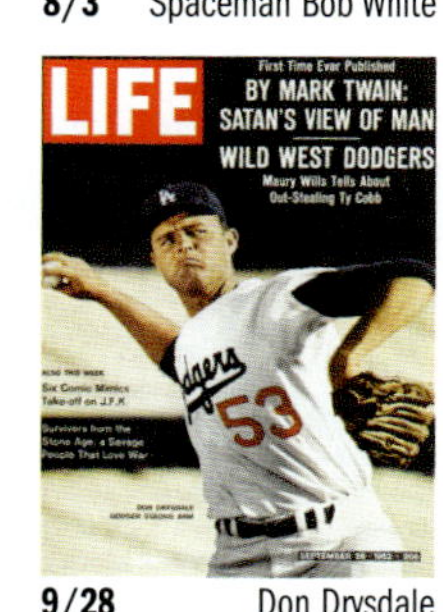
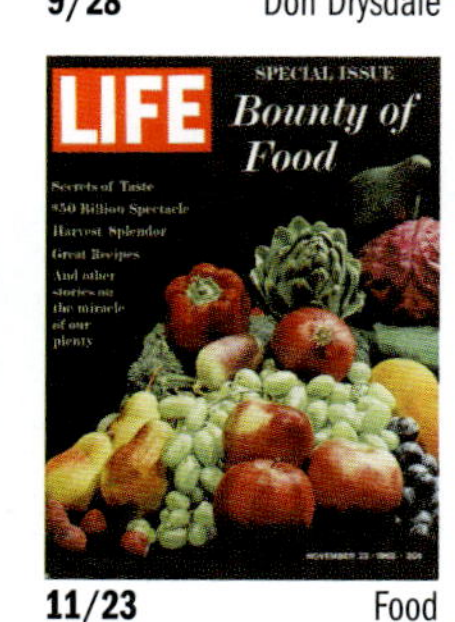
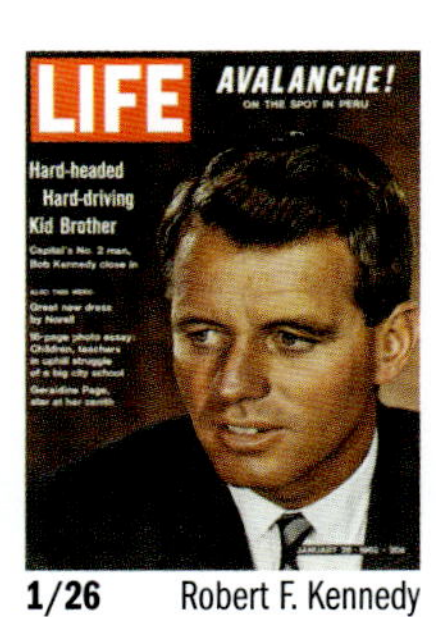
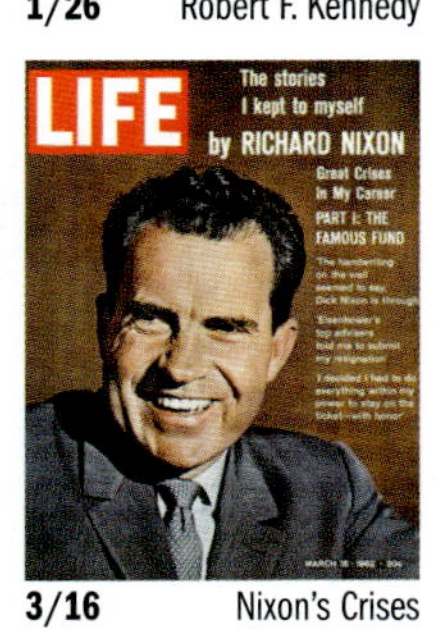
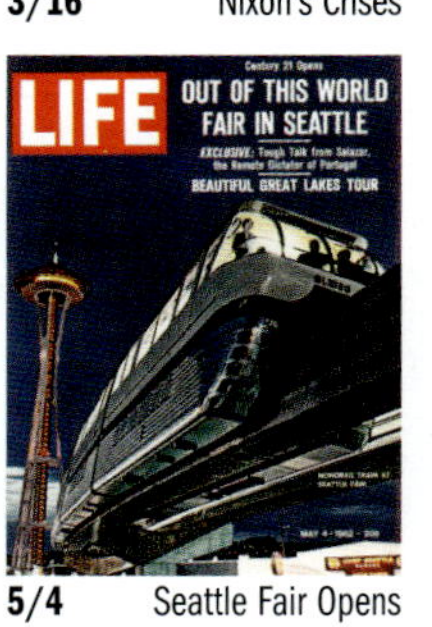
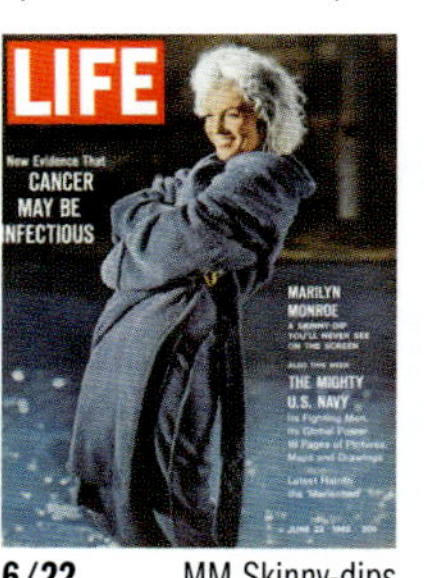
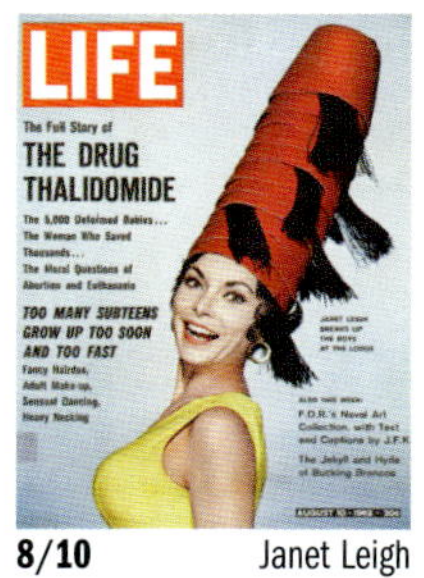
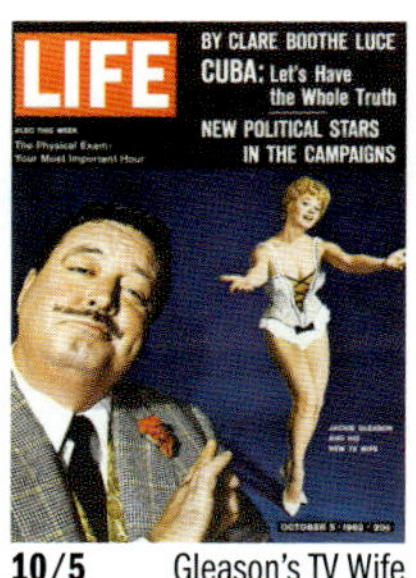
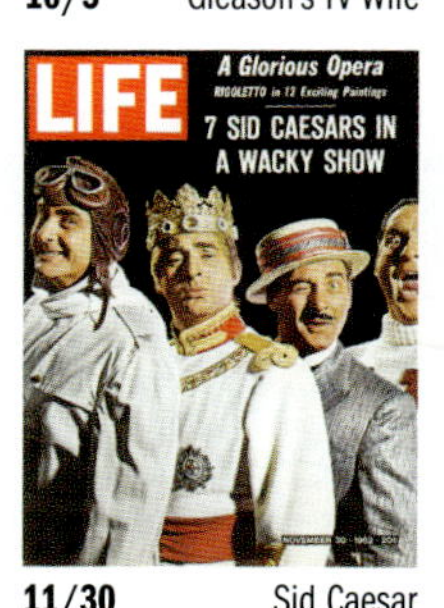
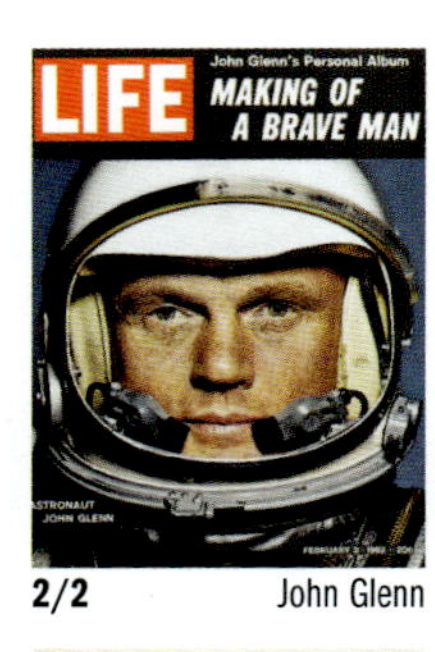
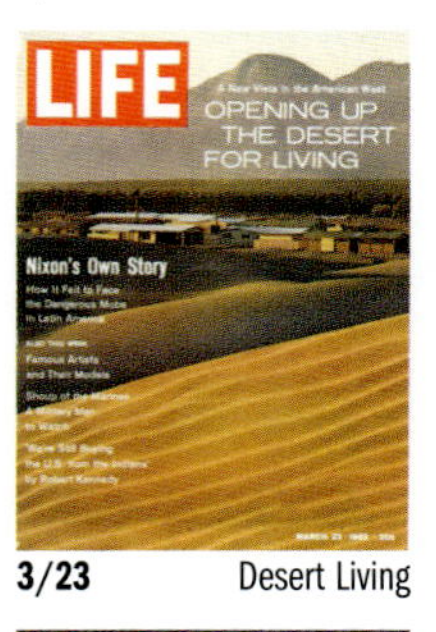
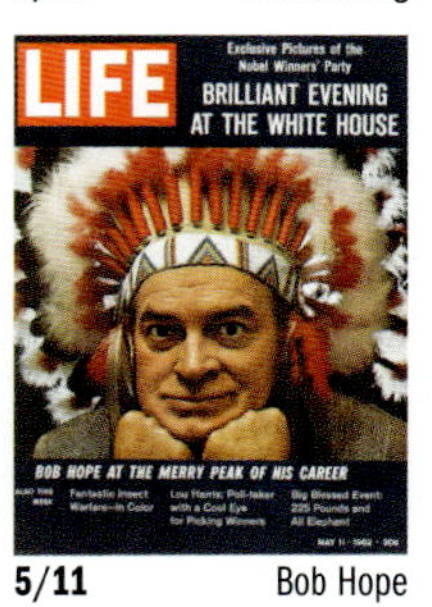
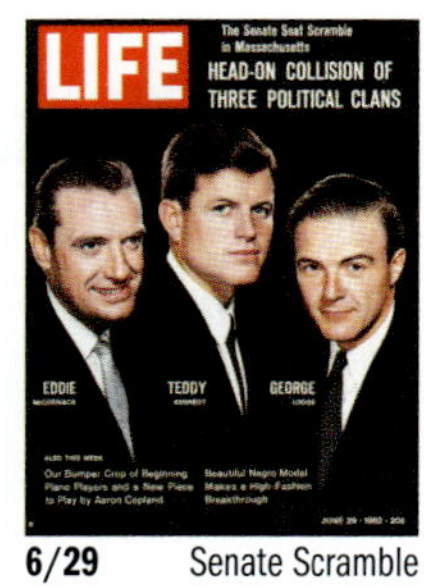
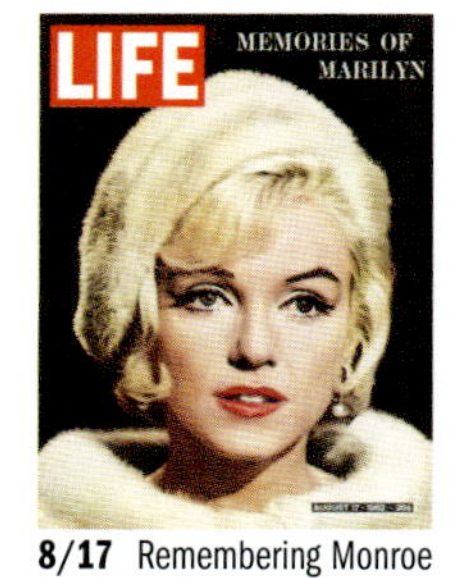
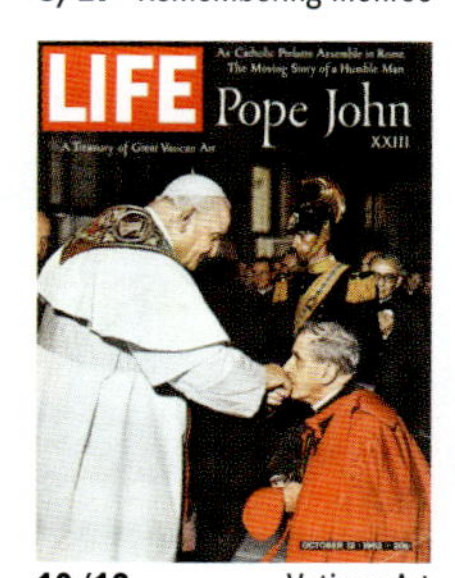
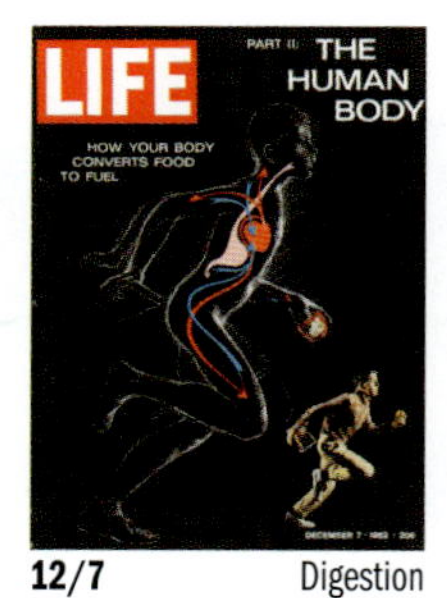
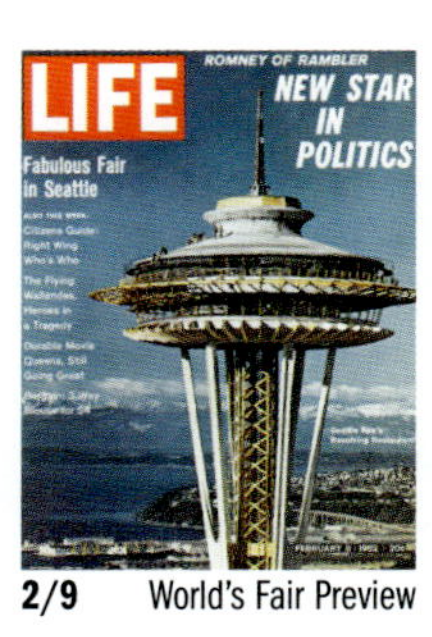
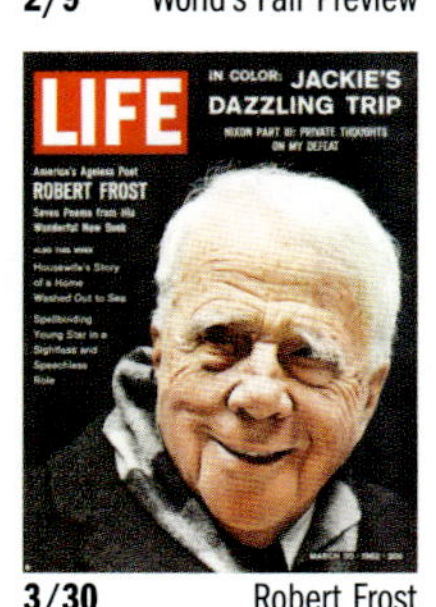
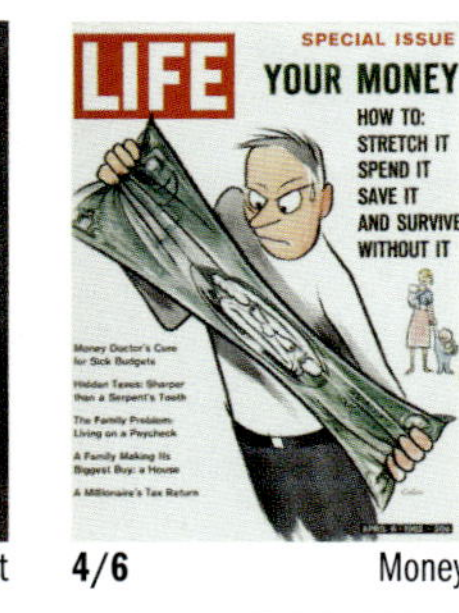
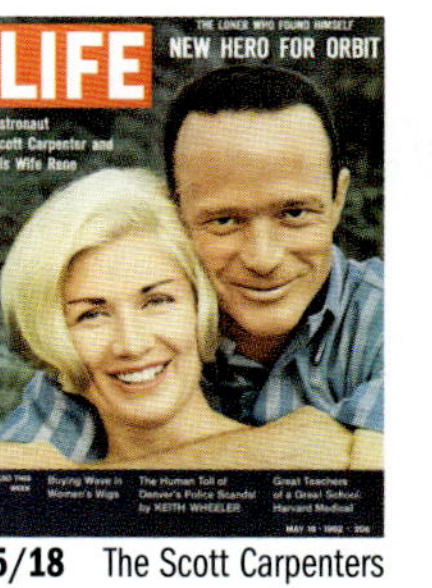
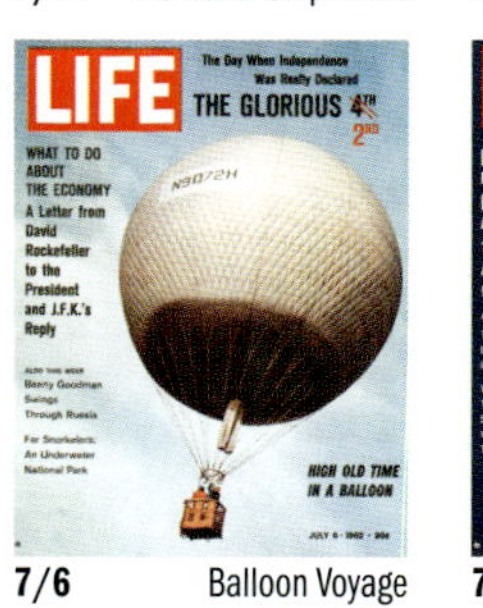
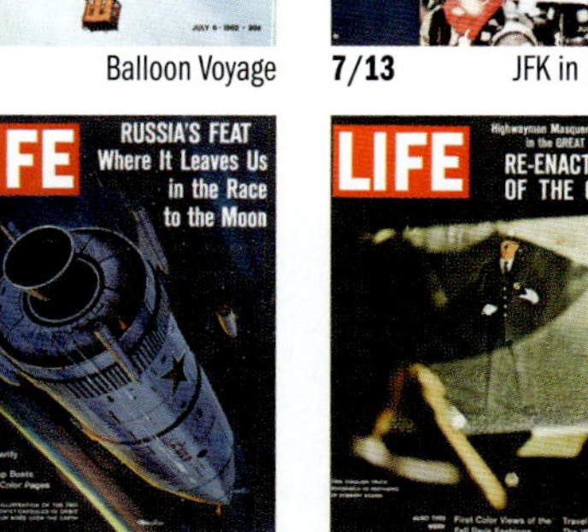
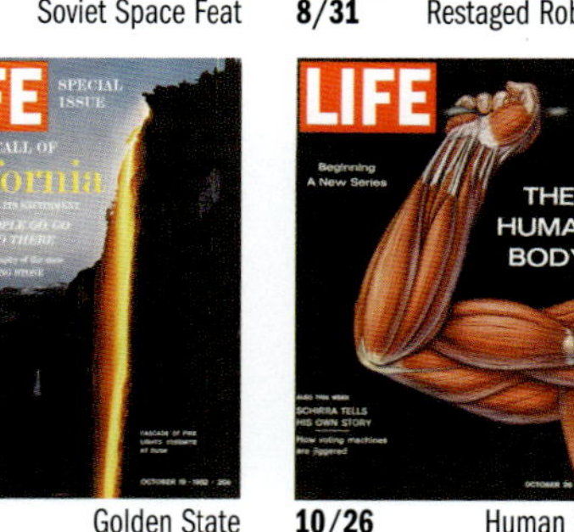
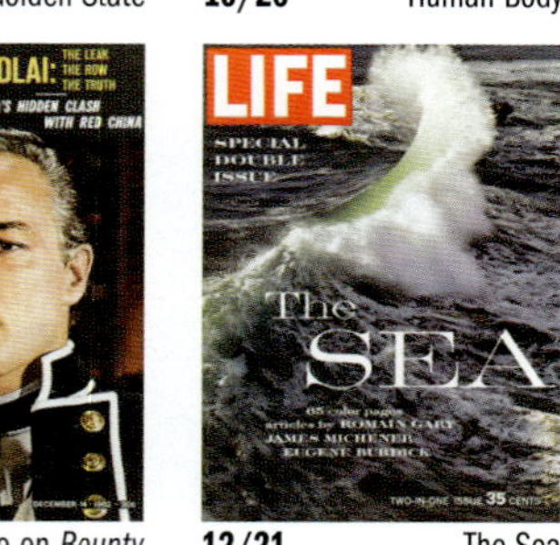
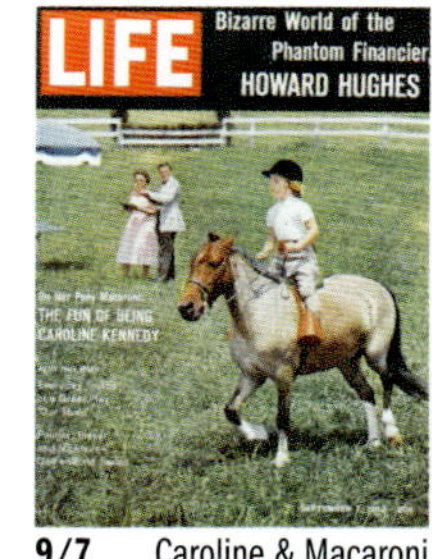
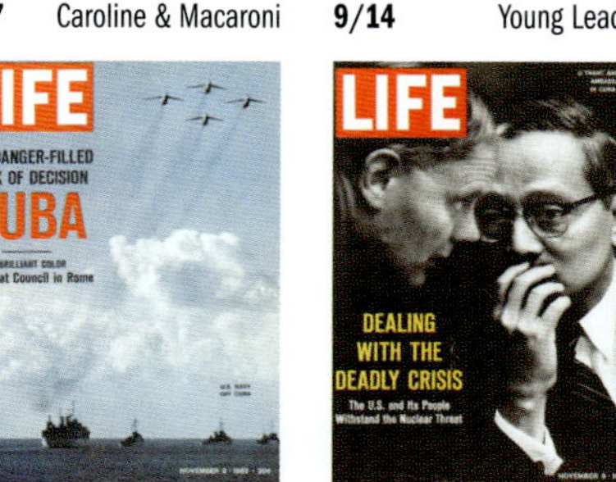
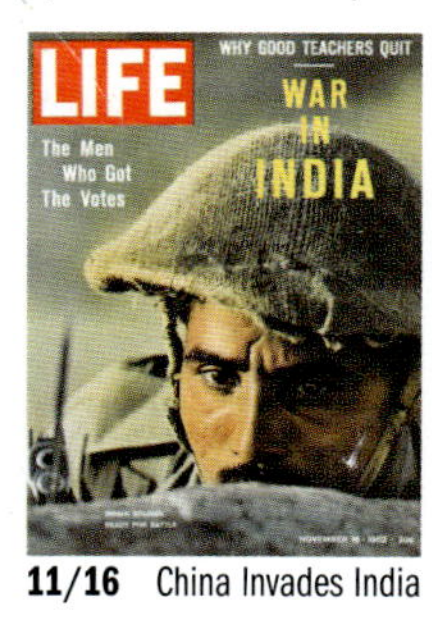
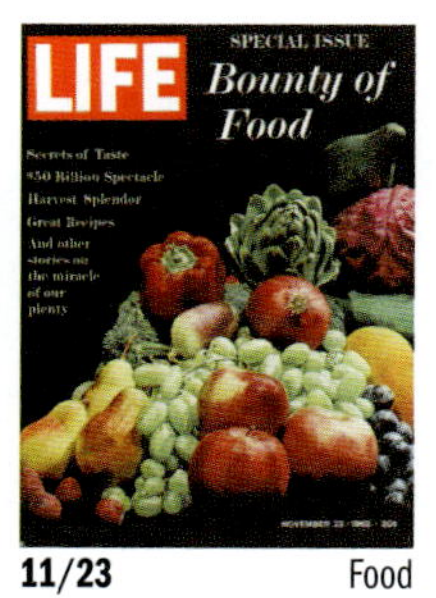
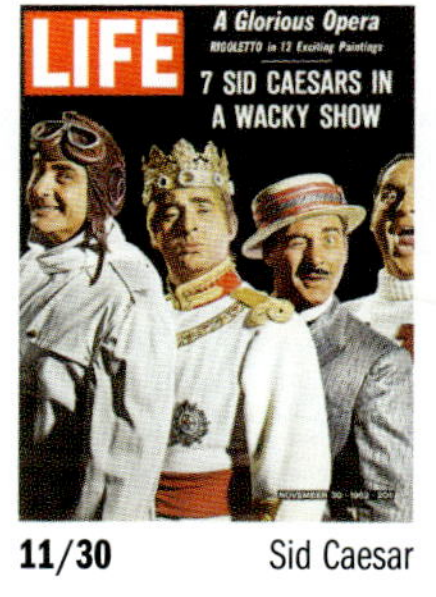

	1/5 Lucille Ball	1/12 Mass Shelters	1/19 Ice Sports	1/26 Robert F. Kennedy	2/2 John Glenn	2/9 World's Fair Preview	2/16 Rock Hudson
	2/23 Shirley MacLaine	3/2 Glenn Returns . . .	3/9 . . . and NYC Cheers	3/16 Nixon's Crises	3/23 Desert Living	3/30 Robert Frost	4/6 Money
	4/13 Burton & Taylor	4/20 Audrey Hepburn	4/27 Moonbound	5/4 Seattle Fair Opens	5/11 Bob Hope	5/18 The Scott Carpenters	5/25 Juan Carlos Weds
	6/1 Wife's Tale	6/8 Market Jolt	6/15 Natalie Wood	6/22 MM Skinny-dips	6/29 Senate Scramble	7/6 Balloon Voyage	7/13 JFK in Mexico
	7/20 H-bomb Tests	7/27 Elsa Martinelli	8/3 Spaceman Bob White	8/10 Janet Leigh	8/17 Remembering Monroe	8/24 Soviet Space Feat	8/31 Restaged Robbery
9/7 Caroline & Macaroni	9/14 Young Leaders	9/21 Iran Earthquake	9/28 Don Drysdale	10/5 Gleason's TV Wife	10/12 Vatican Art	10/19 Golden State	10/26 Human Body
11/2 Missile Crisis	11/9 Negotiation	11/16 China Invades India	11/23 Food	11/30 Sid Caesar	12/7 Digestion	12/14 Brando on *Bounty*	12/21 The Sea

Rachel Carson's *Silent Spring* is published • John Glenn becomes the first American to orbit Earth
The inaugural Wal-Mart store opens in Rogers, Ark. • James Meredith is the first black student at the University of Mississippi
Walter Cronkite becomes the anchor of *CBS Evening News*

1963

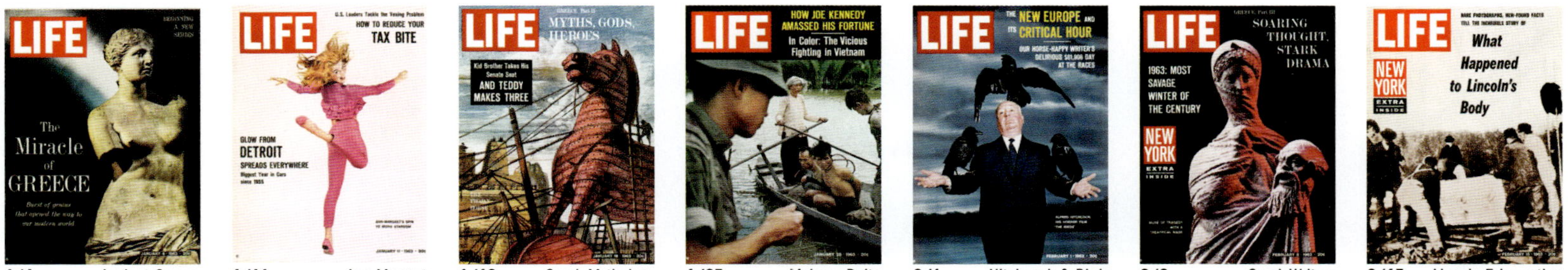

1/4 Ancient Greece

1/11 Ann-Margret

1/18 Greek Mythology

1/25 Mekong Delta

2/1 Hitchcock & *Birds*

2/8 Greek Writers

2/15 Lincoln Exhumation

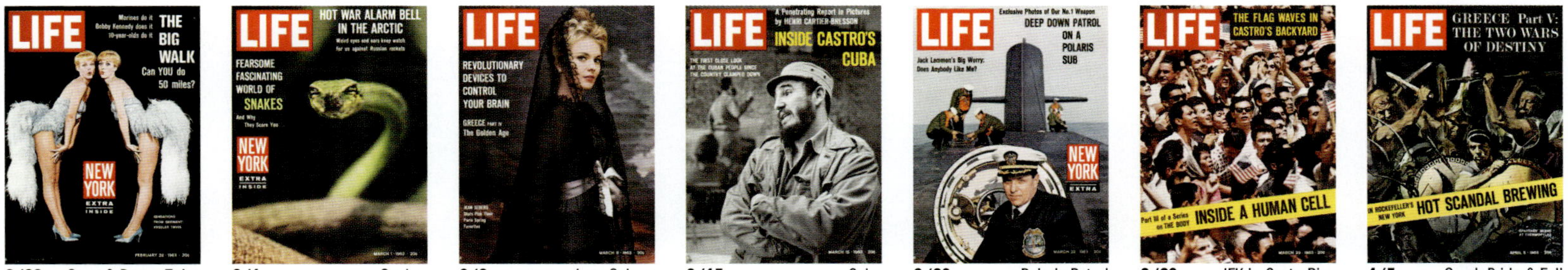

2/22 Song & Dance Twins

3/1 Snakes

3/8 Jean Seberg

3/15 Cuba

3/22 Polaris Patrol

3/29 JFK in Costa Rica

4/5 Greek Pride & Fall

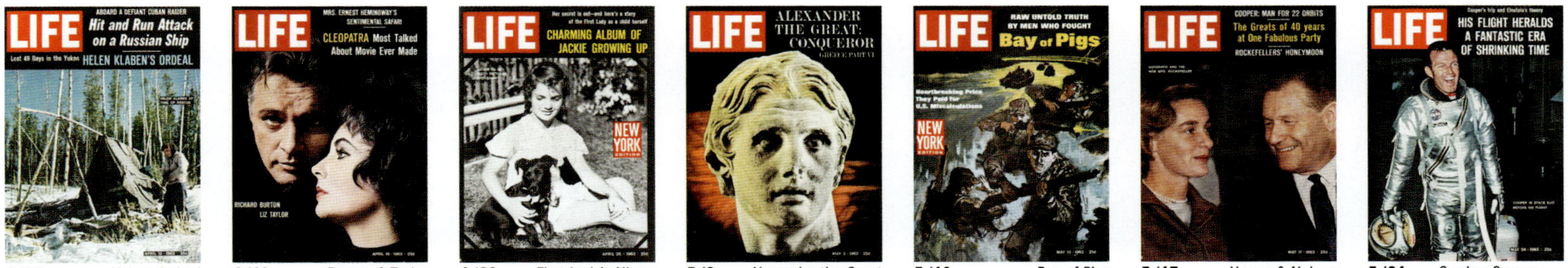

4/12 Yukon Ordeal

4/19 Burton & Taylor

4/26 First Lady's Album

5/3 Alexander the Great

5/10 Bay of Pigs

5/17 Happy & Nelson

5/24 Gordon Cooper . . .

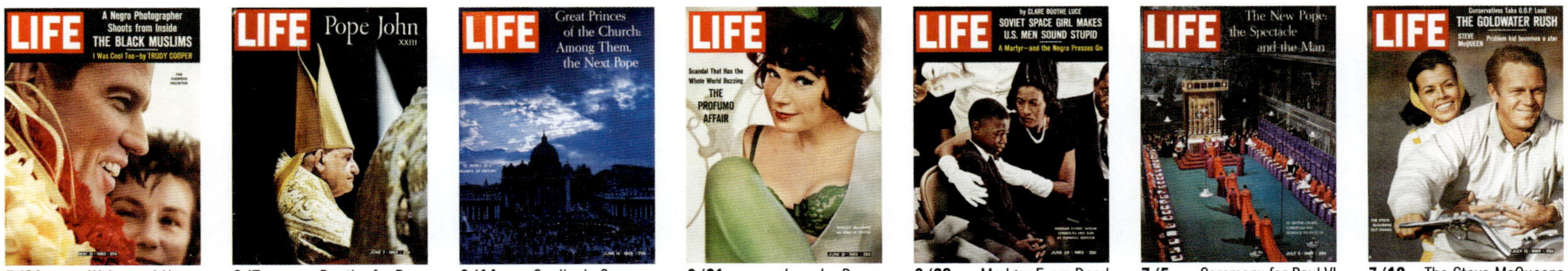

5/31 . . . Welcomed Home

6/7 Death of a Pope

6/14 Cardinals Convene

6/21 *Irma La Douce*

6/28 Medgar Evers Dead

7/5 Ceremony for Paul VI

7/12 The Steve McQueens

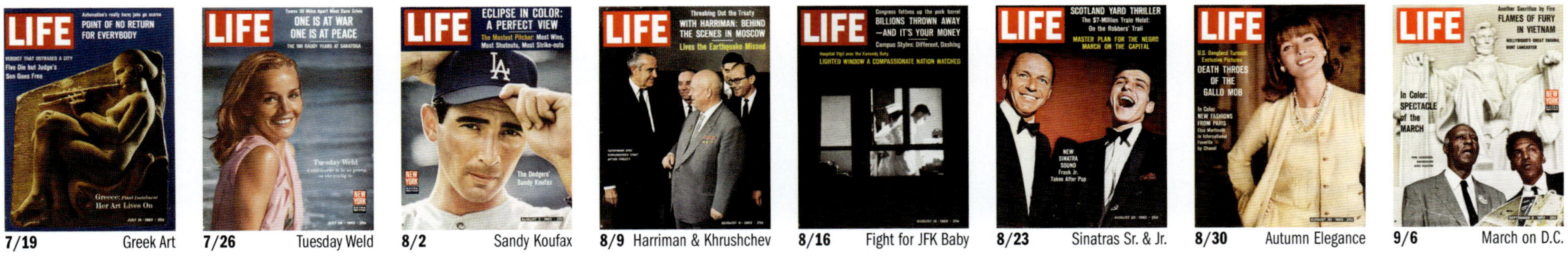

7/19 Greek Art

7/26 Tuesday Weld

8/2 Sandy Koufax

8/9 Harriman & Khrushchev

8/16 Fight for JFK Baby

8/23 Sinatras Sr. & Jr.

8/30 Autumn Elegance

9/6 March on D.C.

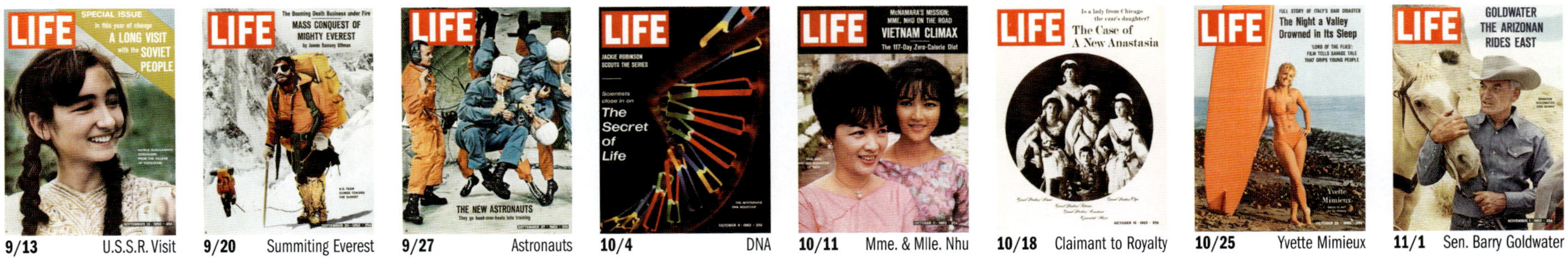

9/13 U.S.S.R. Visit

9/20 Summiting Everest

9/27 Astronauts

10/4 DNA

10/11 Mme. & Mlle. Nhu

10/18 Claimant to Royalty

10/25 Yvette Mimieux

11/1 Sen. Barry Goldwater

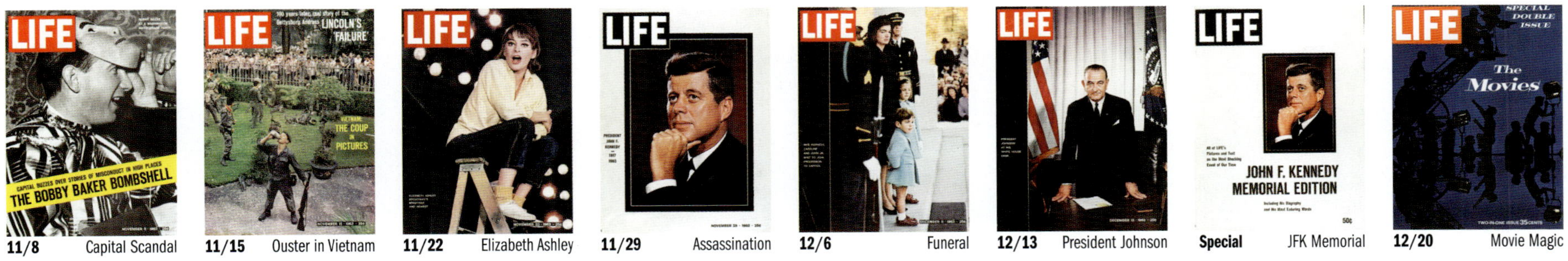

11/8 Capital Scandal

11/15 Ouster in Vietnam

11/22 Elizabeth Ashley

11/29 Assassination

12/6 Funeral

12/13 President Johnson

Special JFK Memorial

12/20 Movie Magic

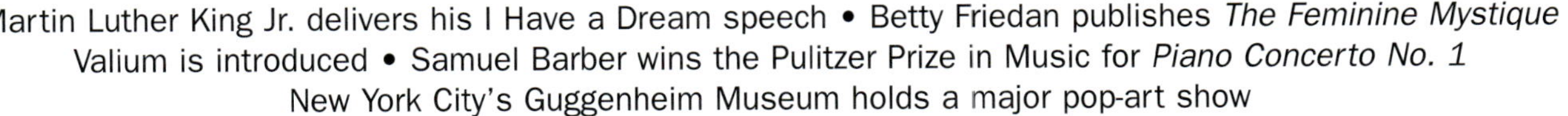

Martin Luther King Jr. delivers his I Have a Dream speech • Betty Friedan publishes *The Feminine Mystique*
Valium is introduced • Samuel Barber wins the Pulitzer Prize in Music for *Piano Concerto No. 1*
New York City's Guggenheim Museum holds a major pop-art show

1964

1/3 Disabled Liner
1/10 MacArthur's Memoirs
1/17 Pope in Holy Land
1/24 Riots in Panama
1/31 Geraldine Chaplin
2/7 Tanganyika Trouble
2/14 Innsbruck Olympics

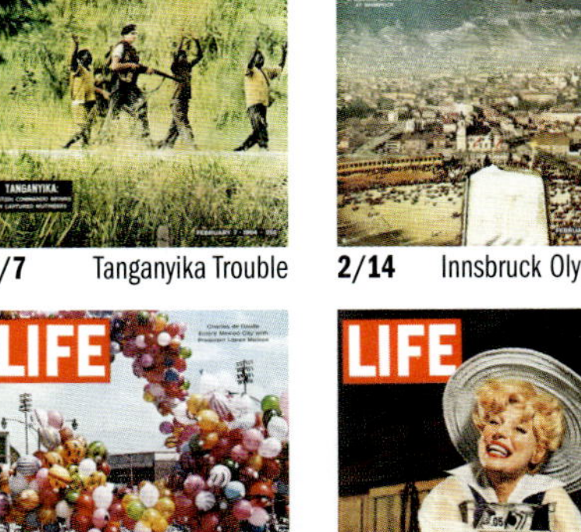

2/21 Lee Harvey Oswald
2/28 Cyprus
3/6 Cassius Clay
3/13 World War I
3/20 Lodge in Vietnam
3/27 De Gaulle in Mexico
4/3 Channing as Dolly

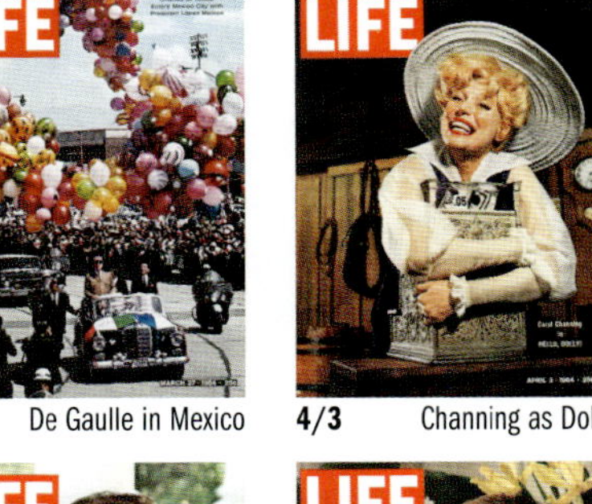

4/10 Alaska Quake
4/17 MacArthur Memorial
4/24 Shakespeare Salute
5/1 N.Y. World's Fair
5/8 Which VP for LBJ?
5/15 Luci Baines Johnson
5/22 Barbra Streisand

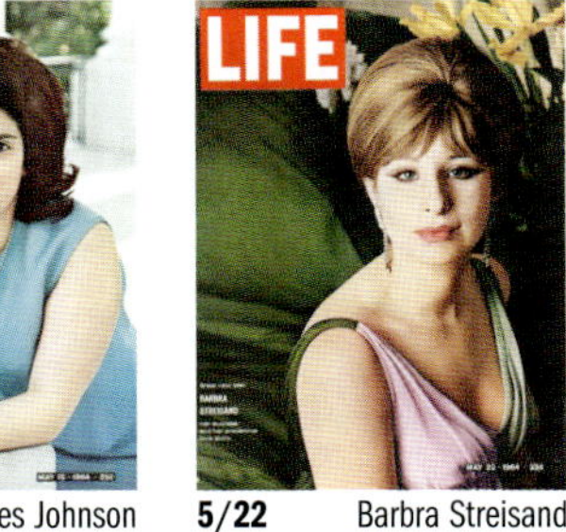

5/29 JFK Exhibit
6/5 Nehru's Funeral
6/12 Patrol in Vietnam
6/19 LBJ's Beagles
6/26 The Scrantons of Pa.
7/3 RFK & Kennedy Kids
7/10 Oswald's Diary

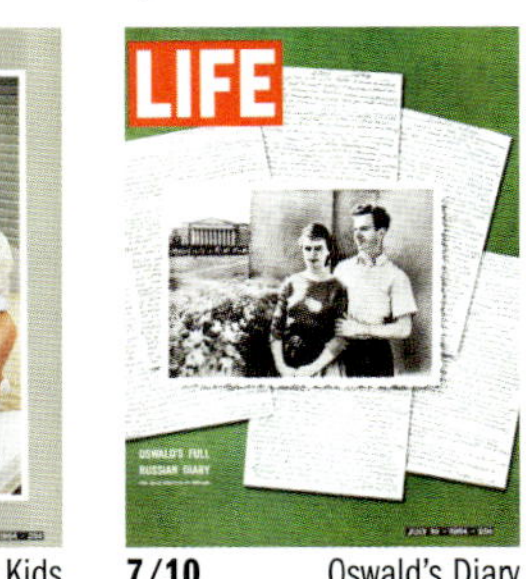

7/17 Carroll Baker
7/24 GOP Nominee & Wife
7/31 Olympic Diver
8/7 Essay on Monroe
8/14 President Johnson
8/21 Vietnam Border
8/28 Beatles' U.S. Return
9/4 LBJ's Convention

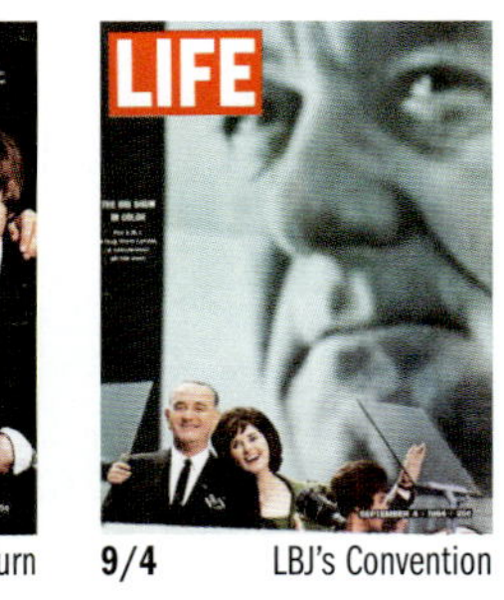

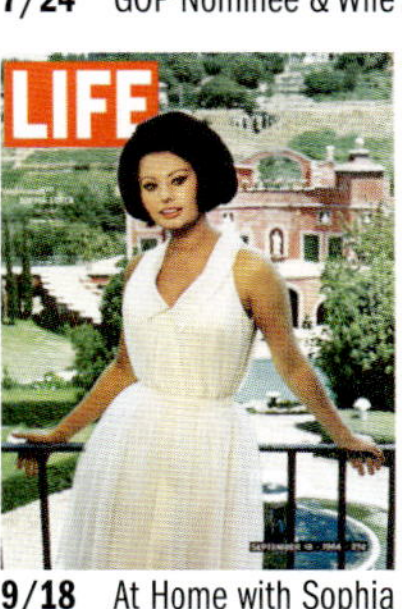
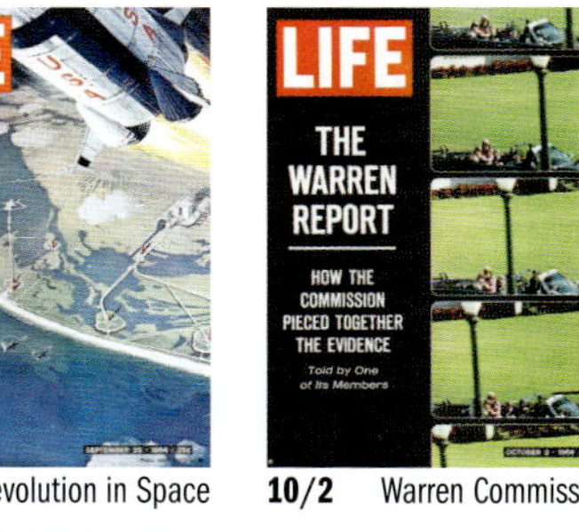
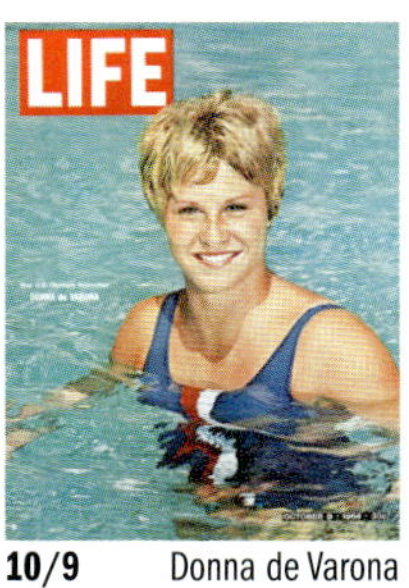
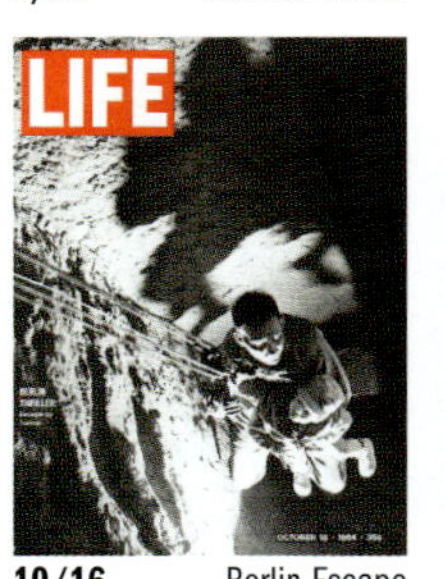
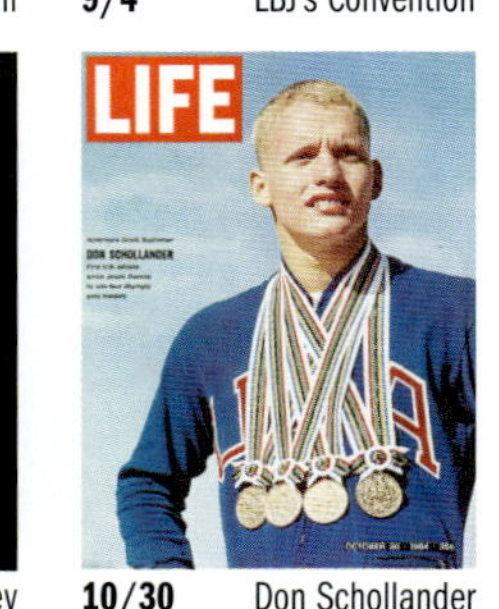

9/11 Japan
9/18 At Home with Sophia
9/25 Revolution in Space
10/2 Warren Commission
10/9 Donna de Varona
10/16 Berlin Escape
10/23 Leonid Brezhnev
10/30 Don Schollander

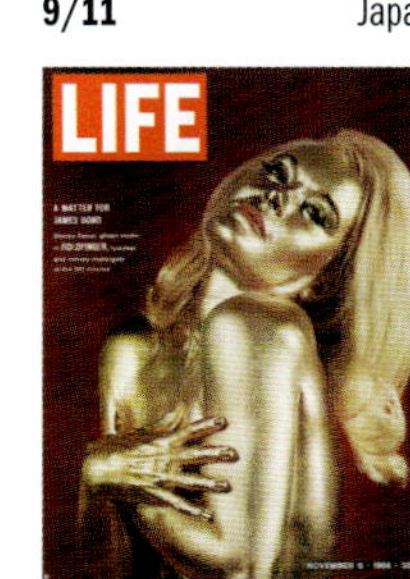
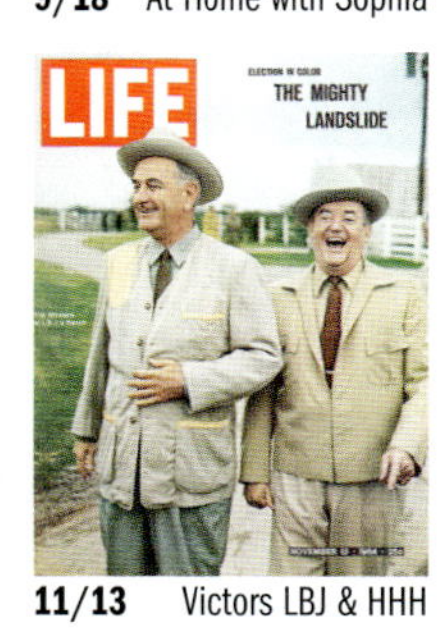
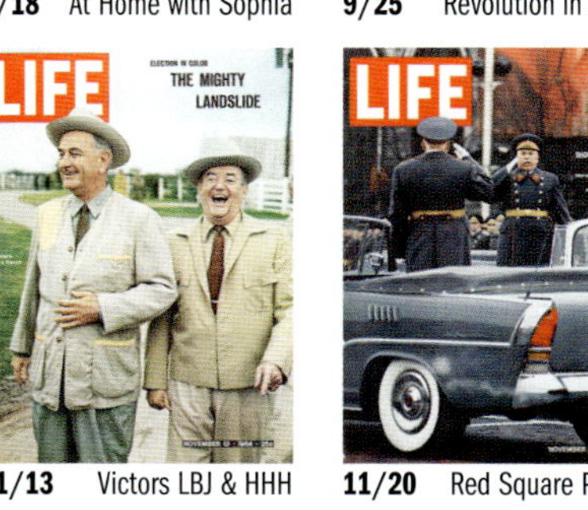
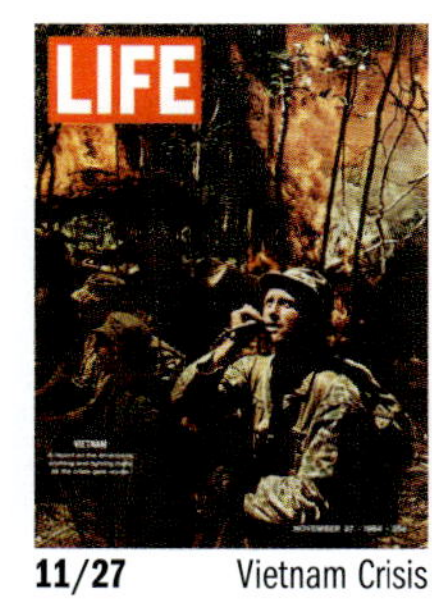
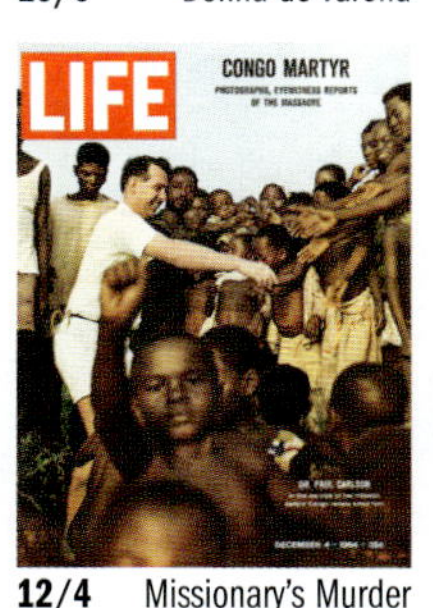
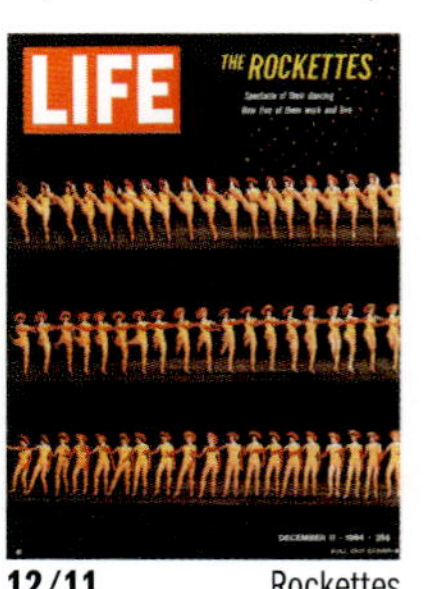
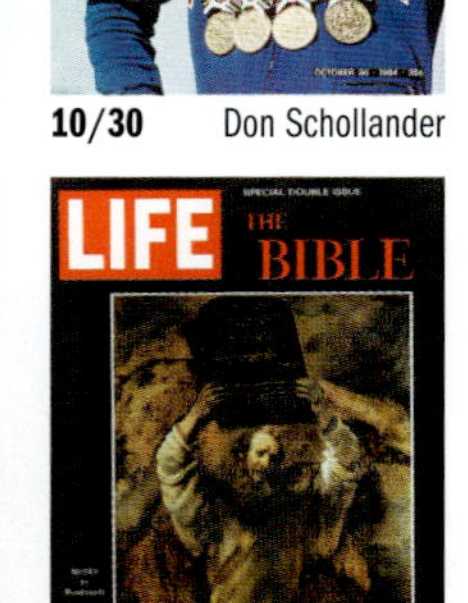

11/6 *Goldfinger*
11/13 Victors LBJ & HHH
11/20 Red Square Parade
11/27 Vietnam Crisis
12/4 Missionary's Murder
12/11 Rockettes
12/18 Liz on Liz
12/25 The Bible

Muhammad Ali knocks out Sonny Liston and becomes heavyweight champ • Elizabeth Taylor divorces Eddie Fisher to wed Richard Burton
Alaska is hit by a 9.2 earthquake, the strongest ever recorded in the U.S.
Poll taxes are abolished by the 24th Amendment • The Verrazano-Narrows, America's longest single-suspension bridge, opens in New York

1965

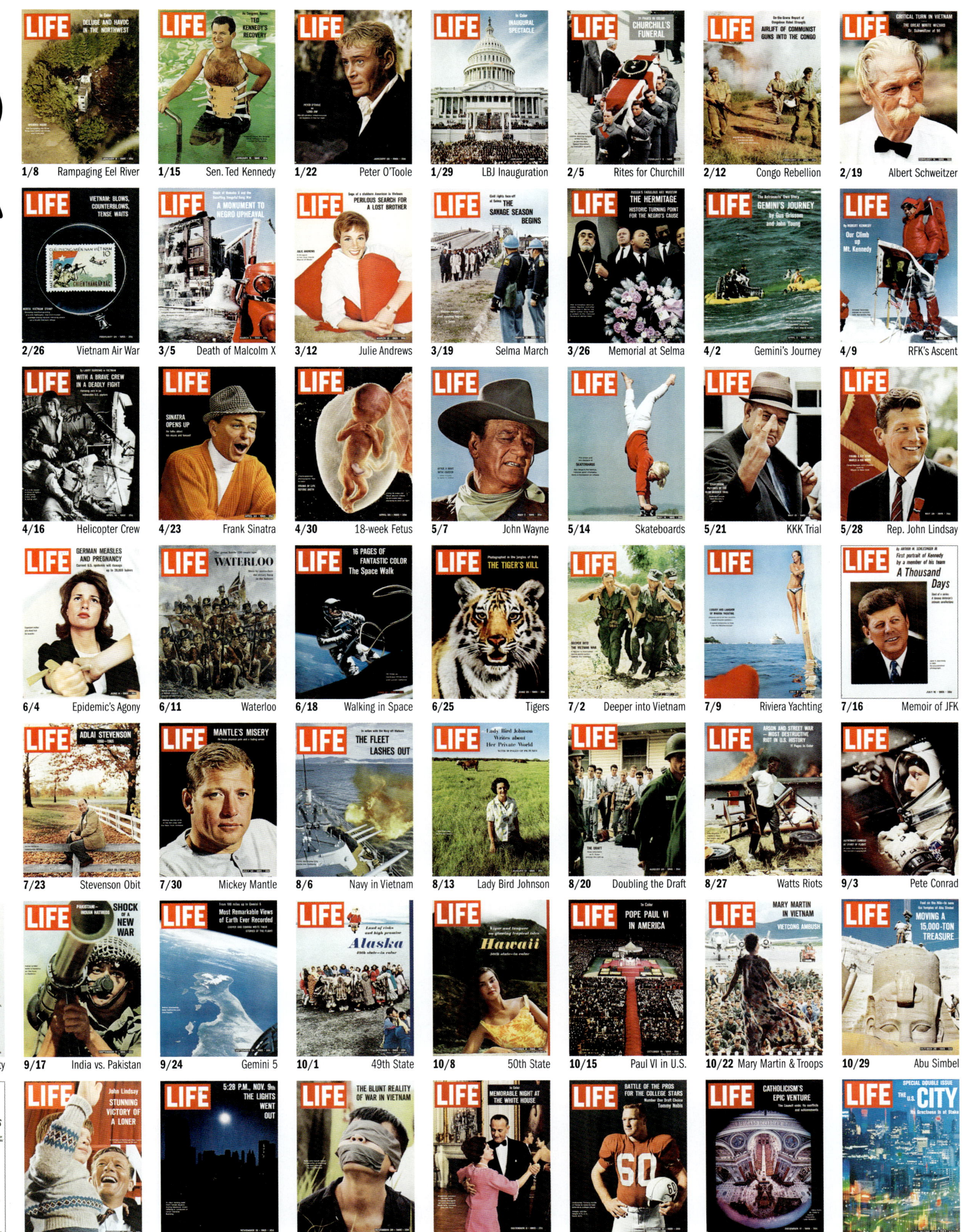

1/8 Rampaging Eel River
1/15 Sen. Ted Kennedy
1/22 Peter O'Toole
1/29 LBJ Inauguration
2/5 Rites for Churchill
2/12 Congo Rebellion
2/19 Albert Schweitzer
2/26 Vietnam Air War
3/5 Death of Malcolm X
3/12 Julie Andrews
3/19 Selma March
3/26 Memorial at Selma
4/2 Gemini's Journey
4/9 RFK's Ascent
4/16 Helicopter Crew
4/23 Frank Sinatra
4/30 18-week Fetus
5/7 John Wayne
5/14 Skateboards
5/21 KKK Trial
5/28 Rep. John Lindsay
6/4 Epidemic's Agony
6/11 Waterloo
6/18 Walking in Space
6/25 Tigers
7/2 Deeper into Vietnam
7/9 Riviera Yachting
7/16 Memoir of JFK
7/23 Stevenson Obit
7/30 Mickey Mantle
8/6 Navy in Vietnam
8/13 Lady Bird Johnson
8/20 Doubling the Draft
8/27 Watts Riots
9/3 Pete Conrad
9/10 Prenativity
9/17 India vs. Pakistan
9/24 Gemini 5
10/1 49th State
10/8 50th State
10/15 Paul VI in U.S.
10/22 Mary Martin & Troops
10/29 Abu Simbel
11/5 JFK Memoir, Part 2
11/12 NYC's Next Mayor
11/19 Blackout
11/26 Horrors of Vietnam
12/3 Margaret & LBJ
12/10 Tommy Nobis
12/17 Vatican II Ends
12/24 The Urban Scene

Medicare is enacted • Ralph Nader publishes *Unsafe at Any Speed*
U.S. ground troops are sent to Vietnam • Mary Quant introduces the miniskirt
The Houston Astrodome opens its doors

1966

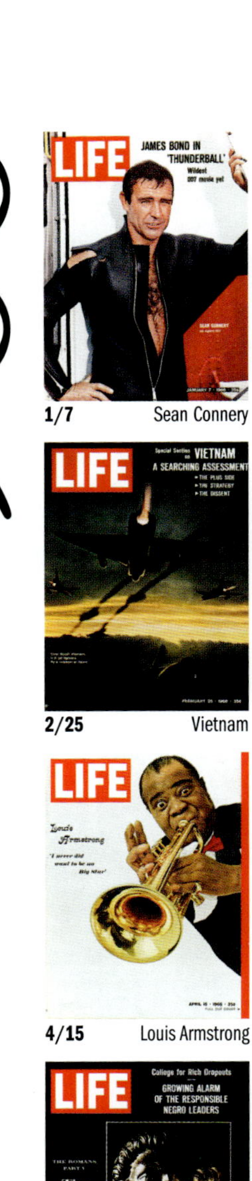
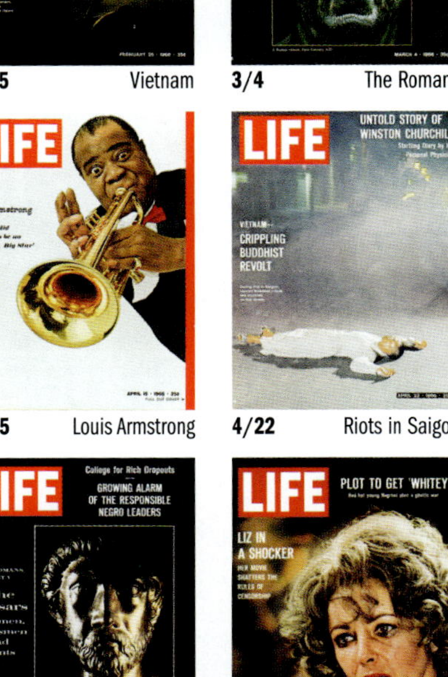
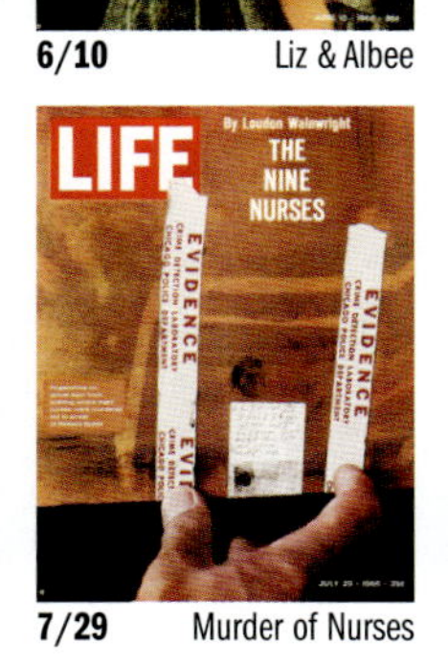
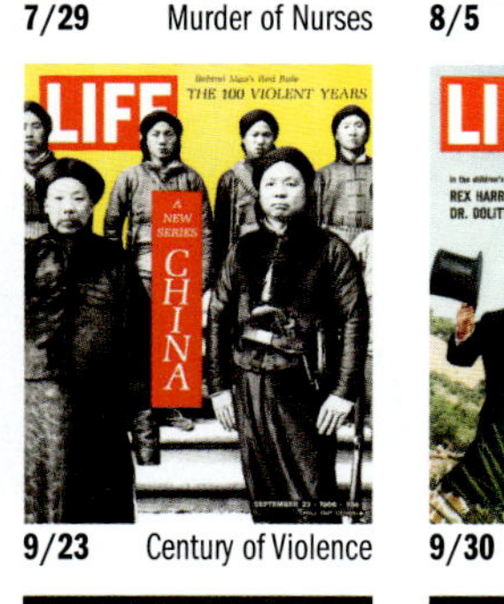
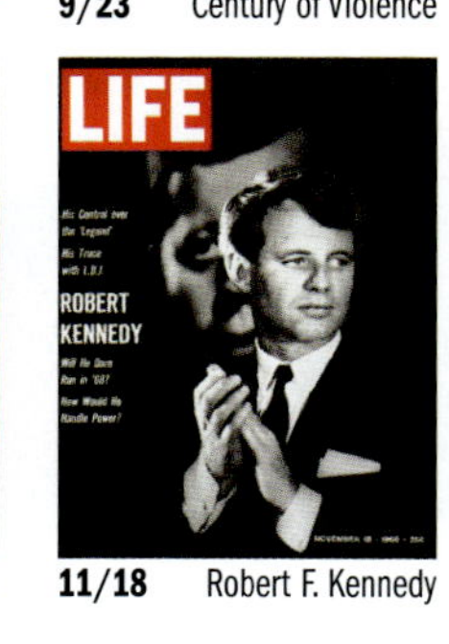
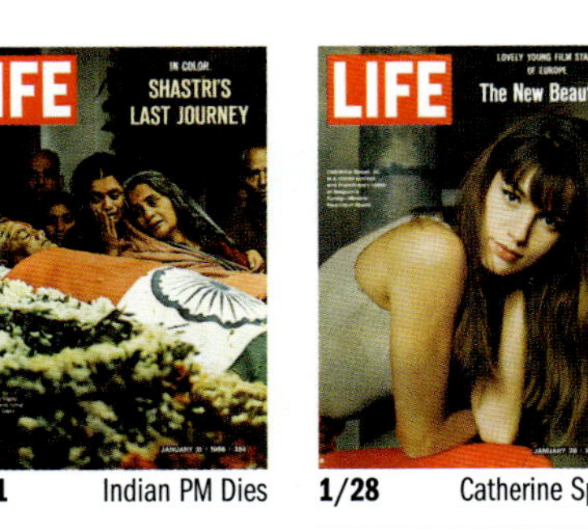
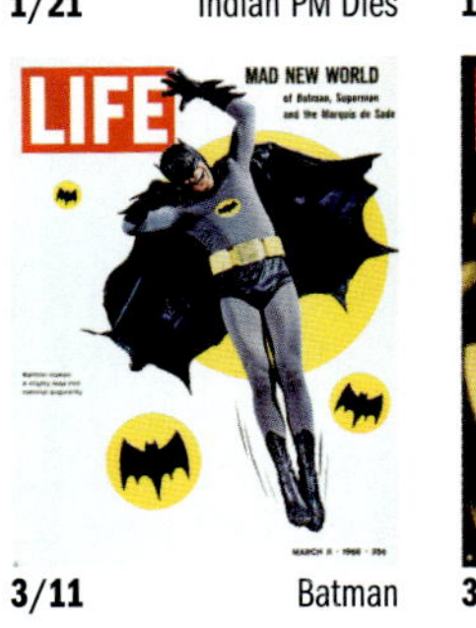
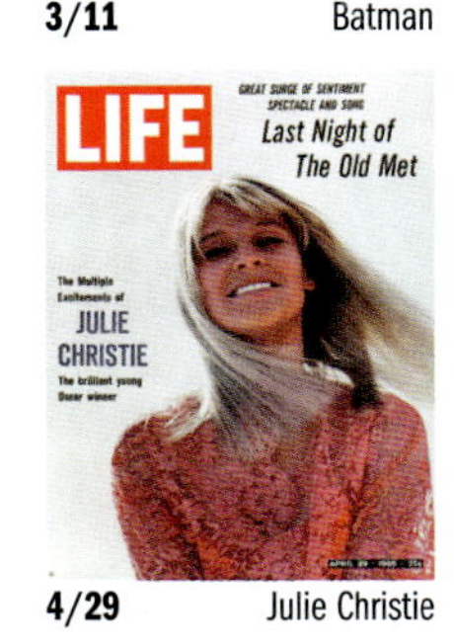
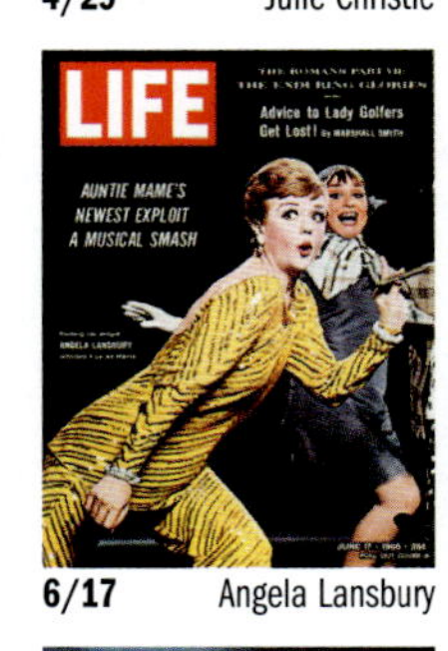
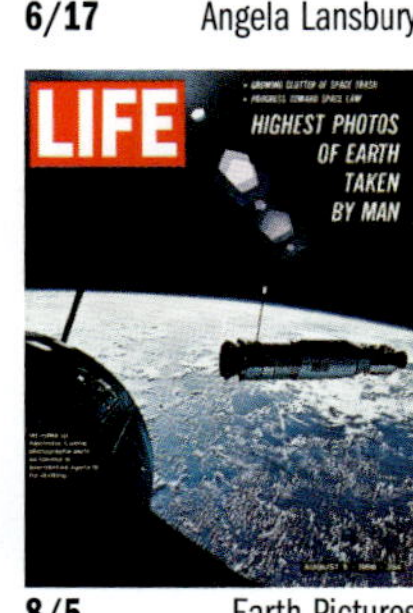
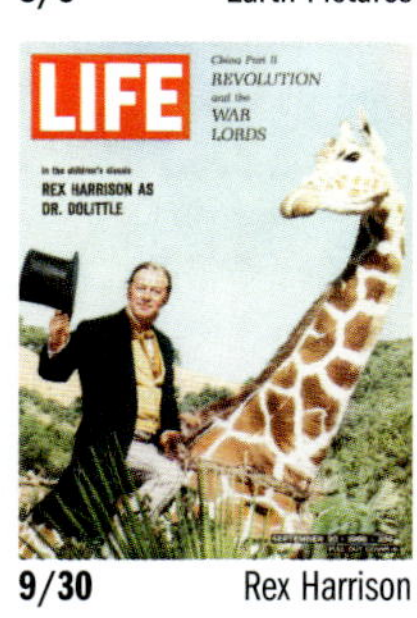
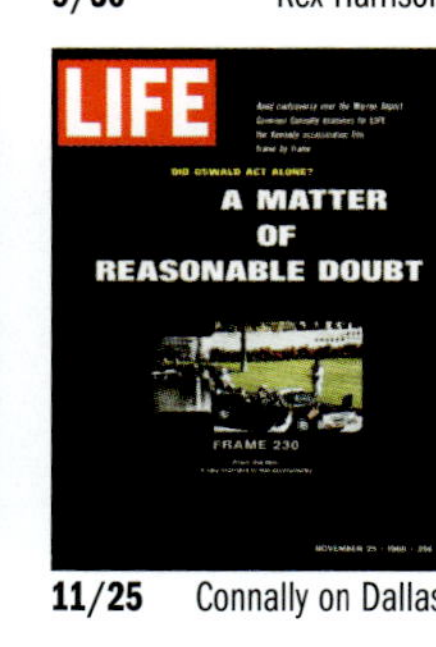
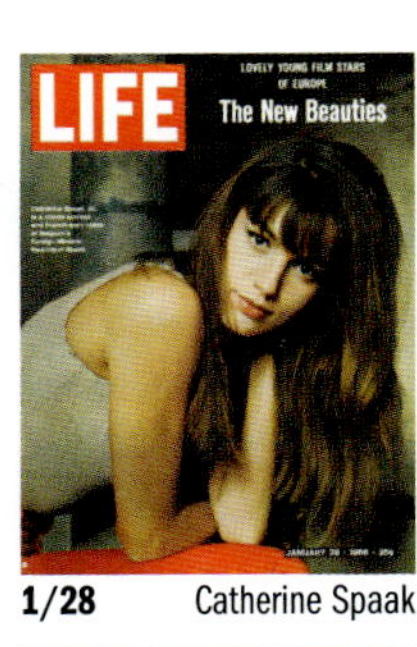
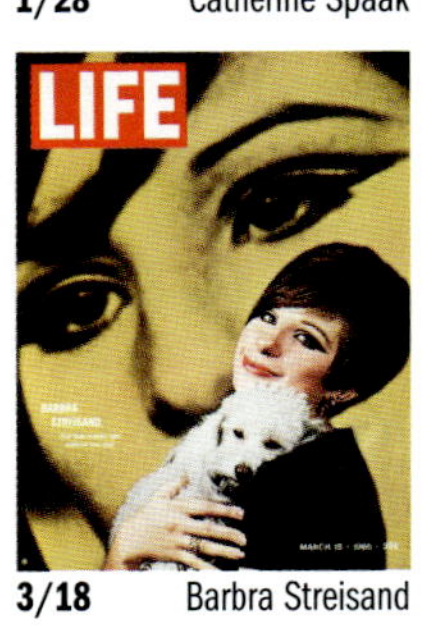
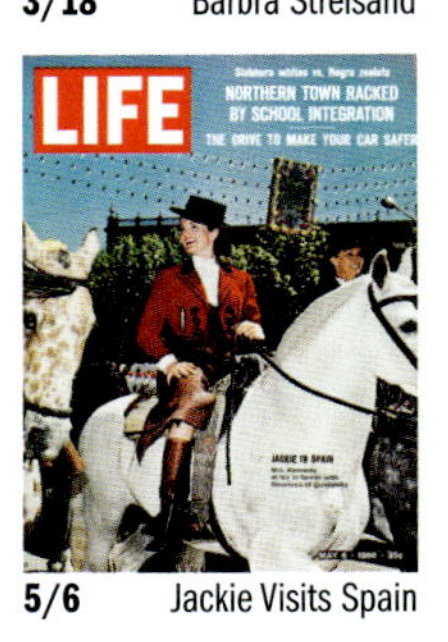
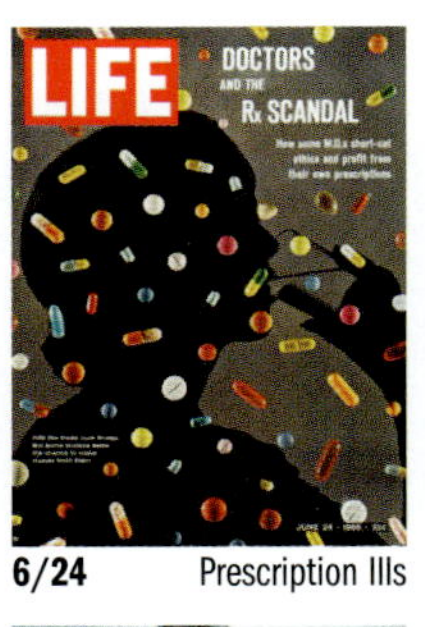
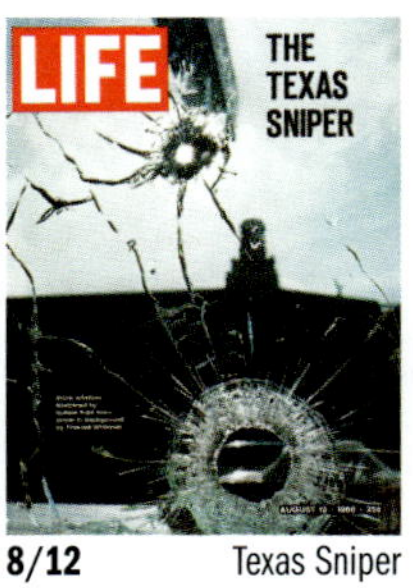
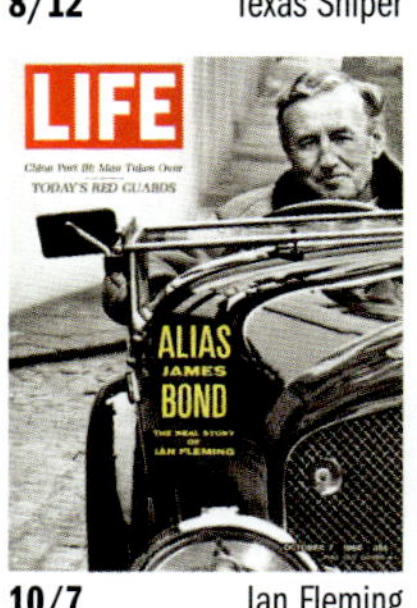
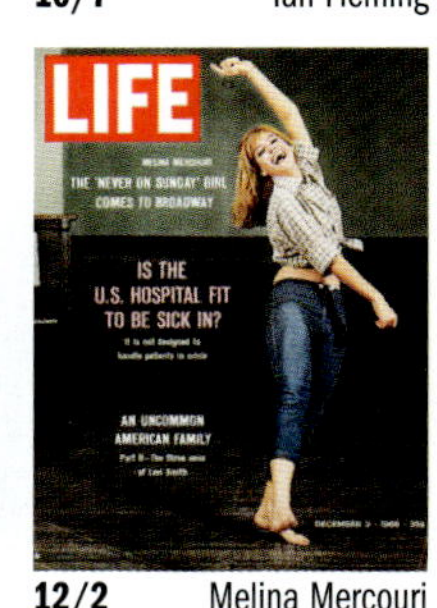
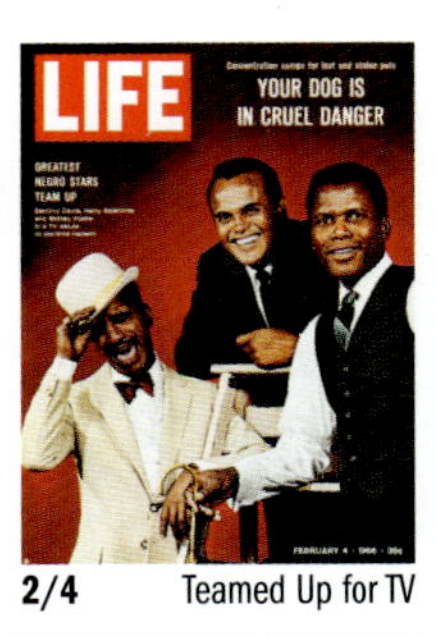
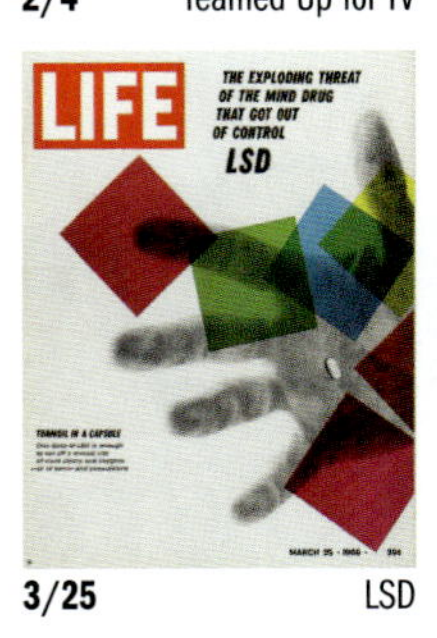
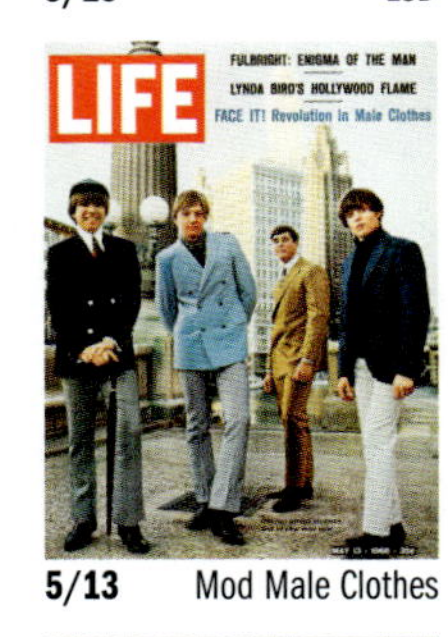
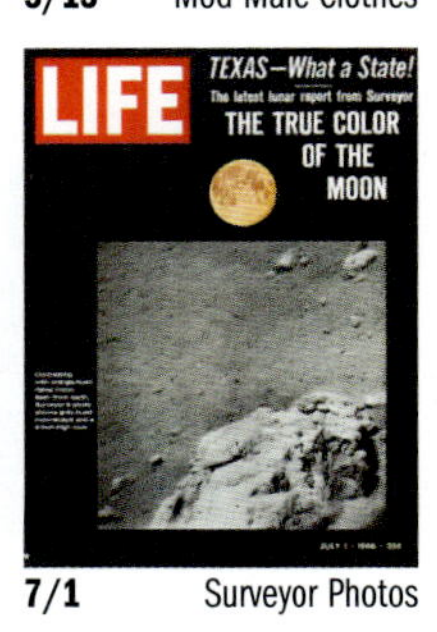
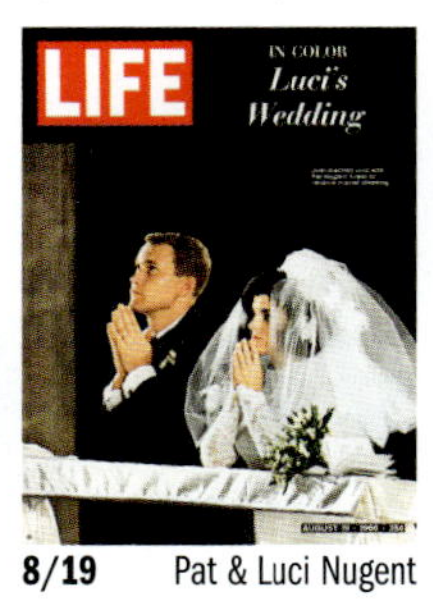
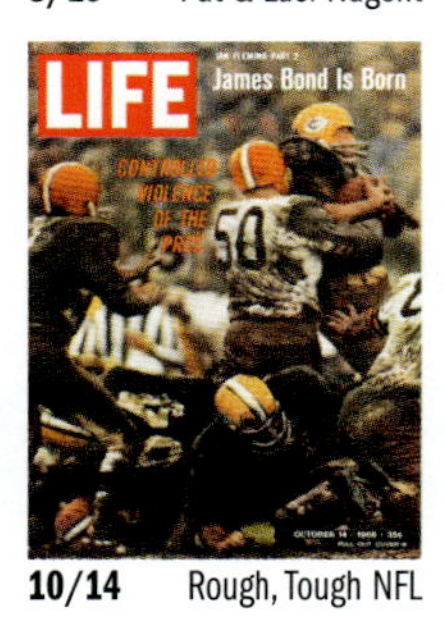
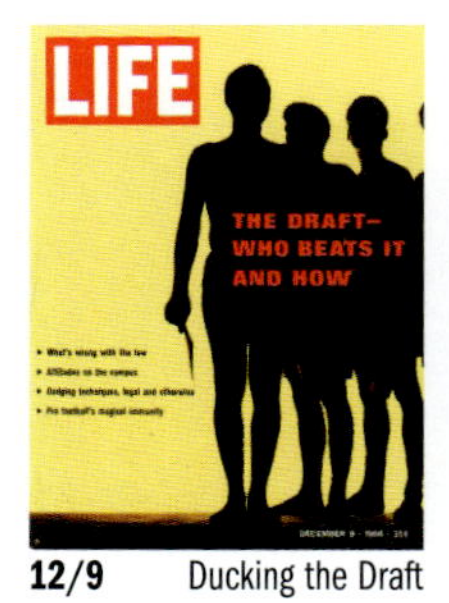
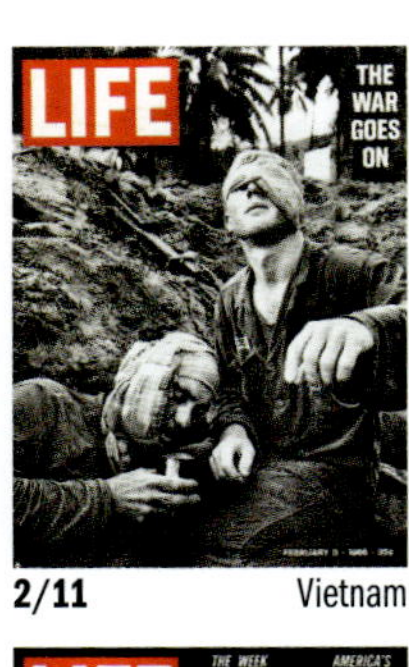
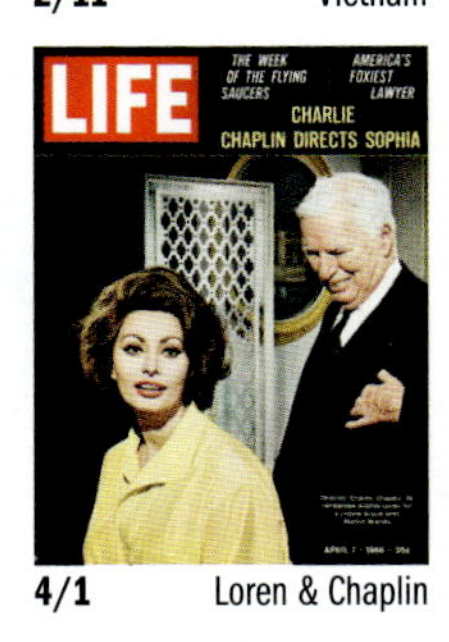
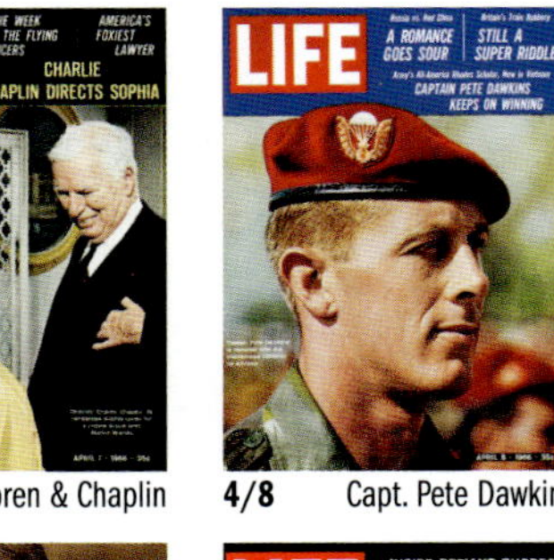
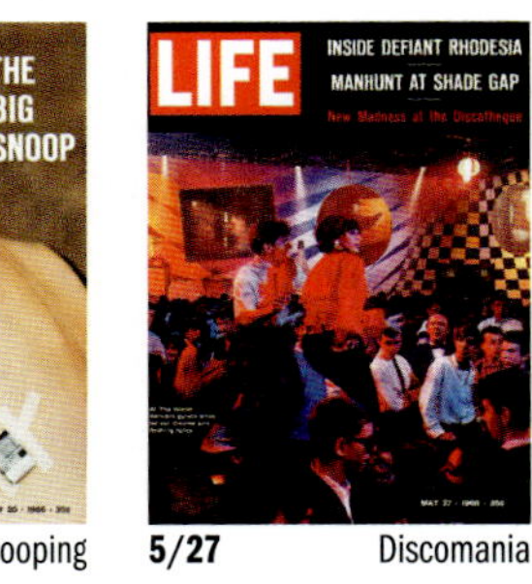
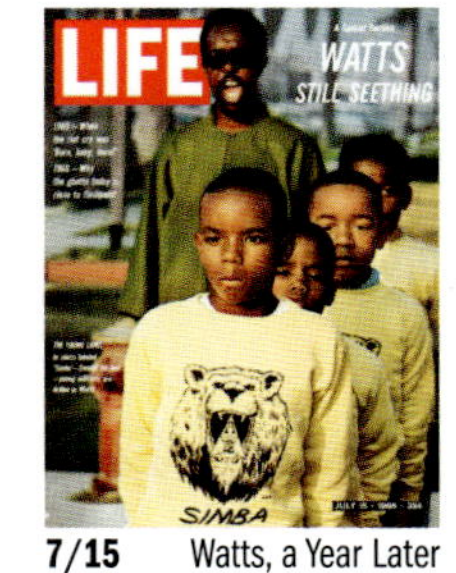
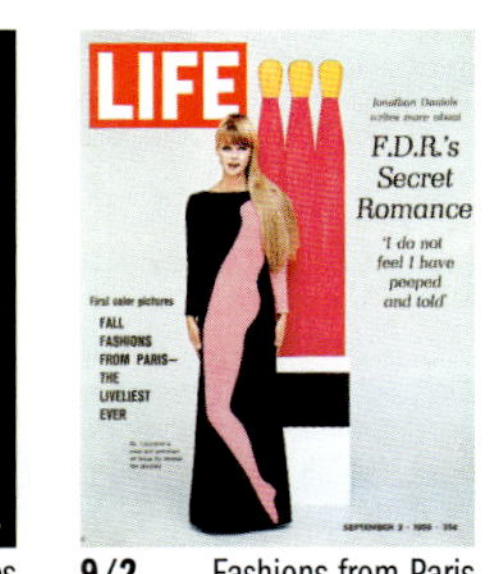
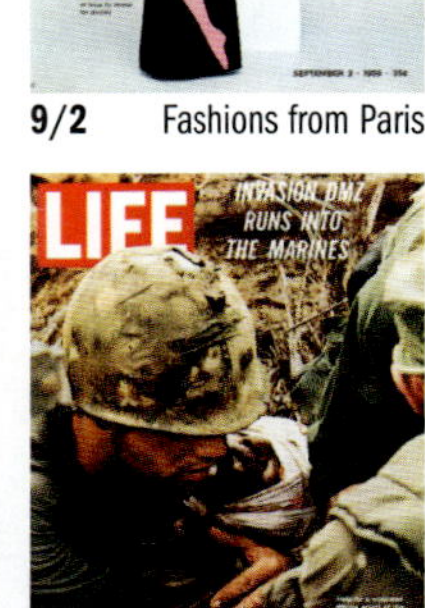
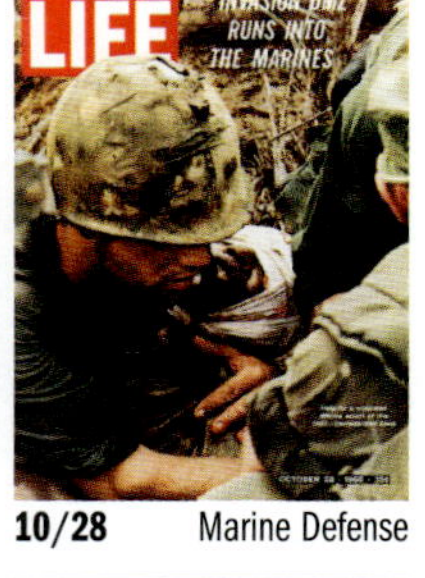

1/7 Sean Connery
1/14 Vietnam's Leaders
1/21 Indian PM Dies
1/28 Catherine Spaak
2/4 Teamed Up for TV
2/11 Vietnam
2/18 Viruses

2/25 Vietnam
3/4 The Romans
3/11 Batman
3/18 Barbra Streisand
3/25 LSD
4/1 Loren & Chaplin
4/8 Capt. Pete Dawkins

4/15 Louis Armstrong
4/22 Riots in Saigon
4/29 Julie Christie
5/6 Jackie Visits Spain
5/13 Mod Male Clothes
5/20 Electronic Snooping
5/27 Discomania

6/3 Rome's Golden Age
6/10 Liz & Albee
6/17 Angela Lansbury
6/24 Prescription Ills
7/1 Surveyor Photos
7/8 Claudia Cardinale
7/15 Watts, a Year Later

7/22 One Second Old
7/29 Murder of Nurses
8/5 Earth Pictures
8/12 Texas Sniper
8/19 Pat & Luci Nugent
8/26 Labor Woes
9/2 Fashions from Paris

9/9 Psychedelic Art
9/16 Sophia Loren
9/23 Century of Violence
9/30 Rex Harrison
10/7 Ian Fleming
10/14 Rough, Tough NFL
10/21 Lindbergh in Africa
10/28 Marine Defense

11/4 LBJ in Vietnam
11/11 Jean-Paul Belmondo
11/18 Robert F. Kennedy
11/25 Connally on Dallas
12/2 Melina Mercouri
12/9 Ducking the Draft
12/16 Damaged Art
12/23 LIFE Is 30

Japanese scientists develop laser radar • TV's first *Star Trek* episode airs
Floods ruin thousands of masterpieces in Venice and Florence • Betty Friedan and others found NOW, the National Organization for Women
The Beatles play their final concert

1967

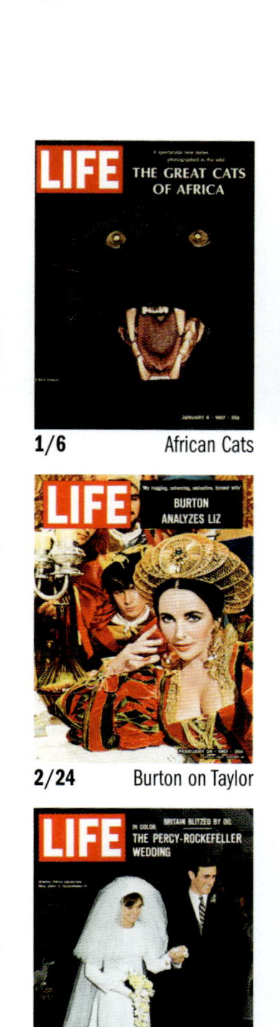
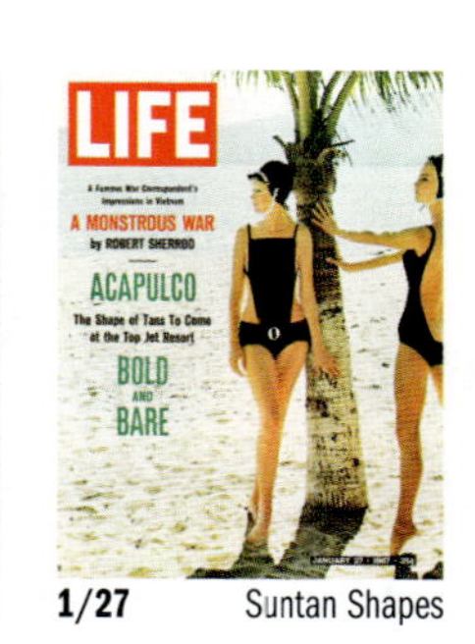
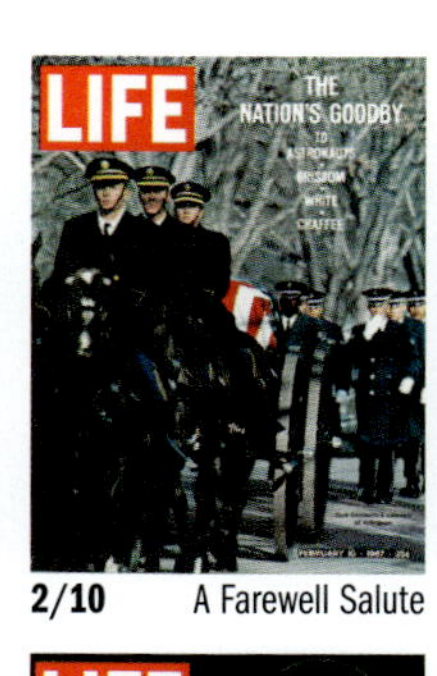

1/6 African Cats · 1/13 Vietcong Heartland · 1/20 Crisis in China · 1/27 Suntan Shapes · 2/3 Tragic Fire · 2/10 A Farewell Salute · 2/17 Underground Art

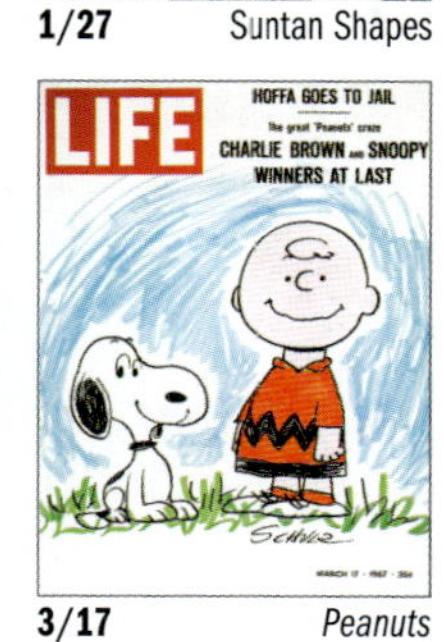
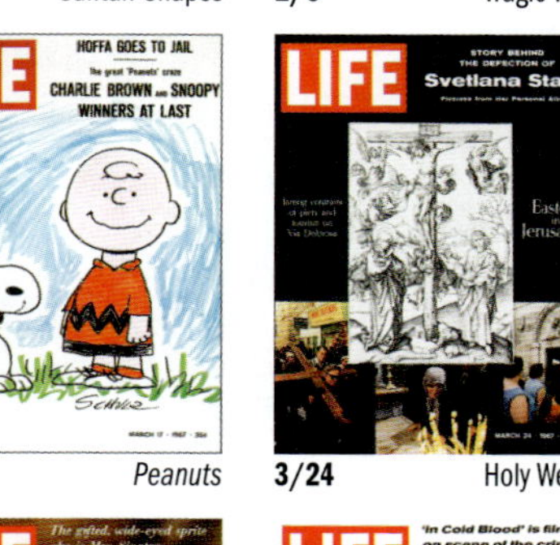
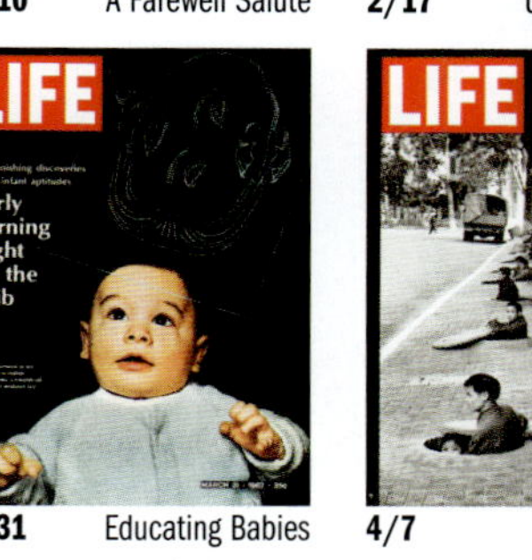

2/24 Burton on Taylor · 3/3 Leonardo's Papers · 3/10 Paratroopers · 3/17 *Peanuts* · 3/24 Holy Week · 3/31 Educating Babies · 4/7 North Vietnam

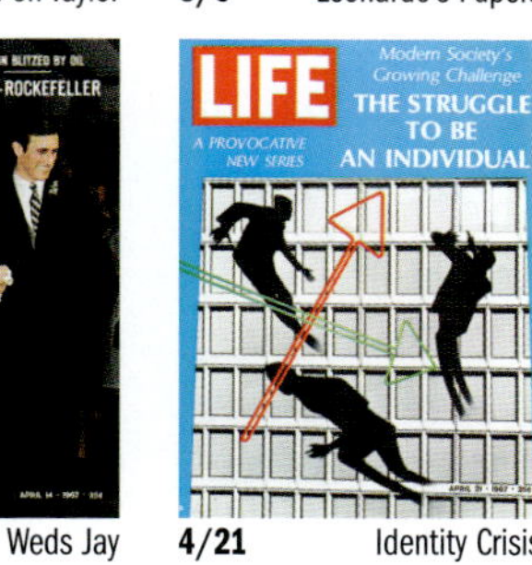
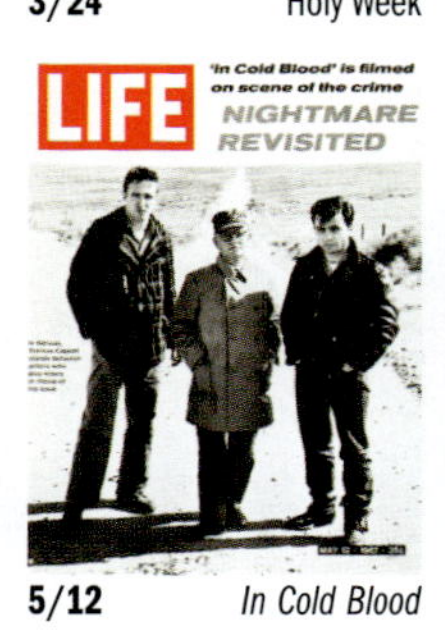
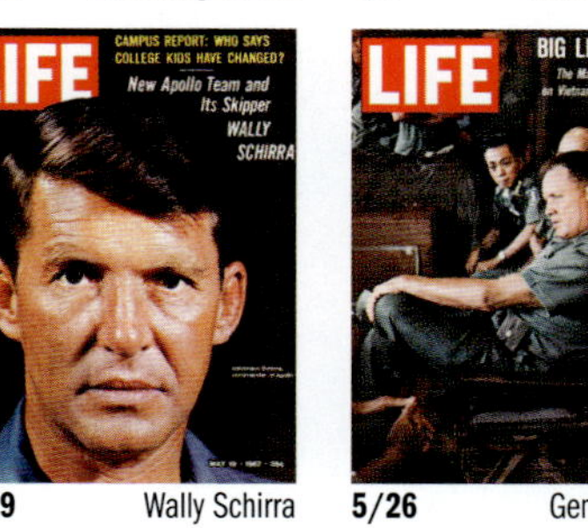
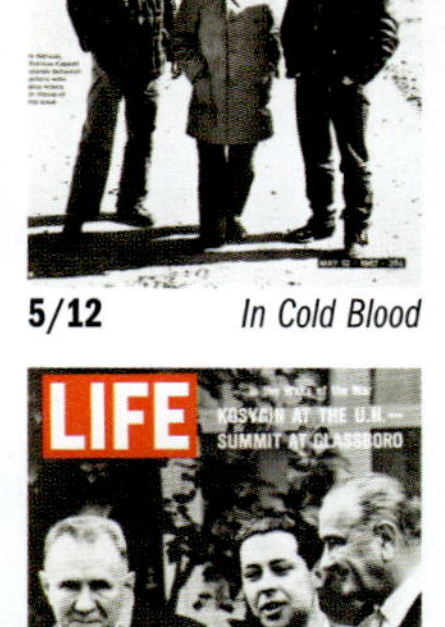

4/14 Sharon Weds Jay · 4/21 Identity Crisis · 4/28 Expo '67 · 5/5 Mia Farrow · 5/12 *In Cold Blood* · 5/19 Wally Schirra · 5/26 General Walt

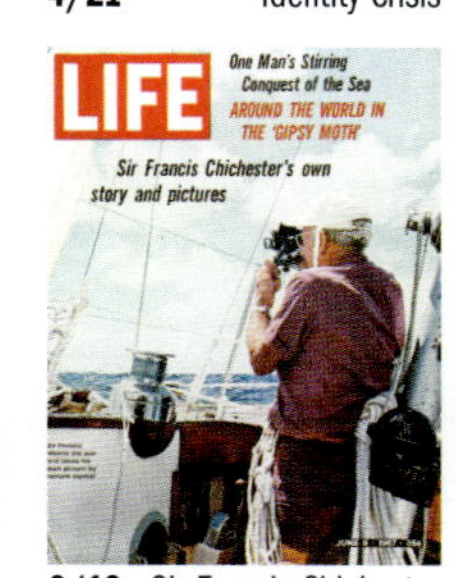
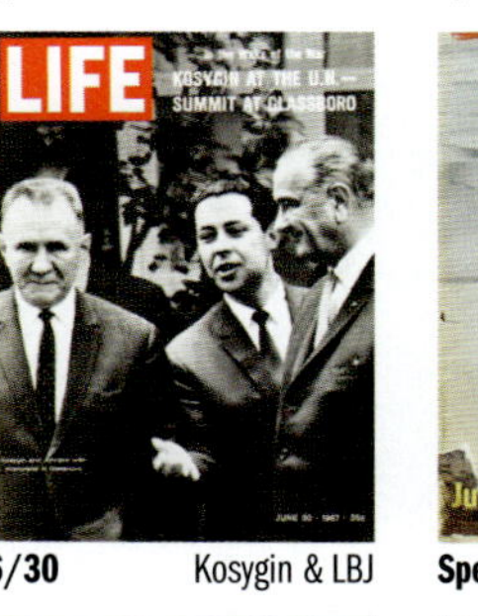
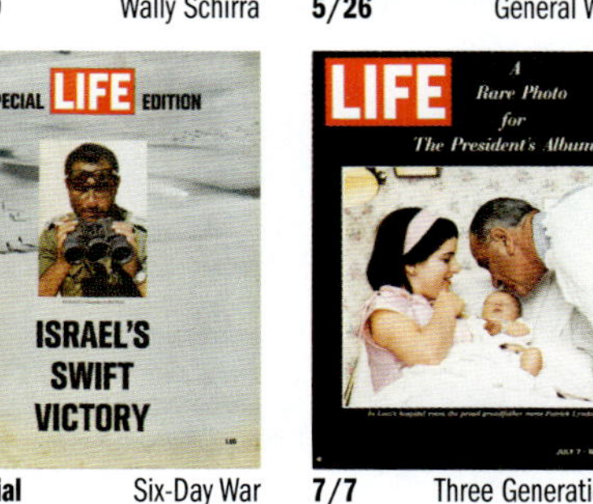

6/2 Escapee's Story · 6/19 Sir Francis Chichester · 6/16 Israeli Onslaught · 6/23 Israeli Victory · 6/30 Kosygin & LBJ · Special Six-Day War · 7/7 Three Generations

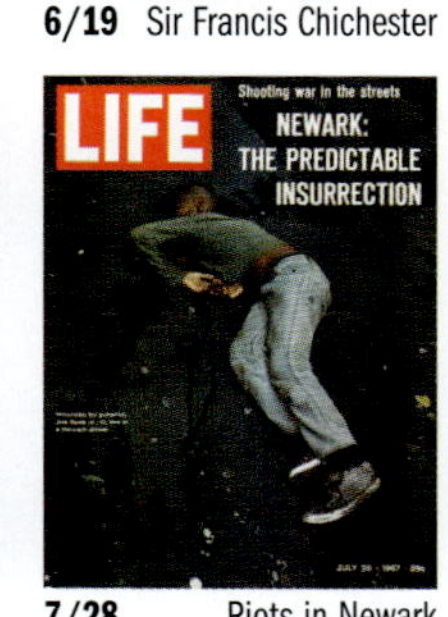
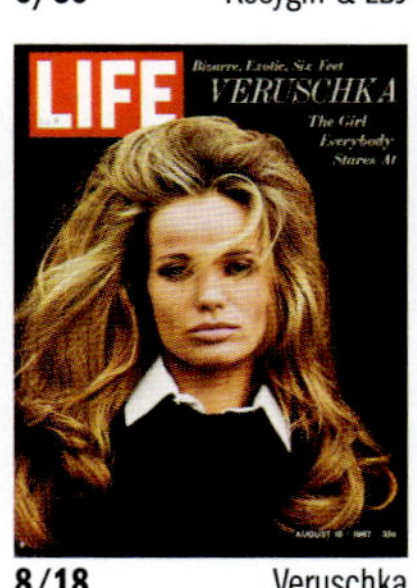
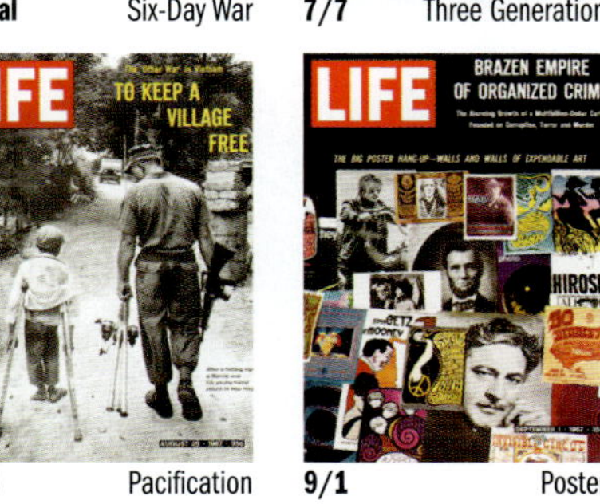
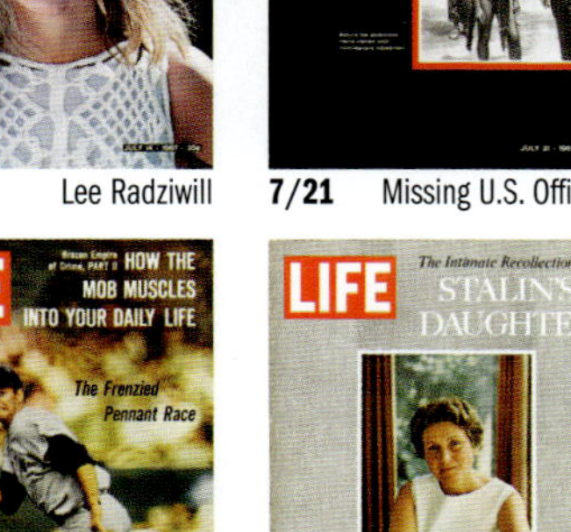

7/14 Lee Radziwill · 7/21 Missing U.S. Official · 7/28 Riots in Newark · 8/4 Riots in Detroit · 8/11 *Forrestal* Disaster · 8/18 Veruschka · 8/25 Pacification · 9/1 Posters

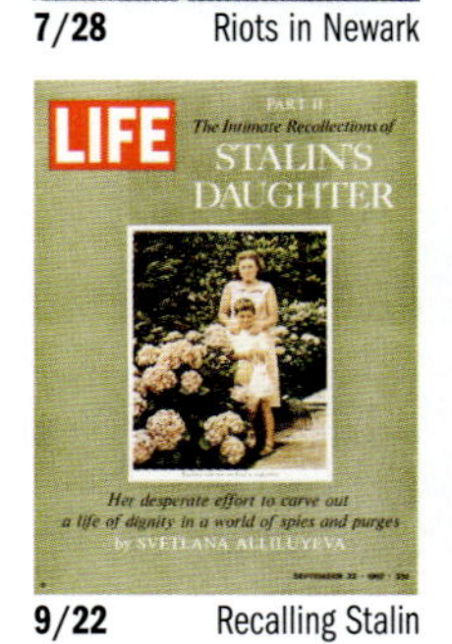
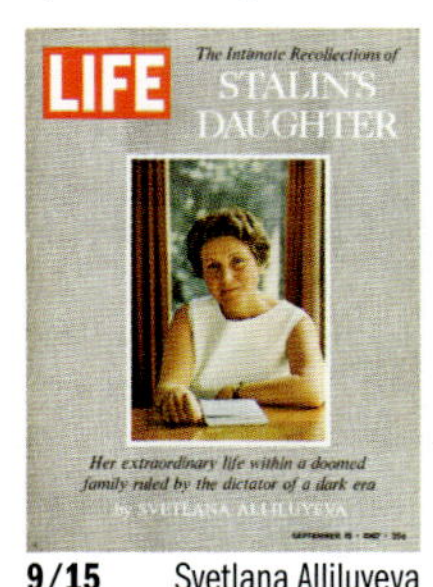
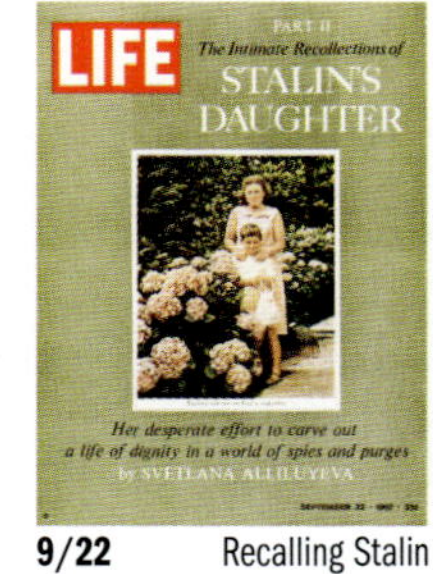
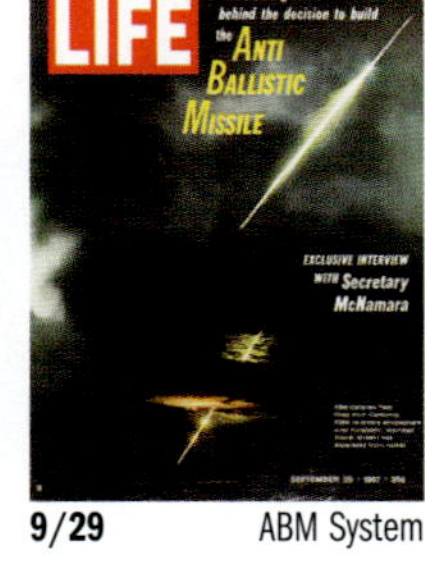
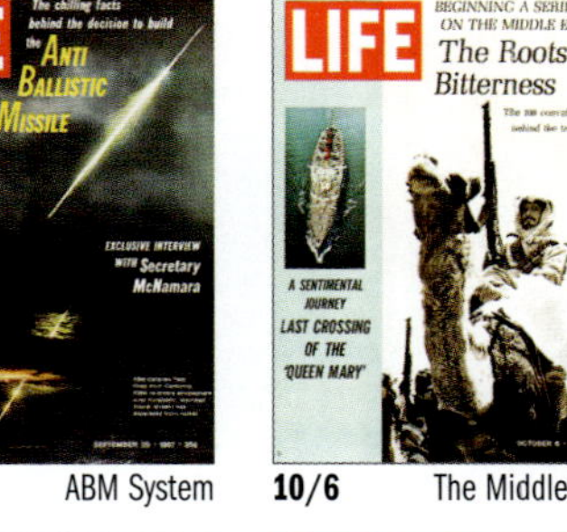
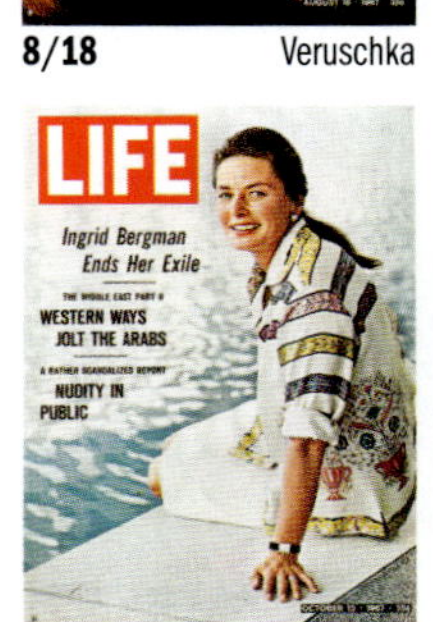
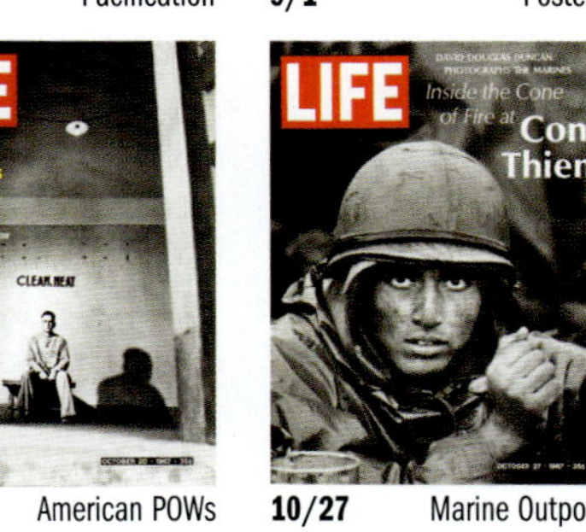

9/8 Carl Yastrzemski · 9/15 Svetlana Alliluyeva · 9/22 Recalling Stalin · 9/29 ABM System · 10/6 The Middle East · 10/13 Bergman Returns · 10/20 American POWs · 10/27 Marine Outpost

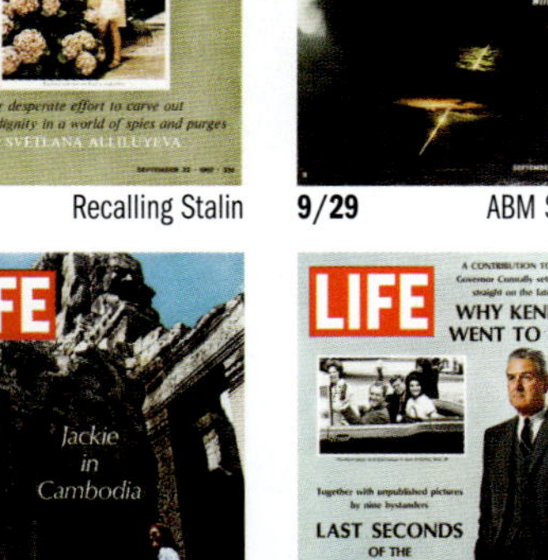
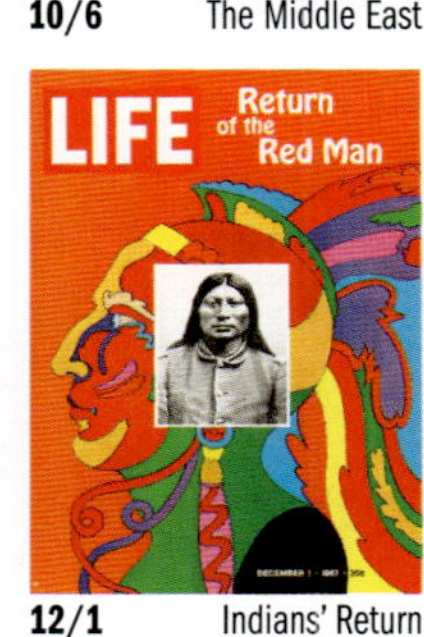
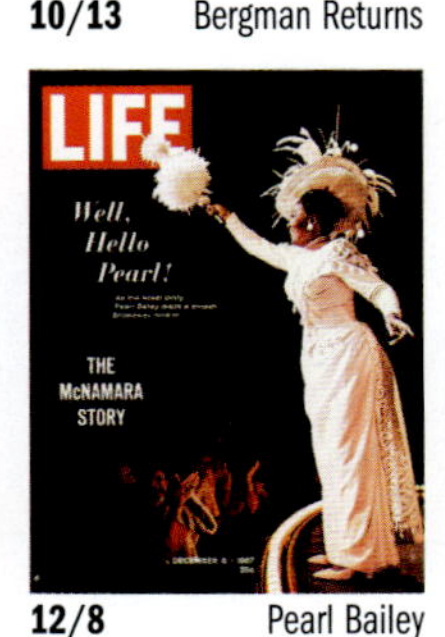
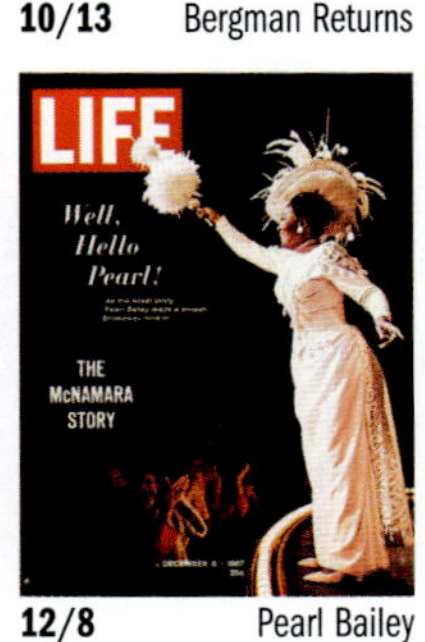
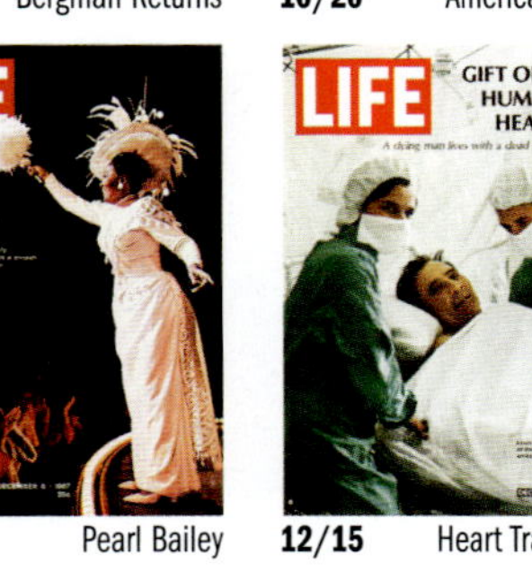
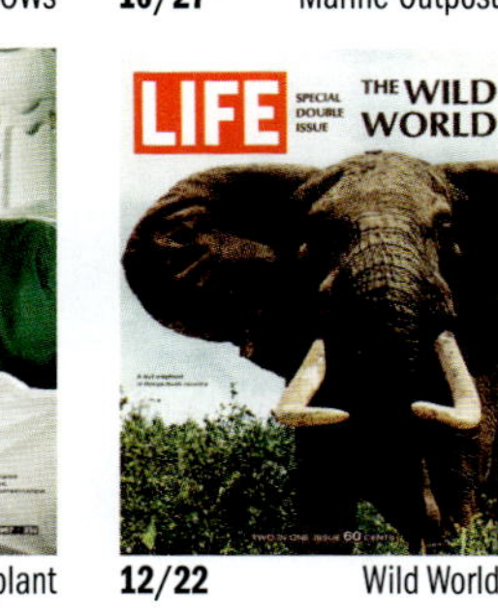

11/3 Runaways · 11/10 U.S.S.R.'s 50th · 11/17 Jackie in Cambodia · 11/24 Connally on JFK · 12/1 Indians' Return · 12/8 Pearl Bailey · 12/15 Heart Transplant · 12/22 Wild World

The Green Bay Packers beat the Kansas City Chiefs in the first Super Bowl • Muhammad Ali refuses to register for the draft
Arthur Penn's *Bonnie and Clyde* opens to mixed reviews
Congress creates the Public Broadcasting System • Thurgood Marshall is sworn in as the first black Supreme Court Justice

1968

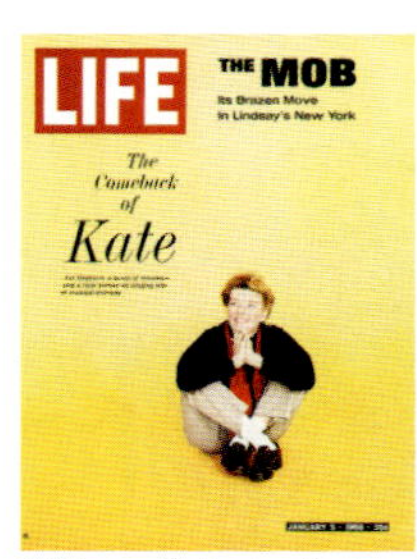

1/5 Katharine Hepburn

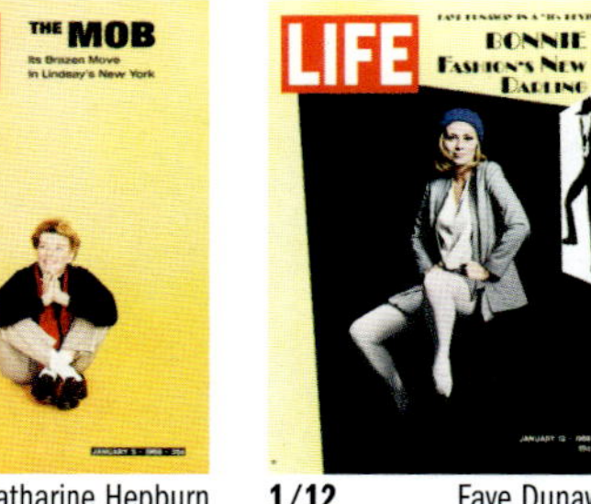
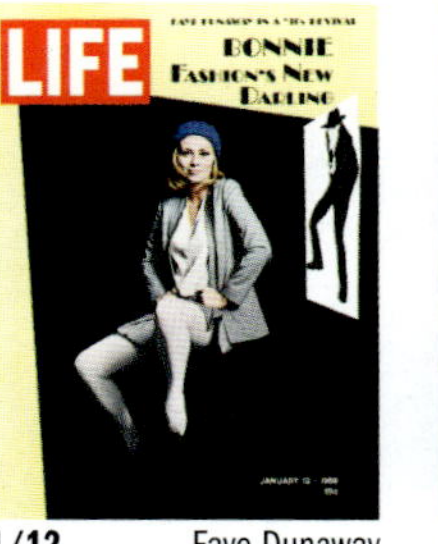

1/12 Faye Dunaway

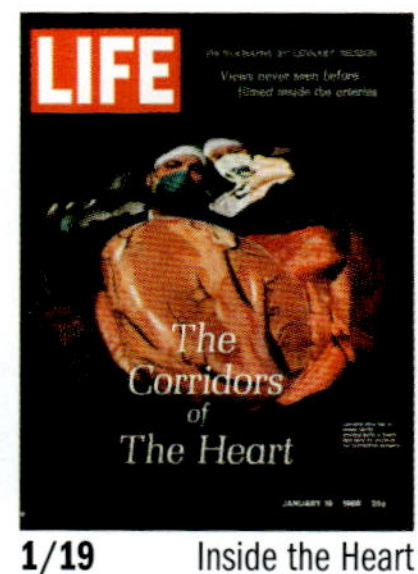

1/19 Inside the Heart

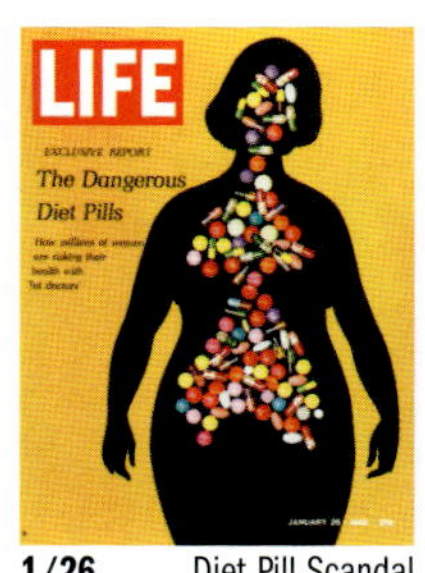

1/26 Diet Pill Scandal

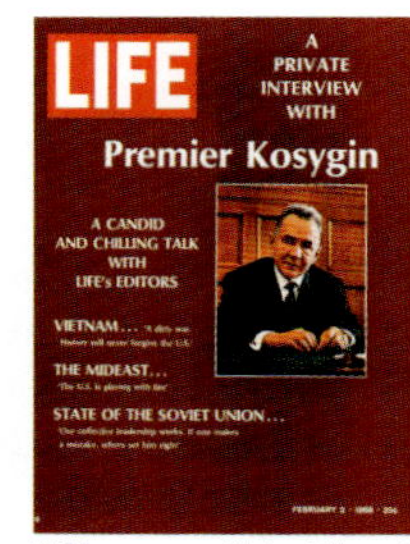

2/2 Aleksei Kosygin

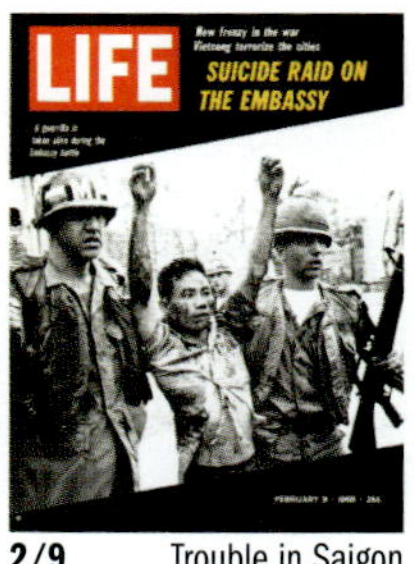

2/9 Trouble in Saigon

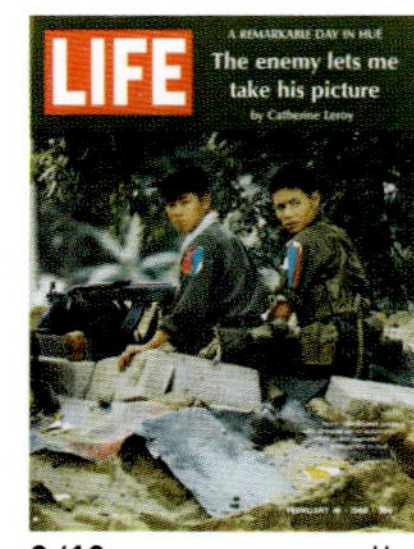

2/16 Hue

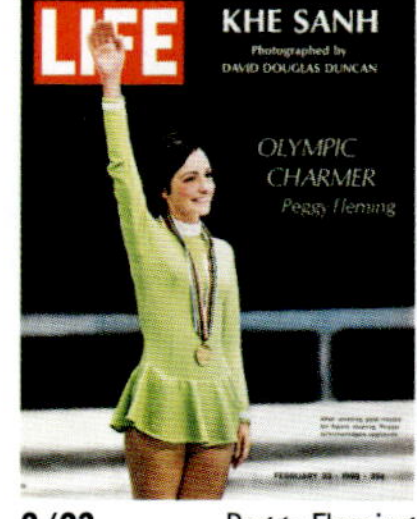

2/23 Peggy Fleming

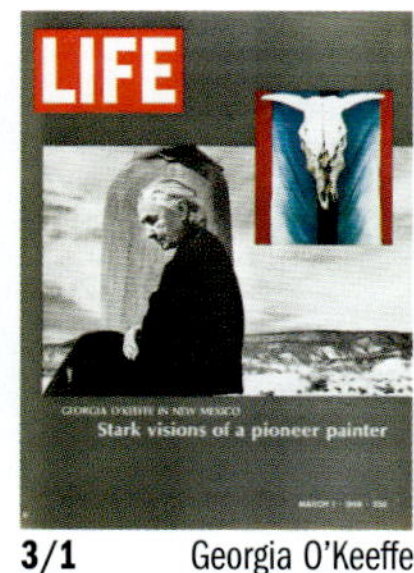

3/1 Georgia O'Keeffe

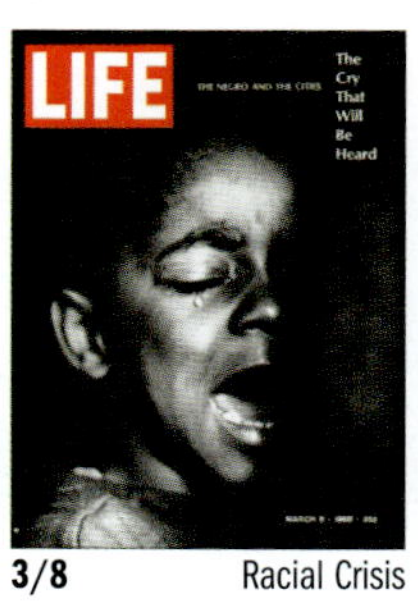

3/8 Racial Crisis

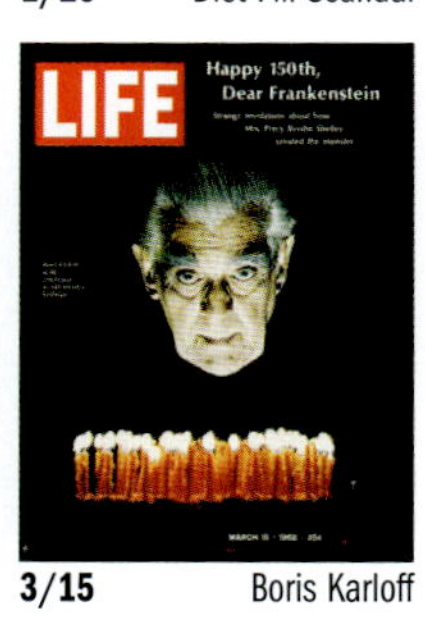

3/15 Boris Karloff

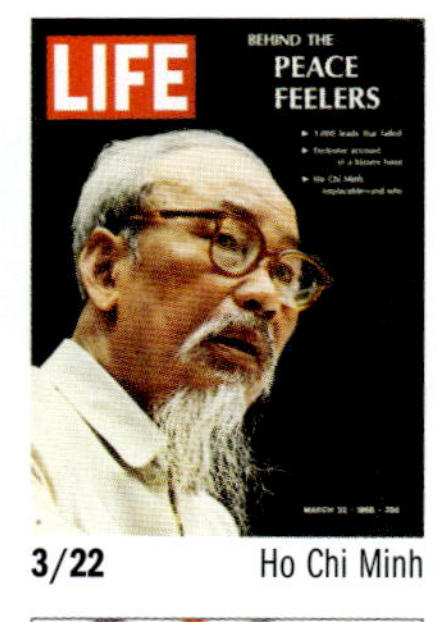

3/22 Ho Chi Minh

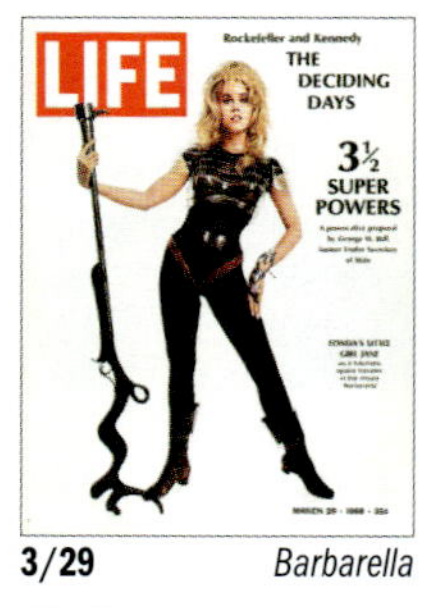

3/29 *Barbarella*

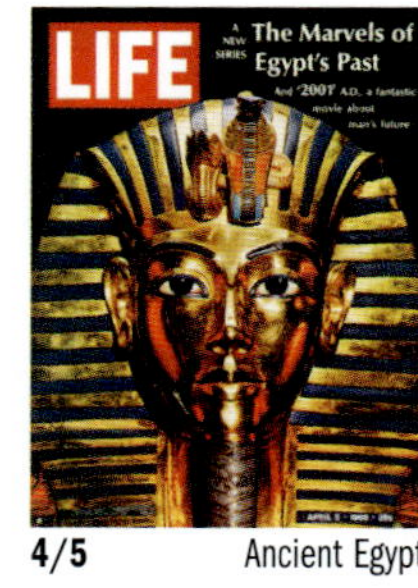

4/5 Ancient Egypt

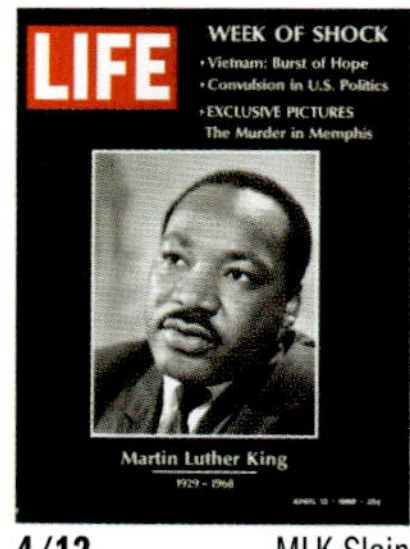

4/12 MLK Slain

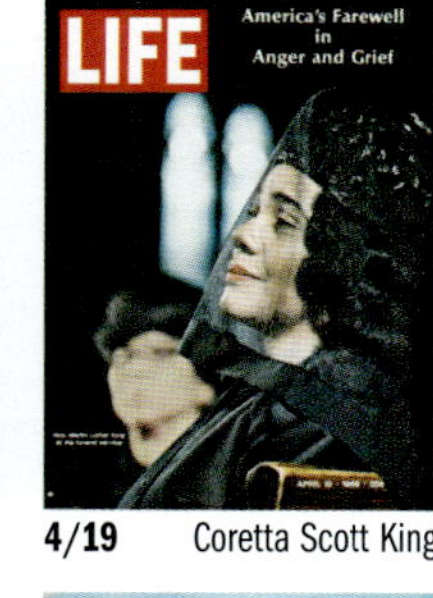

4/19 Coretta Scott King

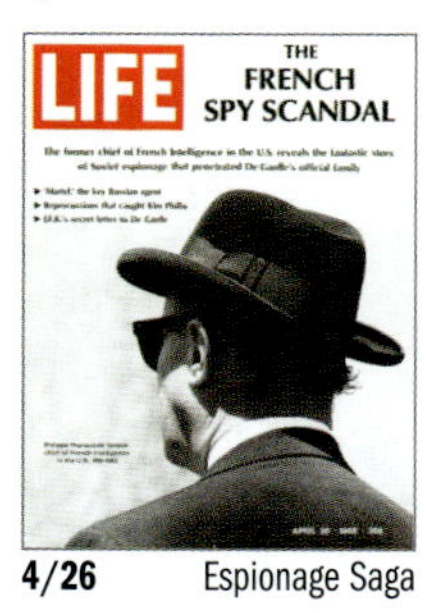

4/26 Espionage Saga

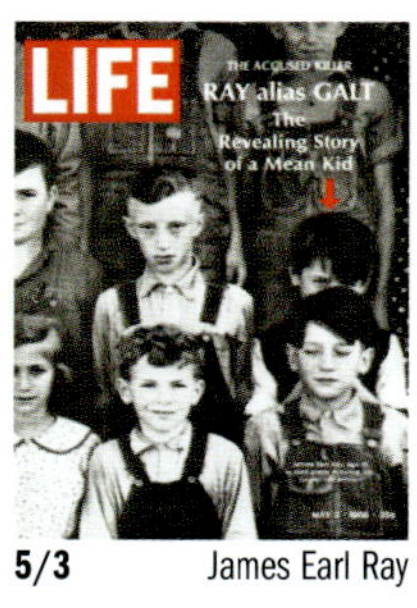

5/3 James Earl Ray

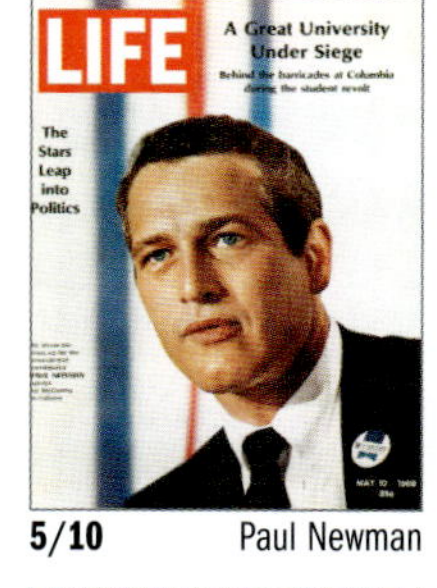

5/10 Paul Newman

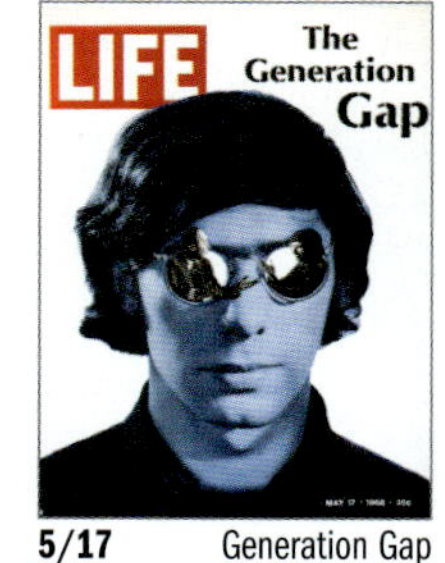

5/17 Generation Gap

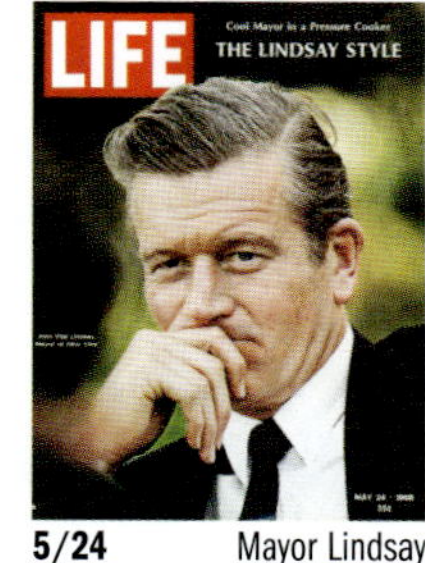

5/24 Mayor Lindsay

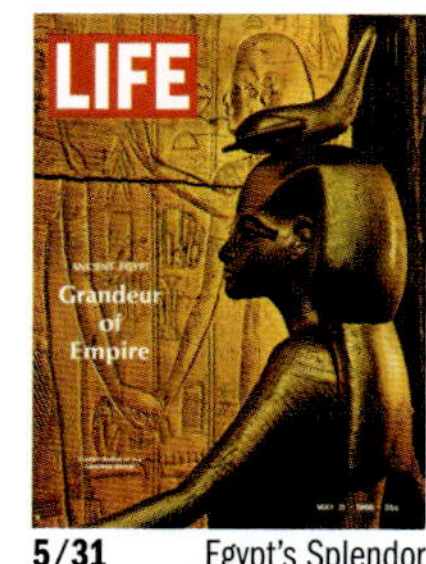

5/31 Egypt's Splendor

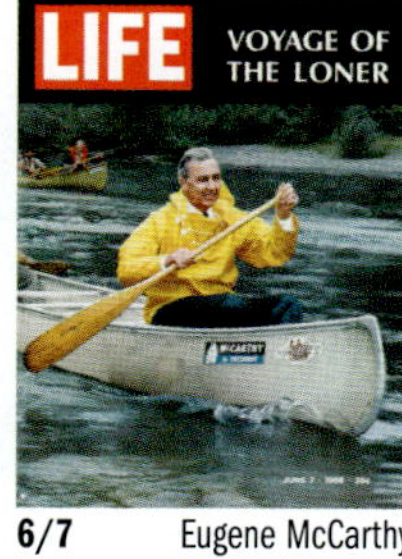

6/7 Eugene McCarthy

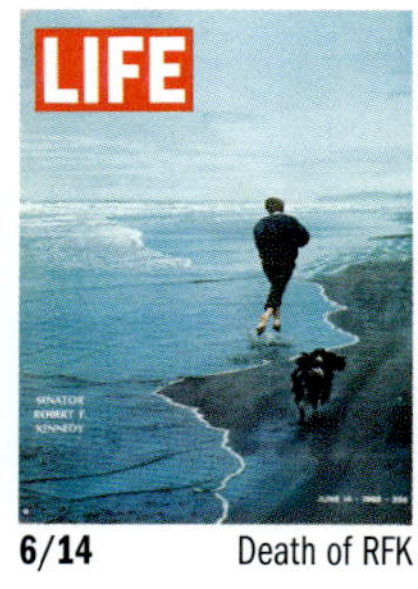

6/14 Death of RFK

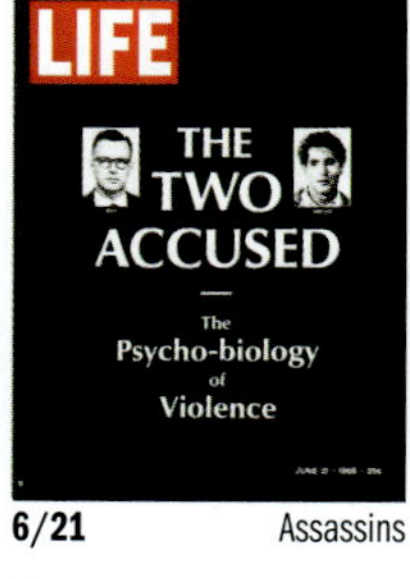

6/21 Assassins

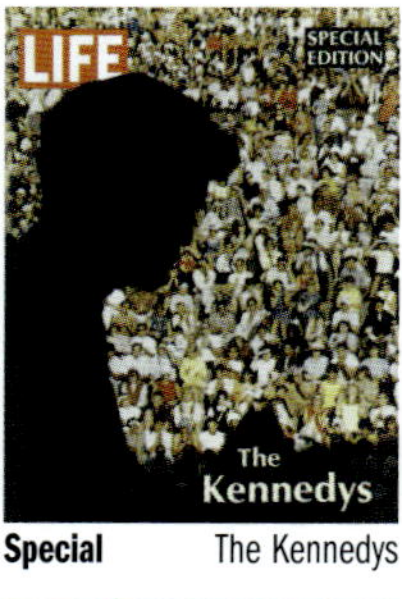

Special The Kennedys

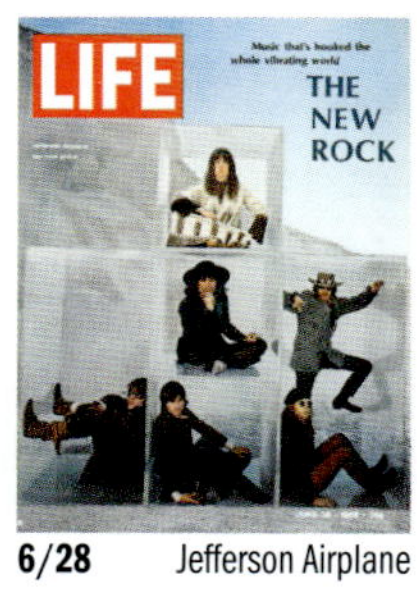

6/28 Jefferson Airplane

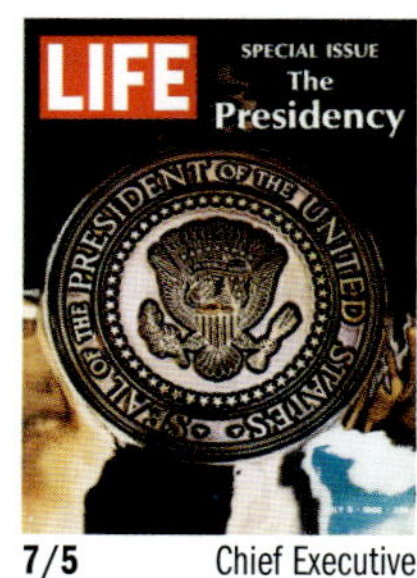

7/5 Chief Executive

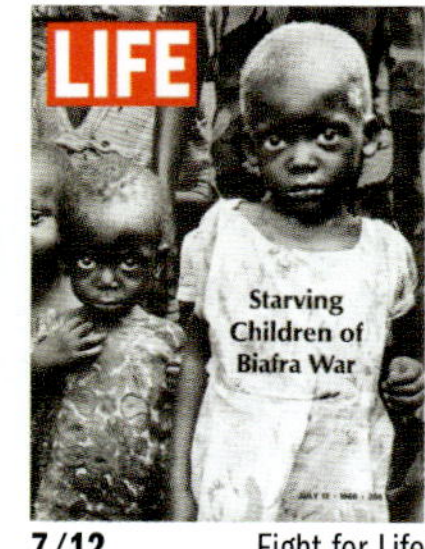

7/12 Fight for Life

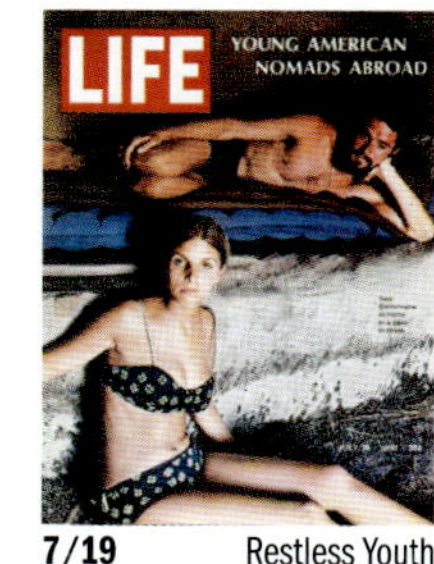

7/19 Restless Youth

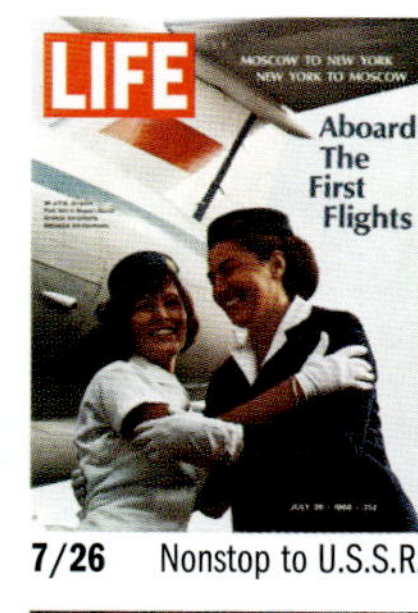

7/26 Nonstop to U.S.S.R.

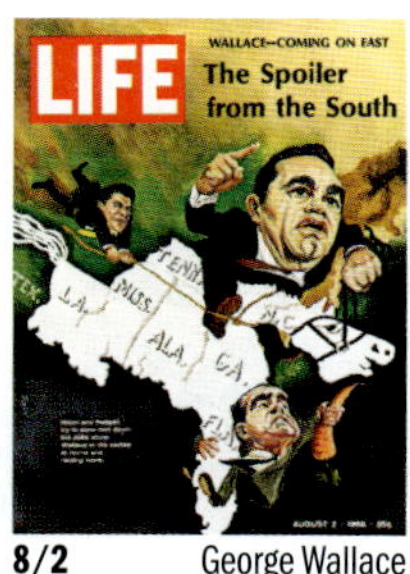

8/2 George Wallace

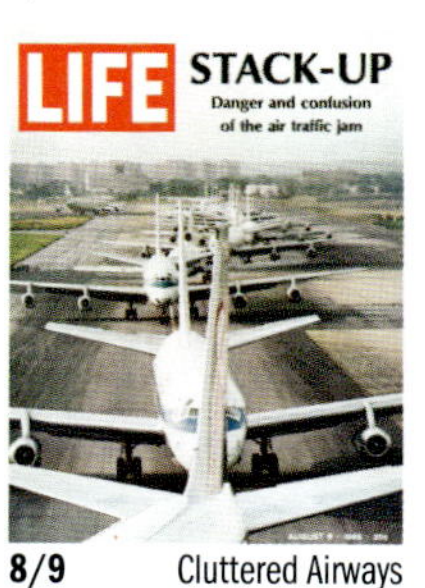

8/9 Cluttered Airways

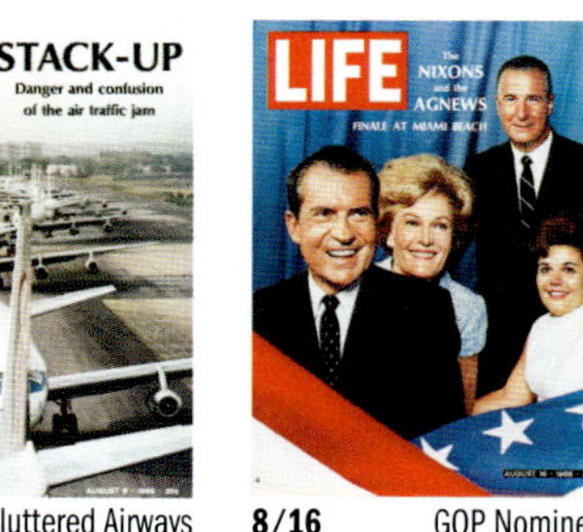

8/16 GOP Nominees

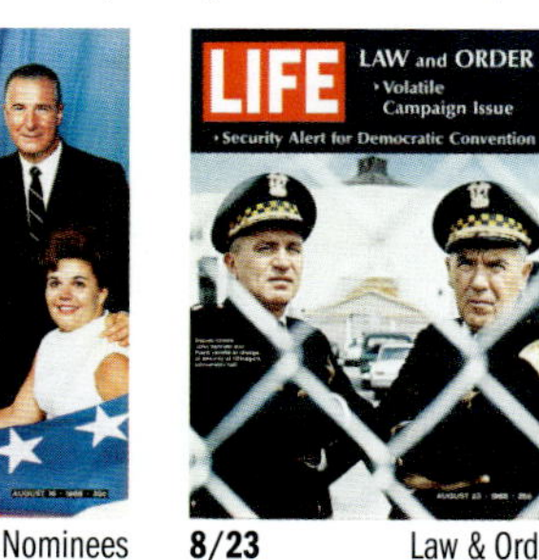

8/23 Law & Order

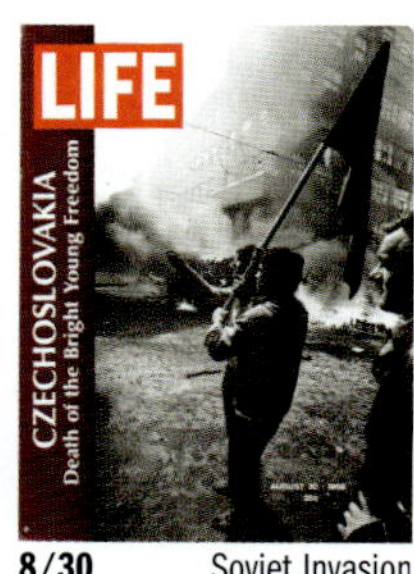

8/30 Soviet Invasion

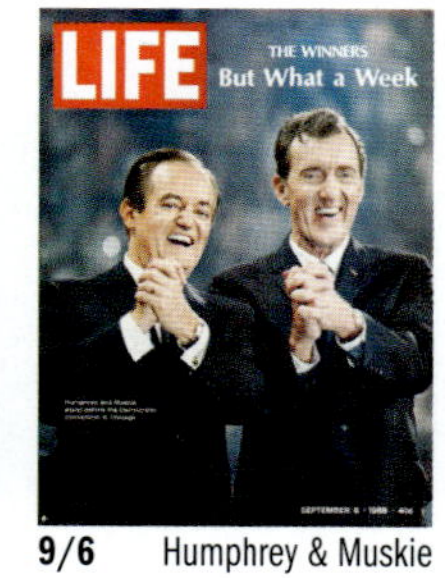

9/6 Humphrey & Muskie

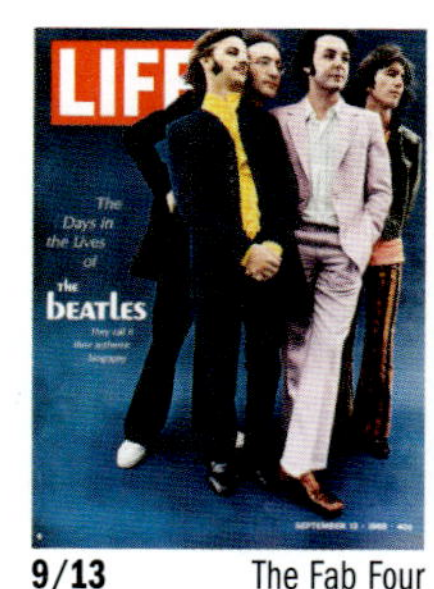

9/13 The Fab Four

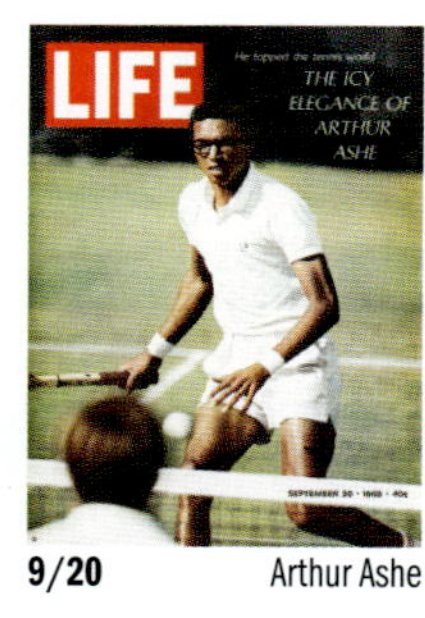

9/20 Arthur Ashe

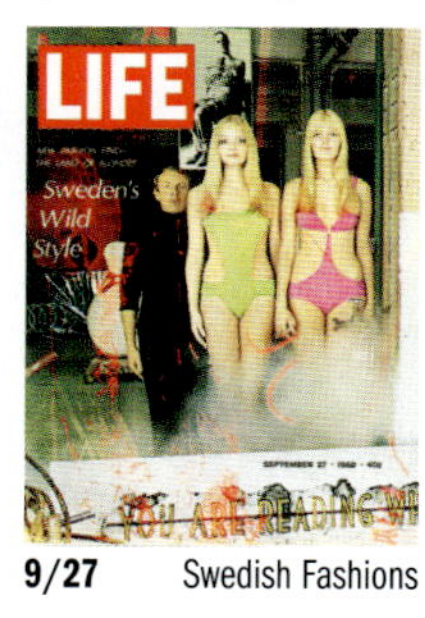

9/27 Swedish Fashions

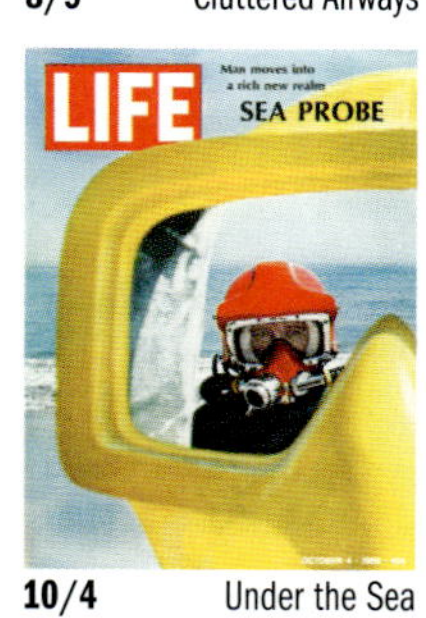

10/4 Under the Sea

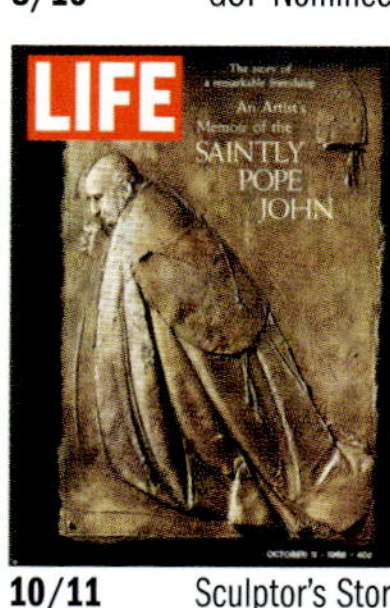

10/11 Sculptor's Story

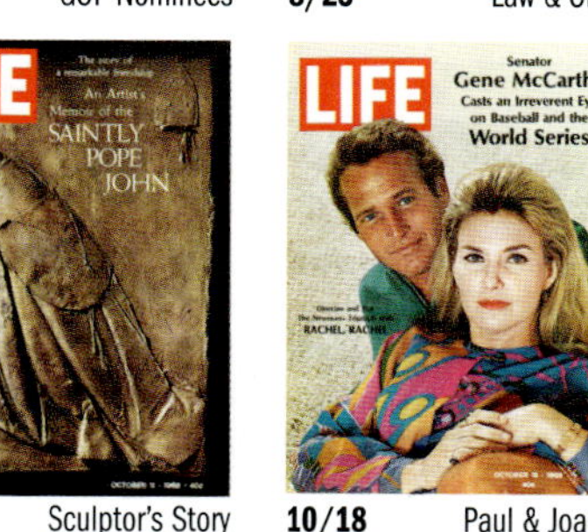

10/18 Paul & Joanne

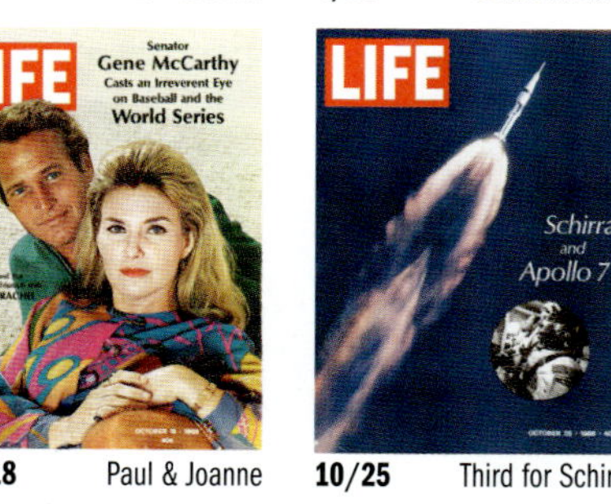

10/25 Third for Schirra

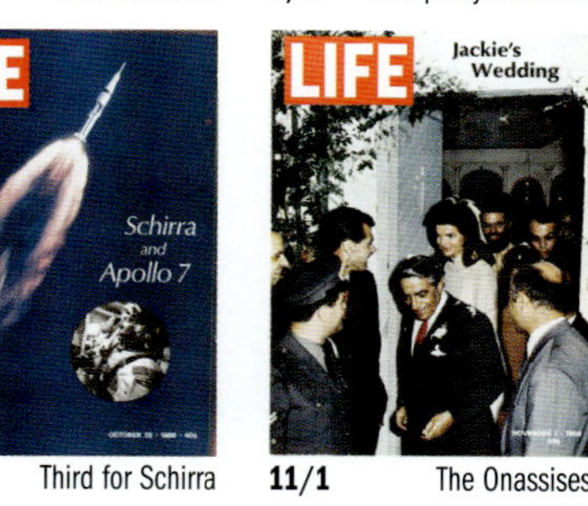

11/1 The Onassises

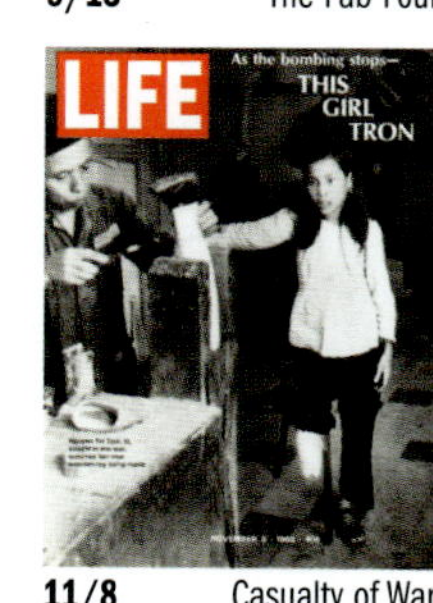

11/8 Casualty of War

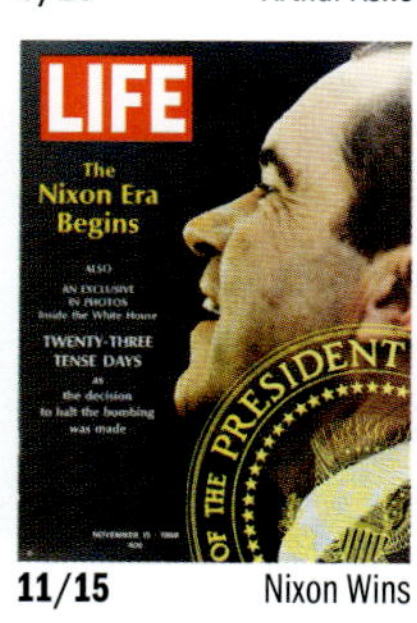

11/15 Nixon Wins

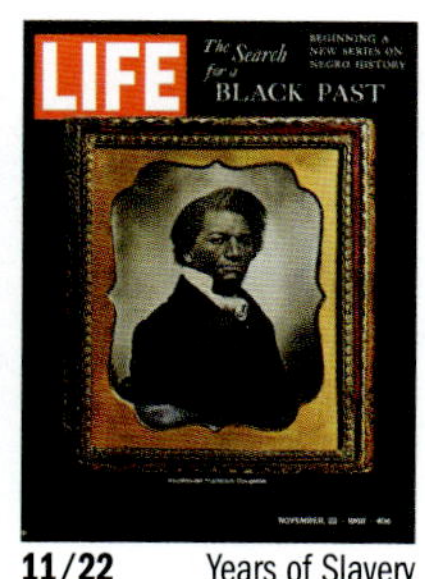

11/22 Years of Slavery

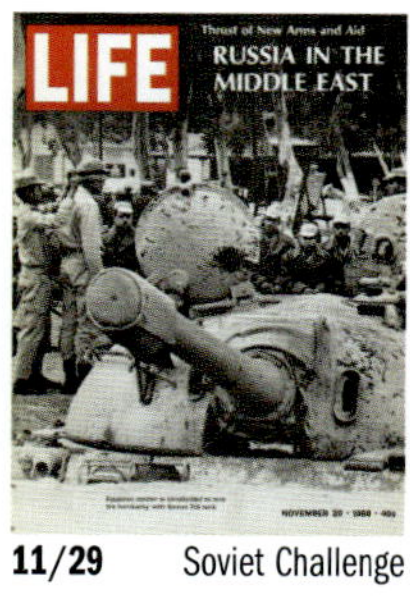

11/29 Soviet Challenge

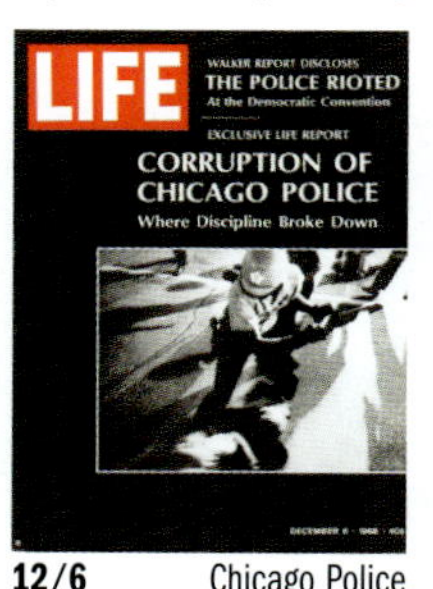

12/6 Chicago Police

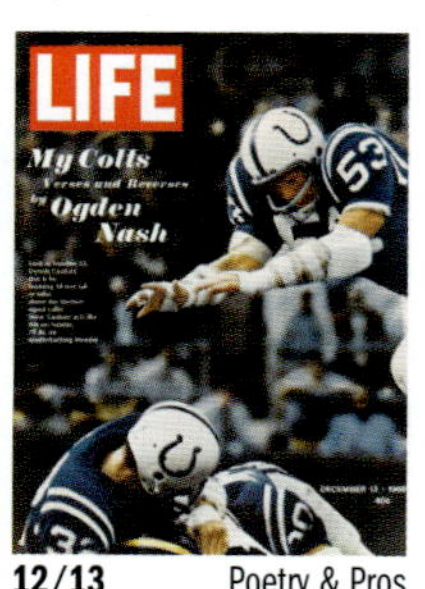

12/13 Poetry & Pros

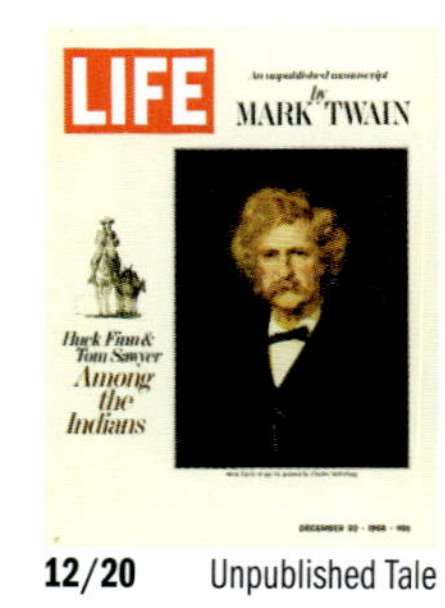

12/20 Unpublished Tale

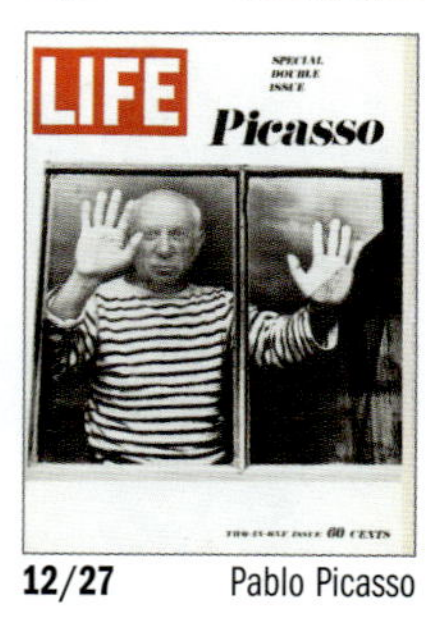

12/27 Pablo Picasso

P, PG, PG-13 and R: The movie rating system is initiated • *60 Minutes* debuts on CBS
North Korean forces seize U.S. intelligence ship *Pueblo*
Tommie Smith and John Carlos deliver black power salute at Mexico City Olympics • Soviet forces invade Czechoslovakia

1969

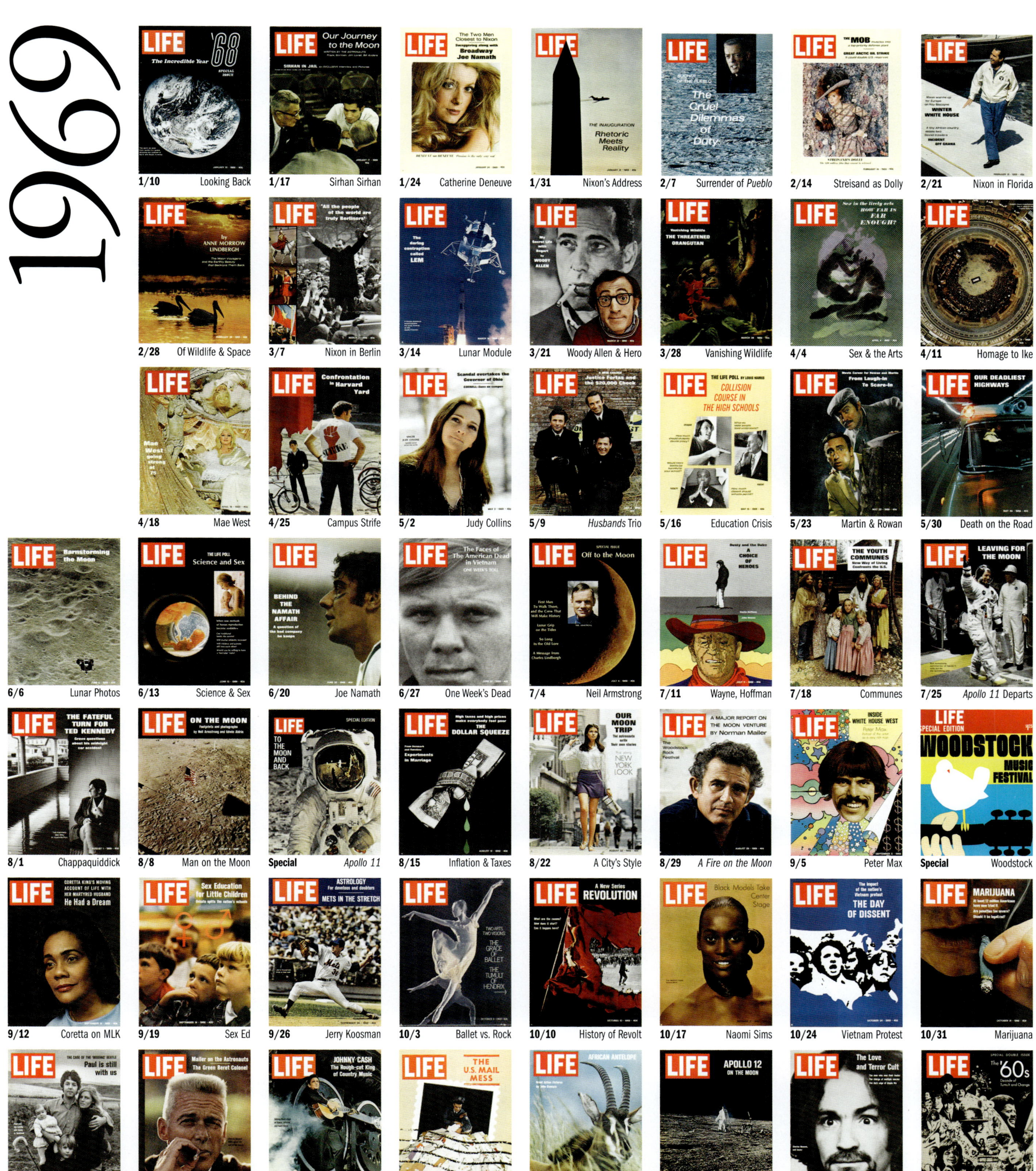

1/10 Looking Back
1/17 Sirhan Sirhan
1/24 Catherine Deneuve
1/31 Nixon's Address
2/7 Surrender of *Pueblo*
2/14 Streisand as Dolly
2/21 Nixon in Florida
2/28 Of Wildlife & Space
3/7 Nixon in Berlin
3/14 Lunar Module
3/21 Woody Allen & Hero
3/28 Vanishing Wildlife
4/4 Sex & the Arts
4/11 Homage to Ike
4/18 Mae West
4/25 Campus Strife
5/2 Judy Collins
5/9 *Husbands* Trio
5/16 Education Crisis
5/23 Martin & Rowan
5/30 Death on the Road
6/6 Lunar Photos
6/13 Science & Sex
6/20 Joe Namath
6/27 One Week's Dead
7/4 Neil Armstrong
7/11 Wayne, Hoffman
7/18 Communes
7/25 *Apollo 11* Departs
8/1 Chappaquiddick
8/8 Man on the Moon
Special *Apollo 11*
8/15 Inflation & Taxes
8/22 A City's Style
8/29 *A Fire on the Moon*
9/5 Peter Max
Special Woodstock
9/12 Coretta on MLK
9/19 Sex Ed
9/26 Jerry Koosman
10/3 Ballet vs. Rock
10/10 History of Revolt
10/17 Naomi Sims
10/24 Vietnam Protest
10/31 Marijuana
11/7 McCartney & Family
11/14 Colonel Rheault
11/21 Johnny Cash
11/28 Postal Mess
12/5 Antelopes
12/12 Moon Visit
12/19 Charles Manson
12/26 End of a Decade

Sesame Street is introduced, with Big Bird as its first star • Mario Puzo's *The Godfather* is a best-seller • Nudie musical *Oh! Calcutta* opens off-Broadway • The first automatic teller machine is installed in a bank in Rockville Centre, N.Y. The supersonic *Concorde* makes its maiden flight

1970

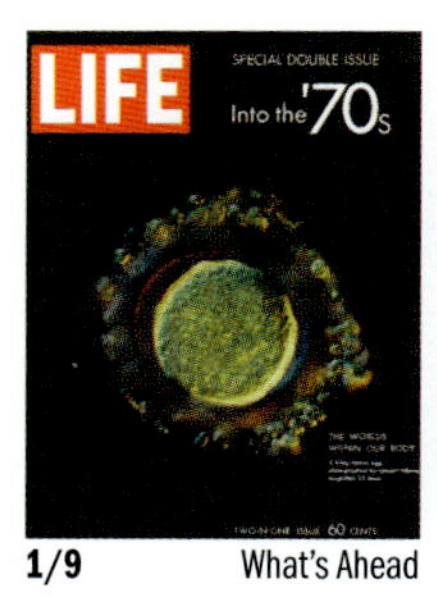
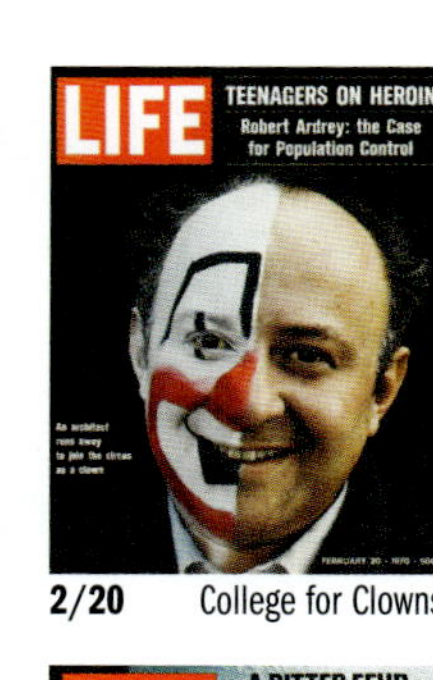
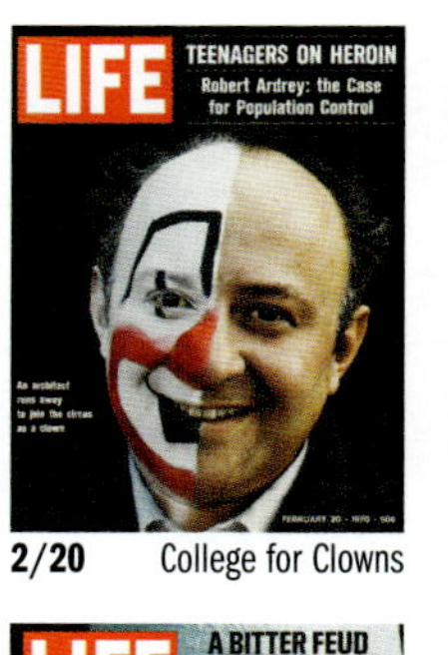
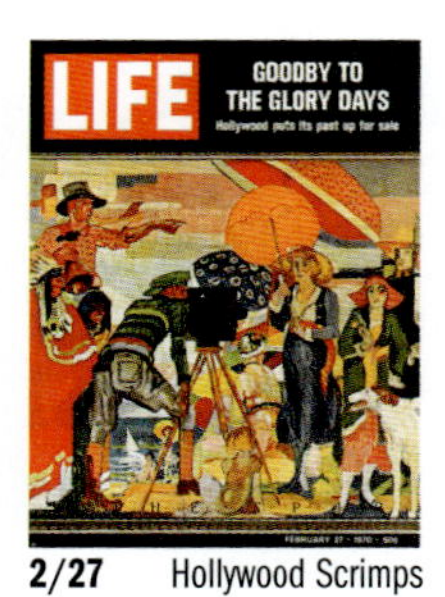

1/9 What's Ahead · 1/23 Johnny Carson · 1/30 Snow Monkeys · 2/6 Robert Redford · 2/13 Survival Tactics · 2/20 College for Clowns · 2/27 Hollywood Scrimps

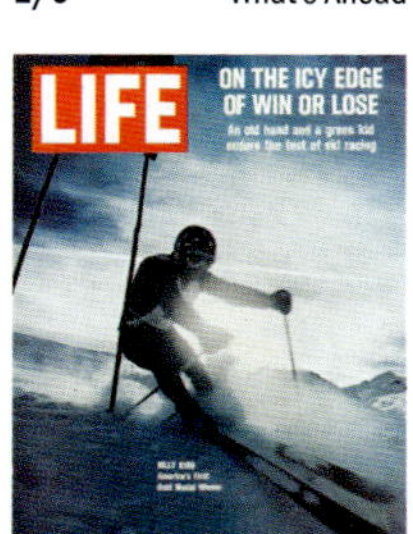
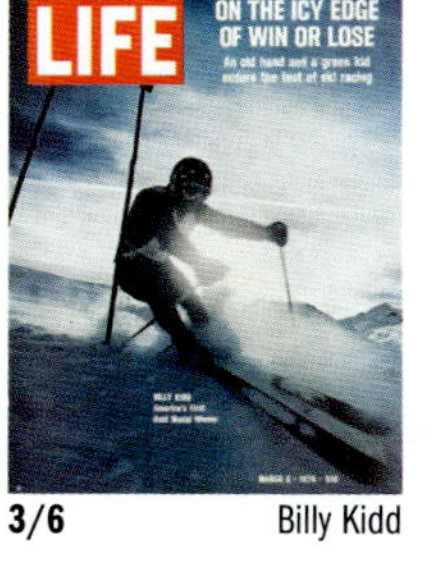
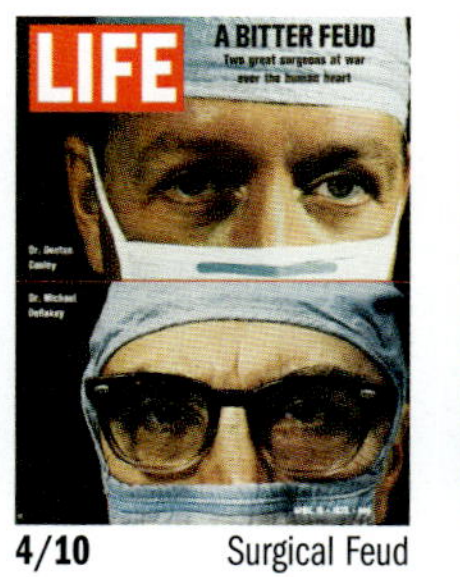
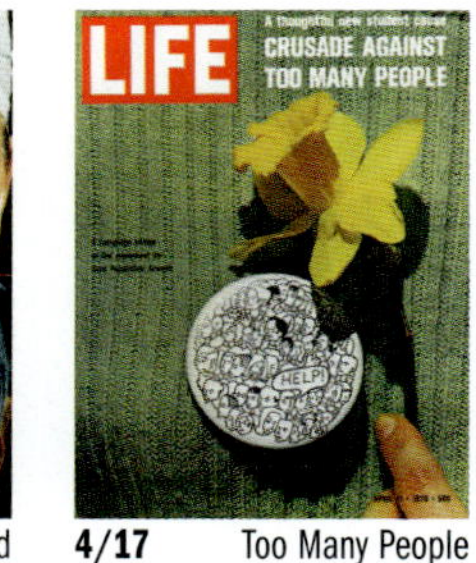

3/6 Billy Kidd · 3/13 Hemlines · 3/20 Dogma & Dissent · 3/27 Credit Cards · 4/3 Lauren Bacall · 4/10 Surgical Feud · 4/17 Too Many People

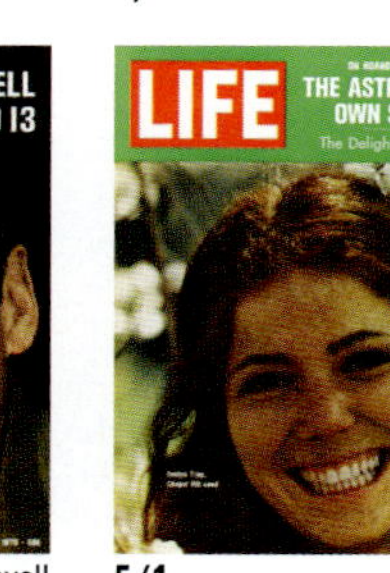
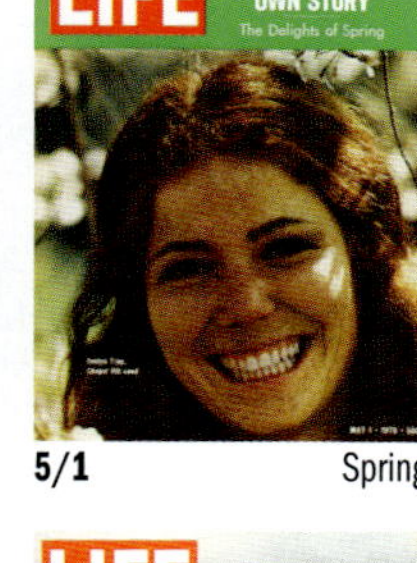
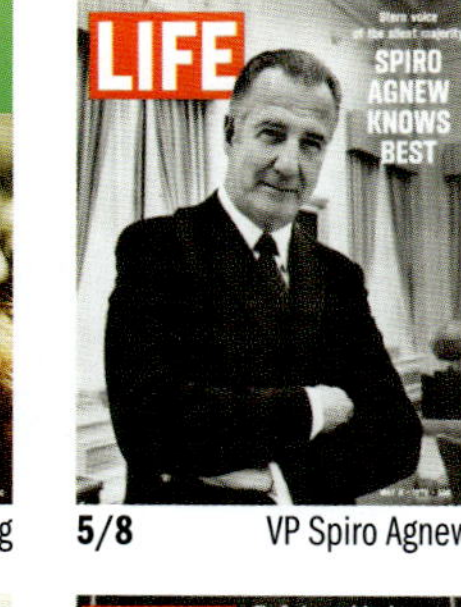
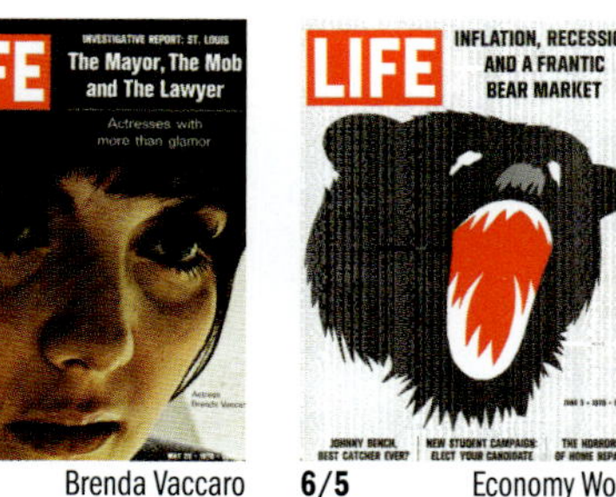

4/24 Jim Lovell · 5/1 Spring · 5/8 VP Spiro Agnew · 5/15 Kent State · 5/22 VA Hospitals · 5/29 Brenda Vaccaro · 6/5 Economy Woes

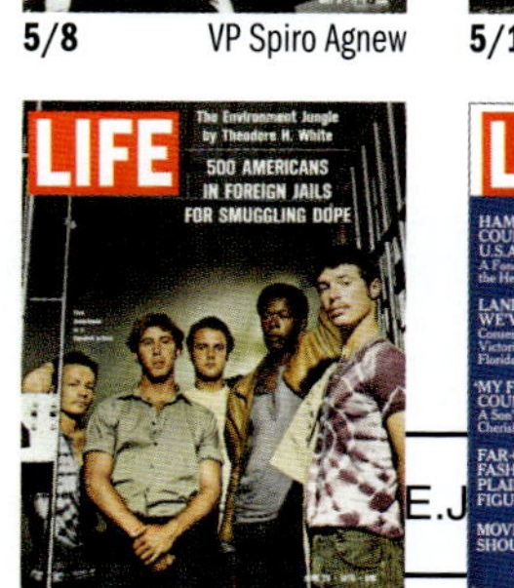
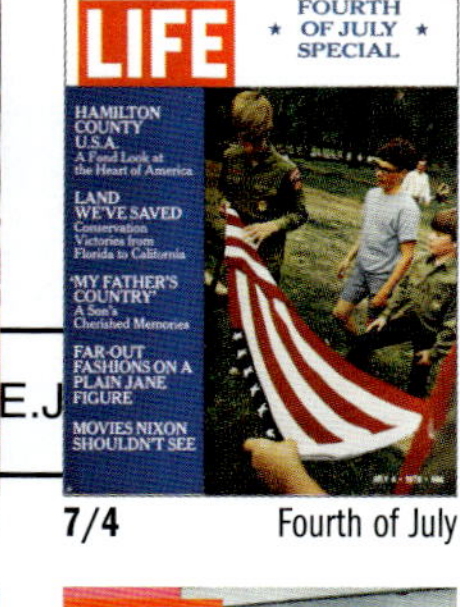
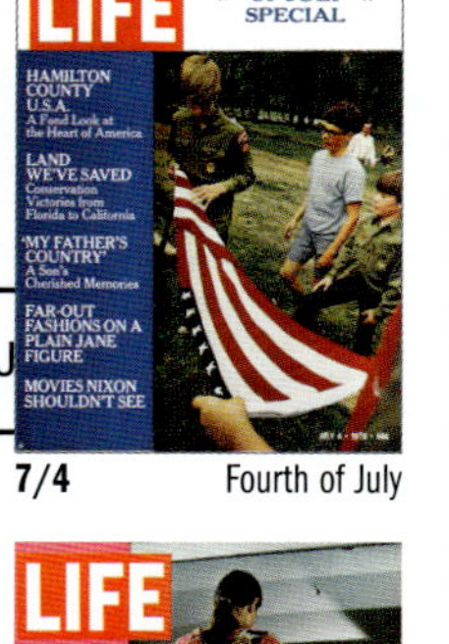
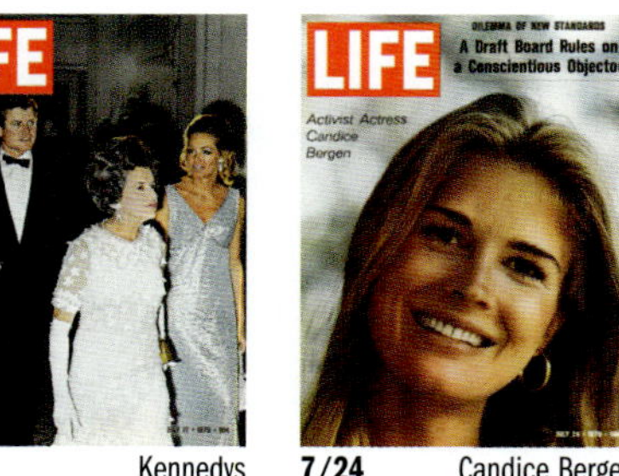

6/12 Student Guerrillas · 6/19 Dennis Hopper · 6/26 Busted Abroad · 7/4 Fourth of July · 7/10 Sun & Surf · 7/17 Kennedys · 7/24 Candice Bergen

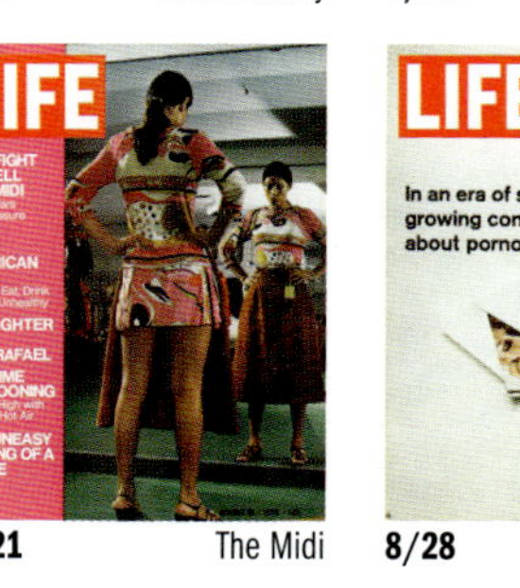
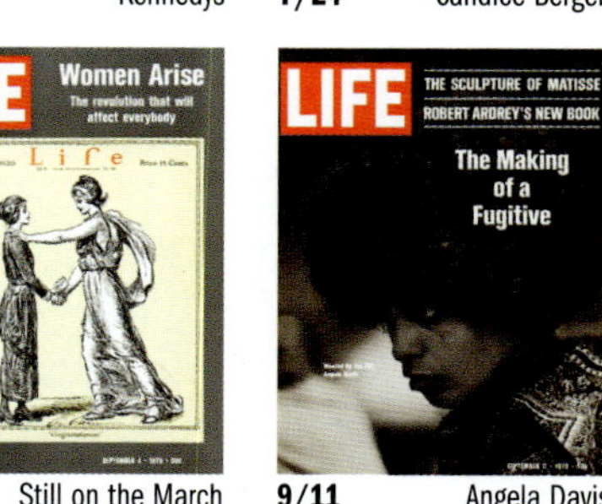
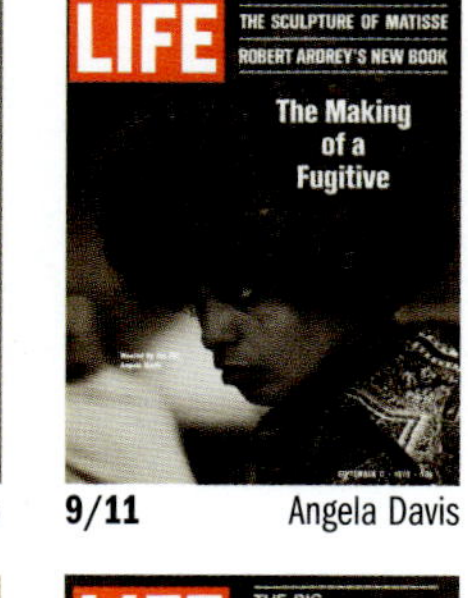

7/31 Bebe Rebozo · 8/7 Insider's Report · 8/14 America Travels · 8/21 The Midi · 8/28 Pornography · 9/4 Still on the March · 9/11 Angela Davis

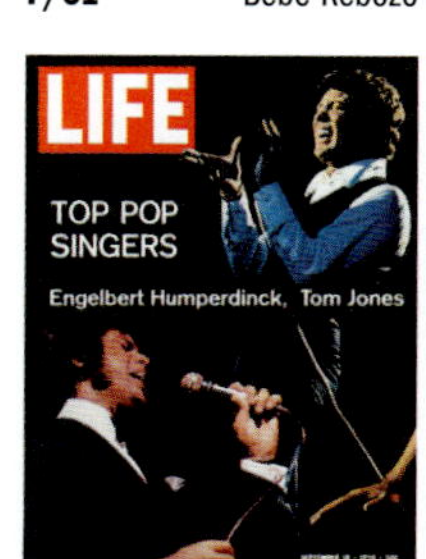
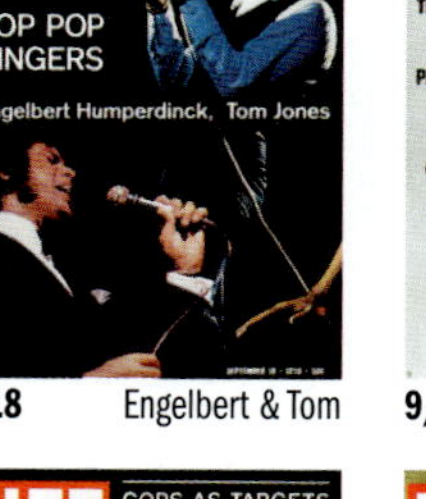
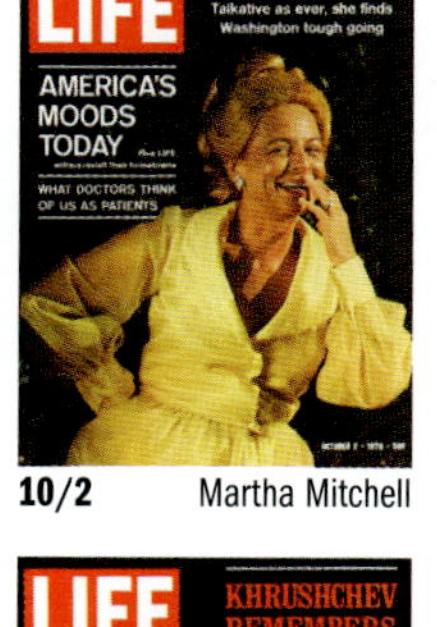
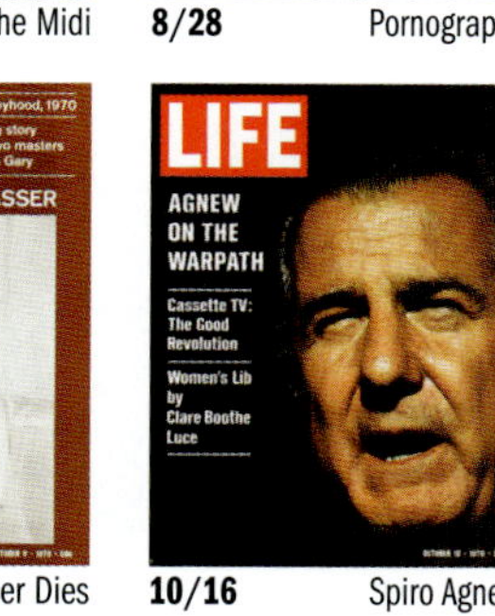
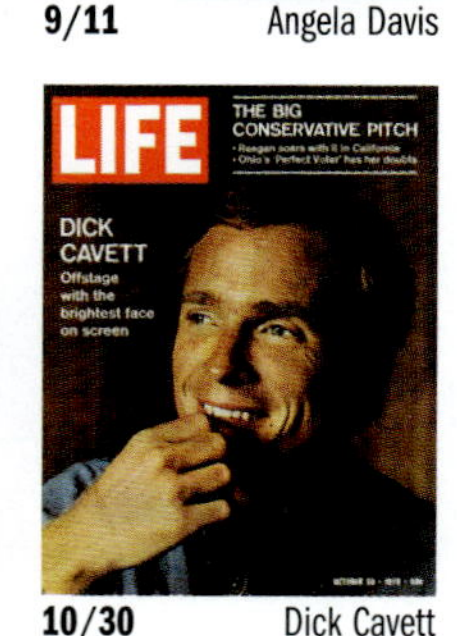

9/18 Engelbert & Tom · 9/25 Dandyism Returns · 10/2 Martha Mitchell · 10/9 Egypt's Nasser Dies · 10/16 Spiro Agnew · 10/23 Muhammad Ali · 10/30 Dick Cavett

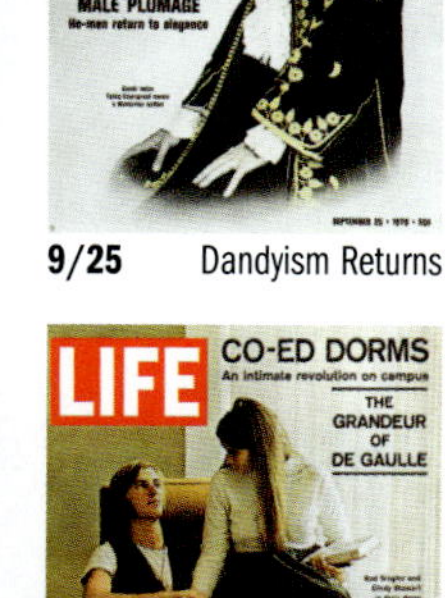
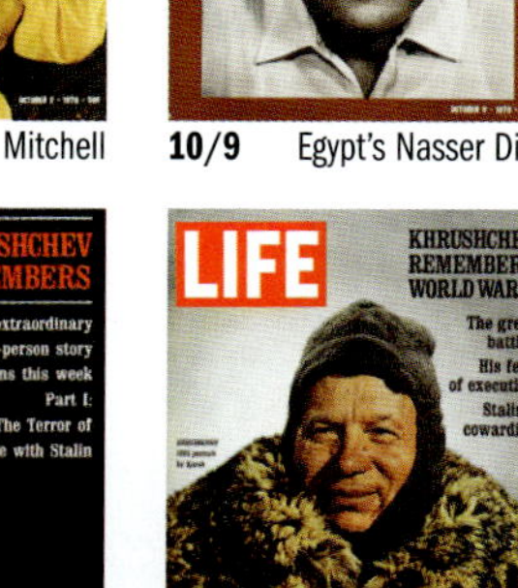
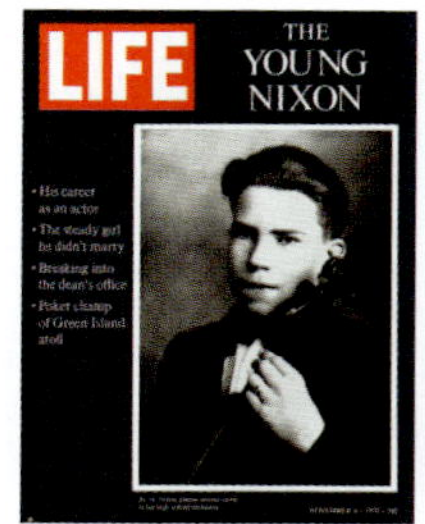
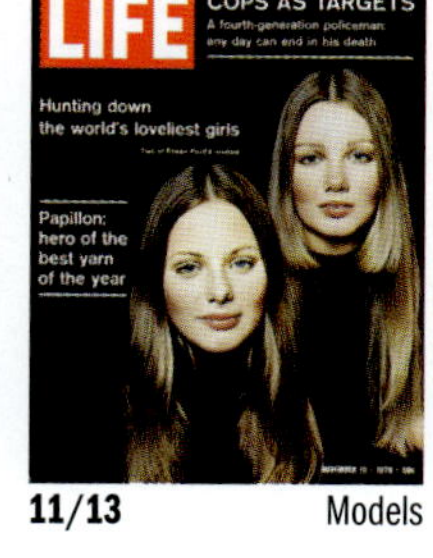
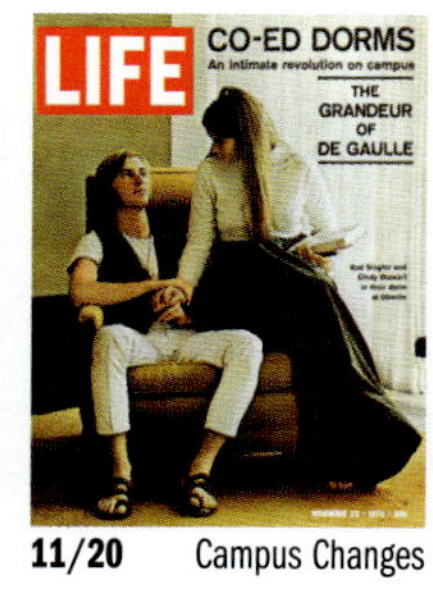
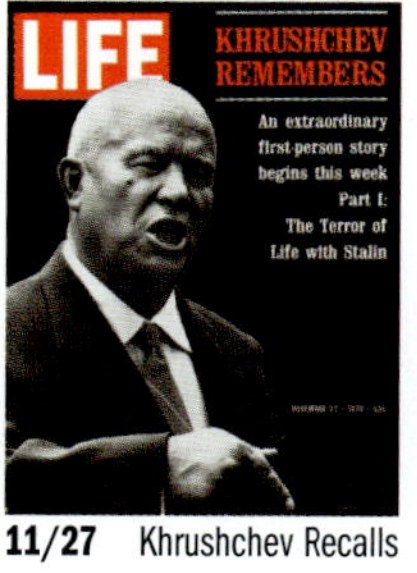
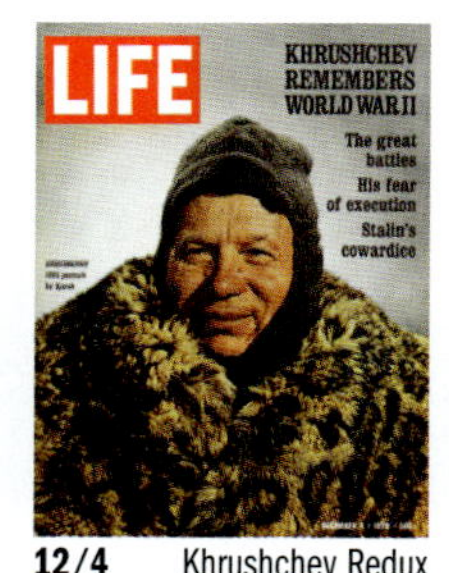
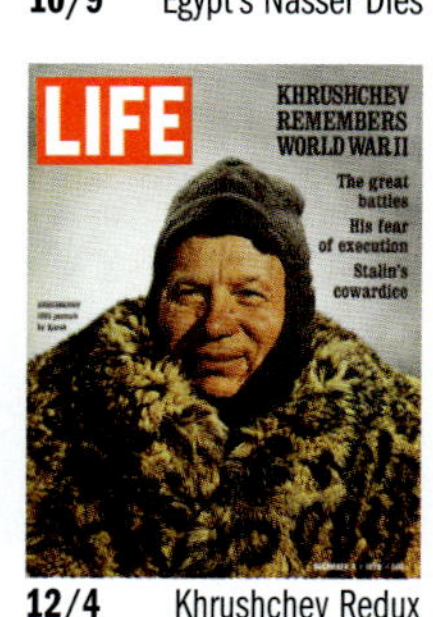
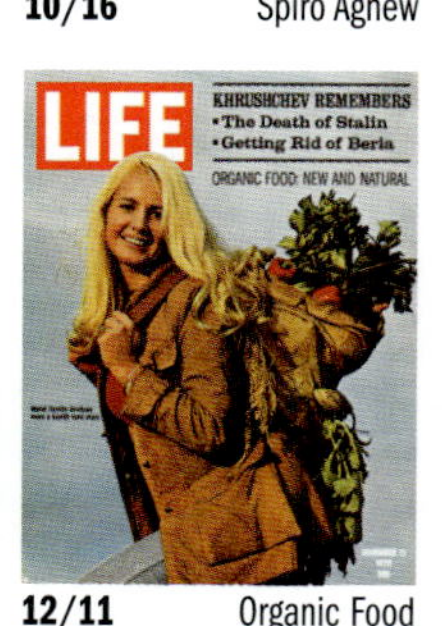
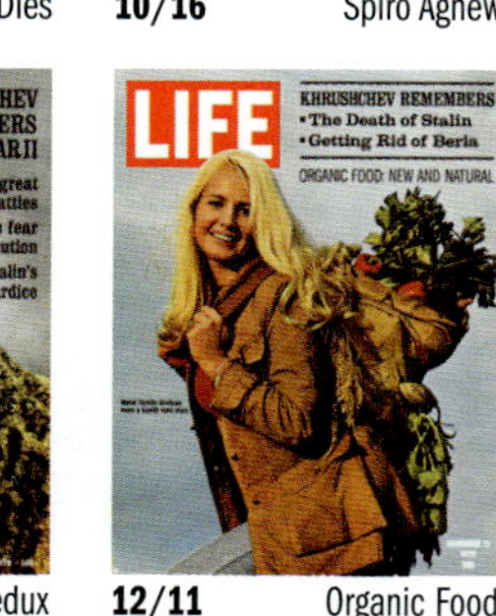
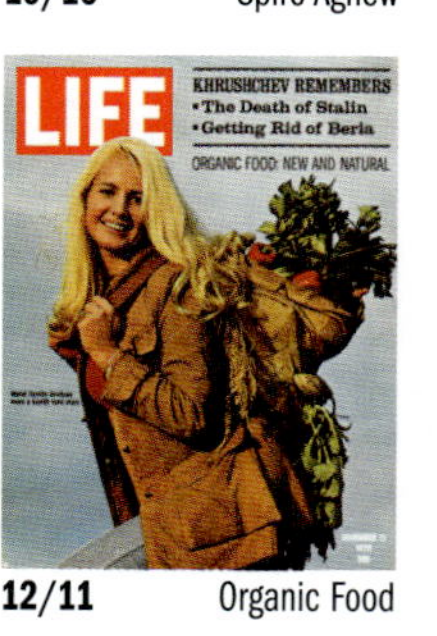
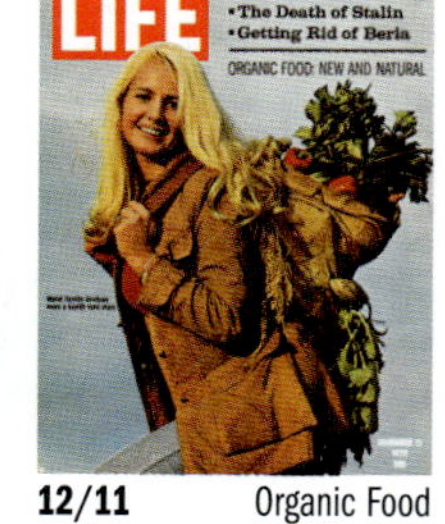
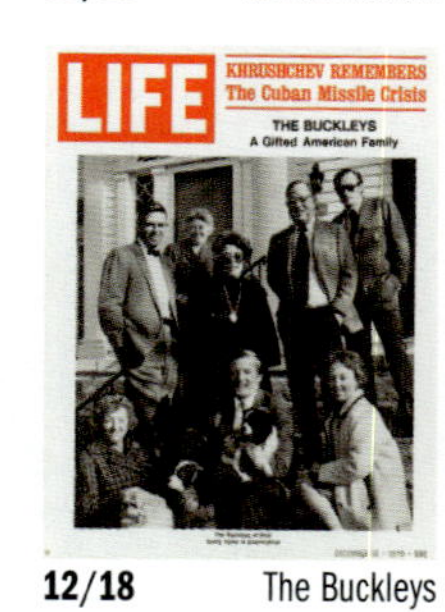
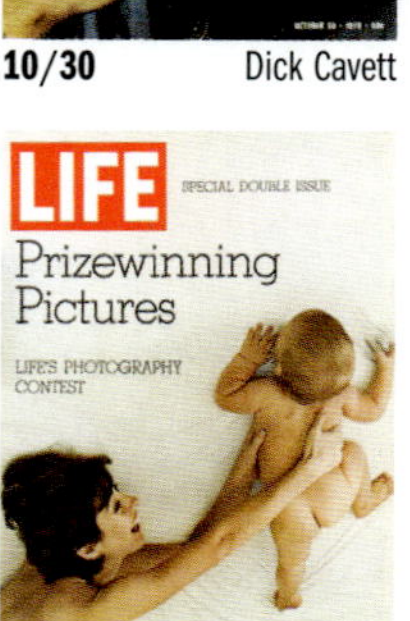
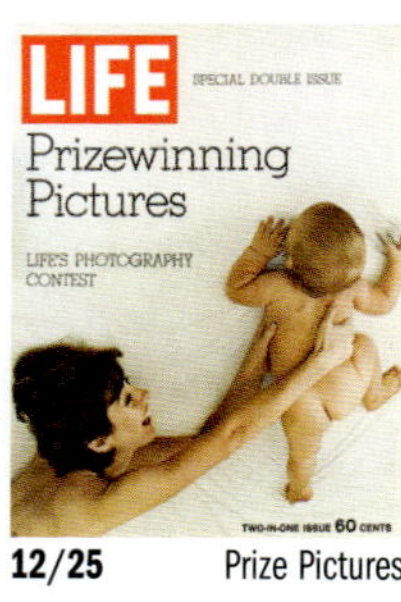

11/6 Nixon's Youth · 11/13 Models · 11/20 Campus Changes · 11/27 Khrushchev Recalls · 12/4 Khrushchev Redux · 12/11 Organic Food · 12/18 The Buckleys · 12/25 Prize Pictures

The U.S. population is 203,302,031 • Cartoonist Garry Trudeau introduces *Doonesbury*
55 runners cross the finish line at the inaugural New York City Marathon • The first Earth Day brings out millions of demonstrators
Monday Night Football premieres

1971

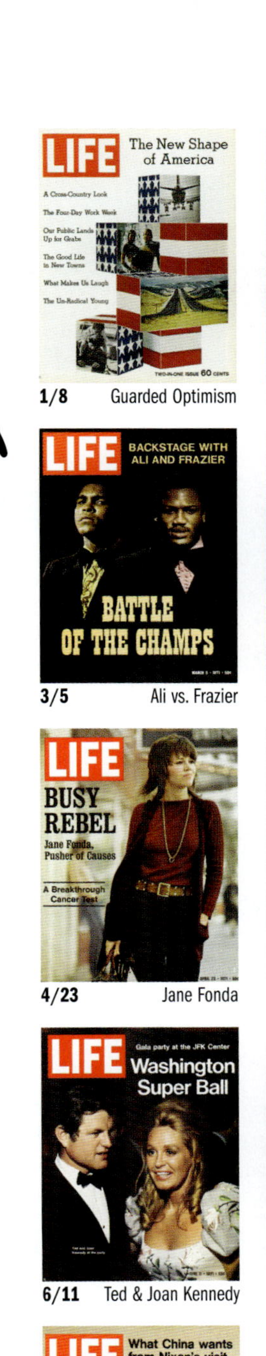
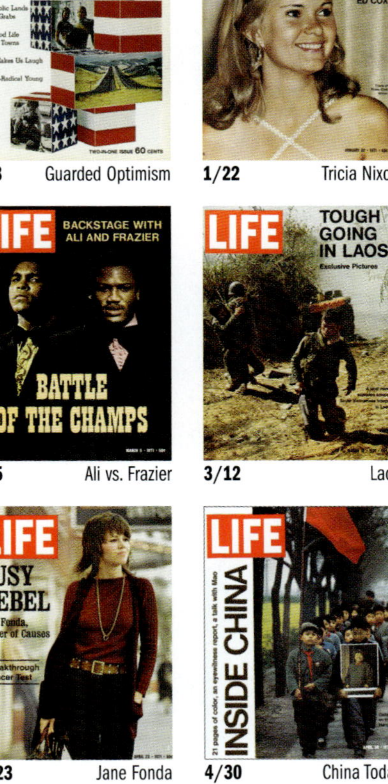

1/8 Guarded Optimism | 1/22 Tricia Nixon | 1/29 Bob Hope | 2/5 The New Army | 2/12 Jackie Onassis | 2/19 Nostalgia | 2/26 Snowmobiles

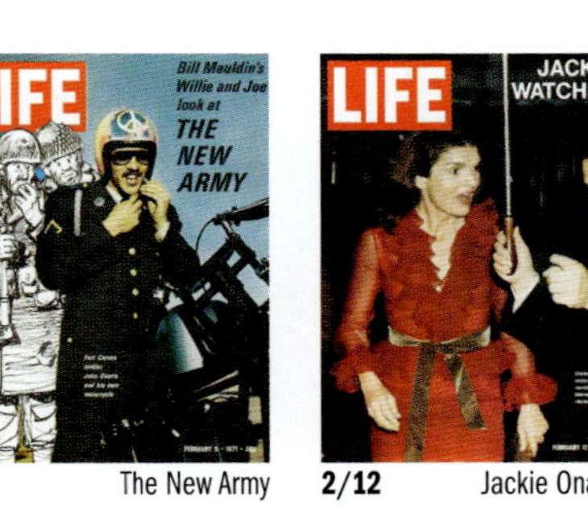
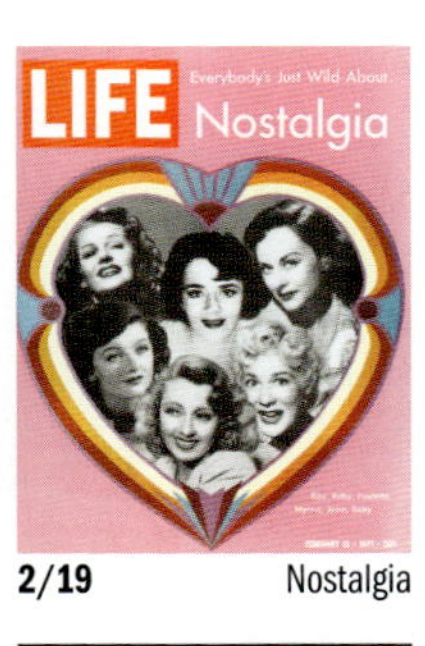
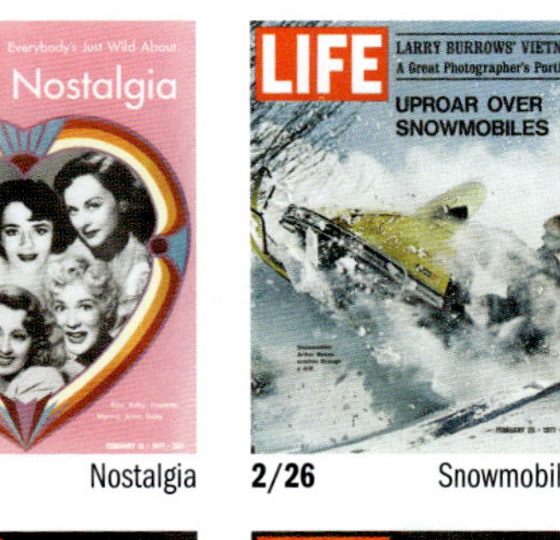

3/5 Ali vs. Frazier | 3/12 Laos | 3/19 Frazier Still Champ | 3/26 Walter Cronkite | 4/2 Student Mothers | 4/9 J. Edgar Hoover | 4/16 The McCartneys

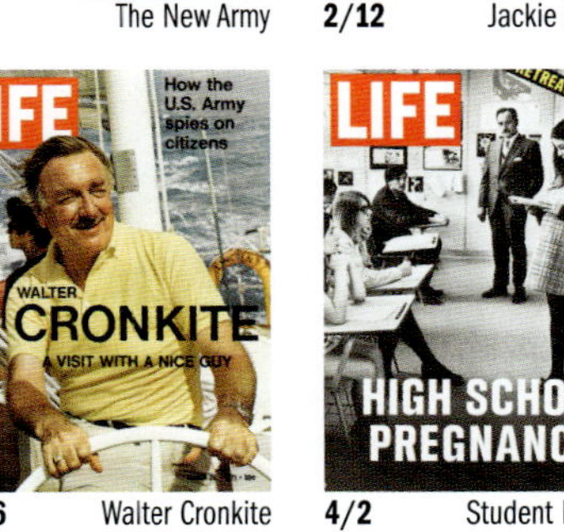
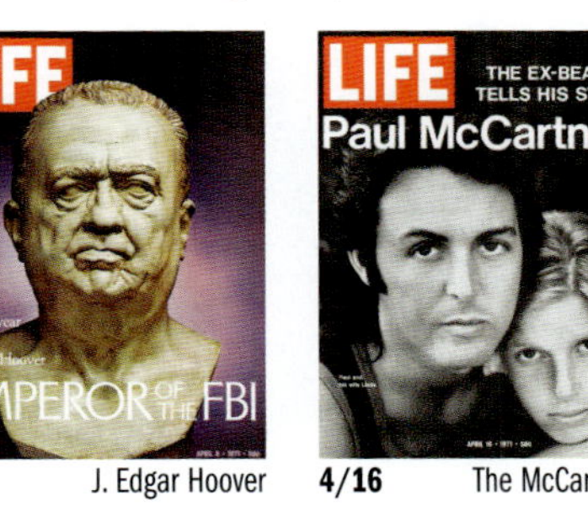
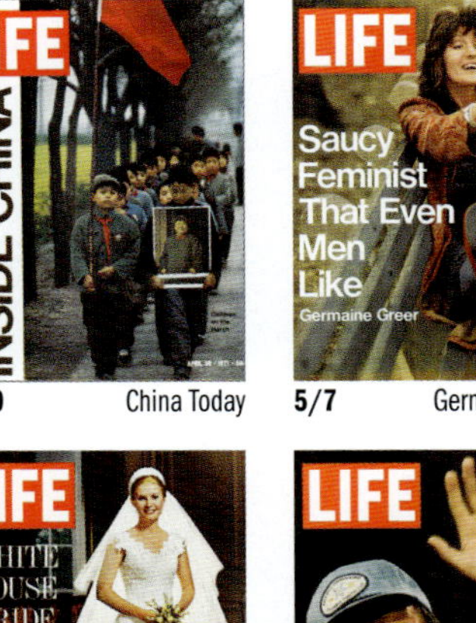

4/23 Jane Fonda | 4/30 China Today | 5/7 Germaine Greer | 5/14 Carol Burnett | 5/21 Citizen LBJ | 5/28 Rock Opera | 6/4 Cristina Ford

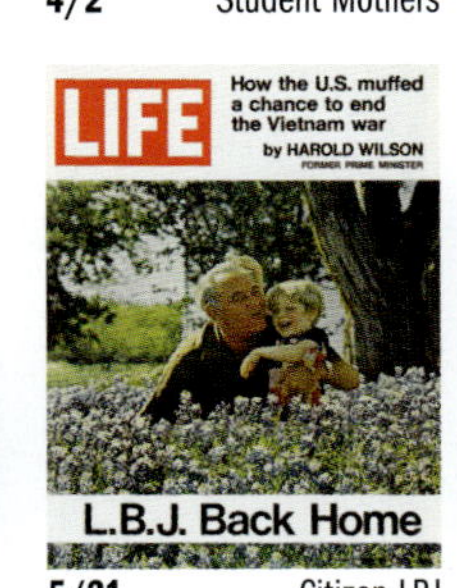
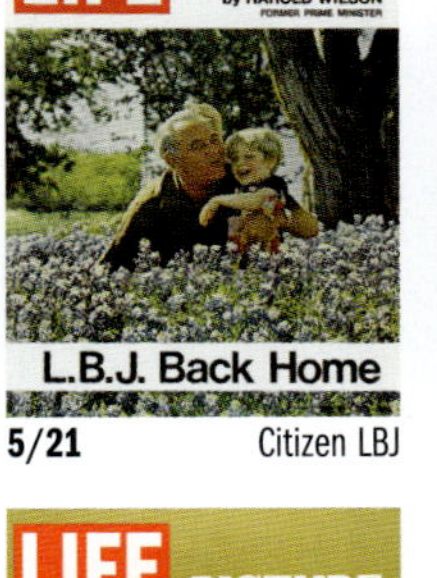
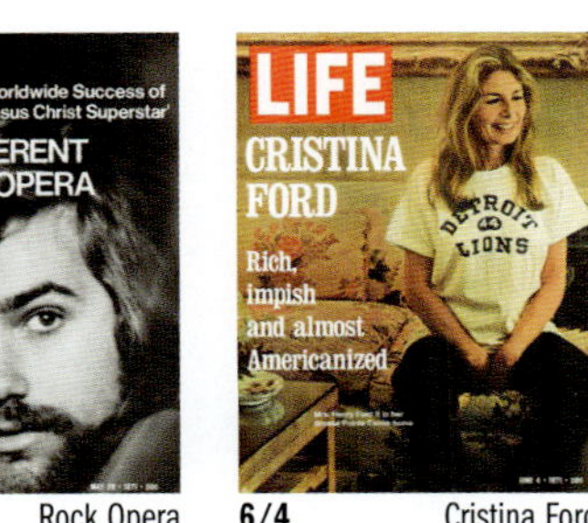
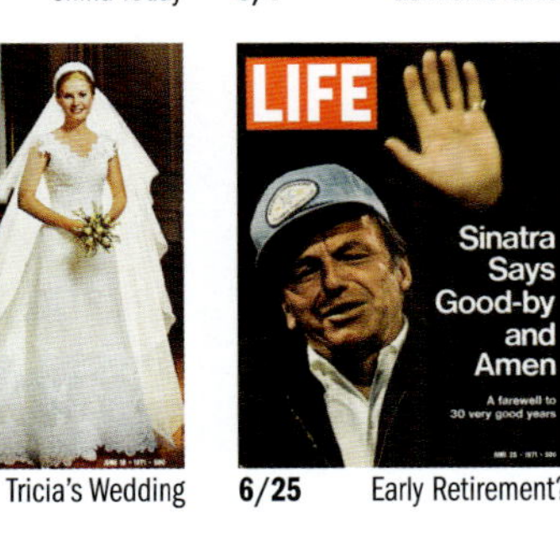
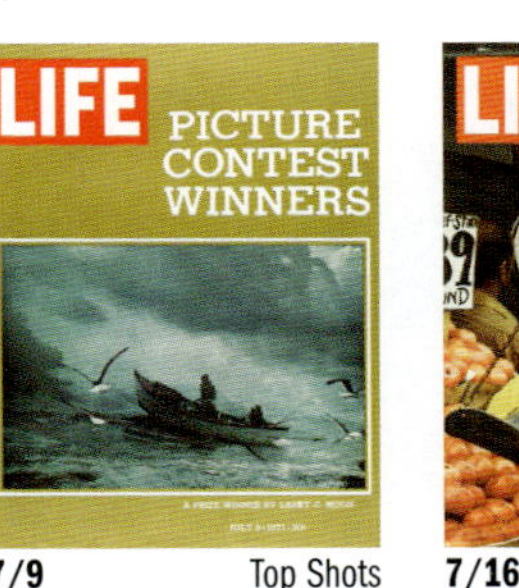
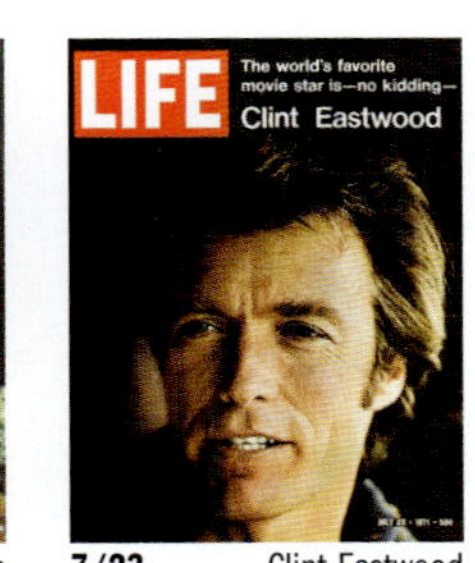

6/11 Ted & Joan Kennedy | 6/18 Tricia's Wedding | 6/25 Early Retirement? | 7/2 Native Americans | 7/9 Top Shots | 7/16 Bess Myerson | 7/23 Clint Eastwood

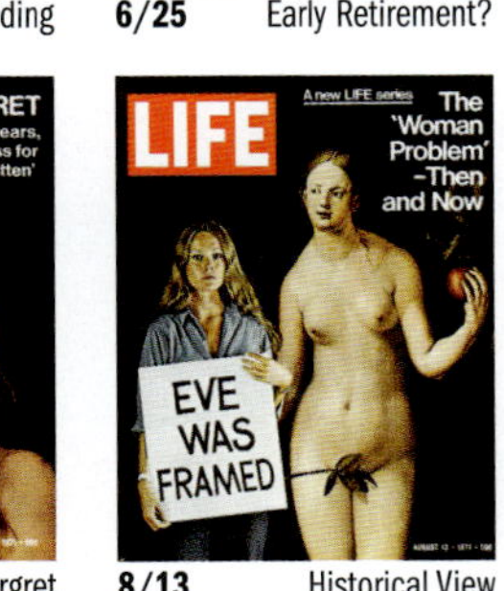
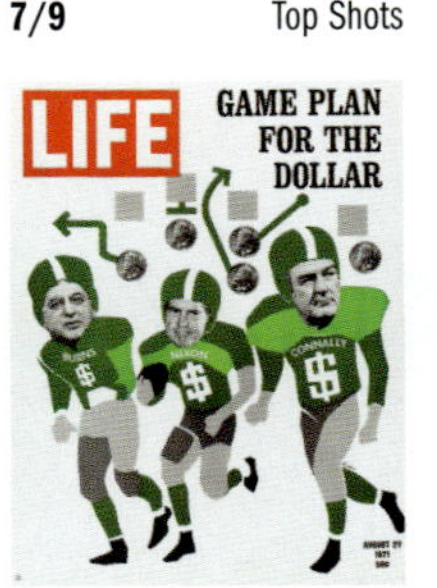
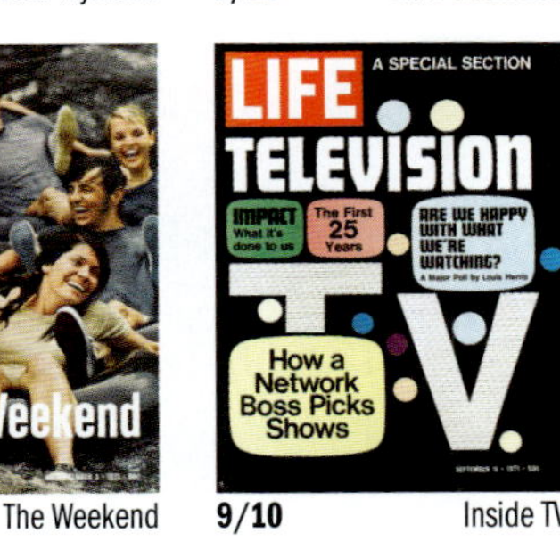
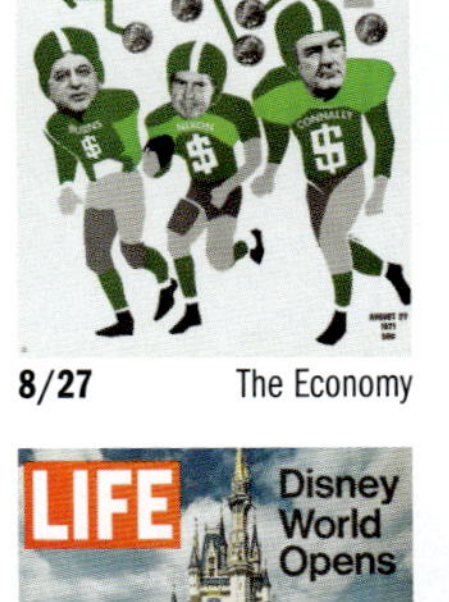

7/30 Chou En-lai | 8/6 Ann-Margret | 8/13 Historical View | 8/20 Princess Anne | 8/27 The Economy | 9/3 The Weekend | 9/10 Inside TV

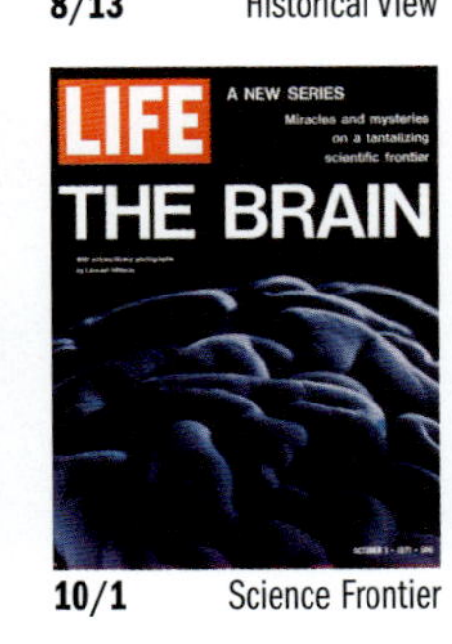
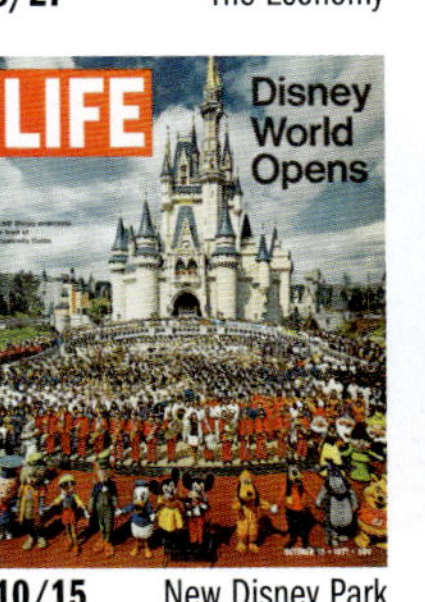
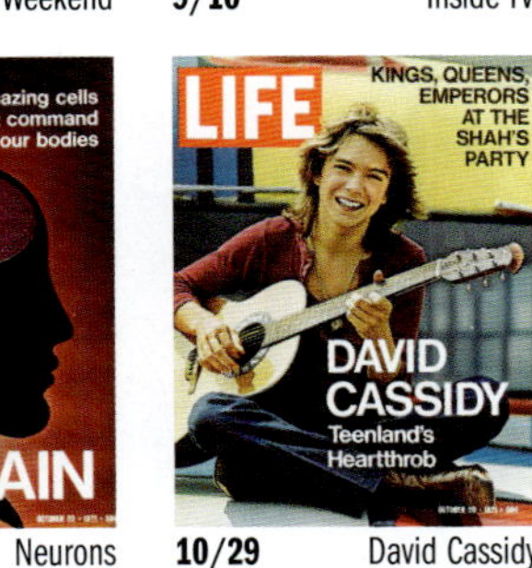
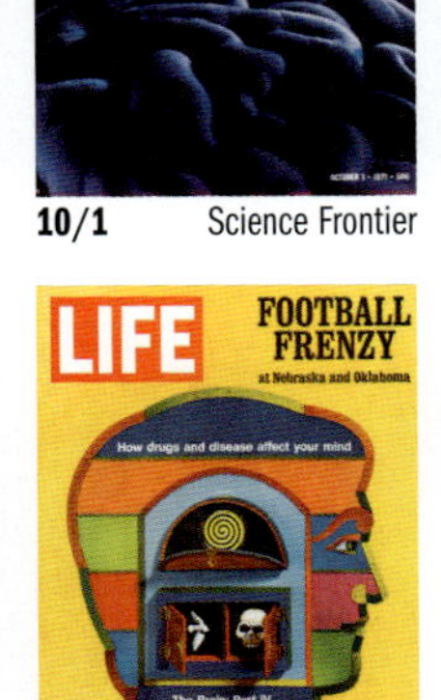
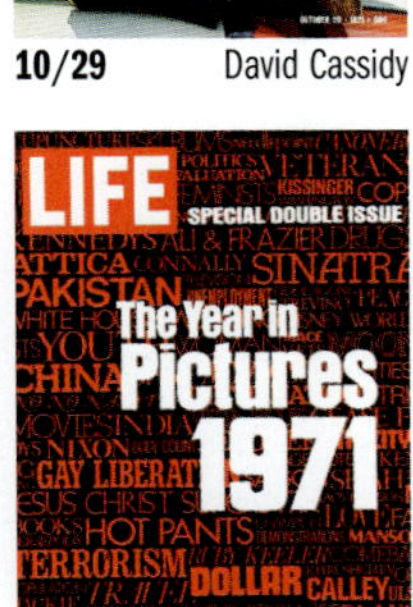

9/17 Reconsideration | 9/24 Rock Families | 10/1 Science Frontier | 10/8 '72 Models | 10/15 New Disney Park | 10/22 Neurons | 10/29 David Cassidy

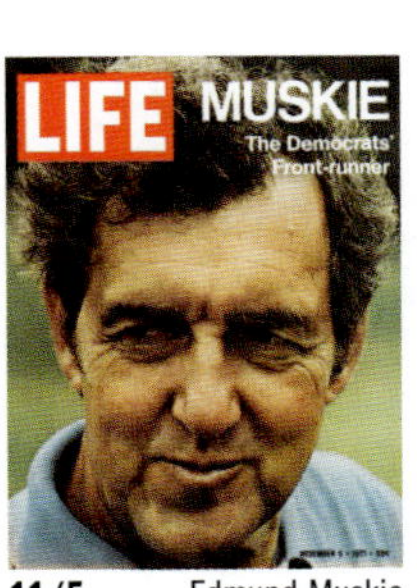
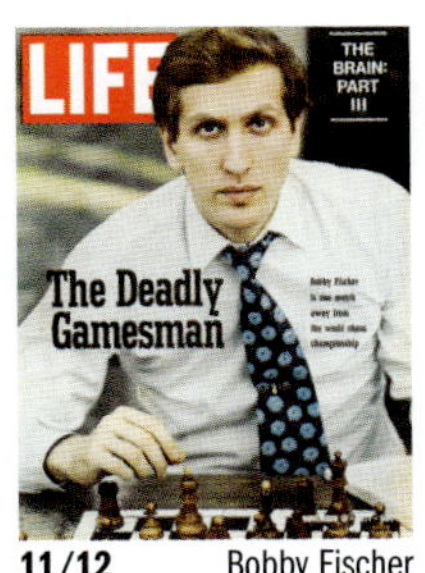
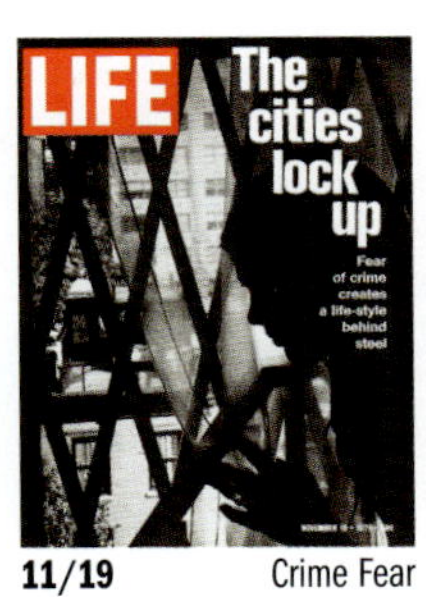
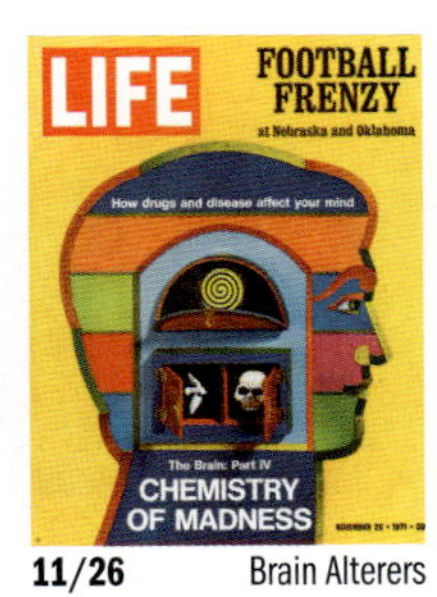
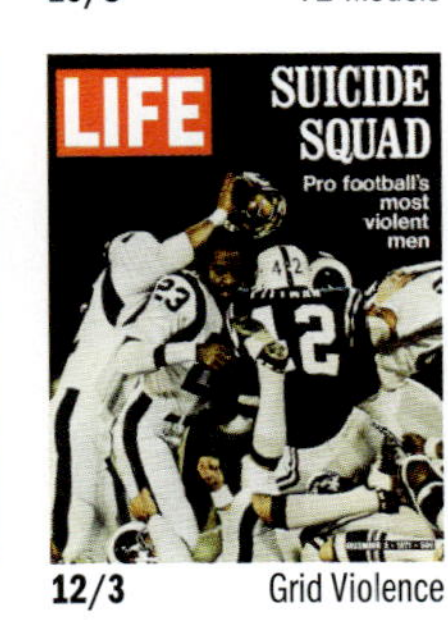
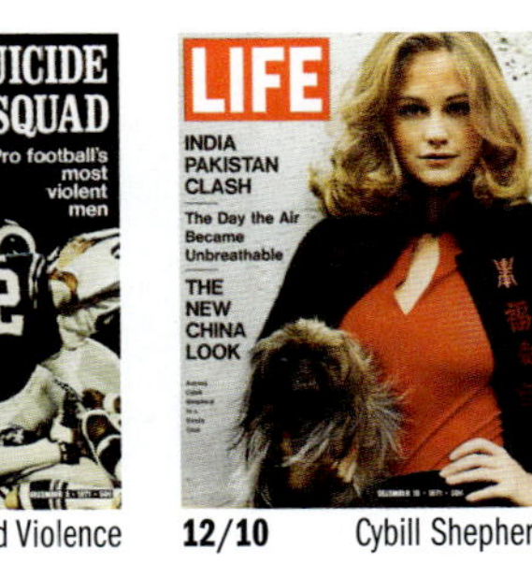
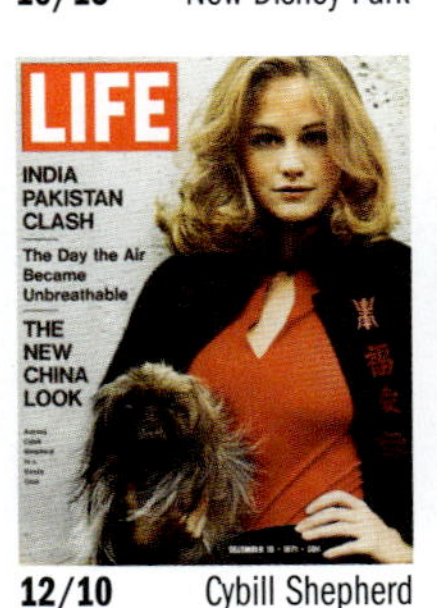
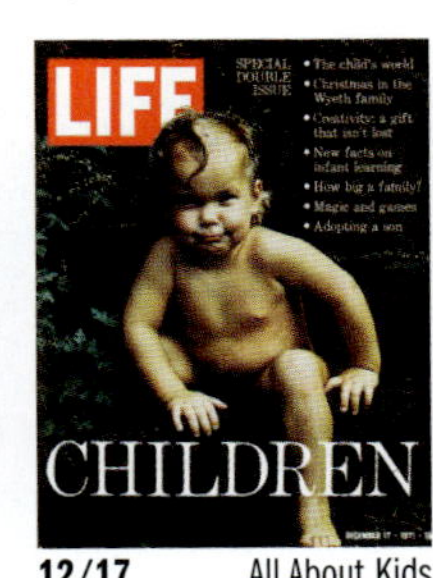

11/5 Edmund Muskie | 11/12 Bobby Fischer | 11/19 Crime Fear | 11/26 Brain Alterers | 12/3 Grid Violence | 12/10 Cybill Shepherd | 12/17 All About Kids | 12/31 Year in Pictures

The 26th Amendment lowers the voting age to 18 • Charles Manson and three cultists are found guilty of killing Sharon Tate
Cigarette ads are banned on TV • CBS broadcasts *All in the Family*
The first segments of the classified Pentagon Papers appear in *The New York Times*

1972

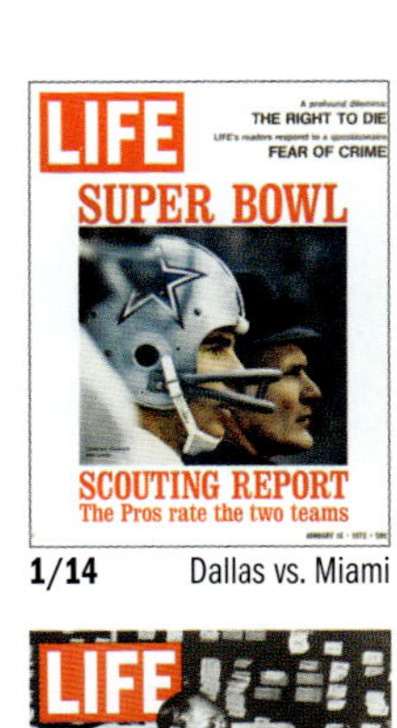

1/14 Dallas vs. Miami

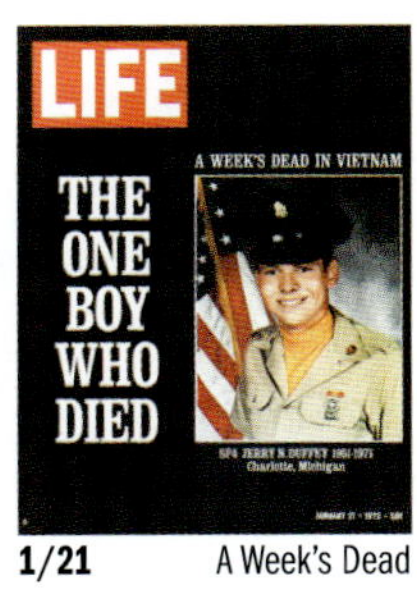

1/21 A Week's Dead

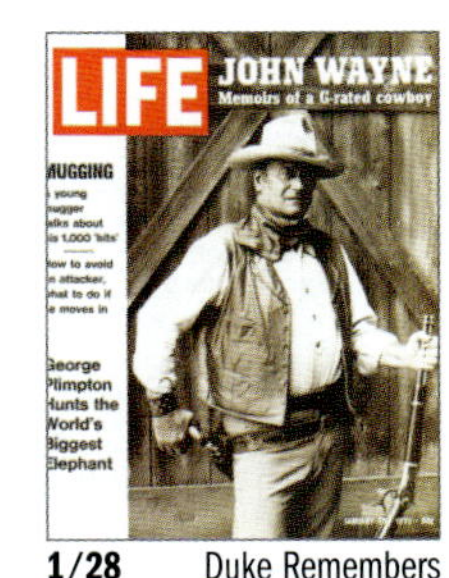

1/28 Duke Remembers

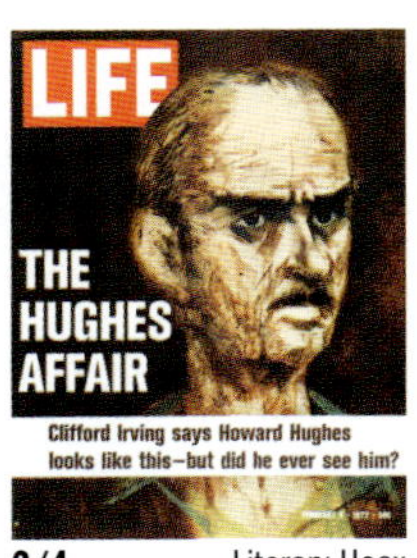

2/4 Literary Hoax

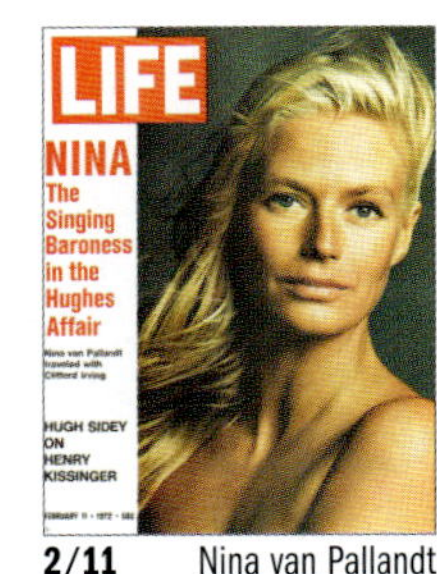

2/11 Nina van Pallandt

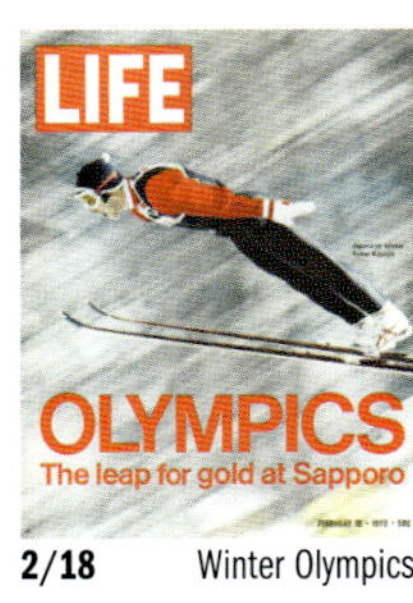

2/18 Winter Olympics

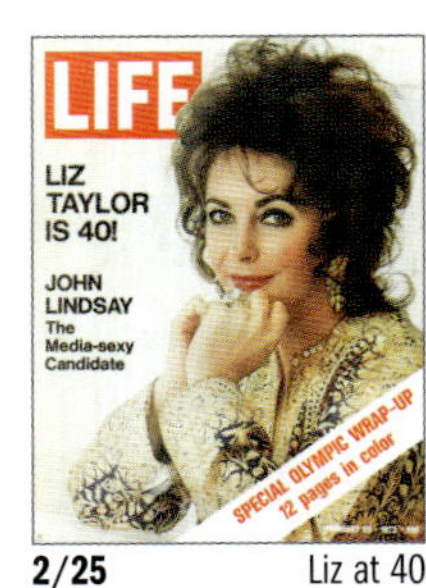

2/25 Liz at 40

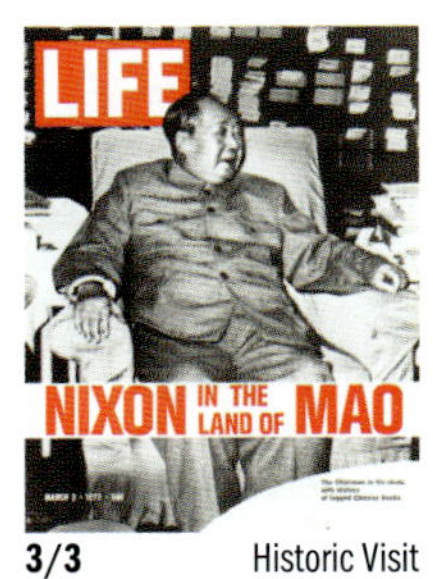

3/3 Historic Visit

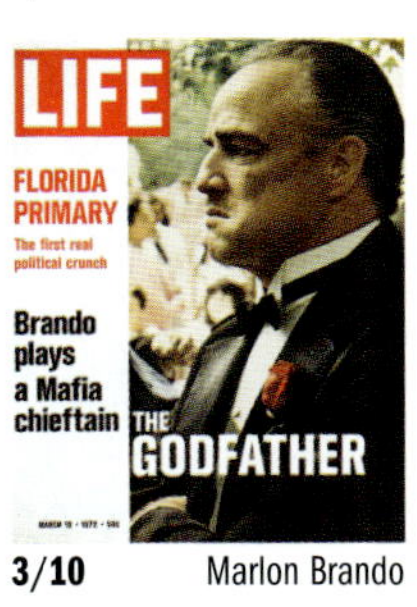

3/10 Marlon Brando

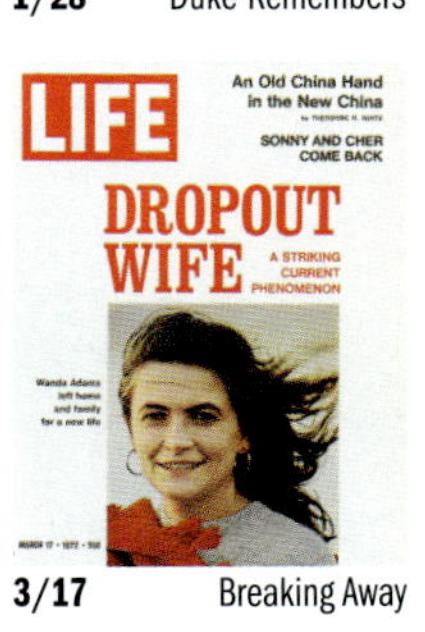

3/17 Breaking Away

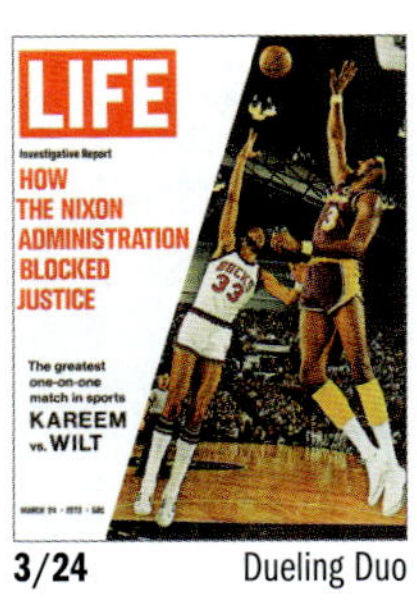

3/24 Dueling Duo

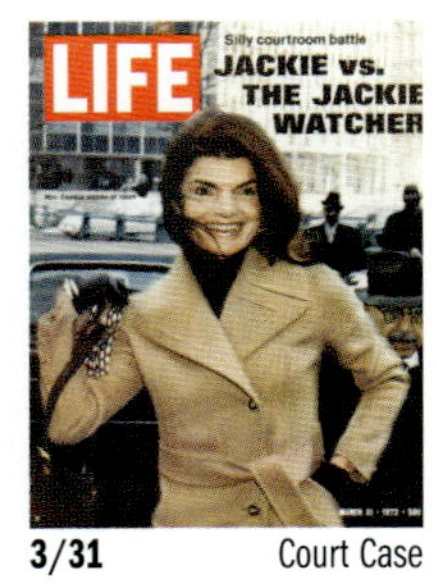

3/31 Court Case

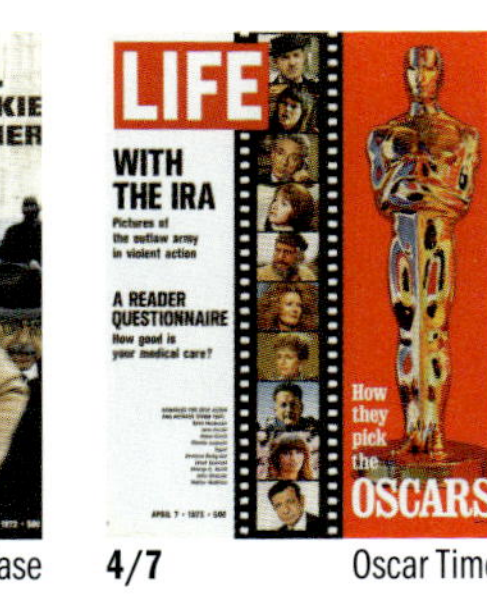

4/7 Oscar Time

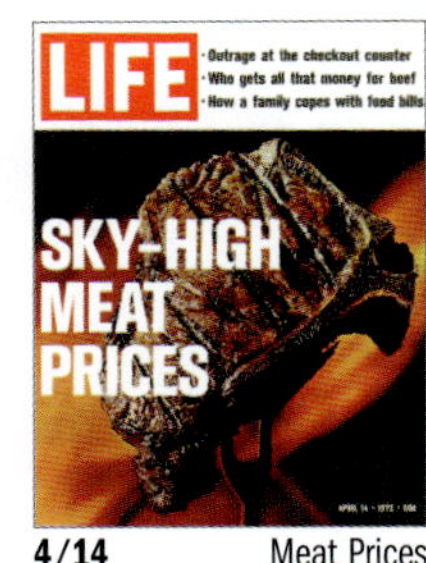

4/14 Meat Prices

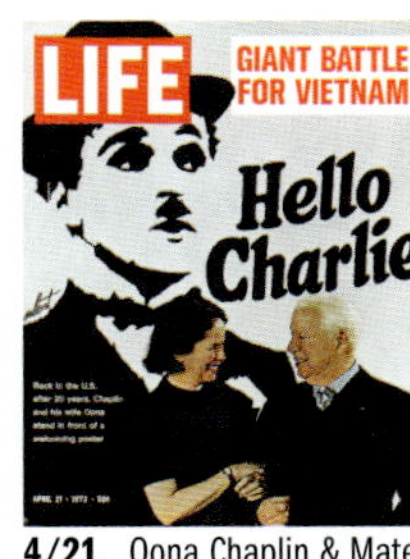

4/21 Oona Chaplin & Mate

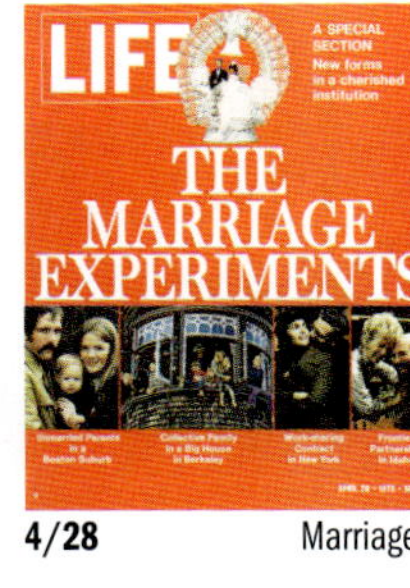

4/28 Marriage

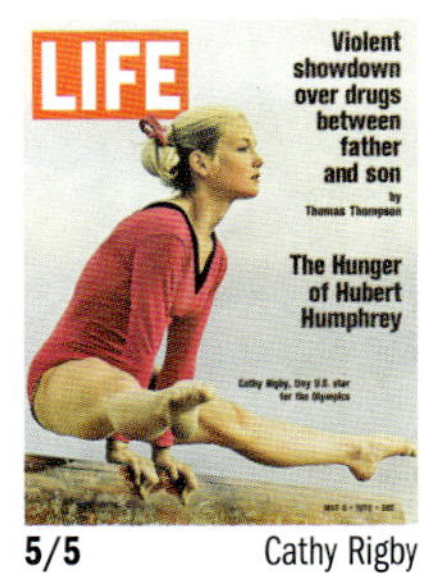

5/5 Cathy Rigby

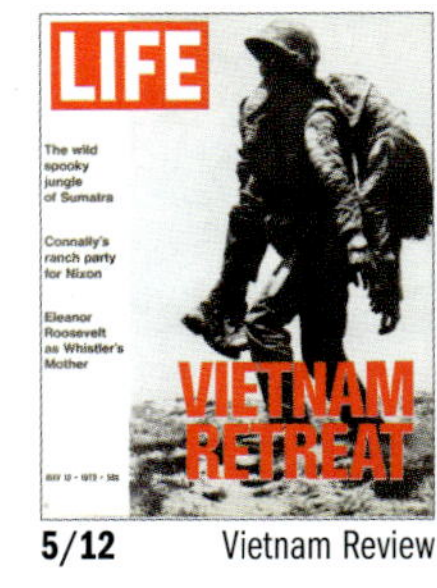

5/12 Vietnam Review

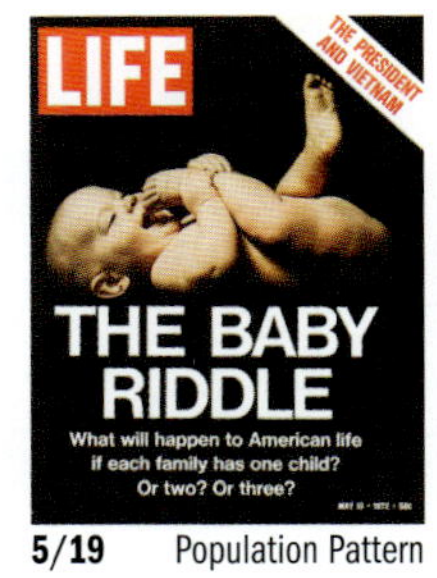

5/19 Population Pattern

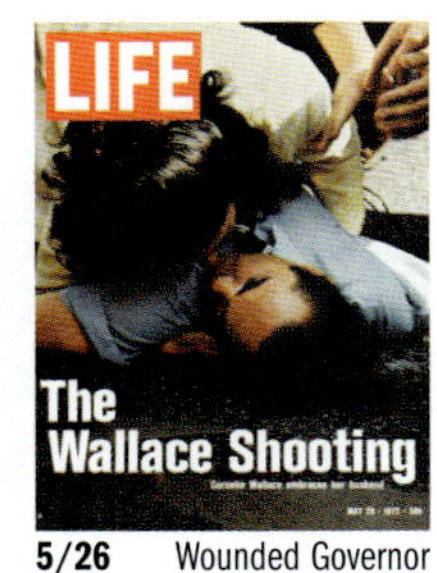

5/26 Wounded Governor

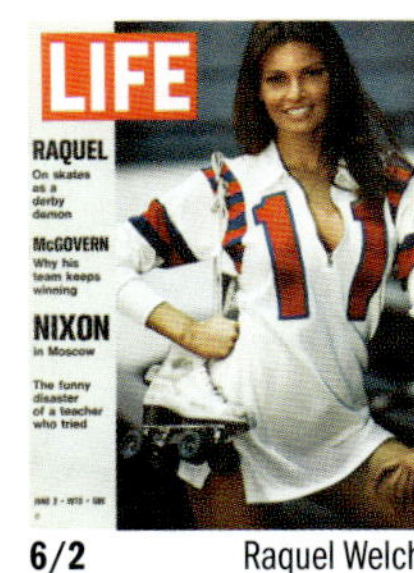

6/2 Raquel Welch

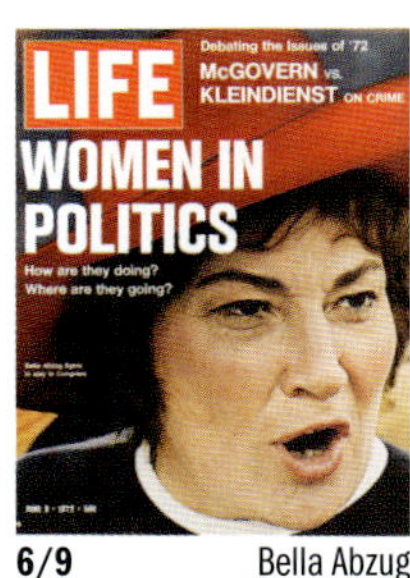

6/9 Bella Abzug

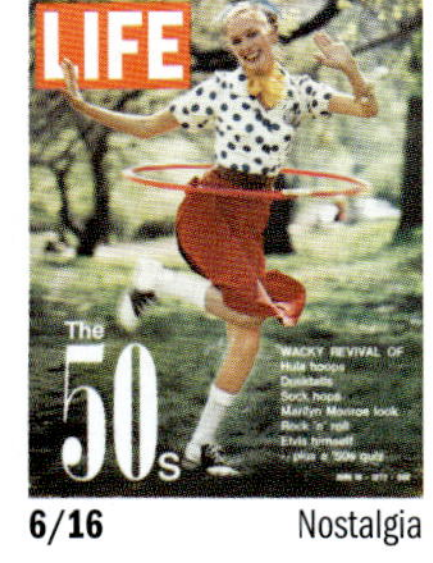

6/16 Nostalgia

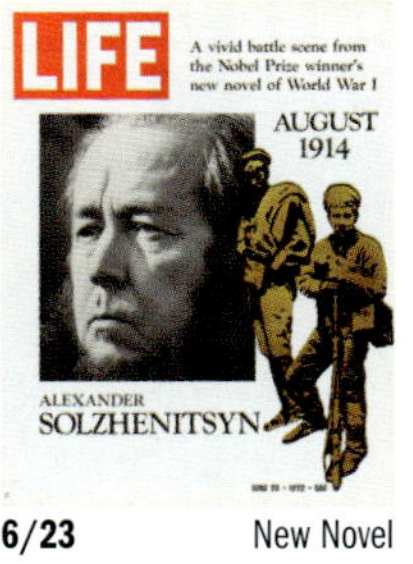

6/23 New Novel

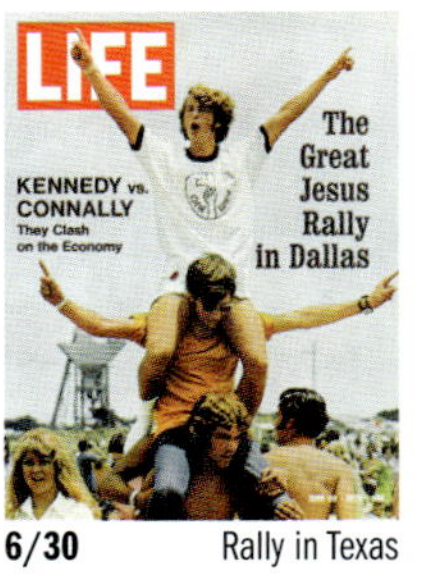

6/30 Rally in Texas

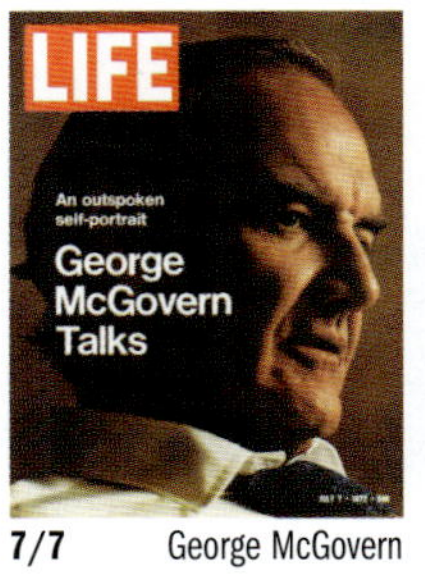

7/7 George McGovern

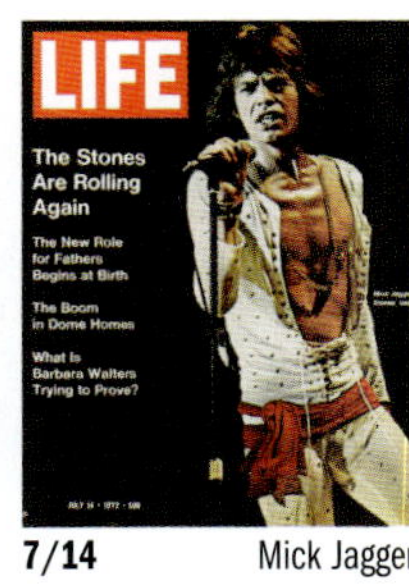

7/14 Mick Jagger

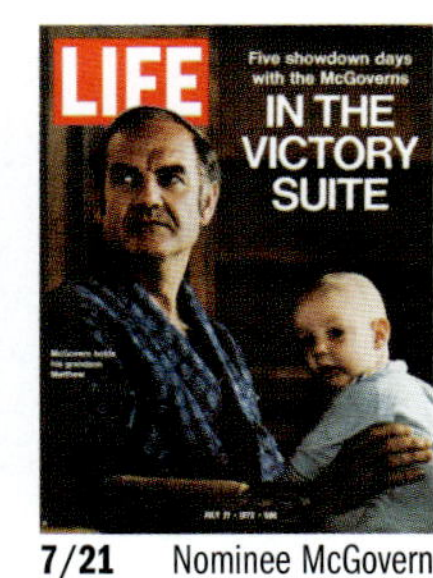

7/21 Nominee McGovern

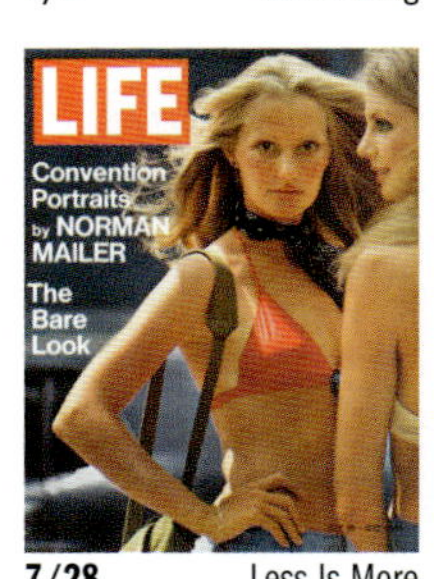

7/28 Less Is More

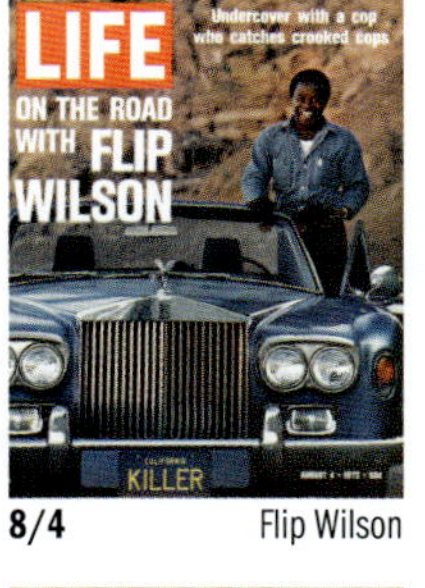

8/4 Flip Wilson

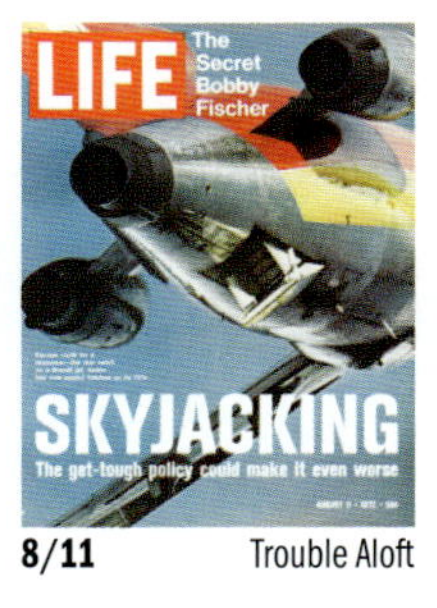

8/11 Trouble Aloft

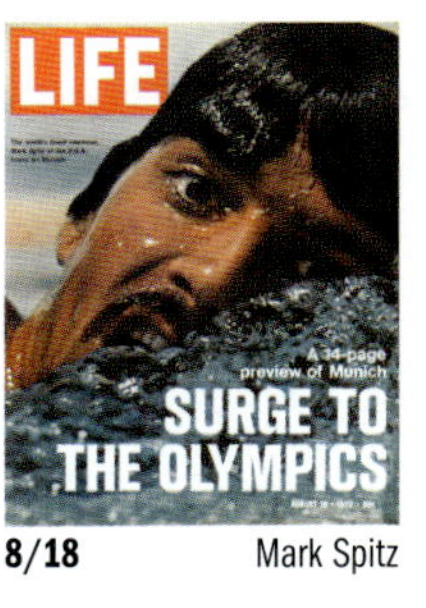

8/18 Mark Spitz

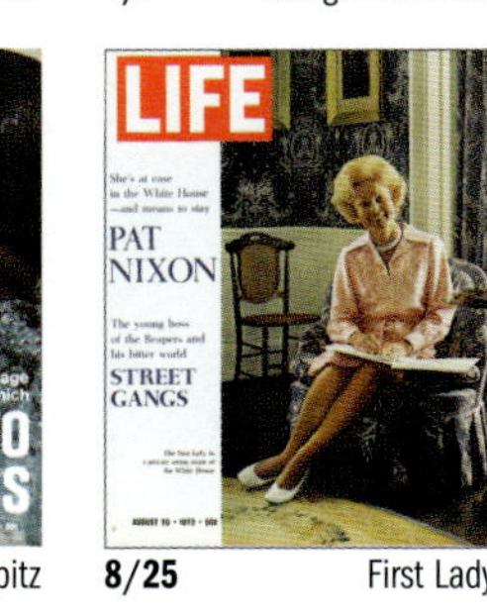

8/25 First Lady

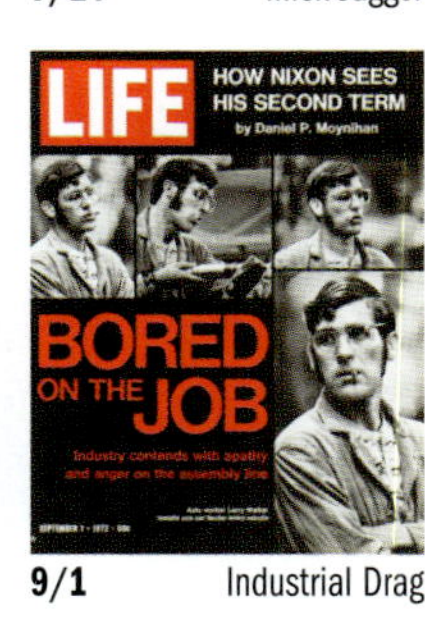

9/1 Industrial Drag

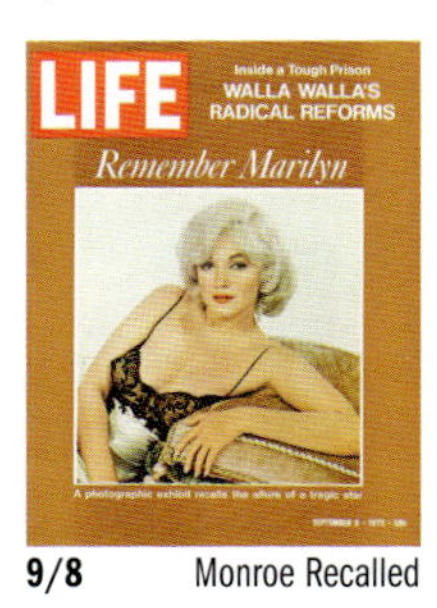

9/8 Monroe Recalled

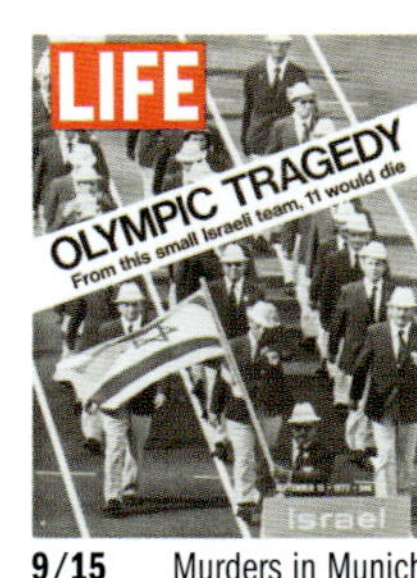

9/15 Murders in Munich

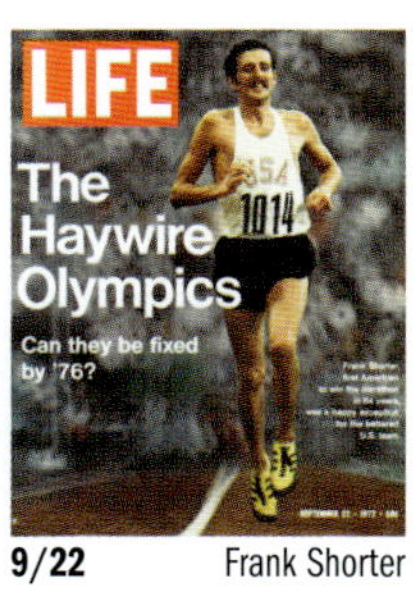

9/22 Frank Shorter

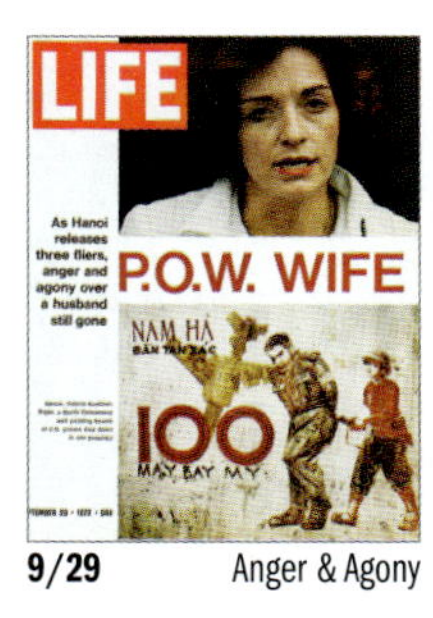

9/29 Anger & Agony

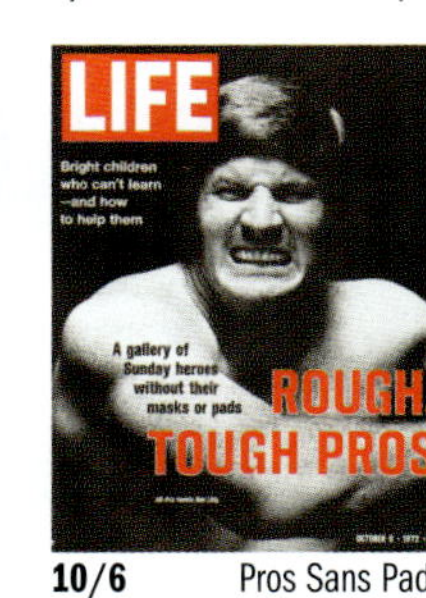

10/6 Pros Sans Pads

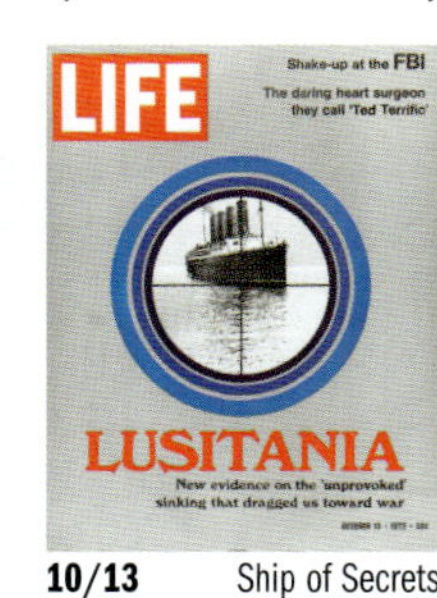

10/13 Ship of Secrets

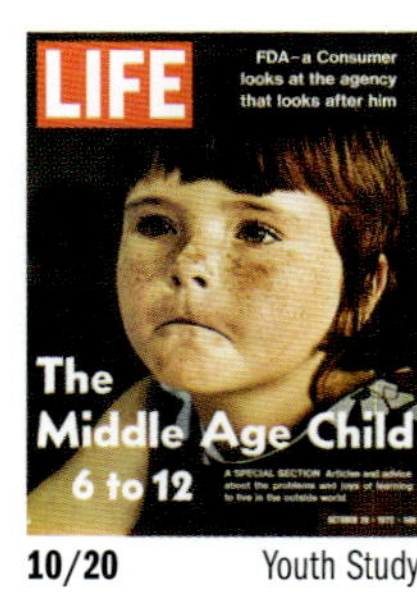

10/20 Youth Study

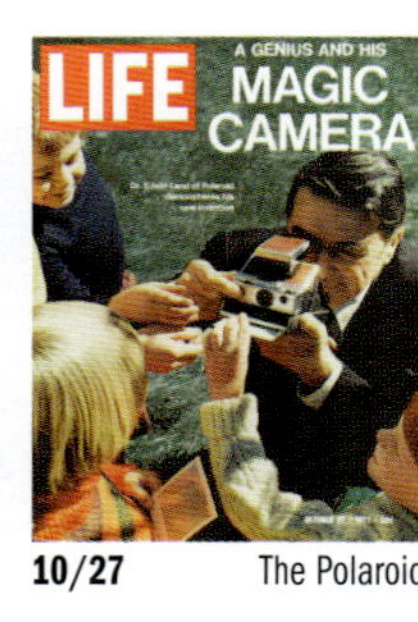

10/27 The Polaroid

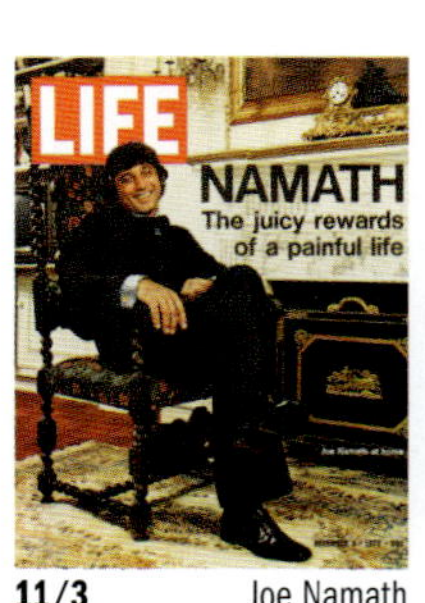

11/3 Joe Namath

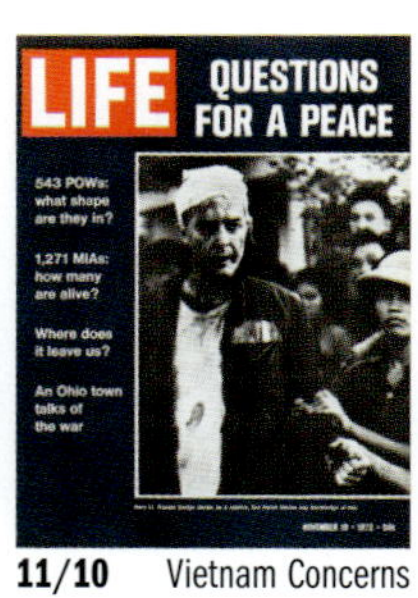

11/10 Vietnam Concerns

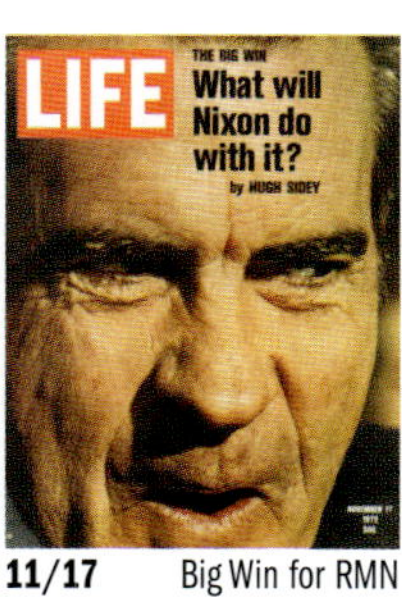

11/17 Big Win for RMN

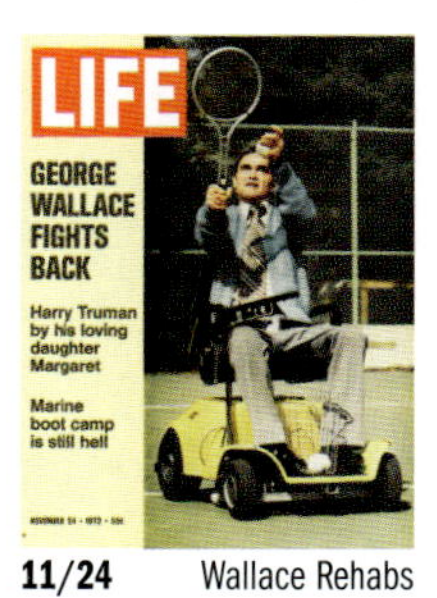

11/24 Wallace Rehabs

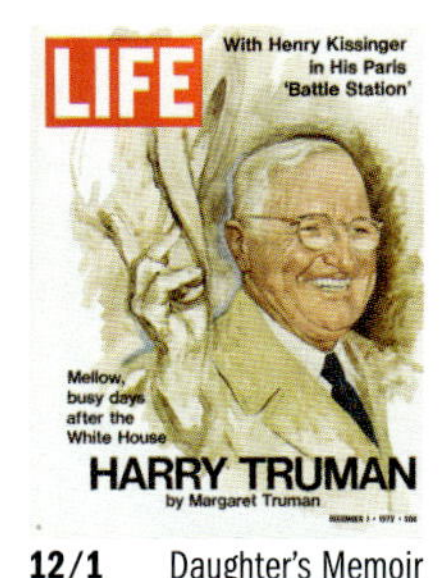

12/1 Daughter's Memoir

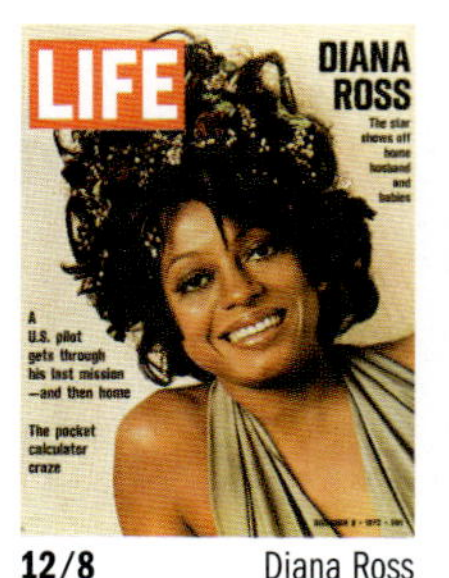

12/8 Diana Ross

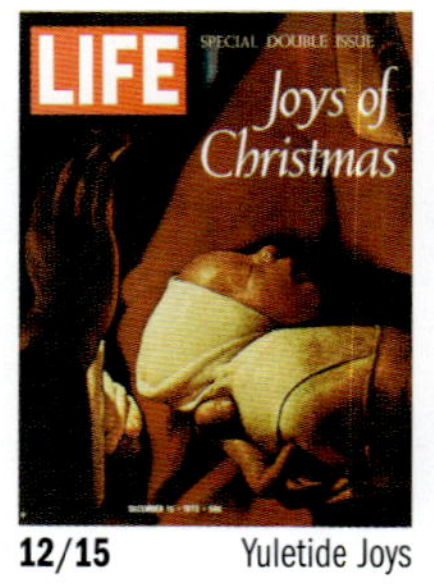

12/15 Yuletide Joys

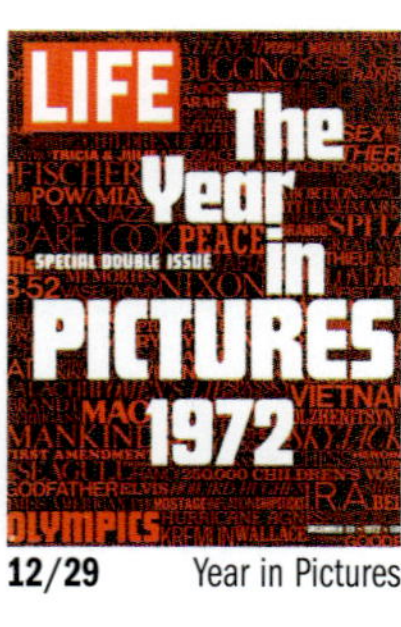

12/29 Year in Pictures

Five are arrested for break-in at Watergate office building in Washington, D.C. • The Goodyear blimp is launched
The Dow Jones Industrial Average closes above 1000 for the first time • The U.S. and U.S.S.R. sign the Strategic Arms Limitation Treaty
Hair closes after 1,752 performances on Broadway

1973

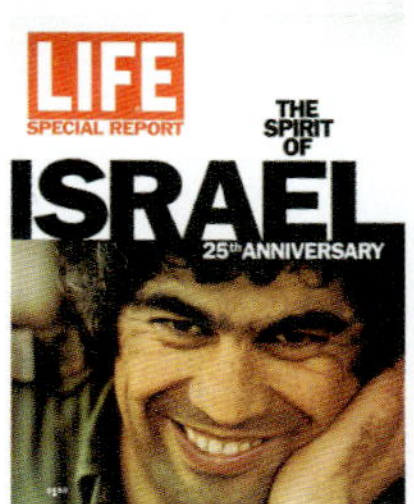

Special Report: Israel

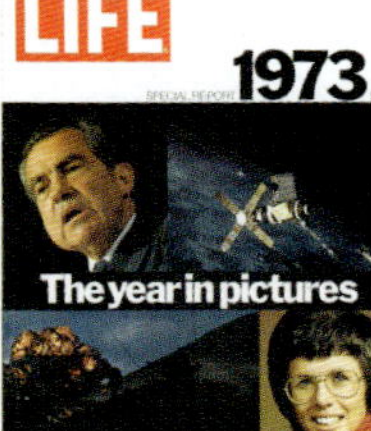

Year in Pictures

Secretariat becomes the ninth horse to win the Triple Crown • After OPEC cuts off oil supplies, gas lines stretch for miles • Peace pact is signed, ending the Vietnam War • The Supreme Court rules on *Roe* v. *Wade* • East and West Germany join the U.N.

1974

Special Report: America

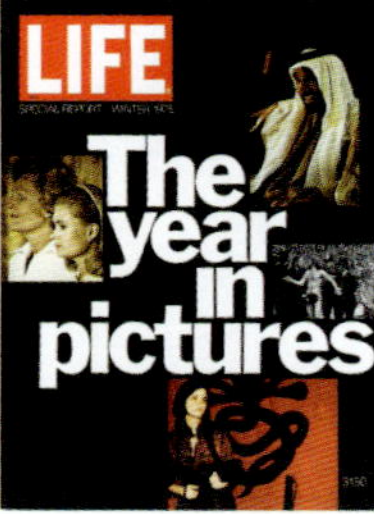

Year in Pictures

Richard Nixon is the first U.S. President to resign • Newspaper heiress Patty Hearst is kidnapped by the Symbionese Liberation Army • The Heimlich maneuver is introduced • Evangelist Jim Bakker founds the Praise the Lord TV ministry

1975

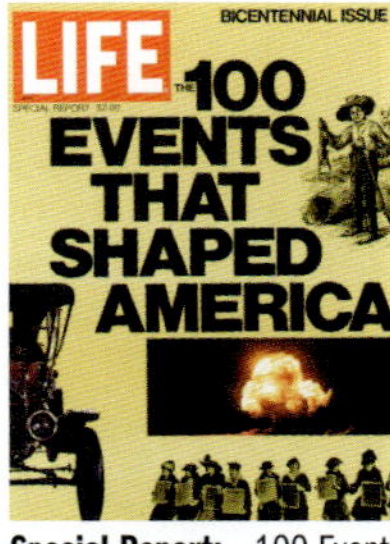

Special Report: 100 Events

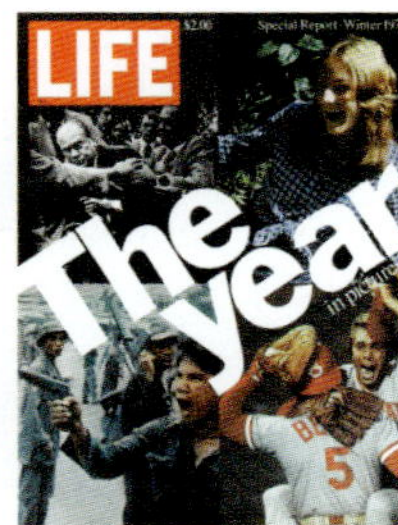

Year in Pictures

More than a million people buy Pet Rocks • Former teamster head Jimmy Hoffa disappears • Beverly Sills makes her Metropolitan Opera debut in Rossini's *The Siege of Corinth* • Thousands of life-size pottery figures from the 3rd century B.C. are found in China • Steven Spielberg's *Jaws* is a summer smash

1976

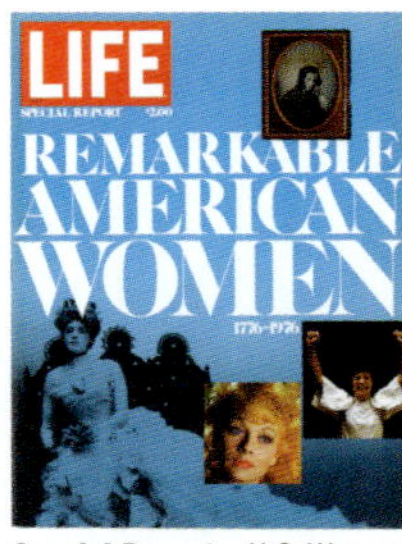

Special Report: U.S. Women

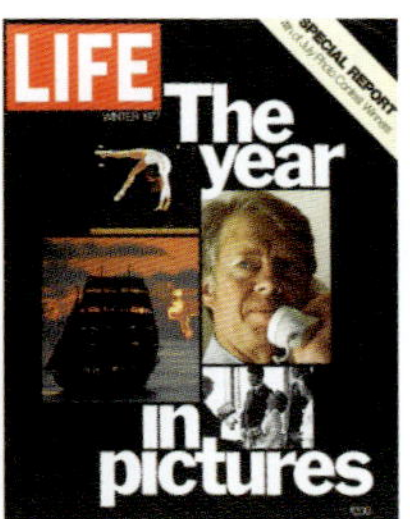

Year in Pictures

Viking lands on Mars, the red planet • Apple II, the first practical personal computer, is introduced • Millions watch "tall ships" enter New York Harbor in honor of Bicentennial • The real Smokey Bear dies in Washington's National Zoo • Lyme disease is first identified in Old Lyme, Conn.

1977

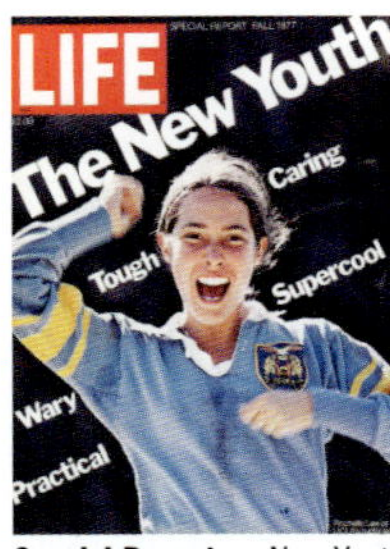

Special Report: New Youth

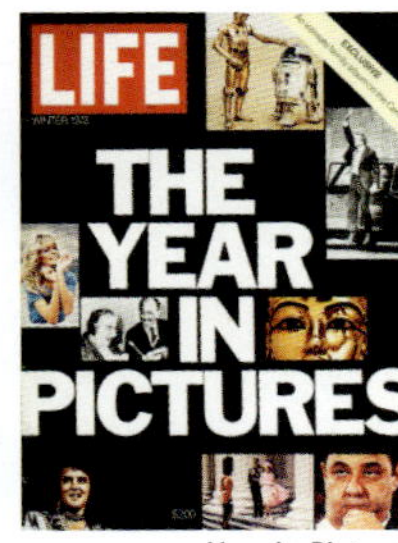

Year in Pictures

Smallpox is eradicated • Alex Haley's *Roots* runs for eight nights on ABC • Fans line up for the first *Star Wars* • The Trans-Alaskan pipeline opens • *Saturday Night Fever* features the Bee Gees' disco music

1978

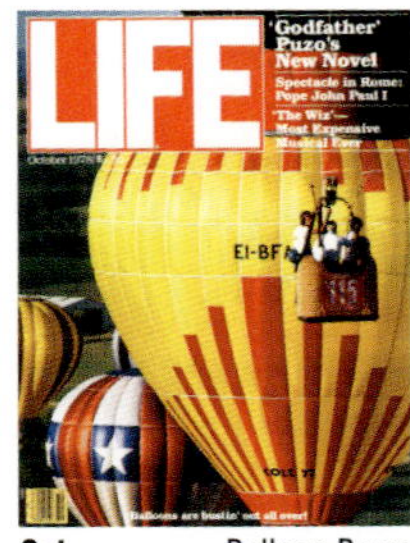

Oct. Balloon Boom

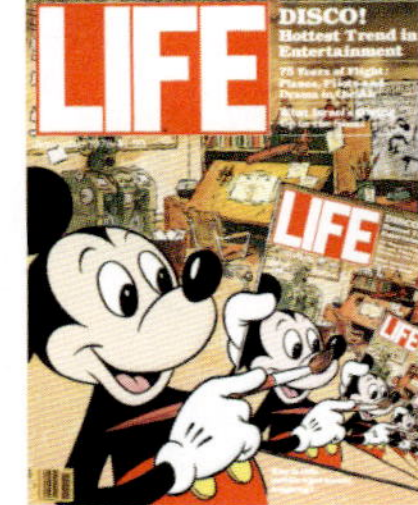

Nov. Mickey Is 50

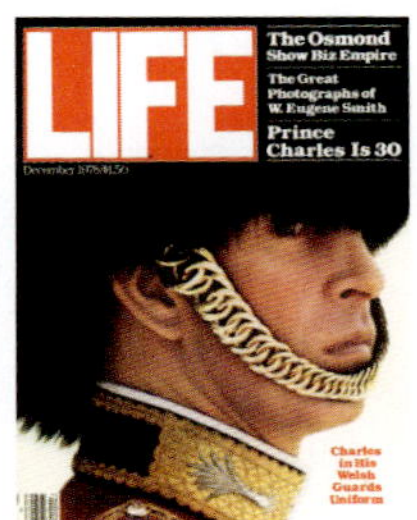

Dec. Prince Charles

Louise Brown, the first test-tube baby, is born in England • Hip-hop becomes a new sensation in the Bronx • U.S. Senate turns the canal over to Panama • Polish Cardinal Karol Wojtyla becomes Pope John Paul II

1979

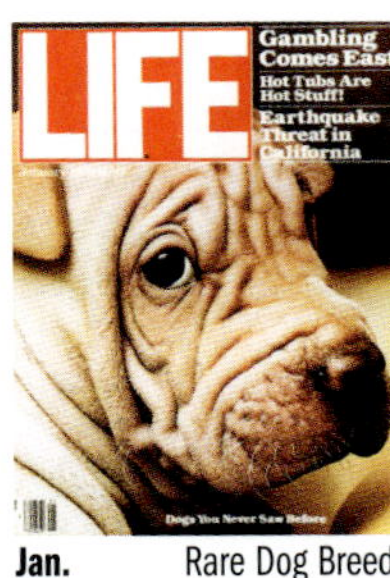

Jan. Rare Dog Breeds

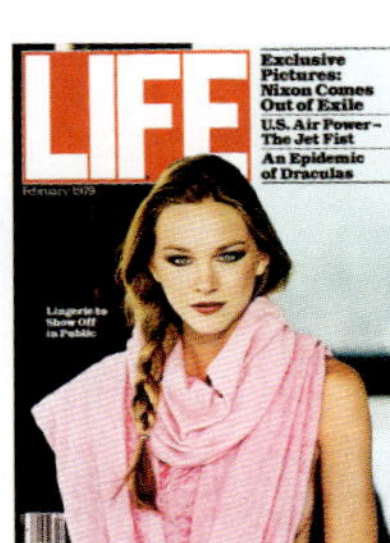

Feb. Lingerie in Public

Mar. Lesley-Anne Down

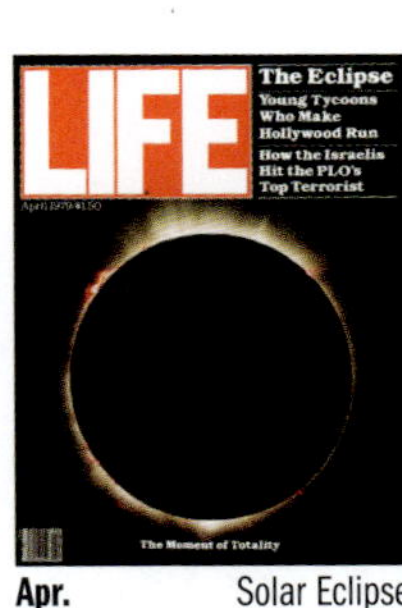

Apr. Solar Eclipse

May Three Mile Island

June Marlon Brando

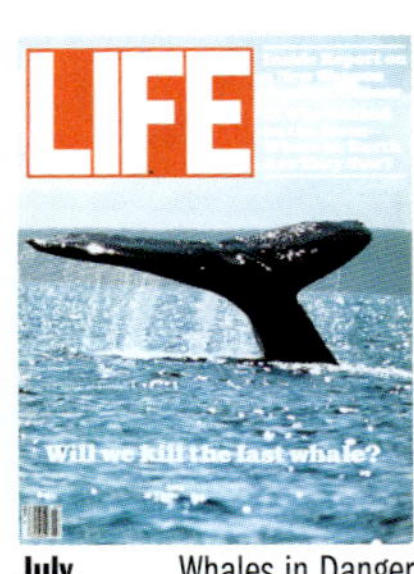

July Whales in Danger

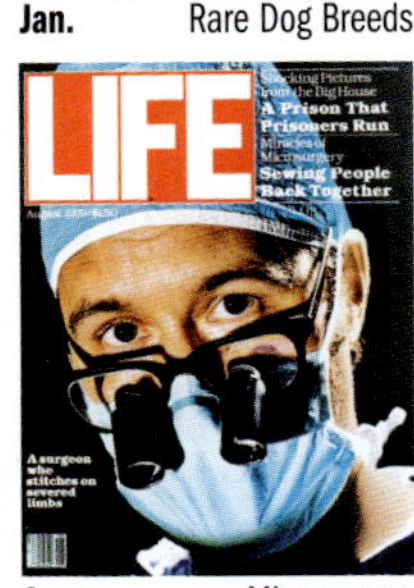

Aug. Microsurgery

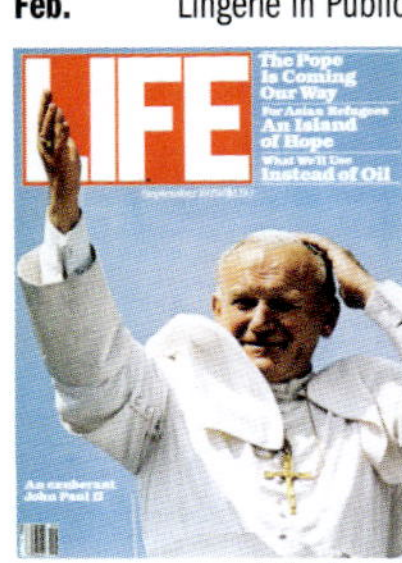

Sept. John Paul II

Oct. Dolly Parton

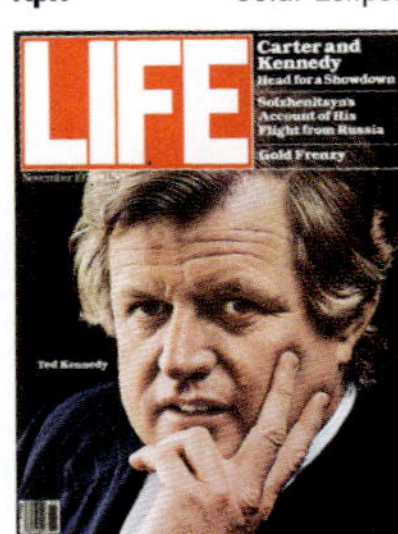

Nov. Sen. Ted Kennedy

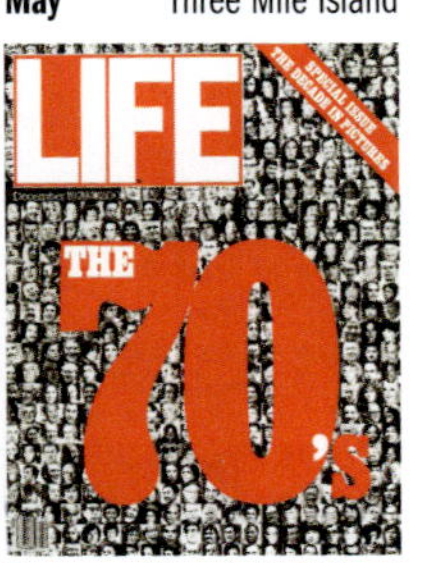

Dec. Decade in Pictures

Mohammed Reza Pahlavi is forced to relinquish Iran's Peacock Throne • Soviet paratroopers land in Afghanistan • Ugandan President Idi Amin flees after being accused of widespread atrocities • The Sony Walkman is introduced

1980

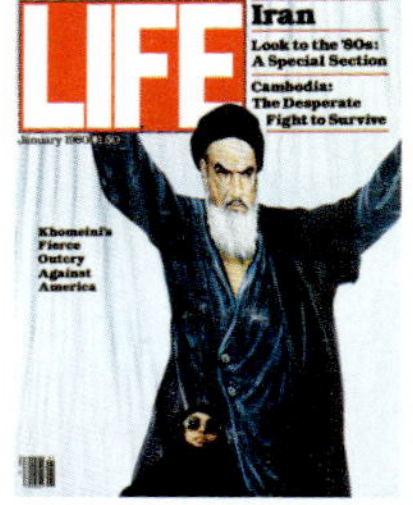
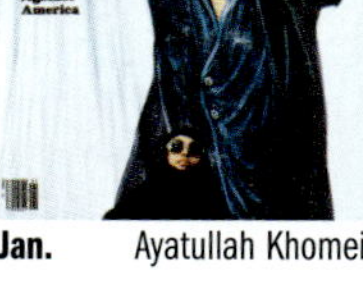
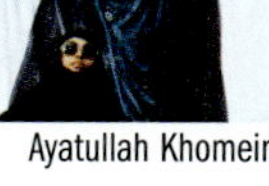

Jan. Ayatullah Khomeini

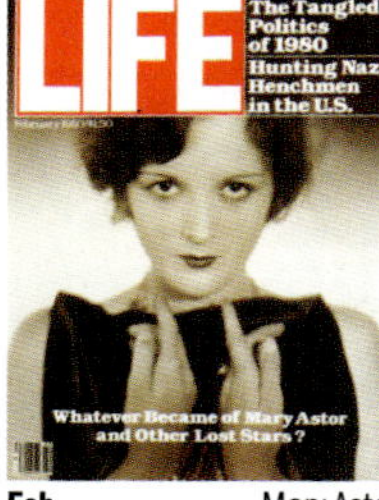

Feb. Mary Astor

Mar. Mickey Rooney

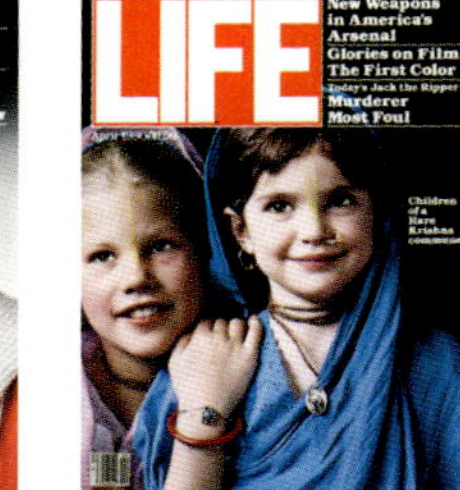

Apr. Hare Krishna Children

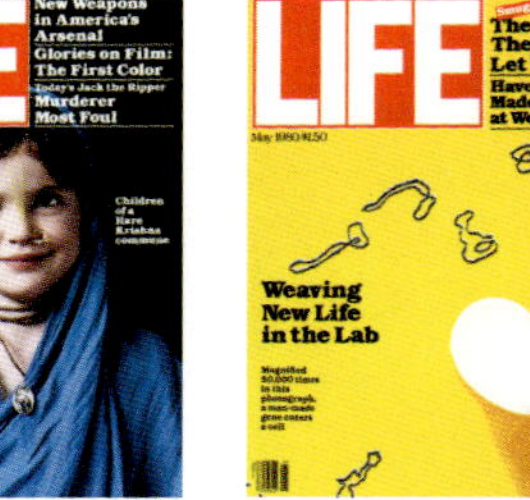

May Gene Splicing

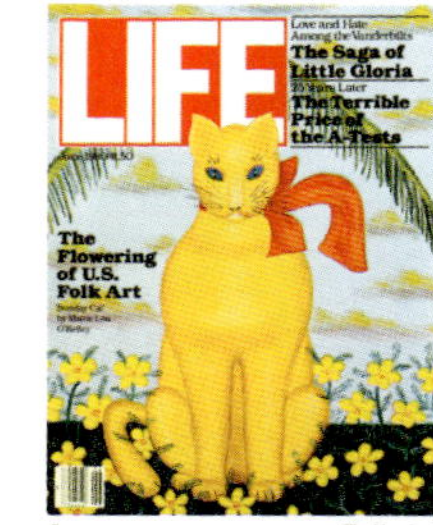

June Folk Art

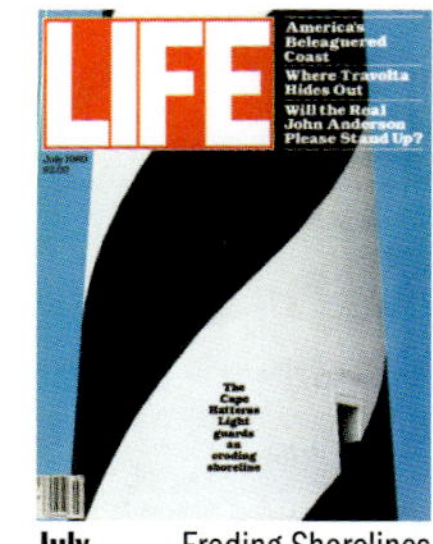

July Eroding Shorelines

Aug. Miss Piggy

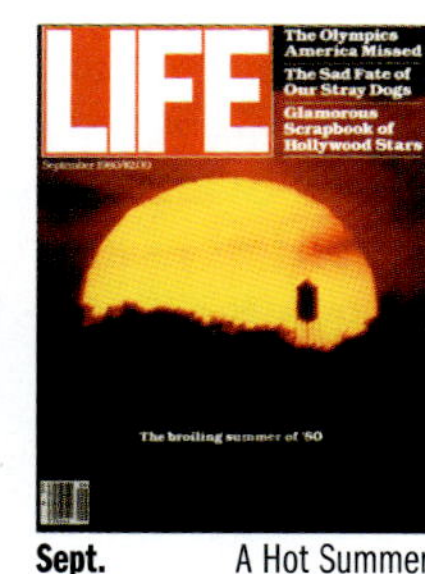

Sept. A Hot Summer

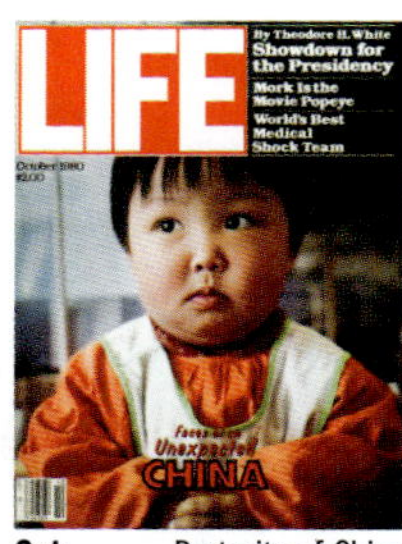

Oct. Portraits of China

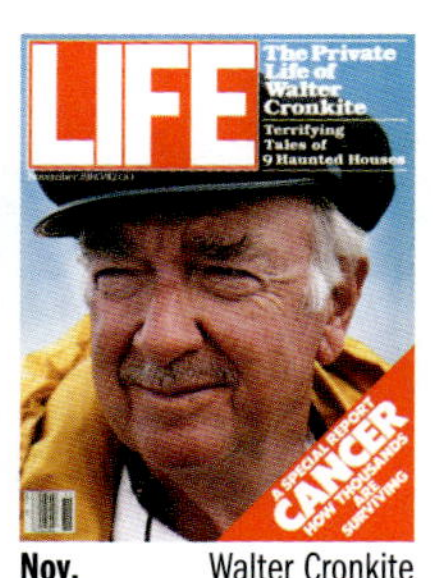

Nov. Walter Cronkite

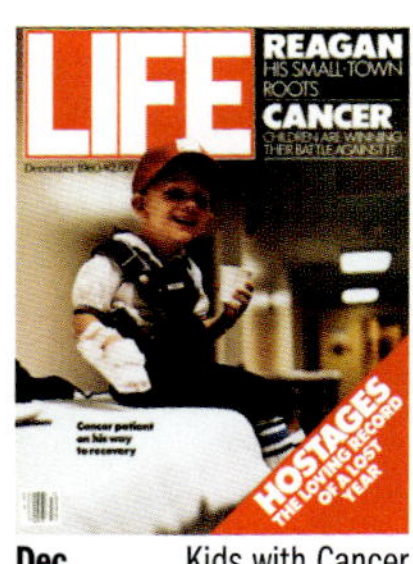

Dec. Kids with Cancer

The U.S. population is 226,542,199
Ted Turner launches CNN as the first all-news network • Roller blades become popular
Post-it Notes are introduced • John Lennon is slain

1981

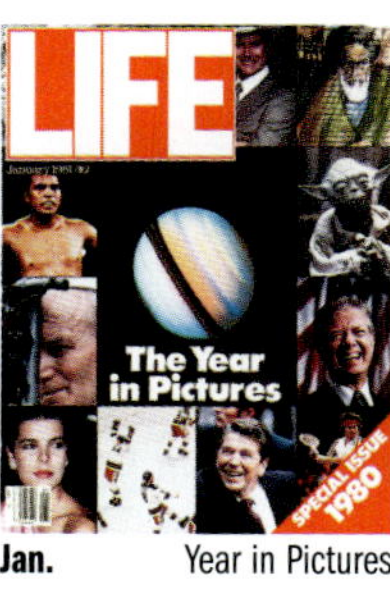

Jan. Year in Pictures

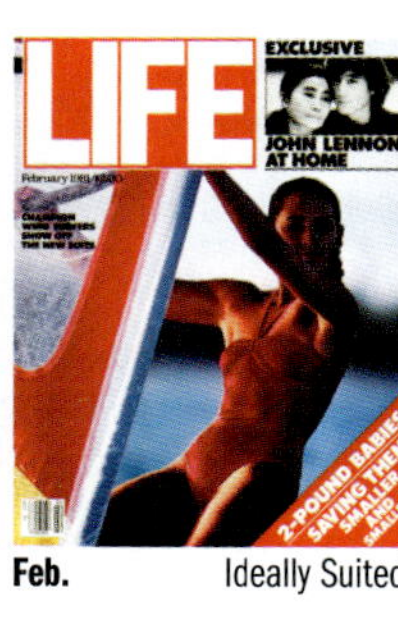

Feb. Ideally Suited

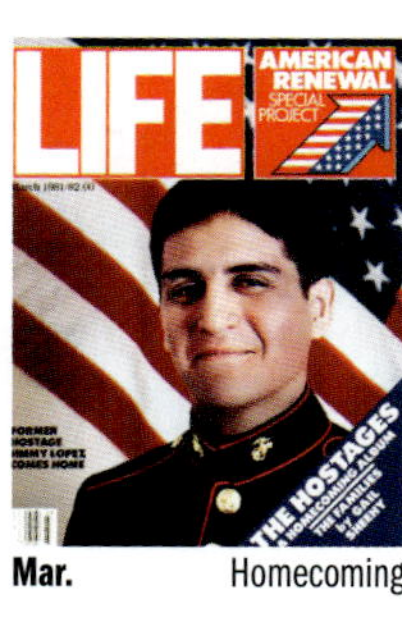

Mar. Homecoming

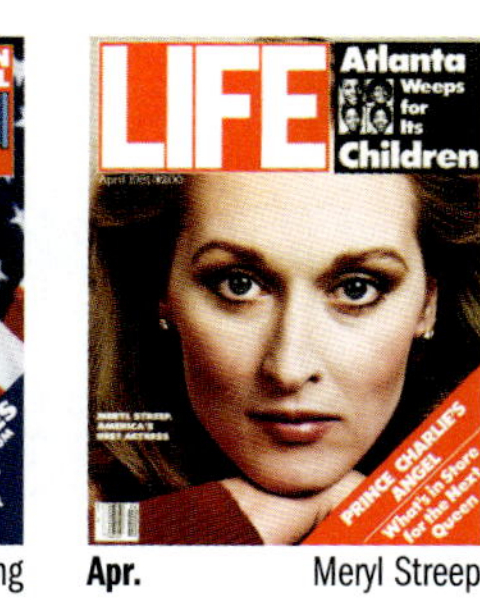

Apr. Meryl Streep

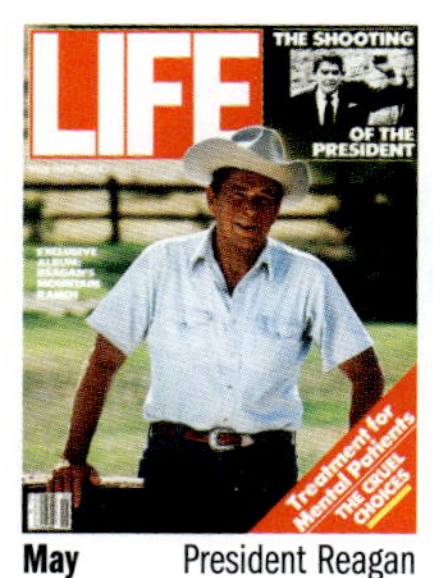

May President Reagan

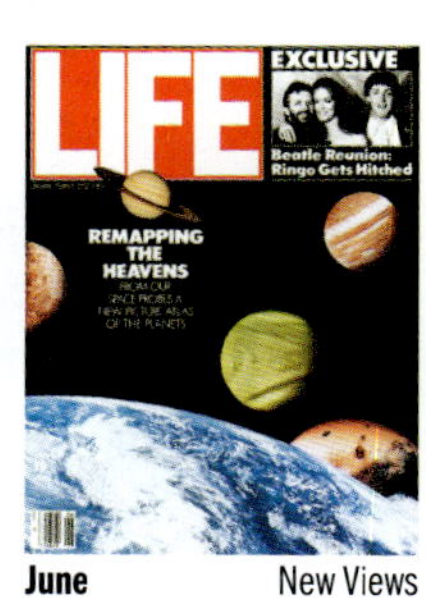

June New Views

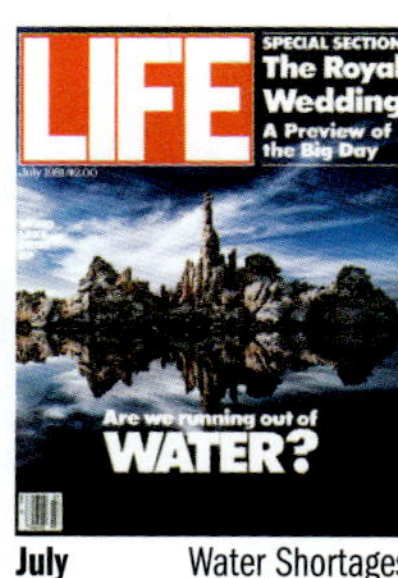

July Water Shortages

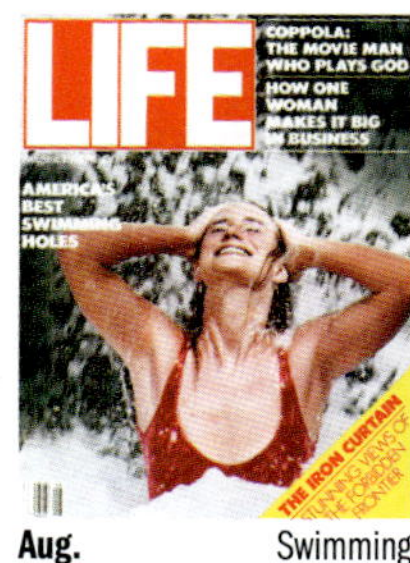

Aug. Swimming

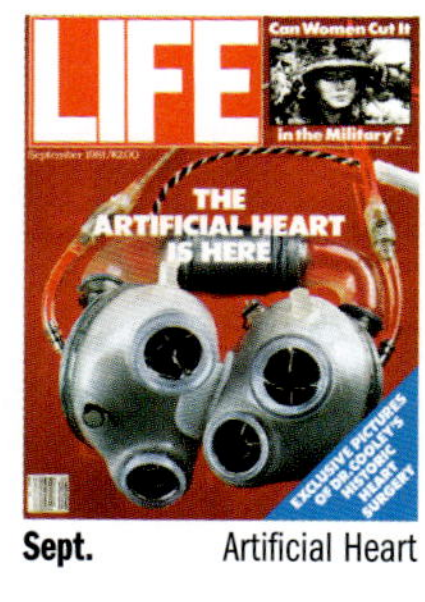

Sept. Artificial Heart

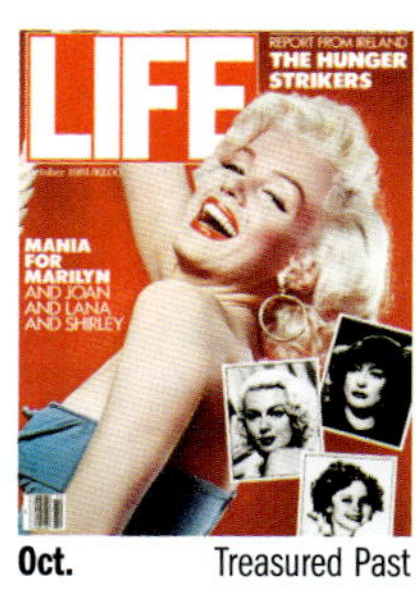

Oct. Treasured Past

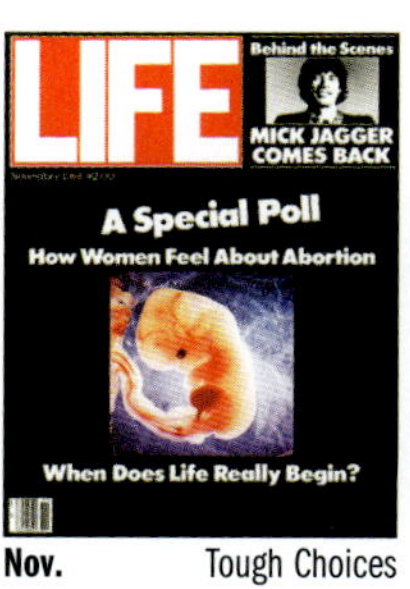

Nov. Tough Choices

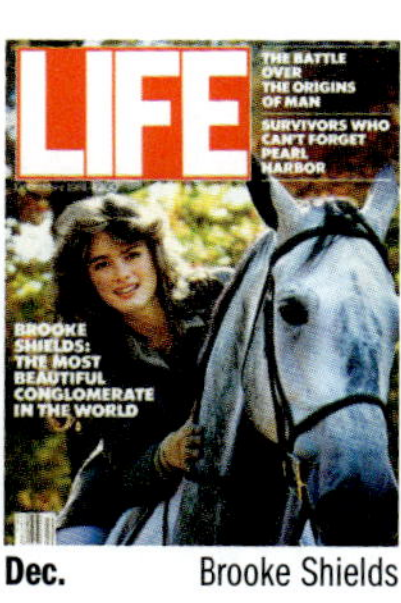

Dec. Brooke Shields

Pope John Paul II survives an assassination attempt in St. Peter's Square • Paul Allen and Bill Gates launch their first PC
Muslim extremists kill Egyptian President Anwar Sadat
Scientists identify the AIDS virus • Sandra Day O'Connor becomes the first woman to sit on the Supreme Court

1982

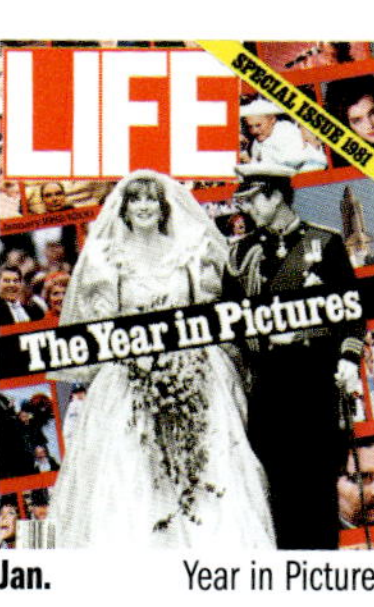

Jan. Year in Pictures

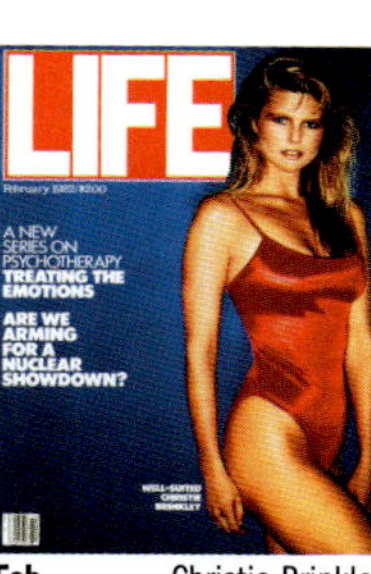

Feb. Christie Brinkley

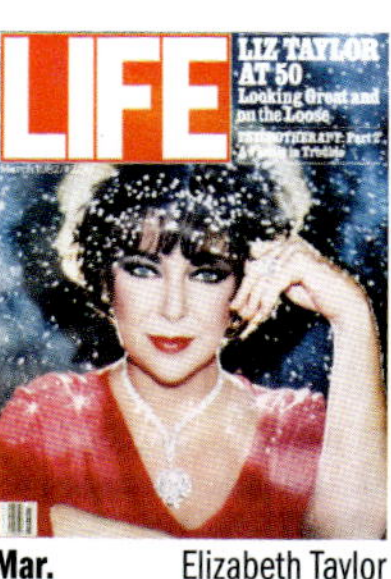

Mar. Elizabeth Taylor

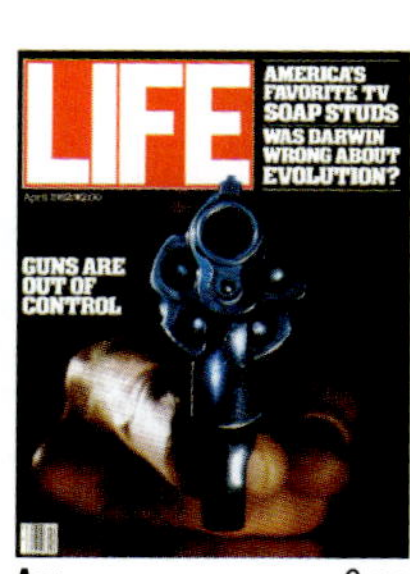

Apr. Guns

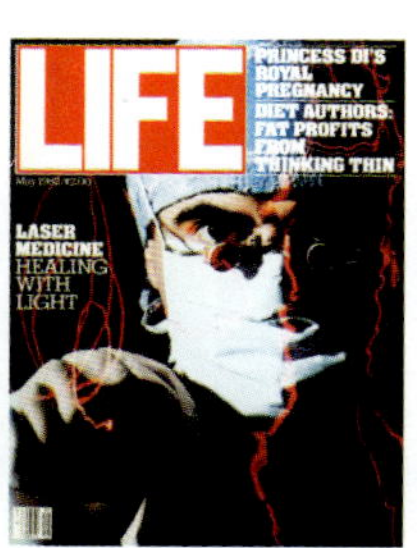

May Laser Medicine

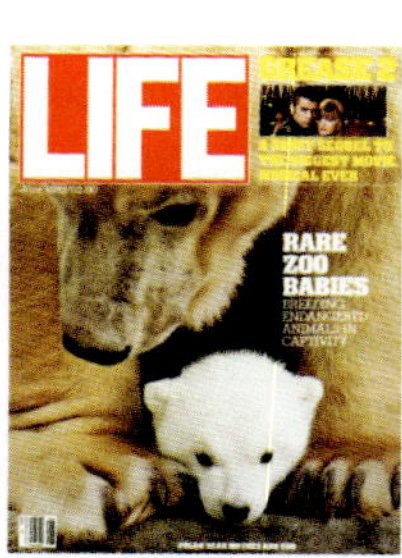

June Zoo Nursery

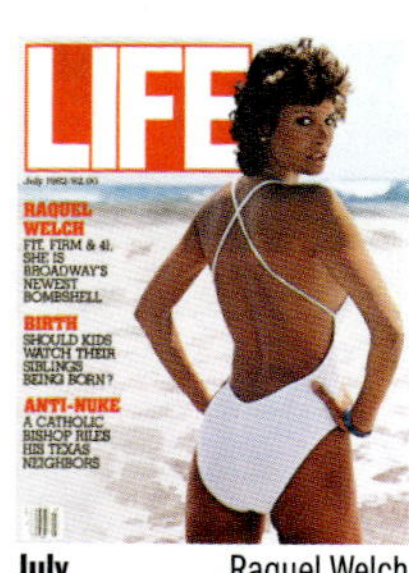

July Raquel Welch

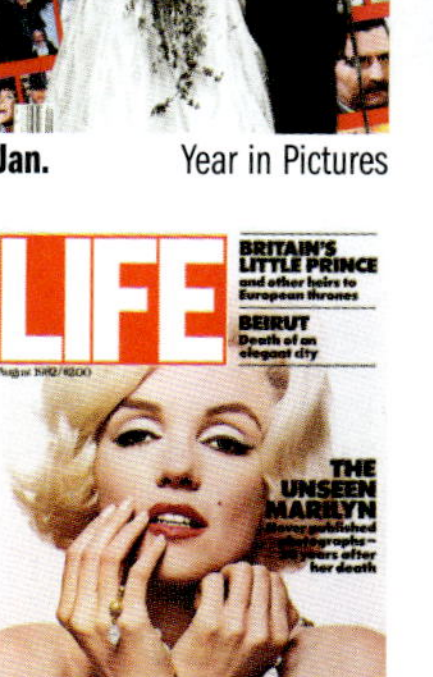

Aug. New Photos

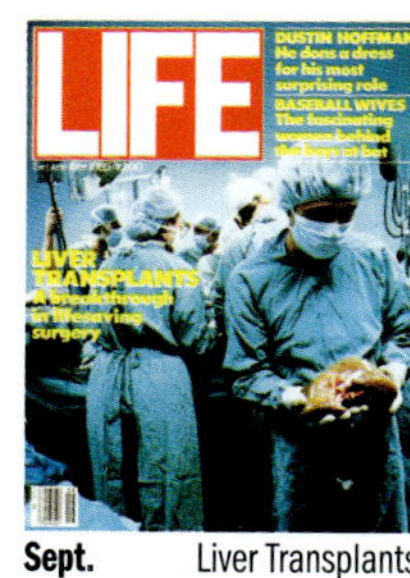

Sept. Liver Transplants

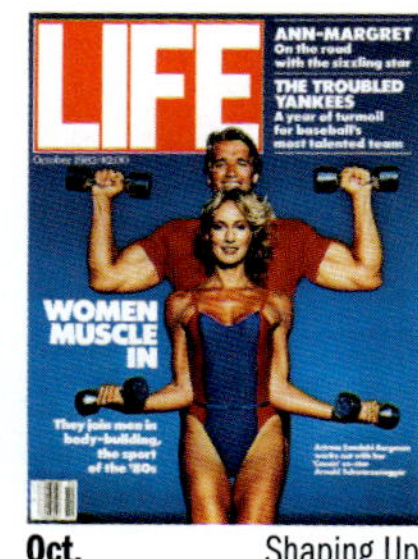

Oct. Shaping Up

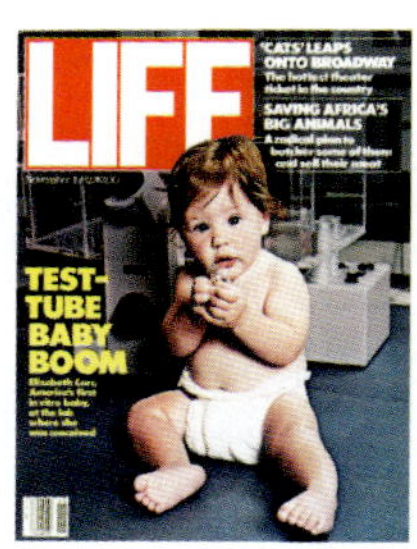

Nov. In-vitro Pioneers

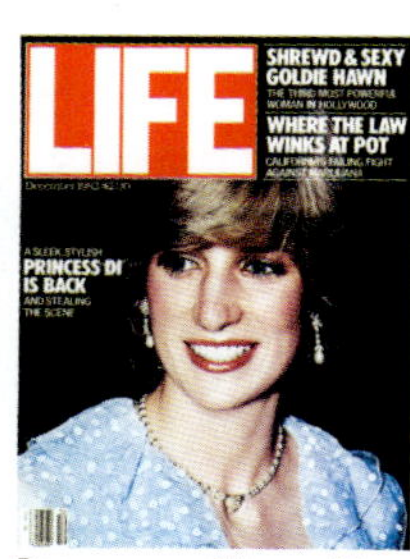

Dec. Princess Diana

The Vietnam Veterans Memorial, with 57,939 names, is dedicated
Barney Clark receives an artificial heart and survives 112 days • The Weather Channel airs on cable TV
Argentina invades the Falkland Islands • AT&T is broken up into 22 companies

1983

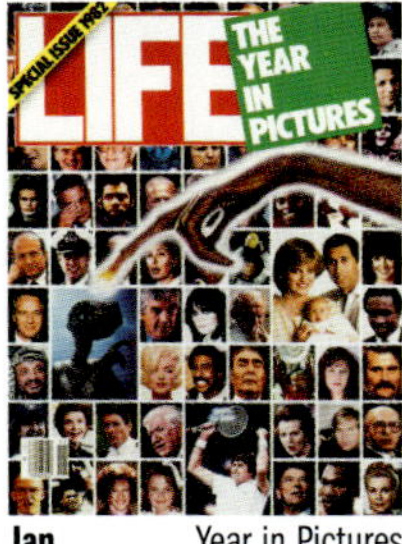
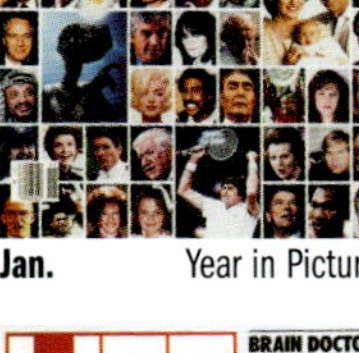
Jan. Year in Pictures

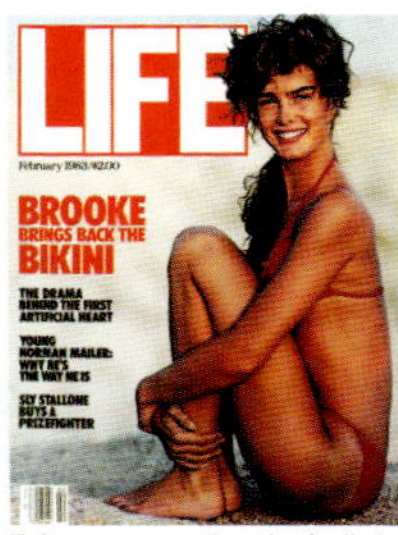
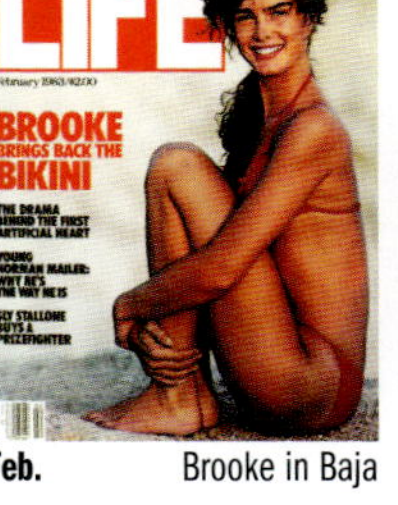
Feb. Brooke in Baja

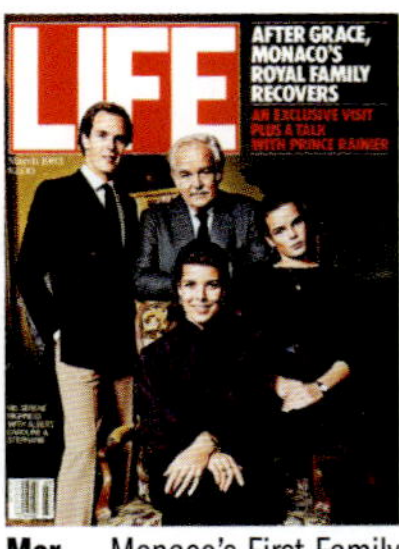
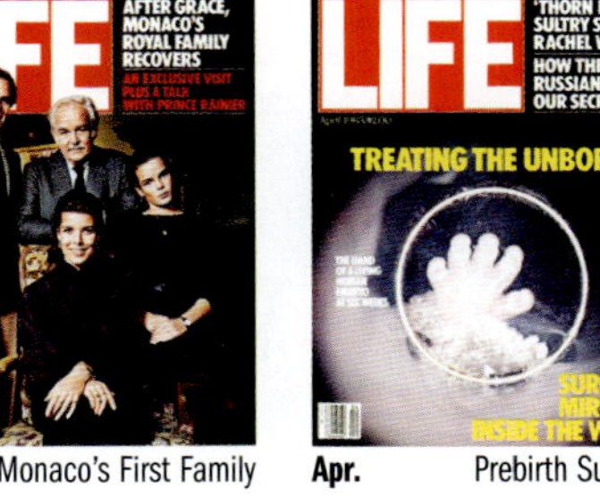
Mar. Monaco's First Family

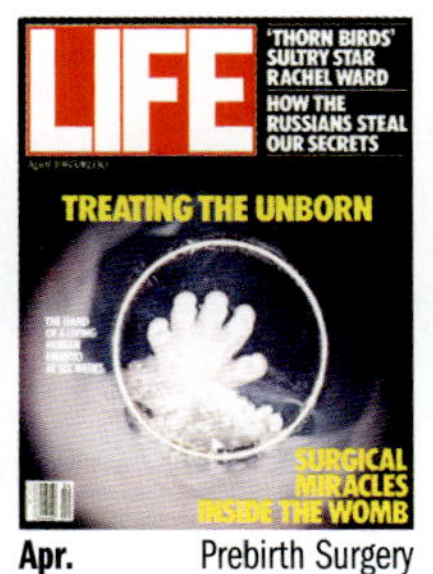
Apr. Prebirth Surgery

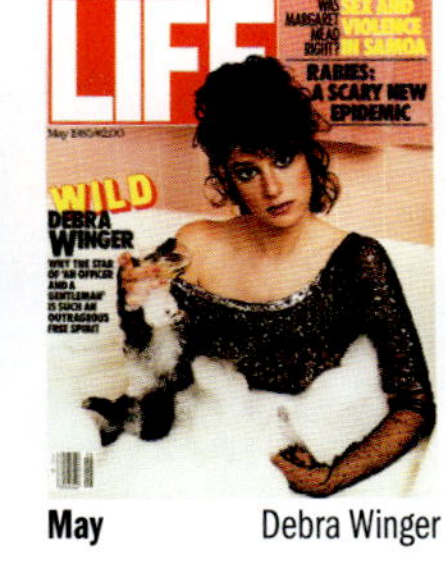
May Debra Winger

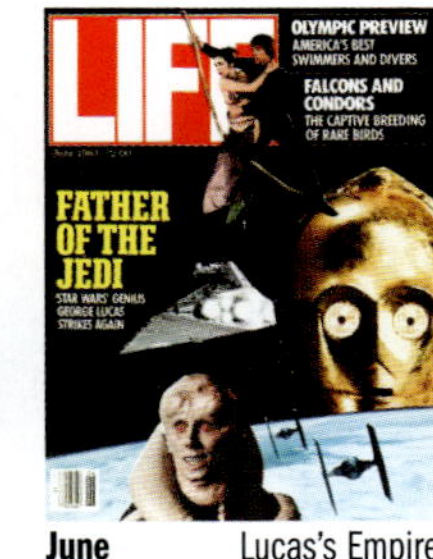
June Lucas's Empire

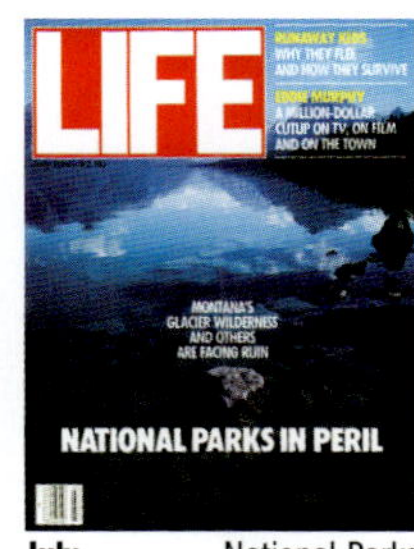
July National Parks

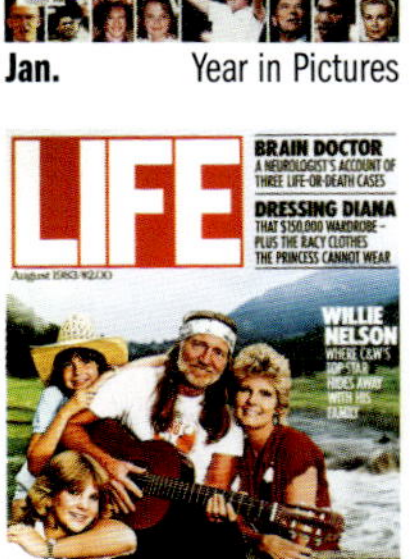
Aug. Willie & Family

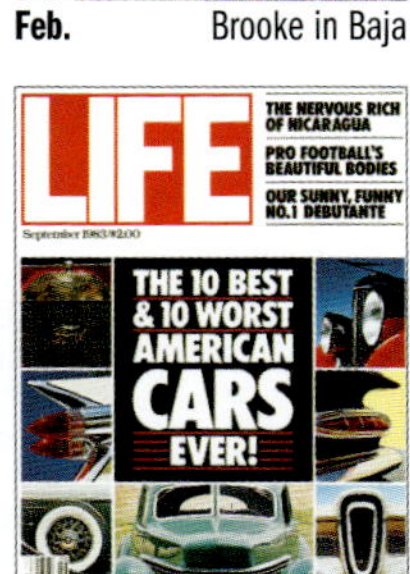
Sept. Cars

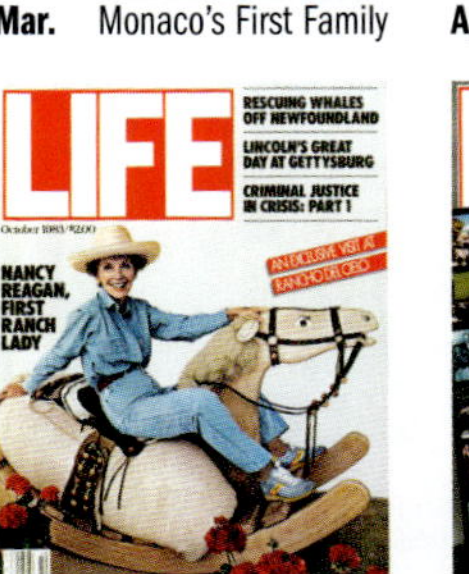
Oct. Nancy Reagan

Nov. 20 Years Ago

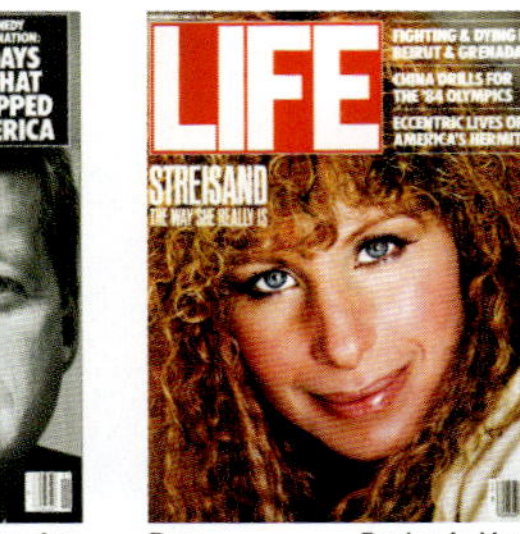
Dec. Barbra's *Yentl*

Sally Ride becomes the first American woman to go into space • President Reagan proposes the Star Wars defense system
A jawbone of *Silvapithecus*, believed to be 16 million years old, is found in Kenya
The Cabbage Patch doll becomes a must-have toy • Bjorn Borg, 26, shocks the tennis world when he announces his retirement

1984

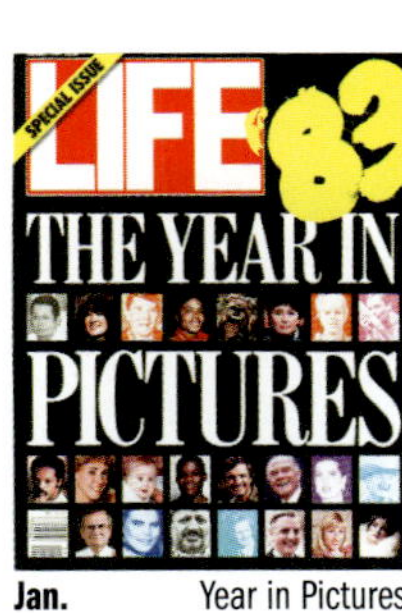
Jan. Year in Pictures

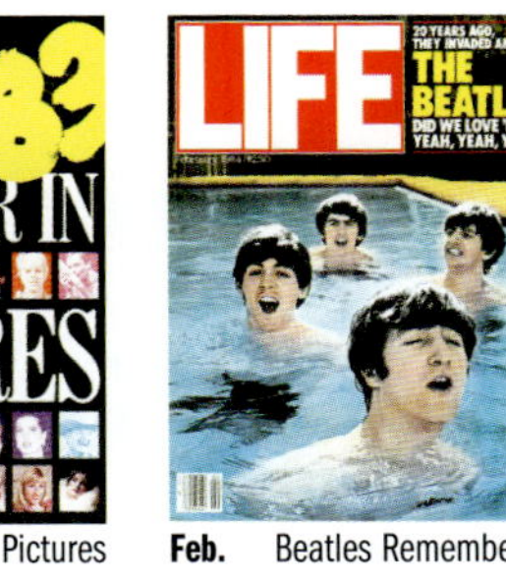
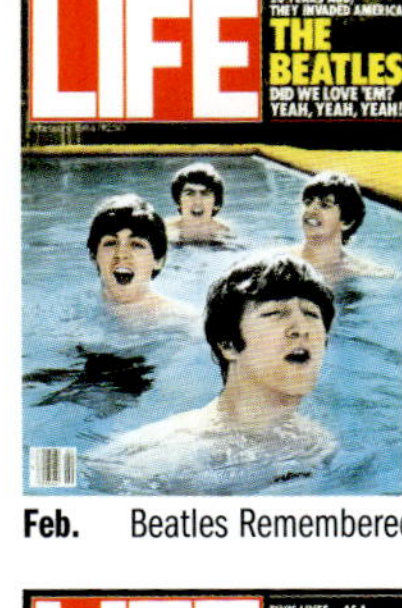
Feb. Beatles Remembered

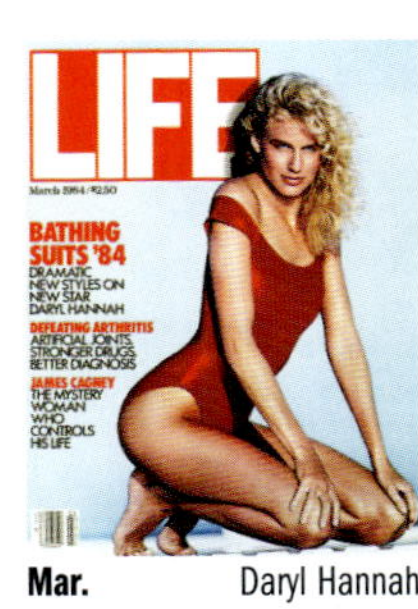
Mar. Daryl Hannah

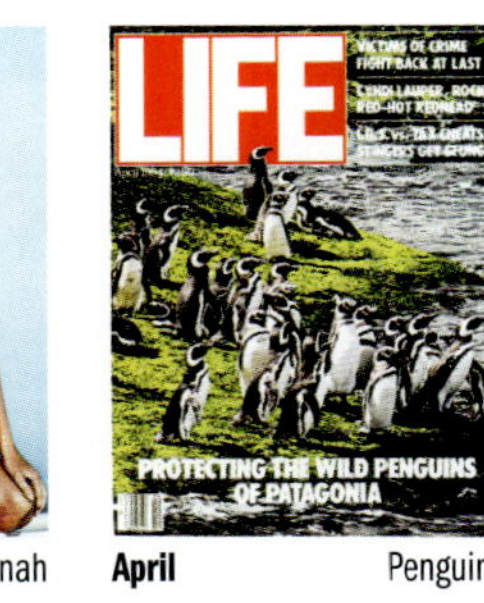
April Penguins

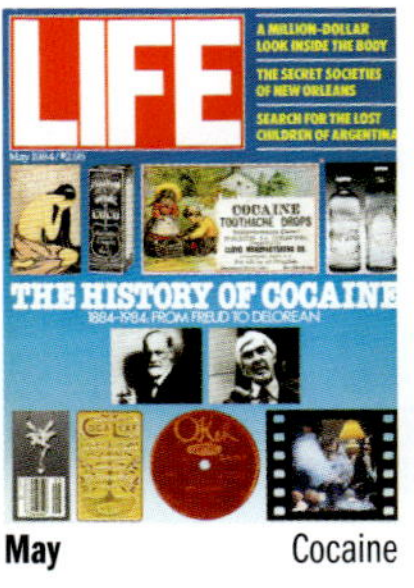
May Cocaine

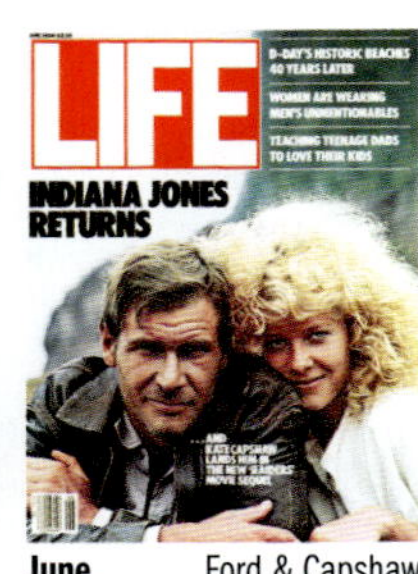
June Ford & Capshaw

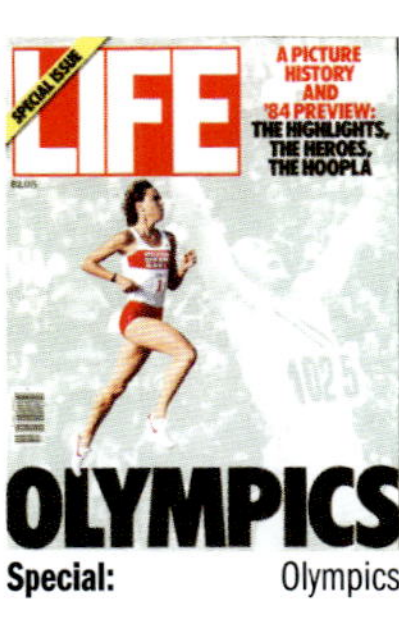
Special: Olympics

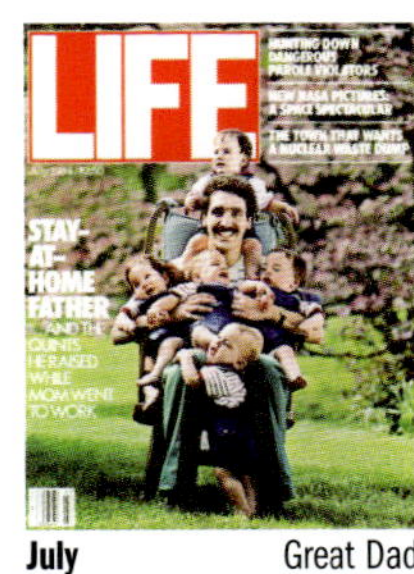
July Great Dad

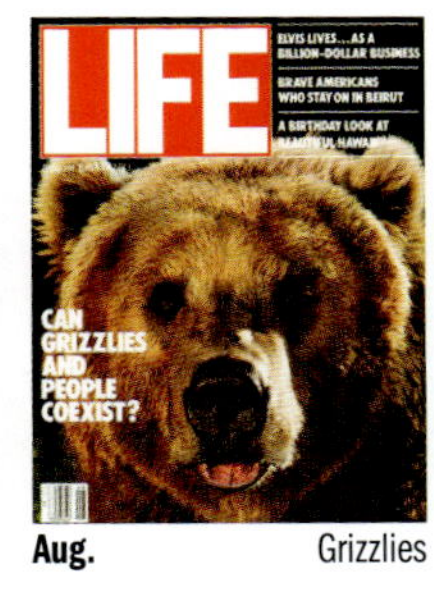
Aug. Grizzlies

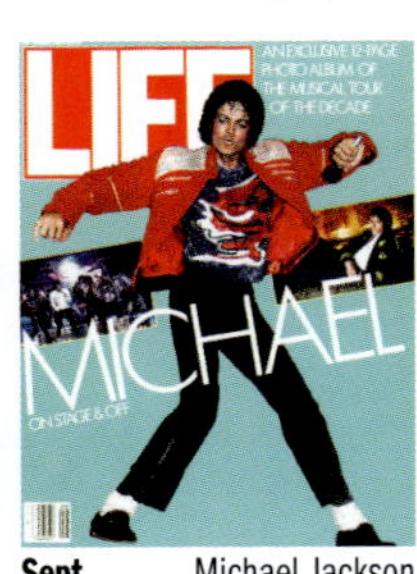
Sept. Michael Jackson

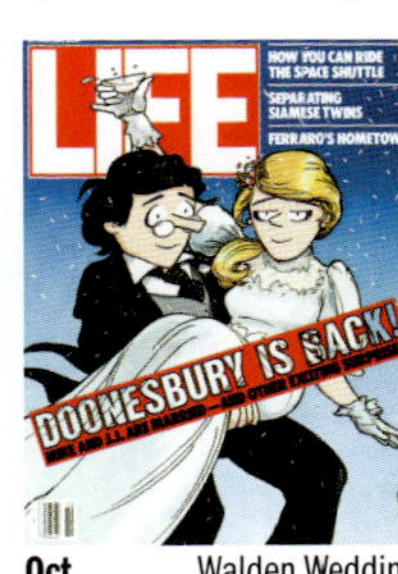
Oct. Walden Wedding

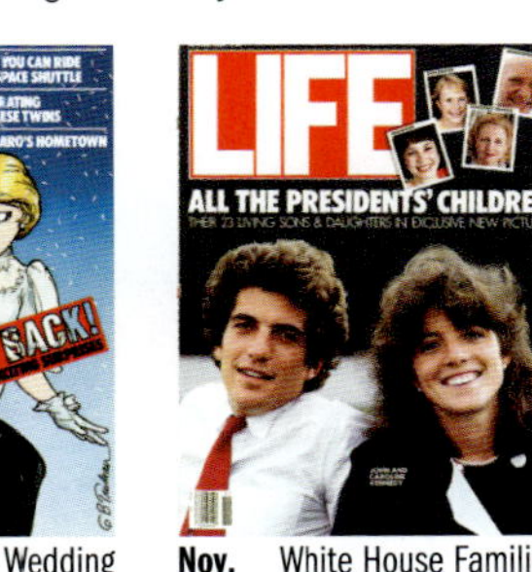
Nov. White House Families

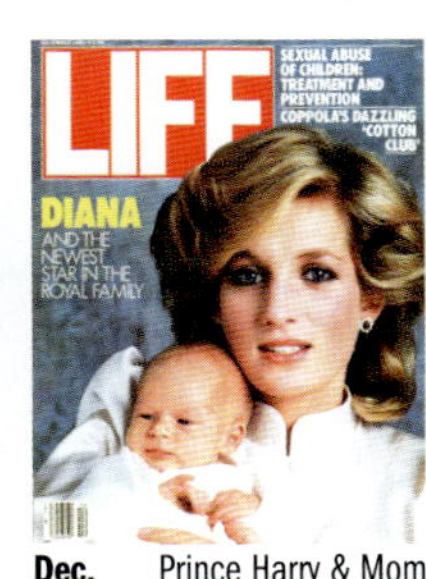
Dec. Prince Harry & Mom

Between 250,000 and 300,000 Americans are homeless • The Soviets boycott the Olympic Games in Los Angeles
China signs an agreement with Great Britain, which will return Hong Kong in 1997
The average price for a single-family home reaches $70,000 • Indian Prime Minister Indira Gandhi is assassinated

1985

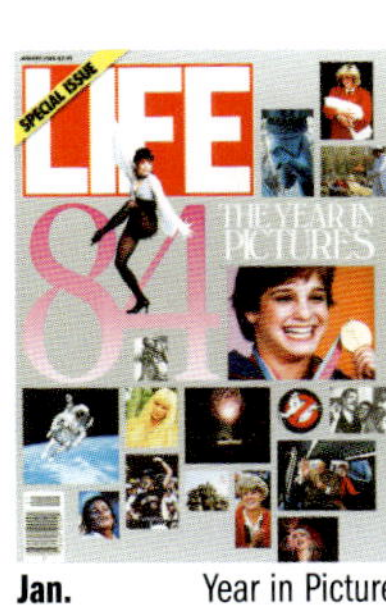
Jan. Year in Pictures

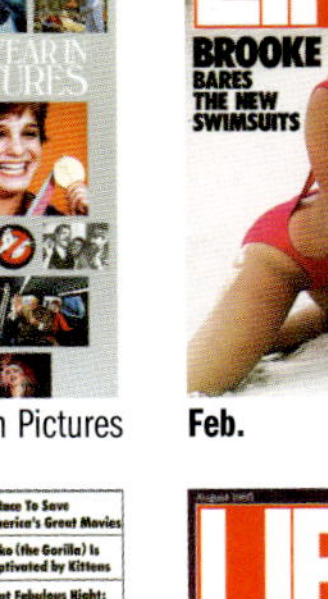
Feb. Princeton Coed

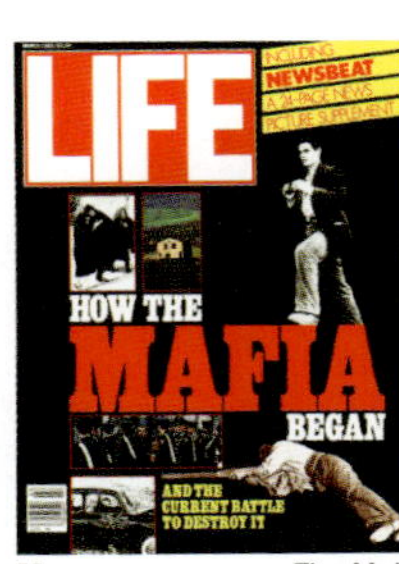
Mar. The Mob

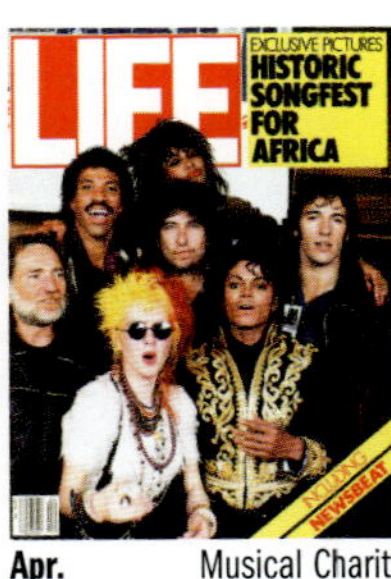
Apr. Musical Charity

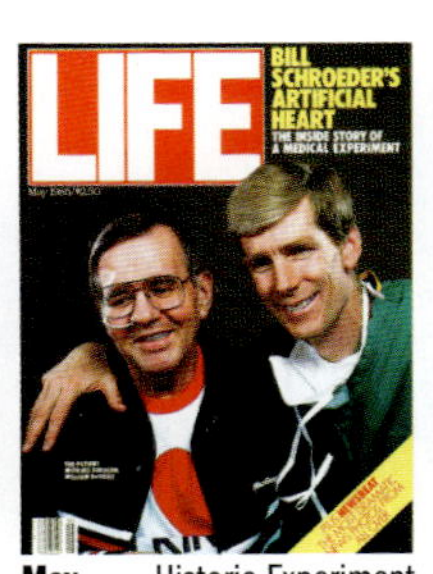
May Historic Experiment

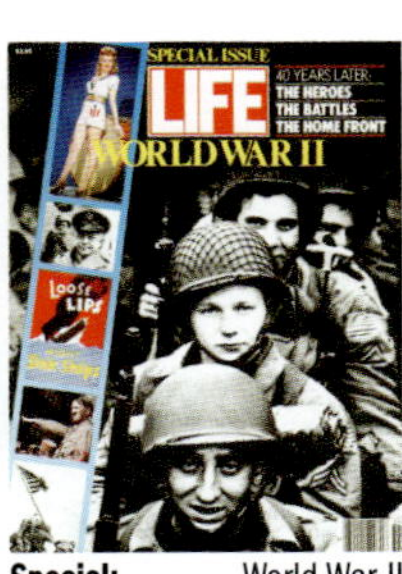
Special: World War II

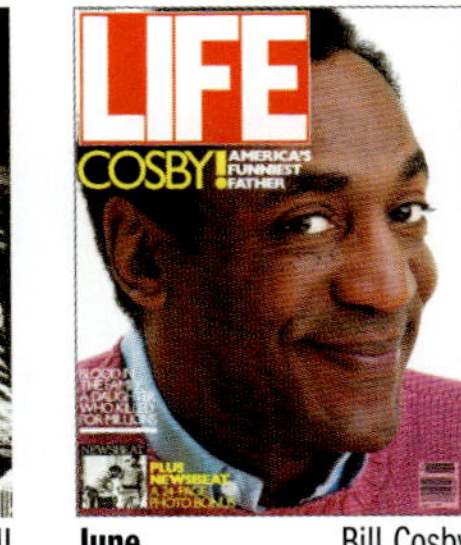
June Bill Cosby

July New Victims

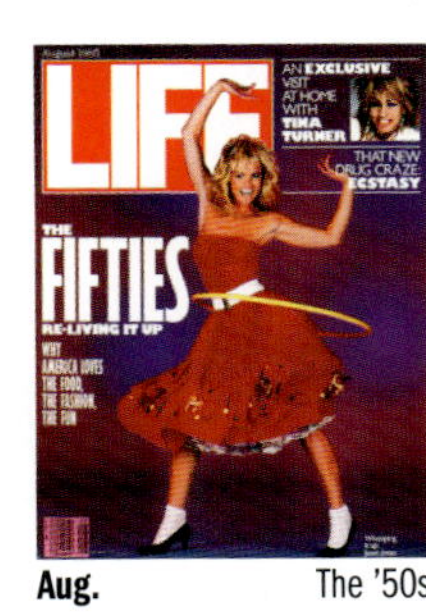
Aug. The '50s

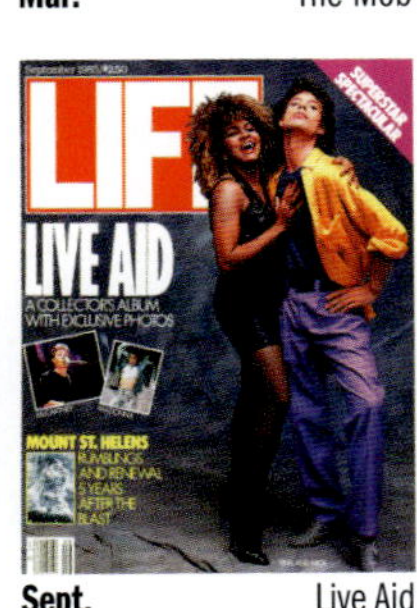
Sept. Live Aid

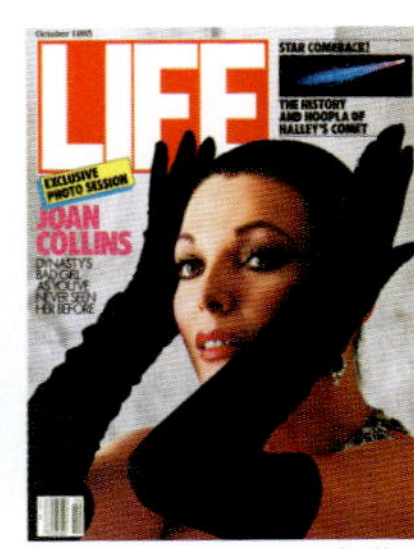
Oct. Joan Collins

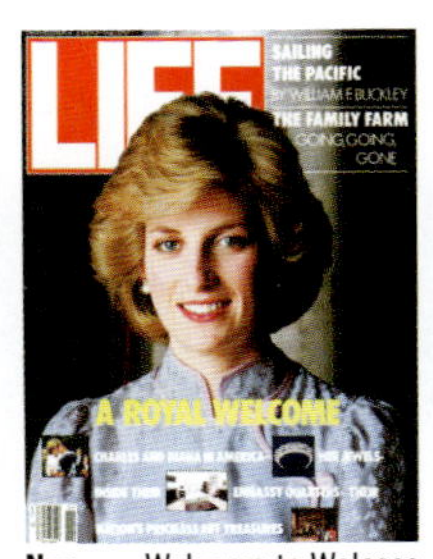
Nov. Welcome to Waleses

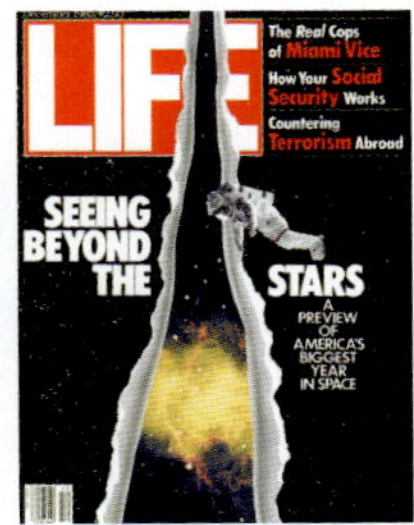
Dec. Space Shots

The sunken *Titanic* is located after 73 years • Reagan and Gorbachev meet in Geneva
The worst freeze in a century ruins 90 percent of Florida's citrus crop • The U.S. is a debtor nation for the first time since 1914
American engineers send 300,000 telephone calls along a single optical fiber

1986

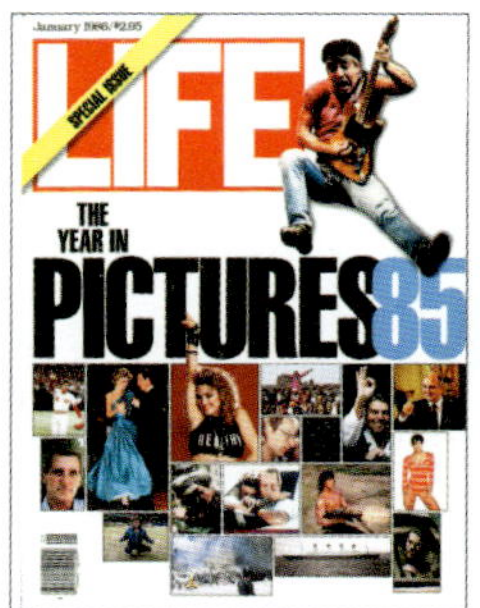
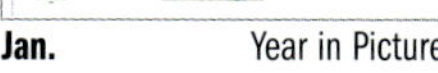
Jan. Year in Pictures

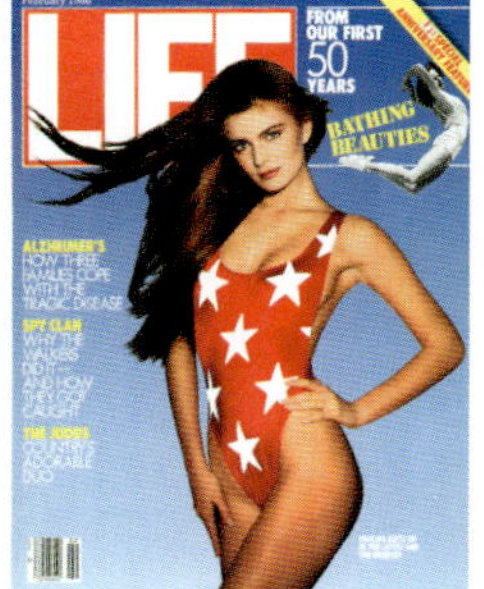
Feb. Swimsuits

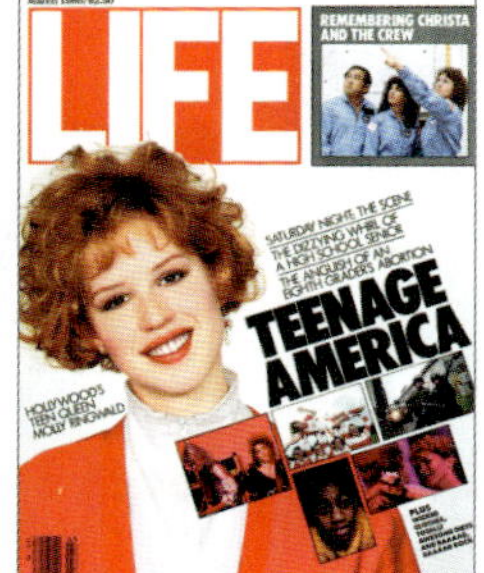
Mar. Molly Ringwald

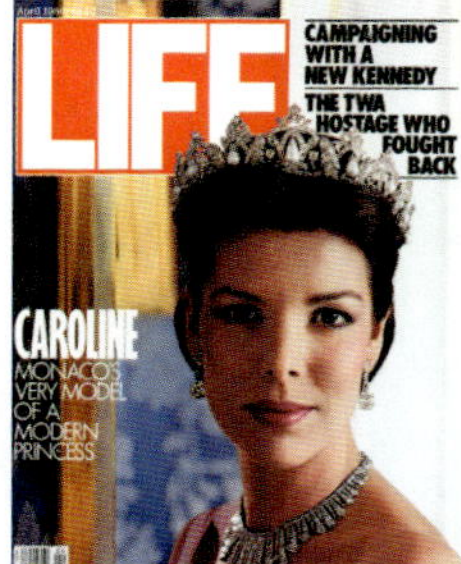
Apr. Princess Caroline

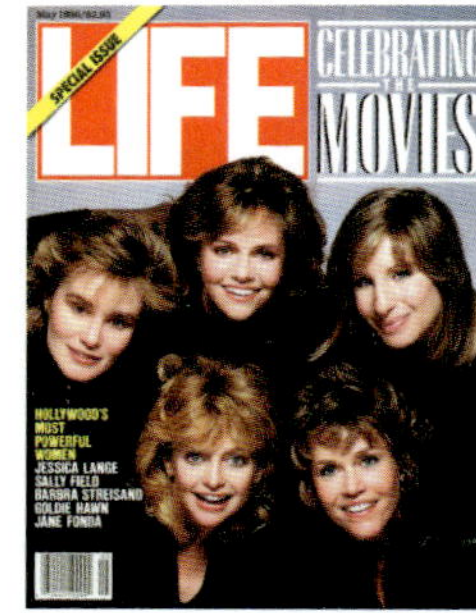
May Hollywood

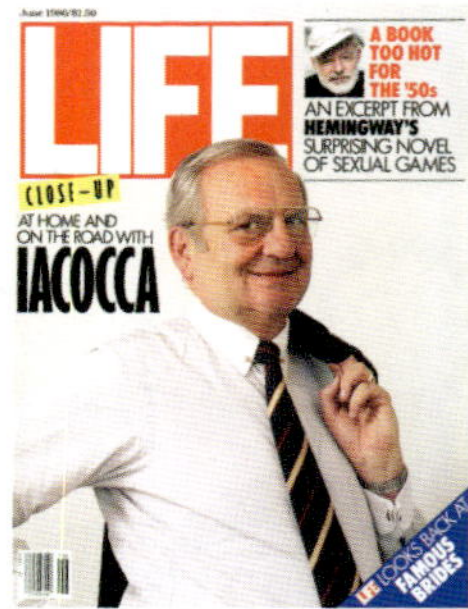
June Lee Iacocca

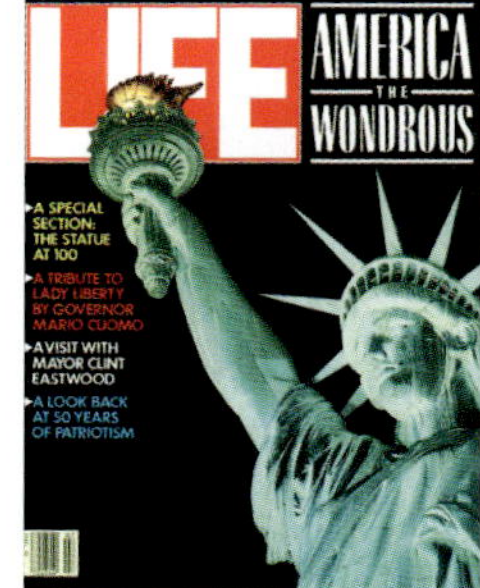
July Portrait of a Lady

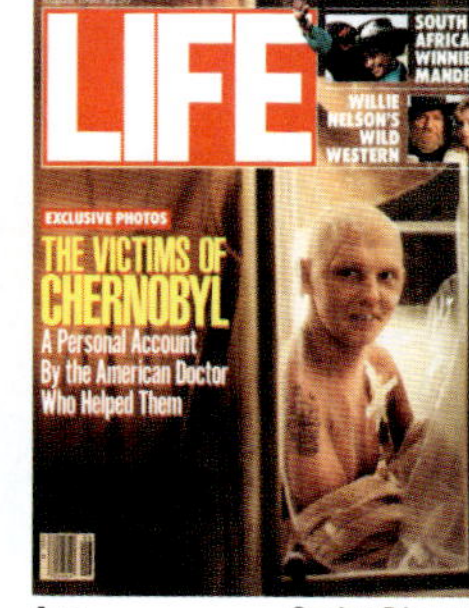
Aug. Soviet Disaster

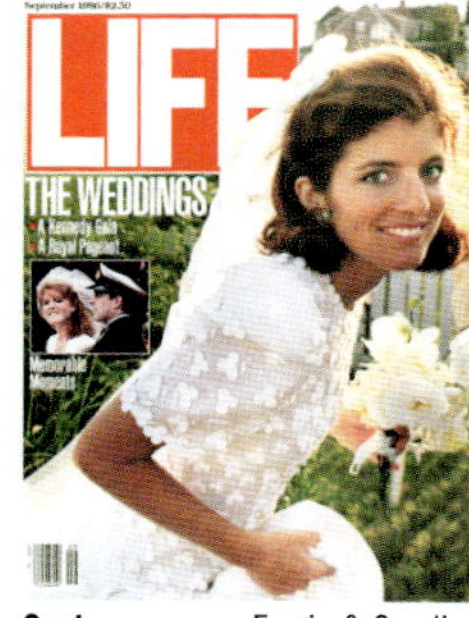
Sept. Fergie & Caroline

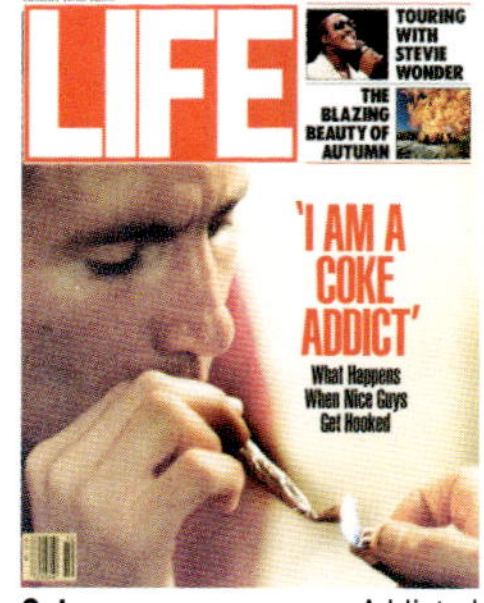
Oct. Addicted

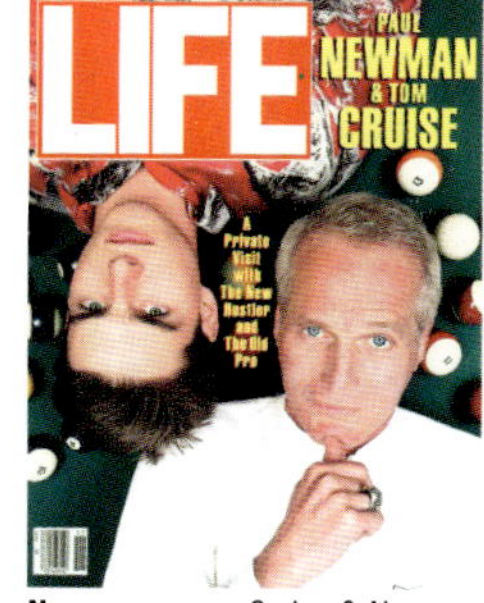
Nov. Cruise & Newman

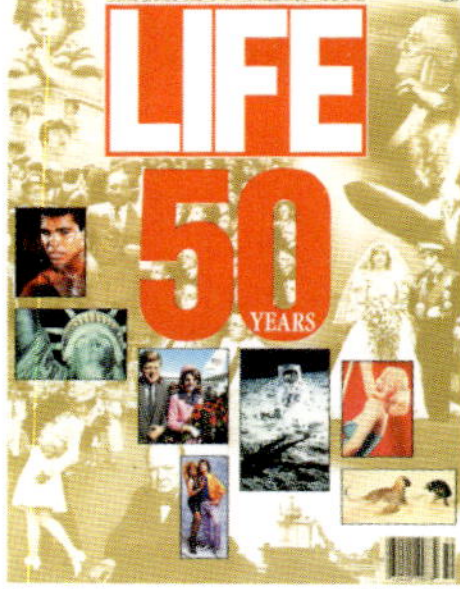
Special: LIFE Is 50

Dec. Madonna

The *Challenger* space shuttle explodes over the Atlantic
Imelda Marcos leaves behind at least 1,060 pairs of shoes when she flees the Philippines
The FDA approves the first vaccine against hepatitis B
Plans for the Chunnel are unveiled
Insider trading shakes Wall Street as Ivan Boesky pleads guilty

1987

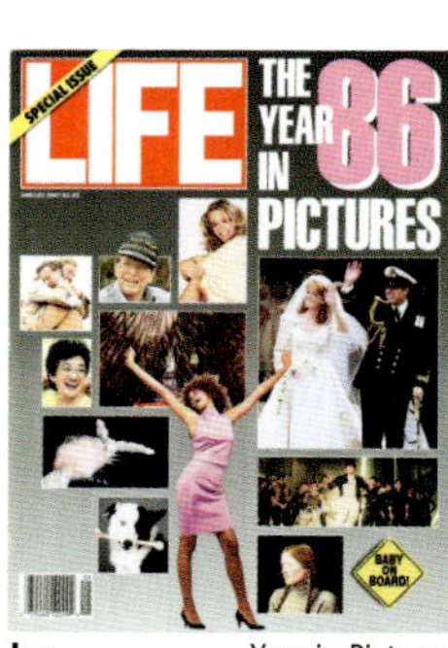
Jan. Year in Pictures

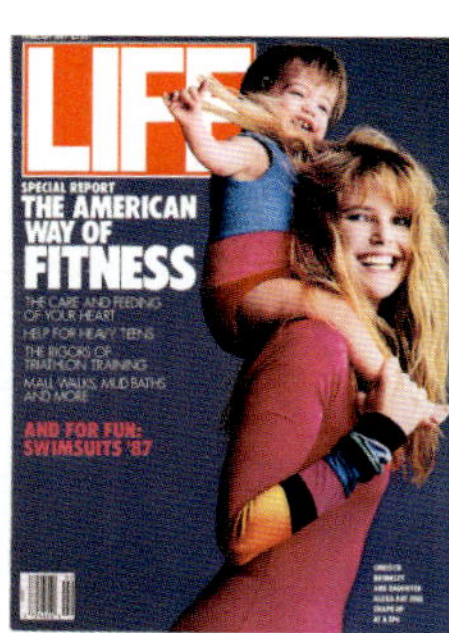
Feb. Alexa & Christie

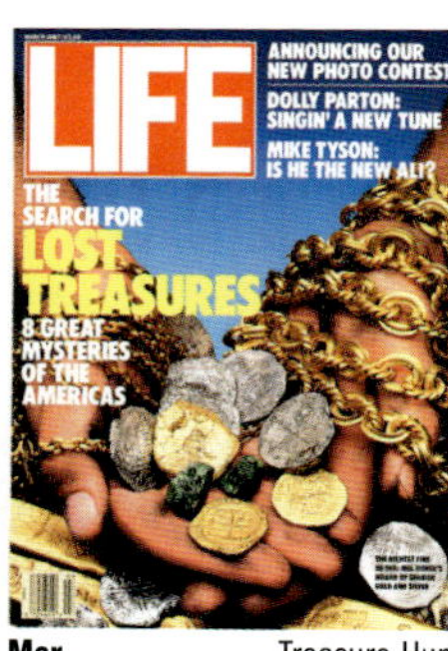
Mar. Treasure Hunt

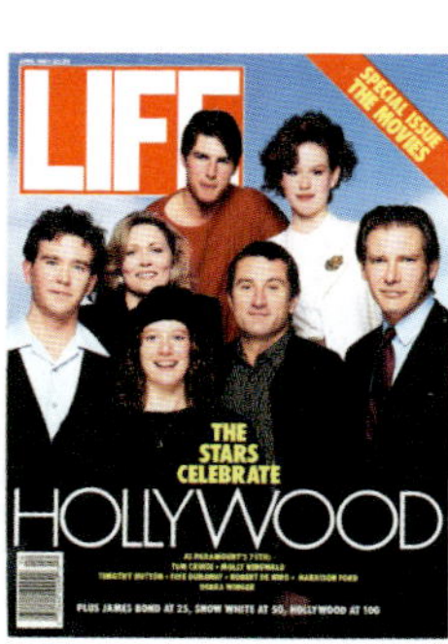
Apr. Hollywood at 100

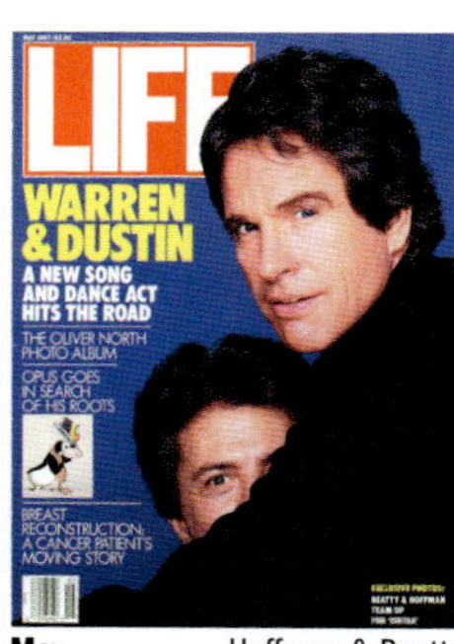
May Hoffman & Beatty

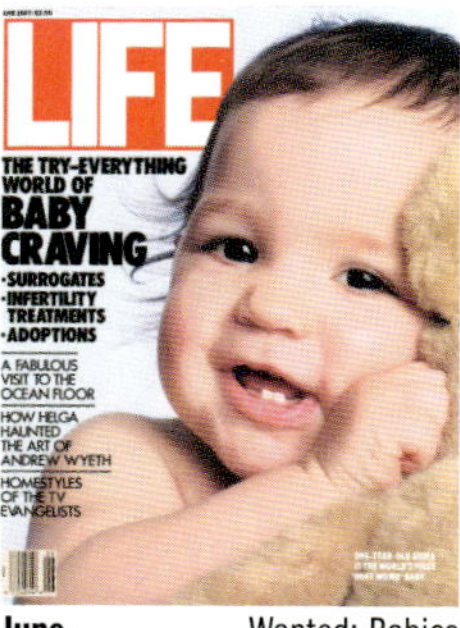
June Wanted: Babies

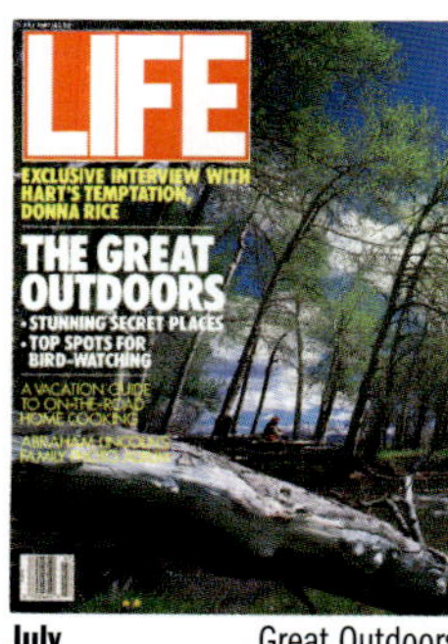
July Great Outdoors

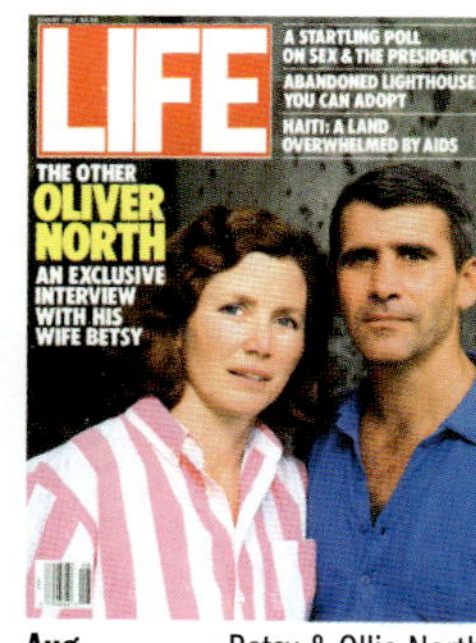
Aug. Betsy & Ollie North

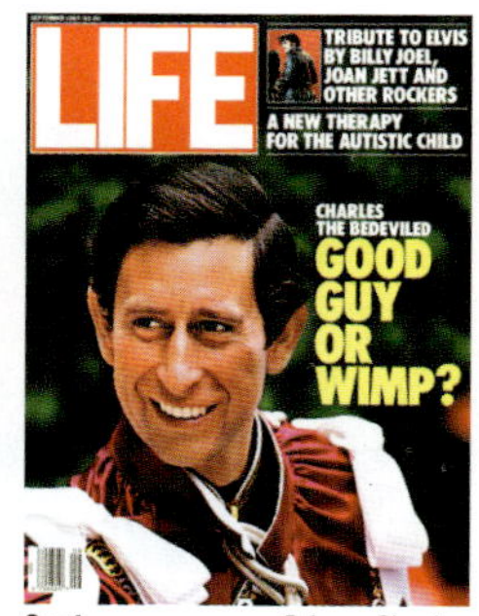
Sept. Prince Charles

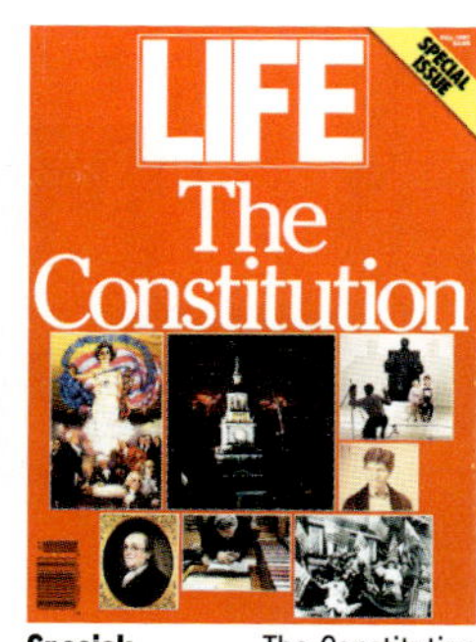
Special: The Constitution

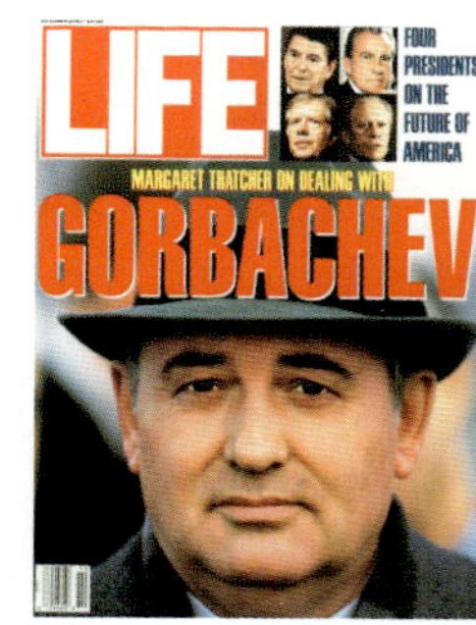
Oct. Soviet Leader

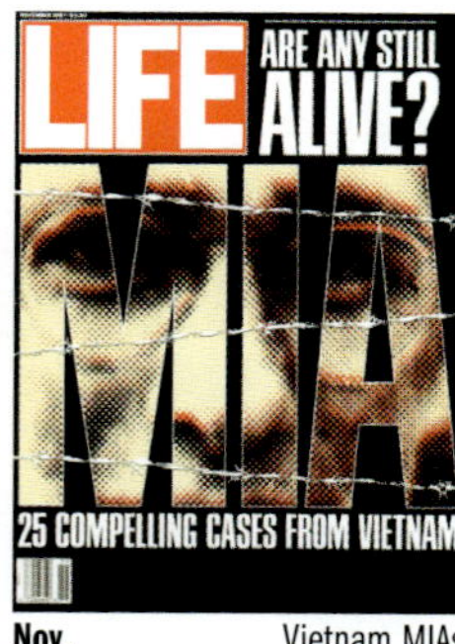
Nov. Vietnam MIAs

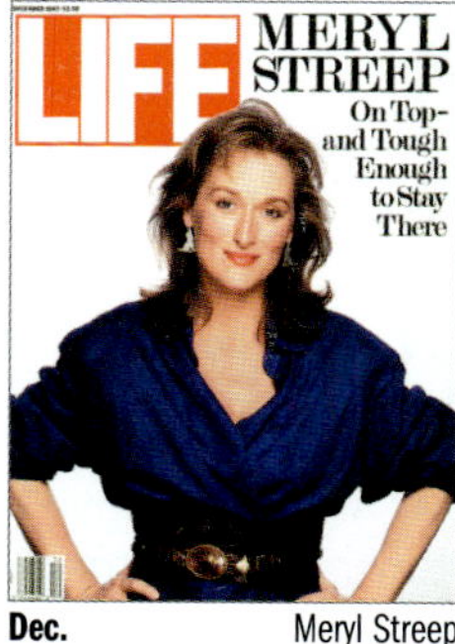
Dec. Meryl Streep

Les Misérables breaks all records for advance ticket sales on Broadway
Democratic presidential hopeful Gary Hart withdraws after affair with a young model
"Baby Jessica" McClure is rescued from a well in Texas
Texaco declares bankruptcy • U.S. and U.S.S.R. agree to destroy intermediate-range missiles

1988

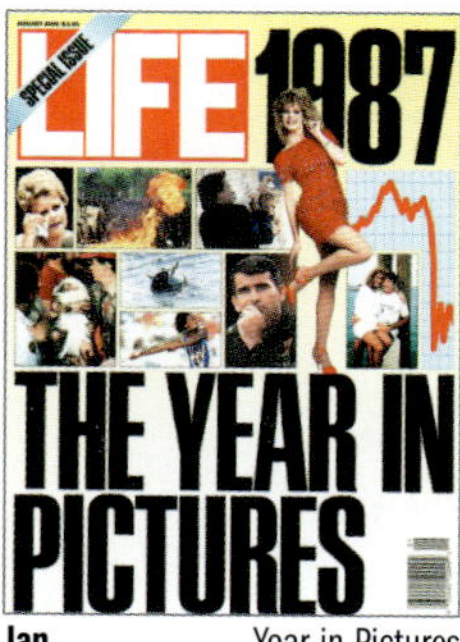

Jan. Year in Pictures

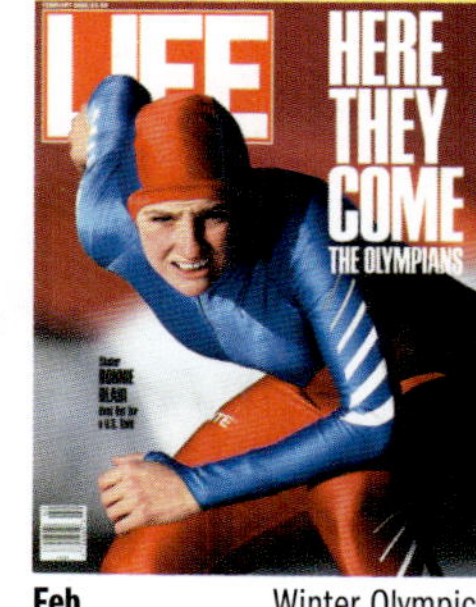

Feb. Winter Olympics

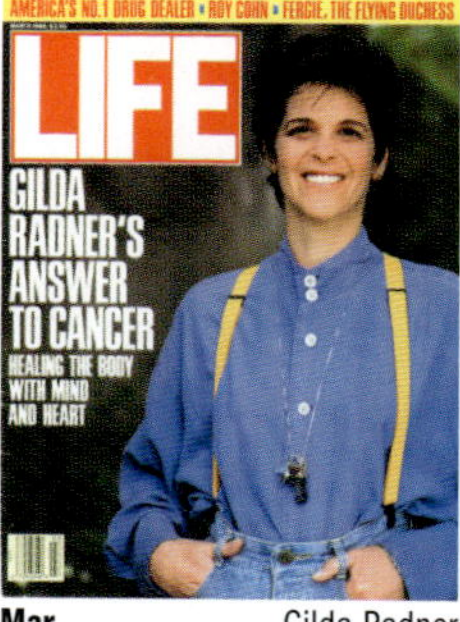

Mar. Gilda Radner

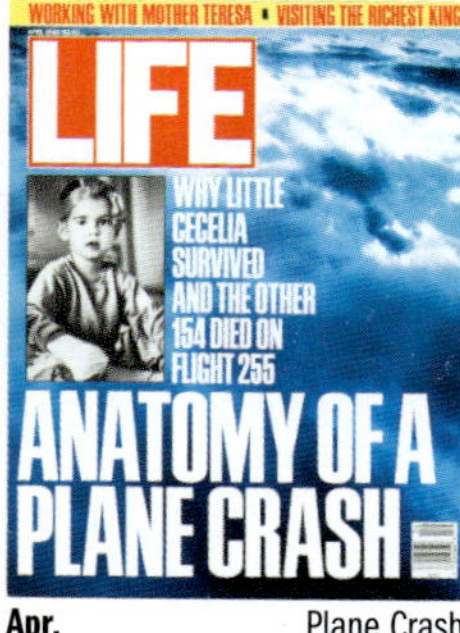

Apr. Plane Crash

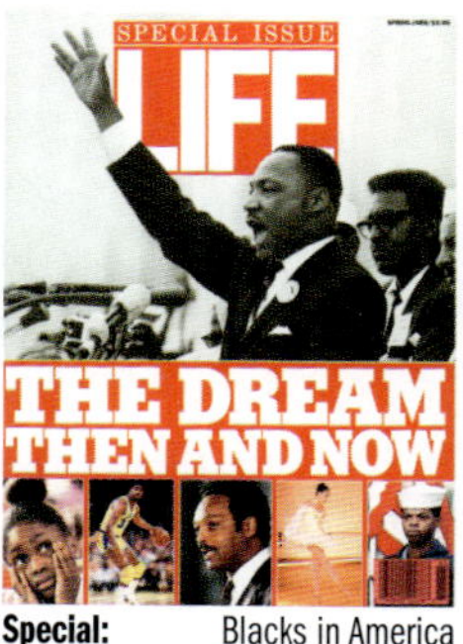

Special: Blacks in America

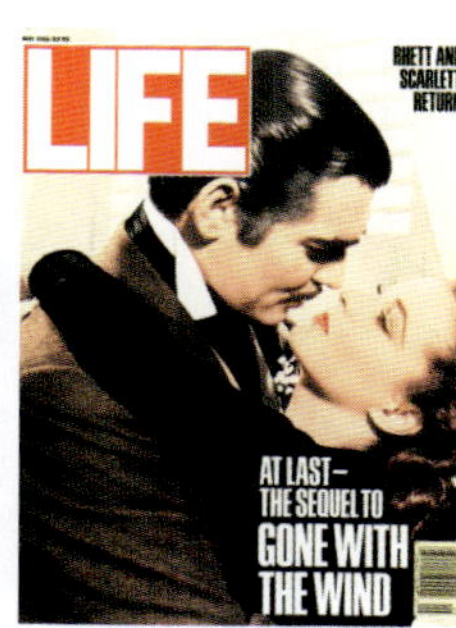

May A Remake

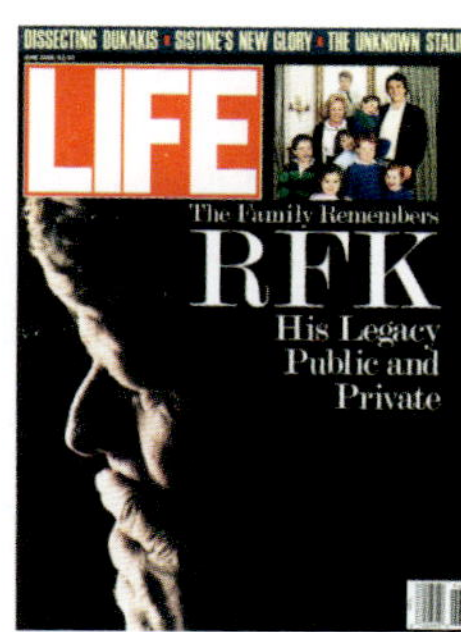

June RFK Tribute

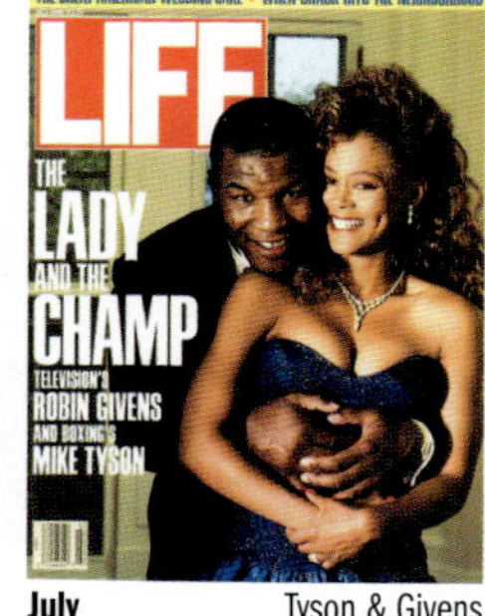

July Tyson & Givens

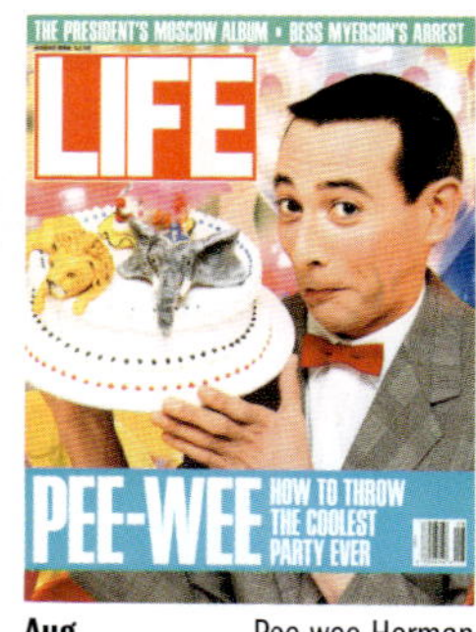

Aug. Pee-wee Herman

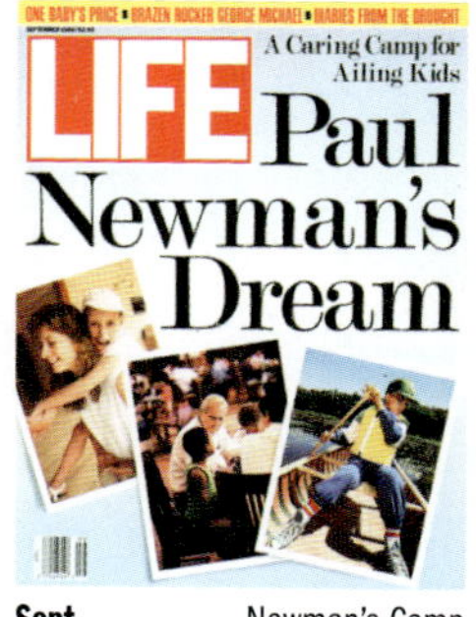

Sept. Newman's Camp

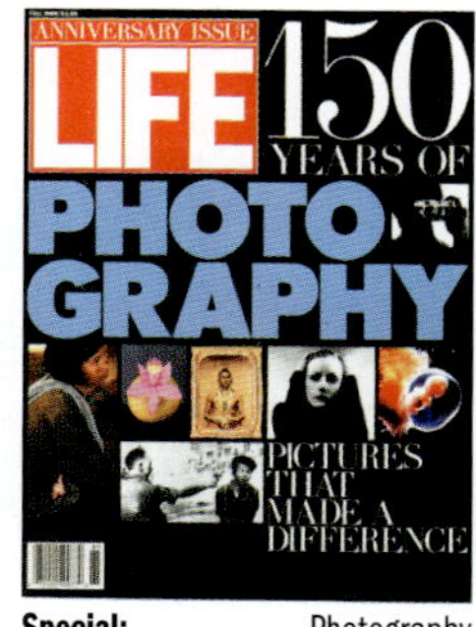

Special: Photography

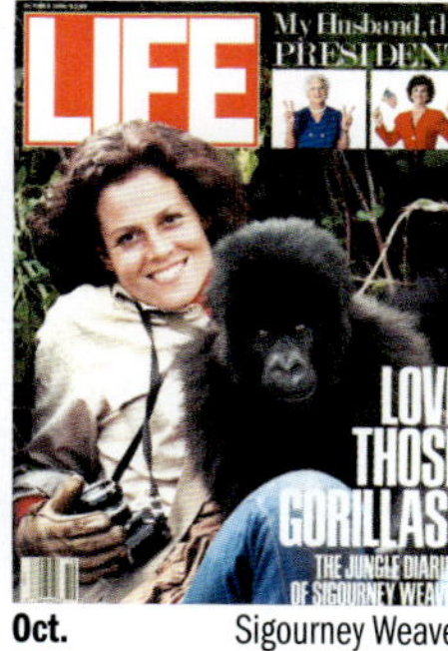

Oct. Sigourney Weaver

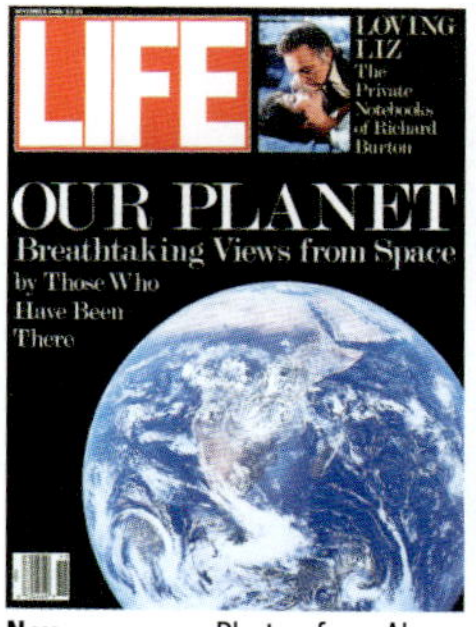

Nov. Photos from Above

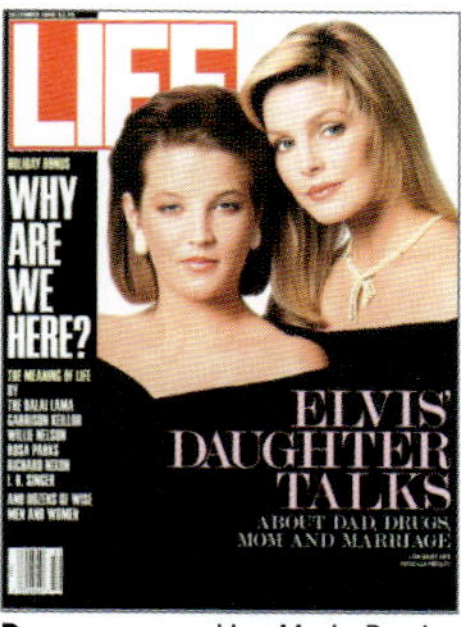

Dec. Lisa Marie Presley

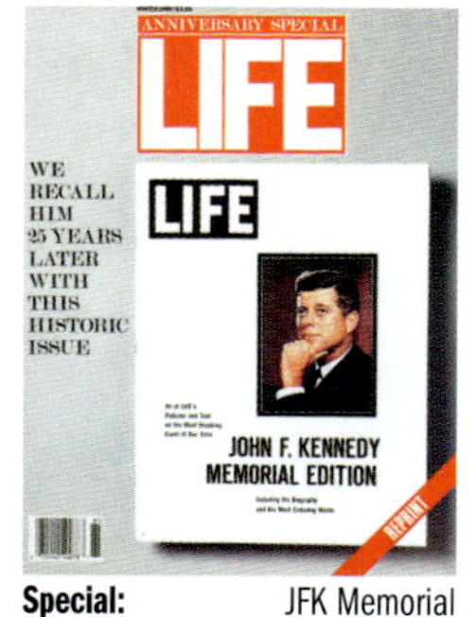

Special: JFK Memorial

The Phantom of the Opera opens on Broadway and wins seven Tonys
Oprah Winfrey becomes TV's richest and most powerful woman
A virus released by a computer hacker infects 6,000 systems in the U.S.
Physicist Stephen Hawking's *A Brief History of Time* is a best-seller
Superman celebrates his 50th birthday

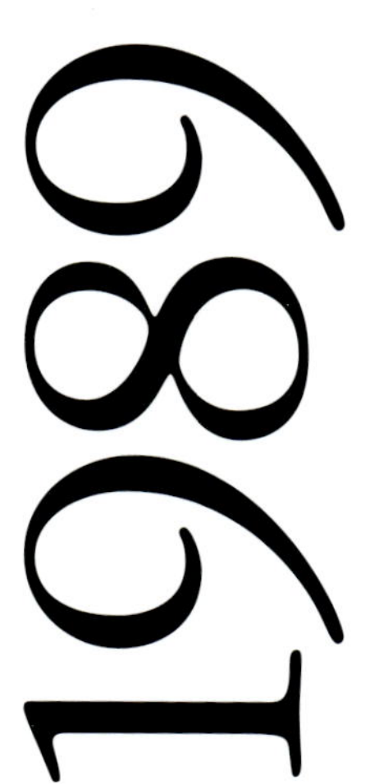

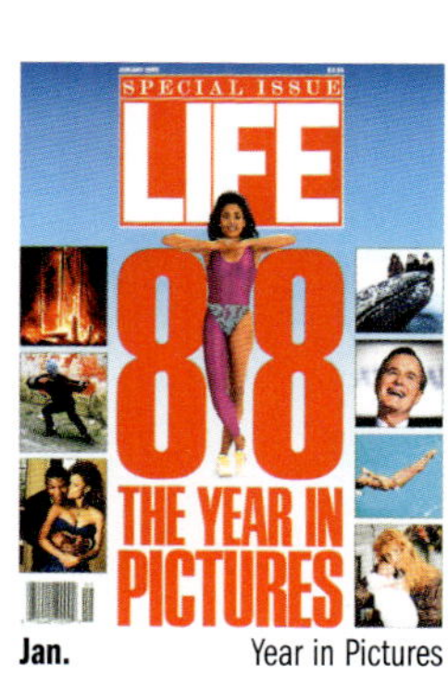

Jan. Year in Pictures

The Berlin Wall comes down • Nations of the world ban trade in ivory
Hundreds are killed in Beijing's Tiananmen Square
The *Exxon Valdez* spills nearly 11 million gallons of oil into Alaska's Prince William Sound
Teenage Mutant Ninja Turtles are the latest craze

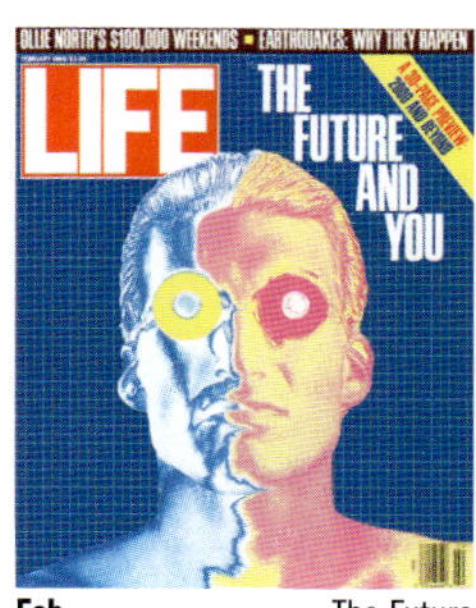

Feb. The Future

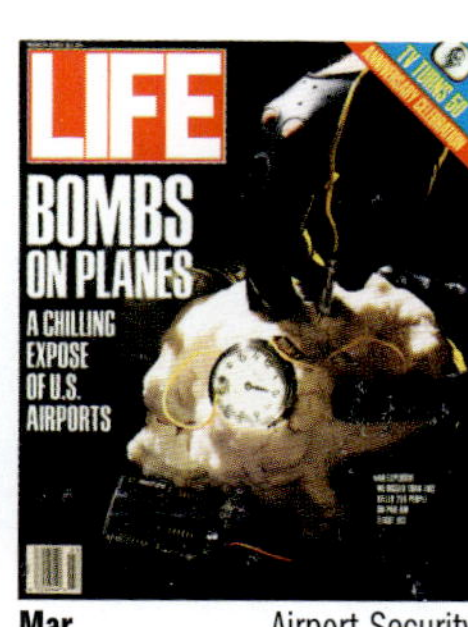

Mar. Airport Security

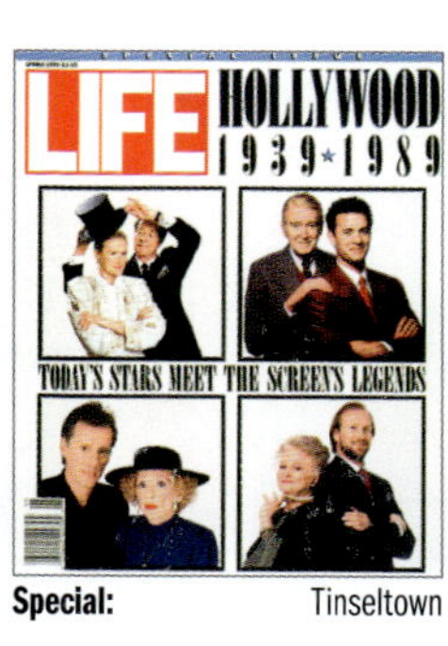

Special: Tinseltown

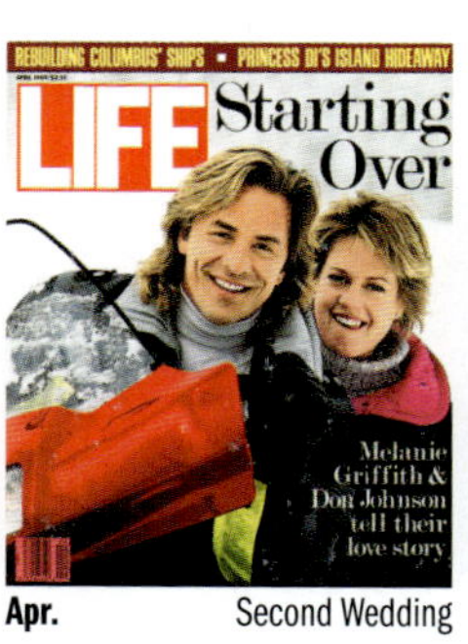

Apr. Second Wedding

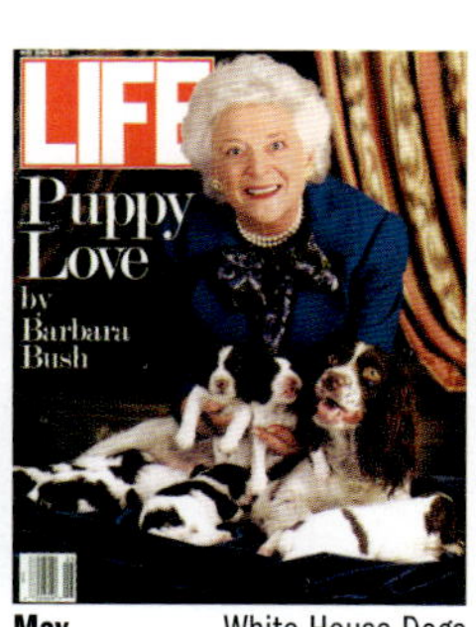

May White House Dogs

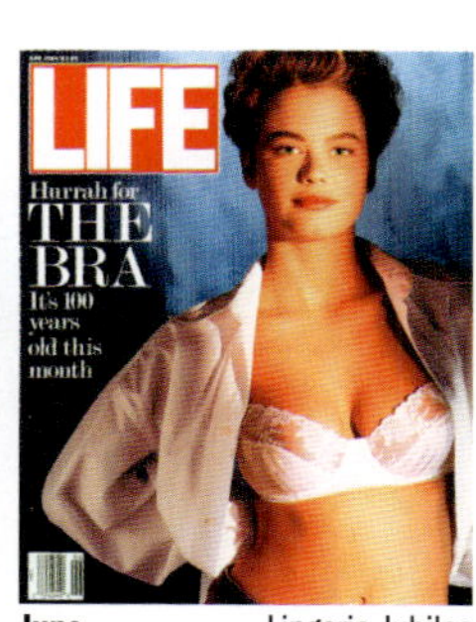

June Lingerie Jubilee

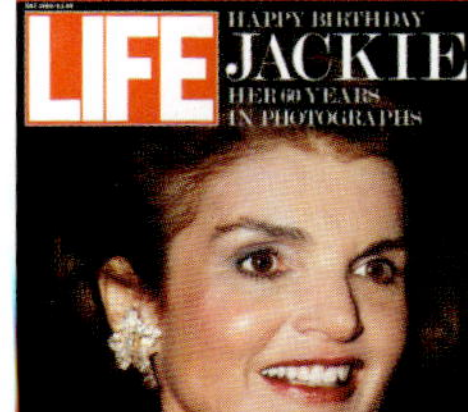

July Jackie's 60th

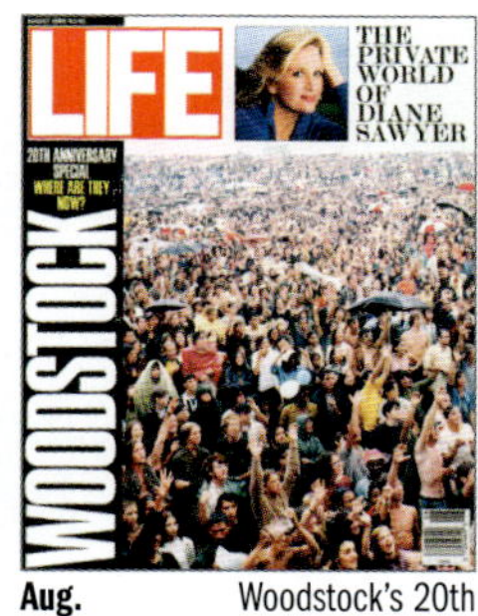

Aug. Woodstock's 20th

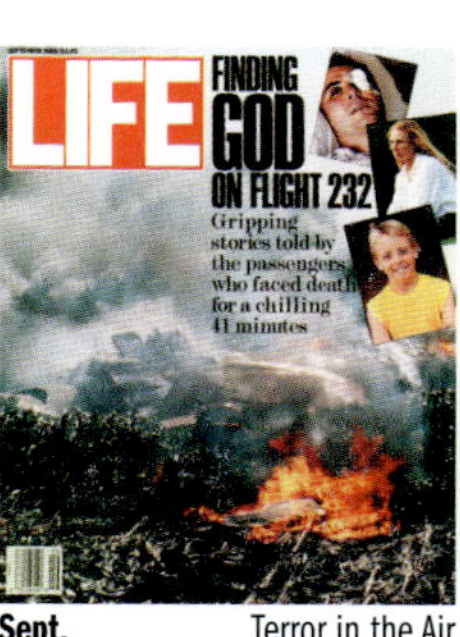

Sept. Terror in the Air

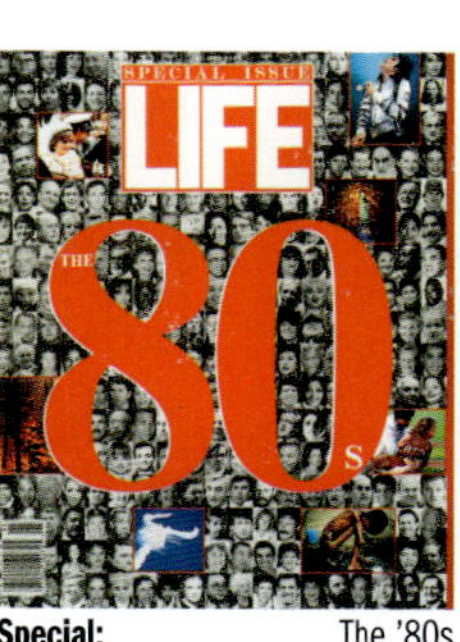

Special: The '80s

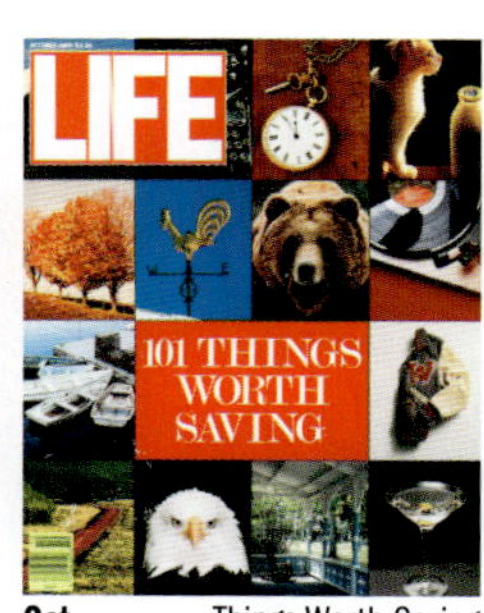

Oct. Things Worth Saving

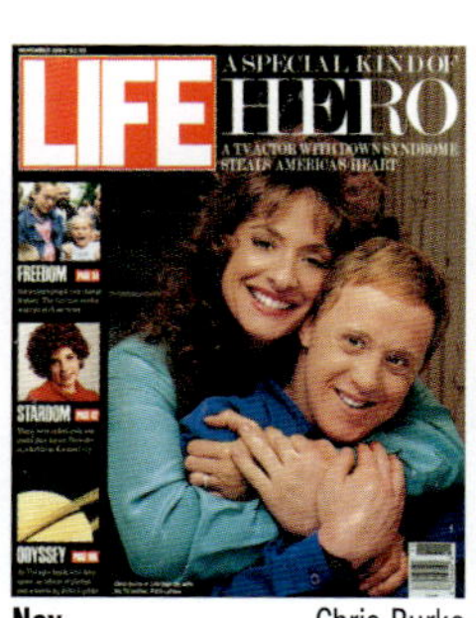

Nov. Chris Burke

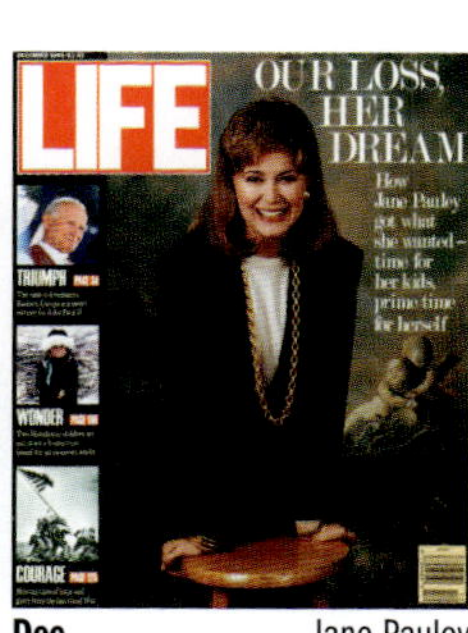

Dec. Jane Pauley

1990

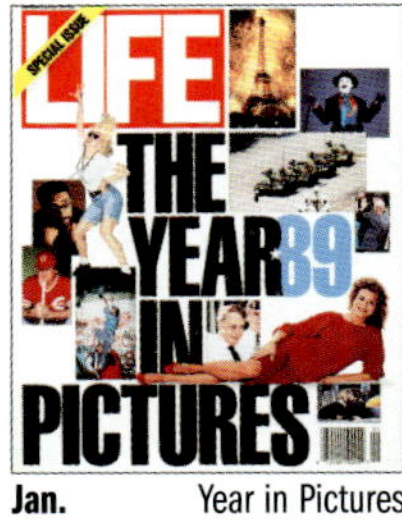

Jan. Year in Pictures

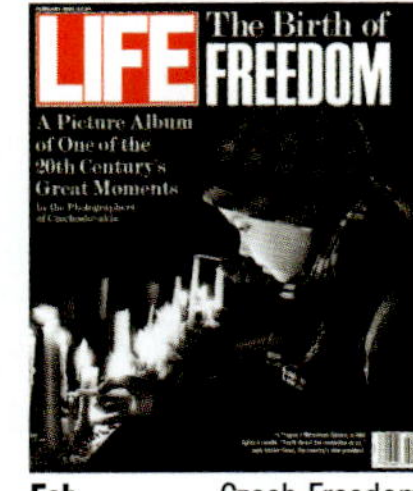

Feb. Czech Freedom

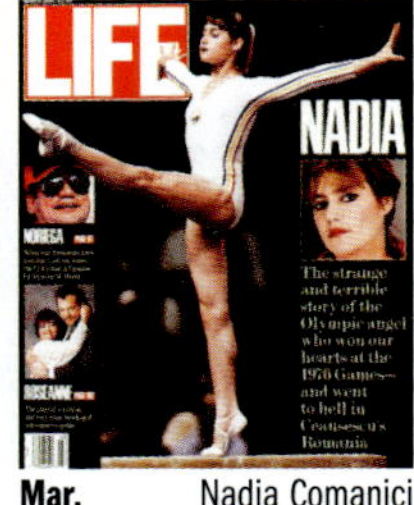

Mar. Nadia Comanici

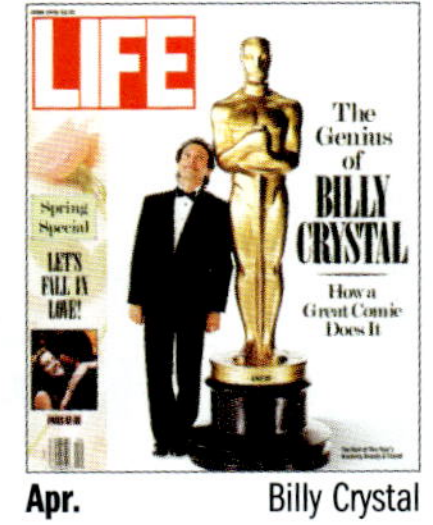

Apr. Billy Crystal

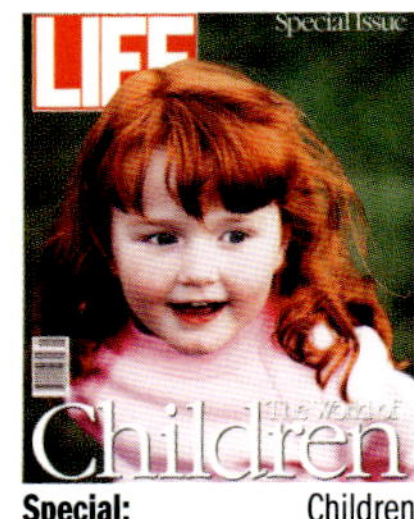

Special: Children

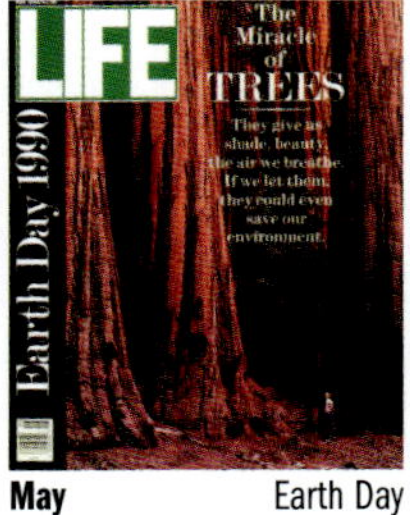

May Earth Day

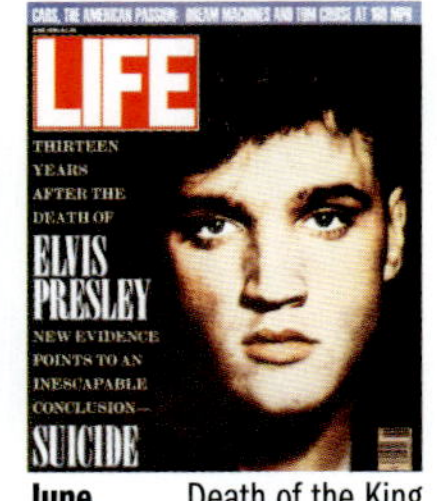

June Death of the King

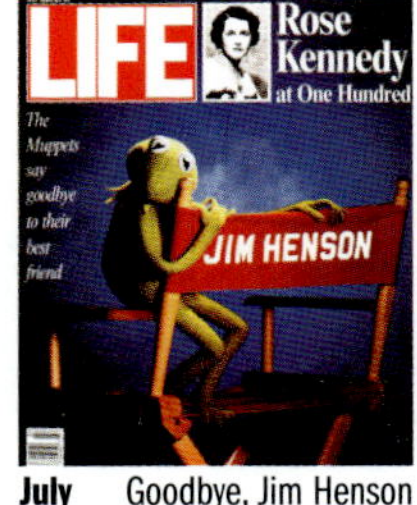

July Goodbye, Jim Henson

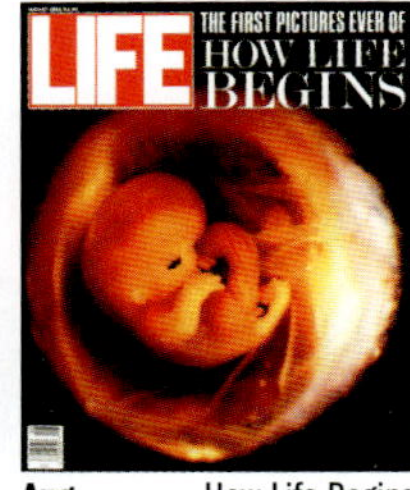

Aug. How Life Begins

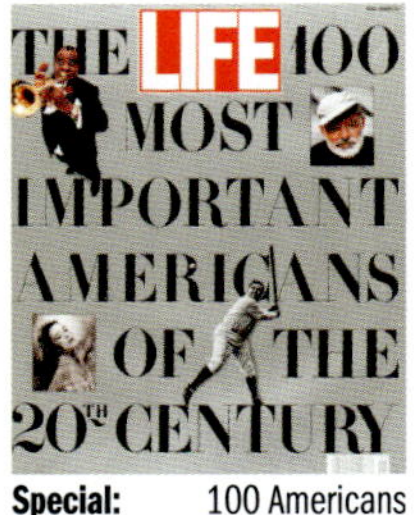

Special: 100 Americans

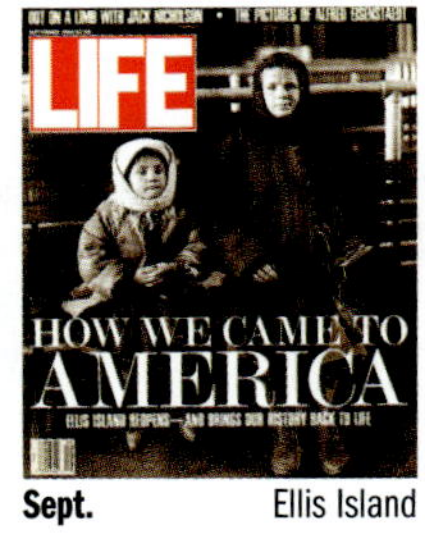

Sept. Ellis Island

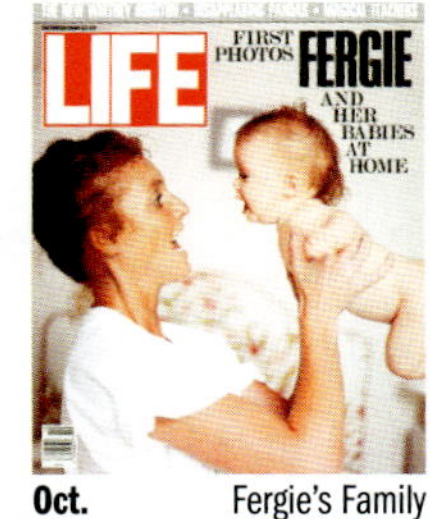

Oct. Fergie's Family

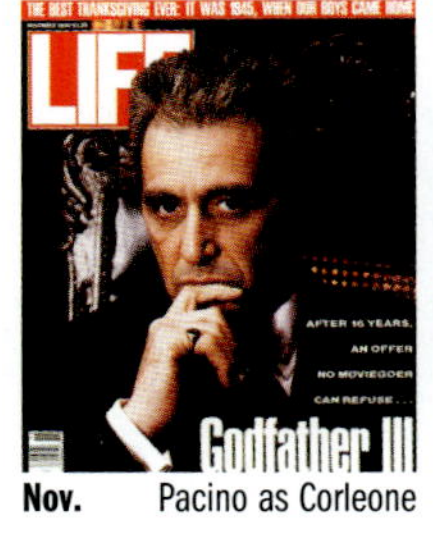

Nov. Pacino as Corleone

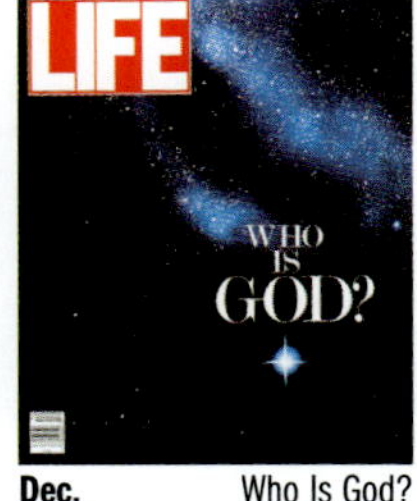

Dec. Who Is God?

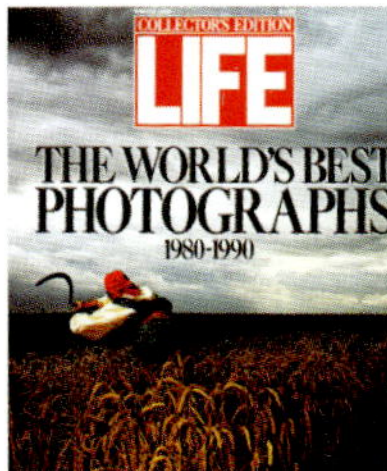

Special: Photography

The U.S. population is 248,718,302
British software consultant Tim Berners-Lee develops the World Wide Web
Smoking is banned on virtually all U.S. domestic flights • The Hubble Space Telescope is put into orbit
Martina Navratilova wins a record ninth singles title at Wimbledon

1991

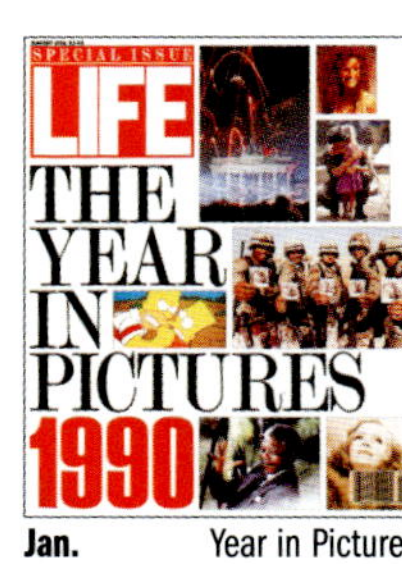

Jan. Year in Pictures

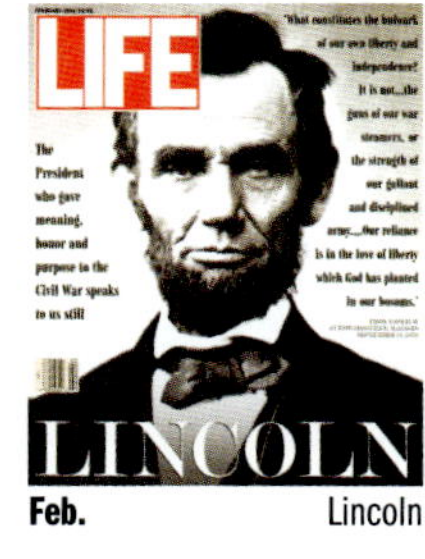

Feb. Lincoln

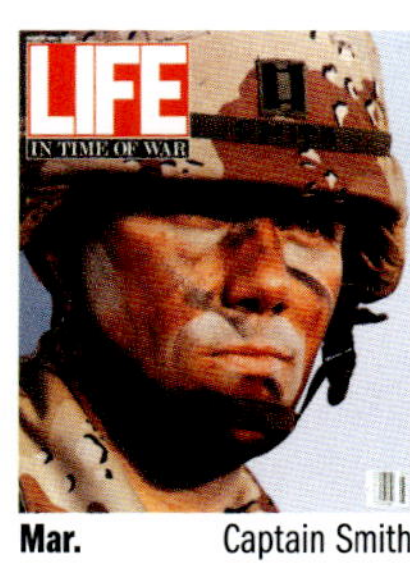

Mar. Captain Smith

NBA star Magic Johnson says he has tested positive for HIV
American Express celebrates 100th anniversary of its Travelers Cheques
Queen Elizabeth II is first British monarch to address U.S. Congress
Video shows L.A. police beating Rodney King in the street
Swiss banks announce that secret numbered accounts will be abolished

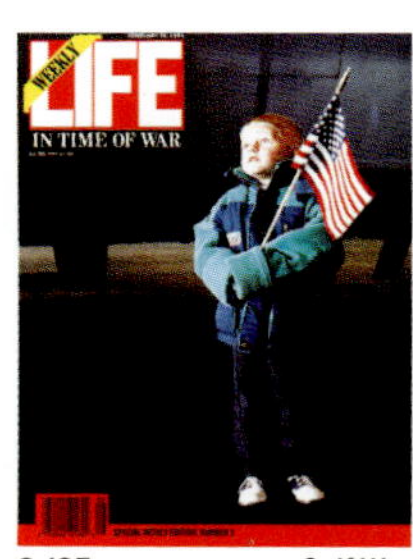

2/25 Gulf War

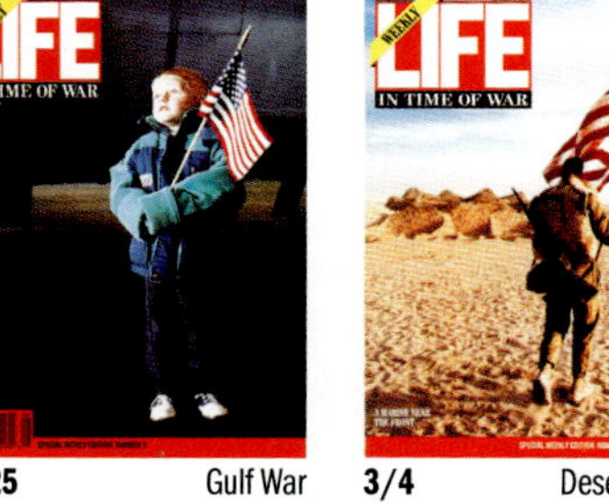

3/4 Desert Storm

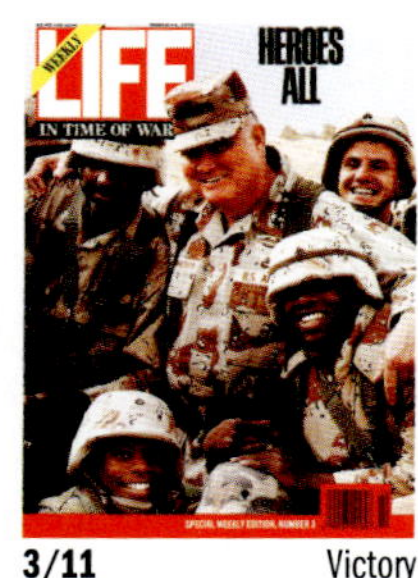

3/11 Victory

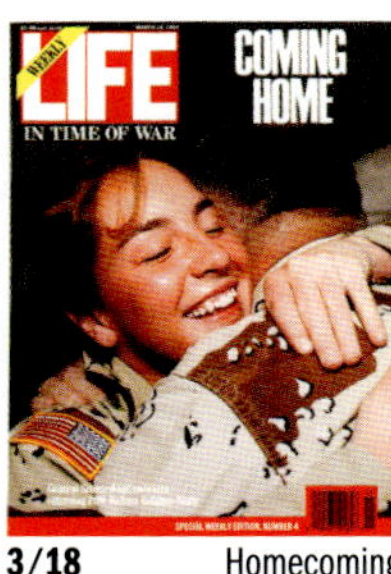

3/18 Homecoming

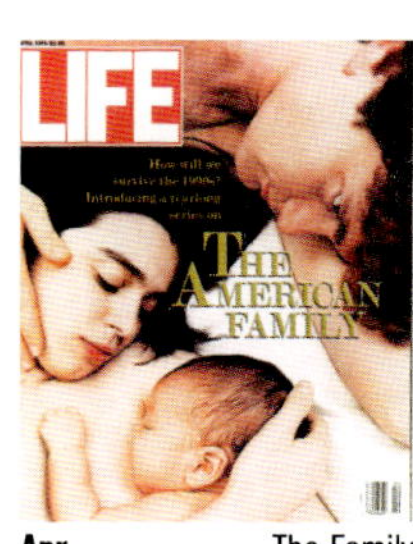

Apr. The Family

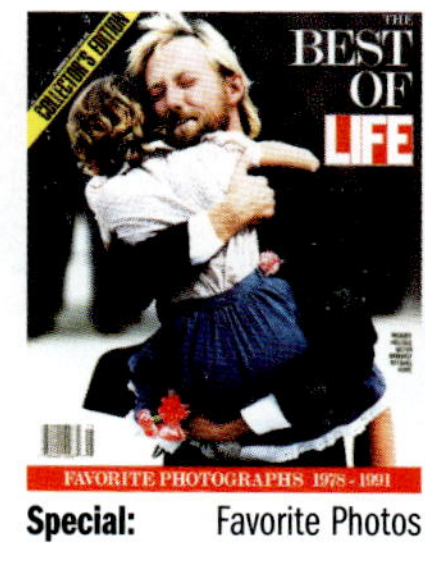

Special: Favorite Photos

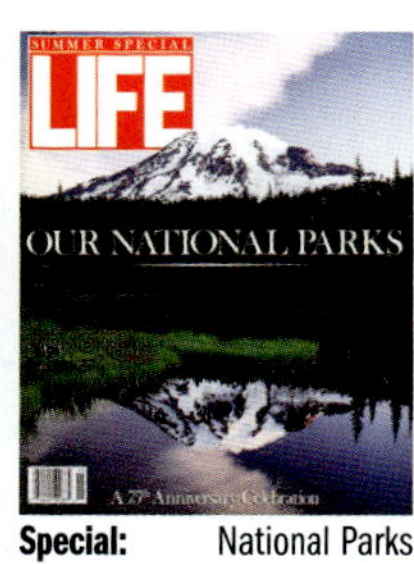

Special: National Parks

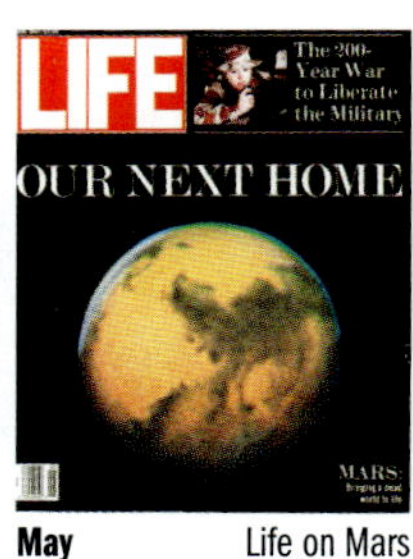

May Life on Mars

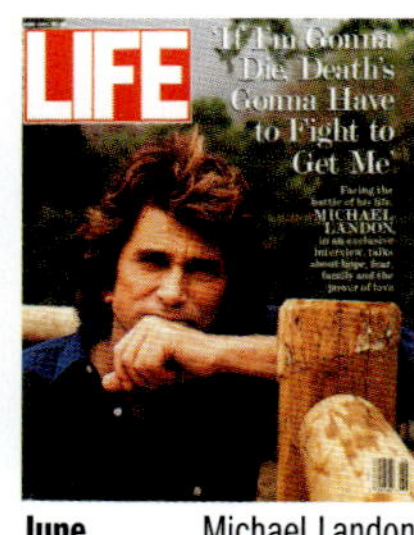

June Michael Landon

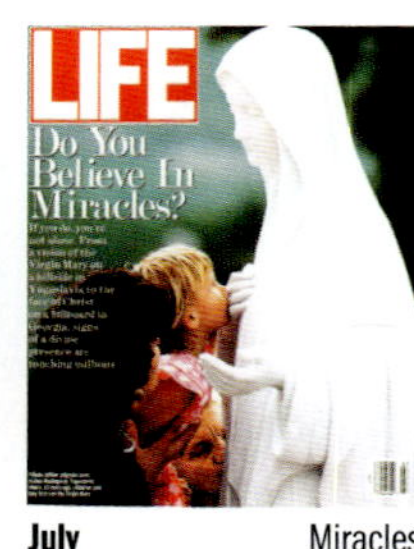

July Miracles

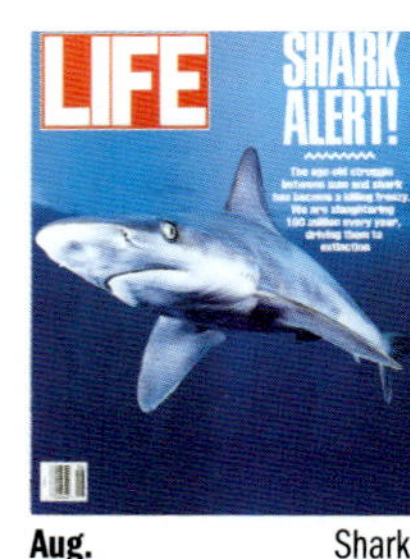

Aug. Sharks

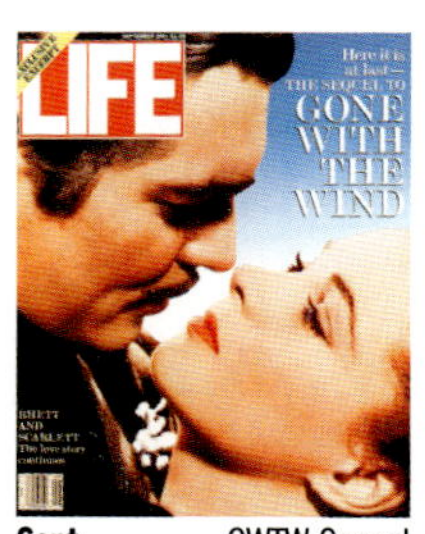

Sept. GWTW Sequel

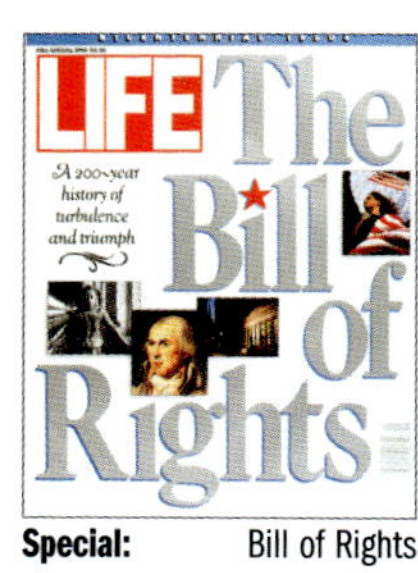

Special: Bill of Rights

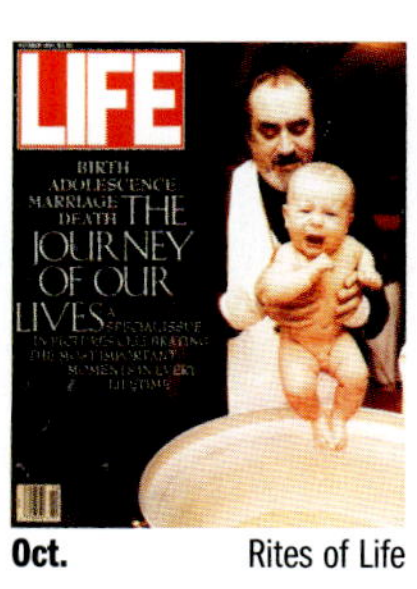

Oct. Rites of Life

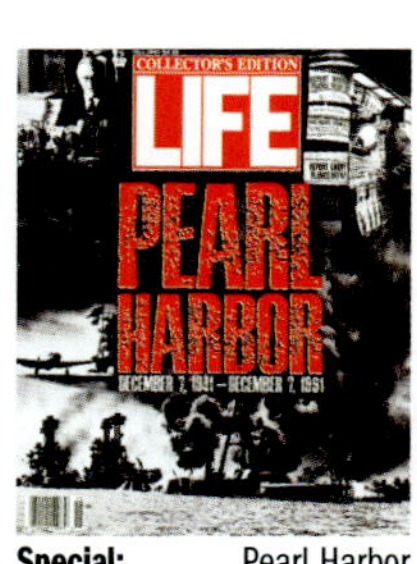

Special: Pearl Harbor

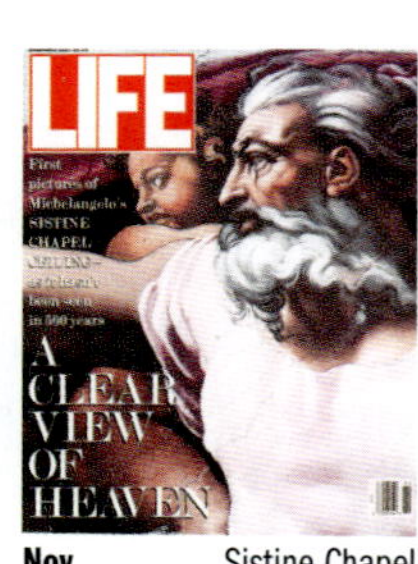

Nov. Sistine Chapel

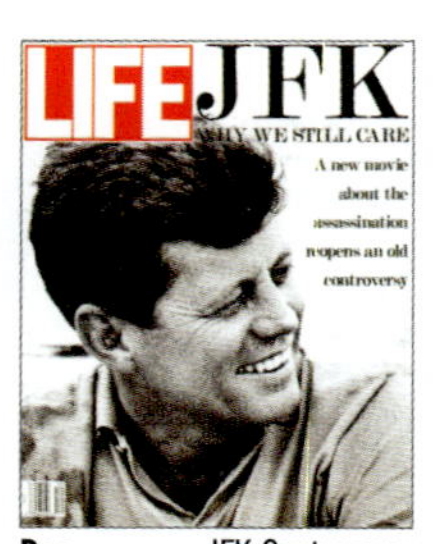

Dec. JFK Controversy

1992

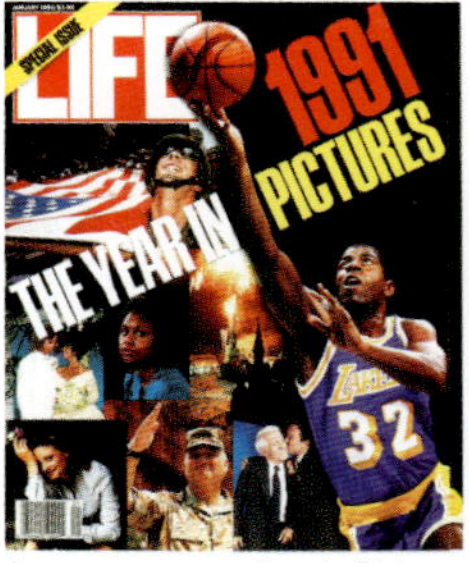

Jan. Year in Pictures

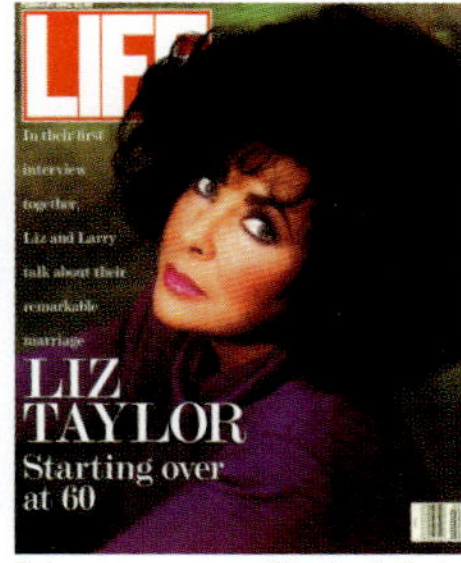

Feb. Elizabeth Taylor

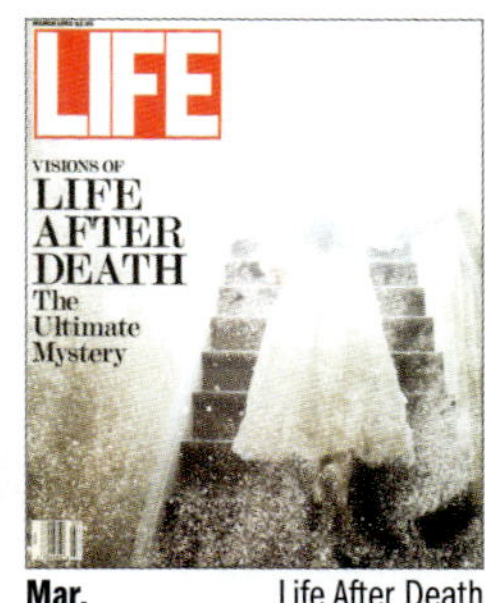

Mar. Life After Death

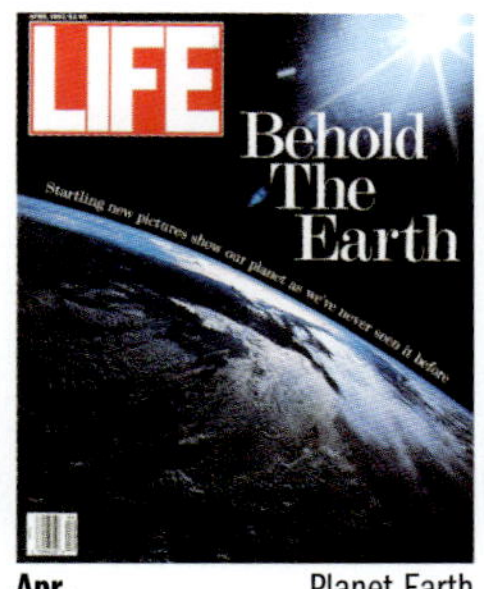

Apr. Planet Earth

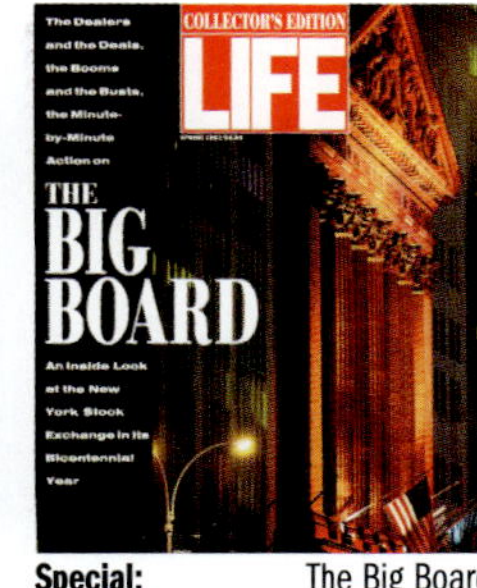

Special: The Big Board

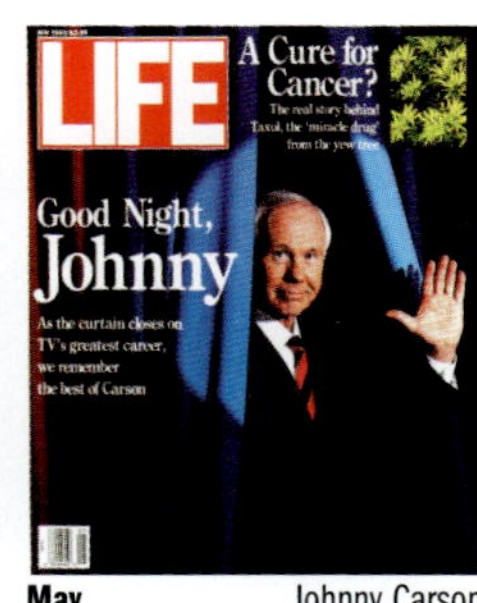

May Johnny Carson

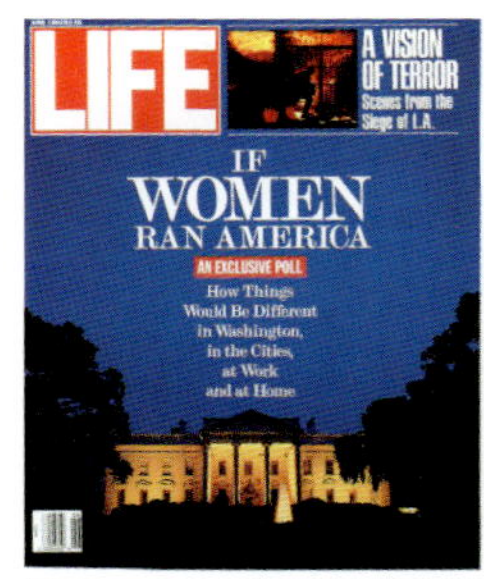

June Women in Politics

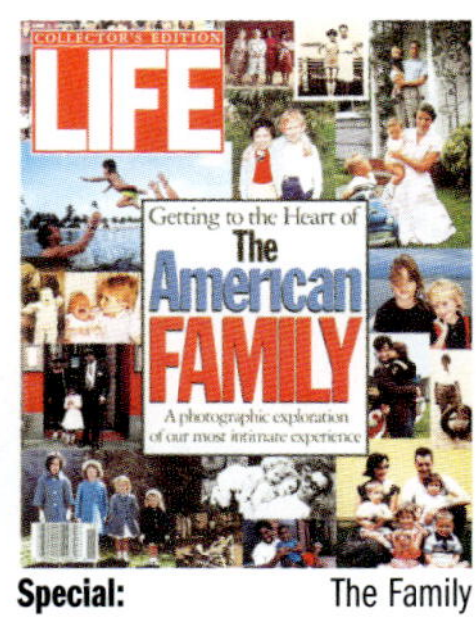

Special: The Family

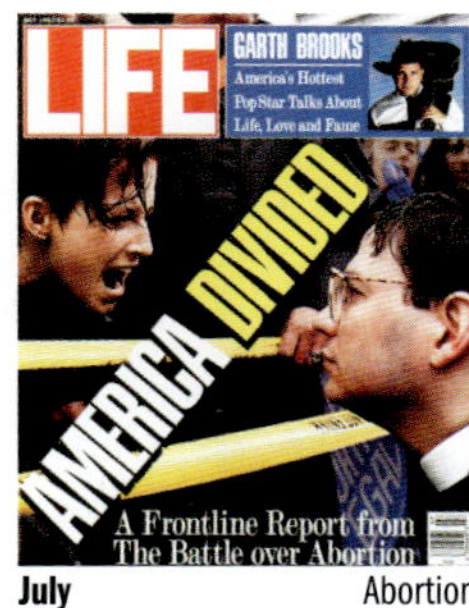

July Abortion

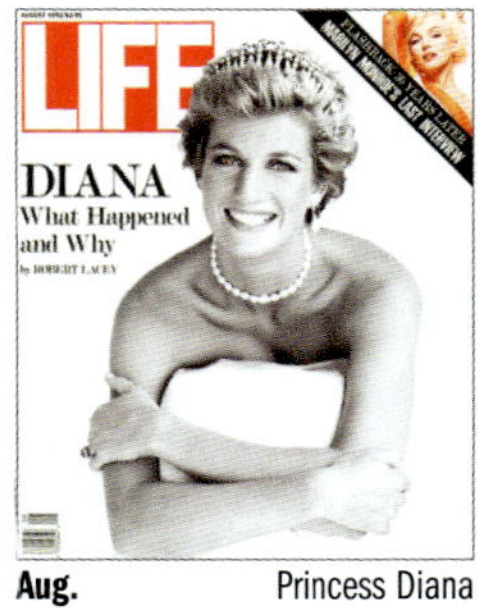

Aug. Princess Diana

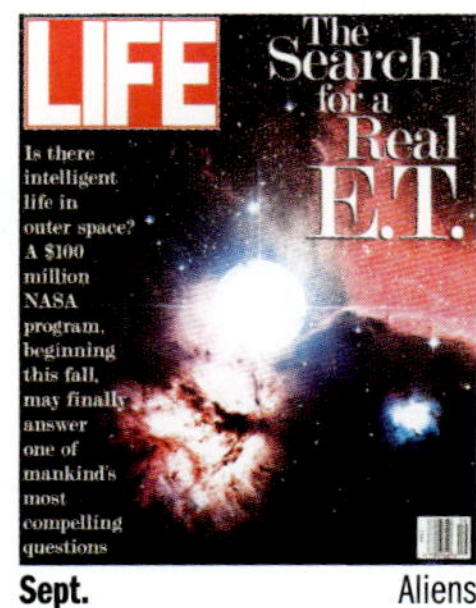

Sept. Aliens

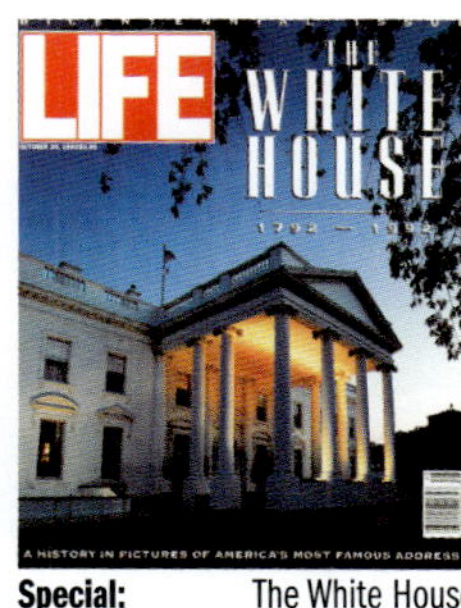

Special: The White House

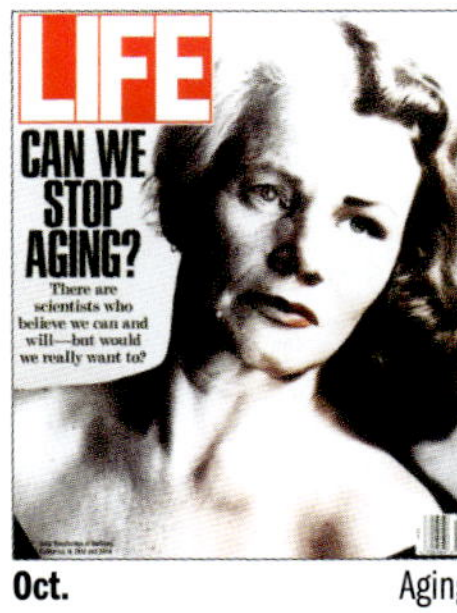

Oct. Aging

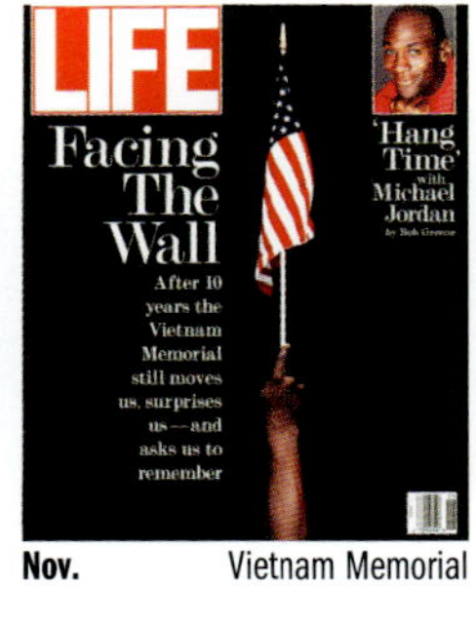

Nov. Vietnam Memorial

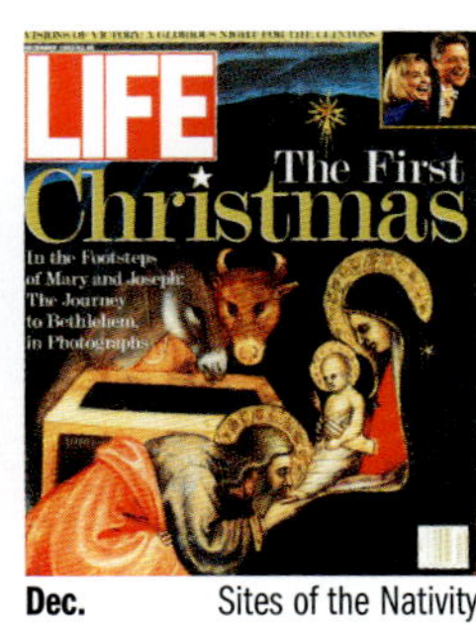

Dec. Sites of the Nativity

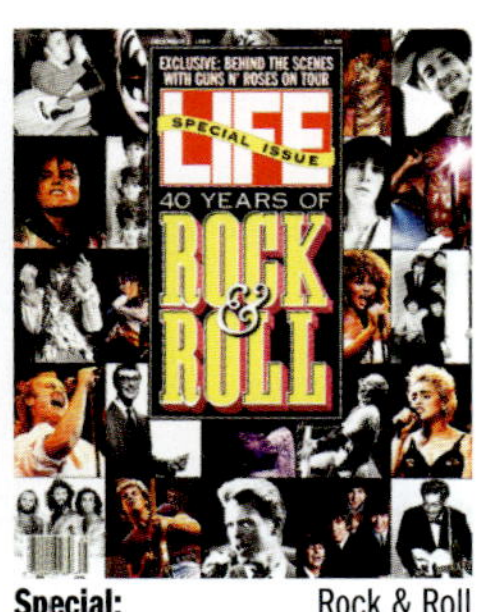

Special: Rock & Roll

John Gotti, the Teflon Don, is convicted of murder and racketeering • Famine kills more than 300,000 in Somalia
The largest shopping mall in the U.S. opens in Bloomington, Minn.
Amy Fisher pleads guilty to shooting Mary Jo Buttafuoco, her lover's wife • Euro Disney opens near Paris

1993

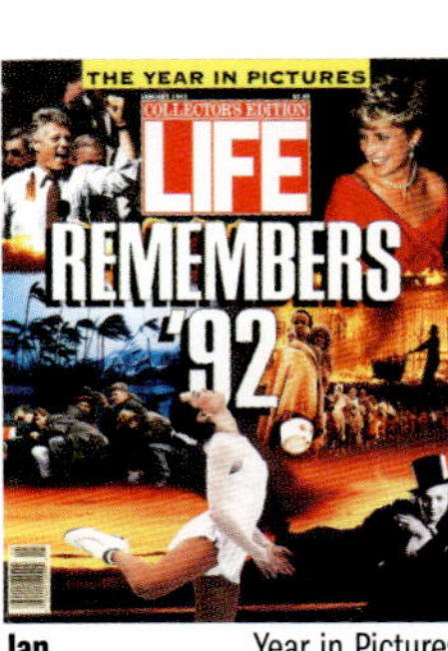
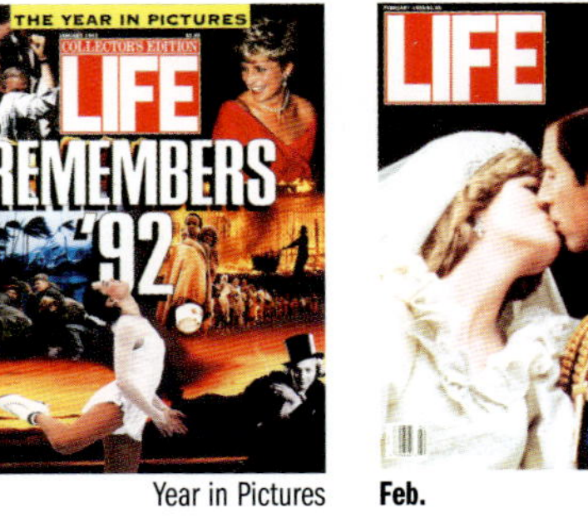

Jan. Year in Pictures

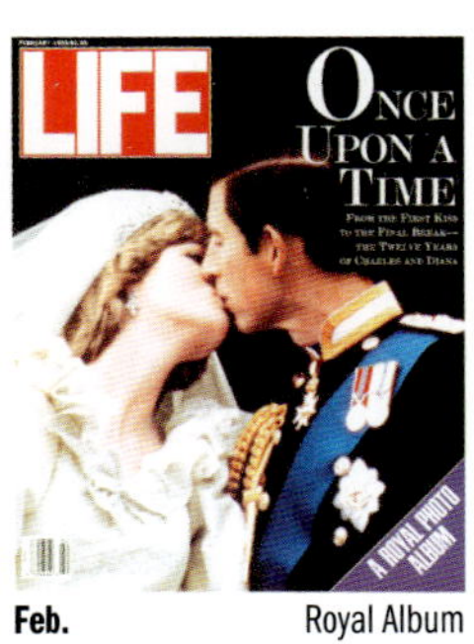

Feb. Royal Album

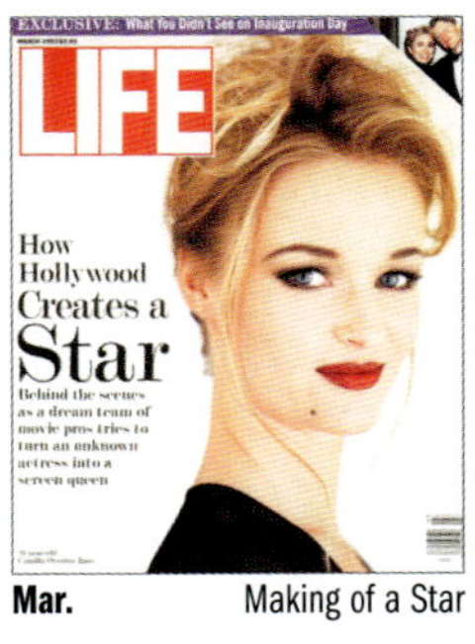

Mar. Making of a Star

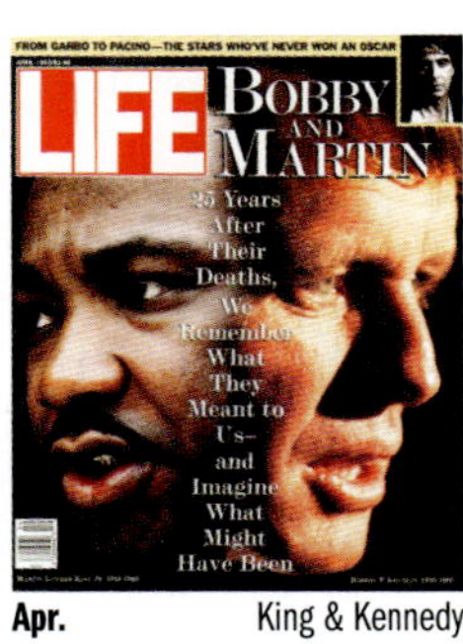

Apr. King & Kennedy

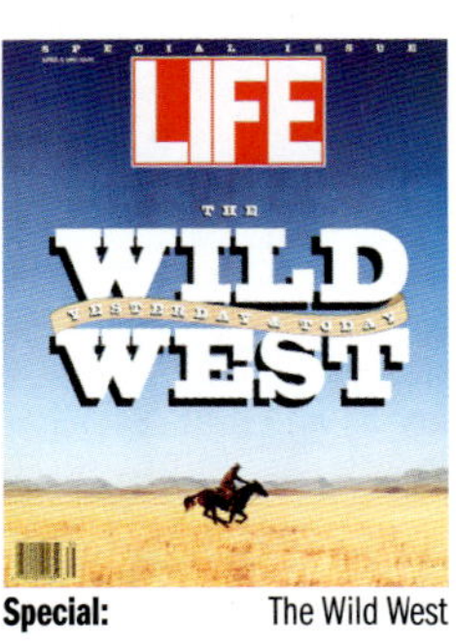

Special: The Wild West

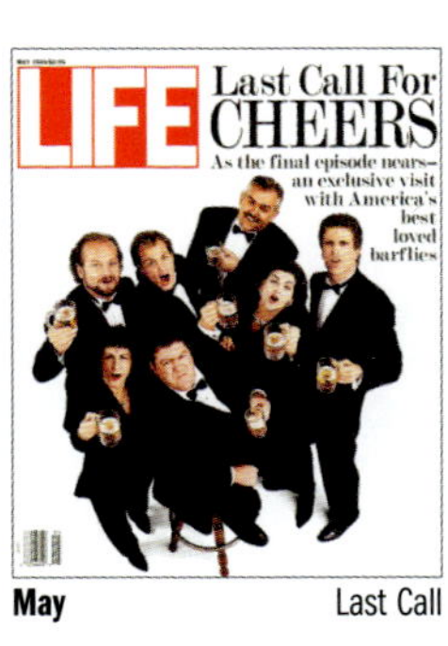

May Last Call

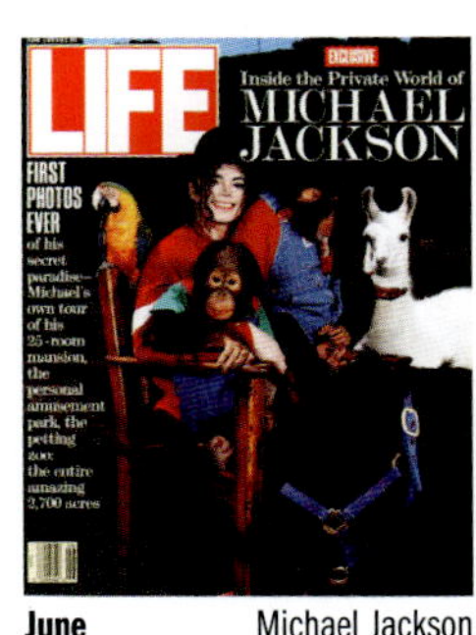

June Michael Jackson

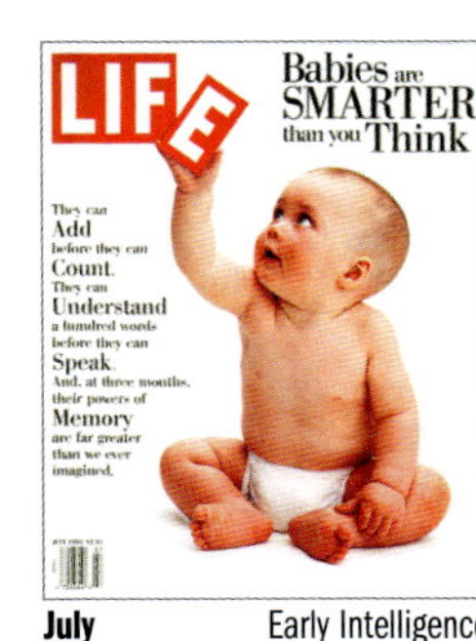

July Early Intelligence

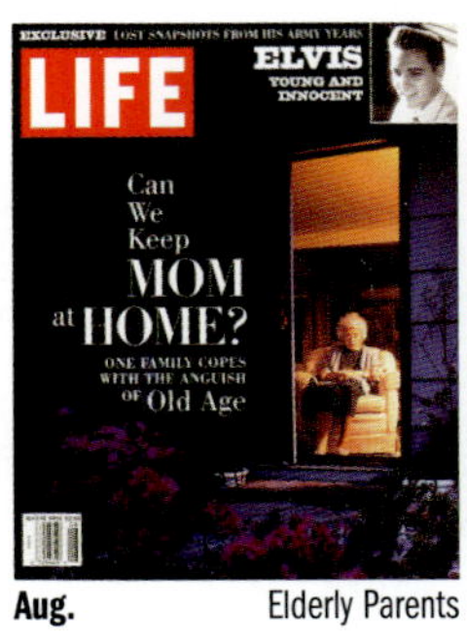

Aug. Elderly Parents

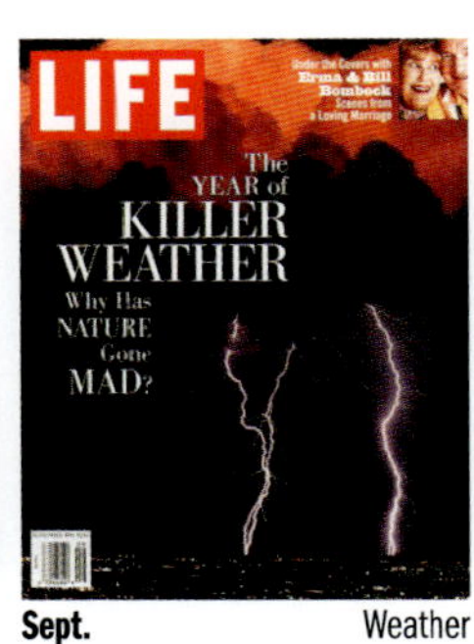

Sept. Weather

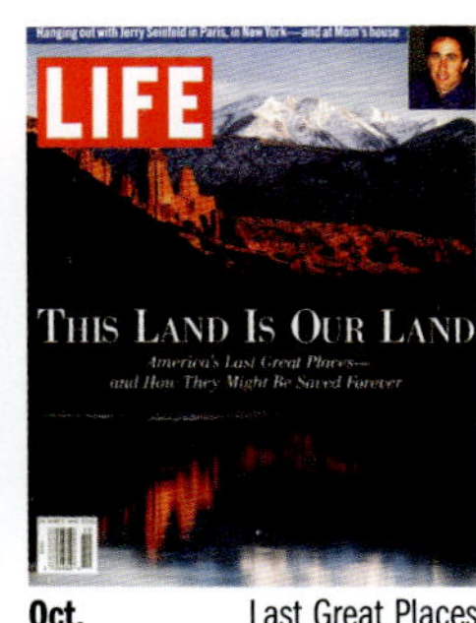

Oct. Last Great Places

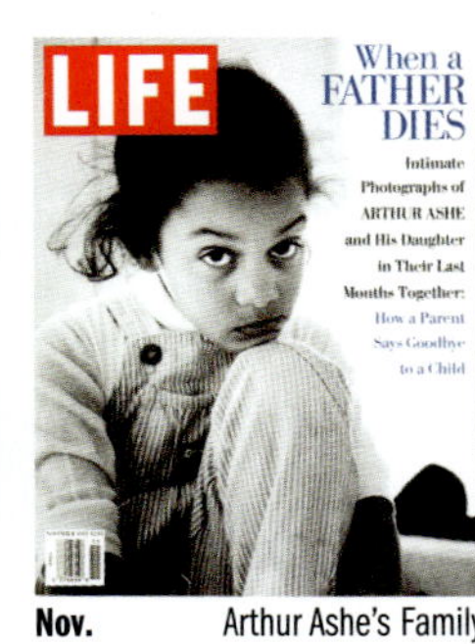

Nov. Arthur Ashe's Family

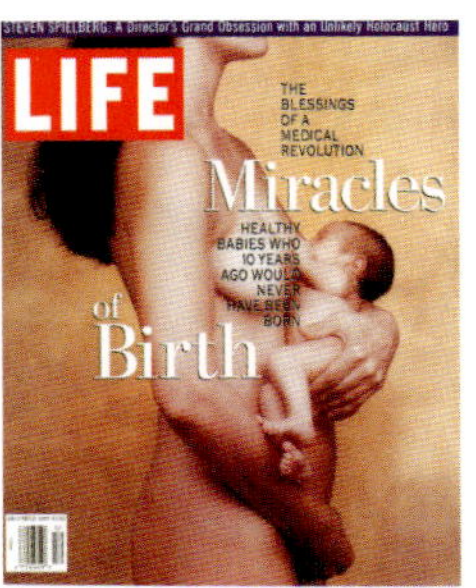

Dec. Miracle Births

The EPA states that secondhand smoke kills some 3,000 nonsmokers annually
Pocket-size phones are a common sight on the streets of American cities
The $1 billion MGM Grand, the world's largest hotel, opens in Las Vegas
New York's World Trade Center is bombed, killing six and injuring more than 1,000
The Missouri and Mississippi rivers overflow, inundating eight Midwestern states

1994

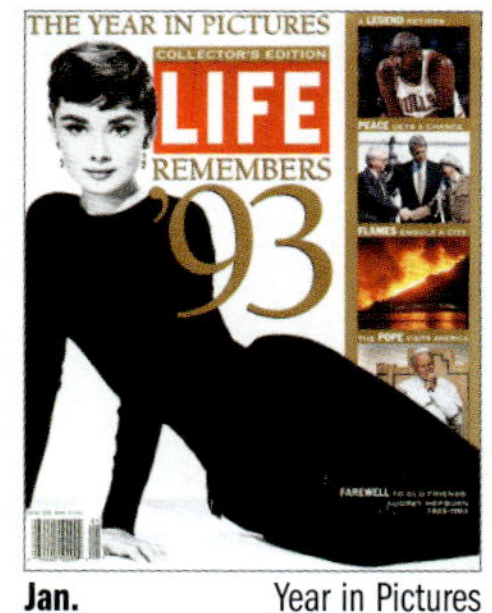

Jan. Year in Pictures

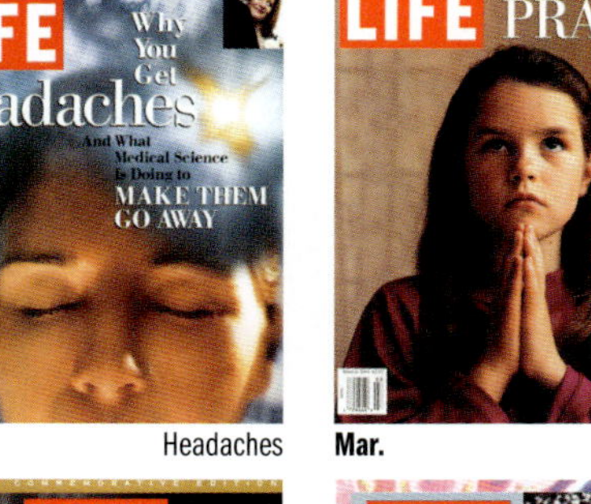

Feb. Headaches

Mar. Prayer

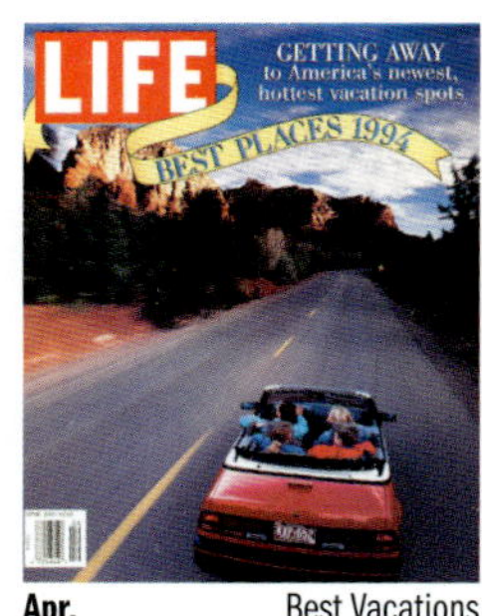

Apr. Best Vacations

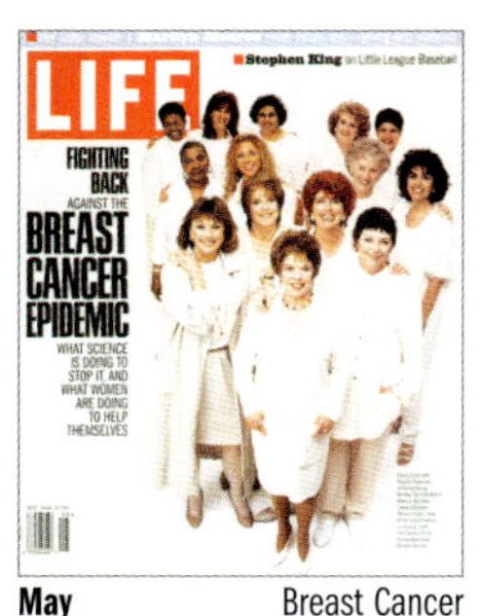

May Breast Cancer

June Dream House

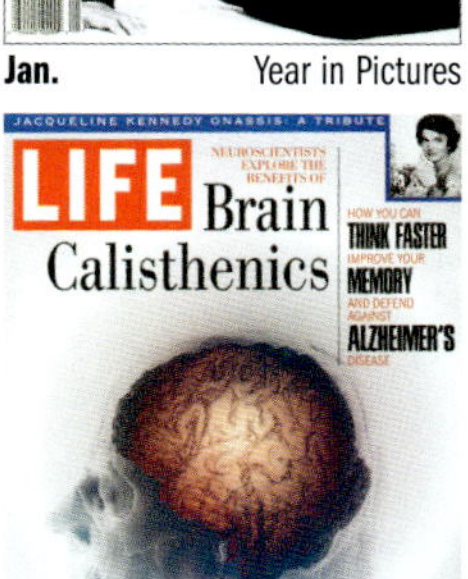

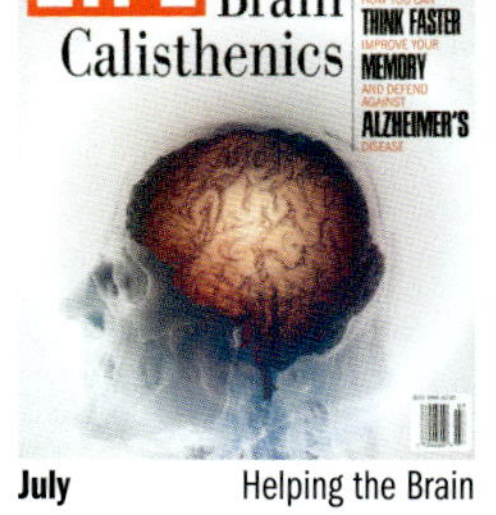

July Helping the Brain

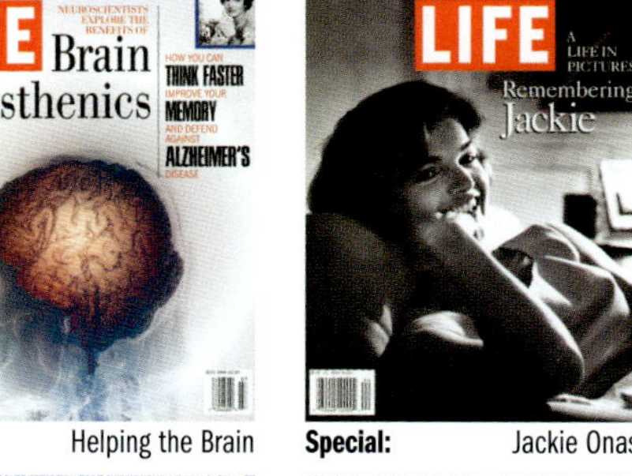

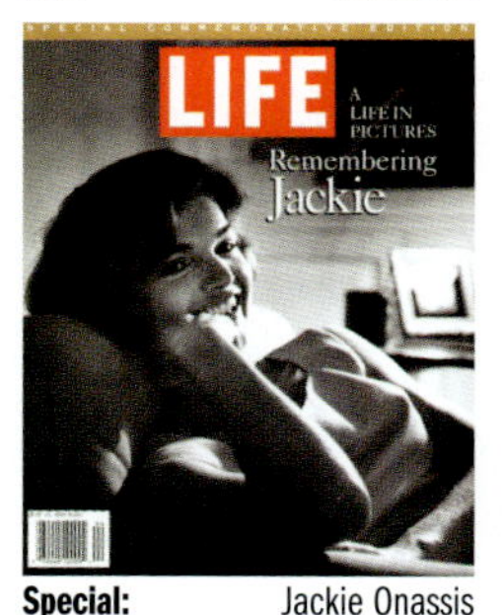

Special: Jackie Onassis

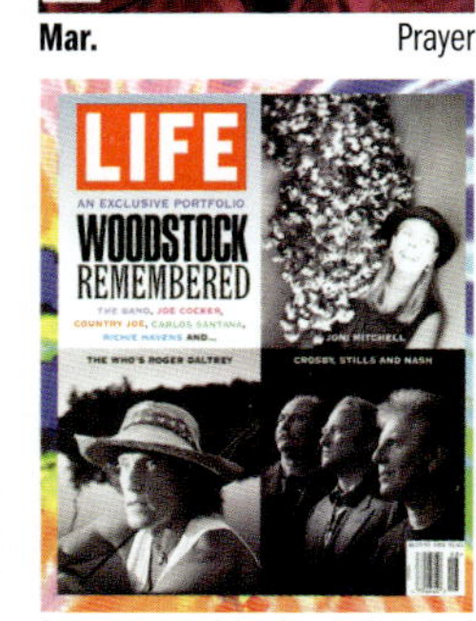

Aug. Woodstock Recalled

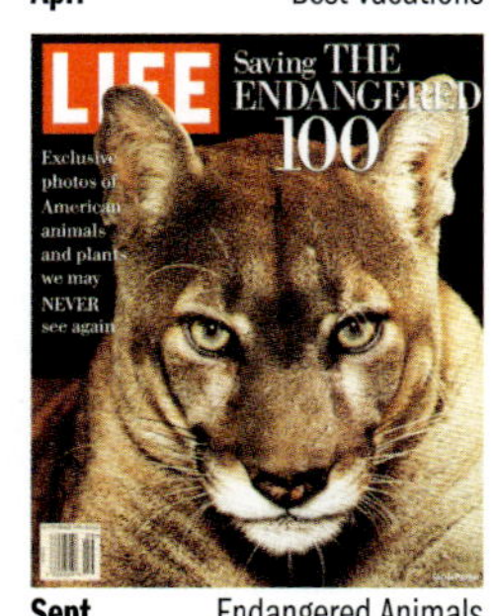

Sept. Endangered Animals

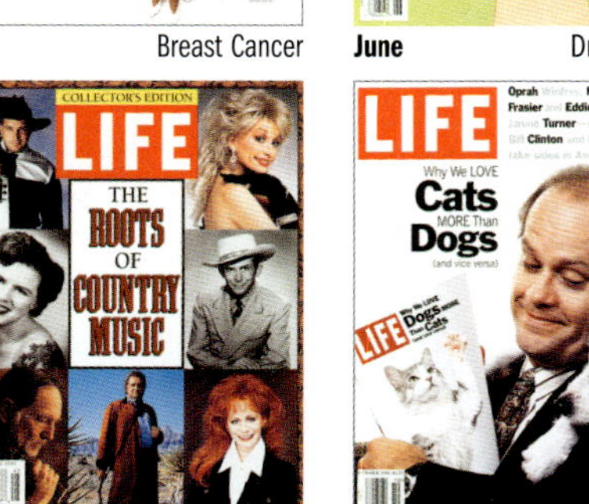

Special: Country Music

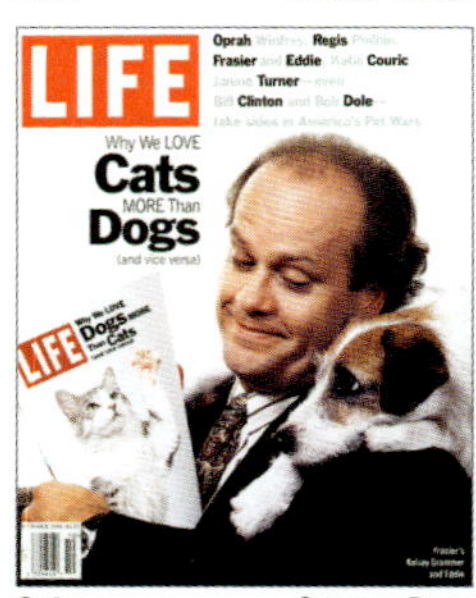

Oct. Cats vs. Dogs

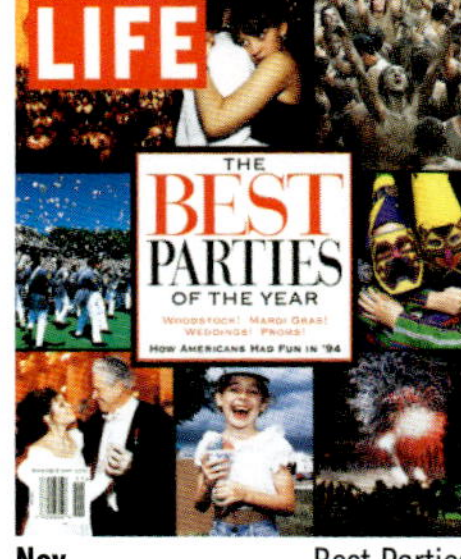

Nov. Best Parties

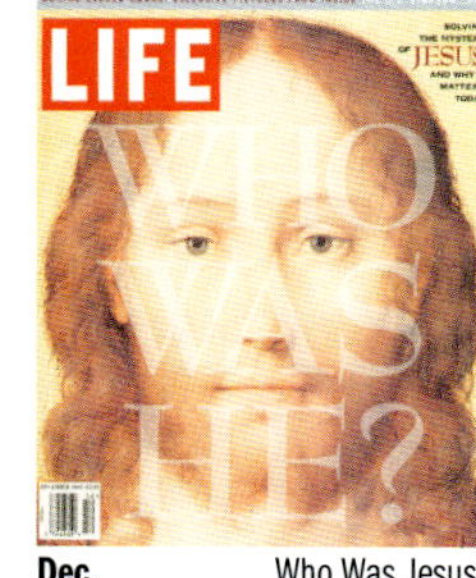

Dec. Who Was Jesus?

Apartheid ends in South Africa and Nelson Mandela is sworn in as president
Civil war between Hutus and Tutsis drive 1.5 million from Rwanda • Tom Hanks makes *Forrest Gump* a household name
Heather Whitestone, a deaf Alabamian, becomes Miss America
CIA agent Aldrich Ames and his wife are convicted of selling secrets to the Kremlin

1995

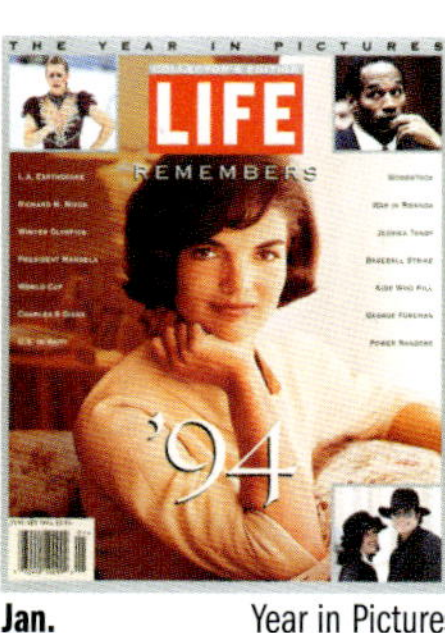

Jan. Year in Pictures

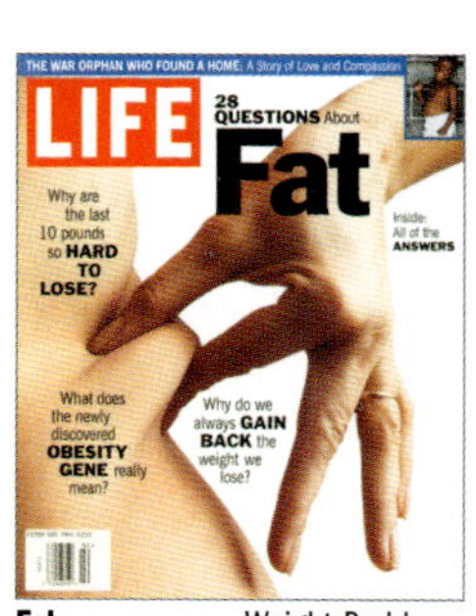

Feb. Weight Problems

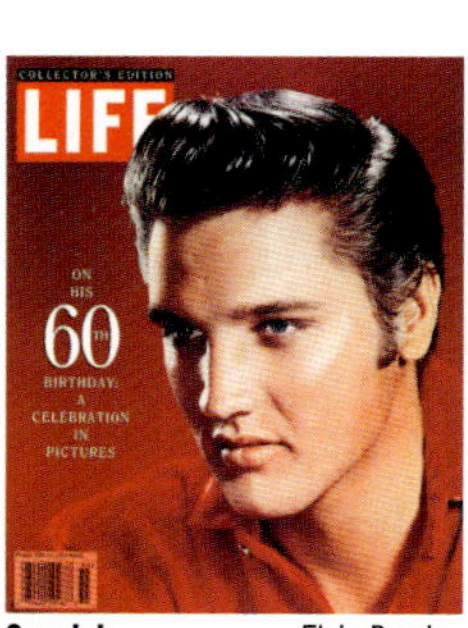

Special: Elvis Presley

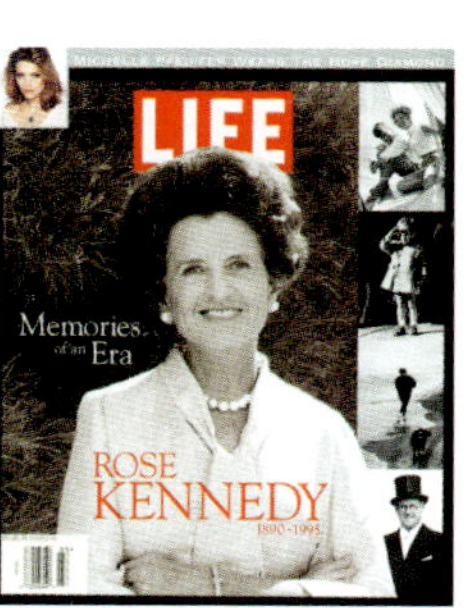

Mar. Rose Kennedy

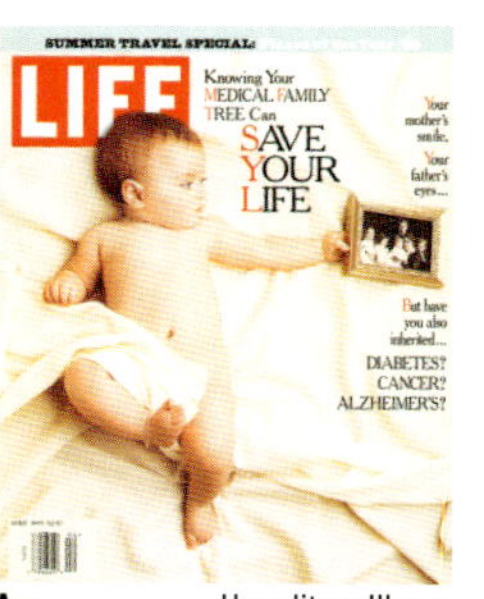

Apr. Hereditary Illness

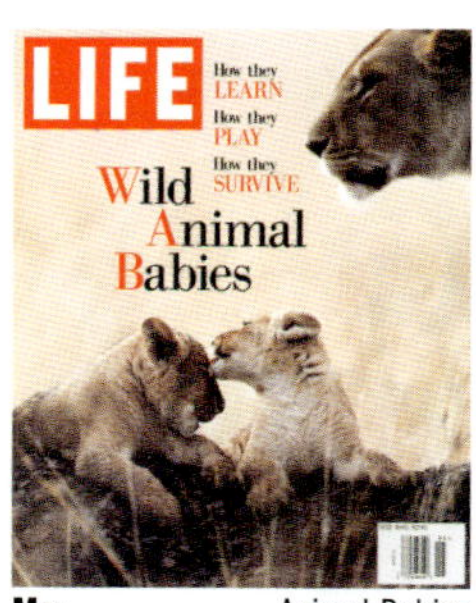

May Animal Babies

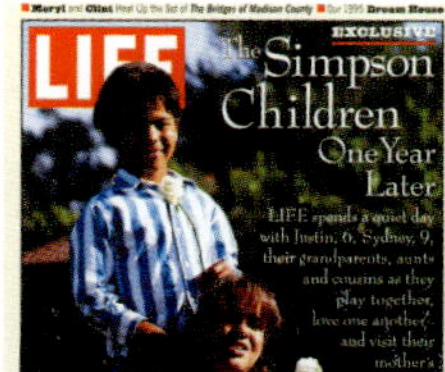

June Simpson Children

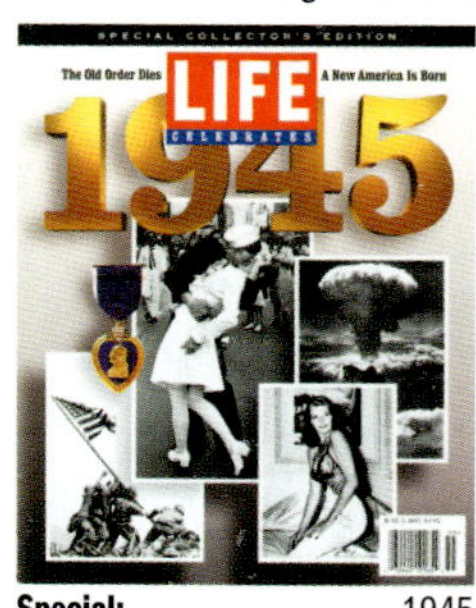

Special: 1945

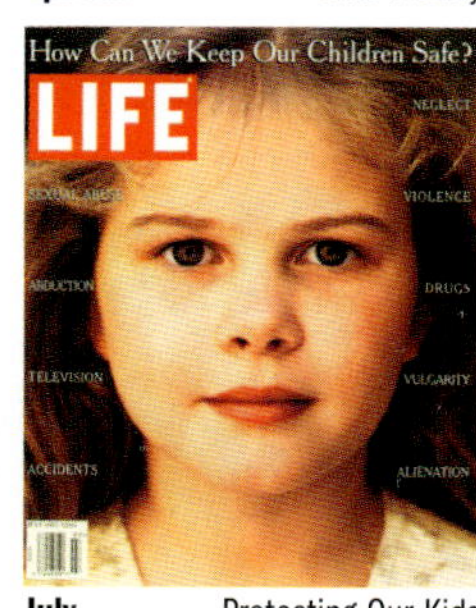

July Protecting Our Kids

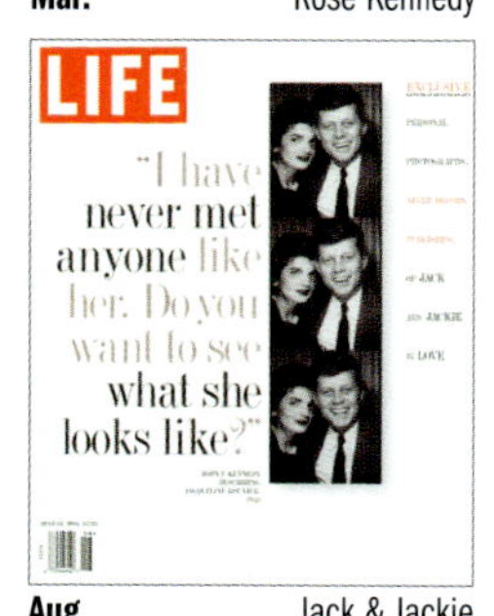

Aug. Jack & Jackie

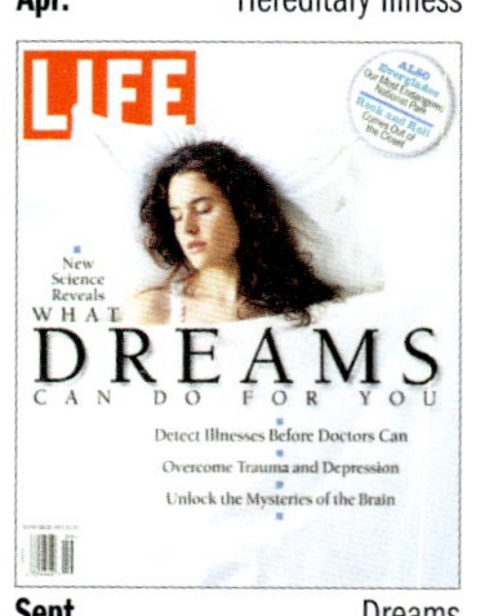

Sept. Dreams

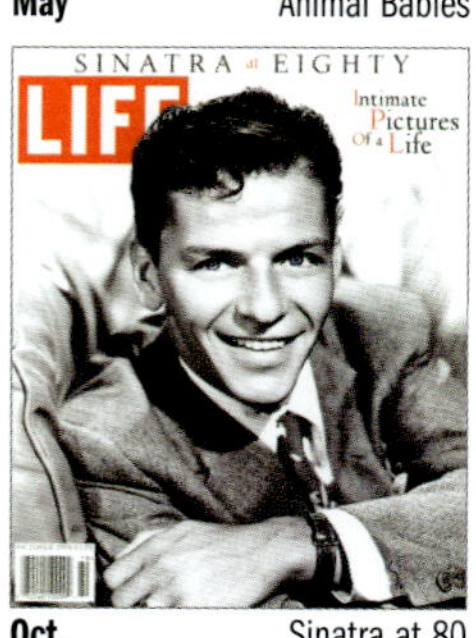

Oct. Sinatra at 80

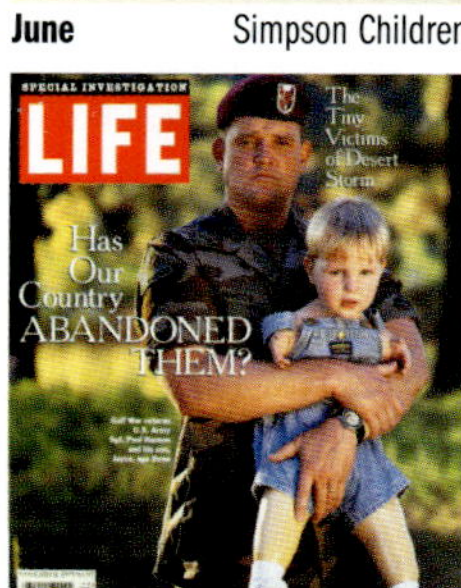

Nov. Gulf War Babies

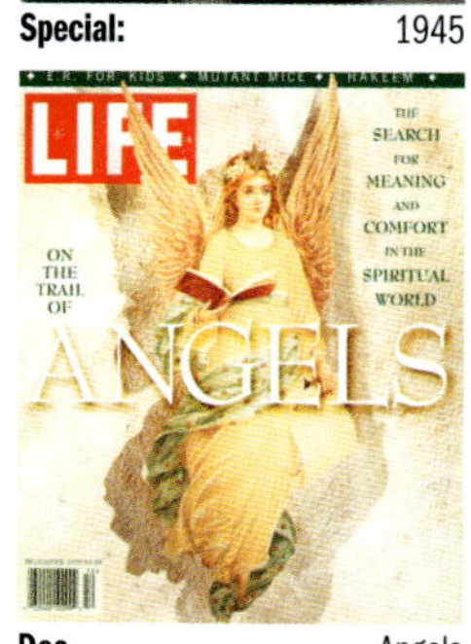

Dec. Angels

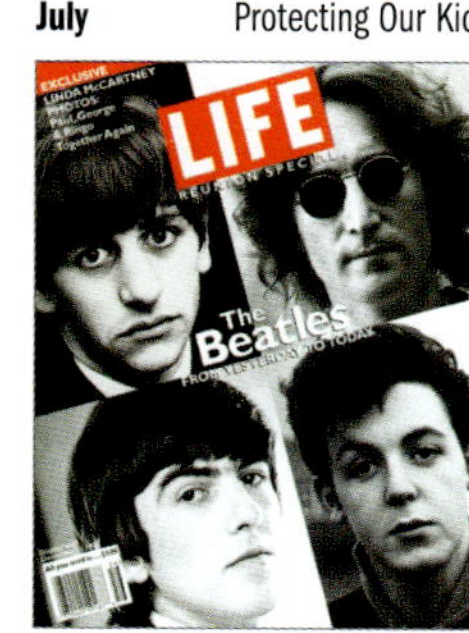

Special: The Beatles

A truck bomb at a federal building in Oklahoma City kills 168 people, 19 of them children
The Rock and Roll Hall of Fame opens in Cleveland • Artist Christo envelops Berlin's Reichstag with a silver cloak
Blue becomes the first new M&M color since 1949
Former *Superman* actor Christopher Reeve is paralyzed after being thrown from a horse

1996

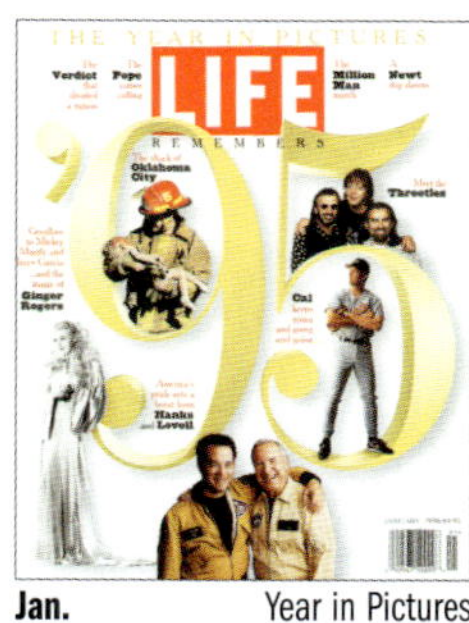
Jan. Year in Pictures

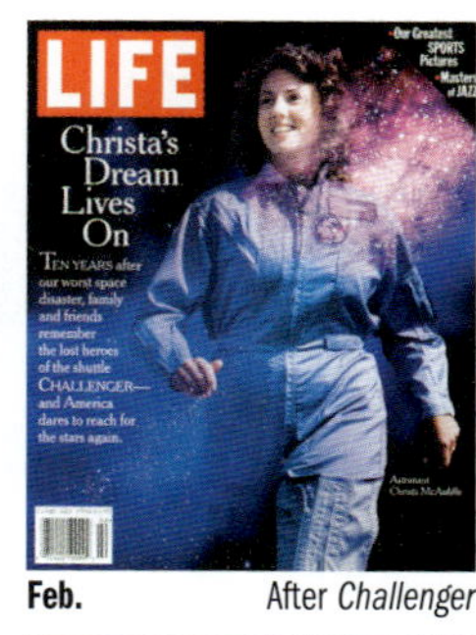
Special: Cars

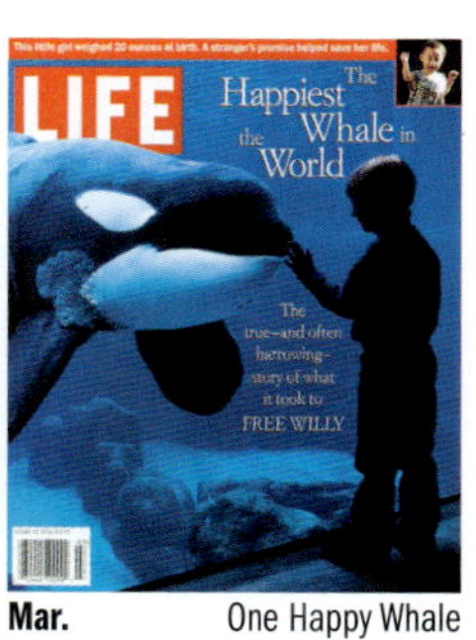
Feb. After *Challenger*

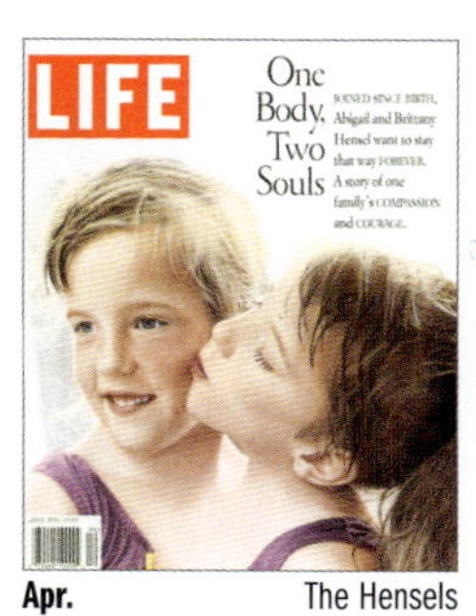
Mar. One Happy Whale

Apr. The Hensels

May Dream House

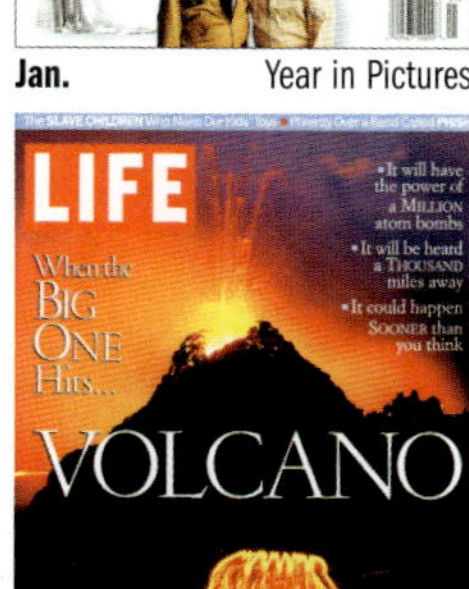
June Volcano

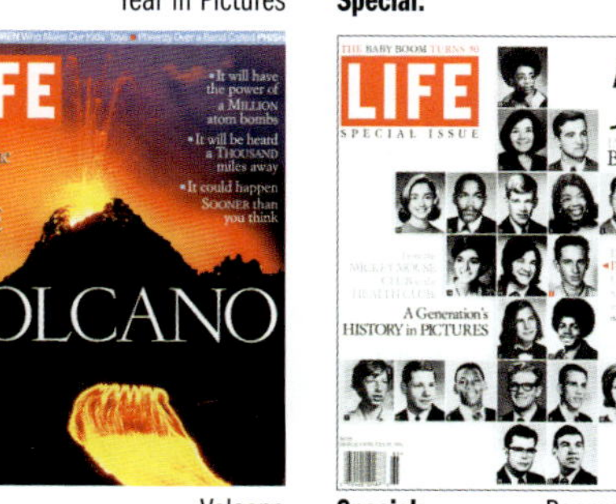
Special: Boomers at 50

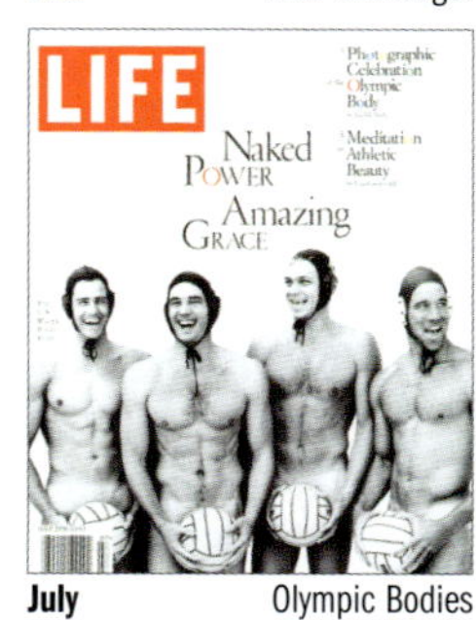
July Olympic Bodies

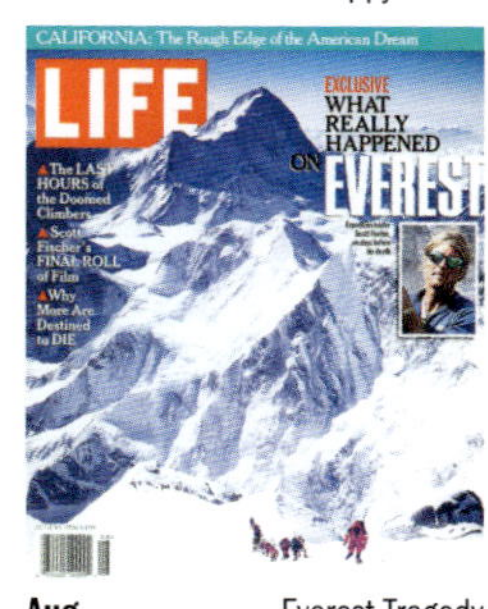
Aug. Everest Tragedy

Sept. Alternatives

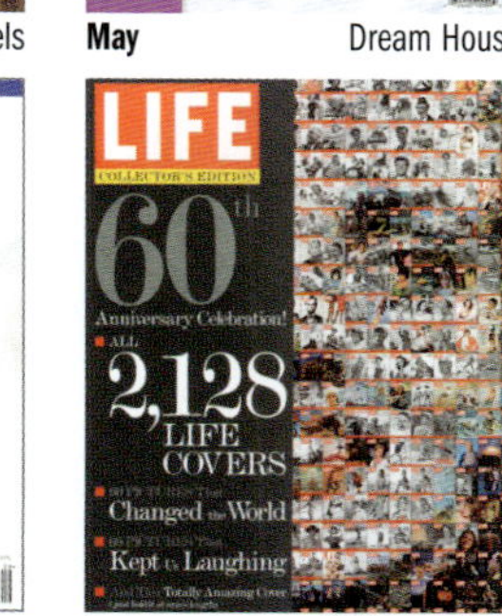
Oct. 60 Years of LIFE

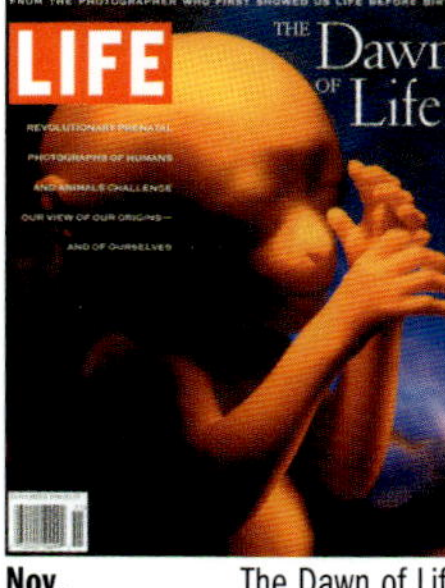
Nov. The Dawn of Life

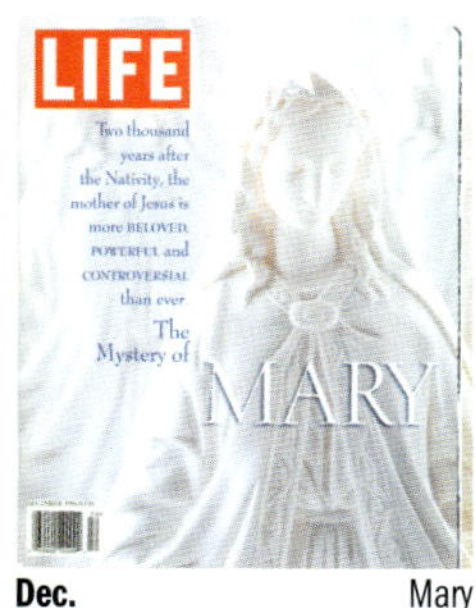
Dec. Mary

Ted Kaczynski, a.k.a. the Unabomber, is arrested in Montana
John F. Kennedy Jr. marries Carolyn Bessette in a small church on Cumberland Island, Ga.
A bomb explodes at the Atlanta Olympic Games, killing one • Kofi Annan of Ghana becomes secretary-general of the U.N.
Prince Charles and Princess Diana say they will end their 15-year marriage

1997

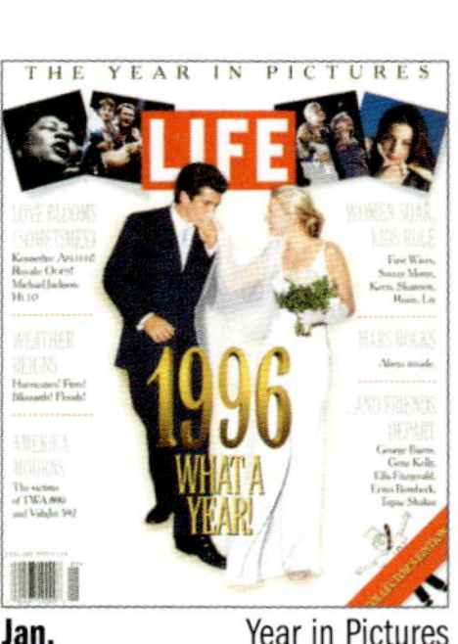
Jan. Year in Pictures

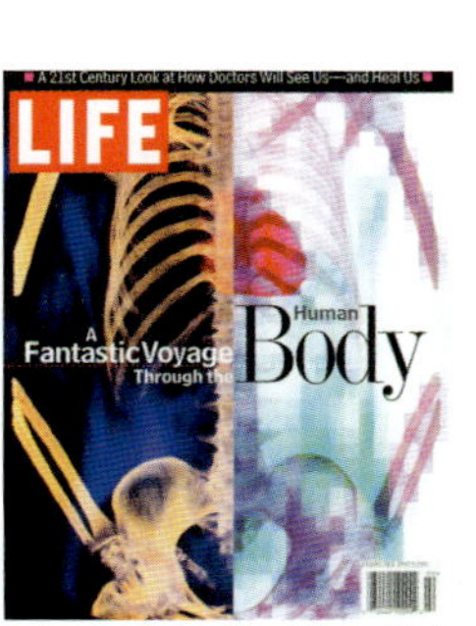
Feb. The Human Body

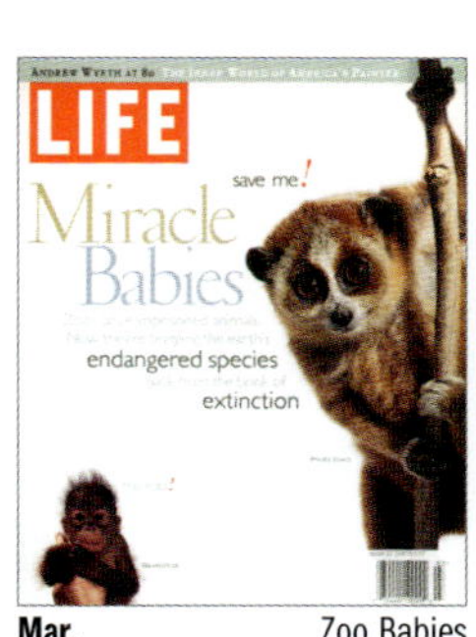
Mar. Zoo Babies

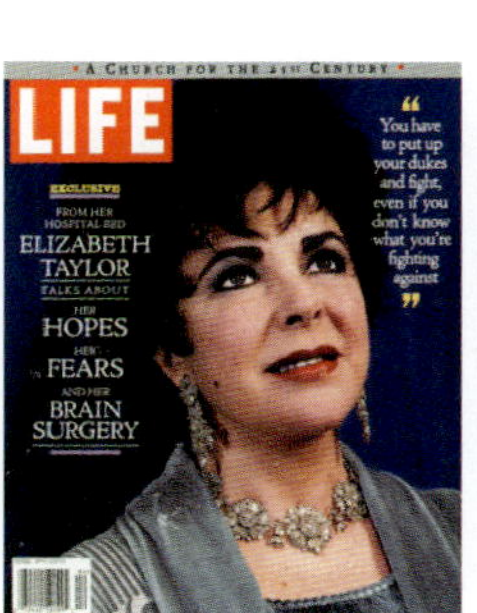
Apr. Elizabeth Taylor

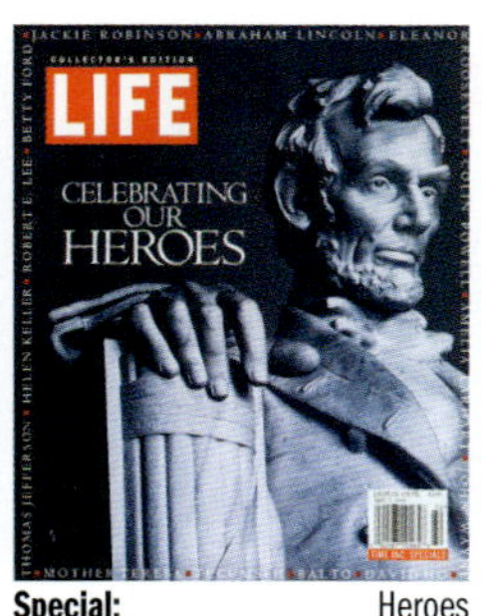
Special: Heroes

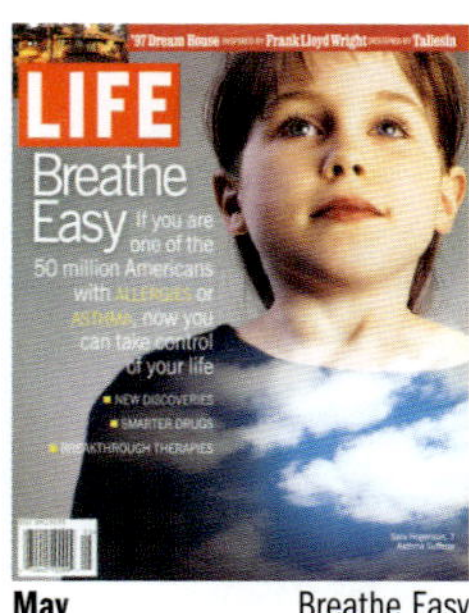
May Breathe Easy

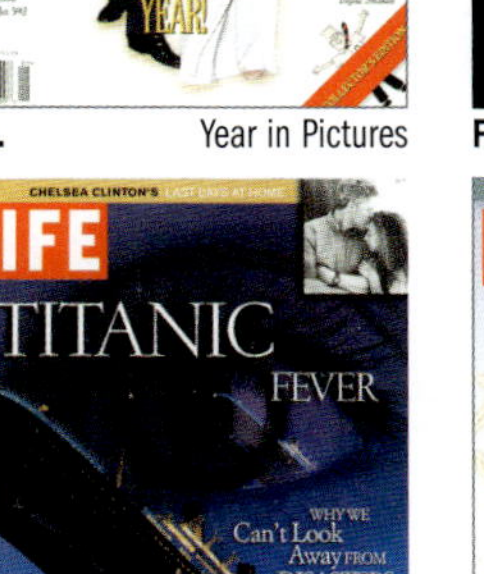
June *Titanic*

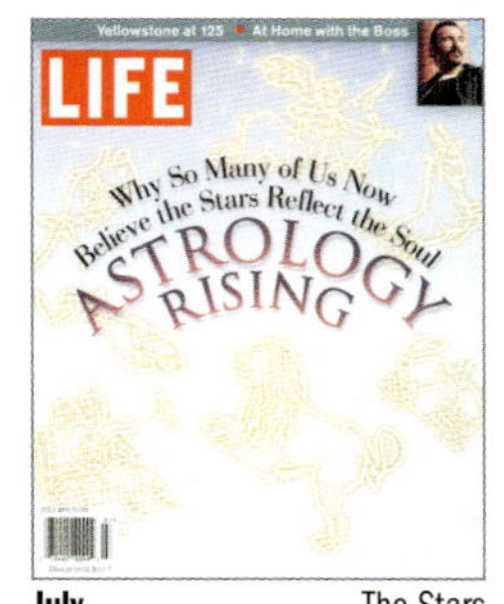
July The Stars

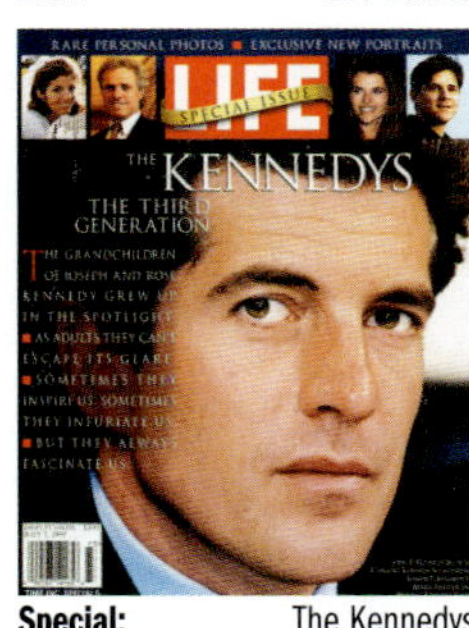
Special: The Kennedys

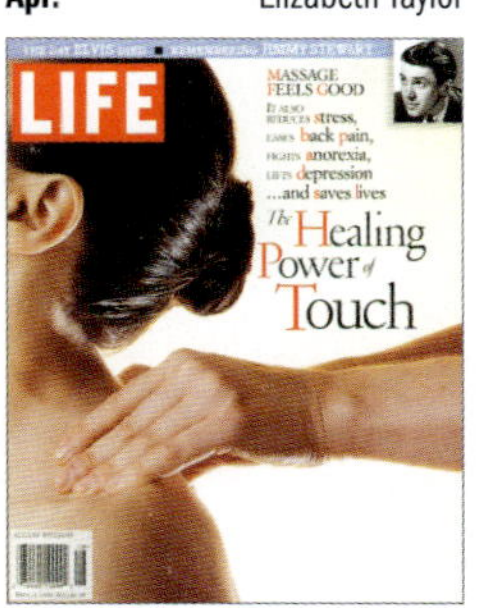
Aug. Massage

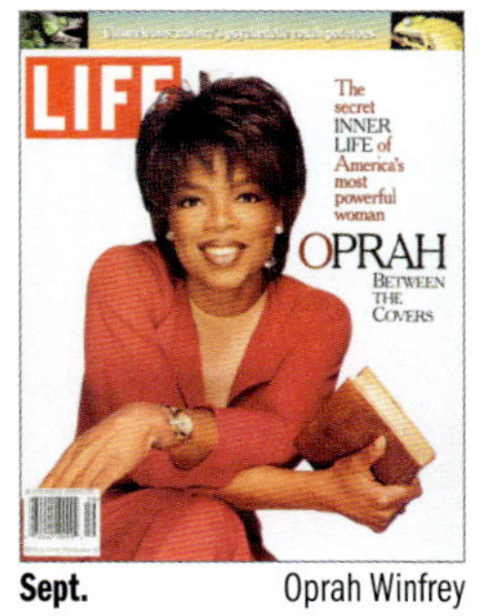
Sept. Oprah Winfrey

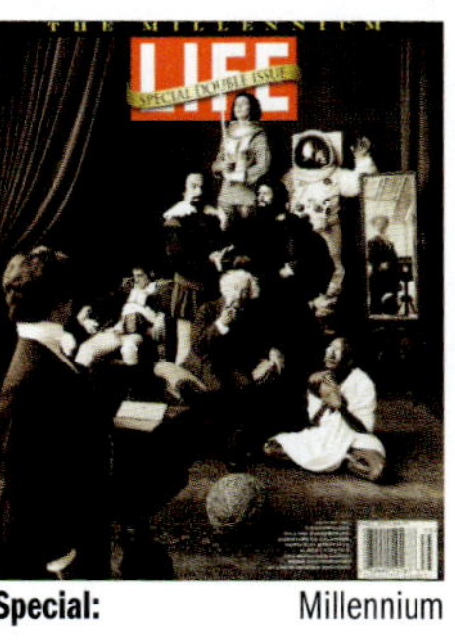
Special: Millennium

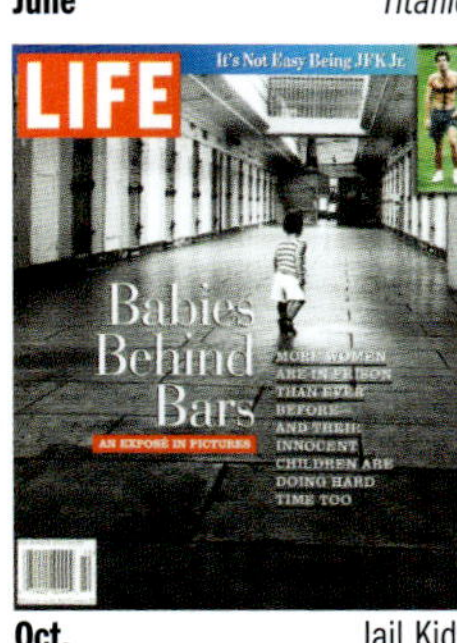
Oct. Jail Kids

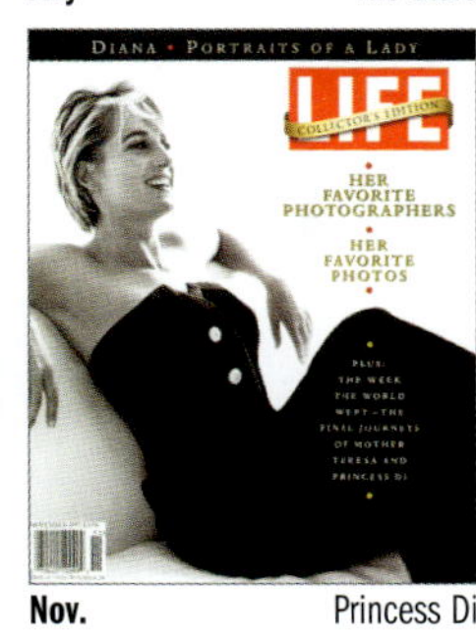
Nov. Princess Di

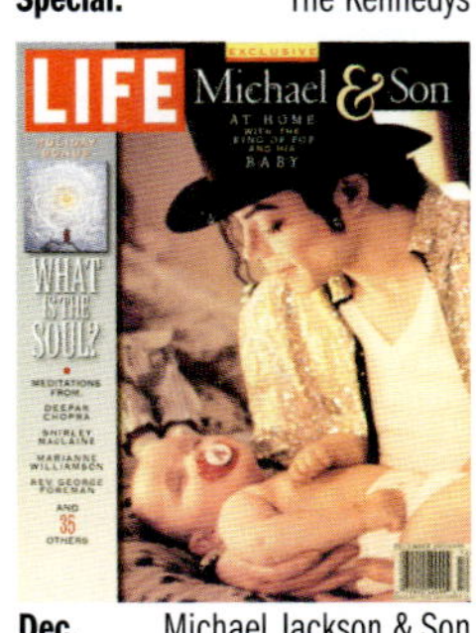
Dec. Michael Jackson & Son

Madeleine Albright is sworn in as the first woman secretary of state
Scottish researchers announce they have cloned a sheep named Dolly • The last F.W. Woolworth store closes its doors
The comet Hale-Bopp is seen by people all over the world as it hurtles through the skies
An Iowa couple gives birth to the first surviving septuplets

1998

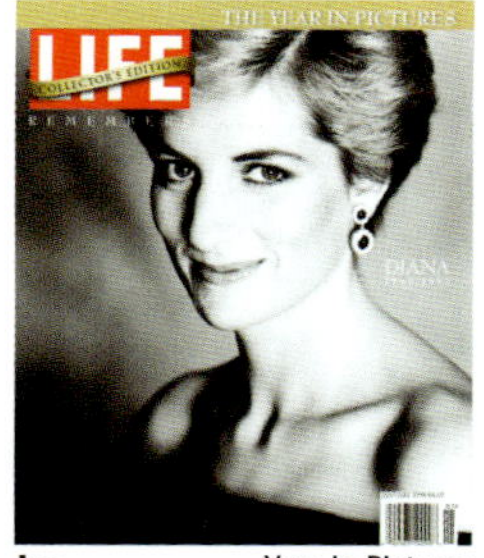

Jan. Year in Pictures

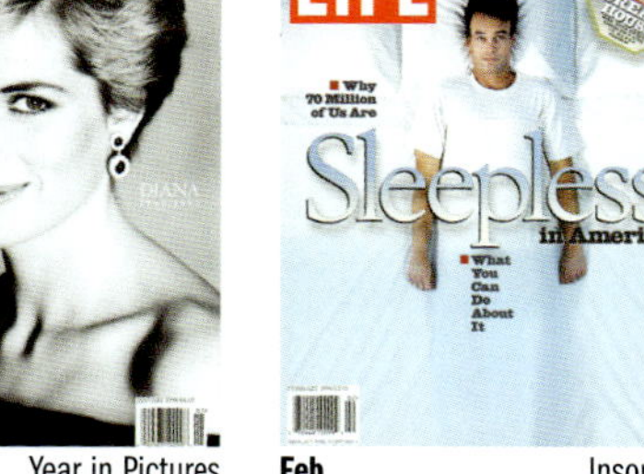

Feb. Insomnia

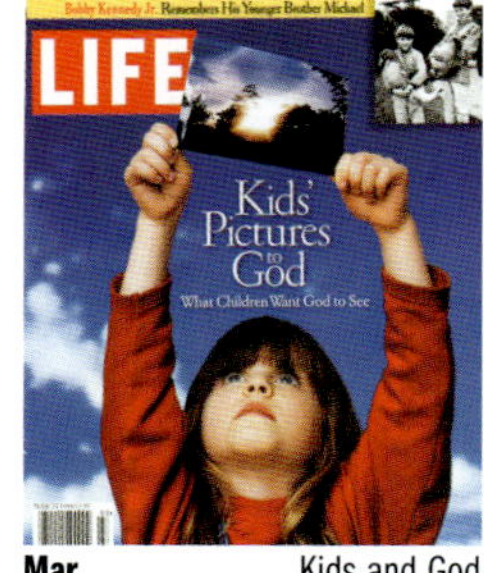

Mar. Kids and God

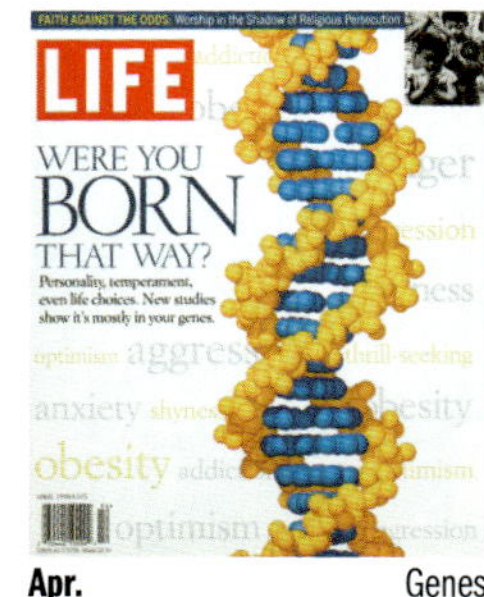

Apr. Genes

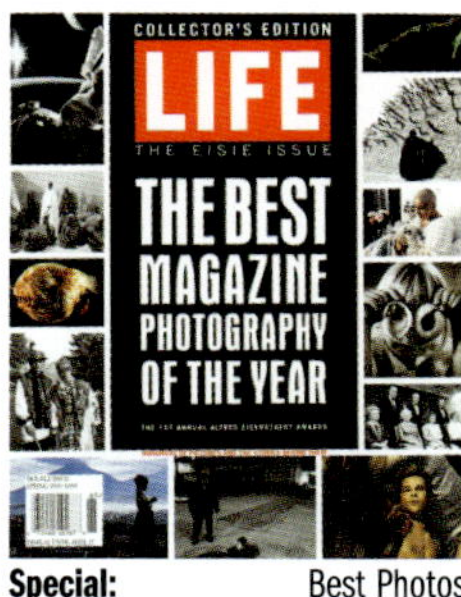

Special: Best Photos

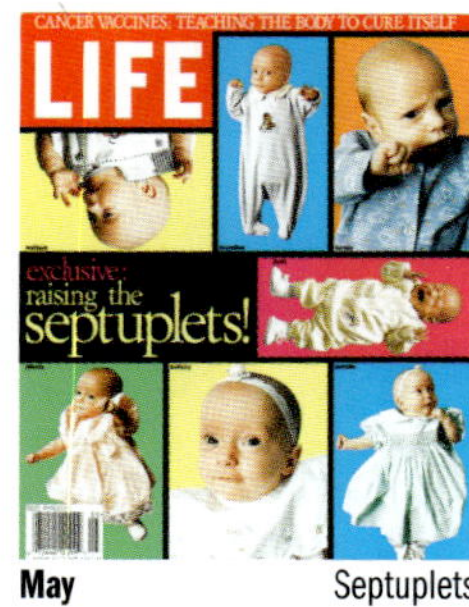

May Septuplets

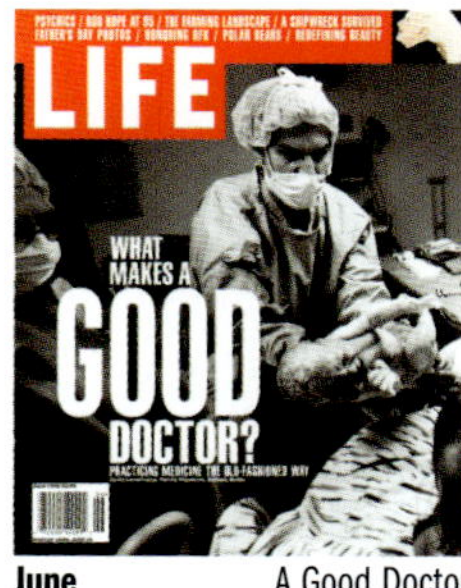

June A Good Doctor

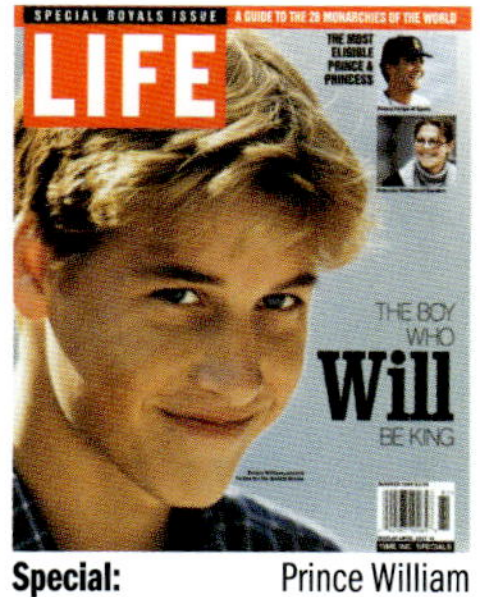

Special: Prince William

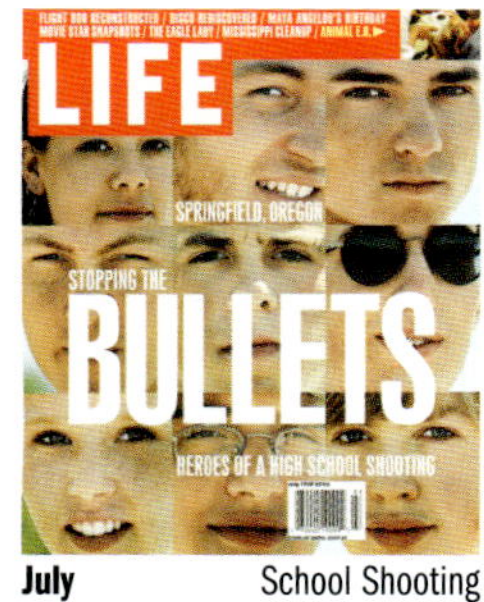

July School Shooting

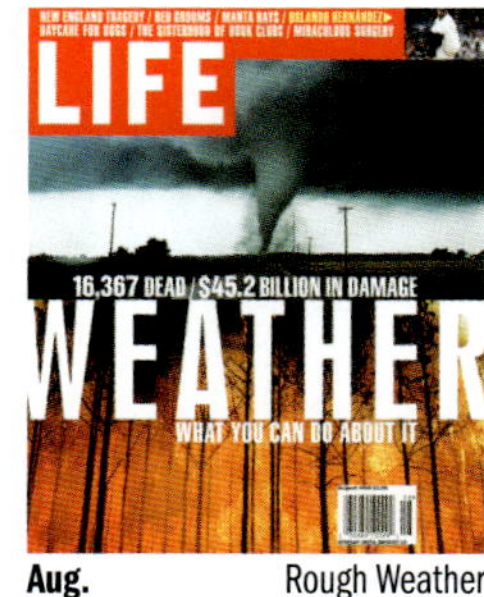

Aug. Rough Weather

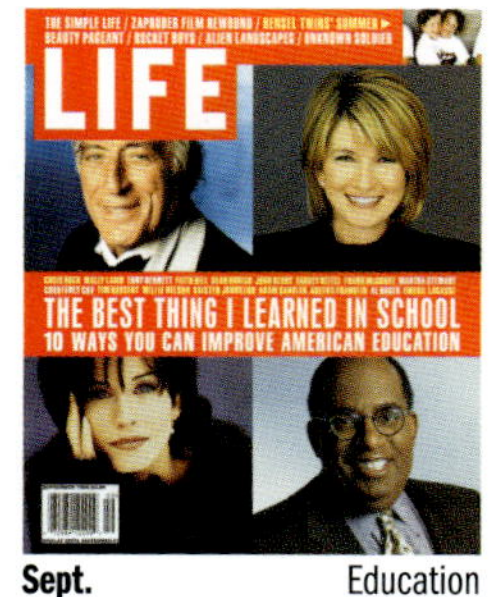

Sept. Education

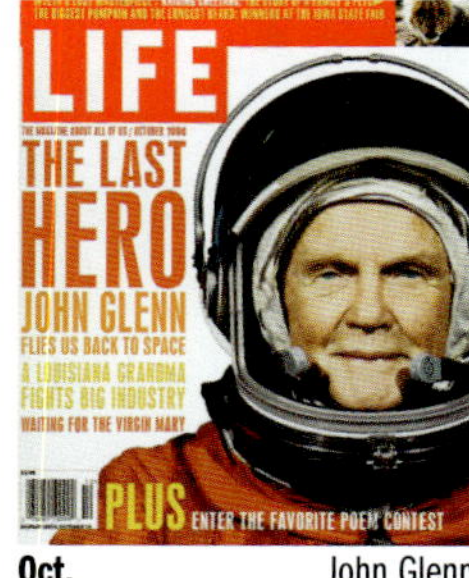

Oct. John Glenn

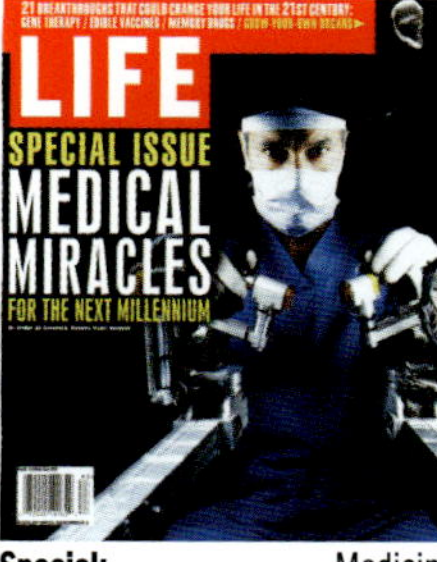

Special: Medicine

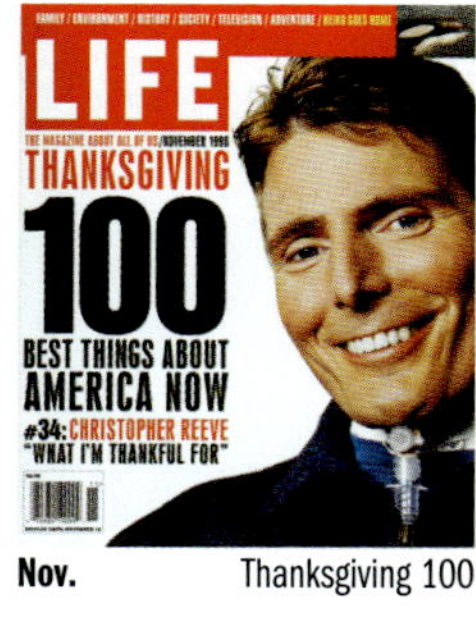

Nov. Thanksgiving 100

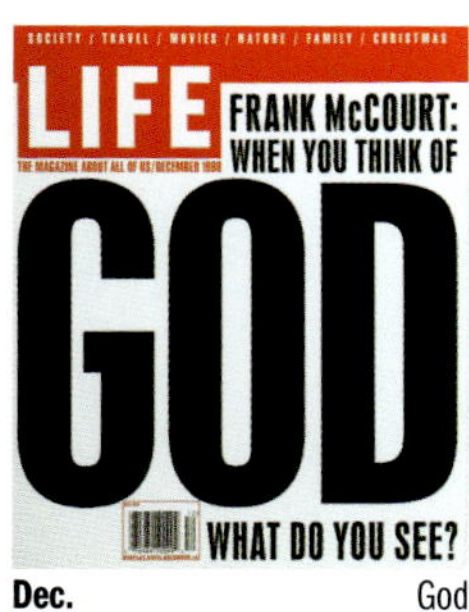

Dec. God

Wrestler Jesse Ventura is elected governor of Minnesota • Viagra goes on sale
98 percent of U.S. homes have at least one TV set • Bill Clinton becomes the second President to be impeached
Fidel Castro welcomes John Paul II, the only pope to visit Cuba

1999

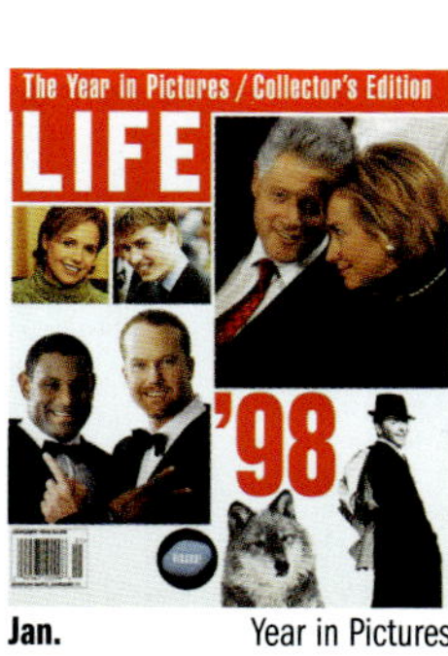

Jan. Year in Pictures

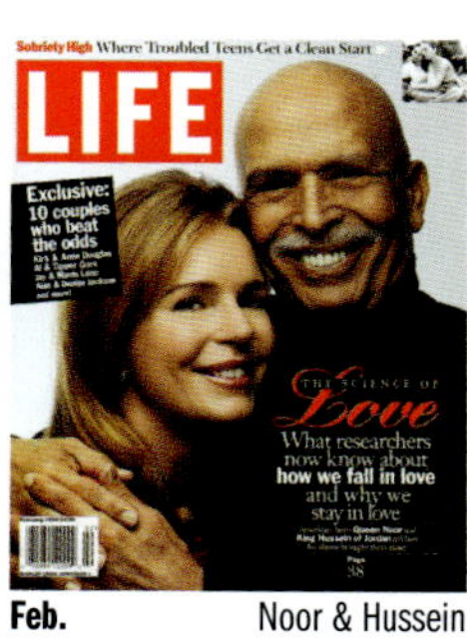

Feb. Noor & Hussein

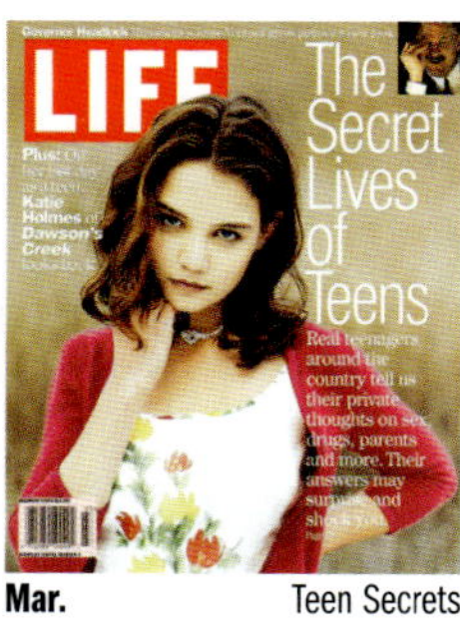

Mar. Teen Secrets

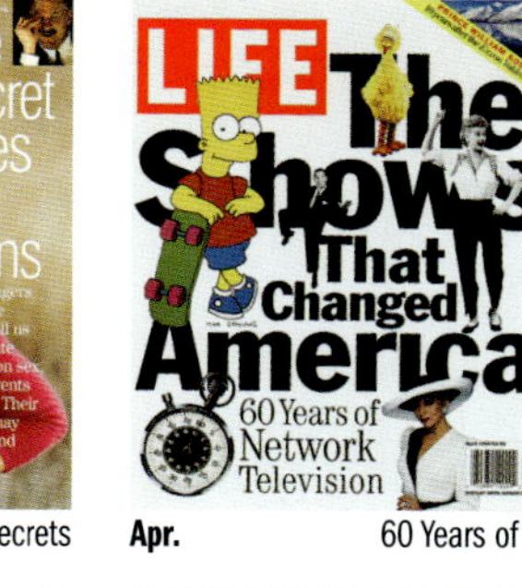

Apr. 60 Years of TV

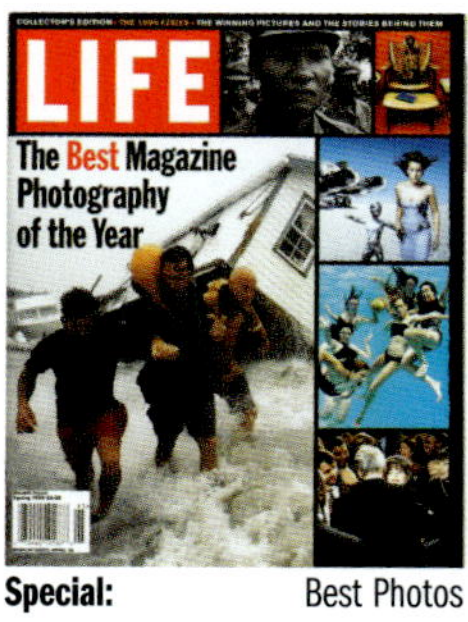

Special: Best Photos

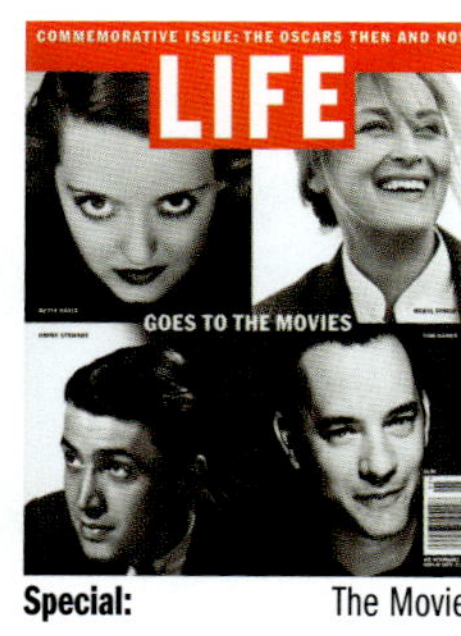

Special: The Movies

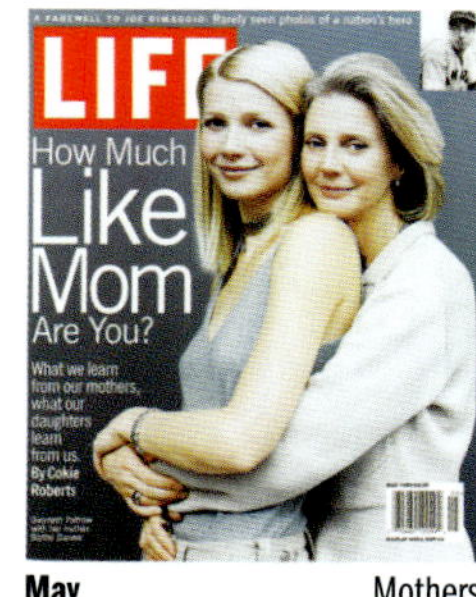

May Mothers

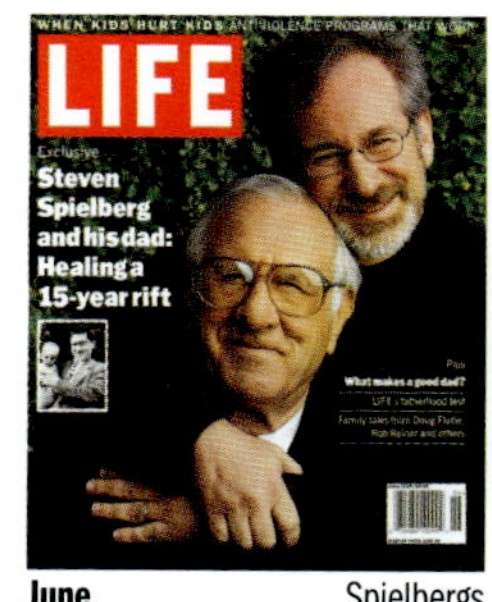

June Spielbergs

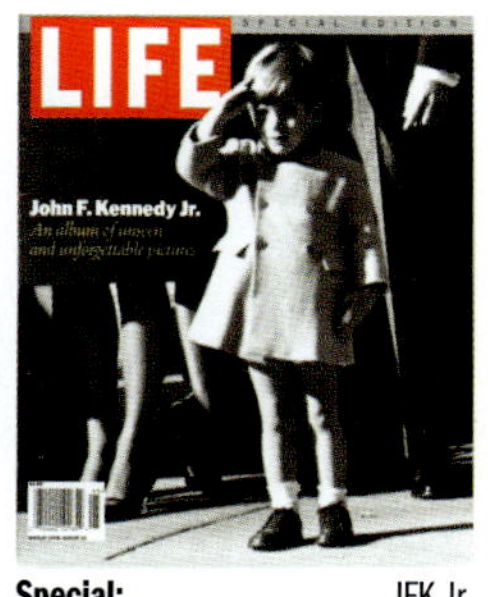

Special: JFK Jr.

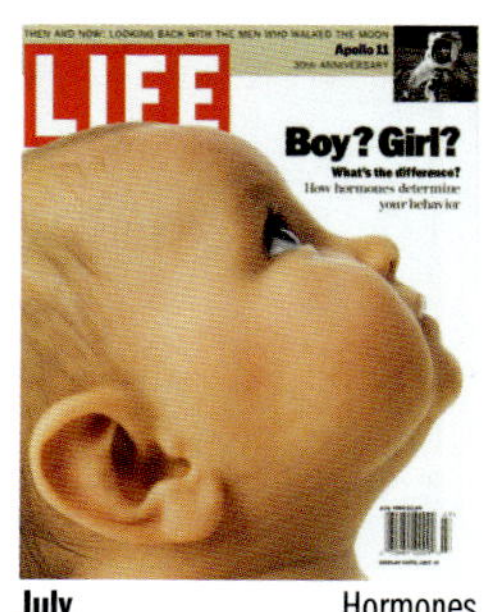

July Hormones

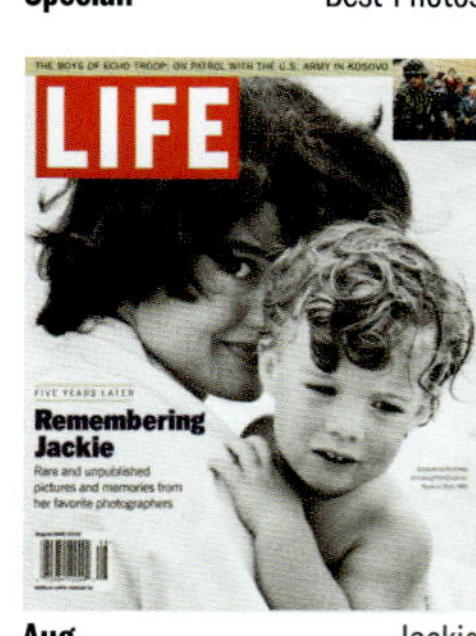

Aug. Jackie

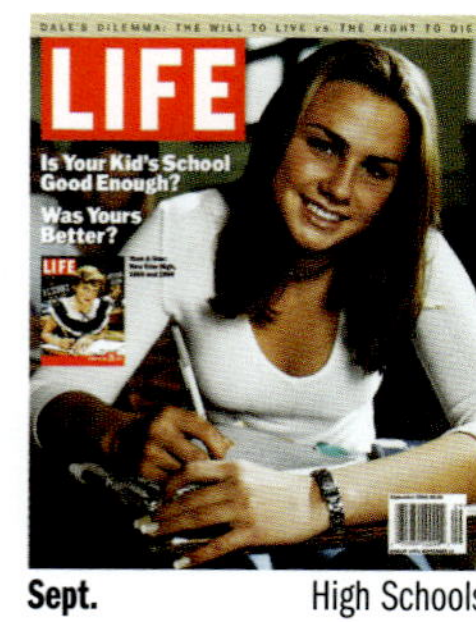

Sept. High Schools

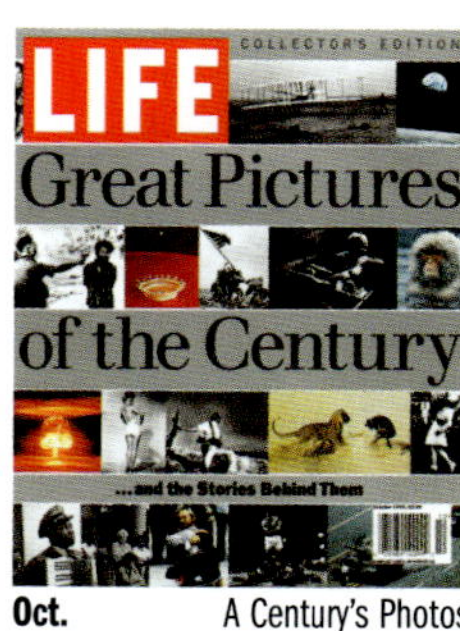

Oct. A Century's Photos

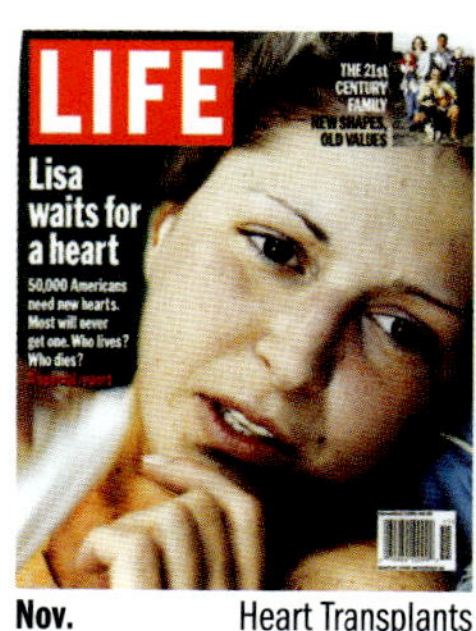

Nov. Heart Transplants

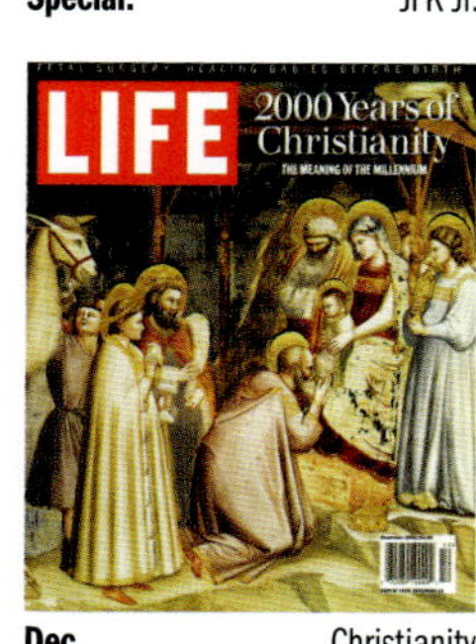

Dec. Christianity

The world population reaches six billion • Two boys kill 13 and themselves at Columbine High School in Littleton, Colo.
A World Trade Organization meeting in Seattle is beset by thousands of protestors
Pokémon fever grips the nation • The U.S. women's soccer team wins the World Cup at the Rose Bowl

2000

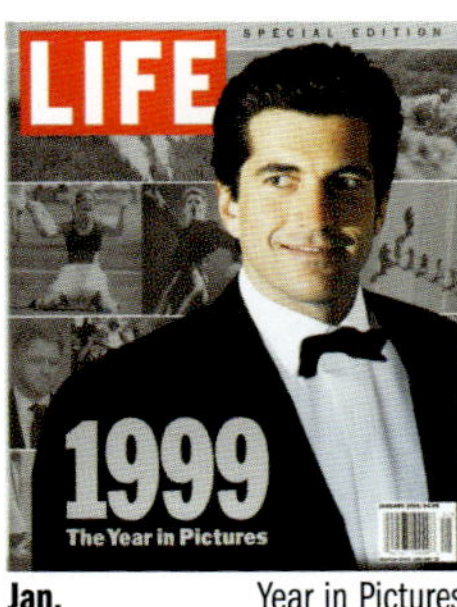

Jan. Year in Pictures

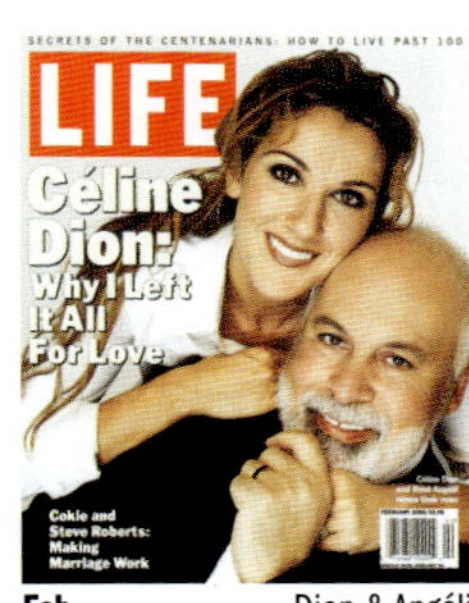

Feb. Dion & Angélil

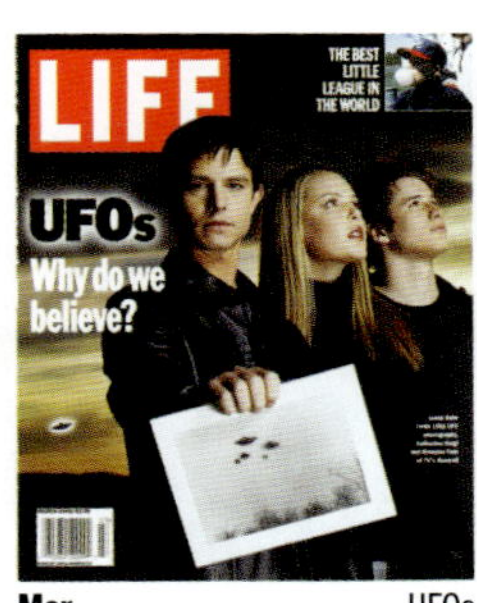

Mar. UFOs

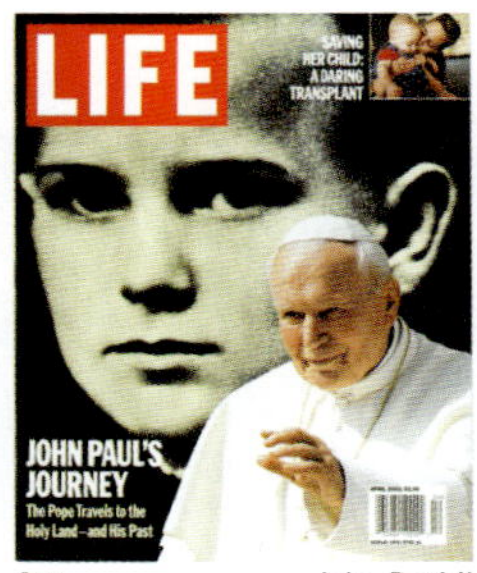

Apr. John Paul II

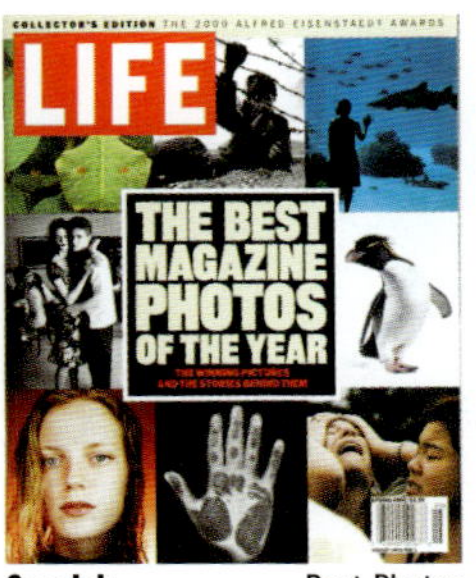

Special: Best Photos

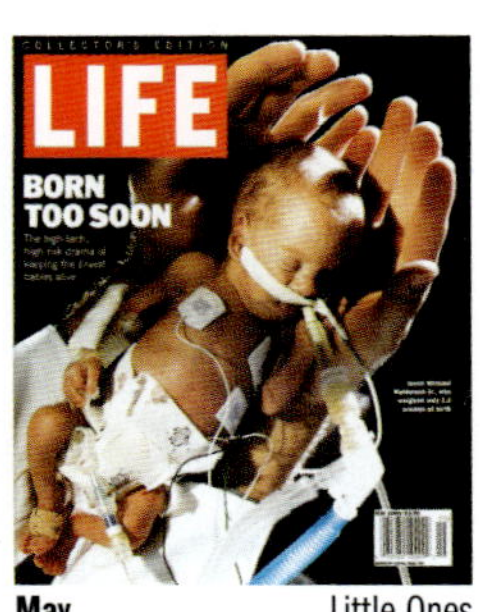

May Little Ones

The U.S. population is 281,423,231 • A special flame travels underwater for the opening of the Sydney Olympic Games
The dreaded Y2K computer bug fails to materialize
The human genome is mapped • Red shoes from *The Wizard of Oz* are auctioned off for $666,000 at Christie's

2001

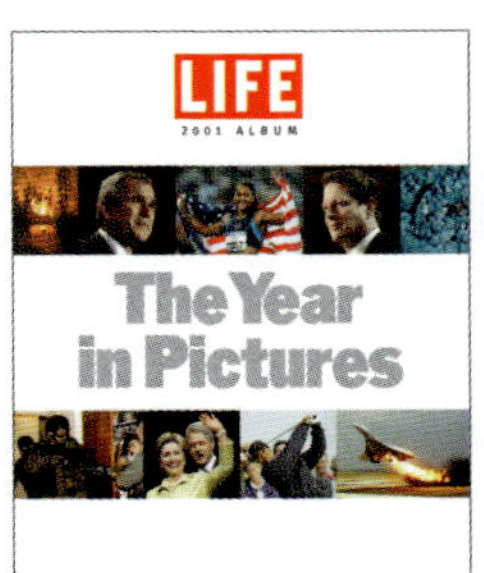

Book: Year in Pictures

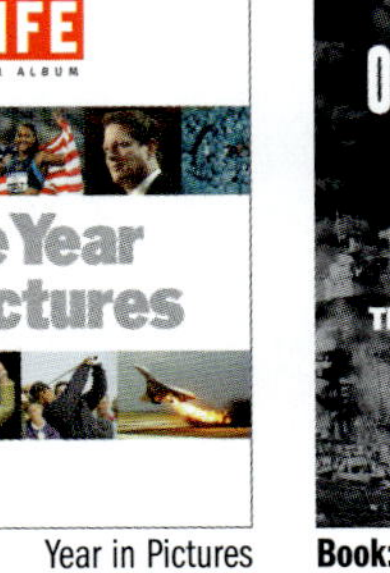
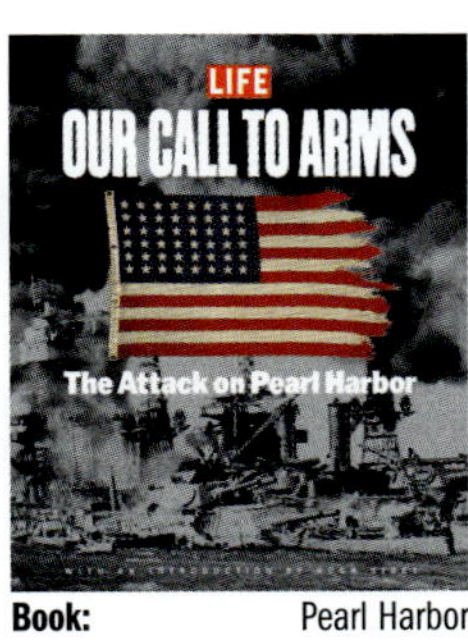

Book: Pearl Harbor

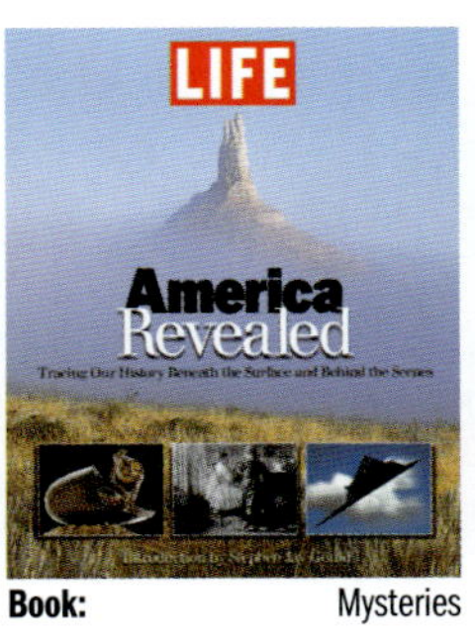

Book: Mysteries

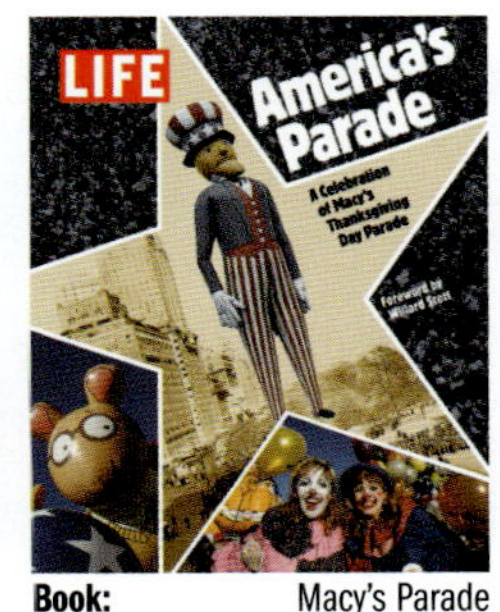

Book: Macy's Parade

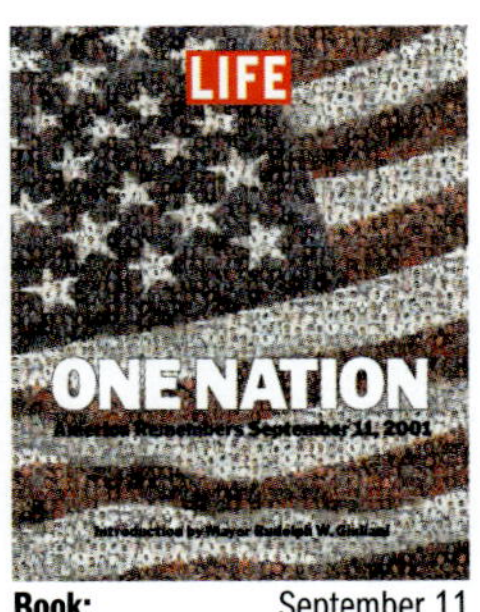

Book: September 11

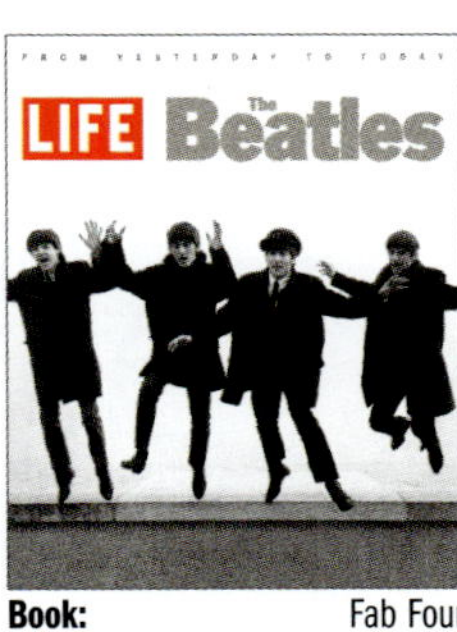

Book: Fab Four

Book: Pope John Paul II

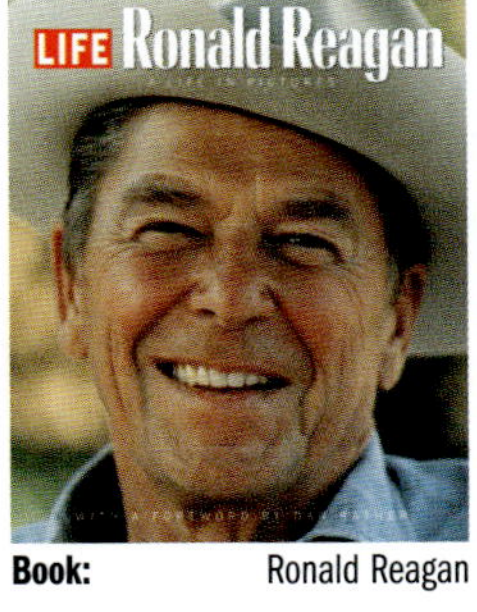

Book: Ronald Reagan

The first Harry Potter film premieres • The average cost of a 30-second Super Bowl ad is $2.3 million
San Francisco Giant Barry Bonds hits 73 home runs
The House votes 265–162 to ban human cloning • 60-year-old Dennis Tito pays $20 million to go on Russian *Soyuz* mission

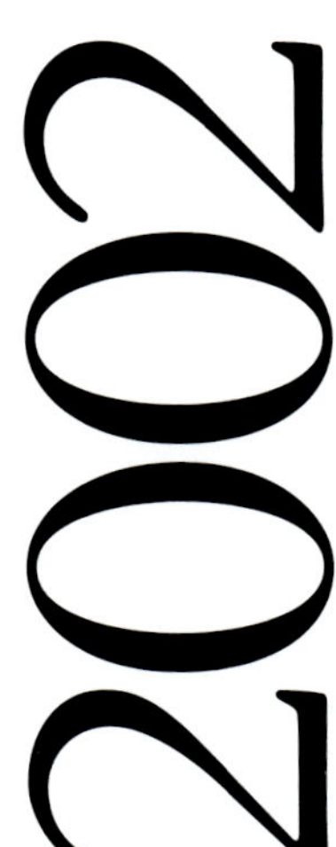

2002

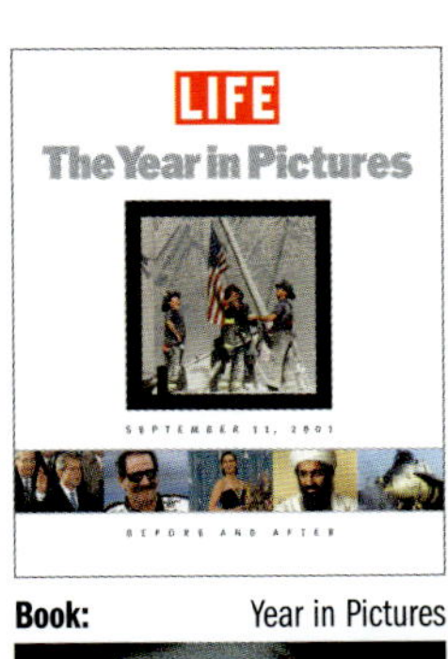

Book: Year in Pictures

Book: Rock & Roll Turns 50

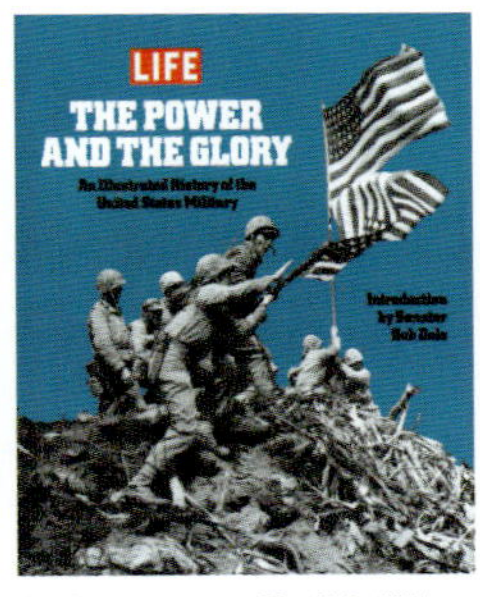

Book: The U.S. Military

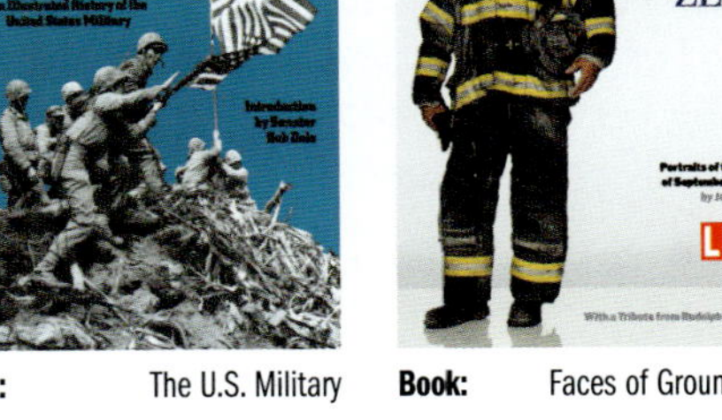

Book: Faces of Ground Zero

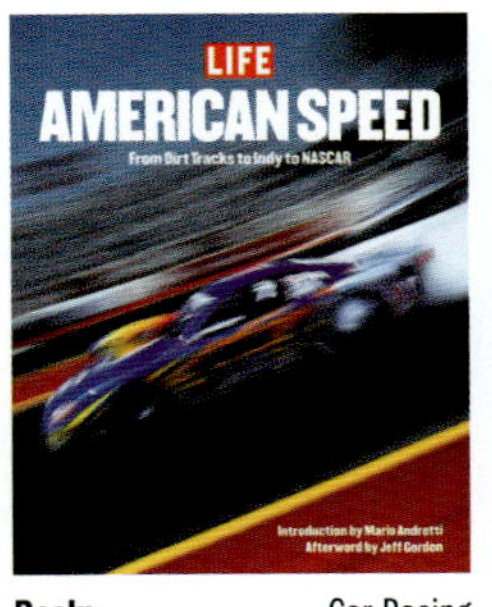

Book: Car Racing

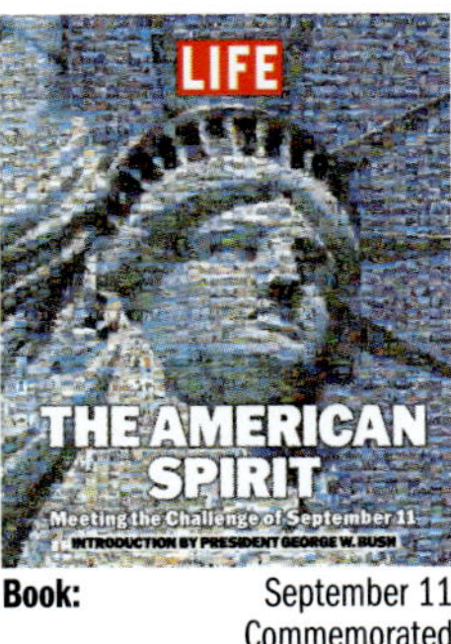

Book: September 11 Commemorated

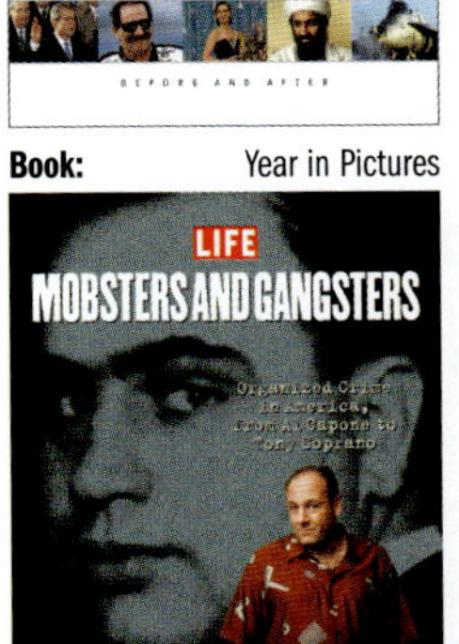

Book: Mobsters and Gangsters

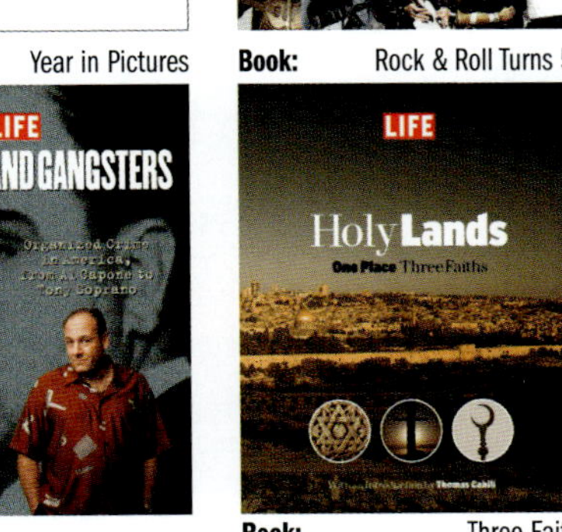

Book: Three Faiths

Euro notes and coins enter circulation, replacing local money • More than one billion cell phones are in use worldwide
Four million chocolate Easter bunnies melt in a warehouse fire in Volketswil, Switzerland
A five-color warning system is devised for ranking terrorist threats • D.C. area beset by snipers

2003

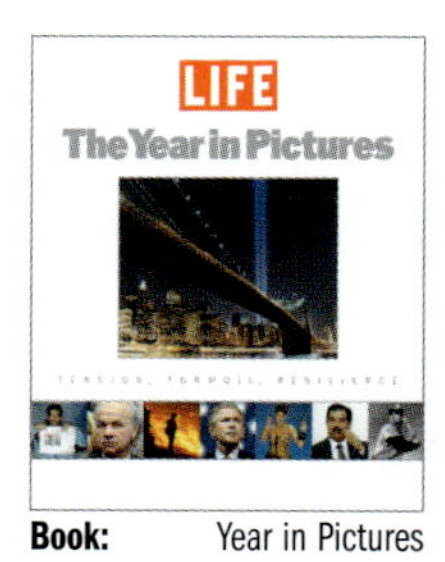

Book: Year in Pictures

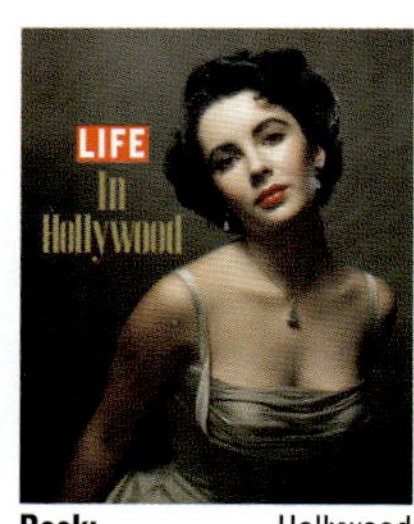

Book: Hollywood

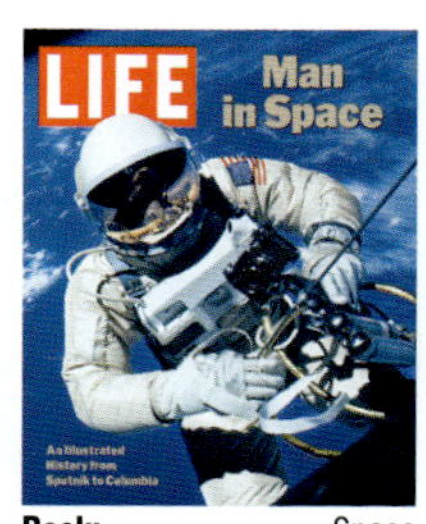

Book: Space

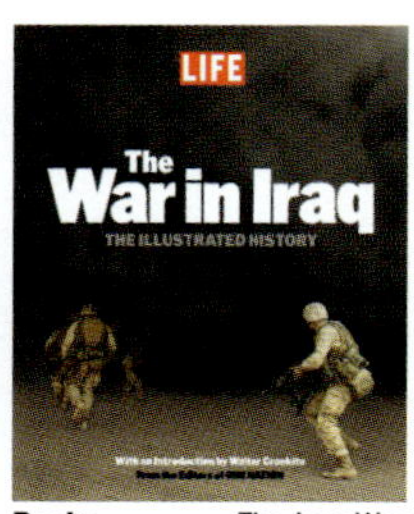

Book: The Iraq War

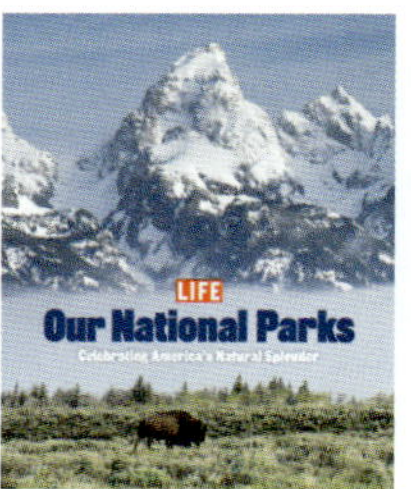

Book: U.S. National Parks

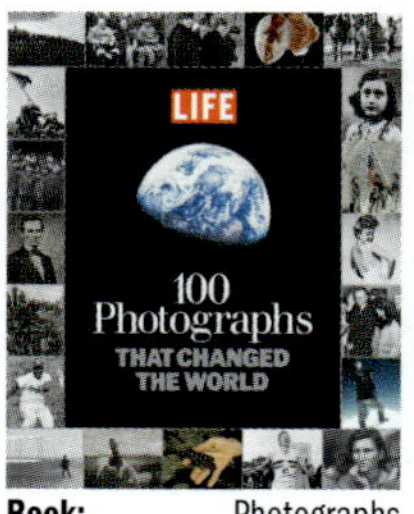

Book: Photographs

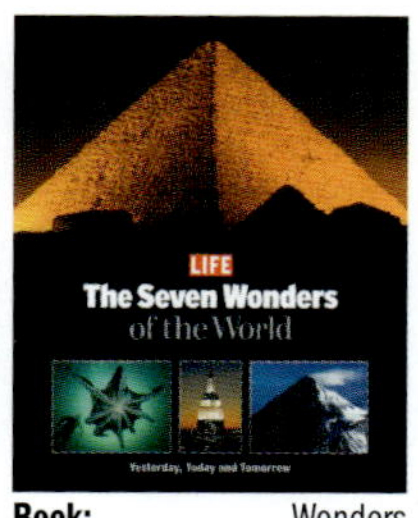

Book: Wonders of the World

Remnants of a Greek vessel dating back 2,300 years are found in the Black Sea
Jason Blair, a 27-year-old reporter for *The New York Times,* resigns owing to plagiarism
The U.N. says more than 40 million have AIDS, many of them in sub-Saharan Africa
A haggard Saddam Hussein is captured in a "spider hole" outside Tikrit, Iraq
SARS (severe acute respiratory syndrome) breaks out in 32 countries, killing 744

2004

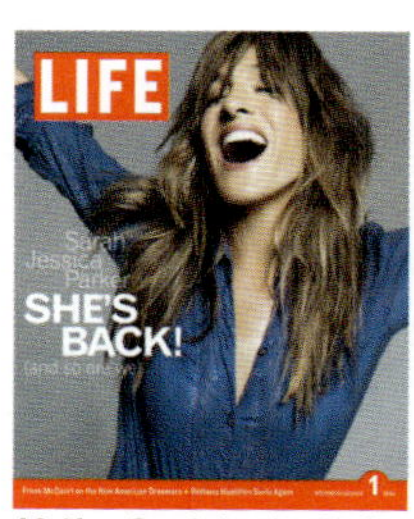

10/1 Sarah Jessica Parker

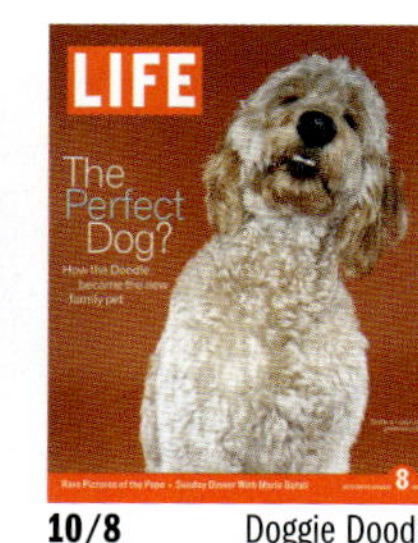

10/8 Doggie Doodle

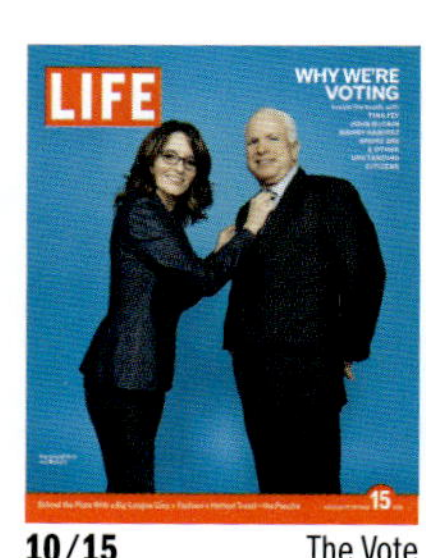

10/15 The Vote

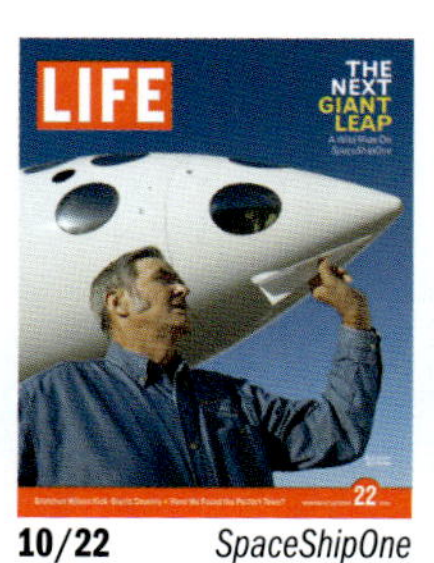

10/22 *SpaceShipOne*

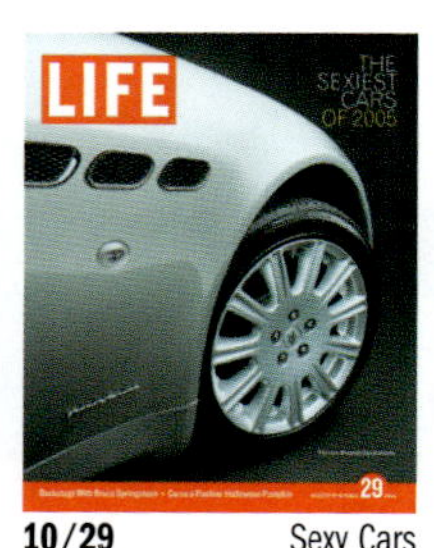

10/29 Sexy Cars

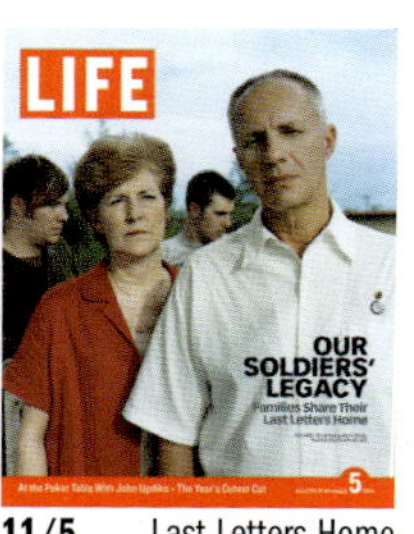

11/5 Last Letters Home

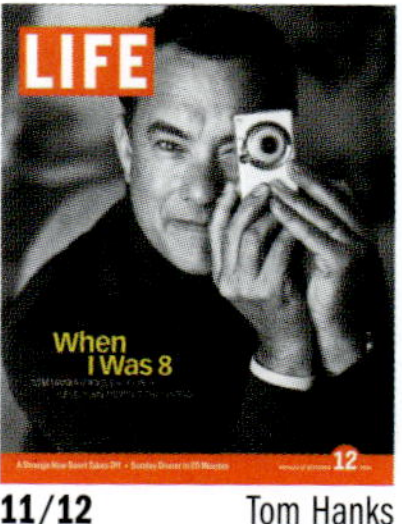

11/12 Tom Hanks

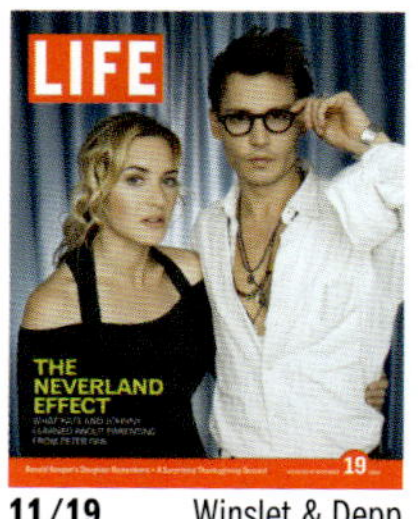

11/19 Winslet & Depp

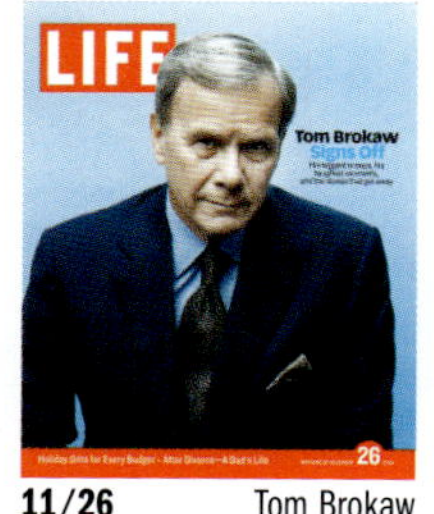

11/26 Tom Brokaw

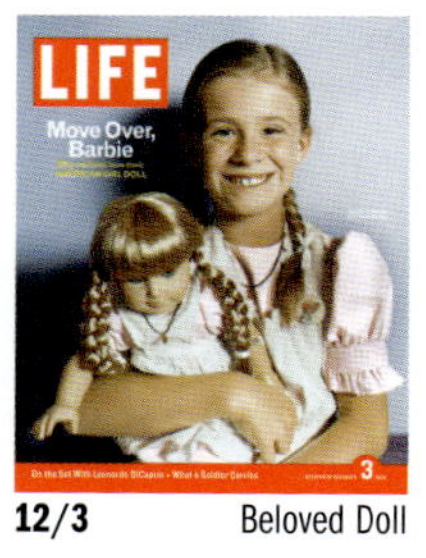

12/3 Beloved Doll

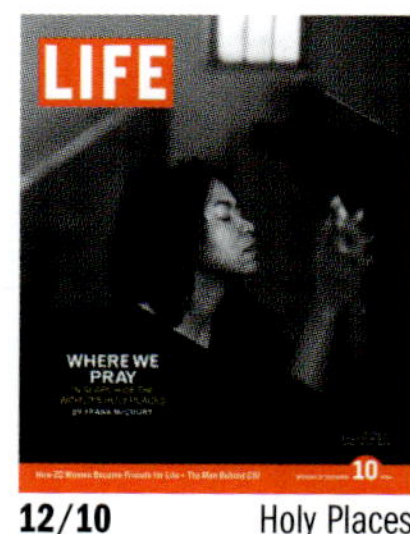

12/10 Holy Places

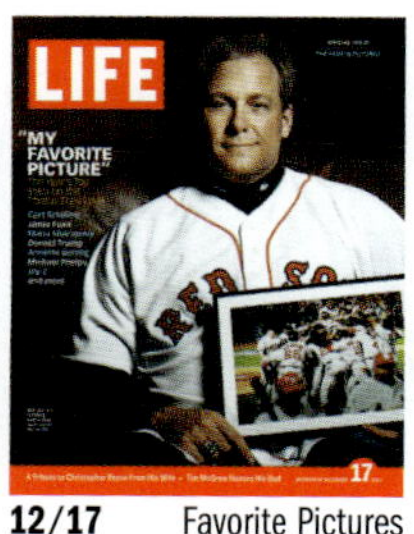

12/17 Favorite Pictures

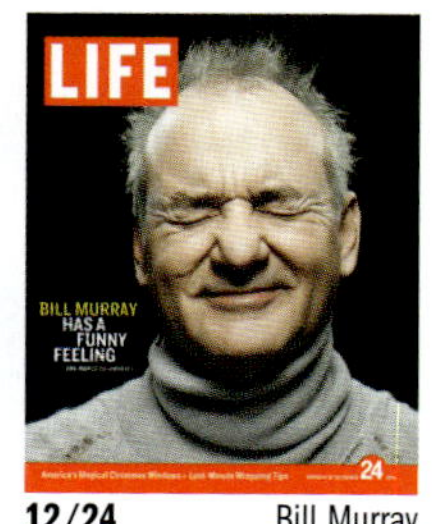

12/24 Bill Murray

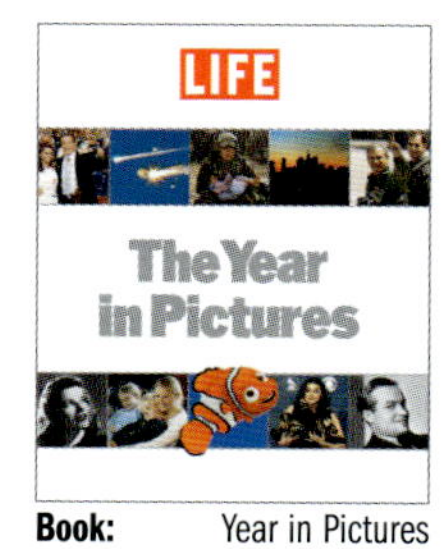

Book: Year in Pictures

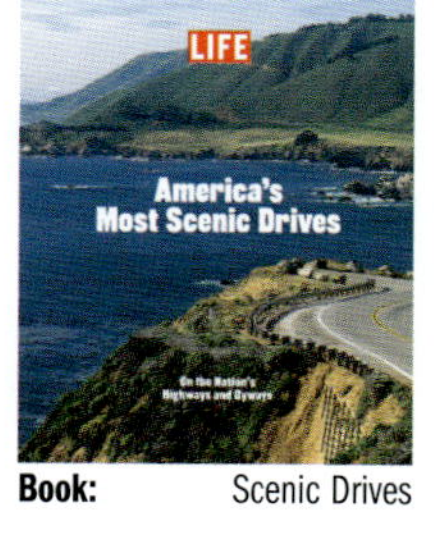

Book: Scenic Drives

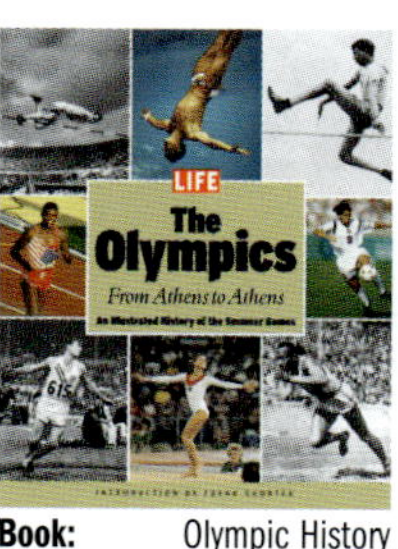

Book: Olympic History

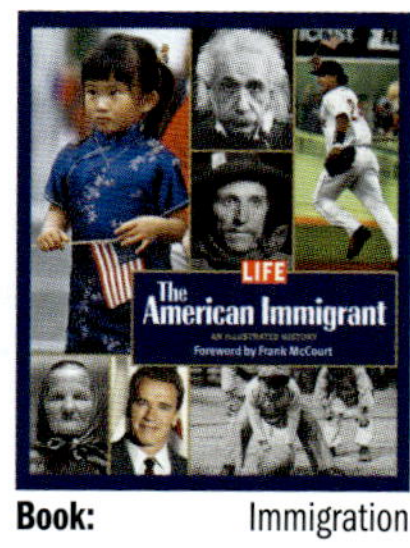

Book: Immigration

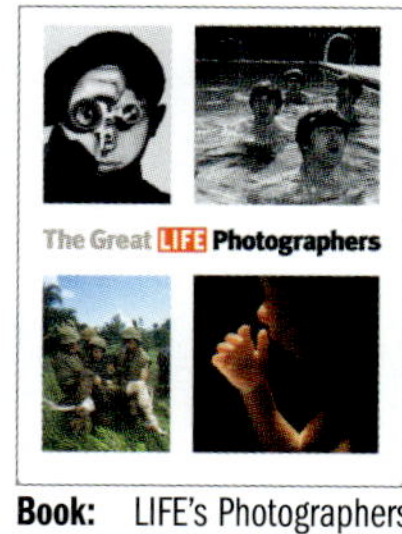

Book: LIFE's Photographers

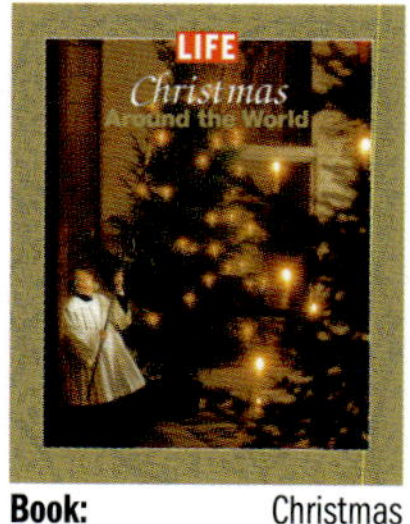

Book: Christmas

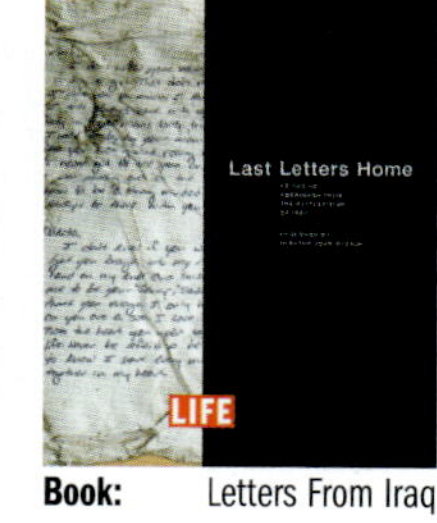

Book: Letters From Iraq

The Salvation Army receives $1.5 billion from deceased McDonald's heiress, Joan Kroc
Martha Stewart is sentenced to five months in prison for obstructing justice, conspiracy and lying
The Lord of the Rings: The Return of the King wins all 11 Oscars for which it is nominated
The Cassini spacecraft sends back spectacular images of Saturn and its rings
Beloved colt Smarty Jones fails in his Triple Crown bid, losing in the Belmont to a long shot

2005

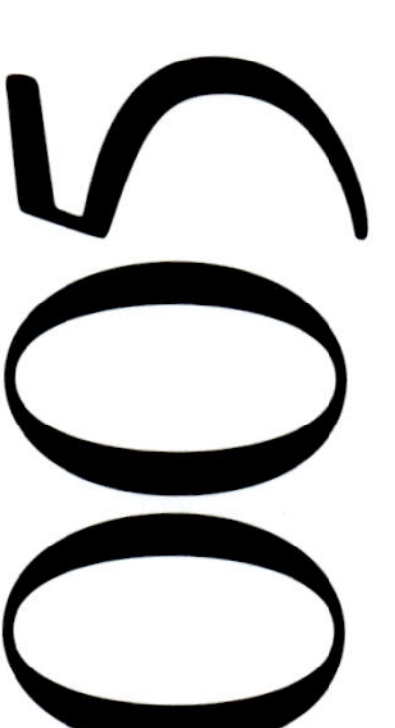

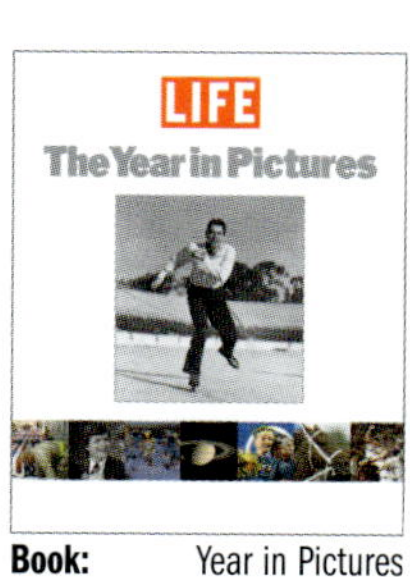

Book: Year in Pictures

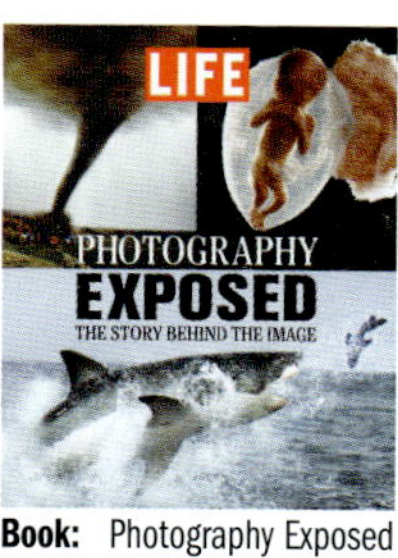

Book: Photography Exposed

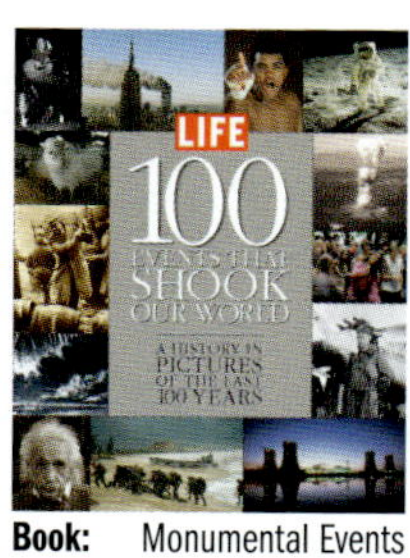

Book: Monumental Events

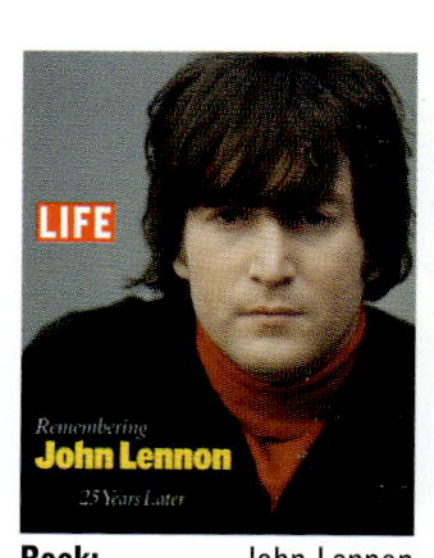

Book: John Lennon

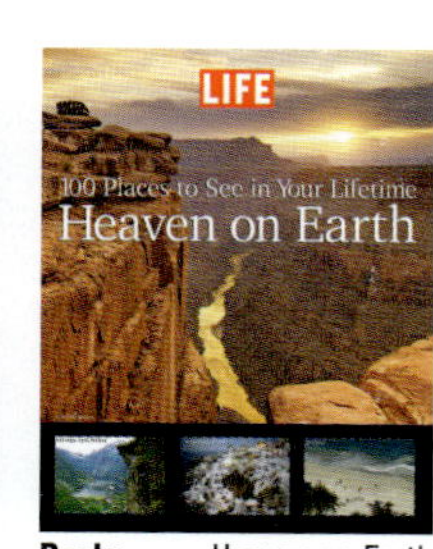

Book: Heaven on Earth

2005

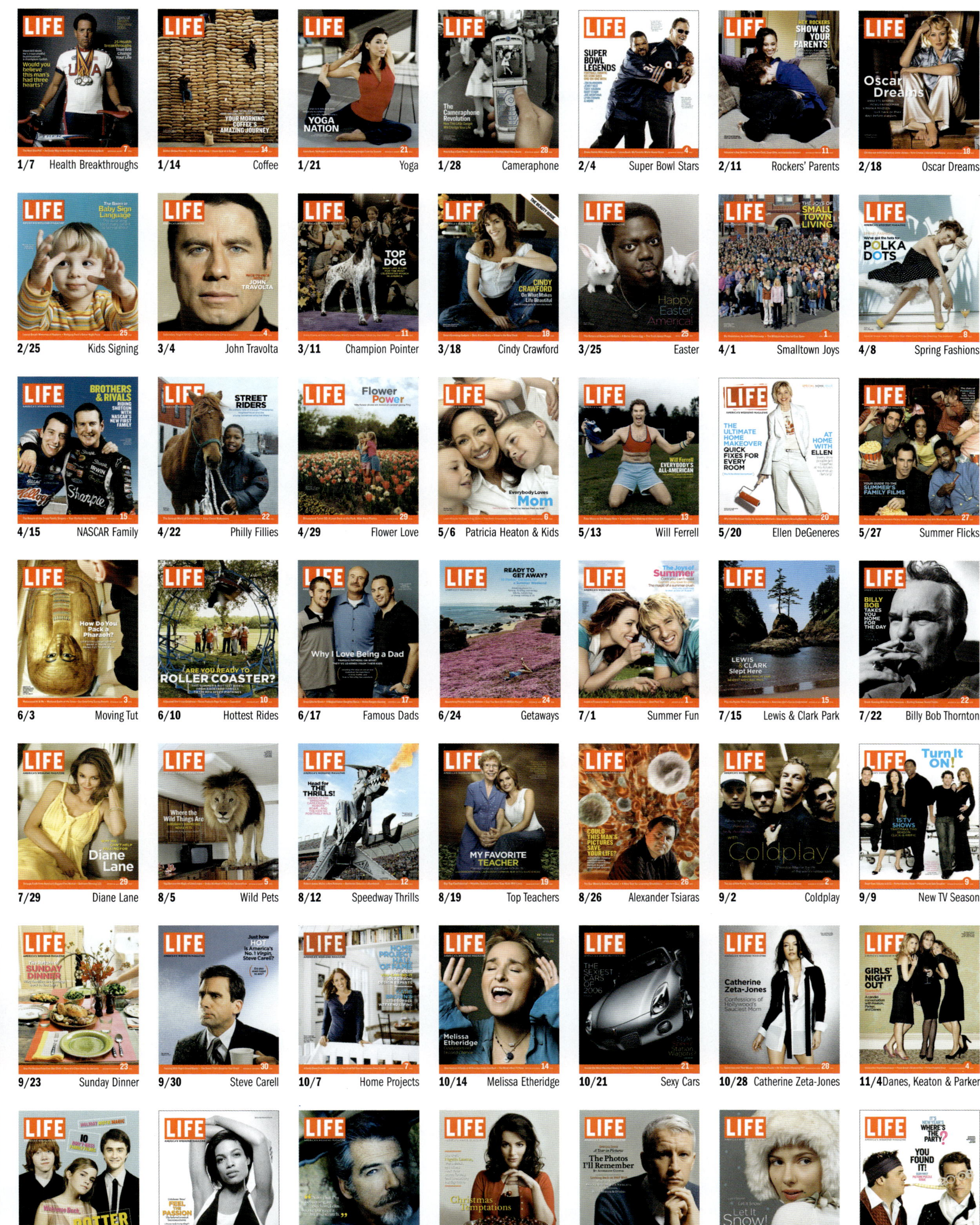

1/7 Health Breakthroughs · 1/14 Coffee · 1/21 Yoga · 1/28 Cameraphone · 2/4 Super Bowl Stars · 2/11 Rockers' Parents · 2/18 Oscar Dreams

2/25 Kids Signing · 3/4 John Travolta · 3/11 Champion Pointer · 3/18 Cindy Crawford · 3/25 Easter · 4/1 Smalltown Joys · 4/8 Spring Fashions

4/15 NASCAR Family · 4/22 Philly Fillies · 4/29 Flower Love · 5/6 Patricia Heaton & Kids · 5/13 Will Ferrell · 5/20 Ellen DeGeneres · 5/27 Summer Flicks

6/3 Moving Tut · 6/10 Hottest Rides · 6/17 Famous Dads · 6/24 Getaways · 7/1 Summer Fun · 7/15 Lewis & Clark Park · 7/22 Billy Bob Thornton

7/29 Diane Lane · 8/5 Wild Pets · 8/12 Speedway Thrills · 8/19 Top Teachers · 8/26 Alexander Tsiaras · 9/2 Coldplay · 9/9 New TV Season

9/16 Elijah Wood · 9/23 Sunday Dinner · 9/30 Steve Carell · 10/7 Home Projects · 10/14 Melissa Etheridge · 10/21 Sexy Cars · 10/28 Catherine Zeta-Jones · 11/4 Danes, Keaton & Parker

11/11 Hot Toys · 11/18 Harry Potter · 11/25 *Rent* · 12/2 Pierce Brosnan · 12/9 Christmas Fare · 12/16 Memorable Photos · 12/23 Scarlett Johansson · 12/30 New Year's Party

German Cardinal Ratzinger is elected pope and takes the name Benedict XVI • John G. Roberts Jr. succeeds William Rehnquist as Supreme Court Chief Justice
Hurricane Katrina blasts the Gulf Coast, killing thousands and devastating New Orleans
Rioting in France leads to state of emergency • The Chicago White Sox win the World Series for the first time since 1917

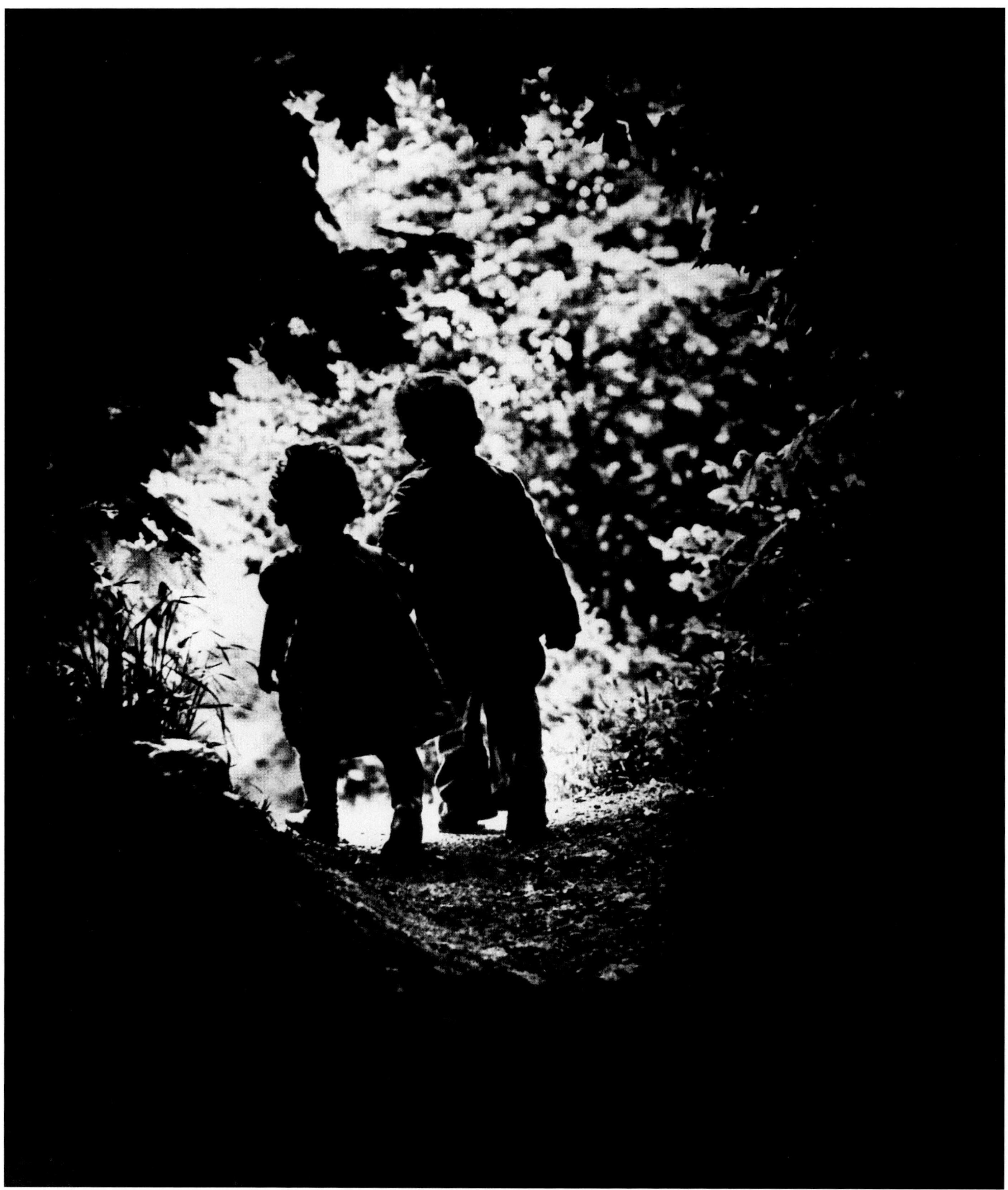

THE WALK TO PARADISE GARDEN

LIFE had a star-studded roster of photographers in World War II, and none shone brighter than W. Eugene Smith, who was known to the troops as "Wonderful" Smith because of his bravado during a series of intense Pacific island invasions. In April 1945 he was badly wounded on Okinawa, and didn't—couldn't—pick up a camera again until May 1946. "The day I again tried for the first time to make a photograph, I could barely load the roll of film into the camera. Yet I was determined that the first photograph would be a contrast to the war photographs and that it would speak an affirmation of life." In *The Walk to Paradise Garden*, we watch as Gene's daughter and son, behind their New York suburban home, make their way from a shrouded place into a world of light. Note that the preposition in the title is *to,* not *in.* Gene Smith is taking us, the observers, the seekers, with him and his children out of the dark despair of Depression and global war and into a land of bright dreams and vivid hopes. Paradise, at least for a while, has been regained.

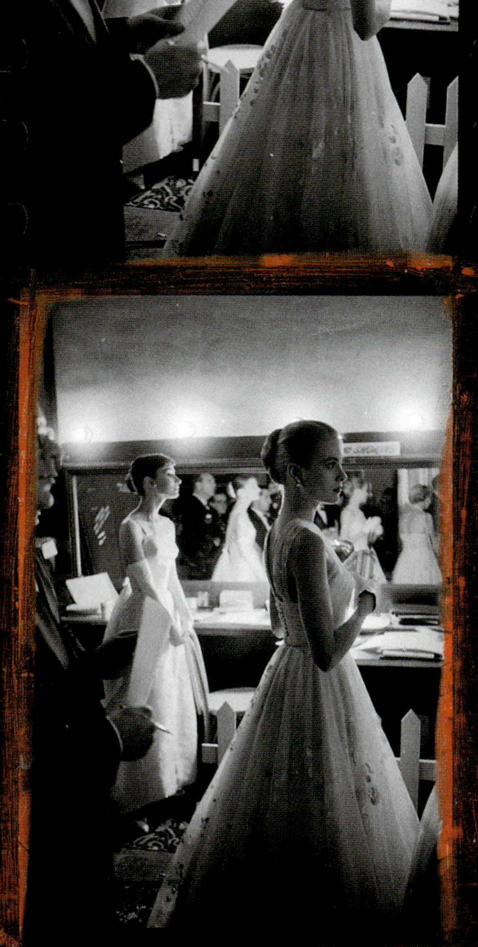
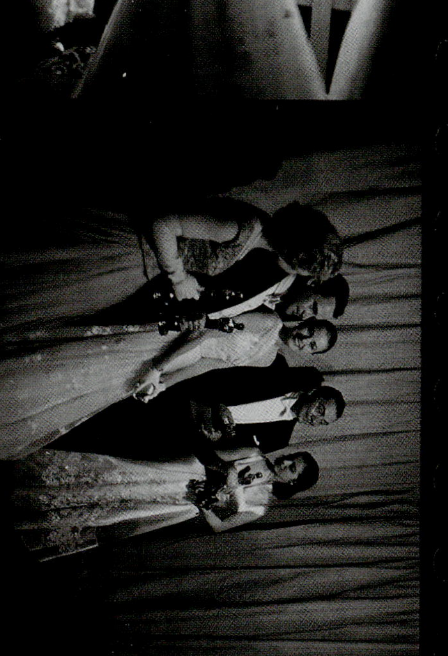
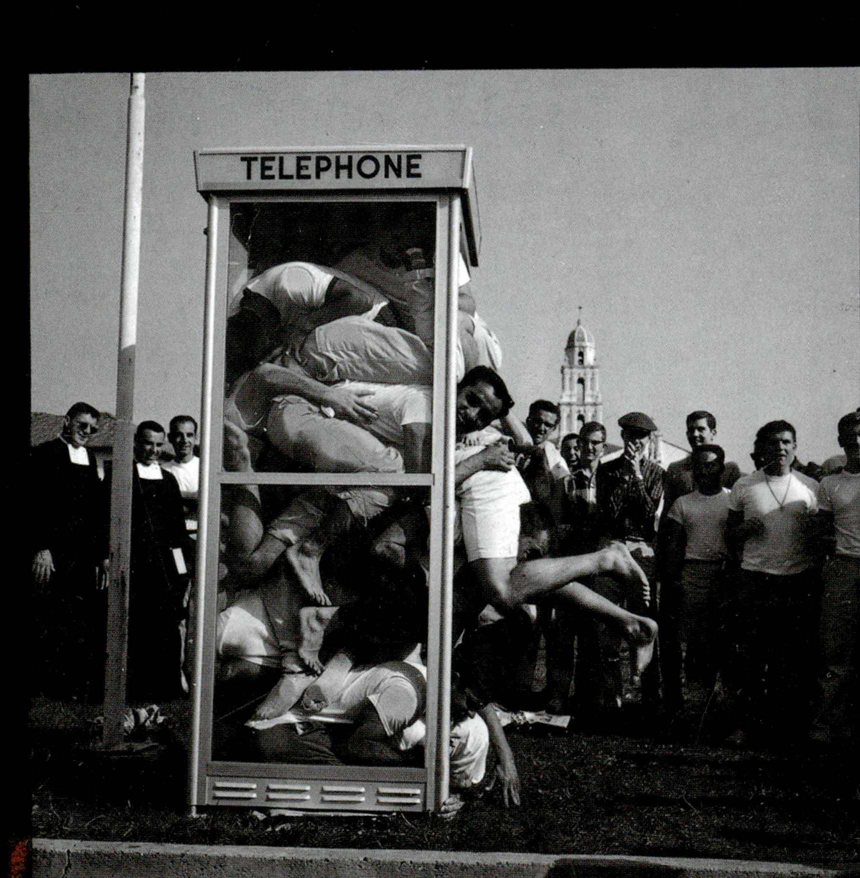
TELEPHONE
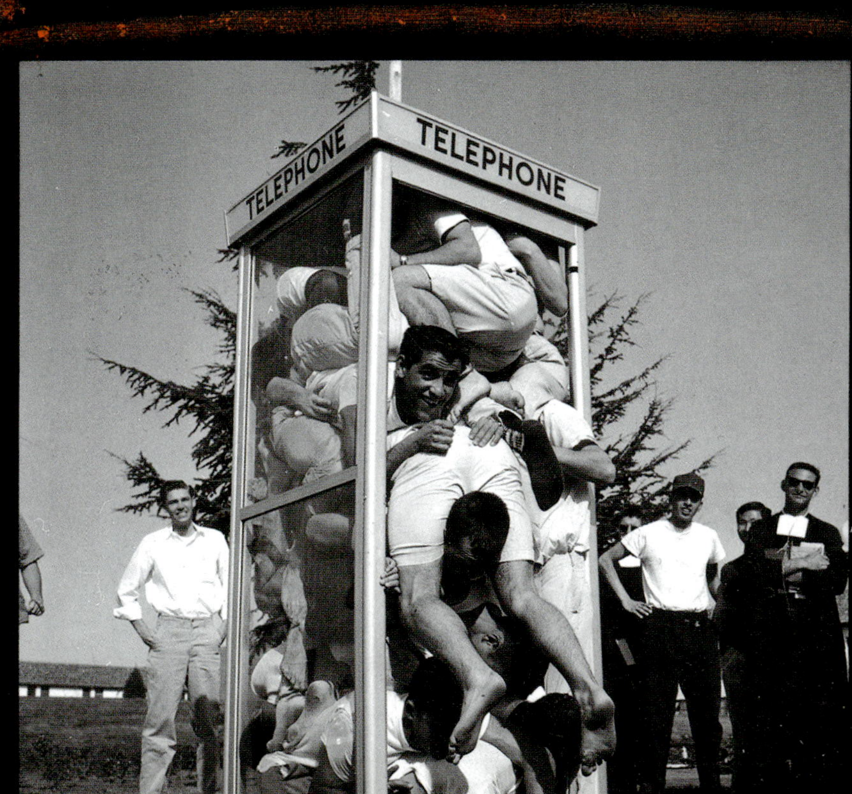
TELEPHONE
TELEPHONE
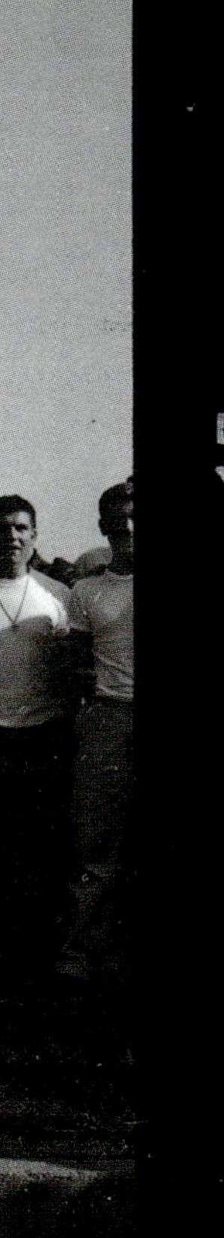
16
SAFETY FILM
SUPER XX
15
14
13
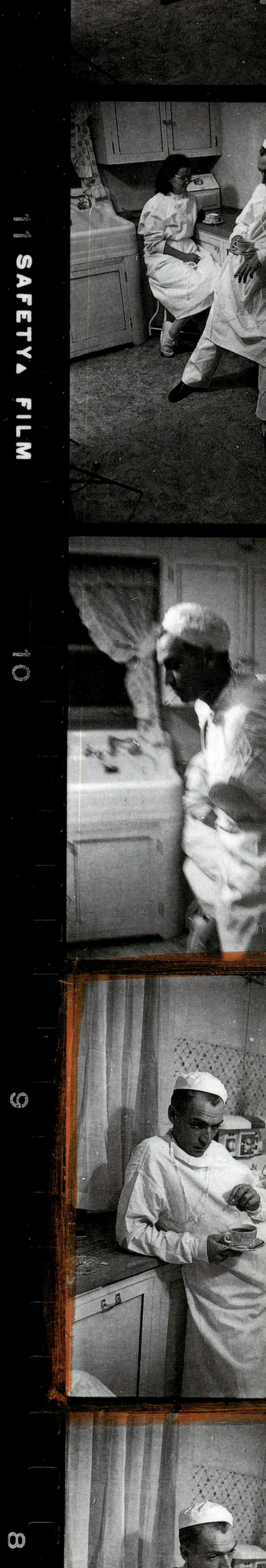